CANADIAN SERIALS DIRECTORY

RÉPERTOIRE DES PUBLICATIONS SÉRIÉES CANADIENNES

1976

Canadian Serials Directory

Répertoire des publications sériées canadiennes

1976

Martha Pluscauskas

University of Toronto Press
TORONTO AND BUFFALO

Toronto and Buffalo

Printed in Canada
Reprinted in 2018

Canadian Cataloguing in Publication Data

Main entry under title:
Canadian serials directory = Répertoire des publications sériées canadiennes, 1976

Text in English and French.
Includes indexes.

ISBN 0-8020-4507-3
ISBN 978-1-4875-7926-5 (paper)

1. Canadian periodicals – Directories.
I. Pluscauskas, Martha. II. Title: Répertoire des publications sériées canadiennes.
Z6954.C2C23 016.051 C77-001094-6E

Données de catalogage avant publication (Canada)

Vedette principale au titre:
Canadian serials directory = Répertoire des publications sériées canadiennes, 1976

Texte en anglais et en français.
Comprend des index.

ISBN 0-8020-4507-3
ISBN 978-1-4875-7926-5 (paper)

1. Périodiques canadiens – Répertoires.
I. Pluscauskas, Martha. II. Titre: Répertoire des publications sériées canadiennes.
Z6954.C2C23 016.051 C77-001094-6F

This book has been published during the
Sesquicentennial year of the University of Toronto

CONTENTS

TABLE DES MATIÈRES

INTRODUCTION

The *Canadian Serials Directory/Répertoire des publications sériées canadiennes* is a bibliographic listing of periodicals and serials presently being published in Canada. As a bibliographic tool it is aimed at librarians and scholars, but it is also an order guide for subscription agencies and booksellers.

A serial is defined as a publication which appears in successive parts bearing numerical, chronological or other sequential designation. The following are examples of serial publications which are included in the *Directory*: periodicals, magazines, annuals, yearbooks and journals, as well as proceedings and transactions of associations and societies. Also included are newspapers of special (i.e. ethnic, labour etc) interest, while general interest newspapers, monographic series, annual reports, company reports and financial statements, university and school calendars, city and telephone directories, and all government publications are excluded.

The information contained in the *Canadian Serials Directory* has been compiled through the cooperation of the National Library of Canada and the Bibliothèque nationale du Québec. Special assistance was given by the staffs of the University of Toronto Library, York University Library, and the Canadian Periodical Publishers' Association.

Listings in the *Directory* are based on information obtained from publishers in response to a detailed questionnaire. Many publishers also supplied a sample of their publication for examination by the editor. The extent of information gathered varies from title to title since some publishers were unable to answer all questions listed in the questionnaire. In such cases, the information was occasionally supplemented by information from other sources such as *Canadiana*, the order files of large library systems and the records of the Canadian Periodical Publishers' Association.

The *Canadian Serials Directory* is divided into three sections.

1 The "List of Serials" is arranged alphabetically by entry as determined by the Anglo-American cataloguing rules. This means that publications are listed under title except in cases where the title is a generic term such as bulletin or newsletter. The latter are listed under the name of the body responsible for their publication. Cross references are provided for alternative titles and/or former titles. The form of the entry has been altered from that used in the first (1972) edition to conform with the bibliographic form recommended by ISBD(S). French language entries are described in French while other entries are described in English. Abbreviations have been avoided except for the citations of indexing and abstracting services. A key to these abbreviations is given following this introduction. All titles listed are verified to be current for the year 1976.

2 The "Subject Index" provides a listing of serials arranged into 155 subject categories. A cross referencing list which precedes the subject index gives the French and English equivalents of the terms used in the list.

3 The "Publisher and Sponsor Index" gives access to each publication both by its official publisher and in many cases by the corporate body or association which sponsored its publication. Addresses have not been included in the index since some publishers give different addresses for different publications. Full mailing information for each serial is therefore given in the "List of Serials" under the main entry.

MARTHA PLUSCAUSKAS
Toronto, October 1976

INTRODUCTION

Le Répertoire des publications sériées canadiennes est une énumération bibliographique des périodiques et des publications en série qui paraissent actuellement au Canada. Il s'agit d'un outil bibliographique destiné aux bibliothécaires et aux savants mais qui peut aussi servir de guide de commande pour les libraires et les services d'abonnements.

Par définition, une publication en série est celle qui doit être publiée par tranches successives portant une désignation numérique, chronologique ou autrement séquentielle. Voici des exemples de publications incluses dans le Répertoire: périodiques, magazines, publications annuelles, annuaires et journaux, aussi bien que mémoires et comptes rendus de travaux d'associations et de sociétés. Sont aussi compris les journaux d'un intérêt particulier (par exemple, les publications ethniques, ouvrières etc.) Ne sont pas compris les journaux d'un intérêt général, les monographies numérotées les rapports annuels, les rapports et états financiers de compagnies, les annuaires des écoles et des universités, les bottins des villes et les annuaires téléphoniques et toutes publications des gouvernements.

Tous les renseignements contenus dans *Le Répertoire des publications seriées canadiennes* ont été recueillis par la Bibliothèque nationale du Canada et la Bibliothèque nationale du Québec. Le personnel de la Bibliothèque de l'Université de Toronto et de l'Université York et The Canadian Periodical Publishers' Association ont prêté une assistance spéciale.

Les inscriptions dans le *Répertoire* sont établies d'après les renseignements reçus des éditeurs en réponse à des questionnaires détaillés. Beaucoup d'éditeurs ont également fourni un example de leur publication pour l'inspection du rédacteur. L'étendue des renseignements recueillis varie selon la publication, étant donné que certains éditeurs ont été incapables de répondre à toutes les questions posées dans le questionnaire. En ce cas, on a complété les renseignements en ayant recours à d'autres sources telles que "Canadiana," les fiches de grandes bibliothèques et de The Canadian Periodical Publishers' Association.

Le Répertoire des publications sériées canadiennes comprend trois parties.

1 La liste de publications en série" est arrangée alphabétiquement selon les règles de catalogage Anglo-américaines. Cela veut dire que les publications sont classées selon leurs titres sauf dans le cas où le titre est un terme générique comme un bulletin ou une circulaire. Ces derniers se classent sous le nom des agences qui les publient. On y trouve également des renvois réciproques pour les titres alternatifs et/ou pour les anciens titres. La forme de l'inscription utilisée dans la première édition (1972) a été modifiée pour être conforme à la forme bibliographique recommandée par ISBD(S). Les publications en langue française sont décrites en français, tandis que toutes les autres le sont en anglais. On a évité les abréviations

sauf dans le cas de citations de services d'indexation et d'analyse des documents. La clef de ces abréviations suit cette introduction. On s'est assuré que tous les titres répertoriés paraissent encore en 1976.

2 "La Liste des matières" donne un classement de publications seriées groupées en 155 catégories de sujets. Une liste de renvois réciproques qui précède la liste de matières donne les termes anglais et français employés dans la liste.

3 "La Liste d'éditeurs et de parrains" donne accès à chaque publication par le nom de son éditeur officiel et aussi dans beaucoup de cas par le nom de la société ou de l'agence qui a parrainé sa publication. Les adresses ne figurent pas dans la liste étant donné que quelques éditeurs donnent une adresse differente pour chaque publication. Les renseignements postaux pour chaque publication seriée se trouvent dans "La liste de publications en série" sous chaque notice principale.

MARTHA PLUSCAUSKAS
Toronto, Octobre 1976

Indexing and Abstracting Services
Services de répertoirage et d'analyse à dépouillement

A.B.C. pol. sci.	Advance bibliography of contents: political science and government
Abstr. anthropol.	Abstracts in anthropology
Abstr. bull. Inst. Pap. Chem.	Institute of Paper Chemistry abstract bulletin
Abstr. crim. pen.	Abstracts on criminology and penology (formerly Excerpta criminogica)
Abstr. Eng. stud.	Abstracts of English studies
Abstr. soc. work	Abstracts for social workers
Alt. press ind.	Alternative press index
Amer. hist. & life	America: history and life
Annu. bib. Engl. lang. & lit.	Annual bibliography of English language and literature
Appl. sci. & tech. ind.	Applied science and technology index
Arct. bibl.	Arctic bibliography
Art ind.	Art index
B.P.I.	Business periodicals index
Biol. abstr.	Biological abstracts
Biol. & agri. ind.	Biological and agricultural index (Formerly Agricultural index)
Bior. index	Bioresearch index
C.I.N.L.	Cumulative index to nursing literature
Can. B.P.I.	Canadian business periodicals index
Can. educ. ind.	Canadian education index = Répertoire canadien sur education
Can. essay & lit. ind.	Canadian essay and literature index
Can. ind.	Canadian periodical index = Index de périodiques canadiens
Can. leg. per. lit.	Index to Canadian legal periodical literature
Canon law abstr.	Canon law abstracts
Cath. ind.	The Catholic periodical and literature index
Chem. abstr.	Chemical abstracts
Cons. index prod. eval. & infor. sources	Consumers index to product evaluations and information sources
Crim. delinq. abstr.	Crime and delinquency abstracts
Curr. ind. j. educ.	Current index to journals in education
Curr. issues com. & fin.	Current issues in commerce and finance
Educ. admin. abstr.	Educational administration abstracts
Educ. ind.	Education index
Employ. rel. abstr.	Employment relations abstracts
Eng. ind.	Engineering index
Environ. abstr.	Environment abstracts
Except. child educ. abstr.	Exceptional child education abstracts
Excerpt. med.	Excerpta medica
Food sci. & tech. abstr.	Food science and technology abstracts
Foreign leg. per.	Index to foreign legal periodicals
Geo. abstr.	Geographical abstracts
Hist. abstr.	Historical abstracts
Hosp. abstr.	Hospital abstracts
Hosp. lit. ind.	Hospital literature index
Hum. ind.	Humanities index
IBZ	Internationale bibliographie der Zeitschriftenliterature
ISI	Institute for scientific information
Ind. med	Index medicus
Int. ind. film period.	International index to film periodicals
Int. labour doc.	International labour documentation

Int. nurs. ind.	International nursing index
Int. pharm. abstr.	International pharmaceutical abstracts
Int. polit. sci. abstr.	International political science abstracts
LLBA	Language and language behaviour abstracts
Leg. per.	Index to legal periodicals
Lib. info. sci. abstr.	Library and information science abstracts (Formerly Library science abstracts)
J. econ. lit.	Journal of economic literature
Lib. lit.	Library literature
MLA abstr.	MLA abstracts of articles in scholarly journals
MLA int. bib.	MLA international bibliography of books and articles on the modern languages and literatures
Manage. ind.	Management index
Math. r.	Mathematical reviews
Meteoro. & geoastrophys. abstr.	Meteorological and geoastrophysical abstracts
Multi-media rev. ind.	Multi-media reviews index
Music ind.	The Music index
North title	Northern titles – New polar index
Nutr. abstr.	Nutrition abstracts and reviews
Ophthal. lit.	Ophthalmic literature
P.A.I.S.	Public affairs information service
PHRA	Poverty and human resources abstracts
Peace res. abstr.	Peace research abstracts journal
Per. art. rel. law	Index to periodical articles related to law
Périodex	Périodex : index analytique de périodiques de langue française
Phil. ind.	The Philosopher's index
Pollut. abstr.	Pollution abstracts
Pop. ind.	Population index
Psych. abstr.	Psychological abstracts
Pub. admin. abstr.	Public administration abstracts and index of articles
RADAR	Répertoire analytique d'articles de revues de Québec
RICS abstr. & reviews	RICS abstracts and reviews
R.I.L.A.	International repertory of the literature of art
RILM	RILM abstracts of music literature
Rel. & theol. abstr.	Religious and theological abstracts
Res. high. educ. abstr.	Research into higher education abstracts
Resources in educ.	Resources in education
Sci. abstr. electr. & elect.	SATRA: Electronics and electrical engineering
Sci. cit. ind.	Science citation index
Soc. sci. cit. ind.	Social sciences citation index
Soc. sci. ind.	Social sciences index
Sociol. abstr.	Sociological abstracts
Sociol. educ. abstr.	Sociology of education abstracts
Theo. rel. index	Theological and religious index
World text. abstr.	World textile abstracts
Writings Am. hist.	Writings on American history
Zentralbl. math.	Zentralblatt für mathematik und ihre grenzgebrete

LIST OF SERIALS

LISTE DES SÉRIES

The ? mark (March 1964-July 1965) *See* Cassette gazette

ABC British Columbia lumber trade directory and year book - *Published by* Progress Publishing Co. (1958) Ltd. 355 Burrard St., Vancouver, B.C. V6C 2G6.
Biennial. Directory, yearbook, book format, 350 p.
$15.75.

L'ABC du motocyclisme / *édité par* Jean-Pierre Belmonte. - *Publié par* Martin Levesque. 423 Sherbourne St., Toronto, Ont. M4X 1K5(adresse d'abonnement: 666, Ste-Croix, Montréal, Qué. H4L 3Y2) 1975-
Annuel. Publication spécialisée, magazine, 128 p. Comprend publicité. Tirage: 25,000
$1.50 par année : $2.00 par année, l'étranger.

ACBLF (1965-1973) *Voir* Association pour l'avancement des sciences et des techniques de la documentation. ASTED nouvelles

A.C.E. newsletter *See* Pacific Association for Continuing Education. P.A.C.E. newsletter

ACMC - AFMC newsletter (October 1963 - January-February 1974) *See* Association of Canadian Medical Colleges. ACMC/AFMC forum

AFV news magazine / *sponsored by* AFV Association ; *edited by* George Bradford. - *Published by* George Bradford. R.R. 2, Preston, Ont. N3H 4R7.
Issued every other month. Association publication, magazine format, 12 p. Includes book reviews. Circulation: 1800
$.50 per issue : $3.00 per year.

AIC review (1969) *See* Agrologist

ARC magazine *See* Arc Arabic Journal

ARTiculator / *edited by* Harriet Scott. - *Published by* The Kingston Arts Council. Performing Arts Office, Queen's University, Kingston, Ont. K7L 3N6, July 1975-
Former title(s): Arts Kingston (to January 1975)
Quarterly. House/company organ, newspaper format, 4 p. Circulation: 5000
$3.00 per year. Controlled circulation.

A voz do imigrante / *édité par* Antonio Leiras Pedroso. - *Publié par* Fédération des organismes portugais du Québec. C.P. 336, Succursale N, Montréal, Qué. H2Y 3M6, avril 1975-
Paraît tous les 15 jours. Ethnic, journal, 16 p. Langue(s): Portugais. Tirage: 11,000
Envoi gratuit.

Abbotsford International Air Show. Newsletter / *edited by* R.C. Thornber. - *Published by* Abbotsford International Air Show Society. P.O. Box 361, Abbotsford, B.C. V2S 4N9.
Issued every other month. Special interest, newsletter format,

L'Abordage - *Publié par* Syndicat du personnel non-enseignant de l'Université du Québec à Rimouski. 300, ave des Ursulines, Rimouski, Qué., mars 1974-
Intermittent (approximativement 15 éditions par an). Publication d'association, bulletin, 8 p.
Tirage: 250
Envoi gratuit.

About unions / *edited by* Si Dardick, Brenda Perry, Jim Best and others. - *Published by* Simon Dardick. 3564B Clark St., Montreal, Que., May 1973-
Former title(s): About unions : Friends of NUSGWUE newsletter (March 1974) Friends of NUSGWUE newsletter (May 1973 - November 1974)
Irregular (approximately 3 to 4 issues per year). Association publication, magazine format, 22 p. Language: English and French. Includes book reviews. Circulation: 1000
ISSN 0315-9922 Voluntary contributions (Institutions $8.00 for 6 issues). Prepayment required.

About unions : Friends of NUSGWUE newsletter (March 1974) *See* About unions

About us / *edited by* Vernon N. Quinn. - *Published by* Silverwood Industries Ltd. P.O. Box 2185, 75 Bathurst St., London, Ont., February 1971-
Former title(s): Cream topics (April 1948-November 1970)
House/company organ, magazine format, 8-12 p. Circulation: 4000
Controlled circulation.

L'Académie *See* The Academy

The Academy = L'Académie / *edited by* Ann J. Nelles. - *Published by* Royal Canadian Academy of Arts. Room 1112, 40 University Ave., Toronto, Ont. M5J 1T1, January 1974-
Irregular (approximately 4 issues per year). Association publication, newsletter format, 8 p. Language: English and French. Circulation: 550
Free.

Academy of Medicine, Toronto. Bulletin / *edited by* H.F. Robertson. - *Published by* Academy of Medicine. 288 Bloor St. W., Toronto, Ont. M5S 1V8, 1927-
Monthly except August. Institutional publication (Universities, schools, etc.), magazine format, 24 p. Circulation: 2800
$12.50 per year. Controlled circulation.

The Acadia bulletin / *edited by* Linda Cann. - *Published by* Associated Alumni. Acadia University. P.O. Box 520, Wolfville, N.S., February 1912-
Quarterly. Alumni publication, magazine format, 28 p. Includes book reviews, advertising. Circulation: 10,000
Controlled circulation.

Acadiensis : journal of the history of the Atlantic Region / *edited by* Phillip A. Buckner. - *Published by* Department of History. University of New Brunswick. Fredericton, N.B., November 1971-
Issued twice a year. Scholarly publication, journal format, 160 p. Language: English and French. Includes book reviews.
Indexed in Hist. abstr.; Amer. hist. and life.
ISSN 0004-5851 $7.20 (Institutions $12.00). 10% discount to agencies.

L'Acayen - *Publié par* L'Acayen. 355 Munroe, Bathurst, N.B.
Mensuel. Magazine,
$6.00 par année : $7.00 par année, l'étranger.

The Accelerator / *edited by* W.A. O'Leary. - *Published by* Ottawa Club. Ontario Motor League. 1354 Richmond Rd., Ottawa, Ont. K2B 7Z3.
Quarterly. Association publication, magazine format, 12 p.
ISSN 0315-3339 Controlled circulation.

Accelerator - *Published by* Saskatchewan Science Teachers Society. P.O. Box 1108, 2317 Arlington Ave., Saskatoon, Sask. S7J 2H8 (Subscription address: c/o Lorne Wilson, 2129 Albert Ave., Saskatoon, Sask. S7J 1J8)
Quarterly. Association publication.
Indexed in Can. educ. index.

Accident fatalities - Canada / *edited by* R.M. Plunkett. - *Published by* Canada Safety Council. 1765 St. Laurent Blvd., Ottawa, Ont. K1G 3S7.
23 p. Circulation: 1200
ISSN 0316-7305 $1.50 per issue.

Des accidents Canada - *Publié par* Conseil canadien de la sécurité. 30, Driveway, Ottawa, Ont. K2P 1C9, 1961-
Publié en anglais: Accident fatalities - Canada.
23 p. Tirage: 250
$1.50 le numéro.

The Accounter / *edited by* W.C. Easton. - *Published by* The Society of Industrial Accountants of Alberta. 400 Herald Bldg, 206 - 7th Ave. S.W., Calgary, Alta. T2P 0W8.
Issued every other month. Association publication, newsletter format, 6 p.
Controlled circulation.

L'Acheteur / *édité par* Jacques Combaluzier. - *Publié par* Maclean-Hunter Ltd. 481 University Ave., Toronto, Ont., 1966-
Mensuel. Magazine, 44 p. Comprend critique de livres. Tirage: 5000
$1.00 le numéro : $12.00 par année. Tirage contrôlé.

Achimowin / *edited by* Yvonne Laboucan. - *Published by* Sagitawa Friendship Centre. P.O. Box 1283, Peace River, Alta. T0H 2X0.
Monthly. Association publication, newsletter format, 6 p. Circulation: 100
Indexed in North. tit.
Subscription included in membership fee.
Controlled circulation.

Across the board / *edited by* Anne C. Cox. - *Published by* Protestant School Board of Greater Montreal. 6000 Fielding Ave., Montreal, Que. H3X 1T4, March 1975-
Former title(s): PSBGM news; Your school reports.
Issued 10 times a year September to June. House/company organ, newsletter format, 8 p.
Circulation: 60,000
Free.

Act news / *edited by* Dorothy Bird. - *Published by* Association of Community Theatres, Central Ontario. 43 Amelia St., Toronto, Ont. M4X 1E3, 1954?-
Former title(s): Newsletter - Central Ontario Drama League.
Issued every other month. Association publication, newsletter format, 20 p. Includes play reviews. Circulation: 1500
$7.00 per year.

Acta criminologica *Voir* Criminologie

Action / *edited by* Jessie E. Wright. - *Published by* Alberta-Northwest Territories Division. The Canadian Red Cross Society. 1504 First St. S.E., Calgary, Alta. T2G 2J5, Spring 1970-
Quarterly. Association publication, magazine format, 12 p. Circulation: 6000

Action / *edited by* Robert J. Skinner. - *Published by* The Pentecostal Assemblies of Canada. 10 Overlea Blvd., Toronto, Ont. M4H 1A5, 1968-
Former title(s): Missionary outlook (1960-1968)
Monthly. Church publication, magazine format, 16 p. Circulation: 17,800
Free.

Action / *edited by* Peter Woodger. - *Published by* Purchasing Management Association of Canada. Suite 1702, 80 Richmond St. W., Toronto, Ont. M5H 2A4, 1970-
Former title(s): Purchasing management newsletter (1970)
Monthly. Association publication, newsletter format, 6 p. Language: English and French ; summaries: English and French.
ISSN 0319-5023 Free to members.

Action : chamber of commerce / *edited by* Gilles Monette. - *Published by* Gilles Monette. Quebec Chamber of Commerce. 500 St. Francis Xavier St., Montreal, Que. H2Y 2T6, April 1974-
Former title(s): Newsletter - The Province of Quebec Chamber of Commerce (October 1965 - December 1973)
Issued twice a month. Association publication, newsletter format, 4 p. Circulation: 2000
ISSN 0315-131X Free.

Action : chambre de commerce / *édité par* Gilles Monette. - *Publié par* La Chambre de commerce de la province de Québec. 500, rue St-François Xavier, Montréal, Qué. H2J 2T6, avril 1974-
Ancien titre: Faits et tendances (avril 1949-décembre 1973)
Bimensuel. Publication d'association, bulletin, 4 p. Tirage: 5000
ISSN 0319-3717 Envoi gratuit.

Action catholique ouvrière (1951-1957) *Voir* Dossiers "vie ouvrière" au service des militants chrétiens du monde ouvrier

L'action nationale / *édité par* Jean Genest. - *Publié par* Librairie Gagné ltée. St-Justin, Cté de Maskinongé, Qué., janvier 1933-
Mensuel. Publication d'association, magazine, 80 p. Comprend critique de livres, publicité. Tirage: 2000
Indexé dans Periodex, Can. ind., RADAR, Hist. abstr.; Amer. hist. and life.
$1.00 le numéro : $10.00 par année. Tarifs spéciaux disponibles. Abonnements payables à l'avance.

Actionews : world vision's heartline to needy world / *edited by* Ian J. Stanley. - *Published by* World Vision of Canada. 410 Consumers Rd., Willowdale, Ont. M2J 1P8.
Former title(s): Heartline.
Issued every other month. Association publication, magazine format, 16 p. Circulation: 25,000
$1.00 per year.

Actrascope / *edited by* Margaret Collier. - *Published by* Association of Canadian Television and Radio Artists (ACTRA). 105 Carlton St., Toronto, Ont. M5B 1M2, March 1968-
Quarterly. Association publication, magazine format, 24 p. Includes book reviews. Circulation: 5200
ISSN 0065-1796 $5.00 per year. Controlled circulation.

Actrascope news / *edited by* Margaret Collier. - *Published by* Association of Canadian Television and Radio Artists (ACTRA). 105 Carlton St., Toronto, Ont. M5B 1M2, July 1973-
Irregular (approximately 8 issues per year). Association publication, magazine format, 20-24 p. Includes book reviews.
ISSN 0315-484X Controlled circulation.

L'Actualité économique / *édité par* Roland Jouandet-Bernadat. - *Publié par* Ecole des hautes études commerciales. 5255, ave. Decelles, Montréal, Qué., avril 1925-
Trimestriel. Publication d'association, 150 p. Comprend index cumulatif. Tirage: 1800
ISSN 0001-771X $3.00 le numéro : $10.00 par année.

L'Actualité économique / *édité par* Roland Jouandet-Bernadat. - *Publié par* Ecole des hautes études commerciales. 5255, ave Decelles, Montréal, Qué. H3T 1V6, avril 1925-
Trimestriel. Publication d'association, revue, 150 p. Langue(s): français ; sommaires: anglais. Comprend critique de livres, index cumulatif. Tirage: 1800
Indexé dans Periodex, Can. ind., RADAR, Soc. sci. cit. ind., Hist. abstr.; Amer. hist. and life, I.B.Z., Arct. bibl.
ISSN 0001-771X $4.00 le numéro : $13.00 par année.

L'Actualité joliettaine - *Publié par* Serge Housseaux. 598 rue St-Viateur, Joliette, Qué., octobre 1974-
Mensuel. Intérêt général, magazine, 40 p. Comprend critique de livres, publicité, index de volumes. Tirage: 5000
$.50 le numéro : $5.00 par année.

Actualité magazine / *édité par* Claude Martin. - *Publié par* Claude Martin. 4059, Hochelaga, Montréal, Qué. H1W 3S4, 1909-
Mensuel. Intérêt général, magazine, 60 p. Comprend critique de livres, critique de films, critique de pièces de théâtre, publicité. Tirage: 141,500
$.75 le numéro : $3.00 par année.

Actualitiés Montréal *See* Current events magazine. Montreal edition

Adaptation : revue d'éducation spécialisée - *Publié par* Lester Toupin. Association des éducateurs specialisés pour inadaptés du Québec. 8147 est, Sherbrooke, Montréal, Qué. H1L 1A7, novembre 1974-
Intermittent (approximativement 4 éditions par an). Publication d'association, journal, 15 p. Comprend critique de livres, publicité. Tirage: 1000
Envoi gratuit.

Addiction Research Foundation. The Journal / *edited by* Gary Seidler. - *Published by* Addiction Research Foundation of Ontario. 33 Russell St., Toronto, Ont., June 1972-
Monthly. Newspaper format, 16 p. Includes advertising. Circulation: 54,816
ISSN 0044-6203 $1.00 per issue : $12.00 per year : $16.00 per year, foreign. Free to Ontario residents.

Addictions / *edited by* Barbara Rutledge. - *Published by* Addiction Research Foundation of Ontario. 33 Russell St. Toronto, Ont. M5S 2S1, 1961-
Former title(s): Alcoholism research (1953-1961)
Quarterly. Magazine format, 72 p. available in microform. Circulation: 50,000
ISSN 0001-8082 $6.00 per year : $10.00 for 2 years : free in Ontario : $6.00 per year, foreign.

Additions and accessions - *Published by* Education Centre Library. Toronto Board of Education. 155 College St., Toronto, Ont. M5T 1P6, 1966-
Irregular (approximately 12 issues per year). Bibliography.
Controlled circulation.

Administration hospitalière et sociale / *édité par* Claude Bertrand. - *Publié par* Fédération des administrateurs des services de santé et services sociaux du Québec. 4237, rue de Bordeaux, Montréal, Qué., 1955-
Ancien titre: L'hôpital d'aujourd'hui.
Intermittent (approximativement 10 éditions par an). Publication d'association, magazine, 40 p. Comprend publicité, index de volumes. *Indexé dans* RADAR.
ISSN 0317-3739 $2.50 le numéro : $10.00 par année : $13.00 par année, l'étranger. Abonnements payables à l'avance.

Administration publique du Canada *See* Canadian public administration

Administrative digest / *edited by* Gary Weiss. - *Published by* Southam Business Publications Ltd. 1450 Don Mills Rd., Don Mills, Ont., 1966-
Monthly. Trade publication, magazine format, 32 p. Includes advertising. Circulation: 20,896
ISSN 0030-0136 $1.00 per issue : $12.00 per year : $1.50 per issue, foreign: $18.00 per year, foreign.

Administrative digest reference manual / *edited by* Gary Weiss. - *Published by* Southam Business Publications Ltd. 1450 Don Mills Rd., Don Mills, Ont.
Annual. Directory, magazine format, 75 p. Includes advertising. Circulation: 21,000
Included in the regular subscription to Administrative digest.

The Administrative scene / *sponsored by* Saskatchewan Council on Educational Administration ; *edited by* K.A. Wilson. - *Published by* Saskatchewan Teachers' Federation. P.O. Box 1108, Saskatoon, Sask., 1970-
Irregular (approximately 3 issues per year). Association publication, newsletter format, 4 p. Circulation: 300
$5.00 per year. Subscription included in membership fee.

The Administrator / *edited by* Robert Wilson. - *Published by* York Administrative Alumni Association. Room 111, Administrative Studies Building, York University, 4700 Keele St., Downsview, Ont., 1969-
Irregular (approximately 2 issues per year). Alumni publication, newsletter format, 4 p. Circulation: 1200
Free.

Adolescence, sport and leisure - *Published by* SIRLS. Faculty of Human Kinetics and Leisure Studies. University of Waterloo. Waterloo, Ont. N2L 3G1.
Quarterly. Bibliography, computer printout, $20.00 per year. $100.00 subscription to SIRLS required.

Adsum / *édité par* Dan Nolan. - *Publié par* BFC Valcartier. Courcelette, Québec G0A 1R0, mai 1972-
Journal, 16 p. Comprend publicité. Tirage: 5000
$.15 le numéro : $5.00 par année. Envoi gratuit.

Adulthood, sport and leisure - *Published by* SIRLS. Faculty of Human Kinetics and Leisure Studies. University of Waterloo. Waterloo, Ont. N2L 3G1.
Quarterly. Bibliography, computer printout, $20.00 per year. $100.00 subscription to SIRLS required.

The Advocate (January 1956 - October 1970) *See* Concerns

The Advocate / *sponsored by* Ontario Association of School Business Officials ; *edited by* P.M. Machetzki and T.R. Moore. - *Published by* London Board of Education. P.O. Box 5873, London, Ont. (Subscription address: Suite N-1201, 252 Bloor St. W., Toronto, Ont. M5S 1V5) 1970?-
Issued every other month. Association publication, newsletter format, 8-12 p. Circulation: 1200
Subscription included in membership fee $25.00. Controlled circulation.

Les affaires / *édité par* M. Jean V. Baltayan. - *Publié par* Publications les affaires inc. 635 est, Henri-Bourassa, Montréal, Qué. H2C 1E4, 1961-
Hebdomadaire. Revue d'entreprise, journal, 32 p. Comprend critique de livres. parution de suppléments.
$.35 le numéro : $12.00 par année : $35.00 par année, l'étranger. Tarifs spéciaux disponibles. Abonnements payables à l'avance.

Affaires universitaires *See* University affairs

Africa now / *edited by* Kerry E. Lovering. - *Published by* Sudan Interior Mission. 3251 Sheppard Ave. E., Agincourt, Ont. M1T 3K1, 1958-
Issued every other month. Church publication, magazine format, 16 p. Circulation: 28,000
Free.

Agent's bulletin (1913-1971) *See* Field record

Agent's news letter *See* Manufacturers Life Insurance Company. News letter

Aggression in sport and physical activity - *Published by* SIRLS. Faculty of Human Kinetics and Leisure Studies. University of Waterloo. Waterloo, Ont. N2L 3G1.
Quarterly. Bibliography, computer printout, $20.00 per year. $100.00 subscription to SIRLS required.

Aging leisure and retirement - *Published by* SIRLS. Faculty of Human Kinetics and Leisure Studies. University of Waterloo. Waterloo, Ont. N2L 3G1.
Quarterly. Bibliography, computer printout, $20.00 per year. $100.00 subscription to SIRLS required.

Agora / *sponsored by* Canadian Association of Special Libraries and Information Services ; *edited by* Anne Woodsworth. - *Published by* Canadian Library Association. 151 Sparks St., Ottawa, Ont., K1P 5E3., 1968-
Quarterly. Association publication, newsletter format, 8 p. Circulation: 710
Subscription included in membership fee. Controlled circulation.

Agricultural Pesticide Society. Proceedings / *edited by* J.A. Scott. - *Published by* Agricultural Pesticide Society. c/o Plant Products Division, Agriculture Canada, Ottawa, Ont. K1A 0C5, 1953-
Annual. Association publication, proceedings of the annual conference, 50 p. Language: English and French ; summaries: English and French. Circulation: 225
ISSN 0065-4485 $5.00.

Agricultural Science *See* Agricultural science

Agricultural science / *edited by* B. Wolfe and Extension Division Staff. - *Published by* Extension Division. University of Saskatchewan. Saskatoon, Sask., January 1974-
Former title(s): Information (1972-1973)
Issued every other month. Institutional publication, sheets, 4 p. Circulation: 4000
$1.00 per year.

Agricultural science - *Published by* Extension Division. University of Saskatchewan. Saskatoon, Sask. S7N 0W0, November 1972-
Former title(s): Agricultural Science; Information; Saskatchewan farm science.
Issued every other month. Institutional publication (Universities, schools, etc.), factsheet, 4 p. Circulation: 1600
Free.

Agriculture / *édité par* Jean-Baptiste Roy. - *Publié par* Ordre des agronomes du Québec. 262 ouest, boul. Henri-Bourassa, Montréal, Qué. H3L 1N6, 1944-
Trimestriel. Publication d'association, magazine, Langue(s): français ; sommaires: anglais.
$1.25 le numéro : $5.00 par année : $5.50 par, année, l'étranger.

Agriculture bulletin / *edited by* J.C. Lees. - *Published by* Public Relations and Publications Committee. Faculty of Agriculture and Forestry. University of Alberta. 326 Assiniboia Hall, Edmonton, Alta. T6G 2E1 (Subscription address: Department of Extension, The University of Alberta, Edmonton, Alta. T6G 2G4) 1962-
Quarterly. Institutional publication (Universities, schools, etc.), magazine format, 16 p. Includes book reviews. available in microform. Circulation: 16,000
Indexed in North. tit., Biol. abstr..
ISSN 0568-9074 Free.

L'Agriculture canadienne / *édité par* Dennis S. Hladysh. - *Publié par* Dennis S. Hladysh. International Harvester Canada. 1190 Blair Rd., Burlington, Ont. L7M 1K9, January 1950-
Ancien titre: Culture canadienne motorisée (1950-1959) Publié en anglais : Canadian farming.
Trimestriel. Revue d'entreprise, magazine, 20 p. Tirage: 25,000
Envoi gratuit. Tirage contrôlé.

Agriculture Institute review (1945) *See* Agrologist

Agrologist / *edited by* W.E. Henderson. - *Published by* Agricultural Institute of Canada. Suite 907, 151 Slater St., Ottawa, Ont. K1P 5H4., June 1934-
Former title(s): AIC review (1969) Agriculture Institute review (1945) Canadian Society of Technical Agriculturists review (1934) Scientific agriculture.
Quarterly. Association publication, magazine format, 40 p. Includes book reviews, advertising, volume index. Circulation: 5000
Indexed in Chem. abstr.
$1.25 per issue ($2.50 for special issues): $6.00 per year: $7.00, foreign (outside the Commonwealth).

Ahoy : an Atlantic magazine for children / *sponsored by* Junior League of Halifax. - *Published by* Ahoy. P.O. Box 3380, Halifax South Post Office, Halifax, N.S., 1976-
Special interest.

Aies annuaire / *édité par* Jacques Laliberté. - *Publié par* Centre d'animation de développement et de recherche en éducation. 1940 est, boul. Henri-Bourassa, Montréal, Qué. H2B 1S2, 1968-
Titre de couverture Annuaire : Association des institutions d'enseignement secondaire.
Annuel. Publication d'association, 160 p.
Tirage: 7000
Envoi gratuit.

Air Pollution Control Association. Quebec Section. Annnual symposium - *Published by* Quebec Section. Air Pollution Control Association. P.O. Box 1000, Varennes, Que., May 1973-
Annual. Association publication, 100 p.
Language: English and French ; summaries: English and French.

L'Ajiste *See* The Hosteller

Alberta amateur *See* VE6

Alberta Association of Registered Nurses. AARN newsletter / *edited by* Brenda Laing. - *Published by* Alberta Association of Registered Nurses. 10256 - 112th St., Edmonton, Alta. T5K 1M6.
Monthly. Association publication, newsletter format, 16 p. Includes advertising, volume index. Circulation: 14,000
$5.00 per year : $6.50 per year, foreign. Free to members.

Alberta Bid Depository. Rules and regulations including trade definitions - *Published by* Alberta Construction Association. 10415 Princess Elizabeth Ave., Edmonton, Alta. T5G 0Y5, 1964-
Annual. Association publication, 110 p.
Circulation: 2000
Free.

The Alberta bowhunter & archer / *edited by* Wm. A. Gillespie. - *Published by* Alberta Bowhunters & Archers Association. c/o 10129 - 90 St., Edmonton, Alta. T5H 1R5, 1968-
Issued every other month. Association publication, newsletter format, 40 p. Includes advertising. Circulation: 300
ISSN 0044-7080 $3.00 per year.

Alberta Catholic directory - *Published by* Western Catholic Reporter. 9537-76th Ave., Edmonton, Alta. T6C 4H7.
Former title(s): The Catholic home annual (1920)
Annual. Directory, church publication, magazine format, 160 p. Language: English. Includes updating service. Circulation: 1400
$2.50 per year. Controlled circulation.

Alberta Certified Nursing Aide Association. Newsletter - *Published by* Alberta Certified Nursing Aide Association. Suite 2, 10830-107th Ave., Edmonton, Alta. T5H 0X3, 1946-
Former title(s): Flyer.
Irregular (approximately 5 issues per year). Association publication, newsletter format, 24-32 p. Circulation: 3400
Subscription included in membership fee.

Alberta Construction Association. Membership roster & buyers guide - *Published by* Alberta Construction Association. 10415 Princess Elizabeth Ave., Edmonton, Alta. T5G 0Y5.
Annual. Association publication, directory, Spiral bound format, 122 p.

Alberta construction industry directory/purchasing guide / *edited by* D.O. Brewer. - *Published by* Sanford Evans Publishing (Alberta) Ltd. Suite 1, 5512 Macleod Trail S.W., Calgary, Alta. T2H 0J5, 1974-
Annual. Trade publication, magazine format, Includes advertising.

Alberta cooperative and farm organization directory - *Published by* Rural Education and Development Association. 9934-106th St., Edmonton, Alta. T5K 1C4.
Association publication, directory.

Alberta corporation manual / *edited by* E.R. Hughes and R.B. Love. - *Published by* Richard De Boo Ltd. 70 Richmond St. E., Toronto, Ont. M5C 2M8.
Issued every other month. Legal articles, 64 p. Includes updating service.
$40.00 per year.

The Alberta counselor / *edited by* Lloyda Allen. - *Published by* Guidance Council. Alberta Teachers' Association. 11010-142 St., Edmonton, Alta.
Irregular (approximately 2 issues per year). Association publication, magazine format, 40 p. Includes book reviews, film reviews.
Circulation: 500
Indexed in Can. educ. ind.
$7.50 per year. Prepayment required.

Alberta English / *sponsored by* English Council of The Alberta Teachers' Association ; *edited by* R. Glenn Martin. - *Published by* Alberta Teachers' Association. Barnett House, 11010-142 St., Edmonton, Alta., November 1969-
Former title(s): The English teacher - (Fall 1961 to March 1969)
Irregular 3-4. Association publication, journal format, 40 p. Includes book reviews.
Circulation: 750
Indexed in Resources in educ., Can. educ. ind.
$5.00 per year. Subscription includes its Newsletter. Prepayment required.

Alberta English notes / *sponsored by* English Council of the Alberta Teachers' Association ; *edited by* Hassan Rushdy. - *Published by* Alberta Teachers' Association. Barnett House, 11010-142 St., Edmonton, Alta., October 1968-
Irregular 3-4. Association publication, newsletter format, 4-8 p. Circulation: 650

Alberta fish and game magazine *See* Fish and game sportsman

Alberta fishing guide / *edited by* George Mitchell. - *Published by* Railton Publications Ltd. 125 Talisman Ave., Vancouver, B.C. V5Y 2L6, 1972-
Annual. Special interest, magazine format, 68 p. Includes advertising, volume index, updating service. Circulation: 20,000
$1.00. Prepayment required.

The Alberta handicapped forum / *edited by* Dwayne Jiry. - *Published by* John Mockler. Alberta Rehabilitation Council for the Disabled. 14443-125th Ave., Edmonton, Alta. T5L 3C4, December 1973-
Former title(s): Handicapped forum (Summer 1972-1973)
Monthly. Institutional publication (Universities, schools, etc.), newspaper format, 16 p. Includes advertising.
$3.00 per year. Subscription voluntary.

Alberta historical review / *edited by* Hugh A. Dempsey. - *Published by* Historical Society of Alberta. P.O. Box 4035, Postal Station C, Calgary, Alta., 1953-
Quarterly. Association publication, magazine format, 32 p. Includes book reviews.
Circulation: 2200
Indexed in Can. ind., Hist. abstr.; Amer. hist. and life, Arct. bibl.
ISSN 0002-4783 $1.25 per issue : $4.00 per year.

Alberta hog journal / *edited by* Ed Schultz. - *Published by* Alberta Hog Producers Marketing Board. 6113-101 Ave., Edmonton, Alta. T6C 4G2, January 1972-
Quarterly. Trade publication, magazine format, 50 p. Includes advertising.
Free. Controlled circulation.

Alberta Home Economics Association. AHEA newsletter / *edited by* R.P. Mallen. - *Published by* Alberta Home Economics Association. P.O. Box 1052, Edmonton, Alta., June 1966-
Quarterly. Association publication, newsletter format, 20 p. Includes book reviews, film reviews. Circulation: 650
$.50 per issue : $2.00 per year.

Alberta Information Retrieval Association. A.I.R.A. - Western Canada A.S.I.S. newsletter / *sponsored by* University of Alberta ; *edited by* Mrs. N. Cooke. - *Published by* Mrs. N. Cooke. Boreal Institute for Northern Studies. University of Alberta. Edmonton, Alta., March 1967-
Irregular (approximately 3 issues per year). Association publication, newsletter format, 5 p.
$2.00 per year. Prepayment required.

The Alberta journal of educational research / *edited by* Thomas E. Kieren. - *Published by* The Faculty of Education. University of Alberta. Edmonton, Alta. T6G 2E1 (Subscription address: Room 949, Education I, University of Alberta, Edmonton, Alta. T6G 2E1) 1955-
Quarterly. Journal format, 80 p. Includes book reviews, advertising, volume index. Back numbers available. Circulation: 750
Indexed in Educ. admin. abstr., Sociol. educ. abstr., Can. educ. ind., Soc. sci. cit. ind., Curr. ind. j. educ., Psych. abstr.
ISSN 0002-4805 $2.00 per issue : $6.00 per year.

Alberta law quarterly (1935-1945) *See* Alberta law review

Alberta law review / *sponsored by* University of Alberta. Faculty of Law. - *Published by* Alberta Law Review. C/o Faculty of Law, University of Alberta, Edmonton, Alta., 1955-
Former title(s): Alberta law quarterly (1935-1945)
Irregular (approximately 3 issues per year). Legal articles, journal format, 125 p. Includes book reviews, advertising, volume index. available in microform. Circulation: 2800
Indexed in Can. leg. per. lit.
ISSN 0002-4821 $4.00 per issue : $12.00 per year.

Alberta learning resources journal / *edited by* Ray Schmidt. - *Published by* The Alberta Teacher's Association. 11010 - 142 St., Edmonton, Alta T5N 2R1, Fall 1975-
Former title(s): Mediator; Alberta school library review.
Irregular (approximately 3 issues per year). Association publication, 50 p. Includes book reviews, film reviews. Circulation: 500
$10.00 per year.

Alberta medical bulletin / *edited by* A.B. Jones. - *Published by* Alberta Medical Association. Suite 304, 9901-108th St., Edmonton, Alta. T5K 1G8, 1935-
Quarterly. Association publication, magazine format, 32 p. Includes advertising. Circulation: 3456
ISSN 0002-4848 Controlled circulation.

Alberta modern language journal / *edited by* Gaston Renaud. - *Published by* Modern Language Council. Alberta Teachers' Association. 11010 - 142 St., Edmonton, Alta. T5N 2R1, April 1962-
Former title(s): Modern language journal (Fall 1973-Spring 1974) Modern and classical language bulletin (1962-Winter 1972-1973)
Irregular (approximately 3 issues per year). Association publication, journal format, 30 p. Includes book reviews, volume index. supplements issued. Circulation: 300
Indexed in Can. educ. ind.
ISSN 0318-5176 $5.00 (University students $2.00).

Alberta Motor Transport Association. AMTA news bulletin / *edited by* The A.M.T.A. Public and Internal Relations Co-ordinator. - *Published by* Alberta Motor Transport Association. 5112 - 3 St. S.E., Calgary, Alta.
Monthly. Association publication, newsletter format, 10-12 p. Includes advertising.
Free to members and others upon request.

Alberta motor transport directory - *Published by* Alberta Motor Transport Association. 5112-3 St. E., Calgary, Alta.
Former title(s): Alberta shippers guide (to 1970)
Annual. Directory, magazine format, 175 p. Includes advertising. supplements issued.
$8.50.

Alberta motorist / *sponsored by* Alberta Motor Association ; *edited by* Brian W. Johnson and Janice A. Bauman. - *Published by* George A. Macdonald. 109 St. & Kingsway Ave., Edmonton, Alta. T5L 4J5, 1923-
Former title(s): The Voice of motordom (1950) Western motordom (1930-1950) Good roads (1923-1930)
Association publication, magazine format, 32 p. Circulation: 165,000
ISSN 0002-4856 Subscription included in membership fee. Controlled circulation Membership.

Alberta music calendar / *sponsored by* Calgary Region Arts Foundation ; *edited by* Gerald Moran. - *Published by* Gerald Moran. 31 Chatham Dr. N.W., Calgary, Alta. T2L 0Z4, February 1970-
Former title(s): Music Calendar (1971-1974) Choir news (1970-1971)
Quarterly. Association publication, newsletter format, 4 p. Circulation: 700
Free.

Alberta new homes / *edited by* Tom Verner. - *Published by* Guide Magazines Ltd. 1105 Granville St., Vancouver, B.C., 1973-
Issued every other month. Trade publication, magazine format, Includes advertising.
$1.00 per issue : $5.00 per year.

Alberta poetry yearbook / *edited by* June L. Fritch. - *Published by* Edmonton Branch. Canadian Authors Association. 13104 - 136th Ave., Edmonton, Alta. T5L 4O3, 1930-
Annual. Special interest, paperbound book format, 80 p.
ISSN 0065-5996 $1.50. Controlled circulation. Prepayment required.

Alberta Polled Hereford Club. Newsletter / *edited by* Betty Elliott. - *Published by* Alberta Polled Hereford Club. Dewberry, Alta. T0B 1G0, February 1955-
Irregular (approximately 5-6 issues per year). Association publication, newsletter format, 4 p.

Alberta school library review *See* Alberta learning resources journal

The Alberta school trustee / *edited by* H.E. Martin. - *Published by* Alberta School Trustees' Association. 311 Royal Alex Place, 10106 - 111 Ave., Edmonton, Alta. T5G 0B4.
Quarterly. Association publication, magazine format, 32 p. Includes book reviews.
Circulation: 2300
Indexed in Can. educ. ind.
ISSN 0002-4880 $.75 per issue : $3.00 per year.

Alberta science education journal / *sponsored by* Science Council. Alberta Teachers Association ; *edited by* W. Holliday. - *Published by* Alberta Teachers' Association. 11010-142nd St., Edmonton, Alta. T5N 2R1.
Former title(s): S.C.A.T. bulletin.
Irregular (approximately 3 or 4 issues per year). Association publication, journal format, 40-50 p.
Indexed in Can. educ. ind.
$8.00 per year. Prepayment required.

Alberta shippers guide (to 1970) *See* Alberta motor transport directory

Alberta Teachers' Association. English council. Newsletter / *sponsored by* English Council of The Alberta Teachers' Association ; *edited by* Tom Gee. - *Published by* Alberta Teachers' Association. Barnett House, 11010-142 St., Edmonton, Alta., Spring 1962-
Irregular (approximately 3 issues per year). Association publication, newsletter format, 8-10 p. Circulation: 700
$5.00 per year. Subscription includes Alberta English. Prepayment required.

Alberta Teachers' Association. Health and Physical Education Council. HPEC runner / *sponsored by* Health and Physical Education Council ; *edited by* Pat Brand and Jim Paul. - *Published by* Alberta Teachers' Association. 11010-142 St., Edmonton, Alta. T5N 2R1.
Former title(s): The Health and Physical Education Council bulletin (1964-1974)
Quarterly. Association publication, magazine format, 50 p. Includes book reviews.
Circulation: 600
Indexed in Can. educ. ind.
ISSN 0318-0433 $1.50 per issue : $5.00 per year.

Alberta Teachers' Association. Industrial Arts and Vocational Education Council. IAVEC communicator - *Published by* Industrial Arts and Vocational Educational Council. Alberta Teachers' Association. 11010-142 St., Edmonton, Alta., 1972-
Former title(s): Newsletter - Alberta Teachers' Association. Industrial Arts and Vocational Education Council.
Annual. Association publication.

Alberta Teachers' Association. Learning Resources Council. Newsletter / *edited by* Rolf C. Seidel. - *Published by* Learning Resources' Council. Alberta Teachers' Association. 11010-142 St., Edmonton, Alta. T5N 2R1.
Irregular (approximately 5-8 issues per year). Association publication, newsletter format, 6 p.
Circulation: 450
Subscription included in membership fee $15.00.

Alberta Teachers' Association. Special Education Council. Newsletter / *edited by* Henry H. Unrall. - *Published by* Special Education Council. Alberta Teachers' Association. 11010-142 St., Edmonton, Alta. T5N 2R1, Spring 1970-
Quarterly. Association publication, newsletter format, 14 p. Includes book reviews.
Circulation: 500
ISSN 0315-3509 $7.50 per year. Controlled circulation.

Alberta Teachers' Association. The ATA magazine / *edited by* T.W. McConaghy. - *Published by* The Alberta Teachers' Association. 11010 - 142nd St., Edmonton, Alta. T5N 2R1, 1920-
Issued every other month. Association publication, magazine format, 40 p.
Circulation: 27,244
Indexed in Can. educ. ind.
$1.25 per issue. $6.00 per year combined with the ATA news.

Alberta Teachers' Association. The ATA news / *edited by* W.S.H. Boston. - *Published by* The Alberta Teachers' Association. 11010 - 142nd St., Edmonton, Alta. T5N 2R1, February 1967-
Issued every other month. Association publication, newspaper format, 8 p.
Circulation: 27,244
$6.00 per year combined with the ATA magazine.

Alberta towline / *edited by* N. Bell and P. Hagler. - *Published by* Edmonton Soaring Club. P.O. Box 472, Edmonton, Alta.
Former title(s): Towline.
Monthly. Association publication, newsletter format, 10 p.
Subscription included in membership fee. Controlled circulation.

Alberta Wilderness Association. Newsletter / *edited by* R.P. Pharis. - *Published by* Alberta Wilderness Association. P.O. Box 6398, Postal Station D, Calgary, Alta. T2P 2E1, 1968-
Quarterly. Association publication, newsletter format, 38-40 p. Includes book reviews.
Circulation: 1900
$5.00 per year. Prepayment required.

The Albertan geographer - *Published by* Department of Geography. University of Alberta. Edmonton, Alta. T6G 2H4, 1965-
Annual. Institutional publication (Universities, schools, etc.), magazine format, 70-80 p.
Circulation: 200
Indexed in North. tit., Arct. bibl.
ISSN 0065-6097 $1.00.

Albert-Westmorland-Kent Regional Library. News = Nouvelles - *Published by* Albert-Westmorland-Kent Regional Library. P.O. Box 708, Moncton, N.B., E1C 8M9, October 1971-
Irregular (approximately 8-10 issues per year). House/company organ, newsletter format, 8 p.
Language: French and English. Circulation: 250
ISSN 0315-355x

Alcan Canada Products Ltd. Alcan news / *edited by* George Hancocks. - *Published by* Alcan Canada Products Ltd. P.O. Box 269, Toronto-Dominion Centre, Toronto, Ont. M5K 1K1.
Irregular (approximately 9-11 issues per year). Special interest, magazine format, 12 p.
Language: English and French. Circulation: 35,000
ISSN 0002-4996 Free. Controlled circulation.

Alcan Canada Products Ltd. Revue Alcan / *édité par* George Hancocks. - *Publié par* Produits Alcan Canada. C.P. 269, Toronto, Ont.
Intermittent (approximativement 9-11 édition par an). Organe interne/officiel, magazine, 12 p.
Envoi gratuit. Tirage contrôlé.

Alcoholism research (1953-1961) *See* Addictions

Alimentation du Quebec / *édité par* Robert Bastin. - *Publié par* Les Editions du marchand québécois. 6841, rue St. Hubert, Montréal, Qué. H2S 2M8, janvier 1961-
Mensuel. Publication spécialisé, journal, 20 p.
Tirage: 12,000
$5.00 par année.

Alive magazine (1969-1974) *See* Alive magazine : literature and ideology

Alive magazine : literature and ideology - *Published by* Alive Production Collective. P.O. Box 1331, Guelph, Ont., 1975-
Former title(s): Alive magazine (1969-1974) Literature and ideology (1969-1974)
$.50 per issue : $5.00 per year.

All about boating / *edited by* Marlene Smith (assistant editor). - *Published by* Sarah Swartz. 136 Adelaide St. E., Toronto, Ont. M5C 1L6, January 1974-
Quarterly. Special interest, magazine format, 35 p. Includes book reviews, advertising, volume index. Circulation: 40,000
ISSN 0317-0403 $2.95 per year : $7.50 for 3 years. Special rates offered.

Allergy information (1964-1970) *See* Allergy Information Association. Newsletter

Allergy Information Association. Newsletter / *edited by* Susan Daglish and Kathleen Miller. - *Published by* AIA Allergy Information Association. 3 Powburn Pl., Weston, Ont. M9R 2C5, 1964-
Former title(s): Allergy information (1964-1970)
Quarterly. Association publication, newsletter format, 14 p. Includes book reviews. available in microform. supplements issued. Cookbook available for $2.00. Circulation: 1500
$.75 per issue : $5.00 per year : $3.00 annual renewal. Prepayment required.

L'Alliance de la fonction publique du Canada. Nouvelles de la semaine - *Publié par* L'Alliance de la fonction publique du Canada. 233, Gilmour, Ottawa, Ont. K2P 0P1, 1967-
Publié en anglais: Public Service Alliance of Canada. Newsletter.
Hebdomadaire. Publication d'association, bulletin, 2 p. Tirage: 4000

Allocations aux organismes nationaux *See* Allocations to national organizations

Allocations to national organizations = Allocations aux organismes nationaux - *Published by* United Way of Canada. P.O. Box 3505, Postal Station C, 55 Parkdale Ave., Ottawa, Ont. K1Y 1E5.
Issued every 3 years. 40 p. Language: English and French.
ISSN 0316-4721

Almanach du peuple - *Publié par* Librairie Beauchemin ltée. 450, ave Beaumont, Montréal, Qué.
Annuel. Magazine,
$2.50 par année.

Almanach éclair *Voir* Almanach moderne

Almanach moderne / *édité par* Paul Rochon. - *Publié par* Les Publications éclaire ltée. 9393, ave. Edison, Anjou, Qué. H1J 1T5, 1956/1957-
Ancien titre: Almanach éclair.
Annuel. Intérêt général, 640 p. Tirage: 134,506
ISSN 0315-2898

Alpine Club of Canada. Montreal Section. Newsletter / *edited by* George Ascroft. - *Published by* Montreal Section. The Alpine Club of Canada. 111 White Rd., Vaudreuil, Que. J7V 5V5.
Irregular (approximately 5 issues per year). Special interest, newsletter format, 6 p.
Free. Controlled circulation.

Alpine Club of Canada. Ottawa Section. Bulletin / *edited by* Mary Lynn Taylor. - *Published by* Ottawa Section. The Alpine Club of Canada. c/o P. Mix, Chairman, Ottawa Section, Apt. 1204, 311 Bell, Ottawa, Ont. K1S 4K1.
Quarterly. Association publication, newsletter format, 5 p.
Subscription included in section membership $5.00. Prepayment required.

Alternative to alienation / *edited by* Bill Holloway and others. - *Published by* Alternative to Alienation. P.O. Box 46, Postal Station M, Toronto, Ont. M6S 4T2, March 1974-
Issued every other month. General interest, newspaper format, 24 p. Includes book reviews, film reviews, play reviews, advertising. Circulation: 3000
ISSN 0315-0984 $3.00 for 12 issues. Prepayment required.

Alternatives : perspectives on society and environment / *edited by* Robert C. Paehlke. - *Published by* Alternatives Inc. c/o Traill College, Trent University, Peterborough, Ont., Summer 1971-
Quarterly. Concerned with environmental and resource problems, journal format, 44 p. Includes book reviews. available in microform. Circulation: 1500
Indexed in Environ. abstr., Pollut. abstr., Alt. press ind., Curr. ind. j. educ.
ISSN 0002-6638 $1.00 per issue.

Alumni / *edited by* Milo Craig. - *Published by* Brandon University Alumni Association. Brandon, Man. R7A 6A, 1975-
Irregular (approximately 2-4 issues per year). Alumni publication, magazine format, 20 p. Includes book reviews. Circulation: 3000
Free. Controlled circulation.

The Alumni bulletin *See* The Alumni journal

The Alumni journal / *edited by* John M. Gordon. - *Published by* Alumni Association. University of Manitoba. Rm 139, University Centre, University of Manitoba, Winnipeg, Man., October 1936-
Former title(s): The Alumni bulletin.
Quarterly. Alumni publication, magazine format, 24 p. Includes book reviews, advertising. Circulation: 33,000
$6.00 per year. Controlled circulation.

Alumni news, Ottawa = Bulletin des anciens, Ottawa / *edited by* Germain Mercier. - *Published by* Alumni Association. University of Ottawa. 143 Willbroad St., Ottawa, Ont. K1N 6N5, December 1950-
Quarterly. Alumni publication, newspaper format, 16 p. Language: English and French ; summaries: English and French.
Free.

The Ambassador / *edited by* Len Lizmore. - *Published by* Publications Commission. Students Administrative Council. University of Windsor. Windsor, Ont., 1939-
Annual. Alumni publication.
$6.00 (Students $5.00).

Ambassador of peace (January 1966-December 1970) *See* Young companion

Amber / *sponsored by* Scotian Pen Guild ; *edited by* Hazel Firth Goddard. - *Published by* Hazel Firth Goddard. P.O. Box 173, Dartmouth, N.S. B2Y 3Y3, January 1973-
Former title(s): Innovator; Pegasus.
Quarterly. General interest, magazine format, 24 p. Circulation: 100
$3.00 per year.

L'Ame de la communauté / *édité par* Normand Décary. - *Publié par* Centre communautaire Tour de David inc. 220, chemin des Vingt, Saint-Basile-le-Grand, Cté Verchères, Qué., avril 1972-
Trimestriel. Publication spécialisée, magazine, 16 p. Tirage: 2000
$.50 le numéro : $2.00 par année : $3.00 par année, l'étranger.

American Self Protection Association. World of ASP / *edited by* Stewart H. Fraser. - *Published by* Stewart H. Fraser. American Self-Protection Association, Inc. P.O. Box 302, Kingston, N.S. B0P 1R0, November/December 1975-
Issued every other month. Association publication, newsletter format, Includes book reviews, advertising.
ISSN 0380-4712 $2.00 per year. Controlled circulation.

American Society for Information Science. Western-Canada Chapter. Annual meeting. Proceedings - *Published by* Western-Canada Chapter. American Society for Information Science. c/o Mrs. G.A. Cooke, 8734 119th St., Edmonton, Alta. T6G 1W8, 1969-
Annual. Association publication, book format, 125 p.
Free to those attending the conference. May be purchased individually.

L'Amérique latine / *édité par* Jill Stocker. - *Publié par* Bureau canadien de l'éducation internationale. 151 rue Slater, Ottawa, Ont. K1P 5H3, 1972-
Publié en anglais: Latin America.
Paraît tous les 2-3 ans. Publication d'association, 40 p.
Envoi gratuit.

Amethyst *See* Mudcreek magazine

Amex-Canada / *edited by* Maryanne Campbell, Jack Colhoun and Dee Knight. - *Published by* Amex-Canada Enterprises. 614 Huron St., Toronto, Ont. (Subscription address: P.O. Box 189, Postal Station P, Toronto, Ont. M5S 2S7) 1969-
Irregular (approximately 9 issues per year). Special interest, magazine format, 39 p.
Indexed in Alt. press ind.
ISSN 0003-1674 $5.00 per year (Institutions $8.00): $7.50 for 2 years.

AmiSol / *edited by* Denise Soulières. - *Published by* Service mond-ami. 25 ouest, rue Jarry, Montréal, Qué. H2P 1S6, septembre 1973-
Former title(s): Jeunes de 3 et 4ième année.
Bimestriel. Publication ecclésiastique, bulletin, 16 p.
ISSN 0318-5737 $.20 le numéro : $1.00 par année. Abonnements payables à l'avance.

L'Ami de Saint-Benoît-du-Lac / *édité par* Le Secrétaire des Amis de Saint-Benoît-du-Lac. - *Publié par* Les Amis de Saint-Benoit-du Lac inc. 10631, Vianney, Montréal, Qué., mars 1962-
Publié à Noel, Päques et Fête de St-Benoît (11 juillet). Publication d'association, bulletin, 18 p. Tirage: 4000
$5.00 par année. Abonnements payables à l'avance.

L'Ami des sourds / *édité par* Joseph Paquin. - *Publié par* Jean Paquin. Institut des sourds de Montréal. 7400, boul. St-Laurent, Montréal, Qué. H2R 2Y1, mars 1908-
Ancien titre: L'Ami des sourds-muets (mars 1908-janvier 1958)
Mensuel excepté en juillet, août et Septembre. Publication d'association, bulletin, 24 p. Tirage: 850
$.25 par numéro : $2.00 par année. A raison d'échange avec autres revues plus quelques numéros en hommage.

L'Ami des sourds-muets (mars 1908-janvier 1958) *Voir* L'Ami des sourds

L'Ami du Frère André / *édité par* Bernard Lafrenière. - *Publié par* Oratoire Saint-Joseph. 3800, chemin Reine Marie, Montréal, Qué. H3V 1H6, novembre 1956-
Publié en anglais: The Friend of Brother André.
Trimestriel. Publication ecclésiastique, bulletin, 4 p.
$.50 par année.

Amigo / *édité par* Jean-Paul Labelle. - *Publié par* Service Mond-Ami. 25 ouest, rue Jarry, Montréal, Qué. H2P 1S6, septembre 1973-
Ancien titre: Jeunes de 5 et 6ième année.
Bimestriel. Bulletin, 16 p. Tirage: 83,000
ISSN 0318-5729 $.20 le numéro : $1.00 par année. Abonnements payables à l'avance.

Among the deep sea fishers / *edited by* Douglas Heath. - *Published by* The International Grenfell Association. Room 701, 88 Metcalfe St., Ottawa, Ont. K1P 5L7, April 1903-
Quarterly. Association publication, magazine format, 24 p. Includes book reviews, advertising. Circulation: 4150
$3.00 per year : 1.50 pounds, U. K.

Amphora - *Published by* The Alcuin Society. P.O. Box 94108, Richmond, B.C. V6Y 2A2, 1967-
Quarterly. Association publication, magazine format, 40 p. Circulation: 275
Indexed in Can. essay and lit. ind.
ISSN 0003-200X $2.50 per issue : $10.00 per year. Special rates offered.

Anagennesis / *edited by* Stelios Fragoulis. - *Published by* Stelios Fragoulis. 4526A Park Ave., Montreal, Que.
Weekly. Ethnic press. Language: Greek.
$.25 per issue.

Analyse de politiques *See* Canadian public policy

L'Ancêtre / *édité par* Esther Oss. - *Publié par* Société de généalogie de Québec. C.P. 2234, Québec, Qué. G1K 7N8, septembre 1974-
Mensuel excepté les mois de juillet, et août. Publication d'association, bulletin, 35 p. Tirage: 400
ISSN 0316-0513 $1.00 le numéro : $5.00 par année : $10.00 par année, l'étranger. Abonnements payables à l'avance.

The Anglican / *edited by* W.N. Turner. - *Published by* Incorporated Synod. Diocese of Toronto. Anglican Church of Canada. 135 Adelaide St. E., Toronto, Ont. M5C 1L8, Easter 1958-
Monthly except July and August. Church publication, newspaper format, 12 p. Includes book reviews, advertising. Circulation: 42,000
$.20 per issue : $2.00 per year.

Anglican Church of Canada. Anglican Church yearbook / *edited by* A.H. Davis. - *Published by* General Synod. Anglican Church of Canada. 600 Jarvis St., Toronto, Ont. M4Y 2J6, 1892-
Annual. Church publication, yearbook, 250 p. Includes advertising. Circulation: 1400
$5.50 per year. Special rates offered.

Anglican Church of Canada. General Synod. Journal of proceedings - *Published by* Anglican Church of Canada. 600 Jarvis St., Toronto, Ont. M4Y 2J6.
Annual. Church publication, journal format, 275 p. Circulation: 500
$8.00. Controlled circulation. Prepayment required.

The Anglican crusader *See* The Crusader

Animal and poultry science seminar / *edited by* Dept. of Animal Science and Dept of Poultry Science. - *Published by* Faculty of Agricultural Sciences. University of British Columbia. Vancouver, B.C. V6T 1W5.
Annual. 50 p.
Free.

Animal Defence League of Canada. News bulletin / *edited by* P.J. Hyde. - *Published by* Animal Defence League of Canada. P.O. Box 713, Ottawa, Ont., K1P 5P8., 1957-
Irregular (approximately 4-5 issues per year). Association publication, newsletter format, 8 p. Circulation: 1000
$2.00 per year.

Animal news = Nouvelles de nos animaux (octobre 1968-hiver 1973) *Voir* La Société canadienne de protection des animaux. Courrier SPCA

Animals voice / *edited by* T.I. Hughes. - *Published by* Ontario Humane Society. Suite 503, 696 Yonge St., Toronto, Ont.
Quarterly. Association publication, newspaper format, 12 p. Circulation: 35,000
Subscription included in membership fee.

Animateur - *Publié par* Chrétiens d'aujourd'hui. 8100, boul. St-Laurent, Montréal, Qué. H2P 2L9, janvier 1970-
Ancien titre: Bulletin des présidents (1966-1969) Bulletin des ligues (1936-1966) Bulletin des directeurs (1911-1917)
Mensuel. Publication d'association, bulletin, 15 p.
$3.00 par année. Abonnements payables à l'avance.

Annales canadiennes d'histoire *See* Canadian journal of history

Annales de l'association (1898-1915) *Voir* Prêtre et pasteur : revue eucharistique du clergé

Annales de Notre-Dame du Sacré-Coeur (janvier 1903-décembre 1964) *Voir* RND (Revue Notre-Dame)

Les Annales de Saint-Joseph du Mont-Royal (janvier 1912-décembre 1943) *Voir* L'Oratoire : au service de la famille chrétienne

Les Annales de Ste Anne de Beaupré *Voir* Ste Anne de Beaupré

Annales des prétres-adorateurs (1915-1937) *Voir* Prêtre et pasteur : revue eucharistique du clergé

The Annals of good St. Anne du Beaupré / *edited by* Eugene Lefebere. - *Published by* Ste Anne de Beaupre Province. The Redemptorist Order. Montmorency, Que., June 1876-
Publised in French: Ste Anne de Beaupré.
Monthly. Church publication, magazine format, 32 p. Includes book reviews.
Circulation: 76,000
$.35 per issue : $3.00 per year. Prepayment required.

Annoosch / *sponsored by* Annoosch Information Centre. - *Published by* A. Robertson. P.O. Box 130, Norway House, Man., June 1973-
ISSN 0318-5761

Annotated guide to health instruction materials in Canada / *edited by* M.E. Palko. - *Published by* Canadian Health Education Specialists Society. P.O. Box 2305, Postal Station D, Ottawa, Ont. K1P 5K0, 1972-
Annual. Association publication, bibliography, paperbound book format, 120 p. supplements issued. Circulation: 3500
$2.50. Prepayment required.

Annuaire *See* Royal Society of Canada. Calendar

Annuaire canadien de droit international *See* Canadian yearbook of international law

Annuaire de l'A.H.C.C *See* Catholic Hospital Association of Canada. C.H.A.C. annual directory

Annuaire de l'exécutif *See* Executive's directory

Annuaire des courses = Racing year book / *édité par* Albert Trottier. - *Publié par* Blue Bonnets Raceway. 7440, boul. Delarie, Montréal, Qué., 1973-
Annuel. Publication spécialisée, 60 p.
Langue(s): français et anglais.
Envoi gratuit.

Annuaire des professeurs de droit *See* Directory of law teachers

Annuaire des sociologues et anthropologues au Canada et leur recherche courante = A Directory of sociologists and anthropologists in Canada and their current research / *édité par* James E. Curtis. - *Publié par* Société canadienne de sociologie et d'anthropologie. C.P. 878, Succursale A, Montréal, Qué. H3C 2V8, 1968-
Annuel. Publication d'association, 153 p.
Langue(s): français et anglais.
$3.50.

Annual directory of chemical engineering research in Canadian universities = Compte rendu annuel de la recherche en génie chimique dans les universités canadiennes / *edited by* D.E. Seborg. - *Published by* Canadian Society for Chemical Engineering. Suite 906, 151 Slater St., Ottawa, Ont. K1P 5H3, 1961-
Annual. Directory, magazine format, 45 p.
Language: English and French.
ISSN 0070-525X $2.00 (Non-members $4.00).

Annual proceedings - International Commission for the Northwest Atlantic Fisheries *See* International Commission for the Northwest Atlantic Fisheries. Annual report

Annual report - The Ontario Cancer Treatment and Research Foundation (1945-1971) *See* Cancer in Ontario

Annual sale of yearlings and mixed stock - *Published by* British Columbia Thoroughbred Breeders' Society. 4023 East Hastings St., North Burnaby, B.C. V5C 2J1, 1952-
Annual. Association publication, 150 p.
Circulation: 2500

Annual survey of clerical employees = Enquête annuelle sur les employés de bureau / *sponsored by* Canadian Manufacturers' Association (Quebec division) : La Chambre de commerce du district de Montréal. - *Published by* Montreal Board of Trade. 6th Floor, Commerce House, 1080 Beaver Hall Hill, Montreal, Que.
Annual. Directory, 20-25 p. Language: English and French.
$3.00 (Non-members $5.00).

Annuelles (1964-1968) *Voir* Annuelles et légumes : résultats des cultures d'essai

Annuelles et légumes : résultats des cultures d'essai / *édité par* Pierre Bourque. - *Publié par* Jardin botanique de Montréal. 4101 est, rue Sherbrooke, Montréal, Qué. H1X 2B2, 1964-
Ancien titre: Annuelles (1964-1968)
Annuel. Notes sur les plantes, brochure, 90 p.
Tirage: 1200
Envoi gratuit.

The Ansul / *edited by* Alison Manzer and Jonnette Watson. - *Published by* Dalhousie Law School. Weldon, Law Building, Dalhousie University, Halifax, N.S.
Quarterly. Legal articles, magazine format, 14 p. Includes advertising. Circulation: 2300
$3.50 per year. Prepayment required.

Anthropologica - *Published by* The Canadian Research Centre for Anthropology. 223 Main St., Ottawa, Ont. K1S 1C4, 0003-5459-
Issued twice a year. 159 p.
$14.00 per year.

Anthropological journal of Canada / *edited by* Thomas E. Lee. - *Published by* Anthropological Association of Canada. 1575 Forlan Dr., Ottawa, Ont., K2C 0R8., January 1963-
Quarterly. Association publication, journal format, 36 p. Language: English (French) ; summaries: English (French). Includes book reviews, advertising, cumulative index.
Indexed in Geo. abstr., Soc. sci. cit. ind., Soc. sci. journal file.
ISSN 0003-5475 $2.00 per issue : $6.00 per year : $7.00 per year, foreign.

Antics / *edited by* Peter H. Roberts. - *Published by* Halifax Antique Car Club. P.O. Box 2302, Halifax, N.S., 1962-
Issued every other month. Association publication, newsletter format, 16-20 p. Includes advertising.
$5.00 per year.

The Antigonish review / *edited by* R.J. MacSween. - *Published by* The Public Relations Department. St. Francis Xavier University. Antigonish, N.S., Spring 1970-
Quarterly. Institutional publication (Universities, schools, etc.), magazine format, 115 p. Includes book reviews, film reviews, volume index. Circulation: 500
Indexed in Can. essay and lit. ind., M.L.A. int. bib., MLA abstr., Abstr. eng. stud.
$1.50 per issue : $5.00 per year. Special rates offered.

Antiques in Ontario : Canadian antiques year book / *edited by* Doris J. Unitt. - *Published by* Clock House Publications. P.O. Box 103, Peterborough, Ont. K9J 6Y5, 1967-
Former title(s): Collect antiques in Ontario (1967-1968)
Annual. Directory, book format, 224 p. Includes advertising. Circulation: 4000
$2.95.

Antológia: Kanadai magyar irók könyve / *edited by* John Miska. - *Published by* Canadian-Hungarian Authors' Association. 3206 South Parkside Dr., Lethbridge, Alta., 1969-
Annual. Ethnic press, journal format, 130 p. Language: Hungarian.
$4.00.

Apartment and building / *edited by* Noel Marples. - *Published by* BKN Publications Ltd. 876 Commercial Dr., Vancouver, B.C. V5L 3Y5, 1971-
Issued every other month. Trade publication, magazine format, Includes advertising.

Aperçu de l'industrie laitière : quelques données - *Publié par* Fédération canadienne des producteurs de lait. 111, rue Sparks, Ottawa, Ont. K1P 5B5.
Publié en anglais: Dairy facts and figures at a glance.
Annuel. Publication d'association.

Apostolat / *édité par* Guy Marchessault. - *Publié par* Missionnaire Oblats de Marie Immaculée. 460 - 1ère rue, Richelieu (Rouville), Qué. J3L 3W2(adresse d'abonnement: 460, 1ère rue, Richelieu, Qué. J3L 3W2) septembre 1929-
Bimestriel. Publication d'association, magazine, 28 p. Tirage: 38,500
$.50 le numéro : $3.00 par année : $3.50 par année, l'étranger.

The 'Appaloosa' (January 1968 to May 1973) *See* The Canadian Appaloosa journal

L'Appel du Sacré-Coeur / *édité par* Armand Desautels. - *Publié par* Les Pères Assomptionnistes. 1679 chemin St-Louis, Québec, Qué., juin 1949-
Mensuelle sauf février et août. Publication ecclésiastique, magazine, 16 p. Comprend critique de livres. Tirage: 11,000
$2.00 par année. Abonnements payables à l'avance.

Applegarth's folly / *edited by* Jill Jamieson, MacLean Jamieson, Michael Niederman and Hilary Bates. - *Published by* Applegarth Follies. 156 Albert St., London, Ont. N6A 1M1, January 25, 1973-
Irregular (approximately 3 issues per year). General interest, magazine format, 140 p. Includes book reviews, cumulative index.
Circulation: 800
ISSN 0316-1412 $4.00 per issue.

Appliance and home entertainment business / *edited by* Alex Watson. - *Published by* Kerrwil Publications Ltd. 30 Eglinton Ave. E., Toronto, Ont. M4P 1B6, September-October 1975-
Issued every other month. Trade publication, magazine format, Includes advertising.
$5.00 per year.

Applicants and applications to Canadian dental schools / *sponsored by* Association of Canadian Faculties of Dentistry ; *edited by* F. Chebib. - *Published by* Council on Education. Canadian Dental Association. 234 St. George St., Toronto, Ont. M5R 2P2, 1964-
Annual. Statistics, 25 p. Includes updating service.
ISSN 0315-2413 Free.

Applicator / *edited by* H.W. Near. - *Published by* The Master Insulator's Association of Ontario Inc. 1 Sparks Ave., Willowdale, Ont. M2H 2W1, January 1972-
Irregular (approximately 4 issues per year). Association publication, newsletter format, 1-2 p.
Free to association members.

Appoint / *édité par* Maryse St-Onge. - *Publié par* Réjeanne Martin. 8020, St-Dominique, Montréal, Qué. H2R 1X9, septembre 1967-
Bimestriel. Magazine, 50 p. Langue(s): française. Tirage: 1800
$5.00 par année : $6.00 par année, l'étranger.

Appraisal Institute. Directory / *edited by* W.T. O'Brien. - *Published by* Appraisal Institute of Canada. Suite 502, 177 Lombard Ave., Winnipeg, Man. R3B 0W5., June 1970-
Annual. Association publication, directory, booklet format, 72 p.
Controlled circulation.

Appraisal Institute of Canada. Appraisal Institute digest / *edited by* W.T. O'Brien. - *Published by* Appraisal Institute of Canada. Suite 302, 177 Lombard Ave., Winnipeg, Man. R3B 0W5., January 1957-
Cover title: Appraisal Institute magazine.
Quarterly. House/company organ, newsletter format, 72 p. Includes book reviews, advertising.
ISSN 0003-7079 $1.50 per issue : $5.00 per year. Controlled circulation.

The Aquarian *See* The Median

Aquarius - *Published by* Haney Correctional Center. Box 1000, Maple Ridge, B.C. V2X 7G4.
Monthly. Institutional publication, magazine format, 35 p. Includes film reviews, play reviews.
Free.

Arab - Canada newsletter / *sponsored by* League of Arab States ; *edited by* Director, Arab Information Centre. - *Published by* Arab Information Centre. Suite 709, 170 Laurier Ave. W., Ottawa, Ont. K1P 5V5, May 1971-
Monthly. Special interest, newsletter format, 4 p. Language: English and French. Includes book reviews.
Free.

Arc Arabic Journal = Le journal "ARC" arabe / *edited by* Salah Allam. - *Published by* Salah Allam. 2112 Frontenac St., Montreal, Que. H2K 2Z3 (Subscription address: P.O. Box 516, Postal Station B, Montreal, Que. H3B 3K3) June 1974-
Former title(s): ARC magazine.
Monthly. Ethnic press, newspaper format, 16 p. Language: Arabic, English and French. Includes book reviews, film reviews, play reviews, record reviews, advertising, volume index, cumulative index, updating service. supplements issued. Circulation: 15,000
$.25 per issue : $3.75 per year : $10.00 per year, foreign.

Arch notes / *edited by* Mike Kirby. - *Published by* Ontario Archaeological Society. P.O. Box 241, Postal Station P, Toronto, Ont. M5S 2S8.
Monthly. Association publication, newsletter format, 5 p. Includes book reviews.
Circulation: 350
Subscription included in membership fee.

Archaeological newsletter / *edited by* A.D. Tushingham. - *Published by* Royal Ontario Museum. 100 Queen's Park, Toronto, Ont. M5S 2C6, May 1965-
Monthly. Special interest, newsletter format, 4 p. Circulation: 2700
Free.

Archidiocèses de Sherbrooke. Annuaire - *Publié par* Archevêché de Sherbrooke. Eglise catholique. C.P. 430, 130, de la Cathédrale, Sherbrooke, Qué., 1950-
Annuel. Organe interne/officiel, 110 p. Tirage: 875
$3.00 le volume.

Architecture concept / *édité par* Helene Geoffrion. - *Publié par* Charles Shewell. Southam Business Publications Ltd. 1450 Don Mills Rd., Don Mills, Ont.(adresse d'abonnement: Architecture/Concept, Suite 201, 310, ave Victoria, Montréal, Qué) 1945-
Bimestriel. Publication spécialisée, magazine, 40 p. Comprend critique de livres, publicité.
Tirage: 3600
Indexé dans Can. ind., RADAR, Can. B.P.I.

L'architecture de paysage Canada - *Publié par* Canadian Society of Landscape Architects. P.O. Box 3304, Postal Station C, Ottawa, Ont. K1Y 4J5, août 1975-
Publié en anglais: Landscape architecture Canada.
Intermittent (approximativement 3 éditions par an). Publication d'association, 4 p.

Archival Association of Atlantic Canada. Newsletter - *Published by* Archival Association of Atlantic Canada. P.O. Box 1228, St. Stephen, N.B. E3L 1T6, December 1973-
Issued 3 times a year. Association publication, newsletter format, 50 p. Circulation: 350
$5.00 per year. Free to some institutions. Prepayment required.

Archives / *édité par* Gilles Héon. - *Publié par* Association des archivistes du Québec. C.P. 159, Haute-Ville, Québec, Qué. G1R 4P3, 1969-
Semestriel. Publication d'association, revue, 80-85 p. Tirage: 500
$2.50 le numéro : $7.00 par année. Tirage contrôlé. Abonnements payables à l'avance.

Arctic / *edited by* M.V. Hambly. - *Published by* McGill-Queen's University Press. 1020 Pine Ave. W., Montreal, Que. H3A 1P2 (Subscription address: Membership secretary, AINA, 1020 Pine Ave. W., Montreal, Que.) (Vol. 1, No. 1) 1948-
Quarterly. Association publication, journal format, 80 p. Includes book reviews, volume index. Circulation: 3500
Indexed in Can. ind., North. tit., Hist. abstr.; Amer. hist. and life, Arct. bibl., Soc. sci. journal file.
ISSN 0004-0843 Free to certain organizations on limited basis. Subscription included in membership fee. Special rates offered. Prepayment required.

Arctic and northern development digest / *edited by* N.J. Walsh. - *Published by* Canadian Century Publishers. P.O. Box 10, Victoria Station, Montreal, Que., June 1969-
Issued every other month. Special interest, magazine format, 40 p. Includes book reviews, advertising. Circulation: 6700
Indexed in North. tit.
$3.00 per year : $5.00 for 2 years : $4.00 per year, foreign : $6.50 for 2 years foreign. Controlled circulation plus subscriptions. Prepayment required.

The Arctic news / *edited by* The Bishop of the Arctic. - *Published by* Diocese of the Arctic. Anglican Church of Canada. 1055 Avenue Rd., Toronto, Ont. M5N 2C8, 1920-
Issued twice a year. Church publication, magazine format, 16 p. Circulation: 4000
Indexed in North. tit.
Free.

Argosy weekly / *edited by* Donald C. Murray. - *Published by* Mount Allison University. Sackville, N.B. E0A 3C0, 1874-
Weekly. Student publication, newspaper format, 12 p. Includes book reviews, film reviews, play reviews, record reviews, advertising. supplements issued. Circulation: 1800
$.10 per issue : $2.00 per year : $.20 per issue, foreign. Controlled circulation.

Argus / *édité par* Madeleine Balcer. - *Publié par* Corporation des bibliothècaires professionnels du Québec. 360, rue Le Moyne, Montréal, Qué. H2Y 1Y3, janvier 1972-
Bimestriel. Publication d'association, bulletin, 25 p. Langue(s): français et anglais. Comprend index de volumes. Tirage: 1000
Indexé dans Lib. lit.
ISSN 0315-9930 $2.00 le numéro : $12.00 par année : $15.00 par année, l'étranger.

Argus / *edited by* R. Wakulich and S. Stewart. - *Published by* Alma Mater Society. Lakehead University. Thunder Bay, Ont. P7B 5E1, September 1965-
Weekly. Student publication, newspaper format, 12 p. Includes book reviews, film reviews, play reviews, record reviews, advertising. Circulation: 3000
$3.50 per year : $3.50 and extra postage, foreign. Free.

The Argus *See* Ontario education

Argus-journal - *Published by* Public Service Alliance of Canada. 233 Gilmour St., Ottawa, Ont. K2P 0P1, August 1966-
Monthly. Association publication, newspaper format, 16 p. Language: French and English. Circulation: 120,000

Ariel: a review of international English literature / *edited by* George Wing. - *Published by* University of Calgary. Calgary, Alta. T2N 1N4, January 1970-
Quarterly. Magazine format, 110 p. Includes book reviews, advertising, volume index. Back numbers on request. Circulation: 1200
Indexed in Hum. ind., M.L.A. int. bib., MLA abstr.
ISSN 0004-1327 $1.50 per issue : $6.00 per year. Special rates offered to agents.

L'Armée de Marie / *édité par* Marie-Paule. - *Publié par* Armée de Marie. C.P. 95, Limoilou, Québec, Qué., septembre 1971-
Mensuel. Publication ecclésiastique, magazine, 20 p.
$2.50 le numéro : $3.00 le numéro, l'étranger ($5.00 par avion).

Arms collecting : the Canadian journal of arms collecting / *edited by* S. James Gooding. - *Published by* Museum Restoration Service. P.O. Box 2037, Postal Station D, Ottawa, Ont. K1P 5W3, February 1963-
Former title(s): The Canadian journal of arms collecting (1963-1972)
Quarterly. Special interest, magazine format, 32 p. Includes book reviews, advertising, volume index. Circulation: 1200
$1.25 per issue : $5.00 per year. Prepayment required.

Around the ring / *edited by* Bryan McGill. - *Published by* University of Victoria. P.O. Box 1700, Victoria, B.C. V8W 2Y2, February 1972-
Weekly. Institutional publication (Universities, schools, etc.), newsletter format, 4 p. Circulation: 1600
Controlled circulation.

The Arrow / *sponsored by* Geography Club ; *edited by* Brian Gallery. - *Published by* Brian O'N. Gallery. Gallery Publications Ltd. 1165 Greene Ave., Westmount, Que. H3Z 2A2.
Issued every other month. Association publication, magazine format, 12 p. Includes advertising.
$5.00 per year. Controlled circulation. Prepayment required.

Art and literary digest (1972) *See* Muskeg review

L'Art dramatique canadien *See* Canadian drama

Art Gallery of Ontario. Extension Department. Circulating exhibition catalogue / *edited by* Olive Koyama. - *Published by* Art Gallery of Ontario. Grange Park, Toronto, Ont. M5T 1G4, Fall 1975-
Annual. Catalogue, 70 p. Circulation: 650

Art magazine / *sponsored by* The Society of Canadian Artists ; *edited by* Pat Fleisher. - *Published by* Art Magazine Incorporated. Suite 19, 2498 Yonge St., Toronto, Ont. M4P 2H8, May 1969-
Former title(s): Journal - Society of Canadian Artists (November 1967-July 1968)
Quarterly. Association publication, magazine format, 72 p. Includes book reviews, film reviews, advertising, cumulative index. Back issues available in zerox. Circulation: 8000
ISSN 0004-3257 $2.00 per issue : $7.00 per year ($4.00 additional per year for first class postage).

Arthur - *Published by* Trent University. Peterborough, Ont. (Subscription address: Bata Library, Trent University, Peterborough, Ont) 1966-
Weekly during the school year. Student publication, newspaper format, 16 p.
$5.00 per year. Free.

Article of the month / *edited by* W.J. Hambly. - *Published by* Canadian Credit Institute. P.O. Box 532, Postal Station F, Toronto, Ont. M4Y 2N1.
Irregular (approximately 10 issues per year). Association publication, newsletter format, 4 p.
Available to members only.

Art-i-fact / *edited by* Anthony Hurst. - *Published by* George A. Harrison. Hamilton and Regional Arts Council. 50 Main St. W., Hamilton, Ont., 1970-
Issued every other month. Special interest, newsletter format, 8-12 p.
$2.50 per year.

Arts and sciences alumni news / *sponsored by* Arts and Science Alumni Association. University of Guelph ; *edited by* Judy Main. - *Published by* Department of Alumni Affairs and Development. University of Guelph. Level 4, University of Guelph, Guelph, Ont.
Quarterly. Alumni publication, newsletter format, 4 p. Circulation: 3500
$4.00 per year. Subscription included in membership fee.

The Arts counsellor / *edited by* Earle Frood. - *Published by* Arts Council of the Nanaimo Regional District. P.O. Box 557, Nanaimo, B.C. V9R 5L5.
Monthly. Special interest, newsletter format, 9 p. Circulation: 700
$2.00 per year.

Arts Kingston (to January 1975) *See* ARTiculator

artscanada / *sponsored by* Canada Council and Ontario Arts Council ; *edited by* Anne Trueblood Brodzky. - *Published by* Society for Art Publications. 3 Church St., Toronto, Ont. M5E 1M2, October 1943-
Former title(s): Canadian art (October 1943-October 1966) Maritime art (October 1940-June 1942)
Issued every other month. Special interest, magazine format, Includes book reviews, film reviews, play reviews, record reviews, advertising, volume index, cumulative index. available in microform. supplements issued. Back issues available. Circulation: 15,000
Indexed in Can. ind., Art ind., Arct. bibl.
ISSN 0004-4113 $3.50 per issue : $18.00 per year : $20.00 per year, foreign. Special rates offered. Prepayment required.

Asbestos producer *Voir* Le Producteur d'amiante

Asia times / *edited by* M. Safri. - *Published by* Asia Publications. Canada Centre Holdings Ltd. 1433 Bloor St. W., Toronto, Ont. M6P 3L6, 1973-
Weekly. Ethnic press. Language: Punjabi. Includes advertising.
$.50 per issue : $6.00 per year.

Aspects / *édité par* Gilles Bellavance. - *Publié par* Gilles Bellavance. C.P. 1400, Québec, Qué., mai 1974-
Semestriel. Revue, 120 p. Tirage: 1000
ISSN 0316-2249 $2.00 le numéro : $8.00 par année : $4.50 le volume : $9.00 par année, l'étranger.

Assessors review / *edited by* Kay McGillivray. - *Published by* Institute of Municipal Assessors of Ontario. 180 Yorkland Blvd., Willowdale, Ont. M2J 1R5, 1945-
Quarterly. Association publication, magazine format, 16 p. Includes volume index. Circulation: 1900
Subscription included in membership fee.

L'Association botanique du Canada. Bulletin *See* Canadian Botanical Association. Bulletin

Association canadienne contre la tuberculose et les maladies respiratoires. Bulletin *See* Canadian Tuberculosis and Respiratory Disease Association. Bulletin

Association canadienne de l'élecricité. Bulletín *See* Canadian Electrical Association. Bulletin

L'Association canadienne de normalisation. ACNOR et le consommateur / *édité par* Sally Southam. - *Publié par* Canadian Standards Association. 178 Rexdale Blvd., Rexdale, Ont., décembre 1970-
Publié en anglais: Canadian Standards Association. CSA and the consumer.
Semestriel. Publication d'association, brochure,

Association canadienne de personnel administratif universitaire. Répertoire *See* Canadian Association of University Business Officers. Directory

Association canadienne d'éducation de langue française. ACELF revue / *édité par* Louis-Albert Vachon. - *Publié par* Association canadienne des éducateurs de langue française. 338, 3 Place Jean Talon, Québec, Qué., décembre 1971-
Intermittent (approximativement 3 éditions par an). Revue, 24 p. Tirage: 2500
Indexé dans Periodex.
$1.00 le numéro : $3.00 par année.

Association canadienne d'éducation de langue française. Bulletin - *Publié par* Association canadienne d'éducation de langue française. 980, chemin St-Louis, Sillery, Qué. G1S 1C7.
Trimestriel. Publication d'association, bulletin, 8 p. Tirage: 1200

Association canadienne des bibliothèques de droit. Bulletin *See* Canadian Association of Law Libraries. Newsletter

Association canadienne des détaillants en quincaillerie. A.C.D.Q. journaliste / *édité par* H.E. Harvey. - *Publié par* Association canadienne des détaillants en quincaillerie. 290 Merton St., Toronto, Ont. M4S 1B2, juin 1966-
Publié en anglais: Canadian Retail Hardware Association. C.R.H.A. reporter.
Mensuel. Publication d'association, bulletin, 6-8 p. Tirage: 1500
Gratuit aux members. Tirage contrôlé.

Association canadienne des écoles universitaires de musique. Journal de l'association canadienne des écoles universitaires de musique / *édité par* Yves Chartier. - *Publié par* Association canadienne des écoles universitaires de musique. Département de musique, Université d'Ottawa, Ottawa, Ont. K1N 6N5, printemps 1971-
Semestriel. Publication d'association, journal, 110 p. Langue(s): français et anglais.
Comprend critique de livres. Tirage: 375
$5.00 le numéro : $7.50 par année : $5.00 le volume : $7.50 2 ans. Abonnements payables à l'avance.

Association canadienne des entraîneurs. Bulletin / *édité par* Gilles Chiasson. - *Publié par* Association canadienne des entraîneurs. 333 River Rd., Vanier, Ont. K1L 8B9, 1973-
Trimestriel. Publication d'association, 16 p. Tirage: 1500
$5.00 par année (Etudiants $3.00), $10.00 par année, l'étranger. Tarifs spéciaux disponibles.

Association canadienne des études latino-américaines. Bulletin / *édité par* Jules Dufour. - *Publié par* Association canadienne des études latino-amèricaines. Bureau 210, Burnside, 151, rue Slater, Ottawa, Ont. H1K 5H3, hiver 1969-
Trimestriel. Publication d'association, bulletin, 8-10 p. Langue(s): anglais, français et espagnol. $6.00 par année.

Association canadienne des professeurs de droit. Annuaire des professeurs de droit *See* Canadian Association of Law Teachers. Directory of law teachers

Association canadienne des professeurs d'université. Bulletin de l'A.C.P.U *See* Canadian Association of University Teachers. C.A.U.T. bulletin

Association canadienne des professeurs d'université. Guide de l'ACPU *See* Canadian Association of University Teachers. Handbook

Association canadienne des sciences de l'information. Nouvelles *See* Canadian Association for Information Science. Newsletter

Association canadienne des Slavistes. Newsletter *See* Canadian Association of Slavists. Newsletter

L'association canadienne des technologistes de laboratoire. Bulletin nouvelles *See* Canadian Society of Laboratory Technologists. News bulletin

Association canadienne du personnel administratif universitaire. Bulletin *See* Canadian Association of University Business Officers. Bulletin

Association canadienne-française de l'Ontario. ACFO-Info - *Publié par* Association canadienne-française de l'Ontario. 204 - 260, rue Dalhousie, Ottawa, Ont. K1N 7E4, septembre 1972-
Trimestriel. Publication d'association, journal, 12 p. Tirage: 12,000
ISSN 0315-1697 Envoi gratuit.

Association de bienfaisance et de retraite de la police de Montréal. Comité de préparation à la retraite / *édité par* Robert Fradet. - *Publié par* Comité de préparation à la retraite. Association de bienfaisance et de retraite de la police de Montréal. 480, rue Gilford, Montréal, Qué. H2J 1N3, juillet 1972-
Intermittent (approximativement 3-4 éditions par an). Publication spécialisée, bulletin, 4 p. ISSN 0317-9206 Envoi gratuit.

Association de la construction de Montréal. Nouvelles : sécurité - *Publié par* Association de la construction de Montréal. 4970, place de la Savane, Montréal, Qué. H4P 1Z6.
Intermittent. Publication d'association, bulletin, Tirage: 2600

Association dentaire canadienne. Conseil des gouverneurs. Délibérations - *Publié par* Association dentaire canadienne. 243, rue St. George, Toronto, Ont. M5R 2P2.
Annuel. Publication d'association, revue, 354 p.

L'Association dentaire canadienne. Journal dentaire *See* Canadian Dental Association. Dental journal

Association des architectes de la province du Québec. Bulletin / *édité par* Laurentin Lévesque. - *Publié par* L'Association des architectes de la province du Québec. 1825 ouest, boul. Dorchester, Montréal, Qué. H3H 1R4, février 1966-
Mensuel. Publication d'association, bulletin, 12 p. Langue(s): français et anglais. Tirage: 1810
ISSN 0316-9200 $9.00 par année. Tirage contrôlé. Abonnements payables à l'avance.

L'association des banquiers canadiens. ABC bulletin *See* The Canadian Bankers' Association. CBA bulletin

L'Association des bibliothécaires du Québec. Bulletin A B Q = Quebec Library Association. QLA bulletin / *édité par* Louise Lefèbvre. - *Publié par* L'Association des bibliothécaires du Québec. c/o Dawson College Library, 1001, est rue Sherbrooke, Montréal, Qué. H2L 1L3, mars 1939-
Trimestriel. Bulletin, 30 p. Langue(s): français et anglais. Comprend critique de livres. Tirage: 350
Abonnement compris avec cotisation des membres.

L'Association des biochimistes des hôpitaux du Québec. Bulletin / *édité par* Michel Pagé. - *Publié par* L'Association des biochimistes des hôpitaux du Québec. L'Hôtel-Dieu de Québec, 11 côte du Palais, Québec, Qué. G1R 2J6, 1964-
Intermittent (approximativement 3 éditions par an). Publication d'association, bulletin, 45 p.
Tirage: 500
Envoi gratuit.

Association des cartothèques canadiennes. Bulletin *See* Association of Canadian Map Libraries. Bulletin

Association des cartothèques canadiennes. Comptes rendus de la conférence annuelle *See* Association of Canadian Map Libraries. Proceedings of the annual conference

Association des collèges communautaires de Canada. Recueil d'études / *édité par* Abram G. Konrad. - *Publié par* Association des collèges communautaires du Canada. 1750 Finch Ave. E., Willowdale, Ont. M2N 5T7.
Annuel. Publication d'association, annuaire.
$5.50 par année.

Association des commissions des écoles bilingues d'Ontario. Service d'information de l'ACEBO (1969-1972) *Voir* Association française des conseils scolaires d'Ontario. Service d'information de l'AFCSO

Association des conseils des médecins et dentistes du Québec. Bulletin de l'A.C.M.D.Q / *édité par* Le Comité de rédaction. - *Publié par* Association des conseils des médecins et dentistes du Québec. 306 est, boul. St-Joseph, Montréal, Qué. H2T 1J2, février 1975-
Intermittent (approximativement 4 éditions par an). Publication d'association, bulletin, 4 p.
Langue(s): français et anglais. Tirage: 10,000 français, 2500 anglais
Envoi gratuit.

Association des enseignants francophones du Nouveau-Brunswick. Nouvelles de l'AEFNB / *édité par* Gérard Snow. - *Publié par* Association des enseignants francophones du Nouveau-Brunswick. C.P. 712, Fredericton, N.B. E3B 5B4, février 1970-
Ancien titre: Bulletin bimensuel de l'AEFNB (septembre 1971-juin 1972)
Bimensuel excepté juillet et août. Publication d'association, bulletin, 8 p. Tirage: 3300
ISSN 0316-8611 Envoi gratuit.

Association des hôpitaux catholiques du Canada. Annuaire des hôpitaux et des foyers membres *See* Catholic Hospital Association of Canada. Directory of member hospitals and homes

L'association des humanités. La Revue de l'Association des humanités *See* The Humanities Association. The Humanities Association review.

Association des infirmières catholiques du Canada. Bulletin des infirmières catholiqués du Canada - *Publié par* Association des infirmières catholiques du Canada. Suite 108, 13 ième rue, Québec, Qué. G1L 2K3, 1933-
Trimestriel. Publication d'association, bulletin, 45 p. Tirage: 3000
$3.00 par année : $3.50 par année, l'étranger.

Association des inspecteurs en santé publique du Québec. Le Journal de L'Association des inspecteurs en santé publique du Québec / *édité par* Jacques Reid. - *Publié par* Association des inspecteurs en santé publique du Québec. C.P. 39, Succursale N, Montréal, Qué. H2X 3M2, janvier 1973-
Bimestriel. Publication d'association, bulletin, 32 p. Tirage: 3000
ISSN 0315-4300 Envoi gratuit.

Association des paysagistes et pépiniéristes du Québec inc. Bulletin - *Publié par* Association des paysagistes et pépiniéristes du Québec inc. C.P. 129, Montréal, Qué. H1X 3B6, 1970-
Intermittent (approximativement 7 éditions par an). Publication d'association, bulletin, 3 p.
Langue(s): français et anglais. Tirage: 200
Envoi gratuit.

Association des pharmaciens des établissements de santé du Québec. Bulletin d'information - *Publié par* Association des pharmaciens des établissements de santé du Québec. C.P. 176, Succursale E, Montréal, Qué. H2T 3A7.
Ancien titre: Bulletin d'information officielle - Société professionelle des pharmaciens d'hôpitaux.
Intermittent (approximativement 6 éditions par an). Publication d'association, 4 p. Tirage: 325
Envoi gratuit.

Association des psychiatres du Canada. Bulletin *See* Canadian Psychiatric Association. Bulletin

L'Association des psychiatres du Canada. La Revue de L'Association des psychiatres du Canada *See* Canadian Psychiatric Association. Canadian Psychiatric Association journal

Association des religieuses enseignantes du Québec. AREQ / *édité par* Marie-Jeanne Alexandre. - *Publié par* Association des religieuses enseignantes du Québec. 2450, chemin Ste-Foy, Québec, Qué. G1V 1T2, septembre-octobre 1957-
Ancien titre: Le bulletin des instituts de religieuses enseignantes du Québec (juin 1959 - juin 1967)
Bimestriel. Publication d'association, revue, 35 p. Comprend critique de livres, critique de pièces de théâtre. parution de suppléments. Tirage: 1500
ISSN 0318-6261 $.50 le numéro : $3.00 par année. Abonnements payables à l'avance.

Association des religieuses enseignantes du Québec. AREQ informations / *édité par* Marie-Jeanne Alexandre. - *Publié par* Association des religieuses enseignantes du Québec. 2450, chemin Ste-foy, Québec, Qué. G1V 1T2, décembre 1975-
Intermittent (approximativement 3-4 éditions par an). Publication d'association, bulletin, 3 p. Tirage: 1500
ISSN 0318-6393 Envoi gratuit pour les membres mais non pour l'association qui paye les frais de poste.

Association des rencontres culturelles avec les détenus. Information-ARCAD / *édité par* Marie-Claude Moisan. - *Publié par* Association des rencontres culturelles avec détenus. 750, croissant Frontenac, Duvernay, Laval, Qué. H7G 4N5, mai 1973-
Trimestriel. Publication d'association, journal, 8 p. Tirage: 5500
Envoi gratuit.

Association des routes et transports du Canada. Nouvelles de l'ARTA / *édité par* Gilbert Morier. - *Publié par* Association des routes et transports du Canada. 1765, boul. St. Laurent, Ottawa, Ont. K1G 3V4, janvier 1975-
Ancien titre: Soit la route; Sur nos travaux.
Publié en anglais: Roads and Transportation Association of Canada. RTAC news l'ARTA.
Intermittent (approximativement 10 éditions par an). Publication d'association, bulletin, 8 p. Comprend critique de livres. Tirage: 350
ISSN 0317-2422 Tirage contrôlé.

L'association des services aux étudiants des collèges et universités du Canada. Le Bulletin *See* Canadian Association of College and University Student Services. The Bulletin

L'Association des universités partiellement ou entièrement de langue française. Bulletin de nouvelles brèves / *édité par* Jean-Marc Leger. - *Publié par* Association des universités partiellement ou entièrement de langue française. Université de Montréal, B.P. 6128, Montréal, Qué. H3C 3J7, 1966-
Bimensuel. Publication d'association, bulletin, 10 p. Tirage: 2500
ISSN 0007-4373 $7.00 par année.

Association des universités partiellement ou entièrement de langue française. AUPELF cahiers - *Publié par* Association des universités partiellement ou entièrement de langue française. Université de Montréal, B.P. 6128, Montréal, Qué. H3C 3J7, 1965-
Annuel. Publication d'association, magazine, 300 p. Tirage: 3000
$10.00 le numéro.

Association des universités partiellement ou entièrement de langue française. AUPELF revue - *Publié par* Association des universités partiellement ou entièrement de langue française. Université de Montréal, B.P. 6128, Montréal, Qué. H3C 3J7, 1963-
Semestriel. Publication d'association, 500 p. parution de suppléments. Tirage: 4000
$4.00 le numéro : $12.00 par année.

Association des universités partiellement ou entièrement de langue française. AUPELF assemblée générale, compte rendu de la conférence triennale / *édité par* Jean-Marc Leger. - *Publié par* Association des universités partiellement ou entièrement de langue française. Université de Montréal, B.P. 6128, Montréal, Qué. H3C 3J7, 1963-
Triennal. Publication d'association, 500 p. Tirage: 1000

Association des universités partiellement ou entièrement de langue française. Séminaire / *edited by* Jean Marc Léger. - *Published by* Association des universités partiellement ou entièrement de langue française. Université de Montréal, C.P. 6128, Montréal, Qué. H3C 3J7, 1972-
Annuel. Publication d'association, magazine, 400 p. Tirage: 3000
$5.00.

L'Association des universities et colleges du Canada. Bibliographie sur l'enseignement supérieur - *Publié par* L'Association des universités et colleges du Canada. 151, rue Slater, Ottawa, Ont. K1P 5N1, 1961-
Trimestriel. Publication d'association, bibliographie, 14 p. Langue(s): français et anglais. Tirage: 100
ISSN 0049-0091 $1.00 le numéro : $4.00 par année. Abonnements payables à l'avance.

Association des universities et colleges du Canada. Délibérations de l'assemblée annuelle *See* Association of Universities and Colleges of Canada. Proceedings of the annual meeting

L'Association féminine d'education et d'action sociale. Revue mensuelle L'A.F.E.A.S *- Publié par* Association féminine d'education et d'action sociale. 515, ave Viger, Montréal, Qué., septembre 1966-
Mensuel. Publication d'association, bulletin, 24 p.
$.35 le numéro : $3.50 par année.

Association for Native Development in the Performing and Visual Arts. Newsletter / *edited by* Gertrude Squire. *- Published by* Association for Native Development in the Performing and Visual Arts. Suite 400, 30 Bloor St. W., Toronto, Ont. M4W 1A2, 1974-
Issued every other month. Association publication, newsletter format, 4 p. Includes play reviews, record reviews. Circulation: 2500
ISSN 0316-8409 Free.

Association for Preservation Technology. APT bulletin / *edited by* E.A. Wylie (Canada) and Lee Wilson (U.S.). *- Published by* Association for Preservation Technology. P.O. Box 2487, Postal Station D, Ottawa, Ont. K1P 5W6, 1968-
Irregular (approximately 4 issues per year). Special interest, magazine format, 125 p. Language: English and French ; summaries: English and French. Includes book reviews. Circulation: 800
$15.00 per year.

Association for Preservation Technology. Communique = Association pour la préservation et ses techniques. Communiqué / *edited by* Martin Eli Weil and Jacques Hebert. *- Published by* Association for Preservation Technology. P.O. Box 2487, Postal Station D, Ottawa, Ont. K1P 5W6, October 1972-
Issued every other month. Association publication, newsletter format, 12 p. Language: English and French. Circulation: 1000
$15.00 per year.

Association for Public Broadcasting in British Columbia. Newsletter / *edited by* Herschel Hardin. *- Published by* Association for Public Broadcasting in British Columbia. P.O. Box 48596, Postal Station H, Vancouver, B.C. V7X 1A3.
Quarterly. Association publication, newsletter format, 3-6 p.
$3.00 per year.

Association for Retarded Children of B.C. newsletter (January 1969-July 1969) *See* The B.C. mental retardation advisor

Association forestière canadienne. Le courrier A.F.C *See* Canadian Forestry Association. C.F.A. news

Association française des conseils scolaires d'Ontario. Service d'information de l'AFCSO *- Publié par* Association françaises des conseils scholaires d'Ontario. 260, rue Dalhousie, Ottawa, Ont., avril 1972-
Ancien titre: Association des commissions des écoles bilingues d'Ontario. Service d'information de l'ACEBO (1969-1972)
Publication d'association.
ISSN 0319-0897

Association internationale des presses universitaires de langue francaise. AIPULF information *- Publié par* Association internationale des presses universitaires de langue francaise. C.P. 6128, Université de Montréal, Montréal, Qué. H3C 3J7, février 1974-
Intermittent. Publication d'association, bulletin, 40 p.
$2.00 le numéro.

Association mathématique du Québec. Bulletin / *édité par* Jean-Berchmans Veilleux. *- Publié par* Association mathématique du Québec. 1415 est, rue Jarry, Montréal, Qué., décembre 1975-
Intermittent (approximativement 5 éditions par an). Publication d'association, bulletin, 64 p. Comprend publicité. Tirage: 1000
$1.50 le numéro : $7.50 par année.
Abonnements payables à l'avance.

L'Association nationale des camionneurs artisans inc. : La Voix de l'ANCAI / *parrainé par* L'Association nationale des camionneurs artisans inc ; *édité par* Danielle Tellier. *- Publié par* Les Publications L & L, inc. 1330, Marier, Drummondville, Qué. J2C 3B4, avril 1973-
Ancien titre: La Voix (avril 1971-février 1973)
Mensuel. Publication d'association, magazine, 48 p. Comprend publicité. Tirage: 4577
ISSN 0317-2937

Association nationale des employés et techniciens en radio diffusion. Nouvelles NABET *See* National Association of Broadcast Employees and Technicians. Canadian Office. NABET news

Association of B.C. Professional Foresters. Annual meeting *- Published by* Association of British Columbia Foresters. 4580 W. 10th Ave., Vancouver, B.C.
Annual. Association publication proceedings of the annual meeting, pamphlet format, 25 p.

Association of Canadian Community Colleges. Yearbook / *edited by* Abram G. Konrad. - *Published by* Association of Canadian Community Colleges. 1750 Finch Ave. E., Willowdale, Ont. M2N 5T7.
Annual. Yearbook, assocation publication.
$5.50.

The Association of Canadian Faculties of Dentistry. Newsletter / *edited by* G.H. Sperber. - *Published by* The Association of Canadian Faculties of Dentistry. Room 3042, Dentistry-Pharmacy Centre, University of Alberta, Edmonton, Alta. T6G 2H7, 1969-
Quarterly. Association publication, newsletter format, 16 p. Circulation: 700
Free to Canadian dental faculty members.

Association of Canadian Fire Marshals and Fire Commissioners. Proceedings / *edited by* Austin Bridges. - *Published by* Association of Canadian Fire Marshals and Fire Commissioners. Department of Public Works, Ottawa, 1925-
Annual. Association publication, 150 p.
Free.

Association of Canadian Map Libraries. Bulletin = Association des cartothèques canadiennes. Bulletin - *Published by* Association of Canadian Map Libraries. c/o National Map Collection, Public Archives of Canada, 395 Wellington St., Ottawa, Ont. K1A 0N3., 1968-
Former title(s): Newsletter - Association of Canadian Map Libraries.
Irregular. Association publication, newsletter format, 35 p. Language: English and French. Includes book reviews.
Free. Available to members only. Controlled circulation.

Association of Canadian Map Libraries. Proceedings of the annual conference = Association des cartothèques canadiennes. Comptes rendus de la conférence annuelle - *Published by* Association of Canadian Map Libraries. National Map Collection, Public Archives of Canada, 395 Wellington St., Ottawa, Ont. K1A 0N3., 1967-
Annual. Association publication, 130 p. Language: English and French. Circulation: 250
ISSN 0066-9474 $5.00.

Association of Canadian Medical Colleges. ACMC/AFMC forum - *Published by* Association of Canadian Medical Colleges. 151 Slater St., Ottawa, Ont. K1P 5H3, March-April 1974-
Former title(s): ACMC - AFMC newsletter (October 1963 - January-February 1974)
Issued every other month. Association publication, newsletter format, 20 p. Language: English and French.
ISSN 0317-5006 Free.

Association of Canadian Schools of Business. Conference proceedings *See* Canadian Association of Administrative Sciences. Conference proceedings

Association of Canadian Underwater Councils. ACUC "1" - *Published by* National Sport and Recreation Centre. 333 River Rd., Vanier, Ont. K1L 8B9, 1960-1970 ; 1973-
Irregular (approximately 6-8 issues per year). Association publication, newsletter format, 25 p. Language: English (French). Circulation: 600
Free to instructors upon written request. Controlled circulation.

The Association of Faculties of Pharmacy. Proceedings of the annual meeting - *Published by* The Association of Faculties of Pharmacy. Faculty of Pharmaceutical Sciences, University of British Columbia, Vancouver, B.C., 1970-
Former title(s): Canadian Conference of Pharmaceutical Faculties proceedings (1944-1969)
Annual. Institutional publication (Universities, schools, etc.), Book format, Language: English (French).
Free in very limited numbers. Controlled circulation.

Association of Polish Engineers in Canada. Bulletin / *edited by* S. Morawski. - *Published by* Association of Polish Engineers in Canada. 269 Windy Oaks Dr., Mississauga, Ont. L5G 1Z8 (Subscription address: Association of Polish Engineers, Toronto Branch, 206 Beverley St., Toronto, Ont. M5T 1Z3) January 1944-
Former title(s): Polish engineering review (1944-1948)
Irregular (approximately 4 issues per year). Association publication, newsletter format, 6 p. Language: Polish. Includes book reviews. Circulation: 500
Free to members only.

Association of Psychologists of the Province of New Brunswick. Journal of The Association of Psychologists of the Province of New Brunswick / *sponsored by* Association of Psychologists of the Province of New Brunswick ; *edited by* André Boudreau. - *Published by* André Boudreau. P.O. Box 275, Caraquet, N.B. E0B 1K0, October 1975-
Former title(s): Bulletin of the New Brunswick Psychological Association.
Irregular (approximately 1-2 issues per year). Association publication, magazine format, 36 p. Language: English and French ; summaries: English and French. Includes advertising. Circulation: 200
$2.00 per issue. Prepayment required.

Association of Registered Nurses of Newfoundland. News bulletin - *Published by* Association of Registered Nurses of Newfoundland. P.O. Box 4185, St. John's, Nfld. A1C 6A1.
Irregular (approximately 5 issues per year). Association publication, newsletter format, 6 p. Controlled circulation.

Association of Registered Professional Foresters of New Brunswick. Papers and reports - *Published by* Association of Registered Professional Foresters of New Brunswick. P.O. Box 23, Fredericton, N.B. E3B 4Y2, 1937-
Annual. Association publication, mimeographed, 30 p.
Controlled circulation.

Association of Superintendents of Insurance of the Provinces of Canada. Conference. Minutes of Proceedings - *Published by* The Office of the Secretary. The Association of Superintendents of Insurance of the Provinces of Canada. 6th floor, 555 Yonge St., Toronto, Ont. M4Y 1Y7.
Annual. Association publication.

Association of Teachers of English of Nova Scotia. Newsletter / *edited by* Linda M. Gorman. - *Published by* Nova Scotia Teachers Union. P.O. Box 1060, Armdale, Halifax, N.S.
Issued every other month. Association publication, newsletter format, 8 p. Includes book reviews.
Controlled circulation.

Association of Teachers of Exceptional Children / *sponsored by* Association of Teachers of Exceptional Children ; *edited by* Fred Atkinson. - *Published by* Nova Scotia Teachers Union. 106 Dutch Village Rd., Halifax, N.S. B3L 4G1.
Irregular (approximately 3 issues per year). Association publication, magazine format, 30 p. Includes book reviews.
Subscription included in membership fee $5.00 per year.

Association of Translators and Interpreters of Ontario. Inform-ATIO - *Published by* Association of Translators and Interpreters of Ontario. 298 Elgin St., Ottawa, Ont. K2P 1M3.
Irregular (approximately 8 issues per year). Association publication, newsletter format, 4-6 p. Language: English and French. Includes book reviews, advertising. Circulation: 500
$5.00 per year.

Association of Universities and Colleges of Canada. Proceedings of the annual meeting = Association des universities et colleges du Canada. Délibérations de l'assemblée annuelle / *edited by* Joan Rondeau. - *Published by* Association of Universities and Colleges of Canada. 151 Slater St., Ottawa, Ont. K1P 5H3.
Annual. Association publication, proceedings of the annual meeting, magazine format, Language: English and French. Circulation: 700
ISSN 0066-9725 $2.00. Controlled circulation. Prepayment required.

Association pour la préservation et ses techniques. Communiqué *See* Association for Preservation Technology. Communique

Association pour l'analyse et la modification du comportement. Bulletin - *Publié par* Service de psychologie. Hôpital St-Jean-de-Dieu. Montréal-Gamelin, Montréal, Qué. H1N 1Z0.
Publication d'association, bulletin,

Association pour l'avancement des sciences et des techniques de la documentation. ASTED nouvelles / *édité par* Denis Rousseau. - *Publié par* Association pour l'avancement des sciences et des techniques de la documentation. 360, rue LeMoyne, Montréal Qué. H2Y 1Y3, 1965-
Ancien titre: ACBLF (1965-1973)
Bimestriel. Bulletin, 32 p. Comprend critique de livres. Tirage: 1200
ISSN 0316-0963 Envoi gratuit aux membres.

L'Association pour l'éducation permanente dans les universités du Canada. Bulletin *See* Canadian Association for University Continuing Education. Bulletin

L'Assurance vie et le fisc - *Publié par* Association des assureurs-vie du Canada. 41 Lesmill Rd., Don Mills, Ont. M3B 2T3, 1959-
Publié en anglais: Life insurance and taxation.
Annuel. Publication spécialisée, livre, 250 p.
$8.50.

Assurances - *Publié par* Gérard Perizeau ltée. 410, rue St-Nicolas, Montréal, Qué. H2Y 2R1, avril 1938-
Trimestriel. Revue d'entreprise, revue, 120 p.
Comprend critique de livres. Tirage: 1000
$1.25 le numéro : $4.00 par année.

Les assurances I.A.R.D. du Canada / *édité par* La section de Toronto de la Société des "fellows". - *Publié par* Bureau d'assurance du Canada. 170 University Ave., Toronto, Ont. M5H 3B3.
Publié en anglais: Facts of the general insurance industry in Canada.
Annuel. Publication spécialisée, booklet format, 36 p.
Envoi gratuit.

L'Assureur-vie du Québec = The Quebec life underwriter / *édité par* Gilbert J. Mullie. - *Publié par* Association provinciale des assureurs-vie du Québec. Suite M-41, 1455, rue Peel, Montréal, Qué., mars 1975-
Ancien titre: Le Trait d'union (avril 1971 - décembre 1974)
Intermittent (approximativement 5 éditions par an). Publication d'association, magazine, 24 p.
Langue(s): français et anglais. Tirage: 5200
Envoi gratuit. Tirage contrôlé.

Asta-Canada notes / *edited by* E.S. Bryant. - *Published by* American Society of Travel Agents, Inc. - Canada (ASTA-CANADA). Suite 306, 116 Albert St., Ottawa, Ont. K1P 5G3, January 1971-
Irregular (approximately 14 issues per year).
Association publication, newsletter format, 2 p.
Free.

Asticou / *édité par* M. Mario Pelletier. - *Publié par* La Société historique de l'ouest du Québec. C.P. 7, Hull, Qué., juin 1968-
Intermittent (approximativement 2 éditions par an). Publication d'association, magazine, 40 p.
Comprend critique de livres. Tirage: 1000
Indexé dans RADAR, Hist. abstr.; Amer. hist. and life.
$2.00 le numéro : $5.00 par année : $2.50 par année. Abonnements payables à l'avance.

Astrolabe / *edited by* C. Wilson. - *Published by* The Navy League of Canada. Suite 910, 85 Range Rd., Ottawa, Ont. K1N 8J6, September 1971-
Irregular (approximately 4 issues per year).
Association publication, newsletter format, 4 p.
Language: English and French. Circulation: 15,000

At Guelph - *Published by* Department of Information. University of Guelph. Guelph, Ont. N1G 2W1, 1969-
Irregular (approximately 4-6 issues per year).
Alumni news, newsletter format, 4 p.
Free.

The Athenaeum - *Published by* Student's Union. Acadia University. Wolfville, N.S. (Subscription address: The Athenaeum, P.O. Box 698, Wolfville, N.S)
Weekly September-April. Student publication, newspaper format, 14 p. Circulation: 3000
$3.50 per year.

Athletica : Canadian track and field magazine / *edited by* David Lach. - *Published by* Athlete's Foot Publishers. P.O. Box 4981, Vancouver, B.C. V6B 4A6, April 1974-
Monthly. Special interest, magazine format, 24 p. Language: English and French. Includes book reviews, advertising. Circulation: 2250
$.75 per issue : $8.50 per year.

The Atlantic advocate / *edited by* J.D. Morrison. - *Published by* University Press of New Brunswick. 49 Phoenix Sq., Fredericton, N.B.
Monthly. General interest, magazine format, 60-80 p. Includes book reviews, volume index.
Circulation: 20,000
Indexed in Can. ind.
$.75 per issue : $6.50 per year. Special rates offered.

Atlantic Baptist / *edited by* George E. Simpson. - *Published by* The Board of Publications. United Baptists Convention of the Atlantic Provinces. P.O. Box 756, Kentville, N.S. B4N 3X9, 1827-
Former title(s): Maritime Baptist.
Monthly. Church publication, newsletter and magazine format, 16 p. Extra editions published. Circulation: 8000
ISSN 0004-6752 $.20 per issue : $3.00 per year : $18.00 per volume. Prepayment required.

Atlantic Canada Economics Association. ACEA papers / *edited by* George J. De Benedetti. - *Published by* Atlantic Canada Economics Association. c/o Dept. of Economics, Mount Allison University, Sackville, N.B. E0A 3C0, 1972-
Annual. Association publication, mimeographed format, 200 p. Circulation: 150
$10.00.

The Atlantic economy : annual review - *Published by* Atlantic Provinces Economic Council. 1 Sackville Place, Halifax, N.S. B3J 1K1, 1967-
Annual. Special interest, journal format, 80-100 p. Circulation: 2000
Controlled circulation.

The Atlantic hosteller / *edited by* Brian Ferguson. - *Published by* Maritime Region. Canadian Youth Hostels Association. 6405 Quinpool Rd., Halifax, N.S., 1950 (?)-
Issued every other month. Association publication, newsletter format, 10 p. Includes advertising. Circulation: 2000
Free to members.

The Atlantic Provinces book review / *edited by* John H. Battye. - *Published by* Saint Mary's University. Halifax, N.S. B3H 3C3, November 1974-
Quarterly. Book reviews, newspaper format, 4 p. Includes book reviews. Circulation: 5000
Free.

Atlantic Provinces Economic Council. APEC newsletter - *Published by* Atlantic Provinces Economic Council. 1 Sackville Place, Halifax, N.S. B3J 1C1, 1958-
Monthly. Special interest, newsletter format, 4 p. available in microform. Circulation: 3000
Indexed in Can. B.P.I.
Controlled circulation.

Atlantic Provinces Inter-University Committee on the Sciences. A.P.I.C.S. newsletter / *edited by* John E. Cary. - *Published by* Atlantic Provinces Inter-University Committee on the Sciences. Suite 500, Duke Tower, Scotia Sq., Halifax, N.S., 1962-
Irregular (approximately 4 issues per year). Newsletter format, 20 p. Circulation: 1100
Free.

Atlantic Provinces Library Association. APLA bulletin - *Published by* Atlantic Provinces Library Association. c/o Dalhousie School of Library Service, Dalhousie University, Halifax, N.S., 1936-
Former title(s): MLA bulletin (1936-1958)
Quarterly. Association publication, magazine format, 28 p. Language: English and French. Includes advertising, volume index, cumulative index. available in microform. Circulation: 600
Indexed in Lib. info. sci. abstr., Can. ind., Lib. lit.
$2.50 per issue : $8.50 per year. Subscription included in membership fee. Prepayment required.

Atlantic Provinces Numismatic Association. Newsletter / *edited by* Vince Mitchell. - *Published by* Atlantic Provinces Numismatic Association. 1635 Edward St., Halifax, N.S. B3H 3H9, May 1965-
Monthly. Association publication, newsletter format, 4 p.
$3.00 per year. Prepayment required.

Atlantic Provinces statistical review - *Published by* Atlantic Provinces Economic Council. 1 Sackville Place, Halifax, N.S. B3J 1K1.
Issued twice a year. Special interest, looseleaf format, 45 p. Includes volume index.

Atlantic report: an analysis of current economic conditions and trends - *Published by* Atlantic Provinces Economic Council. 1 Sackville Place, Halifax, N.S. B3J 1K1, January 1966-
Quarterly. Special interest, magazine format, 12 p. Circulation: 1500
Indexed in Can. B.P.I.
ISSN 0004-6841 Controlled circulation.

Atlantic salmon journal / *edited by* Winnifred Wright. - *Published by* Atlantic Salmon Association. 1405 Peel St., Montreal, Que. H3A 1S5, 1952-
Association publication, journal format, 36 p. Language: English (French). Includes book reviews, advertising. supplements issued. Circulation: 3000
$25.00 per year (Libraries $15.00). Subscription included in membership fee.

The Atlantic shepherd / *edited by* Gloria Logan. - *Published by* Atlantic Region German Shepherd Dog Club. c/o Alison Maitland, RR 4, Armdale, Halifax, N.S. (Subscription address: Mrs. Paul Mueller, 29 Guildwood Cres., Halifax, N.S.) 1966-
Issued every other month. Association publication, magazine format, 20 p.
$1.00 per issue : $3.00 per year. Controlled circulation. Prepayment required.

Atlantic truck transport review / *edited by* Charles R. Allen. - *Published by* Atlantic Provinces Trucking Association. P.O. Box 480, Hartland, N.B., January 1956-
Former title(s): Maritime truck transport review.
Monthly. Association publication, magazine format, 20 p.
$.50 per issue : $5.00 per year.

The Atlantic year book - *Published by* Atlantic Year Book. Gleaner Building, Fredericton, N.B.
Annual. Yearbook, book format,
$6.50.

Atlas steel news (to Spring 1975) *See* Atlas today

Atlas today / *edited by* C. Ohlson. - *Published by* Atlas Steels. Centre St., Welland, Ont.
Former title(s): Atlas steel news (to Spring 1975)
Quarterly. House/company organ, newsletter format, 4-6 p. Includes advertising, updating service.
Free. Controlled circulation.

Atmosphere / *sponsored by* Canadian Meteorological Society ; *edited by* I.D. Rutherford. - *Published by* University of Toronto Press. 5201 Dufferin St., Downsview Ont. M3H 5T8, 1963-
Quarterly. Association publication, magazine format, 40 p. Language: English and French ; summaries: English and French. Includes book reviews, volume index. Extra edition entitled Annual congress published every year. Circulation: 950
Indexed in Metero. and geoastrophys. abstr., North. tit.
$4.00 per issue : $20.00 per year (Institutions $15.00). Prepayment required.

Attitude toward leisure - *Published by* SIRLS. Faculty of Human Kinetics and Leisure Studies. University of Waterloo. Waterloo, Ont. N2L 3G1.
Quarterly. Bibliography, computer printout, $20.00 per year. $100.00 subscription to SIRLS required.

Attitude toward sport and physical activity - *Published by* SIRLS. Faculty of Human Kinetics and Leisure Studies. University of Waterloo. Waterloo, Ont. N2L 3G1.
Quarterly. Bibliography, computer printout, $20.00 per year. $100.00 subscription to SIRLS required.

Au fil des événements / *édité par* Michel Chauveau. - *Publié par* Service des relations publiques. Université Laval. Québec, Qué. G1K 7P4, février 1966-
Hebdomadaire durant l'année académique. Publication d'institution (universités, écoles..), journal, 16 p. Comprend critique de films, critique de pièces de théâtre. Tirage: 19,000
Envoi gratuit.

Au rythme de notre église / *édité par* Gilles Roy. - *Publié par* Gilles Roy. Diocèse de St-Jean. Eglise catholique. C.P. 40, 740, boul. Ste-Foy, Longueuil, Qué., octobre 1970-
Bimestriel. Publication ecclésiastique, bulletin, 4 p. Tirage: 2750
$3.00 par année.

L'Aubelle - *Publié par* L'Ordre des ingénieurs forestiers du Québec. 1415, chemin Ste-Foy, Québec, Qué. G1S 2N7, septembre 1973-
Ancien titre: La Chronique (février 1946-mai 1973)
Intermittent (approximativement 4 éditions par an). Organe interne/officiel, bulletin, 40 p.
ISSN 0316-3733

The Auctioneer / *edited by* Lorne Stout. - *Published by* Auctioneers Association of Alberta. 1306 - 15th St. N.W., Calgary, Alta. T2N 2B6, 1935-
Monthly. House/company organ, magazine format, 32 p. Includes advertising. Circulation: 475
$4.00 per year. Free to members. Controlled circulation. Prepayment required.

The Auctioneer / *sponsored by* Ward-Price, Ltd ; *edited by* June V. Ardiel. - *Published by* College Grenville Ltd. 28 College St., Toronto, Ont., January 1959-
Monthly. House/company organ, newsletter format, 8 p. Includes advertising. Circulation: 21,000
$2.00 per year. Controlled circulation.

The Audio retailer / *edited by* Ernie Weiling. - *Published by* Maclean-Hunter Ltd. 481 University Ave., Toronto, Ont. M5W 1A7, 1973-
Quarterly. Trade publication, magazine format, Includes advertising.
ISSN 0318-0085 $2.00 per issue : $7.00 per year : $11.00 for 2 years : $16.00 for 3 years : $10.00, U.S. and U.K. : $15.00, foreign.

Audio Scene Canada / *edited by* E.A. Weiling. - *Published by* Maclean-Hunter Ltd. 481 University Ave., Toronto, Ont. M5W 1A7, 1964-
Former title(s): Electron ISSN 0013-4759 (February 1964-January 1974)
Monthly. Trade publication, magazine format, Includes advertising.
ISSN 0315-1182 $8.00 per year : $10.00 per year, U.S. and U.K. : $12.00 per year, foreign. Special rates offered.

Audio scene Canada / *edited by* E.A. Welling. - *Published by* E.A. Welling. Maclean-Hunter Ltd. 481 University Ave., Toronto, Ont. M5W 1A7, 1964-
Former title(s): Electron magazine (1964-1974)
Monthly. Trade publication, magazine format, 64 p. Includes book reviews, record reviews, advertising. Circulation: 17,254
$.75 per issue : $8.00 per year : $10.00 per year, U.S. and U.K. : $12.00 per year, foreign.

L'Aujoudhui l'église *Voir* Service de préparation à la vie. Bulletin S.P.V.

Australian news weekly round-up - *Published by* Australian High Commission. 90 Sparks St., Ottawa, Ont. K1P 5B4.
Weekly. House/company organ, newsletter format, 2 p.

Autoclub / *edited by* Andre Gaudet. - *Published by* Quebec Automobile Club. P.O. Box 5600, 871 St. Louis Rd., Quebec, Que. G1K 7T2, 1922-
Quarterly. Trade publication, magazine format, Includes advertising.

Autoclub : le journal de l'automobiliste du Québec - *Publié par* Club automobile du Québec. 871, chemin St-Louis, Québec, Qué. G1K 7T2, juin 1939-
Ancien titre: Service (mars 1928-juin 1939) Revue - Québec Automobile Club = Magazine - Quebec Automobile Club (janvier 1924-mars 1928)
Trimestriel. Publication d'association, magazine, 24 p. Comprend publicité, Mises à jour. Tirage: 56,000
ISSN 0005-0954 Distribué gratuitement aux membres du Club automobile du Québec seulement.

Automatic control theory and applications / *edited by* M.H. Hamza. - *Published by* ACTA Press. P.O. Box 3243, Postal Station B, Calgary, Alta. T2M 4L8, January 1972-
Irregular (approximately 3 issues per year). Special interest, journal format, 24 p. Language: English and French. Includes book reviews, advertising, volume index, cumulative index. Circulation: 500-600
Indexed in Math. r.
ISSN 0315-8934 $10.00 per issue : $28.50 per year.

L'automobile / *édité par* L. Dionne. - *Publié par* French Commercial Publications Division. Publications Wadham Ltd. Suite 3, 5020 de Salaberry, Montréal, Qué., 1939-
Mensuel. Magazine,
$.75 le numéro : $8.00 par année.

Automobile insurance experience - *Published by* Insurance Bureau of Canada. 170 University Ave., Toronto, Ont. M5H 3B3 (Subscription address: 853 York Mills Rd., Don Mills, Ont. M3B 1Y2)
Annual. Trade publication, book format, 200 p. Language: English (French).
ISSN 0317-7815 $10.00 per issue. Controlled circulation.

Automotifs / *édité par* Gary Schlee. - *Publié par* Gulf Oil Canada Ltd. 800 Bay St., Toronto, Ont. M5S 1Y8(adresse d'abonnement: P.O. Box 460, Postal Station A, Toronto, Ont. M5W 1E5)
Publié en anglais: Gulf Canada cartalk.
Intermittent. Organe interne/officiel, bulletin, 4-8 p. Comprend index cumulatif.
Tirage contrôlé.

Automotive, petroleum and TBA marketer (1960-1971) *See* Automotive mass marketer

Automotive Christian / *edited by* Esther F. Fuller. - *Published by* Christian Transportation Inc. 512 Yonge St. (rear), Toronto, Ont. M4Y 1X9, April 1971-
Quarterly. Church publication.

Automotive mass marketer / *edited by* Joe Holliday. - *Published by* Wadham Publications Ltd. Suite 101, 109 Vanderhoof Ave., Toronto, Ont. M4G 2J2, 1960-
Former title(s): Automotive, petroleum and TBA marketer (1960-1971)
Issued twice a year. Trade publication, magazine format, 60 p. Circulation: 5000
$4.00 per issue : $8.00 per year : $6.00 per issue, foreign. Free to the trade. Controlled circulation.

Autosport Canada / *sponsored by* Canadian Automobile Sport Clubs ; *edited by* Doug Mepham. - *Published by* Wheelspin News Inc. 3057 Universal Dr., Mississauga, Ont., L4X 2E2.
Former title(s): Canadian motorsport bulletin.
Monthly. Special interest, magazine format, 40 p. Language: English and French. Includes book reviews, advertising.
$.60 per issue : $6.00 per year.

Aux amis du Père Prévost / *édité par* Valère St-Pierre. - *Publié par* Cause Père Prevost, Pères de la fraternité sacerdotale. C.P. 150, Pointe au Lac, Qué., décembre 1951-
Ancien titre: Le Père Eugène Prévost.
Bimestriel. Publication ecclésiastique, bulletin, 20 p.
$.15 le numéro : $1.00 par année : $1.50 par année, l'étranger.

Avec 'lui' / *édité par* Raoul Dagnon. - *Publié par* Mouvement eucharistique du Canada. 116 ouest, rue Notre Dame, Montréal, Qué. H2Y 1T2, 1972-
Ancien titre: Veillée d'armes.
Bimestriel. Publication ecclésiastique, journal, 8 p. Tirage: 6000
$.30 le numéro : $2.00 par année.

L'Aviculteur québécois / *édité par* Gerard Vincent. - *Publié par* Les Couvoiriers de Québec, inc. C.P. 217, Beloeil, Qué., 1946-
Mensuel.
$3.00 par année.

Avicultural journal / *sponsored by* National Aviculture Association of Canada ; *edited by* June Clough and Doreen Albion (assistant editor). - *Published by* Doreen Albion. 3631 Cedar Hill Rd., Victoria, B.C. V8P 3Z3, May 1975-
Issued every other month. Association publication, magazine format, 24 p. Circulation: 172
ISSN 0317-5650 $1.25 per issue : $1.40 issue per year, foreign. Subscription included in membership fee.

Awards for residential design / *edited by* R.W. Harvey. - *Published by* Canadian Housing Design Council. Rooms 11-15, C.M.H.C. Head Office, Montreal Rd., Ottawa, Ont. K1A 0P7.
Biennial. Association publication, 120 p. Language: English and French.
Free.

Axiom / *edited by* D.T. Murphy. - *Published by* Photo-Atlantic Productions Ltd. P.O. Box 2222, Halifax, N.S., 1973-
Quarterly. Trade publication, magazine format, Includes advertising.
$.75 per issue : $3.00 per year.

B. C. Wildlife Federation. BCWF newsletter / *edited by* George Smith. - *Published by* British Columbia Wildlife Federation. 17655 57th Ave., Surrey, B.C. V3X 1H1, May 22, 1956-
Quarterly. Association publication, newsletter format, 4 p. Includes advertising. Circulation: 14,000
Free to members.

B.B. gazette - *Published by* The Boys' Brigade in Canada, Inc. P.O. Box 151, Montreal, Que., 1900-
Issued every other month. Association publication, magazine format, 42 p.
$2.00 per issue : $6.00 per year. Prepayment required.

B.C. = Hellenic view / *edited by* N. Zapantis. - *Published by* N. Zapantis. 1123 Howe St., Vancouver, B.C. V6Z 1R1, September 1971-
Issued twice a month. Ethnic press, newspaper format, 16 p. Language: Greek.
$.25 per issue : $5.00 per year. Prepayment required.

B.C. agrologists / *edited by* Thomas W. Low. - *Published by* British Columbia Institute of Agrologists. 6626 Hillside Cres., Delta, B.C., 1971-
Monthly. Association publication, newsletter format, 4 p.

B.C. Baptist bulletin *See* The B.C. regular Baptist

B.C. new homes / *edited by* Tom Verner. - *Published by* Guide Magazines Ltd. 1105 Granville St., Vancouver, B.C., 1972-
Former title(s): british columbia new.
Issued every other month. Magazine format, $1.00 per issue : $5.00 per year.

The B.C. professional engineer / *sponsored by* Association of Professional Engineers of B.C ; *edited by* Peter Carson. - *Published by* Western Miner Press Ltd. 305 - 1200 Pender St., Vancouver, B.C. V6E 2S9, 1950-
Former title(s): The Blueprint (August 1943-December 1949)
Monthly. Association publication, magazine format, 32 p. Includes book reviews, advertising. Circulation: 7980
$.50 per issue : $6.00 per year : $3.00 for the August issue.

The B.C. regular Baptist / *edited by* G.R. Dawe. - *Published by* Convention of Regular Baptist Churches of British Columbia. 3358 South East Marine Dr., Vancouver, B.C. V5S 2H6, 1927-
Former title(s): B.C. Baptist bulletin; Western regular Baptist.
Monthly. Church publication, magazine format, 8 p. Includes book reviews.
Circulation: 2500
$.20 per issue : $2.00 (Bulk orders $1.75). Controlled circulation.

B.C. Sports Federation. B.C. Sports Federation newsletter / *edited by* Brian Pound. - *Published by* British Columbia Sports Federation. 1606 West Broadway, Vancouver, B.C. V6J 1X7, January 1974-
Former title(s): Sports British Columbia (to 1973)
Monthly. Association publication, newsletter format, 8 p. Includes book reviews.
Circulation: 1000
Free.

B.C. Teachers' Federation. Special Education Association. Special Education Association newsletter / *sponsored by* Special Education Association. - *Published by* B.C. Teachers' Federation. 105-2235 Burrard St., Vancouver, B.C. V6J 3H9, September 1971-
Former title(s): PATSE Newsletter (to June 1971)
Irregular (approximately 3 issues per year). Association publication, newsletter format, 6 p.
Circulation: 700
Subscriptions are not available.

B.C. Teachers' Federation. Teachers of Home Economics Specialist Association. Newsletter / *sponsored by* Teachers of Home Economics Specialist Association. - *Published by* B.C. Teachers' Federation. 105-2235 Burrard St., Vancouver, B.C. V6J 3H9.
Former title(s): british columbia teachers' federation. teachers.
Irregular (approximately 4 issues per year). Association publication, newsletter format, 10 p. Circulation: 450
Subscriptions are not available. Controlled circulation.

B.C. Tel news / *edited by* Keith C. Matthews. - *Published by* British Columbia Telephone Co. 768 Seymour St., Vancouver, B.C., April 1960-
Former title(s): Telephone talk (1910-1960)
Issued every other week. House/company organ, newspaper format, 6 p. supplements issued.
Free.

B.C.A.M.T. journal *See* Vector: newsletter/journal

B.C.L.A. bulletin (1938-1947, vol. 1-20) *See* British Columbia library quarterly

BCNA newsletter *See* British Columbia Numismatic Association. BCNA news

B.C.P.O. Bulletin de nouvelles *Voir* La Bibliothèque centrale de prêt de l'Outaouais. Les Nouvelles de la bibliothèque centrale de prêt - Région de l'Outaouais

BC Health Association. BCHA activity bulletin / *edited by* Sheila zur Linden. - *Published by* B.C. Health Association. 440 Cambie St., Vancouver, B.C. V6B 2N6, May 1972-
Weekly. Association publication, newsletter format, 1 p.
Controlled circulation.

BC motorist (1961-1974) *See* Westworld : the magazine of travel, leisure and living

B.E.E.P. : business education's exciting publication *See* Manitoba spectra

B.F. Goodrich Canada Ltd. B.F. Goodrich Canada world / *edited by* Bert Coates. - *Published by* B.F. Goodrich Canada Ltd. Kitchener, Ont., 1934-
Former title(s): B.F. Goodrich news (1955-1966) News at B.F. Goodrich (1934-1955)
Issued every other month. House/company organ, newsletter format, 4 p. Language: English and French.
Free.

B.F. Goodrich news (1955-1966) *See* B.F. Goodrich Canada Ltd. B.F. Goodrich Canada world

BNA topics / *edited by* E.H. Hausmann. - *Published by* British North America Philatelic Society. P.O. Box 639, Copper Cliff, Ont. P0M 1N0, 1945-
Monthly. Association publication, magazine format, 20 p. Includes book reviews, volume index. Circulation: 1600
ISSN 0045-3129 $1.00 per issue : $6.50 per year : $10.00 per volume. Subscription included in membership fee. Controlled circulation.

B-A dealer (1950-1968) *See* Gulf Canada dealer news

B-A dealer news (1968) *See* Gulf Canada dealer news

Babsons reports : Canadian investment letter - *Published by* Babsons Canadian Reports Ltd. Harbour Commission Bldg., Toronto, Ont. *Indexed in* Can. B.P.I.

Backtalk / *edited by* Chas. Kibble. - *Published by* British Columbia Chiropractic Association. 106-133 West 15th St., North Vancouver, B.C. V7P 1T4, 1973-
Quarterly. Association publication, newsletter format, 5 p. Circulation: 210

The Badlands of the Red Deer River Valley / *sponsored by* Dinosaur Fossil Museum Society. - *Published by* Big Country News. 327-2nd St. E., Drumheller, Alta.
Annual. Association publication, magazine format, 172-104 p.

Badminton review / *edited by* D.M. Folinsbee. - *Published by* Canadian Badminton Association. 333 River Rd., Vanier City, Ont. K1L 8B9.
Issued every other month. Association publication, newspaper format, 10 p. Language: English and French. Circulation: 18,191
$3.00 per year : $5.00 per year, foreign. Free to members.

La Bagatelle / *édité par* Gisèle Béchard. - *Publié par* Mme Alfred Grenier. Landrienne, Abitibi, Qué. J0Y 1V0, février 1972-
Mensuel (10 nos par an). Organe interne/officiel, revue, 20 p.
$.25 le numéro : $3.00 par année.

Baker Lake prints = Estampes / *sponsored by* Sanavik Co-operative, Baker Lake, N.W.T. - *Published by* Canadian Arctic Producers Ltd. P.O. Box 4130, Postal Station E, Ottawa, Ont. K1S 5B2.
Irregular (approximately 1 issue per year). Catalogue, booklet format, 50 p. Language: English and French.

Baker's journal *See* Bakers journal : the national merchandising and management magazine serving the Canadian baking industry

Bakers journal : the national merchandising and management magazine serving the Canadian baking industry / *edited by* Lance K. LeRay. - *Published by* Roy Kenneth Cooke. Kenroy Publishers Ltd. 451 Beaconsfield Blvd., Beaconsfield, Que., Volume 34, 1974-
Former title(s): Baker's journal.
Issued every other month. Special interest, 32 p. Includes advertising. Circulation: 5000
$1.00 per issue : $10.00 for 2 years : $15.00 per year, foreign.

Balcony square / *sponsored by* Scarborough College Student Council ; *edited by* Len T. Voycey. - *Published by* Scarborough College. 1265 Military Trail, West Hill, Ont., September 1975-
Issued every other week. Student publication, newspaper format, 8 p. Includes book reviews, film reviews, play reviews, record reviews, advertising. Circulation: 5000
Free.

Ballet hoo / *sponsored by* The Royal Winnipeg Ballet ; *edited by* Maggie Morris. - *Published by* Jim Cameron. 289 Portage Ave., Winnipeg, Man. R3B 2B4.
Irregular (approximately 5 issues per year). House/company organ, magazine format, 12 p. $10.00 per year. Controlled circulation.

Bandersnatch - *Published by* John Abbot College. P.O. Box 2000, Ste-Anne-de-Belleview, Que.
Issued twice a month. Student publication. Includes advertising. Circulation: 3800

The Bangladesh / *sponsored by* Bangladesh Village Development Relief Foundation ; *edited by* M.A. Rashid. - *Published by* ABC Publishing. 219 Pine Drive, Barrie, Ont. L4N 4H6, August 1974-
Irregular. Association publication, magazine format, 60 p.
ISSN 0315-2839 $2.00 per issue : $12.00 per year.

Bank Canadian National. Monthly bulletin / *edited by* Paul Morisset. - *Published by* Bank Canadian National. 500 Place d'Armes, Montreal, Que. H2J 2W3, September 1926-
Published in French: Banque canadienne nationale. Bulletin mensuel.
Monthly. General interest, newsletter format, 4 p. Circulation: 25,000
Indexed in Can. B.P.I.
ISSN 0045-1533 Free.

Bank directory of Canada / *sponsored by* Canadian Banker's Association. - *Published by* Houstons Standard Publications Ltd. 30 Duncan St., Toronto, Ont. M5V 2C3, 1907-
Annual. Directory, book format, 270 p.
Includes 5 updating supplements.
$17.00.

Bank of Montreal business review / *edited by* John A. McColl. - *Published by* Bank of Montreal. P.O. Box 6002, Montreal, Que., April 1926-
Published in French as: Banque de Montréal. B de M Revue des affaires.
Monthly. Trade publication, newsletter format, 6 p. Circulation: 140,000
Indexed in P.A.I.S., Can. B.P.I.
Free.

The Bank of Nova Scotia. Monthly review - *Published by* The Bank of Nova Scotia. 44 King St. W., Toronto, Ont. M5H 1E2.
Monthly. Business publication, newsletter format, 4 p. Language: English and French ; summaries: English and French.
Indexed in Can. B.P.I.
ISSN 0005-5328 Free.

Banque Canadienne Nationale. Bulletin mensuel / *édité par* Paul Morisset. - *Publié par* Service des relations publiques. Banque canadienne nationale. 500, Place d'Armes, Montréal, Qué. H2J 2W3, septembre 1926-
Publié en anglais: Bank Canadian National. Monthly bulletin.
Trimestriel. Intérêt général, bulletin, 4 p. Tirage: 78,000
Indexé dans Periodex.
ISSN 0045-1533 Envoi gratuit.

La Banque Canadienne Nationale. Le point BCN - *Publié par* Banque Canadienne Nationale, att: Mlle Céline Paquin. 500 Place d'Armes, Montréal, Qué., novembre 1973-
Ancien titre: Le journal du personnel (printemps 1963-printemps 1973)
Bimestriel. Organe interne/officiel, 24 p. Envoi gratuit.

Banque de Montréal. B de M revue des affaires / *édité par* John A. McColl. - *Publié par* Banque de Montréal. C.P. 6002, Montréal, Qué., 1926-
Publié en anglais: Bank of Montreal. Bank of Montreal business review.
Mensuel. Revue d'entreprise, bulletin, 6 p. Tirage: 140,000

Banque Royale. Bulletin mensuel - *Publié par* La Banque Royale du Canada. C.P. 6001, Edifice la Banque Royale du Canada, Montréal, Qué.
Mensuel. Organe interne/officiel.
Indexé dans Periodex.
Envoi gratuit.

Le Banquier et revue IBC / *édité par* Roland Tessier (directeur). - *Publié par* Association des banquiers canadiens. C.P. 8, Tour de la Bourse, 3920, Place Victoria, Montréal, Qué. H4Z 1A3(adresse d'abonnement: P.O. Box 282, Commercial Union Tower, Toronto Dominion Center, Toronto, Ont. M5K 1K2) janvier-février 1974-
Bimestriel. Publication d'association, magazine, 64 p. Comprend critique de livres, publicité. Tirage: 4895
Indexé dans RADAR.
ISSN 0315-6281 $.50 le numéro : $3.00 par année.

Baobab - *Publié par* Missionnaires comboniens. 7025 boul. Comboni, Brossard, Qué.
Mensuel. Publication d'association, publication ecclésiastique, magazine, 48 p. Tirage: 7000 $2.50 par année. Abonnements payables à l'avance.

The Baptist beacon / *edited by* Sterling Clark. - *Published by* Fundamental Baptist Mission. R.R. 1, Waterford, Ont. N0E 1Y0, November 1973-
Monthly. Church publication, newsletter format, 8 p. Circulation: 500
ISSN 0315-5773 $3.00 per year.

Baptist Convention of Ontario and Quebec. Year book / *edited by* Department of Communications. - *Published by* Baptist Convention of Ontario and Quebec. 217 St. George St., Toronto, Ont. M5R 2M2, 1857-
Former title(s): The Baptist year book (1877-1960) The Baptist register (1874-1876) The Canadian Baptist register (1857-1873)
Annual. Church publication, book format, 270 p. Circulation: 1700
Controlled circulation.

Baptist Federation of Canada. Proceedings, minutes, reports / *edited by* R. Fred Bullen. - *Published by* Baptist Federation of Canada. P.O. Box 901, 91 Queen St., Brantford, Ont., 1970-1973-
Issued every 3 years. Church publication, 250 p.
Free.

The Baptist register (1874-1876) *See* Baptist Convention of Ontario and Quebec. Year book

The Baptist Union of Western Canada. Year book / *edited by* H.A. Renfree. - *Published by* Baptist Union of Western Canada. 4404-16th St. S.W., Calgary, Alta.
Annual. Church publication, yearbook, book format, 230 p. Circulation: 600
ISSN 0067-4087 $2.00.

The Baptist visitor (1884-1927) *See* The Link and visitor

The Baptist year book (1877-1960) *See* Baptist Convention of Ontario and Quebec. Year book

The Barnet marksman / *edited by* Gladys E. Ball. - *Published by* Barnet Rifle Club. 8550 Barnet Highway, Burnaby, B.C., April 1967-
Former title(s): The Barnet newsletter (1967-1968)
Quarterly. Association publication, magazine format, 12-16 p. Circulation: 1000
Free to club members.

The Barnet newsletter (1967-1968) *See* The Barnet marksman

La Barre du jour - *Publié par* La Barre du jour. 665, rue Crevier, Montréal, Qué., 1965-
Trimestriel.
Indexé dans Periodex.
$10.00 par année.

Barreau / *édité par* Léon Bédard. - *Publié par* Barreau du Québec. 84 ouest, rue Notre-Dame, Montréal, Qué. H2Y 1S9, septembre 1969-
Intermittent (approximativement 10 éditions par an). Revue, 16 p. Tirage: 11,000
Gratuit aux membres en règle du Barreau du Québec.

La Barrique : la seule revue française servant l'industrie des boissons alcooliques au Canada / *édité par* Claire Plante-Lambin. - *Publié par* Claire Plante-Lambin. 2949, ave de Saissons, Montréal, Qué. H3S 1W1, avril 1972-
Mensuel. Magazine, 33 p. Tirage: 10,000
ISSN 0315-0399 $.50 le numéro : $7.00 par année : $13.00 par année, l'étranger.

La Base / *édité par* Michel Lauzon. - *Publié par* Centrale des syndicats démocratiques. 188 est, boul. Dorchester, Montréal, Qué., décembre 1972-
Ancien titre: Magazine C.S.D. (décembre 1972)
Intermittent (approximativement 12 éditions par an). Publication politique, revue, 50 p. Tirage: 7000-20,000
Tirage contrôlé.

The Basilian annals / *edited by* Richard J. Allard. - *Published by* The Basilian Press. 95 St. Joseph St., Toronto, Ont. M5S 2R9, January 1975-
Annual. House/company organ, magazine format, 120 p.
Free. Distributed only to members.

Basilian historical bulletin / *edited by* Robert J. Scollard. - *Published by* Basilian Press. 95 St. Joseph St., Toronto, Ont. M5S 2R9, no.1, 1970-
Irregular (approximately 1-4 issues per year). Church publication, Pamphlet, 24-40 p.
Circulation: 150
$.50 per issue.

Bätiment / *édité par* Claude Picher. - *Publié par* Maclean-Hunter Ltd. 625, ave du Président-Kennedy, Montréal, Qué. H3A 1K5, janvier 1926-
Ancien titre: Bätiment-génie-construction (1952-1958) Le constructeur du Québec (1926-1952)
Hebdomadaire. Revue d'entreprise, magazine, 30-70 p. Tirage: 4900
Indexé dans Periodex.
$1.00 le numéro : $8.00 par année : $12.00 par année, France, G.B. : $25.00 par année, l'étranger. Tirage contrôlé. Abonnements payables à l'avance.

Bätiment-génie-construction (1952-1958) *Voir* Bätiment

Batkivschyna = Our country / *edited by* Myron Korolyshyn. - *Published by* Our Country Publishing Company. 362 Bathurst St., Toronto, Ont. M5T 2S6, 1952-
Former title(s): Nasha derzawa = Our state (1952-1956)
Irregular (approximately 1-4 issues per year). Ethnic press, newspaper format, Language: Ukrainian. Includes book reviews, film reviews, advertising.
$.30 per issue : $6.00 per year.

Bayavaya uskalos = Literary magazine / *edited by* S. Khmara. - *Published by* Byelorussian Literary Society, Bayavaya Uskalos. 24 Tarlton Rd., Toronto, Ont. M5P 2M4, 1949-
Annual. Ethnic press, magazine format, 32 p. Language: Byelorussian. Circulation: 500
$1.00.

Beacon / *edited by* Cornelius J. Pasichny. - *Published by* The Basilian Press. 286 Lisgar St., Toronto, Ont. M6J 3G9, March 15, 1966-
Former title(s): Life-Beacon (March 15, 1966 to September 15, 1969)
Issued every other month. Ethnic press, magazine format, 48 p. Includes book reviews.
Circulation: 1300
$.50 per issue : $3.00 per year. Prepayment required.

The Beacon / *edited by* President, Lutheran Collegiate Bible Institute. - *Published by* Lutheran Collegiate Bible Institute. Outlook, Sask., 1939-
Quarterly. Church publication, newsletter format, Circulation: 5500

Beale, Colin. Beale's letter / *edited by* Colin Beale. - *Published by* Colin Beale. 925 West Georgia St., Vancouver, B.C. V6C 1R5, January 1972-
Former title(s): Beale's resource industry newsletter (January 1972)
Issued every other week. Trade publication, newsletter format, 4 p. Circulation: 300
$4.00 per issue : $98.00 per year.

Beale's resource industry newsletter (January 1972) *See* Beale, Colin. Beale's letter

Beauty / *edited by* Audrey Taylor. - *Published by* Intercommunications Ltd. 3rd floor, 2 Elgin Ave., Toronto, Ont (Subscription address: P.O. Box 669, Charles St. P.O., Toronto, Ont.) Fall 1975-
Quarterly. Trade publication, magazine format, $2.50 per issue : $4.50 per issue.

The Beaver - *Published by* Hudson's Bay Company. 79 Main St., Winnipeg, Man. R3C 2P7.
Quarterly. Magazine format, available in microform.
Indexed in North. tit., Hist. abstr.; Amer. hist. and life, Arct. bibl.

Beaverbrook Art Gallery / *edited by* Ian G. Lumsden. - *Published by* Friends of the Beaverbrook Art Gallery. P.O. Box 605, Fredericton, N.B., October 1970-
Quarterly. 16 p.
Subscription included in membership fee.

Beetle / *edited by* Debbie Brioux. - *Published by* Moe Wortzman. Entertainment Publications Incorporated. P.O. Box 5696, Postal Station A, Toronto, Ont., December 1970-
Monthly. Special interest, magazine format, 80 p. Includes book reviews, film reviews, record reviews, advertising. Circulation: 150,000
$.79 per issue : $7.50 per year.

Bell Femme (1965-1975) *See* Communique

Bell news. Eastern ed / *edited by* Michael Dorland. - *Published by* Bell Canada. Room 300, 3737 Metropolitan E., Montreal, Que. H4Z 1A2, 1954-
Former title(s): Blue Bell magazine (1930-1954)
Issued every other week. House/company organ, newspaper format, 8 p. Circulation: 28,500
Free.

Best wishes / *edited by* Myroslava Oleksiuk Baker. - *Published by* Donald Gordon Baker. J.L. Hunt Publications. 37 Hanna Ave., Toronto, Ont. (Subscription address: P.O. Box 8, Postal Station C, Toronto, Ont. M6J 3M8) 1949-
Quarterly. Special interest, magazine format, 68 p. Includes advertising. Circulation: 66,000
ISSN 0005-965X Free. Controlled circulation.

Better boating : Canada's best boating magazine / *edited by* Jim Punfield. - *Published by* S/S/P Publications Limited. 120 Barbados Blvd., Scarborough, Ont. M1J 1L2, January 1965-
Monthly. Special interest, magazine format, 60 p. Includes advertising. Circulation: 25,000
$.75 per issue : $7.00 per year : $7.50 per year, foreign.

Between times / *edited by* Corinne Noonan. - *Published by* Saint Mary's University. Halifax, N.S.
Issued twice a month. Institutional publication (Universities, schools, etc.).

Beverage alcohol reporter / *edited by* J.H. Clarke. - *Published by* Vincent Clarke Publishing Co. Ltd. Unit 9, 1710 Midland Ave., Scarboro, Ont. M1P 3C7, 1949-
Monthly. Trade publication, magazine format,

Bharati / *edited by* Mrs. B. Dhanoya. - *Published by* Asia Publications. Canada Centre Holdings Ltd. 1433 Bloor St. W., Toronto, Ont. M6P 3L6, 1975-
Monthly. Ethnic press, magazine format, Language: Hindu. Includes advertising.
$.50 per issue : $6.00 per year.

Bibliographical Society of Canada. Bulletin / *edited by* Elizabeth Hulse. - *Published by* Bibliographical Society of Canada. 32 Lowther Ave., Toronto, Ont. M5R 1C6, May 1973-
Issued twice a year. Association publication, newsletter format, 6 p.
Available to members only. Controlled circulation.

Bibliographie Canada-CEE (1970-1974) *Voir* Université de Montréal. Centre d'études et de documentation européennes. Bulletin d'information documentaire

Bibliographies in education - *Published by* Canadian Teachers Federation. 110 Argyle Ave., Ottawa, Ont. K2P 1B4, June 1969-
Irregular (approximately 10 issues per year). Bibliography, 30 p. Circulation: 750
Indexed in Resources in educ.
Free distribution list: others $.50 prepaid.

La Bibliothèque centrale de prêt de l'Outaouais. Les Nouvelles de la bibliothèque centrale de prêt - Région de l'Outaouais / *édité par* Jean-Pierre Germain. *- Publié par* Bibliothèque Centrale de prêt de l'Outaouais. C.P. 938, chemin Freeman, Hull, Qué. J8X 3Z2, septembre 1973-
Ancien titre: B.C.P.O. Bulletin de nouvelles. Bimestriel. Publication d'institution (universités, écoles..), bulletin, 35 p. Langue(s): français et anglais. Tirage: 250
ISSN 0316-8441 Envoi gratuit.

Bibliothèque des jeunes naturalistes / *édité par* Dollard Sénécal. *- Publié par* Les Cercles des jeunes naturalistes. 455, rue Saint-Jean, Montréal, Qué., 1932-
Intermittent (approximativement 8-10 éditions par an). Publication d'association, brochure, 4 p. Tirage: 2000
$.10 le numéro : $7.50 le volume : $.20 le numéro, l'étranger.

Bibliothèque publique d'Ottawa. Bulletin *See* Ottawa Public Library. Bulletin

Bibliovision (septembre 1970-avril 1973) *Voir* Le Polariseur

Bielaruski holas = Byelorussian voice / *edited by* M. Ziniak. *- Published by* Federation of Free Byelorussian Journalists. 24 Tarlton Rd., Toronto, Ont. M5P 2M4, November 1974-
Former title(s): Byelaruski emigrant (1949-1952)
Monthly. Ethnic press, newspaper format, 4-6 p. Language: Byelorussian. Includes advertising. Circulation: 2000
$5.00 per year.

Bielarusy u Kanadzie : Fotodocumentation *See* Byelorussian in Canada

Bien-être social canadien (septembre 1949-octobre 1973) *Voir* Digeste social

The Big byte / *edited by* L.S. Easton. *- Published by* Department of Computer Services. University of Calgary. 2920-24 Ave. N.W., Calgary, Alta. T2N 1N4, January 1971-
Monthly. Institutional publication (Universities, schools, etc.), newsletter format, Free.

Big wheel logging news *See* B.C. logging news

Bijou / *édité par* André Robitaille. *- Publié par* La Cie des éditions horlogères canadiennes ltée. Suite 205, 2950 est, rue Masson, Montréal, Qué. H1Y 1X4, janvier 1969-
Ancien titre: La Loupe (1952-1968)
Mensuel. Revue d'entreprise, magazine, 40 p. Tirage: 2300
ISSN 0006-2316 $.75 le numéro : $7.50 par année : $30.00 le volume.

Le Binocle / *édité par* Michel Lalonde. *- Publié par* CEGEP de l'Outaouais. C.P. 220, Hull, Qué., avril 1974-
Mensuel. Publication d'institution (universités, écoles..), journal, 8 p.

Biographical directory of Americans and Canadians of Croation descent / *edited by* Vladimir Markotic. *- Published by* Vladimir Markotic. 2508 - 34th Ave. N.W., Calgary, Alta., 1963-
Former title(s): Hrvati profesori NA Americkim kanadskim visokim skolama.
Irregular. Ethnic press, 200 p.
$15.00 per issue.

Biological Photographic Association. Journal of the Biological Photographic Association / *edited by* Stanley Klosevych. *- Published by* Ottawa Photographic. Biological Photographic Association Inc. P.O. Box 333, Postal Station A, Ottawa, Ont. K1N 8V3, 1932-
Quarterly. Association publication, magazine format, 40 p. Includes book reviews, film reviews, cumulative index. Circulation: 2200
Prepayment required.

Biologie végétale : rapport des activités scientifiques *- Publié par* Camp-ecole Chicobi. Guyenne, Abitibi-ouest, Qué. J0Y 1L0.
Publication d'institution (universités, écoles..), journal,
Tirage contrôlé.

Biomass Energy Institute. Biomass Energy Institute newsletter *- Published by* Biomass Energy Institute. 304-870 Cambridge St., Winnipeg, Man. R3M 3H5, January/February 1972-
ISSN 0315-3223

Bio-nouvelles *- Publié par* Société de biologie de Montréal, inc. 14-230 est, Henri-Bourassa, Montréal, Qué., janvier 1973-
Intermittent (approximativement 8 éditions par an). Publication d'association, bulletin, 10 p. Tirage: 500
Abonnement compris avec carte de membre de la SBM.

Bison (March 1942-June 1971) *See* Contact

Black book : official used car market guide *- Published by* National Auto Research Canada. 79 Ellesmere, Scarborough, Ont.
Issued every other week. Special interest, booklet, 155 p. Language: English and French. Includes updating service. Circulation: 5950
$35.00 per year. Prepayment required.

Black book used truck guide / *edited by* Wm. G. Ward. - *Published by* Wm. G. Ward. National Auto Research Canada. Suite 1A, 67 Ellesmere Rd., Scarborough, Ont.
Issued every other month. Special interest, booklet format, 157 p.
$30.00 per year. Controlled circulation. Prepayment required.

Black book vehicle indentification guide - *Published by* National Auto Research Canada. Suite 1A, 67 Ellesmere Rd., Scarborough, Ont. M1R 4B9.
Annual. Trade publication. Language: English and French.
ISSN 0316-4896 $4.95.

The Black fly - *Published by* The Black Fly. P.O. Box 302, Postal Station P, Thunder Bay, Ont., December 1973-
ISSN 0319-1176

Black images - *Published by* Black Images. P.O. Box 280, Postal Station F, Toronto, Ont. M4Y 2L7.

Blackboard bulletin / *sponsored by* Old Order Amish ; *edited by* Elizabeth Miller. - *Published by* Pathway Publishers. R.R. 4, Aylmer, Ont. N5H 2R3, 1957-
10 issues August-May. Church publication, magazine format, 28 p. Circulation: 6911
$2.00 per year.

The Bleat *See* B.C. dairy goat news

The Block badger (1964 to 1969-70) *See* Press

Blue Bell magazine (1930-1954) *See* Bell news. Eastern ed

The Blue heron - *Published by* Brereton Field Naturalists Club of Barrier. c/o The President, Mrs. J.M. Leigh, R.R. 1, Orillia, Ont., 1957-
Irregular (approximately 2-3 issues per year). Special interest, newsletter format, 16 p. Circulation: 200
$1.00 per year. Free.

Blue jay : a journal of natural history and conservation for Saskatchewan and adjacent regions / *edited by* J. Bernard Gollop. - *Published by* Saskatchewan Natural History Society. P.O. Box 1321, Regina, Sask. S4P 3B8, October-December 1942-
Quarterly. Association publication, magazine format, 64 p. Includes book reviews. Circulation: 2700
Indexed in North. tit.
ISSN 0006-5099 $.75 per issue : $3.00 per year.

Bluebird bulletin / *edited by* Mildred E. Jeffery. - *Published by* British Columbia Division. Canadian Arthritis and Rheumatism Society. 895 West 10th Ave., Vancouver, B.C. N5Z 1L7.
Issued every other month. Association publication, magazine format, 8 p. Circulation: 3000
Free to a selected list.

The Blueprint (August 1943-December 1949) *See* The B.C. professional engineer

Bluewater circle drives : one-day and weekend outings in Southwestern Ontario / *edited by* N.E. Thomson. - *Published by* J.D. Thomson Tourist Promotions Ltd. R.R. 5, Dresden, Ont., 1947-
Annual. Directory, magazine format, 64 p. Includes advertising. Circulation: 21,000
Free. Controlled circulation.

Bluewater vacation guide : Lake Huron, Georgian Bay and Manitoulin Island / *edited by* N.E. Thomson. - *Published by* J.D. Thomson Tourist Promotions Ltd. R.R. 5, Dresden, Ont., 1968-
Annual. Directory, magazine format, 128 p. Includes advertising. Circulation: 31,000
Free. Controlled circulation.

The Board of Trade of Metropolitan Toronto. Journal of the Board of Trade of Metropolitan Toronto / *edited by* J.P. Strimas. - *Published by* J.P. Strimas. The Board of Trade of Metropolitan Toronto. 11 Adelaide St. W., Toronto, Ont., 1900-
Monthly. Association publication, magazine format, 56 p. Circulation: 15,700
Controlled circulation.

Boating news / *edited by* Don Tyrell and Janine Hurley (associate editor). - *Published by* Tyrell Publishing. N. Ft. Cardero St., Vancouver, B.C., July 1970-
Monthly: Special interest, newspaper format, 16 p. Includes book reviews. Circulation: 21,000
$.25 per issue : $3.00 per year. Controlled circulation.

The Body politic gay liberation journal *- Published by* The Body Politic Editorial Collective. 193 Carlton St., Toronto, Ont. (Subscription address: P.O. Box 7289, Postal Station A, Toronto, Ont. M5W 1X9) November 1971-
Issued every other month. Association publication, newspaper format, 28 p. Includes book reviews, film reviews, play reviews, record reviews, advertising. available in microform. Circulation: 4500
Indexed in Alt. press ind.
ISSN 0215-3606 $.35 per issue : $2.25 per year (First class mail $3.25) : $3.00 per year, U.S. : $5.00 per year, overseas air mail.

Body shop / *edited by* Herschel Fenik. *- Published by* Wadham Publications Ltd. Suite 101, 109 Vanderhoof Ave., Toronto, Ont. M46 2J2, January 1970-
Issued every other month. Trade publication, magazine format, 24 p.
$.50 per issue : $3.00 per year : $4.50 per year foreign. Controlled circulation.

Boileau babillard / *édité par* Guy Lorrain. *- Publié par* Service des Loisirs St. Francois de Sales de Laval, att: M. J.-P. Messier. 7100 Mille Iles, St-François, Ville de Laval, Qué., mai 1974-
Mensuel. Publication d'association, bulletin, 16 p. Tirage: 1500
Envoi gratuit.

Bon voyage *- Publié par* Smith Publishing Co. Suite 741, 1010 ouest, rue Ste-Catherine, Montréal, Qué., 1971-
Semestriel. Intérêt général, magazine,

Bonavia, George. The International corner : books, records, films / *edited by* George Bonavia. *- Published by* George Bonavia. P.O. Box 826, Postal Station B, Ottawa, Ont. K1P 5P9, October 1972-
Monthly. Ethnic press, book reviews. Includes book reviews, film reviews, record reviews.
ISSN 0316-6260 Prepayment required.

The Bond record *- Published by* Canadian Daily Quotation Service Ltd. P.O. Box 518, Postal Station K, Toronto, Ont. M4P 2G9.
Annual. Directory, Spiral bound book, 52 p.
$2.00.

Bonne nouvelle / *édité par* Maurice Hébert. *- Publié par* Gabriel Dextraze. Ordre séculier franciscain. 5731, boul. Pie IX, Montréal, Qué. H1X 2B9, 1911-
Ancien titre: L'Echo de St Francois.
Mensuel. Publication ecclésiastique, journal, 12 p. Comprend critique de livres, publicité.
Tirage: 5000
$.20 le numéro : $2.00 par année.

Une Bonne nouvelle pour le transporteur / *édité par* Esther F. Fuller. *- Publié par* Christian Transportation Inc. 512 Yonge St. (rear), Toronto, Ont. M4Y 1X9, 1973-
Publication ecclésiastique.
Envoi gratuit.

Bonne route / *parrainé par* Atelier des sourds ; *édité par* Monique Larocque et Leo MacGillivray. *- Publié par* Marc R. Turcot. 1401, McGill Collège, Montréal, Qué. H3A 1Z5, 1912-
Ancien titre: RACC newsletter.
Intermittent (approximativement 4 éditions par an). Publication d'association, bulletin, 8 p. Langue(s): français et anglais ; sommaires: français et anglais. Tirage: 30,000

Book news / *edited by* Juliet McLaren. *- Published by* Burnaby Public Library. 3127 Thunderbird Cres., Burnaby, B.C. V5A 3G1.
Irregular (approximately 8 issues per year). House/company organ, newsletter format, 4-6 p. Includes book reviews. Circulation: 1000
Free.

The Bookmark / *sponsored by* British Columbia School Librarians' Association ; *edited by* Doug Trounce. *- Published by* British Columbia Teachers Federation. 105-2235 Burrard St., Vancouver, B.C. V6J 3H9, 1959-
Former title(s): Top titles (1972-1973) Occasional papers (1970-1974) Focus on Canada (1970-1973) The Tikinagan (1968-1969) Demonstration school library project newsletter (1972-1973) Newsletter - British Columbia School Librarian's Association (1963-1966)
Monthly. Association publication, magazine format, 20 p. Includes advertising, volume index. supplements issued. Circulation: 800
Indexed in Can. educ. ind.
$11.00 per year. Subscriptions available only to members.

Books for everybody / *sponsored by* Canadian Booksellers Association : Canadian Book Publishers Council : Independent Publishers Association ; *edited by* Fiona Mee. *- Published by* Fiona Mee. Greey de Pencier Publications Ltd. 59 Front St. E., Toronto, Ont. M5E 1B3.
Annual. Catalogue, magazine format, 64 p.
Circulation: 100,000

Books for young people *- Published by* Toronto Public Library Board. 40 Orchard View Blvd., Toronto, Ont. M4R 1B9.
Irregular (approximately 8 issues per year).
Bibliography.
$3.00 per year. Free.

Books in Canada / *edited by* Doug Marshall. - *Published by* Canadian Review of Books, Ltd. 4th floor, 366 Adelaide St. E., Toronto, Ont. M5A 1N4, 1971-
Monthly. Book reviews, magazine format, 32 p. Includes book reviews. Circulation: 45,000
$9.95 per year : $15.00 per year, foreign. Special rates offered.

Books in Canada. : index and microtext - *Published by* McLaren Micropublishing. P.O. Box 972, Postal Station F, Toronto, Ont. M4Y 2N9, May 1971-
Issued 10 times a year. Book reviews, microform format, Includes book reviews. Includes hard copy author-title-reviewer index.
ISSN 0317-4905 $35.00 per year.

The Booster (1925-1931) *See* Ontario dentist

Borden Canada *See* Rapport

Boreal : poesía española en el Canadá / *edited by* Manuel Betanzos - Santos. - *Published by* Boreal. P.O. Box 262, Victoria Stn., Montreal, H3Z 2V5 (Subscription address: Librería Las Américas, Inc., 760 Sherbrooke, Montreal, Que.) June 1965-
Irregular (approximately 4 issues per year). Special interest, magazine format, 20 p. Language: Spanish and others. Includes book reviews. supplements issued. Circulation: 500
$1.00 per issue.

Boreal Institute for Northern Studies Library. Accessions list / *edited by* The Library staff. - *Published by* Boreal Institute for Northern Studies. University of Alberta. Edmonton, Alta. T6G 2E9, January 1971-
Monthly. Catalogue, 15 p.
ISSN 0315-601X Free on request.

Boreal newsletter / *edited by* David C. Norwood. - *Published by* Boreal Institute for Northern Studies. CW 401, Biological Sciences Bldg., The University of Alberta, Edmonton, Alta. T6G 2E9, January 1974-
Irregular (approximately 3 issues per year). Institutional publication (Universities, schools, etc.), newsletter format, 10 p.
ISSN 0315-7105 Free. Controlled circulation.

Le Borroméen : organe de l'Association des anciens du Séminaire de Sherbrooke / *édité par* Rosario Cousineau. - *Publié par* L'Association des anciens. Séminaire de Sherbrooke. 195, rue Marquette, Sherbrooke, Qué., 1931-
Trimestriel. Publication des anciens étudiants, 8 p. Tirage: 5000
Compris dans la cotisation à l'Association des anciens.

Der Bote : ein mennonitisches Familienblatt / *sponsored by* General Conference Mennonite Church ; *edited by* Peter B. Wiens. - *Published by* Heese House of Printing. 716 2nd Ave. N., Saskatoon, Sask., January 1924-
Former title(s): Der Immigrantenbote.
Weekly. Ethnic press, church publication, newspaper format, 12 p. Language: German. Includes book reviews, advertising. supplements issued. Circulation: 8500
$7.00 per year. Prepayment required.

Le Bouscueil - *Publié par* Alliance chorale canadienne. 1052 ouest, ave Laurier, Montréal, Qué., automne 1972-
Intermittent (approximativement 3 éditions par an). Publication d'association, bulletin, 24 p. Tirage: 8000
Envoi gratuit.

Bowline sail and power - *Published by* Dieter Thelen. Flintcom Publishing Co. 57 Glencameron Rd., Thornhill, Ont., 1973-
Monthly. Trade publication, magazine format, Includes advertising.
$12.00 per year : $1.00 per issue outside Ontario.

Bozja beseda = The Word of God / *edited by* Slovenian Missionaries of St. Vincent. - *Published by* John Kopac. 739 Brown's Line, Toronto, Ont., November 1949-
Monthly. Ethnic press, church publication, magazine format, 32 p. Language: Slovenian.
$.50 per issue : $5.00 per year. Controlled circulation.

Branches of Bruce - *Published by* B. Underwood. Bruce Branch. Ontario Genealogical Society. R.R. 2, Port Elgin, Ont. N0H 2C0, February 1971-
Association publication.
ISSN 0319-2032

Branching out / *edited by* Sharon Batt. - *Published by* New Women's Magazine Society. P.O. Box 4098, Edmonton, Alta. T6E 4T1, December 1973-
Issued every other month. Special interest, magazine format, 48 p. Language: English. Includes book reviews, film reviews, play reviews, record reviews, advertising, volume index, updating service. Circulation: 4000
$1.00 per issue : $5.00 per year : $6.00 per year, foreign.

Brandon today / *edited by* Henry Schol. - *Published by* Brandon Chamber of Commerce. P.O. Box 548, 907 Princess Ave., Brandon, Man. R7A 5Z7.
Irregular (approximately 10 issues per year). House/company organ, newsletter format, 6 p. Circulation: 1200

Le Brasier / *édité par* Marie-Hélène Leblanc. - *Publié par* Secteur français. L'Association des guides catholiques. 3827, rue St-Hubert, Montréal, Qué. H2L 4A4, octobre 1941-
Mensuel. Publication d'association, magazine, 16-24 p. Comprend index de volumes. Tirage: 2300
Le numéro $.30 : $3.00 par année.

Bratstvo. Fraternity / *edited by* Alija S. Konjhodzich. - *Published by* Bratstvo/Fraternity. 66 Rusholme Rd., Toronto, Ont. M6J 3H6, April 1954-
Ethnic press. Language: Serbian.
$.30 per issue : $5.00 per year : $6.00 per year, foreign.

Break through - *Published by* Johoso Club of Hamilton. c/o John Howard Society of Hamilton, 228 Bay St. S., Hamilton, Ont.
Quarterly.
$2.00 per year : $3.00 per year, foreign.

Brèches : analyse/fiction / *édité par* André Beaudet. - *Publié par* Les Editions de l'Aurore. 1651, rue Saint-Denis, Montréal, Qué., printemps 1973-
Ancien titre: L'Etrangeté du texte (printemps-été 1975) Sur ferron printemps (1973)
Trimestriel. Publication spécialisée, revue, 110 p. Comprend critique de livres. Tirage: 2000
Indexé dans RADAR.
$3.50 le numéro : $12.00 par année : $14.00 par année, l'étranger.

Breeder and feeder / *edited by* Graeme Hedley. - *Published by* Ontario Beef Improvement Association. 590 Keele St., Toronto, Ont. M6N 3E3, September 1963-
Irregular (approximately 8-10 issues per year). Association publication, newsletter format, 8-12 p. Circulation: 13,000
Free.

Brésil - Sénégal / *édité par* Gérard Ouellet. - *Publié par* Centre Cor Jesu (Frères du Sacré-Coeur de Granby). 4 est, rue Denison, Granby, Qué. J2G 8E3, 1968-
Trimestriel. Publication d'association, publication ecclésiastique, bulletin, 4 p.
Envoi gratuit.

Bricklayer - *Published by* Red Deer College. 56 Ave. and 32 St., Red Deer, Alta. T4N 5H5.
Weekly. Student publication. Includes advertising. Circulation: 1000

The Bride book / *edited by* Audrey Taylor. - *Published by* Elena Domo. Intercommunications Ltd. P.O. Box 669, Postal Station F, Toronto, Ont., 1968-
Quarterly. Magazine format,
$2.00 per year.

Briefly (1966-1967) *See* Doings

Le Brigand : revue missionnaire des Jésuites canadiens-français / *édité par* Louis-Joseph Goulet. - *Publié par* La Procure des missions Jésuites. 1172 ouest, rue Sherbrooke, Montréal, Qué. H3A 1H6, mars 1930-
Bimestriel. Publication ecclésiastique, revue, 24 p. Tirage: 15,000
$.40 le numéro : $2.00 par année.

Bright leaf tobacco journal / *edited by* Guy Goodwin. - *Published by* North Shore Publications. P.O. Box 459, Port Stanley, Ont., 1953-
Irregular (approximately 12 issues per year). Trade publication, magazine format,
$.35 per issue : $2.00 per year : $5.00 per year, foreign.

British Columbia Aberdeen Angus Association. Newsletter / *edited by* Margaret MacGregor. - *Published by* British Columbia Aberdeen Angus Association. R.R.2, Sardis, B.C., 1961-
Issued 8 times a year. Association publication, newsletter format, 2 p. Includes advertising. Circulation: 350-450
Free.

British Columbia Art Teachers' Association. BCATA journal for art teachers / *sponsored by* B.C. Art Teachers' Association. - *Published by* B.C. Teachers' Federation. 105-2235 Burrard St., Vancouver, B.C. V6J 3H9, September 1973-
Former title(s): Perception (Spring 1960-Spring 1972)
Monthly. Association publication, journal format, 25 p. Includes book reviews, film reviews, advertising.
Indexed in Can. educ. ind.
Available to members only. Controlled circulation.

British Columbia Art Teachers' Association. Newsletter / *sponsored by* B.C. Art Teachers' Association. - *Published by* B.C. Teachers' Federation. 105-2235 Burrard St., Vancouver, B.C. V6J 3H9, November 1962-
Irregular (approximately 4 issues per year). Association publication, newsletter format, 20 p. Includes book reviews, film reviews, advertising.
Available to members only. Controlled circulation.

B.C. Artificial Insemination Centre. B.C.A.I. newsletter / *edited by* Gloria Lawson. - *Published by* British Columbia Artificial Insemination Centre. P.O. Box 40, Milner, B.C.
Irregular (approximately 5-6 issues per year). House/company organ, newsletter format, Free.

British Columbia Association for the Mentally Retarded. Conference. Annual conference - *Published by* British Columbia Association for the Mentally Retarded. 221 - 119 West Pender St., Vancouver, B.C. V6B 1S5.
Annual. Association publication, book format, ISSN 0316-9324

British Columbia Association of School Supervisors of Instruction. Newsletter of the British Columbia Association of School Supervisors / *sponsored by* B.C. Association of School Supervisors of Instruction. - *Published by* British Columbia Teachers' Federation. 105-2235 Burrard St., Vancouver, B.C. V6J 3H9.
Issued twice a year. Association publication, newsletter format, 5 p. Circulation: 150
Controlled circulation.

British Columbia Association of Teachers' of Modern Languages. Newsletter (November 1962-November 1969) *See* Elan

B.C. business / *edited by* J.R. Martin. - *Published by* Pacific Rim Publications Ltd. 1132 Hamilton St., Vancouver, B.C. V6B 2S2, 1973-
Former title(s): Business in B.C.
Monthly. Trade publication, magazine format, *Indexed in* Can. B.P.I.
$5.00 per year : $9.00 for 2 years : $12.00 for 3 years.

British Columbia Business Educators' Association. Newsletter / *sponsored by* B.C. Business Educators' Association. - *Published by* British Columbia Teachers Federation. 105-2235 Burrard St., Vancouver, B.C. V6J 3H9, October 1970-
Former title(s): Newsletter - The Commerce Teacher's Association (October 1962-May 1970)
Irregular (approximately 4 issues per year). Association publication, newsletter format, 30 p. Includes book reviews.
Available to members only. Controlled circulation.

The B.C. Catholic / *edited by* G.W. Bartram. - *Published by* Archdiocese of Vancouver. Catholic Church. 150 Robson St., Vancouver, B.C. V6B 2A7, 1931-
Weekly. Church publication, newspaper format, 12 p. Includes book reviews, film reviews, play reviews, advertising. Circulation: 7600
$.15 per issue : $6.50 per year : $7.00 per year, foreign. Controlled circulation.

British Columbia Chamber of Commerce. General policy statements and resolutions - *Published by* British Columbia Chamber of Commerce. Suite 901, 626 West Pender St., Vancouver, B.C. V6B 1V9, June 1975-
Annual. Association publication.
Free.

British Columbia Civil Liberties Association. B.C.C.L.A. news digest / *edited by* Sandra Walton. - *Published by* British Columbia Civil Liberties Association. Suite 206, 207 West Hastings St., Vancouver, B.C. V6B 1L3.
Issued every other month. Association publication, newsletter format, 6 p. Circulation: 450
$.50 per issue : $3.00 per year. Prepayment required.

British Columbia corporation manual / *edited by* Ralph Loltmark. - *Published by* Richard De Boo Ltd. 70 Richmond St. E., Toronto, Ont. M5C 2M8.
Issued every other month. Special interest, 64 p. Includes updating service. supplements issued.
$40.00 per year.

B.C. dairy goat news / *sponsored by* B.C. Goat Breeders Association ; *edited by* Lynn Whitehouse. - *Published by* Lynn Whitehouse. Whitehouse. P.O. Box 262, Dawson Creek, B.C. V1G 4G7, 1921-
Former title(s): Canadian dairy goat news; The Bleat.
Monthly. Association publication, newsletter format, 20 p. Includes advertising. supplements issued. Circulation: 350
ISSN 0319-292X $.25 per issue : $2.50 per year.

British Columbia diocesan post / *edited by* Will Dobson. - *Published by* Diocese of British Columbia. Anglican Church of Canada. 912 Vancouver St., Victoria, B.C., 1964-
Monthly. Church publication, newspaper format, 4 p. Includes book reviews. Circulation: 5500
$1.00 per year. Free.

British Columbia English teacher (1966-1971) *See* British Columbia English Teachers' Association. Journal

British Columbia English Teachers' Association. Journal / *sponsored by* British Columbia English Teachers' Association ; *edited by* Mrs. Lynn Glazier. - *Published by* British Columbia Teacher's Federation. 2235 Burrard St., Vancouver, B.C., February 1973-
Former title(s): Update; British Columbia English teacher (1966-1971) DATE journal (1960-1963)
Issued twice a year. Association publication, magazine format, 100 p. Includes book reviews, advertising. Circulation: 1000
Indexed in Can. educ. ind.
ISSN 0316-0173 $6.00 per year. Subscription included in membership fee.

British Columbia fresh water fishing guide / *edited by* Jim Railton. - *Published by* Railton Publications Ltd. 125 Talisman Ave., Vancouver, B.C., 1946-
Annual. Special interest, magazine format, 82 p. Circulation: 25,000
$1.00. Prepayment required.

British Columbia Fruit Growers Association. Horticultural conference proceedings - *Published by* British Columbia Fruit Growers Association. 1473 Water St., Kelowna, B.C.
Annual. Association publication, newsletter format,

The British Columbia genealogist - *Published by* British Columbia Genealogical Society. P.O. Box 94371, Richmond, B.C., Fall 1971-
Association publication.
ISSN 0315-3835

British Columbia Health Association. Proceedings of the annual conference - *Published by* British Columbia Health Association. 440 Cambie St., Vancouver, B.C. V6B 2N6, 1918-
Annual. Association publication.
Controlled circulation.

Hellenic view *See* B.C.

British Columbia historial news / *edited by* P.A Yandle. - *Published by* British Columbia Historical Association. 3450 West 20th Ave., Vancouver, B.C. V6S 1E4, 1967-
Quarterly. Association publication, magazine format, 25 p. Includes book reviews, cumulative index.
Indexed in Hist. abstr.; Amer. hist. and life.
$1.00 per issue : $3.50 per year.

The B.C. horseman - *Published by* MacDonald's Pub. Co. Langley, B.C., 1971-
ISSN 0315-2855

British Columbia Hospital Association. BCHA news / *edited by* Sheila zur Linden. - *Published by* British Columbia Health Association. 440 Cambie St., Vancouver, B.C. V6B 2N6, August 1972-
Former title(s): British Columbia hospital news (to April 1972)
Issued every other month. Association publication, newsletter format, 8 p.
Circulation: 2500

British Columbia hospital news (to April 1972) *See* British Columbia Hospital Association. BCHA news

British Columbia Institute of Technology. BCIT developments / *edited by* Graham Fane. - *Published by* British Columbia Institute of Technology. 3800 Willingdon Ave., Burnaby, B.C. V5G 3H2, October 1971-
Irregular (approximately 9 issues per year). Institutional publication (Universities, schools, etc.), newsletter format, 3 p. Circulation: 600

British Columbia insurance directory of insurance companies, agents and adjusters / *edited by* William D.S. Earle, and Caroline M. Earle (associate editor). - *Published by* Arbutus Publications Ltd. P.O. Box 35466, Vancouver, B.C. V6M 4G8.
Annual. Directory, coil-bound format, 102 p. Includes advertising. Circulation: 1100
$8.00.

British Columbia library quarterly / *edited by* Ross Carter and Leland Windreich. - *Published by* British Columbia Library Association. 2425 Macdonald St., Vancouver, B.C. V6K 3Y9, 1938-
Former title(s): B.C.L.A. bulletin (1938-1947, vol. 1-20)
Quarterly. Association publication, magazine format, 60 p. Includes book reviews, record reviews, advertising. available in microform.
Circulation: 800
ISSN 0007-053X Free. Available to members only. Controlled circulation.

B.C. logging news / *edited by* Graydon Wheeler. - *Published by* Big Wheel Publications Ltd. 220-1152 Mainland St., Vancouver, B.C. V6B 2T9, 1974-
Former title(s): Big wheel logging news; Truck logger (1943-)
Monthly. Trade publication, magazine format, 60 p. Circulation: 7500
$2.00 per issue : $18.00 per year : $25.00 per year, foreign. Controlled circulation.
Prepayment required.

British Columbia lumberman / *edited by* Brian Martin. - *Published by* Journal of Commerce Ltd. Southam Business Publications Ltd. 2000 West 12th Ave., Vancouver, B.C. V6J 4M8, 1917-
Monthly. Trade publication.
$10.00 per year : $16.00 for 2 years : $14.00 per year, foreign.

British Columbia lumberman's greenbook : a directory of B.C.'s forest industry / *edited by* Jean Sorensen. - *Published by* Tony McDonnell. Journal of Commerce. 2000 W. 12th Ave., Vancouver, B.C.
Annual. Directory, book format, 260 p.
ISSN 0068-1601 $35.00. Controlled circulation.

British Columbia medical journal / *edited by* F.S. Hobbs. - *Published by* British Columbia Medical Association. 1807 West Tenth Ave., Vancouver, B.C. V6J 2A9, January 1959-
Former title(s): Bulletin - Vancouver Medical Association (January 1924 - December 1958)
Monthly. Association publication, journal format, 32 p. Includes book reviews, advertising, volume index. Circulation: 4742
ISSN 0007-0556 $1.00 per issue : $12.00 per year : $15.00 per year, foreign.

British Columbia Medical Library Service. Journal holdings - *Published by* British Columbia Medical Library Service. 1807 West 10th Ave., Vancouver, B.C. V6J 2A9.
Bibliography. supplements issued.

The B.C. mental retardation advisor / *edited by* Arlene R. Rosset. - *Published by* British Columbia Association for the Mentally Retarded. 221 - 119 West Pender St., Vancouver, B.C., October-November 1970-
Former title(s): Association for Retarded Children of B.C. newsletter (January 1969-July 1969) Our children (February 1961-December 1964)
Issued every other month. Association publication, newsletter format, 8 p. Includes book reviews, film reviews. Circulation: 2400
ISSN 0004-9474 Free.

The British Columbia monthly : Canada's national magazine / *edited by* Gerry Gilbert. - *Published by* The British Columbia Monthly. P.O. Box 8884, Postal Station H, Vancouver, B.C. V6B 4E2, July 1972-
Irregular (approximately 1-7 issues per year). Special interest, magazine format, 35 p. Includes book reviews, film reviews, advertising. supplements issued. Circulation: 1000
$2.00 per issue. Prepayment required.

B.C. municipal yearbook / *edited by* Eric (Sandy) Sanderson. - *Published by* Sanderson Publications Ltd. 204-2182 West 12th Ave., Vancouver, B.C. V6K 2N4.
Annual. Statistics, magazine format, 124 p.
Circulation: 2000
$7.00 per issue.

British Columbia music educator / *sponsored by* B.C. Music Educators' Association. - *Published by* British Columbia Teachers Federation. 105-2235 Burrard St., Vancouver, B.C. V6J 3H9, Vol 4, no 1, February 1961-
Issued twice a year. Association publication, journal format, 60 p. Includes book reviews, advertising.
Indexed in Can. educ. ind.
Available to members only. Controlled circulation.

British Columbia Music Educators Association. Newsletter / *sponsored by* British Columbia Music Educators' Association. - *Published by* British Columbia Teachers Federation. 105 - 2235 Burrard St., Vancouver, B.C. V6J 3H9, March 1962-
Former title(s): Drive (January and June 1974)
Irregular (approximately 3 issues per year). Association publication, newsletter format, 10 p. Includes book reviews.
Available to members only. Controlled circulation.

british columbia new *See* B.C. new homes

British Columbia Numismatic Association. BCNA news / *edited by* W.G. Ziegler. - *Published by* British Columbia Numismatic Association. P.O. Box 4311, Vancouver, B.C., 1965-
Former title(s): BCNA newsletter.
Quarterly. Association publication, newsletter format, 3 p.
Controlled circulation.

B.C. outdoors / *edited by* Art Downs. - *Published by* Northwest Digest Ltd. P.O. Box 900, Postal Station A, Surrey, B.C. V3S 4P4.
Issued every other month. General interest, magazine format, 64 p. Circulation: 26,500
$.75 per issue : $3.50 per year : $3.85 per year, foreign.

British Columbia Primary Teachers' Association. Newsletter / *sponsored by* British Columbia Primary Teachers' Association ; *edited by* Mrs. L. Robb. - *Published by* British Columbia Teachers Federation. 105 - 2235 Burrard St., Vancouver, B.C. v6J 3H9.
Issued every other month. Association publication, newsletter format, 30 p. Includes updating service. supplements issued.
Subscription included in membership fee.
Controlled circulation. Prepayment required.

British Columbia Principals' and Vice-Principals' Association. Newsletter / *sponsored by* British Columbia Principals' and Vice-Principals' Association. - *Published by* British Columbia Teachers Federation. 105 - 2235 Burrard St., Vancouver, B.C. V6J 3H9, Vol 4, no 1, September 1962-
Irregular (approximately 4 issues per year). Association publication, newsletter format, 5 p. Includes book reviews.
Indexed in Can. educ. ind.
Available to members only. Controlled circulation.

British Columbia Registered Music Teachers' Association. Provincial newsletter / *edited by* Joan Gosselin. - *Published by* British Columbia Registered Music Teachers' Association. 202 - 1488 Dallas Rd., Victoria, B.C. V8S 1A2, February 1972-
Former title(s): The Music Bulletin (to 1970)
Quarterly. Association publication, newsletter format, 10 p. Circulation: 575
Controlled circulation.

British Columbia salt water salmon guide / *edited by* Jim Railton. - *Published by* Railton Publications Ltd. 125 Talisman Ave., Vancouver, B.C. V5Y 2L6, 1973-
Annual. Special interest, magazine format, 80 p. Includes advertising. Circulation: 20,000
$1.50 per issue.

British Columbia School Counsellors' Association. Newsletter / *sponsored by* B.C. School Counsellors' Association. - *Published by* British Columbia Teachers Federation. 105-2235 Burrard, Vancouver B.C. V6J 3H9, July 1971-
Former title(s): Newsletter - British Columbia Counsellor's Association (October 1960-1971)
Irregular (approximately 5 issues per year). Association publication, newsletter format, 15 p.
Available to members only. Controlled circulation.

British Columbia School Librarians' Association. Index to BCSLA publications / *sponsored by* British Columbia School Librarians' Association ; *edited by* Doug Trounce. - *Published by* British Columbia Teachers' Federation. 105 - 2235 Burrard St., Vancouver, B.C. V6J 3H9, September 1971-
Annual. Index, newsletter format, 6 p. Includes volume index. Circulation: 900
$10.00 per year (Non-members $14.00, students $5.00).

British Columbia School Trustees Association. Report of proceedings / *edited by* Information Services. - *Published by* B.C. School Trustees Association. 1095 Howe St., Vancouver, B.C. V6Z 1P9.
Annual. Association publication, magazine format, Circulation: 500

The B.C. science teacher / *sponsored by* B.C. Science Teachers' Association ; *edited by* Gordon R. Gore. - *Published by* British Columbia Teachers Federation. 105-2235 Burrard St., Vancouver, B.C. V6J 3H9, 1972-
Former title(s): STA news (1960? to 1972)
Irregular (approximately 6 issues per year). Association publication, newsletter format, 30 p. Circulation: 700
Indexed in Can. educ. ind.
$5.00 per year.

B.C. studies / *sponsored by* University of B.C., Simon Fraser University, University of Victoria, The Canada Council and British Columbia Cultural Fund ; *edited by* Margaret Prang and Walter Young. - *Published by* University of British Columbia Press. 2075 Wesbrooke Place, Vancouver, B.C. V6T 1W5 (Subscription address: B.C. Studies, University of B.C., 2075 Wesbrook Place, Vancouver, B.C. V6T 1W5) Winter 1968-69-
Quarterly. Scholarly publication, journal format, 100 p. Includes book reviews, volume index, cumulative index. available in microform. Back numbers available. Circulation: 1000
Indexed in Can. ind., Hist. abstr.; Amer. hist. and life.
ISSN 0005-2949 $3.00 per issue : $5.00 per year.

British Columbia taxation service / *edited by* M.J. O'Keefe. - *Published by* Richard De Boo Ltd. 70 Richmond St. E., Toronto, Ont. M5C 2M8.
Monthly. Special interest, 64 p. Includes updating service.
$35.00 per year.

The B.C. teacher / *edited by* K.M. Aitchison. - *Published by* British Columbia Teachers Federation. 105-2235 Burrard St., Vancouver, B.C. V6J 3H9, 1921-
Issued 5 times a year (every other month October-June). Association publication, magazine format, 40 p. Includes book reviews, advertising, volume index. available in microform. Circulation: 32,000
Indexed in Can. educ. ind.
ISSN 0005-2957 $3.50 per year. Controlled circulation.

British Columbia Teachers' Federation. Newsletter / *edited by* John Hardy. - *Published by* British Columbia Teachers Federation. 105-2235 Burrard St., Vancouver, B.C. V6J 3H9.
Irregular (approximately 12-14 issues per year). Association publication, newsletter format, 4 p. Circulation: 32,000
ISSN 0005-2965 Free. Included with subscription to The B.C. teacher. Controlled circulation.

british columbia teachers' federation. teachers *See* B.C. Teachers' Federation. Teachers of Home Economics Specialist Association. Newsletter

B.C. Tel news careers / *edited by* K.G. Matthews. - *Published by* British Columbia Telephone Co. 10-768 Seymour St., Vancouver, B.C., March 1967-
Irregular (approximately 6 issues per year). House/company organ, newspaper format, 4 p. Free.

British Columbia thoroughbred : an official review of the season - *Published by* British Columbia Thoroughbred Breeders' Society. 4023 East Hastings St., North Burnaby, B.C. V5C 2J1, 1954-
Annual. Association publication, magazine format, 240 p. Includes advertising. supplements issued. Circulation: 3000
$4.00.

B.C. voice / *edited by* Mrs. Deeno Birmingham. - *Published by* British Columbia Voice of Women. P.O. Box 235, Nanaimo, B.C. V9R 5K9, 1963-
Irregular (approximately 6 issues per year). Association publication, newsletter format, 10 p. Includes book reviews. Circulation: 400
$.35 per issue : $2.00 per year. Free to members. Prepayment required.

Broadcaster / *edited by* Virginia Neale. - *Published by* R.G. Lewis Co. Ltd. 77 River St., Toronto, Ont. M5A 3P2, January 1942-
Former title(s): Canadian broadcaster.
Monthly. Trade publication, magazine format, 50 p. Includes record reviews, advertising. available in microform. Circulation: 8000
$2.00 per issue : $15.00 per year : $35.00 for 3 years.

Brotherhood report (April 1971) *See* Native Press

The Brown Swiss bell / *edited by* William J. Lipsey. - *Published by* Canadian Brown Swiss Association. Room 7, 4826 11th St. N.E., Calgary, Alta.
Former title(s): Brown Swiss news; Brown Swiss breeder briefs.
Issued every other month. Association publication, newsletter format, 20 p.

Brown Swiss breeder briefs *See* The Brown Swiss bell

Brown Swiss news *See* The Brown Swiss bell

Browse / *sponsored by* Ontario Dairy Goat Society ; *edited by* Holly Furber. - *Published by* Donald and Holly Furber. R.R. 1 Binbrook, Ont. L0R 1C0, 1953-
10 issues per year. Association publication, magazine format, 22 p. Includes advertising. Includes annual Breeder's directory. Circulation: 500
$.30 per issue : $3.00 per year : $3.50 per year, foreign. Subscription included in membership fee. Prepayment required.

Bruce County historical notes / *edited by* Mrs. Earl Ferris. - *Published by* Bruce County Historical Society. Eskadale Farm, Tiverton, Ont. (Subscription address: R.R. 1 Tiverton, Ont. N0G 2T0) 1958-
Quarterly. Association publication, newsletter format, 4-6 p. Circulation: 470
ISSN 0084-8115

Bruce County Historical Society. Year book / *edited by* Mrs. Earl Ferris. - *Published by* Bruce County Historical Society. Eskadale Farm, Tiverton, Ont. (Subscription address: Mrs. Geo. Downey, Secretary, R.R. 1, Tiverton, Ont. N0G 2T0) 1967-
Annual. Association publication, book format, 50 p.
ISSN 0084-8115 $1.50 per year.

The Bruce Trail news / *edited by* Doug Brown. - *Published by* The Bruce Trail Association. 33 Hardale Cres., Hamilton, Ont. L8T 1X7, 1963-
Irregular (approximately 3 or 4 issues per year). Association publication, newsletter format, 18 p. Circulation: 8000
Subscription included in membership fee
$5.00.

The Brunswickan / *edited by* Susan Manzer and Tom Benjamin (managing ed.). - *Published by* Fredericton Campus. University of New Brunswick. Student Union Building, Fredericton, N.B., 1865-
Former title(s): University monthly (1865-1921)
Weekly. Student publication, newspaper format, 28 p. Includes book reviews, film reviews, play reviews, record reviews, advertising. available in microform.
Circulation: 7000
$3.00 per year. Free to students, faculty, etc. Controlled circulation.

The R.M. Bucke Memorial Society. Conference. Proceedings / *edited by* Raymond H. Prince. - *Published by* R.M. Bucke Memorial Society. 4453 Maisonneuve Blvd. W., Westmount, Que., 1965-
Annual. Association publication, 120 p. Includes book reviews. Circulation: 300
ISSN 0079-9351 $2.75.

The R.M. Bucke Memorial Society newsletter / *edited by* Raymond H. Prince. - *Published by* R.M. Bucke Memorial Society. 4453 Maisonneuve Blvd. W., Montreal, Que., January 1966-
Annual. Association publication, newsletter format, 75 p. Includes book reviews.
Circulation: 300
ISSN 0079-9343 $2.50.

The Buffalo - *Published by* The Manitoba Council. Girl Guides of Canada. 200-267 Edmonton St., Winnipeg, Man. R3C 1S2.
Irregular (approximately 3-4 issues a year). Association publication, newsletter format, 4-6 p. Circulation: 1550

The Builder / *edited by* Nick G. Vanderlee. - *Published by* Empire Life Insurance Co. P.O. Box 1000, Kingston, Ont.
Monthly. House/company organ, magazine format, 16 p. Circulation: 800

Building and management (July 1968-May 1971) *See* Building development

Building development *See* Canadian building

Building development - *Published by* Greey de Pencier Publications Ltd. Grecy Bldg., 56 Esplanade, Toronto, Ont., June 1971-
Former title(s): Building and management (July 1968-May 1971)
ISSN 0316-389X

Building management and maintenance news / *edited by* Peter Logan (publication manager). - *Published by* Logan Brown Communications. 56 Esplanade, Toronto, Ont. M5E 1A7, 1969-
Issued every other month. Trade publication, magazine format, Includes advertising.
$1.00 per issue : $5.00 per year : $10.00 for 3 years.

The Bull and bear / *edited by* David John Robinson. - *Published by* David John Robinson. Suite 402, 110 St. Clair Ave.,· Toronto, Ont. (Subscription address: P.O. Box 751, Postal Station Q, Toronto, Ont. M4T 2N5) February 1972-
Monthly. Trade publication, magazine format, 64 p. Circulation: 15,000
ISSN 0319-1362 $.75 per issue : $9.00 per year. Special rates offered. Prepayment required.

The Bulletin - *Published by* The Marketing Division. The Dominion Life Assurance Company. 111 Westmount Rd. S., Waterloo, Ont., 1925-
Former title(s): The Dominion (January 1919-1925)
Monthly. House/company organ, magazine format, 20 p. Language: English (French).
Circulation: 850
Controlled circulation.

The Bulletin *See* The Teacher

The Bulletin - Canada Safety Council (June 1957-January 1961) *See* Safety Canada

The Bulletin - Canadian Armed Forces Base, Edmonton (June 1969-December 1969) *See* Sealandair

Bulletin - Canadian Association for Health, Physical Education and Recreation (1933-1951) *See* Canadian Association for Health, Physical Education and Recreation. CAHPER journal

Bulletin - Canadian Association of Medical Clinics *See* Group practice in Canada

Bulletin - Canadian Film Institute (January 1955-December 1971) *See* Images

Bulletin - Canadian Operational Research Society (1962?-May 1971?) *See* Canadian Operational Research Society. CORS bulletin

Bulletin - Canadian Society of Landscape Architects *See* Landscape architecture Canada

Bulletin - Canadian Tuberculosis Association (1920-1968) *See* Canadian Tuberculosis and Respiratory Disease Association. Bulletin

Bulletin - Conseil canadien de la sécurité (juillet-decembre 1960) *Voir* La prévention au Canada

The Bulletin - Federation of Ontario Naturalists (1951-1963) *See* Ontario naturalist

The Bulletin - Greater Welland Chamber of Commerce *See* Business beat

Bulletin - London Chamber of Commerce *See* London Chamber of Commerce. Chamber of Commerce news

Bulletin - Occupational Teachers' Specialist Association. (February 1966-December 1974) *See* Secondary Learning Assistance Teachers' Association. Bulletin

Bulletin - Ontario Medical Association (April 1922-June 1943) *See* Ontario medical review

Bulletin - Ontario Secondary School Teachers' Association (January 1921-December 1974) *See* The Forum

Bulletin - Ontario Society for Crippled Children (1970) *See* Horizons

The Bulletin - The Canadian Association for the Mentally Retarded *See* Mental retardation

The Bulletin - The Manitoba Teachers' Society *See* The Manitoba teacher

Bulletin - The Vancouver Art Gallery *See* Vanguard

Bulletin - The Vancouver Art Gallery *See* Vanguard

Bulletin - Vancouver Medical Association (January 1924 - December 1958) *See* British Columbia medical journal

Bulletin - York University. Institute for Behavioral Research (1968-1972) *See* York University. Institute for Behavioural Research. Newsletter

Bulletin APDM (mai 1953-janvier 1974) *Voir* Québec pharmacie

Bulletin bimensuel de l'AEFNB (septembre 1971-juin 1972) *Voir* Association des enseignants francophones du Nouveau-Brunswick. Nouvelles de l'AEFNB

Bulletin d'administration scolaire - *Publié par* Association pour l'avancement de l'administration scolaire. C.P. 6128, Montréal Qué.
Trimestriel. Publication d'association, 30 p. *Indexé dans* Can. educ. ind.

Bulletin de géophysique / *édité par* M. Buist. - *Publié par* Collège Jean-de-Brébeuf. 3200, chemin Ste-Catherine, Montréal, Qué. H3C 1C1, mars 1957-
Semestriel. Publication spécialisée, bulletin, 50 p. Langue(s): anglais et français. Tirage: 330 $2.00 le numéro. Envoi en échange.

Bulletin de l'A.D.Q. (août 1971-décembre 1974) *Voir* Cahiers québécois de démographie

Bulletin de l'ALBLF (1955-1972) *Voir* Documentation et bibliothèques

Bulletin de la Chambre de commerce *Voir* Chambre de commerce française au Canada. Revue de la Chambre de commerce française au Canada

Bulletin de l'agence de presse libre du Québec *Voir* Bulletin populaire

Bulletin de l'Association pour l'analyse et la modification du comportement (décembre 1972-décembre 1973) *Voir* Revue de modification du comportement

Bulletin de l'Eglise unie du Canada *Voir* Credo

Bulletin de l'Eglise Unie du Canada *Voir* Credo : mensuel de l'Eglise Unie du Canada

Bulletin de nouvelles - Corporation des psychologues de la province de Québec (février 1969-septembre 1973) *Voir* Le Psychologue québécois

Bulletin de nouvelles = Newsletter - Corporation professionnelle des médecins du Québec (juillet 1961-mars 1975) *Voir* Corporation professionnelle des médecins du Québec. Bulletin

Bulletin de nouvelles de L'Association pour l'avancement de la thérapie behaviorale en milieu francophone (octobre 1970-janvier 1972) *Voir* Revue de modification du comportement

Bulletin de service *See* Saskatchewan Association of Teachers of French. Bulletin

Le Bulletin des agriculteurs - *Publié par* Lucille Fontaine Davis. 5670 Chauveau St., Montreal, Que. H1N 1H2.
Mensuel. Publication spécialisée.
$4.00 par année.

Bulletin des anciens, Ottawa *See* Alumni news, Ottawa

Bulletin des directeurs (1911-1917) *Voir* Animateur

Bulletin des foyers Notre Dame (1955-1961) *Voir* Couple et famille

Le bulletin des instituts de religieuses enseignantes du Québec (juin 1959 - juin 1967) *Voir* Association des religieuses enseignantes du Québec. AREQ

Bulletin des ligues (1936-1966) *Voir* Animateur

Bulletin des ligues. Section des ligueurs (1936-1965) *Voir* Chrétiens d'aujourd'hui

Bulletin des ligues, section du conseil (septembre 1950-septembre 1965) *Voir* Equipe apostolique

Bulletin des outfitters = Bulletin of the outfitters / *édité par* Louis-Roch Seguin. - *Publié par* L'Association des outfitters du Québec. 2860, chemin des Quatre Bourgeois, Québec, Qué. G1V 1Y3, mars 1974-
Bimestriel. Publication d'association, bulletin, 20-40 p. Langue(s): français et anglais ; sommaires: anglais et français. Tirage: 300
$5.00 le numéro : $50.00 par année. Envoi gratuit. Tirage contrôlé. Abonnements payables à l'avance.

Bulletin des présidents (1966-1969) *Voir* Animateur

Bulletin des relations industrielles (jusqu'en 1951) *Voir* Relations industrielles

Bulletin d'information / *édité par* Marcel B. Archambault. - *Publié par* Ordre des dentistes du Québec. Suite 303, 801 est, rue Sherbrooke, Montréal, Qué. H2L 1K7, juillet 1960-
Intermittent (approximativement 4 éditions par an). Publication d'association, bulletin, 10 p. Langue(s): français et anglais. Tirage: 2000

Bulletin d'information bimestrielle - Service canadien des forêts *Voir* Service canadien des forêts. Revue bimestrielle de recherches

Bulletin d'information officielle - Société professionelle des pharmaciens d'hôpitaux *Voir* Association des pharmaciens des établissements de santé du Québec. Bulletin d'information

Bulletin du collège et des anciens (avril 1954-juin 1969) *Voir* Collège Jean-de-Brébeuf. Bulletin des parents et des anciens

Bulletin économique - *Publié par* Service de recherches economique de la Banque provinciale. 215, rue Saint Jacques, Montréal, Qué. H2Y 1M7, mai-juin 1971-
Bimestriel. Revue d'entreprise, bulletin, 6 p. Langue(s): français et anglais. Tirage: 40,000
Indexé dans Periodex.

Bulletin missionnaire (octobre 1960-février 1962) *Voir* Les Nôtres

Bulletin missionnaire (février 1951-mai 1951) *Voir* Salam

Bulletin missionnaire des Frères de Ste-Croix (septembre 1951-janvier 1953) *Voir* Salam

Bulletin Montraffic = Montraffic news / *édité par* Stan C. Newey. - *Publié par* Traffic Club of Montreal Inc. Room 201, 751 Victoria Sq., Montreal, Que., 1959-
Trimestriel. Publication d'association, bulletin, 16 p. Langue(s): français et anglais. Comprend publicité. Tirage: 1650
Tirage contrôlé.

Bulletin of African Studies = Bulletin des études africaines au Canada *See* Canadian journal of African studies

Bulletin of Canadian petroleum geology / *edited by* Don Glass and Brascan Resources. - *Published by* Canadian Society of Petroleum Geologists. 612 Lougheed Building, Calgary, Alta. T2P 1M7, 1955-
Former title(s): Journal of the Alberta Society of Petroleum Geologists (1953-1962)
Quarterly. Association publication, magazine format, 100 p. Includes advertising, volume index. Circulation: 2000
ISSN 0007-4802 $6.00 per issue : $20.00 per year.

Bulletin of outstanding acquisitions / *edited by* C. Hollyer. - *Published by* Metropolitan Toronto Central Library. 214 College St., Toronto, Ont. M5T 1R3, 1969-
Former title(s): Quarterly bulletin of outstanding acquisitions - Metropolitan Toronto Central Library (1969-1973)
Issued twice a year. Bibliography, magazine format, 12 p. Circulation: 250
Free. Special rates offered.

Bulletin of the C.A.M.R.L. (1942-1973) *See* Canadian Association of Medical Record Libraries. Camrl recorder

Bulletin of the Canadian Society of Education/Societe canadienne pour l'etude de l'education *See* Canadian journal of education

Bulletin of the New Brunswick Psychological Association *See* Association of Psychologists of the Province of New Brunswick. Journal of The Association of Psychologists of the Province of New Brunswick

Bulletin of the outfitters *Voir* Bulletin des outfitters

Bulletin ornithologique - *Published by* Club des ornithologues de Québec, inc. 8191, ave du Zoo, Orsainville, Québec, Qué. G1G 4G4, 1956-
Trimestriel. Association publication, newsletter format, 20 p. Language: French.
ISSN 0007-5265 $6.00 per year.

Bulletin populaire / *édité par* Jacques Massé. - *Publié par* Agence de presse libre du Québec. 2074, rue Beaudry, Montréal, Qué. H2L 3G3, décembre 1973-
Ancien titre: Bulletin de l'agence de presse libre du Québec.
Paraît tous les 15 jours. Publication spécialisée, magazine, 32 p. Comprend critique de livres, critique de films, critique de pièces de théâtre. Tirage: 5000
$.50 le numéro : $12.50 par année. Envoi gratuit. Abonnements payables à l'avance.

Bulletins signaletiques - *Publié par* Informatech France-Québec. Etage E, Place Bonaventure, 20, rue Edison, Montréal, Qué., juin 1975-
Ancien titre: Référence (août-septembre 1970-mars 1975)
Mensuel. Publication spécialisée, bulletin, 15 bulletins, chacun 2 p.

Le Bureau / *édité par* Paul Saint-Pierre. - *Publié par* Brian McKerchar. Maclean-Hunter Ltée. 625, ave Président-Kennedy, Montréal, Qué. H3A 1KA, septembre 1965-
Bimestriel. Revue d'entreprise, magazine, 56 p. Comprend critique de livres. parution de suppléments. Tirage: 7500
Indexé dans Periodex.
$1.50 le numéro : $8.00 par année : $12.00 par année, l'étranger. Tirage contrôlé.

Bureau canadien de l'éducation internationale. Communications *See* Canadian Bureau for International Education. Communications

Bureau of Municipial Research. BMR comment - *Published by* Bureau of Municipal Research. Suite 306, 2 Toronto St., Toronto, Ont. M5C 2B6.
Former title(s): News brief (1966-1970)
Irregular (approximately 12 issues per year). House/company organ, newsletter format, 20 p.
$1.00 per issue : $40.00 per year.

Burlington Fine Arts Association. Newsletter / *edited by* R.H. Boyer. - *Published by* Burlington Fine Arts Association. P.O. Box 866, Burlington, Ont. L7R 3Y7, 1966-
Monthly except June and July. Association publication, newsletter format, 2 p.
Circulation: 200
Free to members.

Bus and truck transport / *edited by* Paul G. Ingram. - *Published by* John Bates. Maclean-Hunter Ltd. 481 University Ave., Toronto, Ont. M5W 1A7, 1925-
Monthly. Magazine format, 65 p. Circulation: 19,804
Indexed in Can. B.P.I.
$1.00 per issue : $10.00 per year : $12.00 per year, U.S. and U.K. : $25.00 per year, foreign.

Business alert / *edited by* Paul J. Mineo. - *Published by* The Canadian Chamber of Commerce. 1080 Beaver Hall Hill, Montreal, Que. H2Z 1T2, 1972-
Published in French: Les Affaires.
Irregular (approximately 8 issues per year). Special interest, newsletter format, 4 p.
Circulation: 3000
$1.25 per year. Controlled circulation.

The Business and professional woman / *edited by* Isabel MacMillan. - *Published by* Canadian Federation of Business and Professional Women's Clubs. Room 115, 56 Sparks St., Ottawa, Ont. K1P 5A9., 1934-
Irregular (approximately 4 issues per year). Association newsletter, magazine format, 21 p. Language: English and French. Includes advertising. Circulation: 5000
$.75 per issue : $2.00 per year. Controlled circulation.

Business beat / *edited by* W.J. Vigars. - *Published by* Greater Welland Chamber of Commerce. 55 Main St. E., Welland, Ont. L3B 3W4, May 1975-
Former title(s): The Bulletin - Greater Welland Chamber of Commerce.
Monthly. Trade publication, newsletter format, 4 p. Includes advertising. Circulation: 500
Controlled circulation.

Business briefs - monthly - *Published by* Windsor Chamber of Commerce. 500 Riverside Dr. W., Windsor, Ont. N9A 5K6, January 1972-
Monthly. House/company organ, newsletter format, 4 p. Includes book reviews.
Circulation: 1100

Business highlights (1974) *See* Byword

Business in B.C *See* B.C. business

Business life in western Canada / *edited by* Donald C. Sylvester. - *Published by* Sylvester Publications Ltd. 2424-2 Ave. S.E., Calgary, Alta. (Subscription address: P.O. Box 6150, Postal Station C, Edmonton, Alta. T5B 4K5) May 1973-
Issued every other month. Trade publication, magazine format, 80 p. Includes advertising. Circulation: 30,000
Indexed in Can. B.P.I., North. tit.
$1.00 per issue : $6.00 per year. Controlled circulation.

The Business quarterly : Canadian management journal / *edited by* Doreen Sanders. - *Published by* School of Business Administration. University of Western Ontario. London, Ont. N6A 3K7, 1933-
Former title(s): Quarterly review of commerce.
Quarterly. Special interest, journal format, 96 p. available in microform. Reprints available.
Indexed in Manage. ind., Can. ind., Can. leg. per. lit., P.A.I.S., B.P.I., Soc. sci. cit. ind., Soc. sci. journal file, Can. B.P.I.
$3.00 per issue : $10.00 per year : $14.00 for 2 years : $18.00 for 3 years.

Business review / *edited by* Rob Weston. - *Published by* University of British Columbia, Commerce Undergraduate Society. Henry Ames Building, University of British Columbia, Vancouver, B.C., 1966-
Annual. Scholarly publication, journal format, 100 p. Circulation: 3500
$2.00.

Butter fat / *edited by* Verlie Bousfield. - *Published by* Fraser Valley Milk Producers' Association. P.O. Box 9100, 6800 Lougheed Highway, Vancouver, B.C. V6B 4G4, 1920-
Issued every other month. Association publication, magazine format, 48 p. Includes advertising, volume index. Circulation: 4000
ISSN 1007-7275 $3.00 per year. Free to members.

Butterworth's Ontario digest : being a statement of the case law of Ontario from 1901 with full annotations - *Published by* Butterworth and Co. (Canada) Ltd. 2265 Midland Ave., Scarborough, Ont.
Irregular (approximately 4 issues per year). Cases, case notes, digest format, supplements issued.

Buyers' market / *edited by* Bob Tyre. - *Published by* Buyers' Market of Canada. P.O. Box 87, 400-259 Portage Ave., Winnipeg, Man. R3C 2G6, 1944-
Issued twice a year. Trade publication.

Byelaruski emigrant (1949-1952) *See* Bielaruski holas

Byelorussian in Canada = Bielarusy u Kanadzie : Fotodocumentation / *sponsored by* Byelorussian Kastus Kalinouski Institute. - *Published by* M. Ziniak. 24 Tarlton Rd., Toronto, Ont.
Irregular. Ethnic press. Language: English and Byelorussian. Circulation: 500

Byelorussian voice *See* Bielaruski holas

Byers Canadian merchandise mart / *edited by* J. Alan Byers. - *Published by* Byers Associates. 1885 Wilson Ave., Weston, Ont. M9M 1A2, 1956-
Former title(s): Canadian merchandise mart (1973)
Annual. Directory, magazine format, 56 p.
Indexed in Can. B.P.I.
ISSN 0068-9238 $5.00.

Byers national industrial directory / *edited by* J. Alan Byers. - *Published by* Byers Associates. 1885 Wilson Ave., Weston, Ont. M9M 1A2, 1928-
Annual. Directory, magazine format, 300 p. Circulation: 9858
ISSN 0068-4600 $17.00 : $20.00, foreign. Controlled circulation.

Byers trade directory / *edited by* J. Alan Byers. - *Published by* Byers Associates. 1885 Wilson Ave., Weston, Ont. M9M 1A2, 1928-
Annual. Directory, 48 p. Circulation: 9593
ISSN 0068-4619 $5.00 : $6.00 foreign. Controlled circulation.

Byers western industrial directory / *edited by* J. Alan Byers. - *Published by* Byers Associates. P.O. Box 2993, Vancouver, B.C. V6B 3X4, 1928-
Annual. Directory, magazine format, 68 p.
ISSN 0068-4627 $10.00.

Byleten' UVAN u kanadi *See* Ukrainian Free Academy of Sciences-UVAN (1949). Byuleten' humanistychnoho viddilu uvan

Byuleten' prezydiyi UVAN *See* Ukrainian Free Academy of Sciences-UVAN (1949). Byuleten' humanistychnoho viddilu uvan

Byword - *Published by* Ottawa Board of Trade. 88 Argyle Ave., Ottawa, Ont. K2E 1B4.
Former title(s): Business highlights (1974)
Monthly. Trade publication, newsletter format, 4 p. Includes advertising.
Subscription included in membership fee.

CAE news / *edited by* F.C. Fraser. - *Published by* CAE Industries Ltd. Suite 1927, 1 Place Ville Marie, Montreal, Que. H3B 2C3, Fall, 1960-
Quarterly. House/company organ, newsletter format, 4 p. Circulation: 4500

CALL news (Spring 1963-June 1966) *See* Canadian Association of Law Libraries. Newsletter

CAMAC. Montreal Committee. Newsletter/bulletin / *sponsored by* CAMAC Montreal Committee. - *Published by* Canadian Amateur Musicians. 2010 Dorchester Blvd. W., Montreal, Que.
Issued every other month. Newsletter format, 4 p. Language: English and French. Circulation: 600
$10.00 per year. Subscription included in membership fee. Controlled circulation. Prepayment required.

C.A.R. weekly : Canadian auto racing news / *edited by* Don Swiston. - *Published by* JWC Publishing. P.O. Box 789, Burlington, Ont. L7P 3Y7, July 1972-
Irregular (approximately 25 issues per year). Special interest, newspaper format, 24 p. Circulation: 14,000
$.25 per issue : $10.00 per year.

C.A.S. news *See* Vancouver Resources Board. Inside the VRB

CASNP bulletin (1972-1974) *See* Canadian Association in Support of the Native Peoples. Bulletin : an independent journal on native affairs

CA magazine / *edited by* Dorothy A. Cooper. - *Published by* Canadian Institute of Chartered Accountants. 250 Bloor St. E., Toronto, Ont. M4W 1G5, 1911-
Former title(s): The Canadian chartered accountant (1911-1972)
Monthly. Magazine format, 75 p. Language: English (French). Includes book reviews, advertising, volume index. Circulation: 38,500
Indexed in P.A.I.S.
$1.50 per issue : $12.00 per year : $33.00 for 3 years. Special rates offered. Prepayment required.

CA newsletter (February 1964 vol. 2. no. 2 - July 1974 vol. 12. no. 1) *See* The Institute of Chartered Accountants of Alberta. CA monthly statement

CDCA (April 1963 - December 1965) *See* De nieuwe weg

CDCA nieuws (January - November 1966) *See* De nieuwe weg

CEDA. current / *sponsored by* CEDA Incorporated ; *edited by* Alex Watson. - *Published by* Kerrwil Publications Ltd. 30 Eglinton Ave. E., Toronto, Ont. M4P 1B6, 1970-
Issued every other month.
$5.00 per year : $8.00 per year, foreign.

CEE electronics directory and Buyers' guide / *edited by* Cliff Hand. - *Published by* Maclean-Hunter Ltd. 481 University Ave., Toronto, Ont. M5W 1A7.
Annual.

CEGEP - ACQ annuaire / *édité par* Jacques Laliberté. - *Publié par* Centre d'animation de développement et de recherche en éducation (CADRE). 1940 est, boul. Henri-Bourassa, Montréal, Qué. H2B 1S2, 1968-
Annuel. Publication d'institution (universités, écoles..), 150 p. Tirage: 2000

CETOF : bulletin de liaison des professeurs de géographie de la région de Québec / *édité par* Jacques Drolet. - *Publié par* La Société des professeurs de géographie du Québec inc. C.P. 9752, Ste-Foy, Québec, Qué. G1V 4C3, janvier 1974-
Intermittent (approximativement 2 éditions par an). Organe interne/officiel, bulletin, 20 p. Tirage: 200
ISSN 0317-0810 Tirage contrôlé.

CE news *See* Encounter : program bulletin

C.F.M.S. newsletter/bulletin *See* Canadian Folk Music Society journal

CFUW newsletter (1970-1973) *See* Canadian Federation of University Women. Bulletin

C.G.A. bulletin / *edited by* V. Macdonald. - *Published by* The Professional Corporation of Certified General Accountants of Quebec. Room 512, 5165 Queen Mary Rd., Montreal, Que. H3W 1X9.
Issued every other month. Association publication, newsletter format, 10 p. Language: English and French. Circulation: 3900
Free.

CGA : the certified general accountant / *edited by* G.W. Fuller. - *Published by* The Certified General Accountants Associations of Canada. 25 Adelaide St. E., Toronto, Ont. M5C 1Y6, July 1967-
Irregular (approximately 5 issues per year). Association publication, magazine format, 44 p. Language: English and French. Includes advertising. Circulation: 20,000
Indexed in Can. B.P.I.
ISSN 0318-742X $1.50 per issue : $6.00 per year.

C.H.A.C. news bulletin *See* Catholic hospital

CHSCO news (to October 1979) *See* The Kernel

CIAO magazine / *edited by* Silvio Ciavardini. - *Published by* CIAO Publishing Co. Suite 1, 2125 Jean Talon St. E., Montreal, Que., 1970-
Monthly. Ethnic press, magazine format, Language: Italian. Includes advertising.
$1.00 per issue : $10.00 per year.

CIL magazine (August 1929-December 1931) *See* Canadian Industries Ltd. C.I.L. contact

C.I.P. news (August 1974-June 1975) *See* Canadian Institute of Planners. Canadian Institute of Planners forum

CIRPHO review *Voir* Cercle international de recherches philosophiques par ordinateur. Revue CIRPHO

CIR journal *See* Real Estate Institute of Canada. Journal

C.I.S. student newsletter *See* Information for candidates

CLU comment / *edited by* Roy Jenkins. - *Published by* The Institute of Chartered Life Underwriters. 41 Lesmill Rd., Don Mills, Ont. M3B 2T3, January 1967-
Issued every other month. Association publication, 4 p. Language: English and French.
Prices vary according to the number of subscriptions. Controlled circulation.

CMA gazette (November 1966-April 1974) *See* Gazette

CNP news, (July 1972-January 1974) *See* South of tuk

COMBO / *edited by* Holly Davidson. - *Published by* The Division of Mission in Canada. United Church of Canada. 85 St. Clair Ave. E., Toronto, Ont. M4T 1M8, January 1972-
Quarterly. Church publication, newsletter format, 8 p. Circulation: 33,000
ISSN 0315-6478

CORS journal (1963-1970) *See* INFOR: Canadian journal of operational research and information processing

COSSIP : Central Ontario Section speaks in print / *sponsored by* Central Ontario Section, Canadian Figure Skating Association ; *edited by* Isabelle F. Hedges. - *Published by* Sport Ontario. 559 Jarvis St., Toronto, Ont. M4Y 2J1 (Subscription address: COSSIP, R.R. 2, Seagrave, Ont. L0C 1G0) 1960-
Issued every other month. Magazine format, 32 p. Circulation: 2000
$2.00 per year. Special rates offered. Prepayment required.

C.P.I. management service / *edited by* Charles Law. - *Published by* Corpus Publishers Services Ltd. 6 Crescent Rd., Toronto, Ont. M4W 1T1, October 1969-
Weekly. Trade publication, newsletter format, 6 p. supplements issued.
ISSN 0315-257X $4.00 per issue : $195.00 per year. Prepayment required.

CPSA newsletter (1971-1972) *See* Canadian Political Science Association. Bulletin

C.R.H.A. news report (1949-1962) *See* Canadian rail

C.S.A. bulletin *See* Challenge in educational administration

C.S.F.S. newsletter (1964-1966) *See* Canadian Society of Forensic Science. Journal

CSF newsletter (1971-1974) *See* Canadian Schizophrenia Foundation. Huxley Institute - CSF newsletter

CSHP Ontario newsletter - Canadian Society of Hospital Pharmacists *See* Hospital pharmacy in Ontario

C.S.P.G. newsletter *See* Canadian Society of Petroleum Geologists. C.S.P.G. reservoir

CTM weekly bulletin / *edited by* Wayne Lahtinen. - *Published by* Wayne Lahtinen. P.O. Box 575, Postal Station F, Toronto, Ont. M4Y 2L8.
Weekly.

CUSSnews / *edited by* Donald Page. - *Published by* Advisory Commitee on Canada-United States Studies. Canadian Institute of International Affairs. 15 King's College Circle, Toronto, Ont. M5S 2V9, February 1974-
Special interest, newsletter format, Circulation: 150
ISSN 0316-6791 $4.25 per year.

CV / II / *edited by* Dorothy Livesay. - *Published by* CV/II. P.O. Box 32, University Centre, University of Manitoba, Winnipeg, Man. R3T 1E0, 1975-
Quarterly.
$4.00 per year.

CW / *edited by* Norman Dahl. - *Published by* Canadian Council on Social Development. P.O. Box 3505, Postal Station C, 55 Parkdale Ave., Ottawa, Ont. K1Y 4G1, 1920-
Former title(s): Canadian welfare.
Issued every other month. Association publication, magazine format, 32 p. Includes advertising. available in microform.
Indexed in Abstr. Soc. work, Soc. sci. journal file.
ISSN 0008-5332 $1.00 per issue : $5.00 per year. Subscription included in membership fee.

Cable communications magazine / *edited by* Bill Pryde. - *Published by* Pryde Publications. Suite 503, 30 Bloor St. W., Toronto, Ont, M4W 1A2, 1934-
Monthly.
$3.00 per issue : $20.00 per year : $25.00 per year, overseas.

Cable TV business (April 1972-February 1973) *See* Communications and cable TV business

Cable TV business and communications business (February 1974-Semptember 1974) *See* Communications and cable TV business

Cadre / *edited by* David MacRae. - *Published by* Student Union. University of Prince Edward Island. Charlottetown, P.E.I.
Weekly. Student publication, newspaper format, 14 p. Includes book reviews, film reviews, record reviews, advertising. Circulation: 1500
$.25 per issue : $5.00 per year : $10.00 per year, foreign. Free to students.

Cahier d'animation missionnaire / *parrainé par* Le Service d'animation missionnaire de la propagation de la foi ; *édité par* Jean-Louis Brouillé. - *Publié par* Propagation de la foi. 1145, chemin de la Canardière, Québec, Qué.
Ancien titre: "Messages" (avril-juin 1957-été 1973)
Trimestriel. Publication ecclésiastique, feuilles détachables sous forme de petit cahier, 32 p. Tirage: 10,000
$.75 le numéro : $3.00 par année : $5.00 par année, l'étranger. Tirage contrôlé.

Cahier des études anciennes - *Publié par* Les Presses de l'Université du Québec. C.P. 250, Succursale N, Montréal, Qué. H2X 3M4, septembre 1972-
Intermittent (approximativement 2 éditions par an). Edition savante, 150 p. Tirage: 700
ISSN 0317-5065 Tirage contrôlé.

Les Cahiers canadiens de musique = The Canada music book / *édité par* Gilles Potvin. - *Publié par* Conseil canadien de la musique/ Canadian Music Council. C.P. 156, Succursale E, Montréal, Qué. H2T 3A7, 1970-
Semestriel. Publication d'association, 200 p. Langue(s): français et anglais ; sommaires: français et anglais. Comprend critique de disques. Tirage: 2000
Indexé dans RADAR.
$3.25 le numéro : $6.00 par année : $3.75 le numéro, l'étranger : $7.00 par année, l'étranger. Envoi gratuit.

Les Cahiers de Cap-Rouge / *édité par* Jean-Pierre Tremblay. - *Publié par* Association des professeurs du campus Notre-Dame-de-Foy de Cap Rouge. 5000, rue St-Félix, Cap Rouge, Qué. G0A 1K0, décembre 1972-
Trimestriel. Publication d'association, 80 p. Comprend critique de livres. Tirage: 1000
Indexé dans RADAR.
$2.00 le numéro : $7.00 par année : $8.00 le volume. Abonnements payables à l'avance.

Les Cahiers de cours de l'holanthrope / *parrainé par* Fondation Cosmos ; *édité par* Gaétan Thibeault. - *Publié par* Gaétan Thibeault. B.P. 3, Jonquière, Qué. G7X 7V8, octobre 1975-
Trimestriel. Publication spécialisée, magazine, 48 p. Tirage: 500
$2.00 le numéro : $6.00 par année.

Les cahiers de droit / *parrainé par* Université Laval. Faculté de droit ; *édité par* J.C. Bonenfant et P.G. Jobin. - *Publié par* Les Presses de l'Université Laval. Pavillon Pouliot, Cité universitaire, Qué., 1954-
Trimestriel. Articles juridiques, revue, 200 p. Langue(s): français et anglais. Comprend critique de livres, index de volumes.Aussi sous microform. Tirage: 1200
Indexé dans RADAR.
ISSN 0007-974X $3.00 le numéro : $10.00 par année. Echanges avec d'autres revues juridiques. Abonnements payables à l'avance.

Cahiers de géographie de Québec - *Publié par* Presses de l'université Laval. C.P. 2447, Québec, Qué., 1966-
Intermittent (approximativement 3 éditions par an).
Indexé dans Hist. abstr., Periodex.
$9.00 par année.

Cahiers de Joséphologie / *parrainé par* Centre de recherche et de documentation sur S. Joseph ; *édité par* Roland Gauthier. - *Publié par* Oratoire Saint-Joseph. 3800, chemin Reine-Marie, Montréal, Qué. H3V 1H6, 1953-
Semestriel. Publication ecclésiastique, revue, 176 p. Comprend critique de livres. Tirage: 1000
$4.00 le numéro : $8.00 par année. Abonnements payables à l'avance.

Cahiers de pastorale scolaire - *Publié par* Faculté de théologie. Université de Sherbrooke. Sherbrooke, Qué., septembere 1971-
Publication d'institution (universités, écoles..).

Les Cahiers du nursing *Voir* Corporation professionnelle des infirmières et infirmiers auxiliaires du Québec. La Revue des infirmières et infirmiers auxiliaires du Québec

Cahiers pédopsychiatriques / *édité par* J.J. Breton, L. Houde, et S. Richer. - *Publié par* Comité d'organisation du carrefour scientifique. Département de Psychiatrie. Hôpital Sainte-Justine. 3100, rue Ellendale, Montréal, Qué. H3S 1W3, printemps 1974-
Intermittent. Publication d'association, revue, 120 p. Comprend critique de livres.
ISSN 0315-9477 $1.25 le numéro.

Cahiers québécois de démographie / *édité par* Diane Vanasse. - *Publié par* Association des démographes du Québec. Suite 304, 3220, chemin de la Gare, Ste-Foy, Qué. G1W 3A7, vol. 4 no. 1 mars 1975-
Ancien titre: Bulletin de l'A.D.Q. (août 1971-décembre 1974)
Trimestriel. Publication d'association, 100 p. Tirage: 250-300
Indexé dans Pop. ind.
$2.50 le numéro : $8.50 par année : $12.00 par année, l'étranger.

Cahiers syndicaux - *Publié par* Congres du travail du Canada. 2841 Riverside Dr., Ottawa, Ont.
Publié en anglais: Notes on unions.
Intermittent. Publication d'association, bulletin, 2 p. Langue(s): anglais et français.
Envoi gratuit.

Calendar almanach "slovo" *See* Vilne slovo annual

Calgary Co-operative Memorial Society Ltd. Newsletter / *edited by* Allan Gibson. - *Published by* Calgary Co-operative Memorial Society Ltd. P.O. Box 6443, Postal Station D, Calgary, Alta. T2P 2E1, 1957-
Issued twice a year. Association publication, newsletter format, 2 p.

The Calgary cord - *Published by* Society for Hearing Handicapped. 401 - 329A 6th Ave. S.W., Calgary, Alta. T2P 0R8, January 1965-
Monthly except July and December. Association publication, newsletter format, 9 p. Includes advertising. Circulation: 150
ISSN 0380-9129 Subscription included in membership fee.

Calgary humane voice / *edited by* Leon Nielsen. - *Published by* Calgary Humane Society for Prevention of Cruelty to Animals. P.O. Box 1011, Calgary, Alta. T2P 2K4, March 1972-
Quarterly. Magazine format, 12 p. Includes book reviews, advertising. Circulation: 2000
Subscription included in membership fee $5.00.

Calgary magazine / *edited by* Charles H. Crawford. - *Published by* Calgary Chamber of Commerce. Suite 273-125, 9 Ave. S.E., Calgary, Alta. T2G 0P6, 1969-
Former title(s): This is Calgary (1969-1971)
Monthly. Special interest, magazine format, 28 p. Includes advertising. Circulation: 10,000
$.50 per issue : $8.00 per year. Controlled circulation.

Calgary Personnel Association. Newsletter / *edited by* Glenda Comery. - *Published by* Calgary Personnel Association. P.O. Box 1237, Calgary, Alta. T2P 1K3, October 1974-
Monthly, September - May. Association publication, newsletter format, 4 p. Includes book reviews, advertising.
Available to Association members and related groups only. Controlled circulation.

Caliper / *edited by* Paul C. O'Neill. - *Published by* Canadian Paraplegic Association. 520 Sutherland Dr., Toronto, Ont. M4G 3V9.
Quarterly. Special interest, magazine format, 16 p. Circulation: 5000
$2.00 per year.

Callboard / *edited by* Gary Russell. - *Published by* Nova Scotia Drama League. 4th floor, Student Union Building, St. Mary's University, Halifax, N.S.
Irregular (approximately 6 issues per year). Association publication, newsletter format, 50 p. Includes book reviews, volume index, cumulative index. Circulation: 300
$2.00 per year. Special rates offered. Prepayment required.

The Calquarium / *edited by* Barrie Templeton. - *Published by* Calgary Aquarium Society. P.O. Box 6116, Postal Station D, Calgary, Alta. T2P 2C7, 1954-
Monthly. Association publication, magazine format, 35 p. Includes advertising. Includes one "show issue" per year. Circulation: 500
$.35 per issue : $4.00 per year. Free on exchange program. Prepayment required.

Calvinist contact / *edited by* D. Farenhorst. - *Published by* Guardian Publishing Co. Ltd. P.O. Box 312, Postal Station B, Hamilton, Ont. L8L 7V7, 1945-
Weekly. General interest, tabloid format, 16 p. Language: English with a few pages in Dutch. Includes book reviews, advertising. Circulation: 10,029
$7.00 per year : $8.00 per year, foreign. Controlled circulation.

Camera Canada / *edited by* Freeman Patterson. - *Published by* National Association for Photographic Art. 10 Shaneen Blvd., Scarborough, Ont. M1R 1B5.
Quarterly. Association publication, magazine and newsletter format, 48 p.
$10.00 per year : $6.00 per year for the magazine alone : $8.80 per year, foreign for the magazine. Subscription included in membership fee. Controlled circulation. Prepayment required.

Camp aérospatial / *édité par* Claude Arsenault. - *Publié par* Conseil de la jeunesse scientifique. 1415 est, rue Jarry, Montréal, Qué., 1972-
Annuel. Publication spécialisée, 60 p. Tirage: 100
Envoi gratuit.

Campgrounds in Canada / *edited by* Gladys Taylor. - *Published by* Tall-Taylor Publishing Ltd. 532 Cleveland Cres., S.E., Calgary, Alta.
Annual. Directory, magazine format, 128 p. Includes advertising.
$2.25.

Camping, caravaning plein air : magazine québecois de l'aventure au grand air / *édité par* Charles Neunier. - *Publié par* Camping, caravaning plein air. 1415 est, rue Jarry, Montréal, Qué. H2E 2Z7, avril 1974-
Mensuel. Publication spécialisée, magazine, 52 p. Comprend critique de livres, critique de films, publicité. Tirage: 25,000
Indexé dans RADAR.
$1.00 le numéro : $9.00 par année. Tirage contrôlé. Tarifs spéciaux disponibles. Abonnements payables à l'avance.

Camping Canada / *edited by* Wayne Patterson. - *Published by* Cana Ltd. 3414 Park Ave., Montreal, Que. H2X 2H5.
Annual. Trade publication, magazine format, Includes advertising.

The Campus / *edited by* Malcolm Curtis. - *Published by* Students' Executive Council. Bishop's University. P.O. Box 1089, Lennoxville, J1M 1Z7, 1944-
Weekly during the academic year. Student publication, newspaper format, 12 p. Includes book reviews, film reviews, play reviews, record reviews, advertising. Circulation: 2100
ISSN 0008-2481 $4.00 per year.

Campus / *edited by* The Director of the News Department. - *Published by* Queen's University. Kingston, Ont. (Subscription address: 131 Union St., Kingston, Ontario) 1968-
Issued every other week. House/company organ, newsletter format, 4 p. Circulation: 5000
Free.

Campus : the national magazine for graduating students / *edited by* Susan Pearce. - *Published by* Whitsed Publishing Ltd. 42 Mercer St., Toronto, Ont. M5V 1H3, 1968-
Issued every other month. Special interest, magazine format, 44 p. Language: English (French). Includes book reviews, film reviews, record reviews, advertising. Circulation: 12,000
$.50 per issue : $3.00 per year. Controlled circulation.

Campus estnion (1961-1971) *Voir* Presse campus

Campus estrien *See* L'Ouvre-boîte

Campus estrien (septembre 1959 - août 1972) *Voir* P C / presse campus

The CanOpener (Fall 1969 to Summer 1971) *See* Carleton University. Alumni Association. The Carleton alumneye

Can crop newsletter / *edited by* J.A. Howard. - *Published by* The Ontario Vegetable Growers' Marketing Board. 209 MacNab St. S., Hamilton, Ont. L8P 3C8.
Irregular (approximately 4-5 issues per year). Association publication, newsletter format, 2 p.

Canada - *Published by* Business Publications Division. Maclean-Hunter Ltd. 481 University Ave., Toronto, Ont. M5W 1A7, March 1971-
ISSN 0318-0158

Canada. Laws. Statutes, etc. Martin's annual criminal code / *edited by* Ian Cartwright - *Published by* Canada Law Book Ltd. 80 Cowdray Court, Agincourt, Ont. M1S 1S5, 1955-
Annual. Legislation, book format, 750 p.
$13.25.

Canada. Laws, statutes, etc. Income tax act annotated / *edited by* H. Heward Stikeman. - *Published by* Richard De Boo Ltd. 70 Richmond St. E., Toronto, Ont. M5C 1M8 2M8, 1975/1976-
Irregular (approximately 2 issues per year). Legislation, 1000 p.
ISSN 0527-7884

Canada : an historical magazine / *sponsored by* McMaster University ; *edited by* David P. Gagan. - *Published by* Holt, Rinehart and Winston of Canada, Limited. 55 Horner Ave., Toronto, Ont. M8Z 4X6, Autumn 1973-
Quarterly. General interest, magazine format, 72 p. Includes book reviews. Circulation: 1100
Indexed in Can. essay and lit. ind., Hist. abstr.; Amer. hist. and life.
ISSN 0315-7601 $2.95 per issue : $9.95 per year ($12.50 for those wishing to be billed).

Canada and the world : for students of world affairs / *edited by* Rupert J. Taylor. - *Published by* Maclean-Hunter Ltd. 481 University Ave., Toronto, Ont. M5W 1A7, September 1970-
Former title(s): World affairs (1935-1970)
Monthly. Special interest, magazine format, 24 p. available in microform. Circulation: 48,000
Indexed in Can. ind.
$.90 per issue : $2.00 per year. Special rates offered.

Canada Armenian press : newsletter / *edited by* A.K. Jizmejian. - *Published by* Armenian Evangelical Church. 34 Glenforest Rd., Toronto, Ont. M4N 1Z8, August 1963-
Quarterly. Church publication, ethnic press, newsletter format, 24 p. Language: Armenian and English. available in microform.
Circulation: 350
Free. Supported by gifts.

Canada corporation manual / *edited by* R.A. Kirgston. - *Published by* Richard De Boo Ltd. 70 Richmond St. E., Toronto, Ont. M5C 2M8.
Issued every other month. Special interest, 64 p. Includes updating service. supplements issued.
$40.00 per year.

Canada estate tax service *See* Provincial succession duties and gift tax service

Canada goose / *edited by* Lorne Daniel and Peter Christensen. - *Published by* Canada Goose. c/o Colloquium Study, University of Lethbridge, Lethbridge, Alta., Fall 1973-
Issued twice a year. Special interest, magazine format, 45 p. Circulation: 150
ISSN 0319-2474 $2.00 per issue.

Canada income tax regulations service / *edited by* A.V. Neil. - *Published by* Richard De Boo Ltd. 70 Richmond St. E., Toronto, Ont. M5C 2M8.
Irregular (approximately 20 issues per year). Special interest, looseleaf format, 16 p. Includes updating service.
$30.00 per year.

Canada Japan / *edited by* N. Gregor Guthrie. - *Published by* Canada Japan Trade Council. Suite 903, 75 Albert St., Ottawa, Ont. K1P 5E7, 1968-
Monthly. Special interest, magazine format, 32 p. available in microform.
ISSN 0576-4343 Free to members.

Canada Japan Trade Council. Newsletter / *edited by* N. Gregor Guthrie. - *Published by* Canada Japan Trade Council. Suite 903, 75 Albert St., Ottawa, Ont. K1P 5E7.
ISSN 0043-4214.
Monthly. Association publication, newsletter format, 12 p. available in microform.
Circulation: 4000
Free.

Canada labour service / *edited by* J.P. Renouf. - *Published by* Richard De Boo Ltd. 70 Richmond St. E., Toronto, Ont. M5C 2M8.
Monthly. Special interest, looseleaf format, 64 p. Includes updating service.
$40.00 per year.

Canada legal directory / *edited by* J.H. Wharton. - *Published by* Canada Bonded Attorney and Legal Directory Ltd. Hayhurst Bldg., 55 Eglinton Ave. E., Toronto, Ont., 1911-
Annual. Directory, 1000 p.
$15.00.

The Canada Lutheran / *edited by* Clyde W. Wentzell. - *Published by* Eastern Canada Synod. Lutheran Church in America. 251 King St. W., Kitchener, Ont.
Irregular (approximately 10 issues per year). Church publication, newsletter format, 8 p. Includes book reviews, advertising. Circulation: 22,000
$2.00 per year.

The Canada music book *Voir* Les Cahiers canadiens de musique

Canada North almanac / *edited by* Donald G. Wood. - *Published by* Research Institute of Northern Canada. P.O. Box 188, Yellowknife, N.W.T. X0E 1H0, May 1975-
Former title(s): Northwest Territories community data book.
Annual. Special interest, 100 p. Includes updating service. Circulation: 4200
ISSN 0319-583X Prepayment required.

Canada nucléaire *See* Nuclear Canada

Canada physiology = Physiologie Canada / *edited by* C. Chapler. - *Published by* The Canadian Physiological Society. Dept. of Physiology, University of British Columbia, Vancouver, B.C., December 1969-
Irregular (approximately 3 issues per year). Association publication, newsletter format, 60 p. Language: English and French. Circulation: 600
Controlled circulation.

Canada poultryman / *edited by* Fred W. Beeson. - *Published by* Farm Papers Ltd. 605 Royal Ave., New Westminster, B.C., 1912-
Monthly. Commodity publication, magazine format, 48 p. Language: English and French. Includes advertising. supplements issued. Circulation: 12,700
\$.50 per issue : \$6.00 per year.

Canada report - *Published by* John S. Crosbie. P.O. Box 5040, Toronto, Ont. M5W 1N4, January 1971-
Weekly. Special interest, newsletter format, 4 p.
\$48.00 per year. Prepayment required.

Canada rides / *edited by* Mary Jo Birrell. - *Published by* Canada Rides Publications. 2912-11 St. S.E., Calgary, Alta. T2G 3G8, 1972-
Issued twice a month. Trade publication, magazine format, Includes advertising.
ISSN 0300-4511 \$1.00 per issue : \$10.00 per year.

Canada ski / *edited by* Larry Grainger. - *Published by* Fred Roberts. 145 Prince Edward Ave., Pointe Claire, Que. H9R 4C9 (Subscription address: P.O. Box 180, Pointe Claire, Que. H9R 4N9) November 1968-
Irregular (approximately 4 issues per year). Magazine format, 32 p. Circulation: 39,878
\$.60 per issue : \$2.00 per year : \$3.50 per year, foreign.

Canada tax cases / *edited by* H.H. Stikeman. - *Published by* Richard De Boo Ltd. 70 Richmond St. E., Toronto, Ont. M5C 2M8.
Issued twice a month. Special interest, looseleaf format, 64 p. Includes updating service.
\$60.00. Includes bound volume at the end of the year.

Canada tax manual / *edited by* A.V. Neil. - *Published by* Richard De Boo Ltd. 70 Richmond St. E., Toronto, Ont. M5C 2M8.
Issued every other month. Special interest, looseleaf format, 56 p. Includes updating service.
\$40.00 per year.

Canada tax service / *edited by* H.H. Stikeman. - *Published by* Richard De Boo Ltd. 70 Richmond St. E., Toronto, Ont. M5C 2M8.
Issued twice a month. Special interest, looseleaf format, 64 p. Includes updating service. supplements issued.
\$125.00 per year.

Canada tax service letter / *edited by* H.H. Stikeman. - *Published by* Richard De Boo Ltd. 70 Richmond St. E., Toronto, Ont. M5C 2M8.
Issued twice a month. Business publication, newsletter format, 6 p.
Included in Canada tax service subscription or purchased separately.

Canada west magazine / *edited by* N.L. Barlee. - *Published by* Canada West Publications. P.O. Box 995, Summerland, B.C.
Quarterly. Magazine format, 36 p. Circulation: 3247
\$1.00 per issue : \$4.00 per year. Prepayment required.

Canada-Belgium-Luxembourg / *édité par* Paul von Emmerik. - *Publié par* Chambre de Commerce Belgo-Luxembourgeoise au Canada. 1, Place Ville Marie, Montréal, Qué. H3B 3R1, 1958-
Trimestriel. Publication spécialisée, magazine, 24 p. Langue(s): français et anglais. Comprend critique de livres, publicité. Tirage: 2000
Envoi gratuit. Tarifs spéciaux disponibles.

Canada-exchange *See* Exchange-Canada

Canadaid : a news report to sponsors and friends / *edited by* Frank J. Whilsmith. - *Published by* Christian Children's Fund of Canada. 1407 Yonge St., Toronto, Ont. M4T 1Y8, 1969-
Issued twice a year. Association publication, pamphlet format, 2-4 p. Circulation: 22,000
Free.

Canadan viesti = Canadian messenger / *edited by* Olli H. Jokisaari. - *Published by* The United Church of Canada. 85 St. Clair Ave. E., Toronto, Ont. M4T 1M8 (Subscription address: 3531 E. 22nd Ave., Vancouver, B.C. V5M 2Z5) 1930-
Monthly. Ethnic press, church publication, magazine format, 16 p. Language: Finnish and English. Circulation: 1400
\$1.00 per year.

Canada's business climate - *Published by* Department of Economic Research. Toronto Dominion Bank. P.O. Box 1, Toronto Dominion Centre, Toronto, Ont. M5K 1A2, Spring 1968-
Former title(s): The Toronto-Dominion Bank chartbook (1959-1968)
Quarterly. Special interest, booklet format, 16 p. Circulation: 28,000
Indexed in Can. B.P.I.
ISSN 0045-4303 Free.

Canada's meat industry / *edited by* L.M. Campbell. - *Published by* Meat Packers Council of Canada. 5233 Dundas St. W., Islington, Ont. M9B 1A6.
Issued every 3 years. Association publication, commodity publication, magazine format, 32 p. Language: English and French.

Canada's packaging market / *sponsored by* Canadian Packaging. - *Published by* Maclean-Hunter Research Bureau. 481 University Ave., Toronto, Ont. M5W 1A7.
Irregular (approximately 1 issue per year). Trade publication, magazine format, 50 p.
ISSN 0317-042X $30.00 per volume.

Canada's who's who of the poultry industry / *edited by* Fred W. Beeson. - *Published by* Farm Papers Ltd. 605 Royal Ave., New Westminster, B.C., 1955-
Directory, magazine format, 106 p. Includes advertising. supplements issued. Circulation: 10,000
$6.00. Prepayment required.

Canada-Suensken - *Published by* Thorwald Wiik. Scandinavian News Co. P.O. Box 653, Postal Station F, Toronto, Ont. M4Y 2N6, 1960-
Issued twice a month. Ethnic press. Language: Swedish.
$.25 per issue : $8.00 per year.

Canadian Aberdeen Angus news / *edited by* R.H. Turner. - *Published by* R.H. Turner. Canadian Aberdeen Angus Association. P.O. Box 277, Lethbridge, Alta. T1J 3Y7, 1952-
Irregular (approximately 10 issues per year). Association publication, magazine format, Circulation: 3800
$5.00 per year. Controlled circulation. Prepayment required.

Canadian actuarial bulletin (1958-1961) *See* Mercer actuarial bulletin

Canadian administrator - *Published by* Department of Educational Administration. University of Alberta. Edmonton, Alta. T6G 2G5.
Irregular (approximately 8 issues per year).

Canadian advertising rates and data / *edited by* Betty Gay. - *Published by* Alan J. Waters. Maclean-Hunter Ltd. 481 University Ave., Toronto, Ont.
Monthly. Special interest, magazine format, 418 p.
$65.00 per year.

Canadian Aeronautics and Space Institute. C.A.S.I. transactions / *edited by* P.A. Cobbett. - *Published by* Canadian Aeronautics and Space Institute. Suite 406, 77 Metcalf St., Ottawa, Ont. K1P 5L6., 1968-
Issued twice a year. Magazine format, 30 p. Back numbers available $8.50 each.
$5.50 per issue : $10.50 per year.

Canadian aeronautics and space journal / *edited by* P.A. Cobbett. - *Published by* Canadian Aeronautics and Space Institute. Suite 406, 77 Metcalfe St., Ottawa, Ont. K1P 5L6, 1954-
Monthly except July and August. Institutional publication (Universities, schools, etc.), journal format, 44 p. available in microform. Back numbers available.
Indexed in I.B.Z.
$2.50 per issue : $20.00 per year : $7.50 per volume : $20.00 per year, foreign : Copies prior to 1974 $4.50 each.

Canadian air comments: a commentary on the application of compressed air - *Published by* Atlas Copco Canada Ltd. 745 Montreal-Toronto Blvd., Dorval, Que. H9S 1A3, 1958-
Former title(s): Compressed air comments (February 1958-May 1967)
Quarterly. House/company organ, magazine format, 16 p. Circulation: 11,000
Free.

Canadian Air Traffic Control Association, Inc. CATCA journal / *sponsored by* Canadian Air Traffic Control Association Inc ; *edited by* P.B. Munnelly. - *Published by* J.M. Livingston. Suite 1216, 1 Nicholas St., Ottawa, Ont. K1N 7B7, 1969-
Issued twice a year. Association publication, magazine format, 32 p. Includes advertising. Circulation: 2000
Free. Controlled circulation.

Canadian aircraft operator / *edited by* R.G. Halford. - *Published by* Robert G. Halford. Canadian Aircraft Operator Publishing Ltd. P.O. Box 669, Streetsville, Ont. L5M ZC2, 1964-
Issued twice a month. Trade publication, magazine format,
$5.00 per year : $8.00 for 2 years : $5.50 per year, U.S.: $6.00 per year, foreign.

The Canadian airline pilot (April 1944-Summer 1970) *See* Pilot

The Canadian almanac and directory / *edited by* Susan Walters. - *Published by* The Copp Clark Publishing Company. 517 Wellington St. W., Toronto, Ont. (Subscription address: Richard de Boo Co., 70 Richmond St. W., Toronto, Ont)
Annual. Directory, book format, 900 p. available in microform. Circulation: 10,000
$22.95.

Canadian alpine journal / *edited by* Moira Irvine. - *Published by* The Alpine Club of Canada. P.O. Box 1026, Banff, Alta. T0L 0C0, 1907-
Annual. Association publication, book format, 100 p. Language: English and French. Includes book reviews, volume index. Circulation: 4000
Indexed in North. tit., Arct. bibl.
ISSN 0068-8207

The Canadian amateur - *Published by* Canadian Amateur Radio Federation. P.O. Box 356, Kingston, Ont. K7L 4W2, January 1973-
ISSN 0318-0867

Canadian Amateur Boxing Association. C.A.B.A. news / *edited by* Gordon Anderson. - *Published by* Canadian Amateur Boxing Association. 333 River Rd., Vanier City, Ont. K1L 8B9, January 1972-
Irregular (approximately 10 issues per year). Association publication, newspaper format, 8 p.
$5.00 per year : $10.00 per year, foreign.

Canadian Amateur Football Association. CAFA football journal / *sponsored by* Canadian Amateur Football Association ; *edited by* Peter T. Mercer. - *Published by* National Sport and Recreation Centre. 333 River Rd., Vanier City, Ont. K1L 8B9, October - November 1974-
Issued every other month. Association publication, magazine format, 24 p. Language: English (French). Circulation: 14,000
$.75 per issue : $3.00 per year.

Canadian Amateur Musicians Southern Ontario Region. CAMMAC newsletter / *edited by* Ray Thompson. - *Published by* Southern Ontario Region. Canadian Amateur Musicians. 403 - 263 Russell Hill Rd., Toronto, Ont. M4V 2T4, 1966-
Monthly. Association publication, newsletter format, 6 p.
Subscription included in membership fee
$10.00 per year.

Canadian Anaesthetists' Society. CAS newsletter / *edited by* A. Dunn. - *Published by* Canadian Anaesthetists' Society. 178 St. George St., Toronto, Ont. M5R 2M7, 1975-
Irregular (approximately 3 issues per year). Association publication, newsletter format, 4-6 p. Language: English and French. Circulation: 1800
Subscription included in membership fee.

Canadian Anaesthetists' Society. The Canadian Anaesthetists' Society journal = Société canadienne d'anesthésistes. Journal de la Société canadienne d'anesthésistes. / *edited by* R.A. Gordon. - *Published by* Canadian Anaesthetists' Society. 478 St George St., Toronto, 1957-
Issued every other month. Association publication, journal format, 100 p. Language: English and French ; summaries: French and English. Includes book reviews, advertising, volume index. available in microform. Circulation: 42,000
Indexed in Ind. med.
ISSN 0008-2856 $4.00 per issue : $20.00 per year.

Canadian and international education = Education canadienne et internationale / *edited by* David Radcliffe. - *Published by* Comparative and International Education Society of Canada. Room S829, 252 Bloor St. W., Toronto, Ont., June 1972-
Issued twice a year. Association publication, magazine format, 120 p. Language: English and French ; summaries: French and English. Includes book reviews. Circulation: 500
Indexed in Can. educ. ind.
ISSN 0315-1409 $3.00 per issue : $6.00 per year.

Canadian and provincial golf records - *Published by* Royal Canadian Golf Association. 696 Yonge St., Toronto, Ont. M4Y 2A7.
Quinquennial. Association publication, magazine format, 44 p. supplements issued.
ISSN 0316-8131 Free. Controlled circulation.

Canadian annual review / *edited by* John Saywell. - *Published by* University of Toronto Press. 5201 Dufferin St., Downsview, Ont. M3H 5T8, 1901-
Annual. Special interest, book format, available in microform.
$30.00 per year.

Canadian antiques collector : a journal of antiques and fine art - *Published by* M.F. Goldenberg. Denmount Publishing Co. Ltd. Suite 404, 200 St. Clair Ave. W., Toronto, Ont. M4V 1R1, 1966-
Former title(s): Canadian collector.
Issued every other month. Special interest, magazine format, 64 p. Includes book reviews, advertising. Circulation: 6000
Indexed in Can. ind.
$2.00 per issue : $10.00 per year : $12.00 per volume : $11.00 per year, foreign.

The Canadian Appaloosa journal / *edited by* Rene Bouthillier. - *Published by* Appaloosa Horse Club of Canada. P.O. Box 3036, Postal Station B, Calgary, Alta. T2M 4L6, May 1973-
Former title(s): The 'Appaloosa' (January 1968 to May 1973) Other title: Appaloosa.
Monthly. Association publication, magazine format, 48 p. Language: English and French. Includes advertising, updating service.
$.75 per issue : $7.50 per year. Special rates offered. Prepayment required.

Canadian Arab world review = La Revue du monde arabe / *edited by* R.R. Kneider. - *Published by* Canadian Arab World Review. 10935 Jeanne Mance St., Montreal, Que. H3L 3C7, 1969-
Monthly. Ethnic press. Language: Arabic, English and French. Includes advertising.
$.50 per issue : $10.00 per year.

Canadian Archaeological Association. Bulletin / *edited by* William D. Finlayson. - *Published by* Canadian Archaeological Association. Archaeological Survey of Canada, National Museum of Man, Ottawa, Ont. K1A 0M8.
Annual. Association publication, magazine format, 120-140 p. Language: English ; summaries: French and English. Includes book reviews, volume index. Circulation: 400
Indexed in North. tit.
$3.00 (Institutions $5.00).

The Canadian archer / *sponsored by* Federation of Canadian Archers. - *Published by* National Centre for Sport and Recreation, Ottawa. 333 River Rd., Vanier City, Ont. K1L 8B9 (Subscription address: P.O. Box 151, St. Norbert, Man. R3V 1L6) February 1949-
Former title(s): Federation of Canadian Archers; Official bulletin - Canadian Archery Association (December 1964-June/July 1969) Toxophilus (March 1959-June/July 1963) The Canadian Bowman (April 1958-December 1958)
Monthly. Association publication, magazine format, 50 p. Circulation: 500
$5.00 per year. Special rates offered to libraries. Controlled circulation. Prepayment required.

The Canadian architect / *edited by* James A. Murray. - *Published by* Southam Business Publications Ltd.,. 1450 Don Mills Rd., Don Mills, Ont. M3B 2X7, 1955-
Monthly.
Indexed in Can. ind., Can. B.P.I.
$2.00 per issue : $12.00 per year.

The Canadian architect product bulletin directory / *edited by* Marketing Communications, Southam Business Publications. - *Published by* Charles Shewell. Southam Business Publications Ltd. 1450 Don Mills Rd., Don Mills, Ont.
Issued twice a year. Directory, magazine format, Includes volume index.
Controlled circulation.

Canadian architect yearbook - *Published by* Southam Business Publications Ltd. 1450 Don Mills Rd., Don Mills, Ont. M3B 2X7, 1955-
Annual. Professional publication. Includes advertising. Issued as the December issue of The Canadian architect.
$2.00.

The Canadian architect's yardstick for costing / *edited by* James A. Murray. - *Published by* The Canadian Architect. Southam Business Publications Ltd. 1450 Don Mills Rd., Don Mills, Ont. M3B 2X7, 1971-
Annual. Yearbook. Includes advertising.
$12.50.

Canadian Armed Forces review *See* Government and military business

Canadian art (October 1943-October 1966) *See* artscanada

Canadian art review *Voir* Racar : revue d'art canadienne

Canadian Arthritis and Rheumatism Society. C.A.R. scope / *edited by* Cecilia E. Long. - *Published by* Canadian Arthritis and Rheumatism Society. 45 Charles St. E., Toronto, Ont. M4Y 1S3.
Issued every other month. Association publication, newsletter format, 6 p.
Free.

Canadian association executive / *edited by* Herb Hardy. - *Published by* Brian Perks. Institute of Association Executive. Suite 206, 660 Eglinton Ave. E., Toronto, Ont., March 1973-
Issued every other month. Association publication, magazine format, 32 p. Includes advertising. Circulation: 1400
Controlled circulation.

Canadian Association for Health, Physical Education and Recreation. CAHPER journal / *edited by* Patricia Rutt (Managing editor). - *Published by* Canadian Association for Health, Physical Education and Recreation. 10th floor, 333 River Rd., Vanier City, Ont. K1L 8B9, October 1933-
Former title(s): Bulletin - Canadian Association for Health, Physical Education and Recreation (1933-1951) Journal - Canadian Association for Health, Physical Education and Recreation (1950-1968)
Issued every other month. Association publication, magazine format, 48 p. Includes book reviews, advertising, volume index. supplements issued. Circulation: 2500
ISSN 0008-2899 $2.50 per issue : $10.00 per year. Subscription included in membership fee. Prepayment required.

Canadian Association for Health Physical Education and Recreation. CAHPER newsletter / *edited by* Patricia Rutt. - *Published by* Canadian Association for Health, Physical Education and Recreation. 10th floor, Tower A, 333 River Rd., Vanier City, Ont. K1L 8B9.
Monthly. Association publication, newsletter format, 6 p. Language: English and French. Includes book reviews. Circulation: 2000

Canadian Association for Humane Trapping. CAHT update - *Published by* Canadian Association for Humane Trapping. P.O. Box 934, Postal Station F, Toronto, Ont. M2Y 2N9.
Irregular. Association publication.

Canadian Association for Information Science. Newsletter = Association canadienne des sciences de l'information. Nouvelles / *edited by* D.M. Heaps. - *Published by* Canadian Association for Information Science. P.O. Box 158, Terminal A, Ottawa, Ont. K1N 8V2, 1973-
Quarterly. Association publication, newsletter format, 10 p. Language: English and French. Circulation: 270
$5.00 per year. Subscription included in membership fee $15.00 per year.

Canadian Association for Israel Philately. C.A.F.I.P. bulletin / *edited by* David Warren. - *Published by* Canadian Association for Israel Philately. P.O. Box 395, Willowdale, Ont. M2N 1Y2, September 1966-
Monthly except July and August. Association publication, magazine format, 10 p. Includes advertising. Circulation: 120
ISSN 0007-7747 $10.00 per year. Prepayment required.

Canadian Association for Laboratory Animal Science. Newsletter / *edited by* Maria Neil. - *Published by* Canadian Association for Laboratory Animal Science. 67 Fentiman, Ottawa, Ont. K1S 0T5, 1969-
Issued every other month. Association publication, newsletter format, 12 p. Language: English and French. Includes book reviews, advertising. Circulation: 1000
$6.00 per year. Prepayment required.

Canadian Association for the Advancement of Netherlandic Studies. CAANS newsletter / *edited by* C.R. Levenson. - *Published by* Canadian Association for the Advancement of Netherlandic Studies. 1103-175 Branson Ave., Ottawa, Ont. K1R 6H2, 1972-
Irregular (approximatley 1-2 issues per year). Association publication, newsletter format, 24 p.
Subscription included in membership fee. Controlled circulation.

Canadian Association for University Continuing Education. Bulletin = L'Association pour l'éducation permanente dans les universités du Canada. Bulletin / *sponsored by* Canadian Association for University Continuing Education ; *edited by* Larry Orton. - *Published by* Canadian Association of Departments of Extension and Summer Schools. Extension Department, Queen's University, Kingston, Ont. K7L 2N6, 1967-
Former title(s): Newsletter - Canadian Association of Departments of Extension and Summer Schools.
Irregular (approximately 3-4 issues per year). Association publication, newsletter format, 6 p. Language: English and French ; summaries: English and French. Includes book reviews. Circulation: 700
Free to members and others interested in adult education.

Canadian Association in Support of the Native Peoples. Bulletin : an independent journal on native affairs / *edited by* Collin Gribbons. - *Published by* Canadian Association in Support of the Native Peoples. Suite 904, 251 Laurier Ave. W., Ottawa, Ont. K1P 5J6, 1974-
Former title(s): I.E.A. bulletin; CASNP bulletin (1972-1974)
Irregular (approximately 4 issues per year). Association publication, newsletter format, 32 p. Includes book reviews, advertising, volume index. available in microform. Circulation: 5000
ISSN 0319-2946 $3.00 per year. Subscription included in membership fee $10.00 per year. Controlled circulation.

Canadian Association of Administrative Sciences. Conference proceedings / *edited by* The Program Chairman. - *Published by* Canadian Association of Administrative Sciences. School of Business, Queen's University, Kingston, Ont., 1973-
Former title(s): Association of Canadian Schools of Business. Conference proceedings.
Annual. Association publication. Language: English and French. Includes volume index. available in microform.
$10.00 per year. Prepayment required.

Canadian Association of College and University Libraries. Newsletter / *sponsored by* Canadian Association of College and University Libraries ; *edited by* Richard Green. - *Published by* Canadian Library Association. 151 Sparks St., Ottawa, Ont. K1P 5E3., 1963-
Irregular (approximately 4-6 issues per year). Association publication, newsletter format, 80 p. Language: English (French). Includes film reviews. Circulation: 950
Subscription included in membership fee. Controlled circulation.

Canadian Association of College and University Libraries. Workshop on Automation. Papers / *sponsored by* Canadian Association of College and University Libraries. - *Published by* Canadian Library Association. 151 Sparks St., Ottawa, Ont. K1P 5E3, 1966-
Annual. Association publication, scholarly publication.
Price varies.

Canadian Association of College and University Student Services. The Bulletin = L'association des services aux étudiants des collèges et universités du Canada. Le Bulletin / *sponsored by* Canadian Association of College and University Student Services ; *edited by* John J. Wine. - *Published by* Council of Associations of University Student Personnel Services. University of Waterloo, Waterloo, Ont. (Subscription address: Counselling Services, University of Waterloo) Spring 1974-
Issued 3 times yearly. Association publication, newsletter format, 16 p. Language: English and French.

Canadian Association of Latin American Studies. CALAS newsletter / *edited by* Jules Dufour. - *Published by* Canadian Association of Latin American Studies. Room 210, Burnside Bldg., 151 Slater St., Ottawa, Ont. K1P 5H3, Winter 1969-
Quarterly. Association publication, newsletter format, 8-10 p. Language: English, French and Spanish.
$6.00 per year.

Canadian Association of Law Libraries. Newsletter = Association canadienne des bibliothèques de droit. Bulletin / *edited by* Rosemary McCormick. - *Published by* Canadian Association of Law Libraries. c/o Bibliothèque de droit. Université de Sherbrooke, Sherbrooke, Qué. J1K 2R1 (Subscription address: Mrs. N. Harvey, York University Law Library, 4700 Keele St., Downsview, Ont. M3J 2R5) June 1970-
Former title(s): CALL news (Spring 1963-June 1966)
Issued every other month. Association publication, newsletter format, 15-20 p. Language: English and French. Includes book reviews, volume index. Circulation: 315
ISSN 0319-5376 $15.00 per year.

Canadian Association of Law Teachers. Directory of law teachers = Association canadienne des professeurs de droit. Annuaire des professeurs de droit / *sponsored by* Canadian Association of Law Teachers ; *edited by* Lyman R. Robinson. - *Published by* Lyman R. Robinson. University of Victoria, P.O. Box 1700, Victoria, B.C. U8W 2Y2.
Annual. Directory, book format, 120 p. Language: English and French.
$4.00.

Canadian Association of Medical Record Libraries. Camrl recorder / *edited by* Janet Milner. - *Published by* Canadian Association of Medical Record Librarians. 187 King St. E., Oshawa, Ont. L1H 1C3, 1973-
Former title(s): Bulletin of the C.A.M.R.L. (1942-1973)
Irregular (approximately 5 issues per year). Association publication, tabloid format, 8 p. Language: English and French. Includes advertising. Circulation: 2700
$2.00 per issue : $7.50 per year : $8.00 per year, U.S. : $9.00 per year, foreign.

Canadian Association of Pathologists. Newsletter / *sponsored by* Canadian Association of Pathologists ; *edited by* D.W. Penner. - *Published by* Health Sciences Centre. 700 William Ave., Winnipeg, Man. R3E 0Z3.
Monthly. Association publication, newsletter format, 15 p. Includes book reviews. Circulation: 530
Free to members.

Canadian Association of Public Libraries. Newsletter / *sponsored by* Canadian Association of Public Libraries ; *edited by* Lynn Matthews. - *Published by* Canadian Library Association. 151 Sparks St., Ottawa, Ont. K1P 5E3, 1973-
Irregular (approximately 3-4 issues per year). Association publication, newsletter format, 10 p. Circulation: 790
Free. Subscription included in membership fee. Controlled circulation.

Canadian Association of Radiologists. Journal / *edited by* D.W. MacEwan. - *Published by* Canadian Association of Radiologists. Suite 806, 1440 St. Catherine St. W., Montreal, Que. H3G 1R8, March 1950-
Quarterly. Association publication, journal format, 100 p. Language: English and French ; summaries: English and French. Includes book reviews, advertising, cumulative index. available in microform. Circulation: 2250
Indexed in Ind. med.
$5.00 per issue : $15.00 per year. Prepayment required.

Canadian Association of Sheet Metal and Air Handling Contractors. CASMAHC news bulletin / *edited by* W.N. McCurdy. - *Published by* Canadian Association of Sheet Metal and Air Handling Contractors. 230 - 3316 Kingsway, Vancouver, B.C.
Monthly. Association publication, newsletter format, 4 p.
$10.00 per year. Free to members.

Canadian Association of Slavists. Newsletter = Association canadienne des Slavistes. Newsletter / *edited by* Peter J. Potichnyj. - *Published by* Canadian Association of Slavists. McMaster University, Hamilton, Ont. L8S 4M4 (Subscription address: Secretary-Treasurer, CAS, McMaster University, Hamilton, Ont. L8S 4M4)
Irregular (approximately 3 issues per year). Association publication, newsletter format, 8 p. Circulation: 400
$.70 per issue : $2.00 per year. Controlled circulation.

Canadian Association of Social Workers. Information / *edited by* Anthony J. Gray. - *Published by* Canadian Association of Social Workers. Suite 400, 55 Parkdale Ave., Ottawa, Ont. K1Y 1E5, March 1971-
Irregular (approximately 6 issues per year). Association publication, newsletter format, 8 p. Language: English and French. Includes advertising. Circulation: 6000
ISSN 0315-3150 $4.00 per year.

Canadian Association of Special Libraries and Information Services. Art Libraries Committee. Newsletter / *sponsored by* Canadian Association of Special Libraries and Information Services ; *edited by* Diana Kraetschmer. - *Published by* Library. Fine Arts Division. University of British Columbia. 2075 Wesbrooke Place, Vancouver, B.C. V6T 1W5, August 1971-
Irregular (approximately 1-2 issues per year). Association publication, newsletter format, 3 p. Controlled circulation.

Canadian Association of University Business Officers. Bulletin = Association canadienne du personnel administratif universitaire. Bulletin / *edited by* K. Clements. - *Published by* Canadian Association of University Business Officers. Suite 1103, 151 Slater St., Ottawa, Ont. K1P 5N1, January 1973-
Irregular (approximately 5 issues per year). Association publication. Language: English (French).
Controlled circulation.

Canadian Association of University Business Officers. Directory = Association canadienne de personnel administratif universitaire. Répertoire - *Published by* Canadian Association of University Business Officers. Room 1103, 151 Slater St., Ottawa, Ont. K1P 5N1.
Annual. Association publication. Language: English and French.
For members only.

Canadian Association of University Teachers. C.A.U.T. bulletin = Association canadienne des professeurs d'université. Bulletin de l'A.C.P.U / *edited by* I. Cinman. - *Published by* Canadian Association of University Teachers. 66 Lisgar St., Ottawa, Ont. K2P 0C1., 1952-
Issued every other month. Association publication, magazine format, 32 p. Language: English and French. Includes book reviews, advertising. available in microform.
Circulation: 18,000
Indexed in Can. educ. ind.
$12.00 per year. Controlled circulation.

Canadian Association of University Teachers. Handbook = Association canadienne des professeurs d'université. Guide de l'ACPU / *edited by* W. Goede. - *Published by* Canadian Association of University Teachers. 66 Lisgar St., Ottawa, Ont. K2P 0C1., 1970-
Annual. Association publication, 300 p. Language: English and French. Includes volume index. available in microform.
Circulation: 17,400
Indexed in Can. educ. ind.
$5.00. Controlled circulation.

Canadian Audubon *See* Nature Canada

Canadian author and bookman / *edited by* Mary Dawe. - *Published by* Edmonton Branch. Canadian Authors Association. 8726-116 St., Edmonton, Alta. T6G 1P7 (Subscription address: 11439-50 Ave., Edmonton, Alta. T6H 0J4) 1921-
Quarterly. Association publication, magazine format, 28 p. Includes book reviews, advertising. available in microform. Circulation: 2118
Indexed in Can. ind., Can. essay and lit. ind.
$1.00 per issue : $4.00 per year : $7.00 for 2 years.

Canadian authors : creative writings by children of Northern Alberta / *sponsored by* ACCESS Television North Alberta ; *edited by* Robert Bell. - *Published by* Children's Services Division. Edmonton Public Library. 7 Winston Churchill Sq., Edmonton, Alta. T5J 2V4, September 1973-
Irregular (approximately 4 issues per year). Special interest, magazine format, 12 p.
Free.

Canadian Authors Association. Vancouver Branch. Bulletin / *edited by* Pixie McGeachie. - *Published by* Vancouver Branch. Canadian Authors Association. 3555 Keswick Ave., Burnaby, B.C. V3J 1M5, 1960?-
Issued 9 times a year, September to May inclusive. Association publication, 3 p. Includes book reviews.
$1.50 per year.

Canadian Authors Association. Winnipeg Branch. Newsletter / *edited by* Joyce Collins. - *Published by* Winnipeg Branch. Canadian Authors Association. 6 Oriole St., Winnipeg, Man. R3T 0K3.
Monthly September to April. Association publication, newsletter format, 4 p.

Canadian automotive trade / *edited by* Ed. Belitsky. - *Published by* Chuck O'Hearn. Maclean-Hunter Ltd. 481 University Ave., Toronto, Ont., 1931-
Published in French: Revue moteur.
Monthly. Trade publication, magazine format, 80 p. Includes advertising.
Indexed in Can. B.P.I.
$1.00 per issue : $10.00 per year : $2.00 per issue, U.S. : $12.00 per year, U.S. & U.K. : $3.00 per issue, foreign. Controlled circulation.

Canadian aviation / *edited by* Hugh G. Whittington. - *Published by* Charles T. Turner. Maclean-Hunter Ltd. 481 University Ave., Toronto, Ont. M5W 1A7, 1928-
Monthly. Trade publication, magazine format, 60 p. available in microform. Circulation: 16,100
Indexed in Can. B.P.I., Peace res. abstr.
ISSN 0008-2953 $1.00 per issue : $10.00 per year : $12.00 per year, U.S. and U.K.: $25.00 per year foreign. Controlled circulation.

Canadian Aviation Historical Society. The C.A.H.S. journal / *edited by* W.J. Wheeler. - *Published by* Canadian Aviation Historical Society. P.O. Box 224, Postal Station A, Willowdale, Ont. M2N 5S8, January 1963-
Former title(s): The Early bird enthusiast (1909-1939)
Quarterly. Association publication, journal format, 32 p. Includes book reviews, volume index. Circulation: 850
ISSN 0007-7771 $9.00 per year. Controlled circulation. Prepayment required.

Canadian Ayrshire review / *edited by* J.C. Drummond. - *Published by* Ayrshire Breeders' Association of Canada. 1160 Carling Ave., Ottawa, Ont. K1Z 7K6., May 1920-
Monthly. Association publication, magazine format, 48 p. Language: English and French. Includes advertising, volume index. Circulation: 3832
$3.00 per year : $4.00 per year, foreign.

The Canadian Band Directors. Newsletter / *edited by* Wilfred L. Manning and Frank McKinnon. - *Published by* The Canadian Band Directors Association (Ontario) Inc. 21 Tecumseh St., Brantford, Ont., November 1970-
Former title(s): The Canadian bandmaster (1957-1967) The Canadian bandsman (1943-1957)
Issued every other month. Association publication, newsletter format, 32 p. Circulation: 300
$15.00 per year. Subscription included in membership fee.

The Canadian bandmaster (1957-1967) *See* The Canadian Band Directors. Newsletter

The Canadian bandsman (1943-1957) *See* The Canadian Band Directors. Newsletter

The Canadian banker (to 1973) *See* The Canadian banker and ICB review

The Canadian banker and ICB review / *sponsored by* Canadian Bankers Association and The Institute of Canadian Bankers ; *edited by* W.G. Ivens. - *Published by* Institute of Canadian Bankers. P.O. Box 282, Toronto-Dominion Centre, Toronto, Ont. M5K 1K2, 1893-
Former title(s): The Canadian banker (to 1973) Published in French: Le banquier et revue IBC.
Issued every other month. Association publication, journal format, 64 p. Language: English and French. Includes book reviews. Circulation: 30,000
Indexed in Can. ind., Can. leg. per. lit., Curr. issues Com. and Fin., P.A.I.S., Can. B.P.I., Soc. sci. journal file.
ISSN 0315-6230 $10.00 per year. Controlled circulation. Special rates offered.

The Canadian Bankers' Association. CBA bulletin = L'association des banquiers canadiens. ABC bulletin / *sponsored by* Canada's 10 Chartered Banks ; *edited by* Canadian Bankers' Association Information and Publications Staff. - *Published by* The Canadian Bankers' Association. P.O. Box 282, Toronto Dominion Centre, Toronto, Ont. M5K 1K2, September 1958-
Former title(s): White bulletin (September 1958-November 1966)
Irregular (approximately 5 issues per year). Association publication, newsletter format, 4-5 p. Language: English and French. Circulation: 26,000 English, 6,000 French
Free.

The Canadian Baptist / *edited by* Harold U. Trinier. - *Published by* Baptist Convention. 217 St. George St., Toronto, Ont. M5R 2M2, 1854-
Former title(s): The Christian messenger (1854-1859)
Irregular (approximately 11 issues per year). Church publication, magazine format, 32 p. Includes book reviews, advertising, cumulative index. Circulation: 17,000
$2.50 per year : $7.00 for 3 years. Prepayment required.

The Canadian Baptist register (1857-1873) *See* Baptist Convention of Ontario and Quebec. Year book

The Canadian Bar Association. Bulletin (to December 1973) *See* National

The Canadian Bar Association. Journal (to December 1973) *See* National

The Canadian bar review = La Revue du barreau canadien / *edited by* J.-G. Castel. - *Published by* The Canadian Bar Association. Suite 320, 90 Sparks St., Ottawa, Ont. K1P 5B4, 1923-
Quarterly. Association publication, journal format, 175 p. Language: English and French. Includes book reviews, advertising, volume index, cumulative index. Back issues available ($3.75 each). Circulation: 17,000
$25.00 per year. Subscription includes 4 individual issues plus the bound volume. Controlled circulation. Prepayment required.

Canadian beekeeping / *sponsored by* Canadian Honey Council ; *edited by* J.H. Arnott. - *Published by* J.H. Arnott and Son. Orono, Ont., July 1968-
Irregular (approximately 8-12 issues per year). Commodity publication, magazine format, 8 p. Circulation: 2500
$5.00 per year : $7.00 per year, foreign.

Canadian Bible Society. Newsletter / *edited by* K. McFrellan. - *Published by* Canadian Bible Society. Suite 200, 1835 Yonge St., Toronto, Ont. M4S 1Y1.
Quarterly. Association publication, newsletter format,

Canadian Biochemical Society. Bulletin / *edited by* E.R. Tustanoff and D.B. Smith. - *Published by* Canadian Biochemical Society. Department of Biochemistry, University of Alberta, Edmonton, Alta.
Issued twice a year. Association publication, newsletter format, 20 p. Language: English and French.
Controlled circulation.

Canadian boating / *edited by* Gary Arthurs. - *Published by* Arthurs Publications Ltd. Suite 204, 5200 Dixie Rd., Mississauga, Ont., 1926-
Former title(s): Canadian power and sail.
Monthly. Special interest, magazine format, Includes advertising.

Canadian Boating Federation. Racing rules and directory - *Published by* Canadian Boating Federation. Suite 901, 67 Yonge St., Toronto, Ont. M5E 1J8.
Annual. Association publication, booklet format, 100 p. Language: English (French). Controlled circulation.

Canadian Book Publishers' Council. Newsletter / *edited by* Jacqueline Nestmann. - *Published by* Canadian Book Publishers' Council. Suite 701, 45 Charles St. E., Toronto, Ont. M4Y 1S2, January 1972-
Monthly. Association publication, newsletter format, 6 p. Circulation: 3000
ISSN 0319-5104 Free.

Canadian books in print / *sponsored by* Canadian Books in Print Committee ; *edited by* Martha Pluscauskas. - *Published by* University of Toronto Press. 5201 Dufferin St., Downsview, Ont. M3H 5T8, 1967-
Annual. Bibliography, book format,
ISSN 0068-8398 Author and title index $35.00 : Subject index $25.00.

Canadian Botanical Association. Bulletin = L'Association botanique du Canada. Bulletin / *edited by* J.K. Morton. - *Published by* Canadian Botanical Association. c/o Dr. J.K. Morton, Department of Biology, University of Waterloo, Waterloo, Ont. N2L 3G1 (Subscription address: c/o Dr. G. Hicks, Department of Biology, Dalhousie University, Halifax, N.S. B3H 4J1) 1968-
Quarterly. Association publication, newsletter format, 12 p. Language: English (French). Includes book reviews. Circulation: 450
ISSN 0008-3046 $1.25 per issue : $5.00 per year. Subscription included in membership. Prepayment required.

The Canadian Bowman (April 1958-December 1958) *See* The Canadian archer

Canadian broadcaster *See* Broadcaster

Canadian building / *edited by* Cliff Fowke. - *Published by* Maclean-Hunter Ltd. 481 University Ave., Toronto, Ont. M5W 1A7, 1951-
Former title(s): Building development.
Monthly. Special interest. Includes advertising.
Indexed in RICS abstr. and reviews, Can. B.P.I.
$1.00 per issue : $10.00 per year : $15.00 for 2 years : $20.00 for 3 years : $12.00 per year, U.S. and U.K. : $25.00 per year, foreign.

Canadian Bureau for International Education. Communications = Bureau canadien de l'éducation internationale. Communications / *edited by* Joan Garnett. - *Published by* Canadian Bureau for International Education. Suite 408, 151 Slater St., Ottawa, Ont. K1P 5H3, November 1966-
Weekly. Special interest, newsletter format, 14-18 p. Language: English and French. Circulation: 500
Free to members. Controlled circulation.

Canadian business / *edited by* Robin Schiele. - *Published by* CB Media Ltd. Suite 710, 1080 Beaver Hall Hill, Montreal, Que. H2Z 1T2.
Monthly. Trade publication, magazine format, Circulation: 46,103
Indexed in Employ. rel. abstr., Int. Labour doc., Manage. ind., Can. ind., P.A.I.S., Can. B.P.I., Peace res. abstr.
$8.00 per year : $9.00 per year, foreign.

Canadian business periodicals index / *edited by* Kwai Ho. - *Published by* Information Access. P.O. Box 34, Postal Station S, Toronto, Ont. M5M 4L6, October 1975-
Monthly with an annual cumulation. Index, magazine format, 64 p. Includes cumulative index.
$350.00 per year.

The Canadian business review / *edited by* Walter E. Duffett. - *Published by* The Conference Board in Canada. Suite 1800, 333 River Rd., Ottawa, Ont. K1L 8B9, Winter 1974-
Quarterly. Trade publication, magazine format, 48 p. Circulation: 9500
Indexed in P.A.I.S., Can. B.P.I.
ISSN 0317-4026 $5.00 per issue : $15.00 per year. Controlled circulation.

Canadian business service : investment reporter / *edited by* Patrick McKeough. - *Published by* Marpep Investment Reports Ltd. 700-133 Richmond St. W., Toronto, Ont. M5H 3M8, 1941-
Weekly. Trade publication, looseleaf format, 8 p. Includes volume index, cumulative index.
$95.00 per year. Prepayment required.

Canadian business service : summary review service / *edited by* Roland Jones. - *Published by* Marpep Investment Reports Ltd. 700 - 133 Richmond St. W., Toronto, Ont. M5H 3M8, 1971-
Weekly. Trade publication, looseleaf reference, 12 p. Includes updating service.
$150.00 per year. Prepayment required.

Canadian business trends : monthly indicators / *edited by* The Business Economics Division. - *Published by* The Conference Board in Canada. Suite 1800, 333 River Rd., Ottawa, Ont. K1L 8B9, 1972-
Monthly. Trade publication, chart-folder format, 10 p.
Rates available on request. Controlled circulation.

Canadian business trends : quarterly indicators / *edited by* The Business Economics Division. - *Published by* The Conference Board in Canada. Suite 1800, 333 River Rd., Ottawa, Ont. K1L 8B9, 1973-
Quarterly. Trade publication, chart-folder format, 10 p.
Rates available on request. Controlled circulation.

Canadian business trends : regional indicators / *edited by* The Business Economics Division. - *Published by* The Conference Board in Canada. Suite 1800, 333 River Rd., Ottawa, Ont. K1L 8B9, 1974-
Quarterly. Trade publication, chart-folder format, 10 p.
Rates available on request. Controlled circulation.

The Canadian camper / *edited by* Jack Morrish. - *Published by* Canadian Family Camping Federation Inc. P.O. Box 397, Rexdale, Ont. M9W 5L4, 1969-
Issued every other month. Association publication, magazine format, 40 p.
Circulation: 1400
ISSN 0045-4729 $.35 per issue : $2.80 per year. Prepayment required.

Canadian camping magazine / *edited by* Helen Stewart. - *Published by* Canadian Camping Association. Suite 203, 102 Eglinton Ave. E., Toronto, Ont. M4P 1M7, 1936-
Quarterly. Association publication, magazine format, 18-20 p. Language: English (French).
Circulation: 200
ISSN 0008-3119 $1.50 per issue : $5.00 per year.

Canadian Cancer Society. Ontario Division. Quarterly newsletter / *edited by* John Simpson. - *Published by* Ontario Division. Canadian Cancer Society. 185 Bloor St. E., Toronto, Ont. M4W 3G5.
Quarterly. Association publication, magazine format, 16 p.
Free.

Canadian Canoe Association newsletter *See* Canoe

Canadian cartographer / *edited by* B.V. Gutsell. - *Published by* B.V. Gutsell. York University, Dept. of Geography, 4700 Keele St., Downsview, Ont. M3J 1P3, 1964-
Former title(s): Cartographer (1964-1967)
Issued twice a year. Official publication of the Canadian Cartographical Association, journal format, Includes book reviews, cumulative index every 2 years. supplements issued.
Circulation: 1500
$6.00 per year. Combined subscription with Canadian cartographer $15.00.

Canadian Catholic Conference. Directory *Voir* Conférence catholique canadienne. Annuaire

Canadian Catholic Historical Association. Study sessions / *edited by* Mrs. J. Lenardon. - *Published by* Canadian Catholic Historical Association. 95 St. Joseph St., Toronto, Ont. M5S 2R9, June 1933-
Former title(s): Report - Canadian Catholic Historical Association (1933-1965)
Annual. Association publication, book format, 220 p. Language: English and French.
Circulation: 300
Indexed in Hist. abstr.; Amer. hist. and life.
$10.00.

Canadian cattlemen (June 1938, Vol. I, No. 1 to May 1969 Vol. 32, No. 5) *See* Cattlemen : the beef magazine

Canadian Ceramic Society. Journal / *edited by* A.G. Sadler. - *Published by* Canadian Ceramic Society. Suite 110, 2175 Sheppard Ave. E., Willowdale, Ont. M2J 1W8.
Annual. Association publication, journal format, 100 p.
Indexed in I.B.Z.
$10.00 per year.

Canadian Chamber of Commerce. Statement of policy / *edited by* C.F. Holloway and R. Haumont. - *Published by* The Canadian Chamber of Commerce. 1080 Beaver Hall Hill, Montreal, Que. H2Z 1T7, 1925-
Published in French: Chambre de commerce du Canada. Déclaration de principes.
Annual. House/company organ, paperbound book, 135-140 p. Language: English and French. Circulation: 8000
$1.00. Free.

Canadian Charolais banner / *edited by* Ted Pritchett. - *Published by* F. Rodney James. P.O. Box 1030, Lacombe, Alta., October 1966-
Monthly. Special interest, magazine format, 100 p. Includes advertising. Circulation: 6100
ISSN 0008-5499 $.50 per issue : $5.00 per year : $9.00 for 2 years : $12.00 for 3 years.

The Canadian chartered accountant (1911-1972) *See* CA magazine

Canadian chemical, pharmaceutical and product directory - *Published by* Lloyd Publications of Canada. P.O. Box 65, West Hill, Ont. M1E 4R4, 1947-
Annual. Directory, magazine format, 100 p.
Circulation: 7000
$10.00 : $13.00, foreign. Prepayment required.

Canadian chemical education / *edited by* R.J. Freisen. - *Published by* The Chemical Institute of Canada. Suite 906, 151 Slater St., Ottawa, Ont. K1P 5H3, 1965-
Irregular (approximately 6 issues per year). "For teachers of chemistry and sciences in high schools, community colleges", magazine format, 24 p. Includes book reviews, advertising.
ISSN 0008-3178 $2.00 per issue : $5.00 per volume : $6.00 per year, foreign. Prepayment required.

Canadian chemical processing / *edited by* Thomas E. Buck. - *Published by* Southam Business Publications Ltd. 1450 Don Mills Rd., Don Mills, Ont. M3B 2X7, 1917-
Former title(s): Canadian chemistry and metallurgy.
Monthly. Trade publication, magazine format, 60 p. Includes book reviews, advertising. Circulation: 11,500
Indexed in Eng. ind., Appl. sci. and tech. ind., Can. B.P.I.
ISSN 0008-3186 $3.00 per issue : $12.00 per year : $20.00 for 2 years : $30.00 per year, U.S. : $48.00 per year, foreign. Controlled circulation.

Canadian chemistry and metallurgy *See* Canadian chemical processing

Canadian chess chat / *edited by* Nathan Divinsky. - *Published by* N. Divinsky. C/o Department of Mathematics, U.B.C., Vancouver, B.C., 1946-
Irregular (approximately 6-12 issues per year). Special interest, magazine format, 24 p. Circulation: 300
$10.00 per year.

Canadian children's annual / *edited by* Robert F. Nielsen. - *Published by* Potlatch Publications. 35 Dalewood Cres. Hamilton, Ont. L8S 4B5, 1975-
Annual. Special interest, 176 p.

Canadian children's literature / *sponsored by* Canadian Childrens Literature ; *edited by* John Sorfleet. - *Published by* Canadian Children's Press. P.O. Box 335, Guelph, Ont., 1975-
Quarterly. Journal format, 100 p. Language: English and French. Includes book reviews, play reviews, advertising. Circulation: 750
ISSN 0319-0080 $2.95 per issue : $9.00 per year.

Canadian children's magazine / *edited by* Evelyn Samuel. - *Published by* Canadian Children's Magazine. 4150 Bracken Ave., Victoria, B.C. V8X 3N8, May 1976-
Quarterly. Special interest, magazine format, 48 p. Includes book reviews, advertising.
$1.25 per issue : $5.00 per year. Prepayment required.

Canadian Chiropractic Association. Journal of Canadian Chiropractic Association / *edited by* D.C. Sutherland. - *Published by* Canadian Chiropractic Association. 1900 Bayview Ave., Toronto, Ont. M4G 3E6, 1957-
Former title(s): Canadian chiropractic journal (1957-1961)
Quarterly. Association publication, magazine format, 40 p. Includes book reviews, advertising, volume index. Circulation: 1600
$4.00 per year. Controlled circulation.

Canadian chiropractic journal (1957-1961) *See* Canadian Chiropractic Association. Journal of Canadian Chiropractic Association

Canadian Church Historical Society. Journal / *edited by* Richard Ruggle. - *Published by* Canadian Church Historical Society. Department of History, Laurentian University, Sudbury, Ont. (Subscription address: 537 Main St., Glen Williams, Ont. L7G 3T1) 1950-
Quarterly. Association publication, magazine format, 26-30 p. Includes book reviews. available in microform. Circulation: 250
ISSN 0008-3208 $1.00 per issue : $4.00 per year.

Canadian churchman / *edited by* J.F. Hames (Managing editor). - *Published by* Anglican Church of Canada. 600 Jarvis St., Toronto, Ont. M4Y 2J6, Summer 1875-
Former title(s): Dominion churchman; Church herald.
Monthly. Church publication, newspaper format, available in microform. Circulation: 280,000
$2.00 per year. Controlled circulation.

The Canadian cinematographer *See* Cinema Canada

Canadian clay and ceramics / *edited by* Harold Taylor. - *Published by* Taylor Enterprises. Suite 110, 2175 Sheppard Ave. E., Willowdale, Ont., April 1928-
Issued every other month. Special interest, magazine format, 20 p. Includes advertising. Circulation: 1450
$1.00 per issue : $6.00 per year : $10.00 per year, foreign. Controlled circulation.

Canadian clothing journal / *edited by* Julius Hayman. - *Published by* Canadian Clothing Journal. Suite 507, 8 Colbourne St., Toronto, Ont., 1950-
Issued twice a month. Trade publication, magazine format,
Indexed in World text. abstr., Can. B.P.I.

The Canadian coach / *edited by* John McConachie. - *Published by* Canadian Interçollegiate Athletic Union (CIAU). 11th Floor, 333 River Rd., Vanier City, Ont. K1L 8B9.
Issued every other month. Association publication, magazine format, 20 p. Includes advertising. Circulation: 1000
$1.00 per issue : $6.00 per year : $8.00 per year, foreign.

Canadian Coach Magazine (October 1965-December 1974) *See* Transit Canada magazine

Canadian coin box magazine - *Published by* Sound Publishing Ltd. 126 - 14th St. W., Owen Sound, Ont.
Monthly. Trade publication.

Canadian coin news *See* Coin, stamp, antique news

Canadian collector *See* Canadian antiques collector : a journal of antiques and fine art

The Canadian College of Teachers. Newsletter / *edited by* Vera Sylvester. - *Published by* The Canadian College of Teachers. P.O. Box 483, Sillery, Que. G1T 2R8.
Irregular (approximately 6 issues per year). Association publication, newsletter format, 8 p. Circulation: 1500

Canadian College of Teachers. The Journal of the Canadian College of Teachers / *edited by* J. Patrick McCluskey. - *Published by* The Canadian College of Teachers. P.O. Box 483, Sillery, Qué. G1T 2R8, 1958-
Annual. Magazine format, 80 p. Circulation: 1500
ISSN 0315-2596 $2.00 per year.

Canadian Commission for UNESCO. Bulletin = Commission canadienne pour l'Unesco. Bulletin / *edited by* Francine Walker. - *Published by* Canadian Commission for UNESCO. 222 Queen St., Ottawa, Ont. K1P 5V9, June 1958-
Irregular (approximately 5 issues per year). Special interest, newsletter format, 8-12 p. Language: English and French. Circulation: 5500

Canadian Committee for Geography. Newsletter / *edited by* J.K. Fraser. - *Published by* Canadian Committee for Geography. Environment Canada, Science Policy Branch, Ottawa, Ont. K1A 0H3, 1966-
Published in French: Comité canadien de géographie. Bulletin de nouvelles.
Quarterly. Association publication, newsletter format, 25 p.
Free.

Canadian communications reports / *edited by* Stephen A. McFarlane. - *Published by* Tele-Connect Publications. Suite 405, 150 Metcalfe St., Ottawa, Ont. K2P 1P1, 1974-
Issued twice a month. Trade publication, newsletter format, 24 p.
$95.00 per year.

The Canadian community publisher / *edited by* Lynn Lashbrook. - *Published by* Canadian Community Newspapers Association. Suite 304, 12 Shuter St., Toronto, Ont. M5B 1A2, 1970-
Monthly. Association publication, newspaper format, 16 p.
$7.00 per year. Free to members.

Canadian community publisher (1970-1973) *See* Publisher

The Canadian composer = Le Compositeur canadien / *sponsored by* Composers, Authors and Publishers Association of Canada Ltd. (CAPAC) ; *edited by* Richard Flohil. - *Published by* Creative Arts Co. Suite 501, 1407 Yonge St., Toronto, Ont. M4T 1Y7, 1965-
Issued 10 times a year. Association publication, magazine format, 48 p. Language: English and French. Includes book reviews, record reviews. available in microform.
Indexed in Can. ind.
$2.00 per year. Controlled circulation.

Canadian computer census / *edited by* Roy J. Whitsed. - *Published by* Canadian Information Processing Society. 42 Mercer St., Toronto, Ont. M5V 1H3.
Annual. Association publication.
$25.00 per copy.

Canadian Conference of Pharmaceutical Faculties proceedings (1944-1969) *See* The Association of Faculties of Pharmacy. Proceedings of the annual meeting

Canadian conservation directory = Guide de la conservation du Canada / *edited by* Theodore Mosquin and Sandra MacDougall. - *Published by* Canadian Nature Federation. 46 Elgin St., Ottawa, Ont. K1P 5K6, 1973/1974-
Former title(s): Directory of natural history, conservation and environment organizations of Canada.
Biennial. Directory, association publication, magazine format, 60 p. Language: English and French. Circulation: 5000
$2.00.

Canadian consulting engineer / *edited by* Russell B. Noble. - *Published by* Southam Business Publications Ltd. 1450 Don Mills Rd., Don Mills, Ont., 1959-
Monthly. Professional publication, magazine format, 70 p. Includes book reviews, advertising. Circulation: 8200
$1.00 per issue : $10.00 per year : $14.00 per year, U.S. : $35.00 per year, foreign. Subscriptions are only accepted from registered professional engineers in consulting engineering practice. Controlled circulation.

Canadian consumer / *edited by* Sandra Thompson. - *Published by* Consumers Association of Canada. Room 801, 251 Laurier Ave. W., Ottawa, Ont. K1P 5Z7, 1971-
Former title(s): Canadian consumer = Le Consommateur (1963-1970) Published in French: Le Consommateur canadian.
Issued every other month. Association publication, magazine format, 40 p. Includes book reviews, cumulative index. available in microform. Circulation: 110,000
Indexed in Can. ind., Can. B.P.I.
ISSN 0008-3275 $.90 per issue : $5.00 per year. Prepayment required.

Canadian consumer = Le Consommateur (1963-1970) *See* Canadian consumer

Canadian contractors equipment magazine / *edited by* Martin Richards. - *Published by* Canadian Contractors Equipment Magazine. Suite 108, 215 Morrish Rd., West Hill, Ont., 1972-
Monthly. Trade publication. Includes advertising.
ISSN 0315-3479 $.50 per issue : $7.00 per year : $13.00 for 2 years.

Canadian controls and instrumentation / *edited by* Tom Kelly. - *Published by* Maclean-Hunter Ltd. 481 University Ave., Toronto, Ont. N5N 1A7, 1961-
Monthly. Trade publication, magazine format, 50 p. Includes book reviews, advertising, volume index. Circulation: 11,000
Indexed in Can. B.P.I.
$1.00 per issue : $10.00 per year : $2.00 per issue U.S. and U.K. : $3.00 per issue, foreign. July buyer's guide: $5.00, $8.00 U.S. and U.K., $9.00 elsewhere. Controlled circulation.

Canadian copper = Cuivre canadien - *Published by* Canadian Copper and Brass Development Association. 1612 - 55 York St., Toronto, Ont. M5J 1R7, 1960-
Former title(s): Canadian copper and brass (1960-1963) Canadian coppermetals (1964-1968)
Quarterly. Special interest, magazine format, 24 p. Language: English and French. Circulation: 15,000
Free.

Canadian copper and brass (1960-1963) *See* Canadian copper

Canadian coppermetals (1964-1968) *See* Canadian copper

Canadian Council of Professional Engineers. Newsbrief = Conseil canadien des ingénieurs. Communiqué / *edited by* L.M. Nadeau. - *Published by* Canadian Council of Professional Engineers. Suite 410, 116 Albert St., Ottawa, Ont. K1P 5G3.
Irregular (approximately 12 issues per year). Association publication, newsletter format, 7 p. Language: English and French ; summaries: English and French. Circulation: 500
$1.00 per issue : $10.00 per year. Prepayment required.

Canadian Council of Teachers of English. Newsletter / *edited by* Evelyn Pearce and Audrey Young. - *Published by* Canadian Council of Teachers of English. c/o Bill Warden, 237 Yonge Blvd., Toronto, Ont. M5M 3J1.
Irregular (approximately 5-6 issues per year). Association publication, newsletter format, 4 p. Circulation: 800-900
Subscription included in membership fee.

The Canadian Council of the Blind. The C.C.B. outlook / *edited by* J.T. Patterson. - *Published by* The Canadian Council of the Blind. 96 Ridout St. S., London, Ont. N6K 3X4, January 1948-
Quarterly. Association publication, Issued in print, braille and talking book format, 32 p. Circulation: 1400 print, 500 braille, 100 talking book
Free.

Canadian Council on Social Development. Canadian Conference on Social Welfare. Proceedings - *Published by* Canadian Council on Social Development. P.O. Box 3505, Postal Station C, 55 Parkdale Ave., Ottawa, Ont. K1Y 1E5, 1938-
Biennial. Special interest. Language: English and French.
ISSN 0068-8509 $2.50 per issue.

Canadian Council woman : keeping you posted / *edited by* Edith Teitelbaum. - *Published by* National Council of Jewish Women of Canada. Suite 2, 300A Wilson Ave., Downsview, Ont. M3H 1S8, Fall 1973-
Irregular (approximately 3 issues per year). Association publication, newsletter format, 8 p.
Free.

Canadian counsellor / *edited by* Myrne Nevison. - *Published by* Canadian Guidance and Counselling Association. Suite 302, 1000 Yonge St., Toronto, Ont., June 1967-
Quarterly. Association publication, magazine format, 72 p. Language: English and French ; summaries: English and French. Includes book reviews, volume index. Circulation: 1500
Indexed in Can. educ. ind., Curr. ind. j. educ., Peace res. abstr., Soc. sci. journal file.
$2.50 per issue : $9.00 per year.

Canadian courier / *edited by* G.O. Hughes. - *Published by* Canadian Hospital Association. 25 Imperial St., Toronto, Ont. M5P 1C1, 1951-
Former title(s): The Record (1951) Le Courrier canadien (1969)
Quarterly. Association publication, newsletter format, 30 p. Circulation: 875
$1.00 per year.

Canadian courses and seminars *See* Short courses and seminars

Canadian Crafts Council. Newsletter = Conseil canadien de l'artisan. Bulletin de nouvelles / *edited by* Patsy Spring. - *Published by* Canadian Crafts Council. Suite 16, 46 Elgin St., Ottawa, Ont. K1P 5K6, Spring 1974-
Monthly, except every two months in the summer and at Christmas. Association publication, newsletter format, 6-12 p. Language: English and French. Includes book reviews, advertising. supplements issued. Circulation: 10,000
$10.00 per year. Prepayment required.

Canadian Cricket Association annual (1959-1970) *See* The Canadian cricketer

The Canadian cricketer / *edited by* K.R. Bullock. - *Published by* Sports Federation of Canada. 333 River Rd., Vanier, Ont. K1L 8B9 (Subscription address: Editor, P.O. Box 1364, Brockville, Ont. K6V 5V6) March 1972-
Former title(s): Canadian Cricket Association annual (1959-1970)
Issued every other month. Association publication, magazine format, 48 p. Includes advertising. Circulation: 4000
$1.00 per issue : $5.00 per year : $5.00 per year, U.S. : $6.00 per year (seamail) foreign : $7.00 per year (airmail), foreign.

Canadian criminal cases / *edited by* Horace Krever. - *Published by* Canada Law Book Ltd. 80 Cowdray Court, Agincourt, Ont. M1S 1S5, 1898-
Weekly. Special interest, magazine format, 64 p. Includes volume index, updating service.
$29.50 per volume. Prepayment required.

Canadian Criminology and Corrections Association. Bulletin - *Published by* Canadian Criminology and Corrections Association. 55 Parkdale Ave., Ottawa, Ont. K1Y 1E5., September 1971-
Former title(s): Correctional process (August 1948-May 1971)
Issued five times a year. Association publication, newsletter format, 16-20 p. Language: English and French.
ISSN 0045-463X Available free to members only. Controlled circulation.

The Canadian curling news / *edited by* George L. Bilych. - *Published by* T.E. Thonger. 1112 Centre St. N., Calgary, Alta. T2E 2R2, 1957-
Issued 8 times a year, October through April and midsummer. Special interest, newspaper format, 12 p. Includes advertising. Circulation: 22,812
$5.00 per year : $7.00 per year, foreign.
Special rates offered. Prepayment required.

Canadian cyclist = Cycliste canadien / *edited by* Kenneth V. Smith. - *Published by* Canadian Cycling Association. 333 River Rd., Place Vanier, Vanier City, Ont. K1L 8B9, January 1973-
Monthly. Association publication, newspaper format, 24 p. Language: English and French. Circulation: 5000
$.50 per issue : $5.00 per year : $6.00 per year, foreign. Controlled circulation.

Canadian dairy and ice cream journal (September 1923-December 1968) *See* Modern dairy

The Canadian dairy farmer / *edited by* Gayle Wykes. - *Published by* Southam Business Publications Ltd. 1450 Don Mills Rd., Don Mills, Ont. M3B 2X7, 1972-
Quarterly. Trade publication. Includes advertising. Inserted in Good farming 4 times a year.

Canadian dairy goat news *See* B.C. dairy goat news

Canadian dancers news / *edited by* Art and Garrie Jackson. - *Published by* Canadian Dancers News. c/o Russ and Grace Hendsbee, 2022 Gatineau View Cr., Ottawa, Ont. (Subscription address: Russ and Grace Hendsbee, 2022 Gatineau View Cr., Ottawa, Ont) 1971-
Quarterly. Special interest, magazine format, 28 p. Includes advertising. Circulation: 900
ISSN 0315-3959 $3.00 per year.

Canadian data processing directory - *Published by* Whitsed Publishing Ltd. 42 Mercer St., Toronto, Ont. M5V 1H3, 1975-
Annual. Directory. Includes advertising.

Canadian datasystems / *edited by* Tom Weissmann. - *Published by* Frank B. Lederer. Maclean-Hunter Ltd. 481 University Ave., Toronto, Ont. M5W 1A7, November 1969-
Monthly. Business publication, magazine format, 90 p. Includes book reviews, advertising, cumulative index, updating service. available in microform. supplements issued. Circulation: 14,500
Indexed in Can. B.P.I.
$10.00 per year. Controlled circulation.

Canadian defence quarterly = Revue canadienne de défense - *Published by* Defence Publications. c/o McAinsh and Co. Ltd., 1835 Yonge St., Toronto, Ont. M4S 1L7, Summer 1971-
Quarterly.
ISSN 0315-3495

Canadian Dental Association. Dental journal = L'Association dentaire canadienne. Journal dentaire / *edited by* Patricia Lundie. - *Published by* Canadian Dental Association. 234 St. George St., Toronto, Ont. M5R 2P2, 1935-
Monthly. Association publication, journal format, 40 p. Language: English and French ; summaries: English and French. Includes advertising, volume index. Back issues available ($2.00 each).
Indexed in Ind. med.
ISSN 0008-3372 $1.50 per issue : $20.00 per year : $22.00 per year, foreign. Controlled circulation.

Canadian Dental Association. Directory - *Published by* Canadian Dental Association. 234 St. George St., Toronto, Ont. M5R 2P2.
Annual. Directory, 200 p. Language: English and French.
$35.00. Controlled circulation.

Canadian Dental Association. Transactions - *Published by* Canadian Dental Association. 234 St. George St., Toronto, Ont. M5R 2P2.
Annual. Association publication, 350 p. Language: English and French.
Controlled circulation.

Canadian Dental Nurses and Assistants Association. Journal / *edited by* L. Masse. - *Published by* Guideline Press Ltd. 3881 Myrtle St., North Burnaby, B.C. V5C 4G1, 1972-
Quarterly. Association publication. Includes advertising.
$10.00 per year : $14.00 per year, foreign.

Canadian Diabetic Association. Quarterly newsletter / *edited by* K.G. Anderson. - *Published by* The Canadian Diabetic Association. 1491 Yonge St., Toronto, Ont. M4T 1Z5, January 1959-
Quarterly. Association publication, newsletter format, 25 p. Includes book reviews, advertising. Circulation: 20,000

The Canadian Diabetic Association. Toronto and District Branch. The Toronto District Diabetic Branch bulletin / *edited by* Carole Hollander. - *Published by* Toronto and District Branch. The Canadian Diabetic Association. Suite 411, 234 Eglinton Ave. E., Toronto, Ont. M4P 1K5, July 1962-
Irregular (approximately 4-5 issues per year). Association publication, newsletter format, 6-8 p.
Free.

The Canadian Dietetic Association. Journal of the Canadian Dietetic Association / *edited by* Kathlyn V. Bettington. - *Published by* Canadian Dietetic Association. 1393 Yonge St., Toronto, Ont. M4T 1Y4, 1935-
Quarterly. Association publication, journal format, 72 p. Language: English and French ; summaries: English and French. Includes book reviews, advertising, volume index.
Circulation: 2600
$1.50 per issue : $6.00 per year. Controlled circulation.

Canadian dimension / *edited by* John Gallagher. - *Published by* Cy Gonick. P.O. Box 1413, Winnipeg, R3C 2Z1, June 1963-
Monthly except summer. General interest, magazine format, 68 p. Includes book reviews, film reviews, advertising. Bound volumes available. Circulation: 8000
Indexed in Can. ind., Can. essay and lit. ind., Hist. abstr.; Amer. hist. and life, Peace res. abstr., Soc. sci. journal file.
$.75 per issue : $6.00 per year : $9.00 per year, foreign. Controlled circulation.

Canadian diving news / *edited by* Morley Eveleigh. - *Published by* Morley Eveleigh. P.O. Box 66, Postal Station T, Toronto, Ont., July 1971-
Monthly. Special interest, magazine format, Language: English (French). Includes book reviews, advertising. Circulation: 4500
$.50 per issue : $4.50 per year. Prepayment required.

Canadian doctor / *edited by* David Elkins. - *Published by* Southam Business Publications Ltd. 310 Victoria Ave., Westmount, Que. H3Z 2M9, October 1935-
Monthly. Professional publication, magazine format, 120 p. Includes book reviews. available in microform.
$2.00 per issue : $12.00 per year . $30.00 per year, foreign. Controlled circulation.

Canadian drama = L'Art dramatique canadien / *edited by* Rota Lister. - *Published by* University of Waterloo. Waterloo, Ont. N2L 3G1 (Subscription address: c/o Department of English, University of Waterloo, Waterloo, Ont. N2L 3G1) March 1975-
Issued twice a year. Special interest, magazine format, 80 p. Language: English and French ; summaries: English and French. Includes book reviews, play reviews, advertising, cumulative index. Circulation: 300
ISSN 0317-9044 $1.50 per issue : $2.00 per year. Prepayment required.

Canadian driver/owner / *edited by* John Bates. - *Published by* Maclean-Hunter Ltd. 481 University Ave., Toronto, Ont. M5W 1A7, 1972-
Quarterly. Trade publication. Includes advertising.
$2.00 per issue : $5.00 per year.

Canadian dry goods review (1891) *See* Style : for Canadian fashion merchandisers

Canadian education (1945-1960) *See* Education Canada

Canadian education and research digest (1959-1960) *See* Education Canada

Canadian Education Association. CEA newsletter / *edited by* Harriett Goldsborough. - *Published by* Canadian Education Association. 252 Bloor St. W., Toronto, Ont. M5S 1V5, November 1946-
Monthly during the school year. Association publication, newsletter format, 6 p. Includes book reviews. Circulation: 7000
Indexed in Can. educ. ind.
ISSN 0008-3445 $.35 per issue : $3.00 per year. Prepayment required.

Canadian Education Association. Convention proceedings - *Published by* Canadian Education Association. 252 Bloor St. W., Toronto, Ont. M5S 1V5, 1892-1945, 1961-
Annual. Association publication, proceedings of the annual convention, magazine format, 96 p. Language: English and French. Circulation: 1000
$3.00. Subscription included in membership fee.

Canadian Education Association. The C.E.A. handbook = Le ki-es-ki / *edited by* Harriett Goldsborough. - *Published by* Canadian Education Association. 8th flr., 252 Bloor St. W., Toronto, M5S 1V5, 1948-49-
Former title(s): Directory of administrative officials in public education - Canada (1948-1970)
Annual. Directory, 144 p. Language: English and French. Circulation: 2000
ISSN 0068-8657 $4.50. Prepayment required.

Canadian education index / *edited by* Carolynn Bett. - *Published by* The Canadian Education Association. 252 Bloor St. W., Toronto, Ont. M5S 1V5.
Issued in three interim issues and annual cumulation. Indexes, magazine format, 132 p. Language: English and French. Includes volume index, cumulative index. available in microform.
ISSN 0008-3453 Interim issues $10.00 each : Annual cumulation $40.00.

Canadian Electrical Association. Bulletin = Association canadienne de l'élecricité. Bulletín / *edited by* R.R. Palin. - *Published by* Canadian Electrical Association. Suite 580, One Westmount Square, Montreal, Que. H3Z 2P9, 1930-
Former title(s): Newsletter - Canadian Electrical Association (1930-1974)
Irregular (approximately 8 issues per year). Association publication, newsletter format, 8 p. Language: English and French. Circulation: 2200
Subscription included in membership fee. Controlled circulation.

Canadian Electrical Association. Newsletter / *edited by* Robin Palin. - *Published by* Canadian Electrical Association. 1 Westmont Sq., Montreal, Que. H3Z 2P9.
Issued 10 times a year. Association publication, newsletter format, 8 p.
Free to members of the Association.

Canadian Electrical Association. Proceedings - *Published by* Canadian Electrical Association. Suite 580, 1 Westmount Sq., Montreal, Que. M3Z 2P9, 1911-
Annual. Association publication, proceedings of the annual meeting, magazine format, 200 p. Includes advertising, volume index.
Free. Available to members only.

Canadian electronics engineering / *edited by* Cliff Hand. - *Published by* Maclean-Hunter Ltd. 481 University Ave., Toronto, Ont. M5W 1A7, 1957-
Monthly. Professional publication, magazine format, 70 p. Includes book reviews, advertising. Circulation: 10,700
Indexed in Eng. ind.
ISSN 0008-3461 $1.00 per issue : $10.00 per year : $2.00 per issue, U.K. : $12.00 per year, U.K. : $3.00 per issue, foreign : $25.00 per year, foreign. Controlled circulation. Prepayment required.

Canadian electronics engineering annual buyers guide and catalog directory / *edited by* Cliff Hand. - *Published by* Maclean-Hunter Ltd. 481 University Ave., Toronto, Ont. M5W 1A7, 1957-
Former title(s): Key to electronics engineering purchasing in Canada.
Annual. Directory, magazine format, 200 p. Includes book reviews, advertising. Circulation: 12,500
Indexed in Eng. ind.
$10.00 per year. Controlled circulation.

The Canadian elk / *sponsored by* B.P.O. Elks of Canada ; *edited by* Ralph Bagley. - *Published by* Lance Publishing Co. Ltd. 620 Dalcota Dr., Winnipeg, Man. R3M 2K3 (Subscription address: 606-294 Portage Ave., Winnipeg, Man. R3C 0B9)
Quarterly. Fraternal organization, newspaper format, 8 p. Circulation: 42,000
$1.00 per year. Subscription included in membership.

Canadian energy news - *Published by* Capital Communications Ltd. Suite 705, 151 Slater St., Ottawa, Ont. K1P 5H3, June 1972-
Monthly. Trade publication, newsletter format, 9 p. Circulation: 140
$50.00 per year. Controlled circulation.

Canadian engineering and industrial year book - *Published by* Lloyd Publications of Canada. P.O. Box 65, West Hill, Ont. M1E 4R4, 1945-
Annual. Directory, magazine format, 210 p. Circulation: 9000
ISSN 0068-8665 $12.00 : $15.00, foreign. Prepayment required.

The Canadian entomologist / *edited by* P.E. Morrison. - *Published by* Entomological Society of Canada. 1320 Carling Ave., Ottawa, Ont. K1Z 7K9, 1862-
Monthly. Association publication, magazine format, 112 p. Language: English and French. Includes volume index. available in microform. supplements issued. Circulation: 2000
Indexed in Biol. abstr., North. tit., I.B.Z., Arct. bibl.
$4.50 per issue : $35.00 per year.

Canadian environmental law news / *edited by* J. Swaigen, J.F. Castrilli, M. Green and D. Estrin. - *Published by* Canadian Environmental Law Association. Suite 303, One Spadina Cres., Toronto, Ont. M5S 2J5, February 1972-
Issued every other month. Association publication, newsletter format, 50 p. Includes book reviews, volume index, cumulative index. Back issues : Vol. I $.75 Vol. II-IV $2.00. Circulation: 700
ISSN 0317-6517 $12.00 per year (Students and senior citizens $6.00 : corporations, law firms, etc $2.00). Special rates offered.

Canadian ethnic studies = Etudes éthniques du Canada / *sponsored by* Canadian Ethnic Studies Association ; *edited by* H.D. Palmer and A. Malycky. - *Published by* Research Centre for Canadian Ethnic Studies. University of Calgary. 2920 - 24 Ave. N.W., Calgary, Alta. T2N 1N4, 1969-
Issued twice a year. Association publication, magazine format, 100 p. Includes book reviews. Circulation: 500
Indexed in M.L.A. int. bib., North. tit., Soc. sci. journal file.
ISSN 0008-3496 $8.00 per issue : $15.00 per year.

Canadian Ethnic Studies Association. Bulletin = Société canadienne d'études éthniques. Bulletin / *edited by* Cornelius J. Jaenen. - *Published by* Canadian Ethnic Studies Association. P.O. Box 370, Postal Station A, Ottawa, Ont. K1N 8V3, July 1974-
Quarterly. Ethnic press, newsletter format, 12 p. Language: English and French. Includes book reviews. Circulation: 700
ISSN 0315-8705 Prepayment required.

Canadian family physician / *edited by* Margaret McCaffery. - *Published by* College of Family Physicians of Canada. 4000 Leslie St., Willowdale, Ont. M2K 2R9, September 1954-
Former title(s): Journal of the College of General Practice of Canada.
Monthly. Professional publication, magazine format, 150 p.
$1.00 per issue : $10.00 per year : $10.00 per year, U.S. : $12.00 per year, foreign.

Canadian far eastern newsletter / *edited by* James G. Endicott. - *Published by* James G. Endicott. 232 Wychwood Ave., Toronto, Ont. M6C 2T3, January 1948-
Monthly. Special interest, newsletter format, Circulation: 1000
$.50 per issue : $4.00 per year.

Canadian farm equipment dealer / *edited by* R.N. Mercer. - *Published by* Southam Business Publications Ltd. 1450 Don Mills Rd., Don Mills, Ont., 1904-
Trade publication, magazine format,
Indexed in Can. B.P.I.
$.75 per issue : $8.00 per year.

Canadian farming / *edited by* Dennis S. Hladysh. - *Published by* Dennis S. Hladysh. International Harvester Canada. 1190 Blair Rd., Burlington, Ont. L7M 1K9.
Former title(s): Tractor farming (1918-1939) Canadian tractor farming (1940-1959)
Published in French: L'Agriculture canadienne.
Quarterly. Trade publication, magazine format, 20 p. Circulation: 135,000
Free.

Canadian federation news / *edited by* P.R. Galsworthy. - *Published by* Canadian Federation of Biological Societies. Room 274, Department of Pharmacology, University of Western Ontario, London, Ont. N6A 3K7.
Annual. Association publication, magazine format, 60 p. Language: English (French).
Controlled circulation.

Canadian Federation of Biological Societies. Proceedings / *edited by* P.R. Galsworthy. - *Published by* Canadian Federation of Biological Societies. Room 274, Department of Pharmacology, University of Western Ontario, London, Ont. N6A 3K7.
Annual. Proceedings of annual meetings, journal format, 200 p. Language: English and French.
$1.00. Controlled circulation.

Canadian Federation of Mayors and Municipalities. Annual conference proceedings - *Published by* Canadian Federation of Mayors and Municipalities. Suite 816, 56 Sparks St., Ottawa, Ont. K1P 5A9 (Subscription address: 220 Laurier Ave. W., Ottawa, Ont. K1P 5J8) 1937-
Annual. Proceedings of annual conference, book format, 150 p. Language: English and French ; summaries: English and French.
$2.50. Prepayment required.

The Canadian Federation of Retail Grocers. Bulletin / *edited by* F.A.B. Ranos. - *Published by* The Canadian Federation of Retail Grocers. P.O. Box 3, 29 Old Oak Rd., Islington, Ont. M9A 4X1.
Monthly. Association publication, newsletter format, 6 p. Circulation: 300
Free on a limited basis. Controlled circulation.

Canadian Federation of University Women. Bulletin / *edited by* Ann Semple. - *Published by* Canadian Federation of University Women. 209A - 151 Slater St., Ottawa, Ont. K1P 5H3.
Former title(s): CFUW newsletter (1970-1973)
Quarterly. Association publication, newsletter format, 4 p. Language: English and French.
Circulation: 10,000
Free.

The Canadian fiction magazine / *edited by* Geoffrey Hancock. - *Published by* Geoffrey Hancock. 3664 W. 2nd Ave., Vancouver, B.C. V6K 1J7 (Subscription address: P.O. Box 46422, Postal Station G, Vancouver, B.C. V6R 4G7) September 1971-
Quarterly. Special interest, magazine format, 120 p. Language: English and French. Includes book reviews, cumulative index. available in microform. Circulation: 1800
Indexed in Can. essay and lit. ind., M.L.A. int. bib.
ISSN 0045-477X $2.00 per issue : $7.00 per year : $8.00 per year, foreign.

Canadian field hockey news / *edited by* Keith Newton. - *Published by* Canadian Field Hockey Association. 333 River Rd., Ottawa, Ont. K1L 8B9, 1964-
Quarterly. Association publication, magazine format, 36 p.
$5.00 per year.

Canadian field-naturalist / *edited by* Lorraine C. Smith. - *Published by* Ottawa Field Naturalists' Club. P.O. Box 3264, Postal Station C, Ottawa, Ont. K1Y 4J5, 1887-
Former title(s): The Ottawa naturalist(1887-1920)
Quarterly. Association publication, magazine format, Language: English (French) ; summaries: English and French. Includes book reviews, volume index. Circulation: 2000
Indexed in Biol. abstr., North. tit., Arct. bibl.
$7.00 per volume (Libraries $12.00).

The Canadian film editor / *edited by* David Nisbet. - *Published by* Canadian Film Editors' Guild. P.O. Box 46, Terminal A, Toronto, Ont. M5W 1A0, April 1974-
Issued every other month. Association publication, magazine format, 36 p. Includes film reviews, advertising. Circulation: 500
$10.00 per year : $10.00 per year, U.S. : $15.00 per year, foreign.

Canadian Film Institute 16 and 35 mm film index (1955-1960) *See* Index of 16mm & 35mm feature length films available in Canada

Canadian financial E-Z directory - *Published by* Canadian Daily Quotation Service Ltd. P.O. Box 518, Postal Station K, Toronto, Ont. M4P 2G9.
Annual. Directory, Spiral bound book, 54 p. supplements issued.
$12.50.

Canadian fisherman and ocean science / *edited by* Allan T. Muir. - *Published by* Muir Publishing Company. Gardenvale, Que. H0A 1B0, January 1914-
Former title(s): Sea harvest and ocean science (June 1969 - December 1970)
Issued every other month. Special interest, magazine format, 48 p. Includes book reviews, advertising. Circulation: 5126
Indexed in Can. B.P.I.
ISSN 0037-0002 $2.00 per issue : $10.00 per year : $14.00 per year, U.K., Commonwealth and U.S. : $17.00 per year, foreign. Controlled circulation.

Canadian flight / *sponsored by* Canadian Owners and Pilots Association ; *edited by* W.N. Peddler. - *Published by* Canadian Flight Publishing Co. P.O. Box 563, Postal Station B, Ottawa, Ont., 1955-
Issued every other month. Magazine format, 32 p. Includes book reviews, advertising. Circulation: 10,000
$4.00 per year. Prepayment required.

Canadian florist, greenhouse and nursery / *edited by* William G. Tolton. - *Published by* Horticulture Publications Ltd. 74 William St., Streetsville, Ont. L5M 1J3, September 1905-
Issued twice a month. Trade publication, magazine format, 38 p. Includes book reviews. Circulation: 2400
$.15 per issue : $3.00 per year : $4.00 per year, foreign. Controlled circulation.

Canadian florist, Keith's directory and horticultural guide / *edited by* W.E. Bowman. - *Published by* Horticulture Publications Ltd. P.O. Box 697, Streetsville, Ont. L5M 2C2, 1932-
Annual. Trade publication. Includes advertising.

Canadian Folk Music Society. Newsletter / *edited by* Michael Cass-Beggs. - *Published by* Canadian Folk Music Society. c/o Beverley Cavanagh, 915 Auden Park Dr., Kingston, Ont. K7M 4T8, July 1965-
Issued twice a year. Association publication, newsletter format,
$1.50 per year. Subscription included in membership fee.

Canadian Folk Music Society journal / *edited by* Edith Fowke. - *Published by* Canadian Folk Music Society. 15 Julien, Pointe Claire, Que. (Subscription address: c/o Beverley Cavanaugh, 915 Auden Park Dr., Kingston, Ont. K7M 4T8) 1973-
Former title(s): C.F.M.S. newsletter/bulletin.
Annual. Association publication, journal format, 56 p. Language: English and French ; summaries: French and English.
$1.50 per year. Subscription included in membership fee $5.00 (Institutions $10.00).

Canadian food and packaging directory - *Published by* Lloyd Publications of Canada. P.O. Box 65, West Hill, Ont. M1E 4R4, 1924-
Annual. Directory, magazine format, 70 p. Circulation: 7000
$10.00 : $13.00, foreign. Prepayment required.

Canadian food industries *See* Food in Canada

Canadian football news / *edited by* Charles Halpin. - *Published by* W.C.C. Publishing Ltd. Suite 217, 1434 St. Catherines St. W., Montreal, Que. H3G 1R7, 1951-
Quarterly. Special interest, magazine format,

Canadian footwear and leather directory - *Published by* Lloyd Publications of Canada. P.O. Box 65, West Hill, Ont. M1E 4R4, 1924-
Annual. Directory, magazine format, 44 p. Circulation: 4500
$7.00 : $10.00, foreign. Prepayment required.

Canadian forest industries / *edited by* Rick Letkman. - *Published by* Fred O'Leary. Southam Business Publications Ltd. 1450 Don Mills Rd., Don Mills, Ont. M3B 2X7, 1882-
Monthly. Business publication, magazine format, 40 p. Includes advertising.
Indexed in Can. B.P.I., North. tit.
$1.00 per issue : $10.00 per year : $16.00 per year, foreign. Controlled circulation.

Canadian forest industries. Directory - *Published by* Fred O'Leary. Southam Business Publications Ltd. 1450 Don Mills Rd., Don Mills, Ont. M3G 2X7.
Annual. Directory, 80 p. Includes advertising.
$10.00 : $16.00, foreign. Controlled circulation.

Canadian Forestry Association. C.F.A. news = Association forestière canadienne. Le courrier A.F.C / *edited by* A.D. Hall. - *Published by* Canadian Forestry Association/ Association forestière canadienne. 185 Somerset St. W., Ottawa, Ont. K2P 0J2, 1968-
Quarterly. Association publication, newsletter format, 4 p. Language: English and French. Circulation: 2200
Controlled circulation.

Canadian forum / *edited by* Michael S. Cross. - *Published by* Survival Foundation. 56 Esplanade St. E., Toronto, Ont. M5E 1A8, 1920-
Monthly. "Independent journal of opinion and the arts, aimed at an intellectual Canadian audience", journal format, 44 p. Includes book reviews, film reviews, advertising, volume index. available in microform. Circulation: 7500
Indexed in Can. ind., Soc. sci. ind., Peace res. abstr., Soc. sci. journal file.
ISSN 0008-3631 $7.50 per year (Students $5.00, Institutions $10.00) : $2.50 extra per year for overseas subscriptions.

The Canadian forwarder / *edited by* Hazel McLaughlin. - *Published by* Progressive Publications Inc. P.O. Box 1475, Sherbrooke, Que., 1958-
Issued every other week. Trade publication, magazine format, 28 p.
$7.50 per year.

Canadian Foundation for Economic Education. Rapport / *edited by* Pamela Hampson. - *Published by* Canadian Foundation for Economic Education. 155 University Ave., Toronto, Ont. M5H 3B7, Autumn 1974-
Published in French: Foundation canadienne d'éducation économique. Rapport.
Quarterly. Association publication, newsletter format, 4 p. supplements issued. Circulation: 8000
$5.00 per year (Organizations $25.00).

The Canadian Free Methodist herald / *edited by* R. Barclay Warren. - *Published by* Jurisdictional Conference. The Free Methodist Church in Canada. 55 Quebec St., Kingston, Ont. K7K 1T8, November 1922-
Irregular (approximately 11 issues per year). Church publication, newspaper format, 4 p.
$.20 per issue : $2.00 per year. Special rates offered.

The Canadian friend : Quaker news and thought / *edited by* J. Elizabeth Hopkins. - *Published by* Home Mission and Advancement Committee. Religious Society of Friends (Quakers). 60 Lowther Ave., Toronto, Ont. M5R 1C7 (Subscription address: 91 1/2 Fourth Ave., Ottawa, Ont. K1S 2L1) 1905-
Issued every other month. Church publication, magazine format, 24 p. Language: English (French). Includes book reviews. Circulation: 600
Indexed in Peace res. abstr.
$.50 per issue : $3.00 per year. Special rates offered to libraries. Prepayment required.

Canadian Friends Service Committee = Secours Quaker Canadien / *edited by* National Coordinator. - *Published by* Canadian Friends Service Committee. 60 Lowther Ave., Toronto, Ont. M5R 1C7.
Issued twice a year. Church publication, newsletter format, 4-6 p. Circulation: 2500

Canadian frontier : a Canadian national history magazine / *edited by* Tom Paterson. - *Published by* Rick Antonson. Nunaga Pub. Co. Ltd. P.O. Box 157, New Westminster, B.C. V3L 4Y4, Spring 1972-
Quarterly. General interest, magazine format, 40 p. Includes book reviews, advertising, volume index. Circulation: 6000
ISSN 0315-0062 $1.00 per issue : $3.50 per year.

Canadian Fruit Wholesalers' Association. Yearbook / *edited by* H.R. Taylor and W. Daman (managing ed.). - *Published by* Canadian Fruit Wholesalers' Association. 1568 Carling Ave., Ottawa, Ont. K1Z 7M5, 1924-
Annual. Association publication, magazine format,

Canadian fruitgrower / *edited by* Dave MacLaren. - *Published by* E. De Sutter. Cash Crop Farming Publications Ltd. 222 Argyle Ave., Delhi, Ont. N4B 2Y2, 1929-
Irregular (approximately 9 issues per year). Commodity publication, magazine format, Circulation: 4479
$.25 per issue : $2.00 per year : $4.00 per year, foreign.

Canadian furniture and furnishings directory *See* Canadian music directory

Canadian furniture and furnishings directory - *Published by* Lloyd Publications of Canada. P.O. Box 65, West Hill, Ont. M1E 4R4, 1924-
Annual. Directory, magazine format, 50 p. Circulation: 6000
$7.00 : $10.00, foreign. Prepayment required.

Canadian Gas Association. Manufacturers' directory / *edited by* The Manufacturers' Section. - *Published by* Canadian Gas Association. 55 Scarsdale Rd., Don Mills, Ont. M3B 2R3.
Biennial. Directory, coil bound format, 200 p. Includes updating service.
Free to members and libraries.

Canadian gas facts / *edited by* E. Patkay (Manager - Statistical Dept.). - *Published by* Statistics Department. Canadian Gas Association. 55 Scarsdale Rd., Don Mills, Ont.
Annual. Statistics, 30 p.
ISSN 0316-3547 Free, single copies : $.30 each for bulk orders. Controlled circulation.

Canadian geographer = Le Géographe canadien / *sponsored by* Canadian Association of Geographers ; *edited by* J.U. Marshall. - *Published by* University of Toronto Press. 5201 Dufferin St., Downsview, Ont. M3H 5T8 (Subscription address: Burnside Hall, McGill University, Montreal, Que)
Quarterly. Association publication.
Indexed in Can ind., Soc. sci journal file, Soc. sci. ind.
$3.75 per issue : $15.00 per year.

Canadian geographical journal / *edited by* David Maclellan. - *Published by* Royal Canadian Geographical Society. 488 Wilbrod St., Ottawa, Ont. K1N 6M8, May 1930-
Irregular (approximately 11 issues per year). Association publication, magazine format, 52 p. Includes book reviews, advertising, volume index. Circulation: 26,581
Indexed in Can. ind., RADAR, P.A.I.S., North. tit., Per. art. rel. law, Hist. abstr.; Amer. hist. and life, I.B.Z., Arct. bibl., Soc. sci. journal file.
ISSN 0315-1824 $1.25 per issue : $9.00 per year : $2.00 per issue, foreign : $9.00 per year, foreign. Membership fee ($8.00) includes subscription.

The Canadian Gideon / *edited by* N.C. Penney. - *Published by* The Gideons International in Canada. 501 Imperial Rd., Guelph, Ont., 1950-
Former title(s): The Torch and trumpet (1935-1950)
Issued every other month. Association publication, magazine format, 40 p. Includes advertising, volume index. Circulation: 3000
$2.50 per year. Prepayment required.

Canadian Gladiolus Society. Annual / *edited by* Grant Wilson. - *Published by* Canadian Gladiolus Society. 1274-129 A St., Ocean Park, B.C., 1921-
Annual. Association publication, 125 p.
$3.50. Controlled circulation.

Canadian golden west / *edited by* Pat Donaldson. - *Published by* Pat Donaldson. 814 16th Ave. N.W., Calgary, Alta. T2M 0J9 (Subscription address: Suite 3, 816 - 15th Ave. S.W., Calgary, Alta.) 1965-
Quarterly. General interest, magazine format, 40-48 p. Includes book reviews, advertising, cumulative index. Circulation: 6047
$1.00 per issue : $3.50 per year : $5.00 per year, foreign. Prepayment required.

Canadian grocer / *edited by* F.M. Shore. - *Published by* Maclean-Hunter Ltd. 481 University Ave., Toronto, Ont. M5W 1A7, 1887-
Monthly. Trade publication, magazine format, 52 p. supplements issued. Circulation: 14,600
Indexed in Can. B.P.I.
$12.00 per year. Controlled circulation. Special rates offered. Prepayment required.

Canadian guernsey breeders' journal / *edited by* Don MacKenzie. - *Published by* Canadian Guernsey Breeders' Association. 368 Woolwich St., Guelph, Ont., 1927-
Irregular (approximately 9 issues per year). Association publication, journal format, 40 p. Includes advertising. Circulation: 1500
$3.00 per year.

Canadian guide : Canada's up-to-the minute gazetteer and shipper's directory / *edited by* Stan C. Newey. - *Published by* International Railway Publishing Co. Ltd. 480 Lagauchetiere St. W., Montreal, Que. H2A 1E3, 1866-
Monthly. Book format, 400 p. Language: English and French. Circulation: 3200
$11.20 per issue : $34.24 per year. Prepayment required.

Canadian guider / *edited by* M. Elizabeth McKay. - *Published by* Girl Guides of Canada. 50 Merton St., Toronto, Ont. M4S 1A3, January 1932-
Irregular (approximately 6 issues per year). Association publication, newsletter format, 4 numbers, 16 p.; 2 numbers, 24 p. Includes book reviews, film reviews, advertising. Circulation: 30,000
ISSN 0300-435x $1.00 per year : $1.25 per year, foreign. All but 600 sent out free.

The Canadian gunner / *edited by* Commanding Officer 3 RCHA. - *Published by* R.C.A. Officers' Regimental Funds. CFB Shilo, Man.
Annual. Military journal, magazine format, 150 p. Includes advertising. Circulation: 2000
$3.00. Controlled circulation.

Canadian Gymastics Federation. C.G.F. monthly bulletin / *edited by* Lewis R. Waller. - *Published by* Canadian Gymnastics Federation. 11th Floor, 333 River Rd., Vanier, Ont. K1L 8B9.
Issued every other month. Association publication, magazine format, 26 p. Circulation: 5000
$3.00 per year : $4.50 per year, foreign. Prepayment required.

Canadian hairdresser / *edited by* Dorothy Anne Miller. - *Published by* Arthurs Publications Ltd. Suite 204, 5200 Dixie Rd., Mississauga, Ont., 1951-
Irregular (approximately 10 issues per year). Trade publication, magazine format,

Canadian handgun / *edited by* W.H. Bush. - *Published by* Ontario Handgun Asociation. 135 Centre St. E., Richmond Hill, Ont. L4C 1A5, 1957-
Irregular (approximately 5 issues per year). Association publication, magazine format, 8 p. Circulation: 4000
Subscription included in membership fee. Controlled circulation.

Canadian hardware, electrical and building supply directory - *Published by* Lloyd Publications of Canada. P.O. Box 65, West Hill, Ont. M1E 4R4, 1954-
Annual. Directory, magazine format, 106 p. Circulation: 8000
$10.00 : $13.00 foreign. Prepayment required.

Canadian hardware-housewares retailing / *edited by* Robert Ferguson. - *Published by* Sentinel Publishing Co. 27 Centrale, La Salle, Que. H8R 3K2.
Monthly. Trade publication. Includes advertising.
Indexed in Can. B.P.I.
$6.00 per year : $10.00 per year, U.S. and U.K. : $15.00 per year, foreign.

Canadian Hemophilia Society. Ontario Chapter. Bulletin / *edited by* Frank Bott. - *Published by* Ontario Chapter. Canadian Hemophilia Society. Suite 510, 30 Bloor St. W., Toronto, Ont. M4W 1A2.
Issued every other month. Association publication, newsletter format, 4 p.
Subscription included in membership fee. Controlled circulation.

The Canadian Hereford digest / *edited by* Keith Gilmore. - *Published by* Gilmore Publications Ltd. 320 - 19th St. S.E., Calgary, Alta. T2E 6J6, 1956-
Monthly, 11 times a year. Special interest, magazine format, 90 p. Language: English (French). Circulation: 12,000
$5.00 per year : $6.00 per year, foreign.

Canadian high news *See* Today's generation

Canadian highway carriers guide / *edited by* Douglas Seip. - *Published by* Southam Business Publications Ltd. 1450 Don Mills Rd., Don Mills, Ont. M3B 2X7, 1972-
Former title(s): Highway carriers guide.
Annual. Trade publication. Includes advertising.
$12.00 per volume.

Canadian historical review / *edited by* Michael Cross. - *Published by* University of Toronto Press. 5201 Dufferin St., Downsview, Ont. M3H 5T8 (Subscription address: Journals Dept. U of T Press, 5201 Dufferin St., Downsview, Ont. M3H 5R8) 1920-
Quarterly. Special interest, journal format, 136 p. Language: English and French. Includes book reviews, advertising, volume index, cumulative index. available in microform.
Circulation: 4000
Indexed in Writings Am. hist., Can. ind., Soc. sci. cit. ind., Hum. ind., Hist. abstr.; Amer. hist. and life, Arct. bibl., Soc. sci. journal file.
ISSN 0008-3755 $12.50 per year. Special rates offered.

Canadian home economics journal / *edited by* Margaret C. Smith. - *Published by* Canadian Home Economics Association. 151 Slater St., Ottawa, Ont. K1P 5H3.
Quarterly. Association publication, magazine format, 36-44 p. Includes book reviews, film reviews, advertising.
$2.00 per issue : $8.00 per year. Controlled circulation.

The Canadian home leaguer: a magazine for women / *edited by* Sucritia Batten. - *Published by* Canadian Home Leaguer. 20 Albert St., Toronto, Ont. (Subscription address: The Home League Dept., 20 Albert St., Toronto, Ont) 1953-
Monthly. Church publication, magazine format, 16 p.
$.20 per issue : $2.00 per year.

Canadian homes / *edited by* A. Harris Mitchell. - *Published by* Southstar Publishers Ltd. The Simpson Tower, 401 Bay St., Toronto, Ont. M5H 2Y8.
Quarterly. Magazine format,

The Canadian horse magazine / *edited by* Philph G. Jones. - *Published by* Rexwood Publishing Co. 48 Belfield Rd., Rexdale, Ont. M9W 1G1, January 1961-
Monthly. Special interest, magazine format, 64 p. Includes advertising. Circulation: 4000
$1.00 per issue : $8.00 per year. Prepayment required.

Canadian hospital (1924-1974) *See* Dimensions in health service

Canadian hospital directory / *edited by* Kaye Finch. - *Published by* Canadian Hospital Association. 25 Imperial St., Toronto, Ont. M5P 1C1, 1953-
Annual. Directory, magazine format, 350 p.
Circulation: 5800
ISSN 0068-8932 $18.00.

Canadian host / *edited by* David Lewis. - *Published by* Canadian Automobile Association. 150 Gloucester St., Ottawa, Ont. K2P 0A6, Summer 1971-
Issued twice a year. Association publication, newsletter format, 4 p.
Controlled circulation.

Canadian hotel, restaurant, institution and store equipment - *Published by* Lloyd Publications of Canada. P.O. Box 65, West Hill, Ont. M1E 4R4, 1926-
Annual. Directory, magazine format, 70 p.
Circulation: 8000
$10.00 per year : $13.00 per year, foreign.
Prepayment required.

Canadian hotel and restaurant - *Published by* Maclean-Hunter Ltd. 481 University Ave., Toronto, Ont. M5W 1A7, 1923-
Former title(s): Canadian hotel review.
Monthly.
Indexed in Can. B.P.I.

Canadian hotel review *See* Canadian hotel and restaurant

Canadian housing statistics / *edited by* A. Stukel. - *Published by* Central Mortgage and Housing Corporation. Montreal Rd., Ottawa, Ont. K1A 0P7., 1955-
Annual. Statistics, 130 p. Language: French and English.

Canadian Hungarian *See* Kanadai magvarsag

Canadian Hungarian News = Kanadai Magyar ujag / *edited by* Gusztav Nemes. - *Published by* The Canadian Hungarian News. 210 Sherbrooke St., Winnipeg, Man., 1924-
Weekly. Ethnic press. Language: Hungarian. Includes advertising.

Canadian Hungarian news annual = Kanadai magyar ujság képes naptara / *edited by* Gusztav Nemes. - *Published by* Canadian Hungarian News. 210 Sherbrooke St., Winnipeg, Man.
Annual. Ethnic press. Language: Hungarian.
$2.00.

Canadian Importers and Traders Association bulletin (1938-1957) *See* The Importers' bulletin

The Canadian independent adjuster / *edited by* William J. MacPherson. - *Published by* Canadian Independent Adjusters' Conference. P.O. Box 51, Postal Station Q, Toronto, Ont. M4T 2L7, Summer 1958-
Quarterly. House/company organ, magazine format, 36 or 32 p. Includes advertising.
ISSN 0008-3828 $3.00 per year.

Canadian index to periodicals and documentary films (1948-1964) *See* Canadian periodical index

The Canadian India times / *edited by* T.J. Samuel. - *Published by* T.J. Samuel. 161 Dalhousie St., Ottawa, Ont. K1N 7C3, July 1967-
Former title(s): India times.
Issued twice a month. Ethnic press, newspaper format, 12 p. Includes book reviews, film reviews, advertising.
$.25 per issue : $6.00 per year.

Canadian industrial equipment news / *edited by* Bill Wallace. - *Published by* Southam Business Publications Ltd. 1450 Don Mills Rd., Toronto, Ont., 1940-
Monthly. Trade publication, magazine format, 65 p.
$1.50 per issue : $13.00 per year : $24.00 for 2 years : $40.00 per year, foreign. Controlled circulation.

Canadian industrial photography *See* Canadian photography

Canadian Industries Ltd. C.I.L. contact / *edited by* The Advertising and Public Department. - *Published by* Canadian Industries Ltd. P.O. Box 10, Montreal, Que. H3C 2R3, August 1929-
Former title(s): CIL magazine (August 1929-December 1931) Published in French: Canadian Industries Ltd. Contact CIL.
Issued every three weeks. House/company organ, newspaper format, 8 p. Language: English and French. Circulation: 11,000
Free.

Canadian Industries Ltd. Contact CIL / *edited by* Roger Brouillet. - *Published by* Canadian Industries Ltd. C.P. 10, Montréal, Qué. H3C 2R3, octobre 1929-
Publié en anglais: Canadian Industries Ltd. CIL contact.
Intermittent (approximativement 16 éditions par an). Organe interne/officiel, journal, 8 p. Language: français et anglais. Includes publicité. parution de suppléments.
Envoi gratuit.

Canadian industry shows and exhibitions / *edited by* Betty Gay. - *Published by* Alan J. Waters. Maclean-Hunter Ltd. 481 University Ave., Toronto, Ont. M5W 1A7.
Annual. Directory, magazine format, 104 p. Circulation: 8500
$8.00. Prepayment required.

Canadian Information Processing Society. CIPS computer magazine / *sponsored by* Canadian Information Processing Society ; *edited by* Roy J. Whitsed. - *Published by* Whitsed Publishing Ltd. 42 Mercer St., Toronto, Ont. M5V 1H3, 1970-
Monthly. Association publication.
Indexed in C.B.P.I.

Canadian Institute of Actuaries. Reports / *edited by* M.B. Hutchison. - *Published by* Canadian Institute of Actuaries. Suite 506, 116 Albert St., Ottawa, Ont. K1P 5G3, 1965-
Irregular (approximately 3 issues per year). Record of general and annual meetings of the Institute held 3 times per year, 150 p. Language: English and French.

Canadian Institute of Actuaries. Year book = Institut canadien des actuaires. Annuaire - *Published by* Canadian Institute of Actuaries. Suite 506, 116 Albert St., Ottawa, Ont. K1P 5G3.
Annual. Yearbook, 135 p. Language: English and French. Circulation: 1200

Canadian Institute of Chartered Accountants. C.I.C.A./I.C.C.A. dialogue / *edited by* Jennifer Grass. - *Published by* Canadian Institute of Chartered Accountants. 250 Bloor St. E., Toronto, Ont., December 1968-
Former title(s): The Institute reports.
Issued every six weeks. Association publication, newsletter format, 4 p. Language: English and French.
Subscription included in membership fee. Controlled circulation.

The Canadian Institute of Chartered Accountants. CICA handbook = L'Institut canadien des comptables agréés Manuel de l'I.C.C.A - *Published by* The Canadian Institute of Chartered Accountants. 250 Bloor St. E., Toronto, Ont. M4W 1G5.
Irregular (approximately 3 issues per year). Association publication. Language: English and French. Includes cumulative index, updating service. Circulation: 55,000
$5.00 per year. Prepayment required.

Canadian Institute of Food Science and Technology. Journal / *edited by* D.W. Stanley. - *Published by* Canadian Institute of Food Science and Technology. Suite 10, 46 Elgin, Ottawa, Ont., K1T 5K6., January 1972-
Former title(s): Journal - Canadian Institute of Food Science and Technology.
Quarterly. Association publication, journal format, 100 p. Language: English and French ; summaries: English and French. Includes volume index. Circulation: 2200
Indexed in ISI.
$25.00 per year : $26.00 per year, foreign. Individual copies available on request. Prepayment required.

The Canadian Institute of Mining and Metallurgy. C.I.M. bulletin / *edited by* E.G. Tapp. - *Published by* The Canadian Institute of Mining and Metallurgy. Suite 906, 1117 St. Catherine St. W., Montreal, Que. H3B 1J3, 1898-
Monthly. Association publication, magazine format, 150 p. Includes book reviews, advertising, volume index, cumulative index. Circulation: 10,500
Indexed in Can. B.P.I.
$15.00 per year.

The Canadian Institute of Mining and Metallurgy. The C.I.M. directory / *edited by* E.G. Tapp. - *Published by* The Canadian Institute of Mining and Metallurgy. Suite 906, 1117 St. Catherine St. W., Montreal, Que. H3B 1J3, 1965-
Annual. Association publication, directory, magazine format, 235 p. Includes advertising. Circulation: 10,500
$25.00. Free to members. Prepayment required.

Canadian Institute of Planners. C.I.P. news = Institut canadien des urbanistes. Nouvelles I.C.U. / *edited by* Elizabeth Katz. - *Published by* Canadian Institute of Planners. Suite 30, 46 Elgin St., Ottawa, Ont. K1P 5K6.
Former title(s): TPIC news = Nouvelles I.U.C.
Monthly. Association publication, newsletter format, 24 p. Language: English and French. Circulation: 1600
$2.00 per issue : $10.00 per year : $12.00 per year, foreign.

Canadian Institute of Planners. Canadian Institute of Planners forum - *Published by* Canadian Institute of Planners. Suite 30, 46 Elgin St., Ottawa, Ont. K1P 5K6, 1923-
Former title(s): C.I.P. news (August 1974-June 1975) T.P.I.C. news (1923-August 1974)
Monthly. Association publication, magazine format, 20 p. Language: English and French. Circulation: 2000
$2.00 per issue : $10.00 per year : $12.00 per year, foreign. Available free to members, subscriptions also available.

Canadian Institute of Realtors journal *See* Real Estate Institute of Canada. Journal

Canadian insurance claims directory / *edited by* Kieran Simpson. - *Published by* University of Toronto Press. 5201 Dufferin St., Downsview, Ont. M3H 5T8, 1933-
Annual. Directory. Includes advertising.
$6.50.

Canadian insurance (incorporating Insurance agent and broker in Canada) / *edited by* Michael F. Steeler. - *Published by* John S. Wyndham. Stone and Cox Ltd. 203 Adelaide St. W., Toronto, Ont. M5H 1X4, 1905-
Monthly. Special interest, magazine format, 45 p. Circulation: 10,337
Indexed in Can. B.P.I.
ISSN 0008-3879 $5.00 per year : $6.00 per year, U.S. and U.K. : $7.00 per year, foreign. Controlled circulation.

The Canadian insurance law service / *edited by* B.C.F. Fraser. - *Published by* Stone & Cox Ltd. 203 Adelaide St. W., Toronto, Ont. M5H 1X4, 1935-
Irregular (approximately 20 issues per year). Law reports, bulletins and repinted pages, Language: English and French. Includes updating service. Circulation: 600
$40.00 per year : $65.00 per volume : $365.00 per set. Prepayment required.

Canadian insurance statistics (annual) / *edited by* Michael Steeler. - *Published by* Stone & Cox Ltd. 203 Adelaide St. W., Toronto, Ont. M5H 1X4.
Annual. Statistics, magazine format, 130 p. Circulation: 11,000
$5.00 : $6.00, foreign. Prepayment required.

Canadian intelligence service / *edited by* Ron Gostick. - *Published by* Canadian Intelligence Publications. P.O. Box 130, Flesherton, Ont. N0C 1E0, January 1951-
Monthly. Special interest, newsletter format, 8 p. Circulation: 5000
$6.00 per year : $7.00 per year, foreign.

Canadian interconnection / *edited by* Jake Koekebakker. - *Published by* Maclean-Hunter Ltd. 481 University Ave., Toronto, Ont. M5W 1A7.
Monthly. Trade publication, newsletter format, 8 p. Includes cumulative index.
$75.00.

Canadian interiors / *edited by* Dand Piper. - *Published by* Ralph Zamsonelli. Maclean-Hunter Ltd. 481 University Ave., Toronto, Ont., April 1964-
Monthly. Trade publication, magazine format, Circulation: 6500
$1.00 per issue : $12.00 per year. Controlled circulation.

Canadian International DX Radio Club. The CIDX messenger / *edited by* R.L. Jennings. - *Published by* CIDX Radio Club. 169 Grandview Ave., Winnipeg, Man., July 1962-
Monthly. Association publication, magazine format, 20 p. Includes book reviews, record reviews. Circulation: 200
$.20 per issue : $5.00 per year : $10.00 per year, foreign.

Canadian issues / *edited by* Paul Koroscil (Simon Fraser University) and Stanley E. McMullin (Waterloo). - *Published by* Association of Canadian Studies. Director, Canadian Studies, University of Waterloo, Waterloo, Ont. N2L 3G1, Spring 1975-
Issued twice a year. Association publication, magazine format, 140 p. Language: English and French.
$4.50 per issue : $10.00 per year : $4.50 per year, foreign. Subscription includes Association membership.

Canadian jaycee / *edited by* James MacLeod. - *Published by* The Canada Jaycees. P.O. Box 550, 39 Leacock Way, Kanata, Ont. K2K 1T1, 1954-
Issued every other month. Association publication, newspaper format, 8 p. Language: English ; summaries: English and French. Includes advertising. Circulation: 8075
ISSN 0576-551X $3.00 per year.

Canadian jersey breeder limited / *edited by* Cameron Honderich. - *Published by* The Canadian Jersey Cattle Club. 343 Waterloo Ave., Guelph, Ont. N1H 3K1, August 1947-
Monthly. Association publication, magazine format, 40 p. Language: English and French. Includes advertising. Circulation: 1400
$5.00 per year : $5.50 per year, foreign.

Canadian jester / *edited by* Julius Hargittay. - *Published by* James Hargittay. Reflections Creative Art. 3605 Ellengale Dr., Mississauga, Ont. L5C 1Z8.
Monthly. General interest. Includes advertising.
$.50 per issue : $4.00 per year.

Canadian jeweller : the jewellery and giftware magazine / *edited by* Dennis Mellersh. - *Published by* George Radford. Maclean-Hunter Ltd. 481 University Ave., Toronto, Ont. M5W 1A7, 1879-
Former title(s): The Trader.
Monthly. Trade publication, magazine format, 66 p.
ISSN 0008-3917 $1.00 per issue : $8.00 per year.

Canadian jewellery and giftware directory - *Published by* Lloyd Publications of Canada. P.O. Box 65, West Hill, M1E 4R4, 1924-
Annual. Directory, magazine format, 70 p. Circulation: 6000
$10.00 : $13.00 foreign. Prepayment required.

Canadian jewellery news - *Published by* Canadian Jewellers' Association. Suite 401, 663 Yonge St., Toronto, Ont. M4Y 2A5.
Association publication.

Canadian Jewish chronicle *See* Canadian Jewish chronicle review

Canadian Jewish chronicle review / *edited by* Arnold Ages. - *Published by* Canadian Jewish news. Suite 209, 4781 Van Horne Ave., Montreal, Que. H3W 1J1.
Former title(s): Canadian Jewish chronicle; Canadian Jewish review; Ottawa Hebrew news; Toronto Jewish voice.
Monthly except August.
$.50 per issue : $2.00 per year.

Canadian Jewish outlook / *edited by* The Advisory Board. - *Published by* Canadian Jewish Outlook. P.O. Box 65, Postal Station B, Toronto, Ont., October 1963-
Monthly. Special interest, magazine format, 16 p. Includes book reviews, play reviews. available in microform. Circulation: 3000
$.35 per issue : $4.00 per year : $6.00 per year, foreign. Prepayment required.

Canadian Jewish review *See* Canadian Jewish chronicle review

Canadian Jewish weekly - *Published by* Canadian Jewish Weekly. 339 Spadina Ave., Toronto, Ont. M5T 2G3.
Issued every other week.

Canadian journal of African studies = Journal canadien des études africaines / *edited by* Mike Mason and Alf Schwartz. - *Published by* Canadian Association of African Studies in Canada/Association canadienne des études africaines. Dept. of Geography, Carleton University, Ottawa, Ont. K1S 5B6, 1967-
Former title(s): Bulletin of African Studies = Bulletin des études africaines au Canada.
Issued 3 times a year. Association publication, journal format, 200 p. Language: English and French ; summaries: French and English. Includes book reviews. Circulation: 650
Indexed in Soc. sci. journal file, Hist. abstr.; Amer. hist. and life, Soc. sci. cit. ind.
ISSN 0008-3968

Canadian journal of agricultural economics / *sponsored by* Canadian Agricultural Economics Society ; *edited by* W.E. Phillips and M.M. Veeman. - *Published by* University of Alberta Press. University of Alberta, Edmonton, Alta. (Subscription address: Suite 907, 151 Slater St. Ottawa, Ont. K1P 5H4)
Irregular (approximately 3 issues per year). Association publication, journal format, 70 p. Language: English (French) ; summaries: French (English). Includes book reviews, advertising, volume index. supplements issued. Circulation: 1200
Indexed in J. econ. lit., Biol. and agri. ind., Soc. sci. journal file.
$10.00 per year.

Canadian journal of agricultural science (1953-1956) *See* Canadian journal of animal science

Canadian journal of agricultural science (1953-1956) *See* Canadian journal of plant science

Canadian journal of agricultural science (1953-1956) *See* Canadian journal of soil science

Canadian journal of animal science / *edited by* Janet McDonald. - *Published by* Agricultural Institute of Canada. Suite 907, 151 Slater St., Ottawa, Ont. K1P 5H4., 1957-
Former title(s): Canadian journal of agricultural science (1953-1956) Scientific agriculture (1920-1952)
Quarterly. Special interest, journal format, 200 p. Language: English and French ; summaries: English and French. Includes volume index. Circulation: 1300
Indexed in ISI, Biol. and agri. ind., Chem. abstr.
ISSN 0008-3984

The Canadian journal of arms collecting (1963-1972) *See* Arms collecting : the Canadian journal of arms collecting

Canadian journal of behavioural science = Revue canadienne des sciences du comportement / *sponsored by* Canadian Psychological Association ; *edited by* Park O. Davidson. - *Published by* University of Toronto Press. 5201 Dufferin St., Downsview, Ont. M3H 5T8 (Subscription address: Business Office, CPA, 1390 Sherbrooke St. W. Montreal, Que. H3G 1K2) January 1969-
Quarterly. Association publication, journal format, 100 p. Includes advertising, volume index. available in microform. Circulation: 1500
Indexed in Abstr. anthropol., LLBA, Soc. sci. cit. ind., Psych. abstr., Soc. sci. journal file.
ISSN 0008-400x $25.00 per year. Prepayment required.

Canadian journal of chemical engineering / *edited by* L.W. Shemilt. - *Published by* Chemical Institute of Canada. Suite 906, 151 Slater St., Ottawa, Ont., K1P 5H3., 1957-
Issued every other month. Trade publication, journal format,
Indexed in Appl. sci. and tech. ind.
ISSN 0008-4034 $8.00 per issue : $40.00 per year : $45.00 per year, foreign.

Canadian journal of comparative medicine = Revue canadienne de médecine comparée / *edited by* R.G. Thomson. - *Published by* Canadian Veterinary Medical Association. 360 Bronson Ave., Ottawa, Ont., K1R 6J3., 1937-
Former title(s): Canadian journal of comparative medicine and veterinary science (1937-January 1968)
Quarterly. Association publication, journal format, 120 p. Language: English and French ; summaries: English and French. Includes book reviews, advertising, volume index. Circulation: 3785
Indexed in Biol. abstr., Nutr. abstr., Ind. med.
$5.00 per year : $10.00 per year, U.S. and U.K. : $12.00 per year, foreign.

Canadian journal of comparative medicine and veterinary science (1937-January 1968) *See* Canadian journal of comparative medicine

Canadian journal of corrections = La revue de criminologie (October 1958-October 1970) *See* Canadian journal of criminology and corrections

Canadian journal of criminology and corrections = Revue canadienne de criminologie / *edited by* Marie-Andrée Bertrand. - *Published by* Canadian Criminology and Corrections Association. 55 Parkdale Ave., Ottawa, Ont. K1Y 1E5., October 1958-
Former title(s): Canadian journal of corrections = La revue de criminologie (October 1958-October 1970)
Quarterly. Association publication, journal format, 120 p. Language: English and French ; summaries: French and English. Includes book reviews, film reviews, advertising, volume index. available in microform. Back numbers available. Circulation: 1600
Indexed in Can. leg. per. lit., Soc. sci. cit. ind., Per. art. rel. law, Psych. abstr., Soc. sci. journal file.
ISSN 0008-4069 $2.50 per issue : $10.00 per year (Students $7.00). Special rates offered. Prepayment required.

The Canadian journal of economics / *sponsored by* Canadian Economics Association ; *edited by* Gideon Rosenbluth. - *Published by* University of Toronto Press. 5201 Dufferin St., Downsview, Ont. M3H 5T8 (Subscription address: University of Toronto Press, Journals Departments, 5201 Dufferin St. Downsview M3H 5T8) February 1968-
Former title(s): Canadian journal of economics and political science (1935-1967)
Quarterly. Association publication, journal format, 141-180 p. Language: English and French ; summaries: English and French. Includes book reviews, volume index. available in microform. Circulation: 4200
Indexed in Can. ind., Soc. sci. ind., Soc. sci. cit. ind., P.A.I.S., Can. B.P.I., Soc. sci. journal file.
ISSN 0008-4085 $15.00 per year : $20.00 per volume. Prepayment required.

Canadian journal of economics and political science (1935-1967) *See* The Canadian journal of economics

Canadian journal of education = Revue canadienne de l'éducation / *edited by* Ronald G. Ragsdale. - *Published by* Canadian Society for the Study of Education. P.O. Box 1000, Edmonton, Alta. T6G 2E1, January 1976-
Former title(s): Bulletin of the Canadian Society of Education/Societe canadienne pour l'etude de l'education.
Quarterly. Association publication, journal format, 96 p. Language: English and French ; summaries: French and English. Includes book reviews. Circulation: 1200
$2.00 per issue : $6.00 per year.

Canadian journal of fabrics (1883-1906) *See* Canadian textile journal

Canadian journal of genetics and cytology = Journal canadien de génétique et de cytologie / *edited by* W.F. Grant. - *Published by* Genetics Society of Canada. Suite 907, 151 Slater St., Ottawa, Ont. K1P 5H4, 1959-
Quarterly. Association publication, magazine format, 250 p. Language: English and French ; summaries: English and French. Includes volume index. supplements issued. Circulation: 1700
Indexed in Biol. abstr., ISI, Biol. and agri. ind., Ind. med., I.B.Z.
ISSN 0008-4093 $7.50 per issue : $30.00 per year. Prepayment required.

Canadian journal of higher education = La Revue canadienne d'enseignement supérieur / *edited by* Robin Ross. - *Published by* Canadian Society for the Study of Higher Education. Suite 8039, 130 St. George St., Toronto, Ont. M5S 2T4, 1971-
Former title(s): STOA (1971-1974)
Issued 3 times a year. Association publication, journal format, 90 p. Language: English and French ; summaries: English and French. Includes book reviews. Circulation: 400
ISSN 0315-6680 $15.00 per year (Students $5.00). Subscription included in membership fee.

Canadian journal of history = Annales canadiennes d'histoire / *sponsored by* University of Saskatchewan and the Canada Council ; *edited by* J. Michael Hayden and others. - *Published by* Journal of History Co. Ltd. P.O. Box 384, Sub Post Office 6, Saskatoon, Sask., March 1966-
Irregular (approximately 3 issues per year). Special interest, magazine format, 120 p. Language: English and French. Includes book reviews. available in microform. Circulation: 700
Indexed in Hum. ind., M.L.A. int. bib., Hist. abstr.; Amer. hist. and life, Soc. sci. journal file.
ISSN 0008-4107 $1.75 per issue : $5.50 per year : $5.50 per year, foreign.

The Canadian journal of history and social science (Fall 1969 - Spring 1974) *See* The History and social science teacher

Canadian journal of history of sport and physical education / *sponsored by* Canadian Association for Health, Physical Education and Recreation ; *edited by* Michael A. Salter. - *Published by* University of Windsor. Windsor, Ont. N9B 3P4 (Subscription address: Faculty of Physical and Health Education, University of Windsor, Windsor, Ont. N9B 3P4) May 1970-
Issued twice a year. Association publication, magazine format, 80 p. Language: French and English. Includes book reviews, cumulative index. Circulation: 500
Indexed in Hist. abstr.; Amer. hist. and life.
$2.00 per issue : $4.00 per year. Prepayment required.

The Canadian journal of hospital pharmacy / *edited by* J.L. Summers. - *Published by* Canadian Society of Hospital Pharmacists. 175 College St., Toronto, Ont. M5T 1P8 (Subscription address: Pharmacy Department, University Hospital, Saskatoon, Sask. S7N 0W8) 1948-
Former title(s): The Hospital pharmacist (1948-1967)
Issued every other month. Association publication, journal format, 44 p. Language: English and French. Includes book reviews, advertising, cumulative index. Circulation: 2500
Indexed in Hosp. abstr.
$2.00 per issue : $10.00 per year.

Canadian journal of information science = Revue canadienne des sciences de l'information / *edited by* F. Dolan. - *Published by* Canadian Association for Information Science. P.O. Box 158, Terminal A, Ottawa, Ont. K1N 8V2, Summer 1976-
Annual. Association publication, magazine format, 100 p. Language: English and French ; summaries: French and English. Circulation: 300
$15.00 (Non-members $20.00).

Canadian journal of linguistics = La Revue canadienne de linguistique / *sponsored by* Canadian Linguistic Association ; *edited by* E.N. Burstynsky. - *Published by* University of Toronto Press. 5201 Dufferin St., Downsview, Ont. M3H 5T8 (Subscription address: c/o Prof. D.A. Wilson, Queen's University, Kingston, Ont. K7L 3N6) 1960-
Issued twice a year. Association publication, journal format, 72 p. Language: English and French. Includes book reviews, volume index. Circulation: 1000
Indexed in Soc. sci. cit. ind., M.L.A. int. bib., Annu. bibl. Engl. lang. and lit., MLA abstr., Hist. abstr.; Amer. hist. and life, I.B.Z. Soc. sci. journal file.
$10.00 per year.

Canadian journal of mathematics = Journal canadien de mathématiques / *sponsored by* Canadian Mathematical Congress ; *edited by* P.G. Rooney and P.H.H. Fantham. - *Published by* University of Toronto Press. 5201 Dufferin St., Downsview, Ont. M3H 5T8, 1949-
Issued every other month. Association publication, journal format, 224 p. Language: English and French. Includes volume index.
Indexed in Zentralbl. math., Math. r., I.B.Z.
$24.00 per volume.

The Canadian journal of medical technology / *edited by* L.D. Mellor. - *Published by* Canadian Society of Laboratory Technologists. P.O. Box 830, 165 Jackson St. E., Hamilton, Ont. L8N 3N8, October 1938-
Issued every other month. Association publication, journal format, 80 p. Language: English and French. Includes book reviews, advertising, volume index. Circulation: 17,000
$2.50 per issue : $11.00 per year : $13.00 per year, foreign. Controlled circulation. Prepayment required.

The Canadian journal of neurological sciences = Le Journal canadien des sciences neurologiques / *edited by* R.T. Ross. - *Published by* R.T. Ross. 1516-233 Kennedy St., Winnipeg, Man. R3C 3J5, January 1974-
Quarterly. Professional publication, journal format, 90 p. Language: English and French ; summaries: English and French. Includes book reviews.
Indexed in Ind. med.
ISSN 0317-1671 $5.00 per issue : $20.00 per year : $21.00 per year, foreign.

Canadian journal of occupational therapy = Revue canadienne d'ergothérapie / *edited by* Rosalie Kupfer-Halstuch. - *Published by* Canadian Association of Occupational Therapists. Suite M19, 4 New St., Toronto, Ont. M5R 1P6.
Quarterly. Association publication, journal format, 65 p. Language: English and French. Includes book reviews, advertising, volume index.
$2.50 per issue : $10.00 per year : $11.50 per year, foreign. Prepayment required.

Canadian journal of ophthalmology / *edited by* C.C. Ewing. - *Published by* Canadian Ophthalmological Society. P.O. Box 8650, Ottawa, Ont., 1966-
Former title(s): Transactions of the Canadian Ophthamological Society (1949, 1954-1966)
Quarterly. Association publication, journal format, 160 p. Language: English and French ; summaries: English and French. Includes book reviews, advertising, volume index.
Circulation: 1350
Indexed in Ophthal. lit., Ind. med., Per. art. rel. law.
ISSN 0008-4182 $20.00 per year : $26.00 per year, foreign.

The Canadian journal of optometry / *edited by* G. Maurice Belanger. - *Published by* The Canadian Association of Optometrists. Suite 2001, 210 Gladstone Ave., Ottawa, Ont. K2P 0Y6, 1938-
Quarterly. Association publication, magazine format, 32 p. Includes book reviews, advertising, volume index. Circulation: 2000
$2.00 per issue : $8.00 per year.

Canadian journal of otolaryngology = Journal canadien d'otolaryngologie / *edited by* P.W. Alberti. - *Published by* Canadian Otolaryngological Society. Suite 405, 600 University Ave., Toronto, Ont. M5G 1Z5, 1972-
Former title(s): Proceedings - Canadian Otolaryngological Society (1971)
Quarterly. Association publication, journal format, 150 p. Language: English and French ; summaries: English and French. Includes book reviews, advertising, volume index. available in microform. supplements issued. Circulation: 900
Indexed in Excerpt. med., Ind. med.
$20.00 per year : $21.00 per year, U.S. : $22.00 per year, foreign.

Canadian journal of pharmaceutical sciences / *edited by* Donald Zuck. - *Published by* Canadian Pharmaceutical Association. 175 College St., Toronto, Ont. M5T 1P8, May 1966-
Quarterly. Association publication, magazine format, 36 p. Language: English and French ; summaries: English and French. Includes advertising, volume index. Circulation: 1000
Indexed in Excerpt. med., Int. pharm. abstr.
ISSN 0008-4190 $4.50 per issue : $15.00 per year. Special rates to members and students.

Canadian journal of plant science / *edited by* Janet McDonald. - *Published by* Agricultural Institute of Canada. Suite 907, 151 Slater St., Ottawa, Ont. K1P 5H4., 1957-
Former title(s): Canadian journal of agricultural science (1953-1956) Scientific agriculture (1920-1952)
Quarterly. Special interest, journal format, 250 p. Language: English and French ; summaries: English and French. Includes volume index.
Circulation: 1500
Indexed in Biol. and agri. ind., I.B.Z., Chem. abstr.
ISSN 0008-4220 $5.00 per issue (Multiuser $8.00) : $14.00 per year (Multiuser $21.50) : $14.50 per year, foreign (Multiuser $23.50).

Canadian journal of psychiatric nursing / *sponsored by* Canadian Association of Psychiatric Nurses ; *edited by* C. Martin. - *Published by* Pennex Limited. 803 - 228 Notre Dame Ave., Winnipeg, Man. (Subscription address: 871 Notre Dame Ave., Winnipeg, Man) 1971-
Issued every other month. Association publication, journal format, 24 p. Includes book reviews, advertising. Circulation: 5000
$1.00 per issue : $5.00 per year : $10.00 per volume : $7.00 per year, foreign. Controlled circulation.

Canadian journal of psychology / *sponsored by* Canadian Psychological Association ; *edited by* P.C. Dodwell. - *Published by* University of Toronto Press. 5201 Dufferin St., Downsview, Ont. M3H 5T8 (Subscription address: CPA, 1390 Sherbrooke St. W., Montreal, Que) 1947-
Quarterly. Association publication, magazine format, 105 p. Language: English and French ; summaries: English and French. Includes advertising, volume index. available in microform.
Indexed in Soc. sci. ind., Soc. sci. cit. ind., Curr. ind. j. educ., Ind. med., Peace res. abstr., Psych. abstr., I.B.Z., Soc. sci. journal file.
ISSN 0008-4255 $5.00 per issue : $20.00 per year.

Canadian journal of public and cooperative economy *Voir* Revue canadienne d'économie publique et coopérative

Canadian journal of public health = Revue canadienne de santé publique / *edited by* Andrew Sherrington. - *Published by* Canadian Public Health Association. 55 Parkdale Ave., Ottawa, Ont. K1Y 1E5.
Issued every other month. Association publication, magazine format, 80 p. Language: English and French ; summaries: English and French. Includes book reviews, volume index. available in microform. Reprints available. Circulation: 5000
Indexed in Soc. sci. cit. ind., Ind. med., Arct. bibl., Hosp. abstr., Soc. sci. journal file.
$2.50 per issue : $12.00 per year : $15.00 per year, foreign. Subscription included in membership fee. Controlled circulation.

The Canadian journal of radiography, radiotherapthy, nuclear medicine = Le Journal canadien de radiographie, radiothérapie, nucléographie / *edited by* A.A. Mattila. - *Published by* Canadian Society of Radiological Technicians. Suite 410, 280 Metcalfe St., Ottawa, Ont. K2P 1R7.
Former title(s): Focal spot.
Issued every other month. Association publication, journal format, 45 p. Language: English and French. Includes book reviews, advertising, volume index.
Indexed in Periodex.
$1.50 per issue : $9.00 per year. Controlled circulation.

The Canadian journal of research in semiotics = Le Journal canadien de recherche sémiotique / *edited by* Pierre A.R. Monod. - *Published by* Canadian Semiotic Research Association. Dept. of Romance Languages, University of Alberta, Edmonton, Alta. T6G 1E2, 1973-
73. Association publication, magazine format, 100 p. Language: English and French ; summaries: French and English. Includes book reviews. Circulation: 300
$2.00 per issue : $6.00 per year. Prepayment required.

Canadian journal of social work education / *edited by* Leonard Rutman. - *Published by* Canadian Association of Schools of Social Work. 151 Slater St., Ottawa, Ont. K1P 5H3, Spring 1975-
Issued 3 times a year (Fall, Spring & Summer). Association publication, journal format, 65 p. Language: English and French ; summaries: French and English. Includes book reviews, advertising. Circulation: 300
ISSN 0316-8565 $14.00 per year.

Canadian journal of soil science / *edited by* Janet McDonald. - *Published by* Agricultural Institute of Canada. Suite 907, 151 Slater St., Ottawa, Ont. K1P 5H4., 1957-
Former title(s): Canadian journal of agricultural science (1953-1956) Scientific agriculture (1920-1952)
Quarterly. Special interest, journal format, 130 p. Language: English and French ; summaries: English and French. Includes volume index. Circulation: 1400
Indexed in Biol. and agri. ind., Chem. abstr.
ISSN 0008-4271 $5.00 per issue (Multiuser $8.00) : $14.00 per year (Multiuser $21.50) : $14.50 per year, foreign (Multiuser $23.50).

Canadian journal of spectroscopy / *sponsored by* The Spectroscopy Society of Canada ; *edited by* I.S. Butler and T. Theophanides. - *Published by* Multiscience Publications Ltd. P.O. Box 1464, Postal Station B, Montreal, Que. H3B 3L2, November 1963-
Former title(s): Canadian spectroscopy (1963-1971)
Issued every other month. Association publication, journal format, 36 p. Language: English and French ; summaries: English and French. Includes book reviews, advertising, volume index.
ISSN 0045-5105 $10.00 per issue : $40.00 per year.

Canadian journal of surgery / *sponsored by* Royal College of Physicians and Surgeons of Canada ; *edited by* L.D. MacLean and C.B. Mueller. - *Published by* Canadian Medical Association. P.O. Box 8650, Ottawa, Ont. K1G 0G8, 1957-
Issued every other month. Association publication, journal format, 100 p. Language: English (French) ; summaries: English and French. Includes book reviews, advertising, volume index. Circulation: 7000
Indexed in Sci. cit. ind., Ind. med.
ISSN 0004-428X $2.50 per issue : $15.00 per year.

Canadian journal of university continuing education / *edited by* Mario Ferland. - *Published by* Canadian Association of Departments of Extension and Summer Schools. Division of Continuing Education, University of Calgary, Calgary, Alta.
Former title(s): Dialogue.
Issued twice a year. Special interest, journal format, 50 p. Language: English and French ; summaries: English and French. Includes book reviews. Circulation: 500

Canadian klaxon / *edited by* Gordon E. Smith. - *Published by* Historic Automobile Society of Canada Inc. P.O. Box 128, 352 Bay St., Orillia, Ont. L3V 6J3.
Issued every other month. Association publication, magazine format, 44 p. Subscription included in membership fee $15.00 per year.

Canadian Kodakery / *edited by* D.M. Dempson. - *Published by* Canadian Kodak Co. Ltd. 3500 Eglinton Ave. W., Toronto Ont. M6M 1V3, 1921-
Monthly. House/company organ, magazine format, 16-20 p. Includes advertising. Circulation: 3500
Free.

Canadian labour = Le travailleur canadien / *edited by* Mary Kehoe (assistant editor). - *Published by* Canadian Labour Congress. 2841 Riverside Dr., Ottawa, Ont. K1V 8N4, 1956-
Quarterly. Association publication, journal format, 60-70 p. Language: English and French. Includes book reviews.
Indexed in Can. ind., Can. leg. per. lit., P.A.I.S., Hist. abstr.; Amer. hist. and life.
ISSN 0008-4336 $1.25 per issue : $5.00 per year. Bulk rate $4.00 per year.

Canadian Labour Comment = Information syndicale - *Published by* Canadian Labour Congress. 2841 Riverside Dr., Ottawa, Ont. K1V 8N4, March 1973-
Issued every other week. Association publication, newsletter format, 4 p. Language: English and French. Circulation: 23,000
Indexed in Can. B.P.I.
ISSN 0316-4780 Free.

Canadian Labour Congress. Memorandum to the Government of Canada - *Published by* Canadian Labour Congress. 2841 Riverside Dr., Ottawa, Ont. K1V 8N4.
Annual. Association publication. Language: English and French.
ISSN 0316-5892

Canadian Labour Congress. Report of proceedings of the convention - *Published by* Canadian Labour Congress. 2841 Riverside Dr., Ottawa, Ont. K1V 8N4.
Annual. Association publication, magazine format, 200 p.

Canadian labour history = Histoire ouvrière canadienne / *sponsored by* Committee on Canadian Labour History ; *edited by* Irving Abella and A.E. LeBlanc. - *Published by* A.E. LeBlanc. Vanier College, 821 Ste. Croix Blvd., Montreal, Que., December 1970-
Issued twice a year. Association publication, newsletter format, 25 p. Language: English and French.
Free.

Canadian Labour Relations Boards. Reports / *edited by* George Adams. - *Published by* Butterworth and Co. (Canada) Ltd. 2265 Midland Ave. Scarborough, Ont. M1P 4S1, 1974-
Monthly. Law reports, booklets, 64 p. Bound volume issued twice a year.

Canadian Ladies Golf Association. Year book / *edited by* L.J. Whamond. - *Published by* Canadian Ladies Golf Association. 333 River Rd., Ottawa, Ont., K1P 8B9.
Annual. Yearbook, magazine format, 132 p. Language: English (French). Circulation: 8000
$1.00 per volume.

The Canadian law list / *edited by* Patricia Egan. - *Published by* Canada Law Book Ltd. 80 Cowdray Court, Agincourt, Toronto, Ont. M1S 1S5, 1883-
Annual. Directory, 1375 p.
$17.00 per year.

The Canadian leader magazine / *edited by* J.F. Mackie. - *Published by* CanYouth Publications Ltd. P.O. Box 5112, Postal Station F, Ottawa, Ont., August/September 1970-
Former title(s): The Scout leader (1922-1970)
Issued 10 times a year. Association publication, magazine format, 40 p. Includes book reviews. Circulation: 32,000
ISSN 0036-9462 $.35 per issue : $3.50 per year.

The Canadian league / *edited by* G. Laviolette. - *Published by* The Catholic Womens' League of Canada. 890 St. James St., Winnipeg, Man. R3G 3J7, 1921-
Quarterly. Association publication, magazine format, 48 p. Includes book reviews.
$.50 per year, with membership. Controlled circulation.

Canadian leathercraft / *edited by* Margaret Monteith. - *Published by* Canadian Society for Creative Leathercraft. 107 Donald St. Barrie, Ont. L4N 1E6, 1951-
Quarterly. Association publication, 8 p.
$5.00 per year. Subscription included in membership fee.

Canadian library *See* Canadian library journal

Canadian Library Association. Proceedings *- Published by* Canadian Library Association. 151 Sparks St., Ottawa, Ont., K1P 5E3., 1946-
Annual. Association publication, 150 p. Circulation: 1700
$6.00 per issue. Free to institutional members of CLA and those registered at the annual conference.

Canadian library bulletin *See* Canadian library journal

Canadian library journal *- Published by* Canadian Library Association. 151 Sparks St., Ottawa, Ont. K1P 5E3, October 1946-
Former title(s): Canadian library; Canadian library bulletin.
Issued every other month. Association publication, magazine format, 80 p. Includes book reviews, advertising, cumulative index. available in microform.
Indexed in Lib lit., Can. ind., Lib. info. sci. abstr., Soc. sci. cit. ind..
$2.00 per issue : $10.00 (Airmail $15.00). Subscription included in membership fee.

Canadian Library Trustees' Association. Newsletter */ sponsored by* Canadian Library Trustees Association ; *edited by* Don Craw. *- Published by* Canadian Library Association. 151 Sparks St., Ottawa, Ont., K1P 5E3., 1967-
Quarterly. Association publication, newsletter format, 12 p. Circulation: 330
Subscription included in membership fee. Controlled circulation.

Canadian life insurance facts */ edited by* F.C. Dimock. *- Published by* The Canadian Life Insurance Association. 44 King St. W., Toronto, Ont. M5H 1E9, 1955-
Annual. Association publication, statistics, booklet format, 36 p. Language: English and French. Includes volume index. Circulation: 20,000
Controlled circulation.

Canadian Linguistic Association. Membership directory and data book memento */ edited by* The Secretary of the Association. *- Published by* Canadian Linguistic Association. English Dept., Queen's University, Kingston, Ont., 1973-
Biennial. Association publication, directory, magazine format, 100 p. Language: English and French. Circulation:
$15.00. Controlled circulation. Prepayment required.

Canadian liquid air review *See* Liquid air review

Canadian literature = Littérature canadienne */ edited by* George Woodcock. *- Published by* University of British Columbia Press. 2075 Westbrook Place, Vancouver, B.C. V6T 1N5, August 1959-
Quarterly. Special interest, journal format, 128 p. Language: English and French. Includes book reviews, advertising, cumulative index. available in microform. Circulation: 2400
Indexed in Can. ind., Hum. ind., M.L.A. int. bib., Annu. bibl. Engl. lang. and lit., Abstr. eng. stud., I.B.Z.
ISSN 0008-4360 $2.00 per issue : $6.50 per year.

Canadian living */ edited by* Margaret Kelly. *- Published by* Canadian Living. C.J. Compton Smith. P.O. Box 1216, Postal Station B, Mississauga, Ont. L4Y 3W5, 1975-
Monthly. General interest, magazine format, $.25. Sold only at grocery stores.

The Canadian log house : a yearbook of current log builder information */ edited by* Mary Mackie. *- Published by* The Canadian log house. P.O. Box 1205, Prince George, B.C. V2L 4V3, Spring 1974-
Annual. Yearbook, magazine format, 64 p. Includes book reviews. Circulation: 5000
ISSN 0315-8756 $3.50 : $5.00, U.S.

Canadian logger and pulpwood contractor */ edited by* Keith F. Pearson. *- Published by* Sentinel Publishing Co. 27 Centrale St., LaSalle, Que., September 1974-
Monthly. Trade publication, newspaper format, 16 p.
$.75 per issue : $6.00 per year : $10.00 per year, foreign. Controlled circulation. Special rates offered.

Canadian luggage and leathergoods news */ sponsored by* Luggage and Leathergoods Association of Canada ; *edited by* Gwen Sands Dempsey. *- Published by* Gwen Sands Publications. 333 King St. W., Toronto, Ont. M5V 1J5, April 1969-
Irregular (approximately 10 issues per year). Trade publication, newspaper format, 16 p. Includes advertising. Circulation: 4700
$5.00 per year. Prepayment required.

Canadian machinery and metalworking */ edited by* Antony Whitney. *- Published by* Maclean-Hunter Ltd. 481 University Ave., Toronto, Ont. M5W 1A7, 1905-
Monthly. Trade publication, magazine format, 100-120 p. Includes book reviews, film reviews, advertising, volume index. Circulation: 10,000
Indexed in Can. B.P.I.
$10.00 per year : $12.00 per year, U.S. and U.K. : $25.00 per year, foreign. Controlled circulation.

Canadian machinist / *edited by* Joseph Hanafin. - *Published by* International Association of Machinists and Aerospace Workers. 302-80 Argyle Ave., Ottawa, Ont., July 1973-
Monthly. Association publication, newspaper format, 8 p. Language: English and French. Circulation: 50,000
$4.00 per year. Controlled circulation.

The Canadian magazine / *edited by* Don Obe. - *Published by* Southstar Publishers Ltd. Suite 1100, 401 Bay St., Toronto, Ont. M5H 2Y8, November 1965-
Weekly. General interest, magazine format, 32 p. Includes advertising. Circulation: 2 million
Indexed in Can. ind.
Roto supplement to 13 newspapers across Canada.

The Canadian manager : the magazine of the professional manager / *edited by* G.E. Muir. - *Published by* Canadian Institute of Management. Suite 303, 51 Eglinton Ave. E., Toronto, Ont. M4P 1G7, September/October 1970-
Former title(s): The Industrial manager (November/December 1965-May/June 1970)
Quarterly. Trade publication, magazine format, 24 p. Language: English and French. Includes advertising. Circulation: 12,000
ISSN 0045-5156 $1.50 per issue : $6.00 per year : $8.00 per year, foreign.

Canadian materials / *edited by* Adèle Ashby. - *Published by* Canadian Library Association. 151 Sparks St., Ottawa, Ont. K1P 5E3, August 1975-
Issued 3 times a year. Book reviews, magazine format, 40 p. Includes book reviews, play reviews, record reviews.
ISSN 0317-4654 $5.00 per year.

Canadian mathematical bulletin = Canadien de mathématiques / *sponsored by* National Research Council ; *edited by* R.D. Bercov and A. Meir. - *Published by* Canadian Mathematical Congress. Suite 15, 3421 Drummond St., Montreal, Que. H3G 1X7, January 1958-
Quarterly. Association publication, journal format, 150 p. Language: English (French). Includes book reviews, volume index. Circulation: 1500
Indexed in Math. r., I.B.Z.
ISSN 0008-4395 $5.00 per issue : $20.00 per year. Subscription included in membership fee. Controlled circulation.

The Canadian Medical Association. Journal / *edited by* W.R. Anderson. - *Published by* The Canadian Medical Association. 1867 Alta Vista Dr., Ottawa, Ont., 1911-
Issued twice a month. Association publication, journal format, 100 p. Language: English and French ; summaries: English and French. Includes advertising, volume index. available in microform. supplements issued. Circulation: 29,428
Indexed in Ind. med., I.B.Z., Hosp. abstr. Hosp. Abstr..
$1.50 per issue : $24.00 per year : $30.00 per year, foreign. Controlled circulation. Special rates offered. Prepayment required.

The Canadian Medical Association. Newfoundland Division. Newsletter / *edited by* John R. Martin. - *Published by* Newfoundland Medical Association. O'Mara-Martin Bldg., Rawlins Cross, St. John's, Nfld.
Issued every other month. Association publication, newsletter format, 20 p. Includes advertising. Circulation: 750
$10.00 per year.

Canadian medical directory / *edited by* Anne Newcombe. - *Published by* Seccombe House. Southam Business Publications Ltd. 1450 Don Mills Road, Don Mills, Ont. M3B 2X7.
Annual. Directory, book format, 800 p. Includes updating service.
$30.00 ($25.00 pre-publication). Prepayment required.

Canadian Mennonite reporter *See* Mennonite reporter

Canadian men's hairstylist and barber / *edited by* Dorothy Anne Miller. - *Published by* Arthurs Publications Ltd. Suite 204, 5200 Dixie Rd., Mississauga, Ont., 1950-
Quarterly. Trade publication, magazine format,

Canadian merchandise mart (1973) *See* Byers Canadian merchandise mart

Canadian messenger *See* Canadan viesti

The Canadian messenger / *edited by* F.J. Power. - *Published by* Jesuit Fathers. 833 Broadview Ave., Toronto, Ont. M4K 2P9, 1891-
Monthly. Church publication. Includes advertising.
$3.00 per year.

Canadian metallurgical quarterly / *edited by* J.M. Toguri. - *Published by* Canadian Institute of Mining and Metallurgy. 906-117 St. Catherine St. W., Montreal, Que. H3B 1H9, 1962-
Quarterly. Association publication, magazine format, 190-300 p. Language: English and French ; summaries: English and French. Includes volume index.
Indexed in I.B.Z.
ISSN 0319-3861 $3.50 per issue : $10.00 per year : $15.00 per year (3.50 per issue), foreign.

Canadian Metric Association newsletter (1973-1975) *See* Metric message

Canadian Middle-East journal = Canadien moyen-orient / *edited by* Joseph Lahoud and Maurice J. Malick (associate editor). - *Published by* Joseph Lahoud. 285 Jean Talon St. E., Montreal, Que. H2R 1S9, June 1966-
Monthly. Ethnic press, newspaper format, 16 p. Language: French, English and Arabic. Includes advertising. Circulation: 2000
$.25 per issue : $10.00 per year : $20.00 per year, foreign.

The Canadian military journal / *edited by* P.E. Parent. - *Published by* Paul E. Parent. Suite 8, 3450 Durocher St., Montreal, Que. H2Y 2E1, July 1934-
Quarterly. Special interest, magazine format, Includes book reviews, advertising. Circulation: 18,598
$3.50 per year : $4.00 per year, U.S. Prepayment required.

Canadian military medals and insignia journal / *sponsored by* Canadian Society of Military Medals and Insignia (1965-1971) ; *edited by* R.W. Irwin. - *Published by* R.W. Irwin. 14 Tamarack Place, Guelph, Ont. N1E 3Y6, September 1965-
Quarterly. Special interest, magazine format, 16 p. Circulation: 200
ISSN 0318-2436 $.50 per issue : $4.00 per year.

Canadian milky way *See* Rapport

The Canadian mineralogist / *edited by* L.J. Cabri and J.L. Jambor. - *Published by* The Mineralogical Association of Canada. c/o Department of Mineralogy, Royal Ontario Museum, 100 Queen's Park, Toronto, Ont. M5Z 2C6, 1955-
Quarterly. Association publication, magazine format, 112 p. Language: English and French ; summaries: English and French. Includes volume index. Circulation: 1500
Indexed in Arct. bibl.
$7.00 per issue (Members $5.00) : $10.00 per year (Students $5.00 ; corporate $20.00). Prepayment required.

Canadian mines handbook / *edited by* F.M. Fielder. - *Published by* Northern Miner Press Ltd. 77 River St., Toronto, Ont. M5A 3P2, September 1929-
Annual. Directory, 400-425 p. available in microform.
$10.00 per year. Prepayment required.

Canadian mining and oil stock charts / *edited by* C.C.R. Tidd. - *Published by* Independent Survey Co. Ltd. P.O. Box 6000, Vancouver, B.C. V6B 4B9, 1957-
Former title(s): Western Mine and Oil Charts.
Monthly. Trade publication, book format, 145 p.
$12.50 per issue : $120.00 per year.

Canadian mining journal / *edited by* Richard Fish. - *Published by* Kevin McCollum. Southam Business Publications Ltd. 310 Victoria Ave., Westmont, Que. H3Z 2M9, 1879-
Monthly. Trade publication, magazine format, 100 p. Includes book reviews, advertising, volume index.
Indexed in Can. B.P.I., North. tit., I.B.Z., Arct. bibl.
$2.00 per issue : $12.00 per year : $30.00 per year, foreign. Controlled circulation.

Canadian mining journal's reference manual & buyers' guide / *edited by* Richard Fish. - *Published by* Southam Business Publications Ltd. 310 Victoria Ave., Westmount, Que. H3Z 2M9, 1891-
Former title(s): Canadian mining manual.
Annual. Trade publication, book format, 180 p. Includes advertising. Circulation: 2948
$20.00 per year (Pre-publication $18.00): $25.00 per year, foreign (Pre-publication $20.00).

Canadian mining manual *See* Canadian mining journal's reference manual & buyers' guide

The Canadian missionary link, (1878-1927) *See* The Link and visitor

The Canadian modern language review / *edited by* Anthony S. Mollica. - *Published by* Ontario Modern Language Teachers' Association. 34 Butternut St., Toronto, Ont. M4R 1T7, Fall 1943-
Quarterly. Association publication, journal format, 96 p. Language: English, French, Spanish, Italian and German. Includes book reviews, volume index. available in microform. supplements issued. Circulation: 3200
Indexed in LLBA, M.L.A. int. bib., Curr. ind. j. educ.
ISSN 0008-4506 $2.50 per issue : $10.00 per year : $11.00 per year, foreign.

The Canadian monarchist (May 1971-October 1972) *See* Monarchy Canada

Canadian mosaic (February 1974-September 1975) *See* Our cultural mosaic

Canadian motorist / *edited by* Jerry Tutujian. - *Published by* Ontario Motor League. 2 Carlton St., Toronto, Ont., January 1914-
Issued 5 times a year. Association publication, magazine format, Circulation: 135,000
$2.00 per year.

Canadian motorsport bulletin *See* Autosport Canada

Canadian municipalities buyers' guide / *edited by* Keith Pearson. - *Published by* Sentinel Publishing Co. 27 Centrale St., La Salle, Que., 1975-
Annual. Includes advertising.
$18.00 : $25.00, foreign. Free distribution to municipal officials.

Canadian Murray Grey Association. Yearbook and breeder's directory - *Published by* The Canadian Murray Grey Association. P.O. Box 605, Red Deer, Alta.
Annual. Association publication, booklet format, 50 p. Includes advertising. Circulation: 500

Canadian Murray Grey news - *Published by* Canadian Murray Grey Association. P.O. Box 605, Red Deer, Alta., 1974-
Quarterly. Association publication, newspaper format, Includes advertising. supplements issued. Circulation: 500
Free.

Canadian music directory - *Published by* Lloyd Publications of Canada. P.O. Box 65, West Hill, Ont. M1E 4R4, 1924-
Former title(s): Canadian furniture and furnishings directory.
Annual. Directory, magazine format, 50 p. Circulation: 5500
$10.00 per year : $13.00 per year, foreign. Prepayment required.

Canadian music educator / *edited by* Duane Bates. - *Published by* Canadian Music Educators. Dept. of Music, Queen's University, Kingston, Ont. K7G 3N6, 1960-
Quarterly. Association publication, journal format, 52 p. Includes book reviews, advertising. Circulation: 1420
Indexed in Can. educ. ind.
ISSN 0008-4549 $10.00 per year : $12.00 per year, foreign. Subscription includes the Newsletter of the Association.

Canadian Music Educators Association. Newsletter / *edited by* Wallace Laughton. - *Published by* Wallace Laughton. Canadian Music Educators. 34 Cameron Rd., St. Catherines, Ont., 1968-
Quarterly. Association publication, newsletter format, 22 p. Includes book reviews, record reviews. Circulation: 1420
$10.00 per year : $12.00 per year, foreign. Subscription includes the Canadian Music Educator.

Canadian music industry directory / *edited by* Walter Grealis. - *Published by* RPM Music Publications Ltd. 6 Brentcliffe Rd., Toronto, Ont. M4G 3Y2, 1965-
Annual. Directory.

Canadian music industry who's who / *edited by* Walter Grealis. - *Published by* RPM Music Publications Ltd. 6 Brentcliffe Rd., Toronto, Ont. M4G 3Y2, September 15, 1975-
Former title(s): Who's who in Canadian talent.
Annual. Directory, magazine format, 84 p. Includes advertising, volume index.
$7.50 per issue. Included free with subscription to RPM Magazine $25.00.

Canadian National Exibition programs - *Published by* Canadian National Exhibition. Exhibition Park, Toronto, Ont. M6K 3C3.
Program.

The Canadian National Institute for the Blind. Kitchener Office. Annual bulletin of services - *Published by* Kitchener Office. The Canadian National Institute for the Blind. 169 Borden Ave. N., Kitchener, Ont. N2H 3J5.
Annual. Association publication.

Canadian nature *See* Nature Canada

Canadian news *See* Kanadské listy

Canadian news facts : the indexed digest of Canadian current events / *edited by* Stephen D. Pepper and Barrie Martland. - *Published by* Marpep Publishing Ltd. 700-133 Richmond St. W., Toronto, Ont., January 1967-
Issued twice a month. Special interest, looseleaf format, 8 p. Includes volume index, cumulative index. Monthly index and quarterly cumulation included.
ISSN 0008-4565 $95.00 per year.

Canadian news synthesis project - *Published by* Canadian News Synthesis. P.O. Box 6300, Postal Station A, Toronto, Ont., November 1972-
Monthly. Newsletter format, 45 p. Circulation: 450
$1.00 per issue : $10.00 per year (Institutions $20.00) : $15.00 per year, foreign.

Canadian newsletter of research on women - *Published by* Department of Sociology. University of Waterloo. Waterloo, Ont., May 1972-
ISSN 0319-4477

Canadian notes and queries = Questions et réponses canadiennes / *edited by* William F.E. Morley. - *Published by* William F.E. Morley. c/o Douglas Library, Queen's University, Kingston, Ont. K7L 5C4.
Irregular (approximately 2 issues per year). Special interest, magazine format, 12 p. Language: English and French. Includes cumulative index. Circulation: 500
ISSN 0576-5803 Free to selected scholars in Canadian studies.

Canadian nuclear technology (1962-December 1967) *See* Canadian research and development

The Canadian numismatic journal / *edited by* Frank Rose. - *Published by* Canadian Numismatic Association. P.O. Box 226, Barrie, Ont. L4M 4T2.
Monthly. Association publication, magazine format, 40 p. Includes book reviews, advertising. Circulation: 3200
ISSN 0008-4573 $1.50 per issue : $15.00 per year : $15.00 per year, foreign. Prepayment required.

The Canadian Numismatic Research Society. The Transactions of the Canadian Numismatic Research Society / *edited by* L. Gingras. - *Published by* The Canadian Numismatic Research Society. 10 Wesanford Place, Hamilton, Ont., January 1965-
Quarterly. Association publication, magazine format, 30 p.
$5.00 per volume. Controlled circulation.

The Canadian nurse / *edited by* Virginia A. Lindabury. - *Published by* Canadian Nurses' Association. 50 The Driveway, Ottawa, Ont. K2P 1E2., 1905-
Monthly. Association publication, magazine format, 64 p. Includes book reviews, advertising. available in microform. Circulation: 80,217
Indexed in C.I.N.L., Hosp. lit. ind., Int. nurs. ind., Ind. med., Hosp. abstr.
$1.00 per issue : $6.00 per year : $10.00 per volume : $6.50 per year, foreign. Controlled circulation. Prepayment required.

Canadian nurseryman (January 1965 - May 1973) *See* Landscape

Canadian Nurses' Association. Library. Current bibliographies - *Published by* Library. Canadian Nurses' Association. 50 The Driveway, Ottawa, Ont. K2P 1E2, 1968-
Irregular (approximately 2 issues per year). Bibliography, sheet format, 6 p. Language: English and French.

Canadian Nurses' Association. Library. Periodical holdings - *Published by* Library. Canadian Nurses Association. 50 The Driveway, Ottawa, Ont., K2P 1E2.
Annual. Catalogue, 52 p.
$1.00 per issue : $6.00 per year : $11.00 for 2 years : $6.50 per year, foreign : $12.00 for 2 years, foreign. Free.

Canadian occupational safety / *edited by* Ernest Harris. - *Published by* Norman H. Parkins. 328 Victoria Ave., Montreal, Que. H3Z 2M8.
Issued every other month. Trade publication, magazine format, 40 p.
ISSN 0008-4611 $5.00 per year : $6.00 per year, U.S.

Canadian office / *edited by* Susan Pearce. - *Published by* Whitsed Publishing Ltd. 42 Mercer St., Toronto, Ont. M5V 1H3, April/May 1975-
Former title(s): Toronto office (1969-March 1975)
Monthly. Trade publication, magazine format, 16 p.
$1.00 per issue : $8.00 per year. Controlled circulation.

Canadian office products and stationary / *edited by* Gary Weiss. - *Published by* Southam Business Publications Ltd. 1450 Don Mills Rd., Don Mills, Ont., 1890-
Other title: Dealer's guide.
Issued every other month. Trade publication, magazine format, 35 p. Includes advertising.
$8.00 per year : $14.00 for 2 years. Controlled circulation.

Canadian office products and stationery : dealer's guide / *edited by* Gary Weiss. - *Published by* Southam Business Publications Ltd. 1450 Don Mills Rd., Don Mills, Ont., 1890's-
Issued every other month. Trade publication, magazine format, 35 p.
$8.00 per year : $14.00 for 2 years.

Canadian office redbook - *Published by* Whitsed Publishing Ltd. 42 Mercer St., Toronto, Ont. M5V 1H3.
Former title(s): Toronto office redbook.
Annual. Trade publication. Includes advertising.

Canadian oil and gas / *edited by* Lewis and Thompson. - *Published by* Butterworth & Co. (Canada) Ltd. 2265 Midland Ave., Scarborough, Ont. M1P 4S1.
Irregular (approximately 10 issues per year). Looseleaf format, Includes updating service.
$185.00 per year.

Canadian oil register / *edited by* Jean Omelusik. - *Published by* C.O. Nickle Publications Co. Ltd. Suite 110, 330-9th Ave. S.W., Calgary, Alta., T2P 1K8.
Annual. Directory, magazine format, 532 p.
$20.00.

Canadian oil register directory / *edited by* Jean Omelusik. - *Published by* C.O. Nickle Publications Co. Ltd. Suite 110, 330-9th Ave. S.W., Calgary, Alta. T2P 1K8.
Annual. Directory, 540 p.
$25.00.

Canadian Opera Guild. Guild news / *edited by* Irene Bartello. - *Published by* Canadian Opera Guild. 35-39 Front St. E., Toronto, Ont. M5E 1B3, Fall 1968-
Quarterly. Association publication, newsletter format, 4 p. Includes book reviews, record reviews. Circulation: 2500
$7.50 per year.

Canadian Operational Research Society. CORS bulletin - *Published by* Canadian Operational Research Society. P.O. Box 5321, Postal Station A, Toronto, Ont. M5W 1N6, July 1971?-
Former title(s): Bulletin - Canadian Operational Research Society (1962?-May 1971?)
Association publication.
ISSN 0315-1417

Canadian Osteopathic Association. Newsletter / *edited by* David A. Patriquin. - *Published by* Canadian Osteopathic Association. 575 Waterloo St. London, Ont. J6B 2R2, November 1960-
Quarterly. Association publication, newsletter format, 40 p.
Free.

Canadian Pacific Ltd. CP rail news / *edited by* J.C. Levebre. - *Published by* Canadian Pacific Ltd. Windsor Station, Montreal, Que. H3C 3E4.
Irregular (approximately 15 issues per year). House/company organ, newspaper format, 4-8 p. Language: English and French. Circulation: 45,000
Free.

Canadian packaging / *edited by* Jim Vernon. - *Published by* Maclean-Hunter Ltd. 481 University Ave., Toronto, Ont. M5W 1A7, 1948-
Monthly.
Indexed in Can. B.P.I.
$1.00 per issue : $10.00 per year : $15.00 for 2 years : $20.00 for 3 years : $25.00 per year, foreign.

Canadian paint and finishing / *edited by* Wm. H. Lurz. - *Published by* M.J. Palmer. Maclean-Hunter Ltd. 481 University Ave., Toronto, Ont. M5W 1A7, 1926-
Former title(s): Canadian paint and varnish; Canadian plating news.
Monthly. Special interest, magazine format, 84 p. Includes advertising, volume index. available in microform. Circulation: 5650
Indexed in Can. B.P.I.
ISSN 0008-4662 $1.00 per issue : $10.00 per year : $12.00 per year, U.S. and U.K. : $25.00 per year, foreign. Controlled circulation. Special rates offered. Prepayment required.

Canadian paint and varnish *See* Canadian paint and finishing

Canadian parachutist : canpara / *edited by* Robin Summerley. - *Published by* Canadian Sport Parachuting Association. P.O. Box 848, Burlington, Ont. L7R 3Y7, March 1968-
Irregular (approximately 9 issues per year). Association publication, magazine format, 16 p. Language: English and French. Includes advertising. Circulation: 3300
ISSN 0319-3896 $.65 per issue : $6.00 per year : $8.00 per year, foreign. Controlled circulation.

Canadian parliamentary guide / *edited by* Pierre G. Normandin. - *Published by* Canadian Parliamentary Guide. P.O. Box 3453, Postal Station C., Ottawa, Ont. K1Y 4J6, 1867-
Annual. Biography, 1000 p. Includes advertising. available in microform.
$10.75.

Canadian patent reporter / *edited by* Gordon F. Henderson. - *Published by* Canada Law Book Ltd. 80 Cowdray Court, Agincourt, Ont. M1S 1S5, 1942-
Monthly. Law reports, magazine format, 100 p. Includes volume index, updating service.
Indexed in Can. leg. per. lit.
$41.50 per volume.

Canadian Peace Research Institute. News report - *Published by* Canadian Peace Research Institute. 119 Thomas St., Oakville, Ont.
Quarterly.

Canadian periodical index = Index des périodiques canadiens / *edited by* Sylvia Morrison. - *Published by* Canadian Library Association. 9th floor, 151 Sparks St., Ottawa, Ont. K1P 5E3, 1948-
Former title(s): Canadian index to periodicals and documentary films (1948-1964)
11 issues per year plus annual cumulation. Index, monthly 75 p. Cumulation 425 p. Language: English and French. Includes cumulative index. 1938-47 available on microfilm. Circulation: 1580
Subscription rates variable, prices quoted on request.

Canadian Periodical Publishers' Association. Newsletter / *edited by* Sheryl Taylor-Munro. - *Published by* Canadian Periodical Publishers' Association. Suite 407, 3 Church St., Toronto, Ont. M5E 1M2, January 1974-
Monthly. Newsletter format, 4-8 p. Circulation: 650
ISSN 0315-0828 $5.00 per year. Free to members.

The Canadian personnel & industrial relations journal / *edited by* J.R. Perigoe. - *Published by* Council of Canadian Personnel Associations. Suite 602, 2221 Yonge St., Toronto, Ont. M4S 2B4, 1954-
Irregular (approximately 6 issues per year). Association publication, magazine format, 60 p. Language: English (French).
Indexed in Can. ind., Can. B.P.I., Soc. sci. journal file.
ISSN 0008-4727 $2.00 per issue : $12.00 per year.

Canadian petroleum / *edited by* James D. Hilborn. - *Published by* Southam Business Publications Ltd. 1450 Don Mills Rd., Don Mills, Ont. M3B 2X7.
Monthly. Trade publication, magazine format, 54 p. Includes book reviews, advertising.
Indexed in Can. B.P.I., North. tit., Arct. bibl.
$1.00 per issue : $10.00 per year : $14.00 per year, foreign. Free. Controlled circulation.

Canadian Petroleum Association. Statistical yearbook - *Published by* Canadian Petroleum Association. 625, 404 - 6th Ave. S.W., Calgary, Alta. T2P 2R9, 1955-
Annual. Statistics, 124 p. Circulation: 450-500
$30.00.

Canadian pharmaceutical journal / *edited by* Arnold V. Raison. - *Published by* Canadian Pharmaceutical Association. 175 College St., Toronto, Ont. M5T 1P8, 1868-
Monthly. Association publication, magazine format, 36 p. Includes book reviews, advertising, volume index. available in microform. Circulation: 13,000
Indexed in Excerpt. med., Int. pharm. abstr., Int. pharm. abstr., Can. B.P.I.
ISSN 0008-4743 $1.50 per issue : $12.00 per year. Special rates offered to students. Controlled circulation. Special rates offered. Prepayment required.

The Canadian philatelist / *edited by* Fred Stulberg. - *Published by* The Royal Philatelic Society of Canada. P.O. Box 4195, Postal Station E, Ottawa, Ont. K1S 5B2.
Issued every other month. Association publication, magazine format, 55 p.
$6.00 per year. Subscribers must be members of the society. Admission fee $1.00.

Canadian photo annual / *edited by* Irvine A. Brace. - *Published by* Maclean-Hunter Ltd. 481 University Ave., Toronto, Ont. M5W 1A7, 1973-
Annual. Magazine format,
$1.50.

Canadian photography / *edited by* Irvine A. Brace. - *Published by* Irvine A. Brace. Maclean-Hunter Ltd. 481 University Ave., Toronto, Ont. M5W 1A7, 1970-
Former title(s): Canadian professional photography; Canadian industrial photography.
Monthly. Trade publication, magazine format, 50 p. Circulation: 7400
ISSN 0031-8582 $2.00 per issue : $8.00 per year : $10.00 per year, foreign. Controlled circulation. Prepayment required.

Canadian Phytopathological Society. C.P.S. news / *edited by* B.H. MacNeill. - *Published by* Canadian Phytopathological Society. Research Station, P.O. Box 1210, Charlottetown, P.E.I. C1A 7M8.
Quarterly. Association publication, newsletter format, 12 p. Language: English and French.
Subscription included in membership fee
$12.00 per year.

Canadian Phytopathological Society. Proceedings / *edited by* B.H. MacNeill. - *Published by* Canadian Phytopathological Society. c/o Department of Environmental Botany, University of Guelph, Guelph, Ont., 1930-
Annual. Association publication, magazine format, 30 p. Circulation: 700
$4.00 per year.

Canadian pit and quarry *Voir* Génie construction

Canadian plains area studies bulletin *See* Canadian plains bulletin

Canadian plains bulletin / *sponsored by* Canadian Plains Research Center ; *edited by* The Director. - *Published by* Canadian Plains Area Studies. University of Saskatchewan. Regina Campus, Regina, Sask. S4S 0A2, December 1973-
Former title(s): Canadian plains area studies bulletin.
Irregular (approximately 4 issues per year). Scholarly publication, newsletter format, 3 p.
Free.

Canadian plastics / *edited by* Antony Anden. - *Published by* Southam Business Publications Ltd. 1450 Don Mills Rd., Don Mills, Ont. M3B 2X7, 1953-
Monthly except July. Trade publication, magazine format, 50 p. Includes advertising. Circulation: 7900
Indexed in Can. B.P.I.
$1.00 per issue : $10.00 per year : $12.00 per year, U.S. : $30.00 per year, foreign. Controlled circulation.

Canadian plastics directory and buyer's guide / *edited by* Antony Anden. - *Published by* Southam Business Publications Ltd. 1450 Don Mills Rd., Don Mills, Ont. M3B 2X7.
Annual. Trade publication, directory, magazine format, 206 p. Includes advertising. Circulation: 7900
$8.00. Controlled circulation.

Canadian plating news *See* Canadian paint and finishing

The Canadian podiatrist / *edited by* Richard Steiner. - *Published by* Dr. F. Weinstein. 406 Tegler Bldg., Edmonton, Alta.
Quarterly. Association publication, journal format, 12-16 p. Includes book reviews, advertising, volume index, cumulative index.
$1.50 per issue : $6.00 per year. Controlled circulation.

Canadian police bulletin *See* Canadian police chief

Canadian police chief / *edited by* Bernard E. Poirier. - *Published by* Canadian Association of Chiefs of Police, Inc. Suite 304, 116 Albert St., Ottawa, Ont. K1P 5G3, 1905-
Former title(s): Canadian police bulletin.
Quarterly. Association publication, magazine format, 48 p. Circulation: 2000
ISSN 0315-2464 Controlled circulation.

Canadian Polish Congress. Information bulletin = Congrès canadien polonais. Bulletin / *edited by* Maria Brodzki. - *Published by* Canadian Polish Congress. 288 Roncesvalles Ave., Toronto, Ont. M6R 2M4, May 1967-
Quarterly. Ethnic press, magazine format, 32 p. Language: Polish.
$1.00 per issue : $4.00 per year.

Canadian Political Science Association. Annual general meeting. Papers - *Published by* Canadian Political Science Association. c/o University of Ottawa, 30 Stewart St., Ottawa, Ont. K1N 6N5., 1970-
Annual. Association publication, proceedings of the annual conference, bound volumes, Language: English and French. Includes volume index, cumulative index. Circulation: 50
$20.00.

Canadian Political Science Association. Bulletin = Société canadienne de science politique. Bulletin / *edited by* Francois-Pierre Gingras. - *Published by* Canadian Political Science Association. University of Ottawa, Ottawa, Ont. K1N 6N5, 1971-
Former title(s): Canadian Political Science Association newsletter (1972-1973) CPSA newsletter (1971-1972)
Issued every other month. Association publication, newsletter format, 40 p. Language: English and French.
$1.00 per issue : $9.00 per year.

Canadian Political Science Association newsletter (1972-1973) *See* Canadian Political Science Association. Bulletin

Canadian pool and patio / *edited by* Peggy Wysong. - *Published by* Southam Business Publications Ltd. 1450 Don Mills Rd., Don Mills, Ont. M3B 2X7, Spring 1975-
Irregular (approximately 4 issues per year). Trade publication, magazine format, 50 p. Includes advertising.
$2.00 per issue : $6.00 per year : $10.00 for 2 years. Free. Controlled circulation.

Canadian ports and seaway directory / *edited by* Douglas W. Seip (Manager/editor). - *Published by* Bruce Wright. Southam Business Publications Ltd. 1450 Don Mills Rd., Don Mills, Ont. M3B 2X7, 1934-
Annual. Directory, magazine format, 175 p. Circulation: 3000
$20.00. Controlled circulation. Prepayment required.

The Canadian postmaster = Le Maître de poste canadien / *edited by* G.A. Meunier. - *Published by* Canadian Postmasters Association. Suite 1204, 130 Albert, Ottawa, Ont., K1P 5G4., 1961-
Irregular (approximately 8-10 issues per year). Association publication, magazine format, 20 p. Language: French and English. Circulation: 8500
ISSN 0008-4794 $1.00 per year.

Canadian poultry review / *edited by* V. Blukm. - *Published by* Donovan Ltd. 6 Adelaide St. E., Toronto, Ont. M5C 1H6, January 1876-
Monthly. Commodity publication, magazine format, 48 p. Circulation: 7000
$4.00.

Canadian power and sail *See* Canadian boating

Canadian power plant worker (1961-1975) *See* The Thermogram

Canadian premiums and incentives / *edited by* Tim Dickson. - *Published by* Maclean-Hunter Ltd. 481 University Ave., Toronto, Ont. M5W 1A7, 1973-
Monthly. Trade publication. Includes advertising.
ISSN 0319-6267 $2.00 per issue : $14.00 per year : $22.00 for 2 years : $29.00 for 3 years : $20.00 per year, U.S. and U.K. : $30.00 per year, foreign.

Canadian printer and publisher / *edited by* W.B. Forbes. - *Published by* Maclean-Hunter Ltd. 481 University Ave., Toronto, Ont. M5W 1A7, 1892-
Monthly.
Indexed in Can. B.P.I.
$2.00 per issue : $15.00 per year : $20.00 per year, U.S. & U.K. : $30,00 per year, foreign.

Canadian process equipment and control news / *edited by* V. Sharp. - *Published by* Canadian Process Equipment and Control News. 745 Mount Pleasant Rd., Toronto, Ont. M4S 2N5, 1972-
Issued every other month. Trade publication. Includes advertising.
ISSN 0318-0859 $8.00 per year : $12.00 for 2 years.

Canadian professional film directory / *edited by* Phil Auguste. - *Published by* Filmcraft Publications & Productions. 116 Earlton Rd., Agincourt, Ont. M1T 2R6, 1973/74-
Irregular (approximately 1 issue per year). Directory, 200 p. Includes advertising. Circulation: 2000
$4.00. Controlled circulation. Prepayment required.

Canadian professional photography *See* Canadian photography

Canadian Psychiatric Association. Bulletin = Association des psychiatres du Canada. Bulletin / *edited by* Lea C. Métivier. - *Published by* Canadian Psychiatric Association. Suite 103, 225 Lisgar St., Ottawa, Ont. K2P 0C6.
Monthly except two months in the summer. Association publication, newsletter format, 10-15 p. Language: English and French.
Free.

Canadian Psychiatric Association. Canadian Psychiatric Association journal = L'Association des psychiatres du Canada. La Revue de L'Association des psychiatres du Canada / *edited by* W.G. Bowden. - *Published by* Canadian Psychiatric Association. Suite 103, 225 Lisgar St., Ottawa, Ont. K2P 0C6., August 1971-
Irregular (approximately 8 issues per year). Directory, journal format, 100 p. Circulation: 850
$3.00 per issue : $95.00 per year. Prepayment required.

Canadian psychological review = Psychologie canadienne - *Published by* Canadian Psychological Association. 1390 Sherbrooke St. W., Montreal, Que. H3G 1K2.
Quarterly.
Indexed in Soc. sci journal file.
$25.00 per year.

Canadian public administration = Administration publique du Canada / *edited by* Donald V. Smiley. - *Published by* The Institute of Public Administration of Canada. 897 Bay St., Toronto, Ont. M5S 1Z7, 1958-
Quarterly. Association publication, journal format, 175 p. Language: English and French ; summaries: English and French. Includes book reviews, volume index, cumulative index. Circulation: 2800
Indexed in Int. polit. sci. abstr., PHRA, Pub. admin. abstr., Can. ind., Can. leg. per. lit., Soc. sci. cit. ind., P.A.I.S., Per. art. rel. law, A.B.C. pol. sci., Soc. sci journal file.
ISSN 0008-4840 $6.00 per issue : $25.00 per year. Prepayment required.

Canadian public policy = Analyse de politiques / *sponsored by* Canadian Economics Association, Canadian Association of Law Teachers, Canadian Political Science Association and the Canadian Sociology and Anthropology Association ; *edited by* John Vanderkamp. - *Published by* Canadian Public Policy. Room 053, Arts Bldg., University of Guelph, Guelph, Ont. N1G 2W1, Winter 1975-
Quarterly. Special interest, magazine format, 150 p. Language: English and French ; summaries: English and French. Includes book reviews. Circulation: 1500
$10.00 per year (Institutions $12.00; students $5.00; members of sponsoring associations $8.00).

Canadian publishers directory - *Published by* Fiona Mee. Greey de Pencier Publications Ltd. 59 Front St. E., Toronto, Ont. M5E 1B3.
Issued twice a year. Special interest, booklet format, 40 p. Includes advertising. Circulation: 8000
Free to subscribers to Quill and Quire. Additional copies $6.00 each.

Canadian Pulp and Paper Association. Air and Steam Improvement Committee. Review (October 1969-January 1971) *See* Canadian Pulp and Paper Association. Environmental Services Office. Review

Canadian Pulp and Paper Association. Environmental Services Office. Review - *Published by* Canadian Pulp and Paper Association. 2300 Sun Life Bldg., Montreal, Que. H3B 2X9, February 1971-
Former title(s): Canadian Pulp and Paper Association. Air and Steam Improvement Committee. Review (October 1969-January 1971)
Association publication.
ISSN 0319-6399

Canadian Pulp and Paper Association. Reference tables / *edited by* Information Office. - *Published by* Canadian Pulp and Paper Association. 2300 Sun Life Bldg., Montreal, Que. H3B 2X9.
Annual. Statistics, brochure format, 35 p. Language: English and French.
ISSN 0317-0934 Free.

Canadian Pulp and Paper Association. Statistical bulletin - *Published by* Canadian Pulp and Paper Association. 2300 Sun Life Bldg., Montreal, Que. H3B 2X9, 1966-
Monthly. Statistics, newsletter format, 4 p. Language: English and French. Circulation: 1200
Free.

Canadian Pulp and Paper Association. Technical Section. Gadget competition entries - *Published by* Pulp and Paper Canada. 2300 Sun Life Building, Montreal, Que. H3B 2X9.
Annual. House/company organ.
Indexed in Soc. sci. journal file.
Controlled circulation.

Canadian Pulp and Paper Association. Technical Section. Proceedings - *Published by* Canadian Pulp and Paper Association. 2300 Sun Life Bldg., Montreal, Que. H3B 2X9.
Annual. Association publication, 560 p.
ISSN 0068-9521 $10.00 (Non-members $30.00). Controlled circulation.

Canadian Pulp and Paper Association. Technical Section. Transactions / *edited by* Sheila Horrocks. - *Published by* Technical Section. Canadian Pulp and Paper Association. 2300 Sun Life Bldg., Montreal, Que. H3B 2X9, 1975-
Former title(s): Papers and discussions - Canadian Pulp and Paper Association. Technical Section.
Quarterly. Association publication, magazine format, 32 p. Includes volume index. Circulation: 4300
Indexed in Abstr. bull. inst. pap. chem.
$30.00 per year.

Canadian Pulp and Paper Association. Woodlands Section. News bulletin - *Published by* Woodlands Section. Canadian Pulp and Paper Association. 2300 Sun Life Bldg., Montreal, Que. H3B 2X9, 1945-
Monthly. Association publication, newsletter format, Includes book reviews. Circulation: 1500
Free.

Canadian pulp and paper industry / *edited by* L. Skory. - *Published by* Wilson Smith. Maclean-Hunter Ltd. 481 University Ave., Toronto, Ont. M5W 1A7.
Monthly. Trade publication, magazine format, 70 p. Includes advertising, volume index. available in microform. Circulation: 9200
Indexed in Can. B.P.I.
$2.00 per issue : $12.00 per year : $3.00 per issue, U.S. and U.K. : $4.00 per issue, foreign : $30.00 per year, foreign. Controlled circulation.

Canadian Quaker history / *edited by* Jadwiga Bennich. - *Published by* Canadian Friends Historical Association. 60 Lowther Ave., Toronto, Ont. M5R 1C7, November 1972-
Quarterly. Association publication, newsletter format, 12 p. Includes book reviews. Circulation: 150
ISSN 0319-3934 $2.00 per issue : $5.00 per year (Senior citizens and students $2.00).

Canadian quarter horse journal / *edited by* A.W. Finn. - *Published by* Golden Arc Publishing and Typesetting Limited. 491 Book Rd. W., Ancaster, Ont. L9G 3L3 (Subscription address: P.O. Box 65, Ancaster, Ont) 1973-
Monthly.
$5.00 per year.

Canadian Racing Pigeon Union. Yearbook - *Published by* Canadian Racing Pigeon Union. R.R. 4, London, Ont. N6A 4B8.
Annual. Association publication, yearbook, booklet format, 150 p.
ISSN 0316-2559 $5.00.

Canadian rail / *edited by* S.S. Worthen. - *Published by* Canadian Railroad Historical Association. P.O. Box 22, Postal Station B., Montreal, Que., 1949-
Former title(s): C.R.H.A. news report (1949-1962)
Monthly. Association publication, magazine format, 36 p. Circulation: 1900
$1.00 per issue : $9.00 per year. Prepayment required.

Canadian real estate annual *See* Real estate development annual

Canadian Real Estate Association. C.R.E.A. reporter / *edited by* E. Mack Parliament. - *Published by* Canadian Real Estate Association. 99 Duncan Mill Rd., Don Mills, Ont. M3B 1Z2, July 1971-
Monthly. Association publication, newspaper format, 8-12 p. Language: English and French. Includes book reviews. available in microform. Circulation: 36,400
Indexed in Can. B.P.I.
ISSN 0315-3843 $.50 per issue : $5.00 per year.

Canadian recreational vehicles ISSN 0319-1028 (1971-1972) *See* Recreational vehicle life

Canadian Red Cross Society. Manitoba Division. News and views / *edited by* Terry Hind. - *Published by* Manitoba Division. Canadian Red Cross Society. 226 Osborne St. N., Winnipeg, Man. R3C 1V4, September 1971-
Quarterly. Association publication, newspaper format, 4 p. Circulation: 6000
Free.

Canadian Red Cross Society. Ontario Division. News bulletin / *edited by* Stanley J. Kjewski. - *Published by* Ontario Division. Canadian Red Cross Society. 460 Jarvis St., Toronto, Ont. M4Y 2H5.
Quarterly. Association publication, newspaper format, 8 p. Circulation: 40,000

Canadian Red Poll Cattle Association. Bulletin / *edited by* G.R. Wagner. - *Published by* Canadian Red Poll Cattle Association. P.O. Box 15, Francis, Sask. S0G 1V0.
Quarterly. Association publication, newsletter format, 10 p. Circulation: 195
Free to members.

Canadian reformed magazine *See* The Clarion : Canadian reformed magazine

Canadian Religious Conference. CRC bulletin / *edited by* Jacques Cloutier. - *Published by* Canadian Religious Conference. 324 Laurier Ave. E., Ottawa, Ont. K1N 6P6, January 1955-
Irregular (approximately 7 or 8 issues a year). Association publication, newsletter format, 8 p. Circulation: 2000
ISSN 0316-8743 $2.00 per year.

Canadian research and development / *edited by* Douglas Dingeldein. - *Published by* Douglas Dingeldein. Maclean-Hunter Ltd. 481 University Ave., Toronto, Ont. M5W 1A7, January 1968-
Former title(s): Canadian nuclear technology (1962-December 1967)
Issued every other month. Special interest, magazine format, 72 p. Includes book reviews, advertising. available in microform. Circulation: 8272
Indexed in Can. B.P.I.
ISSN 0008-493X $1.00 per issue : $8.00 per year : $12.00 per year (U.S. and U.K.) : $25.00 per year, foreign. Controlled circulation.

Canadian research digest (1959-1960) *See* Education Canada

Canadian Retail Hardware Association. CRHA reporter - *Published by* Canadian Retail Hardware Association. 290 Merton St., Toronto, Ont. M4S 1B2, June 1966-
Published in French: ACDQ journaliste.
Monthly. Association publication, newsletter format, 6-8 p. Circulation: 1500
Free to members only. Controlled circulation.

Canadian retailer / *edited by* Judy Johnson. - *Published by* Retail Council of Canada. Suite 723, 74 Victoria St., Toronto, Ont. M5C 2A5.
Monthly. Trade publication, newsletter format, 8 p. Includes book reviews. Circulation: 2400. Controlled circulation.

The Canadian review / *edited by* E.G. Carter. - *Published by* Pomeroy, Carter and Associates Ltd. Suite 344, 85 Hastey Ave., Ottawa, Ont. (Subscription address: P.O. Box 8316, Alta. Vista Terminal, Ottawa, Ont. K1G 3H8) February 1974-
Irregular (approximately 6 issues per year). Magazine format, Circulation: 50,000
ISSN 0315-1190 $.75 per issue. : $7.00 per year.

Canadian review of American studies / *edited by* Robert White. - *Published by* Canadian Association for American Studies. Stong College, York University, Downsview, Ont. M3J 1P3, 1970-
Issued twice a year. Association publication, magazine format, 110 p. Language: English and French. Includes book reviews. Circulation: 500
Indexed in Soc. sci. cit. ind., M.L.A. int. bib., MLA abstr., Hist. abstr.; Amer. hist. and life.
ISSN 0007-7720 $8.00 per year. Subscription included in membership fee. Prepayment required.

Canadian review of comparative literature = Revue canadienne de littérature comparée / *sponsored by* Canadian Comparative Literature Association ; *edited by* Milan V. Dimic. - *Published by* University of Toronto Press. 5201 Dufferin St., Downsview, Ont. M3H 5T8, 1974-
Issued 3 times a year. Association publication, journal format, 102 p. Language: English, French and German. Includes book reviews, volume index. Circulation: 300
Indexed in M.L.A. int. bib.
ISSN 0319-051X $7.50 per year (Institutions $10.00).

Canadian review of sociology and anthropology = Revue canadienne de sociologie et d'anthropologie / *sponsored by* Canadian Sociology and Anthropology Association ; *edited by* Raymond Breton. - *Published by* University of Toronto Press. 5201 Dufferin St., Downsview, Ont. M3H 5T8 (Subscription address: P.O. Box 878, Postal Station A, Montreal, Que. H3C 2V8) 1964-
Quarterly. Association publication, journal format, 240 p. Language: English ; summaries: French. Includes book reviews. available in microform.
Indexed in Soc. sci. cit. ind., North. tit., Per. art. rel. law, Hist. abstr.; Amer. hist. and life, I.B.Z., Arct. bibl., Soc. sci. journal file.
ISSN 0008-4948 $32.00 per year (Institutions $37.00). Subscription included in membership fee. Controlled circulation.

Canadian review of studies in nationalism / *sponsored by* University of Prince Edward Island : Canada Council ; *edited by* Thomas Spira. - *Published by* Canadian Review of Studies in Nationalism. University of P.E.I., Charlottetown, P.E.I. C1A 4P3, Fall 1973-
Issued twice a year. Scholarly publication, journal format, 160 p. Language: English, French, German and Spanish. Includes book reviews. supplements issued. Circulation: 425
$8.00 per year.

Canadian risk management and business insurance / *edited by* Thomas W. Lazenby. - *Published by* Wadham Publications Ltd. Suite 101, 109 Vanderhoof Ave., Toronto, Ont. M4G 2J2, September 1967-
Issued every other month. Trade publication, magazine format, 36-40 p. Includes advertising. Circulation: 7000
$1.00 per issue : $5.00 per year : $7.00 per year, U.S., $7.50 per year, foreign. Controlled circulation.

Canadian road knight - *Published by* Ted Stevens (Publications) Ltd. 50 Crimea St., Guelph, Ont. N1H 2Y6, 1972-
Monthly. Trade publication. Includes advertising.
ISSN 0315-0682 $1.00 per issue : $10.50 per year.

The Canadian rockhound / *sponsored by* The Lapidary Rock and Mineral Society of British Columbia ; *edited by* Cleo M. Sparkes. - *Published by* The Canadian Rockhound. 941 Wavertree Rd., North Vancouver, B.C. V7R 1S4, November 1956-
Issued every other month. Association publication, magazine format, 40 p. Includes book reviews. Circulation: 1500
ISSN 0008-4956 $.65 per issue : $3.50 per volume : $4.00 per year, U.S. : $4.25 per year, foreign.

The Canadian sailing forum / *edited by* T.L. Phillips. - *Published by* Canadian Yachting Association. 333 River Rd., Ottawa, Ont. K1L 8B9, February 1973-
Former title(s): Sailing forum.
Issued every other month. Association publication, magazine format, 32 p. Includes advertising. supplements issued. Circulation: 5000
$1.00 per issue : $4.00 per year : $6.00 for 2 years.

Canadian sales meetings and conventions / *edited by* G. Spark. - *Published by* Southam Business Publications Ltd. 1450 Don Mills Rd., Don Mills, Ont. M3B 2X7, 1972-
Issued every other month.
Indexed in Can. B.P.I.
$8.00 per year : $14.00 for 2 years, $12.00 per year, U.S. : $20.00 per year, foreign.

Canadian scene / *edited by* Ruth Gordon. - *Published by* Canadian Scene. Suite 305, 2 College St., Toronto, Ont. M5G 1K3, March 1951-
Issued every other week. Ethnic press, newsletter format, 8 p. Language: 15 languages. Includes book reviews.
Free to Canada's ethnic press and radio stations.

Canadian Schizophrenia Foundation. Huxley Institute - CSF newsletter / *sponsored by* Huxley Institute for Biosocial Research (New York) and Canadian Schizophrenia Foundation ; *edited by* Mrs. F.H. Kaham. - *Published by* Canadian Schizophrenia Foundation. 2135 Albert St., Regina, Sask. S4P 2V1, January 1974-
Former title(s): CSF newsletter (1971-1974) Schizophrenia newsletter (1969-1971)
Quarterly. Association publication, newsletter format, 12 p. Back issues available except for July, 1974. Circulation: 3500
$2.00 per year. Subscription included in membership fee.

Canadian school journal *See* Ontario education

Canadian School Library Association CSLA on on line / *edited by* Karen Smith. - *Published by* Canadian School Library Association. 151 Sparks St. Ottawa, Ont. K1P 5E3.
Issued 3 times a year. Association publication, newsletter format, 20 p.
Subscription included in membership fee.

The Canadian secretary *See* Communiqué

Canadian serials directory = Répertoire des publications seriées canadiennes / *edited by* Martha Pluscauskas. - *Published by* University of Toronto Press. 5201 Dufferin St., Downsview, Ont. M3H 5T8, 1972-
Biennial. Directory, book format, 500 p. Language: English and French.
$75.00.

Canadian service (1923-1932) *See* Service and indemnity

Canadian service data book / *edited by* Ed Belitsky. - *Published by* Chuck O'Hearn. Maclean-Hunter Ltd. 481 University Ave., Toronto, Ont. M5W 1A7.
Annual. Directory. Includes advertising.
$6.00. Prepayment required.

Canadian service employee / *edited by* Albert G. Hearn. - *Published by* Mutual Press Ltd., Ottawa. 1424 Michael St., Ottawa, Ont. (Subscription address: 14th floor, 67 Yonge St., Toronto, Ont. M5E 1PE) January 1972-
Monthly. Association publication, newsletter format, 8 p. Language: English and French.

Canadian shipping and marine engineering / *edited by* Peter Cale. - *Published by* Malcolm Barnes. Maclean-Hunter Ltd. 481 University Ave., Toronto, Ont. M5W 1A7.
Monthly. Trade publication, magazine format, 50 p. Includes book reviews, advertising.
Indexed in Can. B.P.I.
$1.00 per issue : $10.00 per year : $12.00 per year, U.S. and U.K. : $25.00 per year, foreign. Controlled circulation.

Canadian short story magazine / *edited by* Louis Burke. - *Published by* Louis Burke. 518 - 26th St. Lethbridge, Alta. (Subscription address: P.O. Box 263, Lethbridge, Alta. T1J 3Y5) January 1975-
Quarterly. Special interest, magazine format, 65 p. Includes book reviews, advertising. Circulation: 3250
ISSN 0317-1949 $.85 per issue : $3.00 per year.

Canadian skater / *edited by* Mary Gallant. - *Published by* Canadian Figure Skating Association. 333 River Rd., Ottawa, Ont. K1L 8B9, January 1974-
Former title(s): Canadian skater tabloid (to January 1974)
Quarterly. Association publication, magazine format, 24 p. Language: English (French). Circulation: 3000
$.50 per issue : $2.00 per year. Prepayment required.

Canadian skater tabloid (to January 1974) *See* Canadian skater

Canadian Slavonic papers = Revue canadienne des Slavistes / *sponsored by* Canadian Association of Slavists ; *edited by* R.C. Elwood. - *Published by* Canadian Slavonic Papers. 256 Paterson Hall, Carleton University, Ottawa, Ont. K1S 5B6, 1956-
Quarterly. Special interest, journal format, 150 p. Language: English and French ; summaries: French and English. Includes book reviews, volume index, cumulative index. Circulation: 1000
Indexed in Theo. rel. index, Soc. sci. cit. ind., P.A.I.S., M.L.A. int. bib., MLA abstr., Hist. abstr.; Amer. hist. and life.
ISSN 0008-5006 $3.00 per issue : $12.00 per year.

Canadian Slovak *See* Kanadsky Slovák

Canadian soccer news / *edited by* Eric King. - *Published by* Canadian Soccer Association. 333 River Rd., Vanier, Ont. K1L 8B9, January 1971-
Issued every other month. Association publication, magazine format, 32 p. Language: English and French. Circulation: 1000
$1.00 per issue : $4.00 per year : $5.00 per year, U.S. : $6.00 per year, foreign.

Canadian Society for Cell Biology. CSCB bulletin = Société canadienne de biologie cellulaire. Bulletin / *edited by* V.L. Seligy. - *Published by* Canadian Society for Cell Biology. Dept. of Biology, Carlton University, Ottawa, Ont., September 1974-
Quarterly. Association publication, magazine format, 16 p. Language: English and French. Circulation: 375
$1.50 per issue : $4.00 per year.

Canadian Society for Education through Art. Annual journal / *edited by* Arnel W. Pattemore. - *Published by* Canadian Society for Education through Art. 112 Oakdale Ave., St. Catharines, Ont., 1951/1952-
Annual. Association publication, magazine format, 50 p.
$3.00. Subscription included in membership fee.

Canadian Society for Immunology. Bulletin / *edited by* S. Dubiski. - *Published by* Canadian Society for Immunology. C/o Department of Medicine, University of Manitoba, Winnipeg, Man. (Subscription address: Dr. J. Bienenstock, McMaster University, Medical Centre, 1200 Main St. W., Hamilton, Ont)
Irregular (approximately 2 issues per year). Association publication, newsletter format, 30 p. Language: French and English. Circulation: 400
$15.00 per year. Controlled circulation.

Canadian Society for Mechanical Engineering. Transactions / *edited by* J.T. Rogers. - *Published by* Canadian Society for Mechanical Engineering. 2050 Mansfield St., Montreal, Que. H3A 1Y9, March 1972-
Quarterly. Association publication, 60 p. Language: English and French ; summaries: English and French. Includes volume index, cumulative index. Back issues available. Circulation: 1200
Indexed in Eng. ind.
ISSN 0315-8977 $6.00 per issue (Non-members; libraries, companies and institutions $36.00). Controlled circulation. Prepayment required.

The Canadian Society for the Prevention of Cruelty to Animals. SPCA courier *Voir* La Société canadienne de protection des animaux. Courrier SPCA

Canadian Society for the Study of Education. Bulletin / *sponsored by* Canadian Society for the Study of Education. - *Published by* Faculty of Education. University of Alberta. P.O. Box 1000, Edmonton, Alta. T6G 2E1, January 1974-
Association publication.
ISSN 0315-1166

Canadian Society for the Study of Education. Conference. Proceedings / *edited by* H.T. Coutts. - *Published by* Canadian Society for the Study of Education. P.O. Box 1000, Faculty of Education, University of Alberta, Edmonton, Alta. T6G 2E1.
Annual. Association publication, 164 p.

Canadian Society for the Study of Education. Yearbook = Sociéte canadienne pour l'étude de l'éducation / *edited by* A. Kazipedes. - *Published by* Canadian Society for the Study of Education. P.O. Box 1000, Faculty of Education, University of Alberta, Edmonton, Alta. T3G-2E1, 1974-
Annual. Association publication, booklet format, 75 p. Language: English and French. Circulation: 1600
ISSN 0315-727X $3.00. Controlled circulation.

Canadian Society of Biblical Studies. Bulletin = Société canadienne des études bibliques. Bulletin / *edited by* P.C. Craigie. - *Published by* Canadian Society of Biblical Studies. Religious Studies, Faculty of Arts and Science, University of Calgary, Calgary, Alta. T2N 1N4, 1941-
Annual. Association publication, newsletter format, 25 p. Language: English and French ; summaries: English and French. Circulation: 200
ISSN 0068-970X Distributed to members.

Canadian Society of Clinical Chemists. CSCC newsletter / *edited by* R. Rockerbie. - *Published by* Canadian Society of Clinical Chemists. Suite 906, 151 Slater St., Ottawa, Ont. K1P 5H3.
Issued every other month. Association publication.

Canadian Society of Environmental Biologists. Newsletter = Société canadienne des biologistes de l'environnement. Bulletin / *edited by* G. Adams. - *Published by* Canadian Society of Wildlife and Fishery Biologists. P.O. Box 2292, Postal Station, D, Ottawa, Ont. (Subscription address: P.O. Box 962, Postal Station F, Toronto, Ont. M4Y 2N9) 1958-
Former title(s): Canadian wildlife and fisheries newsletter (1958-1972)
Quarterly. Association publication, newsletter format, 20 p.
Indexed in North. tit.
$5.00 per year. Subscription included in membership fee.

Canadian Society of Exploration Geophysicists. Journal / *edited by* A. Easton Wren. - *Published by* Canadian Society of Exploration Geophysicists. P.O. Box 117, Calgary, Alta. T2P 2G9, December 1965-
Irregular (approximately 1-2 issues per year). Association publication, journal format, 80 p.
ISSN 0008-5022 $7.00 per year.

Canadian Society of Forensic Science. Journal / *edited by* J.A. Churchman. - *Published by* Canadian Society of Forensic Science. 63 Kilbarry Cres., Ottawa, Ont., K1K 0H2., 1968-
Former title(s): C.S.F.S. newsletter (1964-1966)
Quarterly. Association publication, journal format, 40-50 p. Language: English (French). Includes book reviews, volume index.
Circulation: 450
ISSN 0008-5030 $3.75 per issue : $15.00 per year. Controlled circulation. Prepayment required.

Canadian Society of Laboratory Technologists. News bulletin = L'association canadienne des technologistes de laboratoire. Bulletin nouvelles / *edited by* L. Seibel. - *Published by* Canadian Society of Laboratory Technologists. P.O. Box 830, Hamilton, Ont. L8N 3N8, January 1973-
Issued every other month. Association publication, magazine format, 32 p. Language: English and French. Includes book reviews, advertising, volume index. Circulation: 16,500
Subscription included in membership fee.

Canadian Society of Laboratory Technologists. Nova Scotia Branch. The Newsletter / *edited by* R. Lindsay Rankin. - *Published by* Nova Scotia Branch. Canadian Society of Laboratory Technologists. P.O. Box 3102, Halifax South Postal Station, Halifax, N.S.
Issued 3 times per year. Association publication, newsletter format, 26 p. Includes advertising. Circulation: 850
$3.00 per year. Free.

Canadian Society of Microbiologists. Newsletter / *edited by* A.M. Forget and E.C.S. Chan. - *Published by* Canadian Society of Microbiologists. Dept. of Bacteriology and Immunology, The University of Western Ontario, London, Ont. N6A 3K7, July 1952-
Quarterly. Association publication, newsletter format, Language: English and French. Includes book reviews.
Controlled circulation.

Canadian Society of Painters in Water Colour. Annual exhibition catalogue - *Published by* Canadian Society of Painters in Water Colour. 8 York St., Toronto, Ont. M5J 1R2.
Annual. Association publication, brochure format,

Canadian Society of Petroleum Geologists. C.S.P.G. reservoir / *edited by* W.W. Shepheard. - *Published by* Canadian Society of Petroleum Geologists. 612 Lougheed Bldg., Calgary, Alta. T2P 1M7, January 1974-
Former title(s): C.S.P.G. newsletter.
Monthly. Association publication, magazine format, 8 p.
Free to members. Controlled circulation.

Canadian Society of Technical Agriculturists review (1934) *See* Agrologist

Canadian Society of Zoologists. Bulletin - *Published by* Canadian Society of Zoologists. c/o Editor, A.S.M. Saleuddin, York University, 4700 Keele St., Downsview, Ont. M3J 1P3, 1969-
Former title(s): Newsletter - Canadian Society of Zoologists ISSN 0319-6666 (1969-1973)
Quarterly. Association publication, newsletter format, 10 p. Includes book reviews.
Circulation: 1200
Free.

Canadian Sociology and Anthropology Association. Bulletin *Voir* Société canadienne de sociologie et d'anthropologie. Bulletin.

Canadian special truck equipment manual / *edited by* Paul Ingram. - *Published by* Maclean-Hunter Ltd. 481 University Ave., Toronto, Ont. M5W 1A7, 1958-
Annual. Trade publication.

Canadian spectroscopy (1963-1971) *See* Canadian journal of spectroscopy

Canadian sporting goods and playthings directory - *Published by* Lloyd Publications of Canada. P.O. Box 65, West Hill, Ont. M1E 4R4, 1954-
Annual. Directory, magazine format, 106 p. Includes advertising. Circulation: 8000
ISSN 0316-7771 $10.00 per year : $13.00 per year, foreign. Prepayment required.

Canadian sportsman / *edited by* G. Clifford Chapman. - *Published by* G.C. Chapman. 80 Brock St. E., Tillsonburg, Ont., 1870-
Issued twice a month October to May, weekly May to October. Special interest, newspaper format,
$.50 per issue : $8.00 per year : $8.50 per year, foreign : $1.00 special issues.

Canadian Standards Association. C.S.A. quarterly review / *edited by* Sally Southam. - *Published by* Canadian Standards Association. 178 Rexdale Blvd., Rexdale, Ont. M9W 1R3.
Quarterly. Association publication, magazine format, 50 p. Includes book reviews. Circulation: 15,000
ISSN 0007-9065 $2.00 per issue : $7.00 per year.

Canadian Standards Association. CSA and the consumer / *edited by* Sally Southam. - *Published by* Canadian Standards Association. 178 Rexdale Blvd., Rexdale, Ont., December 1970-
Published in French: L'Association canadienne de normalisation. ACNDR et le consommateur.
Issued twice a year. Association publication, pamphlet format, Circulation: 80,000
ISSN 0011-2313

Canadian Standards Association. Directory of CSA certified plumbing products - *Published by* Canadian Standards Association. 178 Rexdale Blvd., Rexdale, Ont. M9W 1R3.
Annual. Association publication, Book format, 200 p.
$10.00 per volume. Prepayment required.

Canadian steam magazine - *Published by* R.L. Coulton. Bentley, Alta., January 1972-
ISSN 0045-5393

Canadian String Teachers Association. Newsletter / *edited by* Lawrence V. Fisher. - *Published by* Canadian String Teachers Association. c/o 3157 Ibbetson Cr., Mississauga, Ont.
Irregular. Association publication, newsletter format, Includes book reviews, film reviews, play reviews, record reviews.

The Canadian student - *Published by* Student Christian Movement of Canada. 736 Bathurst St., Toronto, Ont. M5S 2R4, March 1918-
Issued twice a year. Church publication, newspaper format, 8 p. Includes book reviews. Free.

Canadian sunshine friend / *edited by* Beatrice Cain. - *Published by* Canadian Sunshine Club for Shut-ins & Invalids. 16 Fairview Ave., Toronto, Ont. M6P 3A1, 1944-
Issued every other month. Association publication, newsletter format, 18 p.
ISSN 0045-5415 Free. Available to club membership only.

The Canadian surveyor / *edited by* Harold Jones. - *Published by* The Canadian Institute of Surveying. 512 Rochester St., Ottawa, Ont. K1S 4L9.
Irregular (approximately 5 issues per year). Special interest, journal format, 140 p. Includes book reviews, volume index. Circulation: 2800
Indexed in North. tit.
$4.00 per issue : $25.00 per year.

Canadian swine / *edited by* L.E. McQuay. - *Published by* Canadian Swine Breeders' Association. R.R. 5, Cambridge, Ont. N1R 5S6, 1939-
Quarterly.
Free.

Canadian table tennis news / *edited by* Jose Tomkins. - *Published by* Canadian Table Tennis Association. 333 River Rd., Vanier City, Ottawa, Ont. K1L 8B9, 1965-
Issued every other month. Association publication, newspaper format, 20 p. Language: English and French. Includes book reviews.
$3.00 per year.

Canadian Talent Library. Bulletin / *edited by* Mal Thompson. - *Published by* Standard Broadcasting Ltd. 2 St. Clair Ave. W., Toronto, Ont. M4V 1L6, September 1967-
Monthly. Special interest, newsletter format, 4 p. Includes record reviews.
$2.00 per year. Free to subscribers to CTL, press, etc. Controlled circulation.

Canadian Tax Foundation. Conference report : report of proceedings of the Annual Tax Conference - *Published by* Canadian Tax Foundation. 100 University Ave., Toronto, Ont. M5J 1V6, 1947-
Annual. 700-800 p.
ISSN 0316-3571 Subscription included in membership fee $30.00.

Canadian tax journal / *edited by* John T. McHugh. - *Published by* Canadian Tax Foundation. 100 University Ave., Toronto, Ont. M5J 1V6, January 1953-
Issued every other month. Magazine format, 75-100 p.
Indexed in Can. ind., Can. leg. per. lit., Leg. per., P.A.I.S., Soc. sci. journal file.
ISSN 0008-5111 Subscription included in membership fee $30.00.

Canadian tax news / *sponsored by* Coopers and Lybrand ; *edited by* Donald R. Huggett. - *Published by* Carswell/Methuen Publications. 2330 Midland Ave., Agincourt, Ont. M1S 1P7, May 1973-
Monthly. Trade publication, newsletter format, 12 p. Language: English and French.
Indexed in Can. leg. per. lit.
ISSN 0319-2431 $45.00 per year.

Canadian teacher / *edited by* E.B. Lewis. - *Published by* Lewven Publishing Co. Ltd. P.O. Box 102, Postal Station R, Toronto, Ont., 1883-
Irregular (approximately 10 issues per year).
$1.25 per issue : $12.00 per year.

Canadian Technical Asphalt Association. Proceedings. Annual Conference - *Published by* Canadian Technical Asphalt Association. P.O. Box 1387, Victoria, B.C. V8W 2W3, 1956-
Annual. Association publication. Language: English and French.
$17.50 per year : $15.00 per volume.

Canadian textile directory - *Published by* Lloyd Publications of Canada. P.O. Box 65, West Hill, M1E 4R4, 1926-
Annual. Directory, magazine format, 70 p. Circulation: 7000
$10.00 : $13.00, foreign. Prepayment required.

Canadian textile journal / *edited by* Wm. A.B. Davidson. - *Published by* Canadian Textile Journal Publishing Co. Ltd. 4999 St. Catherine St. W., Montreal, Que., 1883-
Former title(s): Canadian journal of fabrics (1883-1906)
Monthly. Trade publication, magazine format, 94 p. Includes book reviews. Circulation: 3800
Indexed in Can. B.P.I.
$.75 per issue : $6.00 per year : $10.00 per year, foreign. Special rates offered. Prepayment required.

Canadian Textile Seminar. Cahier des conférences / *édité par* J.M. Merriman. - *Publié par* Textile Technical Federation of Canada. Suite 446, 4999 ouest, rue Ste-Catherine, Montréal, Qué. H3Z 1T3, 1948-
Publié en anglais: Book of papers for infotex.
Bienniale. Publication d'association, magazine, 150 p. Tirage: 700

Canadian theatre review / *edited by* Don Rubin. - *Published by* Faculty of Fine Arts. York University. 4700 Keele St., Downsview, Ontario M3V 1P3, January 1974-
Quarterly. Special interest, magazine format, 144 p. Includes book reviews, play reviews, advertising. available in microform.
ISSN 0315-0836 $2.50 per issue : $8.00 per year (Libraries $10.00) : $15.00 for 2 years (Libraries $19.00) : $9.00 per year, foreign.

The Canadian theosophist / *edited by* Mr. and Mrs. T.G. Davy. - *Published by* The Theosophical Society in Canada. P.O. Box 5051, Postal Station A., Toronto, Ont. M5W 1N4, March 1920-
Issued every other month. Association publication, magazine format, 24 p. Includes book reviews, volume index. Circulation: 600
$.50 per issue : $3.00 per year. Prepayment required.

Canadian tobacco grower / *edited by* C.E. Crandon. - *Published by* M.K. Glendinning. Cash Crop Farming Publications Ltd. 222 Argyle Ave., Delhi, Ont. N4B 2Y2, 1952-
Irregular (approximately 10 issues per year).
Commodity publication, magazine format, 66 p. Includes advertising. Circulation: 5000
$.25 per issue : $2.00 per year : $4.00 per year, foreign. Controlled circulation.

Canadian toy fair directory - *Published by* Canadian Toy Manufacturers Association. P.O. Box 294, Kleinburg, Ont. L0J 1C0.
Annual. Directory, 150 p.
Free.

Canadian toy retailing / *edited by* Robert Ferguson. - *Published by* Sentinel Publishing Co. 27 Centrale St., LaSalle, Que. H8R 3K2.
Monthly. Trade publication. Includes advertising.
$6.00 per year : $10.00 per year, U.S. and U.K. : $15.00 per year, foreign.

Canadian tractor farming (1940-1959) *See* Canadian farming

Canadian trade index = Index commercial canadien / *edited by* Nancy Clarke. - *Published by* Canadian Manufacturers' Association. One Yonge St., Toronto, Ont. M5E 1J9, 1900-
Annual. Directory, book format, 1300-1400 p. Language: English (Glossaries: French and Spanish). Circulation: 14,426
$45.00 (Schools and libraries $30.00). Special rates offered (schools, libraries).

Canadian training methods / *edited by* Richard Guerrier. - *Published by* Chesswood House Publishing Ltd. Suite 103, 542 Mount Pleasant Rd., Toronto, Ont. M4S 2M7, 1968-
Issued every other month.
Indexed in Can. educ. ind., Curr. ind. j. educ., Can. B.P.I.
$1.00 per issue : $5.00 per year : $7.00 for 2 years.

Canadian transport / *edited by* Edward H. Finn. - *Published by* Canadian Brotherhood of Railway, Transport, & General Workers. 2300 Carling Ave., Ottawa, Ont.
Monthly. Labour union publication, tabloid format, 8 p. Language: English and French. available in microform. Circulation: 35,000
$5.00 per year.

Canadian transportation and distribution management / *edited by* Douglas W. Seip. - *Published by* Bruce Wright. Southam Business Publications Ltd. 1450 Don Mills Rd., Don Mills, Ont. M3B 2X7, 1898-
Monthly. Trade publication, magazine format, Circulation: 9215
Indexed in Can. B.P.I.
$1.00 per issue : $10.00 per year : $14.00 per year, U.S. : $32.00 per year, foreign. Controlled circulation.

Canadian trapper - *Published by* Canadian Trapper. P.O. Box 705, North Bay, Ont.
Quarterly.

Canadian travel courier / *edited by* John Wardail. - *Published by* Maclean-Hunter Ltd. 481 University Ave., Toronto, Ont. M5W 1A7, 1965-
Issued every other week.
Indexed in Can. B.P.I.
$1.00 per issue : $8.00 per year : $14.00 for 2 years : $18.00 for 3 years : $35.00 per year, foreign (Asia Africa and Pacific Islands $45.00).

Canadian travel news *See* Canadian travel news weekly

Canadian travel news / *edited by* T. Thomas. - *Published by* Southam Business Publications Ltd. 1450 Don Mills Rd., Don Mills, Ont. M3B 2X7, 1961-
Former title(s): Canadian travel news weekly (1972-1974)
Issued every other week.
Indexed in Can. B.P.I.
ISSN 0319-7107 $10.00 per year : $17.00 for 2 years : $12.00 per year, U.S. : $30.00 per year, foreign.

Canadian travel news weekly (1972-1974) *See* Canadian travel news

Canadian travel news weekly - *Published by* Rodney Publications. 2 St. Clair Ave. W., Toronto, Ont., 1972-1974-
Former title(s): Canadian travel news.
ISSN 0319-7093

Canadian travel press / *edited by* Edith Baxter. - *Published by* Baxter Publishing Company. Suite 401, 150 King St. W., Toronto, Ont., 1968-
Issued every other week.
$.50 per issue : $5.00 per year : $10.00 for 3 years: $20.00 per years, foreign.

The Canadian traveller / *edited by* Michael Carreck and Sue Carreck. - *Published by* Ellis Publishing Co. Ltd. Suite 925, 1018 St. Catherine St. W., Montreal, Que. H3B 4B4, 1974-
Irregular (approximately 6 issues per year). Trade publication, magazine format, Includes advertising.

Canadian treasure / *edited by* T.W. Paterson. - *Published by* Stagecoach Pub. Co. Ltd. P.O. 3399, Langley, B.C., Summer 1973-
Quarterly. Special interest, magazine format, 72 p. Includes book reviews, advertising. Circulation: 5000
ISSN 0319-4450 $1.50 per issue : $4.00 per year : $5.25 per year, foreign. Prepayment required.

Canadian Truck Body and Equipment Association. Newsletter - *Published by* Canadian Truck Body and Equipment Association. 19 Sumner Lane, Thornhill, Ont., August 1963-
Irregular (approximately 6 issues per year). Association publication, newsletter format, 2 p. Circulation: 150

Canadian Tuberculosis and Respiratory Disease Association. Bulletin = Association canadienne contre la tuberculose et les maladies respiratoires. Bulletin / *edited by* Ann Hammell. - *Published by* Canadian Tuberculosis and Respiratory Disease Association. 345 O'Connor St., Ottawa, Ont. K2P 1V9, 1920-
Former title(s): Bulletin - Canadian Tuberculosis Association (1920-1968)
Quarterly. Association publication, newsletter format, 16 p. Language: English and French. Circulation: 26,000
$1.00 per year.

Canadian UFO report / *edited by* John Magor. - *Published by* John Magor. P.O. Box 758, Duncan, B.C. V9L 3Y1, January 1969-
Quarterly. "Purpose: to gather and disperse current information on UFO sightings", magazine format, 28 p. available in microform.
ISSN 0008-5243 $1.25 per issue : $5.00 per year : $10.00 per volume : $6.00 per year, foreign (Airmail $6.50).

Canadian underwriter / *edited by* K.E. MacLeod. - *Published by* Wadham Publications Ltd. 109 Vanderhoof Ave., Toronto, Ont. M4G 2J2, 1934-
Monthly. Trade publication, magazine format, 54 p. Includes advertising.
$1.00 per issue : $6.00 per year : $9.00 per year, foreign. Prepayment required.

Canadian union messenger - *Published by* Canadian Union Conference of the Seventh-Day Adventist Church. 1156 King St. E., Oshawa, Ont. L1H 1H8, 1901-
Former title(s): Eastern Canadian messenger (to 1932) Western Canadian tidings (to 1932)
Issued twice a month. Church publication, magazine format, 20 p.
$2.00 per year. Free.

Canadian Union of Public Employees. Journal / *edited by* Norman Simon. - *Published by* Canadian Union of Public Employees. Suite 800, 233 Gilmour St., Ottawa, Ont. K2P 0P5., September 1973-
Irregular (approximately 10 issues per year). Union publication, newspaper format, 12 p. Circulation: 75,000
Free to members.

The Canadian Unitarian / *edited by* Jack Wallace. - *Published by* Canadian Unitarian Council. 175 St. Clair Ave.W., Toronto, Ont. M4V 1P7, Summer 1957-
Irregular (approximately 5 issues per year). Church publication, newsletter format, 4 p.
$.10 per issue. Sold only in bulk to Canadian Unitarian churches and fellowships.

Canadian university and college *See* Educational digest

Canadian University Service Overseas. CUSO forum / *edited by* Hugh Nangle. - *Published by* Canadian University Service Overseas. 10th floor, 151 Slater St., Ottawa, Ont. K1P 5H5, 1969-
Issued every other month. Association publication, newspaper format, 16 p. Includes book reviews, film reviews. Circulation: 8000
ISSN 0318-6830 Free.

Canadian Urban Transit Association. Proceedings of the annual meeting / *edited by* H.E. Brown. - *Published by* Canadian Transit Association. 1138 Bathhurst St., Toronto, Ont. M5H 3H2, 1904-
Annual. Association publication, book format, 100 p.
ISSN 0316-7933 Free to members. Controlled circulation.

Canadian variety merchandise directory - *Published by* Lloyd Publications of Canada. P.O. Box 65, West Hill, Ont. M1E 4R4, 1924-
Annual. Directory, magazine format, 70 p. Circulation: 6000
$10.00 : $13.00, foreign. Prepayment required.

Canadian vending - *Published by* Canadian Vending. P.O. Box 187, 126 14th St. W., Owen Sound, Ont.
Monthly.
Indexed in Can. B.P.I., PAIS.
$7.00 per year.

The Canadian veterinary journal = La revue vétérinaire canadienne / *edited by* O.M. Radostits. - *Published by* Canadian Veterinary Medical Association. 360 Bronson Ave., Ottawa, Ont., K1R 6J3., 1960-
Monthly. Association publication, journal format, 48 p. Language: English and French ; summaries: English and French. Includes book reviews, advertising, volume index. available in microform. Circulation: 4200
Indexed in Biol. abstr., Nutr. abstr., Ind. med.
ISSN 0008-5286 $2.00 per issue : $10.00 per year : $20.00 per volume.

Canadian vocational journal / *edited by* Peter Findlay. - *Published by* Canadian Vocational Journal. Suite 608, 251 Bank St., Ottawa, Ont. K2P 1X3., 1965-
Quarterly. Association publication, magazine format, 44-48 p. Language: English and French ; summaries: English and French. Includes book reviews, advertising. Circulation: 3000
Indexed in Can. educ. ind., Curr. ind. j. educ.
$1.00 per issue : $4.00 per year. Prepayment required.

Canadian volleyball annual and rule book / *edited by* Anton H. Furlani. - *Published by* Canadian Volleyball Association Publications. 78 Tedford Dr., Scarborough, Ont. M1R 1M4.
Annual. Special interest, booklet format, 96 p. Language: English and French. Circulation: 12,000
Special rates offered.

Canadian Volleyball Association. Volleyball technical journal / *edited by* Lorne Sawula. - *Published by* National Volleyball Association. 333 River Rd., Vanier City, Ont. K1L 8B9, January 1974-
Former title(s): Technical Journal - National Volleyball Coaches Association.
Issued 3 times a year. Association publication, magazine format, 60-90 p. Language: English (French). Includes book reviews. Circulation: 500
ISSN 0315-0887 $15.00 per year.

Canadian Warehousing Association. The C.W.A. reporter / *edited by* S.G. Wild. - *Published by* Canadian Warehousing Association. 6 Adelaide St. E., Toronto, Ont. M5C 1H6.
Monthly. Association publication, newspaper format, 6 p.

Canadian weekly industrial stock charts / *edited by* C.C.R. Tidd. - *Published by* Independent Survey Co. Ltd. 1706 W. 1st Ave., Vancouver, B.C. (Subscription address: P.O. Box 6000, Vancouver, B.C. V6B 4B9) July 1958-
Monthly. Special interest, magazine format, 125 p. Includes updating service.
$10.00 per issue : $99.50 per year : $1.00 extra per issue for airmail outside Canada. Special rates offered. Prepayment required.

Canadian weekly law sheet - *Published by* Butterworth & Co. (Canada) Ltd. 2265 Midland Ave., Scarborough, Ont. M1P 4S1.
Weekly. Law reports, newsletter format, 1-2 p.
$35.00 per year.

Canadian weekly mining and oil stock charts / *edited by* C.C.R. Tidd. - *Published by* Independent Survey Co. Ltd. 1706 W. 1st Ave., Vancouver, B.C. (Subscription address: P.O. Box 6000, Vancouver, B.C. V6B 4B9) July 1958-
Former title(s): Eastern mining and oil charts; Western mining and oil charts.
Monthly. Trade publication, magazine format, 170 p. Includes updating service.
$12.50 per issue : $120.00 per year (Airmail outside Canada $1.00 extra). Special rates offered. Prepayment required.

Canadian welder and fabricator / *edited by* D.O. Brewer. - *Published by* S. Steigerwald. P.O. Box 6900, 1077 St. James St., Winnipeg, Man., R3C 3B1.
Monthly. Trade publication, magazine format, 42 p. Includes advertising. Circulation: 8200
$1.00 per issue : $8.00 per year : $10.00 per year, foreign. Controlled circulation. Prepayment required.

Canadian welfare *See* CW

The Canadian western rider / *edited by* A.W. Finn. - *Published by* Golden Arc Publishing and Typesetting Limited. 491 Book Rd. W., Ancaster, Ont. L9G 3L3 (Subscription address: P.O. Box 65, Ancaster, Ont) 1970-
Monthly. Magazine format,
$5.00 per year.

The Canadian white ribbon tidings / *edited by* Grace Fulton. - *Published by* Canadian Woman's Christian Temperance Union. 5592 Dorset St., Burnaby, B.C. V5J 1L5 (Subscription address: Mrs. A.E. Connell, Suite 302, 30 Gloucester St. Toronto, Ont. M4Y 1L6) 1863-
Issued 5 times a year. Association publication, 118 p.
Prepayment required.

Canadian wildlife and fisheries newsletter (1958-1972) *See* Canadian Society of Environmental Biologists. Newsletter

Canadian wings / *edited by* J.K. Norris. - *Published by* J.K. Norris. Nor-Rand Publishing. P.O. Box 3278, Station B, Calgary, Alta. T2M 4L8.
Monthly. Special interest, magazine format, 26-30 p. Includes book reviews, advertising.
$.50 per issue : $5.00 per year.

Canadian wings : aviation directory / *edited by* Marg Kobrinsky. - *Published by* J.K. Norris. Nor-Rand Publishing. 1808 First St. N.W., Calgary, Alta. T2M 4L8 (Subscription address: P.O. Box 3278, Postal Station B, Calgary, Alta. T2M 4L8)
Annual. Directory, magazine format, 45 p. Includes advertising, volume index, updating service. available in microform. Circulation: 2800
$1.00 per year. Controlled circulation. Special rates offered.

Canadian wolf defenders / *sponsored by* Canadian Wolf Defenders ; *edited by* Carol Schurmann. - *Published by* Carol Schurmann. P.O. Box 3480, Postal Station D, Edmonton, Alta. T5L 4J3.
Quarterly. Association publication, newsletter format, 5 p.

Canadian Wood Council. Quarterly reports - *Published by* Canadian Wood Council. 701 - 170 Laurier Ave. W., Ottawa, Ont. K1P 5V5.
Quarterly. Special interest, newsletter format, 4 p.

Canadian Wood Council. Special report - *Published by* Canadian Wood Council. 701 Place Laurier, 170 Laurier Ave. W., Ottawa, Ont. K1P 5V5, August 1971-
ISSN 0315-7032

Canadian wood products / *edited by* Paul Albany. - *Published by* Don Quick Publications. 297 Old Kingston Rd., West Hill, Ont. M1C 2B4, 1900-
Issued every other month. Trade publication. Includes advertising.
Indexed in Can. B.P.I.
$8.00 per year.

Canadian wool grower / *edited by* J.C. Ross. - *Published by* Canadian Co-operative Wool Growers Limited. P.O. Box 790, Carleton Place, Ont. K0A 1J0.
Issued twice a year. Association publication, magazine format, 24 p. Includes advertising.
Circulation: 11,000
$1.00 per year. Free to members.

Canadian worker (1969-1973) *See* The Worker

Canadian World Federalist (1961-1968) *See* World Federalist. Canadian ed

Canadian yearbook of international law = Annuaire canadien de droit international / *sponsored by* International Law Association. Canadian Branch ; *edited by* C.B. Bourne. - *Published by* University of British Columbia Press. 2075 Westbrook Place, Vancouver, B.C. V6T 1W5, 1963-
Annual. Yearbook, 400 p. Language: English and French. Includes book reviews.
ISSN 0069-0058

Canadian Youth Hostels Association. Mid-West Area. Newsletter / *edited by* G. Ivey. - *Published by* Mid-West Area. Canadian Youth Hostels Association. 1854 Portage Ave., Winnipeg, Man. R3J 0G9, 1972-
Quarterly. Association publication, newsletter format, 1 p.
Free.

Canadian Zionist / *edited by* Myer Bick. - *Published by* The Canadian Zionist Federation. Suite 800, 1310 Greene Ave., Montreal, Que. H3Z 2B2, 1934-
Irregular (approximately 10 issues per year). Association publication, magazine format, 44 p. Includes book reviews, advertising.
Circulation: 32,251
$1.00 per year. Special rates offered.

Canadian-American seminar / *sponsored by* University of Windsor ; *edited by* J. Alex Murray. - *Published by* University of Windsor Press. Windsor, Ont. N9B 3P4, 1960-
Former title(s): Seminar on Canadian-American relations.
Annual. Proceedings of the annual conference, 190 p.
$10.30 per year.

Canadian-German folklore - *Published by* Pennsylvania German Folklore Society of Ontario. 43 Melbourne Cr., Waterloo, Ont. N2L 2M4.
Annual. Association publication.

Canadien de mathématiques *See* Canadian mathematical bulletin

Canadien moyen-orient *See* Canadian Middle-East journal

Cancer in Ontario / *edited by* J.O. Godden. - *Published by* The Ontario Cancer Treatment and Research Foundation. 7 Overlea Blvd., Toronto, Ont. M4H 1A8, 1945-
Former title(s): Annual report - The Ontario Cancer Treatment and Research Foundation (1945-1971)
Annual. Association publication, book format, 275 p. Circulation: 17,000
ISSN 0315-9884 Free.

Candid facts / *edited by* John Powell. - *Published by* Canadian Cystic Fibrosis Foundation. Suite 401, 51 Eglinton Ave. E., Toronto, Ont. M4P 1G7, 1964-
Irregular (approximately 4 issues per year). Association publication, newsletter format, 8 p.
Circulation: 11,500
Free.

Canoe / *edited by* Mrs. J.M. Matheson (executive director). - *Published by* Canadian Canoe Association. 333 River Rd., Vanier City, Ont. K1L 8B9, February 1976-
Former title(s): Canadian Canoe Association newsletter.
Quarterly. Association publication, magazine format, 24 p. Language: English and French. Includes book reviews, advertising. Circulation: 2500
$1.25 per issue : $5.00 per year. Prepayment required.

Cape Breton's magazine - *Published by* Cape Breton's Magazine. Wreck Cove, Cape Breton, N.S., 1974-
Irregular. Language: English, Gaelic, French and Micmac. Back issues available.
$4.50 for 6 issues : $8.50 for 12 issues.

Cape Dorset Prints. Estampes - *Published by* Canadian Arctic Producers Ltd. P.O. Box 4130, Postal Station E, Ottawa, Ont. K1S 5B2, October 1975-
Annual. Special interest, 85 p. Language: English and French.

Capilano College communicates *See* The Capilano review

The Capilano review / *edited by* Pierre Coupey. - *Published by* Humanities Division. Capilano College. 2055 Purcell Way, North Vancouver, B.C. V7J 3H5, Spring 1972-
Former title(s): Capilano College communicates.
Issued twice a year. Scholarly publication, journal format, 100 p. available in microform. Circulation: 1000
ISSN 0315-3754 $2.00 per issue : $5.00 for 3 issues (Libraries $6.00) : $6.00 for 3 issues, foreign (Libraries $7.00).

Capt. Lillie's coast guide and radiotelephone directory : British Columbia, Puget Sound and S.E. Alaska Coast Guide / *edited by* Murray D. McLellan. - *Published by* Progress Publishing Co. (1958) Ltd. c310-355 Burrard St., Vancouver, B.C. V6C 2G6, 1936-
Biennial. Directory, book format, 160 p. Includes advertising.
$5.00. 40% discount to booksellers. Special rates offered.

Captain George's penny dreadful / *sponsored by* The Vast Whizzbang Organization ; *edited by* Peter Harris/ Captain George. - *Published by* George Henderson. 594 Markham St., Toronto, Ont. M6G 2L8, December 4, 1968-
Weekly. Special interest, newsletter format, 4 p. Includes book reviews, film reviews. Circulation: 350
$5.00. Controlled circulation.

Capuchins missions : bulletin of the St-Theresa Missionary Center / *edited by* The Capuchin Fathers. - *Published by* St. Theresa Missionary Center. 4387 Ave. Esplanade, Montreal, Que. H3W 1T3, 1965-
Quarterly. Church publication, magazine format, 16 p.
$1.00 per year.

Capucins canadiens / *édité par* P. Armand Bolduc. - *Publié par* Capucins canadiens. 4387 Esplanade, Montréal, Qué., décembre 1961-
Trimestriel. Publication ecclésiastique, bulletin, 8 p. Langue(s): français ; sommaires: anglais. Tirage: 200,000
$1.00 par année.

Careers for graduates = Carrières pour diplômés - *Published by* Development Publications. P.O. Box 84, Postal Station A, Willowdale, Ont. M2N 5S4.
Annual. 56 p. Language: English and French.
ISSN 0318-6229 $1.50.

Caribbean business news / *edited by* Colin Rickards. - *Published by* Victor C. Grunean & Sydney Rosen. 1255 Yonge St., Toronto, Ont. M4W 1Z3, 1969-
Monthly. Trade publication.
$1.00 per issue : $10.00 per year : $12.00 per year, foreign (Airmail $15.00).

Cariboo calling : supplement to the 100 Mile House Free press / *edited by* J.F. Traff. - *Published by* J.F. Traff. P.O. Box 459, 100 Mile House, B.C. V0K 2E0, 1968-
Annual. General interest, newspaper format, 24 p. Includes advertising. Circulation: 8500
Free.

Carillon / *edited by* Don Humphries. - *Published by* Students' Union Saskatchewan. University of Saskatchewan. Regina, Sask.
Weekly. Student publication, newspaper format, 12 p. Includes book reviews, film reviews, play reviews, record reviews, advertising. Circulation: 5000
$10.00 per year.

The Carleton (1945-1971) *See* The Charlatan

Carleton education bulletin / *edited by* Mary Curry. - *Published by* Carleton Board of Education. 133 Greenbank Rd., Ottawa, Ont. K2H 6L3.
Monthly except summer. General interest, newspaper format, 12-16 p. Circulation: 32,000
Free.

Carleton University. Alumni Association. The Carleton alumneye / *edited by* Executive Director of Alumni Affairs. - *Published by* Carleton University, Alumni Association. Colonel By Drive, Ottawa, Ont. K1S 5B6, Winter 1971-
Former title(s): The CanOpener (Fall 1969 to Summer 1971)
Issued twice a year. Alumni newsletter, tabloid format, 20 p.
Free. Controlled circulation.

Les Carnets de zoologie / *édité par* Raymond Cayouette. - *Publié par* La Société zoologique de Québec, inc. 8191 ave du Zoo, Orsainville, Qué. G1G 4G4, 1941-
Trimestriel. Publication d'association, magazine, 16 p. Comprend critique de livres. Tirage: 2000
Indexé dans Periodex.
$.50 le numéro : 2.00 par année. Tarifs spéciaux disponibles. Abonnements payables à l'avance.

Carrefour / *édité par* André J. Hamel. - *Publié par* Association générale des anciens. Université de Sherbrooke. 615, Calixa Lavallée, Qué. G1S 3G7, septembre 1967-
Publication d'association, journal, 11 p. Tirage: 6500

Carrefour chrétien / *édité par* Benoit Beaudoin. - *Publié par* Les Buissonnets inc. 6300, rue St. Denis, Montréal, Que. H2S 2R7, mai 1949-
Ancien titre: Le Sourire (mai 1949-mai 1963)
Mensuel. Publication ecclésiastique, journal, 12 p. parution de suppléments. Tirage: 5000
$.35 le numéro : $3.00 par année : $3.50 par année, l'étranger. Abonnements payables à l'avance.

Carrières pour diplômés *See* Careers for graduates

Carscope / *edited by* Cecilia Long. - *Published by* The Arthritis Society. Suite 420, 920 Yonge St., Toronto, Ont. M4W 3J7, January 1960-
Irregular (approximately 6-8 issues per year). Association publication, newsletter format, 4 p. Circulation: 7100
ISSN 0068-8258

The Cart / *edited by* George Harness. - *Published by* Lord Selkirk Region. Antique Automobile Club of America. 574 Clifton St., Winnipeg, Man. R3J 2E5, June 1972-
Issued every other month. Association publication, newsletter format, 6 p. Circulation: 60

Cartographer (1964-1967) *See* Canadian cartographer

Cartographica / *edited by* B.V. Gutsell. - *Published by* B.V. Gutsell. York University, Dept. of Geography, 4700 Keele St., Downsview, Ont. M3J 1P3.
Irregular (approximately 3 issues per year). Journal format, Issued as a supplement to Canadian cartographer. Circulation: 1500
ISSN 0317-7173 $12.00 per year. Combined subscription with Cartographica $15.00.

Cartologica / *édité par* Yves Tessier. - *Publié par* La Cartothèque. Bibliothèque. Université Laval. Québec, Qué. G1K 1P4, septembre 1969-
Bimestriel. Publication d'association, bulletin, 12 p. Tirage: 250
ISSN 0045-5881 Envoi gratuit. Tirage contrôlé.

Cartoons in the Vancouver Sun / *edited by* L. Norris. - *Published by* The Vancouver Sun Publishing Co. 2250 Granville St., Vancouver, B.C. V6H 3G2, 1952-
Annual. Cartoons, book format, 102 p. Circulation: 27,000

Casagram - *Published by* Canadian Association of School Administrators. Suite N843, 252 Bloor St. W., Toronto, Ont. M5S 1V5, 1970-
Monthly September to June. Association publication. supplements issued.

Casagram : quarterly supplement - *Published by* Canadian Association of School Administrators. Suite N843, 252 Bloor St. W., Toronto, Ont M5S 1V5.
Quarterly. Association publication.

Cash crop farming / *edited by* Dave MacLaren. - *Published by* Cash Crop Farming Publications Ltd. 222 Argyle Ave., Delhi, Ont. N4B 2Y2, 1938-
10 issues per year. Commodity publication, magazine format, Includes advertising. Circulation: 10,737
$.25 per issue : $2.00 per year : $4.00 per year, foreign.

Cassette gazette / *edited by* Deanna Siewert. - *Published by* Alberta Division. Canadian Society of Radiological Technicians. 351 - 18 St. N., Lethbridge, Alta. T1H 3G3, July 1965-
Former title(s): The ? mark (March 1964-July 1965)
Quarterly. Association publication, newsletter format, 30 p. Includes advertising, updating service. Circulation: 1000
$4.00 per year.

Catalogue collectif des périodiques dans les bibliothèques médicales des hôpitaux de Montréal *See* Union list of serials in Montreal hospital libraries

Catalogue des publications périodiques universitaires francophones / *édité par* Jean Marc Léger. - *Publié par* Association des universités partiellement ou entièrement de langue française. B.P. 6128, Montréal, Qué. H3C 3J7, 1964-
Publication d'association, 250 p. Tirage: 2000
$5.00 le numéro.

Catalogue du salon international de la caricature = International Salon of Cartoons / *édité par* Robert LaPalme. - *Publié par* Pavillon de l'Humour. Terre des Hommes Montréal, Qué., 1965-
Annuel. Publication spécialisée, 500 p. Langue(s): français et anglais ; sommaires: français et anglais. Tirage: 1500
ISSN 0316-5450 $15.00 le volume.

Catalogue of current Ontario university recreation and leisure research (1973) *See* Catalogue of Ontario recreation and leisure research

Catalogue of Ontario recreation and leisure research / *edited by* F.W. Martin and D.R. Bigness. - *Published by* Ontario Research Council on Leisure. 23rd Floor, 400 University Ave., Toronto, Ont. M7A 1H9, 1975-
Former title(s): Catalogue of current Ontario university recreation and leisure research (1973)
Annual. Association publication, magazine format, 108 p. Circulation: 4000
Free.

Catalogue of replacement books for children's library collections - *Published by* Toronto Public Library. 40 Orchard View Blvd., Toronto, Ont. M4R 1B9, 1970-
Irregular. Bibliography, 250 p.
$15.00 per year.

Catalogue sélectif de la documentation européenne *Voir* Université de Montréal. Centre d'études et de documentation européennes. Bulletin d'information documentaire

The Catalyst / *edited by* H. Greenspan. - *Published by* Toronto Section. Chemical Institute of Canada. 54 Demaris Ave., Downsview, Ont. M3N 1M1.
Irregular (approximately 7 issues per year). Association publication, newsletter format, 5 p.
Circulation: 1200

Catalyst / *edited by* Etieene Boisjoli. - *Published by* Prison Arts Foundation. 143 Fifth Ave., Brantford, Ont., 1975-
Quarterly. Penal press, magazine format, 20 p.
$5.00 per year : $6.00 per year, foreign. Free to prison addresses everywhere.

The Catholic book review / *edited by* Paul T. Harris. - *Published by* Paul T. Harris. P.O. Box 116, Terminal A, Besserer St., Ottawa, Ont., 1957-
Issued every other month. Book reviews, magazine format, 28 p. Includes book reviews, record reviews.
Free.

Catholic Church. Archdiocese of Ottawa. Directory *Voir* Eglise catholique. Archidiocèse d'Ottawa. Annuaire

The Catholic home annual (1920) *See* Alberta Catholic directory

Catholic hospital / *edited by* Yolande Lapointe (Publications secretary). - *Published by* Catholic Hospital Association of Canada. 312 Daly Ave., Ottawa, Ont. K1N 6G7, 1958-
Former title(s): C.H.A.C. news bulletin.
Published in French: L'Hôpital catholique.
Issued every other month. Association publication, magazine format, 20 p.
Circulation: 3500
ISSN 0008-8099 $3.00 per year.

Catholic Hospital Association of Canada. C.H.A.C. annual directory = Annuaire de l'A.H.C.C / *edited by* Yolande Lapointe (Publications Secretary). - *Published by* Catholic Hospital Association of Canada. 312 Daly Ave., Ottawa, Ont. K1N 6G7., 1958-
Annual. Directory, magazine format, 20 p.
Includes book reviews, advertising, volume index.
ISSN 0008-8099 $3.00 per year.

Catholic Hospital Association of Canada. Directory of member hospitals and homes = Association des hôpitaux catholiques du Canada. Annuaire des hôpitaux et des foyers membres - *Published by* Catholic Hospital Association of Canada. 312 Daly Ave., Ottawa, Ont. K1N 6G7.
Annual. Association publication, directory.
$5.00. Free to members.

The Catholic register / *edited by* Larry Henderson. - *Published by* Canadian Register Ltd. 67 Bond St., Toronto, Ont. M5B 1X6, 1893-
Weekly. Church publication. Includes advertising.
$.20 per issue : $6.00 per year.

The Catholic trustee / *edited by* Chris Asseff. - *Published by* Ontario Separate School Trustees' Association. 38 Berwick Ave., Toronto, Ont. M5P 1H1, 1961-
Quarterly. Association publication, magazine format, 22 p.
Indexed in Can. educ. ind.
Free.

Cattlemen : the beef magazine / *edited by* Harold Dodds. - *Published by* R.W. McGuire. The Public Press Ltd. 1760 Ellice Ave., Winnipeg, Man. R3H 3B6, 1938-
Former title(s): Canadian cattlemen (June 1938, Vol. I, No. 1 to May 1969 Vol. 32, No. 5)
Monthly. Commodity publication, magazine format, 85 p. available in microform.
Circulation: 41,813
$.50 per issue : $4.00 per year : $6.00 per year, foreign. Prepayment required.

Cayuse conserver / *edited by* Norma Bearcroft. - *Published by* The Canadian Wild Horse Society. 1120 Bird Rd., Richmond, B.C., September 1966-
Irregular (approximately 2-4 issues per year). Association publication, magazine format, 30-35 p.
$5.00 per year. Subscription included in membership fee.

Cégepropos / *édité par* Claire Noel. - *Publié par* Fédération des collèges d'enseignement général et professionnel. 1940 est, boul. Henri-Bourassa, Montréal, Qué. H2B 1S2, janvier 1970-
Intermittent (approximativement 10 éditions par an). Publication d'association, bulletin, 48 p. Tirage: 4000
Envoi gratuit.

Central Canada Lutheran *See* Circle 'n dot

Central Ontario Regional Library System. C.O.R.L. comment / *edited by* David Phillips. - *Published by* Central Ontario Regional Library System. 129 Church St. S., Richmond Hill, Ont. L4C 1W4, April 1968-
Monthly. Institutional publication (Universities, schools, etc.), newsletter format, 18 p.
ISSN 0319-2954 Free. Controlled circulation.

Le Centre / *édité par* Serge Privé. - *Publié par* Conseil de la santé et des services sociaux région du Saguenay-Lac-St-Jean. 930 est, rue Jacques-Cartier, Chicoutimi, Qué., août-septembre 1974-
Bimestriel. Organe interne/officiel, bulletin, 2 p. Tirage: 2000
Envoi gratuit.

Centre de recherche en civilisation canadienne-française Bulletin / *édité par* Pierre Savard. - *Publié par* Editions de l'Université d'Ottawa. Bibliothèque générale, 65, rue Hastey, Université d'Ottawa, Ottawa, Ont. K1N 6N5, décembre 1970-
Semestriel. Publication d'institution (universités, écoles..), bulletin, 20 p. Tirage: 1000
Envoi gratuit.

Centre d'équipement et machinerie : le mart / *édité par* Jean-Guy Trinque. - *Publié par* J.-L. Morin. Hexa Inc. Suite 203, 6841 St-Hubert, Montréal, Qué. H2S 2M8, septembre 1971-
Mensuel. Revue d'entreprise, journal, 30 p. Tirage: 12,200
$2.00 par année. Tirage contrôlé.

Centre interuniversitaire d'études européennes. Bulletin *See* Interuniversity Centre for European Studies. Newsletter

Centre stage / *edited by* Brian Wark. - *Published by* The Banff Centre. P.O. Box 1020, Banff, Alta. T0L 0C0 (Subscription address: Information Services, The Banff Centre, P.O. Box 1020, Banff, Alta. T0L 0C0) November 1972-
Issued every other month. Special interest, journal format, 4 p.
Free. Controlled circulation.

Centrescope / *edited by* Estelle Sures. - *Published by* Health Sciences Centre. 800 Sherbrook St., Winnipeg, Man., March 1973-
Issued twice a month. Institutional publication (Universities, schools, etc.), newsletter format, 4-6 p. Circulation: 6000
Free.

Centro gallego de Toronto / *edited by* Jose Maria Martinez. - *Published by* Centro Gallego de Toronto. P.O. Box 506, Postal Station C, Toronto, Ont. M6J 3P6, 1975-
Monthly. Ethnic press. Language: Spanish. Includes advertising.

Les Cercle des jeunes naturalistes. Bulletin de nouvelles / *parrainé par* Hexa Inc ; *édité par* Dollard Senecal. - *Publié par* Les Cercles des jeunes naturalistes. Jardin Botanique, 125, 4101 est, rue Sherbrooke, Montréal, Qué., septembre 1956-
Mensuel. Publication d'association, bulletin, 6-10 p. Tirage: 600
$2.00 par année. Envoi gratuit.

Cercle international de recherches philosophiques par ordinateur. Revue CIRPHO = CIRPHO review / *parrainé par* Cercle international de recherches philosophiques par ordinateur ; *édité par* Venant Cauchy et Alastair McKinnon. - *Publié par* Editions Monmorency. C.P. 6128, Département de philosophie, Université de Montréal, Montréal, Qué. H3C 3Q1, 1973-
Semestriel. Publication d'association, 64 p. Langue(s): français et anglais. Comprend critique de livres. Tirage: 75
ISSN 0317-3569 $2.50 le numéro : $8.00 par année : $8.00 le volume.

Cercles des jeunes naturalistes. Feuillets du club / *parrainé par* Les Cercles des jeunes naturalistes ; *édité par* Dollard Sénécal. - *Publié par* Les Editions des jeunes naturalistes. 455, rue Saint-Jean, Montréal, Qué., janvier 1968-
Mensuel. Publication d'association, brochure, 4 p. Tirage: 5000
ISSN 0045-6179 $.20 le numéro : $2.50 par année : $6.95 le volume. Abonnements payables à l'avance.

Cerebral palsy news - *Published by* Cerebral Palsy Association of British Columbia. 1524 W. 15th, Vancouver B.C. V6J 2K6.
Quarterly. Association publication, newsletter format, 8 p. Includes film reviews. Circulation: 3200

C'est pas un cadeau *See* The Raised roof

Challenge in educational administration / *sponsored by* Council on School Administration ; *edited by* R. Bryce and Ken Ward. - *Published by* Alberta Teachers' Association. 11010-142 St., Edmonton, Alta. T5N 2R1, September 1970-
Former title(s): C.S.A. bulletin.
Quarterly. Association publication, magazine format, 35 p. Circulation: 720
Indexed in Can. educ. ind.
$2.50 per issue : $10.00 per year. Controlled circulation.

Challenge magazine / *edited by* Joseph O'Sullivan. - *Published by* St. Bernard Enterprises. 5th Floor, 2 Lakeview Square, 175 Carlton St., Winnipeg, Man. R3C 3H9 (Subscription address: Challenge Magazine, 1050 Grosvenor Ave., Winnipeg, Man. R3C 3H9) December 1973-
Cover title : Challenge.
Irregular (approximately 10 issues per year). Church publication, magazine format, 24 p. Includes book reviews.
$1.00 per issue : $6.00 per year. Controlled circulation. Special rates offered.

Chamber chat / *edited by* B. Armstrong. - *Published by* Thunder Bay Chamber of Commerce. P.O. Box 2000, 857 North May St., Thunder Bay, Ont. P7C 4Y4, 1973-
Monthly. Trade publication, 8 p. Circulation: 3000
Free. Controlled circulation.

The Chamber link / *edited by* Jean Guerin. - *Published by* Canadian Chamber of Commerce. Suite 710, 1080 Beaver Hall, Montreal, Que. H2Z 1T2.
Published in French: Le Lien.
Issued every other month. House/company organ, newspaper format, 8 p. Language: English and French. Circulation: 5000
$1.00 per year. Free. Controlled circulation.

Chambre de commerce du Canada. Déclaration de principes / *édité par* C.F. Holloway et R. Haumont. - *Publié par* Chambre de commerce du Canada. 1080, côte du Beaver Hall, Montréal, Qué. H2Z 1T2, 1925-
Publié en anglais: Canadian Chamber of Commerce. Statement of policy.
Annuel. Publication d'association, relié, 135 p. Tirage: 8000
Envoi gratuit.

Chambre de commerce française au Canada. Revue de la Chambre de commerce française au Canada - *Publié par* Chambre de Commerce française au Canada. Bureau 826, 1080, côte du Beaver Hall, Montréal, Qué. H2Z 1S8, 1893-
Ancien titre: Bulletin de la Chambre de commerce.
Bimestriel. Publication d'association, magazine, 36 p. Langue(s): français et anglais. Comprend publicité. Tirage: 5000
$.75 le numéro : $4.00 par année : $8.00 par année, l'Etranger.

Champs d'application / *édité par* François-Pierre Déry. - *Publié par* Editions champs d'application inc. C.P. 771, Trois-Rivières, Qué., hiver 1974-
Trimestriel. Publication spécialisée, 56 p. Comprend critique de livres, critique de films, critique de pièces de théâtre, critique de disques. Tirage: 1000
ISSN 0317-3399 $1.50 le numéro : $5.00 par année : $8.00 par année, l'étranger. Envoi gratuit. Tarifs spéciaux disponibles. Abonnements payables à l'avance.

A Chaplin's markings *See* The Pastoral visitor

The Charlatan / *edited by* Peter Birt. - *Published by* Carleton University Students' Association. Colonel By Dr., Ottawa, Ont., September 1971-
Former title(s): The Carleton (1945-1971)
Issued weekly during the academic year. Irregular during the summer. Student publication, newspaper format, 24 p. Includes book reviews, film reviews, play reviews, record reviews, advertising. supplements issued. Circulation: 9000
$7.50 per year (Institutions $10.00). Individual issues are free.

The Charlottes / *edited by* The Publications Committee. - *Published by* Queen Charlotte Islands Museum Society. P.O. Box 130, Masset, B.C. (Subscription address: c/o Miss Agnes Mathers, P.O. Box 2, Sandspit, B.C) 1971-
Issued every 16 months (approximate). Association publication, journal format, 50 p. Special rates offered. Prepayment required.

Charlton coin guide / *edited by* James E. Charlton. - *Published by* Charlton International Publishing Inc. 299 Queen St. W., Toronto, Ont. M5V 1Z9, 1960-
Published in French: Charlton.
Annual. Special interest, magazine format, 70 p. Circulation: 70,000
ISSN 0319-3748

Charlton liste de valeur / *édité par* James E. Charlton. - *Publié par* Charlton International Publishing Inc. 299 ouest, rue Queen, Toronto, Ont. M5V 1Z9, 1960-
Publié en anglais: Charlton coin guide.
Annuel. Publication spécialisée, 70 p.

Chase almanac and fact book / *edited by* A. Butcher. - *Published by* A.W. Chase. Laurentian Laboratories Ltd. 70 Hymus Blvd., Pointe Claire, Que., 1902-
Annual. Almanac, magazine format, 48 p. Includes advertising. Circulation: 500,000

El Chaski / *édité par* Jaime Siles Otazo. - *Publié par* Elchaski enr. 180 est, 6oième rue, Charlesbourg, Qué., décembre 1974-
Mensuel. Publication spécialisée, journal, 8 p. Langue(s): français-espagnol ; sommaires: espagnol-français. Comprend critique de livres, critique de films, critique de pièces de théâtre, critique de disques, publicité. parution de suppléments. Tirage: 1000
$.50 le numéro : $10.00 par année. Tirage contrôlé. Tarifs spéciaux disponibles. Abonnements payables à l'avance.

Chatair / *edited by* D.S. Horton. - *Published by* Chatair. P.O. Box 200, Canadian Forces Base Chatham, Curtis Park, N.B., 1951-
Monthly. Special interest, newspaper format, 24 p. Includes advertising.
$1.50 per year. Free. Controlled circulation.

Chateauguay Valley Historical Society. Journal = Société historique de la vallée de la Châteauguay. Journal / *edited by* Robert McGee. - *Published by* Chateauguay Valley Historical Society. P.O. Box 1114, Huntingdon, Que., 1968-
Annual. Association publication, magazine format, 54 p. Language: English and French.
$3.00.

Chatelaine / *edited by* Doris Anderson. - *Published by* Maclean-Hunter Ltd. 481 University Ave., Toronto, Ont. M5W 1A7, March 1928-
Monthly. General interest, magazine format, 112 p. Includes book reviews, film reviews, advertising, volume index. available in microform. Circulation: 1 million
Indexed in Peace res. abstr., Periodex, Can. ind., RADAR.
$.50 per issue : $4.00 per year.

Check / *edited by* Gary Ruben. - *Published by* Canadian Correspondence Chess Association. 61 Chevron Cres., Scarboro, Ont. M1K 3N6.
Issued every other month. Association publication, newsletter format, 14 p. Language: English and French. Includes book reviews. Circulation: 700
$4.00 per year.

Checkerboard rendez-vous / *édité par* J.L. Gaston Rousseau. - *Publié par* Ralston Purina of Canada, Ltd. 78 rue Guilbault, Longueuil, Qué., octobre 1972-
Bimestriel. Organe interne/officiel, magazine, 20 p. Langue(s): français et anglais. Tirage: 2000
Envoi gratuit. Tirage contrôlé.

The Chelsea journal : a Canadian periodical of social comment, literature and religion / *edited by* A. de Valk. - *Published by* All Seasons Publishing Company. 1437 College Dr., Saskatoon, Sask. S7N 0W6, January 1975-
Issued every other month. General interest, magazine format, 52 p. Includes book reviews, film reviews, play reviews, advertising, volume index, cumulative index. Circulation: 3000
ISSN 0317-2147 $1.50 per issue : $8.00 per year (Students $5.00) : $9.00 per year, foreign. Controlled circulation.

Chem 13 news / *edited by* R.J. Friesen, J.L. Candido and W.A.E. McBryde. - *Published by* Department of Chemistry. University of Waterloo. Waterloo, Ont. N2L 3G1, September 1968-
Monthly except June, July, August. Special interest, newsletter format, 14 p. Includes book reviews. Circulation: 2900
Free on request.

Chemical buyers guide / *edited by* Thomas E. Buck and Rita Tate. - *Published by* Rowan MacDonald. Southam Business Publications Ltd. 1450 Don Mills Rd., Don Mills, Ont. M3B 2X7, 1959-
Annual. Directory, magazine format, 100 p.
ISSN 0069-2891 $7.00. Controlled circulation.

Chemistry in Canada / *edited by* T.H.G. Michael (managing ed.) and D.W. Emmerson (editor). - *Published by* The Chemical Institute of Canada. Suite 906, 151 Slater St., Ottawa, Ont. K1P 5H3., 1949-
Issued 11 times a year. Trade publication. Circulation: 7835
ISSN 0009-3114 $2.00 per issue : $9.00 per year : $15.00 per year, foreign.

Chemistry in Hamilton / *edited by* M. Rowlands. - *Published by* Hamilton Section. Chemical Institute of Canada. c/o Mohawk College A.A. & T., 135 Fennell Ave. W., Hamilton, Ont. (Subscription address: 206-2673 King St, E., Hamilton, Ont, L8K 1y6) September 1972-
Irregular (approximately 4 issues per year). House/company organ, newsletter format, 4 p. Circulation: 300
Free. Controlled circulation.

Chercheurs : bulletin des activités de recherche de l'Université de Montréal - *Publié par* Université de Montréal. 2900, Edouard-Montpetit, Montréal, Qué., octobre 1974-
Mensuel. Edition savante, bulletin, 16 p. Langue(s): français ; sommaires: anglais. Comprend critique de livres. Tirage: 3500
ISSN 0317-1558 Envoi gratuit.

Chess Federation of Canada. Chess Federation of Canada bulletin / *edited by* Les Bunning. - *Published by* Chess Federation of Canada. P.O. Box 7339, Ottawa, Ont., 1974-
Issued every other month. Association publication, magazine format, 36 p. Language: English and French. Includes book reviews. Circulation: 2500
$1.50 per issue : $7.00 per year. Prepayment required.

The Chesterton review / *sponsored by* The G. K. Chesterton Society ; *edited by* J. Ian Boyd. - *Published by* The Chesterton Review. 1437 College Drive, Saskatoon, Sask. S7N 0W6, Fall-Winter 1974-
Irregular (approximately 2 issues per year). Association publication, journal format, 50 p. Includes cumulative index.
$3.00 per year (Institutions $14.00) : 1 pound per year England : $3.25 per year U.S. (Institutions $4.25).

Chevron - *Published by* Federation of Students. University of Waterloo. Waterloo, Ont.
Weekly. Student publication, newspaper format, Includes advertising. Circulation: 13,600

Chicobi (octobre 1968-octobre 1970) *Voir* Journal Chicobi : section information

Childhood, sport and leisure - *Published by* SIRLS. Faculty of Human Kinetics and Leisure studies. University of Waterloo. Waterloo, Ont. N2L 3G1.
Quarterly. Bibliography, computer printout, $20.00 per year. $100.00 subscription to SIRLS required.

The Children's Aid Society of Ottawa. The C.A.S. Record - *Published by* The Children's Aid Society of Ottawa. 1370 Bank St., Ottawa, Ont.
Quarterly. Special interest.

The Children's news / *edited by* The Public Relations Department. - *Published by* The Montreal Children's Hospital. 2300 Tupper St. Montreal, Que. H3H 1P3, 1963-
Irregular (approximately 2-3 issues per year). Institutional publication (Universities, schools, etc.), newsletter format, 6-8 p. Language: English and French.
Free. Controlled circulation.

Chili-Québec informations - *Publié par* Comité de solidarité Québec-Chili. 356 est, rue Ontario, Montréal, Qué., novembre 1973-
Intermittent (approximativement 10 éditions par an). Publication d'association, bulletin, 16 p. Tirage: 1500
$.50 le numéro : $5.00 par année : $6.00 par année, l'étranger. Abonnements payables à l'avance.

Chimo / *edited by* Robert Nixon (program director). - *Published by* Frontier College. 31 Jackes Ave., Toronto, Ont. M4T 1E2.
Issued twice a month. House/company organ, newsletter format, 12 p. Language: English and French. Circulation: 100

China (1919-May 1950) *See* Scarboro missions

Chinatown news / *edited by* Roy Q. Mah. - *Published by* Chinese Publicity Bureau Ltd. 459 E. Hastings St., Vancouver, B.C., September 1953-
Issued twice a month. Ethnic press, magazine format, 36 p. Language: English and Chinese.
$.25 per issue : $5.00 per year : $6.00 per year, foreign.

Chinese express / *edited by* Robert Chow. - *Published by* Chinese Express Ltd. 117A Elizabeth St., Toronto, Ont. M5G 1P8, 1971-
Daily. Ethnic press, newspaper format, Language: Chinese. Includes advertising.

Chinese times / *sponsored by* The Chinese Freemasons Publisher Ltd ; *edited by* Kai Sun Lam. - *Published by* Kwok On Gunn. 116 East Pender St., Vancouver, B.C. (Subscription address: 1 East Pender St., Vancouver, B.C) 1907-
Former title(s): Wah Ying Yat Pa.
Daily. Ethnic press, newspaper format, 8 p. Language: Chinese. Includes advertising. Circulation: 4500
$.15 per issue : $36.00 per year. Prepayment required.

The Chinese voice / *edited by* Kenneth Wu. - *Published by* The Chinese Voice Publishing & Printing Co. Ltd. 233 Main St., Vancouver, B.C. V6A 2S7, 1953-
Daily. Ethnic press. Language: Chinese. Includes advertising.

Chitty's law journal / *edited by* Hugh W. Silverman. - *Published by* Jonah Publications Ltd. 46 Park Hill Rd., Toronto, Ont. M6C 3N1, 1950-
Former title(s): Fortnightly law journal (prior to 1950)
Monthly except July and August. Legal articles, magazine format, 40 p. Includes book reviews, advertising, volume index, cumulative index. Circulation: 800
Indexed in Abstr. crim. pen., Can. leg. per. lit.
$3.50 per issue : $35.00 per year : Bound volume $45.00. Prepayment required.

Chitty's Ontario annual practice *See* The Ontario annual practice

Chivalry / *sponsored by* The Pentecostal Assemblies of Canada ; *edited by* B.T. Parkinson. - *Published by* Crusader Department. 10 Overlea Blvd., Toronto, Ont. M4H 1A5, August 1970-
Monthly, 10 times a year. Church publication, 20 p. Circulation: 1200
$3.00 per year. Controlled circulation. Prepayment required.

Choir news (1970-1971) *See* Alberta music calendar

Chrétiens d'aujourd'hui / *édité par* Rémi Potvin. - *Publié par* La Fédération nationale du mouvement "Chrétiens d'aujourd'hui". 8100, boul. St-Laurent, Montréal, Qué. H2P 2L9, septembre 1966-
Ancien titre: Père d'aujourd'hui (septembre 1965-septembre 1966) Bulletin des ligues. Section des ligueurs (1936-1965)
Mensuel. Publication ecclésiastique, bulletin, 4 p. Tirage: 15,000
$.10 le numéro : $1.00 par année. Abonnements payables à l'avance.

Christian airman / *edited by* Esther F. Fuller. - *Published by* Christian Transportation Inc. 512 Yonge St. (rear), Toronto, Ont. M4Y 1X9, January 1960-
Quarterly. Church publication.

The Christian bus driver / *edited by* Esther F. Fuller. - *Published by* Christian Transportation Inc. 512 Yonge St. (Rear), Toronto, Ont. M4Y 1X9, June 1960-
Quarterly. Church publication, 8 p.

Christian communications / *edited by* John W. Mole. - *Published by* Saint Paul Society. 223 Main St., Ottawa, Ont. K1S 1C4, December 1962-
Quarterly. Church publication, newsletter format, 8 p. Includes book reviews, film reviews, cumulative index. Circulation: 2000
ISSN 0009-5303 $.65 per issue : $2.50 per year. Prepayment required.

Christian family friend *See* Christlicher Familienfreund

The Christian Guardian (1829 - June 1925) *See* Observer

Christian inquirer / *edited by* Ron Marr. - *Published by* International Christian Communications. P.O. Box 339, Ridgeway, Ont. L0S 1N0, November 1970-
Former title(s): The Enquirer (October-December 1971) Happening (November 1970- February 1971)
Monthly, except July. Church publication, tabloid format, 16 p. Includes advertising. Circulation: 50,000
$.35 per issue : $3.00 per year.

The Christian inquirer / *edited by* Ron Marr. - *Published by* Ron Marr. International Christian Communications. P.O. Box 339, Ridgeway, Ont. L0S 1N0, Fall 1970-
Former title(s): The Enquirer (1970-1972)
Monthly. Church publication, newspaper format, 20 p. Circulation: 50,000
$.35 per issue : $3.00 per year. Special rates offered.

The Christian messenger (1854-1859) *See* The Canadian Baptist

Christian railroader / *edited by* Esther F. Fuller. - *Published by* Christian Transportation Inc. 512 Yonge St. (rear), Toronto, Ont. M4Y 1X9, October 1930-
Issued 10 times a year. Special interest, newspaper format, 4 p.
$1.50 for 2 years.

Christian sailor / *edited by* Esther F. Fuller. - *Published by* Christian Transportation Inc. 512 Yonge St., Toronto, Ont. M4Y 1X9, April 1971-
Quarterly. Church publication, 8 p.

The Christian standard / *edited by* E.R. Conley. - *Published by* The Standard Church of America. 195 Perth St., Brockville, Ont., 1917-
Monthly. Church publication, magazine format, 16 p. Circulation: 475
$3.00 per year.

Christlicher Familienfreund = Christian family friend / *edited by* Abe R. Reimer. - *Published by* Evangelical Mennonite Conference. P.O. Box 1268, Steinbach, Man. R0A 2A0, January 1935-
Issued every other week. Church publication, magazine format, 16 p. Language: German. Circulation: 3250
$1.00 per year.

The Chronicle / *edited by* Janet Berton. - *Published by* The Canadian Federation of University Women. Suite 209A, 151 Sparks St., Ottawa, Ont. K1P 5H3, 1919-
Annual. Association publication, magazine format, 32 p. Language: English and French. Circulation: 11,000
Subscription included in membership fee.

The Chronicle - *Published by* Journalism Department. Durham College. P.O. Box 385, Oshawa, Ont., November 1973-
Former title(s): Drum (1969-1972) Durham report (1969-1972)
Issued every other week. Student publication, newspaper format, 8 p.
Free.

La Chronique (février 1946-mai 1973) *Voir* L'Aubelle

Chroniques / *édité par* Laurent-Michel Vacher. - *Publié par* Laurent-Michel Vacher. Revue littéraire les chroniques inc. 1885, rue Wolfe, Montréal, Qué.(adresse d'abonnement: C.P. 747, Succursale N, Montréal, Qué) janvier 1975-
Mensuel. Publication spécialisée, revue, 84 p. Tirage: 1500
$2.00 le numéro : $20.00 par année : $24.00 par année, l'étranger.

Chroniques des grains / *édité par* G. René de Contret. - *Publié par* Office canadien des provendes. C.P. 2250, succursale St-Laurent, Montréal, Qué. H4L 4Y7, novembre 1967-
Publié en anglais: Grain facts.
Paraît tous les 15 jours. Publication d'association, bulletin, 12 p. Langue(s): français et anglais. Tirage: 2089
Envoi gratuit.

Church growth : Canada / *sponsored by* Canadian Theological College ; *edited by* Dennis M. Oliver. - *Published by* Canadian Church Growth Centre. 4400-4th Ave., Regina, Sask. S4T 0H8, March 1974-
Issued 4 times a year. Church publication. Includes book reviews. Circulation: 450
$.50 per issue : $1.00 per year.

Church herald *See* Canadian churchman

Churchwood bulletin - *Published by* Windsor Association for the Mentally Retarded. 870 Ottawa St., Windsor, Ont. N8X 2C8, 1963-
Monthly except July and August. Association publication, newsletter format, 9 p. Circulation: 300
$3.00 per year.

Le Cinéma au Québec : bilan d'une industrie / *édité par* Jean Pierre Tadros. - *Publié par* Jean-Pierre Tadros. Les éditions cinéma Québec. C.P. 309, Station Outremont, Montréal, Qué., février 1975-
Annuaire. Magazine, 300 p. Comprend publicité.
$5.00 par année.

Cinema Canada / *edited by* Jean-Pierre and Connie Tadros. - *Published by* Jean-Pierre Tadros. The Cinema Canada Magazine Foundation. 406 Jarvis St., Toronto, Ont. M4Y 2G6, March 1972-
Former title(s): The Canadian cinematographer.
Monthly. Special interest, magazine format, 54 p. Includes film reviews.
$8.00 (Institutions $15.00) : $10.00 per year, foreign.

Cinéma Québec / *édité par* Jean-Pierre Tadros. - *Publié par* Jean-Pierre Tadros. C.P. 309, Station Outremont, Montréal, Qué., mai 1971-
Mensuel. Publication spécialisée, magazine, 56 p. Comprend critique de films, publicité.
Indexé dans Periodex, RADAR.
$1.00 le numéro : $10.00 par année : $12.00 le volume : $10.00 par année, l'étranger.

Cipher / *sponsored by* Canadian Institute of Quantity Surveyors ; *edited by* Susan Cooke and H. Pedrette (technical editor). - *Published by* Co-Mar Association Management Services Incorporated. Suite 401, 8 Colborne St. Toronto, Ont. M5E 1E1, May 1968-
Quarterly. Association publication, magazine format, 20 p. Language: English and French.

Circle / *sponsored by* National Red Cross Youth Department ; *edited by* Corinne Musgrave. - *Published by* Canadian Red Cross Society. 95 Wellesley St. E., Toronto, Ont. M4Y 1H6, September 1973-
Former title(s): On the move.
Irregular (approximately 5 issues per year). House/company organ, newsletter format, 6-8 p. Language: English and French. Circulation: 17,000
$1.00 per year.

Circle 'n dot / *edited by* K. Lawrence Peterson. - *Published by* Central Canada Synod. Lutheran Church in America. 211-2281 Portage Ave., Winnipeg, Man. R3J 0M1 (Subscription address: 2625 12th Ave., Regina, Sask. S4T 1J1) 1963-
Former title(s): Central Canada Lutheran.
Irregular (approximately 6-8 issues per year). Church publication, newspaper format, 6 p. Includes advertising. Circulation: 8000
Free. Distributed in bulk to member congregations.

Circuit / *edited by* H.K MacDonald. - *Published by* Canadian Electrical Manufacturers Association. 10 Price St., Toronto, Ont.
Irregular (approximately 4-6 issues per year). Association publication, newspaper format, 4 p. Circulation: 5800-6000

Circuit fermé / *parrainé par* Information intérieure de Radio-Canada ; *édité par* Boris V. Volkoff. - *Publié par* Société Radio Canada. 1400 est, boul. Dorchester, Montréal, Qué., septembre 1965-
Bimensuel. Organe interne/officiel, journal, 8 p. Tirage: 7000
Envoi gratuit.

The Citadel Scene - *Published by* Citadel Theatre. 10026-102nd St., Edmonton, Alta. T5J 0V6, 1974/1975-
Irregular. Institutional publication (Universities, schools, etc.).

Cités et villes *Voir* Le Revue municipale

Citizen's Committee for Pollution Control. Newsletter - *Published by* Citizens' Committee for Pollution Control. P.O. Box 38, Burlington, Ont. L7R 3X8, May 1970-
Irregular (approximately 2-3 issues per year). Association publication, newsletter format, 4 p. Free.

Canadian citizen = Le Citoyen canadien *See* Il Cittadino canadese

City magazine - *Published by* Charlottetown Group Publishing Inc. 35 Britain St., Toronto, Ont. M5A 1R7, July 1974-
Irregular (approximately 8 issues per year). Special interest, magazine format, 52 p. Includes book reviews, advertising. Circulation: 3000
ISSN 0315-7911 $1.00 per issue : $7.00 per year (Institutions $15.00), $12.00 per year, foreign. Prepayment required.

City of Ottawa Coin Club. Monthly bulletin / *edited by* Ruth McQuade. - *Published by* City of Ottawa Coin Club. 183 Island Park Drive, Ottawa, Ont. K1Y 0A3, 1968-
Former title(s): The City of Ottawa Institute of Numismatics. The official bulletin for the new City of Ottawa Coin Club (1968-1969)
Monthly. Association publication, newsletter format, 4-5 p. Circulation: 100
$4.00. Subscription included in membership fee.

The City of Ottawa Institute of Numismatics. The official bulletin for the new City of Ottawa Coin Club (1968-1969) *See* City of Ottawa Coin Club. Monthly bulletin

Civic : the public works magazine / *edited by* Walter Jones. - *Published by* Maclean-Hunter Ltd. 481 University Ave., Toronto, Ont. M5W 1A7, 1949-
Former title(s): Civic administration.
Monthly. Reference guide $5.00.
$2.00 per issue : $12.00 per year : $15.00 per year, U.S. and U.K. : $30.00 per year, foreign.

Civic administration *See* Civic : the public works magazine

Civic affairs - *Published by* Bureau of Municipal Research. Suite 306, 2 Toronto St., Toronto, Ont. M5C 2B6, 1948-
Former title(s): Monthly letter - Bureau of Municipal Research.
Quarterly. House/company organ, 20-50 p. available in microform. Circulation: 900
Subscription included in membership fee. Controlled circulation.

Civil Service Association of Ontario. CSAO news / *edited by* John C. Ward. - *Published by* The Civil Service Association of Ontario. 1901 Yonge St., Toronto, Ont., April 1968-
Former title(s): The Trillium; Civil Service Review.
Monthly. Association publication, newspaper format, 5-6 p. Language: English and French. Some back issues available. Circulation: 50,000
Indexed in Can. B.P.I.
Free.

Civil service digest (April 1960-December 1968) *See* New Brunswick Public Employees Association. Newsletter

Civil Service Review *See* Civil Service Association of Ontario. CSAO news

The Civil service review = La revue du service civil - *Published by* Public Service Alliance of Canada. 233 Gilmour St., Ottawa, Ont. K2P 0P1., 1946-
Quarterly. Association publication, magazine format, 72 p. Language: English and French. Includes book reviews, advertising. Circulation: 12,600
$3.00 per year.

Clan Macdonald annual / *edited by* Jennifer Fang. - *Published by* Student Society. Macdonald College. Centennial Centre, P.O. Box 98, Macdonald College, Que.
Annual. Student publication, yearbook, 150 p.
$5.00.

The Clansman news / *edited by* Geroge Mannion. - *Published by* George Mannion. P.O. Box 282, Postal Station AMF, Montreal International Airport, Dorval, Que., 1975-
Issued every other month. Magazine format, 30 p. Language: English and Gaelic. Includes advertising. Circulation: 9000
$6.00.

La Claque : journal des étudiants en sciences - *Publié par* Association générale des étudiants de sciences. Université de Sherbrooke. Boul. Université, Sherbrooke, Qué. J1K 2R1, septembre 1973-
Intermittent (approximativement 10 éditions par an). Edition savante, bulletin, 10 p. Tirage: 500
Envoi gratuit.

The Clarion : Canadian reformed magazine / *edited by* W.W.J. Van Oene. - *Published by* Premier Printing Ltd. 1249 Plessis Rd., Winnipeg, Man. R2C 3L9.
Former title(s): Canadian reformed magazine. Issued every other week. Special interest, magazine format, 16 p. Includes book reviews, advertising, volume index 1976, cumulative index 1973, 1974 & 1975.
$16.50 per year. Prepayment required.

Clarke Institute of Psychiatry. Clarke Institute tabloid / *edited by* Grant Dobson. - *Published by* Clarke Institute of Psychiatry. 250 College St., Toronto, Ont. M5T 1R8, June 1975-
Monthly. Institutional publication (Universities, schools, etc.), newspaper format, 4 p.
Free.

Classical news and views *See* Echos du monde classique

Classmate / *sponsored by* Manitoba Association of Teachers of English ; *edited by* Peter Prystupo. - *Published by* Manitoba Teachers Society. 191 Harcourt St., Winnipeg, Man. R3J 3H2.
Issued three times a year. Association publication, magazine format, 50 p. Includes book reviews. Circulation: 800
ISSN 0315-906X $5.00 per year.

Climatological bulletin / *edited by* B.J. Garnier. - *Published by* Department of Geography (Climatology). McGill University. P.O. Box 6070, Postal Station A, Montreal, Que. H3C 3G1, January 1967-
Issued twice a year. Institutional publication (Universities, schools, etc.), newsletter format, 35 p. Circulation: 350
$5.00 per year : $2.50 per issue. Prepayment required.

Clinical biochemistry / *sponsored by* Canadian Society of Clinical Chemists ; *edited by* D.J. Campbell. - *Published by* The Chemical Institute of Canada. Suite 906, 151 Slater St., Ottawa, Ont. K1P 5H3, 1968-
Issued every other month. Association publication, journal format, 100 p. Includes advertising. Circulation: 1200
ISSN 0009-9120 $5.00 per issue : $18.00 per year : $20.00 per year, foreign. Prepayment required.

Clubs 4-H : programme de l'année - *Publié par* Clubs 4-H Clubs inc. Suite 210, 915 ouest, rue St-Cyrille, Québec, Qué. GVS 1T8.
Annuel. Publication d'association, 100 p. Tirage: 10,000
$.15 le numéro.

Coaching Association of Canada. Bulletin / *edited by* Bette Laderoute. - *Published by* Coaching Association of Canada. 10th Floor, 333 River Rd., Vanier City, Ont. K1L 8B9, January 1973-
Quarterly. Association publication, magazine format, 16 p. Includes book reviews, advertising. Circulation: 7000
$5.00 per year (Students $3.00) : $10.00 per year, foreign. Special rates offered. Prepayment required.

Coda : Canada's jazz magazine / *edited by* John W. Norris. - *Published by* Coda Publications. P.O. Box 87, Postal Station J, Toronto, Ont. M4J 4X8, 1958-
Issued 10 times a year. Special interest, magazine format, 40 p. Includes book reviews, film reviews, record reviews, advertising. available in microform. Circulation: 3300
Indexed in Music ind.
ISSN 0010-017X $7.00 per year.

Cogito Corporation Limited. Bulletin / *edited by* Sheila Burke. - *Published by* Cogito Corporation Limited. Suite 800, 50 Place Cremazie W., Montreal, Que.
Irregular (approximately 4-6 issues per year). Newsletter format, 4 p. Language: English and French. Circulation: 2500
Free.

Cognica - *Published by* SCOC/CGCA. 66 Runnymede Cres., London, Ont. N6G 1Z8.
Irregular (approximately 8 issues per year). *Indexed in* Can. educ. ind.

Coin, stamp, antique news / *edited by* Don Manley. - *Published by* D.B. Thomas. 1567 Sedlescomb Dr., Mississauga, Ont. L4X 1M5, 1962-
Former title(s): Canadian coin news.
Issued twice a month. Special interest, newspaper format, 48 p. Includes updating service. Circulation: 35,000
$.50 per issue : $5.00 per year.

Co-ïncidences / *edited by* François Gallays. - *Published by* Les Editions de l'Université d'Ottawa. 658, ave Hastey, Ottawa, Ont. K1N 6N5, mars 1971-
Former title(s): Incidences (novembre 1962-décembre 1968)
Intermittent (approximativement 3 éditions par an). Publication d'institution (universités, écoles..), revue, 64 p. Tirage: 750
$1.25 le numéro : $3.50 par année.
Abonnements payables à l'avance.

Collect antiques in Ontario (1967-1968) *See* Antiques in Ontario : Canadian antiques year book

Collective bargaining : statistics in education - *Published by* Harold L. Willis and Assoc. 33 Bloor St. E., Toronto, Ont., September 1974-
Former title(s): Collective bargaining in education (1974)
Statistics.

Collective bargaining in education (1974) *See* Collective bargaining : statistics in education

Collective behaviour in sport situations - *Published by* SIRLS. Faculty of Human Kinetics and Leisure Studies. University of Waterloo. Waterloo, Ont. N2L 3G1.
Quarterly. Bibliography, computer printout, $20.00 per year. $100.00 subscription to SIRLS required.

Collectors' choice newsletter / *sponsored by* Collectors' Choice ; *edited by* Mary F. Sutherland. - *Published by* Mary F. Sutherland. 43 Bethune Blvd., Scarborough, Ont. M1M 3B9, February 1972-
Issued every other month. House/company organ, newsletter format, 8 p. Includes book reviews, play reviews.
$6.00 per year.

Collège de hockey BNE / *édité par* S. Clayton. - *Publié par* La Banque de Nouvelle Ecosse. C.P. 4071, Succursale A, 44 ouest, rue King, Toronto, Ont. M5W 1M3, novembre 1971-
Publié en anglais : Scotia Hockey College news.
Mensuel. Publication spécialisée, bulletin, octobre - mai 12 p. ; juin - septembre 4 p. Tirage: 25,000
Tirage contrôlé.

Collège de Ste-Foy. Bibliothèque. Périodiques - *Publié par* Service périodique. Bibliothèque. Collège Sainte-Foy. 2410, chemin Sainte-Foy, Québec, Qué. G1V 1T3, 1973-1974-
Annuel. Biographie, 30 p. Tirage: 325

Collège et famille (janvier 1944-décembre 1969) *Voir* Education et société

Collège Jean-de-Brébeuf. Bulletin des parents et des anciens - *Publié par* Association des anciens. Collège Jean-de-Brébeuf. 3200, chemin Ste-Catherine, Montréal, Qué. H3T 1C1, avril 1954-
Ancien titre: Bulletin du collège et des anciens (avril 1954-juin 1969)
Trimestriel. Publication des anciens étudiants, bulletin, 5 p. Langue(s): français et anglais. Tirage: 4000
Envoi gratuit.

The College of Dental Surgeons of Saskatchewan. Newsletter / *edited by* G.H. Peacock. - *Published by* The College of Dental Surgeons of Saskatchewan. 811 - 105 21st St. E., Saskatoon, Sask. S7K 0B3.
Issued every other month. Association publication, newsletter format, 12 p.

College of Physicians and Surgeons of British Columbia. Medical directory / *edited by* The Registrar of College. - *Published by* College of Physicians and Surgeons of British Columbia. 1706 W. 1st Ave., Vancouver, B.C. (Subscription address: 1807 W. 10th Ave. Vancouver, B.C. V6J 2A9)
Annual. Directory, 244 p.
$10.05.

Collège royal des médecins et chirurgiens du Canada. Annales du collège royal des médecins et chirurgiens du Canada *See* Royal College of Physicians and Surgeons of Canada. Annals of The Royal College of Physicians and Surgeons of Canada

Collège Sainte-Marie. Association des anciens. Bulletin de liaison des anciens de Sainte-Marie / *édité par* Georges-Henri d'Auteuil. - *Publié par* Associations des anciens. Collège Sainte-Marie. 1182, rue Bleury, Montréal, Qué., juin 1942-
Intermittent (approximativement 3 éditions par an). Publication des anciens étudiants, bulletin, 4-8 p. Tirage: 3200
Envoi gratuit.

College times / *edited by* Robert W. Bell. - *Published by* Upper Canada College. 200 Lonsdale Rd., Toronto, Ont.
Annual. School yearbook, magazine format, 144 p. Includes play reviews, advertising. Circulation: 1200
Free. Controlled circulation.

Colloque urbain *See* Urban forum

Colloquium on Scottish studies. Proceedings / *edited by* Alexander H. Brodie. - *Published by* Interdepartmental Committee on Scottish Studies. University of Guelph. Guelph, Ont., 1968-
Irregular (approximately 2 issues per year). Association publication, magazine format, $2.00 per issue. Controlled circulation. Prepayment required.

Colloquium series on transportation (June 1968-June 1970) *See* University of Manitoba. Center for Transportation Studies. Seminar Series on Transportation. Proceedings

Colour Photographic Association of Canada. C.P.A.C. journal / *edited by* Kay F. Elliott. - *Published by* Color Photographic Association of Canada Inc. 165 Yonge Blvd., Toronto, Ont. M5M 3H3, 1951-
Quarterly. Association publication, magazine format, 24 p. Includes book reviews, advertising. Circulation: 1000
ISSN 0319-2280 Subscription included in membership fee $5.00 per year.

Combat / *édité par* Claire Demers. - *Publié par* Bernadette Le Brun. 356 est, ave Mont-Royal, Montréal, Qué., mai 1968-
Bimensuel. Tirage: 3000 391031Tari, journal, 8 p. Comprend critique de livres, critique de films, critique de pièces de théâtre, publicité, index de volumes. parution de suppléments. Tirage: 3000
$.15 le numéro : $3.00 par année : $4.00 par année, l'étranger. Tarifs spéciaux disponibles. Abonnements payables à l'avance.

Comda key / *edited by* Lionel Patterson. - *Published by* Canadian Office Machine Dealer's Association. P.O. Box 117, Markham, Ont. L3P 3J5.
Issued every other month. Association publication, magazine format, 16 p. Language: English and French. Includes advertising. Circulation: 1500
Free. Controlled circulation.

Comdagram / *edited by* Lionel Patterson. - *Published by* Canadian Office Machine Dealer's Association. P.O. Box 117, Markham, Ont. L3P 3J5, September 1970-
Issued every other month. Association publication, newsletter format, 4 p. Language: English and French. Includes advertising. Circulation: 500
Free. Issued to members only. Controlled circulation.

Come all ye / *edited by* Jon N.G. Bartlett. - *Published by* Vancouver Folk Song Society. 1885 Venables St., Vancouver, B.C. V5L 2H6, June 1972-
Monthly. Association publication, magazine format, 22 p. Includes book reviews, record reviews, volume index. Circulation: 75
ISSN 0316-0378 $12.00 per year.

Come and see / *edited by* John van Dijk. - *Published by* Nathanael Literature Distributors. 64 Hills Rd., Ajax, Ont. L1S 2W4.
Issued every other month. Special interest, magazine format, 24 p. Circulation: 2850
ISSN 0316-3040 Free.

Comic art news and reviews (CANAR) / *edited by* John Balge. - *Published by* John Balge. P.O. Box 2005, Postal Station B, Kitchener, Ont., September 1972-
Irregular (approximately 8 issues per year). Special interest, newsletter format, 8 p. Includes book reviews. Circulation: 400
ISSN 0315-0267 $3.00 per volume.

Comité canadien de géographie. Bulletin de nouvelles / *édité par* J.K Fraser. - *Publié par* Comité canadien de géographie. c/o Environment Canada. Science Branch, Ottawa, Ont. K1A 0H3, 1966-
Publié en anglais: Canadian Committee for Geography. Newsletter.
Trimestriel. Publication d'association, bulletin, 25 p.
Envoi gratuit.

Comité de préparation à la retraite / *édité par* Robert Fradet. - *Publié par* Association de bienfaisance et de retraite de la police de Montréal. 480, rue Gilford, Montréal, Qué., juillet 1972-
Intermittent. Organe interne/officiel, bulletin, 4 p.
ISSN 0317-9206 Envoi gratuit.

Comment / *edited by* R. Jenkins. - *Published by* Institute of Chartered Life Underwriters. 41 Lesmill Rd., Don Mills, Ont. M3B 2T3, January 1967-
Issued every other month. Association publication, 4 p. Language: English and French.
$46.75 for minimum order of 25 copies per issue. Available to members only. Minimum order 25 copies. Controlled circulation.

Comment / *edited by* Dennis Roberts. - *Published by* University News Service. Simon Fraser University. Burnaby, B.C. V5A 1S6, April 1969-
Issued every other month. Institutional publication (Universities, schools, etc.), magazine format, 16 p. Circulation: 15,000
Free. Controlled circulation.

Comment on education / *edited by* B.C. Stewart. - *Published by* Guidance Centre. Faculty of Education. University of Toronto. Suite 304, 1000 Yonge St., Toronto, Ont. M4W 2K8.
Irregular (approximately 4 issues per year). Institutional publication (Universities, schools, etc.), 20 p. Circulation: 3000
Indexed in Can. educ. ind.
ISSN 0315-4351 $1.50 per issue : $4.75 per year.

Commerce journal (1933-1970) *See* Widget

Commerceman - *Published by* Commerce Club. Queen's University. Kingston, Ont.
Annual.
Indexed in Can. B.P.I.

Commercial letter / *edited by* M.L. Perry. - *Published by* Canadian Imperial Bank of Commerce. Commerce Court, Toronto, Ont. M5L 1A2, December 1915-
Former title(s): Monthly commercial letter - Canadian Imperial Bank of Commerce (1915-1950) Published in French: Lettre commerciale.
Issued every other month. Trade publication, newsletter format, 8 p.
Indexed in P.A.I.S.
Free.

Commercial news / *edited by* Patricia Copeland. - *Published by* Halifax Board of Trade. P.O. Box 577, Halifax, N.S., March 1921-
Monthly. Association publication, magazine format, 40 p. Circulation: 3000
Indexed in Can. B.P.I.
$5.00 per year.

Commission canadienne pour l'Unesco. Bulletin *See* Canadian Commission for UNESCO. Bulletin

Commission des écoles catholiques de Québec. Bulletin - *Publié par* Commission des écoles catholiques de Québec. 1460, chemin Ste-Foy, Québec, Qué. G1S 2N9.
Intermittent (approximativement 8 éditions par an). Organe interne/officiel, bulletin, 4 p. Tirage: 900
Envoi gratuit.

Common sense economics / *edited by* Robert R. Kerton. - *Published by* University of Waterloo. Waterloo, Ont. N2L 3G1 (Subscription address: Economics Department, University of Waterloo, Waterloo Ont. N2L 3G1) February 1973-
Issued twice a year. Special interest, pamphlet format, 60 p. Includes book reviews.
Indexed in Can. B.P.I.
$2.00 per issue : $3.00 per year : $5.00 for 3 years.

The Commonwealth / *edited by* Angus Ricker. - *Published by* CCF Publishing & Printing Co. Ltd. 1630 Quebec St., Regina, Sask., 1937-
Issued twice a month. Political press, newspaper format, 16 p. Includes book reviews, film reviews, play reviews, record reviews, advertising. Available in microform from Saskatchewan Archives, University of Saskatchewan. Circulation: 15,000
$5.00 per year : $6.00 per year, foreign. Prepayment required.

Communauté / *édité par* Guy Paiement. - *Publié par* Guy Paiement. 362 est, boul. Saint-Joseph, Montréal, Qué, janvier 1974-
Ancien titre: Koinonia (novembre 1971-décembre 1973)
Mensuel. Publication spécialisée, bulletin, 16 p. Comprend critique de livres. Tirage: 450
$.50 le numéro : $5.00 par année.

Communauté chrétienne / *édité par* Richard Guimond. - *Publié par* Communauté chrétienne. 2715, chemin de la Côte Ste-Catherine, Montréal, Qué. H3T 1B6, 1972-
Bimestriel. Revue de pastorale pour des agents de pastorale, 84 p. Comprend critique de livres. Tirage: 2500
Indexé dans Periodex, RADAR.
ISSN 0010-3454 $1.50 le numéro : $7.00 par année (Plus frais d'avion $12.00). Tirage contrôlé. Abonnements payables à l'avance.

Communicate / *edited by* K. Neill Foster. - *Published by* Evangelistic Enterprises Society. P.O. Box 600, Beaverlodge, Alta. T0H 0C0, 1960-
Monthly. Church publication, newspaper format, 16 p. Includes book reviews, advertising. Circulation: 26,500
$.25 per issue : $3.00 per year. Controlled circulation.

Communication / *edited by* A.F. Bailey. - *Published by* The Canadian Public Relations Society, Inc. 220 Laurier Ave. W., Ottawa, Ont. K1P 5Z9, 1970-
Former title(s): PR in Canada (1960-1969)
Issued every other month. Association publication, newsletter format, 12-16 p. Language: English and French. Includes advertising.
Available to members only. Controlled circulation.

Communication, the media, sport and leisure - *Published by* SIRLS. Faculty of Human Kinetics and Leisure Studies. University of Waterloo. Waterloo, Ont. N2L 3G1.
Quarterly. Bibliography.
$20.00 per year. $100.00 subscription to SIRLS required.

Communication-jeunesse / *édité par* Raymond Vézina. - *Publié par* Communication-Jeunesse. C.P. 682, Station Outremont, Montréal, Qué. H2V 4N6, 1971-
Intermittent (approximativement 4 éditions par an). Publication spécialisée, bulletin, 8-12 p.
$5.00 par année.

Communications - The Professional Institute of the Public Service of Canada / *edited by* Charles Levy. - *Published by* Professional Institute of the Public Service of Canada. 786 Bronson Ave., Ottawa, Ont. K1S 4G4, March 1975-
Irregular (approximately 17 issues per year). Association publication, newsletter format, 4 p. Language: English and French.
ISSN 0318-0646 Free to members.

Communications and cable TV business / *edited by* Vic Vickers. - *Published by* Kerrwil Publications Ltd. 30 Eglinton Ave. E., Toronto, Ont. M4P 1B6, November 1974-
Former title(s): Cable TV business and communications business (February 1974-Semptember 1974) Cable TV business (April 1972-February 1973) Communications business (1969-December 1972)
Issued every other month. Trade publication, newspaper format, 16 p. Includes advertising.
Indexed in Can. B.P.I.
$6.00 per year. Controlled circulation.

Communications business (1969-December 1972) *See* Communications and cable TV business

Communications historiques / *édité par* R.P. Gillis. - *Publié par* La Société historique du Canada. 395, rue Wellington, Ottawa, Ont. K1A 0N3, 1922-
Annuel. Publication d'association, revue,. 300 p. Langue(s): français et anglais.
ISSN 0068-8878 $10.00 par année : $6.00 le volume.

Communications Workers of Canada. CWC bulletin / *edited by* Fred W. Pomeroy. - *Published by* Communications Workers of Canada. Suite 301, 25 Cecil St., Toronto, Ont., April 1972-
Monthly. Association publication, newsletter format, 2 p.

The Communicator / *edited by* Howard Langdon. - *Published by* Industrial Teachers' Council. Alberta Teachers Association. 11010-142 St., Edmonton, Alta. T3A 1C4, September 1972-
Former title(s): The IAVEC newsletter & journal.
Irregular (approximately 3 issues per year). Association publication, newsletter format, 24 p. Includes book reviews. Circulation: 500
$1.00 per issue : $5.00 per year.

Communiqué / *edited by* Frank Forcier. - *Published by* Advertising and Sales Executives Club of Montreal. Suite 369, Queen Elizabeth Hotel, Montreal, Que. H3B 4A5.
Monthly. Association publication, newsletter format, 4 p.

Communiqué - *Publié par* Association Canadienne des entraîneurs. 333 River Rd., Vanier, Ont. K1L 8B9.
Publication d'association, journal, Langue(s): français et anglais.

Communiqué / *edited by* M.B. Stuart. - *Published by* Association of Administrative Assistants or Private Secretaries. P.O. Box 976, Adelaide St., Toronto, Ont.
Former title(s): The Canadian secretary; National notes.
Quarterly. Association publication, 10 p. Language: English and French. Circulation: 550
Free. Controlled circulation.

Communique / *edited by* L.E. Laviolette. - *Published by* Canadian Automobile Association. 150 Gloucester St., Ottawa, Ont. K2P 0A6, November 1970-
Quarterly. Association publication, newsletter format, 12 p. Language: English and French. Free. Controlled circulation.

Communiqué / *edited by* Cynthia Steers and Valerie Bruneau. - *Published by* The Children's Aid Society of Ottawa. 1370 Bank St., Ottawa, Ont. K1Y 7Y3, February 1974-
Quarterly. Association publication, newsletter format, Language: English and French.

Communique - *Published by* Communications Union Canada. Suite 16C, 20 Prince Arthur Ave., Toronto, Ont. M5R 1B1, Winter 1975-
Former title(s): Bell Femme (1965-1975)
Quarterly. Trade union publication, newspaper format, 8-12 p. Language: English and French. Free.

Communique / *edited by* Sonya Graham Macdonald. - *Published by* Ontario Association for Children with Learning Disabilities. Suite 322, 88 Eglinton Ave. E., Toronto, Ont. M4P 1B8, 1973-
Quarterly. Association publication, newspaper format, 8 p. Includes book reviews.
Circulation: 3000
Subscription included in membership fee $7.00 per year.

Communique (1970-1973) *See* Progressive Conservative Association of Canada. P.C. bulletin

Communique / *edited by* Keith Oleksuik (copy ed.) and Sally Layton (production ed.). - *Published by* Alumni Association. York University. 4700 Keele St., Downsview, Ont. M3J 1P3.
Former title(s): York University Alumni Association communiqué (1970-1972) The York Communiqué (October 1967-May 1970)
Irregular (approximately 3 issues per year). Alumni publication, magazine format, 16 p.
Circulation: 16,000
Free.

Communique : Canadian studies / *edited by* James E. Page. - *Published by* Association of Canadian Community Colleges. 1750 Finch Ave. E., Willowdale, Ont. M2N 5T7, October 1974-
Irregular (approximately 4-5 issues per year). Association publication, newsletter format, 26 p. Language: English and French.
ISSN 0318-1197 Free. Special rates offered.

Communiqué aux consommateurs = Consumer communique - *Publié par* Association pour la protection automobile. C.P. 117, Succursale E, 292 ouest, boul. St-Joseph, Montréal, Qué., 1975-
Publication d'association, bulletin,

Communiqué de JETRO / *édité par* S. Oue. - *Publié par* L'Organisation du commerce du Japan. C.P. 589, étage F, 50 Frontenac, Place Bonaventure, Montréal, Qué.(adresse d'abonnement: Japan Trade Centre, 151 Bloor St. W., Toronto, Ont. M5S 1S8) avril 1975-
Ancien titre: Echos du Japon (1972-mars 1975)
Mensuel. Publication spécialisée, bulletin, 2 p.
Tirage: 300
Tirage contrôlé.

Communist viewpoint / *edited by* Norman Freed. - *Published by* Progress Books. 487 Adelaide St. W., Toronto, Ont. M5T 1N2, March 1969-
Former title(s): Horizons Autumn 1966-Winter 1969)
Issued every other month. Special interest, journal format, 64 p. Includes book reviews, cumulative index.
Indexed in Hist. abstr., Am. hist. and life.
$.75 per issue : $4.00 per year : $5.00 per year, foreign.

Communitronics / *edited by* T. Jaeger. - *Published by* Canadian Business Publications Co. P.O. Box 750, 660 Trans Canada Hwy., Point Claire, Que., 1973-
Issued every other month. Trade publication, magazine format, Includes advertising.

Community Arts Council of Vancouver / *edited by* W.G. Gerrard. - *Published by* Community Arts Council of Vancouver. 315 West Cordova St., Vancouver, B.C. V6B 1E5.
Irregular (approximately 8-9 issues per year). House/company organ, newsletter format, $5.00 per year (Group subscriptions $10.00).

Community Fund and Councils of Canada. Proceedings of biennal conference - *Published by* Community Funds and Councils of Canada. Canadian Council on Social Development. P.O. Box 3505, Postal Station C, 55 Parkdale Ave., Ottawa, Ont. K1Y 1E5., 1965-
Biennial. Proceedings of the biennial conference. Language: English and French.
ISSN 0315-7571 $3.00. Prepayment required.

Community Funds and Councils of Canada. Allocations to national organizations - *Published by* Community Funds and Councils of Canada. Canadian Council on Social Development. P.O. Box 3505, Postal Station C, 55 Parkdale Ave., Ottawa, Ont. K1Y 4G1, 1956-
Issued every 3 years. Language: English and French.
ISSN 0316-4721 Prepayment required.

Community Planning Association of Canada. National Library. Accessions list / *edited by* Diane Wood. - *Published by* Community Planning Association of Canada. 425 Gloucester St., Ottawa, Ont. K1R 5E9.
Irregular (approximately 12 issues per year). Association publication, bibliography, newsletter format, 8 p. Language: English and French. Includes book reviews. Circulation: 6000
$.35 per issue : $5.00 per year. Prepayment required.

Community Planning Association of Canada. Ontario Division. Ontario division newsletter / *edited by* Janina Milisiewicz. - *Published by* Ontario Division. Community Planning Association of Canada. Suite 307, 68 Yonge St., Toronto, Ont. M5E 1L1.
Issued every other month. Association publication, newsletter format, 8 p. Includes book reviews.
Controlled circulation.

Community Planning Association of Canada. Saskatchewan Division. Saskatchewan Division newsletter / *edited by* P. McAusland. - *Published by* Saskatchewan Division. Community Planning Association of Canada. 202 - 1808 Smith St., Regina, Sask. S4P 2N4.
Irregular (approximately 6 issues per year). Association publication, newsletter format, 6 p. Circulation: 400
$10.00 per year.

Community planning in British Columbia / *edited by* Sharon Fawcett. - *Published by* British Columbia Division. Community Planning Association of Canada. 801-318 Homer St., Vancouver, B.C. V6B 2V3.
Irregular (approximately 3-4 issues per year). Association publication, newsletter format, 5 p. supplements issued. Circulation: 1000
Subscription included in membership fee.

Community planning review = Revue canadienne d'urbanisme / *edited by* Diane Wood. - *Published by* Community Planning Association of Canada. 425 Gloucester St., Ottawa, Ont. K1R 5E9, 1951-
Irregular (approximately 12 issues per year). Association publication, newsletter format, 8 p. Language: French and English ; summaries: French and English.
Indexed in Can. ind.
$.35 per issue : $5.00 per year.

Community schools / *edited by* Myra Novogrodsky. - *Published by* Community Schools Workshop. 171 College St., Toronto, Ont., 1971-
Irregular (approximately 10 issues per year).
$5.00 per year.

Community services in Metropolitan Toronto - *Published by* Community Information Centre of Metropolitan Toronto. 110 Adelaide St. E., Toronto, Ont. M5C 1L1, 1970-
Former title(s): Directory of community services (1962-1968) Directory of health, welfare and recreation services (1938-1960)
Issued approximately every 2 years. Directory, loose leaf format, 225 p. supplements issued. Circulation: 7500
ISSN 0315-0631 $6.00 per issue. Prepayment required.

Community services in Saskatoon : services for the elderly in Saskatoon - *Published by* Community Aid/Resource Centre. 136 Ave. F, Saskatoon, Sask. S7M 1S8.
Biennial. Directory.
Free. Prepayment required.

Comparative health care systems (1973) *See* Journal of comparative sociology

Compendium of pharmaceuticals and specialities (Canada) / *edited by* G.N. Rotenberg. - *Published by* Canadian Pharmaceutical Association. 175 College St., Toronto, Ont. M5T 1P8.
Annual. Directory, 1100 p. Language: English and French.
$20.00.

Competition Canada (January 1971-December 1974) *See* Model aviation Canada

Le Compositeur canadien *See* The Canadian composer

Compressed air comments (February 1958-May 1967) *See* Canadian air comments: a commentary on the application of compressed air

Compte rendu annuel de la recherche en génie chimique dans les universités canadiennes *See* Annual directory of chemical engineering research in Canadian universities

Computer science newsletter (to October 31, 1973) *See* Computernews

Computernews / *edited by* Janet Campbell. - *Published by* Computer Centre. University of Toronto. Room 125, 10 Kings College Rd., Toronto, Ont. M5S 1A1, 1973-
Former title(s): Computer science newsletter (to October 31, 1973)
Monthly. House/company organ, newsletter format, 25 p. Circulation: 1500
ISSN 0315-4661

Computing Canada / *edited by* P. Plesman. - *Published by* Plesman Publications Ltd. 3235-1, Place Ville-Marie, Montreal, Que., May 1975-
Monthly. Special interest, newspaper format, 12 p. Includes advertising. Back issues $.75 each. Circulation: 12,500
ISSN 0319-0161 $7.00 per year. Free to selected job-catagories.

Computing Centre bulletin (December 6, 1968 - April 16, 1971) *See* University of Alberta, Edmonton. Computing Services. Bulletin

Comunita viva / *edited by* Rino Citarella. - *Published by* Photo Press Publishing Co. P.O. Box 429, Postal Station D, Toronto, Ont. M6P 3K1.
Ethnic press, magazine format, 31 p. Language: Italian.
$10.00 per year : $20.00 per year, foreign (Estero) : $50.00 per year (Sostenitore).

Comunita' viva / *edited by* Rino Citarella. - *Published by* Rino Citarella. 1758A Eglinton Ave. W., Toronto, Ont. M6E 2H6, 1972-
Former title(s): Sport vivo.
Issued twice a month. Ethnic press, magazine format, 32 p. Language: Italian. Circulation: 22,000
$.25 per issue : $10.00 per year : $20.00 per year, foreign.

Concept of self in sport and physical activity - *Published by* SIRLS. Faculty of Human Kinetics and Leisure Studies. University of Waterloo. Waterloo, Ont. N2L 3G1.
Quarterly. Bibliography, computer printout, $20.00 per year. $100.00 subscription to SIRLS required.

Concerns / *edited by* David E. Reeve. - *Published by* Alcohol and Drug Concerns Inc. Suite 6038, 15 Gervais Dr., Don Mills, Ont. M3C 1Y8, October 1970-
Former title(s): The Advocate (January 1956 - October 1970) The Temperance advocate (June 1928 to December 1955) The Pioneer (1902 - April 1928)
Quarterly. Directory, newsletter format, 4 p.
ISSN 0045-799X $3.00 per year.

Confédération des loisirs du Québec. Memo CLQ / *édité par* Jean-Eudes Landry. - *Publié par* Confédération des loisirs du Québec. 1414 est, rue Jarry, Montréal, Qué. H2E 2Z7, mars 1973-
Mensuel. Publication d'association, bulletin, 4 p. Tirage: 2500
Envoi gratuit.

Conférence catholique canadienne. Annuaire = Canadian Catholic Conference. Directory / *édité par* Service des relations publiques = Public Information Office. - *Publié par* Claire Dubé. Conférence catholique canadienne. 90, ave. Parent, Ottawa, Ont. K1N 7B1.(adresse d'abonnement: Service des éditions/Publications Service, 90 ave Parent, Ottawa, Ont. K1N 7B1) 1966-
Annuel. Publication ecclésiastique, répetoire, 100 p. Langue(s): français et anglais. Tirage: 2000
$3.00.

Conference of Mennonites in Canada. Bulletin - *Published by* Conference of Mennonites in Canada. 600 Shaftesbury Blvd., Winnipeg, Man., 1965-
Monthly. Church publication, newsletter format, 32 p.

Conference of Mennonites in Canada. Yearbook / *edited by* The Executive of the Conference. - *Published by* Conference of Mennonites in Canada. 600 Shaftesbury Blvd., Winnipeg, Man. R3P 0M4, 1928-
Former title(s): Jahrbuch der Konferenz der Mennoniten in Kanada.
Annual. Church publication, yearbook, 100 p. Language: German and English.
Cost paid by the conference.

Conference religieuse canadienne. Bulletin / *édité par* P. Jacques Cloutier. - *Publié par* La Conférence religieuse canadienne. 324 est, ave Laurier, Ottawa, Ont. K1N 6P6, janvier 1955-
Intermittent (approximativement 8 éditions par an). Publication d'association, bulletin, 8 p. Tirage: 4500
ISSN 0316-8751 $2.00 par année.
Abonnements payables à l'avance.

Confidences : le seul journal d'information sexuelle / *édité par* Lorraine Ross. - *Publié par* Monsieur Yves Aublet. Suite 3, 3535, rue Papineau, Montréal, Qué.(adresse d'abonnement: C.P. 368, Montréal, Qué. H4A 3P7)
Ancien titre: Le Nouveau confidences.
Hebdomadaire. Publication spécialisée, journal, 24 p. Comprend publicité. Tirage: 23,000
ISSN 0317-3607 $.50 le numéro : $25.00 par année.

Congregational libraries newsletter *See* The Rare bird

Congrès canadien polonais. Bulletin *See* Canadian Polish Congress. Information bulletin

Congrès du travail du Canada - *Publié par* Congrès du travail du Canada. 2841 Riverside Dr., Ottawa, Ont.
Annuel. Publication d'association.
ISSN 0036-5892

Congress bulletin / *edited by* Annabelle King. - *Published by* Central Region. Canadian Jewish Congress. 1590 MacGregor Ave., Montreal, Que. H3G 1C5, January 1943-
Irregular (approximately 8 issues per year). Special interest, newspaper format, 16-20 p. Includes book reviews, film reviews, play reviews. Circulation: 25,000
Free. Controlled circulation.

Connection / *edited by* Barbara Pegg. - *Published by* Edmonton Public Library. 7 Sir Winston Churchill Square, Edmonton, Alta. T5J 2V4, April 1973-
Former title(s): News notes - Edmonton Public Library.
Monthly. House/company organ, newsletter format, 8 p.
Free.

Conseil canadien de l'artisan. Bulletin de nouvelles *See* Canadian Crafts Council. Newsletter

Conseil canadien de recherche sur les humanities. Bulletin *See* Humanities Research Council of Canada Canada. Bulletin

Conseil canadien des ingénieurs. Communiqué *See* Canadian Council of Professional Engineers. Newsbrief

Conseil de développement des média communautaires. Bulletin de liason - *Publié par* Conseil de développement des média communautaires. 415-1207, rue Saint-Andrée, Montréal, Qué., été 1973-
Intermittent (approximativement 6 éditions par an). Publication des employés, bulletin, 50 p. Tirage: 300
$6.00 par année.

Conseil de la jeunesse scientifique. Bulletin de liaison du Conseil de la jeunesse scientifique / *édité par* Raymond Blain. - *Publié par* Conseil de la jeunesse scientifique. 1415 est, rue Jarry, Montréal, Qué. H3E 2Z7.
Quadrimestriel. Publication d'association, bulletin, 8 p. Tirage: 12,000
Envoi gratuit.

Conseil de la vie française en Amérique. Le bottin des sociétés patriotiques - *Publié par* Le Conseil de la vie française en Amérique. 75, rue d'Auteuil, Québec, Qué. G1R 4C3, janvier 1963-
Annuel. Publication d'association, 50-60 p.

Conseil du Québec de l'enfance exceptionnelle et Centre d'information sur l'enfance et l'adolescence inadaptées. Documentation C.Q.E.E.-C.I.E.A.I / *édité par* Ginette Charest. - *Publié par* Centre d'information sur l'enfance et l'adolescence inadaptées. Hôpital Sainte-Justine, 3100, rue Ellendale, Montréal, Qué.(adresse d'abonnement: 2765, Côte-Ste-Catherine, Montréal, Qué) novembre 1971-
Intermittent (approximativement 3 éditions par an). Publication d'association, bulletin, 6 p. Tirage: 2000
ISSN 0316-7038 Envoi gratuit.

Conseil du statut de la femme. Bulletin / *édité par* Service d'information. - *Publié par* Conseil du statut de la femme. Chambre 610, 100, place D'Youville, Québec, Qué. G1A 1G4, janvier 1975-
Intermittent (approximativement 9 éditions par an). Publication d'association, bulletin, 14 p. Langue(s): français ; sommaires: français et anglais. Tirage: 3500
Envoi gratuit.

Le Conseiller juridique - *Publié par* Service de police de la communauté urbaine de Montréal. 775, Gosford, Montréal, Qué. H2Y 3C7, août 1974-
Mensuel. Articles juridiques, bulletin, 4 p.

Consensus / *edited by* J. Robitaille. - *Published by* Standards Council of Canada. 1205 - 350 Sparks St., Ottawa, Ont. K1R 7S8, January 1974-
Quarterly. Association publication, magazine format, 12 p. Language: English and French. Includes volume index. Circulation: 8000
Free.

Consensus : a Canadian Lutheran journal of theology / *edited by* Norman J. Threinen. - *Published by* Lutheran Council in Canada. 500 - 365 Hargrave St., Winnipeg, Man. R3B 2K3, January 1975-
Quarterly. Church publication, journal format, 32 p. Includes book reviews. Circulation: 4000
$1.25 per issue : $5.00 per year.

Le Consommateur canadien / *édité par* Sandra Thompson. - *Publié par* Association des consommateurs du Canada. 801, 251 ouest, ave Laurier, Ottawa, Ont. L1P 2Z7.
Publié en anglais: Canadian consumer.
Bimestriel. Publication d'association, magazine, 40 p. Comprend critique de livres, index cumulatif.
Indexé dans Periodex.
$.90 le numéro : $5.00 par année.
Abonnements payables à l'avance.

Constables review *Voir* Police : revue des agents de police

Constat - *Published by* Alberta Construction Labour Relations Association. 10305A Princess Elizabeth Ave., Edmonton, Alta. T5G 0Y5.
Monthly. Association publication, newsletter format, 5 p.
Controlled circulation.

Le constructeur du Québec (1926-1952) *Voir* Bätiment

Construction - *Publié par* L'Association canadienne de la construction. 85, rue Albert, Ottawa, Ont. K1P 6A4.
Publié également en anglais.
Bimestriel. Publication d'association, magazine, 18-20 p.

Construction - *Published by* Canadian Construction Association. 85 Albert St., Ottawa, Ont. K1P 6A4.
Published also in French.
Issued every other month. Association publication, magazine format, 18-20 p.

Construction Alberta news / *edited by* Laurie Watson. - *Published by* Construction Alberta News Ltd. Suite 220, 11 Fairway Dr., Edmonton, Alta. T5J 2S6, 1974-
Issued twice a week. Trade publication, magazine format, Includes advertising.
$1.00 per issue : $50.00 per year.

Construction industries directory *See* Government and the contractor

Construction materials specifier - *Published by* Don Quick Publications. 297 Old Kingston Rd., West Hill, Ont. M1C 2B4, 1975-
Issued every other month. Trade publication, magazine format, Includes advertising.

Construction west - *Published by* J.L. Whitehead. Journal of Commerce Publications. Southam Business Publications Ltd. 2000 W. 12th Ave., Vancouver, B.C.
Monthly. Trade publication. Includes advertising. Supplement to Journal of commerce.

Consumer communique *Voir* Communiqué aux consommateurs

The Consumer interest / *edited by* Kathleen H. Brown. - *Published by* College of Family and Consumer Studies. University of Guelph, Guelph, Ont. N1G 2W1, 1971-
Quarterly. For professionals interested in the consumer field, newsletter format, 4-8 p.
Circulation: 560
ISSN 0045-8252 $1.75 per issue : $5.00 per year (Students $2.50) : $9.00 for 2 years.
Prepayment required.

Consumption of leisure and sport - *Published by* SIRLS. Faculty of Human Kinetics and Leisure Studies. University of Waterloo. Waterloo, Ont. N2L 3G1.
Quarterly. Bibliography, computer printout, $100.00 subscripton to SIRLS required.

Con-Tact / *édité par* Françoise Martin. - *Publié par* L'Association des archivistes médicales du Québec. C.P. 155, 4357, Place Viger, Rock Forest, Sherbrooke, Qué. J0B 2J0, mai 1967-
Trimestriel. Publication d'association, bulletin, 36 p. Tirage: 800
$5.00 par année.

Contact - *Published by* British Columbia Teachers Credit Union. 270-1665 W. Broadway, Vancouver, B.C. V6K 1X1, 1972-
Quarterly. House/company organ, newsletter format, 4-6 p. Circulation: 11,000
Free to members.

Contact / *edited by* John M. Phin. - *Published by* Canadian College of Health Service Executives. 25 Imperial St. Toronto, Ont. M5P 1B9, December 1973-
Institutional publication (Universities, schools, etc.), newsletter format, 4 p. Language: English and French.
Free. Controlled circulation.

Contact / *edited by* John Patton. - *Published by* The Canadian Studies Foundation. 252 Bloor St. W., Toronto, Ont. M5S 1V5, January 1974-
Monthly. Special interest, newsletter format, 4 p. Language: French and English. Circulation: 3500
Free.

Contact / *edited by* Jim Neaves. - *Published by* Family Life Education Council of Edmonton. 10022 - 103 St., Edmonton, Alta. T5J 0X5. Issued every other month. Association publication, magazine format, 12 p. $2.00 per year. Controlled circulation.

Contact / *edited by* Linda Lee. - *Published by* Manitoba Government Employees' Association. 360 McMillan Ave., Winnipeg, Man. R3L 0N2, March 1942-
Former title(s): MGEA news (June 1971-October 1971) Bison (March 1942-June 1971)
Monthly. Association publication, newspaper format, 8 p.
Controlled circulation.

Contact : a military newspaper / *sponsored by* CFB Trenton Base Fund ; *edited by* Joan L. Wright. - *Published by* Joan L. Wright. P.O.Box 40, Astra, Ont., January 1942-
Issued every other week. House/company organ, newspaper format, 16 p. Language: English (French). Circulation: 5000
$1.00 per year : $2.00 per year, foreign. Free. Controlled circulation.

Contact : bulletin of urban and environmental affairs / *sponsored by* University of Waterloo. Faculty of Environmental Studies ; *edited by* N.E.P. Pressman. - *Published by* Graphic Services. University of Waterloo. Waterloo, Ont. N2L 3G1.
Irregular (approximately 6 issues per year). Special interest, newsletter format, 18 p. Includes book reviews, advertising. Circulation: 520
$8.00 per year (Corporations and institutions $10.00 ; Students $4.00). Controlled circulation. Prepayment required.

Contemporary literature in translation / *edited by* Andreas Schroeder. - *Published by* A.P. Schroeder. P.O. Box 3127, Mission City, B.C. V2V 4J3, 1968-
Issued 3 times per year. Special interest, magazine format, 45 p. Includes advertising. available in microform. Circulation: 1500
ISSN 0010-7492 $2.50 per issue : $6.50 per year. Prepayment required.

Contemporary music showcase / *sponsored by* Contemporary Music Showcase Association. - *Published by* Maurice Golah. Madoc Review Ltd. P.O. Box 460, Madoc, Ont. K0K 2K0 (Subscription address: C.M.S.A., 3296 Cindy Cres., Mississauga, Ont. L4Y 3J6) 1970-
Biennial. Association publication, booklet format, 24 p. Circulation: 400
ISSN 0316-893X Free.

Content : Canada's national news media magazine / *edited by* Barrie W. Zwicker. - *Published by* Barry Zwicker. 22 Laurier Ave. Toronto, Ont. M4X 1S3, October 1970-
Former title(s): Content : for Canadian journalists (October 1970-April 1973)
Monthly. Special interest, magazine format, 28 p. Language: English (French). Includes book reviews, film reviews, advertising, volume index, cumulative index. Back issues available $1.00 each. Circulation: 5000
ISSN 0045-835X $.50 per issue : $5.50 per year : $6.50 per year, U.S. : $7.50 per year, foreign. Special rates offered (quantity discount). Prepayment required.

Content : for Canadian journalists (October 1970-April 1973) *See* Content : Canada's national news media magazine

The Continent / *edited by* Tricia Morgan. - *Published by* North American Life Assurance Company. 105 Adelaide St. W., Toronto, Ont. M5H 1R1, September 1929-
Monthly. Employee publication, magazine format, 20 p. Includes book reviews. supplements issued. Circulation: 2000

The Continental times / *edited by* Y. Iwasaki. - *Published by* Y. Iwasaki. P.O. Box 575, Terminal A, 417 Dundas St. W., Toronto, Ont., 1907-
Issued twice a week. Ethnic press. Language: Japanese. Includes advertising.
$11.00 per year.

Continuing education directory : courses, programs and activities, September through December - *Published by* Metropolitan Toronto Library Board. Suite 301, 203 College St., Toronto, Ont. M5T 1P9, 1969-
Former title(s): Continuing education directory for Metropolitan Toronto (1969-1970)
Annual. Directory, 283 p. Circulation: 700
ISSN 0045-8384 $15.00.

Continuing education directory for Metropolitan Toronto (1969-1970) *See* Continuing education directory : courses, programs and activities, September through December

Continuum - *Published by* Osgoode Hall Law School. York University, 4700 Keele St., Downsview, Ont. M3J 1P3, Summer 1973-
Quarterly. Alumni publication, newsletter format, 8 p.
$2.00 per year. Free to alumni $2.00 subscription fee to interested parties. Controlled circulation.

Contrast / *edited by* Errol Townshend. - *Published by* A.W. Hamilton. Contrast Publications Ltd. 28 Lennox St., Toronto, Ont., February 1969-
Weekly. Ethnic publication, newspaper format, 20 p. Includes book reviews, film reviews, play reviews, record reviews, advertising, volume index. available in microform. Circulation: 20,000
$11.00 per year : $13.00 per year, foreign. Special rates offered. Prepayment required.

Conventions and meetings facilities and services in Canada / *edited by* James W. Nuttall. - *Published by* Effective Communications Ltd. 9 Manorpark Court, Willowdale, Ont. M2J 1A1, 1972-
Annual. Directory, magazine format, 180 p. Includes cumulative index. Circulation: 7024
$10.00. Controlled circulation.

Convergence : an international journal of adult education / *edited by* Margaret Gayfer (managing ed.). - *Published by* International Council for Adult Education. 252 Bloor St. W., Toronto, Ont. (Subscription address: P.O. Box 250, Postal Station F, Toronto, Ont. M4Y 2L5) 1968-
Quarterly. Association publication, magazine format, 94 p. Language: English, Spanish, French and Russian. Includes book reviews. Circulation: 2000
$2.00 per issue : $8.00 per year. Prepayment required.

Co-op commentary / *edited by* Bonnie Rose. - *Published by* Co-operative Union of Canada. 111 Sparks St., Ottawa, Ont. K1P 5B5, 1947-
Monthly. House/company organ, newsletter format, 4 p. Circulation: 2500
Controlled circulation.

Coopérateur agricole / *édité par* L.P. Poulin. - *Publié par* Coopérateur féderée de Québec. C.P. 500, Succursale Youville, Montréal, Qué. H2P 2W3, janvier 1972-
Mensuel. Revue d'entreprise, 32 p. Tirage: 34,500
ISSN 0315-1207 $1.00 par année. Abonnements payables à l'avance.

Cooperation Canada / *edited by* W.G. Neddow and Raymond Grenier. - *Published by* Canadian International Development Agency. 122 Bank St., Ottawa, Ont. K1A 0G4, March/April 1972-
Issued every other month. Special interest, magazine format, 32 p. Language: English and French. Circulation: 30,000
Indexed in P.A.I.S.
Free. Controlled circulation.

Co-operative consumer / *sponsored by* Consumer Press Ltd ; *edited by* Dennis W. Adkin. - *Published by* Dennis W. Adkin. 401 - 22 Street E., Saskatoon, Sask., February 1939-
Issued twice a month. Special interest, newspaper format, 12 p. Includes advertising. Circulation: 302,000
$2.00 per year : $3.50 per year, foreign. Controlled circulation. Special rates offered. Prepayment required.

The Co-operative farmer and Maritime dairyman (1895-1910) *See* The Maritime farmer and co-operative dairyman

Copperfield : an independent Canadian literary magazine of the land and the North / *edited by* Douglas Brown. - *Published by* Douglas Brown. P.O. Box 421, Temagimi, Ont. P0H 2H0, November 1969-
Irregular (approximately 2 issues per year). Magazine format, 120 p. Includes book reviews. Circulation: 600
ISSN 0069-9942 $2.00 per issue.

La Coquille / *édité par* Pierre Decary. - *Publié par* Lieutenance de Montréal. L'Ordre équestre du Saint-Sépulcre de Jerusalem. 61, Riverside Dr., Saint Lambert, Qué., mars 1972-
Publication ecclésiastique, 4 p. Comprend publicité.
Envoi gratuit.

Cordweekly - *Published by* Student Union. Sir Wilfred Laurier University. Waterloo, Ont.
Weekly. Student publication, newspaper format, Includes advertising. Circulation: 2800

The Corinthian / *edited by* Jill Wykes. - *Published by* The Canadian Horse Council. 333 River Rd., Ottawa, Ont. K1L 8B9.
Monthly. Association publication, newspaper format, 40 p.
$.75 per issue : $10.00 per year : $.75 per volume. Prepayment required.

The Corinthian / *edited by* Jill Wykes. - *Published by* The Corinthian Publishing Co. Ltd. c/o Humber College, P.O. Box 1900, 205 Humber College Blvd., Rexdale, Ont., 1968-
Monthly. Student publication. Includes advertising.
$.75 per issue : $8.00 per year.

Corn-soy guide / *edited by* Bryan Lyster. - *Published by* R.W. McGuire. The Public Press Ltd. 1760 Ellice Ave., Winnipeg, Man. R3H 0B6, March 1972-
Issued twice a year. Commodity publication, magazine format, 18 p. Issued as a supplement to Country guide. Circulation: 50,000
Included in Country guide subscription. Controlled circulation.

Corporate developments - *Published by* Richard De Boo Limited. 70 Richmond St. E., Toronto, Ont. M5C 2M8, November 1975- Quarterly. Legal articles, newsletter format, 4-6 p.

Corporate insurance in Canada / *edited by* Bobbi Shaw. - *Published by* Stone and Cox Ltd. 203 Adelaide St. W., Toronto, Ont. M5H 1X4, April 1972-
Monthly. Business publication, tabloid format, 12 p. Circulation: 6400
ISSN 0315-8098 $4.00 per year.

Corporate Management Tax Conference - *Published by* Canadian Tax Foundation. 100 University Ave., Toronto, Ont. M5J 1V6, 1972-
Annual. Association publication, 175-200 p. Subscription included in membership fee $30.00.

Corporation professionnelle des diététistes du Québec. Bulletin / *édité par* Andrée Adam. - *Publié par* Corporation professionnelle des diététistes du Québec. Suite 130, 934 est, rue Ste-Catherine, Montréal, Qué. H2L 2E9, 1960-
Intermittent (approximativement 4 éditions par an). Publication d'association, bulletin, 20 p. Envoi gratuit. Tirage contrôlé.

Corporation professionnelle des infirmières et infirmiers auxiliares du Québec. La Revue des infirmières et infirmiers auxiliaires du Québec - *Publié par* Corporation professionnelle des infirmières et infirmiers auxilières du Québec. 1380, rue Gilford, Montréal, Qué. H2J 1R8, mars 1974-
Ancien titre: Les Cahiers du nursing.
Trimestriel. Publication d'association, bulletin, 16 p. Langue(s): français et anglais.
ISSN 0316-411X $4.00 par année : $5.00 par année, l'étranger.

Corporation professionnelle des médecins du Québec. Bulletin = Professional Corporation of Physicians of Quebec. Bulletin - *Publié par* Corporation professionnelle des médecins du Québec. Suite 914, 1440 ouest, rue Ste-Catherine, Montréal, Qué. H3G 1S5, juillet 1961-
Ancien titre: Bulletin de nouvelles = Newsletter - Corporation professionnelle des médecins du Québec (juillet 1961-mars 1975)
Intermittent (approximativement 5-15 éditions par an). Publication d'association, magazine, 52 p. Langue(s): français et anglais. Tirage: 15,000
ISSN 0315-2979 Envoi gratuit.

Corporation professionnelle des médecins du Québec. Bulletin *See* Professional Corporation of Physicians of Quebec. Bulletin

Corporation professionnelle des travailleurs sociaux du Quebéc. Bulletin / *édité par* Francine Hirbour. - *Publié par* Corporation professionnelle des travailleurs sociaux du Québec. Suite 335, 5757 Decelles, Montréal, Qué.
Ancien titre: Elan.
Bimestriel. Publication d'association, bulletin, Langue(s): français et anglais ; sommaires: français.
$25.00 par année : comprend automatiquement un abonnement au Bulletin et à la revue Intervention. Gratuit aux membres de la CORPO.

Corporation service - *Published by* Corporation Service. The Financial Post. 481 University Ave., Toronto, Ont. M5W 1A7, 1928-
Daily, Monday to Friday. Trade publication. $1440.00 per year. Special rates offered.

Corpus administrative index / *edited by* Karen Dunbar. - *Published by* Corpus Publishers Services Ltd. Suite C, 6 Crescent Rd., Toronto, Ont. M4W 1T1, April 1972-
Issued every other month. Directory, magazine format 9-ring binder, 200 p. Includes updating service. supplements issued.
$20.00 per issue : $115.00 per year.
Prepayment required.

Corpus almanac of Canada / *edited by* Margot J. Fawcett. - *Published by* Corpus Publishers Services Ltd. 6 Crescent Rd., Toronto, Ont. M4W 1T1, 1965-
Former title(s): Corpus directory and almanac of Canada.
Annual. Directory, book format, 1000 p. Includes volume index.
ISSN 0315-7083 $23.95 per year.

Corpus directory and almanac of Canada *See* Corpus almanac of Canada

Correctional and criminological literature published in Canada (1964-1966) *See* Correctional literature published in Canada

Correctional literature published in Canada = Ouvrages de criminologie publiés au Canada / *sponsored by* Canadian Criminology and Corrections Association. - *Published by* Canadian Council on Social Development. P.O. Box 3505, Postal Station C, 55 Parkdale Ave., Ottawa, Ont. K1Y 4G1, 1968-
Former title(s): Correctional and criminological literature published in Canada (1964-1966)
Annual. Bibliography, paperbound book, 60 p. Language: French and English.
ISSN 0070-0509 $1.50.

Correctional process (August 1948-May 1971) *See* Canadian Criminology and Corrections Association. Bulletin

Correio portugues / *edited by* Maria Alice Ribeiro. - *Published by* Correio Portugues. 899 College St., Toronto, Ont., 1963-
Issued twice a month. Ethnic press. Language: Portuguese. Includes advertising. Circulation: 8523
$4.00 per year.

Correo Hispano-Americano - *Published by* Carlos Puitti. 175 St. Clair Ave. W., Toronto, Ont. (Subscription address: P.O. Box 25, Postal Station E, Toronto, Ont. M6H 4E1) 1969-
Weekly. Ethnic press. Language: Spanish. Includes advertising.
$7.00 per year.

Corridor - *Published by* Northwest Centre. Ontario Institute for Studies in Education. 10 S. Algoma St., Thunder Bay, Ont. P7B 3A7.
Indexed in Can. educ. ind.

Corriere Canadese = The Canadian courier / *edited by* E. Caprile. - *Published by* Dan Iannuzzi. 1000 Lawrence Ave. W., Toronto, Ont. M6A 1P2, 1954-
Daily, Monday-Thursday. Ethnic press. Language: Italian. Includes advertising. Circulation: 24,316
$39.00 per year.

Corriere commerciale - *Published by* Dan Iannuzzi. Diasons Publications Ltd. 1000 Lawrence Ave. W., Toronto, Ont. M6A 1P2.
Weekly. Ethnic press, trade publication. Language: Italian. Includes advertising. A supplement to Corriere canodese. Circulation: 21,219

Corriere illustrato - *Published by* Il Sole Publications Ltd. 1000 Lawrence Ave. W., Toronto, Ont. M6A 1P2.
Weekly. Ethnic press. Language: Italian. Includes advertising. Circulation: 25,718
$.20 per issue : $10.00 per year.

Cosmetics handbook / *edited by* W.E. Granger. - *Published by* Robert D. Reid. Maclean-Hunter Ltd. 481 University Ave., Toronto, Ont. M5W 1A7, 1966-
Annual. Directory, magazine format, 80 p. Includes advertising. Circulation: 7000
$3.00. Controlled circulation.

Cosmos-express (septembre 1970-mai 1973) *Voir* Le Nouveau cosmos-express

Cost and management / *edited by* D.R. Hicks. - *Published by* Society of Industrial Accountants of Canada. 154 Main St. E., Hamilton, Ont. (Subscription address: P.O. Box 176, Hamilton, Ont. L8N 3C3) 1926-
Issued every other month. Special interest, magazine format, 68 p. Language: English and French. Includes book reviews, advertising, volume index. Circulation: 18,717
Indexed in Can. ind., Can. B.P.I.
$1.50 per issue : $7.50 per year : $10.00 per year, foreign.

La Coulée (juin 1951-septembre 1963) *Voir* L'Equipe

La Coulée / *édité par* Gilles Gauthier. - *Publié par* Sidbec-Dosco Ltée. C.P. 249, 507, Place d'Armes, Montréal, Qué. H3C 2H6, décembre 1972-
Mensuel. Organe interne/officiel, bulletin, 8 p. Tirage: 4000

La Couleur du temps: comment prévoir le temps dans votre région *See* Weather timetable : how to foretell your weather

The Council bulletin / *edited by* Gordon F. Tanner. - *Published by* Saskatchewan Council for Crippled Children and Adults. 1410 Kilburn Ave., Saskatoon, Sask. S7M 0J8, Spring 1973-
Quarterly. Association publication, newspaper format, 8 p. Circulation: 4000
Subscription included in membership $5.00.

Council communicator / *edited by* Ruth Tillman. - *Published by* Canadian Council of Churches. 40 St. Clair Ave. E., Toronto, Ont. M4T 1M9, March 1970-
Issued twice a month. Church publication, newsletter format, 10 p. Includes book reviews, volume index. Circulation: 3000
$.30 per issue : $1.00 per year. Free to selected mailing list.

Council of Atlantic Provincial Employees. CAPE journal - *Published by* CAPE journal. P.O. Box 1085, St. John's, Nfld., 1972-
Irregular (approximately 2 issues per year). Association publication, newspaper format, 8-12 p. Language: English and French. Circulation: 24,000
Free.

Council of Ontario Universities. Research Division. Application statistics - *Published by* Council of Ontario Universities. Suite 8039, 130 St. George St., Toronto, Ont. M5S 2T4, April 1974-
Annual. Institutional publication (Universities, schools, etc.), 40 p.

Council on the Study of Religion. Bulletin / *edited by* Norman E. Wagner. - *Published by* CSR Executive Office. Wilfrid Laurier University, Waterloo, Ont. N2L 3C5, 1970-
Issued 5 times a year. Association publication, magazine format, 60 p. Circulation: 10,000
$1.00 per issue : $4.00 per year.

Countdown: Canadian nursing statistics - *Published by* Canadian Nurses' Association. 50 The Driveway, Ottawa, Ont., K2P 1E2., 1967-
Annual. Statistics, 130 p.
ISSN 0070-1238 $4.00. Prepayment required.

Counterweight - *Published by* Harold Daniels. Counterweight Weight Controls Ltd. Suite 500, 491 Lawrence Ave. W., Toronto, Ont. M5M 1C7, 1972-
Irregular (approximately 10 issues per year). Special interest, magazine format, Includes advertising.
$.50 per issue.

Country estate magazine / *edited by* R. Robson. - *Published by* M. Pembry. Norbry Publishing Ltd. R.R. 1, Terra Cotta, Ont., Winter 1971-
Quarterly. Special interest, magazine format, 24 p. Includes book reviews, advertising. Circulation: 27,500
$.50 per issue : $2.00 per year : $5.00 per year, U.S. : $10.00 per year, foreign. Controlled circulation.

Country guide : the farm magazine / *edited by* Dave Wreford. - *Published by* R.W. McGuire. The Public Press Ltd. 1760 Ellice Ave., Winnipeg, Man. R3H 0B6, June 1909-
Former title(s): The Country guide and nor'west farmer (June 1936-February 1942) The Grain grower's guide (June 1908-March 1928) The Nor'west farmer (1882-1936; absorbed in 1936) Farm and home (1919-1930; absorbed in 1936)
Monthly. Trade publication, magazine format, 52 p. available in microform. supplements issued. Circulation: 262,698
$.35 per issue : $2.00 per year : $3.00 per year, foreign. Prepayment required.

The Country guide and nor'west farmer (June 1936-February 1942) *See* Country guide : the farm magazine

Country life in British Columbia / *edited by* J.R. Armstrong. - *Published by* J.R. Armstrong. Country Life Ltd. 810 - 207 West Hastings, Vancouver, B.C. V6B 1J8, 1915-
Monthly. "Only articles of interest to B.C. farm and ranch subscribers", newspaper format, 32 p. Includes book reviews, advertising. Circulation: 12,000
$1.50 per year : $4.00 per year, foreign.

Couple et famille / *parrainé par* Mouvement couple et famille. - *Publié par* Editions des foyers Notre-Dame. 424, rue St-Sulpice, Montréal, Qué., 1955-
Ancien titre: Eternel triangle (mars 1961-septembre 1968) Bulletin des foyers Notre Dame (1955-1961)
Trimestriel. Publication d'association, bulletin, 30 p. Tirage: 2500
$.75 le numéro : $3.00 par année.

Coupler - *Published by* Employees. Pacific Great Eastern Railway Co. 1095 West Pender St., Vancouver, B.C., October 1959-
Irregular (approximately 10 issues per year). Employee publication, 4 p.
Free.

Courier / *edited by* Don Morrison. - *Published by* British Columbia Corrections Association. Suite 32, 2515 Burrard St., Vancouver, B.C. V6J 3T6.
Quarterly. Association publication, journal format, Circulation: 250
$6.00 per year.

Courier / *edited by* Mrs G.O. Hughes. - *Published by* Canadian Association of Hospital Auxiliaries. P.O. Box 462, Hatzec, B.C. (Subscription address: 25 Imperial St., Toronto, Ont)
Quarterly. Special interest, newsletter format, supplements issued.
$1.00 per year.

Le Courrier du français-cadre : le cycle de l'élémentaire / *édité par* Henri Longpré. - *Publié par* Henri Longpré. 2673 de la Ronde, Québec, Qué., septembre 1974-
Ancien titre: Courrier pédagogique (1970-1974)
Mensuel. Bulletin, 16 p.
$.50 le numéro : $4.00 par année : $4.50 l'étranger, par année.

Le Courrier municipal - *Publié par* Behan Communications Corporation. 71, rue Bank, Ottawa, Ont. K1P 5N2, octobre 1973-
Publié en anglais : Municipal report.
Mensuel. Publication spécialisée, bulletin, 4 p.
$20.00 par année.

Courrier pédagogique (1970-1974) *Voir* Le Courrier du français-cadre : le cycle de l'élémentaire

Cours de perfectionnement - *Publié par* Chambre des notaires du Québec. Suite 1700, 630 ouest, boul. Dorchester, Montréal, Qué. H3B 1T6, février 1962-
Intermittent (approximativement 3 éditions par an). Articles juridiques, 150 p. Tirage: 1500
ISSN 0316-1234 $10.00 le numéro.

Court house echo / *edited by* Gilles H. Senecal. - *Published by* Gilles H. Senecal. 277 Westgate Dr., Rosemere, Que., January 1972-
Weekly. Institutional publication (Universities, schools, etc.), magazine format, 32 p.
Language: English and French. Circulation: 5000
$115.00 per year.

Le Courtier d'assurance / *édité par* Pierre Morin. - *Publié par* L'Association des courtiers d'assurances de la province de Québec. Bureau 150, 550 ouest, rue Sherbrooke, Montréal, Qué. H3A 1C8, 1923-
Ancien titre: The Insurance broker = Le Courtier d'assurances.
Mensuel. Publication d'association, magazine, 32 p. Langue(s): français et anglais. Tirage: 5200
$.50 le numéro : $4.00 par année.
Abonnements payables à l'avance.

Coven / *edited by* Clairie Martin. - *Published by* Journalism Department. Humber College of Applied Arts and Technology. P.O. Box 1900, Rexdale, Ont.
Weekly (September-May). Student publication. Includes advertising.

Craft contacts / *edited by* Barbara Lambert. - *Published by* Craftsmen's Association of British Columbia. 315 West Cordova St., Vancouver, B.C. V6B 1E5 (Subscription address: 801-207 W. Hastings, Vancouver, B.C. V6B 1H7)
Irregular (approximately 10 issues per year). Association publication, newsletter format, Includes advertising. Circulation: 400
$8.50 per year.

Craft dimensions artisanales / *edited by* Gwen Sands. - *Published by* Ontario Chapter. Canadian Guild of Crafts. 29 Prince Arthur Ave., Toronto, Ont. M5R 1B2, 1971-
Issued every other month. Association publication, magazine format, 32 p. Includes book reviews, advertising. supplements issued. Circulation: 2000
$2.00 per issue : $10.00 per year. Subscription included in membership fee.

Craft Ontario / *edited by* Elizabeth Dingman. - *Published by* Ontario Craft Foundation. 7th floor, 8 York St., Toronto, Ont. M5J 1R2.
Monthly. Association publication, Magazine and newsletter format on alternate months, magazine 16p.; newsletter 12 p. Includes book reviews. Circulation: 1500
ISSN 0315-7075 $8.00 per year.

Crafts Canada / *edited by* Gwen Dempsey. - *Published by* Page Publications Ltd. 333 King St. W., Toronto, Ont.
$10.00 per year.

The Craftsman / *edited by* Wilf Wenzel. - *Published by* Old Cabin Crafts Society. 264 Palliser Sq. E., Calgary, Alta. T2G 0P5, 1964-
Issued twice a year. Association publication, newsletter format, 3 p.
Subscription included with membership fee.

Crane Library. Crane Library news / *edited by* Paul E. Thiele. - *Published by* Charles Crane Memorial Library. Brock Hall, University of British Columbia, Vancouver, B.C., October 1970-
Irregular (approximately 3 issues per year). Institutional publication (Universities, schools, etc.), newsletter format, 8 p. Includes updating service. supplements issued. Circulation: 1000
ISSN 0316-7372 Free.

Crane Library. Crane Library update circular / *sponsored by* University of British Columbia. Libraries ; *edited by* Judith C. Thiele. - *Published by* Charles Crane Memorial Library. Brock Hall, University of British Columbia Vancouver, B.C. (Subscription address: 2075 Wesbrook Place, Vancouver, B.C., V6T 1W5) 1972-
Irregular (approximately 4-5 issues per year). Newsletter format, 4 p. Includes updating service.
Free.

Crane Memorial Library. Crane Library News / *edited by* Paul E. Thiele. - *Published by* Crane Memorial Library. University of British Columbia. 2075 Wesbrook Place, Vancouver, B.C. V6T 1W5, October 1974-
Irregular (approximately 3 issues per year). Institutional publication (Universities, schools, etc.), newsletter format, 6 p. Includes book reviews, updating service. Circulation: 1000
Free.

Crawley commentary / *edited by* Graeme Fraser. - *Published by* Crawley Films Ltd. 19 Fairmont, Ottawa, Ont. K1Y 3B5, May 1947-
Issued every other month. House/company organ, newsletter format, 2-3 p. Circulation: 1500
Free. Controlled circulation.

Cream topics (April 1948-November 1970)
See About us

Credit management review / *edited by* W.J. Hambly. - *Published by* Canadian Credit Institute. P.O. Box 532, Postal Station F, Toronto, Ont. M4Y 2N1.
Monthly. Association publication, newsletter format, 2 p. Circulation: 6000
Free. Available to members only. Controlled circulation.

Credit union way / *edited by* A.E. Turner. - *Published by* The Saskatchewan Cooperative Credit Society Ltd. 2625 Victoria Ave., Regina, Sask. S4P 3G8, October 1946-
Issued twice a month. House/company organ, newsletter format, 16 p. Includes book reviews, advertising. Circulation: 5200
$3.00 per year. Special rates offered.

Credo / *édité par* Gérard Gautier. - *Publié par* Eglise unie du Canada. 3480, boul. Décarie, Montréal, Qué. H4A 3J5, 1954-
Ancien titre: Bulletin de l'Eglise unie du Canada.
Mensuel. Publication ecclésiastique, magazine, 32 p. Comprend critique de livres, index de volumes, index cumulatif. Tirage: 2000
$.50 le numéro : $4.00 par année : $5.00 par année, l'étranger. Abonnements payables à l'avance.

Credo : mensuel de l'Eglise Unie du Canada - *Publié par* Gérard Gauthier. 3480, boul. Décarie, Montréal, Qué. H4A 3J5, 1954-
Ancien titre: Bulletin de l'Eglise Unie du Canada.
Mensuel. Publication ecclésiastique, 32 p. parution de suppléments. Tirage: 1500
$.75 le numéro : $4.00 par année : $5.00 par année, l'étranger.

Crest (October 1965 - November 1966) *See* Savant

The Crest : the Salvation Army's youth magazine / *edited by* Ira E. Barrow. - *Published by* Salvation Army Triumph Press. 455 North Service Rd. E., Oakville, Ont. L6H 1A5, February 1956-
Monthly. Special interest, magazine format, 24 p. Circulation: 3450
$.25 per issue : $2.50 per year.

Criminal law quarterly / *edited by* Alan W. Mewett. - *Published by* Canada Law Book Ltd. 80 Cowdray Court, Agincourt, Ont. M1S 1S5, 1958-
Quarterly. Cases, case notes, magazine format, 115 p.
Indexed in Can. leg. per. lit.
$26.50.

Criminologie / *édité par* Denis Szabo (directeur). - *Publié par* Les Presses de L'Université de Montréal. C.P. 6128, Montréal, Qué., janvier 1975-
Ancien titre: Acta criminologica.
Semestriel. Edition savante, revue, 100 p. Langue(s): français ; sommaires: anglais. Tirage: 1500
Indexé dans RADAR, Can. leg. per. lit.
$5.00 le numéro : $8.00 par année : $10.00 le volume. Tirage contrôlé. Abonnements payables à l'avance.

Criminologie made in Canada / *edited by* Yvon Dandurand, Stanley C. Mounsey and Roger F. Fasciaux. - *Published by* Criminilogie made in Canada. P.O. Box 142, Montreal, Que. H1H 5L2, May 1973-
Issued twice a year. Abstracts/summaries, journal format, 110 p. Language: English and French ; summaries: English and French. Includes book reviews. Circulation: 1025
Indexed in Abstr. Crim. pen.
$4.00 per issue : $7.50 per year : $9.50 per year, foreign. Special rates offered.

Crippled civilians quarterly / *edited by* Raymond Byrnes. - *Published by* Society for Crippled Civilians. 234 Adelaide St. E., Toronto, Ont. M5A 1M9.
Quarterly. Association publication, magazine format, 12 p. Circulation: 120,000
Free. Controlled circulation.

Critère / *édité par* Jacques Dufresne. - *Publié par* Collège Ahuntsic. 9155, rue St-Hubert, Montréal, Qué., février 1970-
Semestriel. Edition savante, 225 p. Tirage: 2000
Indexé dans RADAR.
$3.50 le numéro : $6.00 par année. Abonnements payables à l'avance.

The Critical list / *edited by* Jerry Green and Ken Wyman. - *Published by* Jerry Green. 32 Sullivan St., Toronto, Ont., 1975-
Irregular (approximately 6 issues per year). Special interest, magazine format, Includes advertising.

Critical studies in Canadian poetry / *edited by* W. Glenn Clever and Frank M. Tierney. - *Published by* Critical Studies in Canadian Poetry. P.O. Box 5147, Postal Station E, Ottawa, Ont., 1976-

Croatian way *See* Hrvatski put

Croation voice *See* Hrvatski glas

Croation voice annual = Hrvatski glas kalendar / *edited by* Mario Gordan. - *Published by* Croation Voice Publishing Co. Ltd. 325 Logan Ave., Winnipeg, Man. R3A 0P7.
Annual. Yearbook, Book format, 190 p. Language: Croatian. Circulation: 1000
$3.00 per issue.

Croissance - *Publié par* Wood Gundy Limited. P.O. Box 274, Royal Trust Tower, Toronto, Ont. M5K 1M7, novembre 1973-
Publié en anglais: Invest.
Mensuel. Organe interne/officiel, magazine, 16 p.
Tirage contrôlé.

Crop notes (1960-1968) *See* Notes on agriculture

Crops guide / *edited by* D. Wreford. - *Published by* R.W. McGuire. The Public Press Ltd. 1760 Ellice Ave., Winnipeg, Man. R3H 3B6, 1972-
Annual. Commodity publication. Includes advertising. Included in Country guide's subscriptions in Western Canada. Circulation: 168,396

Cross country : a magazine of Canadian-U.S. poetry / *edited by* Ken Norris (Toronto) Robert Galvin (Montreal) and Jim Mele (New York). - *Published by* Cross Country Press. Apt. 14, 1935 Tupper St., Montreal, Que., Winter 1975-
Issued 3 times a year. Special interest, magazine format, 52 p. Language: English and French. Includes book reviews, advertising. Circulation: 500
ISSN 0318-6075 $1.00 per issue : $8.00 for 2 years: $1.50 per issue, foreign. Prepayment required.

Cross trail news / *edited by* Edwin N. Sparshatt. - *Published by* Vancouver Island Western Square Dance Association. 244 Fenton Rd., Victoria, B.C. V9B 1C1.
Issued 5 times per year. Association publication, magazine format, 20 p.
$1.50 per year. Controlled circulation.

Cross-Canada comment / *edited by* George P. Hillmer. - *Published by* William McAdam. Canadian Association of Business Education Teachers (CABET). Curriculum Division, Dept. of Education, Mowat Block, Queen's Park, Toronto, Ont., 1971-
Quarterly. Association publication, newsletter format, 12 p. Language: English (French).
Free to members.

Crossroads / *sponsored by* Ontario Motor League. - *Published by* L.G. Liddle. Tri-County Automobile Club. 836 Courtland Ave. E., Kitchener, Ont.
Quarterly. Association publication, newsletter format, 4 p.
Free to members. Controlled circulation.

Crown's newsletter / *edited by* Kenneth L. Chasse. - *Published by* Ontario Crown Attorneys Association. Crown Attorneys Office, The Court House, 361 University Ave., Toronto, Ont., May 1972-
Monthly. Association publication, newsletter format, 20 p.
Free to prosecutors judges and law schools.

The Crucible / *edited by* Don Galbraith. - *Published by* Science Teachers' Association of Ontario. 123 Heddington Ave., Toronto, Ont. M5N 2K9 (Subscription address: Suite 700, 1261 Bay St., Toronto, Ont)
Irregular (approximately 8 issues per year). Association publication, magazine format, 52 p. Includes book reviews, volume index.
Indexed in Can. educ. ind.
$1.50 per issue : $15.00 per year.

The Crusader / *edited by* R.A. Taylor. - *Published by* The Church Army in Canada. 397 Brunswick Ave., Toronto, Ont.
Former title(s): The Anglican crusader.
Issued twice a year. Church publication, magazine format, 24 p. Circulation: 12,000
Free.

Crux / *edited by* Paul W. Gooch. - *Published by* Graduate Christian Fellowship. 745 Mount Pleasant Rd., Toronto, Ont. M4S 2N5, 1963-
Quarterly. Church publication, journal format, 32 p. Includes cumulative index. Circulation: 600
Indexed in Rel. and theol. abstr.
ISSN 0011-2186 $1.10 per issue : $4.00 per year : $4.25 per year, foreign.

Cuivre canadien *See* Canadian copper

Cul Q / *édité par* Jean Leduc. - *Publié par* Ginette Nault. 980 ouest, rue St-Paul, Montréal, Qué., 1973-
Ancien titre: Let's have a teute (mai 1975) Ecriture-lecture (été-automne 1974)
Semestriel. Publication spécialisée, 100 p. Tirage: 500

Cultural horizons of the deaf in Canada / *edited by* Forrest C. Nickerson. - *Published by* Canadian Cultural Society of the Deaf. 1475 Pacific Ave. W., Winnipeg, Man. R3E 1H1, June 1973-
Issued twice a year. Association publication, magazine format, 32-40 p. Includes play reviews, advertising. supplements issued.
$5.00 for 2 years (Husband-wife $7.50) : $6.00 for 2 years, U.S. (Husband-wife $8.50) : $7.00 for 3 years (Husband-wife $9.50).

Culture canadienne motorisée (1950-1959) *Voir* L'Agriculture canadienne

The Curlew / *sponsored by* Willow Beach Field Naturalists ; *edited by* E.R. McDonald. - *Published by* F. Stephens. Harwood, Ont. (Subscription address: Club Treasurer, 23 Sullivan St., Port Hope, Ont) April 1956-
Issued 10 times a year, none in July or August. Association publication, newsletter format, 5 p. Circulation: 200
ISSN 0011-3093 Subscription included in membership fee. Free on exchange to other clubs.

Curling review / *edited by* Don Fleming. - *Published by* Riegel Publications Ltd. 10623 Kingsway Ave., Edmonton, Alta. T5G 2Z6.
Irregular (approximately 7 issues per year). Special interest, newspaper format, 12-16 p. Circulation: 1300
ISSN 0011-3115 $2.00 per year.

Current Canadian books / *edited by* John R. Grantier. - *Published by* Coutts Library Services. 4290 Third Ave., Niagara Falls, Ont. L2E 4K7, June 1973-
Former title(s): Current Canadian books treated on approval.
Monthly. Bibliography, 20 p. Language: English and French. Includes volume index.
ISSN 0316-9448 $2.00 per issue : $24.00 per year. Controlled circulation.

Current Canadian books treated on approval *See* Current Canadian books

Current events. West coast ed - *Published by* Robert D. Simpson. Current Events Publishing Co. Ltd. 4 - 840 Fort St., Victoria, B.C., 1936-
Monthly. Special interest, magazine format, Includes advertising.
$.50 per issue : $6.00 per year : $8.00 per year, U.S.

Current events magazine. Montreal edition = Actualitiés Montréal / *edited by* Josh Zambrowsky (production manager) and Cheryl Rodeck. - *Published by* James Custy. Suite 725, 1010 St. Catherine St. W., Montreal, Que., 1922-
Monthly. Calendar of events, magazine format, 45 p. Language: English and French.
$1.00 per issue : $9.00 per year.

Current legislative digest : an index-digest of current legislation / *edited by* G.L. Starr and J. Craig Paterson. - *Published by* Current Legislative Digest. P.O. Box 126, Sandwich Postal Station, Windsor, Ont. N9C 3Z1, March 1973-
Weekly while the legislature is in session. Legislation, looseleaf format, Includes cumulative index, updating service. Circulation: 300
$37.50 per legislative session.

Current topics / *edited by* Hugh A. Maclean. - *Published by* The Canadian Life Insurance Association. 44 King St. W., Toronto, Ont. M5H 1E9, 1944-
Irregular (approximately 4 issues per year). Association publication, newsletter format, 4 p. Language: English and French. Includes book reviews. Circulation: 7000
Free. Controlled circulation.

Curriculum council quarterly / *sponsored by* Province Association of Protestant Teachers and Provincial Association of Catholic Teachers ; *edited by* Joe White. - *Published by* Provincial Association of Catholic Teachers. 245 Hymus Blvd., Pointe Claire, Que. H9R 1G6, January 1974-
Irregular (approximately 2 issues per year). Association publication, broad sheet format, 1 p.
Controlled circulation.

Curriculum theory network / *edited by* Joel Weiss. - *Published by* Ontario Institute for Studies in Education. 252 Bloor St. W., Toronto, Ont. M5S 1V6 (Subscription address: Publications Sales Dept., 252 Bloor St. W. Toronto, Ont. M5S 1V6) Summer 1968-
Quarterly. Special interest, journal format, 96 p. Includes book reviews, volume index. Back numbers available. Circulation: 1500
Indexed in Can. educ. ind., Curr. ind. j. educ.
$2.50 per issue : $8.00 per year (Libraries and other institutions $10.00). Prepayment required.

Cutlas / *edited by* Jean Heathcote. - *Published by* Library Automation Services. Library. University of Toronto. 130 St. George St., Toronto, Ont. M5S 1A5, October 1975-
Irregular (approximately 10 issues per year). Institutional publication (Universities, schools, etc.), newsletter format, 10 p.
Free.

Cycle Canada : for and about motorcycling in Canada / *edited by* John Cooper. - *Published by* Martin Levesque. Brave Beaver Pressworks Ltd. 423 Sherbourne St., Toronto, Ont. M4X 1K5 (Subscription address: 81A Front St. E., Toronto, Ont) February 1971-
Monthly. Special interest, tabloid format, 40 p. Includes book reviews, film reviews, advertising. Circulation: 15,000
$.60 per issue : $6.00 per year. Prepayment required.

Cycliste canadien *See* Canadian cyclist

Czas = The Times / *edited by* M.K. Szwej. - *Published by* Polish Press Ltd. 1150 Main St., Winnipeg, Man. R2W 3S6, August 1914-
Weekly. Ethnic press, newspaper format, 8 p. Language: Polish. Includes advertising.
$.20 per issue : $8.00 per year : $9.00 per year, foreign.

DATE journal (1960-1963) *See* British Columbia English Teachers' Association. Journal

DA Vinci / *edited by* Allan Bealy. - *Published by* Vehicule art (Montréal) Inc. P.O. Box 813, Postal Station A, Montreal, Que. H3C 2V5, 1973-
Irregular (approximately 3 issues per year). Special interest, magazine format, 60 p. Circulation: 500
ISSN 0315-9914 $2.00 per issue : $6.00 for 3 issues (Institutions $8.00).

Daily commercial news and construction record / *edited by* Terry McAuloffe. - *Published by* Sidney J. Cohen. Southam Business Publications Ltd. 1450 Don Mills Rd., Don Mills, Ont. (Subscription address: 34 St. Patrick St., Toronto, Ont) 1927-
Daily. Business publication, newspaper format, 16 p. Includes advertising. Circulation: 7800
$.50 per issue : $85.00 per year : $110.00 per year, foreign.

The Daily Ryersonian, (1966-1970) *See* Ryersonian

Dairy facts and figures at a glance - *Published by* Dairy Farmers of Canada. 111 Sparks St., Ottawa, Ont. K1P 5B5.
Published in French: Aperçu de l'industrie quelques donnée.
Annual. Statistics, booklet format, 44 p.

Dairy guide - *Published by* R.W. McGuire. The Public Press Ltd. 1760 Ellice Ave., Winnipeg, Man. R34 0B6, February 1970-
Issued every other month. Special interest, magazine format, 24 p. available in microform. Issued as a supplement to Country guide. Circulation: 33,300
Free to qualified subscribers of Country guide. Controlled circulation.

Dairy policy = Politique laitière - *Published by* Dairy Farmers of Canada. 111 Sparks St., Ottawa, Ont. K1P 5B5.
Annual. Association publication. Language: English and French.

The Dalhousie gazette / *edited by* Mary Pat MacKenzie. - *Published by* Council of the Students. Dalhousie University. Dalhousie Student Union Bldg., University Ave., Halifax, N.S., 1868-
Weekly, September-April. Student publication, newspaper format, 20 p. Includes book reviews, film reviews, play reviews, record reviews, advertising, updating service. supplements issued. Circulation: 9000
$5.00 per year. Free.

Dalhousie Labour Institute for the Atlantic Provinces. Proceedings / *sponsored by* Dalhousie Labour University Committee and Institute of Public Affairs. - *Published by* Institute of Public Affairs. Dalhousie University. Halifax, N.S. B3H 3J5, 1961-
Biennial. Institutional publication (Universities, schools, etc.), 75 p.
ISSN 0316-0688 $2.50.

Dalhousie review / *edited by* Allan R. Bevan. - *Published by* Dalhousie University Press Ltd. Dalhousie University, Halifax, N.S. (Subscription address: Room 4413, Killam Library, Dalhousie University, Halifax, N.S.) April 1921-
Quarterly. Scholarly publication, journal format, 200 p. Includes book reviews, advertising, volume index. available in microform. Back numbers available. Circulation: 1000
Indexed in Can. ind., P.A.I.S., M.L.A. int. bib., Annu. bibl. Engl. lang. and lit., MLA abstr., Abstr. eng. stud., Hist. abstr.; Amer. hist. and life, I.B.Z., Soc. sci. journal file.
$2.00 per issue : $6.00 per year : $15.00 for 3 years. $.50 extra is requested to cover bank charges on non Canadian funds. Prepayment required.

Dalhousie University. Dalhousie alumni news / *edited by* P. Harris. - *Published by* Alumni Association. Dalhousie University. Halifax, N.S.
Irregular (approximately 4-5 issues per year). Alumni publication, magazine format, 18 p. Free. Controlled circulation.

Dalhousie University. Institute of Public Affairs. Library. Industrial Relations Reference Library. Accessions list - *Published by* Library. Institute of Public Affairs. Dalhousie University. Halifax, N.S., January 1966-
Bibliography.
ISSN 0316-0904

Dalhousie University. Institute of Public Affairs. Library. Municipal reference library - *Published by* Library. Institute of Public Affairs. Dalhousie University. 1329 LeMarchant St., Halifax, N.S. B3H 3J5, September 1957-
Annual. Bibliography, 20 p. supplements issued. Circulation: 250
ISSN 0316-5027 Free.

Dalhousie University. Institute of Public Affairs. Library. Urban community and regional development accession list - *Published by* Library. Institute of Public Affairs. Dalhousie University. 1329 LeMarchant St., Halifax, N.S. B3H 3J5, July 1970-
Annual. Bibliography, 40 p. supplements issued. Circulation: 500
ISSN 0316-0882 Free.

Dan Brock's historical almanack of London / *edited by* Daniel J. Brock. - *Published by* Applegarth Follies. 156 Albert St., London, Ont. N6A 1M1, March 27, 1975-
Quarterly. Almanac, book format, 90 p. Includes cumulative index. Circulation: 800
ISSN 0316-1404 $3.95 per issue : $15.80 per year. Prepayment required.

Dance in Canada / *edited by* Susan Cohen. - *Published by* Dance in Canada Association. Suite 103, 314 Jarvis St., Toronto, Ont. M5B 2C5, 1975-
Quarterly. Magazine format, 20 p. Language: English and French. Includes advertising. Circulation: 1000
ISSN 0317-9737 $6.50 per year.

Dartmouth chamber news / *sponsored by* Dartmouth Chamber of Commerce ; *edited by* Clyde Horner. - *Published by* Earle Whynot and Associates Ltd. Trade Mart Bldg., Scotia Square, Halifax, N.S. (Subscription address: 12 Portland St., Dartmouth, N.S. B2Y 1G9)
Quarterly. House/company organ, newsletter format,

Data Processing Institute. Proceedings / *edited by* W.E. Jones. - *Published by* Data Processing Institute. P.O. Box 2458, Postal Station D, Ottawa, Ont.
Annual. Association publication, 486 p. Includes advertising.
$3.00. Prepayment required.

Data Processing Management Association of Toronto. D.P.M.A. Toronto chapter news / *edited by* R.K. McKeon. - *Published by* Data Processing Management Association of Toronto. P.O. Box 116, Postal Station F, Toronto, Ont., 1968-
Monthly except July and August. Association publication, magazine format, 24 p.
Circulation: 400
Controlled circulation.

Dateline Winnipeg / *edited by* C.A. Edson. - *Published by* Better Business Bureau of Metropolitan Winnipeg. 204-365 Hargrave St., Winnipeg, Man. R3B 2K3, 1971-
Irregular (approximately 5 issues per year). Association publication, newsletter format, 3 p.
Circulation: 1200
Free to members and other interested groups. Controlled circulation.

Daugavas vanagu menestraksts : latvijas brivibai un labakai nakotnei / *sponsored by* Latvian Relief Society ; *edited by* Vilis Hazners. - *Published by* Daugavas Vanags Publishing Company. 491 College St., Toronto, Ont. M6G 1A5 (Subscription address: 223 High Park Ave., Toronto, Ont. M6P 2S5) January 1965-
Issued every other month. Association publication, magazine format, 80 p. Language: Latvian. Includes book reviews, film reviews, play reviews, record reviews, advertising, volume index. Circulation: 2900
$1.25 per issue : $6.50 per year. Prepayment required.

David Dunlap doings / *edited by* John F. Heard. - *Published by* David Dunlap Observatory. P.O. Box 360, Richmond Hill, Ont. L4C 4G6.
Institutional publication (Universities, schools, etc.).

Davidsonia / *edited by* Roy L. Taylor and Christopher J. Marchant. - *Published by* The Botanical Garden. University of British Columbia. Vancouver, B.C. V6T 1W5, Spring 1970-
Quarterly. House/company organ, magazine format, 10 p. available in microform.
Circulation: 300
ISSN 0045-9739 $1.00 per issue : $4.00 per year.

Day by day *See* Metro guide

De Hollandse krant : the Dutch newsletter / *edited by* R. Schlyecner. - *Published by* R. Schlyecner. Ethnic Publications Ltd. 1330 Harwood St., Vancouver, B.C. (Subscription address: 2231 Bellevue Ave., Coquitlam B.C) October 1969-
Monthly. Ethnic press, newspaper format, 12 p. Language: Dutch and English. Includes advertising. Circulation: 5000
$.25 per issue : $3.00 per year. Prepayment required.

De Nederlandse courant / *edited by* Thea Schryer. - *Published by* MSM Publishers. P.O. Box 2236, Postal Station B, Scarborough, Ont. M1N 2E9, 1953-
Weekly. Ethnic press. Includes advertising.
$6.00 per year.

De nieuwe weg - *Published by* The Dutch-Canadian Association. P.O. Box 1468, Place Bonaventure, Montreal, Que. H5A 1H5, December 1966-
Former title(s): CDCA nieuws (January - November 1966) CDCA (April 1963 - December 1965)
Monthly. Association publication, ethnic press, magazine format, 32 p. Language: Dutch and English. Includes film reviews, advertising. Circulation: 300
$5.00 per year.

The Deaf Canadian magazine / *edited by* Cliff F. Carbin. - *Published by* The Deaf Canadian. P.O. Box 1016, Calgary, Alta. T2P 2K4, Spring-Summer 1975-
Quarterly. Association publication, magazine format, 24 p. Includes book reviews, film reviews, play reviews, record reviews, advertising. Circulation: 60,000
Indexed in Can. educ. ind.
ISSN 0315-145X Controlled circulation. Special rates offered. Prepayment required.

Debates of the legislative assembly of United Canada / *édité par* Elizabeth Gibbs. - *Publié par* Elaine Naives. Centre d'étude du Québec et centre de recherche en histoire économique du Canada français. 5255, ave Decelles, Montréal, Qué. H3T 1V6, février 1971-
Intermittent (approximativement 2 éditions par an). Legislation, 2000 p. Langue(s): anglais et français.

Decision / *edited by* Stuart Richardson. - *Published by* Sales and Marketing Executives of Montreal Inc. Suite 1, 1414 Crescent St., Montreal, Que. H3G 2B6, 1970-
Monthly. Association publication, newsletter format, 2 p. Circulation: 150
Free to members.

Decks awash / *edited by* Susan Sherk. - *Published by* Extension Service. Memorial University of Newfoundland. 21 King's Bridge Rd., St. John's, Nfld., 1963-
Issued every other month. Special interest, magazine format, 45 p. Circulation: 16,000
Free.

Decor : the Canadian journal for decorating retailers / *sponsored by* Canadian Paint and Wallpaper Dealers' Association ; *edited by* W.H. Metherell. - *Published by* Logan Brown Communications Ltd. Suite 506, 56 Esplanade St. E., Toronto, Ont. M5E 1A7, January 1973-
Issued every other month. Trade publication, magazine format, 32 p. Includes advertising. Circulation: 6534
$1.00 per issue. Free. Controlled circulation.

Décormag : le magazine québécois de décoration / *édité par* Claude Béland. - *Publié par* Ginette Gadoury. Les Publications Décormag inc. 181 est, rue Saint-Paul, Vieux-Montréal, Qué. H2Y 1G8, août 1972-
Mensuel. Magazine, 74 p.
Indexé dans RADAR.
$1.50 le numéro : $13.00 par année : $18.00 par année, l'étranger (Par avion $23.00).

Defending all outdoors / *edited by* P.L. Morck. - *Published by* Alberta Fish & Game Association. 212, 8631 - 109 St., Edmonton, Alta. T6G 1E8, June 1967-
Irregular (approximately 5 issues per year). Association publication, newsletter format, 16 p. Includes advertising. Circulation: 10,000
Indexed in North. tit.
$1.00 per year.

Défience mentale *See* Mental retardation

Definitions of play and games - *Published by* SIRLS. Faculty of Human Kinetics and Leisure Studies. University of Waterloo. Waterloo, Ont. N2L 3G1.
Quarterly. Bibliography, computer printout, $20.00 per year. $100.00 subscription to SIRLS required.

Definitions of sport and leisure - *Published by* SIRLS. Faculty of Human Kinetics and Leisure Studies. University of Waterloo. Waterloo, Ont. N2L 3G1.
Quarterly. Bibliography, computer printout, $20.00 per year. $100.00 subscription to SIRLS required.

Delectus seminum et sporarum quae hortus botanicus Montis Regii pro mutua commutatione offert / *édité par* Normand Cornellier. - *Publié par* Jardin Botanique de Montréal. 4101 est, rue Sherbrooke, Montréal, Qué., 1936/1937-
Ancien titre: Index seminum.
Annuel. Publication spécialisée, 32 p. Langue(s): Latin. Tirage: 800
Envoi gratuit.

Delta-K / *edited by* Edward P. Carriger. - *Published by* Mathematics Council. Alberta Teachers' Association. 11010-142 St., Edmonton, Alta. T5N 2R1.
Irregular (approximately 4 issues per year). Association publication, newsletter format, 25-40 p. Circulation: 500
Indexed in Can. educ. ind.
$6.00 per year.

Dem days Labrador - *Published by* Dem Days Labrador. P.O. Box 589, Goose Bay, Labrador, Nfld.
Quarterly.
$1.00 per year.

Democrat / *sponsored by* National Democratic Party of British Columbia ; *edited by* Soren Bech. - *Published by* Democrat Publishing Co. 1881 East Hastings St., Vancouver, B.C., November 1964-
Monthly. Political press, newspaper format, 16 p. Includes advertising. Circulation: 16,000
$.25 per issue : $3.00 per year.

Democratic commitment / *edited by* R.A.H. Robson. - *Published by* British Columbia Civil Liberties Association. 206-207 W. Hastings St., Vancouver, B.C. V6B 1H7.
Issued every other month. Association publication, newsletter format, 6 p. Circulation: 450
$.50 per issue : $3.00 per year. Prepayment required.

Demography of sport and leisure - *Published by* SIRLS. Faculty of Human Kinetics and Leisure Studies. University of Waterloo. Waterloo, Ont. N2L 3G1.
Quarterly. Bibliography, computer printout, $20.00 per year. $100.00 subscription to SIRLS required.

Demonstration school library project newsletter (1972-1973) *See* The Bookmark

Dental education register / *edited by* Association of Canadian Faculties of Dentistry. - *Published by* Council on Education. Canadian Dental Association. 234 St. George St., Toronto, Ont. M5R 2P2, 1970-
Former title(s): Dental students register.
Annual. Association publication, booklet format, 21 p.
ISSN 0315-2669 Free.

Dental guide / *edited by* S. Marr (managing ed.). - *Published by* Southam Business Publications Ltd. 1450 Don Mills Rd., Don Mills, Ont., 1965-
Annual. Professional publication. Includes advertising. Circulation: 10,209

Dental students register *See* Dental education register

La Dépêche / *édité par* Raymond Hivon. - *Publié par* CEGEP de Trois-Rivières. 3500, rue de Courval, Trois-Rivières, Qué. G9A 5E6, novembre 1974-
Hebdomadaire. Publication d'institution (universités, écoles..), bulletin, 6 p. Tirage: 3000
ISSN 0317-0632 Envoi gratuit.

Der Immigrantenbote *See* Der Bote : ein mennonitisches Familienblatt

Dérives : tiers-monde Québec, une nouvelle conjoncture culturelle / *édité par* Le Comité de rédaction et de direction: Jean-Pierre Durand, Nanie Piou, Jean Jonassaint et Pierre Deschamps. - *Publié par* Jean Jonassaint et Jean-Pierre Durand. 3167, rue Duquesne, Montréal, Qué., septembre-octobre 1975-
Bimestriel. Publication spécialisée, magazine, 40 p. Comprend critique de livres, critique de films, publicité. Tirage: 500
$1.50 le numéro : $8.00 par année : $9.00 par année, l'étranger.

Descant / *edited by* Karen Mulhallen. - *Published by* Descant. P.O. Box 314, Postal Station F, Toronto, Ont. M5S 2S8, 1970-
Issued 3 times a year. Special interest, magazine format, 96-128 p. Includes book reviews. Circulation: 350
Indexed in Can. essay and lit. ind.
$4.00 per year (Institutions $8.00).

Design engineering / *edited by* W.M. King. - *Published by* Maclean-Hunter Ltd. 481 University Ave., Toronto, Ont. M5W 1A7, January 1955-
Monthly. Trade publication, magazine format, 70 p. Includes book reviews, volume index. available in microform. Circulation: 10,700
Indexed in Can. B.P.I., I.B.Z.
$2.00 per issue : $12.00 per year : $15.00 per year, U.S., & U.K. : $30.00, per year, foreign. Controlled circulation.

Design product news / *edited by* J.C. Young. - *Published by* Keith A. Watson. Action Communications Ltd. Suite 233, 4 Lansing Sq., Willowdale, Ont. M2J 1T4, 1973-
Issued every other week. Trade publication. Includes advertising.
$8.00 per year.

Despatch. English ed. / *edited by* The Public Relations Director. - *Published by* Canadian Red Cross Society. 95 Wellesley St. E., Toronto, Ont. M4Y 1H6, January 1940-
Also published in French.
Quarterly. Association publication, magazine format, 16 p. Language: English and French. Circulation: 80,000
Free.

Der Deutsche Katholik in Kanada / *edited by* Karl Schindler. - *Published by* St. Patrick's German Congregation. 131 McCaul St., Toronto, Ont., April 1964-
Monthly. Church publication, ethnic publication, magazine format, 24 p. Language: German.
$3.00 per year.

Deutsch-kanadisches Jahrbuch *See* German-Canadian yearbook

Deux tiers *Voir* L'Escargot

Dialog / *edited by* Joe Rosenblatt. - *Published by* J.D. Publishing Co. Suite 19, 501 Yonge St., Toronto, Ont. M4Y 1Y4, 1969-
Cover title: Jewish dialog.
Quarterly. Special interest, magazine format, 72 p. Includes advertising. Circulation: 6000
$2.50 per issue : $10.00 per year.

Dialogue *See* Canadian journal of university continuing education

Dialogue (mars 1972-octobre 1974) *Voir* Nouveau dialogue

Dialogue / *edited by* Sandra E. Stewart. - *Published by* Saskatchewan Association for the Mentally Retarded. 103 Central Chambers, 219 - 22nd St. E., Saskatoon, Sask. S7K 3N9, October 1966-
Former title(s): Outlook (October 1966-October 1968) Newsletter - Saskatchewan Association for the Mentally Retarded.
Quarterly. Association publication, newsletter format, 8 p. Includes book reviews, film reviews. Circulation: 2500
Free.

Dialogue *See* Scene changes

Dialogue / *edited by* Marie Mullally. - *Published by* United Nurses Inc. Suite 200, 345 Victoria Ave., Montreal, Que. H3Z 2N1.
Quarterly. Association publication. Language: English and French. Includes advertising. Circulation: 11,000
$.85 per issue : $3.00 per year. Free to members.

Dialogue : Canadian philosophical review = Dialogue : revue canadienne de philosophie / *edited by* François Duschesneau and John Woods. - *Published by* Canadian Philosophical Association. Suite 46, 1390 Sherbrooke St. W., Montreal, Que. H3G 1K2, June 1965-
Quarterly. Association publication, journal format, 200 p. Language: English and French. Includes book reviews, advertising, cumulative index. Circulation: 1300
Indexed in Phil. ind., Periodex, Math. r.
ISSN 0012-2173 $5.00 per issue : $16.00 per year (Students $5.00). Special rates offered. Prepayment required.

Dialogue : revue canadienne de philosophie *See* Dialogue : Canadian philosophical review

Dialogue : the voice of the bilingual diocese of Yarmouth, Nova Scotia / *parrainé par* Commission Diocésaine des Communications Sociales ; *édité par* Adrienne Friolet. - *Publié par* Guy Léger. C.P. 278, 53, rue Park, Yarmouth, N.S., février 1967-
Mensuel. Publication ecclésiastique, 12 p. Langue(s): français et anglais. Tirage: 6300
$3.00 par année.

Dick MacLean's guide *See* Vancouver magazine

Did you know? (1939) *See* London Chamber of Commerce. Chamber of Commerce news

Dies und das (December 1965-December 1970) *See* Pazifische Rundschau

Digest, business and law journal / *edited by* W.G. Bowden. - *Published by* A.L. Bowden. 1 - 1311 Portage Ave., Winnipeg, Man. R3G 0V3.
Weekly. Special interest, magazine format, $3.00 per issue : $95.00 per year. Prepayment required.

Digest business and law journal - *Published by* Digest Reporting Service Ltd. 38 Dundas St. E., Toronto, Ont., 1960-
Daily. Trade publication. Includes advertising. $98.00 per year.

Digest business and law journal real estate supplement / *edited by* W.G. Bowden. - *Published by* Digest Reporting Service Ltd. 1 - 1311 Portage Ave., Winnipeg, Man. R3G 0V3, August 1971-
Issued twice a year. Directory, magazine format, 32 p. Circulation: 850
$3.00 per issue : $95.00 per year. Prepayment required.

Digeste social - *Publié par* Conseil canadien de développement social. C.P. 3505, Succursale C, 55, ave Parkdale, Ottawa, Ont. K1Y 4G1, 1949-
Ancien titre: Bien-être social canadien (septembre 1949-octobre 1973)
Parait 5 fois l'an. Publication d'association, revue, 28 p. Comprend critique de livres, publicité.
Indexé dans Periodex.
ISSN 0006-2111 $.60 le numéro : $3.00 par année. Abonnements payables à l'avance.

The Dime bag / *sponsored by* Creative Writing Program. - *Published by* The Dime Bag. Room C222, York Hall, Glendon College, 2275 Bayview Ave., Toronto, Ont. M4N 3M6, 1959-
Former title(s): Ventilator (1959-1963)
Issued twice a year. Special interest, magazine format, 35-40 p. Language: English and French. Circulation: 500
$5.00 per year. Free to Glendon students.

Dimensions / *edited by* Mina H. Caunce. - *Published by* Ontario Métis and Non-Status Indian Association. Suite 208, 5300 Yonge St., Willowdale, Ont.
Monthly. Association publication, magazine format, 24 p. Circulation: 2500
$3.00 per year.

Dimensions in health service / *edited by* B.L.P. Brosseau. - *Published by* Canadian Hospital Association. 25 Imperial St., Toronto, Ont. M5P 1C1, February 1924-
Former title(s): Canadian hospital (1924-1974)
Monthly. Association publication, magazine format, 75 p. Includes book reviews, advertising, volume index, updating service. Circulation: 12,265
Indexed in Ind. med., Can. B.P.I., Hosp. abstr.
$1.00 per issue : $10.00 per year : $15.00 per year, U.S. : $20.00 per year, foreign. Controlled circulation. Prepayment required.

Dimensions nouvelles / *parrainé par* Westroc Industries Ltd. 2650 Lakeshore Highway, Mississauga, Ont. L5J 1K4 ; *édité par* R.E. Davis. - *Publié par* John Brown Publishing Associates Ltd. Suite 4B, 1509 ouest, rue Sherbrooke, Montreal, Qué. H4G 1Z7, 1964-
Publié en anglais: New dimensions.
Bimestriel. Revue d'entreprise, magazine, 16 p. Tirage: 26,000
ISSN 0028-4599 Envoi gratuit.

Dinny's digest / *edited by* Fred C. Scott. - *Published by* Calgary Zoological Society. St. George's Island, Calgary, Alta. T2G 3H4, 1969-
Quarterly. Association publication, magazine format, 20 p. Circulation: 6000
$1.00 per issue : $3.00 per year. Subscription included in membership fee. Special rates offered. Prepayment required.

The Diocesan times / *edited by* L.R. Hines. - *Published by* Diocesan Times Publishing Co. 5732 College St., Halifax, N.S. B3H 1X3, 1946-
Monthly except August and September. Church publication, newspaper format, 8 p. Circulation: 18,000
$.20 per issue : $2.00 per year.

Diocèse de Québec. Annuaire / *édité par* Le secrétariat général. - *Publié par* Diocèse de Québec. Eglise catholique. Grand Séminaire, Cité Universitaire, Ste-Foy, Qué. G1K 7P4.
Annuel. Publication ecclésiastique, 230 p.
$3.00.

Diocèse de Saint-Hyacinthe. Annuaire - *Publié par* La Chancellerie. Evêché de St-Hyacinthe. C.P. 190, Saint-Hyacinthe, Qué., 1966-
Annuel. Publication ecclésiastique, 29 p. parution de suppléments. Tirage: 1000
Envoi gratuit.

Diocèse de Trois-Rivieres. Annuaire - *Publié par* La Chancellerie. Evêché de Trois-Rivieres. C.P. 879, 362, rue Bonaventure, Trois Rivières, Qué. G9A 5J9.
Annuel. Publication ecclésiastique, 90 p.
Tirage contrôlé.

Direction / *sponsored by* Mennonite Brethren Bible College (Winnipeg) Pacific College (Fresno, California) and Tabor College (Hillsboro, Kansas) ; *edited by* Delbert Wiens and Howard Loewen. - *Published by* Christian Press. 159 Henderson Highway, Winnipeg, Man. (Subscription address: 77 Henderson Highway, Winnipeg, Man. R2L 1L1) January 1972-
Former title(s): The Voice of the Mennonite Brethren Bible College (1952-1971) Journal of church and society (1965-1971)
Quarterly. Church publication, magazine format, 32 p. Includes book reviews, cumulative index.
$2.00 per year.

Direction / *edited by* Doreen Wilson. - *Published by* Kitchener Public Library. 85 Queen St. N., Kitchener, Ont. N2H 2H1, September 1971-
Irregular (approximately 8 issues per year). Institutional publication (Universities, schools, etc.), newsletter format, 4 p. Includes book reviews, film reviews, record reviews.
Circulation: 1600
ISSN 0315-3436 Free.

Director's newsletter - United Co-operatives of Ontario *See* United Co-operatives of Ontario. UCO leader

Directory of administrative officials in public education - Canada (1948-1970) *See* Canadian Education Association. The C.E.A. handbook

Directory of associations in Canada = Répertoire des associations du Canada / *edited by* Brian Land. - *Published by* University of Toronto Press. 5201 Dufferin St., Downsview, Ont. M3H 5T8, 1973-
Biennial. Directory, book format, 550 p. Language: English and French.
$37.50.

Directory of Canadian chartered accountants / *edited by* R.E. Hourigan. - *Published by* Canadian Institute of Chartered Accountants. 250 Bloor St. E., Toronto, Ont. M4W 1G5.
Annual. Association publication, directory, 375 p. Circulation: 4000
$20.00. Special rates to members only.

Directory of Canadian community funds and councils *See* Directory of Canadian United Ways and Social Planning Councils

Directory of Canadian data processing services firms *Voir* Répertoire des entreprises canadiennes de services informatiques

Directory of Canadian gas utilities - *Published by* Canadian Gas Association. 55 Scarsdale Rd., Don Mills, Ont. M3B 2R3.
Annual. Directory, 120 p.
$2.00. Controlled circulation.

Directory of Canadian scholars and universities interested in Latin American studies = Repertoire des universitaires et universités se spécialisant dans études latino - américaines au Canada / *edited by* Walter C. Soderlund. - *Published by* Canadian Association of Latin American Studies. Room 210, 151 Slater St. Ottawa, Ont. K1P 5H3, 1970-
Former title(s): Directory of scholars in Latin American teaching and research in Canada.
Annual. Association publication, directory, 60 p. Language: English and French ; summaries: English and French. Includes cumulative index.
Free to members.

Directory of Canadian trust companies - *Published by* The Trust Companies Association of Canada. Suite 400, 11 Adelaide St. W., Toronto, Ont. M5H 1L9.
Annual. Directory, 20 p.
Free.

Directory of Canadian United Ways and Social Planning Councils = Le répertoire des Centraides Canada et des conseils de planification sociale - *Published by* United Way of Canada. P.O. Box 3505, Postal Station C, 55 Parkdale Ave., Ottawa, Ont. K1Y 4G1.
Former title(s): Directory of Canadian community funds and councils.
Annual. Directory, 50 p. Language: English and French.
ISSN 0084-9863 $3.00.

Directory of Canadian welfare services = Répertoire des services sociaux canadiens / *edited by* Dorothy Kearns. - *Published by* Canadian Council on Social Development. P.O. Box 3505, Postal Station C, 55 Parkdale Ave., Ottawa, Ont. K1Y 1E5 4G1.
Biennial. Association publication, directory, 210 p. Language: English and French.
ISSN 0084-9871 $6.50 per issue.

Directory of community services (1962-1968) *See* Community services in Metropolitan Toronto

Directory of community services of Greater Montreal *Voir* Répertoire des services communautaires du grand Montreal

Directory of community services of Hamilton and district - *Published by* Social Planning Council of Hamilton. 153 1/2 King St. E., Hamilton, Ont. L8N 1B1.
Annual. Directory, 225 p.
$3.00.

Directory of education studies in Canada / *edited by* Donat Deiseach. - *Published by* Canadian Education Association. 252 Bloor St. W., Toronto, Ont. M5S 1V5, 1968-69-
Former title(s): Education studies completed in Canadian universities (1960 to 1967-68) Research studies in progress in Canadian Universities (1959)
Annual. Directory, book format, 145 p. Language: English and French ; summaries: English and French. Circulation: 600
ISSN 0070-5454 $6.00.

Directory of family names / *edited by* K.F. Collins. - *Published by* Ottawa Branch. Ontario Genealogical Society. 929 Alpine Ave., Ottawa, Ont. K2B 5R9. (Subscription address: P.O. Box 8346, Ottawa, Ont. K1G 3H8) 1972-
Annual. Association publication, 50 p. Includes updating service. supplements issued. Circulation: 300
$1.00.

Directory of health, welfare and recreation services (1938-1960) *See* Community services in Metropolitan Toronto

Directory of law teachers = Annuaire des professeurs de droit - *Published by* Association of Canadian Law Teachers. Faculty of Law, University of B.C., Vancouver, B.C., 1955-
Annual. Association publication, 100 p. Language: English and French.
$2.00.

Directory of libraries in Northwestern Ontario / *edited by* D. M. Meservier. - *Published by* Northwestern Regional Library System. 910 Victoria Ave., Thunder Bay, Ont., 1970-
Annual. Directory, booklet format, 90 p. Includes volume index. Circulation: 150
$2.00.

Directory of Lutheran churches in Canada / *edited by* Walter A. Schultz. - *Published by* Lutheran Council in Canada. 500 - 365 Hargrave St., Winnipeg, Man. R3K 0P8, 1952-
Annual. Church publication, directory. Includes advertising. supplements issued. Circulation: 1300
ISSN 0316-800X $1.50 per issue.

Directory of municipal governments in Metropolitan Toronto - *Published by* Bureau of Municipal Research. Suite 406, 4 Richmond St. E., Toronto, Ont. M5C 1M6.
Irregular. Directory, booklet format, 32 p.
$2.50.

Directory of natural history, conservation and environment organizations of Canada *See* Canadian conservation directory

Directory of psychologists registered in the Province of Ontario - *Published by* Ontario Board of Examiners in Psychology. P.O. Box 221, Postal Station M, Toronto, Ont., 1962-
Annual. Directory, 95 p.
ISSN 0316-0793 Free on request.

Directory of scholars in Latin American teaching and research in Canada *See* Directory of Canadian scholars and universities interested in Latin American studies

Directory of services for Greater Vancouver - *Published by* Community Information Centre. Crisis Intervention and Suicide Prevention Centre of Canada. 1946 W. Broadway, Vancouver, B.C. V6T 1Z2.
Biennial. Directory, looseleaf format, 240 p.
$10.00.

A Directory of sociologists and anthropologists in Canada and their current research *Voir* Annuaire des sociologues et anthropologues au Canada et leur recherche courante

Discover the bible / *sponsored by* Roman Catholic Archdiocese of Montreal ; *edited by* Robert C. Wilkins. - *Published by* Bible Centre of Montreal. 2000 Sherbrooke St. W., Montreal, Que. H3H 1G4, September 1964-
Former title(s): I discover the bible (1964-1969)
Weekly from September to June. Church publication, newsletter format, 6 p. Includes book reviews, volume index. Circulation: 8000
ISSN 0018-912X $6.00 per year : $6.50 per year, foreign. Special rates offered.

Discovery / *edited by* Keith Wade. - *Published by* Vancouver Natural History Society. P.O. Box 3021, Vancouver, B.C. V6B 3X5.
Quarterly. Association publication, magazine format, 10-20 p. Includes book reviews. Circulation: 1300
$2.00 per year. Prepayment required.

Discovery through art / *sponsored by* Saskatchewan Teachers' Federation ; *edited by* Ruth Caron. - *Published by* Saskatchewan Society for Education through Art. P.O. Box 1108, 2317 Arlington Ave., Saskatoon, Sask. S7K 3N3, April 1972-
Former title(s): SSEA newsletter (1970-1971)
Quarterly. Association publication, journal format, 30-35 p. Includes book reviews. Circulation: 175
Subscription included in membership fee $5.00 per year. Controlled circulation. Prepayment required.

Dispatcher / *edited by* Geo. H. Côté. - *Published by* The Sacro Occipital Research Society International. Suite 11, 3465 Côtes-des-Neiges, Montreal, Que., September 1963-
Issued every other month. Association publication, magazine format, 8 p. Includes updating service. Circulation: 450
$3.00 per issue : $15.00 per year : $13.00 per volume. Prepayment required.

Dive Canada / *edited by* Linda Chambers. - *Published by* Ontario Underwater Council. 559 Jarvis St., Toronto, Ont. M4Y 2J1, Spring 1974-
Issued every other month. Association publication, magazine format, 24 p. Includes book reviews, film reviews, advertising.
$.50 per issue : $3.00 per year. Free to members. Controlled circulation.

Diversions / *edited by* Orlee Lord. - *Published by* Burnaby Creative Writers Society. 6450 Gilpin St., Burnaby, B.C. V5J 2H7 (Subscription address: 5512 Neville St., Burnaby, B.C. V5J 2H7) 1969-
Annual. Association publication, magazine format, 40 p. Circulation: 150
$1.00.

Dividend / *edited by* D.M. Cowls. - *Published by* The Mutual Life Assurance Co. of Canada. 227 King St. S., Waterloo, Ont., February 1951-
Irregular (approximately 9 issues per year). House/company organ, magazine format, 20 p. Circulation: 1000
Free. Controlled circulation.

Dividend record - *Published by* Corporation Service. The Financial Post. 481 University Ave., Toronto, Ont. M5W 1A7.
Weekly. Trade publication, 36 p.
$65.00 per year.

Documentation et bibliothèques / *édité par* Hubert Perron. - *Publié par* Association pour l'avancement des sciences et des techniques de la documentation. 360, rue Le Moyen, Montréal, Qué. H2Y 1Y3, 1955-
Ancien titre: Bulletin de l'ALBLF (1955-1972)
Trimestriel. Publication d'association, bulletin, 50 p. Langue(s): français ; sommaires: Français, anglais, espagnol. Comprend critique de livres, publicité, index de volumes, index cumulatif. Tirage: 1700
Indexé dans RADAR, Lib. lit.
ISSN 0315-2340 $2.00 le numéro : $7.00 par année. Abonnements payables à l'avance.

Dofasco illustrated news / *edited by* Robert P. Strachan. - *Published by* Dominion Foundries & Steel Ltd. P.O. Box 460, Hamilton, Ont. L8N 3V5, 1937-
Issued every six weeks. House/company organ, magazine format, 16 p. Circulation: 30,000
Free.

Dogs in Canada / *edited by* Elizabeth M. Dunn. - *Published by* Elizabeth M. Dunn. 59 Front St. E., Toronto, Ont. M5E 1B3, 1889-
Monthly. Special interest, newspaper format, 28 p. Includes book reviews, advertising. supplements issued. Circulation: 15,000
ISSN 0012-4915 $.60 per issue : $6.00 per year, Canada and U.S. : $7.00 per year, foreign : $11.00 for 2 years : $16.00 for 3 years : $23.00 for 5 years.

Doings / *edited by* Gwen Brooks. - *Published by* Three Schools. 296 Brunswick Ave., Toronto, Ont. M5S 2M7, 1967-
Former title(s): Briefly (1966-1967)
Monthly, 10 times a year. Calendar of events, newsletter format, 5 p.
$7.50 per year. Prepayment required.

The Dome / *edited by* Harvey Linnen. - *Published by* Saskatchewan Government Employees' Association. 1440 Broadway Ave., Regina, Sask. S4P 1E2, 1927-
Issued every other month. Association publication, magazine format, 16 p. Circulation: 15,500
Free to members (Retired members $1.00 per year, non-members $1.50).

The Dominion (January 1919-1925) *See* The Bulletin

Dominion Budgerigar Society. Monthly bulletin / *sponsored by* Dominion Budgerigar Society Inc ; *edited by* Ella Stretton. - *Published by* W.J. Sumison. 2 Caldow Rd., Toronto, Ont. (Subscription address: Robt. Stretton, 159 Cowan Ave., Toronto M6K 2N5)
Monthly except July and August. Association publication, magazine format, 24 p. Includes advertising. Circulation: 110
$6.00 per year. Prepayment required.

Dominion churchman *See* Canadian churchman

Dominion law reports / *edited by* Horace Krever. - *Published by* Canada Law Book Ltd. 80 Cowdray Court, Agincourt, Ont. M1S 1S5, 1912-
Weekly. Law reports, magazine format, 160 p.
$26.50 per volume.

Dominionaire / *edited by* Judy Dekker. - *Published by* Sales Promotion Department Head Office. Dominion Life Assurance Company. 111 Westmount Rd. S., Waterloo, Ont., June 1948-
Irregular (approximately 10 issues per year). House/company organ, newsletter format, 4-6 p. Circulation: 850
Free. Controlled circulation.

Domtar news *See* The News

Données provinciales *See* Provincial results general insurance report : the brown chart

Le Dossier du missionnaire / *édité par* Equipe de l'entraide missionnaire inc. - *Publié par* L'Entraide missionnaire inc. 2295, rue Chambly, Montréal, Qué. H1W 3J6, avril 1972-
Annuel. Publication ecclésiastique, bulletin, 40 p. Tirage: 1500
$.75.

Dossiers "vie ouvrière" au service des militants chrétiens du monde ouvrier / *édité par* Paul-Emile Charland. - *Publié par* Jacques Lemay. Oblats de Marie-Immaculée. 1201, rue Visitation, Montréal, Qué. H2L 3B5, janvier 1974-
Ancien titre: Prêtres et laïcs (janvier 1967-décembre 1973) Prêtre aujourd'hui (1958-1966) Action catholique ouvrière (1951-1957)
Mensuel. Publication ecclésiastique, revue, 64 p. Comprend critique de livres, index de volumes. Tirage: 2500
$1.00 le numéro : $6.50 par année : $6.50 le volume. Envoi gratuit. Tarifs spéciaux disponibles. Abonnements payables à l'avance.

Dow Chemical of Canada Ltd. Sarnia Division. SDN Sarnia Division news / *edited by* Michael Thomas. - *Published by* Sarnia Division. Dow Chemical of Canada, Ltd. P.O. Box 3030, Sarnia, Ont. N7T 7M1, March 1, 1974-
Former title(s): Dow maple leaf (July 1947-January 1970)
Weekly. House/company organ, newsletter format, 4 p. Circulation: 1500
Free. Controlled circulation.

Dow maple leaf (July 1947-January 1970) *See* Dow Chemical of Canada Ltd. Sarnia Division. SDN Sarnia Division news

Drainage Engineers' Conference. Proceedings / *edited by* R.W. Irvin. - *Published by* School of Engineering. Ontario Agricultural College. University of Guelph. Guelph, Ont., 1969-
Annual. Association publication, 50 p.
ISSN 0318-3211 $2.00. Prepayment required.

Drassis *See* Greek Canadian action

Drive (January and June 1974) *See* British Columbia Music Educators Association. Newsletter

Drivers' news letter / *edited by* W.F. Murray. - *Published by* Transportation Safety Association of Ontario. 2 Bloor St. E., Toronto, Ont. M4W 3C2, 1957-
Monthly. Association publication, newsletter format, 2 p. Circulation: 22,000
Controlled circulation.

Driving (1972-1974) *See* Touring and travel

La Drogue / *édité par* P. Robert. - *Publié par* Ordre des pharmaciens du Québec. Bureau 160, 1253, ave McGill College, Montréal, Qué. H3B 2Y5, juin 1970-
Intermittent (approximativement 1 éditions par an). Publication d'association, journal, 8 p.
Tirage: 3000
$3.00 le volume.

Droit de parole - *Publié par* Communication Basse-Ville. 435, rue du Roi, Québec, Qué. G1K 2X4, septembre 1974-
Mensuel. Publication d'association, journal, 8 p. parution de suppléments. Tirage: 10,000
ISSN 0315-9574 $5.00 par année.

Drug merchandising / *edited by* W.E. Granger. - *Published by* Robert D. Reid. Maclean-Hunter Ltd. 481 University Ave., Toronto, Ont. m5W 1A7, 1919-
Former title(s): Druggists weekly (1919-1925)
Monthly. Trade publication, magazine format, 60 p. Includes advertising. Circulation: 7000
Indexed in Can. B.P.I.
$1.00 per issue : $8.00 per year : $12.00 per year, U.S. & U.K. : $25.00 per year, foreign. Controlled circulation.

Druggists weekly (1919-1925) *See* Drug merchandising

The Drum / *edited by* T. Butters. - *Published by* Tom Butters. P.O. Box 1069, Inuvik, Northwest Territories., January 1966-
Weekly. Special interest, newspaper format, 12 p. Circulation: 1400
Indexed in North. tit.
$.10 per issue : $15.00 per year.

Drum (1969-1972) *See* The Chronicle

Duca-post newsletter / *edited by* Bert Kruithof. - *Published by* Duca (Toronto) Credit Union Ltd. P.O. Box 1100, Willowdale, Ont. M2N 5T5, 1960-
Monthly. House organ, newsletter format, 24 p. Language: English and Dutch. Includes book reviews, advertising. Circulation: 6300
Free. Controlled circulation.

Duckological / *edited by* W.G. Leitch. - *Published by* Ducks Unlimited (Canada). 1495 Pembina Highway, Winnipeg, Man. R3T 2E2., 1939-
Irregular (approximately 8 issues per year). Special interest, newsletter format, 4 p. Circulation: 45,000
$10.00 per year. Prepayment required.

Durham report (1969-1972) *See* The Chronicle

Dynamo - *Published by* Kitchener-Waterloo Jaycees. P.O. Box 163, Kitchener, Ont., 1950-
Monthly. Association publication, newsletter format, Includes updating service. Circulation: 50

ERBivore / *edited by* Philip J. Currie. - *Published by* Philip J. Currie. 8198 Ave. De L'Epée, Montreal, Que. H3N 2G1, September 1965-
Former title(s): Fantastic worlds of Burroughs and Kline.
Irregular (approximately 1 issue per year). Special interest, magazine format, 16 p. Includes book reviews, film reviews. supplements issued. Circulation: 300
ISSN 0071-1071 $2.00 for 4 units. Controlled circulation. Prepayment required.

The Early bird enthusiast (1909-1939) *See* Canadian Aviation Historical Society. The C.A.H.S. journal

Early childhood education / *edited by* Joyce B. Krysowaty. - *Published by* Early Childhood Education Council. Alberta Teachers' Association. 11010-142 St., Edmonton, Alta, 1967-
Irregular (approximately 2 issues per year). Association publication.
Indexed in Can. educ. ind.

Earthwords (1970-72) *See* Empty belly : a magazine of poetry and communication

Eastern Canada church news / *edited by* A. Lee Abramson. - *Published by* Gloria Belanger. Unit 26, 120 Sullivan Ave., Ottawa, Ont.
Irregular (approximately 10 issues per year). Church publication, newsletter format, 5 p.

Eastern Canadian messenger (to 1932) *See* Canadian union messenger

Eastern mining and oil charts *See* Canadian weekly mining and oil stock charts

Eastern Ontario farmer / *edited by* S.M. Barker. - *Published by* Bowes Publishers Ltd. 994 Adelaide St. S., London, Ont. N6E 1R6, 1974-
Weekly. Trade publication. Includes advertising. Circulation: 4516
$7.00 per year.

Eastern star quarterly (to 1954) *See* The Freemason

Ebauches / *edited by* Alain Poirier. - *Published by* Association canadienne-française de l'Ontario. Pièce 204, 260, rue Dalhousie, Ottawa, Ont. K1L 5E2, septembre 1973-
Trimestriel. Publication d'association, magazine, 32 p. Includes publicité. Tirage: 4000
$5.00 par année. Envoi gratuit. Tirage contrôlé.

L'Echo - *Publié par* Association des pharmaciens détaillants de la province de Québec. 5115, rue St-Denis, Montréal, Qué. Intermittent (approximativement 5-6 édition par an). Publication d'association.

Echo / *edited by* Henry H. Budd. - *Published by* Briercrest Bible Institute. Caronport, Sask. S0H 0S0, 1939-
Quarterly. Church publication, magazine format, 12 p. Circulation: 10,500
Free.

The Echo / *sponsored by* Dorchester Jaycees ; *edited by* Don Ambrose. - *Published by* The Echo. P.O. Box A, Dorchester, N.B. E0A 1M0, 1968-
Monthly. Association publication, newsletter format, 30 p. Language: English and French. Circulation: 600
Free.

Echo : Armenian tabloid / *edited by* Markar Saraphanian. - *Published by* "S. Zavarian" Toronto Chapter. Armenian Youth Federation. 18 Dupont St., Toronto, Ont. M5R 1V2, February 1972-
Monthly. Ethnic press, magazine format, 40 p. Language: Armenian and English. Includes book reviews, play reviews. Circulation: 600
ISSN 0046-1040 $.50 per issue : $5.00 per year : $10.00 per foreign year.

Echo d'Afrique "se connaître pour s'unir" / *édité par* Yas-Paul Assogba. - *Publié par* Layachi Howsnia. Union générale des étudiants africains à Québec. 665, Saint Oliver, Québec, Qué., novembre 1973-
Mensuel. Publication d'association, revue, 30-40 p. parution de suppléments.
$1.50 le numéro : $10.00 par année : $20.00 par année, l'étranger. Tirage contrôlé.

L'Echo de St Francois *Voir* Bonne nouvelle

Echo magazine (1969-1975) *See* O : publication of the arts

Echo Sacré-Coeur : journal du comité d'école / *édité par* Denise Lestage. - *Publié par* Comité Ecole Sacré-Coeur. 775 Sacré-Coeur, Ste-Hyacinthe, Qué., octobre 1974-
Bimensuel. Publication ecclésiastique, bulletin, Tirage contrôlé.

Echoes / *edited by* Winifred M. Anderson. - *Published by* I.O.D.E. 111 Eglinton Ave. E., Toronto, Ont. M4P 1H9, 1902-
Quarterly. House/company organ, magazine format, 44 p. Includes book reviews, advertising. Circulation: 20,000
$.50 per issue : $2.00 per year. Controlled circulation.

Echos du Japon (1972-mars 1975) *Voir* Communiqué de JETRO

Echos du monde classique = Classical news and views / *edited by* C.M. Wells and S.M. Treggiari. - *Published by* Classical Association of Canada. c/o Department of Classical Studies, University of Ottawa, Ottawa, Ont. K1N 6N5. (Subscription address: University of Ottawa, Ottawa, Ont. K1N 6N5) 1956-
Irregular (approximately 3 issues per year). Association publication, journal format, 34 p. Language: English, French, Latin and Ancient Greek. Includes book reviews, advertising. Circulation: 800
$4.00 per year (Institutions $5.00).

L'Éclair / *édité par* Jacques Robert. - *Publié par* Jacques Robert. C.P. 1123, Waterloo, Qué. J0E 2N0, février 1974-
Mensuel. Intérêt général, journal, Tirage: 3000
$3.00 par année.

Eco log information services / *edited by* Celia Fairclough. - *Published by* Corpus Publishers Services Ltd. 6 Crescent Rd., Toronto, Ont. M4W 1T1.
Monthly. Special interest, 40 p. Includes cumulative index, updating service. supplements issued.
ISSN 0315-5056 $125.00 per year. Prepayment required.

Ecole de médecine vétérinaire. Bibliothèque. Nouvelles acquisitions - *Publié par* Bibliothèque. Ecole de médecine vétérinaire. C.P. 5000, Saint-Hyacinthe, Qué., décembre 1969-
Intermittent. Catalogue.
Envoi gratuit.

Ecole nationale de théâtre du Canada - *Publié par* Ecole nationale de théâtre du Canada. 5030 St-Denis, Montréal, Qué. H2J 2L8.

École ontarienne (1956-1968) *Voir* Entre nous

L'Ecole publique - *Publié par* La Commission des écoles catholiques de Montréal. 3737 est, rue Sherbrooke, Montréal, Qué. H1X 3B3. Publié en anglais: The Public school.
Trimestriel. Publication spécialisée, journal, 12 p. Tirage: 250,000
ISSN 0027-0695 Envoi gratuit.

Eco/log week / *edited by* Victor Von Buchstab. - *Published by* Corpus Publishers Services Ltd. 6 Crescent Rd., Toronto, Ont. M4W 1T1, January 11, 1973-
Weekly. Special interest, newsletter format, 6 p. supplements issued.
Indexed in North. tit.
ISSN 0315-0380 $2.50 per issue : $125.00 per year. Prepayment required.

Economic planning / *edited by* Peter Harsany. - *Published by* Academic Publishing Company. P.O. Box 42, Snowdon Station, Montreal, Que., 1965-
Issued every other month. "For agriculture and related businesses", journal format, 16 p. Includes book reviews. Circulation: 5000
Indexed in P.A.I.S.
$1.00 per issue : $5.00 per year : $6.00 per year, foreign.

Economic review - *Published by* Economic Research Department. Provincial Bank of Canada. 215 St. Jacques St., Montreal, Que. H2Y 1M7, May-June 1971-
Issued every other month. Special interest, newsletter format, 6 p. Language: English and French. Circulation: 40,000
Indexed in Can. B.P.I.

Economics leisure and sport - *Published by* SIRLS. Faculty of Human Kinetics and Leisure Studies. University of Waterloo. Waterloo, Ont. N2L 3G1.
Quarterly. Bibliography, computer printout, $20.00 per year. $100.00 subscription to SIRLS required.

Ecospeak : a quarterly publication of Winnipeg Pollution Probe / *edited by* Stephanie Kostiuk. - *Published by* Winnipeg Pollution Probe. 95 Osborne St., Winnipeg, Man. R3L 1Y4, 1971-
Quarterly. Special interest, magazine format, 44 p. Includes book reviews, advertising. supplements issued. Circulation: 2000
$.60 per issue : $2.00 per year.

Ecouri romanesti = Romanian echo / *edited by* A. Baranga. - *Published by* Romanian Canadian Publishing Co. 1862 Eglinton Ave. W., Toronto, Ont.
Monthly. Ethnic press. Language: Romanian. Includes advertising. Circulation: 800

Ecrits du Canada français / *édité par* Claude Hurtubise. - *Publié par* Ecrits du Canada français. Editions La Presse, 7 ouest, rue Saint-Jacques, Montréal, Qué. H2Y 1X9, 1950-
Intermittent (approximativement 1-4 volumes par an). Publication spécialisée, Recueil d'oeuvres, 255 p. Tirage: 2700
Indexé dans RADAR.
$4.50 le numéro : $14.00 pour 4 numéros. Abonnements payables à l'avance.

Ecriture-lecture (été-automne 1974) *Voir* Cul Q

Ecumenism: a quarterly information bulletin / *edited by* Irénée Beaubien. - *Published by* Office national d'oecuménisme. Room 214, 1452 Drummond St., Montreal, Que. H3G 1V9, 1966-
Published in French: Oecuménisme.
Quarterly. Church publication, newsletter format, 14 p. Circulation: 800
$2.00 per year.

Edge / *edited by* Stan Garrod. - *Published by* Educational Research Institute of B.C. 200-1237 Burrard St., Vancouver, B.C. V6Z 1Z6, 1973-
Issued every other month. Institutional publication (Universities, schools, etc.), newsletter format, 8 p. Includes book reviews. Circulation: 6700
Indexed in Can. educ. ind.
$1.00 per year. Free to schools in B.C.

Edibul (1973-1974) *See* Educatus

The Edmonton culture vulture / *edited by* Vic Yanda. - *Published by* Culture Vulture Publishing Ltd. 9204 A 112 St. Edmonton, Alta. (Subscription address: P.O. Box 1784, Edmonton, Alta.) September 1975-
Weekly. General interest, magazine format, Includes book reviews, film reviews, play reviews, record reviews, advertising. supplements issued. Circulation: 5000
$.75 per issue : $25.00 per year : $45.00 for 2 years, $40.00 per year, foreign. Special rates offered. Prepayment required.

Edmonton monthly newsletter / *edited by* Ellen Sharp and Emily Pickett. - *Published by* Association for the Hearing Handicapped. 11024 - 99th Ave., Edmonton, Alta. T5K 2G1.
Monthly. Association publication, newsletter format, 20 p.
$2.00 per year.

The Edmonton Stamp Club. Bulletin / *edited by* Kim T. Frandsen. - *Published by* Edmonton Stamp Club. P.O. Box 399, Edmonton, Alta.
Issued every other month. Association publication, newsletter format, 25 p. Circulation: 400
$4.00 per year.

Education B.C. / *edited by* Janet E. Willson. - *Published by* B.C. School Trustees Association. 1095 Howe St., Vancouver, B.C. V6Z 1P9, January 1971-
Monthly. Association publication, newspaper format, 8 p. Circulation: 10,000
Indexed in Can. educ. ind.
Free.

Education bulletin *See* University of British Columbia. Faculty of Education. The Journal of education of the Faculty of Education

Education Canada / *edited by* Harriett Goldsborough. - *Published by* Canadian Education Association. 8th floor, 252 Bloor St. W., Toronto, Ont. M5S 1V5, 1945-
Former title(s): Canadian education and research digest (1959-1960) Canadian research digest (1959-1960) Canadian education (1945-1960)
Quarterly. Association journal, magazine format, 48 p. Language: English and French. Includes book reviews, advertising, volume index. available in microform. Circulation: 4692
Indexed in Except. child educ. abstr., PHRA, Educ. ind.
ISSN 0013-1253 $1.25 per issue : $5.00 per year. Subscription included in membership fee. Subscriptions sold to libraries and educational institutions. Prepayment required.

Education canadienne et internationale *See* Canadian and international education

Education et société / *édité par* Robert Picard. - *Publié par* Les Editions Bellarmin. 8100, boul. St-Laurent, Montreal, Qué. H2P 2L9, février 1970-
Ancien titre: Collège et famille (janvier 1944-décembre 1969)
Mensuel, sauf janvier, juin, juillet et août. Publication spécialisée, magazine, 24 p. Comprend critique de livres, publicité, index de volumes. Tirage: 1200
Indexé dans Periodex.
$.65 le numéro : $5.00 par année. Tarifs spéciaux disponibles. Abonnements payables à l'avance.

Education perspectives - *Published by* Education Students' Association. Faculty of Education. University of British Columbia. Room 1, Neville Scarfe Building, Faculty of Education, University of British Columbia, Vancouver, B.C., March 1975-
Annual. Institutional publication (Universities, schools, etc.), journal format, 96 p. Includes advertising.
Free. Controlled circulation.

Education studies completed in Canadian universities (1960 to 1967-68) *See* Directory of education studies in Canada

The Educational ABC's of industry - *Published by* Ernest W. Whelpton. Educational ABCs of Canadian Industry Ltd. 643 Yonge St., Toronto, Ont. M4Y 2A2, 1956-
Special interest, magazine format, Language: English and French. Circulation: 1,285,000
Free.

Educational courier / *sponsored by* Ontario Public School Men Teachers' Federation ; *edited by* Edward Lynas. - *Published by* Federation of Women Teachers' Associations of Ontario. 315-207 Queen's Quay W., Toronto, Ont. M5J 1A7, 1930-
Issued 8 times a year. Association publication, magazine format, 34 p. Includes book reviews, advertising, volume index. Circulation: 54,700
Indexed in Can. educ. ind.
$.50 per issue : $4.00 per year.

Educational digest / *edited by* Robert Smith. - *Published by* MacLean-Hunter Ltd. 481 University Ave., Toronto, Ont. M5W 1A7.
Former title(s): School progress; Canadian university and college.
Monthly. Special interest, magazine format, Includes book reviews, film reviews, record reviews, advertising. available in microform. Circulation: 20,000
$2.00 per issue : $12.00 per year : $15.00 per year, U.S. and U.K.: $30.00 per year, foreign. Controlled circulation.

Educational planning / *edited by* Cicely Watson, Russell Hammond and Mark Scarrah. - *Published by* International Society of Educational Planners. c/o Dept. of Educational Planning, OISE, 252 Bloor St. W., Toronto, Ont. M5S 1V6, May 1974-
Quarterly. Association publication, magazine format, 90-110 p. Includes book reviews, volume index. Circulation: 600-700
$5.00 per issue : $15.00 per volume. Subscription included in membership fee.

Educational programs *Voir* Programmes d'éducation

Educational system and sport - *Published by* SIRLS. Faculty of Human Kinetics and Leisure Studies. University of Waterloo. Waterloo, Ont. N2L 3G1.
Quarterly. Bibliography, computer printout, $20.00 per year. $100 subscription to SIRLS required.

Educatus - *Published by* Education Students' Association. Faculty of Education. University of British Columbia. Rm. 1, Neville Scarfe Bldg., Faculty of Education, University of British Columbia, Vancouver, B.C., September 1974-
Former title(s): Incubs (to 1973) Edibul (1973-1974)
Issued every other week. Student publication, newsletter format, 2 p.
Free.

Eglise canadienne : documents et informations / *édité par* Roland-M. Charland. - *Publié par* Editions Fides. 245 est, boul. Dorchester, Montréal, Qué., janvier 1968-
Mensuel. Publication ecclésiastique, revue, 32 p. Comprend index de volumes. Tirage: 4000
Indexé dans Periodex, RADAR.
ISSN 0013-2322 $.70 le numéro : $7.00 (relie $12.00) : $8.50 par année, l'étranger (Par avion $10.00).

Eglise catholique. Archidiocèse de Montréal. Bottin - *Publié par* La Chancellerie de Montréal. 2000 ouest, rue Sherbrooke, Montréal, Qué. H3H 1Q4.
Annuel. Publication ecclésiastique, Bottin, 225 p.
ISSN 0317-8463 $3.50.

Eglise catholique. Archidiocèse d'Ottawa. Annuaire = Catholic Church. Archdiocese of Ottawa. Directory - *Publié par* Les Archives de L'Archdiocèse d'Ottawa (A.A.O.). Eglise catholique. 256 King Edward, Ottawa, Ont. K1N 7M1, 1927-
Annuel. Publication ecclésiastique, 100 p. Langue(s): français et anglais. Tirage: 600
$2.00 le numéro.

Eglise catholique. Diocèse de Mont-Laurier. Annuaire diocésain / *édité par* M. André Chalifoux. - *Publié par* Service diocésain de pastorale. 750, rue Charette, Mont-Laurier, Qué. J9L 2G2, 1936-
Annuel. Annuaire, 70 p. Comprend Mises à jour. parution de suppléments. Tirage: 275
$1.50.

Eglise catholique. Diocèse de Saint-Jean-de-Québec. Annuaire / *édité par* Secrétariat général du diocèse. - *Publié par* Centre diocésain. C.P. 40, 740, boul. Ste-Foy, Longeuil, Qué. J4K 4X8, 1934-
Bi-annuel. Qy, 150 p.

Eglise catholique. Diocèse de Trois-Rivières. Annuaire - *Publié par* Chancellerie du diocèse de Trois-Rivières. C.P. 879, 362, rue Bonaventure, Trois-Rivières, Qué.
Annuel. Annuaire, publication ecclésiastique, magazine, 90 p.

L'Eglise de Montréal / *édité par* Jean-Paul Rivet. - *Publié par* Archevêché de Montréal. Eglise catholique. 200 ouest, rue Sherbrooke, Montréal, Qué. H3H 3G4, 1882-
Ancien titre: Votre église (mars 1967-décembre 1967) La Semaine religieuse de Montréal (1882-1967)
Hebdomadaire. Publication ecclésiastique, revue, 16 p. Tirage: 2100
$.30 le numéro : $12.00 par année : $14.00 par année l'étranger.

Eglise de Québec (1967-1970) *Voir* Pastorale - Québec : revue de l'église de Québec

Eglise et théologie / *édité par* Léo Laberge. - *Publié par* Université de St-Paul. 223, rue Main, Ottawa, Ont., janvier 1970-
Intermittent (approximativement 3 éditions par an). Publication d'institution (universités, écoles..), revue, 150 p. Langue(s): français et anglais ; sommaires: français et anglais. Tirage: 300
Indexé dans I.B.Z.
$5.00 le numéro : $12.00 par année. Tarifs spéciaux disponibles. Abonnements payables à l'avance.

Ego / *edited by* Ray Lancashire (Ed. dir.). - *Published by* Michael Lands. Harrison-Lands Publications. Suite 311, 1396 St. Catherine St. W., Montreal, Que. H3G 1P6, 1971-
Quarterly. Trade publication. Language: English and French. Includes advertising.
$6.00 per year : $15.00 for 3 years.

Either/Or *See* Mudcreek magazine

Elan / *sponsored by* British Columbia Association of Teachers' of Modern languages. - *Published by* B.C. Teachers' Federation. 105, 2235 Burrard St., Vancouver, B.C. V6J 3H9, February 1970-
Former title(s): British Columbia Association of Teachers' of Modern Languages. Newsletter (November 1962-November 1969)
Irregular (approximately 10 issues per year). Association publication, newsletter format, 10 p. Language: Spanish, English, German and French.
Available to members only. Controlled circulation.

Elan *Voir* Corporation professionnelle des travailleurs sociaux du Quebéc. Bulletin

Elan-image / *edited by* Eileen Collyer. - *Published by* James H. Collyer. Intercol Publishing Company Ltd. 23 McNider, Outremont, Que. H2V 3X4, 1967-
Quarterly. Trade publication. Language: English and French. Includes advertising.

The Elder statesman / *edited by* Anne Woods. - *Published by* Bryon Lawes and Assoc. 301-1587 W. 8th Ave., Vancouver, B.C., 1958-
Irregular (approximately 10 issues per year). Published as an official newspaper for senior citizens, newspaper format, 18 p. Includes book reviews, advertising. Circulation: 17,400
$.20 per issue : $2.00 per year.

L'Electeur / *parrainé par* Parti libéral de Québec ; *édité par* Lucette St-Amant. - *Publié par* Compagnie de publication la réforme ltée. 1010 est, rue Ste-Catherine, Montréal, Qué.
Publication politique.
$.25 le numéro : $2.00 par année. Envoi gratuit.

The Electric power communicator / *edited by* Bill Gusen. - *Published by* Corpus Publishers Services Ltd. 6 Crescent Rd., Toronto, Ont. M4W 1T1, June 1973-
Weekly. Trade publication, newsletter format, 4 p. Includes volume index.
$85.00 per year. Prepayment required.

The Electric power communicator / *edited by* A.I. Reid. - *Published by* Teccom Publications. 3176 Eglinton Ave. E., Scarborough, Ont. (Subscription address: P.O. Box 1010, Postal Station C, Scarborough, Ont. M1H 2X4) June 1973-
Issued every other week. Trade publication, newsletter format, 8 p.
$60.00 per year. Prepayment required.

Electrical business / *edited by* Alex Watson. - *Published by* Kerrwil Publications Ltd. 30 Eglinton Ave. E., Toronto, Ont. M4P 1B6, 1964-
Monthly. Trade publication, newspaper format, 16 p. Circulation: 16,000
Indexed in Can. B.P.I.
ISSN 0013-4244 $.35 per issue : $5.00 per year : $9.00 per year, foreign (Airmail $20.00). Controlled circulation.

Electrical contractor and maintenance supervisor / *edited by* George McNevin. - *Published by* Maclean-Hunter Ltd. 481 University Ave., Toronto, Ont. M5W 1A7.
Monthly. Trade publication, magazine format, 70 p.
$1.00 per issue : $10.00 per year : $12.00 per year, U.S. and U.K. : $25.00 per year, foreign. Controlled circulation.

Electrical engineering : Canadian universities : research abstracts and reports (1962-1964) *See* Electrical engineering research abstracts : Canadian universities

Electrical engineering research abstracts : Canadian universities / *edited by* J. Douglas. - *Published by* Department of Electrical Engineering. University of British Columbia. Vancouver, B.C. V6T 1W5, 1962-
Former title(s): Electrical engineering : Canadian universities : research abstracts and reports (1962-1964)
Annual. Abstracts/summaries, magazine format, 135 p. Language: English and French. Includes volume index.
Controlled circulation.

Electrical equipment news / *edited by* Bryan Barney. - *Published by* Southam Business Publications Ltd. 1450 Don Mills Rd., Don Mills, Ont. M3B 2X7, 1956-
Trade publication. Includes advertising. Circulation: 18,068
$8.00 per year : $14.00 for 2 years : $12.00 per year, U.S. : $30.00 per year, foreign.

Electron ISSN 0013-4759 (February 1964-January 1974) *See* Audio Scene Canada

Electron magazine (1964-1974) *See* Audio scene Canada

Electronic procurement index for Canada / *edited by* Geoff Spark. - *Published by* Southam Business Publications Ltd. 1450 Don Mills Rd. Don Mills, Ont. M3B 2X7, 1953-
Annual. Directory, trade publication, magazine format, 180 p. Includes advertising.
$8.00 : $12.00 foreign. Controlled circulation.

Electronics and communications / *edited by* Geoff Spark. - *Published by* Southam Business Publications Ltd. 1450 Don Mills Rd., Don Mills, Ont. M3B 2X7, 1953-
Monthly. Trade publication, newspaper format, 40 p. Includes advertising.
$1.00 per issue : $12.00 per year : $14.00 per year, foreign. Controlled circulation. Prepayment required.

Electronics communicator / *edited by* Gordon D. Hutchison. - *Published by* Evert Communications. 411-56 Sparks St., Ottawa, Ont. K1P 5A9, May 1970-
Weekly. "Current news and commentary for executives in manufacturing, R & D, governments, universities, telecommunications", newsletter format, 8 p. supplements issued. Circulation: 1000
ISSN 0046-1733 $60.00 per year. Prepayment required.

Elements : translating theory into practice / *edited by* K. Allen Neufeld. - *Published by* Department of Elementary Education. The University of Alberta. Edmonton, Alta. T6G 2E1, September 1969-
Monthly. Institutional publication, newsletter format, 6 p. Includes volume index. Circulation: 1200
Indexed in Can. educ. ind., Curr. ind. j. educ.
ISSN 0046-1792 .35 per issue : $3.00 per year : $5.50 for 2 years : $8.00 for 3 years. Special rates offered. Prepayment required.

Elements of technology / *edited by* Richard Guerrier. - *Published by* Chesswood House Publishing Ltd. Suite 103, 542 Mount Pleasant Rd., Toronto, Ont. M4S 2M7, 1969-
Quarterly. Includes advertising. Circulation: 7906
Indexed in Can. educ. ind.
$4.00 per year : $6.00 for 2 years.

Elite / *edited by* Adrian Waller. - *Published by* David S. Wells. J.E.M. Publications Ltd. 300 Decarie Blvd., Montreal, Que. H4N 2M2, 1974-
Issued every other month. Magazine format, Includes advertising.

The Elizabeth Fry Society. Peel-Halton Branch. Newsletter / *edited by* Margaret McDyre. - *Published by* Peel-Halton Branch. The Elizabeth Fry Society. 33 Main St. N., Brampton, Ont.
Irregular (approximately 5-6 issues per year). Association publication, newsletter format, 3 p. Circulation: 110

Ellipse / *édité par* Richard Giguère et Larry Shouldice. - *Publié par* Ellipse. C.P. 10, Faculté des Arts, Université de Sherbrooke, Sherbrooke, Qué.
Paraît 3 fois par an. Publication spécialisée, revue, Langue(s): français et anglais.
Indexé dans RADAR, Can. essay and lit. ind.
ISSN 0046-1830 $5.00 par année.

Emergency librarian / *edited by* Phyllis Yaffe and Sherrill Cheda. - *Published by* Barbara Clubb. 697 Wellington Cres., Winnipeg, Man. R3M 0A7, September 1973-
Issued 6 times per year. Special interest, magazine format, 26-40 p. Includes book reviews, record reviews. available in microform. Circulation: 500
Indexed in Can. bk. rev. dig.
ISSN 0315-8888 $.75 per issue : $7.00 per year : $9.00 per year, foreign. Prepayment required.

The Emery weal - *Published by* North Hill News Ltd. P.O. Box 3160, Postal Station B, Calgary, Alta. T2M 4L7.
Weekly. Student publication. Includes advertising. Circulation: 3200

Empire Club of Canada. Addresses / *edited by* The President. - *Published by* The Empire Club of Canada. 461 King St. W., Toronto, Ont. M5V 1K7, 1903-1904-
Annual. Association publication, 400 p.
Not available on request or on order. Sent free to every library in Canada above elementary level.

Employee benefit plan bulletin (1951-1958) *See* Mercer actuarial bulletin

Employers' Association of Saskatchewan. Bulletin / *edited by* Ralph Purdy. - *Published by* Employers' Association of Saskatchewan. 1717 - 13th Ave., Regina, Sask. S4P 3A2, 1943-
Irregular (approximately 8 issues per year). Association publication, newsletter format, 2 p. Circulation: 180

Employment opportunities handbook, Canada. English ed. - *Published by* The University and College Placement Association. 254A Main St. N., Markham, Ont. L3P 1Y7, September 1970-
Annual. Association publication, magazine format, 150 p. Circulation: 62,000
ISSN 0316-8972 $4.00 per year. Free to graduates at post-secondary institutions. Controlled circulation.

Employment opportunities handbook = Répertoire des possibilités d'emploi Canada. Bilingual edition - *Published by* University and College Placement Association. P.O. Box 356, Markham, Ont. L3P 3J8, September 1970-
Annual. Special interest, magazine format, 240 p. Language: English and French. Circulation: 62,000
ISSN 0316-8980 $5.00 per year. Free to graduates at post secondary institutions.

Employment opportunities handbook Canada. Western ed. - *Published by* University and College Placement Association. 254A Main St. N., Markham, Ont. L3P 1Y7, September 1970-
Annual. Association publication, magazine format, 150 p. Circulation: 62,000
ISSN 0316-8972 $4.00. Free to graduates of post-secondary institutions. Controlled circulation.

Empty belly : a magazine of poetry and communication / *edited by* Charles Tidler. - *Published by* Orphan Universe Press. P.O. Box 14, Ganges, B.C. V0S 1E0, May 1972-
Former title(s): Earthwords (1970-72) Wordjock (1967-70)
Irregular (approximately 2 issues per year). Special interest, magazine format, 24-32 p. Language: English and French. Includes book reviews. Circulation: 200
$2.50 per issue (Individuals $1.00) : $6.00 per year : $10.00 per year, foreign. Controlled circulation. Special rates offered. Prepayment required.

En église : vie de l'église du diocèse de Chicoutimi / *édité par* Yves Gagnon. - *Publié par* L'abbé Yves Gagnon. Office des communications sociales. Diocèse de Chicoutimi. Eglise catholique. 679, rue Chabanel, Chicoutimi, Qué. G7H 3S5, janvier 74-
Mensuel. Publication ecclésiastique, journal, 4 p. Tirage: 1500
$2.00 par année. Envoi gratuit.

En grande / *édité par* François Aubin. - *Publié par* Société d'énergie de la Baie James. 21iéme étage, 800 est, boul. de Maisonneuve, Montréal, Qué. H2L 4M8, décembre 1973-
Mensuel. Publication d'association, journal, 24 p. Tirage: 7500
Envoi gratuit.

En orbite *Voir* L'Orbite

Encore / *edited by* Andrea Mann. - *Published by* Edmonton Symphony Society. P.O. Box 4232, Edmonton, Alta. T6E 4T2, September 1970-
Irregular (approximately 12 issues per year). Program, magazine format, 16 p. Includes advertising. Circulation: 4000
Free to members.

Encounter : program bulletin / *edited by* Janet Fisher. - *Published by* The Baptist Union of Western Canada. 4404 16th St. S.W., Calgary, Alta. T2T 4H9, January 1970-
Former title(s): CE news.
Irregular (approximately 3-4 issues per year). Church publication, newsletter format, Circulation: 1800
Free.

The End - *Published by* Vanier College. 821 Ste Croix Blvd., St-Laurent, Que.
Issued twice a month. Student publication. Includes advertising. Circulation: 4000

End times messenger / *edited by* Irvin W. Ellis and Robert A. Larden. - *Published by* Apostolic Church of Pentecost of Canada, Inc. c/o Irvin W. Ellis, 4907-84 Avenue N.E., R.R. 6, Calgary, Alta. T2M 4L5 (Subscription address: 4-3026 Taylor St. E., Saskatoon, Sask. S7H 4J2)
Monthly. Church publication, magazine format, 23 p.
$.35 per issue : $3.00 per year : $5.00 for 2 years.

Energy analects / *edited by* Hugh McIntyre. - *Published by* Corpus Publishers Services Ltd. 6 Crescent Rd., Toronto, Ont. M4W 1T1, June 8, 1972-
Weekly. Trade publication, newsletter format, 8 p. supplements issued.
ISSN 0315-1654 $4.00 per issue : $195.00 per year. Prepayment required.

Energy processing / Canada / *edited by* Jim Armstrong. - *Published by* Sanford Evans Publishing (Alberta) Ltd. Suite 1, 5512 Macleod Trail S.W., Calgary, Alta. T2H OJ5, 1908-
Irregular (approximately 8 issues per year). Trade publication. Includes advertising. Circulation: 6751
Indexed in Can. B.P.I.

L'Enfant exceptionnel / *édité par* Jacques Lalumière. - *Publié par* Conseil du Québec de l'enfance exceptionnelle. 2765, chemin Côte Ste-Catherine, Montréal, Qué. H3T 1B5, mai 1965-
Trimestriel. Publication d'association, revue, 32 p. Tirage: 2000
Indexé dans RADAR, Can. educ. ind.
$1.00 le numéro : $3.00 par année.

Engineering / *edited by* K. Gibbons. - *Published by* F.M. Weston. Canadian Technical Publications Ltd. P.O. Box 887, Postal Station F, 36B Prince Arthur Ave., Toronto, Ont. M5R 1A9, 1957-
Trade publication. Includes advertising. Circulation: 61,557
$6.00 per year : $15.00 per year, foreign.

Engineering and contract record / *edited by* T. Brandon Jones. - *Published by* D.R. Mackenzie. Southam Business Publications Ltd. 1450 Don Mills Rd., Don Mills, Ont. M3B 2X7, 1887-
Incorporating: Canadian pit and quarry. Monthly. Trade publication, magazine format, 110 p. Includes book reviews. Circulation: 18,500
Indexed in Can. B.P.I., Arct. bibl.
ISSN 0013-7804 $1.00 per issue : $13.00 per year : $39.00 per year, foreign. Controlled circulation.

Engineering digest / *edited by* W.H. Meyfarth. - *Published by* C.F. Broad. Canadian Engineering Publications Ltd. 46 St. Clair Ave. E., Toronto, Ont. M4T 1N2, 1954-
Monthly except for July and December. Professional publication, magazine format, 68 p. Includes book reviews, advertising, volume index, cumulative index. available in microform. Circulation: 56,375
$2.00 per issue : $15.00 per year : $20.00 per year, foreign. Distributed to registered professional engineers residing in Canada.

The Engineering journal / *edited by* Byron T. Kerr. - *Published by* The Engineering Institute of Canada. 2050 Mansfield St., 700 EIC Building, Montreal, Que. H3A 1Y9, 1918-
Former title(s): Society of Civil Engineers. Transactions (1887-1917)
Irregular (approximately 6 issues per year). Association publication, journal format, 80 p. Language: English (French) ; summaries: English (French). Includes book reviews, advertising, volume index. Circulation: 18,000
Indexed in Eng. ind., I.B.Z., Arct. bibl.
$2.00 per issue : $10.00 per year to EIC members : $14.00 per year (Canada, Br. Commonwealth, France, U.S., Mexico) : $16.00 per year, foreign. Controlled circulation.

Engineering manpower news *Voir* Main d'oeuvre en génie bulletin

The English quarterly / *edited by* Anthony Hopkins and Grace Jolly. - *Published by* Canadian Council of Teachers of English. 2275 Bayview Ave., Toronto, Ont. (Subscription address: 237 Yonge Blvd., Toronto, Ont) 1967-
Quarterly. Association publication, magazine format, 80-100 p. Includes book reviews, advertising, cumulative index. available in microform. Circulation: 1000
Indexed in Can. educ. ind., Curr. ind. j. educ.
ISSN 0013-8355 $15.00 per year. Prepayment required.

English studies in Canada / *sponsored by* Association of Canadian University Teachers of English ; *edited by* Lauriat Lane. - *Published by* University of Toronto Press. 5201 Dufferin St., Downsview, Ont. M3H 5T8 (Subscription address: 5201 Dufferin St., Downsview, Ont. M3H 5T8) 1975-
Quarterly. Association publication, journal format, 150 p.
$12.00 per year. Subscription included in membership fee $12.00 per year.

The English teacher - (Fall 1961 to March 1969) *See* Alberta English

Enquête annuelle sur les employés de bureau *See* Annual survey of clerical employees

The Enquirer (October-December 1971) *See* Christian inquirer

The Enquirer (1970-1972) *See* The Christian inquirer

Les Enseignants / *édité par* Fernand Houde. - *Publié par* Fernand Houde. Le Journal Les enseignements ltée. 767, rue Demers, Saint-Jean, Qué. J3B 4W1, 1970-
Mensuel. Publication spécialisée, journal, 16 p. Comprend critique de livres, critique de pièces de théâtre, publicité. Tirage: 5000
$.35 le numéro : $3.50 par année : $5.00 par année, l'étranger.

L'Enseignement (septembre 1947-juin 1970) *Voir* Ligne directe

Ensemble : journal d'information coopérative / *édité par* Jean-Paul Légaré. - *Publié par* Les Editions Solidarité Inc. 2030, boul. Père Lelièvre, Québec, Qué., janvier 1940-
Paraît tous les 15 jours. Revue d'entreprise, journal, 16 p.Aussi sous microform. Tirage: 21,000
$3.00 par année : $4.00 par année, l'étranger. Abonnements payables à l'avance.

The Enterprise / *edited by* Perry V. Allaby. - *Published by* Canadian Baptist Overseas Mission Board. 217 St. George St., Toronto, Ont. M5R 2M2, September 1974-
Quarterly. Church publication, magazine format, 30 p. Circulation: 5500
$.50 per issue : $2.00 per year.

Enterpriser - *Published by* Alberta Chamber of Commerce. Room 212, 10201-104th St., Edmonton, Alta.
Irregular (approximately 5 issues per year). House/company organ, newsletter format, 6 p.

Entertainer / *edited by* Anna Scott Draper. - *Published by* Entertainer Magazines Inc. 940 Main St. W., Hamilton, Ont. L8S 1B1.
Monthly. Calendar of events, newspaper format, Circulation: 115,000
$.75 per issue : $6.00 per year. Distributed free in certain areas.

Entertainment Atlantic / *edited by* George Topp. - *Published by* Entertainment Atlantic Publications Ltd. P.O. Box 44, Moncton, N.B. E1C 8K6, January 1972-
Monthly. Calendar of events, newspaper format, 28 p. Includes book reviews, film reviews, play reviews, record reviews, advertising. Circulation: Summer 45,000 Winter 25,000
$.40 per issue : $4.00 per year. Free in hotels etc.

Entomological Society of British Columbia. Journal of the Entomological Society of British Columbia / *edited by* H.R. MacCarthy. - *Published by* Entomological Society of British Columbia. 6660 N.W. Marine Dr., Vancouver, B.C. V6T 1X2 (Subscription address: c/o Secretary-treasurer, 2819 Graham St., Victoria, B.C. V8T 3Z3) 1966-
Former title(s): Entomological Society of British Columbia. Proceedings (1906-1965)
Annual. Association publication, journal format, 60 p. Includes book reviews. available in microform.
$4.00 per year. Available on exchange. Prepayment required.

Entomological Society of British Columbia. Proceedings (1906-1965) *See* Entomological Society of British Columbia. Journal of the Entomological Society of British Columbia

Entomological Society of Canada. Bulletin / *edited by* D.C. Eidt. - *Published by* Entomological Society of Canada. 1320 Carling St., Ottawa, Ont. K1Z 7K9, 1969-
Quarterly. Association publication, magazine format, 40 p. Language: English and French. Includes book reviews. available in microform. Circulation: 2000
Indexed in Biol. abstr.
Available only with subscription (membership) to the volume of the Canadian entomologist in which it occurs.

Entomological Society of Canada. Memoirs / *edited by* Paul Morrisson. - *Published by* Entomological Society of Canada. 1320 Carling St., Ottawa, Ont. K1Z 7K9.
Former title(s): Entomological Society of Canada. Supplements of the society.
Irregular (approximately 2-8 issues per year). Association publication, magazine format, 80-500 p. Language: English and French ; summaries: French and English. available in microform. Circulation: 2000
Indexed in Biol. abstr.
Available only with subscription or membership to the volume of Canadian entomologist in which they occur.

Entomological Society of Canada. Supplements of the society *See* Entomological Society of Canada. Memoirs

Entomological Society of Quebec. Annals *Voir* Société entomologique du Québec. Annales.

Entomological Society of Quebec. Memoirs *Voir* Société entomologique du Québec. Mémoires

Entrance requirements for schools of nursing and schools of practical nursing - *Published by* Canadian Nurses' Association. 50 The Driveway, Ottawa, Ont. K2P 1E2, 1971/72-
Annual. Association publication, 6 p.
Language: English and French.

Entre nous / *édité par* Lise Gareau. - *Publié par* Association des enseignants franco-ontariens. Suite 202, 1427, chemin Ogilvie, Ottawa, Ont. K1J 8M7, janvier 1969-
Ancien titre: École ontarienne (1956-1968)
Intermittent (approximativement 6 éditions par an). Publication d'association, revue, 20-24 p. Comprend publicité, index de volumes, Mises à jour. parution de suppléments. Tirage: 5700
$.75 le numéro : $4.00 par année.
Abonnements payables à l'avance.

Entretiens d'oraison : message spirituel / *édité par* Fernande Charbonneau. - *Publié par* Fernande Charbonneau. 4120, ave de Vendôme, Montréal, Qué. H4A 3N1, septembre-octobre 1974-
Bimestriel. Publication spécialisée, bulletin, 16 p.
ISSN 0316-9227 $.40 le numéro : $2.00 par année : $3.00 par année, l'étranger.
Abonnements payables à l'avance.

Envergure *See* Scope

L'Envers du décor / *édité par* Anne Le Dain. - *Publié par* Théâtre du nouveau monde. 84 ouest, rue Ste-Catherine, Montréal, Qué., novembre 1968-
Intermittent (approximativement 7 éditions par an). Organe interne/officiel, journal, 8 p.
Tirage: 10-15,000
Gratuit aux abonnés du Théatre du nouveau monde.

Environment probe : Saskatchewan's environment magazine / *edited by* Mrs. J.F.C. Wright. - *Published by* Saskatoon Environmental Society. P.O. Box 1372, Saskatoon, Sask. S7K 3N9, November 1972-
Issued every other month. Association publication, magazine format, 20 p. Includes book reviews, advertising.
ISSN 0316-0033 $.50 per issue : $3.00 per year.

Environmental Centre of Greater Victoria. Newsletter - *Published by* Environmental Centre of Greater Victoria. Camosun College, 1950 Lansdowne Rd., Victoria, B.C.
Issued every other month. Institutional publication (Universities, schools, etc.), newsletter format, 4-6 p. Circulation: 570

Environmental control newsletter - *Published by* CCH Canadian Ltd. 6 Garamond Ct., Don Mills, Ont. M3C 1Z5.
Issued twice a month. Special interest, looseleaf format, 8 p. Includes volume index. supplements issued.
$70.00 per year : $130.00 for 2 years.
Prepayment required.

Environmental education / *edited by* Margot Reynolds and Doug Torgerson. - *Published by* Pollution Probe. 43 Queen's Park Cres. E., Toronto, Ont., February 1973-
Irregular (approximately 6 issues per year). Association publication, newsletter format, 20 p. Includes book reviews. Circulation: 1000
$2.00 per issue (Institutions $3.00).

Environmental systems industries / *edited by* Thomas W. Lazenby. - *Published by* Frank R. Walker. Wadham Publications Ltd. 109 Vanderhoof Ave., Toronto, Ont. M4G 2V2, 1969-
Former title(s): Hydronic and plumbing industries.
Monthly. Trade publication. Includes advertising. Circulation: 11,739
Indexed in Can. B.P.I.

Envol (1972) *Voir* L'Envol de la danse

L'Envol de la danse / *édité par* Jeanne d'Arc Dubé. - *Publié par* Grands ballets canadiens. 5465, Chemin de la Reine-Marie, Montréal, Qué. H3X 1V5, octobre 1972-
Ancien titre: Envol (1972)
Trimestriel. Publication d'institution (universités, écoles..), magazine, 12 p.
Langue(s): français et anglais. Tirage: 12,000
Envoi gratuit.

L'Envolée dans l'aujourd'hui l'église - *Publié par* Service de préparation à la vie. 6984, rue Fabre, Montréal, Qué. H2E 2B2, septembre 1973-
Mensuel. Publication ecclésiastique, bulletin, 10 p. Tirage: 1100
$.25 le numéro : $5.00 par année.

L'Epicier / *édité par* D. Desjardins. - *Publié par* F. Maurice Shore. Maclean-Hunter Ltd. 481 University Ave., Toronto, Ont.(adresse d'abonnement: 625, ave President Kennedy, Montréal, Qué. H3A 1K5) 1946-
Intermittent (approximativement 10 éditions par an). Comprend publicité. Tirage: 7853
$1.00 le numéro : $8.00 par année : $14.00 2 ans : $10.00 par année, E.U. et France : $25.00 par année, l'étranger.

Epigram - *Published by* Epilepsy Association of Calgary. 2422 - 5th Ave. N.W., Calgary, Alta. T2R 0M8.
Monthly. Association publication, newsletter format, 3 p. Includes book reviews.
Free.

Epilepsy Association of Metropolitan Toronto. Newsletter - *Published by* Epilepsy Association of Metropolitan Toronto. Suite 205, 90 Eglinton Ave. E., Toronto, Ont. M4P 1A6, November 1973-
Quarterly. Association publication, newsletter format, 4 p. Circulation: 1000

The Equestrian Image : Canadian all breeds magazine / *edited by* Pat Mellen. - *Published by* The Equestrian Image. R.R. 5, Fenwick, Ont. L0S 1C0, November 1973-
Monthly. Special interest, magazine format, 48 p. Includes book reviews, film reviews, advertising. supplements issued. Circulation: 3240
ISSN 0319-8731 $.75 per issue : $5.00 per year : $5.50 per year, foreign. Controlled circulation. Special rates offered. Prepayment required.

L'Equipe / *parrainé par* Alcan ; *édité par* Yvon Julien. - *Publié par* Aluminum du Canada Ltée de Beauharnois. C.P. K, Beauharnois, Qué. J6N 1W5, août 1967-
Ancien titre: La Coulée (juin 1951-septembre 1963)
Intermittent (approximativement 10 éditions par an). Organe interne/officiel, magazine, 16 p. Tirage: 300
Envoi gratuit.

Equipe apostolique / *édité par* Remi Potvin. - *Publié par* La Fédération nationale du mouvement chrétien d'aujourd'hui. 8100, boul. St-Laurent, Montréal, Qué. H2P 2L9, septembre 1965-
Ancien titre: Bulletin des ligues, section du conseil (septembre 1950-septembre 1965)
Mensuel. Publication ecclésiastique, bulletin, 4 p. Tirage: 2000
$.10 le numéro : $1.00 par année.

Equipement motorisé plein air *See* Outdoor power products

Equipment journal - *Published by* E.E. Abel. Pace Publishing Ltd. 3049 Jarrow Ave., Mississauga, Ont. L4X 2C6, 1966-
Irregular (approximately 17 issues per year). Trade publication. Includes advertising. Circulation: 18,500
$.50 per issue : $5.50 per year.

Erasmus in English / *edited by* R.M. Schoeffel and P. Tracy. - *Published by* University of Toronto Press. 5201 Dufferin St., Downsview, Ont. M3H 5T8, 1970-
Irregular (approximately 1 issue per year). Special interest, newsletter format, 36 p. Language: English and French. Includes book reviews, volume index. Circulation: 3200
Indexed in M.L.A. int. bib.

L'Erecteur - *Publié par* Pierre Marcheldon. C.P. 500, Trois-Rivières, Qué., septembre 1975-
Ancien titre: Le Journal (septembre 1969-mai 1970 et septembre 1974-mai 1975)
Paraît tous les 15 jours. Publication des étudiants, journal, 8 p. Comprend critique de livres, critique de films, critique de pièces de théâtre, critique de disques, publicité. Tirage: 2000

Erindaliam *See* Medium II

L'Escargot / *édité par* Jacques Fournier. - *Publié par* Service universitaire canadien outre-mer. 4824, chemin de la Côte des Neiges, Montréal, Qué., Juillet 1974-
Ancien titre: Deux tiers.
Bimestriel. Publication d'association, bulletin, 24 p. Tirage: 1300
Envoi gratuit.

Eskimo / *edited by* J.-M. Rousselière. - *Published by* Oblate Fathers of the Churchill-Hudson's Bay Diocese. P.O. Box 10, Churchill, Man. R0B 0E0, 1943-
Irregular (approximately 2 issues per year). Church publication, magazine format, 24-32 p. Language: French and English. Includes book reviews. Circulation: 3000 French 2000 English
Indexed in North. tit.
$.50 per issue : $1.00 per year : $25.00 for the whole collection. Sample sent on request.

Esprit / *edited by* Mary Elizabeth Axtem. - *Published by* Esprit Publishing Co. Limited. 4th floor, 105 Carlton St., Toronto, Ont. M5B 1M2, 1975-
Monthly. Magazine format, 75 p. Includes advertising.
$10.00 per year.

Essays on Canadian writing / *edited by* Jack David. - *Published by* Essays on Canadian Writing. S. 765 Ross Bldg. York University, 4700 Keele St., Downsview, Ont. M3J 1P3, Winter 1974-
Issued twice a year. Special interest, journal format, 80 p. Includes book reviews. Circulation: 600
ISSN 0316-0300 $1.50 per issue : $4.50 per year : $6.00 per year, foreign.

Estampes *See* Baker Lake prints

Estampes *See* Pangnirtung 1975-prints

Estampes esquimaudes d'Holman *See* Holman Eskimo prints 1974

Estate and gift tax handbook *See* Succession duty and gift tax handbook

Estates and trusts quarterly / *edited by* Robert C. Dick. - *Published by* Canada Law Book Ltd. 80 Cowdray Court, Agincourt, Ont. M1S 1S5, September 1973-
Quarterly. Magazine format, 100 p. Includes volume index.
Indexed in Can. leg. per. lit.
$25.00 per year.

Eté au Canada / *édité par* Mary-Lynn Gravel. - *Publié par* Bureau canadien de l'éducation internationale. 151, rue Slater, Ottawa, Ont. K1P 5H3.
Publié en anglais : Summer in Canada.
Annuel.
Envoi gratuit.

Eternel triangle (mars 1961-septembre 1968) *Voir* Couple et famille

L'Etrangeté du texte (printemps-été 1975) *Voir* Brèches : analyse/fiction

Etudes éthniques du Canada *See* Canadian ethnic studies

Etudes françaises dans le monde : bulletin de liaison des départements et centres d'études françaises / *édité par* Jean-Marc Léger. - *Publié par* Association des universités partiellement ou entièrement de langue française. C.P. 6128, Université de Montréal, Montréal, Qué. H3C 3J7, novembre 1972-
Intermittent (approximativement 4 éditions par an). Publication d'association, bulletin, 10 p.
ISSN 0316-2672 $7.00 par année.
Abonnements payables à l'avance.

Etudes internationales - *Publié par* Centre québecois de relations internationals. Pavillion de Koninck, Université Laval, Québec, Qué. G1K 7P4, décembre 1970-
Semestriel. Publication d'institution (universités, écoles..), revue, 150 p. Comprend critique de livres. Tirage: 1500
Indexé dans Periodex, RADAR, Hist. abstr.; Amer. hist. and life.
ISSN 0014-2123 $5.00 le numéro : $10.00 par année : $3.00 le volume. Abonnements payables à l'avance.

Etudes littéraires - *Published by* Presses de l'Université Laval. C.P. 2447, Québec, Qué., 1968-
Irregular (approximately 3 issues per year).
Indexed in Periodex.
$8.00 per year.

Etudes oblates (1942-1973) *Voir* Vie oblate

Etudes pastorales : l'évangélisation et ses défis - *Publié par* Librairie de l'Université de Montréal. C.P. 6128, Montréal, Qué.
Annuel. Publication d'institution (universités, écoles..), Recueil d'articles, 130 p.

Etudes slaves et est-européennes *See* Slavic and East-European studies

Etudiant : the newspaper for Ukrainian Canadian students *See* Student

L'étudiant de l'Ontario *See* The Ontario student

Evaluation and measurement newsletter / *edited by* Dawn Whitmore. - *Published by* Department of Measurement and Evaluation. Ontario Institute for Studies in Education. 252 Bloor St. W., Toronto, Ont.
Irregular (approximately 3 issues per year). Institutional publication (Universities, schools, etc.), newsletter format, 4 p. Circulation: 7200
Indexed in Can. educ. ind.
$1.00 per year. Free to Ontario principals. Prepayment required.

Evangelical Baptist / *edited by* J.R. Armstrong. - *Published by* Fellowship of Evangelical Baptist Churches in Canada. 74 Sheppard Ave. W., Willowdale, Ont., November 1953-
Former title(s): Fellowship Baptist.
Monthly. Church publication, magazine format, 24 p. Includes book reviews, advertising. Circulation: 7000
$.35 per issue : $3.50 per year : $3.75 per year, foreign. Special rates offered. Prepayment required.

Evangelical morning *See* Yevanhel's'kyi ranok

Evangelical recorder / *edited by* Douglas C. Percy. - *Published by* Ontario Bible College. 16 Spadina Rd., Toronto, Ont. M5R 2S8, September 1894-
Former title(s): Recorder.
Quarterly. Special interest, magazine format, 28 p. Includes book reviews.
Free.

Evangelska pravda / *sponsored by* Ukrainian Presbyterian Church ; *edited by* M. Fesenko. - *Published by* M. Fesenko. 26 Robina Ave., Toronto, Ont. M6C 3Y6, January 1939-
Issued every other month. Church publication, ethnic press, magazine format, 24 p. Language: Ukrainian and English. Circulation: 1000
$.75 per issue : $3.50 per year.

Event / *edited by* Robert W. Lowe. - *Published by* Department of English. Douglas College. P.O. Box 2503, New Westminster, B.C., 1971-
Issued 3 times per year. Special interest, magazine format, 100 p. Circulation: 250
ISSN 0315-3770 $2.00 per issue : $5.00 per year. Complimentary copies available.

Events / *edited by* Fred H. Hatch. - *Published by* The Advertising & Sales Club of Toronto. Suite 301B, 19 Richmond St. W., Toronto, Ont. M5H 1Y9.
Monthly. Association publication, newsletter format, 4 p. Circulation: 500
Free to members.

Everybody's money. Canadian edition / *sponsored by* Credit Union National Association Inc ; *edited by* Sharon Stark. - *Published by* John R. Prindle. P.O. Box 800, Station U, Toronto, Ont. (Subscription address: P.O. Box 431, Madison, Wisconsin, 53701, U.S.A) Spring 1960-
Quarterly. "Consumer and money management publication", magazine format, 32 p. Includes book reviews, cumulative index. available in microform. supplements issued. Circulation: 300,000
$.35 per issue : $1.25 per year. Prepayment required.

Excalibur - *Published by* Excalibur Publications. York University. Downsview, Ont.
Weekly. Student publication, newspaper format, Includes advertising. Circulation: 14,000

Exchange / *edited by* V.J. Godin. - *Published by* The Ontario Chamber of Commerce. Suite 501, 330 University Ave., Toronto, Ont. M5G 1R7.
Monthly. Association publication, newsletter format, 20 p. Circulation: 2000
$12.00 per year. Prepayment required.

Exchange-Canada = Canada-exchange / *edited by* Mary-Lynn Gravel. - *Published by* Canadian Bureau for International Education. 151 Slater St. Ottawa Ont. K1P 5H3, Spring 1972-
Quarterly. Association publication, magazine format, 24 p. Language: English and French. Includes cumulative index. Circulation: 1400
Indexed in Can. educ. ind.
ISSN 0315-8543 Free. Available to members only. Sent free to various overseas organizations. Controlled circulation.

Executive / *edited by* Loren J. Chudy. - *Published by* A.P. McVeigh. Southam Business Publications Ltd. 1450 Don Mills Rd., Don Mills, Ont., 1959-
Monthly. Trade publication, magazine format, 68 p. Includes book reviews, advertising. Circulation: 28,000
Indexed in Can. ind., P.A.I.S.
$1.25 per issue : $14.00 per year : $16.00 per year, U.S. : $40.00 per year foreign. Controlled circulation.

Executive compensation in Canada *See* Management compensation in Canada

Executive's directory = Annuaire de l'exécutif - *Published by* A.M. Bougie. Plaza Advertising. Suite 7, 660 Cremazie Blvd. E., Montreal, Que. H2P 1G1.
Annual. Trade publication, magazine format, Language: English and French. Circulation: 70,000

Exile / *edited by* Barry Callaghan. - *Published by* Barry Callaghan. P.O. Box 546, Downsview, Ont.
Quarterly. Special interest, journal format, 145 p.
$2.00 per issue : $7.00 per year.

Exodus - *Publié par* Centre federal de formation. 6099, boul. Livesque, Cité de Laval, Qué.
$1.00 par année.

L'Exploitation minière du Canada - renseignements et statistiques (1967, 1968) *Voir* Les Mines au Canada : renseignements et statistiques

Exploration / *sponsored by* B.C. Social Studies' Teachers' Association. - *Published by* British Columbia Teachers Federation. 105-2235 Burrard St., Vancouver, B.C. V6J 3H9, May 1961-
Irregular (approximately 2 issues per year). Association publication, journal format, 50 p. Includes book reviews.
Indexed in Can. educ. ind.
Available to members only. Controlled circulation.

Export news bulletin / *edited by* J.D. Moore. - *Published by* Canadian Export Association. Suite 1020, 1080 Beaver Hall Hill, Montreal, Que. H2Z 1T7.
Monthly. Special interest, newsletter format, ISSN 0316-7631 $25.00 per year. Subscription includes U.S. news bulletin and Review and digest bulletin. Controlled circulation.

Expos baseball magazine / *edited by* Ronald A. Millichamp. - *Published by* Montreal Baseball Club Ltd. Room 15, 1010 St. Catherine St. W., Montreal, Que. (Subscription address: P.O. Box 500, Postal Station R, Montreal, Que. H2S 3G7) 1969-
Irregular (approximately 4 issues per year). Special interest. Includes advertising.

Expression / *edited by* Peggy White. - *Published by* Ontario Library Association. 2397a Bloor St. W., Toronto, Ont. M6S 1P6, November 1975-
Issued twice a year. Association publication, 40 p. Circulation: 1676
Free to members of OLA. Controlled circulation.

Eyeopener / *edited by* Gary Curtis. - *Published by* Student Union. Ryerson Polytechnical Institute. 380 Victoria St., Toronto, Ont. M5B 1W7.
Weekly. Trade publication. Includes advertising. Circulation: 8500

F.I.I.C. program syllabus - *Published by* The Insurance Institute of Canada. 3rd Floor, 220 Bay St., Toronto, Ont. M5J 1P3.
Former title(s): Syllabus and tuition guide - The Insurance Institute of Canada.
Annual. Association publication, 40 p.
Free.

The FM guide / *edited by* F.E. Calder. - *Published by* The FM Guide. 122 Davenport Rd., Toronto, Ont. M5R 1H9, 1971-
Monthly. Magazine format, Includes advertising.

FRI/CAM journal *See* Real Estate Institute of Canada. Journal

FSA on record *See* On record

FYI (For your information) - *Published by* Concordia University. 1455 de Maisonneuve Blvd. W., Montreal, Que. H3G 1M8.
Former title(s): Transcript (September 1974-April 1975) Issues and events (September 1969-April 1974) September 1975.
Weekly. Institutional publication (Universities, schools, etc.), newspaper format, 8 p.

Fabreries : carnet de l'amateur d'insectes / *édité par* Firmin Laliberté. - *Publié par* Association des entomologistes amateurs du Québec. 2400, chemin Ste-Foy, Quebéc, Qué. G1V 1T2, janvier 1975-
Paraît 10 fois par an. Publication d'association, 12 p. Langue(s): français et anglais. Tirage: 125
ISSN 0318-6725 $2.00 par année.

Face to face with talent - *Published by* Alberta Branch. Association of Canadian Television and Radio Artists (ACTRA). 105 Carlton St., Toronto, Ont.
Biennial. Association publication.

Factotum / *edited by* S.M. Mohan. - *Published by* Queen's University Libraries. Kingston, Ont., April 1965-
Monthly. House/company organ, newsletter format, 10-12 p. Includes book reviews. Back numbers available. Circulation: 350
Free.

Facts and Figures : mining in Canada - *Published by* The Mining Association of Canada. 9th Floor, 20 Toronto St., Toronto, Ont. N5C 2C2, 1964-
Former title(s): Facts and figures about the Canadian mining industry (1964) Published in French: Les mines au Canada.
Annual. Statistics.
Free.

Facts and figures about the Canadian mining industry (1964) *See* Facts and Figures : mining in Canada

Facts and figures of the automotive industry - *Published by* Motor Vehicle Manufacturers' Association. Suite 1602, 25 Adelaide E., Toronto, Ont. M5C 1Y7.
Annual. Statistics.
ISSN 0316-3490 Free.

Facts of the general insurance industry in Canada / *edited by* The Toronto Chapter of the Society of Fellows. - *Published by* Insurance Bureau of Canada. 170 University Ave., Toronto, Ont. M5H 3B3.
Published in French: Les assurances I.A.R.D. au Canada.
Annual. Special interest, booklet format, 36 p. Circulation: 15,000
Free. Nominal charge for volume orders

Facts on fish / *edited by* D.M. Bell. - *Published by* Fisheries Association of B.C. 400-100 W. Pender St., Vancouver, B.C. V6B 1R8.
Monthly. Association publication, newsletter format, 4 p.
Controlled circulation.

Faculty affairs / *sponsored by* Langara Faculty Association ; *edited by* Alan Dawe. - *Published by* Vancouver Community College. 100 W. 49th Ave., Vancouver, B.C. V5Y 2Z6, 1967-
Issued every other week. Association publication, newsletter format, 16 p. Includes book reviews. Circulation: 275
Free. Subscriptions not available.

Faith of our fathers *See* Isien usko

Faits et tendances (avril 1949-décembre 1973) *Voir* Action : chambre de commerce

Families / *edited by* George Hancocks. - *Published by* Ontario Genealogical Society. P.O. Box 66, Postal Station Q, Toronto, Ont. M4T 2L7, August 1962-
Former title(s): OGS bulletin.
Quarterly. Employer publication, magazine format, 32 p. Includes book reviews, advertising, volume index. Circulation: 1700
Indexed in Hist. abstr.; Amer. hist. and life.
ISSN 0030-2945 $2.00 per issue : $12.00 per year.

Famille avertie / *édité par* Guy Maheux. - *Publié par* Guy Mathieu. Ligue de sécurité de la province de Québec. 5576, chemin Upper Lachine, Montréal, Qué. H4A 2A7, septembre 1974-
Trimestriel. Intérêt général, magazine, 32 p. Tirage: 25,000
ISSN 0315-954X $2.95 par année. Tirage contrôlé. Tarifs spéciaux disponibles.

Famille d'aujourd'hui / *édité par* Louise Gravel-Dupuis. - *Publié par* Librairie Beauchemin Ltée. 450, ave. Beaumont, Montréal, Qué. H3N 1T8, mai 1971-
Ancien titre: Votre pharmacien.
Bimestriel. Intérêt général, magazine, 64 p. Comprend critique de livres. Tirage: 200,000
$.35 le numéro : $2.00 par année. Abonnements payables à l'avance.

Family involement - *Published by* Canadian Educational Programs. 41 Madison Ave., Toronto, Ont. M5R 2S2.
Monthly September-April followed by combined May-June and July-August issues. Magazine format, 32 p. Includes book reviews. Back issues available $1.75 each.
ISSN 0319-1443 $1.50 per issue : $15.00 per year.

Family life / *edited by* David L. Wagler. - *Published by* Pathway Publishers. R.R.4, Aylmer, Ont., January 1968-
Issued 11 times a year. Church publication, magazine format, 36 p. available in microform. Circulation: 12,000
$4.00 per year.

Fanfares / *edited by* Anne Selby. - *Published by* Stratford Shakespearean Festival Foundation of Canada. P.O. Box 520, Stratford, Ont. N5A 6V2, March 1967-
Quarterly. Special interest, newsletter format, 4 p.
ISSN 0046-3256 $10.00 per year. Controlled circulation.

Fantastic worlds of Burroughs and Kline *See* ERBivore

The Far point (1968-1973) *See* Northern light

Farm and country / *edited by* John Phillips. - *Published by* John Phillips. Suite 305, 30 Bloor St. W., Toronto, M4W 1A2, 1891-
Former title(s): Rural co-operator (1936-1965) Farmer's sun (1891-1936)
Irregular (approximately 19 issues per year). Special interest, newspaper format, 34 p. Includes book reviews, advertising. supplements issued. Circulation: 89,000
Indexed in Can. B.P.I.
$.25 per issue : $4.00 per year : $5.00 for 2 years : $8.40 for 2 years, foreign. Prepayment required.

Farm and home (1919-1930; absorbed in 1936) *See* Country guide : the farm magazine

Farm focus / *edited by* Edgar Bain. - *Published by* Fundy Group Publications Ltd. P.O. Box 128, Yarmouth, N.S.
Issued twice a month. Trade publication, newspaper format, 40 p. Circulation: 10,300
$.25 per issue : $4.95 per year.

Farm journal - *Published by* Fred Aston. Granby Leader-Mail Reg'd. P.O. Box 8, 237 Main St., Granby, Que., 1969-
Monthly. Includes advertising.
$.20 per issue : $4.50 per year.

Farm light and power / *edited by* W.J. Bradley. - *Published by* Bradley Publications Ltd. Suite 210, 1808 Smith St., Regina, Sask. S4P 2N4, March 1959-
Monthly except July/August and December/January are combined. Trade publication, 28 p. Includes advertising. Circulation: 162,203
$.25 per issue : $2.50 per year. Prepayment required.

Farm news, views and comments - *Published by* N.R.D.C. Agriculture Committee. P.O. Box 5, Bathurst, N.B. E2A 3Z1.
Quarterly. General interest, newsletter format, 6 p.

Farm report / *edited by* J.K. Davy. - *Published by* The Steel Co. of Canada Ltd. 100 King St. W., Hamilton, Ont. L8N 3T1, 1968-
Issued twice a year. Trade publication, newsletter format, 4 p. Language: English and French. Circulation: 35,000
Free.

Farm trends / *edited by* Ron Smith. - *Published by* Len J. Bland. Unifarm. 9934 - 106 St., Edmonton, Alta. T5K 1E1.
Former title(s): Organized farmer (to June 1970)
Monthly. Association publication, magazine format, 32 p. Circulation: 15,000
$1.00 per year.

Farmer forums - *Published by* Saskatchewan Federation of Agriculture. 201 - 2220 Albert St., Regina, Sask. S4P 2V2.
Annual. Association publication, 20 p.
Free. Controlled circulation.

Farmer's sun (1891-1936) *See* Farm and country

Fashion textiles mode (June 1973-March 1975) *See* Fem ego

Fastener facts / *edited by* J.K. Davy. - *Published by* The Steel Co. of Canada Ltd. 100 King St. W., Hamilton, Ont. L8N 3T1, 1972-
Irregular (approximately 3 issues per year). Trade publication, magazine format, 6 p. Language: English and French. Circulation: 13,000
Free.

Feather fancier / *sponsored by* Standard Breed Poultry and Pigeon Associations ; *edited by* C.R. Herrington. - *Published by* Corey R. Herrington. 142B Main St., Erin, Ont. N0B 1T0, March 1945-
Monthly. Association publication, newspaper format, 12-16 p. Language: English and French. Includes advertising. Circulation: 2100
$.50 per issue : $5.00 per year. Prepayment required.

Federal court of Canada service - *Published by* Butterworth & Co. (Canada) Ltd. 2265 Midland Ave., Scarborough, Ont. M1P 4S1, 1970-
Irregular. Looseleaf format, Includes updating service.
$85.00 per year.

Fédération de volleyball du Québec. Bulletin de nouvelles / *édité par* Jean-Pierre Tibi. - *Publié par* Fédération de volleyball du Québec. 881 est, boul. de Maisonneuve, Montréal, Qué. H2L 1Y9, septembre 1970-
Intermittent (approximativement 10 éditions par an). Publication d'association, bulletin, 15 p. Tirage: 1500

Fédération des associations de professeurs des universités du Quebec. FAPUQ information / *édité par* René Serge Larouche. - *Publié par* Fédération des associations de professeurs des universités du Québec. 2715, chemin de la Côte Sainte-Catherine, Montréal, Qué. H3T 1B6.
Publication d'association, journal,

Fédération des associations de professeurs des universités du Québec. FAPUQ nouvelles brèves / *édité par* René Serge Larouche. - *Publié par* Fédération des associations de professeurs des universités du Québec. 2715, chemin de la Côte Ste-Catherine, Montréal, Qué. H3T 1B6, janvier 1973-
74-5. Publication d'association, journal, 16 p. Langue(s): français et anglais. Tirage: 7000
ISSN 0316-5159 Envoi gratuit.

Fédération des CEGEP. Annuaire Cégeps-ACQ / *parrainé par* Fédération des Cégeps : Association des collèges du Québec ; *édité par* Jacques Laliberté. - *Publié par* Centre d'animation de développement et de recherche en éducation. 1940 est, boul. Henri-Bourassa, Montréal, Qué. H2B 1S2.
Annuel. Publication d'association, 144 p.
Envoi gratuit.

Fédération des médecins omnipraticiens du Québec. Nouvelles de la F.M.O.Q - *Publié par* Fédération des médecins omnipraticiens du Québec. Suite 1100, 1440 est, rue Ste-Catherine, Montréal, Qué. H3G 1R8, août 1972-
Intermittent (approximativement 8 éditions par an). Publication d'association, bulletin, 4 p. Langue(s): français et anglais.
Envoi gratuit.

Federation of Canadian Archers *See* The Canadian archer

Federation of Independent School Associations in British Columbia. Fisa spokesman - *Published by* Federation of Independent School Associations in British Columbia. 150 Robson St., Vancouver, B.C. V6B 2A7, 1973-
Irregular (approximately 1-2 issues per year). Association publication, newsletter format, 4-6 p. Circulation: 1500 (direct) and 10,000 (indirect)
Free.

Federation of Women Teachers' Associations of Ontario. FWTAO newsletter / *edited by* Jean Cochrane. - *Published by* Federation of Women Teachers' Associations of Ontario. 1260 Bay St., Toronto, Ont. M5R 2B8.
Irregular (approximately 7 issues per year). Association publication, newspaper format, 4-8 p. Includes book reviews. Circulation: 33,000

Feed and farm supply dealer / *edited by* D.O. Brewer. - *Published by* S. Steigerwald. P.O. Box 6900, 1077 St. James St., Winnipeg, Man. R3C 3B1.
Issued every other month. Trade publication, magazine format, 42 p. Includes advertising. Circulation: 6400
$1.00 per issue : $8.00 per year : $10.00 per year, foreign. Controlled circulation. Prepayment required.

Feeders' day / *edited by* The Chairman, Department of Animal Science. - *Published by* Department of Animal Science. The University of Alberta. Edmonton, Alta., 1945-
Annual. Institutional publication (Universities, schools, etc.), magazine format, 80 p. Circulation: 17,000
Free on request.

Feliciter / *edited by* Pamela Lee MacRae. - *Published by* Canadian Library Association. 151 Sparks St., Ottawa, Ont. KIP 5E3., 1944-
Monthly. Association publication, newsletter format, 32 p. Includes advertising. Circulation: 5000
Indexed in Lib. lit.
Free. Subscription included in membership fee.

Fellowship Baptist *See* Evangelical Baptist

Fellowship year book / *edited by* J.H. Watt. - *Published by* The Fellowship of Evangelical Baptist Churches in Canada. 74 Sheppard Ave. W., Willowdale, Ont. M2N 1M3, October 1953-
Annual. Church publication, 128 p. Includes book reviews, advertising. Circulation: 1500
ISSN 0317-266X $2.50. Special rates offered.

Fellowships and scholarships offered by private donors and foreign governments - *Published by* Association of Universities and Colleges of Canada. 151 Slater St., Ottawa, Ont. K1P 5N1.
Annual. Directory, booklet format,

Fem ego / *edited by* Ray Lancashire. - *Published by* Stephen Harrison. Fashion Textiles Mode Publishing Ltd. 1396 St. Catherine St. W., Montreal, Que. H3G 1P9, June 1975-
Former title(s): Fashion textiles mode (June 1973-March 1975)
Quarterly. Trade publication, magazine format, 100 p. Language: English and French. Includes advertising.
$2.50 per issue : $10.00 per year. Controlled circulation.

Feminist communication collective - *Published by* Feminist Communication Collective. P.O. Box 1238, Place d'Armes, Montreal, Que. H2Y 3K2, 1973-
Association publication, newsletter format, 30 p. Includes book reviews, record reviews, advertising. Circulation: 500
$.35 per issue : $4.00 per year (Libraries and institutions $5.00) : $7.00 per year, foreign.

Femme / *édité par* Claude Charron. - *Publié par* Les Editions Lizon inc. 385, boul. Lebeau, Ville St-Laurent, Qué., 1975-
Mensuel. Intérêt général, magazine, Comprend publicité. Circulation: 80,000
$1.00 le numéro : $10.00 par année : $12.00 par année l'étranger.

Femme d'action. Ottawa / *édité par* Alida St-Amand. - *Publié par* La Fédération des femmes canadiennes-françaises. Suite 312-13, 256, ave. King Edward, Ottawa, Ont. K1N 7M1, octobre 1971-
Trimestriel. Publication d'association, bulletin, 16 p. Tirage: 1000
$.25 le numéro : $1.00 par année : $2.00 par année, l'étranger. Envoi gratuit. Abonnements payables à l'avance.

Festival Lennoxville / *edited by* David Rittenhouse. - *Published by* St. Francis Theatre Corp. P.O. Box 60, Lennoxville, Que. J1M 1Z3, 1972-
Annual. Program. Includes advertising.
Free.

Le feuillet biblique - Parole-dimanche (novembre 1958 - septembre 1970) *Voir* Parole-dimanche

Le feuillet paroissial / *édité par* Marcel Dubois. - *Publié par* Imprimerie Drouin Inc. 815, rue Beaumont, Montréal, Qué. H2N 1W1, juillet 1952-
Hebdomadaire. Publication ecclésiastique, brochure, 4 p. Langue(s): français et anglais. Tirage: 600,000
$5.00 par année. Abonnements payables à l'avance.

Feux verts : nous les marginaux / *édité par* Lafrance Gilles. - *Publié par* Corporation du journal des handicapés. 2222 est, rue Laurier, Montréal, Qué. H2C 1C4.
Bimestriel. Publication spécialisée, journal, 12 p.
$.50 le numéro : $3.00 par année.

The Fiddlehead / *edited by* Roger Ploude. - *Published by* The Fiddlehead. The Observatory, University of New Brunswick, Fredericton, N.B. E3B 5A3, 1945-
Quarterly. Journal format, 150 p. Back issues available $2.00 each.
$1.50 per issue : $6.00 per year : $7.00 per year, U.S.

Field beacon *See* Metropolitan life

Field news / *edited by* Karen Gibson. - *Published by* Sun Life Assurance Co. of Canada. P.O. Box 6075, Montreal, Que. H3C 3G5.
Published in French: Sun Life du Canada compagnie d'assurance-vie. Nouvelles.
Monthly. House/company organ, newsletter format, 16 p. Circulation: 4700
Free.

Field record / *edited by* D.G. Booth (publications editor). - *Published by* The Mutual Life Assurance Co. of Canada. 227 King St. S., Waterloo, Ont. N2J 4C5, June 1971-
Former title(s): Agent's bulletin (1913-1971)
Published in French : Palm arès.
Monthly. House/company organ, magazine format, 20 p. Includes book reviews.
Controlled circulation.

File magazine / *edited by* General Idea (Michael Tims, Ron Gabe and Jorge Saia). - *Published by* Art-Official Inc. 241 Yonge St., 3rd Floor, Toronto, Ont. M5B 1N8, April 1972-
Irregular (approxiamtely 2-3 issues per year). Special interest, magazine format, 80 p. Language: English ; summaries: French, German and Italian (occasionally). Includes book reviews, film reviews, play reviews, advertising. Circulation: 2000
ISSN 0315-2456 $3.00 per issue : $10.00 per year : $15.00 per year Gt. Brit. and Europe : $20.00 per year, foreign. Prepayment required.

Film canadiana. Part 1 - Film, Part 2 - Television / *edited by* Louis Valenzuela, Piers Handlins, Manard Collins. - *Published by* Canadian Film Institute. 1762 Carling Ave., Ottawa, Ont., K2A 2H7., 1972-
Annual. Yearbook, magazine format, Language: French and English. available in microform.
$15.00 per year (Part 1 $9.95, Part 2 $5.95).

Film catalogue : a union catalogue of films, videotapes and filmloops used in the Ontario colleges of applied arts and technology - *Published by* College Bibliocentre Division. Centennial College of Applied Arts and Technology. 20 Railside Rd., Don Mills, Ont. M3A 1A4, 1973-
Irregular. Catalogue.
$25.00 per year.

Film monthly (June 1968-February 1970) *See* Panorama

Films à l'écran - *Publié par* Office des communications sociales. 4635, rue de Lorimier Montréal, Qué. H2H 2B4, janvier 1957-
Hebdomadaire. Critique de films, fiche cartonnée, Tirage: 700
$5.00 par année.

Filo cable / *édité par* Pierre Gosselin. - *Publié par* Cäblerie-Tréfilerie de Shawinigan. Alcan Canada Limitée. C.P. 810, Shawinigan, Qué. G9N 6W3, janvier 1974-
Intermittent (approximativement 4 éditions par an). Organe interne/officiel, journal, 8 p.
Envoi gratuit.

Filter / *edited by* M.E. Wastle (managing editor). - *Published by* Ontario Society of Radiological Technologists. P.O. Box 1054, Brantford, Ont. N3T 5S7.
Monthly except the July August issues are combined. Association publication, magazine format, 32 p. Circulation: 3000
$3.00 per year. Prepayment required.

The Financial post / *edited by* Paul S. Deacon. - *Published by* Maclean-Hunter Ltd. 481 University Ave., Toronto, Ont. M5W 1A7, January 1907-
Weekly. Trade publication, newspaper format, available in microform. Circulation: 148,789
Indexed in Can. ind., Can. B.P.I.
$.50 per issue : $15.00 per year : $30.00 for 3 years : $17.00 per year, foreign : $36.00 for 3 years, foreign. Half price for students and teachers.

The Financial post directory of directors - *Published by* Maclean-Hunter Ltd. 481 University Ave., Toronto, Ont.
Annual. Directory, book format, 730 p.
$30.00.

Financial Post magazine *See* Impetus magazine

Financial post report on conventions, conferences and business meetings (1969-1973) *See* Meetings, conferences and conventions: a Financial post guide

The Financial Post survey of funds / *edited by* Beatrice Graham. - *Published by* The Financial Post. Maclean-Hunter Ltd. 481 University Ave., Toronto, Ont. M5W 1A7.
Former title(s): The Financial Post survey of investment funds.
Annual. Statistics, book format, 350 p. Circulation: 5000
$15.00 per volume.

The Financial post survey of industrials. V. 1 Manufacturing Co. V. 2 Sales and Service Co / *edited by* G.H. Johnson. - *Published by* Maclean-Hunter Ltd. 481 University Ave., Toronto, Ont. M5W 1A7, 1926-
Annual. Trade publication. Includes advertising. Circulation: 22,134
$8.00 per volume : $13.50 for the 2 vol. set.

The Financial Post survey of investment funds *See* The Financial Post survey of funds

Financial post survey of markets / *edited by* Beatrice Hamilton. - *Published by* Maclean-Hunter Ltd. 481 University Ave., Toronto, Ont. M5W 1A7, 1924-
Annual. Trade publication. Includes advertising. Circulation: 7504
$15.00 per volume.

The Financial post survey of mines / *edited by* G.H. Johnson. - *Published by* Maclean-Hunter Ltd. 481 University Ave., Toronto, Ont. M5W 1A7, 1925-
Annual. Trade publication. Includes advertising. Circulation: 17,289
$12.00 per volume.

The Financial post survey of oils / *edited by* G.H. Johnson. - *Published by* Maclean-Hunter Ltd. 481 University Ave., Toronto, Ont. M5W 1A7, 1936-
Annual. Trade publication. Includes advertising. Circulation: 13,877
$11.00 per volume.

Financial statistics : Canada's provinces and representative municipalities - *Published by* Wood Gundy Limited. P.O. Box 274, Royal Trust Tower, Toronto, Ont. M5K 1M7.
Annual. Statistics, booklet format,

Financial times of Canada / *edited by* Don McGillivray. - *Published by* Donald Carlson. 10 Arundel St., Place Bonaventure, Montreal, Que. H5A 1B6 (Subscription address: P.O. Box 6160, Montreal H3C 3K7) 1912-
Weekly. Special interest, newspaper format, 36 p. Includes book reviews, advertising. Circulation: 52,000
Indexed in Can. B.P.I.
$12.00 per year. Prepayment required.

Financial times of Canada perspective on money / *edited by* Gordon Pape. - *Published by* Donald Carlson. Financial Times of Canada. 1885 Leslie St., Don Mills, Ont. M3B 3J4.
Quarterly. Magazine format, Includes advertising. Circulation: 55,358

Fine / *sponsored by* Fine Arts Council, Alberta Teachers Association ; *edited by* James E. Simpson. - *Published by* Alberta Teachers' Association. 11010 - 142 St., Edmonton, Alta., 1964-
Former title(s): M.A.D. (1973)
Issued twice a year. Association publication, magazine format, Includes book reviews. Circulation: 300
Indexed in Can. educ. ind.
$5.00 per year.

Fine print - *Published by* Ecology Action Centre. Room 20-A, Forest Bldg., Dalhousie University, Halifax, N.S.
Quarterly. Institutional publication (Universities, schools, etc.), newsletter format, 4 p. Circulation: 1500
Free.

Fire Control Course. Fire control notes - *Published by* Canadian Forestry Association of British Columbia. Suite 410, 1200 W. Pender St., Vancouver, B.C. V6E 2S9, April 1976-
Biennial. Association publication, magazine format, 140 p. Circulation: 500
$4.00 per volume.

Fire fighting in Canada / *edited by* Ernest Harris. - *Published by* Norman H. Parkins. 328 Victoria Ave., Montreal, Que. H3Z 2M8.
Issued every other month. Trade publication, magazine format, 40 p.
$5.00 per year : $6.00 per year, U.S.

First encounter - *Published by* Student Administrative Council. Mount Allison University. Sackville, N.B., 1969-
Annual. Creative writing, magazine format, $1.75 per issue. Controlled circulation.

Fish and game sportsman / *edited by* Red Wilkinson. - *Published by* Nimrod Publications Ltd. P.O. Box 1654, Regina, Sask. S4P 3C4, 1969-
Former title(s): Saskatchewan sportsman; Alberta fish and game magazine.
Quarterly. Special interest, magazine format, 80 p. Includes advertising. available in microform. Circulation: 12,000
$1.00 per issue : $3.25 per year : $3.75 per year, foreign. Prepayment required.

The Fisherman / *edited by* Harold H. Griffin. - *Published by* The Fisherman Publishing Society. 138 E. Cordova St., Vancouver, B.C. V6A 1K9, 1937-
Issued every other week. Special interest, newspaper format, 12 p. Includes advertising. Circulation: 9500
$.25 per issue : $7.00 per year : $25.00 per volume : $8.00 per year, foreign.

The Fish-eye lens - *Published by* The Ecumenical Institute of Canada. 11 Madison Ave., Toronto, Ont. M5R 2S2, October 1974-
Issued every other month. Church publication, newsletter format, 25 p. Circulation: 500
$3.00 per year.

Fleuriste *Voir* Fleuriste du Québec

Fleuriste du Québec / *édité par* Gilles Domaine. - *Publié par* Gilles Domaine. 541, 8ième ave., Grand-Mère, Qué. Q9T 5K7, 1969-
Ancien titre: Fleuriste.
Paraît 7 fois par an. Publication spécialisée, magazine, Langue(s): français et anglais. Tirage: 1000
$1.50 le numéro : $10.00 par année. Tarifs spéciaux disponibles. Abonnements payables à l'avance.

Flyer *See* Alberta Certified Nursing Aide Association. Newsletter

The Flying quail / *edited by* Rennie Patterson. - *Published by* Model "A" Ford Club of Pembroke. 618 Glenwood Dr., Pembroke, Ont. (Subscription address: P.O. Box 161, Pembroke, Ont. K8A 6X3) January 1973-
Former title(s): Newsletter of the Model A Ford Club of Pembroke.
Monthly. Association publication, newsletter format, 8 p. Circulation: 65
Free to club members and on exchange with other clubs.

Focal spot *See* The Canadian journal of radiography, radiotherapthy, nuclear medicine

Focus / *edited by* Ida Reddy and Peter Rogers. - *Published by* Ontario Library Association. 2397a Bloor St. W., Toronto, Ont. M6S 1P6, May 1975-
Former title(s): OLA newsletter; OLA news.
Monthly. Association publication, newsletter format, 12 p. Includes advertising. Circulation: 1676
ISSN 0318-0247 $8.00 per year outside Ontario. Free to members. Controlled circulation.

Focus / *edited by* Carolyn E. Thomson. - *Published by* The Toronto Camera Club. 587 Mount Pleasant Rd., Toronto, Ont. M4S 2M5.
Irregular (approximately 8 issues per year). Association publication, magazine format, 16 p. Includes book reviews, advertising. Controlled circulation.

Focus : social and preventive medicine / *sponsored by* Community Health Co-operative Federation Ltd ; *edited by* Betsy Naylor. - *Published by* Modern Press. 446 Second Ave. N., Saskatoon, Sask. S7K 2C2, November 1964-
Issued every other month. Association publication, newsletter format, 6 p. Circulation: 5000
$1.20 per year. Free to members.

Focus on beef - *Published by* Richard D. Secord. 1108 Empire Building, Edmonton, Alta. T5J 1V9, May 1971-
Monthly. Special interest, magazine format, 120 p. Includes advertising. Circulation: 10,000
$7.50 per year : $12.00 for 2 years : $10.00 per year, foreign : $12.50 for 2 years. Controlled circulation.

Focus on Canada (1970-1973) *See* The Bookmark

Focus on Winnipeg schools *See* Our schools

Folio / *edited by* Marcy Davies. - *Published by* The Publications Office. The University of Alberta. 326 Assiniboia Hall, The University of Alberta, Edmonton, 1964-
Weekly. Institutional publication (Universities, schools, etc.), newsletter format, 8 p. Free. Controlled circulation.

Fondation canadienne d'éducation économique. Rapport / *édité par* Pamela Hampson. - *Publié par* Fondation canadienne d'éducation économique. 155, av. University, Toronto, Ont. M5H 3B7, automne 1974-
Publié en anglais: Canadian Foundation for Economic Education. Rapport.
Trimestriel. Publication spécialisée, 4 p. Langue(s): français et anglais. parution de suppléments. Tirage: 1000
$5.00 par année (Organization $25.00).

Food in Canada / *edited by* Robert F. Barratt. - *Published by* Maclean-Hunter Ltd. 481 University Ave, Toronto, Ont. M5W 1A7, 1941-
Former title(s): Canadian food industries.
Monthly. Trade publication. Includes advertising. Circulation: 8102
Indexed in Manage. ind., Can. B.P.I.

Forces / *édité par* Jean Sarrazin. - *Publié par* Société d'édition de la revue Forces. a/s Hydro Québec, 75 ouest, boul. Dorchester, Montréal, Qué. H2Z 1A4, mars 1967-
Trimestriel. Publication spécialisée, magazine, 64 p. Langue(s): français et anglais ; sommaires: espagnol, allemand, russe, italien et japonais.
Indexé dans Periodex, RADAR, North. tit., Arct. bibl.
$2.00 le numéro : $6.00 par année : $8.00 par année, l'étranger.

Fore and aft / *edited by* Pat Murphy. - *Published by* Photo-Atlantic Productions Ltd. P.O. Box 2222, Halifax, N.S., 1972-
Quarterly. General interest. Includes advertising.
$1.00 per issue.

Forecaster : Canadian corporate earnings forecasts / *edited by* Winifred Noble. - *Published by* Investor's Digest of Canada Publishing Co. Ltd. 481 University Ave., Toronto, Ont. M5W 1A7.
Quarterly. Special interest, magazine format, 64 p. Circulation: 1000
$12.00 per year.

The Forecaster = Le Prévisionniste / *edited by* M.E.H. Trueman. - *Published by* Meteorology Group. The Professional Institute of the Public Service of Canada. 786 Bronson Ave., Ottawa, Ont. K1S 4G4, 1941-
Quarterly. Association publication, magazine format, 25 p. Language: English and French ; summaries: English and French.
Free to members only.

Foreign focus / *edited by* Dale S. Herendeen. - *Published by* Canadian Theological College. 440 Fourth Ave., Regina, Sask. S4T 0H8, July 1974-
Quarterly. Institutional publication (Universities, schools, etc.), 20 p. Circulation: 1000
$1.00 per year.

Foresterie à tout / *édité par* Jean-Claude Gilbert. - *Publié par* Association des techniciens forestiers du Québec. C.P. 118, St-Rédempteur de Lévis, Qué. G0S 3B0, décembre 1974-
Ancien titre: Le Technicien forestier (octobre 1972-juillet 1974)
Bimestriel. Publication d'association, magazine, 30 p. Comprend publicité. Tirage: 1000
$.75 le numéro : $3.00 par année : $1.25 le numéro. Abonnements payables à l'avance.

The Forestry chronicle / *edited by* J.D. MacArthur. - *Published by* The Canadian Institute of Forestry. P.O. Box 5000, MacDonald College, Que, H0A 1C0, 1925-
Issued every other month. Trade publication. Includes advertising.
$5.00 per issue : $12.00 per year : $15.00 per year, foreign.

Forêt et papier / *edited by* Paul Saint-Pierre. - *Published by* Wilson Smith. Maclean-Hunter Ltée. 625, ave President Kennedy, Montréal, Qué. H3A 1K5 (Subscription address: 481 University Ave, Toronto, Ont. M5W 1A7) 1975-
Trimestriel. Revue d'entreprise, magazine, 52 p. Includes publicité.
$8.00 par année : $12.00 par année, E.U., U.K. et France : $25.00 par année, l'étranger.

La Forêt québecoise (1934-1951) *Voir* Forêt-conservation

Forêt-conservation / *édité par* Pierre Mathieu. - *Publié par* Association forestière québécoise inc. 915 ouest, boul. St Cyrille, Québec, Qué. G1S 1T8.
Ancien titre: La Forêt québecoise (1934-1951)
Paraît 10 fois par an. Publication d'association, magazine, 28 p. Tirage: 6000
Indexé dans Periodex, RADAR.
$10.00 par année : $15.00 par année l'étranger.

Fortnightly crescent Toronto / *edited by* L. Owaisi. - *Published by* Canadian Publications. 338 Hollyberry Trail, Willowdale, Ont. M2H 2P6.
Issued twice a month. Ethnic press. Language: Pakistani and English. Includes advertising. Circulation: 2600
$.20 per issue.

Fortnightly law journal (prior to 1950) *See* Chitty's law journal

Forum / *edited by* Bruce A. Blackburn. - *Published by* Life Underwriters Association of Canada. 41 Lesmill Rd., Don Mills, Ont. M3B 2T3, 1914-
Former title(s): Life underwriters news (1914 - May 1971)
Issued 10 times a year; June-July and August-September are combined issues. Association publication, magazine format, 32 p. Language: English and French. Includes advertising. Some issues contain 8 page insert in French. Circulation: 16,140
$.60 per issue : $6.00 per year. Subscription included in membership fee. Controlled circulation. Prepayment required.

The Forum / *edited by* Mike Crawford. - *Published by* Ontario Secondary School Teachers' Federation. 1260 Bay St., Toronto, Ont. M5R 2B9, February 1975-
Former title(s): Bulletin - Ontario Secondary School Teachers' Association (January 1921-December 1974)
Irregular (approximately 5 issues per year). Association publication, magazine format, 75 p. Includes book reviews, advertising. available in microform. Circulation: 37,000
Controlled circulation.

Forum de nutrition *See* Nutrition forum

Forward / *edited by* Betty Kimber. - *Published by* Grand Division. Sons of Temperance of Nova Scotia. 8 Retreat Ave., Armdale, Halifax, N.S. B3N 1Y2, 1895-
Monthly. Association publication, newspaper format, 4 p.
$1.00 per year : $1.25 per year, foreign.

Forward : democratic monthly *See* Vorwârts

Forze nuove / *edited by* Odoardo Di Santo. - *Published by* Forze Nuove Inc. Suite 1907, 1455 Lawrence Ave. W., Toronto, Ont. M6L 1B1, 1972-
Monthly. Ethnic press. Language: Italian. Includes advertising. Circulation: 6000
$.15 per issue : $3.00 per year.

Foto flash / *edited by* Helen Hancock. - *Published by* National Association for Photographic Art. 10 Shaneen Blvd., Scarborough, Ont. M1R 1B5.
Association publication, newsletter format, Available to members only. Controlled circulation.

Four decades of poetry 1890-1930 - *Published by* Four Decades of Poetry. 231 Lonsmount Dr., Toronto, Ont.
Issued twice a year. Journal format, $5.00 per year.

La Fournée / *édité par* R. Bastin. - *Publié par* J.L. Morin. Hexa inc. Suite 203, 6841, St-Hubert, Montréal, Qué. H2S 2M8.
Bimestriel. Magazine, 40 p.

The Fourth estate / *edited by* A.L. O'Neill. - *Published by* A.L. O'Neill. P.O. Box 3184, Postal Station C, Ottawa, Ont. K1Y 4J4, July 1967-
Monthly. General interest, magazine format, 18 p.
ISSN 0015-9190 $2.00 per year : $3.50 per year, foreign. Controlled circulation.

"Fracture" *See* Pegboard

The Fragment / *sponsored by* The War amputations of Canada ; *edited by* H.C. Chadderton. - *Published by* Southam-Murray. 2973 Weston Rd, Weston Ont., 1920-
Quarterly. Association publication, magazine format, 124 p. Language: English and French. Circulation: 3600
Controlled circulation.

Fraser Valley farm, home and garden / *edited by* Kurt Langmann. - *Published by* Rudy Langmann. Central Valley Star. P.O. Box 220, Aldergrove, B.C. V0X 1A0, 1969-
Monthly. General interest, magazine format, Includes advertising. Circulation: 3289

Fraser's Canadian trade directory - *Published by* R.C. Freeman. 481 University Ave., Toronto, Ont. M5W 1A7, 1913-
Annual. Directory, 2500 p.
ISSN 0071-9277 $55.00.

Fraser's construction and building directory - *Published by* R.C. Freeman. Fraser's Trade Directories. 481 University Ave., Toronto, Ont. M5W 1A7.
Annual. Trade publication. Includes advertising.

Free Estonian *See* Vaba Eestlane

Free flight / *edited by* R.F. Nancarrow. - *Published by* Soaring Association of Canada. P.O. Box 1173, Postal Station B, Ottawa, Ont. K1P 5R2, 1946-
Issued every other month. Association publication, magazine format, 28 p. Includes book reviews, advertising, volume index. Circulation: 1350
$9.00 per year. Subscription included in membership fee. Controlled circulation.

Free press *See* Vapaa sana

Free Press weekly farmer *See* Free Press weekly report of farming : the farmer's business publication

Free Press weekly farmers advocate *See* Free Press weekly report of farming : the farmer's business publication

Free Press weekly prairie farmer *See* Free Press weekly report of farming : the farmer's business publication

Free Press weekly report of farming : the farmer's business publication / *sponsored by* The Winnipeg Free Press ; *edited by* Bruce P. McDonald. - *Published by* Free Press Weekly Ltd. 300 Carlton St., Winnipeg, Man. R3C 3C1., 1884-
Former title(s): Free Press weekly farmer; Free Press weekly farmers advocate; Free Press weekly prairie farmer.
Weekly. Special interest, newspaper format, 36 p. Includes book reviews, advertising, volume index. supplements issued. Circulation: 300,000
$4.00 per year : $7.00 per year, foreign. Special rates offered.

Free word *See* Vilne slovo

Freelance / *edited by* Pat Krause. - *Published by* Saskatchewan Writers' Guild and Saskatchewan Arts Board. P.O. Box 1005, Regina, Sask., S4P 0A0., 1966-
Former title(s): Newsletter - Saskatchewan Writer's Guild (1966-1973)
Issued every other month. Association publication, magazine format, 23 p. Includes book reviews, play reviews.
$1.00 per issue : $6.00 per year. Subscription included in membership fee. Controlled circulation.

The Freemason - *Published by* M.F. Beach. 1330 Danforth Ave., Toronto, Ont. M4J 1M9, 1881-
Former title(s): Masonic light (1954) Eastern star quarterly (to 1954)
Issued every other month. Association publication, magazine format, 36 p. Includes book reviews, advertising. Circulation: 12,000
$1.00 per issue : $3.00 per year.

The Friend of Brother André / *edited by* Bernard Lafreniere. - *Published by* St. Joseph's Oratory. 3800 Queen Mary Rd., Montreal, Que. H3B 1H6, November 1956-
Published in French: L'ami du Frère André.
Quarterly. Church publication, newsletter format, 4 p.
$.50 per year.

Friends of NUSGWUE newsletter (May 1973 - November 1974) *See* About unions

Fringe benefit costs in Canada / *edited by* Frank Feeley. - *Published by* The Thorne Group Ltd. P.O. Box 260, Royal Trust Tower, Toronto-Dominion Centre, Toronto, Ont. M5K 1J9, 1953-
Biennial. Statistics.
$45.00.

From the ground up - *Published by* Aviation Publishers Co. Ltd. P.O. Box 1361, Ottawa B, Ont. K1P 5AO., 1940-
Annual. Training manual, 196 p.
$6.95.

Frozen foods / Canada / *edited by* Robert R. Dickson. - *Published by* Norman A. Goldie. Canadian Hotel and Restaurant. Maclean-Hunter Ltd. 481 University Ave., Toronto, Ont. M5W 1A7, 1973-
Annual. Trade publication. Includes advertising. Circulation: 22,742

Fulcrum / *edited by* J.G. Jenkins and others. - *Published by* Victoria Local. Socialist Party of Canada. P.O. Box 4280, Postal Station A, Victoria, B.C. V8X 3X8, May 1968-
Quarterly. Special interest, magazine format, 16 p.
$.25 per issue : $1.00 per year.

Fulcrum / *edited by* Louis Soulière. - *Published by* Students' Federation. University of Ottawa. Room 035, 85 Hastey Ave., Ottawa, Ont. K1N 5N6.
Irregular (approximately 16 issues per year). Student publication, newspaper format, 10 p. Includes advertising.
$5.00 per year.

Fur and feathers / *sponsored by* Toronto Academy of Veterinary Medicine ; *edited by* A. Dorothy Green. - *Published by* Fur and Feathers. 13 Brant Ave., Mississauga, Ont. L5G 3N9, 1963-
Quarterly. Institutional publication (Universities, schools, etc.), magazine format, 12 p. Language: English. Includes book reviews. Circulation: 6000
$.35 per issue : $1.50 per year : $2.00 per year, foreign. Bulk rates to humane organizations.

Fur trade journal / *edited by* Charles Clay. - *Published by* Clay Publishing Co. Ltd. Oak St., Bewdley, Ont. K0L 1E0, 1923-
Former title(s): Fur trade journal of Canada.
Monthly. Trade publication, magazine format, 12 p. Includes advertising.
ISSN 0016-2973 $.75 per issue : $6.00 per year. Controlled circulation.

Fur trade journal of Canada *See* Fur trade journal

Furniture and furnishings / *edited by* Ronald H. Shuker. - *Published by* Southam Business Publications Ltd. 1450 Don Mills Rd., Don Mills, Ont. M3B 2X7, 1910-
Monthly. Trade publication, tabloid format, 32 p. Language: English and French. Circulation: 10,510
Indexed in Can. B.P.I.
$1.00 per issue : $10.00 per year : $12.00 per year, U.S.

Furniture and furnishings buyers' guide and directory / *edited by* Ronald H. Shuker. - *Published by* Southam Business Publications Ltd. 1450 Don Mills Rd., Don Mills, Ont. M3B 2X7 (Subscription address: $5.00) 1910-
Annual. Directory, tabloid format, 48 p. Circulation: 10,510
Controlled circulation.

The Gallup report - *Published by* The Canadian Gallup Poll Ltd. 45 Charles St. E., Toronto, Ont. M4Y 1S2, December 1941-
Issued twice a week. National opinion surveys, newsletter format, 2 p.
$2.50 per issue : $60.00 per year.

Gam on yachting / *edited by* Karin Larson. - *Published by* Karin Larson. Room 307, 29 Colbourne St., Toronto, Ont. M5E 1E2, June 1957-
Monthly. Special interest, magazine format, 48 p. Includes book reviews, film reviews, advertising. Circulation: 17,000
$.50 per issue : $3.00 per year. Prepayment required.

Garden clippings / *edited by* Mrs. Monty Zary. - *Published by* Saskatoon Horticultural Society. 1208 Wiggins Ave., Saskatoon, Sask.
Irregular (approximately 5 issues per year). Association publication, magazine format, 32 p. Includes book reviews, advertising. Circulation: 3500
$.50 per issue : $2.00 per year. Prepayment required.

Garnet / *edited by* David Gersovitz and David Nayman. - *Published by* Alumni Association. Sir George Williams University. 1455 de Maisonneuve Blvd. W., Montreal, Que., October 1975-
Monthly. Alumni publication, newspaper format, 12 p. Includes advertising. Circulation: 12,000
$8.00 per year : $10.00 per year, foreign. Controlled circulation.

Gaspesian Cultural Association. Newsletter - *Published by* Gaspesian Cultural Association. P.O. Box 50, Shigawake, Que. G0C 3E0, 1971-
Monthly. Association publication, newsletter format, 4-6 p. Circulation: 675
Free.

Gastown and Vancouver today / *edited by* J.R.H. Cruikshank. - *Published by* Cruikshank Communications Ltd. P.O. Box 45, West Vancouver, B.C. V7V 3N3, December 1973-
Monthly. Special interest, magazine format, 32 p. Includes advertising.
$.25 per issue : $3.00 per year. Some paid subscribers. Controlled circulation.

Gateway / *edited by* Greg Neiman. - *Published by* Students' Union. University of Alberta. Students' Union Building, University of Alberta, Edmonton, Alta. T6G 2S7.
67. Student publication, newspaper format, 16 p. Includes book reviews, film reviews, play reviews, record reviews, advertising. Circulation: 18,000
$.10 per issue : $10.00 per year. Free.

Gauntlet / *edited by* Noel Jantzie. - *Published by* University of Calgary, Students' Union. 209 MacEwan Hall, University of Calgary, Calgary, Alta. T2N 1N4, September 1959-
Former title(s): Medium (Spring 1969)
Irregular (approximately 60 issues per year). Student publication, newspaper format, 12 p. Includes book reviews, film reviews, play reviews, record reviews, advertising. supplements issued. Circulation: 8000
$6.00 per year : $12.00 per year, foreign.

Gays of Ottawa. GO info / *edited by* Ron Dayman. - *Published by* Gays of Ottawa. P.O. Box 2912, Postal Station D, Ottawa, Ont. K1P 5K0, July 1972-
Irregular. Special interest, newsletter format, 10 p. Language: English and French.
ISSN 0315-0151 Free.

Gazette / *edited by* Gary J. Sirois. - *Published by* Canadian Museums Association. Room 505, 56 Sparks St., Ottawa, Ont. K1P 5A9 (Subscription address: PO. Box 1328, Postal Station B, Ottawa, Ont. K1P 5R4) November 1966-
Former title(s): CMA gazette (November 1966-April 1974)
Quarterly. Association publication, magazine format, 36-40 p. Language: English and French. Includes book reviews, advertising, volume index. supplements issued. Circulation: 1200
ISSN 0317-6045 $3.00 per issue : $8.00 per year : $8.80 per year, foreign. Free to members of C.M.A. Prepayment required.

Gazette / *edited by* Chris Redmond. - *Published by* Information Services Department. University of Waterloo. Dana Porter Arts Library Bldg., Waterloo, Ont. N2L 3G1, November 1960-
Former title(s): University of Waterloo. Quarterly.
Irregular (approximately 40 issues per year). Institutional publication (Universities, schools, etc.), newspaper format, 8 p. Circulation: 11,000
ISSN 0042-031X

Gazette laurentienne *See* Laurentian University. Laurentian gazette

La Gazzetta : Windsor Italian weekly - *Published by* La Gazzetta Publishing Co. 2110 Spring Garden Rd., Windsor, Ont. N9A 6B5 (Subscription address: 212 Erie St. W., Windsor, Ont. N9A 6B5) October 1972-
Weekly. Ethnic press, newspaper format, 16 p. Language: Italian. Includes book reviews, film reviews, play reviews, record reviews, advertising. Circulation: 4000
$.15 per issue : $7.00 per year : $10.00 per year, foreign.

The Genetics Society of Canada. Bulletin = La Société de génétique du Canada. Bulletin / *edited by* W. Woodbury. - *Published by* Genetics Society of Canada. Central Experimental Farm, Ottawa, Ont. (Subscription address: Suite 907, 151 Slater St., Ottawa, Ont. K1P 5H4) 1969-
Quarterly. Association publication, newsletter format, 10-12 p. Language: English and French. Circulation: 700
ISSN 0316-4357 $1.25 per issue : $5.00 per year. Subscription included in membership fee.

Génie construction / *édité par* Robert Girouard. - *Publié par* Southam Business Publications Ltd. Suite 201, 310, ave. Victoria, Montréal, Qué. H3Z 2M9, 1958-
Ancien titre: Canadian pit and quarry.
Mensuel. Revue d'entreprise. Comprend publicité.
Indexé dans RADAR.
$1.50 le numéro : $13.00 par année.

Le Géographe canadien *See* Canadian geographer

Geolog / *edited by* Lexi Clague. - *Published by* Geological Association of Canada. 7th King St. E., Toronto, Ont. (Subscription address: Business and Economic Service Ltd., Suite 509, 111 Peter St., Toronto, Ont) 1970-
Monthly except July and August. Association publication, magazine format, Language: English and French. Includes book reviews, advertising, updating service. Circulation: 2800
$5.00 per year. Prepayment required.

George Cross news letter: Western Canadian investments / *edited by* George Cross. - *Published by* George Cross. 114-744 W. Hastings St., Vancouver, B.C. V6C 1A5, April 1948-
Issued five days per week (250 per year). Special interest, newsletter format, 4 p. Includes cumulative index.
$.60 per issue : $160.00 per year. Special rates offered. Prepayment required.

The Georgian / *edited by* Kevin Quinn. - *Published by* Day Students' Association. Sir George Williams Campus. Concordia University. 1455 de Maisonneuve Blvd. W., Montreal, Que. H3G 1M8.
Issued twice a week. Student publication, newspaper format, 24 p. Includes book reviews, film reviews, play reviews, record reviews, advertising. supplements issued. Circulation: 16,150
$.10 per issue : $10.00 per year : $17.00 per volume. Free. Controlled circulation.

Geoscience Canada / *sponsored by* Geological Association of Canada ; *edited by* G.V. Middleton. - *Published by* Ainsworth Press Ltd. 65 Hanson, Kitchener, Ont. (Subscription address: Business and Economic Services Ltd., Suite 509, 111 Peter St. Toronto, Ont. M5V 2H1) January 1971-
Former title(s): Proceedings - Geological Association of Canada (1947-1973)
Quarterly. Association publication, magazine format, 40 p. Language: English and French ; summaries: English and French. Includes book reviews, advertising. Circulation: 3000
$3.00 per issue : $10.00 per year.

Geoscope / *edited by* P.G. Burpee. - *Published by* Provincial Association of Geography Teachers. P.O. Box 32, Postal Station NDG, Montreal, Que. J4R 2EB, April 1966-
Issued twice a year. Association publication, magazine format, 60 p. Includes book reviews, advertising. Circulation: 330
Indexed in North. tit.
$4.00 per year. Prepayment required.

German press review / *edited by* Press and Information Counsellor, German Embassy. - *Published by* Embassy of the Federal Republic of Germany. 1 Waverley St., Ottawa, Ont., 1971-
Weekly. Special interest, newsletter format, 5 p. Circulation: 200
Free.

German-Canadian yearbook = Deutsch-kanadisches Jahrbuch / *sponsored by* Historical Society of Mecklenburg Upper Canada Inc ; *edited by* Hartmut Froeschle. - *Published by* University of Toronto Press. 5201 Dufferin St., Downsview, Ont. M3H 5T8 (Subscription address: 34 Beattie Ave., Rexdale, Ont. M9W 2M3) May 1974-
Annual. Yearbook, book format, 260 p. Language: English, German and French.
ISSN 0316-8603 vol. I-$13.00 : vol. II-$16.00.

Germano-Slavica : a Canadian journal of Germanic and Slavic comparative studies / *edited by* J.W. Dyck. - *Published by* Department of Germanic and Slavic Languages and Literatures. University of Waterloo. Waterloo, Ont. N2L 3G1, Spring 1973-
Issued twice a year. Scholarly publication, journal format, 80 p. Language: English, German and Russian. Includes book reviews, advertising. supplements issued. Circulation: 300
Indexed in I.B.Z.
$4.50 per issue : $8.00 per year. Special rates offered.

Gerrish House newsletter (1967-1974) *See* Grand Manan Museum newsletter

Il Giornale di Toronto / *edited by* Pierino Mori. - *Published by* Il Giornale di Toronto Ltd. 2 Ramsden Rd., Toronto, Ont. M6E 2N2.
Weekly. Ethnic press. Language: Italian. Includes advertising. Circulation: 11,600

Glad Tidings Missionary Society. G.T.M.S / *edited by* Raymond H. Gaglardi. - *Published by* Glad Tidings Missionary Society, Inc. 3456 Fraser St., Vancouver, B.C. V5V 4C4, October 1974-
Former title(s): Harvest time (to May 1974)
Monthly. Directory, newspaper format, 8-12 p. Circulation: 1500
$2.00 per year.

Glas Kanadskih srba = Voice of Canadian Serbs - *Published by* Avala Printing and Publishing. 1297 Drouillard Rd., Windsor, Ont.
Weekly. Ethnic press. Language: Serbian. Includes advertising.
$12.00 per year.

Glenbow / *edited by* David Scollard. - *Published by* Glenbow-Alberta Institute. 902-11 Ave. S.W., Calgary, Alta. T2R 0E7, 1975-
Quarterly. Association publication, magazine format, 32 p.
Indexed in North. tit.
$1.50 per issue : $5.00 per year.

Glenhyrst Arts Council. Newsletter / *edited by* Secretary, Glenhyrst Arts Council. - *Published by* Glenhyrst Arts Council. 20 Ava Rd., Brantford, Ont.
Monthly. Association publication, newsletter format, 2 p.
$5.00 per year. Subscription included in membership fee.

Glitter - *Published by* Joyce Barslow. Glitter Happiness Inc. Suite 302, 189 Church St., Toronto, Ont. M5B 1Y7, 1974-
Issued every other month. Magazine format, Includes advertising.
$.75 per issue : $4.00 per year : $7.00 for 2 years : $10.00 for 3 years.

Glitter magazine / *edited by* Joyce Barslow and Lorraine Dewald Kennedy (managing editor). - *Published by* Joyce Barslow. Suite 302, 189 Church St., Toronto, Ont. M5B 1Y7, January 1975-
Issued every other month. General interest, magazine format, 64 p. Includes book reviews, film reviews, play reviews, record reviews, advertising. Circulation: 50,000
ISSN 0316-5965 $.75 per issue : $4.00 per year : $5.00 per year, U.S. : $5.50 per year, foreign.

The Globe and Mail vacation guide / *edited by* Kenneth Craig. - *Published by* Classified Advertising Department. 444 Front St. W., Toronto, Ont. M5V 2S9.
Annual. Directory, magazine format, 56 p.

The Glory hole / *edited by* Ann Geoghegan. - *Published by* Victoria Antique Glass and Bottle Collectors Association. P.O. Box 197, Shawigan Lake, B.C. V0R 2W0, November 1972-
Monthly. Association publication, newsletter format, 8 p. Includes book reviews, advertising. Circulation: 100

Glos Polski-gazeta Polska = Polish voice gazette / *edited by* Zygmunt Rusinek. - *Published by* Polish Voice Publishing Co. 1089 Queen St. W., Toronto, Ont. M6V 1H5, 1908-
Weekly. Language: Polish. Includes advertising. Circulation: 5275
$.25 per issue : $11.00 per year.

Glossa : an international journal of linguistics - *Published by* Department of Modern Languages. Simon Fraser University. Burnaby, B.C. V5A 1S6, 1967-
Issued twice a year. Association publication, magazine format, 250 p. Language: English and French. Includes book reviews, cumulative index. available in microform.
Indexed in LLBA, Curr. ind. j. educ., I.B.Z.
$4.00 per issue : $7.00 per year (Institutions $8.00).

Goed nieuws (May 1958-January 1971) *See* The Windmill herald

The Golden links / *edited by* George E. Dusenbury. - *Published by* Grand Lodge of Manitoba. Independent Order of Odd Fellows. 293 Kennedy St., Winnipeg, Man. R3B 2M7, 1964-
Monthly. Association publication, newsletter format, 6 p. Circulation: 1500
$1.50 per year.

Golden taffy / *sponsored by* Saskatchewan English Teachers' Association. - *Published by* Saskatchewan Teachers' Federation. P.O. Box 1108, 2317 Arlington Ave., Saskatoon, Sask. S7J 2H8.
Annual. Association publication, magazine format, 55 p.
$1.25. Controlled circulation.

Golf and club news *See* Golf Canada

Golf Canada / *edited by* Michael Bartlett. - *Published by* Nik Reitz. Golf and Club News Inc. Suite 404, 56 The Esplanade, Toronto, Ont., 1962-
Former title(s): Golf and club news.
Published April to October inclusive.
Magazine format, 48 p. Includes book reviews, advertising. Circulation: 88,000
$.60 per issue : $4.00 per year.

Golf Québec / *édité par* Gilles Terroux. - *Publié par* Angini inc. C.P. 278, Boucherville, Qué. J4B 5J6, mai 1974-
Intermittent (approximativement 5 éditions par an). Publication spécialisée, magazine, 36 p. Tirage: 8500
ISSN 0315-1344 $2.00 par année.
Abonnements payables à l'avance.

Good farming / *edited by* Gayle Wykes. - *Published by* Southam Business Publications Ltd. 1450 Don Mills Rd., Don Mills, Ont. M3B 2X7, 1949-
Quarterly. Includes advertising. Circulation: 115,261

Good roads (1923-1930) *See* Alberta motorist

Good tidings / *edited by* A. Stanley Bursey. - *Published by* Printing Department. Pentecostal Assemblies of Newfoundland. 57 Thorburn Rd. (P.O. Box 8248), St. John's Nfld. A1B 3N4.
Issued every other month. Church publication, magazine format, 36 p. Circulation: 5000
$.15 per issue : $1.50 per year. Controlled circulation.

The Good work of the Holy Land *Voir* L'Oeuvre de Terre-Sainte

Gospel herald / *sponsored by* Gospel Herald Foundation ; *edited by* Roy D. Merritt and H. Ralph Perry. - *Published by* H. Ralph Perry. Roy D. Merritt. P.O. Box 94, Beamsville, Ont., 1936-
Monthly. Church publication, magazine format, 17-25 p. Includes book reviews, advertising. Circulation: 1700
$.25 per issue : $3.00 per year : $4.00 per volume. Special rates offered. Prepayment required.

Gossip / *edited by* Virginia Stoyanoff (assistant editor). - *Published by* Gossip Ltd. 86 Avenue Rd., Toronto, Ont. M5R 2H2, 1926-
Monthly. Magazine format, Includes advertising.

Government and military business / *edited by* Wain King. - *Published by* Kerrwil Publications Ltd. 30 Eglinton Ave. E., Toronto, Ont. M4P 1B6, 1973-
Former title(s): Canadian Armed Forces review.
Issued every other month. Special interest, newspaper format, 8 p.
$9.00 per year.

Government and the contractor - *Published by* Engineering and Contract Record. 1450 Don Mills Rd., Don Mills, Ont. M3B 2X7, 1958-
Former title(s): Product distribution directory.
Annual. Includes advertising.

Government and the contractor / *edited by* T.B. Jones. - *Published by* D.R. Mackenzie. Southam Business Publications Ltd. 1450 Don Mills Rd., Don Mills, Ont. M3B 2X7, October 1975-
Former title(s): Construction industries directory.
Annual. Trade publication, magazine format, 100 p. Circulation: 18,000
$1.00 per issue. Controlled circulation.

Government purchasing guide / *edited by* R. Gladney. - *Published by* Michael J. Gladney. Gladney Publishing Group. Suite 706, 43 Eglinton Ave. E., Toronto, Ont. M4P 1A2, October 1969-
Issued every other month. Trade publication, magazine format, 24 p.
$4.50 per year. Controlled circulation.

The Grad post / *edited by* David Jones. - *Published by* Graduate Students' Union. University of Toronto. 16 Bancroft Ave., Toronto, Ont. M5S 1C1, September 1973-
Monthly May to August (Issued every other week September to April). Student publication, newspaper format, 4 p. Includes advertising. Circulation: 6000
Free.

Graduate / *edited by* Donald Evans. - *Published by* Department of Information Services. University of Toronto. 45 Willcocks St., Toronto, Ont. M5S 1C7, 1967-
Former title(s): University of Toronto news (1956-1963) Varsity graduate (1948-1967) University of Toronto monthly (1900)
Quarterly. Alumni publication, magazine format, 12 p. Includes book reviews. Circulation: 150,000
Indexed in Can. educ. ind.

The Graduate chronicle (April 1931-October 1948) *See* University of British Columbia. Alumni Association. UBC alumni chronicle

Graffiti / *edited by* Don Vezina. - *Published by* College Council of Students. Confederation College of Applied Arts and Technology. P.O. Box 398, Thunder Bay, Ont. P7C 4W1.
Former title(s): Origin 100.
Issued twice a month. Student publication, newspaper format, 8 p. Includes film reviews, play reviews, advertising. Circulation: 1500
Free.

Grain / *edited by* Caroline Heath. - *Published by* Saskatchewan Writer's Guild. P.O. Box 1005, Regina, Sask. (Subscription address: P.O. Box 1885, Saskatoon, Sask. S1K 3S2) Spring 1973-
Issued twice a year. Special interest, magazine format, 65 p. Circulation: 1000
Indexed in Can. essay and lit. ind.
$1.00 per issue : $2.00 per year : $5.00 for 3 years. Special rates offered.

The Grain grower's guide (June 1908-March 1928) *See* Country guide : the farm magazine

Grains de sel, grains de sable - *Publié par* Le Sablier inc. C.P. 120, Boucherville, Qué. J4B 5E6.
Intermittent (approximativement 4 éditions par an). 16-32 p.
$2.00 par année.

Le Grand journal illustré - *Publié par* Les Publications québecor inc. 4270, ave Papineau, Montréal, Qué. H2H 1T1.
Hebdomadaire. Intérêt général, journal, Comprend publicité. Tirage: 53,712
$.35 le numéro.

The Grand Manan historian / *edited by* L.K. Ingersall. - *Published by* Grand Manan Historical Society. Grand Manan, N.B.
Annual. Association publication, magazine format, 50 p.
$3.00 per issue.

Grand Manan Museum newsletter / *edited by* Eric Allaby. - *Published by* Grand Manon Museum. Grand Harbour, Grand Mawan, N.B. E0G 1X0, January 1975-
Former title(s): Gerrish House newsletter (1967-1974)
Quarterly. Institutional publication (Universities, schools, etc.), newsletter format, 4 p.

The Grande new Dawson and hind quarterly epistle / *edited by* B. Diane Skalenda. - *Published by* Association of Manitoba Museums. 190 Rupert Ave., Winnipeg, Man. R3B 0N2, September 1971-
Quarterly. Association publication, magazine format, 100 p. Includes book reviews. Circulation: 200
Available as part of AMM membership: $3.00 individuals; $5.00 institutions.

Les Grands espoirs / *édité par* H.N. Haken. - *Publié par* Professional Publishing Associates. Suite 409, 30 Bloor St. W., Toronto, Ont. M4W 1A2, 1972-
Publié en anglais: Great expectations.
Trimestriel. Publication spécialisée, magazine, Comprend publicité. Tirage: 77,841
$2.00 par année.

Great expectations / *edited by* H.N. Haken. - *Published by* Professional Publishing Associates. Suite 409, 30 Bloor St. W., Toronto, Ont. M4W 1A2, 1972-
Quarterly. Magazine format, Includes advertising. Circulation: 77,841
$2.00 per year.

The Great Lakes fisherman / *edited by* F.H. Prothero. - *Published by* F.H. Prothero. 542 George St., Port Stanley, Ont. N0L 2A0, November 1973-
Monthly. Trade publication, magazine format, 32 p. supplements issued.
$.50 per issue : $5.50 per year : $5.75 per year, foreign. Prepayment preferred.

Greater Windsor industrial building list (to 1974) *See* Industrial buildings - Windsor and Essex County

Greater Windsor manufacturers directory (1969-1972) *See* Windsor and Essex county manufacturers directory

Greater Winnipeg industrial topics (July 1952-May 1972) *See* Winnipeg industrial topics

Greek Canadian action = Drassis / *edited by* Stylianos Gusmas. - *Published by* Stylianos Gusmas. Suite 3, 8064 Wiseman St., Montreal, Que. H3N 2P1.
Monthly. Ethnic press. Language: Greek. Includes advertising. Circulation: 4000
$.25 per issue : $5.00 per year.

Greek Canadian reportage / *edited by* Anthony Bartzakos. - *Published by* Anthony Bartzakos. Suite 3, 7460 Champagneur, Montreal, Que. H3N 2J9, 1974-
Weekly. Ethnic press. Language: Greek. Includes advertising.
$13.00 per year : $20.00 per year, foreign.

Greek Canadian tribune / *edited by* G. Kandalepas and T. Petritis. - *Published by* G. Papadakis and N. Kalyvitis. 5619 Park Ave., Montreal, Que, 1964-
Weekly. Ethnic press. Language: Greek. Includes advertising. Circulation: 3227

The Green / *sponsored by* Canadian Lawn Bowling Council ; *edited by* Cy English. - *Published by* P. Wilkins. Sports Federation. 333 River Rd., Vanier, Ont. K1L 8B9 (Subscription address: 24 Deer Park Cr., Toronto, Ont. M4V 2C2)
Irregular (approximately 3-4 issues per year). Association publication, magazine format, 24 p.
Free.

The Green and white / *edited by* G. McConnell. - *Published by* Alumni Association. University of Saskatchewan. 107 Memorial Union Building, Saskatoon, Sask. S7M 0W0, 1939-
Quarterly. Alumni publication, magazine format, 32 p. Includes book reviews. Circulation: 26,000
ISSN 0017-3924

Greenhouse newsletter / *sponsored by* Canada Council ; *edited by* J.D. Campbell. - *Published by* Plant Science Department. Faculty of Agriculture. University of Manitoba. Winnipeg, Man. R3T 2N2, January 1972-
Issued twice a year. Institutional publication (Universities, schools, etc.), newsletter format, 5 p.
ISSN 0315-0860 Controlled circulation.

The Greenleaves. B.C. edition - *Published by* L. Paul Masse. Greencrest Industrial Publications Ltd. 541 E. Broadway, Vancouver, B.C. V5T 1X4, 1973-
Issued twice a year. Trade publication. Includes advertising. Circulation: 4711
$12.00 per issue : $20.00 per year.

Greensward / *edited by* E. Seager. - *Published by* Ontario Parks Association. 15 Wintemute St., Fort Erie, Ont. L2A 2N7.
Quarterly. Association publication, newsletter format, 4 p.
$8.00 per year.

Grocery report *See* Retail food report

Group practice in Canada - *Published by* Canadian Association of Medical Clinics. P.O. Box 8244, Ottawa, Ont., January/February 1973-
Former title(s): Bulletin - Canadian Association of Medical Clinics.
Association publication.
ISSN 0319-3209

The Grower / *edited by* W.L. Armstrong. - *Published by* Cash Crop Farming Publications Ltd. 222 Argyle Ave., Delhi, Ont. N4B 2Y2.
Monthly. Commodity publication, newspaper format, Includes advertising. Circulation: 13,000
$2.00 per year.

The Grower / *edited by* Les Armstrong. - *Published by* Ontario Fruit & Vegetable Growers Association. 301 Ontario Food Terminal, 165 The Queensway, Toronto, Ont., 1879-
Monthly. Trade publication. Includes advertising. Circulation: 12,361
$2.00 (Free to members).

Guelph alumnus / *edited by* David G. Smith. - *Published by* Department of Alumni Affairs. University of Guelph. University Centre, Level 4, University of Guelph, Guelph, Ont. N1G 2W1.
Issued every other month. Alumni publication, magazine format, 20 p. Circulation: 30,000

Guidance and Counselling Association newsletter (to June 1967) *See* Guidelines

The Guide / *edited by* Edward Vanderkloet. - *Published by* Christian Labour Association of Canada. 1036 Weston Rd., Toronto, Ont. M6N 3S2, 1952-
Monthly. Association publication, magazine format, 16 or 24 p. Includes book reviews, advertising, volume index. Circulation: 8000
$5.00 per year (airmail $7.50). Special rates offered. Prepayment required.

Guide annuaire des représentants de commerce - *Publié par* L'Association provinciale des conseillers de vente inc. Suite 405, 2950 Masson, Montréal, Qué. H1Y 1X4, 1971-1972-
Annuel. Publication d'association, 170 p.
Envoi gratuit.

Guide de la conservation du Canada *See* Canadian conservation directory

Guide de la cosméticienne / *édité par* X.B. de Lusigny. - *Publié par* Robert D. Reid. Maclean-Hunter Ltd. 481 University Ave., Toronto, Ont. M5W 1A7, 1966-
Annuel. Revue d'entreprise, magazine, 80 p. Comprend publicité. Tirage: 3000
$3.00 le numéro. Tirage contrôlé.

Guide de l'étudiant = Student handbook - *Publié par* Département d'histoire. Université d'Ottawa. 147, rue Wilbrod, Ottawa, Ont. K1N 6N5, 1968-
Annuel. Publication d'institution (universités, écoles..), bulletin, 40 p. Langue(s): français et anglais. Comprend publicité. Tirage: 500
Envoi gratuit.

Guide des institutions Joncas = Joncas institutional guide / *édité par* Robert Joncas. - *Publié par* Paul A. Joncas Inc. 250 ouest, rue Faillon, Montréal, Qué. H2R 2V7.
Annuel. Publication spécialisée. Langue(s): français et anglais. Comprend publicité. Tirage: 8081
$7.50 par année.

Guide du transport par camion = Truck transport guide / *edited by* Liliane Duchesne. - *Published by* Guide du transport par camion inc. Suite 11, 4246 est, Jean Talon, Montréal, Qué. H1S 1J8, 1937-
Annuel. Revue d'entreprise. Language: français et anglais.
$8.00 par année.

Le Guide génétique de l'éleveur - *Publié par* Agence de sélection bovine enr. 30 est, Evêché, Rimouski, Qué.
Intermittent. Publication spécialisée, 40 p.
$1.00 le numéro.

Guide to good food in Metro Vancouver / *edited by* Nathan Divinsky. - *Published by* Nathan Divinsky. Department of Mathematics, University of British Columbia, Vancouver, B.C., 1971-
Annual. Restaurant guide, magazine format, 24 p.
$1.00.

Guide to periodicals and newspapers currently received (1972) *See* Guide to periodicals and newspapers in the public libraries of Metropolitan Toronto

Guide to periodicals and newspapers in the public libraries of Metropolitan Toronto - *Published by* Metropolitan Toronto Library Board. Suite 301, 203 College St., Toronto, Ont. M5T 1R9, 1970-
Former title(s): Guide to periodicals and newspapers currently received (1972) Guide to serials currently received... (1970)
Annual. Bibliography, 318 p. supplements issued. Circulation: 700
ISSN 0315-7288 $15.00.

Guide to serials currently received... (1970) *See* Guide to periodicals and newspapers in the public libraries of Metropolitan Toronto

Guide touristique *See* Tourist guide

Guidelines / *sponsored by* Saskatchewan Guidance and Counselling Association ; *edited by* Don Reimer. - *Published by* Saskatchewan Teachers' Federation. P.O. Box 1108, Saskatoon, Sask. S7J 2H8, Vol. 6 No. 1 January 1968-
Former title(s): Guidance and Counselling Association newsletter (to June 1967)
Quarterly. Association publication, magazine format, 25-30 p. Includes book reviews. Circulation: 100
Indexed in Can. educ. ind.
$10.00 per year.

Guidelines to industrial progress / *edited by* P.C. Trussell. - *Published by* British Columbia Research Council. 3650 Wesbrook Crescent, Vancouver, B.C. V6S 2L2, January 1967-
Monthly. Special interest, newsletter format, 1 p. Circulation: 3000
Free.

Guiding for you : programme, uniform and badges - *Published by* Girl Guides of Canada. 50 Merton St., Toronto, Ont. M4S 1A3.
Issued 6 times per year (September, October, November, January, March, and May).
House/company organ, magazine format, 16 p. Includes advertising. Circulation: 32,000
$.20 per issue : $2.00 per year : $2.25 per year, foreign. Prepayment required.

The Guiding light / *edited by* T.H. Drillen. - *Published by* Northern Regional Development Council. P.O. Box 5, Bathurst, N.B. E2A 3Z1, January 1970-
Quarterly. 10 p.
Free.

Gulf Canada cartalk / *edited by* Gary Schlee. - *Published by* Gulf Oil Canada Ltd. 800 Bay St., Toronto, Ont. (Subscription address: P.O. Box 460, Postal Station A, Toronto, Ont. M5W 1E5) January 1970-
Published in French: Automotifs.
Irregular (approximately 8 issues per year). House/company organ, newsletter format, 4-8 p. Includes cumulative index. A supplement to Gulf Canada dealer news.
Controlled circulation.

Gulf Canada dealer news / *edited by* Gary Schlee. - *Published by* Gulf Oil Canada Ltd. 800 Bay St., Toronto, Ont. (Subscription address: P.O. Box 460, Postal Station A, Toronto, Ont. M5W 1E5) 1943-
Former title(s): B-A dealer news (1968) B-A dealer (1950-1968) Timely station topics (1943-1950) Published in French: Nouvelles Gulf Canada.
Irregular (approximately 8 issues per year). House/company organ, newsletter format, 8 p. supplements issued.
Controlled circulation.

Gulf wings / *edited by* John R. Scott. - *Published by* Canadian Forces Base, Summerside Base Commander. CFB Summerside, P.E.I. C0B 2A0, June 1974-
Monthly. House/company organ, newspaper format, 10 p. Language: English (French). Includes book reviews, advertising. Circulation: 1500
$1.00 per year.

Gun talk / *sponsored by* Saskatchewan Gun Collectors association ; *edited by* Mike McCall. - *Published by* Adventure Press. P.O. Box 1334, Regina, Sask., 1961-
Quarterly. Association publication, magazine format, 50 p.
Controlled circulation.

Gut : magazine of prose, reviews and poetry / *edited by* Alfred Rushton. - *Published by* Alfred Rushton. 389 Berkeley St., Toronto, Ont., March 1973-
Quarterly. Special interest, 20 p. Includes book reviews, film reviews, advertising. Circulation: 2000
$.50 per issue : $3.00 per year : $4.50 per year, foreign.

Hair - *Published by* Audrey Taylor. Intercommunications Ltd. 3rd Floor, 2 Elgin Ave., Toronto, Ont. (Subscription address: P.O. Box 669, Charles St. P.O., Toronto, Ont.) 1965-
Former title(s): Trim.
Quarterly. Trade publication. Includes advertising.

Hamilton Automobile Club. H.A.C. news / *edited by* Alfred U. Oakie. - *Published by* Hamilton Automobile Club. 393 Main St. E., Hamilton, Ont. L8N 1J7, 1956-
Issued 8 times a year. Association publication, newsletter format, 4 p.
Free to members only.

Hamilton journal / *edited by* Rosel Greinwald. - *Published by* Erich O. Reprich. P.O. Box 278, Pickering, Ont. L1V 2R4, 1952-
Weekly. Ethnic press, newspaper format, 16 p. Language: German.
$7.50 per year : $11.50 per year, foreign.

Hamilton place - *Published by* Hamilton Place. Hamilton, Ont. L8P 1H3.
Monthly (September through May). Includes advertising.

Handicapped forum (Summer 1972-1973) *See* The Alberta handicapped forum

Happening (November 1970- February 1971) *See* Christian inquirer

Happy landings - *Published by* Royal Canadian Flying Clubs Association. Suite 207, 2277 Riverside Dr. E., Ottawa, Ont. K1H 7X6, 1962-
Irregular. Association publication.
$.15 per issue.

Harbour and shipping / *edited by* Judy E. Corser. - *Published by* Progress Publishing Co. (1958) Ltd. c301-355 Burrard St., Vancouver, B.C. V6C 2G6, 1918-
Monthly. Trade publication, magazine format, 46 p. Includes advertising. Circulation: 1500
$.75 per issue : $6.00 per year : $10.00 for 2 years : $1.50 for special issues : $10.00 per year, foreign. Controlled circulation.

Hardware handbook / *edited by* John O'Keefe. - *Published by* Maclean-Hunter Ltd. 481 University Ave., Toronto, Ont. M5W 1A7.
Annual. Trade publication, magazine format, 84 p. Includes advertising.
$1.00 per issue : $10.00 per year : $12.00 per year, U.S. and U.K. : $25.00 per year, foreign. Controlled circulation.

Hardware merchandising / *edited by* Starr Smith. - *Published by* Maclean-Hunter Ltd. 481 University Ave., Toronto, Ont. M5W 1A1, 1888-
Former title(s): Hardware merchandising hardware handbook.
Monthly. Trade publication. Includes advertising. Circulation: 8673
Indexed in Can. B.P.I.
$10.00 per year : $12.00 per year, U.S. and U.K.

Hardware merchandising hardware handbook *See* Hardware merchandising

Harlequin / *edited by* Beth McGregor. - *Published by* Harlequin Enterprises Ltd. 240 Duncan Mills Rd., Don Mills, Ont. M3B 1Z4 (Subscription address: Harlequin Reader Service, 649 Ontario St., Stratford, Ont. N5A 3J6) May 1973-
Former title(s): Harlequin's woman (May 1974-March 1975) Harlequin newsletter magazine (May 1973-May 1974)
Monthly. General interest, magazine format, 72 p. Circulation: 85,000
ISSN 0319-0595 $.75 per issue : $9.00 per year.

Harlequin newsletter magazine (May 1973-May 1974) *See* Harlequin

Harlequin's woman (May 1974-March 1975) *See* Harlequin

Harness world = Monde du harnais / *edited by* J.M. Le Page. - *Published by* Harness World Publishing Ltd. P.O. Box 100, Cote-des-Neiges, Montreal, Que. H3S 2S4.
Special interest, magazine format, Language: English and French. Includes advertising. Circulation: 1857

Harvest / *edited by* Lambert Hogenbirk and Judith Nowlan. - *Published by* Student Society. Macdonald College Publications Office. P.O. Box 98, Centennial Centre, Macdonald College, Que. H9X 3M1.
Irregular (approximately 12 issues per year). Student publication. Includes advertising.

Harvest time (to May 1974) *See* Glad Tidings Missionary Society. G.T.M.S

Harvestings from the wheatland / *edited by* Marjorie Allan. - *Published by* Wheatland Regional Library. 806 Duchess St., Saskatoon, Sask. S7K 0R3, August 1967-
Issued twice a year. Institutional publication (Universities, schools, etc.), newsletter format, 15-20 p. Includes book reviews, advertising, updating service. Circulation: 750
$2.00 per issue : $3.00 per year. Controlled circulation.

Health / *edited by* Gordon Bates. - *Published by* Health League of Canada. 76 Avenue Rd., Toronto, Ont. M5R 2H1, Spring 1976-
Quarterly. Special interest, magazine format, 28 p. Circulation: 13,000
$.75 per issue : $3.00 per year. Special rates offered.

The Health and Physical Education Council bulletin (1964-1974) *See* Alberta Teachers' Association. Health and Physical Education Council. HPEC runner

Health car digest / *edited by* John Boyd. - *Published by* Southam Business Publications Ltd. 1450 Don Mills Rd., Don Mills, Ont. M3B 2X7.
Quarterly. Trade publication. Includes advertising. Circulation: 15,790
$10.00 per year.

Health facilities in Metropolitan Toronto / *edited by* George T. Liguori. - *Published by* Metropolitan Toronto Hospital Planning Council. 50 Yorkville Ave., Toronto, Ont. M4W 1L4, 1973-
Issued twice a year. 70 p.
$3.00 per year.

Health rays / *edited by* Donald M. Brown. - *Published by* Nova Scotia Sanatorium. Kentville, N.S., November 1919-
Former title(s): X-ray (1919 to 1927)
Monthly. Special interest, magazine format, 17 p. Circulation: 700
$.25 per issue : $2.00 per year.

Healthful living digest / *edited by* Bill Solar. - *Published by* Health Supply Centre. 414 Graham Ave., Winnipeg, Man. R3C 0L9, 1940-
Issued twice a year. House/company organ, magazine format, 120 p. Includes book reviews, advertising, volume index.
Circulation: 700,000
Free.

Heartline *See* Actionews : world vision's heartline to needy world

Heating, plumbing, air conditioning / *edited by* Nick Hancock. - *Published by* Henry Longstaff. Southam Business Publications Ltd. 1450 Don Mills Rd., Don Mills, Ont. M3B 2X7.
Monthly. Trade publication, newspaper format, 24-32 p. Circulation: 13,500
Indexed in Can. B.P.I.
Controlled circulation.

Heating, plumbing, air conditioning buyers' guide / *edited by* Nick Hancock. - *Published by* Henry Longstaff. Southam Business Publications Ltd. 1450 Don Mills Rd., Don Mills, Ont. M3B 2X7.
Annual. Directory, magazine format, 100 p. Language: English and bilingual version.
$10.00.

Heavy construction news / *edited by* David Judge. - *Published by* A. Bert Sevink. Maclean-Hunter Ltd. 481 University Ave., Toronto, Ont. M5W 1A7, 1956-
Issued every other week. Trade publication. Includes advertising. Circulation: 17,627
Indexed in Can. B.P.I.

Heavy equipment *Voir* Machinerie lourde

The Hebrew journal / *edited by* S.B. Rose. - *Published by* J. Switzman. 304 Adelaide St. W., Toronto, Ont. M5W 1P6.
Weekly. Special interest. Language: Hebrew. Includes advertising. Circulation: 4700
$.15 per issue : $15.00 per year.

Heimskringla (1886-1959) *See* Logberg - heimskringla

Hellenic community voice of Ottawa *See* Koinotiki foni

Hellenic echo / *edited by* Kostas Karatsikis. - *Published by* Kostas Karatsikis and Nick Panos. Hellenic Echo Publishing Co. Ltd. 2932 W. Broadway, Vancouver, B.C. V6K 2G8, 1971-
Issued twice a month. Ethnic press. Language: Greek. Includes advertising. Circulation: 1500
$10.00 per year.

Hellenic free press / *edited by* A. Stambolis. - *Published by* Mrs. Z. Stambolis. 1602 Dupont St., Toronto, Ont. M6P 3S7, 1967-
Weekly. Ethnic press. Language: Greek. Includes advertising.

Hellenic postman / *edited by* Christos El. Kolivas. - *Published by* Hellenic Postman. 3622 St. Lawrence Blvd., Montreal, Que., 1958-
Ethnic press. Language: Greek. Includes advertising.
$.15 per issue : $8.00 per year.

Hellenic tribune / *edited by* D. Zotos. - *Published by* D. Zotos. Zotos Printing and Publishing Co. 795 Carlaw Ave., Toronto, Ont, 1957-
Weekly. Ethnic press. Language: Greek. Includes advertising.
$7.00 per year.

Help for the leper : Raoul Fallereau foundations - *Published by* The Canadian Leprosy Relief Association Inc. P.O. Box 1672, Postal Station B, Montreal, Que. H3B 3L3, 1964-
Published in French: Le Secours aux lépreux. Issued every other month. Association publication, newsletter format, 4 p.
Free.

Herald *See* Visnyk

Heraldry in Canada / *edited by* Strome Galloway. - *Published by* Nancy Poipier. The Heraldry Society of Canada. 588 Gladstone Ave., Ottawa, Ont. K1R 5P3 (Subscription address: 900 Pinecrest Rd., Ottawa, Ont. K2B 6B3) September 1966-
Quarterly. Association publication, magazine format, 36 p. Language: English and French. Includes book reviews. Circulation: 650
$15.00 per year. Prepayment required.

Le Héraut de Saint-Paul / *édité par* Le Diocèse de Saint-Paul (R. Roy). - *Publié par* St-Paul Herald. C.P. 339, Saint-Paul, Alta. T0A 3A0, automne 1972-
Intermittent (approximativement 10 éditions par an). Publication ecclésiastique. Langue(s): français et anglais.

Here and Now = D'ores et déjà - *Published by* Institute of Psychological Research Inc. 34 Fleury St. W., Montreal, Que.
Institutional publication (Universities, schools, etc.).

Heritage Canada quarterly / *edited by* T.J. McDougall. - *Published by* Heritage Canada. P.O. Box 1358, Postal Station B, Ottawa, Ont. K1P 5R4, Winter 1975-
Quarterly. Special interest, magazine format, 40 p. Language: English and French. Includes book reviews, film reviews. Circulation: 8000
Subscription included in membership fee $5.00 (Students and senior citizens $3.00; households $7.00). Special rates offered.

Heritage comics - *Publié par* Jacques Payette et Sidney Simms. Les Editions Héritage inc. 300, boul. Arran, St. Lambert, Montréal, Qué.
Mensuel. Publication spécialisée, magazine, Comprend publicité. Tirage: 218,000
$.25 le numéro.

Hiballer magazine / *edited by* J.M. Siddall. - *Published by* Cy Young. H.B. Publishers Ltd. 1240 W. Pender St., Vancouver, B.C., 1948-
Monthly. Trade publication. Includes advertising. Circulation: 5989
$1.00 per issue : $6.00 per year : $10.00 for 2 years : $7.50 per year, foreign.

Highlights of the East (1936-1944) *See* National news

The High-way / *sponsored by* The Anglican Church of Canada, Diocese of Kootenay ; *edited by* F. Ilene Patterson. - *Published by* Salmon Arm Observer. Salmon Arm, B.C. (Subscription address: P.O. Box 549, Kelowna, B.C)
Issued every other month. Church publication, newsletter format, 4-8 p.
Free.

Highway carriers guide *See* Canadian highway carriers guide

Highway finance (1956-1972) *See* Nation on the move

Highway safety news (January 1961 - February 1969) *See* Safety Canada

Highway Transport Board. Highway Transport Board Bulletin / *edited by* Mrs. D. Myles. - *Published by* Ontario Trucking Association. 555 Dixon Rd., Rexdale, Ont. M9W 1H8, July 1957-
Former title(s): Members' bulletin - Highway Transport Board (January 1940-June 1957)
Weekly. Association publication, newsletter format, 18 p. Circulation: 2050
Circulation restricted to members. Controlled circulation.

L'Histoire au'pays' de Matane : généalogie, biographie, anecdotes, folklore / *édité par* Robert Fournier. - *Publié par* La Société d'histoire de Matane. C.P. 608, Matane, Qué.
Semestriel. Publication d'association, 40-60 p. Tirage: 1000
Indexé dans RADAR.
$.75 le numéro : $1.50 par année. Un certain nombre d'envoi gratuit. Tarifs spéciaux disponibles. Abonnements payables à l'avance.

Histoire ouvrière canadienne *See* Canadian labour history

Histoire sociale *See* Social history

Histoire sociale = Social history - *Published by* Les éditions de l'Université d'Ottawa. University of Ottawa Press, Ottawa, Ont. K1N 6N5.
Issued twice a year.
Indexed in Periodex.
$7.00 per year.

Historia mathematica : international journal of history of mathematics / *sponsored by* Canada Council; *edited by* Kenneth O. May. - *Published by* International Commission on the History of Mathematics. University of Toronto, Toronto, Ont. M5S 1A1, February 1974-
Quarterly. Association publication, 125 p. Includes book reviews, advertising, volume index, cumulative index. Circulation: 1150
Indexed in Math. r., I.B.Z.
ISSN 0315-0860 $6.00 per issue : $10.00 per year (Libraries $22.00). Special rates offered.

Historic Kingston : journal of the proceedings of the Kingston Historical Society / *edited by* William A. Angus. - *Published by* Kingston Historical Society. P.O. Box 54, Kingston, Ont., 1952-
Annual. Association publication, journal format, 80 p. Includes cumulative index. Reprints of Volume 1-10 (1952-1961) available through Mika Publications of Belleville. Circulation: 650
$3.00. Prepayment required.

Historical and Scientific Society of Manitoba. Transactions / *edited by* Mrs. David McDowell. - *Published by* Manitoba Historical Society. Room 211, 190 Rupert Ave., Winnipeg, Man. R3B 0N2.
Annual. Association publication, magazine format, 125-140 p.
Indexed in Hist. abstr.; Amer. hist. and life.
$5.00.

Historical reflections = Réflexions historiques / *edited by* John F.H. New and Gilman M. Ostrander. - *Published by* Department of History. University of Waterloo. Waterloo, Ont. N2L 3G1, Summer 1974-
Issued twice a year. Scholarly publication, journal format, 140 p. Language: English and French. Circulation: 225
Indexed in Hist. abstr.; Amer. hist. and life.
ISSN 0315-7997 $5.00 per issue : $5.00 per year (Institutions $10.00).

Historical Society of Alberta. Whoop-up Country Chapter. Newsletter / *edited by* Alex Johnston. - *Published by* Historical Society of Alberta, Whoop-up Country Chapter. P.O. Box 974, Lethbridge, Alta., 1967-
Issued every other month. Association publication, newsletter format, 4 p. Circulation: 300

The History and social science teacher / *edited by* Donald Bogle. - *Published by* The Ontario History and Social Sciences Teachers' Association. 67 Drakefield Rd., Markham, Ont. L3P 1G9, Fall 1974-
Former title(s): The Canadian journal of history and social science (Fall 1969 - Spring 1974) The History Teacher (1965-1969)
Quarterly. Association publication, journal format, 80 p. Includes book reviews, film reviews, record reviews, advertising. Circulation: 1100
Indexed in Resources in educ., Can. educ. ind.
ISSN 0316-4969 $9.00 per year.

The History Teacher (1965-1969) *See* The History and social science teacher

The Hitching post / *edited by* Janet Fewster. - *Published by* Janet Fewster. The Hitching Post. R.R.1, Kempville, Ont. K0G 1J0, January 1968-
Monthly. Special interest, magazine format, 25-30 p. Includes book reviews, advertising. Circulation: 100
$.25 per issue : $3.00 per year : $3.25 per year, foreign. Prepayment required.

Hi-tension news - *Published by* Canadian Ohio-Brass Co. Ltd. P.O. Box 267, Niagara Falls, Ont. L2E 6T5.
Issued every other month. House/company organ, magazine format, 8 p. Circulation: 1700
Free. Controlled circulation.

Hlas novych = Newcomers' voice (May 1967-December 1972) *See* Kanadské listy

Hobo-Québec : journal d'écritures et d'images / *édité par* Claude Robitaille. - *Publié par* Claude Robitaille. Editions Hobo-Québec. C.P. 464, Succursale C, Montréal, Qué. H2L 4K4, novembre 1972-
Bimestriel. Publication spécialisée, journal, 24 p. Comprend critique de livres, critique de films, critique de pièces de théâtre. Tirage: 2500
$.75 le numéro : $5.00 par année : $1.00 le numéro, l'étranger. Envoi gratuit. Abonnements payables à l'avance.

Hockey amateur de Québec / *édité par* Richard Laliberté. - *Publié par* Hockey amateur du Québec. 3098, rue Edgar, Fabreville, Laval, Qué., 1972-
Intermittent (approximativement 6 éditions par an). Publication spécialisée, magazine, Comprend publicité.
$.50 per issue.

The Hockey news / *edited by* Charles Halpin. - *Published by* Ken McKenzie. W.C.C. Publishing Ltd. Suite 217, 1434 St. Catherine St. W., Montreal, Que. H3G 1R7, 1947-
Irregular (approximately 37 issues per year). Special interest, magazine format, Includes advertising. Circulation: 154,036
$.60 per issue : $9.50 per year.

Hockey pictorial / *edited by* Charles Halpin. - *Published by* Ken McKenzie. W.C.C. Publishing Ltd. Suite 217, 1434 St. Catherine St. W., Montreal, Que. H3G 1R7, 1955-
Irregular (approximately 7 issues per year). Special interest, magazine format, Includes advertising. Circulation: 78,616
$.75 per issue : $4.50 per year.

Hockey's heritage : Hockey Hall of Fame / *edited by* M.H. (Lefty) Reid. - *Published by* Hockey Hall of Fame. Exhibition Park, Toronto, Ont. M6K 3C3, 1969-
Annual. Institutional publication (Universities, schools, etc.), book format, 90 p.
$3.45.

Hog guide - *Published by* R.W. McGuire. 1760 Ellice Ave., Winnipeg, Man., October 1965-
Issued every other month. Special interest, magazine format, 20 p. available in microform. Issued as a supplement to Country guide. Circulation: 36,645
Free to qualified subscribers of Country guide. Controlled circulation.

Hog marketplace quarterly / *edited by* John Philips. - *Published by* Agricultural Publishing Co. Ltd. Suite 305, 30 Bloor St. W., Toronto, Ont. M4W 1A2, 1969-
Quarterly. Trade publication. Includes advertising. Circulation: 33,041

The Holiday host / *edited by* Zdena Baranek. - *Published by* Richard Ballentine. Calendar Magazines Ltd. 65 Front St. E., Toronto, Ont. M5E 1B6, Christmas 1969-
Issued twice a year. General interest, magazine format, 72 p. Includes advertising.
Delivered with Calendar magazines.
Controlled circulation.

Hollandia-news - *Published by* Hollandia Publications. P.O. Box 234, 244 Queen St., Chatham, Ont.
Issued twice a month. Ethnic press. Language: Dutch. Includes advertising. Circulation: 2250
$1.00 per year.

Holman Eskimo prints 1974 = Estampes esquimaudes d'Holman / *sponsored by* Holman Island Eskimo Co-operative. - *Published by* Canadian Arctic Producers Ltd. P.O. Box 4130, Postal Station E, Ottawa, Ont. K1S 5B2.
Irregular (approximately 1 issue per year). Catalogue, 25 p. Language: English and French.

Holos Instytutu. Mohyla Institute. Newsletter / *sponsored by* Mohyla Institute ; *edited by* Walter Mysak. - *Published by* Candra Courier. Candra, Sask. (Subscription address: 1240 Temprance St., Saskatoon, Sask. S7N 0P1) 1962-
Issued every other month. Ethnic press, newsletter format, 8 p. Language: English and Ukrainian.

Holos spasytels = The Redeemer's voice / *sponsored by* Ukrainian Catholic Mission of the Most Holy Redeemer ; *edited by* M. Schudlo. - *Published by* Redeemer's Voice Press. Yorkton, Sask. S3N 2V7, 1921-
Monthly. Magazine format, 64 p. Language: Ukrainian and English. Circulation: 1700
$.50 per issue : $5.00 per year : $7.50 per volume.

Holstein-Friesian journal / *sponsored by* Holstein-Friesian Association of Canada ; *edited by* Hugh J. Colson. - *Published by* Donovan Ltd. Room 904, 6 Adelaide St. E., Toronto, Ont., April 1938-
Monthly. Special interest, magazine format, 145 p. Language: English and French. Includes advertising. Circulation: 17,000
$5.00 per year : $6.00 per year, foreign. Prepayment required.

Home and country / *sponsored by* Alberta Women's Institute ; *edited by* Basilia Heninger. - *Published by* Lethbridge Herald. Lethbridge, Alta. (Subscription address: 7720-106a Avenue, Edmonton, Alta.) 1933-
Quarterly. Association publication, newsletter format, 8 p. Circulation: 2000
$1.00 per year. Group rate to W.I. branches $.50. Prepayment required.

Home and country / *edited by* Basilia Heninger. - *Published by* University of Toronto Press. 5201 Dufferin St., Downsview, Ont. M3H 5T8, 1933-
Quarterly. Association publication, newsletter format, 8 p. Circulation: 2000
$1.00 per year. Group rate to W.I. branches $.50. Prepayment required.

Home and country, W.I.N.S / *edited by* Emily Jardine. - *Published by* Women's Institutes of Nova Scotia. 576v Prince St., Truro, NS. (Subscription address: Boulden Bldg., Nova Scotia Agricultural College, Truro, N.S. B2N 5E3)
Monthly. Newspaper format, 8 p.
$2.00 per year. Prepayment required.

Home echos - *Published by* Home Economics Council. Alberta Teachers' Association. 11010-142 St., Edmonton, Alta.
Irregular (approximately 3 issues per year). Association publication.
Indexed in Can. educ. ind.

Home economics newsletter / *sponsored by* Nova Scotia Home Economics Association ; *edited by* Clara E. Jefferson. - *Published by* Kentville Publishing Co. Ltd. Kentville, N.S., 1928-
Quarterly. Association publication, magazine format, 24-32 p. Includes book reviews. Circulation: 250
$1.00 per issue : $4.00 per year.

Home economics newsletter / *edited by* Isabelle Morrison. - *Published by* Home Educational Section. Ontario Education Association. Suite S904, 252 Bloor St. W., Toronto, Ont. M5S 1V7 (Subscription address: c/o Mrs. Mary Robson, 15 Hawthorn Ave., Toronto, Ont.)
Issued twice a year. Association publication, newsletter format, 40 p. Includes book reviews.
subscription included in membership fee $10.00.

Home goods retailing / *edited by* Helen Bohen. - *Published by* Maclean-Hunter Ltd. 481 University Ave., Toronto, Ont. M5W 1A7.
Monthly. Trade publication, tabloid format, 36 p. Language: English (French).
$1.00 per issue : $10.00 per year. Controlled circulation.

Home Oil Company. Library bulletin / *edited by* Jane Graham. - *Published by* Library. Home Oil Company. 304 Sixth Ave. S.W., Calgary, Alta. T2P 0R4, 1963-
Annual. House/company organ, bulletin format, 15 p.
Free. Controlled circulation.

Homemaker's digest *See* Homemakers magazine

Homemakers magazine / *edited by* Jane Hughes. - *Published by* Edward H. Gittings. Comac Publishing Ltd. Yonge-Eglinton Centre, 2300 Yonge St., Toronto, Ont., June 1966-
Former title(s): Homemaker's digest.
Irregular (approximately 8 issues per year). Magazine format, 135 p. Language: English and French.
Free. $8.00 for 2 years outside free distribution area. Controlled circulation.

Homes and families / *edited by* M.H. Hull. - *Published by* Extension Division. University of Saskatchewan. Saskatoon, Sask., June 1962-
Issued every other month. Institutional publication (Universities, schools, etc.), newsletter format, 4 p. Includes book reviews. supplements issued. Circulation: 480
$1.00 per year.

Homiletic service / *sponsored by* St. Paul University ; *edited by* W.E. O'Meara. - *Published by* Novalis. P.O. Box 498, Postal Station, A, Ottawa, Ont. K1N 8Y5, 1962-
Issued every other month. Special interest, magazine format, 40 p.
$1.30 per issue : $7.50 per year : $9.30 per year, foreign.

Homin ukrainy = Ukrainian echo / *edited by* W. Solonynka. - *Published by* Homin Ukrainy Publishing Co. Ltd. 140 Bathrust St., Toronto, Ont. M5V 2R3.
Weekly. Ethnic press. Language: Ukrainian. Includes advertising. Circulation: 8130

L'Homme nouveau. Edition canadienne / *édité par* Marcel Clément. - *Publié par* Centre américain de l'homme nouveau. Les Editions de l'homme nouveau. 5767, ave Durocher, Montréal, Qué.(adresse d'abonnement: C.P. 425, Outremont, Qué. H2V 4N3) novembre 1972-
Bimensuel. Intérêt général, journal, 16 p. Comprend critique de livres. Tirage: 3000
$.65 le numéro : $14.00 par année : $16.00 par année, l'étranger (Par avion $20.00). Abonnements payables à l'avance.

L'Hôpital catholique / *édité par* Yolande Lapointe. - *Publié par* Catholic Hospital Association of Canada. 312 Daly Ave., Ottawa, Ont. K1N 6G7, 1958-
Ancien titre: O.H.A.C. news bulletin.
Bimestriel. Publication d'association, magazine, Tirage: 3500
ISSN 0315-4858 $3.00 par année.

L'hôpital d'aujourd'hui *Voir* Administration hospitalière et sociale

Horizons / *edited by* Marjorie W. Buckley. - *Published by* Alberta Council on Aging. Room 1104, 10235-124 St., Edmonton, Alta. T5N 1P9, 1968-
Quarterly. Association publication, newsletter format, 4 p. Includes volume index. Circulation: 1750
Indexed in North. tit.
$2.00 per year.

Horizons - *Published by* Ontario Society for Crippled Children. 350 Rumsey Rd., Toronto, Ont. M4G 1R8, November 1970-
Former title(s): Bulletin - Ontario Society for Crippled Children (1970)
Quarterly. Association publication, newspaper format, 4-6 p. Circulation: 15,000
Free.

Horizons Autumn 1966-Winter 1969) *See* Communist viewpoint

Horsing around (newsletter) / *edited by* Madeleine Florent. - *Published by* Ottawa Valley Western Horse Association. P.O. Box 2685, Postal Station D., Ottawa, Ont.
Monthly. Association publication, newsletter format, 5 p. Includes advertising. Circulation: 200
Free. Controlled circulation.

HospitAlta / *edited by* H. Eliot. - *Published by* Alberta Hospital Association. 10025 - 108th St., Edmonton, Alta. T5J 1K9, January 1962-
Monthly. Association publication, newsletter format, 13 p. Circulation: 2500
Free to members.

Hospital administration in Canada / *edited by* John Boyd. - *Published by* Southam Business Publications Ltd. 1450 Don Mills Rd., Don Mills, Ont. M3B 2X7, June 1959-
Monthly. Business publication, magazine format, 72 p. Circulation: 9000
Indexed in Can. B.P.I., Hosp. abstr.
$1.50 per issue : $14.00 per year : $16.00 per year, U.S. : $36.00 per year, foreign.
Controlled circulation.

Hospital chaplaincy bulletin *See* The Pastoral visitor

Hospital highlights / *edited by* Hilary Short. - *Published by* Ontario Hospital Association. 24 Ferrand Dr., Don Mills, Ont. M3C 1H6, 1932-
Quarterly. Association publication, magazine format, 12 p. Circulation: 9000

The Hospital pharmacist (1948-1967) *See* The Canadian journal of hospital pharmacy

Hospital pharmacy in Ontario / *edited by* Charles J. Hartlieb. - *Published by* Ontario Branch. Canadian Society of Hospital Pharmacists. 175 College St., Toronto, Ont., January 1967-
Former title(s): CSHP Ontario newsletter - Canadian Society of Hospital Pharmacists.
Irregular (approximatley 6-16 issues per year). Association publication, newsletter format, 5 p. Circulation: 300
Subscription included in membership fee.
Controlled circulation.

Hospitalité Laurentides / *edited by* Gilles P. Verronneau. - *Published by* Marc Fortin Nord. L'Echo du Norc. Inc. 300, rue Labelle, St.-Jérôme, Qué., 1975-
Issued twice a year. Special interest, magazine format, Language: English and French. Includes advertising. Circulation: 50,000
ISSN 0318-9643 Free distribution in Laurentian hotels and motels.

Hospitality Canada / *edited by* Eric (Sandy) Sanderson. - *Published by* Sanderson Publications Ltd. Suite 204, 2182 12th Ave., Vancouver, B.C. V6K 2N4, 1968-
Monthly. Trade publication. Includes advertising. Circulation: 20,354
$5.00 : $9.00 for 2 years : $10.00 per year, foreign.

The Hosteller = L'Ajiste / *edited by* Richard Desrosiers. - *Published by* St. Lawrence Region. Canadian Youth Hostels Association. 1324 Sherbrooke St. W., Monteal, Que. H3G 1H9, 1960?-
Quarterly. Association publication, newsletter format, 4 p. Language: English and French. Includes advertising. Circulation: 5000
Subscription included in membership fee. Controlled circulation.

L'Hôtellerie magazine / *édité par* H.P. Garceau. - *Publié par* The Council of Hotels and Restaurants Inc. Suite 410, 1500 Stanley St., Montréal, Qué. H3A 1R3, 1926-
Mensuel. Revue d'entreprise. Comprend publicité. Tirage: 5986

Hotuys / *sponsored by* Plast - Ukrainian Youth Association ; *edited by* Tonia Horochowych. - *Published by* Plast Publication. 2445A Bloor St. W., Toronto, Ont. M6S 1P7, 1953-
10 issues a year. Ethnic press, magazine format, 16 p. Language: Ukrainian. Circulation: 1600
ISSN 0046-8061 $.70 per issue : $7.00 per year. Prepayment required.

Hourly wage survey (plant) - *Published by* Quebec Industrial Relations Institute. 630 Sherbrooke St. W., Montreal, Que. H3A 1E4.
Annual. Book format, 250 p. Includes cumulative index, updating service. supplements issued.
Subscription included in membership fee. Controlled circulation.

Houses for sale / *sponsored by* Toronto Home Builders' Association ; *edited by* B.A. Komorowski. - *Published by* Thorn Press Ltd. 135 Railside Rd., Toronto, Ont. (Subscription address: 5218 Yonge St., Willowdale, Ont. M2N 5P6) Spring 1975-
Issued twice a year. Magazine format, $.50 per issue.

Housing and people / *edited by* Jan McClain. - *Published by* Canadian Council on Social Development. P.O. Box 3505, Postal Station C., 55 Parkdale Ave., Ottawa, Ont. K1Y 4G1, June 1970-
Quarterly. Special interest, 16 p. Language: English and French. Includes book reviews, volume index, cumulative index. available in microform. Circulation: 3000
Indexed in P.A.I.S.
$1.00 per issue : $3.00 per year : $3.00 per year, foreign. Special rates offered. Prepayment required.

Hrvati profesori NA Americkim kanadskim visokim skolama *See* Biographical directory of Americans and Canadians of Croation descent

Hrvatski glas = Croation voice / *sponsored by* Croation Peasant Society of Canada ; *edited by* Mario Gordan. - *Published by* Croation Voice Publishing Co. Ltd. 325 Logan Ave., Winnipeg, Man. R3A 0P7, 1929-
Weekly. Ethnic publication, newspaper format, 8 p. Language: Croatian. supplements issued. Circulation: 7900
$.50 per issue : $10.00 per year. Annual almanac $3.00.

Hrvatski glas kalendar *See* Croation voice annual

Hrvatski put = Croatian way / *sponsored by* Croatian Republicans ; *edited by* Rudi Tomic. - *Published by* Rudi Tomic. P.O. Box 78, Postal Station M, Toronto, Ont. M6S 4T2, July 1962-
Former title(s): Nas put = Our way (1962-1972)
Monthly. Ethnic press, newspaper format, 8 p. Language: Croatian. Includes book reviews. Circulation: 3700
$.50 per issue : $5.00 per year. Special rates offered. Prepayment required.

Hsin min kuo = The New republic / *edited by* Shin-Han Hsu. - *Published by* Stanley Owen. The New Republic Printing and Publishing Co. Ltd. P.O. Box 2741, 531 Main St., Vancouver, B.C. V6A 2V1, 1911-
Daily. Ethnic press, newspaper format, 8 p. Language: Chinese. Includes advertising. Circulation: 2500
$36.00 per year.

Huguenot trails / *edited by* Lela F. Common. - *Published by* The Huguenot Society of Canada. 145 Kent St., Hamilton, Ont. L8P 3Z2 (Subscription address: Muriel Tufford, 176 Darling St., Brantford, Ont. N3S 3W6) Spring 1968-
Quarterly. Special interest, magazine format, 8 p. Includes book reviews.
$1.00 per issue : $4.00 per year. Subscription included in membership fee.

Humane viewpoint / *edited by* Stephanie Brown. - *Published by* Toronto Humane Society. 11 Wellesley St. W., Toronto, Ont., October 1974-
Former title(s): T.H.S. newsletter.
Issued every other month. Association publication, tabloid format, 4 p. Circulation: 17,000
ISSN 0316-9014 Free.

Humanist in Canada / *sponsored by* Humanist-Association of Canada ; *edited by* J. Lloyd Breveton. - *Published by* Pacific Northwest Humanist Publications. P.O. Box 157, Victoria, B.C., 1967-
Former title(s): Victoria Humanist (1964-1967)
Quarterly. Magazine format, 48 p. Includes book reviews. available in microform. Back numbers available. Circulation: 1500
ISSN 0018-7402 $.75 per issue : $3.00 per year.

The Humanities Association. The Humanities Association review. = L'association des humanités. La Revue de l'Association des humanités / *edited by* Phillip W. Rogers. - *Published by* The Humanities Association of Canada. c/o Mrs. S.J. Wynne-Edwards, Dept. of English, Queen's University, Kingston, Ont. K7L 3N6, 1951-
Quarterly. Association publication, journal format, 88 p. Language: English and French ; summaries: English and French. Circulation: 650
ISSN 0317-0454 $3.00 per issue : $10.00 per year.

Humanities Research Council of Canada Canada. Bulletin = Conseil canadien de recherche sur les humanities. Bulletin - *Published by* Humanities Research Council of Canada. 415 - 151 Slater, Ottawa, Ont. K1P 5H3, Spring/printemps 1974-
Irregular (approximately 2 issues per year). Newsletter format, 8 p. Language: English and French. Circulation: 7500
Free.

Hungarian journal *See* Magyar hirlap

Hungarian life *See* Magyar Elet

Huron Church news / *edited by* Geoffrey Dibbs. - *Published by* Morse C. Robinson. Diocese of Huron. Anglican Church of Canada. P.O. Box 308, London, Ont., 1950-
Monthly. Church publication, newspaper format, 12 p. Includes book reviews, film reviews, record reviews, advertising. supplements issued. Circulation: 26,000
$1.00 per year.

Huron historical notes / *edited by* Mrs. Tait Clark. - *Published by* Huron County Historical Society. 165 Rattenbury St. E., Clinton, Ont. (Subscription address: Mrs. M. Batkin, 75 Princess St., Clinton, Ont. N0M 1L0) 1965-
Annual. Association publication, magazine format, 40 p.
$2.50. Prepayment required.

Huron soil : crop news / *edited by* Bill Batten. - *Published by* Exeter Times Advocate. Exeter, Ont., 1956-
Annual. Includes advertising.

Huronia tourist guide book - *Published by* Huronia Tourist Association. Simcoe County Bldg., Barrie, Ont.
Annual. Directory, magazine format, 48 p. Includes advertising. supplements issued. Circulation: 65,000
Free.

Huronia winter adventures - *Published by* Huronia Tourist Association. Simcoe County Administration Centre, Midhurst, Ont. L0L 1X0.
Annual. Association publication, newspaper format, 16 p. Includes advertising. Circulation: 30,000
Free.

Hydronic and plumbing industries *See* Environmental systems industries

IAC rendezvous / *edited by* D.A. Gemmell. - *Published by* IAC Ltd. 45 St. Clair Ave. W., Toronto, Ont.
Issued every other month. House/company organ, newsletter format, 16 p. Language: English and French. Circulation: 3700
Controlled circulation.

The IAVEC newsletter & journal *See* The Communicator

I.E.A. bulletin *See* Canadian Association in Support of the Native Peoples. Bulletin : an independent journal on native affairs

IF *See* Industrialization forum

INFOR : journal canadien recherche opérationnelle et d'informatique *See* INFOR: Canadian journal of operational research and information processing

INFOR: Canadian journal of operational research and information processing = INFOR : journal canadien recherche opérationnelle et d'informatique / *sponsored by* Canadian Operational Research Society and Canadian Information Processing Society ; *edited by* R.E.A. Mason. - *Published by* Infor. P.O. Box 2225, Station D, Ottawa, Ont. K1P 5K0, December 1963-
Former title(s): CORS journal (1963-1970)
Issued 3 times a year. Association publication, journal format, 125 p. Language: English and French ; summaries: French. Includes volume index. Circulation: 4000
$7.50 per issue : $15.00 per year : $15.00 per volume. 10% discount to agencies.

IPLO newsletter (1963-1967) *See* Institute of Professional Librarians of Ontario. IPLO quarterly

IPL newsletter (1959-1963) *See* Institute of Professional Librarians of Ontario. IPLO quarterly

ISM : information services Mississauga / *edited by* The Staff of Information Services Department of the Mississauga Public Library. - *Published by* Mississauga Public Library. 110 Dundas St.W., Mississauga, Ont. L5B 1H3, September 1969-
Former title(s): Information services monthly (September 1969-February 1974 inclusive)
Issued every other month. Directory, newsletter format, 15 p.
ISSN 0446-841X $1.00 per issue : $5.00 per year.

I discover the bible (1964-1969) *See* Discover the bible

Ici Radio Canada : programme de la télévision / *édité par* Marguerite Béchard. - *Publié par* M. Beaudry-Béchard. C.P. 6000, Montréal, Qué., 1950-
Ancien titre: La Semaine à Radio-Canada.
Hebdomadaire. Calendrier d'événements, magazine, 16-24 p. Comprend publicité.
Tirage: 10,000
$13.00 par année : $15.00 par année, l'étranger.

Ideas / *edited by* Anne Middleton. - *Published by* Maclean-Hunter Ltd. 481 University Ave., Toronto, Ont. M5W 1A7, 1974-
Issued every other month. Trade publication.
Includes advertising. Circulation: 30,335
$5.00 per year : $10.00 per year, U.S. and U.K. : $20.00 per year, foreign.

Il Cittadino canadese = Canadian citizen = Le Citoyen canadien / *edited by* Michele Pirone. - *Published by* Nick Ciamarra. 6896 St. Lawrence Blvd., Montreal, Que. H2S 3C7, August 1941-
Weekly. Ethnic press, newspaper format, 32 p.
Language: Italian. Includes advertising. supplements issued. Circulation: 50,000
$.15 per issue : $7.00 per year.

Illustrated world review *See* Kepes vilaghirado

Image : illustration médicale Roche - *Publié par* Hoffman-La Roche ltée. 1000, boul. Roche, Vaudreuil, Qué., mai 1963-
Publié en anglais : Image medical illustrated Roche.
Intermittent (approximativement 3 éditions par an). Publication spécialisée, magazine, 32 p.
Comprend publicité. Tirage: 4000
Envoi gratuit aux médecines seulement.

Image medical illustrated Roche - *Published by* Hoffmann-La Roche Ltd. 1000 Roche Blvd., Vaudreuil, Que., May 1963-
Published in French: Image : illustration médicale Roche.
Irregular (approximately 3 issues per year).
General interest, magazine format, 32 p.
Includes advertising. Circulation: 16,000
Free to the medical profession.

Image nation / *edited by* David Hlynsky. - *Published by* Coach House Press. 401 Huron St., Toronto, Ont., 1970-
Irregular (approximately 4 issues per year).
Special interest, magazine format, 62 p.
$3.00 per issue : $10.00 for 4 issues : $3.50 per issue, U.S.

Images / *edited by* Piers Handling. - *Published by* Canadian Film Institute. 1762 Carling Ave., Ottawa, Ont. K2A 2H7, January 1972-
Former title(s): Bulletin - Canadian Film Institute (January 1955-December 1971)
Issued every other month. Association publication, newsletter format, 2 p.
Indexed in Multi-media rev. ind.
ISSN 0316-2451 Controlled circulation.

Impact / *édité par* Richard Doin. - *Publié par* Office des relations publiques. Commission des écoles catholiques de Montréal. 3737 est, rue Sherbrooke, Montréal, Qué. H1X 3B3, décembre 1973-
Bimestriel. Organe interne/officiel, magazine, 16 p. Langue(s): français et anglais. Tirage: 20,000
Envoi gratuit.

Imperial oil review - *Published by* Imperial Oil Ltd. 111 St. Clair Ave. W., Toronto, Ont. M5W 1K3, 1917-
Issued every other month. General interest, magazine format, 32 p. Language: French and English. Circulation: 120,000
Indexed in Periodex, Can. ind., P.A.I.S., North. tit.
Free.

Impetus - *Published by* Manitoba Provincial Council. Greater Winnipeg Regional Council. Boy Scouts of Canada. 148 Colony St., Winnipeg, Man. R3C 1V9, January 1969-
Irregular (approximately 5 issues per year).
Association publication, magazine format, 8 p.
Circulation: 2000
Controlled circulation.

Impetus magazine / *edited by* Ann Rhodes. - *Published by* John Duncan. Maclean-Hunter Ltd. 481 University Ave., Toronto, Ont. M5W 1A7.
Former title(s): Financial Post magazine.
Irregular (approximately 10 issues per year). Trade publication, magazine format, Includes advertising.
Indexed in Can. ind.

Importer and trader (1936-1938) *See* The Importers' bulletin

The Importers' bulletin / *edited by* Keith G. Dixon. - *Published by* Canadian Importers Association Inc. Suite 602, 2180 Yonge St., Toronto, Ont. M4S 2B9, April 1957-
Former title(s): Canadian Importers and Traders Association bulletin (1938-1957) Importer and trader (1936-1938)
Weekly. Association publication, newsletter format, 4-6 p.
ISSN 0318-823X Available to members only.

Impulse / *edited by* Cliff Letovsky. - *Published by* Cliff Letovsky. P.O. Box 901, Postal Station Q, Toronto, Ont. M6S 2V8, February 1972-
Irregular. Special interest, magazine format, 32 p.
Indexed in Can. essay and lit. ind.
ISSN 0315-3894 $1.00 per volume : $1.25 per year, foreign. Controlled circulation. Special rates offered. Prepayment required.

In a nutshell - *Published by* Mental Patients Association. 2146 Yew St., Vancouver, B.C. V6K 3G7, 1971-
Irregular (approximately 6 issues per year). Association publication, newsletter format, 12 p. Includes book reviews, film reviews, play reviews. Circulation: 2000
$4.00 per year. Free. Single issues are free.

In orbit *See* Sun life orbit

In pharmation / *edited by* Frank M. Archer. - *Published by* British Columbia Professional Pharmacists' Society. 1400 - 207 West Hastings St., Vancouver, B.C. V6B 1K5, December 1971-
Irregular (approximately 10 issues per year). Association publication, newsletter format, 4 p. Includes advertising. Circulation: 650
Controlled circulation.

In touch / *edited by* William Goetz. - *Published by* Canadian Bible College. 4400-4th Ave., Regina, Sask. S4T 0H8, September 1972-
Issued every other month. Institutional publication (Universities, schools, etc.), newsletter format, 6 p.
ISSN 0315-5889 Controlled circulation.

Incidences (novembre 1962-décembre 1968) *See* Co-ïncidences

Incubs (to 1973) *See* Educatus

The Independencer / *edited by* Sheila Bresalier. - *Published by* Committee for an Independent Canada. Suite 48, 46 Elgin St., Ottawa, Ont. K1P 5K5, February 1972-
Issued every other month. Association publication, magazine format, 16 p. Includes book reviews, advertising. Circulation: 10,000
ISSN 0315-6087 $5.00 per year.

Independent Lithuania *See* Nepriklausoma Lietuva

Index commercial canadien *See* Canadian trade index

Index de documentation en géographie *Voir* Index des revues de géographie de langue française

Index de l'actualité / *parrainé par* Service d'analyse et d'indexation, Université Laval ; *édité par* Pierre Noreau. - *Publié par* Presses de l'université Laval. Université Laval, Ste-Foy, Qué. G1K 7P4, janvier 1972-
Ancien titre: Index du journal le Devoir (janvier 1966-décembre 1971)
Mensuel plus une refonte annuelle. Index de journaux, 850 p. Tirage: 80
$30.00 le numéro : $360.00 par année (Incluant la refonte).

Index des périodiques canadiens *See* Canadian periodical index

Index des revues de géographie de langue française / *parrainé par* Comité international d'historiens et de géographes ; *édité par* Henri Dorion. - *Publié par* Université du Québec à Chicoutimi. 930 rue Jacques-Cartier, Chicoutimi, Qué., 1973-
Ancien titre: Index de documentation en géographie.
Trimestriel. Index, 60 p. Comprend index cumulatif.
$25.00 par année. Abonnements payables à l'avance.

Index du journal le Devoir (janvier 1966-décembre 1971) *Voir* Index de l'actualité

Index of 16mm & 35mm feature length films available in Canada / *edited by* The C.F.F.S. Index Committee. - *Published by* Canadian Federation of Film Societies. P.O. Box 484, Terminal A, Toronto, Ont. M5W 1E4, January 1947-
Former title(s): The National Film Society of Canada film catalogue (to 1955) Canadian Film Institute 16 and 35 mm film index (1955-1960) Short title : C.F.F.S. index feature length films.
Annual (Spring each year). Association publication, directory, 390 p. Circulation: 250
ISSN 0316-5019 $25.00 per volume.

Index seminum *Voir* Delectus seminum et sporarum quae hortus botanicus Montis Regii pro mutua commutatione offert

Index to Canadian legal periodical literature / *sponsored by* Canadian Association of Law Libraries ; *edited by* Marianne Scott. - *Published by* Index to Canadian Legal Periodical Literature. P.O. Box 386, N.D.G. Station, Montreal, Que. H4A 3P7, ISSN 0316-8891-
Issued every other month. Index, 40 p. Cumulated yearly. Circulation: 300
$30.00 per year.

Index to little magazines of Ontario, 1967- / *edited by* Clarke E. Leverette. - *Published by* Killaly Press. 764 Dalkeith Ave., London, Ont. N5X 1R8, 1972-
Annual. Index, magazine format, 50 p. Circulation: 100
$2.50.

India star / *edited by* R.S. Rania. - *Published by* Asia Publications. 1433 Bloor St. W., Toronto, Ont. M6P 3L6, 1973-
Monthly. Ethnic press, magazine format, Includes advertising. Circulation: 3283
$4.00 per year.

India times *See* The Canadian India times

Indian ed / *edited by* Marilyn Assheton-Smith and Carl Urion. - *Published by* Intercultural Education Program. University of Alberta. 5-109 Education Centre, University of Alberta, Edmonton, Alta. T6G 2E1, Fall 1973-
Quarterly. Institutional publication (Universities, schools, etc.), newsletter format, 6 p. Includes book reviews. Circulation: 800
Indexed in Resources in educ., Can. educ. ind.
$.75 per issue : $2.50 per year.

The Indian missionary record *See* Indian record

The Indian record *See* Indian record

Indian record / *edited by* G. Laviolette. - *Published by* The Oblate Fathers. 1301 Wellington Cres., Winnipeg, Man. R3N 0A9, January 1938-
Former title(s): The Indian record; The Indian missionary record.
Issued every other month. Church publication, magazine format, 16 p.
Indexed in North. tit.
$.50 per issue : $3.00 per year.

The Indian voice / *edited by* Donna Doss. - *Published by* Indian Homemakers Association. 201, 423 W. Broadway, Vancouver, B.C. V5Y 1R4, October 1969-
Monthly. News relating to native people, newspaper format, 12 p. Includes book reviews, film reviews, play reviews, record reviews.
Indexed in North. tit.
$.30 per issue : $3.00 per year.

Indian-ed / *sponsored by* University of Alberta. Department of Educational Foundations Intercultural Education Program ; *edited by* C. Urion, M. Assheton-Smith, K. Toohey and C. Hadler. - *Published by* Education Centre Alberta Department. University of Alberta. Edmonton, Alta. T6G 2G5, October 1973-
Quarterly. Institutional publication (Universities, schools, etc.), newsletter format, 4 p. Includes book reviews. Circulation: 550
ISSN 0318-8647 $1.00 per issue : $3.00 per year.

Industrial buildings - Windsor and Essex County / *edited by* J.R. Moore. - *Published by* Windsor-Essex County Development Commission. 500 Riverside Dr. W., Windsor, Ont. N9A 5K6, 1974-
Former title(s): Greater Windsor industrial building list (to 1974)
Irregular (approximately 2-4 issues per year). Trade publication, newsletter format, 10-12 p. Circulation: 300
Free. Controlled circulation.

Industrial business management / *sponsored by* Saskatchewan Research Council ; *edited by* A.D. Scharf. - *Published by* Industrial Services. 30 Campus Dr., Saskatoon, Sask. S7N 0X1.
Former title(s): Industrial management systems; Industrial management science.
Monthly. Trade publication, magazine format, 8 p. Circulation: 4000
Free. Controlled circulation.

Industrial Developers Association of Canada. Bulletin / *edited by* J.D. Flintoft. - *Published by* Industrial Developers Association of Canada. 457A Sussex, Ottawa, Ont. K1N 6Z4, 1970-
Irregular (approximately 6-8 issues per year). Association publication, newsletter format, 6 p. Includes book reviews. Circulation: 400
$10.00 per year. Free to members.

The Industrial first aid attendant / *edited by* Gus Porcher and Joanne MacGregor. - *Published by* The Industrial First Aid Attendants Association of British Columbia. 201-6111 Cambie St., Vancouver, B.C. V5Z 3B2, January 1943-
Issued every other month. Association publication, magazine format, 16 p. Circulation: 1600
$3.00 per year.

Industrial leasing - *Published by* George Clifford. Maclean-Hunter Ltd. 481 University Ave., Toronto, Ont. M5W 1A7, 1973-
Annual. Trade publication. Includes advertising. Circulation: 14,495
$5.00 per year.

Industrial locations in Canada / *edited by* Don McGillivray. - *Published by* Donald Carlson. Financial Times of Canada. 1885 Leslie St., Don Mills, Ont. M5B 3J4, 1966-
Annual. Directory, tabloid format, 52 p. Includes advertising. Circulation: 100,000
ISSN 0073-7569 Free to subscribers to The Financial times of Canada.

Industrial management science *See* Industrial business management

Industrial management systems *See* Industrial business management

The Industrial manager (November/December 1965-May/June 1970) *See* The Canadian manager : the magazine of the professional manager

The Industrial market of Quebec Province / *sponsored by* Quebec Industrial. - *Published by* Maclean-Hunter Research Bureau. 481 University Ave., Toronto, Ont. M5W 1A7.
Annual. Statistics, 19 p.
ISSN 0317-9001

Industrial relations *Voir* Relations industrielles

Industrialization forum = IF / *edited by* Colin H. Davidson. - *Published by* Aménagement/Architecture. University of Montreal. P.O. Box 6128, Montreal, Que., October 1969-
Published in French.
5 issues per year. Magazine format, 76 p. Includes book reviews, volume index, cumulative index. available in microform. Circulation: 1300
Indexed in RADAR.
ISSN 0019-8927 $2.50 per issue : $25.00 per year (Individuals $12.50 per year).

L'Industrie minière - pilier de l'économie canadienne (1968-1971) *Voir* Les Mines : pilier de l'économie canadienne

Industry digest / *edited by* Gladys Taylor. - *Published by* Tall-Taylor Publishing Ltd. 532 Cleveland Cres., S.E., Calgary, Alta.
Monthly. Trade publication, magazine format, 23 p.
$3.50 per year : $6.00 for 2 years : $9.00 for 3 years.

L'Infirmière canadienne / *édité par* Claire Bigué. - *Publié par* L'Association des infirmières canadiennes. 50, The Driveway, Ottawa, Ont. K2P 1E2., 1959-
Mensuel. Publication d'association, magazine, 48 p. Comprend critique de livres, publicité, index de volumes.Aussi sous microform. Tirage: 34,907
Indexé dans Int. nurs. ind., Periodex, Hosp. abstr.
$1.00 le numéro : $6.00 par année : $11.00 2 ans : $6.50 par année l'étranger (2 ans $12.00). Abonnements payables à l'avance.

Info - *Published by* New Brunswick Association of Registered Nurses. 231 Saunders St., Fredericton, N.B. E3B 1N6, July 1975-
Former title(s): NBARN news (May 1970-May 1975)
Issued every other month. Association publication, newspaper format, 12 p. Language: English and French. Circulation: 6500
$2.00 per year. Prepayment required.

Info / *edited by* Carol Kalbfleisch. - *Published by* Standing Committee on Secondary School Liaison. Ontario Universities Registrars Association. c/o Carol Kalbfleisch, Assistant Liaison Officer, University of Waterloo, Waterloo, Ont.
Issued 3 times a year. Special interest, loose-leaf format,

Info-éducation / *édité par* Aline Foster. - *Publié par* Commission scolaire regionale de Chambly. Suite 500, 6, boul. Désaulniers, St-Lambert, Qué. J4P 1L5, septembre 1966-
Intermittent au besoin. Organe interne/officiel, bulletin, 24 p. Langue(s): français et anglais.

Info-estrie / *édité par* Pierre Lacasse. - *Publié par* Centre de recherche en aménagement régional. Université de Sherbrooke. Sherbrooke, Qué. J1K 2R1, mai 1973-
Intermittent (approximativement 1-2 éditions par an). Publication spécialisée, bulletin, 20 p. Comprend Mises à jour. Tirage: 1000
Envoi gratuit.

Info-parents / *édité par* Jean Castonguay. - *Publié par* Cegep-Saint-Jean-sur-Richelieu. C.P. 310, 30, boul. du Séminaire, St-Jean, Qué., novembre 1974-
Semestriel. Publication d'institution (universités, écoles..), bulletin, 4 p. Tirage: 3000
Envoi gratuit.

Informapec / *édité par* Marcel Blondeau. - *Publié par* Marcel Blondeau. Association provinciale de l'enseignement commercial. 5639, ave Canterbury, Montréal, Qué., janvier 1973-
Intermittent (approximativement 5 éditions par an). Publication d'association, revue, 20 p. Tirage: 500
$15.00 par année. Abonnements payables à l'avance.

Informateur (janvier 1951-août 1956) *Voir* Notre ministère du royaume

Information (1972-1973) *See* Agricultural science

Information *See* Agricultural science

Information / *edited by* Anthony J. Gray. - *Published by* Canadian Association of Social Workers. 55 Parkdale Ave., Ottawa, Ont. K1Y 1E5, March 1971-
Irregular (approximately 6 issues per year). Association publication, newsletter format, 8-12 p. Language: English and French. Includes advertising. Circulation: 6000
ISSN 0315-3150 $4.00 per year.

Information : pastorale du diocèse de Mont-Laurier / *édité par* André Chalifoux. - *Publié par* Service diocésain de pastorale. 750, rue Charette, Mont-Laurier, Qué. J9L 2G2, janvier 1970-
Paraît tous les 15 jours. Publication ecclésiastique, bulletin, 10 p. Comprend publicité, Mises à jour. parution de suppléments. Tirage: 375
$5.00 par année. Abonnements payables à l'avance.

Information bulletin / *sponsored by* Peace and socialism publishers, Prague, Czechoslovakia. - *Published by* Progress Books. 487 Adelaide St. W., Toronto, Ont. M5V 1T4.
Issued twice a month. Supplement to World Marxist review, pamphlet format, 50 p.
Free to subscribers of World Marxist review.

Information bulletin to school trustees / *edited by* Lloyd G. Burton. - *Published by* Ontario School Trustees' Council. Suite 500, 2 Bloor St. W., Toronto, Ont. M4W 3E2, October 1957-
Irregular (approximately 3 issues per year). Association publication, newsletter format, 5 p. Circulation: 3000
Controlled circulation.

Information for candidates - *Published by* The Institute of Chartered Secretaries and Administrators. National office, 34 King St. W., Toronto, Ont. M5H 1R7, 1963-
Former title(s): C.I.S. student newsletter.
Irregular. Institutional publication (Universities, schools, etc.), newsletter format, Free.

L'Information médicale et paramédicale / *édité par* Lorraine Trempe. - *Publié par* L'Information médicale et paramédicale inc. C.P. 219, Montréal, Qué. H3Z 2T2, novembre 1948-
Bimensuel. Publication spécialisée, revue, 52 p. Comprend critique de livres, critique de films, critique de pièces de théâtre. Tirage: 13,000
$10.00 par année. Envoi gratuit aux médecins. Tirage contrôlé.

L'Information nationale / *édité par* Jacques Brault. - *Publié par* La Société St-Jean Baptiste de Montréal. 1182, boul. St-Laurent, Montréal, Qué. H2X 2S5, mars 1952-
Mensuel. Publication d'association, journal, 12-16 p. Tirage: 17,000
Envoi gratuit.

Information services monthly (September 1969-February 1974 inclusive) *See* ISM : information services Mississauga

Information syndicale *See* Canadian Labour Comment

L'information vétérinaire (vol. 1-11; 1959-1969) *Voir* Informations vétérinaires

Informations vétérinaires - *Publié par* Louis-Phillipe Phaneuf. Faculté de Médecine Vétérinaire. Université de Montréal. C.P. 5000, St-Hyacinthe, Qué. J2S 7C6, 1970-
Ancien titre: L'information vétérinaire (vol. 1-11; 1959-1969)
Intermittent. Publication d'institution (universités, écoles..). Tirage: 150-200
Envoi gratuit. Distribution limitée.

Informator / *edited by* Anna Ujejska. - *Published by* Polish Canadian Women's Federation. 271 Benson Ave., Toronto, Ont. M6G 2J9, 1956-
Quarterly. Ethnic press, newsletter format, 20-30 p. Language: Polish. Includes volume index. Circulation: 500
$.50 per issue : $2.00 per year.

L'Ingénieur / *édité par* Madeleine G. Lambert. - *Publié par* Association des diplômés de polytechnique. Campus de l'Université de Montréal. a/s Ecole Polytechnique, C.P. 6079, Succursale A, Montréal, Qué. H3C 3A7, 1915-
Ancien titre: Revue trimestrielle canadienne (1915-1955)
Bimestriel. Publication d'association, magazine, 32 p. Comprend publicité. Tirage: 8600
Indexé dans Periodex, RADAR.
$2.00 le numéro : $10.00 par année : $12.00 par année, l'étranger. Envoi gratuit aux ingénieurs francophones. Tirage contrôlé. Abonnements payables à l'avance.

Inhalation therapy *See* Respiratory technology

Initiatives - *Publié par* La Jeune chambre de Montréal. Suite 206, 1380, Gilford, Montréal, Qué., 1956-
Intermittent (approximativement 5 éditions par an). Revue d'entreprise. Comprend publicité.

Inner life : Toronto's aquarian age newsletter / *edited by* Ero Talvila. - *Published by* Ero Talvila. 214 Glengarry Ave., Toronto, Ont. M5M 1E4, September 1974-
Former title(s): Psychic society newsletter (February 1973-June 1974)
Monthly (except July and August). Special interest, newsletter format, 30 p. Includes book reviews, advertising. Circulation: 750
ISSN 0318-0697 $0.25 per issue : $2.00 per year.

Innis herald : "lets go nummies" / *sponsored by* Innis College Student Society ; *edited by* Barbara Winter. - *Published by* Innis Herald. 63 St. George St., Toronto, Ont.
Monthly. Student publication, newspaper format, 8 p. Language: English and French. Includes book reviews, film reviews, play reviews, record reviews, advertising. available in microform. supplements issued. Circulation: 2000

Les Innovateurs / *édité par* D.H. MacDonald. - *Publié par* La Compagnie Northern Electric Limitée. 1600 ouest, boul. Dorchester, Montréal, Qué. H3H 1R1, mai 1974-
Publié en anglais: The Innovators.
Trimestriel. Organe interne/officiel, magazine, 32 p.
Envoi gratuit. Tirage contrôlé.

Innovator *See* Amber

The Innovators / *edited by* D.H. Macdonald. - *Published by* Northern Electric Company Ltd. 1600 Dorchester Blvd. W., Montreal, Que. H3H 1R1, May 1974-
Published in French: Les Innovateurs.
Quarterly. House/company organ, magazine format, Circulation: 45,000
Controlled circulation.

Inscape : a journal of new Canadian writing / *sponsored by* University of Ottawa. Department of English ; *edited by* John Nause. - *Published by* The Hopkins Club. Department of English, University of Ottawa, Ottawa, Ont. K1N 6N5, 1959-
Quarterly. Special interest, magazine format, 70 p. Includes volume index. Circulation: 1000
$2.00 per issue : $5.00 per volume.

Inside RTAC *See* Roads and Transportation Association of Canada. RTAC news

Insieme : mensile d'informazione e di attualita / *sponsored by* Scalabrini League ; *edited by* Domenico Rodighiero. - *Published by* Domenico Rodighiero. 2875 Sauvé St. E., Montreal, Que. H2B 1C6, April 1973-
Monthly. Ethnic press, newspaper format, 20 p. Language: Italian. Circulation: 16,000
$.25 per issue : $2.00 per year. Free.

Insight / *edited by* Margaret G. Root. - *Published by* Director of Public Relations & Development. Mount Saint Vincent University Vincent. Halifax, N.S. B3M 2J6, December 1971-
Quarterly. Institutional publication (Universities, schools, etc.), magazine format, 24-36 p. Circulation: 6500
$5.00 per year. Free. Controlled circulation. Prepayment required.

Insight / *sponsored by* John Milton Society for the Blind in Canada ; *edited by* Remmelt Hummelen. - *Published by* Salvation Army Triumph Press. 455 North Service Rd., Oakville, Ont., December 1972-
Irregular (approximately 11 issues per year). Church publication, newspaper format, 16 p. Circulation: 2606
Free.

Insight / *edited by* Adeleine Morris. - *Published by* Publicity and Information Services. University of Regina. Room 509, Ad/Hum. Bldg., University of Regina, Sask. S4S 0A2, October 1975-
Former title(s): Podium (to September 1975)
Monthly. Institutional publication (Universities, schools, etc.), magazine format, 8 p. Circulation: 4500
Free.

Insite / *sponsored by* Saskatchewan Industrial Education Association ; *edited by* H. Sweetman. - *Published by* Saskatchewan Teachers' Federation. P.O. Box 1108, Saskatoon, Sask., 1968-
Quarterly. Association publication, magazine format, 40 p. Includes book reviews, advertising. Circulation: 250
Indexed in Can. educ. ind.
$5.00 per year. Subscription included in membership fee.

L'Institut canadien d'éducation des adultes. L'I.C.E.A. bulletin / *édité par* René Diotte. - *Publié par* Institut canadien d'éducation des adultes. Suite 800, 506 ouest, rue Ste-Catherine, Montréal, Qué. H2L 2C7, 1965-
Bimestriel. Publication d'association, bulletin, 8 p. Tirage: 2000
Indexé dans Can. educ. ind.
$4.80 par année. Abonnements payables à l'avance.

Institut canadien des actuaires. Annuaire *See* Canadian Institute of Actuaries. Year book

L'Institut canadien des comptables agréés Manuel de l'I.C.C.A *See* The Canadian Institute of Chartered Accountants. CICA handbook

Institut canadien des urbanistes. Nouvelles I.C.U. *See* Canadian Institute of Planners. C.I.P. news

L'Institut d'assurance du Canada. Communiqué de l'Institut d'assurance du Canada / *édité par* Ella Kolm. - *Publié par* L'Institut d'assurance du Canada. 220 Bay St., Toronto, Ont. M5J 1P3, octobre 1972-
Publié en anglais: The Insurance Institute of Canada. Newsletter.
Trimestriel. Publication d'association, bulletin, 4 p. Tirage: 3300
ISSN 0316-5116 Envoi gratuit. Tirage contrôlé.

Institut de cardiologie de Montréal / *édité par* Nicole B. Tobin. - *Publié par* Institut de cardiologie de Montréal. 5000 est, rue Bélanger, Montréal, Qué. H1T 1C8, septembre 1973-
Trimestriel. Publication d'institution (universités, écoles..), bulletin, 4 p. Tirage: 3000

L'Institut de recherches psychologiques. L'Actualité à l'IRP d'ores et déjà = The Institute of Psychological Research. Here and now : a brief of news from the IPR / *édité par* Jean Marc Chevrier. - *Publié par* Institut de recherches psychologiques inc. 34 ouest, rue Fleury, Montréal, Qué., 1940-
Intermittent. Publication d'association, bulletin, Langue(s): français et anglais.
Envoi gratuit.

l'Institut professionnel du service public du Canada. Journal de l'institut professionnel *See* The Professional Institute of the Public Service of Canada. Journal of the Professional Institute

Institute of Chartered Accountants of British Columbia. News and views / *edited by* J.D. Manson and Mrs. D.O. Gibbs. - *Published by* Institute of Chartered Accountants of British Columbia. 562 Burrard St., Vancouver, B.C. V6C 2K8.
Quarterly. Association publication, newsletter format, 8 p.
Controlled circulation.

Institute of Canadian Bankers. Educational programs / *edited by* Rose Simon. - *Published by* Institute of Canadian Bankers. Suite 3920, Place Victoria, Stock Exchange Tower, Montreal, Que. H4Z 1A3.
Annual. Association publication, directory, 48 p. Language: English and French.
Free.

The Institute of Chartered Accountants of Alberta. CA monthly statement - *Published by* Institute of Chartered Accountants of Alberta. 207 Empire Building, 10080 Jasper Ave., Edmonton, Alta. T5J 1V9, September 1974-
Former title(s): CA newsletter (February 1964 vol. 2. no. 2 - July 1974 vol. 12. no. 1)
Monthly. House/company organ, newsletter format, 4 p. Circulation: 3100
Provided as a service to members and students. Controlled circulation.

Institute of Chartered Engineers of Ontario. News letter / *edited by* R.J. Seyler. - *Published by* The Institute of Chartered Engineers of Ontario. 72 Stevens Cr., Georgetown, Ont. (Subscription address: P.O. Box 415, Downsview, Ont. M3M 3A8) 1954-
Monthly. House/company organ, newsletter format, 3 p.
Controlled circulation.

Institute of Chartered Life Underwriters. C.L.U. comment / *edited by* Roy Jenkins. - *Published by* Institute of Chartered Life Underwriters. 41 Lesmill Road, Don Mills, Ont. M3B 2T3, 1967-
Issued every other month. Association publication, newsletter format, 4 p. Language: English and French.
$46.75 per year for 25 copies (minimum order). Price varies according to quantity. One copy free to each member. Controlled circulation.

Institute of Chartered Life Underwriters. Commentaires CLU / *édité par* Roy Jenkins. - *Publié par* L'Association des assureurs-vie du Canada. 41 Lesmill Rd., Don Mills, Ont., 1967-
Publié en anglais: Institute of Chartered Life Underwriters. CLU comment.
Bimestriel. Publication d'association, bulletin, 4 p. Langue(s): français.
$46.75 pour 25 copies. Tirage contrôlé.

Institute of Chartered Secretaries and Administrators. Canadian Division. Newsletter - *Published by* Institute of Chartered Secretaries and Administrators. National office, 34 King St. W., Toronto, Ont. M5H 1R7.
Issued twice a month. Association publication, newsletter format, 6 p.

Institute of Chartered Secretaries and Administrators. ICSA opportunities bulletins - *Published by* Institute of Chartered Secretaries and Administrators. c/o National Office, 34 King St., W., Toronto, Ont. M5H 1R7, 1974-
Irregular. Association publication, 2 p.
Free.

The Institute of Chartered Secretaries and Administrators. Newsletter - *Published by* The Institute of Chartered Secretaries and Administrators. c/o National Office, 34 King St. W., Toronto, Ont. M5H 1R7, 1966-
Irregular (approximately 5 issues per year). Association publication, magazine format, Free. Distributed to members, licentiates, affiliates and students.

Institute of Professional Librarians of Ontario. IPLO quarterly / *edited by* Lloyd Houser. - *Published by* Institute of Professional Librarians of Ontario. 36B Prince Arthur Ave., Toronto, Ont. M5R 1A9, July 1967-
Former title(s): IPL newsletter (1959-1963) IPLO newsletter (1963-1967)
Quarterly. Association publication, magazine format, 32-40 p. Language: English and French. Circulation: 550
Indexed in Lib. lit.
ISSN 0046-9831 $4.00 per issue : $15.00 per year. Controlled circulation.

The Institute of Psychological Research. Here and now : a brief of news from the IPR *Voir* L'Institut de recherches psychologiques. L'Actualité à l'IRP d'ores et déjà

The Institute reports *See* Canadian Institute of Chartered Accountants. C.I.C.A./I.C.C.A. dialogue

Instrument Society of America. Montreal Section. Newsletter / *edited by* Claudo Leduc. - *Published by* Montreal Section. Instrument Society of Ametrica. Room 105, 5165 Sherbrooke St. W., Montreal, Que.
Monthly. House/company organ, magazine format, 24 p. Language: French and English. Includes advertising. Circulation: 500
Free. Controlled circulation.

The Insurance broker / *edited by* Pierre Morin. - *Published by* Insurance Brokers Association of the Province of Quebec. Room 1570, 550 Sherbrooke St. W., Montreal, Que. H3A 1C8, 1923-
Monthly. Association publication. Language: English and French. Includes advertising. Circulation: 5132
$4.00 per year (Members $3.00).

The Insurance Institute of Alberta. Calgary Chapter. Newsletter - *Published by* The Insurance Institute of Alberta. 601 - 630 - 8th Ave. S.W., Calgary, Alta. T2P 1G6, 1970-
Irregular (approximately 3 issues per year). Association publication, newsletter format, 4 p. Circulation: 450
Free to members.

The Insurance Institute of Canada. Newsletter of the Insurance Institute of Canada / *edited by* Ella Kolm. - *Published by* The Insurance Institute of Canada. 220 Bay St., Toronto, Ont. M5J 1P3, October 1972-
Quarterly. Association publication, newsletter format, 4 p. Language: English and French. Circulation: 9100
ISSN 0316-5116 Free. Controlled circulation.

The Insurance marketer / *edited by* Kenneth E. MacLeod. - *Published by* Wadham Publications Ltd. Suite 101, 109 Vanderhoof Ave., Toronto, Ont. M4G 2J2, 1972-
Annual. Trade publication, magazine format, 50 p. Includes advertising.
$4.00. Controlled circulation. Prepayment required.

The Intelligence crediter / *edited by* John Bilan. - *Published by* J. Bilan. P.O. Box 54, Postal Station B, Toronto, Ont. M5T 2T2, May 1973-
Irregular (approximately 2-4 issues per year). Special interest, magazine format, 32 p. Includes book reviews, advertising. Circulation: 3000
$.50 per issue.

L'Inter *Voir* L'Interdit

Interaction / *edited by* Rob Garrison (managing editor) and Susan Gemmell (assistant editor). - *Published by* Ontario Teachers' Federation. Suite 700, 1260 Bay St., Toronto, Ont. M5R 2B5, November 1974-
Former title(s): OTF reporter; Update from OTF.
Irregular (approximately 8 issues per year). Association publication, newspaper format, 8 p. Language: English (French).
ISSN 0316-3903 Controlled circulation.

Interchange : a journal of educational studies / *edited by* Andrew Effrat and The Board of Student Editors. - *Published by* The Ontario Institute for Studies in Education. 252 Bloor St. W., Toronto, Ont. M5S 1V6, 1970-
Quarterly. Special interest, journal format, 96 p. Includes book reviews, volume index. available in microform. Circulation: 1700
Indexed in Can. educ. ind., Curr. ind. j. educ.
$3.00 per issue : $11.00 per year, institutions (Individuals $9.00; students $5.00).

Intercom / *edited by* J.H. Watt. - *Published by* Fellowship of Evangelical Baptist Churches in Canada. 74 Sheppard Ave. W., Willowdale, Ont. M2N 1M3, October 1968-
Quarterly. Church publication, 8 p.
Circulation: 12,000
Free.

Intercom - *Publié par* Institut national de la recherche scientifique. 2700, rue Einstein, Saint-Foy, Qué., novembre 1970-
Hebdomadaire. Publication d'association, bulletin, 8 p. Tirage: 360
Envoi gratuit.

Intercom / *edited by* Mrs. Sydney Isaacs. - *Published by* Ontario University Registrars' Association. c/o Office of the Registrar, University of Western Ontario, London, Ont., 1973-
Irregular (approximately 6 issues per year). Association publication, newsletter format, 10 p. Circulation: 250
Free to individuals : $25.00 per year to each university. Controlled circulation.

Intercom / *sponsored by* Saskatchewan Business Teachers' Association ; *edited by* Joan Wilkes. - *Published by* Saskatchewan Teachers' Federation. P.O. Box 1108, Saskatoon, Sask. S7J 2H8.
Quarterly. Association publication, journal format, 45 p. Includes book reviews, advertising. Circulation: 200
Indexed in Can. educ. ind.
$5.00 per year. Controlled circulation. Prepayment required.

Interdisciplinary field studies - the zoo - *Published by* Calgary Zoological Society. St. George's Island, Calgary, Alta. T2G 3H4.
Irregular. Association publication.
$2.00 per year.

L'Interdit / *édité par* Michel Guillotte. - *Publié par* L'Association des diplomés de l'Université de Montréal. Bureau 3, 2910, boul. Edouard-Montpetit, Montréal, Qué. H3T 1J7, 1947-
Ancien titre: L'Inter.
Intermittent (approximativement 6 éditions par an). Publication d'association, magazine, 20 p.
$6.00 par année : $8.00 par année, l'étranger.

Interface / *sponsored by* Colleges of Medicine, Dentistry, Nursing and Physiotherapy of the University of Saskatchewan ; *edited by* Jay Barsky and Vic Thackeray. - *Published by* Health Science Students. University of Saskatchewan. Interface, SMS Office, Health Science Bldg., University of Saskatchewan, Saskatoon, Sask., October 1968-
Quarterly. Student publication, magazine format, 20 p. Includes advertising. supplements issued. Circulation: 3000
Free (donations accepted). Controlled circulation.

Interface-1 / *edited by* B. Wrangham. - *Published by* Capital Communications Ltd. Suite 705, 151 Slater St., Ottawa, Ont. K1P 5H3, July 1972-
Monthly. Trade publication, newsletter format, 8 p. Circulation: 100
ISSN 0315-842X $50.00 per year. Controlled circulation.

Interior Designers of Canada. Quarterly newsletter - *Published by* Interior Designers of Canada. 302 - 1008 Homer St., Vancouver, B.C. V6B 2X1.
Quarterly. Association publication, newsletter format, 8 p. Language: English and French. Circulation: 600
Free. Controlled circulation.

The Intermediate naturalist (April 1946-December 1953) *See* The Ontario field biologist

Intermediate teacher / *sponsored by* Provincial Intermediate Teachers' Association. - *Published by* B.C. Teachers' Federation. 105-2235 Burrard St., Vancouver, B.C. V6J 3H9, September 1967-
Former title(s): PITA journal (March 1962-August 1967)
Irregular (approximately 2 issues per year). Association publication, journal format, 75 p. Includes book, film and play lists.
Available to members only. Controlled circulation.

International Air Transport Association. IATA news review - *Published by* International Air Transport Association. 1155 Mansfield St., Montreal, Que. H3B 4A4, 1966-
Irregular (approximately 8-10 issues per year). Association publication, newsletter format, 8 p.
Free. Controlled circulation.

International Atlantic Salmon Foundation. Newsletter / *edited by* W.M. Carter. - *Published by* International Atlantic Salmon Foundation. P.O. Box 429, St. Andrews, N.B. E0G 2X0, 1970-
Former title(s): Quarterly Newsletter - International Atlantic Salmon Foundation.
Issued every other month. Special interest, newsletter format, 4 p. Circulation: 2000
Free.

International business news magazine / *edited by* Wilfred E. LaVergne. - *Published by* International Business News Magazine. 507-283 Portage Ave., Winnipeg, Man. R3B 2B5, January 1975-
Issued every other month. 68 p. Includes book reviews, advertising. supplements issued. Circulation: 10,000
$1.00 per issue : $10.00 per year : $30.00 per year, foreign. Free.

International Canada / *edited by* R.J. Willmot. - *Published by* Canadian Institute of International Affairs. Parliamentary Centre for Foreign Affairs and Foreign Trade. 31 Wellesley St. E., Toronto, Ont. M4Y 1G9, 1970-
Former title(s): Monthly report on Canadian external relations (1962-1969)
Monthly. Institutional publication (Universities, schools, etc.), magazine format, 16-32 p. Circulation: 1350
ISSN 0027-0512 $25.00 per year : $15.00 special rate for subscriptions placed directly with the publisher.

International Commission for the Northwest Atlantic Fisheries. Annual report / *edited by* W.H. Champion. - *Published by* International Commission for the Northwest Atlantic Fisheries. P.O. Box 638, Dartmouth, N.S. B2Y 3Y9, 1951-
Former title(s): Annual proceedings - International Commission for the Northwest Atlantic Fisheries.
Annual. Contains administrative reports, reports of meetings and summaries of research.

International Commission for the Northwest Atlantic Fisheries. List of vessels fishing in the ICNAF convention area / *edited by* V.M. Hodder. - *Published by* International Commission for the Northwest Atlantic Fisheries. P.O. Box 638, Dartmouth, N.S. B2Y 3Y9, 1959-
Issued every three years.

International Commission for the Northwest Atlantic Fisheries. Research bulletin / *edited by* W.H. Champion. - *Published by* International Commission for the Northwest Atlantic Fisheries. P.O. Box 638, Dartmouth, N.S. B2Y 3Y9, 1964-
Annual. Fixed period reports (annual, biennial).
Indexed in Arct. bibl.

International Commission for the Northwest Atlantic Fisheries. Statistical bulletin / *edited by* V.M. Hodder. - *Published by* International Commission for the Northwest Atlantic Fisheries. P.O. Box 638, Dartmouth, N.S. B2Y 3Y9, 1952-
Annual. Statistics, newsletter format,

The International fiction review / *edited by* Saad Elkhadem. - *Published by* The International Fiction Association. c/o Dr. S. Elkhadem, Dept. of German and Russian, University of New Brunswick, Fredericton, N.B., January 1974-
Issued twice a year. Scholarly publication, magazine format, 80 p. Includes book reviews, advertising, volume index. Circulation: 500
ISSN 0315-4149 $3.00 per issue : $6.00 per year.

International journal / *edited by* James Eayrs and Robert Spencer. - *Published by* Canadian Institute of International Affairs. 31 Wellesley St. E., Toronto, Ont., 1946-
Quarterly. Association publication, journal format, 176 p. Language: English and French. Includes book reviews, advertising, volume index. Circulation: 3400
Indexed in Can. ind., Hist. abstr.; Amer. hist. and life, Peace res. abstr., A.B.C. pol. sci.
ISSN 0020-7020 $15.00 per year. Special rate of $12.00 for subscriptions placed directly.

International Microwave Power Institute. IMPI newsletter / *edited by* W.A.G. Voss and P. Bhartia. - *Published by* International Microwave Power Institute. P.O. Box 1556, Edmonton, Alta., February 1973-
Quarterly. Association publication, newsletter format, 30-40 p. Includes book reviews, advertising. Circulation: 700-800
ISSN 0318-0883 $6.00 per year.

International press journal / *edited by* Edward H. Barr. - *Published by* Edward H. Barr. 81 Haig Ave., Scarborough, Ont. M1N 2W2 (Subscription address: P.O. Box 758, Postal Station F, Toronto, Ont) 1956-
Issued every other month. Special interest, newspaper format, 20 p. Circulation: 4832
$10.00 per year.

International Real Estate Federation. Canadian Chapter. IREF newsletter / *edited by* E. Mack Parliament. - *Published by* Canadian Chapter. International Real Estate Federation. 99 Duncan Mill Rd., Don Mills, Toronto, Ont. M3B 1Z2, 1971-
Issued every other month. Association publication, magazine format, 8 p. Circulation: 500
Free on request.

International Salon of Cartoons *Voir* Catalogue du salon international de la caricature

International specification index *See* Spec index international

International view / *edited by* Shanthi Radcliffe. - *Published by* Office on International Education. University of Western Ontario. Stevenson Lawson Bldg., University of Western Ontario, London, Ont., October 1974-
Irregular (approximately 4 issues per year). Institutional publication (Universities, schools, etc.), newspaper format, 4 p. Includes book reviews. Circulation: 2000
Free.

International wheelspin news *See* Wheelspin news : Canada's autosport newsmagazine

Interrobang - *Published by* Fanshaw College. P.O. Box 4005, Terminal C, London, Ont. N5W 5H1.
Weekly. Student publication. Includes advertising. Circulation: 5000

Interuniversity Centre for European Studies. Newsletter = Centre interuniversitaire d'études européennes. Bulletin - *Published by* Interuniversity Centre for European Studies. Pavillon Riverin 6410, P.O. Box 8888, Montreal, Que. H3C 3P8, September 1973-
Issued twice a month during the academic year. Association publication, newsletter format, 10 p. Language: English and French. Includes book reviews. Circulation: 500
$5.00 per year. Prepayment required.

Inter-Varsity in action / *edited by* Betti Erb. - *Published by* Inter-Varsity Christian Fellowship of Canada. 745 Mount Pleasant Rd., Toronto, Ont. M4S 2N5, Summer 1972-
Quarterly. Association publication, newspaper format, 8 p. Language: English (French). Includes book reviews, film reviews. supplements issued.
Free.

Intervention / *édité par* Francine Hirbour. - *Publié par* La Corporation des travailleurs sociaux du Québec. Suite 114, 5757, ave. Decelles, Montréal, Qué., janvier 1975-
Trimestriel. Publication d'association, bulletin, Langue(s): français et anglais. Tirage: 1800
$1.25 le numéro : $4.00 par année (Etudiants $2.00).

Intouch / *edited by* Cherilyn Spraakman. - *Published by* Ontario Physiotherapy Association. 25 Imperial St., Toronto, Ont., May 1974-
Irregular (approximately 3 issues per year). Association publication, newsletter format, Controlled circulation.

Intralogue - *Published by* Lake Erie Regional Library System. 493 Wellington Rd., London, Ont., 1967-
Monthly. House/company organ, newsletter format, 8 p.
Controlled circulation.

Introduction to motorcycling / *edited by* John Cooper. - *Published by* Martin Levesque. Cycle Canada. 81A Front St. E., Toronto, Ont. M5E 1B8 (Subscription address: 666 Ste-Croix, Montreal, Que. H4L 3Y2) 1975-
Annual. Special interest, magazine format, 128 p. Includes advertising. Circulation: 25,000
$1.50 : $2.00, foreign. Sold at newsstands.

Introductions from an island / *edited by* R. Skelton. - *Published by* Department of Creative Writing. University of Victoria. P.O. Box 1700, Victoria, B.C. V8W 2Y2, 1969-
Annual. Student publication, magazine format, 55 p.
$.50. Prepayment required.

Inuit monthly *See* Inuit today

Inuit today / *edited by* Leah Diargencourt. - *Published by* Inuit Tapirisat of Canada. 222 Somerset St. W., Ottawa, Ont. K1P 5G3.
Former title(s): Inuit monthly.
Monthly. , magazine format, 60 p. Language: English and Inuktitut. Circulation: 925
Indexed in North. tit.
$5.00 and $10.00 per year.

Inventaire des recherches sur l'enseignement supérieur au Canada *See* Inventory of research into higher education in Canada

Inventions catalog: inventions for industry - *Published by* Canadian Patents and Development Ltd. 275 Slater St., Ottawa, Ont. K1A 0R3.
Former title(s): Patents handbook (prior to April 1972)
Issued twice a year. "A single listing of abstracts of inventions from government and university sources available for licensing", Revision sheets, 8-10 p.
Free.

Inventory of research into higher education in Canada = Inventaire des recherches sur l'enseignement supérieur au Canada / *edited by* G.F. Houning and A.M. Kristfanison. - *Published by* Association of Universities and Colleges of Canada. 151 Slater St., Ottawa, Ont. K1P 5H3, 1974-
Former title(s): Inventory of research relevant to higher education in Canada (1974)
Annual. Association publication. Language: English and French.
ISSN 0316-1129 $3.00 per issue. Prepayment required.

Inventory of research relevant to higher education in Canada (1974) *See* Inventory of research into higher education in Canada

Investigart : journal of research in art education / *édité par* Elizabeth J. Sacca. - *Publié par* Graduate Division in Fine Art. Concordia University. 1230, rue de la Montagne, Montréal, Qué., printemps 1973-
Semestriel. Publication spécialisée, 70 p.
Langue(s): français et anglais ; sommaires: français et anglais. Tirage: 65
$3.00 par année.

Investor's digest of Canada / *edited by* A.C. Dunbar. - *Published by* N.J. Nankive. The Financial Post. Maclean-Hunter Ltd. 481 University Ave., Toronto, Ont. M5W 1A7, 1969-
Issued twice a month. Trade publication. Includes advertising. Circulation: 2256
$60.00 per year : $85.00 per year, foreign.

Involvement : the family resource magazine / *edited by* Gloria Shephard. - *Published by* Browndale. P.O. Box 19, Postal Station P, Toronto, Ont. M5S 2T3, September 1968-
Issued every other month. General interest, magazine format, 36 p. Includes book reviews, volume index. supplements issued. Back numbers available $1.25 each. Circulation: 4000
ISSN 0047-1380 $1.00 per issue : $5.00 per year.

Is / *edited by* Victor Coleman. - *Published by* The Eternal Network. 101 Kendall Ave., Toronto, Ont. M5R 1L8, Spring 1966-
Former title(s): Island.
Issued 3 times a year. Format varies, 48-210 p. Circulation: 500
$3.00 per issue : $7.50 per year : $4.00 per issue, foreign : $10.00 per year, foreign.

Isien usko = Faith of our fathers / *edited by* Armas Korhonen. - *Published by* Suomi Conference - Canada Area. Lutheran Church in America. 25 Old York Mills Rd., Willowdale, Ont. (Subscription address: 69 Florence Ave., Willowdale, Ont., M2N 1G1) October 1935-
Monthly. Church publication, ethnic press, newspaper format, 8 p. Language: Finnish. Circulation: 2000
$.25 per issue : $3.00 per year.

Iskra = Spark / *edited by* Peter J. Soloreoff. - *Published by* The Union of Spiritual Communities of Christ. P.O. Box 760, Grand Forks, B.C., February 1943-
Former title(s): Sten-gazeta (February 1943-February 1945)
Issued every other week. Religious and cultural publication, magazine format, 32 p. Language: Russian and English. Circulation: 1000
$.50 per issue : $10.00 per year. Prepayment required.

Island *See* Is

The Islander / *edited by* Donn Gardner. - *Published by* Vancouver Island Real Estate Board. P.O. Box 592, 6374 Metral Dr., Nanaimo, B.C. V9R 5L5, January 1974-
Issued every other month. Association publication, newsletter format, 8 p.

Issue / *edited by* John W. Foster. - *Published by* United Church of Canada. 85 St Clair Ave. E., Toronto, Ont., 1974-
Monthly. Church publication, 1 p. Circulation: 80,000
Free.

Issues and events (September 1969-April 1974) *See* FYI (For your information)

It needs to be said : a new look at Canadian literature / *edited by* Jim Smith and others. - *Published by* It Needs to Be Said. P.O. Box 1355, Kingston, Ont., 1974-
Alternative title: The Front.
Quarterly. Special interest, magazine format, 16-20 p. Includes book reviews, play reviews, volume index. Circulation: 1000
$.50 per issue : $2.00 per year (Institutions $5.00) : $1.00 per issue, foreign : $6.00 per year, foreign (Institutions $10.00). Special rates offered (bulk rates to schools).

Italian Chamber of Commerce. Bulletin / *edited by* Sergio Lanzieri. - *Published by* Italian Chamber of Commerce of Montreal. Suite 412, 1255 Phillips Sq., Montreal, Que. H3B 3G1, 1964-
Issued every other month. Special interest, magazine format, 40 p. Language: French and English and Italian. Includes advertising. Subscription included with membership. Controlled circulation.

Italian trade topics - *Published by* Italian Embassy, Office of the Commercial Counsellor. 172 Maclaren St., Ottawa, Ont. K2P 0K9., 1961-
Monthly. House/company organ, pamphlet format, 8 p. Circulation: 5000

ItalyCanada trade / *edited by* Antonio Valeri. - *Published by* The Italian Chamber of Commerce. Suite 313, 159 Bay St., Toronto, Ont. M5J 1J7, 1964-
Former title(s): Italy Canada trade.
Quarterly with a special issue in October. Trade publication, magazine format, 84 p. Language: English and Italian.
Free.

Italy Canada trade *See* ItalyCanada trade

It's happening - *Published by* Children's Services Division. Edmonton Public Library. 7 Sir Winston Churchill Sq., Edmonton, Alberta. Institutional publication (Universities, schools, etc.).
Free.

It's our bag (1969-1972) *See* Venture forth

JETRO communique / *sponsored by* Japan External Trade Organization ; *edited by* S. Oue. - *Published by* Japan Trade Centre. Suite 700, 151 Bloor St. W., Toronto, M5S 1S8, March 1975-
Former title(s): Tradewinds from Japan (June 1970-February 1975)
Monthly. House/company organ, newsletter format, 4 p. Circulation: 2200
Free. Controlled circulation.

JMC chronicle (1951-1971) *See* Jeunesses Musicales of Canada. JMC bulletin

Jabberwocky / *sponsored by* Ontario Arts Council ; *edited by* Mary Stella Johnston. - *Published by* Leslie Cowger. Apt. 612, 35 Charles St. W., Toronto, Ont. M4Y 1R6 (Subscription address: 530 Lakeshore Rd., Sarnia, Ont) June 1974-
Quarterly. Special interest, magazine format, 28 p. Circulation: 300
ISSN 0316-6759 $1.25 per issue : $5.00 per year.

Jahrbuch der Konferenz der Mennoniten in Kanada *See* Conference of Mennonites in Canada. Yearbook

Jameel's journal / *edited by* James Peters. - *Published by* James Peters. 20 Veery Place, Don Mills, Ont. M3C 2E1, November 1972-
Irregular (approximately 2-3 issues per year). Special interest, newsletter format, 4 p. Circulation: 150

Japanese Canadian Citizen's Association. Bulletin / *edited by* Gordon Mayede. - *Published by* Greater Vancouver Japanese Canadian Citizens Association. P.O. Box 2108, Main P.O., Vancouver, B.C. V6B 3T5.
Monthly. Ethnic press, newsletter format, 40 p. Language: English and Japanese. Includes advertising. Circulation: 3450
ISSN 0316-3288 Free to Japanese Canadians and decendants and others.

Je crois : magazine populaire catholique / *édité par* André Daigneault. - *Publié par* Messagers catholiques de la Bible. C.P. 1815, Québec, Qué. G1K 7K7, janvier 1960-
Mensuel. Publication ecclésiastique, magazine, 32 p. Tirage: 17,000
$.30 le numéro : $3.00 par année : $4.00 par année, l'étranger. Tarifs spéciaux disponibles.

Jerusalem times / *edited by* Joseph Almaleh. - *Published by* Jerusalem Times Publishing Co. P.O. Box 65654, Postal Station F, Vancouver, B.C. V5N 5K7, April 1974-
Monthly. Ethnic press, newspaper format, 12 p. Language: English and Arabic. Includes book reviews.
ISSN 0317-0829 $.25 per issue : $4.00 per year : $5.00 per year, foreign.

Le Jeune scientifique (octobre 1962-décembre 1969) *Voir* Québec science

Jeunes de 3 et 4ième année *See* AmiSol

Jeunes de 5 et 6ième année *Voir* Amigo

Jeunes du monde / *édité par* André Roberge. - *Publié par* Jeunesse du monde. 1145, de la Canardière, C.P. 220, Québec, Qué. G1L 4V7.
Mensuel. Organe interne/officiel, bulletin, 12 p. Tirage: 2000
$.40 le numéro : $3.00 par année : $5.00 par année, l'étranger. Envoi gratuit. Tarifs spéciaux disponibles.

Jeunes scientifique / *édité par* Raymond Blain. - *Publié par* Conseil de la jeunesse scientifique. 1415 est, rue Jarry, Montréal, Qué., septembre 1975-
Bimensuel. Publication spécialisée, bulletin, 6 p. Tirage: 2000
ISSN 0319-4779 Envoi gratuit.

Jeunesses musicales du Canada. Bulletin JMC / *édité par* Gaston Germain. - *Publié par* Jeunesses musicales du Canada. 462, chemin Côte Ste-Catherine, Montréal, Qué. H2V 2B4, janvier 1974-
Ancien titre: Journal des Jeunesses musicales du Canada (1951-1971) Publié en anglais: Jeunesses Musicales of Canada. JMC bulletin.
Bimestriel. Publication d'association, bulletin, 4 p. Comprend critique de disques, publicité.Aussi sous microform.
ISSN 0315-2332 Envoi gratuit.

Jeunesses Musicales of Canada. JMC bulletin / *edited by* M. Gaston Germain. - *Published by* Jeunesses musicales of Canada. 462 Côte Ste-Catherine, Montreal, Que. H2V 2B4, January 1974-
Former title(s): JMC chronicle (1951-1971) Published in French: Jeunesses musicales du Canada. Bulletin JMC.
Issued every other month. Association publication, newsletter format, 4 p. available in microform.
ISSN 0317-0489 Free.

Jewish dialogue / *edited by* J. Rosenblatt. - *Published by* J.D. Publishing Co. 501 Yonge St., Toronto, Ont.
Quarterly. Special interest, magazine format, 80 p. Includes advertising. Circulation: 8000
$2.50 per issue : $10.00 per year.

Jewish eagle / *edited by* Joseph Gallay. - *Published by* The Jewish Eagle. Kanader Adler Inc. Suite 218, 4180 De Courtrai, Montreal, Que. H3S 1C3, 1907-
Weekly. Special interest. Includes advertising.
$.20 per issue : $10.00 per year : $12.00 per year, foreign.

The Jewish post / *edited by* Bess Kaplan. - *Published by* Harold Markusoff. P.O. Box 3777, Postal Station B, Winnipeg, Man. R2W 3R6., 1925-
Weekly. Ethnic press, newspaper format, 12-16 p.
$.20 per issue : $7.00 per year.

Jewish standard / *edited by* Julius Hayman. - *Published by* Julius Hayman. Suite 507, 8 Colborne St., Toronto, Ont. M5E 1E1.
Issued twice a month. Special interest, magazine format, Includes advertising.
$5.00 per year.

Jobber news / *edited by* Sam Dixon. - *Published by* Wadham Publications Ltd. 109 Vanderhoof Ave., Toronto, Ont. M4G 2J2, 1932-
Monthly. Special interest, magazine format, 70 p. Circulation: 7924
$.50 per issue : $5.00 per year : $10.00 per year, foreign.

John Howard Society of Ontario. Newsletter / *edited by* D.G. Lennie. - *Published by* John Howard Society of Ontario. 168 Isabella St., Toronto, Ont. M4Y 1P6.
Issued twice a year. Association publication, newsletter format, 8 p. Circulation: 6000
Free with membership and to educational institutions.

Joint Program in Transportation. Newsletter / *sponsored by* University of Toronto-York University ; *edited by* Ann J. Poole. - *Published by* Centre for Urban and Community Studies. 150 St. George St., Toronto, Ont. M5S 1A1, July 1971-
Irregular (approximately 5 issues per year). Special interest, newsletter format, 28 p. Circulation: 950
ISSN 0318-1235

Joncas institutional guide *Voir* Guide des institutions Joncas

Le Journal (septembre 1969-mai 1970 et septembre 1974-mai 1975) *Voir* L'Erecteur

The Journal - *Published by* St. Mary's University. Robie St., Halifax, N.S.
Weekly. Student publication. Circulation: 4500

Journal - Canadian Association for Health, Physical Education and Recreation (1950-1968) *See* Canadian Association for Health, Physical Education and Recreation: CAHPER journal

Journal - Canadian Institute of Food Science and Technology *See* Canadian Institute of Food Science and Technology. Journal

Journal - Society of Canadian Artists (November 1967-July 1968) *See* Art magazine

Journal - The Town Planning Institute of Canada (1920-1931) *See* PLAN Canada

Le journal "ARC" arabe *See* Arc Arabic Journal

Le journal Bell / *édité par* Rose Matton. - *Publié par* Bell Canada. C.P. 23, Tour de la Bourse, Montréal, Qué, 1963-
Paraît tous les 15 jours. Organe interne/officiel, magazine, 8 p. Tirage: 28,500
Envoi gratuit.

Journal canadien de génétique et de cytologie *See* Canadian journal of genetics and cytology

Journal canadien de mathématiques *See* Canadian journal of mathematics

Le Journal canadien de radiographie, radiothérapie, nucléographie *See* The Canadian journal of radiography, radiotherapthy, nuclear medicine

Le Journal canadien de recherche sémiotique *See* The Canadian journal of research in semiotics

Journal canadien des études africaines *See* Canadian journal of African studies

Le Journal canadien des sciences neurologiques *See* The Canadian journal of neurological sciences

Journal canadien d'otolaryngologie *See* Canadian journal of otolaryngology

Journal Chicobi (janvier 1971-mai 1972) *Voir* Journal Chicobi : section information

Journal Chicobi : section information - *Publié par* Camp-ecole Chicobi. Guyenne, Abitibi-ouest, Qué. J0Y 1L0, octobre 1972-
Ancien titre: Journal Chicobi (janvier 1971-mai 1972) Chicobi (octobre 1968-octobre 1970)
Intermittent (approximativement 3-4 éditions par an). Organe interne/officiel, 15 p. Tirage: 275
$1.00 par année. Tirage contrôlé.

Journal Chicobi : section scientifique - *Publié par* Camp-ecole Chicobi. Guyenne, Abitibi-ouest, Qué. J0Y 1L0, octobre 1972-
Intermittent (approximativement 3-4 éditions par an). Bulletin, 20 p. Tirage: 275
Tirage contrôlé.

Le Journal de la marine marchande des Maritimes *See* The Maritimes shipping herald and marine engineering journal

Journal dentaire du Québec / *édité par* Marcel Hebert. - *Publié par* L'Association dentaire de la province de Québec. 1509 ouest, rue Sherbrooke, Montréal, Qué.(adresse d'abonnement: 4290 est, Beaubien, Montréal, Qué)
Mensuel. Publication d'association, magazine, Langue(s): français et anglais ; sommaires: anglais. Comprend critique de livres, publicité. Tirage: 2800
Indexé dans RADAR.
$10.00 par année. Abonnements payables à l'avance.

Journal des Jeunesses musicales du Canada (1951-1971) *Voir* Jeunesses musicales du Canada. Bulletin JMC

Le Journal des stages (stages accessibles aux résidents québécois) - *Publié par* Office Franco-Québécois pour la jeunesse. 290 Place d'Youville, Montréal, Qué. H2Y 2B6, 1970-
Ancien titre: Stages en France.
Trimestriel. Publication spécialisée, bulletin, 8-16 p.

Le journal du personnel (printemps 1963-printemps 1973) *Voir* La Banque Canadienne Nationale. Le point BCN

Journal epiK-KaKouna / *édité par* Yvan Roy. - *Publié par* Service d'information de Cacouna. C.P. 152, Cacouna, Cté Rivière-du-Loup, Qué. G0L 1G0, octobre 1974-
Mensuel sauf juillet et août. Publication spécialisée, journal, 20 p.
ISSN 0319-3918 $.25 le numéro : $2.00 par année. Abonnements payables à l'avance.

Journal l'éclosion - *Publié par* Association étudiante services collectifs inc. 2410, chemin Ste-Foy, Québec, Qué., novembre 1972-
Hebdomadaire. Publication des étudiants, journal, 8 p. Comprend critique de livres, critique de films, critique de disques.
$5.00 par année : $10.00 par année, l'étranger.

The Journal of automatic writing : communications from the spiritual forces / *edited by* William T. Metzger. - *Published by* The Spiritual Press. P.O. Box 464, Don Mills, Ont. M3C 2T3, June 1974-
Monthly (10 issues a year). Special interest, magazine format, 36 p.
ISSN 0315-5412 $1.00 per issue : $6.00 per year : $8.00 per year, foreign. Prepayment required.

Journal of business administration / *edited by* Ilan Vertinsky. - *Published by* Faculty of Commerce and Business Administration. University of British Columbia. Vancouver, B.C., 1969-
Issued twice a year. Institutional publication (Universities, schools, etc.), journal format, 65 p. Includes book reviews. available in microform.
Indexed in Can. B.P.I.
$2.50 per issue : $3.50 per year.

The Journal of Canadian art history : studies in Canadian art, architecture and the decorative arts / *edited by* Donald F.P. Andrus and Sandra R. Paikowsky. - *Published by* Owl's Head Press. Concordia University, H-543, 1488 De Maisonneuve Blvd., Montreal, Que., Spring 1974-
Issued twice a year. Special interest, magazine format, 80 p. Language: English and French. Includes book reviews. Circulation: 1000
Indexed in R.I.L.A.
$8.00 per year.

Journal of Canadian fiction / *sponsored by* Journal of Canadian Fiction Association ; *edited by* John Robert Sorfleet, John G. Moss and David Arnason. - *Published by* Bedrock Press. 2050 Mackay St., Montreal, Que., February 1972-
Quarterly. Special interest, journal format, 200 p. Language: English (French). Includes book reviews.
Indexed in Can. ind., Can. essay and lit. ind., M.L.A. int. bib., Annu. bibl. Engl. lang. and lit., Abstr. eng. stud.
ISSN 0047-2255 $2.95 per issue : $9.00 per year.

The Journal of Canadian petroleum technology / *edited by* E.G. Tapp. - *Published by* The Canadian Institute of Mining and Metallurgy. Suite 906 - 1117 Ste. Catherine St. W., Montreal, Que. H3B 1J3, 1967-
Quarterly. Association publication, magazine format, 100 p. Includes book reviews, advertising, cumulative index. Circulation: 1500
Indexed in North. tit.
$3.00 per issue : $10.00 per year : $15.00 per year, foreign.

Journal of Canadian studies / *edited by* Denis Smith. - *Published by* Trent University. Peterborough, Ont. K9J 7B8.
Quarterly. Scholarly publication, journal format, 64 p. Language: English (French). Circulation: 1250
Indexed in Can. ind., Can. essay and lit. ind., Soc. sci. cit. ind., Hum. ind., Hist. abstr.; Amer. hist. and life, A.B.C. pol. sci.
ISSN 0021-9495 $6.00 per year : $11.00 for 2 years (Institutions: $10.00 per year, $15.00 for 2 years).

Journal of church and society (1965-1971) *See* Direction

Journal of commerce / *edited by* A.H.A. Brown. - *Published by* J.L. Whitehead. Journal of Commerce. 2000 W. 12th Ave., Vancouver, B.C., 1911-
Issued twice a week. Business publication, newspaper format, Monday ed. 23 p. Wednesday ed. 8 p. Includes advertising. supplements issued. Circulation: 9434
$1.50 per issue : $75.00 per year.

Journal of comparative family studies / *edited by* George Kurian. - *Published by* Department of Sociology and Anthropology. University of Calgary. Calgary, Alta. T2N 1N4, Autumn 1970-
Issued twice a year. Special interest, journal format, 120 p. Includes book reviews, advertising, volume index. Circulation: 500
Indexed in Sociol. abstr., Psych. abstr.
$4.00 per issue : $8.00 per year. Special rates offered. Prepayment required.

Journal of comparative sociology / *sponsored by* MRW Management Training and Productivity Motivation, Ltd ; *edited by* A.J.S. Sethi. - *Published by* Canada Sociological Research Centre. 6275 Sundown Cr., Orleans, Ont. (Subscription address: P.O. Box 7305, Ottawa, Ont. K1L 8E4) 1973-
Former title(s): Comparative health care systems (1973)
Annual. Association publication, magazine format, 150-200 p. Includes book reviews, advertising.
$11.50.

Journal of education thought / *edited by* D. McDougall. - *Published by* Faculty of Education. University of Calgary. 2920-24th Ave. N.W., Calgary, Alta. T2N 1N4 (Subscription address: Room 1304, Education Tower, The University of Calgary)
Issued 3 times a year (April August and December). Journal format, 64 p. Includes book reviews, advertising, cumulative index. available in microform. Back issues available $1.00 per copy or group rates.
Indexed in Sociol. educ. abstr., Can. educ. ind., Curr. ind. j. educ.
$1.75 per issue : $5.00 per year : $9.00 for 2 years : $12.00 for 3 years.

Journal of microwave power / *edited by* W.A.G. Voss. - *Published by* International Microwave Power Institute. P.O. Box 1556, Edmonton, Alta. T5J 2N7, 1966-
Quarterly. "An international journal devoted to the industrial, scientific and medical applications of microwaves", journal format, 100 p. Includes advertising, cumulative index. supplements issued.
Indexed in Bior. index, Biol. abstr., Eng. ind., Food sci. and tech. abstr., Sci. abstr.: electr. and elect., North. tit.
$12.50 per issue : $50.00 per year.

Journal of orthomolecular psychiatry / *sponsored by* Academy of Orthomolecular Psychiatry ; *edited by* J. Ross MacLean. - *Published by* Toronto Branch. Canadian Schizophrenia Foundation. 2135 Albert St., Regina, Sask. Q4P 2V1, January 1974-
Former title(s): Schizophrenia (to May 1972) Orhomolecular psychiatry (May 1972-January 1974)
Quarterly. Association publication, journal format, 80 p. Includes book reviews, advertising, volume index. available in microform. Circulation: 1100
ISSN 0317-2029 $4.25 per issue : $17.00 per year.

The Journal of rheumatology / *edited by* Metro A. Ogryzlo. - *Published by* The Journal of Rheumatology Publishing Co. Ltd. 45 Charles St. E., Toronto, Ont. M4Y 1S3, March 1974-
Quarterly. Professional publication, magazine format, 125 p. Includes book reviews, advertising, volume index. supplements issued. Circulation: 1100
ISSN 0315-162X $6.00 per issue : $20.00 per year (Students, interns, residents, fellows in training $10.00), $21.00 per year, foreign.

Journal of student papers in anthropology and sociology *See* Kumtuks review

Journal of the Alberta Society of Petroleum Geologists (1953-1962) *See* Bulletin of Canadian petroleum geology

The Journal of the Canadian Physiotherapy Association (1923-1972) *See* Physiotherapy Canada

Journal of the College of General Practice of Canada *See* Canadian family physician

Joyceville journal - *Published by* Joyceville Institution. P.O. Box 880, Kingston, Ont.
$1.00 per year.

Jubilee : a magazine of Canadian writing / *edited by* Charles Mountford. - *Published by* Coach House, Owen Sound. Owen Sound, Ont. (Subscription address: R.R. 2, Gorrie, Ont. N0G 1X3) September 1974-
Issued twice a year. General interest, magazine format, 60 p. Circulation: 100
$1.75 per issue : $3.00 per year : $4.00 per year, foreign.

Junior Red Cross news (1951-1972) *See* Reach

Justice / *edited by* Si Bresner. - *Published by* International Ladies' Garment Workers' Union. 405 Concord St., Montreal, Que. H3A 1J4, 1936-
Issued every other month. House/company organ, newsletter format, Language: French ; summaries: English, Italian and Greek.

Justinien (1964-1969) *Voir* Revue générale de droit

KVP news / *edited by* Murry A. Lunn. - *Published by* M.A. Lunn. Manitoba Division. Canadian Society of Radiological Technicians. 294 Duffield St., Winnipeg, Man. R3V 2V9., January 1964-
Quarterly. Association publication, newsletter format, 20-26 p. Includes advertising. Circulation: 670
Subscription included in membership fee.

K Ray / *edited by* Ron Sclater. - *Published by* Eastern Canada and the Caribbean District. Kiwanis International. Casa Loma, 1 Austin Terrace, Toronto, Ont. M5R 1X8, 1925-
Issued every other month. Association publication, newsletter format, 6-8 p. Language: English and French. Circulation: 10,000
$1.50 per year.

Kabalarian courier / *edited by* Donalie Graves. - *Published by* Kabalarian Philosphy. 1160 West 10th Ave., Vancouver, B.C.
Issued every other month. Special interest, magazine format, 16 p. Circulation: 1000
Free.

kalendar holosu spasytelia *See* Redeemer's voice almanac

Kalendar svitla = The Light almanac / *edited by* S. Yakymyshyn. - *Published by* The Basilian Press. 286 Lisgar St., Toronto, Ont. M6J 3G9.
Annual. Almanac, book format, 192 p. Language: Ukrainian. Circulation: 4000
$2.00.

Kanadai magvarsag = Canadian Hungarian / *edited by* Stephen Vorosuary. - *Published by* Stephen Vorosuary. 412 Bloor St. W., Toronto, Ont. M5S 1X5, 1950-
Weekly. Ethnic press. Language: Hungarian. Includes advertising. Circulation: 7122

Kanadai Magyar ujag *See* Canadian Hungarian News

Kanadai magyar ujság képes naptara *See* Canadian Hungarian news annual

Kanadiysky farmer = The Canadian farmer / *edited by* Dr. Martynowich. - *Published by* Trident Press. P.O. Box 3629, Postal Station B, Winnipeg, Man., 1903-
Weekly. Ethnic press, newspaper format, 8 p. Language: Ukrainian. Includes book reviews, advertising. Circulation: 9500
$.20 per issue : $10.00 per year : $11.00 per year, foreign. Prepayment required.

Kanadiysky ranon = Canadian morning *See* Yevanhel's'kyi ranok

Kanadské listy = Canadian news / *edited by* Mike Janecek. - *Published by* Club of Newcomers of Czech and Slovak Origin in Canada. Klub novych - Newcomers Club. 388 Atwater Ave., Mississagua, Ont. L5G 2A3, January 1973-
Former title(s): Hlas novych = Newcomers' voice (May 1967-December 1972)
Monthly. Ethnic press, newsletter format, 6 p. Language: Czech and Slovak. Includes book reviews. Circulation: 1200-1500

Kanadski srbobran = The Canadian srbobran / *edited by* Lazar Stoysich. - *Published by* Serbian League of Canada. 335 Britannia Ave., Hamilton, Ont. L8H 1Y4, September 1951-
Weekly. Ethnic press, newspaper format, 6 p. Language: Serbian. Includes advertising. Circulation: 8000
$.25 per issue : $10.00 per year. Special rates offered.

Kanadsky Slovák = Canadian Slovak / *edited by* Marián Jankovsky. - *Published by* Canadian Slovak League. 61 Golden Blvd. W., Welland, Ont. (Subscription address: 400 A Queen St. W, Toronto, Ont) 1941-
Weekly. Ethnic publication, newspaper format, 8 p. Language: Slovak with some English. Includes book reviews, advertising. Circulation: 2500
$.15 per issue : $8.00 per year : $10.00 per year, foreign.

The Kanata standard / *edited by* R.G. Andoff and F.C. Boyd. - *Published by* Kanata-Beaverbrook Community Association. P.O. Box 13061, Kanata, Ont. K2K 1X3, 1965-
Issued every other week. Association publication, newspaper format, 12 p. Includes book reviews, play reviews, advertising.
$3.00 per year.

Karaki - *Published by* Karaki. Apt. 1, 2821 Irma St., Victoria, B.C., V9A 1S3.
Issued twice a year.
$1.50 per issue.

Kaszebe / *edited by* Walter Markiewicz. - *Published by* Polish Canadian Courier. P.O. Box 161, Postal Station P, Toronto, Ont., November 1974-
Irregular. Ethnic press, newspaper format, Language: Kashubian, Polish, and English. Circulation: 1000

Kateri. Edition française / *édité par* Henri Béchard. - *Publié par* Henri Béchard. C.P. 70, Caughnawaga, Qué. J0L 1B0, décembre 1957-
Trimestriel. Publication spécialisée, magazine, 36 p. Comprend publicité, Mises à jour. Tirage: 4100
$1.00 par année. Abonnements payables à l'avance.

Keith's florist directory and horticultural guide / *edited by* W.G. Tolton. - *Published by* Horticulture Publications Ltd. P.O. Box 697, 245 Queen St. S., Streetsville, Ont., 1905-
Issued every other week. Directory, magazine format, 36 p. Includes book reviews, advertising. Circulation: 2400
$.15 per issue : $3.00 per year : $4.00 per year, foreign. Prepayment required.

The Kensington market - *Published by* Richard Norman. 3563 Eglinton Ave. W., Toronto, Ont. M6M 1V8.
24 p.
$1.00 per issue.

Kepes vilaghirado = Illustrated world review / *edited by* Margaret Janossy. - *Published by* Andrew Laszlo. Illustrated World Review. 6 Alcina Ave., Toronto, Ont.
Monthly. Language: Hungarian. Includes advertising.

The Kernel / *edited by* J.G. Ballantyne. - *Published by* The Canada Starch Company Ltd. 1 Place du Commerce, Nun's Island, Montreal, Que.
Former title(s): CHSCO news (to October 1979)
Monthly. House/company organ, newsletter format, 4 p.
Controlled circulation.

Kerygma / *édité par* H. Charbonneau. - *Publié par* Institut des sciences missionnaires. Université Saint-Paul. 223 Main St., Ottawa, Ont. K1S 1C4, 1967-
Semestriel. 96 p. Langue(s): français et anglais.
ISSN 0023-0693 $4.00 le numéro : $8.00 par année.

Key to electronics engineering purchasing in Canada *See* Canadian electronics engineering annual buyers guide and catalog directory

Key to Toronto / *edited by* Elizabeth M. Dunn. - *Published by* Key Publishers Ltd. 59A Front St. E, Toronto, Ont. M5E 1B3.
Monthly. Calendar of events, magazine format, 132 p. Includes film reviews, advertising. Circulation: 75,000
$.75 per issue : $7.00 per year : $9.00 per year, foreign. Controlled circulation.

Keystone / *edited by* Catherine J. Kenny. - *Published by* Board of Publications. Wilfrid Laurier University. Waterloo, Ont.
Annual. Yearbook, student publication, 175 p.
$6.00.

Khristianin (the Christian) / *edited by* John K. Huk. - *Published by* Toronto Christian Mission. P.O. Box 220, Postal Station N, Toronto, Ont. M8V 3T2, January 1968-
Monthly except August. Special interest, magazine format, 18 p. Language: Russian. Circulation: 600
$2.00 per year. Free to those unable to pay subscription.

Khrystiansky visnyk = The Christian herald / *edited by* M. Podworniak. - *Published by* The Ukrainian Evangelical Baptist Convention of Canada. 787 Toronto St., Winnipeg, Man. R3E 1Z7., September 1942-
Issued every other month. Church publication, magazine format, 24 p. Language: Ukrainian.
$.50 per issue : $3.00 per year.

Le ki-es-ki *See* Canadian Education Association. The C.E.A. handbook

Kin / *edited by* B.R. Causton. - *Published by* The Association of Kinsmen Clubs. P.O. Box 40, Thornhill, Ont. L3T 3N1, 1920-
Issued every other month. Association publication, magazine format, Includes advertising. Circulation: 16,415
$3.00 per year.

Kinesis / *edited by* Joanne Lazenby. - *Published by* Vancouver Status of Women. 2029 West Fourth Ave., Vancouver, B.C. V6J 1N3, August 1971-
Former title(s): Vancouver Status of Women newsletter.
Monthly. Special interest, newspaper format, 20 p. Includes book reviews, film reviews. Circulation: 1000
ISSN 0317-9095 $.25 per issue : $3.00 per year (Organizations $10.00). Prepayment required.

Kiro santé : le magazine des gens en santé / *édité par* Roger Charland. - *Publié par* Roger Charland. C.P. 35, Plessisville, Qué. G6L 2Y6, novembre 1974-
Bimestriel. Publication spécialisée, magazine, 36 p. Tirage: 8100
ISSN 0317-0519 $1.00 le numéro : $3.00 par année. Abonnements payables à l'avance.

Kitchener journal / *edited by* Rosel Greinwald. - *Published by* Erich O. Reprich. P.O. Box 278, Pickering, Ont. L1V 2R4, 1952-
Weekly. Ethnic press, newspaper format, 16 p. Language: German.
$7.50 per year : $11.50 per year, foreign.

Kitchener-Waterloo Probe. K.W. Probe news / *sponsored by* K.W. Probe. - *Published by* Kitchener-Waterloo Probe. Environment 202, University of Waterloo, Waterloo, Ont. N2L 3G1.
Irregular (approximately 3-4 issues per year). Association publication, 6-8 p. Circulation: 100
$5.00 per year. Subscription included in membership fee. Special rates offered. Prepayment required.

Kitimat - Kemano ingot / *edited by* G. Blair Parkhurst. - *Published by* Aluminum Company of Canada Ltd. P.O. Box 1800, Kitmat, B.C., August 1954-
Weekly. House/company organ, newsletter format, 4 p. supplements issued. Circulation: 3000

KiwaNews : Western Canada district / *edited by* George Bothwell. - *Published by* Western Canada District. 849 Kildonan Dr., Winnipeg, Man. R2K 2G3, January 1968-
Former title(s): Western Canada District news (to January 1968)
Irregular (approximately 5 issues per year). Association publication, 4 p.
$.50 per year. Controlled circulation.

Know Canada - *Published by* Terry Art Ltd. 643 Yonge St., Toronto, Ont. M4Y 2A2.
Issued twice a year. Magazine format, 60 p.
$3.00 per volume.

Koinonia (novembre 1971-décembre 1973) *Voir* Communauté

Koinotiki foni = Hellenic community voice of Ottawa / *sponsored by* Hellenic Community Voice of Ottawa ; *edited by* Kostas Zygoumis. - *Published by* Hellenic Postman. 3622 St. Lawrence Blvd., Montreal, Que (Subscription address: 1315 Prince of Wales, Ottawa, Ont.)
Monthly. Ethnic press, newspaper format, 8 p. Language: Greek. Includes book reviews, advertising.
$5.00 per year.

Kolping Society. Kolping bulletin / *edited by* Karl Lange. - *Published by* Karl Lange. 1736 E. 46th Ave., Vancouver, B.C.
Monthly. Association publication, newsletter format, 8 p. Language: German. Includes advertising. Circulation: 100
Free to members.

Kombe / *édité par* Wilfrid Rejean. - *Publié par* Gérard-Roger Saint Victor. 125, rue Renaud, Chomedey, Laval, Qué., juin 1973-
Intermittent (approximativement 3 éditions par an). Publication spécialisée, magazine, 20 p. Comprend critique de films, critique de pièces de théâtre, critique de disques.
$.50 le numéro : $2.00 par année. Abonnements payables à l'avance.

The Korean journal / *edited by* Young-Rin Ryu. - *Published by* Korean Journal. 257 Olive Ave., Willowdale, Ont. M2N 4P5.
Weekly. Ethnic press. Includes advertising. Circulation: 600

Kredytova Kooperatyva Pivnichnoho Vinnipegu. Biuleten = North Winnipeg Credit Union Limited. Bulletin / *edited by* Andrew Kachor. - *Published by* North Winnipeg Credit Union Ltd. 544 Selkirk Ave., Winnipeg, Man. R2W 2M9., September 1959-
Quarterly. Newsletter format, 8 p. Language: Ukrainian ; summaries: English.
Free to members.

Krzyk = Outcry / *edited by* Vanusz Uiberall. - *Published by* Canadian Photopress Publishing Ltd. P.O. Box 113, Postal Station M, Toronto, Ont. M6S 4T2, 1974-
Monthly. Ethnic press. Language: Polish. Includes advertising. Circulation: 2300
$.50 per issue : $6.00 per year.

Kumtuks review / *edited by* D. Rowe and T.R. Hickman. - *Published by* Alma Mater Society. University of Victoria. Dept. of Anthropology and Sociology, University of Victoria, Victoria, B.C., Spring 1972-
Former title(s): Journal of student papers in anthropology and sociology.
Annual. Special interest, magazine format, 100 p.
ISSN 0318-2894 $2.50 (Institutions $5.00).

Kurier Poisko-Kanadyjski *See* The Polish Canadian courier

Kurier polsko-kanadyjski = Polish Canadian courier - *Published by* W. Markiewicz. 36 Robina Ave., Toronto, Ont. M6C 3Y6.
Weekly. Ethnic press, newspaper format,
$.20 per issue : $7.50 per year.

K-W Women's Place newsletter (September 1973-July 1975) *See* Strength

The Kyloe cry / *edited by* Nancy Irene Pease. - *Published by* Canadian Highland Cattle Society. R.R. 6, Shelburne, Ont. L0N 1S0, 1968-
Quarterly. Association publication, newsletter format, 8-10 p.
$5.00 per year : $10.00 per year, foreign. Prepayment required.

LU week (January 1967-April 1974) *See* Lakehead University. LU week 2

La Tribuna Italiana = The Italian tribune / *edited by* Camillo Carli. - *Published by* La Tribuna Italiana Co. 257 Dante St., Montreal, Que. H2S 1K3, 1963-
Monthly. Ethnic press. Language: Italian. Includes advertising. Circulation: 23,000
$.25 per issue : $3.00 per year : $4.00 per year, U.S. : $7.00 per year, foreign.

La Voce del popolo = The People's voice / *edited by* Michele Pirone. - *Published by* Mario Barone. Cosmo Maciocia. 5796 Jean Talon E., St. Leonard, Montreal, Que, 1968-
Weekly. Ethnic press. Language: Italian. Includes advertising.
$.15 per issue : $5.00 per year.

Lâânekaare postipoiss / *edited by* Valdeko Weemees. - *Published by* Vancouver Estonian Society. 6520 Oak St., Vancouver, B.C., 1953-
Former title(s): Lâânekarr.
Issued every other month. Association publication, magazine format, 24 p. Language: Estonian. Includes book reviews, film reviews, play reviews, record reviews. Circulation: 450

Lâânekarr *See* Lâânekaare postipoiss

Labatt news / *edited by* B. James Barlow. - *Published by* Labatt Breweries of Canada Ltd. 150 Simcoe St., London, Ont. N6A 4M3, 1938-
Former title(s): Spearhead (1938-1945)
Monthly. House/company organ, newspaper format, 8 p. Circulation: 5200

Laboratory equipment guide *See* Laboratory guide : directory issue of Laboratory product news

Laboratory guide : directory issue of Laboratory product news / *edited by* Rita Tate. - *Published by* Southam Business Publications Ltd. 1450 Don Mills Rd., Don Mills, Ont. M3B 2X7.
Former title(s): Laboratory equipment guide.
Annual. Directory, magazine format, 100 p. Includes advertising. Circulation: 14,500 Controlled circulation.

Laboratory product news / *edited by* Rita Tate. - *Published by* Southam Business Publications Ltd. 1450 Don Mills Rd., Don Mills, Ont. M3B 2X7, March 1971-
Issued every other month. Directory, magazine format, 28 p. Includes advertising.
$2.00 per issue : $8.00 per year : $30.00 per year, foreign. Controlled circulation.

Labour arbitration cases / *edited by* C.G. Simmons. - *Published by* Canada Law Book Ltd. 80 Cowdray Court, Agincourt, Ont. M1S 1S5, 1948-
Monthly. Special interest, magazine format, 108 p.
$30.00 per volume.

Labour challenge / *edited by* George Addison. - *Published by* Labor Challenge Publishing Association. P.O. Box 5595, Postal Station A, Toronto, Ont., February 1970-
Issued every other week. Special interest, newspaper format, 12 p. Includes book reviews. available in microform. Circulation: 3000
$.25 per issue : $4.00 per year : $5.50 per year, foreign.

Labour review / *edited by* Ed Cosgrove. - *Published by* Ontario Federation of Labour. Suite 202, 15 Gervais Dr., Don Mills, Ont., 1957-
Issued every other month. Association publication, newsletter format, 12 p.

Lacrosse-the Canadian game / *edited by* John Tobias. - *Published by* Canadian Lacrosse Association. 333 River Rd., Ottawa, Ont. K1L 8B9, May 1975-
Issued every other month. Association publication, magazine format, 32 p. Language: English and French. Includes book reviews, advertising. Circulation: 2000
$3.00 per year : $.50 per volume. Special rates offered.

Lakehead University. LU week 2 / *edited by* Michael O'Dwyer. - *Published by* Lakehead University. Oliver Rd., Thunder Bay, Ont. P7B 5E1, January 1967-
Former title(s): LU week (January 1967-April 1974)
Issued every other week. Institutional publication (Universities, schools, etc.), newspaper format, 4 p. Includes book reviews. Circulation: 3000

Lakehead University. Review / *edited by* P. Wesley and M. O'Dwyer (managing editor). - *Published by* Lakehead University. Thunder Bay, Ont. P7B 5E1, 1968-
Issued twice a year. Scholarly publication, magazine format, 155 p. Includes book reviews, volume index. Circulation: 200
Indexed in M.L.A. int. bib.
$1.75 per issue : $3.50 per year. Prepayment required.

Lambda - *Published by* Lambda Publications. Laurentian University. Sudbury, Ont.
Weekly. Student publication. Includes advertising. Circulation: 3000

The Lance - *Published by* Publications Commission. Students' Administrative Council. University of Windsor. Windsor, Ont.
Weekly. Student publication. Includes advertising. Circulation: 8300

Land compensation reports / *edited by* Arnold S. Weinrib. - *Published by* Canada Law Book Ltd. 80 Cowdray Court, Agincourt, Ont. M1S 1S5, 1971-
Irregular (approximately 8 issues per year). Cases, case notes, magazine format, 100 p.
$30.00 per volume.

Landmarks / *edited by* Diane Coble. - *Published by* The Winnipeg Real Estate Board. 1315 Portage Ave., Winnipeg, Man.
Issued 10 times a year. House/company organ, 15 p. Includes advertising.
Free. Controlled circulation.

Landscape / *edited by* Gwen Stupple. - *Published by* Gwen Stupple. Carlisle Business Service. Carlisle, Ont. L0R 1H0.
Monthly. Trade publication. Includes advertising. Circulation: 2543

Landscape = Paysage Canada / *edited by* Bryan F. Sutton. - *Published by* Canadian & Ontario Nursery Trades Association. 1568 Carling Ave., Ottawa, Ont. K1Z 7M5, January 1964-
Former title(s): The Nurseryman (1964) Canadian nurseryman (January 1965 - May 1973)
Issued every other month. Special interest, magazine format, 32 p. Language: English (French). Includes book reviews, advertising. Circulation: 2200
ISSN 0315-4874 $6.00 per year : $10.00 for 2 years : $12.00 for 3 years.

Landscape = Paysage Canada / *edited by* Bryan Sutton. - *Published by* Canadian Nursery Trades Association. 1568 Carling Ave., Ottawa, Ont. K1Z 7M5, 1960-
Issued every other month. Association publication. Includes advertising. Circulation: 2150
$6.00 : $10.00 for 2 years : $12.00 for 3 years.

Landscape architecture Canada / *edited by* Moura Quayle. - *Published by* Canadian Society of Landscape Architects. P.O. Box 3304, Postal Station C, Ottawa, Ont., August 1975-
Former title(s): Bulletin - Canadian Society of Landscape Architects. Published in French: L'Architecture du paysage Canada.
Irregular (approximately 3 issues per year). Association publication, 4 p.

Landscape Ontario / *edited by* Tom Harkness. - *Published by* Landscape Ontario. Suite 203, 4569 Sheppard Ave. E., Agincourt, Ont. M1S 1V3, 1967-
Issued every other month. Trade publication. Includes advertising. Circulation: 1000
$12.00 per year.

The Last post / *edited by* Drummond Burgess. - *Published by* Canadian Journalism Foundation. Suite 302, 454 King St., W., Toronto, Ont., 1969-
Irregular (approximately 8 issues per year). General interest, magazine format, 52 p. available in microform. Back issues available. Circulation: 15,000
Indexed in Alt. press ind., Can. essay and lit. ind..
ISSN 0023-8651 $.75 per issue : $5.00 per year (Institutions $7.00).

The Latest word from the Nova Scotia Museum / *edited by* Barbara B. Shaw. - *Published by* Nova Scotia Museum. 1747 Summer St., Halifax, N.S. B3H 3A6, December 1967-
Irregular (approximately 6 issues per year). Institutional publication, newsletter format, 4 p.
Free. Controlled circulation.

Latin America / *edited by* Jill Stocker. - *Published by* Canadian Bureau for International Education. Suite 408, 151 Slater St., Ottawa, Ont. K1P 5H3, 1972-
Published in French: L'Amerique Latine.
Issued every 2-3 years. Special interest, booklet format, 40 p.
Free.

Latvija Amerika / *edited by* Kriss Sidars. - *Published by* Latvija Amerika Publishing Ltd. 125 Broadview Ave., Toronto, Ont.
Weekly. Ethnic press, newspaper format, 20 p. Language: Latvian. Circulation: 2600
$.50 per issue : $21.00 per year : $17.00 per year, foreign.

Laurentian Communiqué (vol 1, no. 1, November 1967 - vol. 2, no. 3, June 1969) *See* Laurentian University. Laurentian journal

Laurentian University. Laurentian gazette = Gazette laurentienne / *edited by* Jean Baxter. - *Published by* Laurentian University. Ramsey Lake Rd., Sudbury, Ont. P3E 2C6, October 1974-
Monthly. Institutional publication (Universities, schools, etc.), newsletter format, 6 p. Language: English and French. Circulation: 1100
Free.

Laurentian University. Laurentian journal = Université laurentienne. Journal laurentien / *edited by* Jean Baxter. - *Published by* Laurentian University. Ramsey Lake Rd., Sudbury, Ont. P3E 2C6, November 1969-
Former title(s): Laurentian Communiqué (vol 1, no. 1, November 1967 - vol. 2, no. 3, June 1969)
Issued every other month. Institutional publication (Universities, schools, etc.), tabloid format, 4-8 p. Language: English and French. Circulation: 8000
Free.

Laurier campus / *edited by* Barry Lyon. - *Published by* Wilfrid Laurier University. 75 University Ave. W., Waterloo, Ont., June 1962-
Former title(s): Waterloo Campus (June 1962-December 1974)
Quarterly. Alumni publication, magazine format, 12 p. Circulation: 13,500
$5.00 per year. Controlled circulation.

Laval administration / *parrainé par* Corporation des relations étudiants et administrateurs. - *Publié par* Faculté des sciences de l'administration. Université Laval. Québec, Qué. G1K 7P4.
Publication des étudiants. Tirage: 4000

Laval théologique et philosophique / *parrainé par* Université Laval. Facultés de théologie et de philosophie ; *édité par* Paul-Emile Langevin (théologie) et Emmanuel Trépanier (philosophie). - *Publié par* Les Presses de l'Université Laval. C.P. 2447, Québec, Qué., 1945-
Parait 3 fois par an. Edition savante, revue, 112 p. Langue(s): français et anglais. Comprend critique de livres. Tirage: 1200
Indexé dans RADAR, Cath. ind., M.L.A. int. bib.
$2.50 le numéro : $7.00 par année : $8.00 par année, l'étranger. Tarifs spéciaux disponibles. Abonnements payables à l'avance.

Lavalin / *édité par* Francois Fauteux. - *Publié par* Groupe Lavalin. 1130 ouest, rue Sherbrooke, Montréal, Qué., juillet 1975-
Mensuel. Publication d'association, bulletin, 12 p. Langue(s): français ; sommaires: anglais. Tirage: 2000
Envoi gratuit.

Law mountain globe *See* Logberg - heimskringla

The Law Society of Upper Canada. Gazette / *edited by* John D. Honsberger. - *Published by* Law Society of Upper Canada. Osgoode Hall, Toronto, Ont. (Subscription address: Suite 501, 85 Richmond St. W., Toronto, Ont. M5H 2C9)
Quarterly. Association publication, journal format, 100 p.
$3.00 per issue : $10.00 per year.

The Lawyer's phone book - *Published by* Canada Law Book Ltd. 80 Cowdray Court, Agincourt, Ont. M1S 1S5.
Annual. Directory, 350 p.
$8.00 per year.

Le Beaver / *edited by* David E. Williams. - *Published by* David E. Williams. R.R. 3, P.O. Box 7, Sutton Rd., Williams Lake, B.C., February 1972-
Former title(s): Q.P.S. bulletin; Q.C.C. bulletin.
Quarterly. Special interest, magazine format, 24 p. Includes book reviews, film reviews, advertising.
$.75 per issue : $2.00 per year : $3.00 per year, foreign.

Le Courrier canadien (1969) *See* Canadian courier

Le Métis / *edited by* Barbara Bruce-Linnemann. - *Published by* Manitoba Métis Federation. 301-374 Donald St., Winnipeg, Man. R3B 2J2.
Monthly. Association publication, newspaper format, 8 p. Language: English and French. Includes book reviews, advertising. supplements issued.
Indexed in North. tit.
$3.00 per year. Free. Controlled circulation. Prepayment required.

Learning and development - *Published by* Centre for Learning and Development. McGill University. P.O. Box 6070, Montreal, Que. H3C 3G1, September 1969-
Irregular (approximately 6 issues per year). Association publication, newsletter format, 4-6 p.
Indexed in Can. educ. ind.
$.50 per issue : $2.50 per year. Available free on campus. Prepayment required.

Learning resources / *edited by* Richard Guerrier. - *Published by* Richard Guerrier. Chesswood House Publishing Ltd. Suite 103, 542 Mt. Pleasant Rd., Toronto, Ont. M4S 2M7.
Quarterly. Special interest. Includes advertising. Circulation: 13,784
Indexed in Can. educ. ind.
$5.00 per year : $7.00 for 2 years.

L'Eco d'Italia / *edited by* Cesare Tofini. - *Published by* L'Eco d'Italia Company. 1665 Commercial Dr., Vancouver, B.C. V5L 3Y3, 1955-
Weekly. Ethnic press, newspaper format, 12 p. Language: Italian ; summaries: English and French. Circulation: 5000
$.15 per issue : $9.00 per year.

The Lectern / *edited by* J. Peters and Eric Wright. - *Published by* Ryerson Faculty Association. 50 Gould St., Toronto, Ont., April 1975-
Issued every other month. House/company organ, newsletter format, 4 p.
Free. Controlled circulation.

The Legal secretary's newsletter / *sponsored by* The Legal Secretary's Reverence Service ; *edited by* Katherine Moore and Gail Parry. - *Published by* Moore/Parry Ltd. 3390 West 41st Ave., Vancouver, B.C. V6N 3E4, November 1973-
Monthly. Special interest, newsletter format, 8 p. Circulation: 1000
$2.50 per issue : $35.00 per year.

Legion magazine / *edited by* Lorne Manchester. - *Published by* Royal Canadian Legion. 405 Gilmour St., Ottawa, Ont. K2P 0R7., May 1926-
Former title(s): The Legionary (May 1926-December 1968)
Monthly. Association publication, magazine format, 54 p. Includes book reviews, advertising. Circulation: 450,000
$.35 per issue : $3.00 per year : $3.50 per year, foreign.

The Legionary (May 1926-December 1968)
See Legion magazine

Leisure, ideology and philosophy - *Published by* SIRLS. Faculty of Human Kinetics and Leisure Studies. University of Waterloo. Waterloo, Ont. N2L 3G1.
Quarterly. Bibliography, computer printout, $20.00 per year. $100.00 subscription to SIRLS required.

Leisure, sport and the life cycle - *Published by* SIRLS. Faculty of Human Kinetics and Leisure Studies. University of Waterloo. Waterloo, Ont. N2L 3G1.
Quarterly. Bibliography, computer printout, $20.00 per year. $100.00 subscription to SIRLS required.

Leisure and movement / *sponsored by* Saskatchewan Teachers' Federation ; *edited by* Marcel Gallays. - *Published by* Saskatchewan Physical Education Association. P.O. Box 1108, 2317 Arlington Ave., Saskatoon, Sask. S7J 2H8.
Quarterly. Association publication, journal format, 25-30 p. Includes book reviews.
$5.00 per year. Subscription included in membership fee. Controlled circulation. Prepayment required.

Leisure and social stratification - *Published by* SIRLS. Faculty of Human Kinetics and Leisure Studies. University of Waterloo. Waterloo, Ont. N2L 3G1.
Quarterly. Bibliography, computer printout, $20.00 per year. $100.00 subscription to SIRLS required.

Leisure and sport in a cross-national and cross-cultural perspective - *Published by* SIRLS. Faculty of Human Kinetics and Leisure Studies. University of Waterloo. Waterloo, Ont. N2L 3G1.
Quarterly. Bibliography, computer printout, $20.00 per year. $100.00 subscription to SIRLS required.

Leisure as the arts - *Published by* SIRLS. Faculty of Human Kinetics and Leisure Studies. University of Waterloo. Waterloo, Ont. N2L 3G1.
Quarterly. Bibliography, computer printout, $20.00 per year. $100.00 subscription to SIRLS required.

Leisure as time - *Published by* SIRLS. Faculty of Human Kinetics and Leisure Studies. University of Waterloo. Waterloo, Ont. N2L 3G1.
Quarterly. Bibliography, computer printout, $20.00 per year. $100.00 subscription to SIRLS required.

Leisurewheels / *edited by* Gladys Taylor. - *Published by* Tall-Taylor Publishing Ltd. 532 Cleveland Cres., S.E. Calgary, Alta., July 1969-
Former title(s): Travel/leisure (July 1969-June 1972)
Monthly. Trade publication, magazine format, 40 p. Includes advertising. supplements issued. Circulation: 10,000
$3.50 per year : $4.50 per year, foreign. Controlled circulation.

Leisurewheels and mobile homes / *edited by* Gladys Taylor. - *Published by* Tall-Taylor Publishing Ltd. 532 Cleveland Cres., S.E., Calgary, Alta.
Monthly. Special interest, magazine format, 70 p. Includes advertising.
$.50 per issue : $3.50 per year : $6.00 for 2 years : $9.00 for 3 years.

Leisurewheels campgrounds directory - *Published by* Gladys Taylor. Tall-Taylor Publishing Ltd. 532 Cleveland Cresc. S.E., Calgary, Alta. T2G 4A9, 1971-
Annual. Special interest, magazine format, Includes advertising. Circulation: 5000

Lemko news / *edited by* Iwan Eliashewsky. - *Published by* Organization for the Defence of Lemkivschyna. P.O. Box 964, Adelaide St. P.O., Toronto, Ont.
Monthly. Ethnic press. Language: Ukrainian. Includes advertising.
$.25 per issue.

Lemko news annual / *edited by* M. Fedak. - *Published by* Organization for the Defence of Lemkivschyna. P.O. Box 964, Adelaide St. P.O., Toronto, Ont.
Annual. Ethnic press. Language: Ukrainian. Includes advertising.
$3.00 per year.

Lennox and Addington Historical Society. Paper and records - *Published by* Lennox and Addington Historical Society. Dundas St. W., Napanee, Ont., 1912-
Association publication. Language: 200. Vol. 2 available as a reprint $6.00.
Vol. 14 $2.50.

Let's have a teute (mai 1975) *Voir* Cul Q

The Letter leaflet *See* Living message

Lettre commerciale / *édité par* M.L. Perry. - *Publié par* Banque de commerce canadienne impériale. Commerce Court, Toronto, Ont. M5L 1A2.
Publie en anglais: Commercial letter.
Bimestriel. Bulletin, 8 p.
Indexé dans Peirodex.
Envoi gratuit.

La Lettre de l'Abbé Gravel / *édité par* Pierre Gravel. - *Publié par* M. le curé Pierre Gravel. 1515, ave de la Ronde, Québec, Qué., mars 1970-
Ancien titre: La Lettre de Michelle de S. Antoine.
Mensuel. Publication ecclésiastique, bulletin, 4 p. Tirage: 150
$5.00 par année.

La Lettre de Michelle de S. Antoine *Voir* La Lettre de l'Abbé Gravel

Lettres du Bengale (janvier 1951) *Voir* Salam

Liaison / *édité par* John V. Titley. - *Publié par* Canadian Cement Lafarge Ltd. 606, Cathcart, Montréal, Qué. H3B 1L7, 1970-
Publié aussi en anglais.
Intermittent (approximativement 3 éditions par an). Organe interne/officiel, magazine, 20 p. Comprend critique de livres.
Envoi gratuit.

Liaison / *édité par* La Direction générale. - *Publié par* Centre Hospitalier de l'Université Laval. 2705, boul. Laurier, St-Foy, Qué. G1V 4G2, novembre 1970-
Intermittent (approximativement 10 éditions par an). Publication d'institution (universités, écoles..), 8 p. Tirage: 1200
ISSN 0317-3682 Envoi gratuit.

Liaison (1967-June 1970) *See* Service

Liaison. Edition française / *edited by* Marc Bernier (directeur) Gaston J. Stratford (adjoint à la rédaction). - *Published by* Section de l'information. Service des relations publiques. Université de Sherbrooke. Bureau 503, Pavillion central, Université de Sherbrooke, Sherbrooke, Qué.
Hebdomadaire de septembre-avril. Publication d'institution (universités, écoles..), bulletin, 8 p.
Envoi gratuit.

Liaison. English edition / *edited by* John V. Tittley. - *Published by* Canadian Cement Lafarge Ltd. 606 Cathcart, Montreal, Que. H3B 1L7, 1970-
French edition available.
Issued 3 times a year. House/company organ, magazine format, 20 p. Includes book reviews.
Free.

Liaudies balsas = People's voice / *edited by* John Yla. - *Published by* Lithuanian Press Association. 160 Claremont St., Toronto, Ont. M6J 2M8, 1932-
Issued every other week. Ethnic press, newspaper format, 8 p. Language: Lithuanian.
$.20 per issue : $5.00 per year : $7.00 per year, foreign.

Libération / *édité par* Alain Beiner. - *Publié par* Libération enr. B.P. 641, Succursale N, Montréal, Qué., avril 1971-
Mensuel. Publication politique, journal, 12 p. Tirage: 5000
$.25 le numéro : $2.00 par année : $3.50 par année, l'étranger.

Liberation Support Movement. LSM news - *Published by* LSM Information Center. P.O. Box 94338, Richmond, B.C., Spring 1974-
Quarterly. Political press, magazine format, 40 p. Includes book reviews, record reviews. Circulation: 4000
ISSN 0315-1840 $.50 per issue : $2.00 per year (Institutions $4.00) : foreign add $1.00 for postage.

Libertarian option : freedom or tyranny / *edited by* Marshall Bruce Evoy. - *Published by* Libertarian Enterprises of Canada. P.O. Box 5159, Postal Station A, Toronto, Ont. M5W 1N5, January 1973-
Former title(s): Option.
Issued every other month. Special interest, magazine format, 24 p. Includes book reviews, film reviews, play reviews, advertising. Circulation: 2000
$1.10 per issue : $6.50 per year : $6.75 per year, U.S.: $8.00 per year, foreign. Prepayment required.

Liberté / *édité par* Jean Guy Pilon (directeur). - *Publié par* Liberté. 5120, Chemin de la Côte St-Antoine, Montréal, Qué. H4A 1R9, février 1959-
Bimestriel. Edition savante, magazine, 128 p. Comprend critique de livres. Tirage: 3000
ISSN 0024-2020 $3.00 le numéro : $10.00 par année. Abonnements payables à l'avance.

Library information bulletin / *edited by* Bruce Peel. - *Published by* The Library. University of Alberta. Library Administration, University of Alberta Library, Edmonton, Alta. T6G 2E1, October 1968-
Former title(s): Library staff information (bulletin) (June 1960-December 1971)
Irregular. Institutional publication (Universities, schools, etc.), magazine format, 5 p.
Free. Controlled circulation.

Library research news / *sponsored by* Mills Memorial Library, McMaster University ; *edited by* Wm. Ready. - *Published by* McMaster University Library Press. Mills Memorial Library, McMaster University, Hamilton, Ont. L8S 4L6, Winter 1968-1969-
Irregular (approximately 3 issues per year). Special interest, magazine format, 40 p.
ISSN 0024-2527 $1.00 per issue.

Library staff information (bulletin) (June 1960-December 1971) *See* Library information bulletin

Library staff information (bulletin) (June 15, 1960, no. 1, - December 17, 1971) *See* University of Alberta, Edmonton. Library. Library staff bulletin

The Licensed victualler / *edited by* Bob Lewis. - *Published by* John Warbutton. L.V. Publications Ltd. 190 Nantucket Blvd., Scarborough, Ont. M1P 2N9, 1975-
Issued every other month. Trade publication. Includes advertising. Circulation: 12,517
$10.00 per year : $16.00 per year, foreign.

Lien - *Publié par* Association des assureurs-vie du Canada. 41 Lesmill Rd., Don Mills, Ont. M3B 2T3.
Publication d'association.

Le Lien / *édité par* Jean Guerin. - *Publié par* Chambre de commerce du Canada. 1080, côte du Beaver Hall, Montréal, Qué. H2Z 1T2.
Publié en anglais: The Chamber link.
Intermittent (approximativement 6 éditions par an). Publication spécialisée, journal, 8 p. Tirage: 5000
$1.00 par année. Tirage contrôlé.

Life in Red Cross / *edited by* Joan Wallace. - *Published by* British Columbia - Yukon Division. Canadian Red Cross Society. 4750 Oak St., Vancouver, B.C. V6H 2N9, April 1966-
Quarterly. Association publication, newsletter format, 4 p. Circulation: 1200
Free.

Life insurance and taxation / *edited by* Roy Jenkins and R.L. Kayler. - *Published by* Life Underwriters Association of Canada. 41 Lesmill Rd., Don Mills, Ont. M3B 2T3, 1959-
Published in French: L'Assurance vie et le fisc.
Annual. Association publication. Language: English and French.
$7.50.

Life insurance in Canada / *edited by* Stuart Brooks. - *Published by* Wadham Publications Ltd. Suite 101, 109 Vanderhoof Ave., Toronto, Ont. M4G 2J2, January 1974-
Issued every other month. Trade publication, magazine format, 32 p. Includes advertising.
Indexed in Can. B.P.I.
$1.00 per issue : $5.00 per year : $8.00 per year, foreign. Controlled circulation. Special rates offered. Prepayment required.

Life Underwriters Association of Canada. The LUAC monitor / *edited by* R.L. Kayler. - *Published by* Life Underwriters Association of Canada. 41 Lesmill Rd., Don Mills, Ont. M3B 2T3, June 1957-
Irregular (approximately 4 issues per year). Association publication, newsletter format, 4 p. Language: English and French. Circulation: 16,500
$.10 per issue. Free to members. Controlled circulation.

Life underwriters news (1914 - May 1971) *See* Forum

Life-Beacon (March 15, 1966 to September 15, 1969) *See* Beacon

Lifeline : a meeting place for writers, illustrators and publishers / *edited by* Douglas C. Pollard. - *Published by* Highway Book Shop. 300,000 Yonge St., Cobalt, Ont. P0J 1C0, July 1974-
Monthly. Special interest, newsletter format, 16 p.
ISSN 0316-0602 $1.00 per issue : $15.00 per year.

Lifeliner / *edited by* E.L. Bean. - *Published by* Royal Life Saving Society Canada. 550 Church St., Toronto, Ont.
Quarterly. Association publication, newsletter format, 4 p. Language: English and French. Circulation: 11,000

Life-style, leisure and sport - *Published by* SIRLS. Faculty of Human Kinetics and Leisure Studies. University of Waterloo. Waterloo, Ont. N2L 3G1.
Quarterly. Bibliography, computer printout, $20.00 per year. $100.00 subscription to SIRLS required.

Lighthouse - *Published by* Atlantic Institute of Education. 5244 South St., Halifax, N.S.
Quarterly. Association publication, magazine format, Back issues available.
Indexed in Can. educ. ind.
ISSN 0316-5108 Free.

Ligne directe / *édité par* Pierre L. Desaulniers. - *Publié par* Centrale de l'enseignement du Québec. 2336, Chemin Ste-Foy, Qué. G1V 1S5, janvier 1973-
Ancien titre: L'Enseignement (septembre 1947-juin 1970)
Mensuel. Publication d'association, magazine, 48 p. Comprend critique de livres, publicité, index de volumes, index cumulatif.Aussi sous microform. parution de suppléments. Tirage: 23,000
Indexé dans RADAR, Can. educ. ind.
ISSN 0046-211X $2.50 par année : $3.50 par année, l'étranger. Abonnements payables à l'avance.

Ligne directe sur le Montréal international / *édité par* Michel Gagné et Francis Millien. - *Publié par* Club sportif Montréal international. C.P. 1976, Succursale St-Michel, Montréal, Qué. H2A 3M3, octobre 1974-
Mensuel. Publication d'association, bulletin, 16 p. Comprend publicité. Tirage: 2000
$5.00 par année. Abonnements payables à l'avance.

Like it is / *edited by* Ron Scammel. - *Published by* Gary C. Price. Student Enterprises and Assistance League. P.O. Box 250, Postal Station P, Toronto, Ont. M5S 2T9.
Quarterly. Student publication, magazine format, Includes advertising.

Lillooet District Historical Society bulletin / *edited by* Renee Chipman. - *Published by* Lillooet District Historical Society. P.O. Box 305, Lillooet, B.C. V0K 1V0 (Subscription address: P.O. Box 441, Lillooet, B.C. V0K 1V0) May 1973-
Quarterly. Association publication, newsletter format, 8 p.
$.25 per issue (Students) : $5.00 per year. Controlled circulation.

The Limousin leader and stockman's recorder / *edited by* Harald Gunderson. - *Published by* Sage Brush Ventures Ltd. Suite 200, 304-8th Ave., S.W. Calgary, T5P 1C2.
Monthly. Includes advertising. Circulation: 4716

The Line / *edited by* C.A. Harry Gazey. - *Published by* Power System Division. McGraw-Edison of Canada Ltd. 3595 St. Clair Ave. E., Scarborough, Ont. M1K 1M1.
Quarterly. House/company organ, magazine format, 20 p.
Free. Controlled circulation.

Le Lingot / *édité par* Ludovid-D. Simard. - *Publié par* Service des relations publiques. Alcan. C.P. 370, 340, rue Davis, Arvide, Qué. G7S 4K9, février 1943-
Ancien titre: La Sentinelle (décembre 1936-janvier 1943)
Paraît tous les 15 jours. Organe interne/officiel, journal, 16 p. Langue(s): français et anglais.
$.10 le numéro : $3.00 par année.

Linguistic Circle of Manitoba and North Dakota. Proceedings / *sponsored by* Linguistic Circle of Manitoba and North Dakota ; *edited by* J.J. Gahan. - *Published by* Faculty of Arts. University of Manitoba. c/o Slavic Studies Department, University of Manitoba, Winnipeg, Man. R3T 2N2, 1959-
Annual. Scholarly publication, booklet format, Circulation: 500
ISSN 0075-9597

Link / *sponsored by* BCIT Student Association ; *edited by* Bruce O'Kabe. - *Published by* British Columbia Institute of Technology. 3700 Willingdon Ave., Burnaby, B.C., September 1974-
Issued twice a month. Student publication, newspaper format, 12 p. Includes film reviews, play reviews, record reviews, advertising. Circulation: 4000

Link / *edited by* Hans Jewinski. - *Published by* Missing Link Press. 78 Chelwood Rd., Scarborough, Ont. M1K 2K8.
$5.00 per year.

The Link and visitor / *edited by* Mrs. Perry Allaby. - *Published by* The Baptist Women's Missionary Society of Ontario and Quebec. 217 St. George St., Toronto, Ont. M5R 2M2, September 1878-
Former title(s): The Canadian missionary link, (1878-1927) The Baptist visitor (1884-1927)
Monthly except July and August. Church publication, magazine format, 16-24 p. Includes advertising, volume index. Circulation: 8300
$2.00 per year. Prepayment required.

Lionage / *edited by* J.F. Wilson. - *Published by* District A. Lions International. 1407 Yonge St., Toronto, Ont. M4T 1Y7.
Irregular (approximately 5 issues per year). Association publication, magazine format, Includes advertising. Circulation: 19,823
$3.00 (Members $1.25).

Liquid air review / *edited by* I. MacFadden. - *Published by* Canadian Liquid Air Ltd. 1210 Sherbrooke St. W., Montreal, Que. H3A 1H8, 1952-
Former title(s): Canadian liquid air review.
Quarterly. House/company organ, magazine format, 12 p.
Controlled circulation.

Liscio e busso / *edited by* Umberto Taccola. - *Published by* Riviera Printers and Publishers Inc. 210 Mozart St. W., Montreal, Que. H3S 3C7, 1974-
Monthly. Ethnic press. Language: Italian. Includes advertising. Circulation: 48,800
$.25 per issue : $7.00 per year.

List of certified fuel burning equipment and fuels handling equipment / *edited by* The Certification Division. - *Published by* Canadian Standards Association. 178 Rexdale Blvd., Rexdale, Ont. M9W 1R3.
Annual. Association publication, book format, 100-120 p.
Prepayment required.

Listings magazine / *edited by* Wes Lore. - *Published by* Toronto Real Estate Board. 1883 Yonge St., Toronto, Ont. M4S 1Y7.
Issued every other month. Trade publication, magazine format, 36 p. Circulation: 9000

Literary magazine *See* Bayavaya uskalos

Literature and ideology (1969-1974) *See* Alive magazine : literature and ideology

Literature and ideology (1969-1974) *See* New literature and ideology

Litter letter (March 1970-April 1970) *See* Newslitter

Littérature canadienne *See* Canadian literature

The Little daily (1950-1952) *See* Ryersonian

Little justice little joy *See* United Church of Canada. Committee on the Church and International Affairs. Report to the General Council of the United Church of Canada

The Little paper / *edited by* Neville Cheeseman. - *Published by* The Society of Saint John the Evangelist. Bracebridge, Ont., 1928-
Issued every other month. Church publication, newsletter format, 12-16 p.
$1.00 per year.

The Little weekly, (1950-1952) *See* Ryersonian

Liturgie de glorie. Edition complète - *Publié par* Les Moniales Bénédictines du Précieux-Sang. 300, boul. Paquette, Mont-Laurier, Qué. J9L 1J9, mars 1965-
Hebdomadaire. Publication ecclésiastique, brochure, 48 p. Tirage: 7000
$8.00 par année.

Liturgie de glorie. Edition dominicale - *Publié par* Les Moniales Bénédictines du Précieux-Sang. 300, boul. Paquette, Mont-Laurier, (Labelle), Qué. J9L 1J9, mars 1965-
Hebdomadaire. Publication ecclésiastique, brochure, 24 p. Tirage: 11,000
$8.00 par année.

Liturgie et vie chrétienne / *édité par* André Gignac. - *Publié par* Dominicains du Canada. 2715, chemin de la Côte Ste-Catherine, Montréal, Qué. H3T 1B6, janvier 1956-
Trimestriel. Publication ecclésiastique, 96 p. Comprend critique de livres. Tirage: 1500
Indexé dans RADAR.
$5.00 par année. Abonnements payables à l'avance.

Liubystok : a Ukranian magazine of literature, arts and literary criticism / *edited by* Petro Rojenko. - *Published by* Petro Rojenko. 281 Garden Ave., Toronto, Ont. M6R 1J4.
Quarterly. Ethnic press, booklet format, 16 p. Language: Ukrainian.
$.30 per issue.

Living message / *edited by* Rita Baker. - *Published by* The Anglican Church of Canada. 600 Jarvis St. Toronto, Ont. M4Y 2J6, 1889-
Former title(s): The Letter leaflet.
Monthly except July and August. Church publication, magazine format, 36 p. Includes book reviews, film reviews, advertising.
Circulation: 14,000
$2.00 per year : $2.50 per year, foreign. Prepayment required.

Living with Christ / *sponsored by* Saint Paul University ; *edited by* Stephen Somerville. - *Published by* Novalis. P.O. Box 498, Postal Station A, Ottawa, Ont. K1N 8Y5.
Irregular (approximately 8 issues per year). Church publication, pamphlet format, 160 p.
$2.50 per year : $4.00 per year, foreign.

Livre canadien / *édité par* Roland M. Charland. - *Publié par* Office des communications sociales. 4635, rue de Lorimer, Montréal, Qué., janvier 1970-
Mensuelle excepté juillet et août. Calendrier événements, revue, 36 p. Comprend critique de livres. Tirage: 1200
$5.00 par année. Abonnements payables à l'avance.

Livre de poche du fonctionnaire / *édité par* Gérard Langlois. - *Publié par* Editions de 9 à 5. C.P. 2233, Québec, Qué. G1K 7N8, mai 1974-
Annuel. Intérêt général, 384 p. Tirage: 10,000
$2.00.

Livre et auteurs québécois : revue critique / *parrainé par* Université Laval. Département des littératures ; *édité par* M. Clément Moisan. - *Publié par* Presses de l'Université Laval. Université Laval, Québec, Qué., 1961-
Annuel. Edition savante, livre, 400 p. Comprend critique de livres. Tirage: 3000
Indexé dans RADAR.
$5.00 le numéro.

The Locomotive engineer / *edited by* W.A. Rice. - *Published by* Brotherhood of Locomotive Engineers. Suite 512, Varette Bldg., 130 Albert St., Ottawa, Ont. K1P 5G4, 1867-
Former title(s): Locomotive engineers journal (1867-1956)
Weekly. House/company organ, newspaper format, 8 p. Language: English and French. Includes book reviews.
$.10 per issue : $4.50 per year.

Locomotive engineers journal (1867-1956) *See* The Locomotive engineer

Lodestone / *edited by* Lando Klassen. - *Published by* Lodestone Security Society. 33067 First Ave., Mission City, B.C. V2V 1G2, October 1973-
Monthly 10 times a year. Church publication, newspaper format, 12 p. Includes book reviews, film reviews, record reviews, advertising, volume index.
$.25 per issue : $3.00 per year.

Lodgistiks / *sponsored by* Divine Order of the Lodge ; *edited by* David UU. - *Published by* Derwyddon Press. Lodge North, P.O. Box 764, Kingston, Ont. K7L 4X6, October 1972-
Irregular (approximately 2 issues per year). Special interest, magazine format, 60 p.
Circulation: 100-500
ISSN 0315-0623 $3.00 per issue.

Lögberg (1888-1959) *See* Logberg - heimskringla

Logberg - heimskringla = Law mountain globe / *edited by* Caroline Gunnarsson. - *Published by* Lögberg-Heimskringla Publishing Co. Ltd. 512-265 Portage Ave., Winnipeg, Man. R3B 2B2, 1886-
Former title(s): Heimskringla (1886-1959) Lögberg (1888-1959)
Weekly. Ethnic press, newspaper format, Language: Icelandic and English. Includes book reviews, advertising.
$.15 per issue : $10.00 per year : $15.00 per volume.

Logos / *sponsored by* Ukrainian Catholic Mission of the Most Holy Redeemer ; *edited by* S.S. Shawel. - *Published by* Redeemer's Voice Press. P.O. Box 220, 165 St. Catherine St., Yorkton, Sask. S3N 2V7, January 1950-
Quarterly. Church publication, ethnic press, magazine format, 96 p. Language: Ukrainian and English. Circulation: 350
$2.00 per issue : $7.50 per year.

Loisard / *édité par* Richard Leclerc. - *Publié par* Richard Leclerc. 4315A, rue Doré, St-Hubert, Qué., mars 1974-
Trimestriel. Publication spécialisée, bulletin, 27 p. Langue(s): français et anglais. Comprend publicité. Tirage: 11,000
Envoi gratuit.

Loisir plus : magazine québécois du loisir / *édité par* Antoine Godbout. - *Publié par* Confédération des loisirs du Québec. 1415 est, rue Jarry, Montréal, Qué. H2E 2Z7(adresse d'abonnement: Periodica, C.P. 220, Ville Mont-Royal, Qué. H3P 3C4) septembre 1972-
Mensuel. Publication d'association, magazine, 24 p. Tirage: 2500
Indexé dans RADAR.
ISSN 0380-4291 $.75 le numéro : $6.00 par année. Abonnements payables à l'avance.

Loisirs jeunesse / *édité par* André Bernard. - *Publié par* Les Editions publi ltée. 5609, des Pensées, Montréal-Nord, Qué.(adresse d'abonnement: C.P. 71, Succursale R, Montréal, Qué. H2S 3K8) février 1974-
Semestriel. Publication spécialisée, 60 p.
$1.00 le volume : $1.25 par année, E.U. : $1.50 par année, l'étranger.

Loisirs mieux / *édité par* Jean Pouliot. - *Publié par* Haut commissariat à la jeunesse, aux loisirs et aux sports. Edifice "G", 7e étage, 1035, de la Chevrotière, Québec, Qué. G1A 1J4, février 1975-
Intermittent (approximativement 10 éditions par an). Bulletin, 8 p. Tirage: 600
Envoi gratuit.

London Chamber of Commerce. Chamber of Commerce news / *edited by* Hugh Smith. - *Published by* London Chamber of Commerce. P.O. Box 3295, 299 King St., London, Ont. N6A 4K3, 1939-
Former title(s): Bulletin - London Chamber of Commerce; Did you know? (1939)
Monthly. House/company organ, newsletter format, Circulation: 2100
Free.

The London hi riser / *edited by* Nancy Millar. - *Published by* Lorne Millar. Pinpoint Publications. 1356 Collingwood Ave., London, Ont. N6K 2M1, June 1973-
Issued twice a month. General interest, newspaper format, 12 p. Includes advertising. Circulation: 13,550
Controlled circulation.

Long time coming : Canadian Lesbian-Feminist newspaper / *edited by* Jackie Manthorne. - *Published by* Jackie Manthorne. 3595 St. Urbain St., Montreal, Que. (Subscription address: P.O. Box 218, Postal Station E, Montreal, Que) July 1973-
Monthly. Special interest, magazine format, 35 p. Language: English and French. Includes book reviews, record reviews, advertising. Circulation: 500
$.50 per issue : $5.00 per year (Institutions $10.00) : $10.00 per year, foreign.

The Lookout / *edited by* Anthony Hawkins. - *Published by* C.F.B. Esquimalt. Esquimalt, B.C., 1955-
Former title(s): Maritime command (Pacific) lookout; Pacific command lookout; Nader Outlook.
Issued twice a month. Military publication, newspaper format, 16 p. Circulation: 3000
$3.00 per year.

L'ora di Ottawa / *edited by* Mario Colonnese. - *Published by* Mario Colonnese. 542 Booth St., Ottawa, Ont. K1R 7L2, November 1968-
Ethnic press, newspaper format, 12 p. Language: Italian ; summaries: Italian. Circulation: 2000
$5.00 for 2 years : $10.00 for 2 years, foreign. Controlled circulation. Prepayment required.

La Loupe (1952-1968) *Voir* Bijou

L'Outaouais hosteller - *Published by* Canadian Youth Hostels Association. 75 Nicholas St., Ottawa, Ont. K1N 7B9, April 1964-
Issued every other month. Association publication, newsletter format, 2 p. Includes advertising. Circulation: 1300
Free.

L'Ouvre-boîte - *Published by* Association fédérative des étudiants de l'Université de Sherbrooke. Université de Sherbrooke. Sherbrooke, Qué., septembre 1974-
Former title(s): Presse campus; Campus estrien.
Hebdomadaire. Publication des étudiants, journal-dossier,
Envoi gratuit.

The Loyalist gazette / *edited by* E.J. Chard. - *Published by* E.J. Chard. The United Empire Loyalists' Association of Canada. Dominion Headquarters, 23 Prince Arthur Ave., Toronto, Ont. M5R 1B2, Spring 1963-
Issued twice a year. Association publication, magazine format, 20 p. Includes book reviews. supplements issued.
Indexed in Hist. abstr.; Amer. hist. and life.
$.75 per issue : $1.50 per year : $3.00 for 2 years. Supplements $.50 each. Prepayment required.

Loyola news - *Published by* Students' Association. Loyola University. 6931 Sherbrooke St. W., Montreal, Que.
Weekly. Student publication, newspaper format, Includes advertising. Circulation: 8000

Luggage and leathergoods news / *edited by* William Schabas. - *Published by* Gwen P. Demsey. Page Publications Ltd. 333 King St. W., Toronto Ont. M5V 1J5.
Irregular. Trade publication. Includes advertising. Circulation: 4376
$5.00 per year.

Lumber and Building Materials Association of Ontario. LBMAO reporter / *edited by* Herbert C. Hardy. - *Published by* The Lumber and Building Materials Association of Ontario. 660 Eglinton Ave. E., Toronto, Ont. M4G 2K2, 1917-
Former title(s): O.R.L.D.A. bulletin (1957-1972) Monthly bulletin - Lumber and Building Materials Association of Ontario (1917-1956)
Issued every other month. Association publication, magazine format, 30 p. Includes advertising.
Free to members of the Association. Controlled circulation.

Luminus / *edited by* Paul F. Vavasour. - *Published by* Alumni Office. Memorial University of Newfoundland. St. John's, Nfld. A1C 5S7, Winter 1971-
Quarterly. Political press, magazine format, 20 p. Circulation: 8600

Lumo / *edited by* G. duTemple. - *Published by* Kanada Esperanto Association. 51 B, Commercial Centre, Roxboro, Que. H8Y 2N3, 1957-
Quarterly. Association publication, journal format, 16 p. Language: Esperanto. Includes book reviews. Circulation: 250
$2.00 per year. Prepayment required.

Lusitano / *edited by* José Simoes Silvestre. - *Published by* José Simoes Silvestre. 60 Duluth St. E., Montreal, Que., 1964-
Issued twice a month. Ethnic press. Language: Portuguese. Includes advertising.
$5.00 per year.

Lustucru / *parrainé par* Société d'histoire des Iles Percées, Boucherville ; *édité par* Paul-Henri Chagnon. - *Publié par* Paul-Henri Chagnon. 540, rue Notre-Dame, Boucherville, Qué., novembre 1974-
Annuel. Publication d'association, bulletin, 30-38 p. Tirage: 1000

Lutheran Church in America. Canada Section. Convention minutes - *Published by* N.A. Berner. Canada Section. Lutheran Church in America. 600 Jarvis St., Toronto, Ont. M4Y 2J6.
Biennial. Church publication, booklet format, 45 p.
ISSN 0317-0063

Lutheran Church in America. Central Canada Synod. Convention. Minutes / *edited by* The Synod Secretary. - *Published by* Central Canada Synod. Lutheran Church in America. Suite 221, 2281 Portage Ave., Winnipeg, Man., 1963-
Annual. Church publication, 100 p.
Circulation: 700
Free.

Lutheran Church in Canada. Directory / *edited by* Walter A. Schultz. - *Published by* Lutheran Council in Canada. 500-365 Hargrave St., Winnipeg, Man. R3B 2K3, 1952-
Annual. Church publication, directory, 68 p. Includes advertising. Circulation: 1400
ISSN 0316-800X $1.50.

Lyman's British North America postage stamp retail catalogue / *edited by* J.K. MacRory. - *Published by* J.K. MacRory. P.O. Box 23, Postal Station V, Toronto, Ont. M6R 3A4.
Annual. Catalogue, booklet format, 64 p.
Circulation: 50,000
$1.75 per year. Available free to libraries and universities only. Special rates offered.

M / *édité par* Bill Bantey. - *Publié par* Musée des beaux-arts de Montréal. 1193, Place Phillips, Montréal, Qué., juin 1969-
Trimestriel. Publication d'institution (universités, écoles..), magazine, 40 p. Langue(s): français et anglais. Comprend publicité, index de volumes, index cumulatif. Tirage: 8000
$1.00 le numéro : $3.50 par année. Abonnements payables à l'avance.

M.A.D. (1973) *See* Fine

MARN (to 1972) *See* Nurscene

MBBM news = Nouvelles MCMB / *edited by* Alan B. Furniss. - *Published by* Macmillan Bloedel Ltd. 1075 W. Georgia St., Vancouver, B.C. V6E 3R9 (Subscription address: P.O Box 335, Postal Station A, Vancouver, B.C. V6C 2M7) 1946-
Former title(s): Sylvaply news (1946-1971)
Quarterly. Trade publication, magazine format, 16 p. Language: English and French ; summaries: Japanese and Swedish. Circulation: 25,000
ISSN 0039-7652 Controlled circulation.

MD of Canada / *edited by* W.C. Gibson. - *Published by* MD Publication (Canada) Ltd. 1310 Greene Ave., Westmount, Que. H3Z 2B3, January 1960-
Monthly. General interest, magazine format, 130 p. Includes book reviews, film reviews, play reviews, advertising. Circulation: 27,000
$1.50 per issue : $12.00 per year : $14.50 per year, foreign. Controlled circulation.

MGEA news (June 1971-October 1971) *See* Contact

M.G.H. bulletin (1951-1960) *See* The Montreal General Hospital. The Montreal General Hospital news

M.G.H. newsletter (1960-1965) *See* The Montreal General Hospital. The Montreal General Hospital news

MLA bulletin (1936-1958) *See* Atlantic Provinces Library Association. APLA bulletin

M.P.s at work *See* Ottawa report

MPs at work - *Published by* New Democratic Party. 301 Metcalfe St., Ottawa, Ont.
Monthly. House/company organ, newsletter format, 25 p. Circulation: 450
$12.00 per year.

MS Canada / *edited by* Deanna F. Kaufman. - *Published by* Multiple Sclerosis Society of Canada. 1220 Yonge St., Toronto, Ont. M4T 1W1, February 1974-
Quarterly. Association publication, newsletter format, 8 p. Circulation: 8000
ISSN 0316-1131 $2.00 per year.

The MTF bulletin (1923-1924) *See* The Manitoba teacher

M C Q : music Canada quarterly magazine / *edited by* David Farreil. - *Published by* Joseph Paul Publications. Unit 7, 2585 Drew Rd., Malton, Ont. L4T 1G1, 1970-
Quarterly. Special interest, magazine format, Includes advertising.
$.75 per issue : $2.50 per year : $5.00 for 2 years : $7.00 for 3 years.

Ma caisse populaire / *édité par* Claude Moguin. - *Publié par* La Fédération de Québec des caisses populaires Desjardins. 150, ave des Commandeurs, Lévis, Qué. G6V 6P8, juin 1952-
Trimestriel. Organe interne/officiel, magazine, 24 p. Tirage: 300,000
$.10 le numéro : $.40 par année.

Macdonald Institute - Family and Consumer Studies. Alumni Association. Alumni news / *sponsored by* Macdonald Institute - Family and Consumer Studies. Alumni Association Studies ; *edited by* Lyn Seivert and Joan Styan. - *Published by* Department of Alumni Affairs and Development. University of Guelph. University Centre Level, University of Guelph, Guelph, Ont.
Quarterly. Alumni newsletter, newsletter format, 8 p. Circulation: 1500
$4.00 per year.

The MacDonald journal / *edited by* Gordon Bachman. - *Published by* R.J. Cooke Ltd. 58 Madsen Ave., Beaconsfield, Que.
Monthly. Special interest, magazine format, 23 p. Includes advertising.
$7.00 for 2 years: $10.00 for 2 years, foreign.

McGill daily - *Published by* Students' Society. McGill University. 3480 McTavish St., Montreal, Que.
Daily, September-March. Student publication, newspaper format, 8 p. Includes book reviews, film reviews, play reviews, record reviews, advertising. supplements issued.
$9.00 per year.

McGill dental review / *edited by* D. Bridger and A. Fischel. - *Published by* Dental Students' Society. Faculty of Dentistry. McGill University. c/o Dental Clinic, Montreal General Hospital, Montreal, Que. H3G 1A4, 1935-
Irregular (approximately 3 issues per year). Professional publication, business, Includes advertising.

McGill journal of education / *edited by* Margaret Gillett. - *Published by* Faculty of Education. McGill University. 3700 McTavish St., Montreal, Que., Spring 1966-
Issued twice a year. Scholarly publication, journal format, 110 p. Language: English and French. Includes book reviews, film reviews, cumulative index. available in microform.
Indexed in Resources in educ., Sociol. educ. abstr.
$2.00 per issue : $3.00 per year : $5.00 for 3 years.

McGill law journal / *edited by* Laura Falk Scott. - *Published by* Faculty of Law. McGill University. 3644 Peel St., Montreal, Que. H3A 1W9, 1952-
Quarterly. Legal articles, journal format, 150 p. Language: English and French. Includes book reviews, advertising, volume index, updating service. supplements issued. Circulation: 2000
Indexed in Soc. sci. cit. ind., Leg. per.
$3.50 per issue : $10.00 per year. Controlled circulation. Special rates offered. Prepayment required.

McGill medical journal / *edited by* J. Thomas Bulger. - *Published by* Medical Students Society. McGill University. 3655 Drummond St., Montreal, Que. H3G 1Y6, 1931-
Quarterly. Professional publication, journal format, 20 p. Circulation: 7500
ISSN 0024-905X $5.00 per volume.

McGill reporter / *edited by* Ginny Jones. - *Published by* Information office. McGill University. P.O. Box 6070, Postal Station A, Montreal, Que. H3C 3G1, September 1968-
Weekly. Institutional publication (Universities, schools, etc.), newspaper format, 4 p. Language: English (French). Circulation: 11,200
ISSN 0580-8537 Free on campus.

McGill University. Computing Centre. Newsletter / *edited by* Kathryn Hubbard, A.M. Valenti and Barbara Fox. - *Published by* Computing Centre. McGill University. P.O. Box 6070, Postal Station A, Montreal, Que. H3G 3G1 (Subscription address: c/o Joan Brown, Room 223, Burnside Hall, Montreal, Que) April 1969-
Monthly. Institutional publication (Universities, schools, etc.), newsletter format, 6 p. Includes cumulative index.
Free. Controlled circulation.

McGill University. Mechanical Engineering Laboratory. Technical note - *Published by* Department of Mechanical Engineering. McGill University. P.O. Box 6000, Postal Station A, Montreal, Que. H3C 3G1, 1962-
Irregular (approximately 6 issues per year). 65 p.
Free of charge under 50 pages. Cost of handling, mailing over 50 pages.

McGoldrick's handbook of Canadian customs tariff and excise duties - *Published by* McMullin Publishers Ltd. 417 St. Peter St., Montreal, Que. H2Y 2M4.
Annual. Customs and excise information, 1300 p.
$21.00.

Machinerie lourde = Heavy equipment / *édité par* Marcel Poirier. - *Publié par* Gérard Privé. Association des propriétaires de machinerie lourde du Québec, inc. 2500A, rue Bellechasse, Montréal, Qué., 1970-
Ancien titre: Revue travaux mécanisés.
Mensuel. Publication d'association, magazine, 24 p. Comprend publicité. Tirage: 4766
Envoi gratuit. Tirage contrôlé.

The Machinist (1946-1973) *See* The Machinist Canada

The Machinist Canada / *edited by* Joseph Hanafin. - *Published by* International Association of Machinists and Aerospace Workers. International Association of Machinists and Aerospace Workers. Room 302, 80 Argyle Ave., Ottawa, Ont. K2P 1B5, July 1973-
Former title(s): The Machinist (1946-1973)
Monthly. Association publication, newspaper format, Language: English and French. Circulation: 50,000
$4.00 per year.

Le Maclean / *édité par* Jean Paré. - *Publié par* Lloyd M. Hodgkinson. Maclean-Hunter Ltd. 481 University Ave., Toronto, Ont. M5W 1A7(adresse d'abonnement: 625, ave President-Kennedy, Montréal, Qué. H3A 1K5) 1961-
Paraît tous les 15 jours. Intérêt général, magazine, Comprend publicité. Tirage: 150,702
Indexé dans Periodex, Can. ind., RADAR.

Maclean's / *edited by* Peter C. Newman. - *Published by* Maclean-Hunter Ltd. 481 University Ave., Toronto, Ont. M5W 1A7, 1905-
Issued every other week. General interest, magazine format, Includes advertising. Circulation: 725,519
Indexed in Can. ind., P.A.I.S., Peace res. abstr.

McMaster alumni news (1931-1965) *See* McMaster news

McMaster news / *edited by* Dennis A. Carson. - *Published by* Alumni Association. McMaster University. Hamilton, Ont. L8S 4K1, 1895-
Former title(s): McMaster alumni news (1931-1965) The McMaster graduate (1895-1930)
Quarterly. Alumni publication, magazine format, 20 p.
Free to graduates.

McMaster University. Publications of the faculty and staff / *edited by* M. Zack. - *Published by* McMaster University. Hamilton, Ont., 1971-
Annual. Bibliography, 55 p.
Free. Controlled circulation.

MacMillan Bloedel Building Materials. MBBM news / *sponsored by* MacMillan Bloedel Building Materials ; *edited by* Alan B. Furniss. - *Published by* MacMillan Bloedel Ltd. P.O. Box 335, Postal Station A, Vancouver, B.C. V6E 2M7, 1950-
Former title(s): MacMillan Bloedel building materials news (July 1971-July 1973) Syladly news (1950-1973)
Quarterly. Special interest, magazine format, 16 p. Language: English and French. Circulation: 28,000
Free.

MacMillan Bloedel building materials news (July 1971-July 1973) *See* MacMillan Bloedel Building Materials. MBBM news

MacMillan Bloedel Ltd. MB & PR newsletter, (May 1964-December 1966) *See* MacMillan Bloedel Ltd. MacMillan Bloedel news

MacMillan Bloedel Ltd. MacMillan Bloedel news / *edited by* Tom Williams. - *Published by* MacMillan Bloedel Ltd. 1075 West Georgia St., Vancouver, B.C. V6E 3R9, January 1967-
Former title(s): MacMillan Bloedel Ltd. MB & PR newsletter, (May 1964-December 1966)
Monthly. House/company organ, newsletter format, 8 p. Circulation: 24,000
Controlled circulation.

Madame / *edited by* Robert Juster. - *Published by* Robert Juster. Les Editions de la Femme Inc. Suite 620, 1440 St. Catharine St. W., Montreal, Que. H3G 1S2, 1974-
Monthly. Special interest, magazine format, Includes advertising. Circulation: 47,461
$1.00 per issue : $10.00 per year.

Magazine advertising summary service / *edited by* Freeda Andreas. - *Published by* Magazine Association of Canada. Suite 300, 1240 Bay St., Toronto, Ont. M5R 2A7.
Quarterly. Special interest, 280 p. Includes cumulative index. supplements issued.
$80.00 per year. Prepayment required.

Magazine C.S.D. (décembre 1972) *Voir* La Base

Magazine madame : le magazine de la québécoise / *édité par* Louise Pilon-Juster. - *Publié par* Les Editions de la femme inc. Suite 620, 1440 ouest, rue Ste-Catherine, Montréal, Qué. H3G 1S2, mai 1974-
Mensuel. Intérêt général, magazine, 72 p. Tirage: 50,000
$1.00 le numéro : $10.00 par année.

Magazine sur scène - *Publié par* Perfecta Plus enr. Bureau 300, 1454 de la Montagne, Montréal, Qué. H3Q 1Z4, 1971-
Intermittent (approximativement 20 éditions par an). Publication spécialisée, magazine, 40 p.
$1.50 le numéro.

The Magnet / *edited by* R.J. Hollywood. - *Published by* Greater Barrie Chamber of Commerce. 2 Fred Grant St., Barrie, Ont. L4M 3G6, September 1972-
Monthly except August. House/company organ, newsletter format, 4 p.
Free.

Magyar Elet = Hungarian life - *Published by* Andrew Publishing. Patria Publising Co. Ltd. 6 Alcina Ave., Toronto, Ont. M6G 2E8, 1948-
Weekly. Ethnic press. Language: Hungarian. Includes advertising. Circulation: 8255
$13.00 per year.

Magyar hirlap = Hungarian journal / *edited by* George Stirling. - *Published by* Hungarian Journal Publishing Co. 33 Ledbury St., Toronto, Ont., 1974-
Weekly. Ethnic press, magazine format, Language: Hungarian. Includes advertising. Circulation: 4000
$.30 per issue : $15.00 per year.

Main d'oeuvre en génie bulletin = Engineering manpower news / *édité par* L.M. Nadeau. - *Publié par* Conseil canadien de la main d'oeuvre en génie. 401-116, rue Albert, Ottawa, Ont. K1P 5G3, avril 1974-
Intermittent (approximativement 4-6 éditions par an). Publication d'association, bulletin, 4 p. Langue(s): français et anglais. Tirage: 500
$1.00 le numéro : $10.00 par année.

Maineline : all about Maine-Anjou - *Published by* Maine-Anjou Canada Ltd. Petroleum Bldg., 720, 310-9th Ave. S.W., Calgary, Alta., July 1974-
Monthly. Trade publication, magazine format, 40 p. Includes advertising. Circulation: 3000
ISSN 0316-8581 $5.00 per year : $9.00 for 2 years : $10.00 per year foreign. Controlled circulation.

Maintenant - *Publié par* Les Editions maintenant inc. 2715, cote St-Catherine, Montréal, Qué H3T 1B5, 1962-
Mensuel. Comprend publicité.
Indexé dans RADAR.
$1.00 le numéro : $8.50 par année.

La Maison (Centre francophone de Toronto) - *Publié par* Jeanne Bryan. La Maison (Centre francophone de Toronto). 64 Charles St. E., Toronto, Ont. M4Y 1T1, avril 1968-
Ancien titre: Maison française à Toronto (avril 1968-décembre 1971) Maison française de Toronto (janvier 1972-juin 1974)
Mensuel. Intérêt général, bulletin, 2 p. Comprend critique de livres, publicité. Tirage: 800
$.50 le numéro : $5.00 par année. Abonnements payables à l'avance.

Maison française à Toronto (avril 1968-décembre 1971) *Voir* La Maison (Centre francophone de Toronto)

Maison française de Toronto (janvier 1972-juin 1974) *Voir* La Maison (Centre francophone de Toronto)

Le Maître de poste canadien *See* The Canadian postmaster

Le Maître imprimeur / *édité par* Hélène Lagadec. - *Publié par* L'Association des maîtres-imprimeurs de Montréal inc. 480 est, ave Mont-Royal, Montréal, Qué. H2J 1W4, janvier 1937-
Mensuel. Publication d'association, magazine, 24 p. Tirage: 2600
Indexé dans RADAR.
$2.00 par année. Envoi gratuit. Tirage contrôlé.

Makara / *edited by* Karen Muntean. - *Published by* The Pacific Women's Graphic Arts Co-operative Association. 1011 Commercial Dr., Vancouver, B.C.
Issued every other month. Association publication.
$6.00 per year.

The Malahat review / *edited by* Robin Skelton. - *Published by* University of Victoria. P.O. Box 1700, Victoria, B.C. V8W 2Y2, January 1967-
Quarterly. "International quarterly of life and letters", journal format, 140 p. Includes book reviews. Back numbers available.
Indexed in Can. essay and lit. ind., M.L.A. int. bib., Annu. bibl. Engl. lang. and lit.,.
$1.50 per issue : $5.00 per year.

Man underwater / *edited by* Debby Quinn. - *Published by* Gary Tennenhouse. Manitoba Underwater Council. 482 Belmont Ave., Winnipeg, Man. R2V 0Z3 (Subscription address: P.O. Box 711, Winnipeg, Man. R3C 2K3) 1974-
Former title(s): Manitoba Underwater Council Newsletter.
Monthly, 10 times a year. Association publication, 14 p. Circulation: 700
$5.00 per year. Prepayment required.

Management compensation in Canada / *edited by* H.V. Chapman and Associates Ltd. - *Published by* H.V. Chapman and Associates Ltd. Suite 300, 1491 Yonge St., Toronto, Ont., 1961-
Former title(s): Executive compensation in Canada.
Annual. "Compensation data for senior business executives", 250 p.
ISSN 0315-5420

Management Compensation Survey - *Published by* Quebec Industrial Relations Institute. 630 Sherbrooke St. W., Montreal, Que. H3A 1E4.
Annual. Newsletter format, 20 p. Includes cumulative index.
Subscription included in membership fee. Controlled circulation.

Management digest / *edited by* Catherine Harris. - *Published by* Ontario Federation of Agriculture. Suite 502, 387 Bloor St. E., Toronto, Ont. M4W 1H9.
Monthly. Trade publication, 8 p. Language: English and French.
$35.00 per year.

Mandat *See* Mandate

Mandate / *edited by* Nora Neilson. - *Published by* R.C. Plant. Committee on Education and Stewardship. Division of Communications. United Church of Canada. Suite 213, 85 St. Clair Ave. E., Toronto, Ont. (Subscription address: Distribution Services, 47 Coldwater Road, Don Mills, Ont) October 1969-
Quarterly. Church publication, magazine format, 24 p. Circulation: 40,000
$6.00 per year for 10 subscriptions. Sent free to selected subscribers. Special rates offered.

Mandate = Mandat - *Published by* Canadian Federation of Independent Business. 15 Coldwater Rd., Don Mills, Ont. M3B 3J1, January 1972-
Monthly. Association publication, newsletter format, 2 p. Language: English and French. Circulation: 30,000
Free to members.

Manitoba archaeological newsletter / *edited by* Walter M. Hlady. - *Published by* Manitoba Archaeological Society. P.O. Box 1171, Winnipeg, Man. R3C 2Y4., 1964-
Quarterly. Association publication, newsletter format, 30 p. Includes book reviews, cumulative index. Circulation: 550
$5.00 per year. Prepayment required.

Manitoba Association of School Trustees. Newsletter / *edited by* Ed. J. Martens. - *Published by* Manitoba Association of School Trustees. 191 Provencher Blvd., Winnipeg, Man. R2H 0G4, June 1965-
Issued twice a month. Association publication, newsletter format, 4 p. Circulation: 975
Free. Controlled circulation.

Manitoba Buddhist bulletins - *Published by* Manitoba Buddhist Association, Inc. 825 Winnipeg Ave., Winnipeg, Man. R3E 0R5, October 1955-
Monthly. Church publication, newsletter format, 8 p. Language: English and Japanese. Includes book reviews. Circulation: 190
$2.00 per year. Free.

Manitoba builders' directory *See* Manitoba construction industry directory : purchasing guide

Manitoba Business Education Teachers Association. BETA journal / *sponsored by* Manitoba Business Education Teachers' Association ; *edited by* Heather Cunningham. - *Published by* Manitoba Teachers Society. 191 Harcourt St. at Portage Ave., Winnipeg, Man. R3J 3H2.
Quarterly. Association publication, journal format, 35 p.
ISSN 0318-2118 $5.00 per year. Prepayment required.

Manitoba construction industry directory : purchasing guide / *edited by* D.O. Brewer. - *Published by* S. Steigerwald. P.O. Box 6900, 1077 St. James St., Winnipeg, Man. RC3 3B1.
Former title(s): Manitoba builders' directory.
Annual. Directory, magazine format, 152 p. Includes advertising. Circulation: 3200
$4.00. Controlled circulation. Prepayment required.

The Manitoba consumer / *edited by* Susan Hayward. - *Published by* Lance Publishing Co. Ltd. 620 Dakota St., Winnipeg, Man.
Annual. Association publication, newspaper format, 4 p.
Subscription included in membership fee.

The Manitoba co-operator / *edited by* W.E. Morriss. - *Published by* Manitoba Pool Elevators. Room 908, 220 Portage Ave., Winnipeg, Man. R3C 0A5, 1943-
Weekly. Trade publication. Includes advertising. Circulation: 41,405
$.10 per issue : $3.00 per year.

The Manitoba counsellor / *sponsored by* School Counsellors' Association of Manitoba ; *edited by* Dave Little. - *Published by* Manitoba Teachers' Society. 191 Harcourt St., Winnipeg, Man. R3J 3H2.
Issued every other month. Association publication, magazine format, 40-50 p.
Indexed in Biol. abstr.
$5.00 per year. Prepayment required.

Manitoba entomologist / *edited by* W.J. Turnock. - *Published by* Entomological Society of Manitoba. c/o Department of Agriculture, Norquay Building, 25 Dafoe Rd., Winnipeg, Man. R3T 2M9, 1967-
Former title(s): Proceedings - Entomological Society of Manitoba (1945-1966)
Annual. Association publication, magazine format, 80 p. Includes book reviews. Circulation: 225
Indexed in Chem. abstr.
ISSN 0076-3810 $6.00.

Manitoba Farm Vacations Association. Newsletter / *edited by* Marguerite Manning. - *Published by* Manitoba Farm Vacations Association. 385 St. Mary Ave., Winnipeg, Man. R3C 0N1.
Quarterly. Association publication, newsletter format, 3 p.
Free.

Manitoba geography teacher (1968-1974) *See* Manitoba social sciences teacher

Manitoba Highway News / *sponsored by* Manitoba Trucking Association ; *edited by* J. Veitch. - *Published by* D.W. Friesen. Altona, Man. (Subscription address: 66E Polo Park, Winnipeg, Man. R3G 0W4)
Issued every other month. Association publication, magazine format, 32 p.
Circulation: 4000
$.75 per issue : $6.00 per year.

Manitoba Historical Society. Newsletter - *Published by* Manitoba Historical Society. Room 211, 190 Rupert Ave., Winnipeg, Man. R3B 0N2.
Monthly. Association publication, newsletter format, 3 p.
Free to members.

Manitoba Historical Society. Transactions / *edited by* Mrs. David McDowell. - *Published by* Manitoba Historical Society. Suite 211, 190 Rupert Ave., Winnipeg, Man. R3B 0N2.
Annual. Association publication, 120-140 p.
$5.00. Free with membership.

Manitoba industrial topics (May 1941-August 1950) *See* Winnipeg industrial topics

Manitoba journal of education / *edited by* J.A. Riffel. - *Published by* Manitoba Educational Research Council. Department of Educational Administration, University of Manitoba, Winnipeg, Man. R3T 2N2, November 1965-
Issued twice a year. Association publication, journal format, 50 p.
Indexed in Can. educ. ind.
$1.50 per issue : $3.00 per year : $3.25 per year, U.S.

Manitoba law journal / *edited by* W.G. Gibson. - *Published by* Faculty of Law. University of Manitoba. Robson Hall, University of Manitoba, Winnipeg, Man. R3T 2N2, 1962-
Former title(s): Manitoba Law School journal (1962-1965)
Issued twice a year. Scholarly publication, journal format, 200 p. Includes book reviews, volume index. Circulation: 900
Indexed in Can. leg. per. lit., Leg. per.
$4.00 per issue.

Manitoba Law School journal (1962-1965) *See* Manitoba law journal

Manitoba Library Association. Bulletin / *edited by* The Public Relations Committee. - *Published by* Manitoba Library Association. Room 301, 190 Rupert St., Winnipeg, Man. R3B 0N2, 1952-
Quarterly. Association publication, newsletter format, 35 p. Includes book reviews.
Circulation: 325
$5.00 per year (Institutions $10.00).

The Manitoba mathematics teacher / *sponsored by* Manitoba Association of Mathematics Teachers ; *edited by* Celia Baron. - *Published by* Manitoba Teachers' Society. 191 Harcourt St., Winnipeg, Man. R3J 3H2.
Quarterly. Association publication, magazine format, 40 p.
ISSN 0315-9167 $5.00 per year. Prepayment required.

The Manitoba medical register - *Published by* College of Physicians and Surgeons of Manitoba. 371 Broadway Ave., Winnipeg, Man. R3C 0T9.
Annual. Association publication. supplements issued.
$25.00 : supplements $7.50 each. Controlled circulation.

Manitoba motorist / *sponsored by* Manitoba Motor League. - *Published by* Howes, Waldon Associates Ltd. Suite 18, 399 Berry St., Winnipeg, Man. R3V 1N6, 1958-
Issued twice a month. Association publication, magazine format, Includes advertising.
Circulation: 34,900

The Manitoba music educator / *sponsored by* Manitoba Music Educators' Association ; *edited by* Morna-June Morrow. - *Published by* Manitoba Teachers Society. 191 Harcourt St., Winnipeg, Man. R3J 3H2., 1961-
Quarterly. Association publication, magazine format (October, February and May) newsletter format (September), Magazine 48 p., newsletter 8 p. Language: English (French). Includes book reviews, record reviews.
Circulation: 425
ISSN 0315-9116 $5.00 per year. Subscription included in membership fee.

Manitoba nature / *sponsored by* Zoological Society of Manitoba ; *edited by* Robert E. Wrigley. - *Published by* Manitoba Naturalists' Society. 214 - 190 Rupert Ave., Winnipeg, Man. R3B 0N2, 1966-
Former title(s): Zoolog (1966-1972)
Quarterly. Association publication, magazine format, 36 p. Includes advertising, volume index. Circulation: 4000
Indexed in North. tit.
ISSN 0315-5064 $.85 per issue : $2.50 per year. Prepayment required.

Manitoba New Democrat / *edited by* Allan Cohen. - *Published by* Manitoba Section. New Democratic Party. 656 Broadway Ave., Winnipeg, Man. R3C 0X3.
Irregular (approximately 10 issues per year). Political press, newspaper format, 16 p.
Circulation: 13,000
$.25 per issue : $2.00 per year.

Manitoba pageant / *edited by* William Frazer. - *Published by* Manitoba Historical Society. Room 211, 190 Rupert Ave., Winnipeg, Man. R3B 0N2, April 1956-
Quarterly. Association publication, magazine format, 24 p.
Indexed in Hist. abstr.; Amer. hist. and life.
$2.00 per year.

The Manitoba professional engineer / *edited by* E.A. Speers and The Bulletin Committee. - *Published by* Association of Professional Engineers of the Province of Manitoba. 710-177 Lombard Ave., Winnipeg, Man. R3B 0W9.
Issued every other month. Association publication, magazine format, 15 p.
Available to members only.

Manitoba School Library Audio Visual Association. M.S.L.A.V.A. journal / *sponsored by* Manitoba School Library - Audio Visual Association ; *edited by* Dave Jenkinson. - *Published by* Manitoba Teachers' Society. 191 Harcourt St., Winnipeg, Man. R3J 3H2.
Issued every other month. Association publication, magazine format, 40-50 p.
Circulation: 350
Indexed in Can. educ. ind.
ISSN 0315-9124 $5.00 per year. Prepayment required.

Manitoba social sciences teacher - *Published by* Manitoba Teachers' Society. 191 Harcourt St., Winnipeg, Man., 1974-
Former title(s): Manitoba geography teacher (1968-1974)
Association publication.

Manitoba social worker / *edited by* Kim Clare. - *Published by* Manitoba Association of Social Workers. 429 Rosseau Ave. W., Winnipeg, Man. R2C 1X6, November 1971-
Monthly (9 times a year). Association publication, newsletter format, 12 p.
$.40 per issue : $3.00 per year.

Manitoba spectra / *sponsored by* Manitoba Business Education Teachers' Association ; *edited by* Heather Cunningham. - *Published by* Manitoba Teachers' Society. 191 Harcourt St., Winnipeg, Man.
Former title(s): B.E.E.P. : business education's exciting publication.
Issued twice a year. Association publication, magazine format, 35 p.
$5.00 per year. Prepayment required.

The Manitoba teacher - *Published by* The Manitoba Teachers' Society. 191 Harcourt St., Winnipeg, Man. R3J 3H2., 1919-
Former title(s): The MTF bulletin (1923-1924) The Bulletin - The Manitoba Teachers' Society.
Monthly except July and August. Association publication, tabloid format, 8-12 p. Includes advertising. supplements issued. Circulation: 17,000
Indexed in Can. educ. ind.
$3.00 per year. Controlled circulation. Prepayment required.

Manitoba theatre centre - *Published by* Manitoba Theatre Centre. 174 Market Ave., Winnipeg, Man. R3B 0P8, 1961-
Irregular (approximately 6 issues per year). Program. Includes advertising.

Manitoba Trucking Association. M.T.A. ship by truck directory / *edited by* J. Veitch. - *Published by* Manitoba Trucking Association. 66E Polo Park Shopping Centre, Winnipeg, Man. (Subscription address: 1355 Portage Ave., Winnipeg, Man)
Annual. Directory, magazine format, 154 p. supplements issued. Circulation: 1600
$5.00.

Manitoba Underwater Council Newsletter *See* Man underwater

Manitoba Women's Institute. Institute news / *edited by* Gwen Parker. - *Published by* Manitoba Women's Institute. 1981 Portage Ave., Winnipeg, Man. R3J 0J9, 1928-
Quarterly. Association publication, magazine format, 12 p. Circulation: 2600
Subscription included in membership fee
$1.00.

Manitoban - *Published by* Students' Union. University of Manitoba. Winnipeg, Man., 1913-
Issued twice a week. Student publication, newspaper format, 12 p. Includes book reviews, film reviews, advertising. supplements issued. Circulation: 10,000
$10.00 per year.

Manoir-écho / *édité par* Louis Fandrich. - *Publié par* Manoir Notre-Dame de Gräce. 5319, ave Notre-Dame de Gräce, Montréal, Qué. H4A 1L2, septembre 1964-
Ancien titre: Manoir-express.
Mensuel septembre-juin. Journal, Comprend critique de films, publicité, index de volumes.
Tirage: 16,000

Manoir-express *Voir* Manoir-écho

Manpower and unemployment research in Africa - *Published by* Centre for Developing-Area Studies. McGill University. 3437 Peel St., Montreal, Que. H3A 1W7, April 1968-
Issued twice a year. Institutional publication (Universities, schools, etc.), newsletter format, 75 p. Language: English and French. Includes book reviews, advertising. supplements issued.
Indexed in P.A.I.S.
$1.75 per issue : $3.00 per year : Free to persons or institutions in developing countries. Controlled circulation. Special rates offered.

Manual of the textile industry of Canada / *edited by* W.A.B. Davidson. - *Published by* Canadian Textile Journal Publishing Co. Ltd. 4999 St. Catherine St. W., Montreal, Que., 1928-
Annual. Directory, magazine format, 250 p. Includes updating service. Circulation: 3800
$7.50.

Manufacturers Life Insurance Company. ManuLife news / *edited by* Lucy C. Drunewych. - *Published by* Manufacturers Life Insurance Company. 200 Bloor St. E., Toronto, Ont. M4W 1E4, December 1971-
Weekly. House/company organ, newsletter format, 8 p. Includes book reviews, film reviews, play reviews. supplements issued. Circulation: 4600
Free. Controlled circulation.

Manufacturers Life Insurance Company. News letter / *edited by* Sheila Herbert. - *Published by* Manufacturers Life Insurance Company. 200 Bloor St. E., Toronto, Ont. M4W 1E4, 1902-
Former title(s): Agent's news letter.
Monthly and quarterly issues. House/company organ, magazine format, Monthly 40p., quarterly 32 p. Circulation: 3500

Marguerite G. Bagshaw Theatre Committee. Newsletter - *Published by* Toronto Public Library. 40 Orchard View Blvd., Toronto, Ont. M4R 1B9, September 1973-
Annual. Institutional publication (Universities, schools, etc.), newsletter format, 5 p.

The Marian news *See* The Median

Marianews *See* The Median

Marine and outdoor trades / *edited by* N.J. Arthurs. - *Published by* Arthurs Publications Ltd. Suite 204, 5200 Dixie Rd., Mississauga, Ont. L4W 1E4, 1955-
Quarterly. Trade publication. Includes advertising. Circulation: 5319

The Mariner / *sponsored by* Gospel Text Publishers ; *edited by* Enos Brubacher. - *Published by* Letter Service. 58 Scott St., Kitchener, Ont. K0J 1T0 (Subscription address: R.R. 6, Eganville, Ont) April 1969-
Quarterly. Church publication, newsletter format, 4 p.
Free.

Maritime affairs bulletin / *edited by* F.B. Caldwell. - *Published by* The Navy League of Canada. Suite 910, 85 Range Rd., Ottawa, Ont. K1N 8J6, December 1969-
Quarterly. Association publication, newsletter format, 8 p. supplements issued. Circulation: 2750
Controlled circulation.

Maritime art (October 1940-June 1942) *See* artscanada

Maritime Art Association news / *edited by* Mischa German-van Eck. - *Published by* Maritime Art Association. 25 Rupert St., Amherst, N.S., September 1965-
Irregular (approximately 1-2 issues per year). Association publication, newsletter format, 4 p. Controlled circulation.

Maritime Baptist *See* Atlantic Baptist

Maritime command (Pacific) lookout *See* The Lookout

Maritime co-operator / *edited by* Zita Cameron. - *Published by* Maritime Co-operative Printers Ltd. P.O. Box 1178, Antigonish, N.S., 1931-
Monthly. House/company organ. Includes advertising. Circulation: 21,604
$2.25 per year : $2.50 per year, foreign.

The Maritime express / *edited by* R.D. Tennant. - *Published by* Scotian Railroad Society, Inc. P.O. Box 798, Armdale Postal Station, Halifax, N.S. B3G 4K5, June 1968-
Quarterly. Association publication, magazine format, 16 p. Includes book reviews, cumulative index.
ISSN 0047-5963 Subscription included in membership fee $10.00 per year for associate membership : $11.00 per year for regular membership. Prepayment required.

The Maritime farmer and co-operative dairyman / *edited by* James M. Thomson. - *Published by* R.D. Robinson Ltd. P.O. Box 2350, St. John, N.B., October 1895-
Former title(s): The Co-operative farmer and Maritime dairyman (1895-1910)
Issued twice a month. Special interest, tabloid format, 24 p. Includes book reviews, advertising, volume index, cumulative index. Circulation: 10,200
$.75 per year : $2.00 for 3 years. Prepayment required.

Maritime Lumber Bureau log - *Published by* Maritime Lumber Bureau. P.O. Box 459, Amherst, N.S. B4H 4A1.
Monthly. Trade publication, newsletter format, Circulation: 400
$18.00 per year.

The Maritime professional (1966-1970) *See* National news

Maritime sediments / *edited by* B.R. Pelletier. - *Published by* B.R. Pelletier. c/o Bedford Institute of Oceanography, Box 1006, Dartmouth, N.S. B2Y 4A2, 1965-
Irregular (approximately 3 issues per year). Scholarly publication, magazine format, 40 p. Language: English and French. Includes book reviews, volume index. Circulation: 530
Indexed in Arct. bibl.
$3.00 per issue : $8.00 per year.

The Maritime singer *See* The Windwing

Maritime truck transport review *See* Atlantic truck transport review

The Maritimes shipping herald and marine engineering journal = Le Journal de la marine marchande des Maritimes / *edited by* Edoardo Weis. - *Published by* Saint John School of Marine Technology. P.O. Box 1137, 115 Prince William St., Saint John, N.B. E2L 2B4, April 1974-
Irregular (approximately 9 issues per year). Institutional publication (Universities, schools, etc.), magazine format, 70 p. Language: English and French. Includes advertising. Circulation: 10,000
ISSN 0315-4289 $1.00 per issue : $7.00 per year : $8.00 per year, foreign.

Mark 11 : the sales and marketing management magazine / *edited by* Harry Weston. - *Published by* Weston Publishing Co. Ltd. Suite 102, 109 Railside Rd., Don Mills, Ont. M3A 1B5.
Irregular (approximately 8 issues per year). Trade publication, magazine format, 32 p. Includes advertising. Circulation: 10,244
$1.00 per issue : $8.00 per year : $12.00 per year, foreign.

Market research facts and trends - *Published by* Maclean-Hunter Research Bureau. 481 University Ave., Toronto, Ont. M5W 1A7, 1960-
Monthly. Trade publication, newsletter format, 4 p. Circulation: 4100
ISSN 0025-360X Free.

Marketing / *edited by* Colin Muncie. - *Published by* Andrew L. Rodgers. Maclean-Hunter Ltd. 481 University Ave., Toronto, Ont. M5W 1A7, 1908-
Weekly. Trade publication, magazine format,
Indexed in Can. B.P.I.
$.50 per issue : $14.00 per year : $17.00 per year.

Le Marketing social / *parrainé par* Les Editions marketing social inc ; *édité par* Robert Germain. - *Publié par* Roger Falardeau. 976, ave Moncton, Québec, Qué. G1S 2Y5, juillet-aout 1973-
Bimestriel. Revue d'entreprise, magazine, 52 p. Tirage: 6960
Indexé dans Periodex, RADAR.
$1.50 le numéro : $9.00 par année : $12.00 par année, l'étranger. Tarifs spéciaux disponibles. Abonnements payables à l'avance.

Martlet / *edited by* Gregory Middleton. - *Published by* Alma Mater Society. University of Victoria. P.O. Box 1700, University of Victoria, Victoria, B.C.
Weekly. Student publication, newspaper format, 16-20 p. Includes book reviews, film reviews, play reviews, record reviews, advertising. Circulation: 5500
$5.00 per year : $7.50 per year, foreign. Prepayment required.

Masonic light (1954) *See* The Freemason

Mass line / *edited by* Haridal S. Bains. - *Published by* Communist Party of Canada (Marxist-Leninist). P.O. Box 666, Postal Station C, Montreal, Que. (Subscription address: National Publications Centre, P.O. Box 727, Adelaide Station, Toronto, Ont) 1968-
Irregular. Political press, newspaper format, 40 p. Language: English and French.

Materials handling and distribution market in Canada. Annual - *Published by* Stewart R. Conway. Materials Management and Distribution Magazine. 481 University Ave., Toronto, Ont. M5W 1A7.
Annual. Trade publication, 36 p.
Prepayment required.

Materials handling handbook and directory of buying sources / *edited by* Jack Homer. - *Published by* S.R. Conway. Maclean-Hunter Ltd. 481 University Ave., Toronto, Ont., 1958-
Annual. Magazine format, 90 p. Includes advertising.
$2.00. Controlled circulation.

Materials handling in Canada *See* Materials management and distribution

Materials management and distribution / *edited by* Jack Homer. - *Published by* S.R. Conway. Maclean-Hunter Ltd. 481 University Ave., Toronto, Ont. M5W 1A7, 1957-
Former title(s): Materials handling in Canada. Monthly. Trade publication, magazine format, 60 p. Includes advertising.
Indexed in Can. B.P.I.
$1.00 per issue : $10.00 per year : $12.00 per year, foreign. Controlled circulation.

Matricule - *Publié par* Université Laval. Porte 1362, pavillon Pollack, Université Laval, Québec, Qué. G1K 7P4.
Hebdomadaire. Publication des étudiants, journal, 8 p.

Matrix : new Canadian writing / *edited by* Nigel Spencer. - *Published by* The English Department. Champlain Regional College. P.O. Box 510, Lennoxville, Que., Spring 1975-
Issued twice a year. Special interest, newsletter format, 40 p. Includes book reviews. Circulation: 1000
ISSN 0318-3610 $1.00 per issue : $2.00 per year.

The McGill engineer / *edited by* Ralph Bischoff and Anna Cullinan. - *Published by* Engineering Undergraduate Society. McGill University. McConnell Engineering Building, McGill University, Montreal, Que.
Annual. Student publication, magazine format, 90 p. Includes advertising. Circulation: 2000
Free. Controlled circulation.

The McGill news / *edited by* Louise Abbott. - *Published by* The Graduates' Society. McGill University. 3605 Mountain St., Montreal, Que. H3G 2M1, 1919-
Quarterly. Alumni publication. Includes advertising. Circulation: 35,000
$5.00 per year.

The McMaster graduate (1895-1930) *See* McMaster news

MeDal / *edited by* C.M. Bethune. - *Published by* Dalhousie Medical Alumni Association. Sir Charles Tupper Medical Bldg., Halifax, N.S., 1968-
Annual. Alumni publication, magazine format, ISSN 0318-0735 Free. Controlled circulation.

Mechanical contractor / *sponsored by* Plumbing and Mechanical Contracting Industry in British Columbia ; *edited by* V.J. Traynor. - *Published by* MDI Plumbing and Heating Planning Centre Ltd. 1128 West Georgia St., Vancouver, B.C. V6E 3H9, 1964-
Irregular (approximately 5 issues per year). Trade publication, magazine format, 24 p. Circulation: 5600
Free. Controlled circulation.

Mechanical Contractors Association of Windsor. Monthly newsletter / *edited by* Robert S. Dufty and Frederick Smith. - *Published by* Mechanical Contractors Association of Windsor. 1076 Crawford Ave., Windsor, Ont. N9A 5C9, 1972-
Monthly. Association publication, newsletter format, 2-3 p.

La Mèche / *édité par* Jacques Spooner. - *Publié par* Syndicat des travailleurs de l'enseignement du nord-ouest québécois. C.P. 6000, Rouyn, Qué. J9X 5M6, juin 1975-
Mensuel. Publication d'association, revue, 16 p. Comprend publicité. Tirage: 4000
$2.00 par année.

Le Médecin du Québec / *édité par* Georges Boileau. - *Publié par* Les Editions le Caducée inc. Suite 1100, 1440 ouest, rue Ste-Catherine, Montréal, Qué.
Mensuel. Publication spécialisée. Comprend publicité. Tirage: 12,105
Indexé dans RADAR.

Médecine moderne du Canada / *édité par* John A. Kellen. - *Publié par* Southam Business Publications Ltd. 1450 Don Mills Rd., Don Mills, Ont. M3B 2X7.
Publié en anglais: Modern medicine of Canada.
Mensuel. Publication spécialisée, magazine, 100 p. Comprend critique de livres, publicité. Tirage: 32,405
$2.00 le numéro : $12.00 par année : $30.00 par année, l'étranger. Envoi aux "personnes qualifiées".

Media Club of Canada. Newspacket - *Published by* Media Club of Canada. P.O. Box 504, Postal Station B, Ottawa, Ont. K1P 5P6, August 1971-
Association publication.
ISSN 0380-559X

The Media message / *edited by* Fred Johnston. - *Published by* Lorra Hines. Association for Media and Technology in Education in Canada. Secretary of EMAC/ETRAC, Duncan McArthur Hall, Queen's University, Kingston, Ont.
Quarterly. Association publication, magazine format, 25-35 p. Language: English and French. Includes book reviews, advertising. Circulation: 600
Indexed in Can. educ. ind.
$15.00 per year. Available to members only. Controlled circulation.

Mediaeval studies / *edited by* Virginia Brown. - *Published by* Pontifical Institute of Mediaeval Studies. 59 Queen's Park Cres. E., Toronto, Ont. M5S 2C4, 1939-
Annual. Scholarly publication, journal format, 400 p. Language: English and French. Includes cumulative index.
Indexed in I.B.Z.
ISSN 0076-5872 $14.65. Special rates offered.

The Median / *sponsored by* Marianopolis College ; *edited by* J. David Sloan, Margaret Curran and Sandra Vokaty. - *Published by* Student Society Typesetting. McGill University, 3647 Peel St., Montreal, Que. H3A 1X1, October 1974-
Former title(s): The Marian news; The Aquarian; Marianews.
Issued every other week. Student publication, newspaper format, 4 p. Includes film reviews, record reviews, advertising. Circulation: 1080
Free.

Mediator *See* Alberta learning resources journal

Medical aspects of human sexuality. Canadian edition / *edited by* M. Powell. - *Published by* J.E. Knox. 1 Heath St. W., Toronto, Ont. M4V 1T2 (Subscription address: P.O. Box 685, Don Mills, Ont. M3C 2T6) October 1971-
Issued every other month. Professional publication, magazine format, Circulation: 22,000
$2.00 per issue : $20.00 per year : $35.00 per volume : $30.00 per year, foreign. Controlled circulation.

Medical Council of Canada. Annual announcements / *edited by* The Registrar, The Medical Council of Canada. - *Published by* Medical Council of Canada. P.O. Box 8234, 1867 Alta Vista Dr., Ottawa, Ont. K1G 3H7, 1940-
Annual. Association publication, 74 p.
Free.

Medical education news / *edited by* A.M. Bryans. - *Published by* Health Sciences Office of Education. Queen's University. Kingston, Ont. K7L 3N6, 1974-
Former title(s): Nexus.
Quarterly. Institutional publication (Universities, schools, etc.), newsletter format, 4 p.
Free. Controlled circulation.

The Medical post / *edited by* Earl Damude. - *Published by* Murray Mark. Maclean-Hunter Ltd. 481 University Ave., Toronto, Ont., September 1965-
Issued every other week. Professional publication, newspaper format, 48 p. Includes book reviews, advertising. available in microform. Circulation: 28,000
$12.00 per year : $20.00 per year, U.S. & U.K. : $25.00 per year, foreign. Controlled circulation.

Medium (Spring 1969) *See* Gauntlet

The Medium / *edited by* Richard Skidmore. - *Published by* Student Institute. Nova Scotia Teachers College. Nova Scotia Teachers College, P.O. Box 810, Truro, N.S. B2N 5G5.
Issued twice a month. Student publication, newspaper format, 8 p. Includes book reviews, film reviews, play reviews, advertising. Circulation: 500
$.10 per issue : $.80 per year. Controlled circulation.

The Medium - *Published by* Saskatchewan Association of Educational Media Specialists. 2317 Arlington Ave., Saskatoon, Sask., M. Hepp-
Former title(s): Saskatchewan School Librarian.
Quarterly. Association publication, journal format, 30-40 p. Includes book reviews, film reviews. Circulation: 204
Indexed in Can. educ. ind.
Subscription included in membership fee $5.00 per year.

Medium II / *edited by* Gregg-Michael Troy. - *Published by* Students Administrative Government. Erindale College. University of Toronto. Room 5005, 3359 Mississauga Rd., Mississauga, Ont., September 1974-
Former title(s): Erindaliam.
Weekly. Student publication, newspaper format, 8-12 p. Includes book reviews, film reviews, play reviews, record reviews, advertising. Circulation: 7000
$3.00 per year. Free to members of the university.

Meetings, conferences and conventions: a Financial post guide / *sponsored by* The Financial Post ; *edited by* Ann Rhodes. - *Published by* John Duncan. Maclean-Hunter Ltd. 481 University Ave., Toronto, Ont. M5W 1A7, 1969-
Former title(s): Financial post report on conventions, conferences and business meetings (1969-1973)
Annual. Directory, magazine format, 60 p.
Included in subscription to the Financial post. Controlled circulation.

Mega communications - *Publié par* Gilles Saint-Marie & Associés Inc. 1454, de la Montagne, Montréal, Que. H3G 1Z6, avril 1973-
Paraît tous les 15 jours. Publication spécialisée, 4 p.
$15.00 le numéro : $45.00 pour 24 numéro : $80.00 pour 48 numéros.

Meie elu = Our life / *edited by* H. Rebane and S. Veidenbaum. - *Published by* Estonian Publishing Co. Toronto Ltd. 958 Broadview Ave., Toronto, Ont. M4K 2R6, March 1950-
Weekly. Ethnic press, newspaper format, 8-12 p. Language: Estonian. Includes book reviews, play reviews, advertising. available in microform.
$.35 per issue : $18.00 per year : $19.00 per year, U.S. : $22.00 per year, overseas. Prepayment required.

Meliorist / *sponsored by* University of Lithbridge. Students' Union. - *Published by* Production Department. Student Society Council. University of Lethbridge. Lethbridge, Alta., September 1968-
Weekly. Student publication, newspaper format, 8 p. Includes film reviews, record reviews, advertising. Circulation: 1500
$10.00 per year.

Members' bulletin - Highway Transport Board (January 1940-June 1957) *See* Highway Transport Board. Highway Transport Board Bulletin

Mémoire présenté au Premier Ministre du Canada et membres du cabinet - *Publié par* Fédération canadienne de l'agriculture. 111 Sparks, Ottawa, Ont. K1P 5B5.
Publié en anglais: Presentation to the Prime Minister and members of parliament.
Annuel. Publication d'association, 53 p.

Mémoires - *Publié par* Jardin Botanique de Montréal. 4104 est, rue Sherbrooke, Montréal, Qué. H1X 2B2, 1940-
Intermittent. Recueil des travaux sur plantes, bulletin, Langue(s): français et anglais.

Memorial University of Newfoundland. Serials holdings in the libraries of Memorial University of Newfoundland, St. John's Public Library, and College of Trades and Technology - *Published by* Memorial University of Newfoundland. St. John's, Nfld. A1C 5S7, 1964-
Former title(s): Serials holdings in the libraries of Memorial University of Newfoundland and St John's Public Library (1969-1973) Serials holdings in the libraries at Memorial University of Newfoundland (1968) Serial holdings in the library of Memorial University of Newfoundland (1964-1966)
Annual. Catalogue, paperbound book,
Free to selected libraries and institutions.

Mennonite Brethren herald / *edited by* Harold Jantz. - *Published by* Board of Publications. Canadian Mennonite Brethren Conference. 159 Henderson Highway, Winnipeg, Man. R2L 1L4., 1962-
Issued every other week. Church publication, magazine format, Includes book reviews, advertising, volume index. supplements issued. Circulation: 9400
$.25 per issue : $6.00 per year : $10.00 per volume. Controlled circulation. Prepayment required.

Mennonite mirror / *edited by* R.H. Vogt. - *Published by* Brock Publishers Ltd. 203-818 Portage Ave., Winnipeg, Man. R3G 0N4, October 1971-
Monthly. Ethnic press, magazine format, 24 p. Language: English and German. Includes book reviews, play reviews, advertising.
$.50 per issue : $4.00 per year. Controlled circulation.

Mennonite reporter / *edited by* David Kroeker. - *Published by* Mennonite Publishing Service. Waterloo, Ont. N2L 3G6, August 1971-
Former title(s): Canadian Mennonite reporter.
Issued every other week. Church publication, newspaper format, 14 p. Includes book reviews, film reviews, play reviews, advertising, volume index. supplements issued. Circulation: 6700
$7.00 per year : $20.00 per volume (bound-stitched), $13.00 per year, foreign (airmail). Controlled circulation. Prepayment required.

Mennonite review *See* Mennonitische Rundschau

Mennonitische Rundschau = Mennonite review / *sponsored by* Canadian Conference of Mennonite Brethren Churches ; *edited by* Erich L. Ratzlaff. - *Published by* The Christian Press. 159 Henderson Highway, Winnipeg, Man. R2L 1L4, 1877-
Former title(s): Nebraska ansiedler (1877-1880)
Weekly. Ethnic press, church publication, newspaper format, 16 p. Language: German. Includes book reviews, advertising. Circulation: 5400
$.15 per issue : $6.00 per year. Prepayment required.

Menorah - egyenloseg / *edited by* George Egri. - *Published by* Menorah-Egyenloseg. 105 Almore Ave., Downsview, Ont.
Weekly. Ethnic press. Language: Hungarian. Includes advertising.

Men's wear of Canada / *edited by* Robert G. Webb. - *Published by* MacLean-Hunter Ltd. 481 University Ave., Toronto, Ont. M5W 1A7, 1909-
Monthly. Directory, magazine format, 60 p. Language: English and French. Includes advertising. supplements issued. Circulation: 6494
$1.00 per issue : $10.00 per year : $ 12.00 per year, U.S. and U.K. : $25.00 per year, foreign.

Mental retardation = Défience mentale / *edited by* R.G. Anglin. - *Published by* Canadian Association for the Mentally Retarded. York University Campus, Kinsmen NIMR Building, 4700 Keele St., Downsview, Ont. M3J 1P3, January 1958-
Former title(s): The Bulletin - The Canadian Association for the Mentally Retarded.
Quarterly. Association publication, magazine format, 48 p. Language: English and French. Includes book reviews. Circulation: 14,000
$.50 per issue : $2.00 per year. Prepayment required.

Mercer actuarial bulletin - *Published by* William M. Mercer Ltd. 7 King St. E., Toronto, Ont. M5C 1A2, January 1951-
Former title(s): Employee benefit plan bulletin (1951-1958) Canadian actuarial bulletin (1958-1961)
Monthly. House/company organ, newsletter format, 2 p. Language: English (French). Circulation: 6000
Free. Controlled circulation.

Message de vérité / *édité par* Jean-Paul Berney. - *Publié par* Publications chrétiennes. 230, rue Lupien, Cap de la Madeleine, Qué., 1960-
Trimestriel. Publication ecclésiastique, magazine, 24 p. Tirage: 20,000
$1.00 par année.

Message métrique *See* Metric message

Messager de Marie Reine des Coeurs *Voir* Regard de foi : revue mariale d'actualité

Le Messager de Saint-Antoine / *édité par* Viateur Pleau. - *Publié par* Pères Capucins. Ermitage St-Antoine, Lac Bouchette, Cté Roberval, Qué.(adresse d'abonnement: Lac Bouchette, Qué. G0W 1V0)
Mensuel. Publication ecclésiastique, revue, 30 p.

"Messages" (avril-juin 1957-été 1973) *Voir* Cahier d'animation missionnaire

Messenger of the Sacred Heart of Jesus / *edited by* F.J. Power. - *Published by* Apostleship of Prayer. 68 Broadview Ave., Toronto, Ont. M4K 2P9, 1890-
Monthly. Church publication, magazine format, 24 p. Circulation: 22,000
$.25 per issue : $2.50 per year.

Meta / *édité par* P.A Clas. - *Publié par* Les Presses de l'Université de Montréal. C.P. 6128, Montréal, Qué. H3C 3J7, 1955-
Trimestriel. Edition savante, revue, 100 p. Langue(s): français et anglais ; sommaires: français et anglais. Comprend publicité. Tirage: 2000
Indexé dans RADAR, Curr. ind. j. educ.
ISSN 0026-0452 $2.00 le numéro : $7.00 par année. Envoi gratuit. Abonnements payables à l'avance.

Metalworking management / *edited by* Julian Chadwick. - *Published by* Don Quick Publications. 297 Old Kingston Rd., West Hill, Ont. M1C 2B4, 1938-
Monthly. Trade publication. Includes advertising. Circulation: 9321
$.75 per issue : $8.00 per year.

Metalworking production and purchasing / *edited by* James C. Young. - *Published by* Keith A. Watson. Action Communications Ltd. Suite 233, 4 Lansing Square, Willowdale, Ont. M2J 1T4.
Irregular. Trade publication. Includes advertising.

Métiers d'art informe (1974-1975) *Voir* Signe

Metric message = Message métrique / *edited by* Guy W. Richard. - *Published by* The Canadian Metric Association. P.O. Box 35, Fonthill, Ont. L0S 1E0, June 1975-
Former title(s): Canadian Metric Association newsletter (1973-1975)
Quarterly. Association publication, newsletter format, 4 p. Language: English and French. Circulation: 700
ISSN 0318-6385 $5.00 per year : $9.00 for 2 years : $5.25 per year, U.S. Prepayment required.

Metro guide / *edited by* Herb Aslin. - *Published by* Aslin Advertising Company. P.O. Box 481, Halifax, N.S. B3J 2R7.
Former title(s): Day by day; This week in Halifax.
Monthly except the December January issues are combined. Special interest, magazine format, 70 p. Circulation: 30,000
Free.

Metro telecaster and entertainment guide / *edited by* Edith Muise. - *Published by* Fundy Group Publications Ltd. P.O. Box 128, 2 Second St., Yarmouth, N.S. B5A 4B1, 1974-
Weekly. Special interest, newspaper format, 28 p. Includes advertising. Circulation: 50,000
Controlled circulation.

Metropolitan life / *edited by* Dean Jones. - *Published by* Public Relations Division. Metropolitan Life. 180 Wellington St., Ottawa, Ont. K1P 5A3, October 1974-
Former title(s): Field beacon.
Issued twice a month. House/company organ, newsletter format, 8 p. Language: English and French.
Free to employees. Controlled circulation.

Metropolitan Toronto Library Board. Business Library. Selected list of new titles - *Published by* Metropolitan Toronto Library Board. 214 College St., Toronto, Ont. M5T 1R3, 1967-
Monthly. Bibliography, newsletter format, 6-10 p. Circulation: 250
ISSN 0316-7321 Free.

Metropolitan Toronto Library Board. Languages Co-ordinator. Books... / *edited by* Languages Co-ordinator. - *Published by* Metropolitan Toronto Library Board. 214 College St., Toronto, Ont. M5T 1R3, 1967-
Quarterly. Lists of additions of books in other languages broken up by individual language.

Le Meunier québécois / *édité par* René Blanchard et Benoit Giard. - *Publié par* L'Association professionnelle des meuniers du Québec. Suite 4, Parc Samuel Holland, Québec, Qué. G7S 3R3, 1966-
Mensuel. Publication d'association, journal, 24 p. Comprend publicité. Tirage: 15,442
$3.00 par année : $5.00 (3 ans).

Micro notes / *edited by* J.D. Currie. - *Published by* Canadian Micrographic Society. P.O. Box 6084, Postal Station J, Ottawa, Ont. K2A 1T1, September 1972-
Quarterly. Association publication, magazine format, 20 p. Includes advertising.
$20.00 per year. Controlled circulation.

Microscopical Society of Canada. Bulletin = Société de microscopie du Canada. Bulletin / *edited by* F.W. Doane. - *Published by* Microscopical Society of Canada. c/o F.W. Doane, School of Hydiene, Room 79, 150 College St., Toronto, Ont. M5S 1A1.
Quarterly. Association publication, newsletter format, 32 p. Includes book reviews.
$5.00 per year.

The Midden / *edited by* Nick Russell. - *Published by* Archaeological Society of British Columbia. c/o Centennial Museum, Vancouver, B.C., November 1968-
Former title(s): Newsletter of the Archaeological Society of British Columbia (November 1968 - October 1970)
Issued every other month except August. Association publication, newsletter format, 18 p. Includes book reviews. Circulation: 220
$5.00 per year.

Milk break / *edited by* Verlie Bousfield. - *Published by* Fraser Valley Milk Producers' Association. P.O. Box 9100, Vancouver, B.C. V6B 4G4, June 1975-
Monthly. Association publication, newsletter format, 4 p. Circulation: 1500
Controlled circulation.

The Mill news letter / *sponsored by* Victoria College ; *edited by* John M. Robson and Michael Laine. - *Published by* University of Toronto Press. 5201 Dufferin St., Downsview, Ont. M3H 5T8 (Subscription address: Deparment of English, Victoria College, University of Toronto, Toronto, Ont) Fall 1965-
Issued twice a year. Scholarly publication, newsletter format, 20 p. Includes book reviews. Circulation: 660
Free.

Mineralogical Association of Canada. Newsletter / *edited by* F.J. Wicks. - *Published by* The Mineralogical Association of Canada. Royal Ontario Museum, 100 Queen's Park Cres., Toronto, Ont. M5S 2C6, 1958-
Issued twice a year. Association publication, newsletter format, 12 p.
Free to members.

Les Mines : pilier de l'économie canadienne - *Publié par* L'Association minière du Canada. 9ième étage, 20, rue Toronto, Toronto, Ont. M5C 2C2, 1973-
Ancien titre: L'Industrie minière - pilier de l'économie canadienne (1968-1971)
Publication d'association, magazine, 60 p. Tirage: 20,000
ISSN 0317-9524 Envoi gratuit.

Les Mines au Canada : renseignements et statistiques - *Publié par* L'Association minière du Canada. 9ième étage, 20, rue Toronto, Toronto, Ont. M5C 2C2, 1969-
Ancien titre: L'Exploitation minière du Canada - renseignements et statistiques (1967, 1968) Publié en anglais: Facts and figures : mining in Canada.
Annuel. Publication d'association, brochure, 40 p. Tirage: 10,000
Envoi gratuit.

Mini pegg / *edited by* A.C. Milroy. - *Published by* Association of Professional Engineers, Geologists, and Geophysicists of Alberta. 215 One Thornton Court, Edmonton, Alta. T5J 2E7, May 1972-
Monthly except December and July. Association publication, newspaper format, 8 p. Includes advertising. Circulation: 9600
$5.00 per year. Controlled circulation.

Mining : what it means to Canada - *Published by* The Mining Association of Canada. 9th Floor, 20 Toronto St., Toronto, Ont. M5C 2C2, 1964-
Former title(s): What the mining industry means to Canada (1964-1967) Published in French: Les mines : pilier de l'économie canadienne.
Annual. Association publication.
Free.

Mining exploration and development review, British Columbia-Yukon / *edited by* F.G. Higgs. - *Published by* British Columbia & Yukon Chamber of Mines. 840 West Hastings St., Vancouver, B.C. V6C 1C8.
Annual. Association publication, magazine format, 50 p. Circulation: 3000
ISSN 0318-1766 $2.00 per year. Free to members. Prepayment required.

Le Mirabel - *Publié par* Le Mirabel. C.P. 276, St-Jérôme, Qué. J7Z 5L3.
Hebdomadaire.

Miss Chatelaine / *edited by* Mildred Istona. - *Published by* Maclean-Hunter Ltd. 481 University Ave., Toronto, Ont. M5W 1A7.
Irregular (approximately 7 issues per year). Special interest, magazine format, Includes book reviews, film reviews, record reviews, advertising. Circulation: 160,000
$2.50 per year.

The Missing link magazine / *edited by* Greg Gatenby and Hans Jewinski. - *Published by* Missing Link Press. 78 Chelwood Rd., Scarborough, Ont. M1K 2K8.
Quarterly.
$1.50 per issue : $4.00 per year.

Mission '75 / *sponsored by* The Society for the Propagation of the Faith and The National Missionary Council ; *edited by* Gerald Curry. - *Published by* Pontifical Missionary Union. Suite 16, 46 Elgin St., Ottawa, Ont. K1P 5K6, March 1974-
Quarterly. Church publication, magazine format, 28 p.
$3.00 per year. Controlled circulation.

The Missionary messenger / *edited by* Ken Johnson. - *Published by* Fundamentalist Baptist Publications of Canadian Baptist Missions. P.O. Box 40, Postal Station J, Calgary, Alta. T2A 4X4, December 1971-
Monthly. Special interest, newspaper format, 12-16 p. Includes advertising.
$.25 per issue : $3.00 per year.

Missionary outlook (1960-1968) *See* Action

The Missionary Sisters of the Immaculate Conception. MIC mission news / *edited by* Madeline Maillet. - *Published by* The Missionary Sisters of the Immaculate Conception. P.O. Box 157, Laval des Rapides, Laval, Que. H7N 4Z4, January 1974-
Former title(s): The Precursor (January 1923-December 1973)
Issued every other month. Church publication, newsletter format, 6 p.
ISSN 0315-9655 $2.00 per year : $3.00 for 2 years : $8.00 for 5 years : $50.00 for life.

Missions d'Afrique / *édité par* Adrien Fontaine. - *Publié par* Les Pères blancs d'Afrique. 180, chemin Ste-Foy, Québec, Qué. G1R 4R2, janvier 1904-
Bimestriel. Publication ecclésiastique, magazine, 32 p.
$2.00 par année. Abonnements payables à l'avance.

Missions des franciscains / *édité par* Edouard Otis. - *Publié par* Procure des missions. Franciscains. 2080 ouest, boul. Dorchester, Montréal, Qué., janvier 1923-
Ancien titre: Les Missions franciscaines.
Bimestriel. Publication ecclésiastique, bulletin, 6 p.
$1.00 par année.

Missions étrangères : magazine d'information missionnaire / *édité par* Jean-Denis Tremblay. - *Publié par* Jean Greffard. Société des missions-étrangères. 59 rue Desnoyers, Pont-Viau, Ville de Laval, Qué.(adresse d'abonnement: C.P. 69, L.D.R., Port-Viau, Ville de Laval, Qué) janvier 1941-
Bimestriel. Publication d'association, publication ecclésiastique, magazine, 32 p. Tirage: 53,000
$.35 le numéro : $2.00 par année. Tirage contrôlé. Abonnements payables à l'avance.

Les Missions franciscaines *Voir* Missions des franciscains

Missions Saint-Viateur / *édité par* Laurent Pilon. - *Publié par* Les Clercs de Saint-Viateur. 2715, chemin de la Côte Ste-Catherine, Montréal, Qué. H3T 1B6, fevrier 1949-
Trimestriel. Organe interne/officiel, bulletin, 16 p. Tirage: 1000
$2.00 par année.

Missisquoi County Historical Society. Missisquoi / *edited by* Doris Jones McIntosh. - *Published by* Missisquoi County Historical Society. P.O. Box 186, Stanbridge East, Que., 1911-
Subtitle varies.
Annual. Association publication, book format, 175 p. Language: English and French ; summaries: English and French.
$5.00 per volume.

Mississauga library link / *edited by* Edna Toth. - *Published by* Mississauga Library System. 110 Dundas St. W., Mississauga, Ont. L5B 1H3, December 1973-
Monthly September to May, inclusive. Institutional publication (Universities, schools, etc.), newspaper format, 4 p. Circulation: 6000
$1.00 per year. Individual issues are free.

Mitre (1893-1970) *See* New mitre : literary magazine of Bishop's University

Mobile home and recreational vehicle industry / *edited by* Charles Clay. - *Published by* Clay Publishing Co. Ltd. Bewdley, Ont. K0L 1E0, 1954-
Monthly. Trade publication, magazine format, 12 p. Includes advertising.
ISSN 0026-7171 $.75 per issue : $6.00 per year. Controlled circulation.

Mobile home directory / *edited by* Gladys Taylor. - *Published by* Tall-Taylor Publishing Ltd. 532 Cleveland Cres., S.E., Calgary, Alta.
Annual. Directory, magazine format, 48 p. Includes advertising.

Mobile homes Canada / *edited by* Gladys Taylor. - *Published by* Tall-Taylor Publishing Ltd. 532 Cleveland Cres., S.E., Calgary, Alta.
Monthly. , magazine format, 30 p. Language: English and French. Includes advertising.

Mobile living in Canada / *edited by* John Carruthers. - *Published by* John Carruthers. Mobile Publications Ltd. P.O. Box 3097, Postal Station B, Calgary, Alta. T2M 4L6, 1964-
Monthly. Special interest, tabloid format, 16 p. Includes book reviews, advertising. Circulation: 10,000
$.50 per issue : $5.00 per year : $9.00 per year, foreign. Controlled circulation. Special rates offered.

Moccasin telegraph / *sponsored by* Canadian School Library Association ; *edited by* Karen Smith. - *Published by* Canadian Library Association. 151 Sparks St., Ottawa, Ont. K1P 5E3.
Quarterly. Association publication, journal format, 65 p. Includes book reviews. supplements issued. Circulation: 700
Subscription included in membership fee. Controlled circulation.

Moccasin telegraph / *sponsored by* Northern Stores Dept. - Hudson's Bay Company ; *edited by* V.H. Tower. - *Published by* Hudson's Bay Company. 77 Main St., Winnipeg, Man. R3C 2R1 (Subscription address: Hudson's Bay House, 77 Main St., Winnipeg, Man. C3C 2R1) August 1941-
Issued twice a year. House/company organ, magazine format, 60 p. Language: English and French. Circulation: 5000
Free. Controlled circulation.

Model aviation Canada / *edited by* John McNicol. - *Published by* Model Aeronautics Association of Canada. 4612 Howard Ave., Windsor, Ont. (Subscription address: P.O. Box 9, Oakville, Ont) January 1975-
Former title(s): Competition Canada (January 1971-December 1974)
Irregular (approximately 10 issues per year). Association publication, newsletter format, 24 p. Includes advertising.
ISSN 0315-2200 $10.00 per year. Prepayment required.

Modern and classical language bulletin (1962-Winter 1972-1973) *See* Alberta modern language journal

Modern dairy / *edited by* I. Macnab. - *Published by* Maccan Publishing Company. Suite 203, 702 Weston Rd., Toronto, Ont. M6N 3R2, 1923-
Former title(s): Canadian dairy and ice cream journal (September 1923-December 1968)
Issued every other month. Magazine format, 28 p. Includes advertising. Circulation: 2582
ISSN 0026-7651 $1.50 per issue : $10.00 per year : $22.00 per year, foreign : $30.00 for 2 years, foreign. Special issues and back issues $2.50 each.

Modern drama / *sponsored by* Graduate Centre for Study Drama. University of Toronto. - *Published by* A.M. Hackkert Ltd. 554 Spadina Cres., Toronto, Ont. M5S 2J9.
Quarterly.
Indexed in Hum. ind.
$9.00 per year.

Modern language journal (Fall 1973-Spring 1974) *See* Alberta modern language journal

Modern medicine of Canada / *edited by* John A. Kellen (medical editor). - *Published by* Southam Business Publications Ltd. 1450 Don Mills Rd., Don Mills, Ont. M3B 2X7, 1946-
Published in French: Médecine moderne du Canada.
Monthly. Professional publication, magazine format, 100 p. Includes book reviews, advertising. Circulation: 32,405
$2.00 per issue : $12.00 per year : $30.00 per year, foreign.

Modern power and engineering / *edited by* Bruce Glassford. - *Published by* Maclean-Hunter Ltd. 481 University Ave., Toronto, Ont. M5W 1A7 (Subscription address: P.O. Box 9100, Postal Station A, Toronto, Ont) 1906-
Monthly. Business publication, magazine format, 100 p. Includes book reviews, advertising.
Indexed in Can. B.P.I.
$15.00 per year : $20.00 per year, foreign. Controlled circulation.

Modern purchasing / *edited by* W. Gallagher. - *Published by* Peter I. Volny. Maclean-Hunter Ltd. 481 University Ave., Toronto, Ont. M5W 1A7, 1959-
Includes advertising. Circulation: 8398
$1.00 per issue : $10.00 per year : $15.00 for 2 years : $20.00 for 3 years, $12.00 U.S. and U.K. : $25.00 per year, foreign.

Modern wood (1959-1973) *See* Treated wood perspectives

Modernist studies / *edited by* Shirley Rose (Alta.) and Ernest Griffin (York). - *Published by* Department of English. University of Alberta. Edmonton, Alta. T6G 2E1, 1974-
Issued twice a year.
$11.75 per year.

Modersmaalet = Mother tongue / *edited by* Erik Melander. - *Published by* Danish Canadian Press. P.O. Box 323, Oakville, Ont., 1956-
Issued every other week. Ethnic press, newspaper format, 16-20 p. Language: Danish. Circulation: 4000
$.30 per issue : $6.00 per year.

Modicum / *edited by* J. Brender à Brandis. - *Published by* Brandstead Press. Carlisle, Ont., 1969-
Irregular (approximately 1 issue per year). Special interest, newsletter format, 8 p. Language: English and French and Latin. Circulation: 150
$1.50 per volume.

Moko / *edited by* R.T. Robertson. - *Published by* Canadian Association for Commonwealth Literature and Language Studies. Department of English, University of Saskatchewan, Saskatoon, Sask. S7N 0W0 (Subscription address: Mrs. A. Steele, Secretary CACLALS Library, University of Calgary, Calgary, Alta) March 1973-
Issued twice a year. Association publication, newsletter format, 20 p. supplements issued. Circulation: 80
$5.00 per year. Prepayment required.

Moloda Ukraina = Young Ukraine / *sponsored by* Ukrainian Democratic Youth Association ; *edited by* M. Hawrysh. - *Published by* P. Rodak. 12 Minstrel Dr., Toronto, Ont. M8Y 3G4 (Subscription address: P.O. Box 8, Postal Station E, Toronto, Ont) 1950-
Monthly. Ethnic press, magazine format, 28 p. Language: Ukrainian.
$6.00 per year.

Mon bébé / *édité par* J.L. Morin. - *Publié par* Les Publications mon bébé inc. Suite 203, 6841, rue St-Hubert, Montréal, Qué. H2S 2M8, 1951-
Intermittent (approximativement 2 éditions par an). Intérêt général, magazine, 68 p. Tirage: 44,000
$.50 le numéro : $1.00 l'numéro. l'étranger.

Mon frère et moi / *édité par* Homer Laplante. - *Publié par* Homer Laplante. Association Missionnaire de Marie Immaculée (AMMI). C.P. 721, Winnipeg, Man. R3C 2K3., juin 1968-
Publié en anglais: My brother and I.
Trimestriel. Publication ecclésiastique, bulletin, 24 p. Tirage: 2000
ISSN 0316-0785 Pour associés seulement.

Mon mariage : et mon nouveau foyer / *édité par* Marcelle Jacques. - *Publié par* Jean P. Héroux. 3454, rue St-Denis, Montréal, Qué. H2X 3L3, 1948-
Trimestriel. Publication spécialisée, magazine, 116 p. Tirage: 20,000
$1.00 le numéro : $2.50 par année. Abonnements payables à l'avance.

The Monarchist (October 1970-May 1971) *See* Monarchy Canada

Monarchy Canada / *sponsored by* The Monarchist League of Canada ; *edited by* Arthur Bousfield. - *Published by* John L. Aimers. 611-10 Rosemount Ave., Westmount, Que. H3Y 3K4 (Subscription address: 2 Wedgewood Cres, Ottawa, Ont. K1B 4B4) October 1970-
Former title(s): The Canadian monarchist (May 1971-October 1972) The Monarchist (October 1970-May 1971)
Issued 5 times a year. Special interest, magazine format, 16 p. Language: English and French. Includes book reviews, advertising. Circulation: 3500
ISSN 0319-4019 $1.00 per issue : $5.00 per year : $9.00 per year in the Commonwealth : $10.00 per year, foreign. Prepayment required.

Monchanin / *édité par* Jacques Langlais. - *Publié par* Robert Vachon (directeur). Centre Monchanin. 4917, rue St-Urbain, Montréal, Qué. H2T 2W1.
Ancien titre: Monchanin information (janvier 1968-mars-avril 1972)
Bimestriel. Edition savante, revue, 32 p. Langue(s): français et anglais. Comprend critique de livres, index de volumes, index cumulatif. Tirage: 1000
$1.00 le numero : $4.00 par année : $1.25 le numéro, l'étranger : $5.00 par année, l'étranger. Tarifs spéciaux disponibles. Abonnements payables à l'avance.

Monchanin information (janvier 1968-mars-avril 1972) *Voir* Monchanin

Monday morning - *Published by* Second Century Canada Pub. Inc. 52 St. Clair Ave. E., Toronto, Ont. M4T 1N4, 1967-
Irregular (approximately 5 issues per year).

Monday report on retailers / *edited by* G. Barry Kay. - *Published by* Maclean-Hunter Ltd. 481 University Ave., Toronto, Ont. M5W 1A7.
Weekly. Trade publication, newsletter format, 8 p. Includes volume index.
$159.00 per year. Special rates offered.

Le Monde de l'électricité / *édité par* Jean Racine. - *Publié par* F. Guibert. Les Publications industrielles ltée. Suite 5, 1509 ouest, rue Sherbrooke, Montréal, Qué. H3G 1L7, 1965-
Mensuel. Comprend publicité. Tirage: 15,266

Monde du harnais *See* Harness world

Monde nouveau, présence nouvelle (septembre 1968-juin 1972) *Voir* Le Prêtre

Il Mondo / *edited by* Filippo Ciaccio. - *Published by* Il Mondo Publishing and Broadcasting Ltd. P.O. Box 186, Postal Station H, Toronto, Ont., 1967-
Issued twice a month. Ethnic press. Language: Italian. Includes advertising.
$.15 per issue : $6.00 per year.

The Monograph / *edited by* Paul F. Thomas. - *Published by* Ontario Association for Geographic and Environmental Education. Suite S904, 252 Bloor St. W., Toronto, Ont., 1950-
Quarterly. Association publication, 32 p. Includes advertising. Circulation: 1000
Indexed in Can. educ. ind.
ISSN 0048-1793 $1.50 per issue : $6.00 per year.

Monthly bulletin - Lumber and Building Materials Association of Ontario (1917-1956) *See* Lumber and Building Materials Association of Ontario. LBMAO reporter

Monthly business analysis / *edited by* Jacques J. Singer. - *Published by* W.A. Beckett Associates. Suite 808, 40 St. Clair Ave. W., Toronto, Ont. M4V 1M2, July 1960-
Monthly. Business publication, newsletter format, 21 p. Circulation: 200
$90.00 per year (Second copy price $20.00). Prepayment required.

Monthly commercial letter - Canadian Imperial Bank of Commerce (1915-1950) *See* Commercial letter

Monthly letter - Bureau of Municipal Research *See* Civic affairs

Monthly newsprint report - *Published by* Canadian Pulp and Paper Association. 2300 Sun Life Building, Montreal, Que. H3B 2X9.
Monthly. Association publication, statistics, looseleaf format, 4 p.
ISSN 0316-4268 Free.

Monthly report on Canadian external relations (1962-1969) *See* International Canada

Montraffic news *Voir* Bulletin Montraffic

Montreal - Courier / *edited by* Bernd Laengin. - *Published by* Courier Press Ltd. Suite 304, 455 Spadina Ave., Toronto, Ont. M5S 2G9, 1907-
Weekly. Ethnic press, newspaper format, 16 p. Language: German. available in microform.
$.25 per issue : $9.00 per year : $12.00 per year, foreign. Prepayment required.

Montreal Board of Trade. Bulletin - *Published by* Montreal Board of Trade. 6th Floor, Commerce House, 1080 Beaver Hall Hill, Montreal Que. H4A 3M3.
Monthly. Association publication, newsletter format, 20 p. Language: English and French. Circulation: 8500
Free. Subscription included in membership fee.

Montreal calendar magazine / *edited by* Jim Chouinard. - *Published by* Calendar Magazines Ltd. 65 Front St. E., Toronto, Ont. M5E 1B6, October 1971-
Monthly. Magazine format, 48 p. Includes film reviews, play reviews, advertising. Circulation: 95,000
$.75 per issue : $9.00 per year. Controlled circulation.

Montreal Catholic School Commission. Monthly news (1969) *See* The Public school

Montréal ce mois-ci : l'agenda du mieux-vivre / *édité par* Michelle Labrèche. - *Publié par* Richard Ballentine Ltd. Calendar Magazines. 65 Front St. E., Toronto, Ont. M5E 1B6(adresse d'abonnement: Suite 1502, 1115 ouest, rue Sherbrooke, Montréal, Qué) octobre 1974-
Mensuel. Calendrier d'événements, magazine, 48 p. Comprend critique de films, critique de pièces de théâtre. Tirage: 131,000
$.75 le numéro : $9.00 par année. Tirage contrôlé.

Montreal Construction Association. Newsletter : safety - *Published by* Montreal Construction Association. 4970 Place de la Savane, Montreal, Que. H4P 1Z6.
Irregular (approximately 10 issues per year). Association publication, newsletter format, 4 p. Circulation: 2600

The Montreal General Hospital. The Montreal General Hospital news - *Published by* The Montreal General Hospital. 1650 Cedar Ave., Montreal, Que. H3G 1A4, 1965-
Former title(s): M.G.H. newsletter (1960-1965) M.G.H. bulletin (1951-1960)
Quarterly. Institutional publication (Universities, schools, etc.), magazine format, 20 p. Circulation: 6000

Montreal scene - *Published by* Derek A. Price. The Montreal Star (1973) Ltd. P.O. Box 4005, Place d'Armes, Montreal, Que. H2Y 1M6.
Weekly. General interest, magazine format, Includes advertising. A supplement to the Montreal Star. Circulation: 226,390

Montreal Teachers Association. M.T.A. - the teacher / *edited by* Sylvia Gold. - *Published by* Montreal Teachers Association. 5485 Sherbrooke St. W., Montreal, Que. H4A 1W1.
Irregular (approximately 6 issues per year). Association publication, newspaper format, 16 p. Circulation: 4000
Free. Controlled circulation.

Montreal Women's Yellow Pages = Les Pages jaunes des femmes de Montréal - *Published by* Women's Information and Referral Centre. 3595 St. Urbain, Montreal, Que., 1973-
Annual. Special interest, magazine format, 50 p. Language: English and French. Circulation: 10,000
$1.00 (Institutions $2.00) : $2.00, foreign. Prepayment required.

Montrealer Nachrichten / *edited by* Rosel Greinwald. - *Published by* Eric O. Reprich. German Publications Ltd. P.O. Box 278, Pickering, Ont. L1V 2R4.
Weekly. Ethnic press. Language: German. Includes advertising. Circulation: 11,400
$7.50 per year.

Montrealer Zeitung / *edited by* Rosel Greinwald. - *Published by* Erich O. Reprich. P.O. Box 278, Pickering, Ont. L1V 2R4, 1952-
Weekly. Ethnic press, newspaper format, 16 p. Language: German.
$7.50 per year : $11.50 per year, foreign.

Moongoose / *edited by* Ralph Alfonso. - *Published by* Ralph Alfonso. 5252 Borden Ave., Montreal, Que. H4V 2T1, 1971-
Annual. Special interest, magazine format, 30 p.
$1.00 : $1.50 foreign. Controlled circulation.

Il Mormoratore / *edited by* Tony Baccari. - *Published by* Tony Baccari. P.O. Box 394, Calgary, Alta. T2S 0A7, 1970-
Monthly. Ethnic press, newspaper format, 12 p. Language: Italian and English.
$.35 per issue : $3.00 per year.

Mosaic : a journal for the comparative study of literature and ideas / *sponsored by* University of Manitoba ; *edited by* R.G. Collins and John Wortley. - *Published by* University of Manitoba Press. Winnipeg, Man. R3T 2N2 (Subscription address: 208 Tier Bldg., University of Manitoba, Winnipeg, Man. R3T 2N2) October 1967-
Quarterly. Scholarly publication, journal format, 180 p. Language: English and French. Includes volume index, cumulative index, updating service. supplements issued. Back issues $1.75 each. Circulation: 1500
Indexed in Can. ind., Can. essay and lit. ind.
ISSN 0027-1276 $3.00 per issue : $10.00 for 4 issues : $18.00 for 8 issues.

Mosaico / *edited by* Luigi Pautasso. - *Published by* ItCan Media Inc. 4800 Dufferin St., Downsview, Ont. M3H 5S9, 1974-
Monthly. Ethnic press, magazine format, Language: English and Italian. Includes advertising. Circulation: 61,921
$6.00 per year.

Mosport competition magazine / *edited by* Chuck Williams. - *Published by* Mosport Park Ltd. 1905 Avenue Rd., Toronto, Ont. M5M 3Z9.
Monthly. Special interest, magazine format, 60 p. Includes advertising.
$5.00 per year.

Motel Association of Alberta. MAA news bulletin / *edited by* G.G. Marshall. - *Published by* Motel Association of Alberta. P.O. Box 5262, Postal Station E, Edmonton, Alta. T5P 4C5, January 1955-
Former title(s): Motor Courts and Resorts Association news (to December 1974)
Monthly. Trade publication, newsletter format, 6 p.
Subscription included in membership fee.

Moteris : lietuviy motery zurnalas = Woman : Lithuanian women's magazine / *edited by* Nora Kulpaviciene. - *Published by* Lithuanian Catholic Women's Association. 1011 College St., Toronto, Ont. M6H 1A8, 1955-
Issued every other month. Ethnic press, magazine format, 29 p. Language: Lithuanian.
$6.00 per year.

Mother tongue *See* Modersmaalet

Mothercraft newsletter - *Published by* Canadian Mothercraft. 450 Maclaren St., Ottawa, Ont. K1R 5K6.
Issued every other month. Association publication, newsletter format, 4 p. Includes book reviews. Circulation: 200
Subscription included in membership fee $6.00 per year.

Motion / *edited by* P.M. Evanchuck, C. Wittgens and J. McLarty. - *Published by* P.M. Evanchuck. P.O. Box 5558, Postal Station A, Toronto Ont. M5W 1N7.
Issued every other month. Special interest, magazine format, 50 p. Language: English (French). Includes book reviews, film reviews, play reviews, advertising. Circulation: 10,000
ISSN 0315-6966 $.75 per issue : $4.00 per year : $5.00 per year, foreign. Controlled circulation.

Motivation and incentive in sport - *Published by* SIRLS. Faculty of Human Kinetics and Leisure Studies. University of Waterloo. Waterloo, Ont. N2L 3G1.
Quarterly. Bibliography, computer printout, $20.00 per year. $100.00 subscription to SIRLS required.

Moto journal / *édité par* Jean-Pierre Belmonte. - *Publié par* Martin Levesque. Cycle Canada. 3rd floor, 81 A Front St. E., Toronto, Ont.(adresse d'abonnement: 666, Ste-Croix, Montréal, Qué. H4L 3Y2) 1972-
Mensuel. Publication spécialisée, journal, 32 p. Comprend critique de livres, critique de films, publicité. Tirage: 12,000
$.60 le numéro : $6.00 par année.
Abonnements payables à l'avance.

Motoneige magazine / *édité par* Gustave Rousseau. - *Publié par* Madeleine Lemire. Les Editions Rousseau. Suite 201, 3009 boul. de la Concorde, Duvernay, Ville de Laval, Qué, 1969-
Intermittent (approximativement 4 éditions par an). Magazine, Comprend publicité. Tirage: 39,994
$.75 le numéro.

Motoneigiste canadien / *édité par* Marc Castro. - *Publié par* Andre C. Gagnon. CRV Publishing Co. Ltd. Suite 221, 3414, ave Park, Montréal, Qué. H2X 2H5.
Semestriel. Magazine, Comprend publicité.

Motor carrier / *edited by* J.B. Tompkins. - *Published by* Westrade Publications Ltd. Suite 202, 1089 West Broadway, Vancouver, B.C., 1940-
Former title(s): Motor transport.
Monthly. Trade publication. Includes advertising. Circulation: 750
$5.00 per year : $8.00 for 2 years : $10.00 for 3 years.

Motor Courts and Resorts Association news (to December 1974) *See* Motel Association of Alberta. MAA news bulletin

Motor in Canada / *edited by* Ralf Neuendorff. - *Published by* Sanford Evans Publishing Ltd. P.O. Box 6900, 1077 St. James St., Winnipeg, Man. R3C 3B1., 1915-
Monthly. Trade publication, business, Includes advertising. Circulation: 13,073
$1.00 per issue : $8.00 per year : $14.00 for 2 years : $18.00 for 3 years.

Motor transport *See* Motor carrier

Motor transport factbook / *edited by* J.B. Tompkins. - *Published by* J.B. Tompkins. WesTrade Publications Ltd. Suite 202, 1089 West Broadway, Vancouver, B.C., 1960-
Annual. Trade publication. Includes advertising. Circulation: 750
$3.00.

Motor truck / *edited by* Barry M. Holmes. - *Published by* Wadham Publications Ltd. Suite 101, 109 Vanderhoof Ave., Toronto, Ont. M4G 2J2, 1934-
Monthly. Trade publication, newspaper format, 32 p.
Indexed in Can. B.P.I.
$.75 per issue : $8.00 per year : $12.00 per year, foreign. Controlled circulation.

Motor vehicle data book / *edited by* C.B. Wagner. - *Published by* Sanford Evans Publishing Ltd. 1077 St. James St., Winnipeg, Man. R3C 3B1.
Annual. Statistics, book format, 500 p.

Motor Vehicle Safety Association. M.V.S.A. news letter / *edited by* J. Heward Winchester. - *Published by* Motor Vehicle Safety Association. 1200 Eglinton Ave. E., Don Mills, Ont. M3C 1J2, 1948-
Irregular (approximately 10 issues per year). Association publication, newsletter format, 2 p.

Motorways miler / *sponsored by* Manitoba Motor League ; *edited by* R.N. Waldon. - *Published by* Howes, Waldon Associates Ltd. 18-399 Berry St., Winnipeg, Man. R3J 1N6, 1958-
Issued every other month. House/company organ, magazine format, 16 p. Circulation: 36,000
$.75 per issue : $3.00 per year : $5.00 per volume : $5.00 per year, foreign.

Motosports / *édité par* Jean Bertrand. - *Publié par* Jean Bertrand. 360, boul. Lévesque, ch. 104 Pont-Viau, Laval, Qué. H7G 4P4(adresse d'abonnement: C.P. 60, Duvernay, Laval, Qué. H7E 4P4) mars 1975-
Mensuel. Publication spécialisée, magazine, 40 p. Tirage: 25,000
ISSN 0319-2229 $.75 le numéro : $6.00 par année.

Motosports : cycling-camping-snowmobiling - *Published by* Jean Bertrand. P.O. Box 60, Duvernay, Laval, Que., 1975-
Monthly. Trade publication, magazine format, Includes advertising.
$.60 per issue : $5.00 per year.

Mount Allison record / *sponsored by* Mount Allison University ; *edited by* Linda (Collins) Ross. - *Published by* Mount Allison Federated Alumni. P.O. Box 1140, Sackville, N.B. E0A 3C0, 1916-
Quarterly. Alumni publication, magazine format, 28-32 p. Includes advertising. Circulation: 7000-11,000
$5.00 per year.

The Mountain breeze / *edited by* Elizabeth Robertson. - *Published by* Edmonton Section. Alpine Club of Canada. 1007-11135 83 Ave., Edmonton, Alta.
Monthly. Association publication, newsletter format, 3 p.
$2.00 per year. Controlled circulation. Special rates offered. Prepayment required.

Mouthful - *Published by* Saskatchewan Division. Canadian Red Cross Society. 2571 Broad St., Regina, Sask. S4P 3B4.
Quarterly. Association publication, newsletter format, 9 p.

Mouthpiece / *edited by* Brent Thrall. - *Published by* Canadian National Institute for the Blind. 1929 Bayview Ave., Toronto, Ont. M4G 3E8, 1970-
Quarterly. Institutional publication (Universities, schools, etc.), newsletter format, 3 p.

Mouvement / *édité par* Michèle Fleury. - *Publié par* Association des professionels de l'activité physique du Québec. 1415 est, rue Jarry, Montréal, Qué., janvier 1966-
Trimestriel. Publication d'association, revue, 80 p. Comprend mises à jour. parution de suppléments. Tirage: 3000
Indexé dans Periodex, RADAR, Can. educ. ind.
$3.00 le numéro : $10.00 par année : $11.00 par année, l'étranger. Tarifs spéciaux disponibles. Abonnements payables à l'avance.

Mouvement - *Publié par* L'Association des professionnels de l'activité physique du Québec. P.O. Box 9875, Québec, Qué., 1966-
Trimestriel. Comprend publicité.
Indexé dans Periodex, RADAR, Can. educ. ind.

Mudcreek magazine / *edited by* J.T. Lovesy-Light and Alex Morton (1975 guest editor). - *Published by* Student's Union. Acadia University. Wolfville, N.S., 1955-
Former title(s): Amethyst; Either/Or.
Annual. Student publication, magazine format, 50-75 p. Circulation: 1000
$1.00.

The Multinational - *Published by* Capital Communications Ltd. Suite 705, 151 Slater St., Ottawa, Ont. K1P 5H3, November 1973-
Quarterly. Trade publication, newsletter format, 8 p. Circulation: 50
$25.00 per year. Controlled circulation.

The Municipal news / *edited by* The Executive Director. - *Published by* Newfoundland and Labrador Federation of Municipalities. P.O. Box 5756, 197 Water St., St. John's, Nfld. A1C 5X3, Winter 1973-
Irregular (approximately 4 issues per year). Association publication, newsletter format, 12 p. Circulation: 2000
Free. Controlled circulation.

Municipal Officers' Association of British Columbia. Proceedings and minutes of the annual conference / *edited by* R.N. Chester. - *Published by* Municipal Officers' Association of British Columbia. 14245 - 56th Ave., Surrey, B.C.
Annual. Association publication, spiral bound, 80-90 p. Circulation: 400
ISSN 3116-4179 Controlled circulation.

Municipal open line / *edited by* Elizabeth A. Vaughan. - *Published by* Union of Nova Scotia Municipialities. Suite 134, Roy Building, 1657 Barrington St., Halifax, N.S. B3J 2A1, March 1974-
Monthly. Association publication, newsletter format, 7 p.
$1.75 per year (Bulk mailing to members $1.00 per issue). Prepayment required.

Municipal report - *Published by* Information Ottawa. P.O. Box 5738, Postal Station F, Ottawa, Ont., October 1973-
Published in French: Le Courrier municipal.
Monthly. Special interest, newsletter format, 4 p.
$20.00 per year.

Municipal world / *edited by* M.J. Smither. - *Published by* Municipal World Ltd. P.O. Box 399, 360 Talbot St., St. Thomas, Ont. N5P 3V3, 1891-
Monthly. Business publication, magazine format, 28 p. Includes book reviews, advertising, volume index.
$1.35 per issue : $13.50 per year.

Muscle mag. International ed / *edited by* Robert Kennedy. - *Published by* Health Culture. Unitone, 270 Rutherford Rd. S., Brampton, Ont., 1974-
Quarterly. Special interest, magazine format, 110 p.
$1.25 per issue : $5.00 per year : $2.00 per issue, foreign. Prepayment required.

Muscular dystrophy reporter / *edited by* Frank J. Murphy. - *Published by* British Columbia Chapter. The Muscular Dystrophy Association of Canada. 2281 Chapman Way, North Vancouver, B.C. V7H 1W2, January 1958-
Quarterly. Association publication, newspaper format, 8 p. Language: English and French. Circulation: 9000
Free.

Muse / *edited by* John Goundrey and others. - *Published by* Council of the Students' Union. Memorial University of Newfoundland. St. John's, Nfld. (Subscription address: P.O. Box 118, Memorial University, St John's, Nfld.) 1936-
Weekly. Student publication, newspaper format, 16 p. Includes book reviews, film reviews, play reviews, record reviews, advertising. Circulation: 5000
$4.00 per year.

Muséogramme *See* Museogramme

Museogramme = Muséogramme / *edited by* Gary J. Sirois. - *Published by* Canadian Museums Association. Room 500, 56 Sparks St., Ottawa, Ont. K1P 5A9 (Subscription address: P.O. Box 1328, Postal Station B, Ottawa, Ont. K1P 5R4) April 1973-
Monthly. Association publication, newsletter format, 4-8 p. Language: English and French. Circulation: 2200
$.50 per issue : $5.00 per year. Available free to members only.

Museum round-up / *edited by* John E. Kyte. - *Published by* British Columbia Museums Association. c/o British Columbia Provincial Museum, Parliament Bldgs., Victoria, B.C. V8W 1A1, January 1961-
Quarterly. Association publication, magazine format, 40 p. Includes book reviews. Circulation: 300
ISSN 0045-3005 $1.50 per issue : $6.00 per year. Prepayment required.

The Music Bulletin (to 1970) *See* British Columbia Registered Music Teachers' Association. Provincial newsletter

Music Calendar (1971-1974) *See* Alberta music calendar

Musical notes / *edited by* John Conrad. - *Published by* Central Ontario Musicians' Association. 125 Union St. E., Waterloo, Ont., 1965-
Irregular (approximately 6 issues per year). Association publication, magazine format, 4-6 p. Includes advertising. Circulation: 1575

Muskeg review / *edited by* Diane Schoemperlen. - *Published by* Arts and Literary Society. Student Union. Lakehead University. Oliver Rd., Thunder Bay, Ont. P7B 5E1, Fall 1972-
Former title(s): Art and literary digest (1972)
Annual. Special interest, magazine format, 50 p.
$1.00 per year.

The Musk-ox / *edited by* William Barr. - *Published by* Institute for Northern Studies. University of Saskatchewan. University of Saskatchewan, Saskatoon, Sask. S7N 0W0.
Issued twice a year. Special interest, magazine format, 75-80 p. Includes book reviews. Back numbers available.
Indexed in North. tit., Arct. bibl.
$2.00 per issue : $3.00 per year (Libraries, companies, institutions, etc. $5.00 per year) : Back issues $3.00 each.

Mutualist / *edited by* D.G. Booth. - *Published by* Mutual Life Assurance Co. of Canada. 227 King St. S., Waterloo, Ont. N2J 4C5, March 1971-
Published in French: Mutualiste.
Irregular (approximately 7 issues per year). House/company organ, magazine format, 36 p. Circulation: 3000
Free. Controlled circulation.

Mutualiste / *édité par* D.G. Booth. - *Publié par* Co. Life Assurance Company of Canada. 227 King St. S., Waterloo, Ont. N2J 4C5, 1971-
Publié en anglais: Mutualist.
Intermittent (approximativement 7 éditions par an). Organe interne/officiel, magazine, 36 p. Envoi gratuit. Tirage contrôlé.

My brother and I / *edited by* Lomer Laplante. - *Published by* Missionary Association of Mary Immaculate. P.O. Box 721, Winnipeg, Man. R3C 2K3., October 1968-
Published in French: Mon frère et moi.
Issued twice a year. Church publication, newsletter format, 24 p. Circulation: 250
ISSN 0316-8913 Free to associates.

My i svit = We and the world / *edited by* Mykola Kolankiwsky. - *Published by* Mykola Kolankiwsky. Niagara Falls Art Gallery & Museum, Queen Elizabeth Way, Niagara Falls, Ont., 1950-
Issued every other month. Ethnic press, magazine format, 64 p. Language: Ukrainian. Includes book reviews, advertising. Circulation: 2000
$1.00 per issue : $6.00 per year. Prepayment required.

N.B. heart beat - *Published by* New Brunswick Division. Canadian Heart Foundation. 28 Germain St., Saint John, N.B. E2L 2E5.
Quarterly. Association publication, newsletter format, 7 p.

NBARN news (May 1970-May 1975) *See* Info

NGEA bulletin - Newfoundland Association of Public Employees *See* Newfoundland Association of Public Employees. Nape news

NSTU newsletter *See* The Teacher

NSTU teacher *See* The Teacher

NWA on record *See* On record

Nachrichten aus Kanada / *edited by* Martin Theurer and Annette Fischer. - *Published by* Montreal Office. Canadian German Chamber of Industry and Commerce Inc. Suite 1110, 2015 Peel St., Montreal, Que. H3A 1T8, 1971-
English edition has title: Trade newsletter.
Monthly. Association publication, 15 p. Language: German.
$25.00 per year : 45 deutschmarks per year, foreign.

Nader Outlook *See* The Lookout

Napao : a Saskatchewan anthopology journal / *edited by* Urve Linnamae. - *Published by* Department of Anthropology and Archaeology. University of Saskatchewan. Saskatoon, Sask. S7N 0W0, April 1968-
Annual. Scholarly publication, journal format, 50-60 p. Includes book reviews. Circulation: 400
Indexed in North. tit.
$2.00 per issue : $4.00 per volume.

Narodniarsky kalendar = National calendar / *edited by* Ted Baker - Pekarovic. - *Published by* Canadian Slovak Benefit Society. P.O. Box 61, Postal Station C, Toronto, Ont., 1957-
Annual. Association publication, yearbook, book format, 120 p. Language: Slovak. Includes advertising. Circulation: 1000
$2.00 per year : $2.50 per year, foreign. Prepayment required.

Nas put = Our way (1962-1972) *See* Hrvatski put

Nase hlasy = Our voices / *edited by* Milo Kominek. - *Published by* Our Voices Publishing and Printing. 106 Howard Park Ave., Toronto, Ont. M6R 1V6.
Weekly. Ethnic press. Language: Czech. Includes advertising. Circulation: 2124
$7.00 per year : $8.00 per year, U.S. : $9.00 per year, foreign.

Nasha derzawa = Our state (1952-1956) *See* Batkivschyna

Nasha meta = Our aim / *sponsored by* Ukrainian Catholic Epurchy of Toronto ; *edited by* Peter Chomyn. - *Published by* Our Aim Publishing Company. 278 Bathurst St., Toronto, Ont. M5T 2S3, 1949-
Weekly. Church publication, newspaper format, 8 p. Language: Ukrainian. Includes book reviews, advertising. Circulation: 3500
$.25 per issue : $10.00 per year. Special rates offered. Prepayment required.

Nation en mouvement *See* Nation on the move

Nation on the move = Nation en mouvement - *Published by* Roads and Transportation Association of Canada. 1765 St. Laurent Blvd., Ottawa, Ont. K1G 3V4, 1956-
Former title(s): Highway finance (1956-1972)
Annual. Association publication. Language: English and French. Circulation: 1200
$3.00 per year. Controlled circulation.

National / *edited by* W.W. Holland. - *Published by* The Canadian Bar Association. Suite 320, 90 Sparks St., Ottawa, Ont. K1P 5B4, 1974-
Former title(s): The Canadian Bar Association. Journal (to December 1973) The Canadian Bar Association. Bulletin (to December 1973)
Monthly. Legal articles, newspaper format, 16 p. Language: English and French. Includes advertising. Circulation: 17,000
Indexed in Crime delinq. abstr.
ISSN 0315-2286 $5.00 per year. No agency subscriptions. Prepayment required.

National Association of Broadcast Employees and Technicians. Canadian Office. NABET news = Association nationale des employés et techniciens en radio diffusion. Nouvelles NABET / *edited by* Jiacomo Papa. - *Published by* National Association of Broadcast Employees and Technicians. Room 735, 1010 St-Catherine St. W., Montreal, Que. H3B 3R3.
Issued every other month. Association publication, newsletter format, 4 p.

National Association of Canadian Credit Unions. NACCU briefs / *edited by* G.M. MacKenzie. - *Published by* National Association of Canadian Credit Unions. P.O. Box 800, Postal Station U, Toronto, Ont. M8Z 5R2, January 1970-
Weekly. Association publication, newsletter format, 1 p. Circulation: 1000
Free.

National bang : Canada's humour and erotica review / *edited by* Bob Berke. - *Published by* Mom Publications Group Ltd. P.O. Box 24, Snowdon Station, Montreal, Que., September 1974-
Monthly. Special interest, newspaper format, 32 p. Includes book reviews, film reviews, play reviews, advertising.
$6.00 for 10 issues : $10.00 for 16 issues.

National calendar *See* Narodniarsky kalendar

National Chinchilla Breeders of Canada. Monthly bulletin / *edited by* John D.W. Clarke. - *Published by* National Chinchilla Breeders of Canada. P.O. Box 640, Carleton Place, Ont., January 1947-
Former title(s): National Chincilla breeder (1947-1950)
Monthly. Association publication, magazine format, 32 p. Language: English and French. Includes advertising. Circulation: 563
$1.00 per issue : $7.00 per year.

National Chincilla breeder (1947-1950) *See* National Chinchilla Breeders of Canada. Monthly bulletin

National Council of Canadian Labour. NCCL briefs / *edited by* Clive Thomas. - *Published by* National Council of Canadian Labour. Suite 10, 53 Queen St., Ottawa, Ont. K1P 5C5, May 1971-
Former title(s): National labour journal (to 1970)
Irregular (approximately 4 issues per year). Association publication, newsletter format, 4 p. Circulation: 4000

National Council of Canadian Labour. NCCL information / *edited by* Clive Thomas. - *Published by* National Council of Canadian Labour. Suite 10, 53 Queen St., Ottawa, Ont. K1P 5C5, May 1971-
Former title(s): National labour journal (to December 1970)
Irregular (approximately 4 issues per year). House/company organ, newsletter format, 4 p. Circulation: 4000

The National Council of Women of Canada. Annual year book - *Published by* The National Council of Women of Canada. Room 20, 270 MacLaren St., Ottawa, Ont. K2P 0M3.
Annual. Association publication, yearbook, 140 p. Circulation: 500
$3.00 per issue.

The National Council of Women of Canada. NCWC newsletter - *Published by* The National Council of Women of Canada. Room 20, 270 MacLaren St., Ottawa, Ont. K2P 0M3.
Quarterly. Association publication.
$1.25 per year.

The National Council of Women of Canada. Yearbook - *Published by* The National Council of Women of Canada. Room 20, 270 MacLaren St., Ottawa, Ont. K2P 0M3.
Quarterly. Association publication, 125 p.
$3.00 per year.

National Farmers Union. Newsletter - *Published by* National Farmers Union. 250-c 2nd Ave. S., Saskatoon, Sask.
Issued every other week. Association publication, newsletter format, 4 p.
Free. Available to members. Controlled circulation.

The National Film Society of Canada film catalogue (to 1955) *See* Index of 16mm & 35mm feature length films available in Canada

The National finances : an analysis of the revenue and expenditures of the Government of Canada - *Published by* Canadian Tax Foundation. 100 University Ave., Toronto, Ont. M5J 1V6, 1954-
Annual. Association publication, 275 p.
ISSN 0077-4529 Subscription included in membership fee $30.00 per year.

National Hockey League. National Hockey League guide / *edited by* Ron Andrews. - *Published by* National Hockey League. 922 Sun Life Building, Montreal, Que. H3B 2W2, 1964/1965-
Annual. House/company organ, 600 p.
ISSN 0316-8174 $3.50.

National Hockey League. Official rule book of the National Hockey League - *Published by* National Hockey League. Information and Statistics Bureau, 920 Sun Life Bldg., Montreal, Que. H3B 2W2.
Annual. Special interest, pamphlet format, 82 p.

National Indian Brotherhood of Canada. Library and Information Services. Weekly acquisitions / *edited by* Brian Deer. - *Published by* National Indian Brotherhood. Suite 1610, 130 Albert St., Ottawa, Ont. K1P 5G4, January 1975-
Weekly. Catalogue, sheet format, 1-2 p.
ISSN 0317-7858 Free (apply to librarian).

National labour journal (to 1970) *See* National Council of Canadian Labour. NCCL briefs

National labour journal (to December 1970) *See* National Council of Canadian Labour. NCCL information

The National list of advertisers / *edited by* Betty Gay. - *Published by* Alan J. Waters. Maclean-Hunter Ltd. 481 University Ave., Toronto, Ont. M5W 1A7, 1939-
Annual. Directory, 500 p. Includes advertising.
$15.00. Prepayment required.

The National music teacher / *edited by* Alf Carlson. - *Published by* The National Professional Music Teachers' Association. 2285 East 61st Ave., Vancouver, B.C. V5P 2K5, January 1974-
Monthly. Association publication, magazine format, 16 p. Includes book reviews, advertising. Circulation: 100
$.50 per issue : $5.00 per year.

National news / *edited by* Peggy Wright. - *Published by* Maritime Professional Photographers' Association (Atlantic Division of the Professional Photographers of Canada Inc.). 6292 Quinpool Rd., Halifax, N.S. B3L 1A5, July 1973-
Former title(s): The Maritime professional (1966-1970) Highlights of the East (1936-1944)
Monthly. Special interest, newsletter format, 1 p. Circulation: 170

National news of the blind / *edited by* Brent Thrall. - *Published by* Canadian National Institute for the Blind. 1929 Bayview Ave., Toronto, Ont. M4G 3E8, 1942-
Issued twice a year. Institutional publication (Universities, schools, etc.), newsletter format, 8 p. Language: English and French.

National newsletter (June 1972-July 1974) *See* Rights and freedoms

National newsletter - YWCA of Canada *See* YW resource

National Northern Development Conference. Proceedings - *Published by* National Northern Development Conference. 10985-124 St., Edmonton, Alta. (Subscription address: P.O. Box 3113, Postal Station A, Edmonton, Alta.) 1958-
Issued every 3 years. Special interest, magazine format, 175 p. Circulation: 2000 Controlled circulation.

National notes *See* Communiqué

National Pensioners and Senior Citizens Federation. National pensioners and senior citizens news / *edited by* J.V. VanWaggoner. - *Published by* The National Pensioners and Senior Citizens Federation. 105-4th St., Toronto, Ont. M8Y 2Y4, January 1969-
Quarterly. Association publication, newsletter format, 23 p. Language: English and French. Circulation: 2100
$.25 per issue : $1.00 per year.

The National police gazette : America's oldest magazine / *sponsored by* Good Earth Corporation ; *edited by* Nat K. Perlow. - *Published by* Joseph Azaria. 1229 Mountain St., Montreal, Que. H3G 1Z2 (Subscription address: 21 Elm St., P.O. Box 704, Rouses Point, N.Y. 12979 and 521 Fifth Ave., N.Y., N.Y. 10017) 1845-
Monthly. General interest, magazine format, 74 p.
$.75 per issue : $7.50 per year : additional charge of $1.50 per year to South America and $2.00 for foreign. Prepayment required.

National reference book / *edited by* Philip B. Gurvich. - *Published by* Canadian Newspaper Services International Ltd. 96 Eglinton Ave. E., Toronto, Ont. M4P 1C5.
Biennial. Special interest. Includes advertising.

National retailer / *edited by* R.E. Walker. - *Published by* Retail Merchants' Association of Canada (Saskatchewan) Inc. 120-3rd Ave. N., Saskatoon, Sask. STK 2H6, 1912-
Former title(s): Western retailer (1912-1962)
Issued every other month. Association publication, magazine format, 20 p. Includes book reviews, advertising. Circulation: 3200
ISSN 0028-002X $.25 per issue : $3.00 per year : $3.50 per year, foreign. Prepayment required.

National Student aid information service - *Published by* National Student Aid Information Services. 1554 Knareswood Dr., Mississauga, Ont. L5H 2M1.
Annual. Book format, supplements issued.

Native Brotherhood of Indians and Metis. Native brotherhood newscall / *edited by* Merve L. Akan. - *Published by* Native Brotherhood of Indians and Metis. P.O. Box 160, Prince Albert, Sask.
Quarterly. Published by and for the inmates of the Saskatchewan penetentiary, Prince Albert, Sask, newsletter format, 37 p.
Free.

The Native people / *edited by* George LaFleur. - *Published by* Alberta Native Communications Society. 11427-Jasper Ave., Edmonton, Alta. T5K 0M6, April 1969-
Weekly. Association publication, tabloid format, 12-16 p. Language: English, Cree and Chipewyan. Includes book reviews, film reviews, play reviews, record reviews, advertising. available in microform. supplements issued. Circulation: 9000
Indexed in Can. ind., North. tit.
$.25 per issue : $10.00 per year. Special rates offered to Alberta natives.

Native Press - *Published by* Indian Brotherhood of N.W.T. P.O. Box 2338, Yellowknife, N.W.T., April 1971-
Former title(s): Brotherhood report (April 1971)
Issued twice a month. Newspaper format, 16-20 p. Includes book reviews, film reviews, advertising. Circulation: 4500
Indexed in North. tit.
$.20 per issue : $6.00 per year. Controlled circulation (3000) to native families in western NWT.

Native voice / *sponsored by* Native Brotherhood of B.C ; *edited by* Diana Recalma. - *Published by* Native Voice Publishing Society. 517 Ford Building, 193 East Hastings, Vancouver, B.C., 1946-
Monthly. Association publication, newspaper format, 8 p. Circulation: 2500
$5.00 per year.

Natural fauna / *edited by* David MacWilliam. - *Published by* David MacWilliam. 3440 Upper Terrace, Victoria, B.C. V8R 6E7, Fall 1974-
Annual. Special interest, magazine format, 65 p.
ISSN 0315-9051 $1.00.

Le Naturaliste / *parrainé par* Les Cercles des jeunes naturalistes ; *édité par* Dollard Senecal. - *Publié par* Les Editions des jeunes naturalistes. 4101 est, rue Sherbrooke, Montréal, Qué. H1X 2B2, 1963-
Mensuel (octobre-mai). Publication ecclésiastique, magazine, 32 p. Comprend index de volumes. Tirage: 9000
Indexé dans Periodex, RADAR.
ISSN 0028-078X $.75 le numéro : $5.00 par année : $7.00 par année, l'étranger.

Le Naturaliste canadien : revue d'écologie et de systématique / *parrainé par* Université Laval ; *édité par* G. Wilfrid Corrivault. - *Publié par* Les Presses de l'Université Laval. C.P. 2447, Québec, Qué. G1K 7R4, 1868-
Bimestriel. Edition savante, journal, 180 p. Langue(s): français et anglais ; sommaires: français et anglais. Comprend index cumulatif.
Tirage: 1400
Indexé dans Periodex, RADAR, I.B.Z., Arct. bibl.
ISSN 0028-798X $4.00 le numéro : $12.00 (Collectif $24.00).

Nature Canada / *edited by* Theodore Mosquin. - *Published by* Canadian Nature Federation. 46 Elgin St., Ottawa, Ont. K1P 5K6., January 1972-
Former title(s): Canadian Audubon; Canadian nature.
Quarterly. Association publication, magazine format, 52 p. Includes book reviews, advertising. available in microform.
Circulation: 22,756
Indexed in Can. ind., North. tit.
$2.50 per issue : $10.00 per year : $10.00 per year, foreign. Subscription included in membership fee ($8.00). Prepayment required.

Nature is fun / *edited by* Hazel Bird. - *Published by* Willow Beach Field Naturalists. c/o Mrs. Hazel Bird, Harwood, Ont. K0K 2H0, November 1971-
Monthly. Association publication, mimeographed, 9 p. Circulation: 125
Free.

Nebraska ansiedler (1877-1880) *See* Mennonitische Rundschau

Nebula / *edited by* Ken Stange. - *Published by* Nebula. 509 Lakeshore Dr., North Bay, Ont., 1975-
Issued twice a year. Special interest, magazine format, 57 p. Includes advertising.
ISSN 0317-2104 $1.25 per issue : $5.00 for 2 years.

Nepriklausoma Lietuva = Independent Lithuania / *sponsored by* Lithuanian League of Canada = Remejy Klubas ; *edited by* Frank P. Pansestaites. - *Published by* Independent Lithuania Printing Company Ltd. 7722 George St., La Salle, Que., 1941-
Weekly. Ethnic press, newspaper format, 8 p. Language: Lithuanian.
$.25 per issue : $9.50 per year : $10.00 per year, foreign.

New Alberta Liberal / *edited by* Len Stahl. - *Published by* The Liberal Party in Alberta. 912 Macleod Bldg., Edmonton, Alta., April 1972-
Quarterly. Political press, newspaper format, 4 p. Includes advertising. supplements issued.
Circulation: 2500

New breed / *edited by* Clifford Bunnie. - *Published by* Metis Society of Saskatchewan. Suite 4, 1846 Scarth St., Regina, Sask. S4P 2G3, 1970-
Monthly. Association publication, magazine format, 20 p.
$.50 per issue : $6.00 per year.

New Brunswick Public Employees Association. Newsletter / *edited by* Harold L. Lockhart. - *Published by* The New Brunswick Employees Association. P.O. Box 95, Fredericton, N.B. E3B 4Y2, November 1970-
Former title(s): Public employees journal (July 1969-September 1971) Civil service digest (April 1960-December 1968)
Irregular (approximately 5 issues per year). Association publication, newsletter format, 4 p.
Circulation: 5000
Free.

New Canada / *sponsored by* Canadian Liberation Movement. - *Published by* New Canada Publications. P.O. Box 41, Postal Station E, Toronto, Ont. (Subscription address: P.O. Box 6088, Postal Station A, Toronto, Ont)
Monthly. Political press, newspaper format, 16 p. Includes book reviews, play reviews. available in microform.
$.25 per issue : $3.00 per year : $1.50 per volume.

The New Canadian / *edited by* Ken Mori (Japanese section), K. Tsumura (English section). - *Published by* T. Umezuki. 479 Queen St. W., Toronto, Ont. M5V 2A9, 1939-
Issued twice a week. Ethnic press, newspaper format, 8 p. Language: Japanese and English.
$.20 per issue : $14.00 per year : $15.00 per year, foreign.

New Canadian film / *edited by* Jean-Pierre Bastien. - *Published by* La Cinématique québécoise. 360 McGill St., Montreal, Que. H2Y 2E9, March 1968-
Published in French: Nouveau cinema canadien.
Issued 5 times a year. Special interest, magazine format, 32 p. available in microform.
Circulation: 2000
$.50 per issue : $2.50 per volume : $5.00 for 2 years. Special rates offered. Prepayment required.

The New Captain George's whizzbang : the Canadian magazine of popular culture / *sponsored by* Memory Lane Publications ; *edited by* Peter Harris. - *Published by* Captain George Henderson. 594 Markham St., Toronto, Ont., December 1968-
Quarterly. Special interest, magazine format, 32 p. Includes book reviews, film reviews. Circulation: 2000
$.60 per issue : $5.00 for 10 issues. Prepayment required.

New days *See* Nowi dni

The New Democrat / *edited by* Terry O'Connor. - *Published by* New Democratic Party of Ontario. 3 Church St., Toronto, Ont. M5E 1M2, 1961-
Issued every other month. Political press, newspaper format, 12 p. Language: English (French). Includes advertising. Circulation: 20,000
$1.25 per year.

New equipment news / *edited by* D.H. Graham. - *Published by* C.F. Broad. Canadian Engineering Publications Ltd. 46 St. Clair Ave. E., Toronto, Ont. M4T 1N2, 1940-
Monthly. Trade publication, tabloid size magazine, 52 p. Includes advertising.
$12.00 per year : $20.00 per year, foreign. Controlled circulation.

The New freeman / *sponsored by* Roman Catholic Bishop of Saint John Diocese, New Brunswick ; *edited by* Robert G. Merzetti. - *Published by* Arthur J. Gilbert. New Freeman Publishing Co. Ltd. c/o Chancery Office, Waterloo St., Saint John, N.B. (Subscription address: P.O. Box 609, Saint John, N.B) January 1900-
Weekly. Special interest, tabloid format, 16 p. Includes advertising. Circulation: 6039
$.20 per issue : $8.00 per year : $9.00 per year, foreign. Prepayment required.

New generation *See* Nor serount

New homeland *See* Nouy domov

New homes and apartments guide / *edited by* B.A. Komorowski. - *Published by* Toronto Home Builders Association. 5218 Yonge St., Willowdale, Ont. M2N 5P6.
Issued twice a year. Special interest, magazine format, 68 p. Includes advertising. Circulation: 10,000
$.50 per issue.

New horizon / *edited by* Christa Freiler. - *Published by* Alberta Association for the Mentally Retarded. 12225-105 Ave., Edmonton, Alta. T5N 0Y3.
Quarterly. Association publication, magazine format, 32 p. Circulation: 1200
$1.00 per year : $2.00 per year, foreign.

New Korea times / *edited by* C.L. Chun. - *Published by* C.L. Chun. P. O. Box 261, Postal Station O, Toronto Ont., 1973-
Weekly. Ethnic press. Language: Korean. Includes advertising.
$7.00 per year.

The New life / *edited by* Rev. and Mrs. Frank Uhlir. - *Published by* Temple Pastures Mission. R.R. 1, Pointe Gatineau, Que. J8T 4Y6, September 1953-
Issued every other month. Church publication, magazine format, 16 p. Circulation: 600
Free. Supported by voluntary contributions.

New literature and ideology - *Published by* Norman Bethune Institute. P.O. Box 727, Adelaide Station, Toronto, Ont., 1969-
Former title(s): Literature and ideology (1969-1974)
Quarterly. Magazine format, 100 p.
$2.25 per issue : $5.00 per year.

New mitre : literary magazine of Bishop's University / *edited by* Herbert Bailey. - *Published by* Students' Executive Council. Bishop's University. P.O. Box 1098, Bishop's University, Lennoxville, Que. J1M 1Z7, 1893-
Former title(s): Mitre (1893-1970)
Annual. Student publication, magazine format, 60-80 p. Includes book reviews, play reviews, advertising.
ISSN 0315-7458 $2.00.

The New nation / *sponsored by* Indian and Metis Friendship Centre ; *edited by* Jack McDonald. - *Published by* New Nation. 17-388 Donald St., Winnipeg, Man. (Subscription address: 590 Main St., Winnipeg, Man. R3B 1C9)
Monthly. "The newspaper of the native people", newspaper format, 12 p.
$3.00 per year.

The New outlook (June 1925 - April 1939) *See* Observer

New pathway annual - *Published by* New Pathway Publishers Ltd. P.O. Box 230, Postal Station M, Toronto, Ont. M6S 4T3.
Annual. Ethnic press. Language: Ukrainian. Includes advertising.
$1.50 per year.

New republic / *edited by* Robert Chow. - *Published by* P. Mor. Chinese Express Ltd. 117A Elizabeth St., Toronto, Ont. M5G 1P8, 1971-
Daily. Ethnic press. Language: Chinese. Includes advertising.

The New review : a journal of East-European history (1965-1974) *See* New review of East-European history

New review of East-European history / *edited by* M. Mladenovic, O.S. Pidhainy and N. Lypowecky. - *Published by* Alexandra Pidhainy. P.O. Box 31, Postal Station E, Toronto, Ont. M6H 4E1, 1961-
Former title(s): The New review : a journal of East-European history (1965-1974)
Quarterly. Special interest, magazine format, 64 p. Includes book reviews, advertising. Circulation: 1000
Indexed in Hist. abstr.; Amer. hist. and life.
$2.50 per issue : $10.00 per year.

New season / *edited by* The Extension Librarian. - *Published by* Extension Services Dept. Saint John Regional Library. 20 Hazen Ave., Saint John, N.B. E2L 3G8, September 1973-
Irregular (approximately 3-4 issues per year). Institutional publication (Universities, schools, etc.), newsletter format, 6 p. Includes book reviews, record reviews.
Free.

New Thursday / *edited by* Gary Botting. - *Published by* Red Deer College Press. P.O. Box 5005, Red Deer, Alta. T4N 5H5, 1969-
Former title(s): Thursday (1969-1973)
Annual. Institutional publication (Universities, schools, etc.), magazine format, 64 p. Includes book reviews. Circulation: 500
$2.00 per year. Special rates offered.

New trail / *edited by* Jeanette Rothrock. - *Published by* Publications Office. The University of Alberta. 326 Assiniboia Hall, University of Alberta, Edmonton, Alta. T6G 2E1, 1942-
Issued every other month. Institutional publication (Universities, schools, etc.), magazine format, 8 p. Circulation: 50,000
ISSN 0028-6907 Free.

The Newfoundland amateur / *edited by* John Tessier. - *Published by* Society of Newfoundland Radio Amateurs Inc. P.O. Box 1226, St. John's, Nfld. A1C 5M9, January 1960-
Former title(s): SONRA news (January 1960-April 1968)
Monthly. Association publication, newsletter format, 4 p. Includes advertising. Circulation: 400
ISSN 0048-0177 $1.00 per year. Prepayment required.

Newfoundland and Labrador business directory and buyers guide / *edited by* Eric-A. MacEwen. - *Published by* Maritime Directories Inc. P.O. Box 2039, St. John's Nfld.
Annual. Trade publication, magazine format, 300 p. Includes advertising, updating service. Circulation: 5000
$5.00. Prepayment required.

Newfoundland and Labrador Provincial Libraries. Newsletter / *edited by* Joan M. Wheeler. - *Published by* Newfoundland Public Libraries Board. Allandale Road, St. John's, Nfld., June 1975-
Former title(s): Newsletter - Newfoundland and Labrador Regional Libraries (to 1972)
Quarterly. Institutional publication (Universities, schools, etc.), newsletter format, 20 p.
Free.

Newfoundland and Labrador Women's Institutes. Monthly newsletter - *Published by* Newfoundland and Labrador Women's Institutes. P.O. Box 4056, St. John's Nfld. A1C 5Y2.
Issued every other month. Association publication, 15 p.

Newfoundland Association of Public Employees. Nape news / *edited by* Peter Fenwick. - *Published by* Newfoundland Association of Public Employees. P.O. Box 1085, 249 Duckworth St., St. John's, Nfld. A1C 5M5.
Former title(s): NGEA bulletin - Newfoundland Association of Public Employees.
Issued every other month. Association publication, newspaper format, 12-16 p. Circulation: 10,000
Free.

Newfoundland medical directory - *Published by* Newfoundland Medical Board. P.O. Box 5279, 247 Queen's Rd., St John's, Nfld.
Annual. Directory.

Newfoundland Medicial Association. Newsletter / *edited by* John R. Martin. - *Published by* Newfoundland Medical Association. O'Mara-Martin Building, St. John's, Nfld. A1C 2E4.
Issued every other month. Association publication, newsletter format, 24 p. Includes advertising, updating service. Circulation: 650
$6.00 per year.

Newfoundland Status of Women Council. Newsletter - *Published by* Newfoundland Status of Women Council. P.O. Box 6072, St. John's, Nfld. A1C 5X8, 1974-
Association publication.
ISSN 0315-2324

Newfoundland surveyor / *edited by* A. Reid. - *Published by* Association of Newfoundland Land Surveyors. P.O. Box 4155, St. John's, Nfld. A1C 5Z7.
Irregular (approximately 2-4 issues per year). Association publication, magazine format, 20-50 p. Includes advertising.
Free. Controlled circulation.

Newfoundland Teachers' Association. N.T.A. journal / *edited by* Heber E. Walters. - *Published by* Newfoundland Teachers' Association. 3 Kenmount Rd., St. John's, Nfld. A1B 1W1.
Issued twice a year. Association publication. Includes advertising.
$3.00 per year.

Newfoundland Teacher's Association. School Library/Audio Visual Council. Newsletter - *Published by* Newfoundland Teachers' Association. 3 Kenmount Rd., St. John's Nfld., Spring 1974-
Association publication.
ISSN 0315-7830

The News / *edited by* Don Canning. - *Published by* Corporate Communications. Domtar Limited. P.O. Box 7210, Montreal, H3C 3M1, September 1966-
Former title(s): Domtar news.
Issued every other month. House/company organ, newspaper format, 8 p. Circulation: 20,000
Free to a selected 300.

NewsNewsNews / *edited by* Harvey Linnen. - *Published by* Saskatchewan Government Employees' Association. 1440 Broadway Ave., Regina, Sask. S4P 1E2 (Subscription address: Free to all members ($1.00 per year for retired members) : $1.50 for non-members) 1974-
Issued twice a month. Association publication, newsletter format, 2 p. Circulation: 15,500
ISSN 0316-8433 Subscription includes The Dome.

News and reviews / *edited by* Brian Miller. - *Published by* Nova Scotia Credit Union League. 6074 Lady Hammond Rd., Halifax, N.S. (Subscription address: P.O. Box 1674, Halifax, N.S. B3J 3A6) December 1957-
Monthly. Association publication, newsletter format, 8 p. Includes advertising. Circulation: 2500
Controlled circulation.

News and views (September 1962-June 1975) *See* The Reporter

News at B.F. Goodrich (1934-1955) *See* B.F. Goodrich Canada Ltd. B.F. Goodrich Canada world

News brief (1966-1970) *See* Bureau of Municipial Research. BMR comment

News from the Canadian North / *edited by* Pat Potts. - *Published by* Institute for Northern Studies. University of Saskatchewan, Saskatoon, Sask. S7N 0W0, 1972-
Former title(s): News from the north ISSN 0380-5441 (1971)
Monthly. Institutional publication (Universities, schools, etc.), magazine format, 55 p. Includes volume index.
ISSN 0380-545X $25.00 per year.

News from the north ISSN 0380-5441 (1971) *See* News from the Canadian North

News letter - Community Planning Association of Canada. Nova Scotia Division *See* Plans : planning information exchange for N.S.

News magazine - Regina Chamber of Commerce *See* Regina

News media guide - *Published by* University of Waterloo. Waterloo, Ont., 1972/73-
Former title(s): OQAA news media guide (1970-1972)
Association publication.

News notes - Edmonton Public Library *See* Connection

News of Québec / *edited by* Arnold J. Reynolds. - *Published by* Christian Publications Registered. 230 Lupien, Cap de la Madeleine, Que., 1944-
Quarterly. "Reports on religious events in the province of Quebec", magazine format, 32 p. Circulation: 14,000

Newscap / *edited by* Joan Anderson. - *Published by* The Ontario Association of Education Administrative Officials. Suite N-1201, 252 Bloor St. W., Toronto, Ont. M5S 1V5, 1969-
Irregular (approximately 5 issues per year). Association publication, newsletter format, 6 p. Circulation: 700
Free.

News-facts (1950-1954) *See* Northern neighbours : the magazine of socialism in action

Newsletter - Alberta Teachers' Association. Industrial Arts and Vocational Education Council *See* Alberta Teachers' Association. Industrial Arts and Vocational Education Council. IAVEC communicator

Newsletter - Association of Canadian Map Libraries *See* Association of Canadian Map Libraries. Bulletin

Newsletter - B.C. Association of Teachers of Classics *See* Vexillum

Newsletter - British Columbia Counsellor's Association (October 1960-1971) *See* British Columbia School Counsellors' Association. Newsletter

Newsletter - British Columbia School Librarian's Association (1963-1966) *See* The Bookmark

Newsletter - Canadian Association of Departments of Extension and Summer Schools *See* Canadian Association for University Continuing Education. Bulletin

Newsletter - Canadian Electrical Association (1930-1974) *See* Canadian Electrical Association. Bulletin

Newsletter - Canadian Society of Zoologists ISSN 0319-6666 (1969-1973) *See* Canadian Society of Zoologists. Bulletin

Newsletter - Central Ontario Drama League *See* Act news

Newsletter - Early Childhood Education Council *See* Trail blazers

Newsletter - Newfoundland and Labrador Regional Libraries (to 1972) *See* Newfoundland and Labrador Provincial Libraries. Newsletter

The Newsletter - Nova Scotia Society of Medical Radiological Technicians *See* Scotian rays

Newsletter - Ontario Folkdance Association *See* Ontario folkdancer : newsletter

Newsletter - Professional Corporation of Physicians of Quebec = Bulletin de nouvelles - Corporation professionnelle des médecins du Québec (July 1961-July 1975) *See* Professional Corporation of Physicians of Quebec. Bulletin

Newsletter - Saskatchewan Association for the Mentally Retarded *See* Dialogue

Newsletter - Saskatchewan Writer's Guild (1966-1973) *See* Freelance

Newsletter - Society for Biblical Literature. Section for Ugaritic Studies *See* Newsletter for ugaritic studies

Newsletter - The Commerce Teacher's Association (October 1962-May 1970) *See* British Columbia Business Educators' Association. Newsletter

Newsletter - The Province of Quebec Chamber of Commerce (October 1965 - December 1973) *See* Action : chamber of commerce

Newsletter - Vancouver Museums and Planetarium Association *See* SNAUQ

A Newsletter called Fred / *edited by* Tony Meyie. - *Published by* The Ontario Film Association, Inc. P.O. Box 521, Barrie, Ont., 1972-
Former title(s): OFA bulletin (1948-1970) The Reel thing (1971-1972) Short title: Fred. Monthly September through June. Association publication, newsletter format, 6 p. Includes book reviews, film reviews, advertising. ISSN 0315-6923 Subscription included in membership fee $10.00. Controlled circulation.

Newsletter for ugaritic studies / *sponsored by* Canadian Society of Biblical Studies ; *edited by* P.C. Craigie. - *Published by* Programme in Religious Studies. The University of Calgary, Calgary, Alberta, T2N 1N4, April 1972-
Former title(s): Newsletter - Society for Biblical Literature. Section for Ugaritic Studies.
Irregular (approximately 3 issues per year). Association publication, newsletter format, 8 p. Includes book reviews. Back sets available for $3.00. Circulation: 200
Free.

Newsletter nutrition = Bulletin de nouvelles (1967-1972) *See* Nutrition forum

Newsletter of the Archaeological Society of British Columbia (November 1968 - October 1970) *See* The Midden

Newsletter of the Model A Ford Club of Pembroke *See* The Flying quail

Newslitter / *sponsored by* Outdoors Unlittered (B.C.) Incorp. ; *edited by* Marilyn Corbin. - *Published by* Outdoors Unlittered (Alberta). 1 - 9930 - 106th St., Edmonton, Alta., December 1970-
Former title(s): Litter letter (March 1970-April 1970)
Monthly except July and August. Association publication, newsletter format, 4 p. Includes book reviews, film reviews. Circulation: 7800
$3.00 per year. Available free to schools and non-profit organizations.

Newspacket - *Published by* Stephen Leacock Associates. P.O. Box 854, Orillia, Ont., 1970-
Annual. Association publication, newsletter format, 4 p. Circulation: 1500
Free to members of the Association.

Newsprint data - *Published by* Canadian Pulp and Paper Association. 2300 Sun Life Building, Montreal, Que. H3B 2X9, 0068-9491-
Annual. Association publication, statistics, magazine format, 16 p.
Free.

Next year country : Saskachewan's only newsmagazine / *sponsored by* Saskatchewan Waffle ; *edited by* Patricia Gallagher. - *Published by* Next Year Country. P.O. Box 3446, Regina, Sask., October 1972-
Issued every other month. General interest, magazine format, 32-40 p. Includes book reviews, film reviews, play reviews, record reviews, advertising. available in microform. Circulation: 5000
ISSN 1315-758X $.75 per issue : $4.00 per year (Institutions $6.00) : $5.00 per volume (Institutions $10.00).

Nexus *See* Medical education news

Niagara news / *sponsored by* Niagara College. Journalism Department. - *Published by* A. Jelbert. Niagara College of Applied Arts. Woodlawn Rd., Welland, Ont., December 1971-
Issued every other week during the school year. Student publication, newspaper format, 8 p. Includes play reviews. Circulation: 2000
Free.

Nineteenth century theatre research / *edited by* L.W. Conolly and J.P. Wearing. - *Published by* L.W. Conolly. J.P. Wearing. Department of English, University of Alberta, Edmonton, Alta. T6G 2E1, 1973-
Issued twice a year. Scholarly publication, magazine format, 62 p. Includes book reviews, advertising. Circulation: 350
ISSN 0316-5329 $6.50 per year.

Nor serount = New generation / *edited by* Stephen Tchilingirian. - *Published by* Holy Trinity Armenian Church. 14 Woodlawn Ave. W., Toronto, Ont. M4I 1G7, February 1955-
Monthly. Church publication, magazine format, 40 p. Language: Englisn and Armenian. Includes advertising. Circulation: 600
$.50 per issue : $3.00 per year. Prepayment required.

Norlac news (1934-1968) *See* Northern news

Norman Mackenzie Art Gallery. The NMAG - *Published by* Norman Mackenzie Art Gallery. University of Saskatchewan, Regina Campus, Regina, Sask. S4S 0A2, September 1974-
Issued every other month. Institutional publication (Universities, schools, etc.), newspaper format,
Free. Distributed through a mailing list.

Norrona = The Norseman / *edited by* Gunnar Warolin. - *Published by* Norrona Publishing Company. 8594 Sunbury Place, Delta, B.C. V4C 3Y7, 1910-
Issued twice a month. Ethnic press, tabloid format, 12 p. Language: Norwegian. Includes advertising.
$.25 per issue : $5.00 per year : $7.00 per year, foreign. Controlled circulation. Prepayment required.

The North American Scotsman / *edited by* A.J. MacLeod. - *Published by* A.J. MacLeod & G.S. Tuck. 172 Martindale Rd., St. Catherines, Ont. (Subscription address: 62 Centre St., St. Thomas, Ont.) May 1969-
Irregular (up to 12 issues per year). Ethnic press, magazine format, 36 p. Language: English and Gaelic. Includes book reviews, record reviews. Circulation: 2000
$.75 per issue : $5.00 per year : $6.00 per year, foreign. Prepayment required.

North and South Saanich Agricultural Society. Fall exhibition. Prize list - *Published by* North and South Saanich Agricultural Society. C/o Mrs. E. Hutt, 7013 East Saanich Road, Saanichton, B.C.
Annual. Fall fair prize list, 140 p.

North country (December 1973-July 1974) *See* Ontario report

North wind / *edited by* S. Walsh. - *Published by* The North Wind (Society for Creative Anachronism in B.C.). P.O. Box 65583, Vancouver, B.C. V5N 5K5, 1975-
Monthly. Special interest, magazine format, 8 to 24 p. Language: English (French). Includes book reviews, film reviews. supplements issued.
ISSN 0316-6953 $4.00 per year.

North Winnipeg Credit Union Limited. Bulletin *See* Kredytova Kooperatyva Pivnichnoho Vinnipegu. Biuleten

Northern air / *edited by* Karen Labuik. - *Published by* North Central Saskatchewan Regional Library. 145-12 St. E., Prince Albert, Sask., February 1969-
Quarterly. House/company organ, newsletter format, 35 p. Includes book reviews. Circulation: 200
Free.

Northern journey / *edited by* Craig Campbell, Valerie Kent, David McDonald and Fraser Sutherland. - *Published by* Northern Journey Press. P.O. Box 4073, Postal Station E, Ottawa, Ont. K1S 5B1, 1970-
Issued twice a year. Special interest, magazine format, 120 p. Includes book reviews. Circulation: 800
Indexed in Can. essay and lit. ind.
ISSN 0315-3630 $1.95 per issue : $3.75 per year.

The Northern light - *Published by* Newfoundland Tuberculosis & Respiratory Disease Association Inc. P.O. Box 5250, St. John's, Nfld. A1C 5W1, April 1949-
Issued twice a year. Association publication, magazine format, 25-30 p. Circulation: 2100
Free.

Northern light (1927-1933) *See* Northern news

Northern light / *edited by* George Amabile and Mhari Mackintosh (assistant editor). - *Published by* University of Manitoba Press. 605 Fletcher Argue Bldg., University of Manitoba, Winnipeg, Man. R3T 2N2, 1968-
Former title(s): The Far point (1968-1973)
Issued twice a year. Magazine format, 72 p. Includes book reviews, advertising. Circulation: 1000
Indexed in Can. essay and lit. ind., M.L.A. int. bib.
$1.50 per issue : $3.25 per year. Prepayment required.

Northern lights - *Published by* Northern Lights. Berens River, Man. R0B 0A0.
Monthly. General interest, mimeographed sheets, 10 p.
Indexed in North. tit.
$1.00 per year (Non local subscribers $1.75).

Northern lights: almanac *See* Pivnichne siayvo

The Northern miner / *edited by* J.W. Carrington. - *Published by* Northern Miner Press Ltd. 77 River St., Toronto, Ont. M5A 3P2, 1915-
Weekly. Special interest, newspaper format, 28 p. Includes advertising. available in microform. Circulation: 25,000
Indexed in Can. B.P.I., North. tit.
$.75 per issue : $15.00 per year.

Northern neighbours : the magazine of socialism in action / *edited by* Herbert Dyson Carter. - *Published by* Northern Neighbours Publishing Association. Box 1000, Gravenhurst, Ont. P0C 1G0, January 1950-
Former title(s): News-facts (1950-1954)
Monthly. "Developments in all fields in the U.S.S.R.", magazine format, 28 p. Includes book reviews, advertising. available in microform. supplements issued. Circulation: 12,500
ISSN 0029-3199 $.50 per issue : $3.00 per year. Prepayment required.

Northern news / *edited by* Mrs. Hilary Blair. - *Published by* The Northern Life Assurance Company of Canada. 380 Wellington St., London, Ont., January 1969-
Former title(s): Norlac news (1934-1968) Northern light (1927-1933)
Quarterly. House/company organ, newsletter format, 12 p.
Free.

Northern Ontario Art Association. Bulletin / *edited by* Pauline Melhorn. - *Published by* Northern Ontario Art Association. Apt. 2, 3 Government Rd. E., Kirkland Lake, Ont., 1953-
Irregular (approximately 3 issues per year). Association publication, newsletter format, 15-20 p.
Free. Controlled circulation.

Northern prospectives / *edited by* Edie Van Alstine. - *Published by* Canadian Arctic Resources Committee. Rm. 20, 46 Elgin St., Ottawa, Ont. K1P 5H3, January 1973-
Monthly. Association publication, newsletter format, 8 p. Circulation: 3500
Free.

Northern reporter - *Published by* Capital Communications Ltd. Suite 705, 151 Slater St., Ottawa, Ont. K1P 5H3, November 1973-
Quarterly. Special interest, newsletter format, 8 p. Circulation: 50
$25.00 per year. Controlled circulation.

Northern titles : KWIC index / *edited by* Mrs G.A. Cooke. - *Published by* Boreal Institute for Northern Studies. The University of Alberta, Edmonton, Alta. T6G 2E9, 1972-
Monthly with an annual cumulation. Index, computer print out format, Journal codes included with subscription. Circulation: 50
$35.00 per year (including the annual cummulation) : $30.00 for annual cumulation only. By exchange or subscription.

The Northian / *edited by* Tim Jones. - *Published by* Society for Indian and Northern Education. University of Saskatchewan. Saskatoon, Sask. S7N 0W0, 1964-
Quarterly. Journal format, 42 p. Includes book reviews. available in microform. Circulation: 900
Indexed in Can. educ. ind., Curr. ind. j. educ., North. tit.
ISSN 0029-3253 $5.00 per year.

Northpoint / *edited by* Stephen C. Geneja. - *Published by* Association of Certified Survey Technicians & Technologist of Ontario. 6070 Yonge St., Willowdale, Ont., July 1963-
Quarterly. Association publication, magazine format, 34 p. Circulation: 1250
$2.00 per issue : $8.00 per year. Controlled circulation.

Northwest Canada echoes / *edited by* Q.W. Riegel. - *Published by* A.W. Riegel. Northwest Canada Conference Evangelical Church. 2801-13 Ave. S.E., Medecine Hat, Alta.
Monthly. Church publication, magazine format, 16 p. Includes book reviews. Circulation: 900
$1.50 per year.

Northwest sportsman / *edited by* Jim Railton. - *Published by* Railton Publications Ltd. 125 Talisman Ave., Vancouver, B.C. V5Y 2L6, 1945-
Issued every other month. Special interest, magazine format, 40 p. Includes advertising. Circulation: 10,000
$.60 per issue : $3.00 per year : $3.50 per year, foreign.

Northwest Territories community data book *See* Canada North almanac

Northwest Territories Teachers Association. NWTTA members' handbook / *edited by* W.C. Nettleton. - *Published by* Northwest Territories Teachers' Association. P.O. Box 2340, Yellowknife, N.W.T. X0E 1H0, 1972-
Annual. Association publication, magazine format, 35 p.
$2.00 per year.

Northwest Territories Teachers' Association. NWTTA newsletter / *edited by* R. Armstrong. - *Published by* Northwest Territories Teachers' Association. P.O. Box 2340, Yellowknife, N.W.T. X0E 1H0, 1953-
Issued every other month. Association publication, newspaper format, 17 p.
$2.00 per year.

Northwest travel guide. Alaska - Yukon highway / *edited by* J.H. Bell. - *Published by* Travelina Ltd. Suite 101, 1265 Beach Ave., Vancouver, B.C.
Annual. Special interest, magazine format, Includes advertising.

Northwestern Alberta gymkhana / *edited by* Marilyn Bossert. - *Published by* Northwestern Alberta Gymkhana Association. P.O. Box 402, Edson, Alta. T0E 0P0, 1967-
Issued every other month. Association publication, newsletter format, 10 p. Circulation: 80
$.35 per issue : $2.00 per year.

The Nor'west farmer (1882-1936; absorbed in 1936) *See* Country guide : the farm magazine

Nos écoles / *édité par* Le Service de l'information. - *Publié par* Conseil des écoles séparées catholiques d'Ottawa. 140, rue Cumberland, Ottawa, Ont. K1N 7G9, juin 1974-
Intermittent (approximativement 3 éditions par an). Publication spécialisée, bulletin, 4 p.
Envoi gratuit.

Nos jeunes - *Publié par* Service de l'information. Conseil des écoles séparées catholiques d'Ottawa. 140, rue Cumberland, Ottawa, Ont. K1N 7G9, mai 1974-
Publié en anglais: Our youth.
Intermittent (approximativement 13 éditions par an). Organe interne/officiel, bulletin, 2 p.
ISSN 0315-1974 Envoi gratuit.

Notes, news and comments - *Published by* Canadian Mathematical Congress. Suite 15, 3421 Drummond St., Montreal, Que., March 1969-
Monthly. Association publication, newsletter format, 13 p. Language: English and French. Circulation: 1100
ISSN 0045-5164 $5.00 per year. Controlled circulation. Prepayment required.

Notes on agriculture / *sponsored by* Ontario Agricultural College ; *edited by* W.S. Young. - *Published by* University of Guelph. 157 Johnston Hall, University of Guelph, Guelph, Ont. N1G 2W1, February 1965-
Former title(s): Crop notes (1960-1968)
O.A.C. farmers week (1969)
Quarterly. Institutional publication, magazine format, 18 p. Circulation: 6000
Free. Controlled circulation.

Notes on unions - *Published by* Canadian Labour Congress. 2841 Riverside Dr., Ottawa, Ont. K1V 8N4.
Published in French: Cahiers syndicaux.
Irregular. Association publication, newsletter format, 2 p. Language: English and French.
Free.

Notre Dame University of Nelson. NDU news / *edited by* Stephen M. Bowell. - *Published by* Notre Dame University of Nelson. 820 Tenth St., Nelson, B.C. V1L 3C7, October 1973-
Issued twice a month except monthly during May, June, July and August. Institutional publication (Universities, schools, etc.), newsletter format, 12 p.
Free.

Notre langue, notre culture - *Publié par* Le Conseil français. Alberta Teachers' Association. 11010-142 St., Edmonton, Alta. T5N 2R1, 1970-
Paraît tous les 15 jours. Publication d'association.
Indexé dans Can. educ. ind.

Notre ministère du royaume - *Publié par* Canadian Branch. Watch Tower Bible and Tract Society. 150, ave Bridgeland, Toronto, Ont. M6A 1Z5, janvier 1956-
Ancien titre: Informateur (janvier 1951-août 1956)
Mensuel. Publication ecclésiastique, bulletin, 4 p. Tirage: 7995
Tirage contrôlé.

Notre-Dame du Cap (1973) *Voir* Souvenir du bon Père Frédéric, O.F.M. Nouvelle série annuelle

Les Nôtres / *édité par* Joseph Fabien. - *Publié par* Les Pères Montfortains et les Filles de la sagesse. 665, rue de l'Église, Dorval, Qué. H9S 1R4, octobre 1960-
Ancien titre: Bulletin missionnaire (octobre 1960-février 1962)
Trimestriel. Bulletin, 8 p. Tirage: 8000
$.25 le numéro : $1.00 par année : $2.00 par année, l'étranger.

Nous / *édité par* René Homier-Roy. - *Publié par* P.S. Azzaria. Nous magazine ltée. 1390 ouest, rue Sherbrooke, Montréal, Qué., juin 1973-
Mensuel. Intérêt général, magazine, 72 p. Comprend critique de livres, critique de films, critique de pièces de théâtre, critique de disques, publicité. Tirage: 64,000
Indexé dans RADAR.
$1.25 le numéro : $10.00 par année : $12.00 par année, l'étranger.

Nous fiances / *édité par* Guy Cousin. - *Publié par* Les Publications Cousin-Poupart-Turmel inc. 6285, ave Cairns, Anjou, Montréal, Qué., 1966-
Trimestriel. Magazine, Comprend publicité. Tirage: 15,842
$1.50 le numéro : $4.00 par année.

Nouveau cinéma canadien / *édité par* Jean-Pierre Bastien. - *Publié par* Jean-Pierre Bastien. La Cinémathèque canadienne. 360, rue McGill, Montréal, Qué. H2Y 2E9, mars 1968-
Publié en anglais : New Canadian film.
Bimestriel. Publication spécialisée, magazine, 32 p.Aussi sous microform. Tirage: 1500
$.50 le numéro : $5.00 pour 2 ans : $2.50 le volume. Tarifs spéciaux disponibles.
Abonnements payables à l'avance.

Le Nouveau confidences *Voir* Confidences : le seul journal d'information sexuelle

Le Nouveau cosmos-express / *édité par* Gaétan Thibeault. - *Publié par* Les Citoyens du Cosmos. C.P. 3, 57 St-Dominique, Jonquière, Qué. G7X 7V8, juillet 1975-
Ancien titre: Cosmos-express (septembre 1970-mai 1973)
Mensuel. Publication spécialisée, magazine, 8 p. Comprend critique de livres, publicité. Tirage: 2000
$1.00 le numéro : $8.00 par année.
Abonnements payables à l'avance.

Nouveau dialogue / *édité par* Andre Charron. - *Publié par* Service incroyance et foi. 2930, rue Lacombe, Montréal, Qué. H3T 1L4, no. 10-2, janvier 1975-
Ancien titre: Dialogue (mars 1972-octobre 1974)
Trimestriel. Publication spécialisée, bulletin, 32 p. Tirage: 1500
ISSN 0317-1442 $.75 le numéro : $3.00 par année.

Le Nouveau pouvoir - *Publié par* Fédération nationale des enseignants québécois. 1001, rue St-Denis, Montréal, Qué., novembre 1969-
Intermittent (approximativement 3-4 éditions par an). Publication d'association, 8-16 p.

Nouvelle optique : recherches haïtiennes et caraïbéennes / *édité par* Hérard Jadotte. - *Publié par* Editions nouvelle optique. C.P. 1824, Succursale B, Montréal, Qué. H3B 3L4, janvier 1971-
Trimestriel. Edition savante, revue, 150 p. Comprend critique de livres, publicité. Tirage: 2000
Indexé dans RADAR.
$3.00 le numéro : $9.00 par année : $10.00 par année, l'Europe : $13.50 par année, l'Afrique. Tarifs spéciaux disponibles. Abonnements payables à l'avance.

Nouvelles *See* Albert-Westmorland-Kent Regional Library. News

Les Nouvelles de la brasserie / *édité par* André Godard. - *Publié par* La Brasserie Labatt Ltée au Québec. 305, ave Lepage, Dorval, Qué. H9S 3G1, 1956-
Intermittent (approximativement 4-6 éditions par an). Organe interne/officiel, bulletin, 4-8 p. Tirage: 1200
Envoi gratuit.

Nouvelles de sécurité routière (août 1961-février 1969) *Voir* La prévention au Canada

Nouvelles Gulf Canada - *Publié par* Gulf Oil Canada Ltd. 800 Bay St., Toronto, Ont., 1943-
Intermittent (approximativement 8 éditions par an). Organe interne/officiel.

Nouvelles MCMB *See* MBBM news

Nouvellettes (1935-1962) *See* Prevention

Nouy domov = New homeland / *edited by* Bretislav Kroulik. - *Published by* Masaryk Memorial Institute. 212 Cowan Ave., Toronto, Ont.
Weekly. Language: Czech. Includes advertising. Circulation: 4500
$8.00 per year.

Nova Scotia Bird Society. Newsletter / *edited by* Phyllis R. Dobson (editor-in-chief) and R.G.B. Brown (managing editor.). - *Published by* Nova Scotia Bird Society. 1747 Summer St., Halifax, N.S. B3H 3A6, March 1959-
Quarterly. Association publication, magazine format, 50 p. Includes book reviews, volume index. Circulation: 500
$1.00 per issue : $4.00 per year.

Nova Scotia farmer - *Published by* Nova Scotia Federation of Agriculture. P.O. Box 784, Truro, N.S., September 1970-March 1975-
Association publication.
ISSN 0380-5999

Nova Scotia historical quarterly / *edited by* W.H. McCurdy. - *Published by* Petheric Press Ltd. P.O. Box 1102, Halifax, N.S., 1971-
Quarterly. "Matters of historical interest as they relate to the province of Nova Scotia", journal format, 100 p. Includes book reviews, volume index. Circulation: 450
Indexed in Hist. abstr.; Amer. hist. and life.
ISSN 0300-3728 $3.00 per issue : $10.00 per year.

Nova Scotia Historical Society. Collections of the Nova Scotia Historical Society - *Published by* Nova Scotia Historical Society. Public Archives, Halifax, N.S., 1879-
Issued approximately every 3 years. Association publication, book format, 170-370 p.
Indexed in Hist. abstr.; Amer. hist. and life.

Nova Scotia Historical Society. Genealogical newsletter / *edited by* Ross Graves. - *Published by* Genealogical newsletter. P.O. Box 865, Middleton, N.S., February 1972-
Quarterly. Association publication, newsletter format, 10 p. Circulation: 350
$.50 per year.

Nova Scotia Labour-Management Study Conference. Points of agreement, proceedings, and addresses / *sponsored by* Nova Scotia Joint Labour-Management Study Committee. - *Published by* Institute of Public Affairs. Dalhousie Univesity, Halifax, N.S. B3H 3J5, 1962-
Irregular (approximately 1 issue per year). Special interest, 100 p.
$2.00 per volume.

The Nova Scotia medical bulletin / *edited by* A.J. Buhr. - *Published by* The Medical Society of Nova Scotia. Sir Charles Tupper Medical Bldg., University Ave., Halifax, N.S., 1922-
Issued every other month. Association publication, magazine format, 36 p. Includes advertising, volume index. Circulation: 1150
$2.00 per issue : $10.00 per year. Controlled circulation. Prepayment required.

Nova Scotia School Boards Association. Conference. Proceedings and annual reports / *edited by* E.J. Reyno. - *Published by* Nova Scotia School Boards Association. Room 124, Roy Bldg., Halifax, N.S. B3J 2A1, January 1970-
Issued every other month. Association publication, newsletter format, 4 p.

Nova Scotia Technical College. Newsletter / *sponsored by* Department of Public Relations ; *edited by* Mary L. Barker. - *Published by* Department of Public Relations. Nova Scotia Technical College. Box 1000, Halifax, N.S., 1968-
Monthly. House/company organ, newsletter format, 4-6 p. Circulation: 300
Free. Controlled circulation.

Nowi dni = New days / *edited by* M. Dalney. - *Published by* Nowi Dni Co. Ltd. 28 Northcliffe Blvd., Toronto, Ont.
Monthly. Ethnic press. Language: Ukrainian. Includes advertising.

Nuclear Canada = Canada nucléaire / *edited by* J.A. Weller. - *Published by* Canadian Nuclear Association. Suite 1120, 65 Queen St. W., Toronto, Ont. M5H 2M5.
Monthly. Association publication, magazine format, 16 p. Language: English and French. ISSN 0317-168X Subscription included in membership fee.

Nuclear science research report - *Published by* McMaster University. 1280 Main St. W., Hamilton, Ont. L1S 4K1.
Annual. Abstracts, journal format, 200 p.

Nugget - *Published by* The Northern Alberta Institute of Technology. 11762 - 106 St., Edmonton, Alta. T5J 2R1.
Weekly. Student publication. Includes advertising. Circulation: 4000

Nurscene / *edited by* J.L. Cummings. - *Published by* Manitoba Association of Registered Nurses. 647 Broadway Ave., Winnipeg, Man. R3C 0X2, July 1974-
Former title(s): MARN (to 1972)
Irregular (approximately 8 issues per year). Association publication, newsletter format, 6 p. Circulation: 7650
$3.00 per year. Free to registered members.

The Nurseryman (1964) *See* Landscape

Nurses news - *Published by* Manitoba Association of Licensed Practical Nurses. 431 St. Annes Rd., Winnipeg, Man. R2M 3C7.
Issued every other month. Association publication, newsletter format, 8-12 p. Controlled circulation.

Nursing orderly / *edited by* Paul Wolff and John Nimich. - *Published by* Alberta Association of Registered Nursing Orderlies. 10112-124th St., Edmonton, Alta. T5N 1P6.
Irregular (approximately 3 issues per year). Association publication, magazine format, 16 p. supplements issued. Circulation: 725
Subscription included in membership fee.

Nursing papers / *edited by* Moyra Allen. - *Published by* School of Nursing. McGill University, 3506 University St., Montreal, Que. H3A 2A7, 1969-
Quarterly. Institutional publication (Universities, schools, etc.), magazine format, 32 p. Language: English and French. Includes advertising, volume index. Circulation: 550
Indexed in C.I.N.L.
$1.50 per issue : $6.00 per year.

The Nutcracker / *edited by* A.M. Mardiros, B. Mardiros and J.G. Packer. - *Published by* The Woodsworth-Irvine Socialist Fellowship. R.204 - 10529 Jasper Ave. Edmonton, Alta. (Subscription address: P.O. Box 1602, Edmonton, Alta) November 1974-
Monthly. Political press, magazine format, 10 p. Includes book reviews, film reviews, play reviews. Circulation: 550
$.25 per issue : $1.00 per year.

Nutrition forum = Forum de nutrition / *edited by* J. Edgar Monagle. - *Published by* Nutrition Society of Canada. c/o Agriculture Canada, Research Station, 107 Science Cr., University Campus, Saskatoon, Sask. S7N 0X2, 1967-
Former title(s): Newsletter nutrition = Bulletin de nouvelles (1967-1972)
Issued twice a year. Association publication, newsletter format, 20 p. Language: English and French. Includes book reviews.
Subscription included in membership fee.

Nya Svenka pressen = Swedish press / *edited by* Sture Wermee. - *Published by* Swedish Press Society. Suite 1009, 207 W. Hastings St., Vancouver, B.C. V6B 1H7.
Issued twice a month. Ethnic press. Language: Swedish. Includes advertising.

O.A.C. farmers week (1969) *See* Notes on agriculture

OFA bulletin (1948-1970) *See* A Newsletter called Fred

OGS bulletin *See* Families

O.H.A.C. news bulletin *Voir* L'Hôpital catholique

OLA news *See* Focus

OLA newsletter *See* Focus

O.P.A. quarterly *See* The Ontario psychologist

O : publication of the arts / *edited by* Anna Wadon. - *Published by* "O" Publication of the Arts. 226 Roncesvales Ave., Toronto, Ont. M6R 2L7, Summer 1975-
Former title(s): Echo magazine (1969-1975)
Quarterly. Ethnic press, magazine format, 27 p. Language: English and Polish. Includes advertising.
$1.50 per issue : $5.00 per year.

OQAA news media guide (1970-1972) *See* News media guide

ORCSSB (June 1971) *See* Ottawa's Catholic schools

O.R.D.A. bulletin (December 1952-September 1962) *See* Ontario pharmacist

O.R.L.D.A. bulletin (1957-1972) *See* Lumber and Building Materials Association of Ontario. LBMAO reporter

OTF reporter *See* Interaction

OUAA media Guide *See* Ontario Universities Athletic Association. Directory

O Jornal portugues - *Published by* Saudade Publications. 788 Dundas St. W., Toronto, Ont. M6V 1V1, 1968-
Weekly. Ethnic press. Language: Portuguese. Includes advertising. Circulation: 7692

O Mensageiro / *edited by* Henrique Cipriano. - *Published by* Mário Cipriano. 7746 Sparbrook Cres., Vancouver, B.C., 1968-
Issued twice a week. Ethnic press. Language: Portuguese. Includes advertising.

Obiter dicta / *edited by* Paul Brace and others. - *Published by* Legal and Literary Society. Osgoode Hall Law School. Room 118D, 4700 Keele St., Downsview, Ont.
Issued every other week during the academic year. Student publication, newspaper format, 16 p. Includes book reviews, film reviews, play reviews, record reviews, advertising. Circulation: 2000
Free.

Oblate life *Voir* Vie oblate

L'Observateur *See* The Observer

Observation-opinion-orientation (printemps 1967-printemps 1974) *Voir* Poumons

Observer / *sponsored by* The United Church of Canada ; *edited by* A.C. Forrest. - *Published by* A.C. Forrest. The United Church Publishing House. 85 St. Clair Ave. E., Toronto, Ont. M4T 1M8, March 1939-
Former title(s): The New outlook (June 1925 - April 1939) The Christian Guardian (1829 - June 1925)
Monthly. Church publication, magazine format, 56 p. Includes book reviews, film reviews, play reviews, advertising. Circulation: 302,300
ISSN 0041-7238 $.50 per issue : $5.00 per year : $6.50 per year, foreign. Prepayment required.

The Observer = L'Observateur - *Published by* Paramount Retirement Counselling Ltd. 2800 Francis Hughes Ave., Vimont, Laval, Que. H7L 3J5, February 1972-
Monthly. Special interest, newsletter format, 8 p.
ISSN 0316-9111 Part of a postretirement programme for companies or associations. A sliding fee scale is charged, it is not available to individual subscribers. Controlled circulation.

Observer's handbook / *edited by* John R. Percy. - *Published by* The Royal Astronomical Society of Canada. 252 College St., Toronto, Ont. M5T 1R7, 1907-
Annual. Association publication, paperback book, 100 p.
$3.00.

Occasional papers (1970-1974) *See* The Bookmark

Occidente / *edited by* G. Derin. - *Published by* Occidente. 1756A Eglinton Ave. W., Toronto, Ont.
Monthly. Ethnic press. Language: Italian. Includes advertising. Circulation: 20,000

Oecuménisme / *parrainé par* Centre d'oecuménisme ; *édité par* Irénée Beaubien. - *Publié par* Conférence catholique canadienne. 2065 ouest, rue Sherbrooke, Montréal, Qué. H3H 1G6, février 1966-
Ancien titre: Oecuménisme en marche (décembre 1964-janvier 1965) Publié en anglais: Ecumenism.
Intermittent (approximativement 4 éditions par an). Publication d'association, bulletin, 14-16 p.
$.50 le numéro : $2.00 par année. échange gratuit. Abonnements payables à l'avance.

Oecuménisme en marche (décembre 1964-janvier 1965) *Voir* Oecuménisme

L'Oeof - *Publié par* Ariel Borremans. 5378, rue Durocher, Montréal, Qué.
Publication spécialisée.
$.40 le numéro.

L'Oeuvre de Terre-Sainte = The Good work of the Holy Land / *édité par* Le Commissaire de Terre Sainte. - *Publié par* Commissariat de Terre-Sainte. 160, ave Stanley, Ottawa, Ont. K1M 1P1, 1969-
Annuel. Publication d'association, magazine, 32 p. Langue(s): anglais et français. Tirage: 14,000
Envoi gratuit.

Office des communications sociales. OCS nouvelles / *édité par* Lucien Labelle. - *Publié par* Office des communications sociales. 4635, rue de Lorimer, Montréal, Qué. H2H 2B4, 1971-
Mensuel. Publication d'association, bulletin, 20 p. Tirage: 550
$3.00 par année.

Office des communications sociales. OCS-nouvelles / *édité par* Lucien Labelle. - *Publié par* Office des communications sociales. 4635, rue de Lorimier, Montréal, Qué. H2H 2B4, 1971-
Mensuel. Publication spécialisée, bulletin, 20 p. Tirage: 525
$3.00 par année.

Office equipment and methods / *edited by* Arden Gayman. - *Published by* Maclean-Hunter Ltd. 481 University Ave., Toronto, Ont. M5W 1A7.
Monthly. Business publication, magazine format, 60 p. Circulation: 16,900
Indexed in Can. B.P.I.
$2.00 per issue : $10.00 per year : $12.00 per year, U.S. and U.K. : $25.00 per year, foreign : $5.00 for special issues. Controlled circulation.

Official bulletin - Canadian Archery Association (December 1964-June/July 1969) *See* The Canadian archer

Official Ontario 'ship by truck' directory / *sponsored by* Ontario Trucking Association ; *edited by* A.W. James. - *Published by* Mil-Mac Publications Ltd. 230 Adelaide St. W., Toronto, Ont., 1932-
Annual. Directory, 400 p. Circulation: 6500
$7.50 : $8.00, foreign.

Oilweek / *edited by* Vic Humphreys. - *Published by* Gordon H. Reid. Maclean-Hunter Ltd. 481 University Ave., Toronto, Ont., 1949-
Weekly. Business publication, magazine format, 50 p. available in microform. Circulation: 10,200
Indexed in Can. B.P.I., North. tit., Arct. bibl.
$2.00 per issue : $16.00 per year : $20.00 per year, U.S.A. and U.K., $55.00 per year, foreign.

Okuruk / *edited by* John Groarke. - *Published by* North Hill News Ltd. P.O. Box 3160, Postal Station B, Calgary, Alta. T2M 4L7 (Subscription address: Suite 516, 816-7th Ave. S.W., Calgary, Alta. T2P 1A1)
Issued every other month. General interest, newspaper format, 8 p. Circulation: 4100
Indexed in North. tit.
Free.

Old times / *edited by* J.H. Biggar. - *Published by* Alumni Association. Upper Canada College. 200 Lonsdale Rd., Toronto, Ont. M4V 1W6, 1940-
Irregular (approximately 3 issues per year). Alumni publication, newsletter format, 36 p. Includes advertising. Circulation: 6700

Olifant / *edited by* John R. Allen. - *Published by* American Canadian Branch. Société Rencevals. University of Manitoba. Winnipeg, Man., October 1973-
Published in October, December, March and May. Association publication, journal format, 80 p. Language: English and French. Includes book reviews, volume index. Circulation: 250
$1.50 per issue : $5.00 per volume.

The Olympians - *Published by* Publinova. 421 Vitré St. W., Montreal, Que. H2Z 1G6, September 1974-
Published in French: Les Olympiens.
Irregular. Special interest, booklet format, 100 p.
$.25 per issue.

Olympress 1976 *Voir* Olympresse 1976

Olympresse 1976 = Olympress 1976 / *édité par* Alain Guilbert. - *Publié par* Division des communications. COJO Montréal 1976. C.P. 1976, Montréal, Qué. H3C 3A6, octobre 1973-
Mensuel. Publication spécialisée, magazine, 20 p. Langue(s): français et anglais. Comprend publicité. Tirage: 17,000
Envoi gratuit.

L'Om - *Publié par* Yomega. 4361, Charlemagne #3, Montréal, Qué. H1X 2H2, janvier 1974-
Trimestriel. Publication d'association, journal, 4-8 p.
$.25 le numéro.

On continuing practice / *edited by* B.P. DesRoches. - *Published by* Ontario College of Pharmacy. 483 Huron St., Toronto, Ont. M5R 2R4, October 1973-
Quarterly. Institutional publication (Universities, schools, etc.), newsletter format, 28 p. Includes book reviews, cumulative index. Circulation: 5200
ISSN 0315-1042 $1.00 per issue : $3.00 per year : $1.25 per issue, foreign : $4.00 per year, foreign. Controlled circulation.

On est là *Voir* Service de préparation à la vie. Bulletin S.P.V.

On line / *sponsored by* Canadian School Library Association ; *edited by* Karen Smith. - *Published by* Karen Smith. 57 Hampton Cres., London, Ont. N6H 2N7, September 1974-
Irregular (approximately 5 issues per year). Association publication, newsletter format, 20 p. Circulation: 570
Free. Subscription included in membership fee.

On record - *Published by* Family Service Association of Metropolitan Toronto. 22 Wellesley St. E., Toronto, Ont. M4Y 1G3, May 1958-
Former title(s): NWA on record; FSA on record.
Irregular (approximately 4 issues per year). Association publication, newsletter format, 4 p.
$2.00 per year. Controlled circulation.

On the move *See* Circle

150 books of the last three years - *Published by* Toronto Public Library. 40 St. Clair Ave. E., Toronto, Ont. M4T 1M9, 1930-
Annual. Bibliography, magazine format, 32 p.
$.50 per year. Volume discount available.

One world / *sponsored by* Alberta Social Studies Specialist Council. - *Published by* Alberta Teachers' Association. 11010-142 St., Edmonton, Alta. T5N 2R1.
Irregular (approximately 3 issues per year). Association publication, magazine format, 60-65 p. Includes book reviews. Circulation: 1200
Indexed in Can. educ. ind.
$6.00 per year. Prepayment required.

Only paper today : a bi-monthly devoted to writing about art in Ontario / *sponsored by* Nightingale Arts Council ; *edited by* Vic d'Or and the O.P.T. Editorial Collective. - *Published by* The Eternal Network. 85 St. Nicholas St., Toronto, Ont. M4Y 1W8, October 1973-
Former title(s): Proof only.
Issued every other month. Special interest, newspaper format, 12 p. Includes book reviews. Circulation: 2000
$10.00 per year (Institutions $25.00). Free.

Onomastica / *edited by* J.B. Rudnyckyi. - *Published by* Canadian Institute of Onomastic Sciences. P.O. Box 3504, Postal Station B, Winnipeg, Man. R2W 3R4, 1951-
Issued twice a year. Association publication, magazine format, 32-320 p. Language: Multilingual. Includes book reviews. supplements issued. Circulation: 1000
$2.00-$10.00 per issue.

The Ontarian - *Published by* University of Guelph. Guelph, Ont. N1G 2W1.
Weekly. Student publication. Includes advertising. Circulation: 8500

Ontario - Courier / *edited by* Bernd Laengin. - *Published by* Courier Press Ltd. Suite 304, 455 Spadina Ave., Toronto, Ont. M5S 2G9, 1907-
Weekly. Ethnic press, newspaper format, 16 p. Language: German. available in microform.
$.25 per issue : $9.00 per year : $12.00 per year, foreign. Prepayment required.

Ontario Agricultural College. Alumni news / *sponsored by* Ontario Agricultural College. Alumni Association ; *edited by* Bill Tolten. - *Published by* Department of Alumni Affairs and Development. University of Guelph. Guelph, Ont.
Irregular (approximately 8 issues per year). Alumni publication, newsletter format, 12 p. Circulation: 6300
$5.00 per year.

Ontario Agricultural College. Department of Land Resource Science. Research and Advisory Service. Progress report / *sponsored by* Ontario Ministry of Agriculture and Food ; *edited by* L.R. Webber, and D.B. Hons. - *Published by* Department of Soil Science. University of Guelph. Guelph, Ont., 1954-
Former title(s): Progress report - University of Guelph. Department of Soils (1954-1971)
Irregular (approximately 1 issue per year). Institutional publication (Universities, schools, etc.), 70 p. Includes volume index. Circulation: 750
Free.

The Ontario amateur / *edited by* Lawrence Purdy. - *Published by* Radio Society of Ontario, Inc. P.O. Box 334, Toronto, Ont. M8Z 5P7, 1965-
Issued every other month. Association publication, magazine format, 30 p. Includes advertising.
Subscription included in membership fee. Controlled circulation.

Ontario Amateur Softball Association. O.A.S.A. bulletin - *Published by* Ontario Amateur Softball Association. 709 Fernhill, Blvd., Oshawa, Ont.
Issued twice a month. Association publication, newsletter format, 2 p.
$2.00 per year. Prepayment required.

The Ontario annual practice / *edited by* James J. Carthy. - *Published by* Canada Law Book Ltd. 80 Cowdray Court, Agincourt, Ont. M1S 1S5.
Former title(s): Chitty's Ontario annual practice.
Annual. 835 p.
$15.00 per year.

Ontario archaeology / *sponsored by* Ontario Archaeological Society ; *edited by* William M. Hurley. - *Published by* Wilfrid Laurier University Press. Dr. N. Wagner, Wilfrid Laurier University, Waterloo, Ont. (Subscription address: P.O. Box 241, Postal Station P, Toronto, Ont) 1954-
Issued twice a year. Association publication, magazine format, 50 p. Circulation: 400
$3.00 per issue : $5.00 per year.

Ontario Association for Curriculum Development. Annual conference. Proceedings / *edited by* Sheilagh Dubois. - *Published by* Ontario Association for Curriculum Development. 1260 Bay St., Toronto, Ont.
Annual. Association publications, proceedings of the annual conference, 130 p. Circulation: 1000

Ontario Association of Children's Aid Societies. Journal / *edited by* Ruth Doehler. - *Published by* Ontario Association of Children's Aid Societies. Suite 502, 663 Yonge St., Toronto, Ont. M4Y 2A4, 1958-
Monthly except July and August. Association publication, magazine format, 16 p. Language: English (French). Includes book reviews, advertising. Circulation: 13,000
$.35 per issue : $3.00 per volume. Special rates to members. Prepayment required.

Ontario Association of Corrections and Criminology. Bulletin / *edited by* Peter Kiviloe and Alex Chunak. - *Published by* Ontario Association of Corrections and Criminology. 168 Isabella St., Toronto, Ont., Fall 1974-
Association publication.

Ontario Association of Geomorphologists. Handbook / *edited by* B.D. Fahey. - *Published by* Department of Geography. University of Guelph. Guelph, Ont., 1973-
Biennial. Association publication, 90 p. Controlled circulation.

Ontario business corporations act and regulations - *Published by* Richard De Boo Ltd. 70 Richmond St. E., Toronto, Ont. M5C 2M8.
Annual. Legislation, 200 p.
ISSN 0316-689X $3.75.

Ontario Business Education Association. OBEA newsletter / *edited by* Anthony Holt. - *Published by* Ontario Business Education Association. c/o Anthony Holt, East York Collegiate Institute, 650 Cosburn Ave., Toronto, Ont. M4C 2V2.
Issued twice a year. Association publication.

Ontario camping news (March 1974-August 1974) *See* The Outdoor news

Ontario campus culture newsletter / *sponsored by* Ontario Campus Cultural Association ; *edited by* Barry Cole. - *Published by* Performing Arts Office. Queen's University. Kingston, Ont. K7L 3N6, September 1973-
Quarterly. Association publication, newsletter format, 16 p. Circulation: 100
Subscription included in membership fee
$25.00 per year. Controlled circulation.

Ontario Cancer Treatment and Research Foundation. Proceedings of The Clinical Conference / *edited by* J.O. Godden. - *Published by* The Ontario Cancer Treatment and Research Foundation. 7 Overlea Blvd., Toronto, Ont. M4H 1A8.
Biennal. Proceedings of the biennial conference, bound book format, 140-250 p. Circulation: 350
ISSN 0315-9884 Free.

Ontario Catholic directory / *edited by* F.M. Coulter. - *Published by* Newman Foundation of Toronto. 89 St. George St., Toronto, Ont. M5S 2E8, 1915-
Annual. Directory, magazine format, 145 p. Includes advertising. Circulation: 8210
ISSN 0078-4702 $3.25. Special rates offered.

The Ontario churchman / *edited by* J.B. Peever. - *Published by* The Ontario Churchman. 90 Johnson St., Kingston, Ont. K7L 1X7, January 1959-
Monthly. Church publication, newspaper format, 4-8 p.
$1.50 per year.

Ontario corporation manual / *edited by* R.A. Kingston. - *Published by* Richard De Boo Ltd. 70 Richmond St. E., Toronto, Ont. M5C 2M8.
Monthly. Legislation, 64 p. Includes updating service. supplements issued.
$40.00.

The Ontario cottager / *edited by* Charles Clay. - *Published by* Clay Publishing Co. Ltd. Bewdley, Ont. K0L 1E0, 1971-
Former title(s): Recreation property.
Issued every other month. Special interest, magazine format, Includes advertising. Circulation: 3611
$.75 per issue : $4.00 per year : $7.00 for 2 years.

Ontario Council for Leadership in Educational Administration. OCLEA / *edited by* H. Donald Joyce. - *Published by* Ontario Council for Leadership in Educational Administration. Suite N1201, 252 Bloor St. W., Toronto, Ont. M5S 1V5, June 1974-
Quarterly. Association publication, magazine format, 16 p. Circulation: 10,000
Indexed in Can. educ. ind.
ISSN 0315-792x Free. Controlled circulation.

Ontario Credit Union. News / *edited by* Dennis Collins. - *Published by* Ontario Credit Union League. Credit Union Dr., Toronto, Ont. M4A 2A1, 1943-
Monthly. House/company organ, magazine format, 16 p. Circulation: 20,000
Indexed in Can. B.P.I.
$1.00 per year.

Ontario Curling Association. Annual / *edited by* Leon Sykes. - *Published by* Ontario Curling Association. Suite 203, 85 Eglinton Ave. E., Toronto, Ont. M4P 1H5, 1875-
Annual. Association publication, magazine format, 160 p.
Free.

Ontario dentist / *sponsored by* Ontario Dental Association ; *edited by* K.N. Munro. - *Published by* Scholar House Publications. 1 Heath St. W., Toronto, Ont., 1932-
Former title(s): The Booster (1925-1931)
Monthly. Association publication, journal format, 40 p. Includes book reviews.
ISSN 0300-5275 $2.00 per issue : $18.00 per year : $24.00 per year, foreign (Airmail $12.00 extra).

The Ontario digest / *edited by* John Carruthers. - *Published by* Association of Professional Engineers of Ontario. 1027 Yonge St., Toronto, Ont. M4W 3E5.
Irregular (approximately 10 issues per year). Association publication, magazine format, 32 p. Included in the Ontario edition of Engineering digest.
Available to members only. Controlled circulation.

The Ontario doctor's wife / *edited by* Wilma Breakwell. - *Published by* Ontario Medical Wives' Association. 240 St. George St., Toronto, Ont. M5R 2P4, 1953-
Quarterly. Association publication, magazine format, 24 p. Includes book reviews, advertising. Circulation: 1500
ISSN 0030-2880 Subscription included in membership fee.

Ontario education / *edited by* Jack MacDonald. - *Published by* Ontario Public School Trustees' Association. Suite 303, 4195 Dundas St. W., Toronto, Ont. M8X 1Y4, 1969-
Former title(s): Canadian school journal; The Argus.
Issued 5 times a year. Association publication, magazine format, 32 p. Includes book reviews, advertising. Circulation: 3300
Indexed in Can. educ. ind.
$1.00 per issue : $4.00 per year : $5.00 per year, foreign. Special rates offered. Prepayment required.

Ontario educational review / *edited by* H. Brown and B. Gaouette. - *Published by* Ontario Educational Association. Suite S904, 252 Bloor St. W., Toronto, Ont. M5S 1V7, 1965-
Quarterly. Association publication, newspaper format, 8 p. Circulation: 60,000
Subscription included in membership fee $10.00 a year.

Ontario Federation of Labour. Constitution - *Published by* Ontario Federation of Labour. Suite 202, 15 Gervais Dr., Don Mills, Ont. M3C 1Y8.
Annual. Association publication, pamphlet format, 10 p.

Ontario Federation of Labour. Convention. Report of proceedings - *Published by* Ontario Federation of Labour. Suite 202, 15 Gervais Dr., Don Mills, Ont. M3C 1Y8.
Annual. Association publication, magazine format,

Ontario Federation of Labour. Convention. Resolutions - *Published by* Ontario Federation of Labour. Suite 202, 15 Gervais Dr., Don Mills, Ont. M3C 1Y8.
Annual. Association publication, magazine format,

Ontario Federation of Labour. Legislative proposals to the government of Ontario - *Published by* Ontario Federation of Labour. Suite 202, 15 Gervais Dr., Don Mills, Ont. M3C 1Y8.
Annual. Association publication, magazine format, 25 p.

The Ontario field biologist / *edited by* Barbara Wilkins. - *Published by* Toronto Field Naturalists' Club. 1164 Broadview Ave., Toronto, Ont. (Subscription address: 49 Craighurst Ave., Toronto, Ont. M4R 1J9) April 1946-
Former title(s): The Intermediate naturalist (April 1946-December 1953)
Issued twice a year. Association publication, journal format, 48 p. Circulation: 800
Indexed in Arct. bibl.
ISSN 0078-4834 $1.25 per issue : $2.50 per year.

Ontario fisherman and hunter / *edited by* Burt Myers. - *Published by* Ontario Fisherman and Hunter Publishing Co. 7 Guardsman Rd., Thornhill, Ont. L3T 2A1, 1969-
Monthly. Special interest, magazine format, Includes advertising. Circulation: 21,652

Ontario folkdancer : newsletter / *edited by* Heidi Fiebig. - *Published by* Ontario Folkdance Association. 43 Cynthia Rd., Toronto, Ont. M6N 2P8 (Subscription address: 400 Durie St. Toronto, Ont. M6S 3G4) December 1969-
Former title(s): Newsletter - Ontario Folkdance Association.
Monthly except July and August. Association publication, newsletter format, 20 p. Includes record reviews, advertising. supplements issued. Circulation: 400
$.30 per issue : $2.50 per year. Subscription included in membership fee.

Ontario forests / *edited by* J.D. Coats. - *Published by* Ontario Forestry Association. 150 Consumers Rd., Willowdale, Ont. M2J 1P9, December 1959-
Former title(s): The Ontario tree farmer (December 1959-December 1969)
Quarterly. Association publication, magazine format, 20 p. Circulation: 1300
ISSN 0048-1785 $10.00 per year. Prepayment required.

Ontario Genealogical Society. Newsleaf / *edited by* Eula C. Lapp. - *Published by* Ontario Genealogical Society. P.O. Box 66, Postal Station Q, Toronto, Ont. M4T 2L7, 1971-
Quarterly. Association publication, newsletter format, 12 p. Includes book reviews. Circulation: 1200
$8.00 per year. Subscription included in membership fee. Controlled circulation.

Ontario geography / *edited by* Nigel Waters. - *Published by* Department of Geography. University of Western Ontario. London, Ont., 1967-
Annual. Scholarly publication, includes thesis abstracts for U.W.O. M.A. and PHD's, journal format, 110 p. Includes book reviews. Circulation: 600
ISSN 0078-4850 $1.75.

The Ontario grape grower - *Published by* Ontario Editorial Bureau. Ontario Grape Growers' Marketing Board. P.O. Box 745, St. Catherines, Ont.
Published in French: Le producteur de raisin d'Ontario.
Quarterly. Association publication, newsletter format, 4 p.
Free. Controlled circulation.

Ontario gymnast / *edited by* Michael J. Scanlan and Mary McKeigan. - *Published by* The Ontario Gymnastic Federation. 559 Jarvis St., Toronto, Ont. M4Y 2J1, September 1974-
Issued every 6 weeks. Association publication, newsletter format, 12 p. Includes advertising. Circulation: 1000
$5.00 per year. Prepayment required.

Ontario Health Record Association. OHRA news and views / *sponsored by* Ontario Health Record Association ; *edited by* Fran Emerson. - *Published by* Ontario Hospital Association. 24 Ferrand Dr., Don Mills, Ont., 1968-
Quarterly. Association publication, newsletter format, 12 p.

Ontario Historical Society. Bulletin - *Published by* Ontario Historical Society. 1466 Bathurst St., Toronto, Ont. M5R 3J3.
Issued twice a year. Association publication, newsletter format, 2 p.
Free.

Ontario Historical Society. Museums Section. Newsletter - *Published by* Ontario Historical Society. 1466 Bathurst St., Toronto, Ont. M5R 3J3, 1960-
Issued 5 times a year. House/company organ, newsletter format,
Available as part of membership.

Ontario history / *edited by* P.G. Cornell and K. McLaughlin. - *Published by* The Ontario Historical Society. 1466 Bathurst St., Toronto, Ont. M5R 3J3, 1901-
Quarterly. Association publication, magazine format, 68 p. supplements issued. Circulation: 2000
Indexed in Can. ind., Hist. abstr.; Amer. hist. and life.
$1.50 per issue : $5.00 per year. Prepayment required.

Ontario home buyers guide / *edited by* G. Stelljes. - *Published by* Stelljes Publications Ltd. 45 Charles St. E., Toronto, Ont. M4Y 1S2, 1970-
Issued twice a month. Magazine format, Includes advertising. Circulation: 21,170
$.50 per issue.

Ontario homes buyers guide to private sales / *edited by* Michael R. Ryan. - *Published by* Ontario Homes Private Sale Consultants. 45 Charles St. E., Toronto, Ont. M4V 1S2, December 1970-
Former title(s): Ontario homes magazines (April 1975) Toronto homes magazine (1970-1974)
Monthly. Special interest, newspaper format, 8-16 p. Circulation: 1500
$1.00 per issue : $10.00 per year. Controlled circulation.

Ontario homes magazines (April 1975) *See* Ontario homes buyers guide to private sales

Ontario industrial arts bulletin / *edited by* Jack Holowatch. - *Published by* Ontario Industrial Arts Association. c/o Keith McLaren, 38 Patina Dr., Willowdale, Ont. M2H 1R1.
Issued twice a year. Association publication, magazine format, 40 p. Includes book reviews, film reviews, advertising, volume index.
Indexed in Can. educ. ind.
$15.00 per year. Controlled circulation.

Ontario Industrial Development Council Inc. Newsletter / *edited by* Dianne Moore. - *Published by* Ontario Industrial Development Council Inc. 9835 Esplanade, Windsor, Ont. N8R 1J7, 1971-
Irregular (approximately 5-10 issues per year). Association publication, newsletter format, 1-2 p.
Subscription included in membership fee. Controlled circulation.

Ontario Industrial Development Council Inc. OIDC newsletter and press clippings / *edited by* Dianne Moore. - *Published by* Ontario Industrial Development Council Inc. 9835 Esplanade, Windsor, Ont. N8R 1J7, 1973-
Monthly. Association publication, newsletter format, 10-15 p. Circulation: 150
Subscription included in membership fee
$25.00 per year. Controlled circulation.

Ontario Institute for Studies in Education. News and notes / *edited by* Frank Quinlan. - *Published by* Ontario Institute for Studies in Education. 252 Bloor St. W., Toronto, Ont. M5S 1V6, July 1972-
Monthly. Institutional publication (Universities, schools, etc.), newsletter format, 4 p. Circulation: 1000
Free.

Ontario Institute for Studies in Education. Office of the Coordinator of Field Development. Newsletter / *edited by* Mark Holmes. - *Published by* Ontario Institute for Studies in Education. 252 Bloor St. W., Toronto, Ont. M5S 1V6, September 1971-
Irregular (approximately 10 issues per year). Institutional publication (Universities, schools, etc.), newsletter format, 2 p. Language: English and French.

Ontario Insurance Agents' and Brokers' Association. News / *edited by* Herb T. Baker. - *Published by* Ontario Insurance Agents' & Brokers' Association. Suite 1228, 67 Yonge St., Toronto, Ont. M5E 1J8.
Monthly. Association publication, newsletter format, 6 p. Circulation: 2885
$6.00 per year. Free to a special listing. Special rates offered. Prepayment required.

Ontario journal and tax sale register / *edited by* L.T. Dunlop. - *Published by* Sovereign Publishing Co. 1st Floor, 110 Church St., Toronto, Ont. M5C 2G6, 1963-
Issued every other month. Special interest, magazine format, 40 p. Circulation: 9000
$1.00 per issue : $4.98 per year. Prepayment required.

The Ontario land surveyor / *edited by* Andrew Gibson. - *Published by* The Association of Ontario Land Surveyors. 6070 Yonge St., Willowdale, Ont. M2M 3Z3.
Quarterly. Association publication, magazine format, 32 p. Includes book reviews, advertising. Circulation: 1000
Subscription included in membership fee.

Ontario mathematics gazette / *sponsored by* Ontario Association of Mathematics Education ; *edited by* W. Eames and J.S. Griffith. - *Published by* W. Eames and J.S. Griffith. Lakehead University (Subscription address: 247 Bright St. Sarnia, Ont. N7T 4E9)
Irregular (approximately 3 issues per year). Association publication, magazine format, 60-100 p.
$2.00 per issue : $5.00 per year.

Ontario medical review / *edited by* Ronald E. Brownridge. - *Published by* Ontario Medical Association. 240 St. George St., Toronto, Ont. M5R 2P4, April 1922-
Former title(s): Bulletin - Ontario Medical Association (April 1922-June 1943)
Monthly. Association publication, magazine format, 66 p. Includes book reviews, advertising. Circulation: 12,396
$1.00 per issue : $10.00 per year. Available to members only. Controlled circulation. Prepayment required.

Ontario milk producer / *edited by* David A. McGrath. - *Published by* Ontario Milk Marketing Board. P.O. Box 4027, Postal Station A, Toronto, Ont. M5W 1K2, June 1925-
Monthly. House/company organ, magazine format, 40 p. Language: English and French. Includes advertising. supplements issued. Circulation: 24,893
$.75 per issue : $6.00 per year : $12.00 per year, foreign.

Ontario Mortgage Brokers Association. Monthly letter / *edited by* Chas T. James. - *Published by* Ontario Mortgage Brokers Association. Suite 510, 6 Adelaide St. E., Toronto, Ont. M5C 1H6, 1965-
Monthly. Association publication, newsletter format, 5 p.
Free.

Ontario Motor League news / *edited by* Denis W. Savoie. - *Published by* Craig Ainslie. Essex County Automobile Club. 1215 Ouellette Ave., Windsor, Ont., April 1965-
Quarterly. Association publication, magazine format, 12 p. Circulation: 39,000
Free.

Ontario Municipal Recreation Association. OMRA newsletter / *edited by* Pat Artkin. - *Published by* Ontario Municipal Recreation Association. 559 Jarvis St., Toronto, Ont. M4Y 2J1, April 1970-
Quarterly. Association publication, newsletter format, 6 p. Circulation: 1500
Free to members.

Ontario native experience / *edited by* Susan Daybutch. - *Published by* Ontario Federation of Indian Friendship Centres. Suite 203, 234 Eglinton Ave. E., Toronto, Ont. M4P 1K5, June 1973-
Monthly. Special interest, newspaper format, 12 p. Includes book reviews, film reviews, play reviews, record reviews, advertising. Circulation: 9000
Indexed in North. tit.
ISSN 0380-1519 $5.00 per year (Organizations $10.00).

Ontario naturalist / *edited by* Judith Parsons. - *Published by* Federation of Ontario Naturalists. Suite 49, 1262 Don Mills Rd., Don Mills, Ont. M3B 2W7, 1932-
Former title(s): The Bulletin - Federation of Ontario Naturalists (1951-1963)
Issued every other month. Association publication, magazine format, 40-48 p. Includes book reviews, advertising. Circulation: 11,500
Indexed in North. tit.
$1.00 per issue : $12.00 per year (Students and libraries $6.00, families $14.00). Subscription included in membership fee. Prepayment required.

Ontario nursing home news - *Published by* Ontario Nursing Home Association. Suite 109, 5803 Yonge St., Willowdale, Ont. M2M 3V5.
Quarterly. Association publication, newsletter format, 4 p. Circulation: 1500
Free.

Ontario Petroleum Institute. Annual conference proceedings - *Published by* Ontario Petroleum Institute Inc. P.O. Box 396, Chatham, Ont. N7M 5K5.
Annual. Association publication, proceedings of the annual meeting.
$12.00.

Ontario pharmacist / *edited by* R.B. Franceschini. - *Published by* Ontario Pharmacists' Association. Suite 804, 99 Avenue Rd., Toronto, Ont. M5R 2G5, September/October 1962-
Former title(s): O.R.D.A. bulletin (December 1952-September 1962)
Monthly. Association publication, newsletter format, 2-4 p. Includes updating service. Circulation: 1700

Ontario pipeline - *Published by* Ontario Section. American Water Works Association. 3190 Mavis Rd., Mississauga, Ont., March 1971-
Irregular (approximately 3 issues per year). Association publication, magazine format, 50 p. Circulation: 2000
ISSN 0380-1624 Free.

Ontario Plumbing Inspectors Association. Annual conference. Report - *Published by* Ontario Plumbing Inspectors Association. P.O. Box 812, 184 Regent St., Niagara on the Lake, Ont.
Annual. Association publication, newsletter format, 20 p.
Controlled circulation.

The Ontario psychologist / *edited by* J. Ricks. - *Published by* Ontario Psychological Association. 245 Old Forest Hill Rd., Toronto, Ont. M6C 2H5, 1969-
Former title(s): O.P.A. quarterly.
Issued every other month. Association publication, journal format, 60 p. Includes book reviews, advertising. Circulation: 980
Indexed in Psych. abstr.
$2.00 per issue : $12.00 per year.

Ontario Public School Men Teachers' Federation. News / *edited by* W.G. McMillan. - *Published by* Ontario Public School Men Teachers' Federation. 1260 Bay St., Toronto, Ont. M5R 2B7, 1940-
Issued 8 times per year. Association publication, newspaper format, 14 p.
Circulation: 16,000
Subscription included in membership fee.
Controlled circulation.

The Ontario Registered Music Teachers' Association. Ormata notes - *Published by* The Ontario Registered Music Teachers' Association. 318 Paliser Cres., S., Richmond Hill, Ont. L4C 1R8.
Irregular (approximately 3-4 issues per year). Association publication, newsletter format,

Ontario report / *edited by* Paul Craven. - *Published by* Ontario Report Editorial Board. P.O. Box 6851, Postal Station A, Toronto, Ont. (Subscription address: Report, P.O. Box 1776, Brantford, Ont) January 1975-
Former title(s): North country (December 1973-July 1974)
Issued every other month. General interest, newsletter format, 40 p. Includes book reviews, film reviews, advertising. supplements issued. Circulation: 2000
ISSN 0371-1043 $.75 per issue : $4.00 per year (Institutions $7.00), $7.00 per year, foreign.

Ontario reports / *sponsored by* Law Society of Upper Canada ; *edited by* Horace Krever. - *Published by* Canada Law Book Ltd. 80 Cowdray Court, Agincourt, Ont. M1J 1S5, 1931-
Weekly. Cases, case notes, magazine format, 60 p. Includes advertising.
$26.00 per volume : $27.50 per year, foreign.

Ontario Research Foundation. Newsletter / *edited by* J.A. McPherson. - *Published by* Ontario Research Foundation. Sheridan Park, Mississauga, Ont. L5K 1B3.
Irregular (approximately 6 issues per year). House/company organ, newsletter format, 1 p.
Circulation: 7000
Free.

The Ontario review : a North American journal of the arts / *edited by* Raymond J. Smith. - *Published by* The Ontario Review. 6000 Riverside Dr. E., Windsor, Ont. N8S 1B6, Fall 1974-
Issued twice a year. Special interest, magazine format, 110 p. Includes book reviews, advertising. Circulation: 500
ISSN 0316-4055 $2.50 per issue : $5.00 per year : $5.50 per year, foreign.

Ontario Ringette Association. Official rules - *Published by* Ontario Ringette Association. 559 Jarvis St., Toronto, Ont. M4Y 2J1, 1974/1975-
Annual. Association publication, booklet format, 32 p.
ISSN 0316-7615 $.50 per volume.

Ontario Safety League. OSL news / *edited by* Terry Thompson. - *Published by* Ontario Safety League. 409 King St. W., Toronto, Ont. M5V 1K1.
Quarterly. Association publication, 4 p.
Circulation: 2000
Free. Controlled circulation.

Ontario Shade Tree Council. Newsletter / *edited by* R.H. Stretton. - *Published by* Ontario Shade Tree Council. 7241 Jane St., Concord, Ont. L4K 1A9, 1964-
Issued every other month. Association publication, newsletter format, 6-8 p. Includes advertising. Circulation: 300
Controlled circulation.

The Ontario showcase / *edited by* J. Daniel Taylor. - *Published by* The Ontario Showcase Publishing Company, Ltd. P.O. Box 1000, Ridgetown, Ont. N0P 2C0, July 1965-
Monthly. House/company organ, magazine format, 100 p. Includes advertising.
Circulation: 3286
$.75 per issue : $6.00 per year : $7.00 per year, foreign. Prepayment required.

Ontario Society for Education through Art. Journal / *edited by* Karl Schutt. - *Published by* Ontario Society for Education through Art. 339 Wilbrod St., Ottawa, Ont. K1N 6M4.
Irregular (approximately 3 issues per year). Association publication, journal format, 150 p. Language: English (French). Includes book reviews. Circulation: 200
$9.00 per year : $3.50 per volume.

Ontario Society for Medical Technologists. Newsletter / *edited by* Neville J. Bryant. - *Published by* Ontario Society of Medical Technologists. Suite 320, 88 Eglinton Ave. E., Toronto, Ont. M4P 1B8, 1963-
Quarterly. Association publication, newsletter format, 50 p.
$8.00 per year.

Ontario Speech and Hearing Association. Journal / *edited by* Robert M. Kroll. - *Published by* Ontario Speech and Hearing Association. 80 Gwendolen Cres., Willowdale, Ont. (Subscription address: Association House, Medical Sciences Building, Taddle Creek Rd., Toronto, Ont) 1965-
Annual. Association publication, journal format, 30 p. Circulation: 300
$3.00. Prepayment required.

Ontario statute citator. Bill service - *Published by* Canada Law Book Ltd. 80 Cowdray Court, Agincourt, Ont. M1S 1S5.
Irregular (approximately 8-10 issues per year). Legislation, looseleaf format,
$36.00 per year.

The Ontario student = L'étudiant de l'Ontario / *edited by* Chris Harries. - *Published by* Ontario Federation of Students. Suite 9, 794 Bathurst St., Toronto, Ont.
Irregular (approximately 7-8 issues per year). Association publication, newspaper format, 8 p.
Free.

Ontario Swimming Pool Association. OSPA news / *edited by* Anna Socket. - *Published by* Ontario Swimming Pool Association. Suite 210, 61 Alness St., Downsview, Ont. M3J 2H2, 1970-
Quarterly. Association publication, magazine format, 32 p.
Free.

Ontario taxation service / *edited by* A.V. Neil. - *Published by* Richard De Boo Ltd. 70 Richmond St. E., Toronto, Ont. M5C 2H8.
Monthly. Legislation, 64 p. Includes updating service.
$35.00 per year.

The Ontario technologist / *edited by* Judith A. Landell. - *Published by* Ontario Association of Certified Engineering Technicians and Technologists. 50 Holly St., Toronto, Ont. M4X 1L7, 1958-
Issued every other month. Association publication, magazine format, 24 p.
$10.00 per year.

Ontario tennis / *edited by* David Kentish and Allan Ryan. - *Published by* Ontario Lawn Tennis Association. 559 Jarvis St., Toronto, Ont. M4Y 2J1.
Irregular (approximately 5 issues per year). Association publication, newspaper format, 12 p. Includes advertising. Circulation: 15,000
$1.00 per year. Controlled circulation.

The Ontario tree farmer (December 1959-December 1969) *See* Ontario forests

Ontario Trucking Association. OTA news round-up / *edited by* J. O. Goodman. - *Published by* Ontario Trucking Association. 555 Dixon Rd., Rexdale, Ont. M9W 1H8, June 1974-
Weekly. Association publication, newsletter format, 6 p. Circulation: 2050
Controlled circulation.

Ontario Universities Athletic Association. Directory = Ontario Women's Intercollegiate Athletic Association. Directory / *edited by* Paul G. Condon. - *Published by* Ontario Universities Athletic Association. c/o University of Waterloo, Waterloo, Ont.
Former title(s): OUAA media Guide.
Annual. Association publication, 90 p.

Ontario Veterinary Association. OVA newsletter / *edited by* Rendle Bowhess. - *Published by* Ontario Veterinary Association. 33 Cork St. W., Guelph, Ont. N1H 6N9.
Irregular (approximately 10 issues per year). Association publication, newsletter format, 12 p.
Free. Controlled circulation.

Ontario Veterinary College. Alumni bulletin / *sponsored by* Ontario Veterinary College. Alumni Association ; *edited by* Trevor Jones. - *Published by* Department of Alumni Affairs. Ontario Veterinary College. Guelph, Ont.
Quarterly. Alumni publication, newsletter format, 8 p. Circulation: 2400
$5.00 per year.

Ontario water skier / *edited by* Wendy Horne. - *Published by* Ontario Region. Canadian Water Ski Association. 559 Jarvis St., Toronto, Ont. M4Y 2J1, February 1974-
Former title(s): Whatchamacallit (1970-1973)
Association publication, newsletter format, 48 p. Includes advertising, volume index, cumulative index. Circulation: 2000
$1.00 per year. Prepayment required.

Ontario Weekly Newspapers Association. Bulletin / *edited by* Mary Cann. - *Published by* Ontario Weekly Newspapers Association. P.O. Box 451, Oakville, Ont.
Monthly. Association publication, 8-12 p. Circulation: 800

Ontario Women's Intercollegiate Athletic Association. Directory *See* Ontario Universities Athletic Association. Directory

The Opal / *edited by* Janet Small. - *Published by* Ontario Puppetry Association. 10 Skyview Cres., Willowdale, Ont. M2J 1B8, September/October 1962-
Issued every other month. Special interest, magazine format, 12-16 p. Includes book reviews, play reviews, advertising. supplements issued. Circulation: 125
ISSN 0030-3062 $5.00 per year. Subscription included in membership fee.

The Open door newsletter / *edited by* Peggy Williams. - *Published by* Canada Grains Council. 400 - 177 Lombard Ave. Winnipeg, Man. R3B 0W5, 1970-
Issued every other month. Association publication, newsletter format, 4 p. Circulation: 3000
$1.00 per year. Prepayment required.

Open letter / *edited by* Frank Davey. - *Published by* The Coach House Press. 401 Huron St. (rear), Toronto, Ont. M5S 2G5 (Subscription address: 395 Elm Rd., Toronto, Ont. M5M 3W3)
Irregular (approximately 4 issues per year). "Literary criticism", book format, 100 p. Circulation: 500
Indexed in Can. essay and lit. ind.
$2.00 per issue : $7.25 per year.

Opera Canada - the music theatre magazine / *edited by* Ruby Mercer. - *Published by* Canadian Opera Association. 35/39 Front St. E., Toronto, Ont. M5E 1B3, February 1970-
Issued 6 times per year. Association publication, magazine format, 40 p. Includes book reviews, record reviews, advertising. Circulation: 5500
$1.50 per issue : $7.50 per year : $6.00 per volume. Special rates offered.

Operating results of independent specialty and department stores - *Published by* Retail Council of Canada. Suite 723, 74 Victoria St., Toronto, Ont. M5C 2A5.
Biennial. Association publication, 26 p.
$4.00.

Opérations forestières - *Publié par* Fred O'Leary. Southam Business Publications Ltd. 1450 Don Mills Rd., Don Mills, Ont. M3B 2X7, 1965-
Mensuel. Publication spécialisée, magazine, 55 p. Comprend critique de livres, publicité. Tirage: 4200
$8.00 par année.

Opinion canada / *edited by* Charles Delafield. - *Published by* Canada Committee. Suite 925, 1407 Peel St., Montreal, Que. H3A 1T1, June 1972-
Monthly except July and August. General interest, magazine format, 24 p. Language: English and French ; summaries: English and French. Circulation: 10,400
ISSN 0315-808X $1.00 per issue : $10.00 per year.

Opportunities unlimited - *Published by* Automotive Industries Association of Canada. 1306 Wellington St., Ottawa, Ont. K1Y 3B2, 1974-
Irregular. Association publication, magazine format, Language: French and English.

Option *See* Libertarian option : freedom or tyranny

Oracle / *edited by* Dick Capling. - *Published by* Ontario Association for Continuing Education. 7th floor, 8 York St., Toronto, Ont. M5J 1R2, September 1971-
Issued every other month. Association publication, newsletter format, 12 p. Includes book reviews, advertising.
Subscription included in membership fee $20.00 (Corporate membership $50.00). Controlled circulation. Prepayment required.

Orah magazine / *edited by* B.M. Bloomfield. - *Published by* Hadassah-WIZO Organization of Canada. 1310 Greene Ave., Montreal, Que. H3Z 2B2, 1959-
Monthly. Association publication, magazine format, 28 p.
$2.00 per year.

Oral health / *edited by* James M. Kerr (chairman of editorial board). - *Published by* Southam Business Publications Ltd. 1450 Don Mills Rd., Don Mills, Ont. M3G 2X7, 1910-
Monthly. "Original communications and abstracts on recent advances in dentistry", magazine format, 50-60 p. Includes advertising.
$1.50 per issue : $12.00 per year : $18.00 per year, U.S. : $30.00 per year, foreign. Controlled circulation.

L'Oratoire : au service de la famille chrétienne / *édité par* Réal Fréchette. - *Publié par* Oratoire Saint-Joseph. 3800, chemin Reine-Marie, Montréal, Qué., janvier 1912-
Ancien titre: Les Annales de Saint-Joseph du Mont-Royal (janvier 1912-décembre 1943)
Mensuel. Publication ecclésiastique, revue, 32 p. Comprend critique de livres, publicité. Tirage: 73,000
$.35 le numéro : $3.00 par année. Abonnements payables à l'avance.

Orbit : ideas about teaching and learning / *edited by* H.P.H. Oliver. - *Published by* The Ontario Institute for Studies in Education. 252 Bloor St. W., Toronto, Ont. M5S 1V6, October 1969-
5 issues bi-monthly, October - June. Magazine format, 28 p. Language: English (French). available in microform. Circulation: 7000
Indexed in Can. educ. ind., Curr. ind. j. educ.
$1.00 per issue : $3.00 per year. 5000 copies free to publicly supported schools in Ontario; 1500 by subscription; 500 selected free distribution.

L'Orbite / *édité par* Yvon Desautels. - *Publié par* Sun Life du Canada. C.P. 6075, Montréal, Qué. H3C 3G5, mars 1972-
Ancien titre: En orbite. Publié en anglais: Sun life orbit.
Paraît 8 fois par an. Organe interne/officiel, magazine, 16 p. Tirage: 2000
Envoi gratuit au GEGEP et universités.

Orchestra Canada / *edited by* Jack Edds. - *Published by* The Ontario Federation of Symphony Orchestras and The Association of Canadian Orchestras. Suite 503, 151 Bloor St. W., Toronto, Ont. M5S 1T6.
Issued every other month. Association publication, newsletter format, 8 p. Language: English and French. Includes advertising. Circulation: 1000
$2.00 per year.

Orchestra letter - *Published by* Secretariat. Ontario Federation of Symphony Orchestras. Suite 503, 151 Bloor St. W., Toronto, Ont., 1972-
Irregular (approximately 6 issues per year). Association publication, newsletter format, 14-16 p. Language: English and French.
$5.00 per year.

Order of divine service / *sponsored by* Anglican Church of Canada ; *edited by* J.G. McCausland. - *Published by* Society of St. John the Evangelist. Cowley-Bracebridge Press. P.O. Box 660, Bracebridge, Ont. P0B 1C0, 1952-
Annual. Church publication, 75-80 p. Circulation: 2000
$1.65.

Order of Nurses of Quebec. News and notes *Voir* Ordre des infirmières et infirmiers du Québec. Notes et nouvelles

Order of St. John. Ontario Council. Bulletin / *edited by* Christina Sclanders. - *Published by* Ontario Council. St. John Ambulance. 46 Wellesley St. E., Toronto, Ont. M4Y 1G5.
Quarterly. Association publication, newsletter format, 10 p. Circulation: 800
Free. Controlled circulation.

Ordre des infirmières et infirmiers du Québec. Notes et nouvelles = Order of Nurses of Quebec. News and notes / *édité par* Alice Pelletier. - *Publié par* Ordre des infirmières et infirmiers du Québec. 4200 ouest, boul. Dorchester, Montréal, Qué. H3Z 1V4.
Trimestriel. Publication d'association, magazine, 36 p. Langue(s): français et anglais. Tirage: 50,000

L'Ordre des ingénieurs forestiers du Québec. Textes des études présentées au congrès annuel - *Publié par* L'Ordre des ingénieurs forestiers du Québec. 1415, Chemin Sainte-Foy, Québec, Qué. G1S 2N7, 1921-
Annuel. Publication d'association, 100 p. Tirage: 1200

D'ores et déjà *See* Here and Now

Organic Growers Co-operative. Newsletter / *edited by* Stewart H. Fraser. - *Published by* Organic Growers Co-Operative. P.O. Box 493, Middleton, N.S. B0S 1P0, August 1974-
Monthly. Association publication, newsletter format, 16-20 p. Includes book reviews, advertising. Circulation: 300
ISSN 0317-0527 $6.00 per year. Prepayment required.

Organization for Rehabilitation through Training. Canadian ORT reporter - *Published by* Canadian ORT Organization (ORT Canada). Suite 208, 5165 Sherbrooke St. W., Montreal, Que. H4A 1T6, 1970-
Issued twice a year. Association publication, newsletter format, 4 p. Circulation: 8000
Free.

Organized farmer (to June 1970) *See* Farm trends

Orhomolecular psychiatry (May 1972-January 1974) *See* Journal of orthomolecular psychiatry

Orient / *édité par* Lucien Coutu. - *Publié par* Missions des Pères de Sainte-Croix. 4961, rue Coronet, Montréal, Qué. H3V 1C9, mai 1953-
Bimestriel. Publication ecclésiastique, magazine, 32 p. Tirage: 12,500
$.20 le numéro : $1.00 par année.

Orientation professionnelle = Vocational guidance / *édité par* André Lacombe. - *Publié par* La Corporation professionnelle des conseillers d'orientation du Québec. 1895, ave de La Salle, Montréal, Qué. H1V 2K4, octobre 1964-
Trimestriel. Publication d'association, magazine, 85 p. Langue(s): français et anglais ; sommaires: français. Comprend critique de livres. Tirage: 1500
Indexé dans RADAR, Can. educ. ind.
$3.00 le numéro : $12.00 par année : $13.00 par année, l'étranger. Tarifs spéciaux disponibles. Abonnements payables à l'avance.

Orienteering Canada / *sponsored by* Recreation Canada ; *edited by* Bob Kaill. - *Published by* Canadian Orienteering Federation. 333 River Rd., Vanier City, Ont., January 1968-
Quarterly. Association publication, newsletter format, 30 p. Circulation: 2000
Free.

Origin 100 *See* Graffiti

Origins : a magazine based on creative writing / *edited by* H. Barrett, J. Straub and Len Dickey. - *Published by* Origins. P.O. Box 72, Postal Station E, Hamilton, Ont. L8S 4K9, 1967-
Quarterly. Magazine format, 32 p.
ISSN 0048-2234 $.60 per issue : $2.00 per volume.

Ortocourier = Ortocourrier / *édité par* Philippe Päquet. - *Publié par* ORTO (Olympics Radio and Television Organization - Organization de radio télévision des olympiques). C.P. 76, Succursale H, Montréal, Qué. H3G 1J3, été 1975-
Intermittent. Publication spécialisée, magazine, Langue(s): français et anglais. Tirage: 9000
Envoi gratuit.

Ortocourrier *Voir* Ortocourier

Osgoode Hall law journal / *edited by* Kathleen Swinton. - *Published by* Osgoode Hall Law School. York University. 4700 Keele St., Downsview, Ont. M3J 1P3, 1958-
Issued 3 times a year. Legal articles, journal format, 200 p. Includes book reviews, advertising, volume index. available in microform. Back numbers available.
Circulation: 1100
Indexed in Can. leg. per. lit., Leg. per.
ISSN 0030-6185 Special rates to graduates.

Osler Library newsletter / *edited by* E.H. Bensley. - *Published by* Osler Library. McGill University. Montreal, Que., June 1969-
Issued 3 times a year. Institutional publication (Universities, schools, etc.), newsletter format, 4 p.
Free.

Other side - *Published by* Lambton College. P.O. Box 969, Sarnia, Ont. N7T 7K4.
Issued twice a month. Student publication. Includes advertising. Circulation: 1000

Other voices / *edited by* Jane Johnson. - *Published by* Alice in Wonderland Press. 100 Dutchess Ave., London, Ont. N6C 1N6, May 1965-
Former title(s): The Poets workshop.
Issued twice a year. Special interest, magazine format, 25-30 p. Includes book reviews.
Circulation: 150
$1.50 per issue : $3.00 per year.

The Other woman - *Published by* The Other Woman. P.O. Box 928, Postal Station Q, Toronto, Ont., May 1972-
Issued every other month.
Indexed in Alt. press ind.
$3.00 per year (Institutions $10.00).

Ottawa bibliothèque publique. Périodiques *See* Ottawa Public Library. Periodicals

Ottawa Civil Service Recreational Association. R A news / *edited by* J. Harber. - *Published by* Ottawa Civil Service Recreational Association. 2451 Riverside Dr., Ottawa, Ont. K1H 7X7, 1942-
Irregular (approximately 9 issues per year). Association publication, newspaper format, 20 p. Includes book reviews, advertising.
Circulation: 34,500
$2.00 per year. Free to members.

Ottawa commercial report / *edited by* B. Wrangham. - *Published by* Capital Communications Ltd. Suite 705, 151 Slater St., Ottawa, Ont. K1P 5H3, February 1973-
Monthly. Trade publication, newsletter format, 8 p. Circulation: 650
$50.00 per year.

Ottawa ethnic groups directory / *edited by* George Bonavia. - *Published by* G. Bonavia. P.O. Box 826, Postal Station B, Ottawa, Ont. K1P 5P9, 1972-
Annual. Directory, 40 p.
Free.

Ottawa Hebrew news *See* Canadian Jewish chronicle review

Ottawa jewish bulletin (1936-1973) *See* Ottawa jewish bulletin and review

Ottawa jewish bulletin and review / *edited by* Joseph Peimer. - *Published by* Jewish Community Council of Ottawa. 151 Chapel St., Ottawa, Ont. K1N 7Y2, June 1974-
Former title(s): Ottawa jewish bulletin (1936-1973)
Monthly. Ethnic press, newspaper format, 8 p. Includes book reviews, film reviews, play reviews. Circulation: 2500
Free. Controlled circulation.

Ottawa law review - *Published by* Common Law Section. Faculty of Law. University of Ottawa. 57 Copernicus St., Ottawa, Ont., 1966-
Issued 3 times a year. Legal articles, journal format, 250 p. Language: English and French. Includes book reviews, volume index. available in microform. Circulation: 1000
Indexed in Can. leg. per. lit., Leg. per., P.A.I.S.
$3.00 per issue : $9.00 per year.

The Ottawa naturalist(1887-1920) *See* Canadian field-naturalist

Ottawa Public Library. Bulletin = Bibliothèque publique d'Ottawa. Bulletin / *edited by* The Office of the Assistant Director. - *Published by* Ottawa Public Library. 120 Metcalfe St., Ottawa, Ont. K1P 5M2, 1966-
Monthly except July and August. Institutional publication (Universities, schools, etc.), newsletter format, 5 p.
Free.

Ottawa Public Library. Periodicals = Ottawa bibliothèque publique. Périodiques / *edited by* Ottawa Public Library. - *Published by* Ottawa Public Library. 120 Metcalfe St., Ottawa, Ont. K1P 5M2, 1973-
Annual. Catalogue, 92 p. Language: French and English.
$1.00.

Ottawa R and D report - *Published by* Capital Communications Ltd. Suite 705, 151 Slater St., Ottawa, Ont. K1P 5H3, April 1972-
Monthly. Special interest, newsletter format, 9 p. Circulation: 200
$50.00 per year. Controlled circulation.

Ottawa report / *edited by* Frank Ratcliffe. - *Published by* Canadian Wildlife Federation. 1673 Carling Ave., Ottawa, Ont. K2A 1C4, September-October 1975-
Issued every other month. Association publication, newsletter format, 12 p. Language: English and French. Includes volume index. Circulation: 7000
Free.

Ottawa report - *Published by* New Democratic Party. 301 Metcalfe St., Ottawa, Ont. K2P 1R9.
Former title(s): M.P.s at work.
Issued twice a month. Political press, newsletter format, 4 p. Language: English and French. Circulation: 8000

Ottawa's Catholic schools - *Published by* Ottawa Roman Catholic Separate School Board. 140 Cumberland St., Ottawa, Ont. K1N 7G9, April 1974-
Former title(s): Our children and our schools (December 1971-June 1973) ORCSSB (June 1971)
Issued twice a year. House/company organ, newspaper format, 8 p.
Free.

Oui, notre musique existe *See* Yes, there is Canadian music

Our aim *See* Nasha meta S

Our children (February 1961-December 1964) *See* The B.C. mental retardation advisor

Our children / *edited by* Elizabeth H. Marsh. - *Published by* Children's Aid Society of Metro Toronto. 33 Charles St. E., Toronto, Ont. M4Y 1R9.
Issued 3 times a year. House/company organ, magazine format, 14 p.
$2.00 per year.

Our children and our schools (December 1971-June 1973) *See* Ottawa's Catholic schools

Our country *See* Batkivschyna

Our cultural mosaic / *edited by* Leon Regan. - *Published by* Fellowship Publishers Resources Pool. P.O. Box 858, Postal Station A, Scarborough, Ont., February 1974-
Former title(s): Canadian mosaic (February 1974-September 1975)
Irregular (approximately 3-4 issues per year). Ethnic press, magazine format, 32 p. Language: English and 1 other language on 1 or 2 pages. Includes book reviews, film reviews, play reviews.
$5.00 for 12 issues. Prepayment required.

Our family / *sponsored by* Marian Press ; *edited by* A. James Materi. - *Published by* Oblate Fathers of St. Mary's Province of Canada. P.O. Box 249, Battleford, Sask. S0M 0E0, January 1949-
Monthly. Church publication, magazine format, 32 p. Includes film reviews, advertising. Circulation: 9424
$.40 per issue : $4.00 per year : $7.00 for 2 years : $10.00 for 3 years : $5.00 per volume. Special rates offered. Prepayment required.

Our generation / *edited by* C. George Benello and others. - *Published by* Our Generation. 3934 rue St. Urbain, Montreal, Que., September 1961-
Quarterly. Special interest, magazine format, 80 p. Includes book reviews. available in microform. Circulation: 3000
Indexed in Can. essay and lit. ind.
$1.50 per issue : $6.00 per year (Institutions $12.00).

Our Lady of the Cape / *edited by* Raymond Latraverse. - *Published by* Oblate Fathers of Mary Immaculate. National Shrine of Our Lady of the Cape, Cap-de-la-Madeleine, Que., 1941-
Quarterly. Church publication, magazine format, 32 p. Circulation: 7000
$.50 per issue : $2.00 per year.

Our life *See* Meie elu

Our schools / *edited by* Harold A. Marshall. - *Published by* Winnipeg School Division No. 1. 1577 Wall St. E., Winnipeg, Man. R3E 2S5, November 1972-
Former title(s): Focus on Winnipeg schools.
Monthly except July and August. Special interest, magazine format, 16-56 p.
Circulation: 30,000
Controlled circulation.

Our voices *See* Nase hlasy

Our youth - *Published by* Roman Catholic Separate School Board. 140 Cumberland St., Ottawa, Ont. K1N 7G9, May 1974-
Published in French: Nos jeunes.
Irregular (approximately 13 issues per year).
House/company organ, newsletter format, 2 p.
ISSN 0315-1974 Free.

Out front - *Published by* Kalay Foundation Society. 1636 West 1st Ave., Vancouver, B.C., 1970-
Monthly.

Outcry *See* Krzyk

Outdoor Canada / *edited by* Sheila Kaighin. - *Published by* Ron Kaighin. Suite 201, 181 Eglinton Ave. E., Toronto, Ont. M4P 1J9, December 1972-
Issued every other month. Special interest, magazine format, 80 p. Includes book reviews, advertising. Circulation: 45,000
Indexed in Can. ind.
ISSN 0315-0542 $.75 per issue : $3.50 per year : $4.25 per year, foreign : $7.45 for 2 years, foreign. Prepayment required.

Outdoor careers / *edited by* Charles Clay. - *Published by* Clay Publishing Co. Ltd. Oak St., Bewdley, K0L 1E0, 1971-
Quarterly. Magazine format, 12 p.
ISSN 0316-3431 $1.25 per issue : $4.00 per year. Prepayment required.

The Outdoor news / *edited by* Valerie Fulton. - *Published by* The Outdoor news. 302 Bridgeland Ave. (Rear), Toronto, Ont. M6A 1Z4, September 1974-
Former title(s): Ontario camping news (March 1974-August 1974)
Monthly. Special interest, newspaper format, 16 p.
$.35 per issue : $3.50 per year : $4.00 per year, foreign.

Outdoor power products = Equipement motorisé plein air / *edited by* Starr Smith. - *Published by* Peter J. Watkins. Maclean-Hunter Ltd. 481 University Ave., Toronto, Ont. M5W 1A7.
Issued 6 times per year. Special interest, magazine format, 45 p. Language: English and French ; summaries: English and French. Includes advertising. Circulation: 7000
Indexed in Can. B.P.I.
$1.00 per issue : $8.00 per year : $12.00 per year, USA and UK : $25.00 per year, foreign. Special rates offered. Prepayment required.

The Outlook / *edited by* J.E. Sharp. - *Published by* British Columbia and Yukon Provincial Council. Boy Scouts of Canada. 719 W. 16th Ave., Vancouver, B.C. V1T 6M7, Fall 1973-
Quarterly. Association publication, newsletter format, 14 p. Circulation: 2000
$2.00 per year. Controlled circulation.

Outlook (October 1966-October 1968) *See* Dialogue

Outlook *See* The Saskatchewan Indian

Ouvrages de criminologie publiés au Canada *See* Correctional literature published in Canada

L'Ouvrier *See* The Worker

Ovo. Edition français - *Publié par* Ovo Magazine. 404, rue St.-Henri, Montréal, Qué.
Publié aussi en anglais.
Bimestriel. Publication spécialisée.
$1.50 le numéro : $7.00 par année : $8.00 par année, E.U. : $10.00 par année, l'europe.

Ovo. English ed - *Published by* Ovo Magazine. 404, rue St.-Henri, Montréal, Qué.
Published also in French.
Issued every other month. Special interest.
$1.50 per issue : $7.00 for 6 issues : $8.00 for 6 issues, U.S. : $10.00 for 6 issues, foreign.

Ovul : revue socio-culturelle de l'Outaouais / *édité par* Pierre L'Heureux. - *Publié par* Ovul. C.P. 127, Succursale A, Ottawa, Ont., juillet 1973-
Ancien titre: The Pod ISSN 0315-7237 (février 1973-juin 1973)
Mensuel. Intérêt général, magazine, 24 p. Comprend critique de films, critique de pièces de théâtre, publicité. parution de suppléments. Tirage: 1100
ISSN 0315-7229 $.60 le numéro : $5.00 par année. Tarifs spéciaux disponibles. Abonnements payables à l'avance.

Owl / *edited by* Annabel Slaight and Mary Anne Brinckman. - *Published by* The Young Naturalist Foundation. 59 Front St. E., Toronto, Ont., 1976-
Former title(s): The Young Naturalist (to 1975)
Association publication.
$6.00 per year.

PATSE Newsletter (to June 1971) *See* B.C. Teachers' Federation. Special Education Association. Special Education Association newsletter

P.C. bulletin / *sponsored by* Progressive Conservative Party of Canada ; *edited by* Hugh Segal. - *Published by* Confederation Publishing. 178 Queen St., Ottawa, Ont. K1P 5E1.
Monthly. Political press, newspaper format, 4 p. Language: English and French. supplements issued. Circulation: 17,320
$10.00 per year. Prepayment required.

PITA journal (March 1962-August 1967) *See* Intermediate teacher

PLAN / *édité par* Vasco Varoujean. - *Publié par* Ordre des ingénieurs du Québec. 1100-2075, rue de l'Université, Montréal, Qué. H3A 1K8, 1962-
Mensuel. Publication d'association, journal, 15 p. Langue(s): français et anglais ; sommaires: français et anglais. Comprend publicité. Tirage: 21,500
Envoi gratuit. Tirage contrôlé.

PLAN Canada / *edited by* G. Spragge. - *Published by* Canadian Institute of Planners. Suite 30, 46 Elgin St., Ottawa, Ont. K1P 5K6, 1959-
Former title(s): Journal - The Town Planning Institute of Canada (1920-1931)
Irregular. Association publication, journal format, 80 p. Language: English and French. Circulation: 1750
$4.00 per issue : $10.00 for 3 issues, $12.00 for 3 issues foreign.

PR in Canada (1960-1969) *See* Communication

PSBGM news *See* Across the board

P C / presse campus - *Publié par* Fédération des étudiants. Université de Sherbrooke. Centre Social, Local 117, Sherbrooke, Qué., septembre 1972-
Ancien titre: Campus estrien (septembre 1959 - août 1972)
Publication des étudiants, 8 p. Comprend critique de films. Tirage: 2000
Envoi gratuit.

Pacific affairs : an international review of Asia and the Pacific / *sponsored by* The Canada Council and the University of British Columbia ; *edited by* William L. Holland. - *Published by* University of British Columbia Press. 2075 Westbrook Place, Vancouver, B.C. V6T 1W5, 1928-
Quarterly. Scholarly publication, journal format, 150 p. Includes book reviews, volume index. available in microform.
Indexed in Hum. ind., P.A.I.S., Hist. abstr.; Amer. hist. and life, A.B.C. pol. sci.
$3.00 per issue : $10.00 per year.

Pacific Association for Continuing Education. P.A.C.E. newsletter / *edited by* M.E. Lamoureux. - *Published by* Pacific Association for Continuing Education. 4533 Bellevue Dr., Vancouver, B.C. V6R 1E4, 1972-
Former title(s): A.C.E. newsletter.
Irregular (approximately 5-6 issues per year). Association publication, newsletter format, 35 p. Includes book reviews. Circulation: 400
Subscription included in membership fee
$10.00 per year. Prepayment required.

Pacific command lookout *See* The Lookout

The Pacific hosteller - *Published by* Pacific Region. Canadian Youth Hostels Association. 1406 West Broadway, Vancouver, B.C. V6H 1H4.
Quarterly. Association publication, newsletter format, 6 p. Circulation: 7000
Free. Controlled circulation.

Pacific review *See* Pazifische Rundschau

Pacific tribune / *edited by* Maurice Rush. - *Published by* Tribune Publishing Co. Ltd. Mezz. 3-193 E. Hasting , Vancouver, B.C., 1935-
Weekly. "News and analysis of the B.C. labour movement", newspaper format, 12 p. Includes book reviews. Circulation: 3600
$.15 per issue : $6.00 per year : $8.00 per year, foreign.

The Pacific troller *See* Pacific Trollers' Association. Newsletter

Pacific Trollers' Association. Newsletter / *edited by* Marv Ellis. - *Published by* Pacific Trollers' Association. P.O. Box 94336, 806 Granville Ave., Richmond, B.C. V6Y 2A8, May 1973-
Former title(s): The Pacific troller.
Irregular (approximately 11-15 issues per year). Association publication, newsletter format, 10 p. Circulation: 900
Free. Controlled circulation.

Pacific yachting : power and sail in British Columbia / *edited by* Gerry Kidd. - *Published by* Interpress Publications Ltd. 1520 Albern St., Vancouver, B.C. V6G 1A3.
Former title(s): Pacific yachting journal (August 1968-August 1969)
Monthly. Special interest, magazine format, 90 p. Includes book reviews, advertising. Circulation: 20,000
$1.00 per issue : $8.50 per year : $11.00 per year, U.S. : $15.00 per year, foreign.

Pacific yachting journal (August 1968-August 1969) *See* Pacific yachting : power and sail in British Columbia

Paediatric patter (1968-1969) *See* What's new

Les Pages jaunes des femmes de Montréal *See* Montreal Women's Yellow Pages O

Palliser Wheat Growers Association. Newsletter / *edited by* D.E. Campbell. - *Published by* Palliser Wheat Growers Association. 3829 Albert St., Regina, Sask. S4S 3R4, July 1971-
Former title(s): Western wheatman (Spring 1970-June 1971)
Monthly. Association publication, newsletter format, 4 p.
$20.00 per year.

Palmarès / *édité par* D.G. Booth. - *Publié par* La Mutuelle du Canada. 227 King St. S., Waterloo, Ont. N2J 4C5, juin 1971-
Publié en anglais: Field record.
Mensuel. Organe interne/officiel, magazine, 20 p. Comprend critique de livres.
Tirage contrôlé.

Pangnirtung 1975-prints = Estampes / *sponsored by* Pangnirtung Co-operative, Pangnirtung, N.W.T. - *Published by* Canadian Arctic Producers Ltd. P.O. Box 4130, Postal Station E, Ottawa, Ont. K1S 5B2.
Irregular (approximately 1 issue per year). Catalogue, 50 p. Language: English and French.

Panjab / *edited by* I. Ellahie. - *Published by* Asia Publications. Canada Centre Holdings Ltd. 1433 Bloor St. W., Toronto, Ont. M6P 3L6, 1975-
Monthly. Ethnic press. Language: Urdu. Includes advertising.
$.50 per issue : $6.00 per year.

Panorama / *edited by* Betty Peterson. - *Published by* Society of Canadian Cine Amateurs. 4653 Dundas St. W., Islington, Ont. M9A 1A4, March 1970-
Former title(s): Film monthly (June 1968-February 1970)
Monthly. Association publication, magazine format, 16-20 p. Includes book reviews, film reviews, advertising.
$.40 per issue : $4.00 per year. Free to Society members. Prepayment required.

Papers and discussions - Canadian Pulp and Paper Association. Technical Section *See* Canadian Pulp and Paper Association. Technical Section. Transactions

Le Papetier / *édité par* Jacques Trépanier. - *Publié par* Conseil des producteurs de pâtes et papiers du Québec. Bureau 502, 500 est, Grande-Allée, Québec, Qué. G1R 2J7, janvier 1964-
Intermittent (approximativement 5 éditions par an). Revue d'entreprise, journal, 12 p.

Parachute : revue d'art contemporain / *parrainé par* Centre de documentation en art contemporain ; *édité par* France Morin, Chantal Pontbriand et George Bogardi. - *Publié par* Artdata enr. C.P. 730, Station N, Montréal, Qué., octobre 1975-
Trimestriel. Publication spécialisée, magazine, 40 p. Langue(s): français et anglais.
$2.50 le numéro : $9.00 par année : $2.50 le volume : $10.00 par année, l'étranger.

Paraclite / *edited by* B.G. Hallam. - *Published by* New Brunswick Division. Canadian Paraplegic Association. Room 302, 212 Queen St., Fredericton, N.B.
Issued every other month. Association publication, newsletter format, 8 p.
$2.00 per year.

Paragraphic / *edited by* Canadian Paraplegic Association. - *Published by* British Columbia Division. Canadian Paraplegic Association. 780 S.W. Marine Dr., Vancouver, B.C. V6P 5Y7, 1960-
Quarterly. Association publication, newsletter format, 8 p.
$2.00 per year.

Parikiaka news / *edited by* Nick Tsolakis. - *Published by* Parikiaka News. 8247 Querbes Ave., Montreal, Que. H3N 2C3.
Monthly. Ethnic press. Language: Greek. Includes advertising. Circulation: 6000

Park news / *edited by* Terry Green. - *Published by* National and Provincial Parks Association of Canada. Suite 18, 43 Victoria St., Toronto, Ont. (Subscription address: Suite 308, 47 Colborne St., Toronto, Ont. M5E 1E3) 1965-
Quarterly. Association publication, magazine format, 32 p. Circulation: 2000
Indexed in North. tit.
ISSN 0553-3066 $10.00 per year. Subscription included in membership fee.

Parks and recreation in Canada (1953-1969) *See* Recreation Canada

Parks for tomorrow - *Published by* National and Provincial Parks Association of Canada. Suite 18, 43 Victoria St., Toronto, Ont. (Subscription address: Suite 308, 47 Colborne St., Toronto, Ont. M5E 1E3) 1972-
Irregular (approximately 4-6 issues per year). Association publication, newsletter format, 2 p. Circulation: 2000
Subscription included in membership fee.

Parole-dimanche / *édité par* Pierre Bougie. - *Publié par* Centre biblique de Montréal. 2000 ouest, rue Sherbrooke, Montréal, Qué. H3H 1G4, novembre 1958-
Ancien titre: Le feuillet biblique - Parole-dimanche (novembre 1958 - septembre 1970)
Hebdomadaire. Publication ecclésiastique, bulletin, 6 p. Comprend index de volumes. Tirage: 11,000
ISSN 0018-912X $7.00 : $7.50 par année, l'étranger. Tarifs spéciaux disponibles.

Participation in sport and leisure activies - *Published by* SIRLS. Faculty of Human Kinetics and Leisure Studies. University of Waterloo. Waterloo, Ont. N2L 3G1.
Quarterly. Bibliography, computer printout, $20.00 per year. $100.00 subscription to SIRLS required.

Partners in child care / *edited by* Jane McNally. - *Published by* Catholic Children's Aid Society of Metropolitan Toronto. 26 Maitland St., Toronto, Ont. M4Y 1C6, Spring 1967-
Quarterly. House/company organ, magazine format, 12 p. Circulation: 2000

The Pastoral visitor / *sponsored by* Anglican Church of Canada. Diocese of Toronto ; *edited by* R.K. Downey. - *Published by* Pastoral Visitor Editorial Committee. 135 Adelaide St. E., Toronto, Ont. M5C 1L8 (Subscription address: 1509 Applewood Rd., Mississauga, Ont. L5E 2M2) January 1971-
Former title(s): Hospital chaplaincy bulletin; A Chaplin's markings.
Monthly, 11 issues per year. Church publication, pamphlet format, 4 p. Circulation: 17,000
$4.40 per year. Bulk rate schedule available on request.

Pastorale - Québec : revue de l'église de Québec / *parrainé par* Le Service de pastorale du diocèse de Québec ; *édité par* Denis Duval. - *Publié par* Diocèse de Québec. Grand Séminaire, Cité Universitaire, Québec, Qué. G1K 7P4, janvier 1971-
Ancien titre: Eglise de Québec (1967-1970)
Paraît tous les 15 jours. Publication ecclésiastique, magazine, 24 p. Comprend critique de livres, critique de disques, publicité. Tirage: 2700
$.50 le numéro : $10.00 par année.

Patent and Trademark Institute of Canada. Bulletin / *edited by* R.D. Frayne. - *Published by* Patent and Trademark Institute of Canada. P.O. Box 1298, Postal Station B, Ottawa, Ont. K1P 5R3, March 1962-
Irregular (approximately 2-4 issues per year). Association publication, magazine format, 48 p. Circulation: 560
$5.00 per issue : $25.00 per year. Free to college libraries. Subscription includes Its Newsletter. Prepayment required.

Patent and Trademark Institute of Canada. Newsletter - *Published by* Patent and Trademark Institute of Canada. P.O. Box 1298, Postal Station B, Ottawa, Ont. K1P 5R3, January 1967-
Irregular (approximately 6 issues per year). Association publication, newsletter format, 12 p. Circulation: 560
$1.00 per issue : $25.00 per year. Free Subscription includes its Bulletin. Prepayment required.

Patents handbook (prior to April 1972) *See* Inventions catalog: inventions for industry

Pathfinder - *Published by* North West Region. Canadian Youth Hostels Association. 10922-88 Ave., Edmonton, Alta., 1963-
Irregular (approximately 3-4 issues per year). Association publication, newsletter format, 4 p. Circulation: 3200
Free to members.

The Patrician / *edited by* The Regimental Adjutant Princess Patricia's Canadian Light Infantry. - *Published by* Princess Patricia's Canadian Light Infantry. c/o Regimental Adjutant, Currie Barracks, Calgary, Alta. T3E 1T8, 1934-
Annual. Special interest, 180 p. Circulation: 1300
ISSN 0316-4942 $3.00 per volume.

Pattern and probe *See* Western management/Pattern and probe

Pax regis / *sponsored by* Westminster Abbey ; *edited by* Andrew Keber. - *Published by* Seminary of Christ the King. Mission, B.C. V2V 4J2, June 1942-
Issued twice a year. Church publication, magazine format, 20 p. Circulation: 1800
$.50 per issue : $1.00 per year.

Paysage Canada *See* Landscape

Paysage Canada *See* Landscape

Pazifische Rundschau = Pacific review / *edited by* Baldwin Ackermann. - *Published by* Ackerman's Advertising & News Ltd. P.O. Box 2033, Vancouver, B.C. V6B 3R6, December 1965-
Former title(s): Dies und das (December 1965-December 1970)
Issued twice a month. Ethnic press, newspaper format, 16 p. Language: German. Includes book reviews, film reviews. Circulation: 10,050
$.15 per issue : $3.00 per year : $4.00 per year, foreign.

Peace research / *edited by* Committee of the Canadian Peace Research Institute. - *Published by* Canadian Peace Research Institute. 119 Thomas St., Oakville, Ont. L6J 3A7, 1969-
Quarterly. Association publication, journal format, 20 p. Circulation: 1500
Indexed in Hist. abstr.; Amer. hist. and life.
Free.

Peace research abstracts journal / *edited by* Alan G. Newcombe and Hanna Newcombe. - *Published by* Canadian Peace Research Institute. 119 Thomas St., Oakville, Ont. (Subscription address: 25 Dundana Ave., Dundas, Ont.) 1964-
Monthly. Institutional publication (Universities, schools, etc.), journal format, 200 p. Includes volume index. supplements issued. Peace research abstracts supplement (coding manual) supplied without charge with each volume of twelve issues. Circulation: 461
ISSN 0031-3599 $6.00 per issue : $75.00 per year : $78.75 per year, U.S.

Peace research reviews / *edited by* Alan G. Newcombe and Hanna Newcombe. - *Published by* Canadian Peace Research Institute. 119 Thomas St., Oakville, Ont. (Subscription address: 25 Dundana Ave., Dundas, Ontario) 1967-
Irregular. Institutional publication (Universities, schools, etc.), journal format, 100 p. Circulation: 450
Indexed in I.B.Z., A.B.C. pol. sci.
ISSN 0079-0346 $2.00 per issue : $10.00 per volume. 16.6% discount on orders over 10 copies; $1.50 per issue; $7.00 per volume when payment accompanies the order.

The Peak / *edited by* John Toor (coordinator). - *Published by* Peak Publications Society. Simon Fraser University, Burnaby, B.C. V5A 1S6, September 1966-
Weekly. Student publication, newspaper format, 20 p. Includes book reviews, film reviews, play reviews, record reviews, advertising. available in microform.
Circulation: 8000
$2.50 per semester : $7.50 per year : $12.00 per year, foreign. Controlled circulation.

Pegasus *See* Amber

Pegboard / *edited by* Stephen J. Gee. - *Published by* Gatineau Zone. Quebec Division. Canadian Ski Patrol System. 288 Richmond Rd., Westboro, Ont.
Former title(s): "Fracture".
Monthly. House/company organ, magazine format, 36 p. Circulation: 275
Free. Controlled circulation.

The Pegg / *edited by* A.C. Milroy. - *Published by* Association of Professional Engineers, Geologists, and Geophysicists of Alberta. 215 One Thornton Court, Edmonton, Alta. T5J 2E7, 1950-
Issued twice a week. Association publication, magazine format, 80 p. Includes advertising.
Circulation: 12,000
$5.00 per year. Free. Controlled circulation.
Prepayment required.

The Pelican / *edited by* Nancy Rodrigues. - *Published by* The Canada Life Assurance Company. 330 University Ave., Toronto, Ont., March 1974-
Issued every other week. House/company organ, newspaper format, 8 p.
Controlled circulation.

The Pentecostal testimony / *edited by* Joy E. Hansell. - *Published by* The Pentecostal Assemblies of Canada. 10 Overlea Blvd., Toronto, Ont. M4H 1A5, December 1920-
Monthly. Church publication, magazine format, 28 or 32 p. Includes advertising. Circulation: 17,634
$.33 per issue : $4.50 per year.

People's Canada daily news / *edited by* Hardial Bains. - *Published by* Norman Bethune Institute. P.O. Box 727, Adelaide Station, Toronto, Ont., 1970-
Daily. 4 p.
$.25 per issue : $6.00 per month : $60.00 per year : $8.00 per month, foreign : $80.00 per year, foreign.

People's forest - *Published by* Peoples Wood Producers Board. 37 13th St. E., Prince Albert, Sask., 1974-
Annual. House/company organ.

People's voice *See* Liaudies balsas

Perception (Spring 1960-Spring 1972) *See* British Columbia Art Teachers' Association. BCATA journal for art teachers

Père d'aujourd'hui (septembre 1965-septembre 1966) *Voir* Chrétiens d'aujourd'hui

Le Père Eugène Prévost *Voir* Aux amis du Père Prévost

Le Père Frédéric *Voir* Souvenir du bon Père Frédéric, O.F.M. Nouvelle série annuelle

Performing arts in Canada / *edited by* Arnold Edinborough. - *Published by* George Hencz. 2nd Floor, 52 Avenue Rd., Toronto, Ont. M5R 2G3, 1961-
Quarterly. Special interest, magazine format, 52 p. Includes book reviews, play reviews, record reviews, advertising. available in microform. Circulation: 30,000
Indexed in Can. ind.
$1.00 per issue : $3.00 per year.

Performing arts magazine / *edited by* Arnold Edinborough. - *Published by* George Hercz. Canadian Stage and Arts Publications Ltd. 52 Avenue Rd., Toronto, Ont. M5R 2G3, 1961-
Quarterly. Special interest, magazine format, Includes advertising. Circulation: 34,874
$1.00 per issue : $3.00 per year : $5.00 for 2 years : $4.00 per year, foreign : $6.00 for 2 years, foreign.

Perhaps you can help : volunteer job description for all ages / *edited by* Jean F. Matthews and Barbara Crawford. - *Published by* Volunteer Bureau of Social Planning and Research Council, Hamilton and District. 153 1/2 King St. E., Hamilton Ont. L8N 1B1, Spring 1975-
Annual. Directory, 40 p.
$1.00. Special rates offered.

Personality and sport - *Published by* SIRLS. Faculty of Human Kinetics and Leisure Studies. University of Waterloo. Waterloo, Ont. N2L 3G1.
Quarterly. Bibliography, computer printout, $20.00 per year. $100.00 subscription to SIRLS required.

Personnel guide to Canada's travel industry / *edited by* Edith Baxter. - *Published by* Baxter Publishing Company. 150 King St. W., Toronto, ont.
Issued twice a year. Trade publication. Includes advertising.
$5.00 per issue.

Perspective *See* Spectrum

Perspectives / *édité par* Pierre Gascon. - *Publié par* Perspectives inc. 231, St-Jacques, Montréal, Qué., septembre 1959-
Hebdomadaire. Magazine, 32 p. Tirage: 550,000
Diffusé par six journaux quotidiens dans leur édition du samedi.

Perspectives / *sponsored by* Saskatchewan Council of Social Studies Teachers ; *edited by* John Schaller. - *Published by* Saskatchewan Teachers' Federation. 2317 Arlington Ave., Saskatoon, Sask., 1964-
Former title(s): Social science teachers newsletter.
Quarterly. Association publication, journal format, 40 p. Includes book reviews, volume index. Circulation: 165
Indexed in Can. educ. ind.
ISSN 0316-3334 $6.00 per year. Prepayment required.

Perspectives des bois traités *See* Treated wood perspectives

Perspectives on curriculum / *edited by* A.T. Pearson. - *Published by* Faculty of Education. University of Alberta. Edmonton, Alta. T6G 2E7 (Subscription address: The University of Alberta Bookstore, Edmonton, Alberta) 1971-
Annual. Institutional publication (Universities, schools, etc.), journal format, 180 p. Circulation: 100
$2.00.

Peterborough Historical Society. Bulletin / *edited by* John MacKelvie. - *Published by* Peterborough Historical Society. P.O. Box 143, Centennial Museum, Peterborough, Ont. K9J 6Y5, 1967-
Monthly. Association publication, newsletter format, 4 p.
$3.00 per year.

Petite revue du tiers-ordre et des intérêts du Coeur de Jésus (février 1884-janvier 1975) *Voir* La Revue franciscaine

Le Phare / *édité par* William Henri Frey. - *Publié par* L'Association des Eglises baptistes évangéliques au Canada. 10211, Basile Routhier, Montréal, Qué. H2G 2C5(adresse d'abonnement: 7181, rue Ouimet, Verdun, Qué. H4H 2J3) mai 1956-
Mensuel. Publication ecclésiastique, magazine, 16 p. Tirage: 4500
$.50 le numéro : $2.00 par année.

Phi zéro : revue étudiante de philosophie - *Publié par* Service de documentation. Université de Montréal. C.P. 6128, 2910, Edouard Montpetit, Montréal, Qué. H3C 3J7, janvier 1973-
Paraît 3 fois par an. Edition savante, revue, 120 p. Tirage: 175
Indexé dans RADAR.
$.90 le numéro : $2.00 par année. Abonnements payables à l'avance.

Le Philanthrope *See* The Philanthropist

The Philanthropist = Le Philanthrope / *sponsored by* The Canadian Bar Association ; *edited by* Bertha Wilson. - *Published by* University of Toronto Press. 5201 Dufferin St., Downsview, Ont. M3H 5T8 (Subscription address: Suite 1700, 4 King St. W., Toronto, Ont. M5H 1B9) Fall 1972-
Irregular (approximately 2 issues per year). Association publication, magazine format, 65 p.
$3.00 per issue.

Philippine-Canadian free press / *edited by* Mike R. Ligon. - *Published by* Philippine Canadian Free Press. 374 College St., Toronto, Ont. M5T 1S6.
Monthly. Ethnic press. Language: Philippino and English. Includes advertising.
$.15 per issue : $1.80 per year.

Philippines / *édité par* Gérard Lefebvre. - *Publié par* Le Centre Cor Jesu d'Ottawa. 328, rue Chapel, Ottawa, Ont. K1N 7Z3., juin 1963-
Trimestriel. Publication ecclésiastique, bulletin, 4 p. Langue(s): français et anglais.
$1.00 par année.

Philosophiques : revue de philosophie / *édité par* Yvon Lafrance. - *Publié par* Editions Bellarmin. 8100, boul. Saint-Laurent, Montréal, Qué. H2P 2L9, avril 1974-
Semestriel. Edition savante, revue, 175 p. Comprend critique de livres. Tirage: 127
ISSN 0316-2923 $5.00 le numéro : $8.00 par année (Institutions $10.00). Abonnements payables à l'avance.

Phoenix / *sponsored by* The Classical Association of Canada ; *edited by* T.M. Robinson. - *Published by* University of Toronto Press. 5201 Dufferin St., Downsview, Ont. M3H 5T8 (Subscription address: Secretary/Treasurer, Trinity College, Toronto, Ont. M5S 1H8) 1946-
Quarterly. Journal format, 108 p. Language: English and French. Includes book reviews, advertising, volume index, cumulative index. supplements issued. Back numbers available. Circulation: 1200
Indexed in Curr. ind. j. educ., I.B.Z.
$3.75 per issue : $10.00 per year : $15.00 per volume. Volumes 1-12 $10.00 per volume; $3.75 per issue. Prepayment required.

Photo Atlantic / *edited by* Pat Pritchard. - *Published by* Photo-Atlantic Productions Ltd. P.O. Box 2222, Halifax, N.S., 1970-
Annual. Magazine format, Includes advertising.
$1.95 per year.

Le Photographe professionnel / *édité par* Laurent Granger. - *Publié par* Association des photographes professionnels de la province de Québec. Suite 403, 477, St-Francois Xavier, Montréal, Qué. H2Y 2T2, janvier 1962-
Bimestriel. Publication d'association, magazine, 36 p. Tirage: 1200

Physics in Canada = La Physique au Canada / *edited by* R.L. Clarke. - *Published by* Canadian Association of Physicists. Suite 903, 151 Slater St., Ottawa, K1P 5H3, 1945-
Issued every other month. Association publication, magazine format, 30 p. Language: English and French. Includes book reviews, advertising. Circulation: 2120
$2.00 per issue : $10.00 per year. Controlled circulation. Prepayment required.

Physiologie Canada *See* Canada physiology

Physiothérapie Canada *See* Physiotherapy Canada

Physiotherapy Canada = Physiothérapie Canada / *edited by* Joan Cleather. - *Published by* The Canadian Physiotherapy Association. 469 Stanstead Cres., Montreal, Que. H3R 1Y1 (Subscription address: 25 Imperial St., Toronto, Ont. M5P 1B9) 1923-
Former title(s): The Journal of the Canadian Physiotherapy Association (1923-1972)
Irregular (approximately 5 issues per year). Association publication, Journal, 60-70 p. Language: English ; summaries: French. Includes book reviews, advertising, volume index. Circulation: 4980
ISSN 0300-0508 $7.00 per year : $13.00 for 2 years : $19.00 for 3 years : $9.00 per year, foreign : $17.00 for 2 years, foreign : $25.00 for 3 years, foreign. Prepayment required.

La Physique au Canada *See* Physics in Canada

Phytoprotection / *édité par* Irénée Rivard. - *Publié par* La Société de protection des plantes du Québec. Complexe Scientifique, D-L-63, 555 boul. Henri IV, Ste-Foy, Qué.
Ancien titre: Rapport annuel de La Société de protection des plantes du Québec (1908-1963)
Intermittent (approximativement 3 éditions par an). Publication d'association, magazine, 50 p. Comprend critique de livres, index cumulatif. parution de suppléments. Tirage: 1000
$5.00 le numéro : $5.00 par année : $15.00 le volume. Abonnements payables à l'avance.

Picaro - *Published by* Students' Union. Mount St. Vincent University. Halifax, N.S.
Issued twice a month. Student publication. Includes advertising. Circulation: 2000

Pilot / *edited by* Roger Burgess-Webb. - *Published by* Canadian Air Line Pilots' Association, Montreal. 9675 Cote de Liesse Rd., Dorval, Que. H9P 1A3, April 1944-
Former title(s): The Canadian airline pilot (April 1944-Summer 1970)
Quarterly. Association publication, magazine format, 44 p. Includes advertising, volume index. Circulation: 3300
$5.00 per year. Prepayment required.

The Pioneer (1902 - April 1928) *See* Concerns

Pioneer Christian monthly / *edited by* P.J. Yff. - *Published by* The Council of the Reformed Churches in Canada. 201 Paradise Rd. N., Hamilton, Ont. L8S 3T3, 1950-
11 issues per year July/August issue combined. Church publication, 32 p. Language: English and Dutch. Includes book reviews, film reviews, advertising, volume index. Circulation: 2530
$.50 per issue : $5.00 per year. Prepayment required.

Pivnichne siayvo = Northern lights: almanac / *edited by* Yar Slavutych. - *Published by* Slavuta Publishers. 72 Westbrook Dr., Edmonton, Alta. T6J 2E1, 1964-
Irregular. Ethnic press, Almanac, 180 p. Language: Ukrainian. Includes book reviews. Circulation: 500
$5.00 per issue.

Placowka nad pacifikem: - *Published by* B.C. Branch. Polish Combatant's Association in Canada. 1134 Kingsway St., Vancouver, B.C. V5V 3C8, 1951-
Issued every other month. Association publication, newsletter format, 18 p. Language: Polish. Circulation: 250

The Plainsman / *edited by* R. Cote. - *Published by* Base Commander. Canadian Forces Base, Moose Jaw. P.O. Box 33, Bushell Park, Sask. S0H 0N0, November 1968-
Issued twice a month. House/company organ, newspaper format, 10 p. Includes advertising. Circulation: 800
$1.50 per year.

Plan Canada - *Published by* Town Planing Institute of Canada. Suite 49, 46 Elgin St., Ottawa, Ont. K1P 5K2.
Quarterly.
$3.00 per issue : $10.00 per year (Non-members $4.00) : $12.00 per year, foreign.

Plan Canada news / *edited by* Anastasia Erland. - *Published by* Foster Parents Plan of Canada. 153 St. Clair Ave. W., Toronto, Ont. M4V 1P8, June 1974-
Issued twice a year. House/company organ, newspaper format, 4 p.
Free.

El Planeta / *edited by* Luis S. Valdés. - *Published by* Luis S. Valdés. 983 College St. W., Toronto, Ont., 1974-
Weekly. Ethnic press. Language: Spanish. Includes advertising.
$10.00 per year.

Planning Institute of British Columbia. PIBC newsletter / *edited by* Deane Strongitharm. - *Published by* Planning Institute of British Columbia. P.O. Box 24835, Postal Station C, Vancouver, B.C. V5T 4E9, October 1959-
Irregular (approximately 10 issues per year). Institutional publication (Universities, schools, etc.), newsletter format, 24 p. Circulation: 280
Free to members : $10.00 per year to non-member. Controlled circulation. Special rates offered.

Plans : planning information exchange for N.S. - *Published by* N.S. Division. Community Planning Association of Canada. P.O. Box 211, Halifax, N.S., 1971-
Former title(s): News letter - Community Planning Association of Canada. Nova Scotia Division.
Irregular (approximately 6 issues per year). Newsletter format,
$10.00 per year (Students $4.00). Subscription included in membership fee.

Plans on display bulletin / *edited by* The Secretary. - *Published by* Niagara Construction Association. P.O. Box 983, 34 Scott St., St. Catharines, Ont. L2R 6Z4.
Weekly. Association publication, newsletter format, 2 p.
Free (circulated to members only). Controlled circulation.

Plant - *Published by* Dawson College. 350 Selby St., Montreal, Que.
Weekly. Student publication. Includes advertising. Circulation: 7000

Plant administration and engineering *See* Plant management and engineering

Plant management and engineering / *edited by* John Davies. - *Published by* George Clifford. Maclean-Hunter Ltd. 481 University Ave., Toronto, Ont. M5S 1A6.
Former title(s): Plant administration and engineering.
Monthly. Trade publication, magazine format, 90 p. Includes book reviews, advertising. supplements issued. Circulation: 12,000
Indexed in Can. B.P.I.
ISSN 0315-9183 $1.00 per issue : $10.00 per year : $12.00 per year, U.S. And U.K. : $25.00 per year, foreign. Free to management. Controlled circulation.

Plastatistics / *edited by* E.R. Evason. - *Published by* The Society of the Plastics Industry of Canada. 1262 Don Mills Rd., Don Mills, Ont. M3B 2W7, June 1971-
Monthly. Association publication, scholarly publication, newsletter format, 7 p.
$25.00 per year. Special rates offered.

Plastics directory of Canada / *sponsored by* Canadian Plastics ; *edited by* Antony Anden. - *Published by* Southam Business Publications Ltd. 1450 Don Mills Rd., Don Mills, Ont.
Other title: Canadian plastics and a buyers guide.
Annual. Directory, magazine format, 250 p.
$10.00. Controlled circulation.

Plasticwords / *edited by* E.R. Evason. - *Published by* The Society of the Plastics Industry of Canada. 1262 Don Mills Rd., Don Mills, Ont., November 1966-
Monthly. Association publication, newsletter format, 12 p.
$25.00 per year. Special rates offered.

Plastovy shliakh / *sponsored by* Plast - Ukrainian Youth Association ; *edited by* W. Sochanivskyj. - *Published by* Plast Publication. 2445 A Bloor St. W., Toronto, Ont. M6S 1P7, October 1930-
Quarterly. Ethnic press, magazine format, 64 p. Language: Ukrainian. Circulation: 1400
$2.00 per issue : $8.00 per year. Prepayment required.

Playboard / *edited by* Steven Chitty. - *Published by* Harold Schiel. Archway Publishers Ltd. 7560 Lawrence Dr., Burnaby, B.C. V5A 1T6, October 1966-
Monthly. Calendar of events, magazine format, 12-42 p. Includes play reviews, advertising.
$10.00 per year. Free. Controlled circulation.

Pleasure seeker (December 1973 - April 1975) *See* Seeker

Plein air / *édité par* Charles Meunier. - *Publié par* Charles Meunier. 1415 est, rue Jarry, Montréal, Qué. H2E 1A7.
Publié en anglais: Outdoor magazine.
Comprend publicité.

Pleins feux sur la francophonie... - *Publié par* Association canadienne d'éducation de langue française. 980, chemin St-Louis, Sillery, Qué. G1S 1C7.
Annuel. Publication d'association, magazine, 25 p. Tirage: 10,000

Plomberie-chauffage et climatisation le guide de l'acheteur / *édité par* R. Allaire. - *Publié par* Henry Longstaff. Southam Business Publications Ltd. Suite 201, 310, ave Victoria, Montréal, Qué. H3Z 2M9.
Annuel. Revue d'entreprise. Comprend publicité.
$5.00 par année.

Plumbers pot - *Published by* Engineering Undergraduate Society. McGill University. McConnell Engineering Building, McGill University, Montreal, Que., 1904-
Irregular (approximately 10 issues per year). Student publication. Includes advertising.

The Pod ISSN 0315-7237 (février 1973-juin 1973) *Voir* Ovul : revue socio-culturelle de l'Outaouais

Podium (to September 1975) *See* Insight

Poetry - Windsor = Windsor poésie / *edited by* A. Amprimoz, W. Schiller and A. van den Hoven. - *Published by* French Department. University of Windsor. P.O. Box 6, Sandwich P.O., Windsor, Ont., December 1974-
Irregular (approximately 3 issues per year). Special interest, magazine format, 22 p. Language: English and French ; summaries: English and French. Circulation: 75
$2.50 per year.

Poetry Canada / *edited by* Leona M. Gom. - *Published by* League of Canadian poets. 3323-W. 3rd Ave., Vancouver, B.C. V6R 1L3, 1968-
Irregular (approximately 4 issues per year). Newsletter format, 8 p.
ISSN 0316-036x Subscription included in membership fee. Controlled circulation.

The Poets workshop *See* Other voices

Poilitics leisure and sport - *Published by* SIRLS. Faculty of Human Kinetics and Leisure Studies. University of Waterloo. Waterloo, Ont. N2I 3G1.
Quarterly. Bibliography, computer printout, $20.00 per year. $100.00 subscription to SIRLS required.

Le Point / *édité par* Maurice Chartrand. - *Publié par* La Revue commerce. 1080, Beaver Hall Hill, Montréal, Qué. H2Z 1T1, 1968-
Annuel. Revue d'entreprise. Comprend publicité. Tirage: 29,136

Points west / *edited by* H.A. Renfree. - *Published by* Baptist Union of Western Canada. 4404-16th St. S.W., Calgary, Alta. T2T 4H9, 1968-
Irregular (approximately 4 issues per year). Church publication, newsletter format, 16 p. Circulation: 14,000
Free.

Le Polariseur / *parrainé par* Commission scolaire régionale du Cuivre ; *édité par* Norman Fink. - *Publié par* Service des bibliothèques : Service des centres de documentation. C.P. 908, Rouyn, Qué. J9X 3C5(adresse d'abonnement: 55, des Oblats, Rouyn, Qué) avril 1974-
Ancien titre: Bibliovision (septembre 1970-avril 1973)
Intermittent (approximativement 5 éditions par an). Publication spécialisée, bulletin, 40 p. Comprend critique de livres, critique de pièces de théâtre, publicité. Tirage: 30
$1.50 le numéro.

Police : revue des agents de police = Constables review / *édité par* Lucien Champeau. - *Publié par* Fraternité des policiers de la communauté urbaine de Montréal inc. 480, rue Gilford, Montréal, Qué. H2J 1N3, février 1946-
Mensuel. Publication d'association, revue, 32 p. Langue(s): français et anglais ; sommaires: français et anglais. Tirage: 6850
$5.00 par année : $7.00 (relié). Envoi gratuit aux membres de l'association.

Police dossiers / *édité par* G.-A. Parent. - *Publié par* Les Ecrits du palais enr. Chambre 819, 1117 ouest, rue Ste-Catherine, Montréal, Qué., février 1975-
Intermittent (approximativement 3-4 éditions par an). Publication spécialisée, magazine, 32 p. Tirage: 28,500
$1.00 le numéro.

Polish Canadian courier *See* Kurier polsko-kanadyjski

The Polish Canadian courier = Kurier Poisko-Kanadyjski / *edited by* W. Markiewicz. - *Published by* W. Markiewicz. 36 Robina Ave., Toronto, Ont. M6C 3Y6 (Subscription address: P.O. Box 161, Postal Station P, Toronto, Ont) 1972-
Weekly. Ethnic press. Language: Polish and English. Includes advertising.
$.15 per issue : $7.50 per year.

Polish engineering review (1944-1948) *See* Association of Polish Engineers in Canada. Bulletin

Polish voice gazette *See* Glos Polski-gazeta Polska

Politique laitière *See* Dairy policy

Polyfacts / *edited by* Charles Law. - *Published by* Corpus Publishers Services Ltd. 6 Crescent Rd., Toronto, Ont. M4W 1T1, February 26, 1973-
Weekly. Special interest, newsletter format, 6 p. supplements issued.
ISSN 0315-2588 $2.00 per issue : $95.00 per year. Prepayment required.

Polysar progress. Plastics edition / *edited by* Dick With. - *Published by* Polysar Limited. Sarnia, Ont. N7T 7M2, 1974-
Issued every other month. House/company organ, newsletter format, 8 p.
Free.

Polysar progress. Rubber and latex edition / *edited by* Rod Wiechers. - *Published by* Polysar Limited. Sarnia, Ont. N7T 7M2, 1965-
Issued every other month. House/company organ, newsletter format, 8 p.
Free.

Le Polyscope - *Publié par* Association des étudiants de polytechnique inc. (AEP inc.). Campus de l'Université de Montréal, C.P. 6079, Succursale A, Montréal, Qué. H3C 3A7, septembre 1967-
Hebdomadaire. Publication des étudiants, journal, 12 p. Comprend critique de pièces de théâtre, critique de disques, publicité. Tirage: 10,000
$3.00 par année.

Pools, parks and rinks / *edited by* Geoff Spark. - *Published by* Allan Carin. Southam Business Publications Ltd. 1450 Don Mills Rd., Don Mills, Ont. M3B 2X7, 1958-
Issued every other month. Trade publication. Includes advertising. Circulation: 3772
$1.50 per issue : $8.00 per year.

El Popular / *edited by* Alberto Pintos. - *Published by* Ralph Janowitzer. 486 College St., Toronto, Ont. (Subscription address: P.O. Box 1108, Adelaide St. Station, Toronto, Ont. M5C 2K5) 1970-
Issued twice a week. Ethnic press. Language: Spanish. Includes advertising.
$.25 per issue : $14.00 per year.

Le Portage - *Publié par* Conseil canadien des arts populaires. Suite 300, 8607, boul. St-Laurent, Montréal, Qué. H2P 2N2, 1974-
Mensuel. Bulletin, 8 p. Comprend publicité. Envoi gratuit.

Portfolio strategy - *Published by* Nesbitt, Thomson & Co. Ltd. 355 St. James St. W., Montreal, Que. H2Y 1P1, November 1974-
Quarterly. Trade publication, 50 p. Controlled circulation.

Ports and shipyards *See* Shipping register

The Post / *edited by* Arlette Straessle. - *Published by* Canadian Association for Children with Learning Disabilities. 1390 Sherbrooke St. W., Montreal, Que. H3G 1K2.
Quarterly. Association publication, newspaper format, 4 p. Includes book reviews. Circulation: 4000
$8.00 per year. Free to members. Prepayment required.

Postal Christian witness / *edited by* Esther F. Fuller. - *Published by* Christian Transportation Inc. 512 Yonge St. (rear), Toronto, Ont. M4Y 1X9, April 1964-
Quarterly. Church publication.

Postup = Progress / *edited by* S. Izyk. - *Published by* Progress Printers and Publishers. 418 Aberdeen Ave., Winnipeg, Man. R2W 1V7, 1958-
Weekly. Ethnic press. Language: Ukrainian and English. Includes advertising. Circulation: 5982
$.20 per issue : $8.00 per year : $9.00 per year, foreign.

Poumons - *Publié par* Société du timbre de Noël du Québec inc. 264, rue Chénier, Québec, Qué. G1K 1R2.
Ancien titre: Observation-opinion-orientation (printemps 1967-printemps 1974)
Trimestriel. Publication d'association, bulletin, 16 p. Tirage: 5100
Envoi gratuit. Publication distribuée gratuitement grâce aux souscriptions au Timbre de Noël.

Power protection / *edited by* J.M. McLaren. - *Published by* The Boiler Inspection and Insurance Company of Canada. 8 King St. E., Toronto, Ont. M5C 1B5, June 1951-
Irregular. House/company organ, magazine format, 24 p. Circulation: 7000
Free.

Prairie forum : journal of the Canadian Plains Research Centre / *edited by* Alexander H. Paul. - *Published by* Canadian Plains Research Centre. University of Regina. University of Regina, Regina, Sask., 1975-
Issued twice a year. Institutional publication (Universities, schools, etc.), magazine format, 100-150 p. Language: English ; summaries: English and French. Includes book reviews.
ISSN 0317-6282 $10.00 per year. Prepayment required.

The Prairie garden : Western Canada's only gardening annual / *edited by* Phyllis Thomson. - *Published by* Winnipeg Horticultural Society. P.O. Box 517, Winnipeg, Man. R3C 2J3.
Annual. Association publication, magazine format, 150 p. Back issues $1.50 each. Circulation: 10,000
ISSN 0315-6850 $2.00 per year.

Prairie messenger : Saskatchewan Catholic weekly / *sponsored by* St. Peter's Abbey, Muenster, Sask ; *edited by* Michael M. Pomedli. - *Published by* St. Peter's Press. Muenster, Sask. S0K 2Y0, May 1923-
Weekly. Church publication, newspaper format, 16 p. Includes book reviews, film reviews, play reviews, record reviews, advertising, volume index. Circulation: 12,200
$.15 per issue : $6.00 per year : $7.00 per year, foreign. Special rates offered.

The Prairie overcomer / *edited by* T.S. Rendall and L.E. Maxwell (Contributing Editor). - *Published by* Prairie Bible Institute. Three Hills, Alta. T0M 2A0, 1927-
Monthly. Church publication, magazine format, 60 p. Includes book reviews, volume index. Circulation: 42,000
$3.00 per year. Special rates offered.

Pravoslavnyi tserkovnyi kalendar' = The Orthodox Church calendar / *edited by* Archbishop Sylvester. - *Published by* Basilian Press. 286 Lisgar St., Toronto, Ont. M6T 3G9 (Subscription address: 474 Palmerston Blvd., Toronto, Ont. M6G 2P1) January 1976-
Annual. Church publication, 220 p. Language: Russian.
$6.00 per issue.

Le Précurseur / *édité par* Réjane Gaudet. - *Publié par* Soeurs missionnaires de l'Immaculée Conception. C.P. 157, Succursale Laval des Rapides, Ville de Laval, Qué., mai 1920-
Bimestriel. Publication ecclésiastique, magazine, 36 p. Tirage: 53,000
ISSN 0315-9671 $.50 le numéro : $2.00 par année. Tarifs spéciaux disponibles. Abonnements payables à l'avance.

The Precursor (January 1923-December 1973) *See* The Missionary Sisters of the Immaculate Conception. MIC mission news

Presbyterian Church in Canada. General Assembly. Acts and proceedings / *sponsored by* Presbyterian Church in Canada. - *Published by* Thorn Press Ltd. 135 Railside Rd., Don Mills, Ont. (Subscription address: 50 Wynford Dr., Don Mills, Ont. M3C 1J7)
Annual. Church publication, 700 p.
$5.50.

Presbyterian comment / *sponsored by* Committee of Presbyterian Ministers and Laymen ; *edited by* W. Stanford Reid. - *Published by* W. Stanford Reid. 25 Bellevue St., Guelph, Ont. N1G 1E9, 1960-
Quarterly. Church publication, magazine format, 4 p. Circulation: 450
Free.

Presbyterian record / *sponsored by* The Presbyterian Church in Canada ; *edited by* DeCourcy H. Rayner. - *Published by* The Record Committee. 50 Wynford Dr., Don Mills, Ont. M3C 1J7, January 1876-
Monthly except August. Magazine format, 36 p. Includes book reviews, advertising, volume index. Circulation: 90,176
$3.00 per year. Special rates.

Présence / *édité par* Robert Levy. - *Publié par* Association sépharade francophone. 4735, chemin côte Ste-Catherine, Montréal, Qué. H3W 1M1, septembre 1969-
Trimestriel. Publication d'association, journal, 16 p. Tirage: 4000
Envoi gratuit.

Présence francophone : revue littéraire / *édité par* Léo A. Brodeur. - *Publié par* Centre d'études des littératures d'expression française (CELEF). Faculté des arts, Université de Sherbrooke, Sherbrooke, Qué.
Semestriel. Publication d'institution (universités, écoles..), revue, 200 p. Comprend critique de livres, publicité, index cumulatif. Tirage: 1500
Indexé dans RADAR.
$4.00 le numéro : $8.00 par année : $8.00 par année, l'étranger.

Presentation to the Prime Minister and members of parliament - *Published by* Canadian Federation of Agriculture. 111 Sparks St., Ottawa, Ont., K1P 5B5.
Published in French: Memoire présenté au Premier Ministre du Canada et membres du cabinet.
Annual. Association publication, booklet format, 53 p.

The Press - *Published by* Brock University. St. Catharines, Ont. L2S 3A1.
Weekly. Student publication. Includes advertising. Circulation: 3000

Press / *edited by* John Isaac. - *Published by* Students Union Inc. Brock University. St. Catharines, Ont.
Former title(s): The Block badger (1964 to 1969-70)
Weekly. Student newsletter, newspaper format, 16 p. Includes book reviews, film reviews, play reviews, record reviews, advertising. Circulation: 3000
$3.00 per year.

Presse campus - *Publié par* Association fédérative des étudiants université de Sherbrooke. Local 110, centre social, Université de Sherbrooke, Sherbrooke, Qué. J1K 2R1, septembre 1975-
Ancien titre: Campus estnion (1961-1971)
Paraît tous les 15 jours. Publication des étudiants, journal, 8 p. Comprend critique de films, publicité. Tirage: 2000

Presse campus *See* L'Ouvre-boîte

Press-information / *édité par* Jean-Paul Belleville. - *Publié par* L'Université du Québec à Trois-Rivières. C.P. 500, Trois-Rivières, Qué., mars 1969-
Paraît tous les 15 jours. Organe interne/officiel, journal, 8 p. Tirage: 4000
Envoi gratuit.

Le Prêtre / *édité par* Roger Marien. - *Publié par* L'Oeuvre des vocations. Diocèse de Montréal. Eglise catholique. 1105 est, boul. Gouin, Montréal, Qué. H2C 1B3, mai 1951-
Ancien titre: Monde nouveau, présence nouvelle (septembre 1968-juin 1972)
Trimestriel. Publication ecclésiastique, bulletin, 4 p. Circulation: 20,000
Envoi gratuit.

Prêtre aujourd'hui (1958-1966) *Voir* Dossiers "vie ouvrière" au service des militants chrétiens du monde ouvrier

Prêtre et pasteur : revue eucharistique du clergé / *édité par* Jean Malo. - *Publié par* Jean Malo. Pères du Très Saint Sacrement. 4450, rue St-Hubert, Montréal, Qué. H2J 2W9, janvier 1898-
Ancien titre: Revue eucharistique prêtres-adorateurs clergé (1937-1972) Annales des prétres-adorateurs (1915-1937) Annales de l'association (1898-1915)
Mensuel. Revue, 56 p. Comprend critique de livres. Tirage: 2426
$1.50 le numéro : $7.50 par année : $8.00 le volume : $15.00 par année, l'étranger (Par avion).

Prêtres et laïcs (janvier 1967-décembre 1973) *Voir* Dossiers "vie ouvrière" au service des militants chrétiens du monde ouvrier

Prévenir / *edited by* Fernand Lortie. - *Published by* Association de sécurité des industriels forestiers du Québec, inc. Suite 60, 580 est, Grande-Allée, Québec, Qué. G1R 2K2, janvier/février 1975-
Bimestriel. Publication d'association, bulletin, 4 p. Tirage: 2000
gratuit aux membres de l'association.

Prevention / *edited by* Jean I. Sabanes. - *Published by* Industrial Accident Prevention Association. Suite 812, 50 Place Cremazie, Montreal, Que. H2P 2T5, January 1962-
Former title(s): Nouvellettes (1935-1962)
Monthly. Association publication, magazine format, 16 p. Language: French and English ; summaries: French and English. Includes updating service. Circulation: 22,000
ISSN 0048-5233 Free.

La prévention au Canada / *édité par* Jude des Chênes. - *Publié par* Conseil canadien de la sécurité. 1765, boul. St-Laurent, Ottawa, Ont. K1G 3V4, juillet 1960-
Ancien titre: Nouvelles de sécurité routière (août 1961-février 1969) Bulletin - Conseil canadien de la sécurité (juillet-decembre 1960)
Publié en anglais: Safety Canada.
Publication d'association, magazine, 8-12 p. Comprend critique de livres, critique de films.
Tirage: 3000
ISSN 0048-8968

Le Prévisionniste *See* The Forecaster

Price book for community pharmacy / *edited by* Arnold V. Raison. - *Published by* Canadian Pharmaceutical Association. 175 College St., Toronto, Ont. M5T 1P8.
Issued twice a year. Association publication, book format, 142 p. Includes updating service.
Circulation: 1500
$12.00 per issue. Prepayment required.

Prie avec l'Eglise (1936-1960) *Voir* Prions en église. Edition dominicale

Prime areas / *sponsored by* British Columbia Primary Teachers' Association ; *edited by* Lorna Robb. - *Published by* British Columbia Teachers' Federation. 2235 Burrard St., Vancouver, B.C.
Irregular (approximately 3 issues per year). Association publication, magazine format, 75 p. Includes book reviews, updating service.
Indexed in Can. educ. ind.
$6.00 per year. Subscription included in membership fee. Prepayment required.

Prince Edward Island Heritage Foundation - *Published by* Prince Edward Island Heritage Foundation. P.O. Box 922, 2 Kent St., Charlottetown, P.E.I.
Irregular (approximately 5 issues per year). Association publication, newsletter format, 8 p.
$2.00 per year.

Prince Edward Island Public Service Association, Inc. Association news / *edited by* James M. Brady. - *Published by* Prince Edward Island Public Service Association, Inc. P.O. Box 1116, 51 University Ave., Charlottetown, P.E.I. C1A 7M8, November 1961-
Issued every other month. Association publication, newspaper format, 4 p.
Free to members.

Prince Edward Island Women's Institute. Institute news / *edited by* Louise Maichbank. - *Published by* Prince Edward Island Women's Institute. P.O. Box 1058, Charlottetown, P.E.I. C1A 7M4, 1928-
Quarterly. Association publication, newspaper format, 8 p.
$1.00 per year. Controlled circulation.

Principals journal / *sponsored by* British Columbia Principals' and Vice-Principals' Association ; *edited by* W. Melville. - *Published by* British Columbia Teachers' Federation. 2235 Burrard St., Vancouver, B.C., November 1974-
Issued 10 times a year. Association publication, newsletter format, 75 p.
$10.00 per year.

Printaction - *Published by* John A. Young. Youngblood Co. P.O. Box 469, Agincourt, Ont., 1971-
Monthly. Trade publication, tabloid format, 16 p. Includes advertising.
$1.00 per issue : $10.00 per year : $16.00 for 3 years. Controlled circulation.

Prions en église. Edition complète / *édité par* Gilles Comeau. - *Publié par* Novalis, Université St. Paul. 223, rue Main, Ottawa, Ont. K1S 1C4(adresse d'abonnement: C.P. 498, Succursale A, Ottawa, Ont. K1N 8Y5) décembre 1974-
10 numéros par année. Publication ecclésiastique, brochure, 175 p. Tirage: 180,000
$3.00 par année (Par avion $6.10).

Prions en église. Edition dominicale / *édité par* Gilles Comeau. - *Publié par* Novalis, Université St. Paul. 223, rue Main, Ottawa, Ont. K1S 1C4(adresse d'abonnement: C.P. 498, Succursale A, Ottawa, Ont. K1N 8Y5) juin 1936-
Ancien titre: Prie avec l'Eglise (1936-1960)
Hebdomadaire. Publication ecclésiastique, brochure, 30 p. Tirage: 470,000
$4.90 (envoi de 100 ex.).

Priorities - *Published by* Women's Committee of B.C. New Democratic Party. 3485 West 15th Ave., Vancouver, B.C. V6R 2Z2, January 1973-
Monthly. Political press, newsletter format, 32 p. Includes book reviews. Circulation: 1000
$.35 per issue : $3.00 per year (Commercial $6.00), $4.00 per year, foreign (Commercial $8.00).

Prism - *Published by* School of Social Work. Carleton University. Ottawa, Ont., 1975-

Prisme / *édité par* Marcel Gilbert. - *Publié par* Centre de recherche industrielle du Québec. C.P. 9038, Ste-Foy, Qué. G1V 4C7, avril 1974-
Mensuel. Publication d'institution (universités, écoles..), 4 p. Tirage: 300
ISSN 0316-5361

Pro motion / *sponsored by* British Columbia Physical Education Teachers' Association. - *Published by* British Columbia Teachers' Federation. 105-2235 Burrard St., Vancouver, B.C. V6J 3H9, Vol 2, no 3, June 1962-
Irregular (approximately 4 issues per year). Association publication, newsletter format, 15 p.
Available to members only. Controlled circulation.

Pro tem - *Published by* Glendon Campus. York University. 2275 Bayview Ave., Toronto, Ont.
Weekly. Student publication, newspaper format, Includes advertising. Circulation: 5000

The Probe - *Published by* Pollution Probe London. 322 Queens Ave., London, Ont. N6B 1X4.
Irregular (approximately 4 issues per year). Association publication, newspaper format, 4 p. Includes book reviews. Circulation: 3500
$3.00 per year.

Probe bulletin - *Published by* Pollution Probe at the University of Toronto. Toronto, Ont. M5S 1A1.
Issued every other month. Association publication, newsletter format, 1 p.
Circulation: 1000
Subscription included in membership fee $10.00.

Proceedings - Canadian Otolaryngological Society (1971) *See* Canadian journal of otolaryngology

Proceedings - Entomological Society of Manitoba (1945-1966) *See* Manitoba entomologist

Proceedings - Geological Association of Canada (1947-1973) *See* Geoscience Canada

Product distribution directory *See* Government and the contractor

Le Producteur d'amiante = Asbestos producer / *édité par* Richard Michon. - *Publié par* Association des mines d'amiante du Québec. Chambre 412, 5 Place Ville Marie, Montréal, Qué. H3B 2G2(adresse d'abonnement: C.P. 1643, Succursale B, Montréal, Qué. H3B 3L3) octobre 1954-
Mensuel. Publication d'association, bulletin, 16 p. Langue(s): français et anglais. Tirage: 12,000

Le Producteur de lait / *édité par* Noël Fortin. - *Publié par* Noël Fortin. La Coopérative des producteurs de lait de Montréal. 275, ave Walnut, St. Lambert, Qué.(adresse d'abonnement: 6200, boul. Pelletier Brosseade, Qué) 1962-
Mensuel. Publication d'association, magazine, 20 p. Tirage: 2904
$3.50 par année. Tirage contrôlé.

Le Producteur de raisin d'Ontario - *Publié par* Ontario Grape Growers' Marketing Board. P.O. Box 252, 52 Scott St., St. Catharines, Ont.
Publié en anglais: The Ontario grape grower. Intermittent. Revue d'entreprise, bulletin, 4 p. Tirage contrôlé.

Production machinery and equipment / *edited by* Vincent J. Sharp. - *Published by* George H. Windsor. Five Windsors Publishing Co. Ltd. P.O. Box 775, Oakville, Ont. L6J 5C1, 1971-
Issued every other month. Trade publication, digest format, 76 p. Includes advertising.
ISSN 0315-2057 $1.00 per issue : $5.00 per year : $7.00 per year, U.S. : $25.00 per year, foreign. Controlled circulation.

Professional Corporation of Physicians of Quebec. Bulletin *Voir* Corporation professionnelle des médecins du Québec. Bulletin

Professional Corporation of Physicians of Quebec. Bulletin = Corporation professionnelle des médecins du Québec. Bulletin / *edited by* Roger Béard. - *Published by* Professional Corporation of Physicians of Quebec. 1440 St. Catherine St. W., Montreal, Que. H3G 1S5, July 25, 1961-
Former title(s): Newsletter - Professional Corporation of Physicians of Quebec = Bulletin de nouvelles - Corporation professionnelle des médecins du Québec (July 1961-July 1975)
Irregular (approximately 5-15 issues per year). Association publication, magazine format, 52 p. Language: English and French. Circulation: 15,000
ISSN 0315-2979 Free.

Professional development bulletin / *edited by* R.M. Stuart. - *Published by* Alberta Teachers' Association. 11010-142 St., Edmonton, Alta. T5N 2R1, September 1961-
Irregular (approximately 5 issues per year). Association publication, newsletter format, 2 - 20 p. Circulation: 3500
Free.

The Professional engineer in New Brunswick / *edited by* Dawson B. Lawrence. - *Published by* Association of Professional Engineers of the Province of New Brunswick. 123 York St., Fredericton, N.B. E3B 3N6, 1950-
Annual. Association publication, journal format, 35 p. Includes advertising. Circulation: 1400

The Professional engineer in Nova Scotia / *edited by* J.J. Laffin. - *Published by* Association of Professional Engineers of Nova Scotia. P.O. Box 129, 1828 Upper Water St., Halifax, N.S. B3J 2M4.
Irregular (approximately 3 issues per year). Association publication, magazine format, 40 p.

The Professional forester / *edited by* M.R. Innes. - *Published by* Ontario Professional Foresters Association. Suite 34, 10235 Yonge St., Richmond Hill, Ont. L4C 3B4.
Irregular (approximately 5 issues per year). Association publication, newsletter format, 6 p.

The Professional Institute of the Public Service of Canada. Journal of the Professional Institute = l'Institut professionnel du service public du Canada. Journal de l'institut professionnel / *edited by* Charles Levy. - *Published by* Professional Institute of the Public Service of Canada. 786 Bronson Ave., Ottawa, Ont. K1S 4G4, 1921-
Former title(s): Professional public service.
Irregular (approximately 10 issues per year). Association publication, journal format, 32 p. Language: English and French. Circulation: 17,000
$3.00 per year. Controlled circulation.

Professional journal of early childhood education - *Published by* Association for Early Childhood Education. Suite 6, 60 St. Clair Ave. W., Toronto, Ont. M4V 1M7, October 1975-
Irregular (approximately 2 issues per year). Association publication, journal format, 100 p. $2.00 per issue.

Professional Photographers of Canada. National news / *sponsored by* Professional Photographers of Canada ; *edited by* Peter Jansen. - *Published by* Peter Jansen. 566 Enniskillen Ave., Winnipeg, Man., 1970-
Issued every other month. Association publication, magazine format, 40 p.

Professional public service *See* The Professional Institute of the Public Service of Canada. Journal of the Professional Institute

Professional Recreation Society of B.C. Newsletter / *sponsored by* Professional Recreation Society of B.C ; *edited by* Gene Shuter and Anne Thomson. - *Published by* British Columbia Recreation Association. c/o 1600 West Broadway, Vancouver, B.C. V5N 1W1.
Issued every other month. Association publication, newsletter format, 6 p.
Subscription included in membership fee $25.00 per year.

Profile index to Canadian provincial and municipal publications / *edited by* Louise Fast. - *Published by* Micromedia Limited. P.O. Box 34, Postal Station S, Toronto, Ont. M5M 4L6, January 1973-
Monthly. Index, magazine format, 20 p. Language: English and French. Includes cumulative index.
$75.00 per year.

Programmes d'éducation = Educational programs / *édité par* Rose S. Schwartz. - *Publié par* Institut des banquiers canadiens. Suite 3920, Place Victoria, Montréal, Qué., 1967-
Intermittent (approximativement 1 édition par an). Publication spécialisée, 48 p. Langue(s): français et anglais. Tirage: 30,000
Envoi gratuit.

Programmes d'été à l'étranger *See* Summer programmes abroad

Progress *See* Postup

Progress against cancer : national newsletter / *edited by* Barbara Kilvert. - *Published by* Canadian Cancer Society. 25 Adelaide St. E., Toronto, Ont. M5C 1Y2.
Quarterly. Newsletter format, 8 p. Circulation: 30,000
Free.

Progress report - University of Guelph. Department of Soils (1954-1971) *See* Ontario Agricultural College. Department of Land Resource Science. Research and Advisory Service. Progress report

Progress '75 / *sponsored by* Sault Ste. Marie and District Chamber of Commerce. - *Published by* R. Harris. P.O. Box 1043, Sault Ste. Marie, Ont. (Subscription address: 360 Grt. Northern Rd., Sault Ste. Marie, Ont.)
Annual. Association publication, newspaper format, 12 p.
Free.

The Progression - *Published by* Canadian Progress Club. Suite 532, 67 Yonge St., Toronto, Ont. M5E 1J8, December 1971-
Irregular (approximately 3 issues per year). Association publication, newsletter format, 24 p. Includes advertising. Circulation: 1000
Free.

The Progressive (1923-1924) *See* Western producer : a weekly newspaper serving Western Canadian farmers

Progressive Conservative Association of Canada. P.C. bulletin / *edited by* Hugh Segal. - *Published by* National Progressive Conservative Headquarters. 178 Queen St., Ottawa, Ont. K1P 5E1, December 1973-
Former title(s): Communique (1970-1973)
Monthly. Political press, newspaper format, 8 p. Language: English and French.
Free. Controlled circulation.

Promin / *edited by* N.L. Kohuska. - *Published by* Ukrainian Women's Association of Canada. A25, 11024-82 Ave., Edmonton, Alta. T6G 0T2 (Subscription address: P.O. Box 3551, Postal Station B, Winnipeg, Man. R2W 3R4) 1960-
Monthly. Ethnic press. Language: Ukrainian and English. Includes advertising. Circulation: 2654
$.60 per issue : $6.00 per year.

Proof only *See* Only paper today : a bi-monthly devoted to writing about art in Ontario

Propagation de la foi (février 1924-novembre-décembre 1970) *Voir* Univers

Propane/Canada / *edited by* Jim Armstrong. - *Published by* Sanford Evans Publishing (Alberta) Ltd. Suite 1, 5512 MacLeod Trail S.W., Calgary, Alta. T2H 0J5, 1908-
Irregular (approximately 5 issues per year). Trade publication. Includes advertising. Circulation: 5523

Le Propriétaire de Laval / *édité par* Fernand Bélanger. - *Publié par* Le Propriétaire de Laval. C.P. 102, Duvernay, Laval, Qué., mai 1969-
Hebdomadaire. Publication des étudiants, journal, 20 p. Comprend critique de livres, publicité. parution de suppléments. Tirage: 32,000
$3.00 (12) : $5.00 (24). Tirage contrôlé. Tarifs spéciaux disponibles. Abonnements payables à l'avance.

Prospectives : revue d'information et de recherche en éducation / *édité par* Jacques Laliberté. - *Publié par* Centre d'animation de développement et de recherche en éducation. 1940 est, boul. Henri Bourassa, Montréal, Qué. H2B 1S2, 1964-
Intermittent (approximativement 5 éditions par an). Publication d'association, Revue de recherches, 40 p. Comprend publicité, index cumulatif. Tirage: 13,000
Indexé dans Periodex, RADAR, Can. educ. ind.
$1.50 le numéro : $6.00 par année. Envoi gratuit aux institutions et membres du CADRE.

Prospectors and Developers Association. P.D.A. digest - *Published by* Prospectors and Developers Association. Suite 406, 25 Adelaide St. W., Toronto, Ont. M5H 1N3.
Issued twice a month. Association publication, newsletter format, 8 p.
Free.

Protect yourself / *edited by* Marcel Lecours. - *Published by* Roland Charbonneau. 7th flr., 800 Place d'Youville, Québec, Qué., April 1973-
Published in French: Protégez-vous.
Monthly. General interest, newsletter format, 8 p. Circulation: 5000

Protée : revue des arts, des lettres et des sciences humaines - *Publié par* Département des sciences humaines. Université du Québec à Chicoutimi. Chicoutimi, Qué., décembre 1970-
Semestriel. Edition savante, revue, 100 p. Tirage: 300
Indexé dans RADAR.
ISSN 0300-3523 $2.00 le numéro : $4.00 par année. Abonnements payables à l'avance.

Protégez-vous - *Publié par* Roland Charbonneau. Office de la protection du consommateur. 7e étage, 800, Place d'Youville, Qué. G1A 1L8, avril 1973-
Publié en anglais: Protect yourself.
Mensuel. Intérêt général, bulletin, 8 p. Tirage: 25,000
Envoi gratuit.

The Provincial / *edited by* Bruce McLean. - *Published by* British Columbia Government Employees' Union. 4925 Canada Way, Burnaby, B.C. V5G 3W3, Summer 1947-
Irregular (approximately 10 issues per year). Association publication, magazine format, 16 p. Circulation: 32,000
Free. Controlled circulation.

Provincial and municipal finances - *Published by* Canadian Tax Foundation. 100 University Ave., Toronto, Ont. M5J 1V6, 1971-
Former title(s): Provincial finances (1963-1969)
Biennial. Association publication, 250 - 300 p.
ISSN 0317-946X Subscription included in membership fee $30.00.

Provincial finances (1963-1969) *See* Provincial and municipal finances

Provincial Intermediate Teachers' Association. PITA news / *sponsored by* Provincial Intermediate Teachers' Association. - *Published by* British Columbia Teachers' Federation. 105-2235 Burrard St., Vancouver, B.C. V6J 3H9, November 1962-
Irregular (approximately 5 issues per year). Association publication, newsletter format, 10 p. Includes book, film and play lists.
Available to members only.

Provincial Judges Association of British Columbia. Newsletter / *edited by* Alfrid Watts. - *Published by* Provincial Judges Association of British Columbia. 4470 Ross Crescent, West Vancouver, B.C. V7W 1B2, May 1972-
Issued every other month. Association publication, newsletter format, 8 p.
Circulation: 130

Provincial Lawn Bowling Association of Ontario. P.L.B.A. annual / *edited by* Mark Gilliland. - *Published by* Provincial Lawn Bowling Association of Ontario. Apt. 203, 87 St. George St., Brantford, Ont., 1930-
Annual. Association publication, 240 p.
Free to members.

Provincial notes / *edited by* A. Thompson. - *Published by* Ontario Provincial Council. Boy Scouts of Canada. 9 Jackes Ave., Toronto, Ont. M4T 1E2.
Irregular (approximately 5 issues per year). House/company organ, newsletter format, 8-10 p. Includes updating service. Circulation: 8000
Free to key personnel in Scouting. Controlled circulation.

Provincial results general insurance report : the brown chart = Données provinciales - *Published by* Stone and Cox Ltd. 203 Adelaide St. W., Toronto, Ont. M5H 1X4.
Annual. Statistics, spiral bound book format, 50 p.
$25.00.

Provincial succession duties and gift tax service / *edited by* A.V. Neil. - *Published by* Richard de Boo Ltd. 70 Richmond St. E., Toronto, Ont. M5C 2M8.
Former title(s): Canada estate tax service.
Issued every other month. Special interest, looseleaf format, 48 p. Includes updating service.
$30.00 per year.

Provincial taxation service / *edited by* A.V. Neil. - *Published by* Richard De Boo Ltd. 70 Richmond St. E., Toronto, Ont. M5C 2H8.
Monthly. Legislation, 64 p. Includes updating service.
$35.00 per year.

Psychiatric Hospital Patients' Welfare Association. Newsletter / *edited by* G. Tori Salter. - *Published by* The Psychiatric Hospital Patients' Welfare Association. P.O. Box 39, Postal Station J, Toronto, Ont. M4J 4X8, 1969-
Quarterly. Association publication, newsletter format, 4 p.
Free to members.

Psychic society newsletter (February 1973-June 1974) *See* Inner life : Toronto's aquarian age newsletter

Psychologie canadienne *See* Canadian psychological review

Le Psychologue québécois - *Publié par* Corporation des psychologues de la province de Québec. 1484 est, rue Fleury, Montréal, Qué., janvier 1974-
Ancien titre: Bulletin de nouvelles - Corporation des psychologues de la province de Québec (février 1969-septembre 1973)
Intermittent (approximativement 4-6 éditions par an). Publication d'association, journal, 14-16 p.
$2.00 le numéro : $1.00 par année : $13.00 par année, l'étranger.

Public employees journal (July 1969-September 1971) *See* New Brunswick Public Employees Association. Newsletter

The Public school / *edited by* André Cloutier. - *Published by* Public Relations Department. Internal Relations Bureau. The Montreal Catholic School Commission. 3737 Sherbrooke St. E., Montreal, Que. H1X 3B3, 1969-
Former title(s): Montreal Catholic School Commission. Monthly news (1969) Published in French: L'école publique.
Issued every other month. House/company organ, newspaper format, 8 p. Circulation: 45,000
ISSN 0027-0695 Free.

Public Service Alliance of Canada. Weekly newsletter / *edited by* Jean-Pierre Pouliot. - *Published by* Public Service Alliance of Canada. 233 Gilmour St., Ottawa, Ont. K2P 0P1, May 1967-
Published in French: Alliance de la fonction publique du Canada. Nouvelles de la semaine.
Weekly. Association publication, newsletter format, 2 p. Circulation: 30,000
Free.

Publisher - *Published by* Canadian Community Newspapers Association. P.O. Box 5166, Postal Station F, 63 Grenfell Cr., Ottawa, Ont., 1973-
Former title(s): Canadian community publisher (1970-1973)
Monthly. Association publication, newspaper format, 16 p.
$7.00 per year (Free to members).

Pulp and paper Canada / *edited by* C.F.B. Stevens. - *Published by* National Business Publications Ltd. 310 Victoria Ave., Montreal, Que. H3Z 2M9, 1903-
Former title(s): Pulp and paper magazine of Canada.
Monthly. Trade publication, magazine format, 120 p. Includes advertising, cumulative index.
Indexed in Can. B.P.I.
$2.00 per issue : $12.00 per year : $3.00 per issue, foreign : $30.00 per year, foreign. Controlled circulation.

Pulp and paper Canada business directory / *edited by* C.F.B. Stevens. - *Published by* Southam Business Publications Ltd. 310 Victoria Ave., Westmount, Que. H3Z 2M9, 1907-
Former title(s): Pulp and paper directory of Canada.
Annual. Directory, book format, 300 p.
$20.00 ($18.00 prepublication): $25.00, foreign ($20.00 prepublication). Controlled circulation.

Pulp and paper Canada reference manual and buyers' guide / *edited by* C.F.B. Stevens. - *Published by* Southam Business Publications Ltd. 310 Victoria Ave., Westmount, Que. H3Z 2M9, 1930-
Former title(s): Pulp and paper manual of Canada.
Annual. Directory, book format, 200 p.
$20.00 ($18.00 prepublication). Controlled circulation.

Pulp and paper directory of Canada *See* Pulp and paper Canada business directory

Pulp and paper magazine of Canada *See* Pulp and paper Canada

Pulp and paper manual of Canada *See* Pulp and paper Canada reference manual and buyers' guide

Pulp and paper report - *Published by* Canadian Pulp and Paper Association. 2300 Sun Life Building, Montreal, Que. H3B 2X9. Annual. Association publication, statistics, 5 p. Language: English and French. Circulation: 5000

La Pulpe : revue outaouaise de bandes dessinées / *édité par* Jean-Emmanuel Allard. - *Publié par* Cinésources 10. C.P. 80, succursale A, Ottawa, Ont. K1N 8V1, octobre 1973-
Bimestriel. Magazine, 40 p. Tirage: 2000
$1.00 le numéro : $5.00-$10.00 par année.

Pulse / *edited by* Paul Roland Hill. - *Published by* London Branch. Canadian Institute of Management. P.O. Box 3441, Terminal A, London, Ont. N6A 4K8, September 1973-
Issued every other month except during the summer. Association publication, newsletter format, 10 p. Circulation: 400

Pulse : the film and TV newsletter / *sponsored by* York University ; *edited by* Rick Harris. - *Published by* Rick Harris. P.O. Box 5268, Terminal A, Toronto, Ont. M5W 1N5, October 1974-
Monthly. Special interest, magazine format, 32 p. Includes book reviews, film reviews, record reviews, advertising. Circulation: 3000
ISSN 0316-3857 $.60 per issue : $5.00 per year : $10.00 per volume : $7.00 per year, foreign.

Purchasing in Western Canada / *sponsored by* Purchasing Management Association of Canada. B.C. District ; *edited by* Richard E. Cope. - *Published by* Western Miner Press Ltd. Suite 305, 1200 W. Pender St., Vancouver, B.C. V6E 2S9, September 1949-
Monthly. Trade publication, magazine format, $5.00 per issue.

Purchasing management newsletter (1970) *See* Action

Pythian record / *edited by* Joseph Dougal. - *Published by* Domain of British Columbia. Knights of Pythias, Grand Lodge. 7931 - 12th Ave., New Westminster, B.C. V3N 2K8, 1923-
Quarterly. Association publication, newsletter format, 6 p. Circulation: 2400
Free to members.

Q.C.C. bulletin *See* Le Beaver

Q.P.S. bulletin *See* Le Beaver

The Quad : student yearbook of Bishop's University / *edited by* Debi Walsh. - *Published by* Students Executive Council. Bishop's University. P.O. Box 1098, Bishop's University, Lennoxville, Que. J1M 1Z7.
Annual. Yearbook, magazine format, 200 p. Includes film reviews, play reviews, advertising. Circulation: 500
$5.00.

Quaestiones entomologicae / *sponsored by* The Strickland Memorial Trust Fund ; *edited by* George E. Ball. - *Published by* Department of Entomology. University of Alberta. Edmonton, Alta. T6G 2E3, January 1965-
Quarterly. Special interest, journal format, 300-400 p. Includes book reviews, volume index. available in microform. supplements issued. Back numbers available. Circulation: 300
ISSN 0033-5037 $3.00 per issue : $8.00 per year. Back volumes $6.00, single issues $1.50.

Quarry / *edited by* W.J. Barnes. - *Published by* Quarry Magazine. P.O. Box 1061, Kingston, Ont. K7L 4Y5, 1965-
Quarterly. Special interest, magazine format, 80 p. Language: English and French. Includes book reviews, advertising. Circulation: 650
Indexed in Can. essay and lit. ind.
ISSN 0033-5266 $1.50 per issue : $6.00 per year : $1.75 per issue, foreign : $7.00 per year, foreign.

Quart de rond = Quarter round / *édité par* Donald McMahon. - *Publié par* Donald McMahon. Association des détaillants de bois et matériaux de construction du Québec. Suite 301, 5960 est, rue Jean Talon, Montréal, Qué. H1S 1M2, décembre 1959-
Bimestriel. Publication d'association, journal, 28 p. Langue(s): français et anglais. Tirage: 2000
Envoi gratuit.

Quarter round *Voir* Quart de rond

Quarterly bulletin of outstanding acquisitions - Metropolitan Toronto Central Library (1969-1973) *See* Bulletin of outstanding acquisitions

Quarterly Newsletter - International Atlantic Salmon Foundation *See* International Atlantic Salmon Foundation. Newsletter

The Quarterly of Canadian studies : for the secondary school / *sponsored by* New Civics Studies Group ; *edited by* Andrew Z. Kerekes. - *Published by* Ian J. Collins. P.O. Box 816, Postal Station F, Toronto, Ont., 1971-
Quarterly. Association publication, journal format, 64 p. Includes book reviews, advertising, volume index, cumulative index. supplements issued.
Indexed in Can. educ. ind., Can. essay and lit. ind.
$2.00 per issue : $6.00 per year : $7.00 per year, foreign.

Quarterly review of commerce *See* The Business quarterly : Canadian management journal

Quartier libre - *Publié par* Association générale des étudiants du CEGEP de Rosemont. 6400, 16eme Ave, Montréal, Qué., avril 1974-
Intermittent (approximativement 6 éditions par an). Bulletin, 16 p. Tirage: 1500
Envoi gratuit.

Le Québec astronomique / *édité par* Jean-Louis Neault. - *Publié par* La Société d'astronomie de Montréal. 3860 est, rue Rachel, Montréal, Qué.
Mensuel. Publication d'association, magazine, 12 p. Tirage: 350
$.75 le numéro : $6.00 par année.
Abonnements payables à l'avance.

Québec chasse et pêche / *parrainé par* Publications plein air inc ; *édité par* André Y. Croteau. - *Publié par* Henri Poupart. 3580, rue Masson, Montréal, Qué. H1X 1S2, octobre 1971-
Mensuel. Magazine, 84 p. Reliure. Tirage: 37,469
Indexé dans Periodex, RADAR.
$1.25 le numéro : $10.00 par année : $15.00 par année, U.S. : $18.00 par année, l'étranger.
Tirage contrôlé. Abonnements payables à l'avance.

Québec construction / *édité par* Michel Durand. - *Publié par* Publications les affaires inc. 635 est, Henri-Bourassa, Montréal, Qué. H2C 1E4, 1971-
Hebdomadaire. Comprend publicité. Tirage: 4346
$30.00 pour 6 mois : $48.00 par année.

Quebec corporation manual / *edited by* L.B. Gravel and J.A. Grant. - *Published by* Richard De Boo Ltd. 70 Richmond St. E., Toronto, Ont. M5C 2M8.
Issued every other month. Legislation, 64 p. Includes updating service. supplements issued.
$40.00 per year.

Quebec Farmers' Association. Newsletter / *edited by* Joan Habel. - *Published by* Quebec Farmers' Association. P.O. Box 237, MacDonald College, Ste-Anne-de-Bellevue, Que. H9X 3M1, November 1973-
Monthly. Association publication, newsletter format, 15 p.
Subscription included in membership fee $10.00.

Quebec home and school news : the voice of the parent in education / *edited by* Winifred Potter. - *Published by* Quebec Federation of Home & School Associations. 4795 St. Catherine St. W., Montreal, Que. H3Z 1S8.
Issued every other month except summer (5 per year). Special interest, 16 p. Includes advertising. Circulation: 18,000
$2.00 per year.

Québec horticole - *Publié par* G. Vincent. L'Association des technologistes agricoles inc. C.P. 308, St-Hyacinthe, Qué. J2S 7B6.
Mensuel. Publication d'association, 20 p. Tirage: 5200
Abonnements payables à l'avance.

Quebec Industrial Relations Institute. Management information bulletin - *Published by* Quebec Industrial Relations Institute. 630 Sherbrooke St. W., Montreal, Que. H3A 1E4.
House/company organ, newsletter format, 30 p. Includes cumulative index, updating service. supplements issued.
Subscription included in membership fee.
Controlled circulation.

Le Québec industriel : revue industrielle du Canada français / *édité par* Robert Henry. - *Publié par* Jean Michel Chagnon. Maclean-Hunter Ltd. 481 University Ave., Toronto, Ont., janvier 1946-
Mensuel. Revue d'entreprise, magazine, 70 p. Comprend publicité.Aussi sous microform.
Indexé dans Periodex.
$1.50 le numéro : $12.00 par année : $18.00 par année, E.U. : $30.00 par année, l'étranger.
Tirage contrôlé.

Quebec Library Association. QLA bulletin *Voir* L'Association des bibliothécaires du Québec. Bulletin A B Q

The Quebec life underwriter *Voir* L'Assureur-vie du Québec

Le Québec littéraire / *édité par* Yvon Boucher. - *Publié par* Guérin. 4574, rue Saint-Denis, Montréal, Qué. H2J 2L3, septembre 1974-
Intermittent (approximativement 1-2 éditions par an). Publication spécialisée, magazine, 300 p. Comprend critique de livres.
$5.00 le numéro : $1.00 par année.

Québec pharmacie / *édité par* George Roy. - *Publié par* L'Association québécoise des pharmaciens propriétaires. 5115, rue St-Denis, Montréal, Qué. H2J 2M1, 1953-
Ancien titre: Bulletin APDM (mai 1953-janvier 1974)
Mensuel. Publication d'association, magazine, 32 p. parution de suppléments.
$.75 le numéro : $6.00 par année : $10.00 par année, l'étranger par année. Tirage contrôlé. Abonnements payables à l'avance.

Québec road transport *Voir* Transport routier du Québec

Québec science / *parrainé par* Université du Québec ; *édité par* Jean-Marc Gagnon. - *Publié par* Jean-Marc Gagnon. Les Presses de l'Université du Québec. C.P. 250, Sillery, Qué. G1T 2R1, janvier 1970-
Ancien titre: Le Jeune scientifique (octobre 1962-décembre 1969)
Mensuel. Intérêt général, magazine, 52 p.Aussi sous microform. Tirage: 13,000
Indexé dans Periodex, RADAR.
$1.25 le numéro : $10.00 par année : $15.00 par année, l'étranger. Tirage contrôlé. Abonnements payables à l'avance.

Quebec taxation service / *edited by* A.V. Neil. - *Published by* Richard de Boo Ltd. 70 Richmond St. E., Toronto, Ont. M5C 2H8.
Issued every other month. Legislation, 64 p. Includes updating service.
$35.00 per year.

The Quebecer (1954-1967) *See* Service

Queen St. magazine : a multi-media journal for the arts / *edited by* Angelo Sgabellone. - *Published by* Goathair Press. 396a Queen St. W., Toronto, Ont. (Subscription address: P.O. Box 25, Postal Station B, , Toronto, Ont. M5T 2W1) March 1973-
Irregular (approximately 3 issues per year). Special interest, magazine format, 48 p. Includes book reviews, film reviews, play reviews, record reviews, advertising. Circulation: 5000
$1.00 per issue : $5.00 per year : $3.00 per volume : $8.00 per year, foreign. Controlled circulation.

Queen's College journal *See* Queen's journal

Queen's gazette / *edited by* Information officer, Queen's University. - *Published by* Queen's University. Kingston, Ont. (Subscription address: News Department, 131 Union St., Kingston, Ont. K7L 3N6) January 1969-
Weekly. House/company organ, newsletter format, 4 p. Includes volume index, cumulative index. supplements issued.
Free.

Queen's intramural law journal (1969-1971) *See* Queen's law journal

Queen's journal / *edited by* D. McClelland and S. Yarnell. - *Published by* Alma Mater Society. Queen's University. Students' Union, Queens's University, Kingston, Ont., 1873-
Former title(s): Queen's College journal.
Issued twice a week. Student publication, newspaper format, 16 p. Includes book reviews, film reviews, play reviews, record reviews, advertising. Circulation: 9500
$7.50 per year.

Queen's law journal / *sponsored by* The Queen's Law Students Society ; *edited by* Stephen Sibold. - *Published by* Faculty of Law. Queen's University. Kingston, Ont. (Subscription address: The Carswell Co. Ltd., 2330 Midland Ave., Agincourt, Ont) 1971-
Former title(s): Queen's intramural law journal (1969-1971)
Issued twice a year. Student publication, journal format, 270 p. Includes book reviews, advertising. Circulation: 400
Indexed in Can. leg. per. lit., Leg. per.
ISSN 0048-6310 $3.00 per issue : $6.00 per year.

Queen's quarterly: a Canadian review / *sponsored by* Queen's University of Kingston ; *edited by* Kerry McSweeney. - *Published by* Quarterly Committee of Queen's University. 40 Queen's Quarterly, Queen's University, Kingston, Ont. K7L 3V2, 1893-
Quarterly. Scholarly publication, journal format, Includes book reviews, advertising, volume index, cumulative index. available in microform. Back numbers available. Circulation: 1800
Indexed in Can. ind., Can. educ. ind., P.A.I.S., M.L.A. int. bib., Annu. bibl. Engl. lang. and lit., MLA abstr., Hist. abstr.; Amer. hist. and life, Peace res. abstr., I.B.Z., Arct. bibl.
$2.00 per issue : $8.00 per year : $8.50 per year, foreign.

The Queen's University alumni review / *edited by* Catherine Perkins Morton. - *Published by* Alumni Association. Queen's University. Kingston, Ont. K7L 3N6, March 1927-
Issued every other month. Alumni newsletter, magazine format, 36 p. Circulation: 31,300
Free to graduates.

Query / *sponsored by* Saskatchewan Reading Council ; *edited by* George and Shirley Haines. - *Published by* Saskatchewan Teachers' Federation. P.O. Box 1108, Saskatoon, Sask. S7K 3N3, Winter 1970-
Quarterly. Association publication, journal format, Includes book reviews. Circulation: 300
Indexed in Can. educ. ind.
$5.00 per year. Subscription included in membership fee. Controlled circulation.

Quest / *edited by* Nicholas Steed. - *Published by* Hugh J. Rosser. Comac Publishing Ltd. 2300 Yonge St., Yonge-Eglinton Centre, Toronto, Ont. M4P 1E4, 1971-
Issued every other month. General interest, magazine format, Includes advertising. Circulation: 635,035

Questions et réponses canadiennes *See* Canadian notes and queries

Quetico newsletter / *edited by* A.S.L. Barnes. - *Published by* The Quetico Foundation. Suite 305, 200 Bay St., Toronto, Ont., November 1955-
Issued twice a year. Special interest, newsletter format, 8-10 p. supplements issued. Circulation: 650-700
Free.

Quick Canadian facts: the Canadian pocket encyclopedia / *edited by* C.J. Harris. - *Published by* C.J. Harris. Quick Canadian Facts Ltd. P.O. Box 99, Postal Station M, Toronto, Ont. M6S 4T2, 1945-
Annual. Book format, 176 p.
$4.50 hardcover : $1.50 paperback.

Quill / *edited by* Cliff Ranger. - *Published by* Student's Union Inc. Brandon University. Brandon, Man. R7A 5A7.
Weekly during the school year. Student publication, newspaper format, 8 p.
$2.50 per year.

Quill and quire / *edited by* Fiona Mee. - *Published by* Fiona Mee. Greey de Pencier Publications Ltd. 59 Front St. E., Toronto, Ont. M5E 1B3, April 1935-
Monthly. Trade publication, newspaper format, 32 p. Includes book reviews, advertising, cumulative index. available in microform. Circulation: 12,500
Indexed in Can. ind.
$1.00 per issue : $12.00 per year : $14.00 per year, U.S. : $16.00 per year, foreign.

Le Quincailler / *édité par* Zavier B. Delusigny. - *Publié par* J. Peter Watkins. Maclean-Hunter Ltd. 481 University Ave., Toronto, Ont. M5W 1A7(adresse d'abonnement: 625, ave President Kennedy, Montréal, Qué) 1887-
Mensuel. Revue d'entreprise. Comprend publicité. Tirage: 4150
$1.00 le numero : $8.00 par année : $12.00 par année, E.U., R.U. et France : $25.00 par année, l'étranger.

Quincentario Hispano / *edited by* M.F. Medina. - *Published by* Rafael Medina. 591 W. 17th Ave., Vancouver, B.C.
Issued twice a month. Ethnic press. Language: Spanish. Includes advertising.

RACC newsletter *Voir* Bonne route

RCC master index - *Published by* Radio College Publications. 461 King St. W., Main Floor, Toronto Ont. M5V 1K8.
Annual. Directory. Circulation: 4000
$1.00 per issue.

RCC television, radio, hi-fi service manual - *Published by* Radio College Publications. 461 King St. W., Toronto, Ont. M5V 1K8.
Monthly. Special interest, service manual, 110 p. Circulation: 3500

RIA digest = RIA news / *edited by* Mrs. J. Hewer. - *Published by* Society of Industrial Accountants. 154 Main St. E., Hamilton, Ont.
Issued every other month. Association publication, newsletter format, 12 p. Language: English and French. Includes book reviews, advertising, volume index, cumulative index, updating service. available in microform. Circulation: 31,000
$1.50 per issue : $7.50 per year : $10.00 per year.

RIA news *See* RIA digest

RLS : Regional language studies....Newfoundland / *edited by* William Kirwin. - *Published by* Folklore and Language Archive. Memorial University of Newfoundland. St. John's, Nfld. A1C 5S7, October 1968-
Annual. Institutional publication (Universities, schools, etc.), magazine format, 33 p. Circulation: 200
ISSN 0079-9335 Free.

RND (Revue Notre-Dame) / *parrainé par* Les Missionnaires du Sacre-Coeur ; *édité par* Paul Desaulniers. - *Publié par* La Corporation des missionnaires du Sacré-Coeur. 2215 Marie-Victorin, Québec, Qué.(adresse d'abonnement: C.P. 400, Sillery, Qué. G1T 1J6) janvier 1903-
Ancien titre: Revue Notre Dame du Sacré-Coeur (janvier 1965-décembre 1968) Annales de Notre-Dame du Sacré-Coeur (janvier 1903-décembre 1964)
Mensuel, juillet et août jumeté. Publication ecclésiastique, magazine, Tirage: 90,000 ISSN 0035-3795 $.35 le numéro : $3.00 par année : $3.50 par année, l'étranger. Tirage contrôlé. Tarifs spéciaux disponibles.

RPM weekly / *edited by* Walter Grealis. - *Published by* Walter Grealis. 6 Brentcliffe Rd., Toronto, Ont. M4G 3Y2, February 1964-
Weekly. Trade publication, magazine format, 32 p. Includes book reviews, record reviews, advertising.
$.60 per issue : $25.00 per year : $60.00 per year, foreign. Prepayment required.

Rabbits in Canada / *edited by* Charles Clay. - *Published by* Clay Publishing Co. Ltd. Oak St., Bewdley, Ont. K0L 1E0, 1965-
Former title(s): The Thumper.
Issued every other month. Trade publication, magazine format, 10 p. Includes advertising.
$.75 per issue : $5.00 per year. Prepayment required.

Racar : revue d'art canadienne = Canadian art review / *édité par* Nicolas Gyenes et Claude Bergeron. - *Publié par* Société pour promouvoir la publication en histoire de l'art au Canada. Université Laval, Québec, Qué. G1K 7P4, automne 1974-
Semestriel. Publication d'association, magazine, 60 p. Langue(s): français et anglais. Comprend critique de livres. parution de suppléments. Tirage: 1500
$4.00 le numéro : $8.00 par année : $9.00 par année, l'étranger. Abonnements payables à l'avance.

Racing year book *Voir* Annuaire des courses

Racquets Canada / *sponsored by* Canadian Lawn Tennis Association : Canadian Squash Racquets Association. - *Published by* Canadian Athletic Program Service Ltd. 643 Yonge St., Toronto, Ont., January 1972-
Issued every other month. Association publication, magazine format, 64 p.
$.75 per issue : $4.50 per year.

Raincoast chronicles / *sponsored by* Raincoast Historical Society ; *edited by* Howard White. - *Published by* Harbour Publishing. P.O. Box 119, Madeira Park, B.C., May 1972-
Irregular (approximately 2 issues per year). Association publication, magazine format, 56 p. Includes book reviews, record reviews. Circulation: 5000
$1.75 per issue : $5.00 per year : $6.00 per year, foreign.

The Raised roof = C'est pas un cadeau / *edited by* Dorothy O'Connell. - *Published by* The Canadian Organization of Public Housing Tenants. 69 Sparks St., Ottawa, Ont.
Irregular (approximately 9 issues per year). Association publication, newsletter format, 8 p. Language: English and French. Circulation: 800
$5.00 per year.

Random thoughts / *edited by* Robert D. Migliardi. - *Published by* International Plastic Modellers Society / Canada. P.O. Box 626, Postal Station B, Ottawa, Ont. K1P 5P7, July 1964-
Monthly. Association publication, magazine format, 12 p. Includes book reviews, volume index. Index must be requested each time. Circulation: 2000
$4.00 per year : $4.75 per year, foreign.

Ranok = Morning *See* Yevanhel's'kyi ranok

Rapeseed Association of Canada. Meeting. Proceedings - *Published by* Rapeseed Association of Canada. Room 501, 191 Lombard Ave., Winnipeg, Man. R3B 0X1, 1970-
Annual. Association publication.

Rapeseed digest / *edited by* Rapeseed Association of Canada. - *Published by* Rapeseed Association of Canada. Room 501, 191 Lombard Ave., Winnipeg, Man. R3B 0X1, September 1966-
Monthly. Association publication, newsletter format, 7 p. Circulation: 3000
$25.00 per year.

Rapport / *edited by* Ona Spidell. - *Published by* Experiment in International Living of Canada / Expérience de vie internationale du Canada. 380 Ridout St. N., London, Ont. N6A 2P4 (Subscription address: 34 Wayne Dr.,Kitchener, Ont)
Quarterly. Association publication, newsletter format, 6 p. Language: English and French.
$5.00 per year.

Rapport = Borden Canada / *edited by* Ray Smith. - *Published by* The Borden Company, Ltd. 1275 Lawrence Ave. E., Don Mills, Ont., 1934-
Former title(s): Canadian milky way.
Quarterly. House/company organ, newsletter format, 8 p. Language: English and French.
Controlled circulation.

Rapport annuel de La Société de protection des plantes du Québec (1908-1963) *Voir* Phytoprotection

Rapport des stages - *Publié par* Camp-ecole Chicobi. Guyenne, Abitibi-ouest, Qué. J0Y 1L0, automne 1969-
Annuel. Rapport,
Tirage contrôlé.

Rapport sur l'industrie des pâtes et papier / *édité par* Bureau de renseignement. - *Publié par* L'Association canadienne des producteurs de pâtes et papiers. 2300, Immeuble Sun Life, Montréal, Qué. H3B 2X9.
Annuel. Publication d'association, Dépliant, 6 p. Langue(s): français et anglais.
Envoi gratuit.

The Rare bird / *edited by* Rhoda Stein. - *Published by* Congregational Libraries Association of British Columbia. c/o the Editor, Mrs. M. Brown, 101-7201 Granville, Vancouver, B.C. V6P 4X6, November 1971-
Former title(s): Congregational libraries newsletter.
Quarterly. Association publication, newsletter format, 8 p. Includes book reviews, film reviews, play reviews, record reviews.
Circulation: 235-250
$2.00 per year.

Rassembler / *édité par* Gilles Comeau. - *Publié par* Novalis, Université St. Paul. 223, rue Main, Ottawa, Ont. K1N 8Y5(adresse d'abonnement: C.P. 498, Succursale A, Ottawa, Ont. K1N 8Y5) décembre 1940-
Ancien titre: Service homilétique (décembre 1940-décembre 1970)
Bimestriel. Publication ecclésiastique, magazine, 44 p. Tirage: 4000
$6.50 par année : $8.30 par année, l'étranger (par avion).

Rassembler - *Publié par* Novalis - Université Saint-Paul. 223, rue Main, Ottawa, Ont. K1S 1C4(adresse d'abonnement: C.P. 498, Succursale A, Ottawa, Ont. K1N 8Y5) décembre 1940-
Ancien titre: Service homilétique (décembre 1940-décembre 1970)
Publication ecclésiastique, magazine, 44 p. Comprend critique de films. Tirage: 4000
$6.50 par année : $8.30 par année, l'étranger (par avion). Abonnements payables à l'avance.

Reach / *edited by* Hazel D. Lawrence. - *Published by* Saskatchewan Division. Canadian Red Cross Youth. 2571 Broad St., Regina, Sask. S4P 0B3.
Former title(s): Junior Red Cross news (1951-1972)
Issued every other month. Association publication, newsletter format, 2 p.
Free to members.

Reader's digest / *edited by* Charles W. Magill. - *Published by* Reader's Digest Association (Canada) Limited. 215 Redfern Ave., Montreal, Que. H3Z 2V9, 1943-
Monthly. General interest, magazine format, 230-250 p. Circulation: 1,225,475
$.75 per issue : $7.46 per year : $9.97 per year, foreign.

Real estate development annual / *edited by* Don Long. - *Published by* D.G. Brydges. Maclean-Hunter Ltd. 481 University Ave., Toronto, Ont. M5W 1A7, 1969-
Former title(s): Canadian real estate annual.
Annual. Directory, magazine format, 140 p. Includes advertising. Circulation: 9500
$20.00. Controlled circulation.

Real Estate Institute of Canada. Journal / *edited by* Cherry Carnon. - *Published by* Institute of Real Estate Management. 99 Duncan Mill Rd., Don Mills, Ont. M3B 1Z2.
Former title(s): FRI/CAM journal; CIR journal; Canadian Institute of Realtors journal.
Issued every other month. Association publication, newsletter format, 8 p.
Circulation: 2800
$6.50 per year : $7.50 per year, foreign.

Real estate trends in Metropolitan Vancouver - *Published by* Real Estate Board of Greater Vancouver. 1101 W. Broadway, Vancouver, B.C. V6H 1G2, 1958-
Annual. Trade publication, magazine format, 100 p. Includes updating service. Circulation: 2000
$10.00.

Real living / *sponsored by* The Pentecostal Assemblies of Canada ; *edited by* Robert M. Argue. - *Published by* The Testimony Press. 10 Overlea Blvd., Toronto, Ont. M4H 1A5, 1964?-
Quarterly. Church publication, pamphlet format, 16 p. Circulation: 7000
$1.20 per year : $.15 per volume. Quantity prices available.

Réalisons : ensemble des objectifs scolaires du Québec chez nous / *édité par* Serge Forget. - *Publié par* Association des commissions scolaires laurentiennes (Zone 10). 493, chemin Ste-Marguerite, Sainte Adèle, Comté de Prévost, Qué., mai 1973-
Mensuel. Bulletin, 10 p. Tirage: 600
Envoi gratuit.

Recherche et documentation / *parrainé par* Comité de direction scientifique du centre de documentation en sciences humaines ; *édité par* Louis Le Borgne. - *Publié par* Centre de documentation en sciences humaines. C.P. 8888, Montréal, Qué., mai 1974-
Intermittent (approximativement 1-2 éditions par an). Edition savante, bulletin, 10 p. Tirage: 400
Envoi gratuit.

Recherches amérindiennes au Québec / *édité par* Sylvie Vincent. - *Publié par* Robert Myre et Pierre Bélanger. Société de recherches amérindiennes au Québec. Bureau 40, 417, rue St-Pierre, Montréal, H2Y 2M4, avril 1971-
Intermittent (approximativement 5 éditions par an). Publication d'association, magazine, 64 p. Comprend critique de livres, index de volumes. Tirage: 1500
Indexé dans RADAR, North. tit.
$15.00 par année : $16.00 par année, l'étranger. Envoi gratuit. Tarifs spéciaux disponibles. Abonnements payables à l'avance.

Recherches sociographiques / *parrainé par* Université Laval. Département de sociologie ; *édité par* Fernaud Dumont et Jean-Charles Falardeau. - *Publié par* Les Presses de l'Université Laval. Université Laval, Québec, Qué. G1K 7P4, janvier-mars 1960-
Intermittent (approximativement 3 éditions par an). Edition savante, revue, 135 p. Comprend critique de livres. Tirage: 1300
Indexé dans Periodex, RADAR, Hist. abstr.; Amer. hist. and life.
$3.00 le numéro : $8.00 par année : $9.00 par année, l'étranger.

Reclamation / *edited by* D.R. Broadfoot. - *Published by* Canadian Water Resources Association. P.O. Box 1322, Regina, Sask. S4P 3B8, July 1961-
Former title(s): Western Canada reclamation.
Quarterly. Association publication, newsletter format, 8 p. Circulation: 1200
$10.00 per year. Subscription included in membership fee. Controlled circulation.

The Record (1951) *See* Canadian courier

The Record / *edited by* W.H.A. Horne. - *Published by* Trinity College School. Port Hope, Ont.
Student publication. Includes advertising.
$12.00 per year.

Record of new issues - *Published by* Corporation Service. The Financial Post. 481 University Ave., Toronto, Ont. M5W 1A7.
Annual. Trade publication, 40 p. supplements issued.
$2.00.

Record of predecessor and defunct companies - *Published by* Corporation service. The Financial Post. 481 University Ave., Toronto, Ont. M5W 1A7, 1974-
Irregular (approximately 1 issue per year). Trade publication, 130 p. supplements issued.
$6.00 per volume.

Record of warrants - *Published by* The Financial Post Corporation Service. Maclean-Hunter Ltd. 481 University Ave., Toronto, Ont. M5W 1A7.
Annual. Special interest, 50 p.
$4.00 per volume.

Record week / *edited by* Joey Cee. - *Published by* Joey Cee. Record Week Ltd. Joseph Paul Publications. Unit 7, 2585 Drew Rd., Mississauga, Ont. L4T 1G1, 1975-
Weekly. Special interest. Includes advertising.
$.75 per issue : $40.00 per year.

Recorder *See* Evangelical recorder

The Recorder / *edited by* John R. Harrison. - *Published by* Ontario Music Educators' Association. 18 Hillavon Dr., Islington, Ont. M9B 2P5 (Subscription address: 4 Clareville Cres., Willowdale, Ont. M2J 2C1)
Quarterly. Association publication, magazine format, 48 p. Language: English (French). Includes book reviews, advertising. Circulation: 1000
$1.50 per issue : $6.00 per year.

Records and proceedings of the Committee on Archives of the United Church of Canada *See* United Church of Canada. Committee on Archives. Bulletin

Recreation Canada / *edited by* Art Drysdale. - *Published by* Canadian Parks/Recreation Association. 333 River Rd., Vanier, Ont., K1L 8B9., 1953-
Former title(s): Parks and recreation in Canada (1953-1969)
Issued every other month. Association publication, magazine format, 60-70 p. Language: English and French ; summaries: English and French. Includes book reviews, film reviews, advertising, volume index, cumulative index. available in microform. Circulation: 2700
$2.00 per issue : $7.50 per year : $10.00 per year, foreign. Controlled circulation. Prepayment required.

Recreation property / *edited by* Charles Clay. - *Published by* Clay Publishing Co. Ltd. Oak St., Bewdley, Ont. K0L 1E0, 1971-
Issued every other month. Trade publication, magazine format, 12 p. Includes advertising.
ISSN 0315-0518 $.75 per issue : $4.00 per year. Prepayment required.

Recreation property *See* The Ontario cottager

Recreation reporter / *edited by* Les Spooner. - *Published by* British Columbia Recreation Association. 1200 W. Broadway, Vancouver, B.C. V6J 1X7, 1971-
Issued every other month. Special interest, magazine format, 40 p. Includes book reviews, advertising. Circulation: 1000
$.75 per issue : $4.50 per year. Controlled circulation. Special rates offered. Prepayment required.

Recreational vehicle life / *edited by* Wayne Paterson. - *Published by* Andre C. Gagnon and Wm. E. Taylor. CRV Publishing Co. Ltd. Suite 221, 3414 Park Ave., Montreal, Que. H2X 2H5, 1973-
Former title(s): Canadian recreational vehicles ISSN 0319-1028 (1971-1972)
Irregular (approximately 5 issues per year). Trade publication, magazine format, Includes advertising. Circulation: 132,045
ISSN 0319-101X $3.00 per year : $5.00 for 2 years : $5.00 per year, foreign : $9.00 for 2 years, foreign.

Recreational vehicles trade - *Published by* Andre C. Gagnon and Wm. C. Taylor. CRV Publishing Co. Suite 221, 3414 Park Ave., Montreal, Que. H2X 2H5.
Former title(s): Véhicules de récréation : trade ISSN 0317-5294 (1971-1972)
Issued every other month. Trade publication. Language: English and French. Includes advertising. Circulation: 14,781
ISSN 0317-5308 $6.00 per year.

Recueil des films - *Publié par* Office des communications sociales. La Compagnie de publication rurale inc. 4635, rue de Montréal, Qué. Qué. H2H 2B4, 1956-
Annuel. Publication spécialisée, 225 p. Comprend critique de films. Tirage: 1500
$4.00 le volume.

Redbook / *edited by* V.M. Hodder. - *Published by* International Commission for the Northwest Atlantic Fisheries. P.O. Box 638, Dartmouth, N.S. B2Y 3Y9, 1958-
Annual. House/company organ.
ISSN 0074-2643 Controlled circulation.

Redeemer's voice almanac = kalendar holosu spasytelia / *sponsored by* Ukrainian Catholic Mission of the Most Holy Redeemer ; *edited by* R. Chomiak. - *Published by* Redeemer's Voice Press. 165 Catherine St., Yorkton, Sask. S3N 2V7, 1934-
Annual. Church publication, magazine format, 112 p. Language: Ukrainian and English.
$1.50 per issue. Prepayment required.

The Reel thing (1971-1972) *See* A Newsletter called Fred

Référence (août-septembre 1970-mars 1975) *Voir* Bulletins signaletiques

Reflections from Lakeland / *edited by* Catherine M. O'Neil. - *Published by* Lakeland Library Region. P.O. Box 813, 1791-110 St., North Battleford, Sask. S9A 2Y2, June 1973-
Quarterly. Institutional publication (Universities, schools, etc.), newsletter format, 25 p. Includes book reviews.
Free.

Reflector / *edited by* Nik L. Burton. - *Published by* Student Association. Mount Royal College. Calgary, Alta. T3E 6K6, Fall 1967-
Former title(s): Royal reflector (1963-1967)
Issued twice a month. Student publication, newspaper format, 12 p. Includes book reviews, film reviews, play reviews, record reviews, advertising. Circulation: 3000
$6.20 per year.

The Reflector beam / *edited by* Henry Vollbrecht. - *Published by* The Antique and Classic Car Club of Canada. P.O. Box 1304, Postal Station A, Toronto, Ont. M5W 1G7.
Monthly 10 times a year. 8 p.
Subscription with membership only $15.00 per year.

Reflexion (December 1968-March 1971) *See* Reflexion 2 : primera revista de cultura hispanica en Canada

Reflexion 2 : primera revista de cultura hispanica en Canada / *edited by* Angel Lopez-Fernandez and Miguel A. Giella (managing editor). - *Published by* G. Carrero. S. Hermengildo 12, Madrid, Spain (Subscription address: P.O. Box 8578, Postal Station B, Ottawa, Ont. K1P 5A0) May-August 1972-
Former title(s): Reflexion (December 1968-March 1971)
Issued 3 times a year. Ethnic publication, magazine format, 180 p. Language: Spanish, English and French. Includes book reviews, play reviews, advertising. Circulation: 800
$2.00 per issue : $6.00 per year : $8.00 per year, foreign.

Réflexions historiques *See* Historical reflections

Regard de foi : revue mariale d'actualité / *parrainé par* Les Pères Montfortians ; *édité par* Jean-Paul Michaud. - *Publié par* Odilon Demers. 5875 est, rue Sherbrooke, Montréal, Qué. H1N 1B6, avril 1904-
Ancien titre: Messager de Marie Reine des Coeurs.
Bimestriel. Publication ecclésiastique, magazine, 24 p. Tirage: 9000
$3.00 par année. Tirage contrôlé. Tarifs spéciaux disponibles. Abonnements payables à l'avance.

Regards : official organ of the Social Credit Party of Canada / *sponsored by* Social Credit Party of Canada ; *edited by* Pierre Dallaire. - *Published by* Pierre Dallaire. P.O. Box 1391, Postal Station B, Ottawa, Ont. K1P 5A0, September 1959-
Monthly. Magazine format, 24 p. Language: English and French. Includes book reviews, advertising.
$.25 per issue : $2.00 per year. Prepayment required.

Regards sur Israël / *édité par* Michel Solomon. - *Publié par* Comité Canada-Israël. Bureau 906, 1310, ave Greene, Montréal, Qué. H3Z 2A5, décembre 1972-
Intermittent (approximativement 7-8 éditions par an). Publication d'association, bulletin, 16 p. Tirage: 3500
Envoi gratuit.

Regina / *edited by* Sean W. Quinlan. - *Published by* Regina Chamber of Commerce. 2145 Albert St., Regina, Sask. S4P 2V1, September 1972-
Former title(s): News magazine - Regina Chamber of Commerce.
Monthly. Association publication, magazine format, 24 p. Includes advertising. Circulation: 5000
ISSN 0315-212X $5.00 per year. Free to chamber members. Controlled circulation.

Regina : visitor and buyers guide *See* Regina : visitor information guide

Regina : visitor information guide - *Published by* Regina Chamber of Commerce. 2145 Albert St., Regina, Sask. S4P 2V1.
Former title(s): Regina : visitor and buyers guide.
Annual. Association publication, magazine format, 34 p. Circulation: 5000
$5.00. Free to chamber members.

Register of post-graduate dissertations in progress in history and related subjects / *sponsored by* Public Archives of Canada and the Canadian Historical Association ; *edited by* P. Yurkin. - *Published by* Canadian Historical Association. C/o Public Archives, Ottawa, Ont. K1A 0N3, 1966-
Annual. Directory, magazine format, 110 p. Language: English and French. Circulation: 800
ISSN 0068-8088 $2.00.

Registered Nurses Association of British Columbia. RNABC news / *edited by* J.R. Miller. - *Published by* Registered Nurses Association of British Columbia. 2130 West 12th Ave., Vancouver, B.C. V6H 2N3.
Issued every other month. Association publication, magazine format, 24 p. Includes book reviews, cumulative index. Circulation: 17,000
Controlled circulation.

Registered Nurses Association of Nova Scotia. R.N.A.N.S. bulletin / *edited by* Dorothy Gray Miller. - *Published by* The Registered Nurses' Association of Nova Scotia. 6035 Coburg Rd., Halifax, N.S., November 1964-
Irregular (approximately 5-6 issues per year). Association publication, magazine format, 12 p.
Free to members. Controlled circulation.

Regroupement de chercheurs en histoire des travailleurs québécois. Bulletin RCHTQ / *édité par* James D. Thwaites. - *Publié par* Regroupement de chercheurs en histoire des travailleurs québécois. Université du Québec, 300, ave. des Ursulines, Rimouski, Qué. G5L 3A1, février 1974-
Paraît 3 fois par an. Publication d'association, revue et bulletin, Comprend critique de livres. Tirage: 250
$3.00 (Institutions $5.00). Abonnements payables à l'avance.

The Rehab tab / *edited by* Jack Wallace. - *Published by* The Rehabilitation Society of Calgary for the Handicapped. 1112 Memorial Dr. N.E., Calgary, Alta. T2E 4Z2.
Monthly. Association publication, newsletter format, 10 p. Circulation: 254
Subscription included in membership fee $1.00 per year.

Rehabilitation digest / *edited by* Wilfrid B. Race. - *Published by* Canadian Rehabilitation Council for the Disabled. Suite 2110, One Yonge St., Toronto, Ont. M5E 1E8, Summer 1969-
Quarterly. Special interest, magazine format, 20 p. Includes book reviews, film reviews. Circulation: 1560
Indexed in Except. child educ. abstr., Excerpt. med.
$.75 per issue : $3.00 per year.

Relations : revue d'intérêt général / *édité par* Irénée Desrochers. - *Publié par* Les Editions Bellarmin. 8100, boul. St-Laurent, Montréal, Qué. H2P 2L9, janvier 1941-
Mensuel. Intérêt général, magazine, 32 p. Comprend critique de livres, critique de films, critique de pièces de théâtre, publicité. Tirage: 7427
Indexé dans Periodex, Can. ind., RADAR, Hist. abstr.; Amer. hist. and life.
$.75 le numéro : $8.00 par année. Tirage contrôlé. Tarifs spéciaux disponibles. Abonnements payables à l'avance.

Relations industrielles = Industrial relations / *parrainé par* Université Laval. Département des relations industrielles ; *édité par* Gérard Dion. - *Publié par* Presses de l'Université Laval. C.P. 2442, Université Laval, Québec, Qué. G1R 7R4, septembre 1945-
Ancien titre: Bulletin des relations industrielles (jusqu'en 1951)
Trimestriel. Edition savante, magazine, 200 p. Langue(s): français et anglais ; sommaires: anglais et français. Comprend critique de livres, index de volumes. Tirage: 2000
$3.50 le numéro : $12.00 par année : $13.00 par année, l'étranger.

Relay / *edited by* Patricia A. Holting. - *Published by* Electrical Contractors Association of British Columbia. 2727 Boundary Rd., Vancouver, B.C. V5M 3Z7, Summer 1966-
Monthly. Association publication, newsletter format, 4 p.

Le Rempart / *édité par* Dianne Perreault. - *Publié par* Les Publications des grands lacs. 2418 Central, Windsor, Ont., novembre 1966-
Tous les 15 jours. Journal, 8 p.
$.15 le numéro : $4.00 par année.

Rendez-vous 76 Montréal / *édité par* Alain Guilbert. - *Publié par* Comité organisateur des jeux olympiques de Montréal. C.P. 1976, Montréal, Qué., août 1973-
Intermittent. Publication spécialisée, magazine, 32-48 p. Langue(s): français et anglais. Tirage: 40,000
Envoi gratuit.

Répertoire de l'édition au Québec / *édité par* J.-Z.-Léon Patenaude (administrateur) et Guy Boivin (coordonnateur). - *Publié par* Edi-Québec inc. 436 est, rue Sherbrooke, Montréal, Qué. H2L 1J6, 1972-
Annuel. Bibliographie, 475 p. Comprend index de volumes. parution de suppléments. Tirage: 1200
$40.00 le numéro. Abonnements payables à l'avance.

Répertoire des associations du Canada *See* Directory of associations in Canada

Le répertoire des Centraides Canada et des conseils de planification sociale *See* Directory of Canadian United Ways and Social Planning Councils

Répertoire des cours d'été (et cours permanents pour étrangers) / *édité par* Jean Marc Léger. - *Publié par* Université de Montréal, Association des universités partiellement ou entièrement de langue française. C.P. 6128, Montréal, Qué., 1966-
Publication d'association, 125 p. Tirage: 2500

Répertoire des entreprises canadiennes de services informatiques = Directory of Canadian data processing services firms / *édité par* Jacques Clairoux. - *Publié par* Currie Coopers and Lybrand Ltd./Ltée. 630 ouest, boul. Dorchester, Montréal, Qué. H3B 1W8, 1971-
Annuel. Répetoire, 28 p. Langue(s): français et anglais. Tirage: 2000
Envoi gratuit.

Répertoire des études supérieures et des équivalences de titres, de diplômes et de périodes d'études entres les universités de langue française / *édité par* Jean Marc Léger. - *Publié par* Association des universités partiellement ou entièrement de langue française. C.P. 6128, Montréal, Qué. H3C 3J7, 1966-
Publication d'association. Tirage: 1000

Répertoire des possibilités d'emploi Canada. Bilingual edition *See* Employment opportunities handbook

Répertoire des publications seriées canadiennes *See* Canadian serials directory

Répertoire des services communautaires de la région de Québec / *parrainé par* Accueil, information et référence (actions-24) ; *édité par* Marie-Louise Makdissi. - *Publié par* Centraide - Québec. C.P. 130, St-Sauveur, 180, rue Blouin, Ville Vanier, Qué. G1K 6V7.
Ancien titre: Répertoire des services communautaires du diocèse de Québec.
Annuel. Publication spécialisée, 118 p.
Envoi gratuit.

Répertoire des services communautaires du diocèse de Québec *Voir* Répertoire des services communautaires de la région de Québec

Répertoire des services communautaires du grand Montreal = Directory of community services of Greater Montreal - *Publié par* Centre de référénce du grand Montréal. Suite 54, 759 square Victoria, Montreal, Que. H2Y 2J7.
Paraît tous les 18 mois. Tirage: 4000

Répertoire des services sociaux canadiens *See* Directory of Canadian welfare services

Répertoire des thèses de doctorat soutenues devant les universités de langue française / *édité par* Jean Marc Léger. - *Publié par* Association des universités partiellement ou entièrement de langue français. C.P. 6128, Montréal, Qué. H3C 3J7, 1970-
Semestriel. Publication d'association, 150 p.
Tirage: 800
Abonnements payables à l'avance.

Repertoire des universitaires et universités se spécialisant dans études latino - américaines au Canada *See* Directory of Canadian scholars and universities interested in Latin American studies

Répertoire général des universités membres de l'A.U.P.E.L.F - *Published by* Association des universités partiellement ou entièrement de langue française. C.P. 6128, Montréal, Qué. H3C 3J7, 1966
Répertoire, 500 p.

Report - Canadian Catholic Historical Association (1933-1965) *See* Canadian Catholic Historical Association. Study sessions

Report of National Convents of P.H. Tenants / *edited by* Dorothy O'Connell. - *Published by* Canadian Organization of Public Housing Tenants. 69 Sparks St., Ottawa, Ont., May 1974-
Biennial. Association publication, 50 p.
Language: French and English. Circulation: 400
$2.50.

A Report on advertising revenues in Canada - *Published by* Maclean-Hunter Research Bureau. 481 University Ave., Toronto, Ont. M5W 1A7.
Irregular (approximately 1 issue per year).
Trade publication, 14 p.
ISSN 0315-9779 $6.50 per volume.

A Report on Canada - *Published by* Maclean-Hunter Ltd. 481 University Ave., Toronto, Ont. M5G 1X1.
Annual. Statistics.
ISSN 0315-968X $10.00.

The Reporter / *edited by* Patrick J. O'Neill. - *Published by* Ontario English Catholic Teachers' Association. 6th floor, 1260 Bay St., Toronto, Ont. M5R 2B4, September 1975-
Former title(s): The Review (December 1945-June 1975) News and views (September 1962-June 1975)
Monthly except July and August. Association publication, magazine format, 40 p. Includes book reviews, advertising. Circulation: 18,855
$3.00 per year.

The Reporter / *edited by* Sheila Kenyon. - *Published by* Ontario Welfare Council. Suite 404, 1240 Bay St., Toronto, Ont. M5R 2A7, January 1954-
Quarterly. Association publication, magazine format, 6 p. Circulation: 900
$.35 per issue : $1.00 per year.

Reporting classroom research / *edited by* Phyllis Hooker and James Paton. - *Published by* Ontario Educational Research Council. 1260 Bay St., Toronto, Ont. M5R 2B1, 1972-
Issued 4 times a year, 2 in spring 2 in fall. Institutional publication (Universities, schools, etc.), newsletter format, 8 p. Language: English ; summaries: English and French. Circulation: 7000
ISSN 0315-369X $.50 per issue : $2.00 per year. Free to all schools in Ontario and members of the Council.

Reports - Saskatoon Board of Trade *See* Saskatoon

Reports on family law / *edited by* David M. Steinberg. - *Published by* Carswell Company Ltd. 2330 Midland Ave., Agincourt, Ont. M1S 1P7, 1971-
Monthly. Legal articles, book format, 130 p. Circulation: 120
Indexed in Can. leg. per. lit.
$30.00 per volume.

Repository / *edited by* Bob Atkinson and John Harris. - *Published by* Repository Press. R.R. 7, Buckhorn Rd., Prince George, B.C. V2N 2J5, January 1972-
Former title(s): Seven persons repository (1972-1974)
Quarterly. Special interest, magazine format, 60 p. Back issues available. Circulation: 400
ISSN 0317-0845 $1.00 per issue : $3.00 per year.

Requiem : science fiction fantastique / *édité par* Norbert Spehner. - *Publié par* Norbert Spehner. 455, rue St-Jean, Longueuil, Qué. J4H 2Z3, octobre 1974-
Trimestriel. Publication spécialisée, magazine, 24 p. Comprend critique de livres, critique de films. Tirage: 1000
ISSN 0317-5324 $.75 le numéro : $4.00 par année : $5.00 par année, l'étranger (service par avion).

Requirements for secondary school leaving certificates and for admission to university and teacher training - *Published by* Canadian Education Association. 252 Bloor St. W., Toronto, Ont. M5S 1V5.
Issued every 2 or 3 years. Directory, booklet format, 32 p.
$2.00.

Requirements for teaching certificates in Canada - *Published by* Canadian Education Association. 252 Bloor St. W., Toronto, Ont. M5S 1V5.
Issued every 2 or 3 years. Directory, spiral bound charts,
ISSN 0080-1437 $2.50.

Res gestae / *edited by* R.L. Smith. - *Published by* Yale Book Company Ltd. 34 Butternut St., Toronto, Ont. M4K 1T7, 1933-
Issued twice a month October to May. Special interest, newsletter format, 1 p., Christmas ed. 4 p. Language: Latin. Circulation: 3500
$2.00 per year. Minimum of 4 subscriptions to one address.

Research and studies / *edited by* Caroline Midgley. - *Published by* Carleton University, Information Office. Colonel By Dr., Ottawa, Ont., K1S 5B6., 1970-
Biennial. Abstracts/summaries, book format, 400 p.
Free.

Research McGill / *edited by* Elizabeth Skelton-Pasmore. - *Published by* Research McGill. McGill University. P.O. Box 6070, Montreal, Que. H3C 3G1, January 1973-
Monthly, 10 times a year.
Abstracts/summaries, magazine format, 20 p. Circulation: 1100
Free.

Research studies in progress in Canadian Universities (1959) *See* Directory of education studies in Canada

Réseau / *édité par* Pierre Tétu. - *Publié par* Direction générale des relations publiques. Université du Québec. 2875, boul. Laurier, Québec, Qué., octobre 1969-
Mensuel. Publication d'institution (universités, écoles..), magazine, 20-24 p. Tirage: 25,000
Envoi gratuit.

Resort and motel / *edited by* Ronald J. Cooke. - *Published by* Ronald J. Cooke Ltd. 58 Madison Ave., Beaconsfield, Que. H9W 4T7, 1966-
Issued every other month. Special interest, magazine format, 22 p. Includes advertising. Circulation: 7235
$1.00 per issue : $10.00 for two years : $12.00 for three years : $15.00 for two years, foreign.

Resources Exchange Project. Newsletter / *sponsored by* Pacific Community Self-Development Society ; *edited by* Greg Welsh. - *Published by* Resources Exchange Project (B.C.). P.O. Box 195, Victoria, B.C. V8W 2M6, June 1972-
Issued twice a month. Special interest, newsletter format, 7 p. Circulation: 600
Free to REP participants. Controlled circulation.

Resources exchange project (British Columbia). Library list - *Published by* Resources Exchange Project (B.C.). P.O. Box 195, Victoria, B.C., 1972-
ISSN 0316-7313

Resources Exchange Project (N.S.). Newsletter - *Published by* Resources Exchange Project (N.S.). P.O. Box 912, Middleton, N.S., 1973-
ISSN 0317-9141

Resources exchange project newsletter / *edited by* Gregory Welsh. - *Published by* Pacific Community Self-Development Society. P.O. Box 195, Victoria, B.C. V8W 2M6, 1972-
Issued twice a month. Special interest, newsletter format, 8 p. Circulation: 650
Controlled circulation.

Resources protection / *edited by* Robert Arculli. - *Published by* J.R. Graham. Walgram Publishing Ltd. 18 Cedarbank Cres., Don Mills, Ont. M3B 3A4, 1972-
Irregular (approximately 10 issues per year). Includes advertising.
$1.50 per issue : $10.00 per year : $15.00 per year, U.S. and U.K. : $25.00 per year, foreign.

Respiratory technology / *edited by* John Unrav. - *Published by* Canadian Society of Respiratory Technologists. 203-818 Portage Ave., Winnipeg, Man. R3G 0N4.
Former title(s): Inhalation therapy.
Quarterly. Association publication, magazine format, 32 p. Circulation: 2750
$6.00 per year. Controlled circulation.

The Respiratory Technology Society of Ontario. Quarterly newsletter / *edited by* John G. Wegener. - *Published by* The Respiratory Technology Society of Ontario. Respiratory Technology Department, Toronto Institute of Medical Technology, 222 Saint Patrick St., Toronto, Ont. M5T 1V4, March 1974-
Quarterly. Association publication, newsletter format, 7 p. Includes advertising, updating service. supplements issued. Circulation: 500
$1.00 per issue : $3.00 per year. Prepayment required.

Resultats techniques *See* Underwriting results : the blue chart

Resumé / *edited by* Kempton L. Matte. - *Published by* The National Dairy Council of Canada. 365 Laurier Ave. W., Ottawa, Ont. K1P 5K2, September 1973-
Monthly. Association publication, newsletter format, 20 p. Language: English and French. Circulation: 750
$10.00 per year.

Resume (May 1969-May 1971) *See* Shaver focus

Retail food report / *edited by* Alastair Smith. - *Published by* Retail Council of Canada. Suite 723, 74 Victoria St., Toronto, Ont. M5C 2A5, May 1974-
Former title(s): Grocery report.
Monthly. Association publication, newsletter format, 6 p.
Subscription included in membership fee. Available to members only.

Retail wages and salaries in Canada - *Published by* Retail Council of Canada. Suite 723, 74 Victoria St., Toronto, Ont. M5C 2A5.
Annual. Directory, magazine format, 26 p.
$3.50.

Retailers' group service bulletin - *Published by* Retail Merchants' Association of Canada (Saskatchewan) Inc. 3rd Ave., and 22nd St., Saskatoon, Sask., 1946-
Monthly. Association publication, newsletter format, 4 p.
$2.00 per year.

The Retired teacher / *sponsored by* Nova Scotia Retired Teachers Association ; *edited by* Robert C. Swim. - *Published by* Nova Scotia Teachers Union. P.O. Box 1060, Ormdale, Halifax, N.S., 1965-
Irregular (approximately 3 issues per year). Association publication, newsletter format, 35 p. Circulation: 900
Free.

Réveil missionnaire / *parrainé par* Bureau de Presse IMC ; *édité par* Aventino Oliveira. - *Publié par* Les Missionnaires de la Consolata. 2381 ouest, boul. Gouin, Montréal, Qué. H3M 1B5, 1966-
Mensuel. Publication ecclésiastique, magazine, 12 p. Comprend publicité. Tirage: 20,000
ISSN 0034-6284 $1.00 par année. Tarifs spéciaux disponibles.

The Review (December 1945-June 1975) *See* The Reporter

Review and digest bulletin / *edited by* J.D. Moore. - *Published by* Canadian Export Association. Suite 1020, 1080 Beaver Hall Hill, Montreal, Que. H2Z 1T7.
Monthly. Association publication, newsletter format, 4 p.
ISSN 0319-3233 $25.00 per year. Subscription includes Export news bulletin and U.S. newsbulletin. Controlled circulation.

The Reviewing librarian / *edited by* Larry Moore, Fay Blostein, Dennis Doherty and Anita Newman. - *Published by* School Libraries Division. Ontario Library Association. 2397a Bloor St. W., Toronto, Ont. M6S 1P6, November 1974-
Issued every other month except July. 20, magazine format, 20 p. Includes book reviews, film reviews, record reviews, cumulative index. Circulation: 450
ISSN 0318-0948 $1.50 per issue : $6.00 per year : $12.00 if purchased with The Revolting librarian. Subscription included in membership fee. Prepayment required.

The Revolting librarian / *edited by* Larry Moore. - *Published by* School Libraries Division. Ontario Library Association. 2397a Bloor St. W., Toronto, Ont. M6S 1P6, October 1973-
Former title(s): SL newsletter (October 1969-May 1974)
Issued every other month. Association publication, newsletter format, 16-20 p. Includes updating service. supplements issued. Circulation: 450
ISSN 0316-8840 $1.50 per issue : $8.00 per year : $12.00 if purchased with The Reviewing librarian. Free. Subscription included in membership fee. Prepayment required.

Revue - Québec Automobile Club = Magazine - Quebec Automobile Club (janvier 1924-mars 1928) *Voir* Autoclub : le journal de l'automobiliste du Québec

Revue annuelle de photographie de l'Université Laval / *édité par* Club photo optica. - *Publié par* Yvon Lirette. Service des Loisirs. Université Laval. 1362, pavillon Pollack, Université Laval, Québec, Qué. G1K 7P4, juin 1974-
Annuel. Publication d'association, revue, 32 p. Tirage: 2000
ISSN 0315-6141 $1.00 par année : $1.50 par année, l'étranger.

Revue canadienne de biologie / *parrainé par* Université de Montréal ; *édité par* Jules Brodeur. - *Publié par* Les Presses de l'Université de Montréal. C.P. 6128, Montréal, Qué. H3C 3J7, 1942-
Trimestriel. Edition savante, revue, 80 p. Langue(s): français et anglais ; sommaires: français et anglais. Comprend publicité. Tirage: 800
Indexé dans RADAR, Ind. med., I.B.Z.
ISSN 0035-0915 $4.00 le numéro : $12.00 par année. Tirage contrôlé. Abonnements payables à l'avance.

Revue canadienne de criminologie *See* Canadian journal of criminology and corrections

Revue canadienne de défense *See* Canadian defence quarterly

Revue canadienne de l'éducation *See* Canadian journal of education

La Revue canadienne de linguistique *See* Canadian journal of linguistics

Revue canadienne de littérature comparée *See* Canadian review of comparative literature

Revue canadienne de médecine comparée *See* Canadian journal of comparative medicine

Revue canadienne de santé publique *See* Canadian journal of public health

Revue canadienne de sociologie et d'anthropologie *See* Canadian review of sociology and anthropology

Revue canadienne d'économie publique et coopérative = Canadian journal of public and cooperative economy / *parrainé par* Centre canadien international de recherches et d'information sur l'économie publique et coopérative ; *édité par* Georges Davidovic. - *Publié par* Departement d'économie. Sir George Williams Campus. Université Concordia. 1455 ouest, de Maisonneuve, Montréal, Qué. H3G 1M8, juillet-décembre 1968-
Ancien titre: Revue du CIRIEC canadien = CIRIEC Canadian review (juillet-décembre 1968-janvier-décembre 1973)
Intermittent (approximativement 2 éditions par an). Publication d'association, revue, 175 p. Langue(s): français et anglais ; sommaires: français et anglais. Comprend critique de livres, index de volumes. Tirage: 500
$2.50 le numéro : $5.00 par année : $5.50 par année, l'étranger. Tarifs spéciaux disponibles. Abonnements payables à l'avance.

La Revue canadienne d'enseignement supérieur *See* Canadian journal of higher education

Revue canadienne d'ergothérapie *See* Canadian journal of occupational therapy

Revue canadienne des sciences de l'information *See* Canadian journal of information science

Revue canadienne des sciences du comportement *See* Canadian journal of behavioural science

Revue canadienne des sciences pures et appliquées *See* Science forum : a Canadian journal of science and technology

Revue canadienne des Slavistes *See* Canadian Slavonic papers

Revue canadienne d'urbanisme *See* Community planning review

La Revue commerce / *édité par* Maurice Chartrand. - *Publié par* La Revue Commerce. 1080, Côte du Beaver Hall, Montréal, Qué. H2Z 1S8, 1898-
Mensuel. Publication spécialisée, magazine, 100 p. Tirage: 29,000
$1.00 le numéro : $10.00 par année : $15.00 par année, l'étranger. Abonnements payables à l'avance.

Revue de droit - *Publié par* Faculté de Droit. Université de Sherbrooke. Sherbrooke, Qué. J1R 2R1, 1970-
Annuel. Articles juridiques, revue, 300 p. Langue(s): français et anglais. Tirage: 1200
Indexé dans Periodex, Can. leg. per. lit., Leg. per.
$6.00 par année : $7.00 par année, l'étranger. Abonnements payables à l'avance.

La Revue de géographie de Montréal / *parrainé par* Université de Montréal. - *Publié par* Les Presses de l'Université de Montréal. C.P. 6128, Montréal, Qué. H3C 3J7, 1947-
Trimestriel. Edition savante, revue, 112 p. Langue(s): français ; sommaires: français et anglais. Comprend publicité. Tirage: 1000
Indexé dans Periodex, Can. ind., RADAR, Hist. abstr.; Amer. hist. and life.
$5.00 le numéro : $15.00 par année. Tirage contrôlé. Abonnements payables à l'avance.

La Revue de l'arpenteur-géomètre / *édité par* J. Roland Pelletier. - *Publié par* Ordres des arpenteurs-géomètres du Québec. 917, Mgr. Grandin, Ste-Foy, Qué. G1V 3X8, janvier 1973-
Trimestriel. Publication d'association, 3 numéros de 64 p. ; 1 de 144 p. Tirage: 1200
Indexé dans RADAR.
Envoi gratuit.

Revue de l'Université d'Ottawa / *édité par* Gaston Carrière. - *Publié par* Les Editions de l'Université d'Ottawa. 65, rue Hastey, Ottawa, Ont. K1N 6N5, 1931-
Trimestriel. Publication d'institution (universités, écoles..), magazine, 144 p. Langue(s): français et anglais. Comprend critique de livres, index de volumes, index cumulatif. Tirage: 900
Indexé dans Can. ind., RADAR, Cath. ind., Can. educ. ind., M.L.A. int. bib., Hist. abstr.; Amer. hist. and life, Peace res. abstr., I.B.Z., Arct. bibl.
$4.00 le numéro : $10.00 par année. Abonnements payables à l'avance.

Revue de modification du comportement / *parrainé par* Association des spécialistes en modification du comportement ; *édité par* Jean-Marie Boisvert. - *Publié par* Service de psychologie, Hôpital St-Jean-de-Dieu, att: M. J.-M. Boisvert. Montréal-Gamelin, Montréal, Qué. H1N 1Z0, octobre 1970-
Ancien titre: Bulletin de nouvelles de L'Association pour l'avancement de la thérapie behaviorale en milieu francophone (octobre 1970-janvier 1972) Bulletin de l'Association pour l'analyse et la modification du comportement (décembre 1972-décembre 1973)
Trimestriel. Publication d'association, bulletin, 25 p.
Indexé dans RADAR.
$2.50 le numéro : $8.00 par année. Abonnements payables à l'avance.

La Revue des fermières / *édité par* Pierrette Paré Walsh. - *Publié par* Les Editions Pénélope. 1200, ave Allen, Laval, Qué. H7W 1G9, novembre/décembre 1974-
Bimestriel. Publication d'association, magazine, 40 p. Tirage: 57,000
$5.00 par année.

Revue des sciences de l'éducation / *édité par* André Girard. - *Publié par* Doyens des facultés francophones des sciences de l'éducation. C.P. 6203, Succursale A, Montréal, Qué. H3C 3T3, printemps 1975-
Trimestriel. Publication d'association, revue, 100 p. parution de suppléments. Tirage: 2000
$4.00 le numéro : $10.00 par année.

La Revue Desjardins / *édité par* Claude Moquin. - *Publié par* La Fédération des caisses populaires Desjardins. 150, ave des Commandeurs, Lévis, Qué. G6V 6P8, 1935-
Bimestriel. Organe interne/officiel, magazine, 40 p.Aussi sous microform. Tirage: 20,000
ISSN 0035-2284 $.60 le numéro : $3.50 par année.

Revue d'histoire de la Gaspésie / *édité par* Claude Allard. - *Publié par* Editions Gaspésiennes. C.P. 680, Gaspé, Qué. G0C 1R0, janvier-mars 1963-
Trimestriel. Publication d'association, magazine, 70 p. Langue(s): français et anglais. Tirage: 1600
Indexé dans RADAR, Hist. abstr.; Amer. hist. and life.
$5.00 par année.

Revue d'histoire de la Société historique Nicolas-Denys / *édité par* Eloi DeGräce. - *Publié par* Société historique Nicholas Denys. Case 6, Site 19, Bertrand, N.B. E0B 1J0, juin 1970-
Trimestriel. Publication d'association, magazine, Comprend critique de livres. Tirage: 500
$1.50 le numéro : $5.00 par année (Institutions $10.00). Abonnements payables à l'avance.

Revue d'histoire de l'Amérique française / *édité par* Pierre Savard. - *Publié par* Institut d'histoire de l'Amérique française. 261, ave Bloomfield, Montréal, Qué. H2V 3R6, juin 1947-
Trimestriel. Publication d'association, revue, 160 p. Comprend critique de livres.Aussi sous microform. Tirage: 800
Indexé dans Periodex, Can. ind., RADAR, Hist. abstr.; Amer. hist. and life.
$3.00 le numéro : $10.00 par année : $3.50 le numéro, l'étranger : $12.00 par année l'étranger.

La Revue du barreau canadien *See* The Canadian bar review

Revue du CIRIEC canadien = CIRIEC Canadian review (juillet-décembre 1968-janvier-décembre 1973) *Voir* Revue canadienne d'économie publique et coopérative

La Revue du monde arabe *See* Canadian Arab world review

La Revue du notariat / *parrainé par* La Chambre des notaires du Québec ; *édité par* Roger Comtois. - *Publié par* La Revue du notariat. C.P. 130, Outrement, Qué. H2V 4M8, 1898-
Mensuel. Articles juridiques, revue, 60 p. Langue(s): français et anglais ; sommaires: français. Comprend index de volumes.
Indexé dans RADAR, Can. leg. per. lit.
$1.00 le numéro : $10.00 par année.

La revue du service civil *See* The Civil service review

La Revue économique de l'Université de Moncton *Voir* Université de Moncton. La Revue de l'Université de Moncton

Revue eucharistique prêtres-adorateurs clergé (1937-1972) *Voir* Prêtre et pasteur : revue eucharistique du clergé

La Revue franciscaine / *parrainé par* L'Ordre séculier franciscain ; *édité par* Richer Beaubien. - *Publié par* L'Ordre Laïc de St-François. 2080 ouest, boul. Dorchester, Montréal, Qué. H3H 1R6.
Ancien titre: Petite revue du tiers-ordre et des intérêts du Coeur de Jésus (février 1884-janvier 1975)
Bimestriel. Publication ecclésiastique, publication d'association, magazine, 36 p. Comprend critique de livres. Tirage: 8000
$.50 le numéro : $3.00 par année : $4.00 par année, l'étranger. Tirage contrôlé. Abonnements payables à l'avance.

Revue générale de droit / *parrainé par* Faculté de droit de l'Université d'Ottawa. Section de droit civil ; *édité par* Alain Bisson. - *Publié par* Les Editions de l'Université d'Ottawa. 65, ave Hastey, Ottawa, Ont. K1N 6N5, 1970-
Ancien titre: Justinien (1964-1969)
Semestriel. Publication ecclésiastique, revue, 250 p. Comprend critique de livres, index de volumes, index cumulatif. Tirage: 750
Indexé dans Periodex, Can. leg. per. lit., Leg. per.
$3.00 le numéro : $5.00 par année. Abonnements payables à l'avance.

La Revue hippique - *Publié par* Jean Laurin. 185, boul. Je me Souviens, Ste-Rose, Laval, Qué.
Mensuel. Publication spécialisée, magazine, 50 p.
$.75 le numéro : $6.00 par année.

Revue information / *edited by* Claude M. Poirier. - *Published by* Fédération des principaux du Québec. 7000, boul. Joseph-Reraud, Anjou, Montréal, Qué. H1K 3V5, janvier 1963-
Mensuel. Publication ecclésiastique, bulletin, 24 p. Tirage: 4200
Indexed in Can. educ. ind.
$6.00 par année. Abonnements payables à l'avance.

La Revue juridique thémis de l'Université de Montréal / *édité par* André Poupart. - *Publié par* Les Editions thémis (1951-1965). C.P. 6201, 3101 Marie Guyard, Montréal, Qué. H3C 3T1, 1951-
Ancien titre: Thémis (1951-1965)
Trimestriel. Articles juridiques, revue, 200 p. Langue(s): français et anglais. Comprend critique de livres, publicité, index de volumes, index cumulatif. Tirage: 1800
Indexé dans RADAR, Can. leg. per. lit., Leg. per.
$4.00 le numéro : $10.00 par année. Abonnements payables à l'avance.

Revue machinerie lourde / *édité par* Gerard Privé. - *Publié par* Gérard Privé. Association des propriétaires de machinerie lourde du Quebec, inc. 2500A, Belle chasse, Montréal, Qué. H1Y 1H8, 1970-
Ancien titre: Travaux mécanisés du Québec.
Revue d'entreprise. Comprend publicité.
Tirage: 4224

Revue moteur / *édité par* Bruno Poirier. - *Publié par* Chuck O'Hearn. Maclean-Hunter Ltd. 481 University Ave., Toronto, Ont.
Revue d'entreprise, magazine, 60 p. Comprend publicité.
$1.00 le numéro : $10.00 par année : $12.00 par année, E.U. et R.U. Tirage contrôlé.

Le Revue municipale - *Publié par* La Revue municipale inc. Suite 203, 6841, rue St-Hubert, Montréal, Qué., 1923-
Ancien titre: Cités et villes.
Mensuel. Comprend publicité. Tirage: 10,535
Indexé dans RADAR.

Revue Notre Dame du Sacré-Coeur (janvier 1965-décembre 1968) *Voir* RND (Revue Notre-Dame)

Revue 1 + éditions de luxe / *édité par* Gilles Gheerbrant. - *Publié par* Editions Gilles Gheerbrant. 2130, Crescent, Montréal, Qué. H3G 2B2, mars 1972-
Intermittent (approximativement 3-4 éditions par an). Publication spécialisée, 2 p. Langue(s): français et anglais.

La Revue scolaire / *édité par* Mario LaLiberté. - *Publié par* Jean Gilles Jutras. Fédération des commissions scolaires catholiques du Québec. C.P. 490, 1001, Bégon, Ste-Foy, Québec, Qué. G1V 4C7, décembre 1948-
Mensuel. Magazine, 36 p. Comprend critique de livres, publicité. Tirage: 6000
Indexé dans Periodex, RADAR, Can. educ. ind.
$.60 le numéro : $6.00 par année.
Abonnements payables à l'avance.

Revue Suisse-Canada *See* Swiss Canadian review

Revue travaux mécanisés *Voir* Machinerie lourde

Revue trimestrielle canadienne (1915-1955) *Voir* L'Ingénieur

La Revue uranus enr'g / *édité par* Jacques Cyr. - *Publié par* Les Editions Gémini Enr'g. 8523, rue St-Denis, Montréal, Qué. H2P 2H4, juin 1973-
Bimestriel. Publication spécialisée, magazine, 24 p. Tirage: 3000
$.75 le numéro : $5.00 par année : $2.95 le volume.

La revue vétérinaire canadienne *See* The Canadian veterinary journal

Le Richelieu / *édité par* Françoise Penven. - *Publié par* La Société Blaquière. 2403, rue Bourojogme, Chambly, Qué.
Hebdomadaire. Intérêt général, journal, 28 p. Langue(s): français (anglais). Comprend critique de pièces de théâtre, publicité. Tirage: 17,200
$10.00 par année. Tirage contrôlé.

The Right hand / *edited by* William Randall. - *Published by* Northwest Printing & Lithographing Ltd. P.O. Box 3278, Postal Station B, Calgary, Alta. T2M 4L8.
Issued every other month. House/company organ, magazine format, 16 p.
$.75 per issue : $3.50 per year.

Rights and freedoms / *edited by* Mono Corbus. - *Published by* Canadian Federation of Civil Liberties and Human Rights Associations. 302-14 Metcalfe St., Ottawa, Ont. K1P 5L1, June 1972-
Former title(s): National newsletter (June 1972-July 1974)
Irregular (approximately 8 issues per year). Association publication, newspaper format, 12 p. Language: English and French ; summaries: English and French.
$5.00 per year.

Le Rimouskois / *édité par* M. Ernie Wells. - *Publié par* Les Editions du Bas St-Laurent Inc. 212, Cathédrale, Rimouski, Qué.(adresse d'abonnement: C.P. 460, Rimouski, Qué)
Hebdomadaire. Intérêt général, journal, 36 p. Comprend critique de livres, publicité. Tirage: 11,000
$9.00 par année : $5.00 par année, l'étranger.
Abonnements payables à l'avance.

Il Rincontro / *edited by* Tony Vellone. - *Published by* Tony Vellone. 7092 St-Laurent Blvd., Montreal, Qué. H2S 3E2, 1971-
Monthly. Ethnic press. Language: Italian. Includes advertising. Circulation: 3500
$.25 per issue : $5.00 per year.

Road and wheel *See* Roads and Transportation Association of Canada. RTAC news

Road runner / *edited by* B.J. McCaffery. - *Published by* Ontario Good Roads Association. P.O. Box 128, 354 Talbot St., St. Thomas, Ont. N5P 3T7, January 1973-
Issued 3 times a year. Association publication, newsletter format, 4 p. Circulation: 2300
Free.

Roads and Transportation Association of Canada. Proceedings - *Published by* Roads and Transportation Association of Canada. 1765 St. Laurent Blvd., Ottawa, Ont. K1G 3V4, 1950-
Annual. Association publication, book format, 350 p.

Roads and Transportation Association of Canada. RTAC news / *edited by* Gilbert Morier. - *Published by* Roads and Transportation Association of Canada. 1765 St. Laurent Blvd., Ottawa, Ont. K1G 3V4, January 1975-
Former title(s): Road and wheel; Inside RTAC. Published in French: Association des routes et transports du Canada. Nouvelles de l'ARTC.
Irregular (approximately 10 issues per year). Association publication, newsletter format, 8 p. Includes book reviews. Circulation: 2000
ISSN 0317-1280 Free. Controlled circulation.

Roads and Transportation Association of Canada. Technical bulletin - *Published by* Roads and Transportation Association of Canada. 1765 St. Laurent Blvd., Ottawa, Ont. K1G 3V4, 1955-
Irregular (approximately 3 issues per year). Association publication.

Rock climbing in Ontario / *edited by* Jim Mark. - *Published by* Toronto Section. The Alpine Club of Canada. 85 Fallingbrook Rd., Scarborough, Ont.
Association publication, guide book, 96 p. Circulation: 300
$4.00 per volume.

Romanian echo *See* Ecouri romanesti

Room of one's own : a feminist journal of literature and criticism / *edited by* Gayla Reid and Gail van Varseveld. - *Published by* Growing Room Collective. 1918 Waterloo St., Vancouver, B.C. V6R 3G6, March 1975-
Quarterly. Special interest, magazine format, 80 p. Includes book reviews. Circulation: 800
ISSN 0316-1609

La Rotonde / *édité par* Denis Vézina. - *Publié par* Fédération des étudiants. Université d'Ottawa. 035-85, ave Hastey Chambre, Ottawa, Ont. K1N 5N6.
Publié en anglais: Fulcrum.
Paraît tous les 15 jours. Publication des étudiants, journal, 16 p. Tirage: 10,000
$5.00 par année. Abonnements payables à l'avance.

Rotunda / *edited by* John Campoide. - *Published by* The Royal Ontario Museum. 100 Queen's Park, Toronto, Ont. M5S 2C6 (Subscription address: Information services, Royal Ontario Museum) 1968-
Quarterly. Institutional publication, magazine format, 40 p. Includes volume index. Circulation: 500
Indexed in Hist. abstr.; Amer. hist. and life.
ISSN 0035-8495 $1.25 per issue : $4.00 per year. Special rates offered. Prepayment required.

Rouge et noir (1880-1888) *See* The Trinity University review : a journal of literature, college thought and events

The Roughneck / *edited by* Michael McLaughlin. - *Published by* Lloyd Gilmour. Commercial Publications Ltd. 202, 528-9 Ave. S.W., Calgary, Alta. T2P 1L4, 1952-
Monthly. Trade publication. Includes advertising. Circulation: 7104
$4.00 per year.

Roundtable / *edited by* Walter A. Schultz. - *Published by* Lutheran Council in Canada. 500 - 365 Hargrave St., Winnipeg, Man. R3B 2K3, January 1968-
Irregular (approximately 5 issues per year). Church publication, newsletter format, 6 p. Circulation: 1200
Controlled circulation.

The Roundup / *edited by* J.H. Grey. - *Published by* Canadian Forces Base, Calgary. Currie Barracks, Calgary, Alta. T3E 1T8.
Weekly. House/company organ, newspaper format, 8 p.
$7.50 per year.

Routes du Québec (janvier 1971-janvier 1975) *Voir* Routes et transports

Routes et transports - *Publié par* Association québécoise du transport et des routes. C.P. 6079, Succursale A, Ecole polytechnique, Campus de l'Université de Montréal, Montréal, Qué. H3C 3J7, janvier 1971-
Ancien titre: Routes du Québec (janvier 1971-janvier 1975)
Intermittent (approximativement 3 éditions par an). Publication d'association, magazine, 48 p.
$5.00 le numéro : $15.00 par année. Abonnements payables à l'avance.

The Royal Astronomical Society of Canada. Journal / *edited by* Ian Halliday. - *Published by* The Royal Astronomical Society of Canada. 252 College St., Toronto, Ont. M5T 1R7, 1907-
Issued every other month. Association publication, journal format, 56 p. Language: English and French ; summaries: English and French. Includes book reviews, volume index, cumulative index. available in microform.
Circulation: 2900
Indexed in I.B.Z.
$3.00 per issue : $15.00 per year.

The Royal Bank of Canada. Monthly letter / *edited by* John R. Heron. - *Published by* The Royal Bank of Canada. P.O. Box 6001, Montreal, Que. H3C 3A9, December 1943-
Monthly. General interest, newsletter format, 4 p. Language: English and French.
Circulation: 700,000
Indexed in P.A.I.S., Can. B.P.I.
Free.

Royal Botanical Gardens, Hamilton, Ont. Annual meteorological summary / *edited by* W. John Lamoureux. - *Published by* Royal Botanical Gardens. P.O. Box 399, Hamilton, Ont. L8N 3H8, 1971-
Annual. Special interest, 10-11 p.

The Royal Canadian College of Organists. Quarterly / *edited by* Alan Jackson. - *Published by* The Royal Canadian College of Organists. Suite 300A, 212 King St. W., Toronto, Ont. M5H 1K5.
Quarterly. Association publication, magazine format, 50 p.
$1.50 per volume. Subscription included in membership fee.

Royal College of Physicians and Surgeons of Canada. Annals of The Royal College of Physicians and Surgeons of Canada = Collège royal des médecins et chirurgiens du Canada. Annales du collège royal des médecins et chirurgiens du Canada / *edited by* Jacques Robichon. - *Published by* The Royal College of Physicians and Surgeons of Canada. 74 Stanley Ave., Ottawa, Ont. K1M 1P4, January 1968-
Quarterly. Association publication, magazine format, 90 p. Language: English and French. Includes advertising, volume index.
Circulation: 14,800
$1.25 per issue : $5.00 per year.

Royal Conservatory of Music of Toronto. Bulletin - *Published by* Royal Conservatory of Music of Toronto. 273 Bloor St. W., Toronto, Ont.
Irregular (approximately 3 issues per year). Institutional publication, newsletter format,
Circulation: 20,000
Free.

Royal reflector (1963-1967) *See* Reflector

Royal Society of Canada. Calendar = Annuaire / *edited by* The Honorary Secretary of the Society. - *Published by* Royal Society of Canada. 395 Wellington St., Ottawa, Ont. K1A 0N4, 1968-
Annual. Yearbook, 80 p. Language: English and French.
ISSN 0317-3631 $1.50 per volume.

Royal Society of Canada. Proceedings / *sponsored by* The Royal Society of Canada ; *edited by* A.G. McKay. - *Published by* University of Toronto Press. 5201 Dufferin St., Downsview, Ont. M3H 5T8 (Subscription address: The Royal Society of Canada, 395 Wellington St., Ottawa, Ont. K1A 0N4) 1882-
Annual. Association publication, paperback book, 105 p. Language: English and French. available in microform.
$4.50.

The Royal Society of Canada. Transactions / *sponsored by* The Royal Society of Canada ; *edited by* A.G. McKay. - *Published by* University of Toronto Press. 5201 Dufferin St., Downsview, Ont. M3H 5T8 (Subscription address: 395 Wellington St., Ottawa, Ont. K1A 0N4) 1882-
Annual. Proceedings of annual meeting, paperback book, 300 p. Language: English and French. available in microform.
Indexed in Hist. abstr.; Amer. hist. and life.
$8.00.

Rune / *edited by* E.J. Carson, Brian Henderson and S. Solecki. - *Published by* The Student Council. St. Michael's College. P.O. Box 299, Toronto, Ont. M5S 1J4 1J4, Spring 1974-
Irregular (approximately 1-2 issues per year). Student publication, magazine format, 70-100 p. Includes book reviews. Circulation: 1000
$1.00 per issue. Special rates offered.

The Runic report (October 1972-February 1975) *See* Sojourn: the magazine for Nova Scotians

The Running board / *sponsored by* Edmonton Antique Car Club ; *edited by* Ray Holman. - *Published by* Ray Holman. 9119-14 Ave., Edmonton, Alta. (Subscription address: P.O. Box 102, Edmonton, Alta) 1962-
Monthly. Association publication, newsletter format, 4 p. Includes advertising.
$10.00 per year. Controlled circulation.

Rural co-operator (1936-1965) *See* Farm and country

Rural Education and Development Association. Information services bulletin / *edited by* Jack Muzer. - *Published by* Rural Education & Development Association. 9934 - 106th St., Edmonton, Alta. T5K 1C4.
Annual. Association publication, 8 p.

Rushes / *edited by* Jesse Frayne. - *Published by* Toronto Film-makers Co-op. 67 Portland St., Toronto, Ont. M6R 2K9, 1971-
Irregular (approximately 4 issues per year). Special interest, booklet format, 47 p. Includes film reviews, advertising. Circulation: 350
$3.00 per year. Free.

Russell : the journal of the Bertrand Russell Archives / *edited by* Kenneth Blackwell. - *Published by* McMaster University Library Press. Mills Memorial Library, Macmaster University, Hamilton, Ont., Spring 1971-
Quarterly. Special interest, newsletter format, 32 p. Includes book reviews. Circulation: 360
Indexed in Phil. ind.
ISSN 0036-0163 $.75 per issue : $3.00 per year (Institutions $4.00) : $3.50 and $4.50 per year, foreign.

Ryersonian / *edited by* John McCallam (managing editor). - *Published by* J.D. MacFarlane. Ryerson Polytechnical Institute. 50 Gould St., Toronto, Ont. M5B 1E8, January 1949-
Former title(s): The Daily Ryersonian, (1966-1970) The Little daily (1950-1952) The Little weekly, (1950-1952)
Issued 4 times a week September-April. Student publication, newspaper format, 10 p. Includes book reviews, film reviews, play reviews, record reviews, advertising. supplements issued. Circulation: 3000
$10.00 per year.

S.C.A.T. bulletin *See* Alberta science education journal

SCOOP - *Published by* Civil Service Co-operative Credit Society Ltd. 400 Albert St., Ottawa, Ont. K1R 5B2., October 1970-
Quarterly. House/company organ, newsletter format, 4 p. Language: English and French. Circulation: 55,000
ISSN 0315-839X Free.

SCRLS newsletter (to February 1973) *See* Scurrilous news letter

SEM (service des écrivains de Montréal) / *édité par* Edmond Robillard. - *Publié par* Les Publications SEM inc. Bureau 502, 2767, boul. Edouard-Montpetit, Montréal, Qué., janvier/février 1975-
Bimestriel. Intérêt général, magazine, 64 p. Tirage: 20,000
$1.25 le numéro : $6.00 par année : $1.25 le volume : $8.00 par année, l'étranger (Par avion $15.00).

The S.G.T. (1960-1967) *See* Sask Tel news

SL newsletter (October 1969-May 1974) *See* The Revolting librarian

SMEA bulletin (1958-1970) *See* Saskatchewan Music Educators' Association. Saskatchewan Music Educators newsletter

SMEA journal (1971-1972) *See* Saskatchewan Music Educators' Association. Saskatchewan Music Educators newsletter

SMTS journal *See* Saskatchewan Mathematics Teachers' Society. News/journal

SMTS newsletter *See* Saskatchewan Mathematics Teachers' Society. News/journal

SNAUQ / *edited by* P.A Yandle. - *Published by* Vancouver Museums & Planetarium Association. 1100 Chestnut St., Vancouver B.C. V6J 3J9, September 1973-
Former title(s): Newsletter - Vancouver Museums and Planetarium Association.
Irregular (approximately 2-6 issues per year). Association publication, newsletter format, 25 p. Circulation: 3000
$1.00 per issue. Subscription included in membership fee.

SONRA news (January 1960-April 1968) *See* The Newfoundland amateur

SPK W Kanadzie - *Published by* Polish Combatant's Association in Canada Inc. 206 Beverly St., Toronto, Ont. M5T 1Z3, 1963-
Quarterly. Ethnic press, magazine format, 32 p. Language: Polish and English. Circulation: 2600

SSEA newsletter (1970-1971) *See* Discovery through art

STA news (1960? to 1972) *See* The B.C. science teacher

STOA (1971-1974) *See* Canadian journal of higher education

Saddlebag / *edited by* Jean Andryiszyn. - *Published by* Calgary Exhibition and Stampede. P.O. Box 1060, Calgary, Alta., February 1970-
Quarterly. House/company organ, newsletter format, 4 p.
Free.

Safe-t-line bulletin / *sponsored by* The Accident Prevention Association of Ontario. - *Published by* Electrical Utilities Safety Association of Ontario Inc. 81 Kelfield St., Rexdale, Ont. M9W 5A3, 1959-
Monthly. Association publication, newsletter format, 4 p. Circulation: 2000
Free.

Safety Canada / *edited by* Rick Green. - *Published by* Canada Safety Council. 1765 Blvd. St. Laurent, Ottawa, Ont. K1G 3V4, June 1957-
Former title(s): Highway safety news (January 1961 - February 1969) The Bulletin - Canada Safety Council (June 1957-January 1961) Published in French: Le prévention au Canada.
Monthly, 11 months a year. Association publication, magazine format, 8 or 12 p. Includes book reviews, film reviews, record reviews. Circulation: 13,000
ISSN 0048-8968 Free.

Le Saguenay médical / *édité par* Wilfrid Lachance. - *Publié par* Wilfrid Lachance. Hôpital de Chicoutimi inc. Chicoutimi, Qué. G7H 5H6, 1952-
Trimestriel. Publication d'institution (universités, écoles..), revue, 50-60 p. Comprend publicité, index de volumes. Tirage: 1800
Envoi gratuit.

Sailing forum *See* The Canadian sailing forum

St. Catharines and District Arts Council. Bulletin / *sponsored by* St. Catharines and District Arts Council ; *edited by* Peter Harris. - *Published by* Rodman Hall Arts Centre. 109 St. Paul Cres., St. Catherines, Ont., 1960-
Monthly. Association publication, 1 p. Circulation: 1100
$1.00 per issue : $9.00 per year.

Saint Francis Xavier University. St. F.X. newsletter / *edited by* Robert P. Doherty. - *Published by* Saint Francis Xavier University. Antigonish, N.S. B0H 1C0, September 1973-
Weekly. Institutional publication (Universities, schools, etc.), newsletter format, 8 p.

St. John Ambulance. Ontario Council. Bulletin / *edited by* Christina Sclanders (Director of Communication). - *Published by* Ontario Council. St. John Ambulance. 46 Wellesley St. E., Toronto, Ont. M4Y 1G5.
Quarterly. House/company organ, newsletter format, 10 p. Circulation: 800
Free. Controlled circulation.

St. John Ambulance in Canada. St John news - *Published by* St. John Ambulance. 321 Chapel St., Ottawa, Ont. K1N 7Z2., March 1975-
Quarterly. Association publication, newsletter format, 8 p. Language: English and French. Circulation: 1000

St. John's Board of Trade. News and Views / *edited by* Keith D. Mullins. - *Published by* St. John's Board of Trade. P.O. Box 5127, St. John's, Nfld. A1C 5V5.
Monthly. Trade publication, newsletter format, 12 p. Circulation: 3000
ISSN 0316 9146 Free.

Saint John's Edmonton report / *sponsored by* The Company of the Cross ; *edited by* Ted Byfield. - *Published by* Keith Bennett. Saint John's Edmonton Report Ltd. 11224 142 St., Edmonton, Alta. T5M 1T9, November 1, 1973-
Weekly. General interest, magazine format, 30 p. Includes book reviews, play reviews, advertising. Circulation: 20,000
$.50 per issue : $15.00 per year.

St. Leonard's Society of Canada. News & views / *edited by* Jerry Hames. - *Published by* The Saint Leonard's Society of Canada. 1787 Walker Rd., Windsor, Ont. N8W 3P2, February 1969-
Irregular (approximately 3 issues per year). Association publication, newsletter format, 4-6 p.

St. Thomas More College. Library. History collection : Canadian Catholic Church / *edited by* Alphonse de Valk. - *Published by* Library. St. Thomas More College. 1437 College Dr., Saskatoon, Sask. S7N 0W6, 1971-
Annual. Catalogue. Language: English and French. Circulation: 300
ISSN 0315-3371 Free. Controlled circulation.

St. Thomas More College. Library. Periodicals and serials in the Shannon Library - *Published by* Library. St. Thomas More College. 1437 College Dr., Saskatoon, Sask. S7N 0W6, 1968-
Annual. Yearbook.
Free.

Saint-Sulpice du Canada / *édité par* René Marinier. - *Publié par* Les Prêtres du Saint-Sulpice du Canada. 116 ouest, rue Notre-Dame, Montréal, Qué. H2Y 1T2, mars 1961-
Intermittent (approximativement 2 éditions par an). Publication d'association, publication ecclésiastique, bulletin, 4 p. Tirage: 6000
Envoi gratuit.

Saison : rapport des stages - *Publié par* Camp-école Chicobi. Guyenne, Abitibi-ouest, Qué. J0Y 1L0.
Publication d'institution (universités, écoles..).
Tirage contrôlé.

Salam / *édité par* Faustin Laplante. - *Publié par* Les Presses Elite. 3744, Jean-Brillant, Montréal, Qué.(adresse d'abonnement: 1242, Redpath Cres., Montréal, Qué. H3G 2K1) mars 1953-
Ancien titre: Bulletin missionnaire des Frères de Ste-Croix (septembre 1951-janvier 1953)
Bulletin missionnaire (février 1951-mai 1951)
Lettres du Bengale (janvier 1951)
Trimestriel. Publication ecclésiastique, bulletin, 4 p. Tirage: 1200
$1.00 par année. Tirage contrôlé.
Abonnements payables à l'avance.

Salary categories for Canadian teachers / *edited by* Geraldine Channon. - *Published by* Canadian Teachers' Federation. 110 Argyle Ave., Ottawa, Ont. K2P 1B4.
Bienniel.
$.50 per issue.

Salary survey (office) - *Published by* Quebec Industrial Relations Institute. 630 Sherbrooke St. W., Montreal, Que. H3A 1E4.
Annual. Book format, 250 p. Includes cumulative index.
Subscription included in membership fee.
Controlled circulation.

Salt water salmon fishing guide / *edited by* Jim Railton. - *Published by* Railton Publications Ltd. 125 Talisman Ave., Vancouver, B.C. V5Y 2L6, 1973-
Annual. Special interest, magazine format, 70 p. Circulation: 20,000
$1.50.

Il Samaritano : la voca cattolica / *edited by* Benito Framarin. - *Published by* Italmedia Services. 1000 Lawrence Ave., W., Toronto, Ont., 1975-
Weekly. Ethnic press. Language: Italian.
Includes advertising. Circulation: 32,000

Sand patterns / *edited by* Betty Campbell. - *Published by* Sand Patterns Publications. P.O. Box 321, Charlottetown, P.E.I. C1A 7K7, 1972-
Quarterly. Association publication, magazine format, 50 p. Circulation: 200
ISSN 0316-5167 $1.00 per issue : $4.00 per year. Subscription included in membership fee $5.00.

Sanford Evans gold book of snowmobile data and used prices / *edited by* C.B. Wagner. - *Published by* Sanford Evans Publishing Ltd. P.O. Box 6900, 1077 St. James St., Winnipeg, Man. R3C 3B1, September 1973-
Annual. Trade publication, magazine format, 66 p.
ISSN 0318-9422 $5.00 per year.

Sanford Evans gold book of used car prices / *edited by* C.B. Wagner. - *Published by* Sanford Evans Publishing Ltd. 1077 St. James St., Winnipeg, Man. R3C 3B1.
Monthly. Trade publication, 166 p.
$3.00 per issue : $29.00 per year.

Sarracenia / *edited by* Virginia A. Weadock. - *Published by* C.E.R.S.E. Université du Québec. P.O. Box 8888, Montreal, Que. H3C 3P8, August 1959-
Biennial. "For the use of students and research workers in the field of environmental sciences", 75 p. Language: English and French.
ISSN 0080-6463 $1.70.

Sask Tel news / *edited by* Ted Cholod. - *Published by* Saskatchewan Telecommunications. 2350 Albert St., Regina, Sask. S4P 2Y4, January 1960-
Former title(s): The S.G.T. (1960-1967)
Monthly. House/company organ, newspaper format, 6-8 p. Circulation: 3400

The Saskatchewan administrator / *sponsored by* Saskatchewan Council on Education Administration ; *edited by* Kevin A. Wilson. - *Published by* Saskatchewan Teachers' Federation. 2317 Arlington Ave., Saskatoon, Sask. S7J 2H8 (Subscription address: Room 3073, Education Building, University of Saskatchewan, Saskatoon, Sask. S7N 0W0) 1967-
Quarterly. Association publication, journal format, 35 p. Includes book reviews.
Circulation: 350
$1.00 per issue : $5.00 per year. Subscription included in membership fee. Controlled circulation. Prepayment required.

Saskatchewan Anti-Tuberculosis League. Saskatchewan Anti-Tuberculosis League news quarterly / *edited by* Carol B. Copeland. - *Published by* Saskatchewan Anti-Tuberculosis League. Fort San., Sask. (Subscription address: 25 Qu'Appelle Court, Saskatoon, Sask. S7K 1C2) Spring 1970-
Former title(s): The Valley echo (December 1919-December 1969)
Quarterly. Association publication, newsletter format, 4 p. Circulation: 2659
Free. Controlled circulation.

Saskatchewan archaeology newsletter / *edited by* G. Watson. - *Published by* Saskatchewan Archaeological Society. 857 Elphinstone St., Regina, Sask.
Irregular (approximately 4 issues per year). Association publication, newsletter format, 24 p.
$1.50 per issue : $3.00 per year.

Saskatchewan Association of Teachers of French. Bulletin = Bulletin de service / *sponsored by* Saskatchewan Association of Teachers of French ; *edited by* Daniel Gerle. - *Published by* Saskatchewan Teachers' Federation. P.O. Box 1108, 2317 Arlington Ave., Saskatoon, Sask., Fall 1974-
Irregular (approximately 4 issues per year). Association publication, 5 p. Language: English and French. Circulation: 241
$3.00 per year. Controlled circulation.

Saskatchewan Association of Teachers of French. SATF newsletter / *edited by* Dan Gerle. - *Published by* Saskatchewan Association of Teachers of French. P.O. Box 1108, 2317 Arlington Ave., Saskatoon, Sask. S7K 3N3, 1964-
Quarterly. Association publication, newsletter format, 6-8 p. Includes book reviews. Circulation: 225
Subscription included in membership fee $3.00 per year. Controlled circulation. Prepayment required.

Saskatchewan bar review *See* Saskatchewan law review

Saskatchewan care / *sponsored by* Saskatchewan Association of Special Care Homes ; *edited by* Mrs. M. Betteridge. - *Published by* Saskatchewan Association of Housing & Nursing Homes. P.O. Box 442, Saskatoon, Sask. (Subscription address: 200-2505-11th Avenue, Regina, Sask.)
Quarterly. House/company organ, newsletter format, 12 p. Circulation: 650
$2.00 per year. Controlled circulation.

Saskatchewan Coordinating Council on Social Planning. Newsletter / *edited by* Executive Director. - *Published by* Saskatchewan Coordinating Council on Social Planning. 314 Avenue Bldg., 220 3rd Ave. S., Saskatoon, Sask. S7K 1M1, November 1974-
Irregular (approximately 7 issues per year). Association publication, 6 p. Circulation: 80
Free. Controlled circulation.

Saskatchewan farm science *See* Agricultural science

Saskatchewan Genealogical Society. Bulletin / *edited by* Robert L. Pittendrigh. - *Published by* Saskatchewan Genealogical Society. P.O. Box 1894, Regina, Sask. S4P 3E1, April 1970-
Quarterly. Association publication, magazine format, 45 p. Includes book reviews, volume index. supplements issued. Back numbers available: 1970-74 $5.00. Circulation: 200
$2.00 per issue : $7.50 per year. Prepayment required.

Saskatchewan history / *edited by* D.H. Bocking. - *Published by* Saskatchewan Archives Board. University of Saskatchewan. Library Building, University of Saskatchewan, Saskatoon, Sask. S7N 0W0, 1948-
Issued 3 times a year, January, May and October. Special interest, magazine format, 40 p. Includes book reviews. available in microform.
Indexed in Can. ind., Hist. abstr.; Amer. hist. and life.
$1.00 per issue : $3.00 per year.

Saskatchewan humanitarian / *edited by* P.F. Baines. - *Published by* Saskatchewan Society for Prevention of Cruelty to Animals. 518 Avenue K South, Saskatoon, Sask. S7M 2E2.
Former title(s): Saskatoon humanitarian.
Irregular (approximately 5 issues per year). Association publication, newsletter format, 16-24 p. Includes advertising. Circulation: 1800
$.35 per issue : $2.00 per year. Prepayment required.

The Saskatchewan Indian / *edited by* Lucille Bell. - *Published by* Federation of Saskatchewan Indians. 1114 Central Ave., Prince Albert, Sask. S6V 5J2.
Former title(s): Outlook. Supplement title: Our way.
Issued twice a month. General interest, newspaper format, 16 p. Circulation: 13,000
Indexed in North. tit.
$5.00 per year.

Saskatchewan journal of educational research and development / *sponsored by* Saskatchewan Educational Research Association ; *edited by* Kevin A. Wilson. - *Published by* University of Saskatchewan. Saskatoon, Sask. S7N 0W0 (Subscription address: Room 3073, Education Building, University of Saskatchewan, Saskatoon, Sask. S7M 0W0) 1970-
Issued twice a year. Special interest, journal format, 64 p. Includes book reviews.
Circulation: 2000
Indexed in Can. educ. ind.
$1.25 per issue : $2.50 per year. Prepayment required.

Saskatchewan law review - *Published by* College of Law. University of Saskatchewan. Saskatoon, Sask. S7N 0W0.
Former title(s): Saskatchewan bar review.
Annual.
Indexed in Leg. per.

Saskatchewan Liberal - *Published by* Saskatchewan Liberal Publications Ltd. 2625-3rd Ave., Regina, Sask. S4T 0C8.
Monthly. Political press, 8 p.
$1.00 per year.

Saskatchewan library / *edited by* Rawia Jones. - *Published by* Saskatchewan Library Association. P.O. Box 3388, Regina, Sask. S4P 3H1, 1945-
Issued twice a year. Association publication, magazine format, Includes book reviews, advertising, volume index.
Indexed in Lib. info. sci. abstr.
$1.50 per issue : $3.00 per year. Subscription included in membership fee. Controlled circulation.

Saskatchewan Mathematics Teachers' Society. News/journal / *sponsored by* Saskatchewan Mathematics Teachers' Society ; *edited by* James E. Beamer and Rodger Servranckx. - *Published by* Saskatchewan Teachers' Federation. P.O. Box 1108, 2317 Arlington Ave., Saskatoon, Sask.
Former title(s): SMTS journal; SMTS newsletter.
Irregular (approximately 4 issues per year). Association publication, magazine format, 40 p. Includes book reviews, film reviews.
Circulation: 350
Indexed in Can. educ. ind.
$5.00 per year. Prepayment required.

Saskatchewan medical quarterly / *edited by* E.H. Baergen. - *Published by* Saskatchewan Medical Association. 211 4th Ave., Saskatoon, Sask. S7K 1N1, 1937-
Quarterly. Association publication, journal format, 40 p. Includes advertising. Circulation: 1200
Free to members.

The Saskatchewan motorist / *edited by* G.M. Butler. - *Published by* Centax of Canada. 1440 Scarth St., Regina, Sask., 1951-
Issued every other month. Association publication, newsletter format, 16 p.
Circulation: 69,000
Subscription included in membership fee.

Saskatchewan Music Educators' Association. Saskatchewan Music Educators newsletter / *sponsored by* Saskatchewan Music Educators' Association ; *edited by* Monte Anderson. - *Published by* Saskatchewan Teachers' Federation. P.O. Box 1108, 2317 Arlington Ave., Saskatoon, Sask. S7K 3N3, 1965-
Former title(s): SMEA bulletin (1958-1970) SMEA journal (1971-1972)
Quarterly. Association publication, newsletter format, 6-8 p. Includes book reviews.
Circulation: 250
Subscription included in membership fee
$15.00 per year. Controlled circulation. Prepayment required.

Saskatchewan Natural History Society. Newsletter / *edited by* Bill and Joyce Anaka. - *Published by* Saskatchewan Natural History Society. P.O. Box 1321, Regina, Sask. S4P 3B8.
Quarterly. Association publication, newsletter format, 12 p. Circulation: 2800
$3.00 per year. Subscription included in membership fee.

Saskatchewan Physical Education Association. SPEA newsletter / *sponsored by* Saskatchewan Teachers Federation ; *edited by* Marcel Gallays. - *Published by* Saskatchewan Teachers' Education Association,. P.O. Box 1108, Saskatoon, Sask. S7K 3N3.
Quarterly. Association publication, newsletter format, 3-4 p. Includes book reviews.
Circulation: 250
$5.00 per year. Controlled circulation. Prepayment required.

The Saskatchewan poetry book - *Published by* Saskatchewan Poetry Society. 3104 College Ave., Regina, Sask. S4N 1V7, 1936-
Biennial. Special interest, booklet format, 44 p. Back issues available.
ISSN 0080-6560 $1.25.

The Saskatchewan professional engineer - *Published by* Association of Professional Engineers of Saskatchewan. 220, 2220 12th Ave., Regina, Sask. S4P 0M8.
Irregular (approximately 4 issues per year). Association publication, newsletter format, 4 p.
Circulation: 1700

Saskatchewan Psychiatric Nurses' Association. Newsletter / *edited by* H. Beauregard. - *Published by* Saskatchewan Psychiatric Nurses' Association. Suite 6, 1651-11th Ave., Regina, Sask. S4P 0H5.
Quarterly. Association publication, newsletter format, 11 p.
Subscription included in membership fee. Controlled circulation.

Saskatchewan Red Poll Cattle Club. Annual newsletter / *sponsored by* Canadian Red Poll Cattle Association ; *edited by* G.R. Wagner. - *Published by* G.R. Wagner. P.O. Box 15, Francis, Sask. S0G 1V0.
Irregular (approximately 1-2 issues per year). Association publication, newsletter format, 2 p. Circulation: 85
Free.

Saskatchewan Registered Nurses' Association. News bulletin / *edited by* Heather Buchan. - *Published by* Saskatchewan Registered Nurses' Association. 2066 Retallack St., Regina, Sask. S4T 2K2, 1969-
Issued every other month. Association publication, newsletter format, 12 p.
Circulation: 9000
$5.00 per year. Controlled circulation.

Saskatchewan School Librarian *See* The Medium

Saskatchewan School Trustees Association. SSTA newsletter / *edited by* L.I. Thorson. - *Published by* Saskatchewan School Trustees Association. 570 Avord Tower, Regina, Sask. S4P 0R7, 1964-
Issued twice a month. Association publication, newsletter format, 3 p. Circulation: 1100
Free. Subscription included in membership fee.

Saskatchewan Science Teachers' Society. SSTS newsletter / *edited by* Lorne Wilson. - *Published by* Saskatchewan Teachers' Federation. P.O. Box 1108, 2317 Arlington Ave., Saskatoon, Sask. S7J 2H8.
Irregular (approximately 2 issues per year). Association publication, journal format, 4-6 p. Includes book reviews. Circulation: 400
$5.00 per year.

Saskatchewan sportsman *See* Fish and game sportsman

Saskatchewan Stockgrowers Association. Publication / *edited by* Jack Migowsky and Don Perrin. - *Published by* Saskatchewan Stock Growers Association. P.O. Box 534, Maple Creek, Sask. S0N 1N0, June 1, 1972-
Monthly. Association publication, newspaper format, 4-8 p. Includes advertising.
Circulation: 2000
$2.00 per year. Prepayment required.

Saskatchewan Teachers' Federation. Saskatchewan bulletin / *edited by* Gary Genge. - *Published by* Saskatchewan Teachers' Federation. P.O. Box 1108, 2317 Arlington Ave., Saskatoon, Sask. S7K 3N3.
Twice a month except in July and August. Association publication, newspaper format, 8 p. Includes book reviews, advertising.
Circulation: 17,000
Indexed in Can. educ. ind.
$.35 per issue : $3.50 per year.

Saskatchewan Wildlife Federation. S.W.F. news / *edited by* Edward A. Begin. - *Published by* Saskatchewan Wildlife Federation. P.O. Box 788, Moose Jaw, Sask. S6H 4P5, March 1973-
Irregular (approximately 5 issues per year). Association publication, newsletter format, 8 p. Includes advertising. Circulation: 22,000
$.60 per year.

Saskatoon / *edited by* B. Salloum. - *Published by* Saskatoon Board of Trade. Hotel Bessborough, Saskatoon, Sask. S7K 3G8, September 1974-
Former title(s): Reports - Saskatoon Board of Trade.
Irregular. House/company organ, magazine format, 24 p. Includes advertising.

Saskatoon humanitarian *See* Saskatchewan humanitarian

Saskatoon Public Library. Preface / *edited by* Anne Smart. - *Published by* Saskatoon Public Library. 311 23rd St. E., Saskatoon, Sask., S7K 0J6.
Irregular (approximately 10 issues per year). Institutional publication (Universities, schools, etc.), magazine format, 14 p. Circulation: 600
Free.

Saturday night / *edited by* Robert Fulford. - *Published by* Edgar Cowan. New Leaf Publications Ltd. 80 Richmond St. E., Toronto, Ont. M5C 2P1, 1887-
Monthly. General interest, magazine format, 90 p. Includes book reviews, film reviews, play reviews, record reviews, advertising.
Circulation: 100,000
Indexed in Can. ind., P.A.I.S.
$1.00 per issue : $8.00 per year : $9.00 per year, foreign.

Sault Ste. Marie and District Chamber of Commerce. Chamber newsletter / *edited by* Fred T. Loader. - *Published by* Sault Ste. Marie & District Chamber of Commerce. 360 Great Northern Rd., Sault Ste. Marie, Ont. P6B 4Z7, 1970-
Monthly. Association publication, newsletter format, 6 p. Circulation: 800
Free.

Savant - *Published by* Journalism Department. Vancouver City College. Langara Campus, 100 W. 49th Ave., Vancouver, B.C. V5Y 2Z6, September 1965-
Former title(s): Vancouver City College news; Crest (October 1965 - November 1966)
Issued weekly in the Spring; every other week in the Fall. Student publication, newspaper format, 10 p. Includes book reviews, film reviews, play reviews, record reviews, advertising.
$2.60 per year. Controlled circulation.

Scan / *edited by* P. Coslett. - *Published by* Sarnia Construction Association. P.O. Box 545, 907 Devine St., Sarnia, Ont., 1965-
Weekly. Association publication, newsletter format, 1 p. Circulation: 200
Free to members.

Scandinavian Canadian businessman / *edited by* Erik Melander. - *Published by* EM Publications. P.O. Box 306, Oakville, Ont., 1969-
Monthly. Ethnic press, magazine format, 36-44 p. Language: English and Scandinavian. available in microform. Circulation: 3000
$.50 per issue : $5.00 per year.

Scandinavian centre news / *edited by* Leslie L. Morris. - *Published by* Scandinavian Centre Co-operative Association Ltd. 14220-125 Ave., Edmonton, Alta. T5L 3C2, November 1958-
Monthly. Association publication, ethnic press, newspaper format, 12 p. Includes book reviews, film reviews, advertising. Circulation: 3000
$6.00 per year : $50.00 for life membership. Controlled circulation.

Scarboro missions / *edited by* Gerald Curry. - *Published by* Scarboro Foreign Mission Society. 2685 Kingston Rd., Scarborough, Ont. M1M 1M4, October 1919-
Former title(s): China (1919-May 1950)
Monthly with a combined issue for July/August. Church publication, magazine format, 32 p.
$.25 per issue : $2.00 per year.

Scarborough fair : an anthology of literature / *edited by* Jars Balan. - *Published by* The Library. Scarborough College. University of Toronto. Room S302B, 1255 Military Trail, West Hill, Ont., 1973-
Annual. Special interest, book format, 100-144 p. Circulation: 5000
ISSN 0318-1499 Free.

Scarlet and gold / *edited by* E.A. Macdonald. - *Published by* Vancouver Division. Veterans' Association. Royal Canadian Mounted Police. 675 W. Hastings St., Vancouver, B.C. V6B 1N2, 1919-
Annual. Trade publication. Includes advertising.
$3.00 per year.

Scene changes / *edited by* Donald Schrank. - *Published by* Theatre Ontario. 7th floor, 8 York St., Toronto, Ont. M5J 1R2, October 1974-
Former title(s): Dialogue.
Monthly. Special interest, magazine format, 20 p. Includes play reviews, advertising.
Circulation: 2000
$.75 per issue : $7.50 per year. Prepayment required.

La Scène musicale / *édité par* Nancy Gyokeres. - *Publié par* BMI Canada Ltd. 41 Valleybrook Dr., Don Mills, Ont. M3B 2S6, September 1967-
Published in French: La scène Musicale.
Bimestriel. Special interest, magazine format, 20 p. Comprend record reviews. Circulation: 10,000
Free. Controlled circulation.

Schizophrenia (to May 1972) *See* Journal of orthomolecular psychiatry

Schizophrenia newsletter (1969-1971) *See* Canadian Schizophrenia Foundation. Huxley Institute - CSF newsletter

Scholarly publishing : a journal for authors and publishers / *edited by* Eleanor Harman and Ian Montagnes (associate editor). - *Published by* University of Toronto Press. 5201 Dufferin St., Downsview, Ont. M3H 5T8, October 1969-
Quarterly. Special interest, magazine format, 96 p. Includes book reviews, advertising, volume index, cumulative index. Circulation: 1200
Indexed in Lib. lit., M.L.A. int. bib., Hist. abstr.; Amer. hist. and life, I.B.Z.
ISSN 0336-634X $4.50 per issue : $15.00 per year : $20.00 per volume (hardbound).

School Board news / *edited by* E.J. Reyno. - *Published by* Nova Scotia School Boards Association. Room 124, Roy Bldg., Halifax, N.S. B3J 2A1, January 1970-
Former title(s): School Board newsletter (November 1957)
Issued every other month. Association publication, newsletter format, 4 p.
Indexed in Can. educ. ind.
Free.

School Board newsletter (November 1957) *See* School Board news

School guidance worker / *edited by* C.L. Bedal. - *Published by* Guidance Centre. Faculty of Education. University of Toronto. Suite 304, 1000 Yonge St., Toronto, Ont. M4W 2K8.
Issued every other month. Institutional publication (Universities, schools, etc.), magazine format, 64 p. Includes book reviews, volume index, cumulative index. Circulation: 700
Indexed in Can. educ. ind.
$1.75 per issue : $7.50 per year.

School progress *See* Educational digest

The School trustee / *edited by* L.I. Thorson. - *Published by* Saskatchewan School Trustees Association. 570 Avord Tower, Regina, Sask. S4P 0R7, 1930-
Issued 5 times a year. Association publication, magazine format, 20 p. Includes advertising. Circulation: 4190
Indexed in Can. educ. ind.
$3.00 per year. Controlled circulation.

Science affairs / *edited by* Charles E. Jersch. - *Published by* Youth Science Foundation. Suite 302, 151 Slater St., Ottawa, K1P 5H3.
Quarterly. Association publication, magazine format, 24 p. Includes film reviews, advertising.
$1.00 per issue : $2.50 per year.

Science et esprit : revue théologique et philosophique / *parrainé par* Jesuites au Québec. Les Facultés de théologie et de philosophie ; *édité par* Gilles Langevin. - *Publié par* Les Editions Bellarmin. 8100, boul. St-Laurent, Montréal, Qué. H2P 2L9, 1948-
Ancien titre: Sciences ecclésiastiques (1948-1969)
Paraît 3 fois par an. Edition savante, revue, 150 p. Comprend critique de livres. Tirage: 375
Indexé dans RADAR.
$3.00 le numéro : $7.00 par année. Abonnements payables à l'avance.

Science forum : a Canadian journal of science and technology = Revue canadienne des sciences pures et appliquées / *edited by* David Spurgeon. - *Published by* University of Toronto Press. 5201 Dufferin St., Downsview, Ont. M3H 5T8, February 1968-
Issued every other week. Scholarly publication, magazine format, 32 p. Language: English and French. Includes book reviews, advertising.
Indexed in Sci. cit. ind., Can. ind., North. tit.
ISSN 0036-8393 $1.75 per issue : $10.00 per year : $18.00 for 2 years : $24.00 for 3 years.

Sciences ecclésiastiques (1948-1969) *Voir* Science et esprit : revue théologique et philosophique

Sciences religieuses *See* Studies in religion

Scientific agriculture *See* Agrologist

Scientific agriculture (1920-1952) *See* Canadian journal of animal science

Scientific agriculture (1920-1952) *See* Canadian journal of plant science

Scientific agriculture (1920-1952) *See* Canadian journal of soil science

Scitec bulletin / *edited by* Jean-Louis Meunier. - *Published by* Association of the Scientific, Engineering & Technological Community of Canada. Suite 202, 151 Slater St., Ottawa, Ont. K1P 5H1, April 1970-
Former title(s): Scitec bulletin newsletter.
Quarterly. Association publication, newsletter format,
ISSN 0318-0166 $10.00 per year.

Scitec bulletin newsletter *See* Scitec bulletin

Scope / *edited by* J.K. Davy. - *Published by* The Steel Co. of Canada Ltd. 100 King St. W., Hamilton, Ont. L8N 3T1, 1964-
Issued 3 times a year. Trade publication, magazine format, 8 p. Language: English and French.
Free.

Scope : recreational vehicle and camping news / *edited by* "Uncle Bob" Chatfield. - *Published by* Merton Publications Ltd. R.R. 3, London, Ont. N6A 4B7, 1965-
Issued 8 times a year. Special interest, magazine format, 80-100 p.
$.75 per issue : $4.00 per year.

Scope = Envergure / *edited by* Jeane Kotick. - *Published by* Canadian Council of Christians and Jews. Room 506, 229 Yonge St., Toronto, Ont. M5B 1N9, Fall 1948-
Issued twice a year. Association publication, newsletter format, 4-6 p. Language: English (French). Includes book reviews, advertising. Circulation: 10,000
Free.

Scotiabank Hockey College. Scotiabank Hockey College news / *edited by* S. Clayton. - *Published by* Scotiabank Hockey College. P.O. Box 4071, Postal Station A, 44 King St. W., Toronto, Ont. M5H 1E3, November 1971-
Published in French: Collège de hockey BNE.
Monthly. House/company organ, newsletter format, October-May 12 p ; June-September 4 p. Circulation: 100,000
Free. Controlled circulation.

The Scotian / *edited by* R.S. Bell. - *Published by* Sons of Scotland Benevolent Association. 19 Richmond St. W., Toronto, Ont., September 1966-
Quarterly. Association publication, newsletter format, 20 p. Language: English and Scottish. Circulation: 9100
Free.

Scotian rays / *edited by* Barbara O'Regan and Phyllis Johnston. - *Published by* Nova Scotia Society of Medical Radiological Technicians. 25 Edgehill Rd., Armdale, Halifax, N.S. B3N 1G5, The First edition (September 1970-June 1971)-
Former title(s): The Newsletter - Nova Scotia Society of Medical Radiological Technicians.
Irregular (approximately 4 issues per year). Association publication, newsletter format, 28 p. Includes advertising.
$2.00 per year. Subscription included in membership fee.

Scottish tradition / *edited by* W.L. Straka. - *Published by* Conference on Scottish Studies. Department of History, University of Guelph, Guelph, Ont., Fall 1970-
Issued twice a year. Scholarly publication, magazine format, 70 p. Includes book reviews. Circulation: 150
$2.50 per issue : $5.00 per year.

Scott's industrial directory. Western Section : Western Canada manufacturers directory / *edited by* J.M. Haight. - *Published by* Penstock Publications Ltd. P.O. Box 365, Oakville, Ont. L6L 5M5.
Biennial. Directory, 650 p.
$60.00.

The Scout / *edited by* Linda Boys. - *Published by* Brandon Indian and Metis Friendship Centre. 836 Lorne Ave., Brandon, Man. R7A 0T8, May 1965-
Monthly. Ethnic press, newsletter format, 8 p. Circulation: 400
$1.00 per year. Free to Indians.

Scout du Québec / *édité par* Florian Bernard. - *Publié par* Association des éclaireurs Baden-Powel inc. 16, Place du Fort, Repentigny, Qué., octobre 1974-
Bimestriel. Publication d'association, magazine, 20 p. Tirage: 6000
$1.00 le numéro : $5.00 par année : $7.00 par année, l'étranger. Tarifs spéciaux disponibles. Abonnements payables à l'avance.

The Scout leader (1922-1970) *See* The Canadian leader magazine

Scouting in Prince Edward Island - *Published by* Prince Edward Island Council. Boy Scouts of Canada. P.O. Box 533, 100 Upper Prince St., Charlottetown, P.E.I. C1A 4T3.
Irregular (approximately 4 issues per year). Association publication, newsletter format, 6-8 p.
Free.

Scouting times - *Published by* Newfoundland Council. Boy Scouts of Canada. P.O. Box 4175, 15 Terra Nova Rd., St. John's, Nfld. A1C 5Z7.
Monthly. Association publication, newsletter format, 5 p.

Scripture search program inc. / *edited by* E.A. Forbes. - *Published by* Scripture Search Program Inc. P.O. Box 940, Sussex, N.B. E0E 1P0, June 1967-
Monthly. Questions on scripture, Questionnaires,
No definite price is set.

Scurrilous news letter - *Published by* South Central Regional Library System. 220 Dundurn St. S., Hamilton, Ont. L8P 4K7, March 1973-
Former title(s): SCRLS newsletter (to February 1973)
Monthly (July and August issues are combined). Institutional publication (Universities, schools, etc.), newsletter format, 12 or 16 p. Circulation: 600
Free.

Sea harvest and ocean science (June 1969 - December 1970) *See* Canadian fisherman and ocean science

Sealandair / *edited by* H.E. Matties. - *Published by* Canadian Forces Base, Edmonton. Sealandair, C.F.B. Edmonton, Lancasser Park, Alta. T0A 2H0, December 1969-
Former title(s): The Bulletin - Canadian Armed Forces Base, Edmonton (June 1969-December 1969)
Issued every other week. House/company organ, newspaper format, 16 p. Language: English (French). Circulation: 3500
$.10 per issue : $2.00 per year. Prepayment required.

Seaports and shipping world / *edited by* Brian Gallery. - *Published by* Gallery Publications Ltd. 1165 Greene Ave., Westmount, Que. H3Z 2A2, 1937-
Monthly. Trade publication, magazine format, 52 p. Includes advertising. Circulation: 2800
Indexed in Can. B.P.I.
$10.00 per year : $20.00 per year, foreign. Controlled circulation.

Search lamp / *edited by* E.A. Forbes. - *Published by* Scripture Search Program Inc. P.O. Box 940, Sussex, N.B. E0E 1P0, September 1966-
Quarterly. Bible lessons, magazine format, 35 p.
$3.00 per year.

The Second mile / *edited by* William Pope. - *Published by* Lancelot Press Ltd. P.O. Box 2020, Windsor, N.S. B0N 2T0, October 1973-
Issued every other month. Special interest, magazine format, 32 p. Circulation: 800
$.75 per issue : $5.00 per year.

Second penny / *edited by* Una Leepart. - *Published by* Saskatchewan Women's Institutes. Extension Division, University of Saskatchewan, Saskatoon, Sask. S7M 0W0, 1963-
Issued every other month. Association publication, newsletter format, 8 p.
$.50 per year. Controlled circulation. Prepayment required.

Secondary Learning Assistance Teachers' Association. Bulletin / *sponsored by* Secondary Learning Assistance Teachers' Association. - *Published by* British Columbia Teachers' Federation. 105-2235 Burrard St., Vancouver, B.C. V6J 3H9, January 1975-
Former title(s): Bulletin - Occupational Teachers' Specialist Association. (February 1966-December 1974)
Irregular (approximately 2 issues per year). Association publication, newsletter format, 10 p. Includes film reviews.
Available to members only. Controlled circulation.

Le Secours aux lépreux : Foundations Raoul Follereau - *Publié par* Le Secours aux Lépreux (Canada) Inc. C.P. 1672, Succursale B, Montréal, Qué. H3B 3L3.
Publié en anglais: Help for the leper.
Bimestriel. Publication spécialisée, bulletin, 4 p.
Envoi gratuit.

Secours Quaker Canadien *See* Canadian Friends Service Committee

Seed / *edited by* Dennis R. Klinck. - *Published by* Ousia publishing. P.O. Box 3184, Sherwood Park, Alta. T8A 2A6, February 1974-
Monthly. Scholarly publication, magazine format, 8 p. Includes book reviews.
$.60 per issue : $7.00 per year : $9.00 per year, foreign. Prepayment required.

Seed scoop / *edited by* O.M. Clayton. - *Published by* Canadian Seed Growers Association. P.O. Box 8455, 237 Argyle St., Ottawa, Ont.
Quarterly. Association publication, newsletter format, 8 p. Language: English and French. Circulation: 10,500
Free. Controlled circulation.

Seeker / *edited by* Serge Lavoie. - *Published by* S. Lavoie. Seeker Publishing Co. P.O. Box 82, Sarnia, Ont., May 1975-
Former title(s): Pleasure seeker (December 1973 - April 1975)
Weekly. General interest, magazine format, 32 p. Includes book reviews, film reviews, play reviews, record reviews. Circulation: 10,000
$.10 per issue : $5.00 per year.

Seer / *edited by* Warren Clements. - *Published by* Winters College Student Council. York University. Room 029A, Winter's College, York University, 116, 4700 Keele St., Downsview, Ont., 1967-
Issued from September to March. Student publication, newspaper format, 16 p. Includes film reviews, record reviews. supplements issued. Circulation: 4000
$3.00 per year. Free. Controlled circulation.

Segregation and discrimination in sport - *Published by* SIRLS. Faculty of Human Kinetics and Leisure Studies. University of Waterloo. Waterloo, Ont. N2L 3G1.
Quarterly. Bibliography, computer printout, $20.00 per year. $100.00 subscription to SIRLS required.

Select bibliography on higher education / *sponsored by* The Library, Association of Universities and Colleges of Canada ; *edited by* Hazel J. Roberts and Beatrice Tobias. - *Published by* Association of Universities and Colleges of Canada. 151 Slater St., Ottawa, Ont. K1P 5N1.
Quarterly. Bibliography, 14 p. Language: English and French. Circulation: 85
ISSN 0049-0091 $4.00 per year. Prepayment required.

Select home designs / *edited by* Brian Thorn. - *Published by* The Building Centre. 382 W. Broadway, Vancouver, B.C. V5Y 1R2, 1948-
Issued twice a year. Magazine format, Includes advertising. Circulation: 25,612
$1.50 per issue.

Selected list of acquisitions (August-September 1973-December 1973) *See* Selected list of reference acquisitions

A selected list of acquisitions for reference use / *edited by* The Theatre Section staff. - *Published by* Theatre Section. Metropolitan Toronto Central Library. 214 College St., Toronto, Ont. M5T 1R3, 1968-
Irregular (approximately 8 issues per year). Bibliography, sheet format, 8 p. Circulation: 100
Free.

Selected list of acquisitions for reference use (April 1970-July 1973) *See* Selected list of new titles

A selected list of acquisitions for reference use (January 1969-July 1973) *See* Selected list of reference acquisitions

Selected list of new titles / *edited by* D.A. Watt. - *Published by* General Information Centre. Metropolitan Toronto Central Library. 214 College St., Toronto, Ont. M5T 1R3, January 1974-
Monthly except July and August. Institutional publication (Universities, schools, etc.), newsletter format, 3 p.
ISSN 0316-7410 Free.

Selected list of new titles / *edited by* M. DeMarco and A. Salam. - *Published by* Social Sciences Section. Metropolitan Toronto Central Library. 214 College St., Toronto, Ont. M5T 1R3, July 1969-
Issued every other month. Bibliography, 12 p.
Free. Controlled circulation.

Selected list of new titles / *edited by* The Staff of the Municipal Reference Library. - *Published by* Municipal Reference Library. Metropolitan Toronto Central Library. 214 College St., Toronto, Ont. M5T 1R3 (Subscription address: Municipal Reference Library, City Hall, Toronto, Ont. M5H 2N1) April 1970-
Former title(s): Selected list of acquisitions for reference use (April 1970-July 1973)
Monthly. Bibliography, 12 p. Language: English. Circulation: 700
Free.

Selected list of new titles / *edited by* The Science and Technology Library staff. - *Published by* Science and Technology Library. Metropolitan Toronto Central Library. 214 College St., Toronto, Ont. M5T 1R3 (Subscription address: 229 College St., Toronto, Ont. M5T 1R4) November 1969-
Irregular (approximately 4 issues per year). Bibliography, 10 p. Circulation: 300
Free.

Selected list of recent acquisitions - *Published by* Music Library. Metropolitan Toronto Central Library. 214 College St., Toronto, Ont. M5T 1R3 (Subscription address: Music Library, 559 Avenue Rd., Toronto, Ont. M4V 2J7) 1969-
Irregular (approximately 3 to 4 issues per year). Bibliography, 7 p. Circulation: 87
Free.

Selected list of reference acquisitions / *edited by* The Fine Art staff. - *Published by* Fine Art Section. Metropolitan Toronto Central Library. 214 College St., Toronto, Ont. M5T 1R3, January 1969-
Former title(s): Selected list of acquisitions (August-September 1973-December 1973) A selected list of acquisitions for reference use (January 1969-July 1973)
Issued every other month. Bibliography, 8 p. Circulation: 60

Selection du Reader's Digest / *édité par* Denise Supernant. - *Publié par* Reader's Digest Association (Canada) Limited. 215 Redfern Ave., Montreal, Que. H3Z 2V9, 1947-
Mensuel. Intérêt général, magazine, 200-230 p. Tirage: 269,239
$.75 le numéro : $7.46 par année : $9.97 par année, l'étranger.

A Selection of choice inns and restaurants of Nova Scotia and en route - *Published by* Jean U. Matheson. Kentville Pub. Co. Ltd. P.O. Box 430, Kentville, N.S., June 1961-
Annual. "A selection of inns, restaurants, antique and gift shops etc. in Eastern Canada and northeastern United States", book format, 64 p.
$1.00.

Selling travel / *edited by* John Stephenson. - *Published by* John Stephenson. Travelcom Inc. 111 Pears Ave., Toronto, Ont. M5R 1S9, June 1975-
Former title(s): Vacation.
Monthly. Special interest, magazine format, 48-64 p. Circulation: 16,901
$8.00 per year. Controlled circulation.

La Semaine à Radio-Canada *Voir* Ici Radio Canada : programme de la télévision

La Semaine commerciale : organe officiel des intérêts commerciaux et financiers du grand Québec / *parrainé par* Sokeédit ltée. - *Publié par* J.M. Pouliot. C.P. 301, Succursale B, Québec, Qué. G1K 7B1, août 1894-
Hebdomadaire. Revue d'entreprise, magazine, 32 p. Tirage: 5000
Tirage contrôlé. Abonnements payables à l'avance.

La Semaine religieuse de Montréal (1882-1967) *Voir* L'Eglise de Montréal

Semeuse de joie / *édité par* Le Directeur du bureau d'Apostolat. - *Publié par* Oblats de Marie-Immaculée. 460, 1ière rue, Richelieu, Qué. J3L 3W2, janvier 1959-
Trimestriel. Publication ecclésiastique, brochure, 16 p. Tirage: 2700
$.50 par année.

Semiconductor devices / *edited by* W. Drobny. - *Published by* Key Advertising Service Ltd. 99 Doncaster Ave., Willowdale, Ont.
Former title(s): Semiconductors and integrated circuits.
Annual. Catalogue, magazine format, 40 p.

Semiconductors and integrated circuits *See* Semiconductor devices

Seminar : a journal of Germanic studies / *sponsored by* Canadian Association of University Teachers of German and The Germanic Section of the Australian Universities Language and Literature Association ; *edited by* Michael S. Batts. - *Published by* University of Toronto Press. 5201 Dufferin St., Downsview, Ont. M3H 5T8, 1965-
Quarterly. Association publication, journal format, 64 p. Language: English, French and German. Includes book reviews, advertising, volume index. Circulation: 750
Indexed in I.B.Z.
ISSN 0037-1939 $6.00 per year : $5.00, per year, Australia.

Seminar on Canadian-American relations *See* Canadian-American seminar

Senca - *Published by* Student Federation Council. Third Floor Sports Centre 1750 Finch Ave. E., Willowdale, Ont. M2N 5T7.
Issued twice a month. Student publication. Circulation: 3500

Senior cylinders / *edited by* Alex Farmer. - *Published by* Antique Automobile Club of Ottawa, Inc. P.O. Box 2525, Postal Station D, Ottawa, Ont. K1P 5W6, 1965-
Quarterly. Association publication, magazine format, 10 p. Includes book reviews.
Subscription to members only $10.00 per year. Controlled circulation.

Sentinel / *sponsored by* Loyal Orange Association in Canada ; *edited by* Gordon Keyes. - *Published by* British America Publishing Co. Ltd. 94 Sheppard Ave., Willowdale, Ont. M2N 1M5, 1875-
Monthly except July and December. Association publication, magazine format, 24 p. Circulation: 6000
$.40 per issue : $4.00 per year : $5.00 per year, foreign. Controlled circulation. Prepayment required.

Sentinela / *edited by* Gabriel Sousa. - *Published by* Gabriel Sousa. P.O. Box 65532, Postal Station F, Vancouver, B.C., November 1972-
Issued twice a month. Ethnic press, newspaper format, 12 p. Language: Portugese. Includes advertising. Circulation: 2000
$.20 per issue : $5.00 per year : $8.00 per year, foreign. Prepayment required.

La Sentinelle (décembre 1936-janvier 1943) *Voir* Le Lingot

Séquences : revue de cinéma / *édité par* Léo Bonneville. - *Publié par* Séquences. 4635, rue de Lorimier, Montréal, Qué. H2H 2B4, 1954-
Trimestriel. Publication spécialisée, magazine, Comprend critique de films. Tirage: 1500
$1.00 le numéro : $3.50 par année.

Serena Canada. Bulletin mensuel / *édité par* Bernard Fortin. - *Publié par* Serena Canada. 6646, St-Denis, Montréal, Qué. H2S 2R9, avril 1966-
Mensuel. Publication d'association, bulletin, 20 p. Comprend critique de livres. parution de suppléments.
$.40 le numéro : $4.00 par année.
Abonnements payables à l'avance.

Serena Canada newsletter / *edited by* Georges LeGal. - *Published by* Serena Canada. 55 Parkdale Ave., Ottawa, Ont. K1Y 1E5, January/February 1974-
Former title(s): Serena Inc. Serena newsletter(1972-1974)
Quarterly. Association publication, newsletter format, 20 p. Includes book reviews.
Free.

Serena Inc. Serena newsletter(1972-1974) *See* Serena Canada newsletter

Serial holdings in the library of Memorial University of Newfoundland (1964-1966) *See* Memorial University of Newfoundland. Serials holdings in the libraries of Memorial University of Newfoundland, St. John's Public Library, and College of Trades and Technology

Serial titles in the pure and applied sciences - University of Windsor. Library (1963-1974) *See* University of Windsor. Library. List of serials held in the University of Windsor Library

Serials holdings in the libraries at Memorial University of Newfoundland (1968) *See* Memorial University of Newfoundland. Serials holdings in the libraries of Memorial University of Newfoundland, St. John's Public Library, and College of Trades and Technology

Serials holdings in the libraries of Memorial University of Newfoundland and St John's Public Library (1969-1973) *See* Memorial University of Newfoundland. Serials holdings in the libraries of Memorial University of Newfoundland, St. John's Public Library, and College of Trades and Technology

Serviam : organe interne du parti de l'Unité nationale du Canada - *Publié par* Parti de l'Unité nationale du Canada. C.P. 120, Succursale R, Montréal, Qué. H2S 3K6.
Ancien titre: Unité nationale (1954)
Intermittent (approximativement 10 éditions par an). Publication politique, bulletin, 20 p. Langue(s): français et anglais.
$4.00 par année. Abonnements payables à l'avance.

Service (mars 1928-juin 1939) *Voir* Autoclub : le journal de l'automobiliste du Québec

Service / *edited by* C.R. Watson. - *Published by* Quebec Credit Union League. 17 Ronald Dr., Montreal, Que. H4X 1M9, June 1970-
Former title(s): Liaison (1967-June 1970) The Quebecer (1954-1967)
Irregular (approximately 10 issues per year). House/company organ, newsletter format, 8 p. Language: French and English. Circulation: 1200
$1.00 per year. Controlled circulation.

Service and indemnity / *edited by* M.J. Hutton and J.B. Miln. - *Published by* The Canadian Indemnity Co. 333 Main St., Winnipeg, Man. R3C 1C3, March 1923-
Former title(s): Canadian service (1923-1932)
Monthly. House/company organ, newsletter format, 8 p.
Free.

Service canadien des forêts. Revue bimestrielle de recherches / *parrainé par* Service canadien des forêts ; *édité par* T.G. Harvey. - *Publié par* Joseph D. Armand. Place Vincent Massey, 351, boul. St Joseph, Hull, Qué. K1A 0H3, 1966-
Ancien titre: Bulletin d'information bimestrielle - Service canadien des forêts.
Bimestriel. Notes sur les recherches en sciences forestières et produits forestiers, magazine, 8-12 p. Comprend index de volumes. Tirage: 2300
Envoi gratuit.

Service de préparation à la vie. Bulletin S.P.V. - *Publié par* Secrétariat Général du S.P.V. 10215, Sacré-Coeur, Montréal, Qué.
Ancien titre: On est là; L'Aujoudhui l'église.
Paraît tous les 15 jours. Publication ecclésiastique, bulletin, 10 p. Tirage: 2000
$.25 le numéro : $5.00 par année. Abonnements payables à l'avance.

Service homilétique (décembre 1940-décembre 1970) *Voir* Rassembler

Service homilétique (décembre 1940-décembre 1970) *Voir* Rassembler

Service social / *parrainé par* Ecole de service social de l'Université Laval ; *édité par* Simone Paré. - *Publié par* Presses de l'Université Laval. Québec, Qué. G1K 7R4, 1951-
Intermittent (approximativement 2-3 éditions par an). Publication d'institution (universités, écoles..), revue, simple 100p. ; double 200 p. Comprend critique de livres. Tirage: 1000
Indexé dans Periodex, RADAR.
$2.50 le numéro simple : $4.50 le numéro double : $6.00 par année : $7.00 par année, l'étranger. Abonnements payables à l'avance.

Service station and garage management / *edited by* Joe Holliday and Herschel Fenik. - *Published by* Wadham Publications Ltd. 109 Vanderhoof Ave., Toronto, Ont. M4G 2J2, 1956-
Former title(s): Service station management (1956-1971)
Monthly. Special interest, magazine format, 30-40 p. Includes book reviews.
Indexed in Can. B.P.I.
$.75 per issue : $8.00 per year : $10.00 per year, foreign. Controlled circulation.

Service station management (1956-1971) *See* Service station and garage management

La Settimana / *edited by* V. Ricciardi. - *Published by* V. Ricciardi. Grobar Publishing. Suite 402, 2333 Dundas St. W., Toronto, Ont. M6R 1X7, 1975-
Weekly. Ethnic press, Italian p. Includes advertising.
$.25 per issue.

Seven persons repository (1972-1974) *See* Repository

Sex Information and Education Council of Canada. Sieccan newsletter / *edited by* F. Michael Barrett. - *Published by* Sex Information and Education Council of Canada. 423 Castlefield Ave., Toronto, Ont. M5N 1L4, Spring 1966-
Irregular (approximately 2 issues per year). Association publication, newsletter format, 36 p. Includes book reviews, film reviews. Circulation: 1500
$2.50 per year.

The Shantyman / *edited by* George M. Bowman. - *Published by* Shantymen's Christian Association of North America. 3251 Sheppard Ave. E., Agincourt, Ont. M1T 3K1, July 1923-
Monthly. Special interest, newspaper format, 8 p. Circulation: 22,000
$2.00 per year.

Shaver focus - *Published by* Shaver Poultry Breeding Farms Ltd. P.O. Box 400, Cambridge Ont. N1R 5V9, July 1971-
Former title(s): Resume (May 1969-May 1971)
Quarterly. Trade publication, newsletter format, 4 p.
ISSN 0315-6915 Controlled circulation.

The Sheaf / *edited by* Dianne Rogers. - *Published by* Students Union. University of Saskatchewan. Memorial Union Building, University of Saskatchewan, Saskatoon, Sask. S7N 0W0, 1910-
Issued twice a week. Student publication, newspaper format, 12 p. Includes book reviews, film reviews, play reviews, record reviews, advertising. Circulation: 11,000
$6.00 per year.

Shell News *See* Sphere

The Shepherd / *edited by* O. Summerfield. - *Published by* Foothills Lutheran Press. 806 Third Street N.E., Calgary, Alta., 1924-
Irregular (approximately 11 issues per year). Church publication. Includes advertising.
4.00 per year : $7.00 for 2 years.

The Sheridan sun / *edited by* John Fennell. - *Published by* Sheridan College of Applied Arts and Technology. 1430 Trafalgar Rd., Oakville, Ont. L6H 2L1, 1970-
Weekly (September-April). Student publication. Includes advertising. Circulation: 2000

The Shillelagh / *edited by* Vicki Cram. - *Published by* The Student Association. St. Patrick's College. Carleton University. Colonel By Drive, Ottawa, Ont. K1S 1N4.
Issued twice a month. Student publication. Includes advertising.

Shing Wah daily news / *sponsored by* Shing Lea Association ; *edited by* H.B. Giong. - *Published by* William C. Wong. Shing Wah Association. 12 Hagerman St., Toronto, Ont., 1922-
Daily. Ethnic press, newspaper format, 8 p. Language: Chinese. Includes film reviews, advertising.
$.10 per issue : $36.00 per year.

Shipping register / *edited by* O.J. Silva. - *Published by* J.W. McManus. 1434 St. Catherine St. W., Montreal, Que., 1917-
Former title(s): Ports and shipyards.
Irregular (approximately 6 issues per year). Trade publication. Ports and shipyards ed. and Montreal port guide and directory are issued as annual supplements.

Shoe and leather journal / *edited by* P.L. Butt. - *Published by* Rowan MacDonald. Southam Business Publications Ltd. 1450 Don Mills Rd., Don Mills, Ont. M3B 2X7, 1888-
Monthly. Trade publication. Includes advertising. Circulation: 5374
$1.00 per issue : $12.00 per year.

Shop / *edited by* A. Carin. - *Published by* Southam Business Publications Ltd. 1450 Don Mills Rd., Don Mills, Ont. M3B 2X7, 1945-
Monthly. Trade publication, magazine format, 48 p. Includes book reviews.
$1.00 per issue : $10.00 per year : $20.00 per year.

Short courses and seminars / *edited by* Harry T. Kane. - *Published by* Development Publications. P.O. Box 84, Postal Station A, Willowdale, Ont. M2N 5S4, June 1973-
Former title(s): Canadian courses and seminars.
Issued twice a year. Directory, magazine format, 80 p. Includes advertising. Circulation: 3100
$2.00 per issue : $4.00 per year.

Shorthorn news / *edited by* Carrie C. Fisk. - *Published by* Canadian Shorthorn Association. Gummer Building, Guelph, Ont. N1H 2S8, 1940-
Issued every other month. Special interest, magazine format, 54-60 p. Includes advertising. Circulation: 4200
$2.00 per year : $2.50 per year, foreign.

Signal / *édité par* Yves R. Mondoux. - *Publié par* La Ligue de sécurité de la province de Québec. 5576, chemin Upper Lachine, Montréal, Qué. H4A 2A7, novembre 1974-
Intermittent (approximativement 10 éditions par an). Publication d'association, bulletin, 6 p. Langue(s): français et anglais.
ISSN 0037-4911

Signal pour l'évangélisation par des communautés évangéliques / *parrainé par* La Rencontre ; *édité par* Christian Beaulieu. - *Publié par* Editions du Renouveau. C.P. 1815, Québec, Qué. G1K 5K7(adresse d'abonnement: C.P. 1096, Québec, Qué. G1K 7B5) février 1970-
Mensuel. Bulletin, 16 p.
$.30 le numéro : $3.00 par année.
Abonnements payables à l'avance.

Signe - *Publié par* Métiers d'Art du Québec Inc. 4547, rue St-Denis, Montréal, Qué., juillet/août 1975-
Ancien titre: Métiers d'art informe (1974-1975)
Mensuel. Publication d'association, bulletin, 20 p. Tirage: 4000
ISSN 0317-6573 $6.00 par année.

Silhouette / *edited by* Don Sancton. - *Published by* McMaster Students' Union Inc. Hamilton Hall, McMaster University, Hamilton, Ont.
Weekly during the school year. Student publication, newspaper format, 16 p. Includes book reviews, film reviews, play reviews, record reviews, advertising. Circulation: 10,000
$12.00 per year. Free.

Simgames : a Canadian guide to simulations and games / *edited by* Guy LeCavalier and Patricia LeCavalier. - *Published by* Guy Le Cavalier. P.O. Box 381, Postal Station A, Ottawa, Ont. K1M 8V4, October 1973-
Quarterly. Special interest, newsletter format, 4 p. Includes book reviews, advertising. Circulation: 200
$.50 per issue : $2.00 per year (Institutions $4.00) : $4.75 per year, foreign. Prepayment required.

Simmental scene / *edited by* R.D. Secord. - *Published by* Simmental Canada Ltd. 120-310-9 Ave. S.W., Calgary, Alta. T2P 1K5, March 1973-
Monthly. Trade publication, magazine format, 100 p. Includes advertising. Circulation: 5000
$7.50 per year : $12.50 for 2 years : $10.00 per year, foreign.

Simon Fraser University. Library. Information bulletin - *Published by* Library. Simon Fraser University. Burnaby, B.C., 1967-
Monthly. Institutional publication (Universities, schools, etc.), newsletter format, 1 p.
Free. Controlled circulation.

Simon Fraser University : SFU information for secondary school and college students / *edited by* A.C. McMillan. - *Published by* Admissions Office. Simon Fraser University. Burnaby, B.C. V5A 1S6.
Annual. Institutional publication (Universities, schools, etc.), pamphlet format, 45 p.
Free.

16mm films = Films 16mm / *edited by* The Ottawa Public Library. - *Published by* The Ottawa Public Library. 120 Metcalfe St., Ottawa, Ont. K1P 5M2.
Annual. Catalogue, 63 p. Language: English and French
$1.00 per issue.

Films 16mm *See* 16mm films

16mm films available from the public libraries of Metropolitan Toronto - *Published by* Metropolitan Toronto Library Board. Suite 301, 203 College St., Toronto, Ont. M5T 1P9, 1968-
Former title(s): 16mm sound films available from the public libraries of Metropolitan Toronto (1968)
Annual. Catalogue, book format, 414 p. supplements issued. Circulation: 1000
ISSN 0315-7326

Ski Canada journal / *edited by* Clive Hopson. - *Published by* Terry M. Whelpton. 643 Yonge St., Toronto, Ont. M4Y 2A2.
Issued every other month. Special interest, magazine format, 64 p.
$.75 per issue : $3.37 per year.

Ski Quebec / *édité par* Denis Duquet. - *Publié par* Quebec Division. Canadian Ski Association. Publisysteme Inc. 305, Deslauriers, Ville St. Laurent, Qué. H4N 1W2.
Intermittent (approximativement 4 éditions par an). Publication d'association, magazine, Comprend publicité. Tirage: 36,000
$.75 le numéro : $3.00 par année.

Ski runner / *edited by* Arthur C. Benson. - *Published by* Toronto Ski Club. 8 Colborne St., Toronto, Ont., 1926-
Irregular (approximately 6 issues per year). Association publication, magazine format, 20 p.
$3.00 per year.

Ski trails west - *Published by* Toby Nakamura and Associates Ltd. 216 East 6 Ave., New Westminster, B.C.
Monthly. Special interest, magazine format, Includes advertising.
$.60 per issue : $4.00 per year.

Ski ventures / *edited by* L.B. Fuller. - *Published by* Ski East Association. 306A Youville Sq., Montreal, Que. H2Y 2B6.
Annual. Association publication, newspaper format, 12 p. Language: English (French).
Free.

Ski-mag / *edited by* Roger Labonte. - *Published by* Les Publications Norco Inc. 306-5890 Monkland, Notre Dame de Grace, Montreal, Que. H4A 1G2, 1972-
Irregular (approximately 5 issues per year). Special interest, magazine format, Language: English and French. Includes advertising. Circulation: 9925
$.75 per issue : $4.50 per year.

Skylark / *sponsored by* Saskatchewan English Teachers' Associaton ; *edited by* Mildred A. Rose and Joan G. Smith (Chairmen of editorial board). - *Published by* Saskatchewan Teachers' Federation. P.O. Box 1108, 2317 Arlington Ave., Saskatoon, Sask. S7J 2H8.
Quarterly. Association publication, magazine format, 50-100 p. Includes book reviews, film reviews, play reviews. Circulation: 500
Indexed in Can. educ. ind.
$1.00 per issue : $8.00 per year. Prepayment required.

Slavic and East-European studies = Etudes slaves et est-européennes / *sponsored by* Eastern Canada Centre of Slavic and East European Specialists. - *Published by* Les Presses de l'Université Laval. Québec, Qué. (Subscription address: c/o Dept. of Political Science, McMaster University, Hamilton, Ont. L8S 4M4)
Association publication. Back issues available $8.00 per volume.
Indexed in Hist. abstr.; Amer. hist. and life.
$3.00 per year.

Slipara vortaro / *edited by* R. Eichholz. - *Published by* Esperanto Press. 2040 Springbank Rd., Mississauga, Ont. L5H 3N6, 1968-
Annual. A supplementary dictionary, sheet format, 144 p. Language: Esperanto (with translations into English, French and German). Circulation: 500
$.90. Prepayment required.

Slovak voice *See* Slovensky hlas

Slovenian country *See* Slovenska drzava

Slovenska drzava = Slovenian country / *edited by* Vladimir Mauko. - *Published by* Slovenian National Federation of Canada. 646 Euclid Ave., Toronto, Ont.
Monthly. Ethnic press. Language: Slovenian. Includes advertising. Circulation: 4160

Slovenski Jezuiti v Kanade / *edited by* Vincent Danco. - *Published by* Slovak Jesuit Fathers. P.O. Box 600, Cambridge, Ont. N1R 5W3, 1954-
Annual. Church publication, yearbook, magazine format, 64 or 32 p. Language: Slovak ; summaries: English. Includes book reviews.
Free.

Slovensky hlas = Slovak voice / *edited by* Ted Baker - Pekarovich. - *Published by* Canadian Slovak Benefit Society. P.O. Box 61, Postal Station C, Toronto, Ont., March 1949-
Monthly. Association publication, ethnic press, newspaper format, 8 p. Language: Slovak. Includes book reviews, advertising. Circulation: 1400
$.25 per issue : $2.00 per year : $2.50 per year, foreign.

Slovo na storozhi = Word on guard = La parole en gard / *edited by* J.B. Rudnyckyi. - *Published by* Ukrainian Language Association. P.O. Box 3504, Postal Station B, Winnipeg, Man., 1964-
Monthly. Association publication, magazine format, 32-48 p. Language: Ukrainian. supplements issued. Circulation: 1000
$1.00 per issue : $12.00 per year.

The Small voice / *edited by* Lloyd G. Cumming. - *Published by* The United Church Renewal Fellowship. 304 - 7 Vancouver St., Barrie, Ont. L4M 4M1, 1968-
Quarterly. Church publication, magazine format, 35-40 p. Circulation: 2000
$2.00 per year.

Snowmobile annual / *edited by* David B. Lamb. - *Published by* Leisure Publications. Suite 503, 56 The Esplanade, Toronto, Ont. M5E 1A7, 1974-
Annual. Special interest, magazine format, Includes advertising.

Snowmobile trade / *edited by* Keith Pearson. - *Published by* Rene Lejeune. Sentinel Publishing Co. 27 Centrale, La Salle, Que. H8R 3K2, 1972-
Trade publication. Includes advertising. Circulation: 15,514
$6.00 per year : $10.00 per year U.S. and U.K. : $15.00 per year, foreign.

Social development / *edited by* Valerie Bachynsky. - *Published by* Canadian Council on Social Development. P.O. Box 3505, Postal Station C, 55 Parkdale, Ottawa, Ont. K1Y 4G1, January 1972-
Issued every other month. Association publication, newsletter format, 4 p.
ISSN 0316-313X Subscription included in membership fee.

Social history *See* Histoire sociale

Social history = Histoire sociale / *edited by* Fernand Ouellet (directeur). Julian Gwyn (Assistant editor). - *Published by* University of Ottawa Press. 65 Hastey St., Ottawa, Ont. K1N 6N5, April 1968-
Issued twice a year (May and November). Scholarly publication, magazine format, 225 p. Language: English and French. Includes book reviews, advertising. Circulation: 400
Indexed in Hist. abstr.; Amer. hist. and life.
$7.00 (Individuals $5.00). Special rates offered. Prepayment required.

Social science teachers newsletter *See* Perspectives

Social thought / *edited by* Grant Maxwell and Tony Clarke. - *Published by* Canadian Catholic Conference. 90 Parent Ave., Ottawa, Ont. K1N 7B1.
Monthly except July and August issues are combined. Special interest, 12 p. Includes book reviews, film reviews.
$0.75 per issue : $4.00 per year : $6.00 per year, foreign.

The Social worker = Le Travailleur social / *edited by* Anthony J. Gray. - *Published by* Canadian Association of Social Workers. 55 Parkdale, Ottawa, Ont. K1Y 1E5, 1932-
Quarterly. Association publication, magazine format, 60 p. Language: English and French ; summaries: French and English. Includes book reviews, cumulative index. Circulation: 6000
Indexed in Periodex.
$2.00 per issue : $7.50 per year (Student $4.00 per year).

Socialist press (April 1941 - July 1951) *See* Socialist press bulletin

Socialist press bulletin / *edited by* National Executive Committee, Socialist Labour Party of Canada. - *Published by* Socialist National Executive Committee. Socialist Labour Party of Canada. P.O. Box 123, Adelaide St., Toronto, Ont. M5C 2J1, February 1956-
Former title(s): Socialist press (April 1941 - July 1951)
Monthly. Political press, newsletter format, 8 p. available in microform. Circulation: 500
Free.

Socialization and leisure - *Published by* SIRLS. Faculty of Human Kinetics and Leisure Studies. University of Waterloo. Waterloo, Ont. N2L 3G1.
Quarterly. Bibliography, computer printout, $20.00 per year. $100.00 subscription to SIRLS required.

Socialization and sport - *Published by* SIRLS. Faculty of Human Kinetics and Leisure Studies. University of Waterloo. Waterloo, Ont. N2L 3G1.
Quarterly. Bibliography.
$100.00 subscription to SIRLS required.

Société canadienne d'anesthésistes. Journal de la Société canadienne d'anesthésistes. *See* Canadian Anaesthetists' Society. The Canadian Anaesthetists' Society journal

Société canadienne de biologie cellulaire. Bulletin *See* Canadian Society for Cell Biology. CSCB bulletin

La Société canadienne de protection des animaux. Courrier SPCA = The Canadian Society for the Prevention of Cruelty to Animals. SPCA courier / *édité par* Xavier De Lusigny. - *Publié par* La Société canadienne de protection des animaux. 5215 ouest, rue Jean Talon, Montréal, Qué. H4P 1X4, janvier 1974-
Ancien titre: Animal news = Nouvelles de nos animaux (octobre 1968-hiver 1973)
Trimestriel. Publication d'association, journal, 8 p. Langue(s): français et anglais. Tirage: 10,000
$5.00 par année. Envoi gratuit. Abonnements payables à l'avance.

Société canadienne de science politique. Bulletin *See* Canadian Political Science Association. Bulletin

Société canadienne de sociologie et d'anthropologie. Bulletin. = Canadian Sociology and Anthropology Association. Bulletin / *édité par* Lorna Marsden. - *Publié par* La Société canadienne de sociologie et d'anthropologie. C.P. 878, Succursale A, Montréal, Qué. H3C 2V8.
Trimestriel. Publication d'association, bulletin, 15 p. Langue(s): anglais et français.
$1.00 per issue : $4.00 per year.

Société canadienne des biologistes de l'environnement. Bulletin *See* Canadian Society of Environmental Biologists. Newsletter

Société canadienne des études bibliques. Bulletin *See* Canadian Society of Biblical Studies. Bulletin

Société canadienne d'études éthniques. Bulletin *See* Canadian Ethnic Studies Association. Bulletin

Sociéte canadienne pour l'étude de l'éducation *See* Canadian Society for the Study of Education. Yearbook

La Société de génétique du Canada. Bulletin *See* The Genetics Society of Canada. Bulletin

Société de microscopie du Canada. Bulletin *See* Microscopical Society of Canada. Bulletin

Société de philosophie du Québec. Bulletin / *parrainé par* Société de philosophie du Québec ; *édité par* Raymond Brouillet. - *Publié par* Université du Québec à Trois-Rivières. C.P. 500, Trois-Rivières, Qué.(adresse d'abonnement: 2910, boul. Edouard-Montpetit, Montréal, Qué) octobre 1974-
Trimestriel. Publication d'association, bulletin, 50 p.
$5.00 par année.

Société entomologique du Québec. Annales. = Entomological Society of Quebec. Annals - *Publié par* Société entomologique du Québec. Station de recherches, C.P. 457, Saint-Jean, Qué. J3B 6Z8(adresse d'abonnement: Michel Letendre, Complexe Scientifique, D-1-59, 2700, rue Einstein, Ste-Foi, Qué. G1A 1E6) décembre 1956-
Paraît 3 fois par an. Publication d'association, revue, 50 p. Langue(s): français et anglais ; sommaires: français et anglais. Comprend critique de livres. Tirage: 800
$5.00 par année. Abonnements payables à l'avance.

Société entomologique du Québec. Mémoires = Entomological Society of Quebec. Memoirs - *Publié par* Rodolfe O. Paradis. Société entomologique du Québec. Station de recherches, C.P. 457, Saint-Jean, Qué. J3B 6Z8(adresse d'abonnement: Michel Letendre, Complexe Scientifique, D-1-59, 2700, rue Einstein, Ste-Foy, Qué. G1A 1E6) février 1968-
Intermittent. Publication d'association, Bulletin sur un subject déterminé, 180 p. Langue(s): français et anglais ; sommaires: français et anglais. Tirage: 800
Il faut être abonné aux Annales ($5.00 par année) pour recevoir les Mémoires.

Société généalogique canadienne-française. Mémoires / *édité par* R.P. Julien Déziel. - *Publié par* Société généalogique canadienne-française. C.P. 335, Place d'Armes, Montréal, Qué. H2Y 3H1, 1943-
Trimestriel. Publication d'association, bulletin, 64 p. Comprend critique de livres.
$6.00 par année (Sociétés $7.00) : $7.00 par année, l'étranger. Abonnements payables à l'avance.

La Société historique acadienne. Les Cahiers / *édité par* Jean Daigle. - *Publié par* La Société historique acadienne. C.P. 2363, Succursale A, Moncton, N.B. E1C 8J3, 1961-
Trimestriel. Edition savante, revue, 48 p. Comprend critique de livres. Tirage: 700
$2.00 le numéro : $5.00 par année. Abonnements payables à l'avance.

Société pour l'étude de l'architecture au Canada. Nouvelles *See* Society for the Study of Architecture in Canada. News

Society for Animals in Distress. Newsletter / *edited by* Alan McGinn. - *Published by* Society for Animals in Distress. 603 St. Clair Ave. W., Toronto, Ont. M6C 1A3, June 1971-
Quarterly. Association publication, newsletter format, 12 p.
Free.

Society for the Study of Architecture in Canada. News = Société pour l'étude de l'architecture au Canada. Nouvelles / *edited by* Gront Head. - *Published by* Society for the Study of Architecture in Canada. P.O. Box 2935, Postal Station D, Ottawa, Ont. K1P 5W9, January/February 1975-
Issued every other month. Association publication, newsletter format, 12 p. Language: English and French.
$12.00 per year.

Society of Civil Engineers. Transactions (1887-1917) *See* The Engineering journal

Society of Manufacturing Engineers. Chapter 42. Monthly programme / *edited by* V.A. Skinner. - *Published by* Hamilton District Chapter No. 42. Society of Manufacturing Engineers. 183 Darlington Dr., Hamilton, Ont. L9C 2M4.
Monthly. Association publication, magazine format, 16 p. Includes advertising. Circulation: 160
Free.

Socio-history of sport and leisure in ancient and medieval times - *Published by* SIRLS. Faculty of Human Kinetics and Leisure Studies. University of Waterloo. Waterloo, Ont. N2L 3G1.
Quarterly. Bibliography, computer printout, $20.00 per year. $100.00 subscription to SIRLS required.

Socio-history of sport and leisure renaissance to modern times - *Published by* SIRLS. Faculty of Human Kinetics and Leisure Studies. University of Waterloo. Waterloo, Ont. N2L 3G1.
Quarterly. Bibliography, computer printout, $20.00 per year. $100.00 subscription to SIRLS required.

Sociological inquiry - *Published by* National Honor Society. 252 Bloor St. W., Toronto, Ont.
Issued twice a year.
Indexed in Hist. abstr.
$6.00 per year.

Sociologie et sociétés : revue thématique / *parrainé par* Université de Montréal ; *édité par* Jacques Dofny. - *Publié par* Les Presses de l'Université de Montréal. C.P. 6128, Montréal, Qué. H3C 3J7, 1969-
Semestriel. Edition savante, revue, 168 p. Comprend publicité. Tirage: 1000-3000
Indexé dans Periodex, RADAR.
ISSN 0038-030X $5.00 le numéro : $8.00 par année. Tirage contrôlé. Abonnements payables à l'avance.

Sociology of play and games - *Published by* SIRLS. Faculty of Human Kinetics and Leisure Studies. University of Waterloo. Waterloo, Ont. N2L 3G1.
Quarterly. Bibliography, computer printout, $20.00 per year. $100.00 subscription to SIRLS required.

Socitété historique de la vallée de la Châteauguay. Journal *See* Chateauguay Valley Historical Society. Journal

Soit la route *Voir* Association des routes et transports du Canada. Nouvelles de l'ARTA

Sojourn: the magazine for Nova Scotians / *edited by* Kenneth T. Langille. - *Published by* Runic Publications. 1491 South Park St., Halifax, N.S., March 1975-
Former title(s): The Runic report (October 1972-February 1975)
Monthly. General interest, magazine format, 64-96 p. Language: English (French). Includes book reviews, film reviews, play reviews, advertising, volume index. Circulation: 15,000
$.50 per issue : $6.75 per year : $.65 per issue, foreign. Controlled circulation. Prepayment required.

Solidaire - *Published by* Solidaire. P.O. Box 461, Postal Station N, Montreal, Que.
Indexed in Alt. press ind.
$2.00 for 4 issues.

Sono : sonorisation au Canada - *Publié par* Paul Saint-Pierre. Maclean-Hunter Ltée. 625, ave Président-Kennedy, Montréal, Qué. H3A 1K5, hiver 1973-
Semestriel. Publication spécialisée, magazine, 64 p. Comprend critique de disques. Tirage: 15,000
Indexé dans Periodex, RADAR.
$.60 le numéro : $1.00 par année.

Sound Canada / *edited by* Jim Smith. - *Published by* Chimo Media Ltd. 21 Prince Andrew Pl. Don Mills, Ont. M3C 2H2, February 1971-
Monthly except January and July. Special interest, magazine format, 64 p. Includes record reviews, advertising. Circulation: 30,000
$.75 per issue : $4.00 per year.

The Sounding board / *edited by* Richard G. Cross. - *Published by* Vancouver Board of Trade. 5th Floor, 1177 W. Hastings St., Vancouver, B.C. V6E 2K3.
Twice a month. House/company organ, newsletter format, 4 p. Includes advertising. Circulation: 3300
Free. Controlled circulation.

Sounds about Sunday / *edited by* Gordon A. Walker. - *Published by* Lord's Day Alliance of Canada. 2160 Yonge St., Toronto, Ont. M4S 2A9, September 1972-
Issued twice a year. Association publication, newsletter format, 4 p. Circulation: 12,000

Le Sourire (mai 1949-mai 1963) *Voir* Carrefour chrétien

South east Alberta - *Published by* Medicine Hat & District Tourist Council. P.O. Box 605, Medicine Hat, Alta. T1A 7G5, June 1968-
Annual. Special interest, booklet format, 16 p. Circulation: 30,000
Free.

South of tuk / *edited by* Karl Vaughan. - *Published by* Karl Vaughan. P.O. Box 1267, Postal Station A, Toronto, Ont. M5W 1G7, November 1971-
Former title(s): CNP news, (July 1972-January 1974) The Spadina express (November 1971-June 1972)
Weekly. Special interest, newsletter format, 4 p. Includes book reviews, film reviews, advertising, cumulative index. supplements issued. Back copies are available only to Vol. 4, No. 4. Circulation: 571
$.15 per issue : $6.25 per year : $12.00 per year, foreign. Bonus subscription, 52 issues and 6-90 minute tapes $24.00. Prepayment required.

South Western Ontario Square Dance Association. S.W.O.S.D.A. bugle / *edited by* Tom and Addie Parmenter. - *Published by* South Western Ontario Square Dance Association. 271 Briscoe St. E., London, Ont. N6C 1Y5 (Subscription address: Walt Warner, 117 Empress Ave., London, Ont. N6H 1N1) 1966-
Monthly, September to April. Association publication, newsletter format, 20 p. Circulation: 400
$.35 per issue : $2.50 per year. Prepayment required.

Southam building guide / *edited by* Olga Markovich. - *Published by* Southam Business Publications Ltd. 1450 Don Mills Rd., Don Mills, Ont., 1920-
Monthly. Trade publication, magazine format, Circulation: 16,000
$12.00 per year : $32.00 per year, foreign.

Souvenir du bon Père Frédéric, O.F.M. Nouvelle série annuelle / *édité par* Romain Légaré. - *Publié par* Editions du bon Père Fréderic. 890, St-Maurice, Trois-Rivières, Qué., 1971-
Ancien titre: Le Père Frédéric; Notre-Dame du Cap (1973)
Annuel. Publication ecclésiastique.
$1.00.

Sou'wester = The voice of Atlantic Canada's fishing and marine industry / *edited by* Len Pace. - *Published by* Fundy Group Publications Ltd. P.O. Box 128, Yarmouth, N.S.
Issued twice a month. Trade publication, newspaper format, 24 p. Includes advertising.

The Soviet Union today / *sponsored by* Novosti Press Agency, Moscow, USSR ; *edited by* Alexei Flerovsky (Moscow) and Victor Mikheev (Ottawa). - *Published by* USSR Embassy in Canada. 285 Charlotte St., Ottawa, Ont. (Subscription address: Apt. 1108, 400 Stewart St., Ottawa, Ont. K1N 6L2)
Monthly. General interest, magazine format, 46 p. Language: English and French. Includes book reviews, film reviews, play reviews, advertising. supplements issued.
Indexed in North. tit.
$.50 per issue : $3.00 per year. Special rates offered.

Sovremennik (the contemporary) : Russian national review in Canada / *edited by* G. Zhekulin, E. Bobrow-Zuckert and L. Fabricius. - *Published by* Sovremennik Publishing Association Inc. 9 Garnet Ave., Toronto, Ont. M6G 1V6, 1958-
Issued twice a year. Ethnic press, magazine format, 160-180 p. Language: Russian ; summaries: English and Russian. Includes book reviews. Circulation: 1000
$15.00 per year. Prepayment required.

The Spadina express (November 1971-June 1972) *See* South of tuk

Spark *See* Iskra

Speak up : for political and economic realism - *Published by* Speak Up. P.O. Box 272, Postal Station B, Toronto, Ont. M5T 2W2.
Monthly. Special interest, newspaper format, 16 p.
$.50 per issue : $5.00 per year.

Spearhead (1938-1945) *See* Labatt news

Spec index international = International specification index / *edited by* Bryan S. Rogers. - *Published by* A. Bert Sevink. Maclean-Hunter Ltd. 481 University Ave., Toronto, Ont. M5W 1A7.
Annual. Trade publication. Language: English, French, Spanish and Portuguese. Includes advertising. Circulation: 40,000
$15.00 per year.

Special education in Canada / *edited by* Eric Haughton. - *Published by* Canadian Committee. The Council for Exceptional Children. 6450 Thorold Stone Rd., Niagara Falls, Ont. L2J 1B3 (Subscription address: c/o John McRae, Parkview Secondary School, 1 Danforth Ave., Toronto, Ont. M4K 1M8)
Issued 4 times a year (November, February, April and Summer). Association publication, magazine format, 36 p. Includes book reviews, film reviews, advertising, volume index.
Indexed in Can. educ. ind., Curr. ind. j. educ.
Prepayment required.

Special Libraries Association. Montreal Chapter. Bulletin / *edited by* E.A. MacLean. - *Published by* Montreal Chapter. Special Libraries Association. Blacker-Wood Library, McGill University, Montreal, Que. H3A 1Y1, 1935-
Quarterly. Association publication, newsletter format, Circulation: 350
$2.00 per year.

Specification associate / *edited by* Stuart Frost. - *Published by* Construction Specifications Canada. Suite 301, 1027 Yonge St., Toronto, Ont. M4W 2K2, 1959-
Issued every other month. Trade publication. Includes advertising. Circulation: 3931
$2.00 per issue : $10.00 per year.

Spectrum - *Published by* Society for Pollution and Environmental Control. 1095 West 7th Ave., Vancouver, B.C. (Subscription address: 2007 West 7th Ave., Vancouver, B.C. V6J 1M9)
Former title(s): Perspective.
Issued every other month. Association publication, newspaper format, 8 p.
Circulation: 3000
Prepayment required.

Spectrum / *edited by* Daryl Cook, Nancy Davies and Muriel Peck. - *Published by* Guidance Centre. Faculty of Education. University of Toronto. 1000 Yonge St., Toronto, Ont. M4W 2K8, 1972-
Annual. Special interest, 116 p.
ISSN 0315-078X $2.25 per issue.

Spéléo-Québec / *édité par* Gérard Dubuc. - *Publié par* Société québécoise de spéléologie. C.P. 336, Succursale Delorimier, Montréal, Qué. H2H 2N7, janvier 1974-
Trimestriel. Publication d'association, bulletin, 80 p. Comprend critique de livres. Tirage: 600
$1.50 le numéro : $3.00 par année : $4.00 le volume. Tarifs spéciaux disponibles. Abonnements payables à l'avance.

Sphere / *edited by* Derek Hayter. - *Published by* Shell Canada Ltd. 505 University Ave., Toronto, Ont. M5G 1X4, January 1970-
Former title(s): Shell News. Published in French: Sphère.
Issued every other month. House/company organ, magazine format, 28 p. Circulation: 8000
Free.

Sphère - *Published by* Shell Canada Ltd. 505 University Ave., Toronto, Ont. M5G 1X4, janvier 1970-
Publié en anglais: Sphere.
Bimestriel. Organe interne/officiel, magazine, 28 p. Tirage: 1000
Envoi gratuit.

The Sphinx / *edited by* Aydon Charlton. - *Published by* English Departmet. University of Regina. Regina, Sask. S4S 0A2.
Issued twice a year.
$3.00 per year.

The Spiker / *edited by* Ian Stoddart. - *Published by* Canadian Volleyball Association Publications. 333 River Rd., Vanier, Ont. K1L 8B9.
Quarterly. Association publication, magazine format, 28 p. Circulation: 5000
$1.00 per issue : $3.00 per year : $5.00 per volume : $5.00 per year, foreign.

Split level / *edited by* Harry Peters and Barry Chamish. - *Published by* Split Level Publishing House. P.O. Box 791, Winnipeg, Man. R3C 2N4, October 1974-
Issued twice a year. Special interest, magazine format, 24 p.
$1.00 per issue : $1.50 per year.

Spoke - *Published by* Conestoga College. 299 Doon Valley Dr., Kitchener, Ont. N2C 3W5 (Subscription address: 299 Doon Valley Dr., Kitchener, Ont. N2C 3W5)
Issued twice a month. Student publication. Includes advertising. Circulation: 2000

Sport / *edited by* Aurel Hamran. - *Published by* Sport. P.O. Box 5956, Postal Station A, Toronto, Ont. M5W 1P3, May 1972-
Weekly. Ethnic press, newspaper format, 8 p. Language: Hungarian and English. Circulation: 3000
$.35 per issue : $15.00 per year.

Sport, ideology and philosophy - *Published by* SIRLS. Faculty of Human Kinetics and Leisure Studies. University of Waterloo. Waterloo, Ont. N2L 3G1.
Quarterly. Bibliography, computer printout, $20.00 per year. $100.00 subscription to SIRLS required.

Sport, leisure and deviant behaviour - *Published by* SIRLS. Faculty of Human Kinetics and Leisure Studies. University of Waterloo. Waterloo, Ont. N2L 3G1.
Quarterly. Bibliography, computer printout, $20.00 per year. $100.00 subscription to SIRLS required.

Sport, leisure and life style in Canada - *Published by* SIRLS. Faculty of Human Kinetics and Leisure Studies. University of Waterloo. Waterloo, Ont. N2L 3G1.
Quarterly. Bibliography, computer printout, $20.00 per year. $100.00 subscription to SIRLS required.

Sport and social institutions excluding politics and education - *Published by* SIRLS. Faculty of Human Kinetics and Leisure Studies. University of Waterloo. Waterloo, Ont. N2L 3G1.
Quarterly. Bibliography, computer printout, $20.00 per year. $100.00 subscription to SIRLS required.

Sport and social stratification - *Published by* SIRLS. Faculty of Human Kinetics and Leisure Studies. University of Waterloo. Waterloo, Ont. N2L 3G1.
Quarterly. Bibliography, computer printout, $20.00 per year. $100.00 subscription to SIRLS required.

Sport and the small group - *Published by* SIRLS. Faculty of Human Kinetics and Leisure Studies. University of Waterloo. Waterloo, Ont. N2L 3G1.
Quarterly. Bibliography, computer printout, $100.00 subscription to SIRLS required.

Sport as a macro-social system - *Published by* SIRLS. Faculty of Human Kinetics and Leisure Studies. University of Waterloo. Waterloo, Ont. N2L 3G1.
Quarterly. Bibliography, computer printout, $20.00 per year. $100.00 subscription to SIRLS required.

Sport illustré - *Publié par* Raymond Dulude. 208, chemin St. Jean, La Prairie, Qué., 1968-
Bimensuel. Publication spécialisée, magazine, Comprend publicité. Tirage: 31,850
$.50 le numéro : $10.00 par année.

Sport occupations and career patterns *- Published by* SIRLS. Faculty of Human Kinetics and Leisure Studies. University of Waterloo. Waterloo, Ont. N2L 3G1.
Quarterly. Bibliography, computer printout, $20.00 per year. $100.00 subscription to SIRLS required.

Sport vivo *See* Comunita' viva

Sporthirado = Sportnews */ edited by* G. Super. *- Published by* Gary Super. 277 Wychwood Ave., Toronto, Ont.
Weekly. Ethnic press. Language: Hungarian. Includes advertising. Circulation: 7450
$.30 per issue : $14.50 per year.

Sporting goods Canada */ edited by* James Rennie. *- Published by* Maclean-Hunter Ltd. 481 University Ave., Toronto, Ont. M5W 1A7.
Trade publication. Includes advertising. Circulation: 8928
Indexed in Can. B.P.I.
$2.00 per issue : $10.00 per year : $3.00 per issue, foreign (except U.S. and U.K.), $12.00 per year, U.S. and U.K. : $25.00 per year, foreign.

Sportnews *See* Sporthirado

Sports, recreation and fitness */ edited by* Liz Roach. *- Published by* Fitness and Sports Publishing Ltd. 224 Yorkland Blvd., Willowdale, Ont. M2J 1R5, 1974-
Monthly. Special interest, magazine format, Includes advertising. Circulation: 9783
$6.00 per year : $10.00 per year, foreign.

Sports British Columbia (to 1973) *See* B.C. Sports Federation. B.C. Sports Federation newsletter

Sports/Famille */ édité par* Marcel Ouellet. *- Publié par* Sales & Markets Inc. 10, 549 rue Parthenais, Montréal, Qué., janvier 1966-
Mensuel. Publication spécialisée, journal, 20-32 p. Tirage: 43,000
$.35 le numéro : $4.00 par année : $5.00 par année, l'étranger. Tarifs spéciaux disponibles. Abonnements payables à l'avance.

Sportsland magazine */ edited by* Mel Dagg. *- Published by* Bob McKay. The Springfield Leader Ltd. Lac du Bonnet, Man. R0E 1A0 (Subscription address: Suite 204, 435 Berry St., Winnipeg, Man. R3J 1N6) 1972-
Monthly. Special interest, magazine format, Includes advertising. Circulation: 25,000
$.60 per issue : $5.00 per year : $6.00 per year, U.S.

The Spotlight */ edited by* Harry Blake-Knox. *- Published by* Harry Blake-Knox. 81-83 Hillbrow Ave., Grand Beach, Man. R0E 0S0, 1957-
Issued twice a month. Special interest, newspaper format, 24 p. Includes book reviews, film reviews, play reviews, record reviews, advertising. Circulation: 1200
$.15 per issue : $2.00 per year. Prepayment required.

The Spotlight: news and views on Catholic education */ edited by* Patrick H. Fogarty. *- Published by* Federation of Catholic Education Associations of Ontario. 67 Bond St., Toronto, Ont. M5B 1X5, 1967-
Irregular (approximately 2 issues per year). Church publication, newsletter format, 4 p.
$.20 per issue. Controlled circulation.

The Spread */ edited by* Gerhard Wetzel. *- Published by* Toronto Stock Exchange. 234 Bay St., Toronto, Ont. M5J 1R1, March 1974-
Issued every other month. House/company organ, newsletter format, 8 p. Circulation: 1300
Controlled circulation.

The Spruce log */ edited by* Ken Hutchinson. *- Published by* Spruce Falls Power and Paper Co., Ltd. P.O. Box 100, Kapuskasing, Ont.
Issued every other month. House/company organ, magazine format, 20 p. Circulation: 3500-4000
Free. Controlled circulation.

Stage de biochimie */ édité par* Alain Robert. *- Publié par* Conseil de la jeunesse scientifique. 1415 est, rue Jarry, Montréal, Qué., 1973-
Annuel. Publication spécialisée, 60 p. Tirage: 100
Envoi gratuit.

Stages en France *Voir* Le Journal des stages (stages accessibles aux résidents québécois)

Le Stagiaire */ édité par* A. Lemieux. *- Publié par* Office Franco-Québécois pour la jeunesse. Suite 1150, 555 ouest, boul. Dorchester, Montréal, Qué., 1970-
Trimestriel. Publication d'association, journal, 12-16 p. Tirage: 35,000
Envoi gratuit.

The Standardbred record */ edited by* Barbara Waples. *- Published by* Barbara Waples. P.O. Box 730, Maple, Ont. L0J 1E0, January 1971-
Weekly. Special interest, magazine format, 24 p. Circulation: 2000
$12.00 per year.

Standards Canada / *edited by* Sally Southam. - *Published by* Canadian Standards Association. 178 Rexdale Blvd., Rexdale, Ont. M9W 1R3, 1970-
Quarterly. Association publication, newsletter format, 4 p. Language: English and French. Circulation: 15,000
ISSN 0038-965X Free.

The Stanley Cup records and statistics - *Published by* Ron Andrews. 920 Sun Life Building, Montreal, Que. H3B 2W2.
Annual. Statistics.

Stanstead County Historical Society. Journal / *edited by* A.E. Curtis. - *Published by* Stanstead County Historical Society. P.O. Box 210, Stanstead, Que. J0B 3E0, 1965-
Biennial. Association publication, magazine format, 64 p. Circulation: 600
ISSN 0081-4369 $3.50.

Star-Standard intercom / *edited by* George Burman. - *Published by* The Montreal Star (1973) Ltd. 245 St. James St. W., Montreal, Que. H2Y 1M6, June 1972-
Issued every other month. House/company organ, newspaper format, 12-16 p. Limited supply of back copies.
Free to staff and retired staff. Controlled circulation.

Station reporter / *edited by* P.W. McCarthy. - *Published by* Retail Gasoline Dealers Association of Nova Scotia. P.O. Box 171, 12 Portland St., Dartmouth, N.S., October 1968-
Quarterly. Association publication, magazine format, 20 p.
Subscription included in membership fee.

Statistical handbook / *edited by* Peggy Williams. - *Published by* Canada Grains Council. 400 - 177 Lombard Ave. Winnipeg, Man., 1974-
Annual. Statistics, 270 p. Circulation: 3000
$5.00 per year.

Statistical review of plumbing and heating in Canada - *Published by* Canadian Institute of Plumbing & Heating. Suite 305, 785 Plymouth Ave., Montreal, Que. H4P 1B3.
Annual. Association publication, magazine format, 25 p.

Statistiques : les infirmières au Canada - *Publié par* L'Association des infirmières canadiennes. 50, The Driveway, Ottawa, Ont. K2P 1E2, 1973-
Annuel. Publication d'association, statistiques.
ISSN 0315-2618 $5.00 le numéro.

Status of women news / *edited by* Moira Armour. - *Published by* National Action Committee on the Status of Women in Canada. 121 Avenue Rd., Toronto, Ont. M5R 2G3, Winter 1973-
Irregular (approximately 5 issues per year). Association publication, newsletter format, 32 p. Language: English and French. Includes book reviews. Back issues available.
$3.00 per year.

Ste Anne de Beaupré / *édité par* Bernard Mercier. - *Publié par* La Corporation du T.S. Rédempteui (CSSR). Montmorency, Qué., 1874-
Ancien titre: Les Annales de Ste Anne de Beaupré. Publié en anglais: The Annals of good St. Anne de Beaupré.
Mensuel. Publication ecclésiastique, magazine, 48 p. Comprend critique de livres. Tirage: 132,000
$.35 le numéro : $3.00 par année. Abonnements payables à l'avance.

Steel in homes / *edited by* J.K. Davy. - *Published by* The Steel Co. of Canada Ltd. 100 King St. W., Hamilton, Ont. L8N 3T1, 1966-
Irregular (approximately 3 issues per year). Trade publication, magazine format, 16 p. Language: English and French.

Steel in transportation / *edited by* J.K. Davy. - *Published by* The Steel Co. of Canada Ltd. 100 King St. W., Hamilton, Ont. L8N 3T1, 1973-
Former title(s): Streets and highways.
Irregular (approximately 3 issues per year). Trade publication, magazine format, 8 p. Language: English and French. Circulation: 9000
Free.

Stelco flashes / *edited by* Garry W. Smith. - *Published by* The Steel Co. of Canada Ltd. 100 King St. W., Hamilton, Ont. L8N 3T1, 1936-
Irregular (approximately 8 issues per year). House/company organ, newsletter format, 8 p. Language: English and French. Circulation: 29,000

Sten-gazeta (February 1943-February 1945) *See* Iskra

Stimulus (1966-1974) *See* Stimulus/The gallery

The Stimulus gallery (1972-1974) *See* Stimulus/The gallery

Stimulus/The gallery / *edited by* Dean Walker. - *Published by* Robert F. Bale. Stimulus Publishing Co. Ltd. Suite 202, 67 Yonge St., Toronto, Ont. M5E 1J8, 1966-
Former title(s): Stimulus (1966-1974) The Stimulus gallery (1972-1974)
Issued every other month. Trade publication, magazine format, 48 p. Includes advertising. *Indexed in* Can. B.P.I.
$3.00 per issue : $17.00 per year : $20.00 per year, foreign. Controlled circulation.

Stone and Cox general insurance year book - *Published by* Stone & Cox Ltd. 203 Adelaide St. W., Toronto, Ont. M5H 1X4.
Annual. Yearbook, book, 480 p. Includes advertising. Circulation: 1000
$12.00.

Stone and Cox life insurance tables = Stone and Cox tables d'assurance-vie - *Published by* Stone & Cox Ltd. 203 Adelaide St. W., Toronto, Ont. M5H 1X4.
Annual. Universal rate manual, perfect bound book, 630 p. Language: English and French. Circulation: 5000
$8.25 per year.

Stone and Cox tables d'assurance-vie *See* Stone and Cox life insurance tables

Stop press / *edited by* Diane Shatz. - *Published by* Society to Overcome Pollution. 1361 Greene Ave., Montreal, Que. H3Z 2A5, 1971-
Issued every other month. Association publication, newsletter format, 8 p. Circulation: 1500
$.10 per issue : $5.00 per year.

Straight talk! / *edited by* Attila Marschalko. - *Published by* Western Guard Party. P.O. Box 544, Scarborough, Ont. M1K 5C4.
Irregular (approximately 10 issues per year). Association publication, magazine format, 18 p.
$5.00 per year.

Stratford Festival Canada / *edited by* Publicity Department, Stratford Festival. - *Published by* Publicity Department. Stratford Shakespearean Festival Foundation of Canada. P.O. Box 520, Stratford, Ont. N5A 6V2, 1953-
Issued twice a year. Special interest, brochure, Free.

Stratford Festival (souvenir program) / *sponsored by* Rothmans of Pall Mall Canada Ltd ; *edited by* Anne Selby. - *Published by* Stratford Shakespearean Festival Foundation of Canada. P.O. Box 520, Stratford, Ont. N5A 6V2, 1953-
Annual. Special interest, magazine format, 60 p.
ISSN 0085-6770 $1.50. Prepayment required.

The Stratford Festival story / *edited by* Publicity Department, Stratford Festival. - *Published by* Stratford Shakespearean Festival Foundation of Canada. P.O. Box 520, Stratford, Ont. N5A 6V2, 1954-
Annual. Special interest, magazine format, ISSN 0085-6789 Free.

Stratford International Film Festival - *Published by* Stratford Shakespearean Festival Foundation of Canada. P.O. Box 520, Stratford, Ont. N5A 6V2, 1965-
Annual. Special interest, newsletter format, ISSN 0081-5950 Free.

Streets and highways *See* Steel in transportation

Strength / *edited by* The Publications Collective. - *Published by* Kitchener-Waterloo Woman's Place. 25 Dupont St. E., Waterloo, Ont. N2J 2G8, September 1975-
Former title(s): K-W Women's Place newsletter (September 1973-July 1975)
Monthly. Special interest, magazine format, 18 p. Includes book reviews, film reviews. supplements issued. Circulation: 200
$.25 per issue : $5.00 per year.

The Structurist / *edited by* Eli Bornstein. - *Published by* Eli Bornstein. Department of Art. University of Saskatchewan. P.O. Box 378, Saskatoon, Sask. S7M 0W0, 1960-
Annual (single issues) Biennial (double issues). Magazine format, 100 p. available in microform. Circulation: 1200
ISSN 0081-6027 $5.00 per single issue : $9.00 per double issue. Prepayment required for new subscribers.

Student = Etudiant : the newspaper for Ukrainian Canadian students / *edited by* A. Szuch and L. Szuch. - *Published by* Ukrainian Canadian University Students' Union. Suite 4, 394 Bloor St. W., Toronto, Ont. M5S 1X4, 1968-
Issued every other month. Ethnic press, student publication, newspaper format, 24 p. Language: English, Ukrainian and French. Includes book reviews, advertising.
$1.00 per issue : $4.00 per year. Prepayment required.

Student handbook *Voir* Guide de l'étudiant

Student mathematics / *edited by* W.W. Sawyer. - *Published by* Faculty of Education. University of Toronto. Room 373, 371 Bloor St. W., Toronto, Ont. M5S 2R7, 1970-
Annual. Special interest, pamphlet format, $.20 per year.

Student statistics / *edited by* The Statistics and Research Section. - *Published by* Office of Statistics and Records. University of Toronto. 167 College St., University of Toronto, Toronto, Ont., 1963/1964-
Annual. Statistics, book format, 200-250 p. Includes volume index. Circulation: 200
ISSN 0315-209X Controlled circulation.

Studia canonica / *edited by* Francis G. Morrisey. - *Published by* Faculty of Canon Law. Saint Paul University. 223 Main St., Ottawa, Ont. K1S 1C4, 1967-
Issued twice a year. Legal articles, journal format, 180 p. Language: English and French. Includes book reviews, volume index. Circulation: 575
Indexed in Canon law abstr., Can. leg. per. lit., I.B.Z.
ISSN 0039-310X $2.50 per issue : $5.00 per year.

Studies in religion = Sciences religieuses / *sponsored by* Canadian Corporation for Studies in Religion/Corporation canadienne des sciences religieuses ; *edited by* Michel Campbell. - *Published by* University of Toronto Press. 5201 Dufferin St., Downsview, Ont. M3H 5T8 (Subscription address: c/o H.M. Rumscheidt, Atlantic School of Theology, 640 Francklyn St., Halifax, N.S) 1971-
Quarterly. Scholarly publication, journal format, 112 p. Language: English and French. Includes book reviews, advertising, volume index. Circulation: 950
Indexed in M.L.A. int. bib., MLA abstr.
$10.00 per year.

Stuffed crocodile / *edited by* Clarke E. Leverette. - *Published by* Killaly Press. 764 Dalkeith Ave., London, Ont. N5X 1R8, February 1972-
Quarterly. General interest, magazine format, 24 p. Includes volume index. available in microform. Circulation: 300
ISSN 0315-0496 $1.00 per issue : $8.00 for 2 years.

Style : for Canadian fashion merchandisers / *edited by* Pat Porth. - *Published by* Maclean-Hunter Ltd. 481 University Ave., Toronto, Ont. M5W 1A7, 1949-
Former title(s): Style wear (1891-1949) Canadian dry goods review (1891)
Monthly. Trade publication, magazine format, 60 p. Includes advertising. available in microform. supplements issued. Circulation: 12,500
$12.00 per year. Controlled circulation.

Style wear (1891-1949) *See* Style : for Canadian fashion merchandisers

Succession duty and gift tax handbook - *Published by* Gene @g. Stewart. Southam Business Publications Ltd. 70 Richmond St. E., Toronto, Ont. M5C 2M8.
Former title(s): Estate and gift tax handbook.
Annual. Special interest, 600 p.
$18.75.

Sudentenbote = Sudeten herald / *edited by* William Wanka. - *Published by* Western Canadian Sudeten, German Alliance. P.O. Box 231, Pouce Coupe, B.C. V0C 2C0, July 1965-
Issued every other month. Ethnic press, newsletter format, 30 p. Language: German. Circulation: 400
$.50 per issue : $3.00 per year : $5.00 per year, foreign.

Sudeten herald *See* Sudentenbote

Sumkivets' / *edited by* Yaroslaw Lozowchuk. - *Published by* National Executive. Canadian Ukrainian Youth Asaociation. 718-416 Main St., Winnipeg, Man., 1967-
Quarterly. Ethnic press, magazine format, 52 p. Language: Ukrainian and English. Includes book reviews, film reviews, record reviews.
$1.00 per issue : $3.00 per year. Prepayment required.

The Summary / *sponsored by* Evan Shute Foundation for Medical Research ; *edited by* E.V. Shute. - *Published by* Webber Pharmaceuticals. 14 Ronson Dr., Rexdale, Ont., 1949-
Annual. Special interest, magazine format, 50 p. Circulation: 25,000
Free.

Summer gazette - *Published by* University of Western Ontario. Centralized Advertising Bureau, University of Western Ontario, London, ont.
Irregular (approximately 10 issues per year). Institutional publication (Universities, schools, etc.). Circulation: 4000

Summer in Canada / *edited by* Mary-Lynn Gravel. - *Published by* Canadian Bureau for International Education. Suite 408, 151 Slater St., Ottawa, Ont. K1P 5H3.
Published in French: Eté au Canada.
Annual. Special interest, 100 p.
Free.

Summer programmes abroad = Programmes d'été à l'étranger - *Published by* Canadian Bureau for International Education. 151 Slater St., Ottawa, Ont. K1P 5H3.
Annual. Directory.

Summer weekend seminar - *Published by* Ontario Federation of Labour. Suite 202, 15 Gervais Dr., Don Mills, Ont.
Annual. Association publication, 25 p.

Sun Life du Canada compagnie d'assurance-vie. Nouvelles / *édité par* Karen Gibson. - *Publié par* Cie d'assurance-vie. Sun Life du Canada. C.P. 6075, Montréal, Qué.
Publié en anglais: Field news.
Bimestriel. Organe interne/officiel, bulletin, 8 p. Tirage: 1200
Envoi gratuit.

Sun life orbit / *edited by* Yvon Desautels. - *Published by* Sun Life Assurance Co. of Canada. P.O. Box 6075, Montreal, Que. H3C 3G5, March 1972-
Former title(s): In orbit; Sun life review.
Published in French: L'orbite.
Irregular (approximately 8 issues per year). House/company organ, magazine format, 16 p. Circulation: 4500
Free. Available to college and university libraries.

Sun life review *See* Sun life orbit

Sunday sun television / *edited by* Peter Worthington and Ed Monteith. - *Published by* Douglas Creighton. The Toronto Sun. 333 King St, E., Toronto, Ont.
Weekly. Special interest, magazine format, Includes advertising.

The Supplement / *edited by* Donna Nebenzahl. - *Published by* Quebec Association for Children with Learning Disabilities. Suite 8, 4820 Van Horne Ave., Montreal, Que. H3W 1J3, 1972-
Irregular (approximately 3 issues per year). Association publication, 46-50 p. Language: English (French). Includes book reviews.
$1.75 per issue (Members $1.25) : $5.00 per year (Members $3.00). Prepayment required.

Supply post / *edited by* T.R.C. (Ken) Kenward. - *Published by* The Northwestern Supply Post Ltd. 3535 W. 28th Ave., Vancouver, B.C. (Subscription address: P.O. Box 6616, Postal Station G, Vancouver, B.C)
Trade publication. Includes advertising.

Supreme Court of Canada reports service - *Published by* Butterworth and Co. (Canada) Ltd. 2265 Midland Ave., Scarborough, Ont. M1P 4S1.
Irregular. Looseleaf format, Includes updating service.
$45.00 per year.

Sur ferron printemps (1973) *Voir* Brèches : analyse/fiction

Sur nos travaux *Voir* Association des routes et transports du Canada. Nouvelles de l'ARTA

Sur une note de musique et d'information. (mai 1974) *Voir* Sur une note d'information

Sur une note d'information - *Publié par* L'Orchestre symphonique de Québec. 745 ouest, boul. St.-Syrille, Québec, Qué. G1S 1T3.
Ancien titre: Sur une note de musique et d'information. (mai 1974)
Mensuel. Bulletin, 8 p. Tirage: 13,000
Envoi gratuit.

Survey of consumer buying intentions / *edited by* L.J. Murphy. - *Published by* The Conference Board in Canada. Suite 1800, 333 River Rd., Ottawa, Ont., August 1975-
Quarterly. Trade publication, 40 p.
$18.00 per issue : $48.00 per year.

Survey of corporate securities *See* Survey of industrials

Survey of industrials - *Published by* The Financial Post. Maclean-Hunter Ltd. 481 University Ave., Toronto, Ont. M5W 1A7, 1926-
Former title(s): Survey of corporate securities.
Annual. Trade publication, 2v., 450 p. Includes advertising, volume index.
$14.95 per year : $9.00 per volume. Special rates offered.

Survivre - *Publié par* Association du diabète de la province de Québec. Suite 240, 934 est, rue Ste-Catherine, Montréal, Qué.
Trimestriel. Publication d'association.
Indexé dans Periodex.
$3.00 par année.

Svenka pressen *See* Swedish press

Svitlo = The Light / *sponsored by* The Order of Saint Basil the Great in Canada ; *edited by* Orest F. Kupranec. - *Published by* The Basilian Press. 286 Lisgar St., Toronto, Ont., May 1938-
Monthly. Ethnic press, magazine format, 40 p. Language: Ukrainian. Circulation: 5000
$.50 per issue : $5.00 per year : $7.00 per volume.

Swedish press *See* Nya Svenka pressen

Swedish press = Svenka pressen / *edited by* Sturee Warmee. - *Published by* Sturee Warmee. 570 Cardero St., Vancouver, B.C., 1932-
Issued twice a month. Ethnic press, newspaper format, 6 p. Language: Swedish and English. Includes book reviews, advertising.
$.25 per issue : $5.00 per year.

Sweep / *edited by* K. Dobbin. - *Published by* Canadian Ski Patrol System. 1439 Begin St., St. Laurent, Que.
Quarterly. Special interest to skiers, newsletter format, 10 p. Language: English and French.
Free.

Swiss Canadian news / *sponsored by* Swiss Club Toronto ; *edited by* Jack Walder. - *Published by* Swiss Print. 64 Racine Rd., Rexdale, Ont. (Subscription address: P.O. Box 823, Postal Station Q, Toronto, Ont)
Monthly. Association publication, magazine format, 29 p. Language: English, German and French.
Available to members only. Controlled circulation.

Swiss Canadian review = Revue Suisse-Canada / *sponsored by* Swiss Federal Government ; *edited by* Hans Aebischer. - *Published by* Consulat General of Switzerland. 1572 McGregor Ave., Montreal, Que., 1973-
Former title(s): Swiss Quebec journal.
Quarterly. Ethnic press, magazine format, 28 p. Language: French, English and German. Includes advertising.
Free.

Swiss Quebec journal *See* Swiss Canadian review

Swiss-Canadian Chamber of Commerce, Inc. Journal / *edited by* H.P. Decker. - *Published by* Swiss-Canadian Chamber of Commerce, Inc. 1572 McGregor Ave., Montreal, Que. H3G 1C4, October 1971-
Quarterly. Trade publication, magazine format, 27 p. Language: English and French.
Circulation: 1150
$.75 per issue.

The Sword - *Published by* Student Union. Notre Dame University of Nelson. P.O. Box 20, Nelson, B.C.
Issued twice a month. Student publication, newspaper format, 20 p. Includes book reviews, film reviews, play reviews, record reviews, advertising.
$2.50 per year. Free to Notre Dame University Students. Special rates offered.

Syesis / *edited by* Robert F. Scagel. - *Published by* British Columbia Provincial Museum. Parliament Bldgs., Victoria, B.C. V8W 1A1, 1968-
Annual. Scholarly publication, journal format, 275 p. Includes book reviews. supplements issued. Circulation: 500
Indexed in North. tit., Hist. abstr.; Amer. hist. and life.
$5.00.

Syladly news (1950-1973) *See* MacMillan Bloedel Building Materials. MBBM news

Syllabus and tuition guide - The Insurance Institute of Canada *See* F.I.I.C. program syllabus

Sylvaply news (1946-1971) *See* MBBM news

Synchro Canada / *edited by* Joyce P. Coffin. - *Published by* Canadian Amateur Synchronized Swimming Association. 18 Harlowe Cres., Ottawa, Ont. K2H 5P1.
Former title(s): Syncronized Canada.
Quarterly. Association publication, magazine format, 35 p. Language: English (French).
Circulation: 450
ISSN 0317-0578 $1.50 per issue : $5.00 per year. Special rates offered to clubs.

Syncronized Canada *See* Synchro Canada

Syndicat des fonctionnaires provinciaux du Québec inc. Journal SFPQ / *édité par* Marcel Ledoux. - *Publié par* Syndicat des fonctionnaires provinciaux du Québec inc. 155 est, boul. Charest, Québec, Qué., mars 1970-
Intermittent (approximativement 10-12 éditions par an). Publication d'association, magazine, 24 p.
Envoi gratuit.

Synoptic / *sponsored by* Business Education Council. Teachers' Association ; *edited by* Betty Graham and Lucy Milne. - *Published by* Alberta Teachers' Association. Barnett House, 11010-142 St., Edmonton, Alta. T5N 2R1.
Quarterly. Association publication, magazine format, 20-40 p.
Indexed in Can. educ. ind.
$5.00 per year. Prepayment required.

T.H.S. newsletter *See* Humane viewpoint

T.P.I.C. news (1923-August 1974) *See* Canadian Institute of Planners. Canadian Institute of Planners forum

TPIC news = Nouvelles I.U.C *See* Canadian Institute of Planners. C.I.P. news

T.S. Eliot newsletter : international survey of Eliot scholarship / *sponsored by* York University ; *edited by* Shyamal Bagchee. - *Published by* Shyamal Bagchee. Department of English, Ross Building, 765 S., York University, Downsview, Ont. M3J 1P3, Spring 1974-
Issued twice a year. Scholarly publication, newsletter format, 20 p. Includes book reviews.
ISSN 0315-1174 $2.00 per issue : $5.00 for 2 volumes (Institutions $6.00) : $5.50 for 2 volumes, foreign (Institutions $7.00).

T.V. - radio supplement : TV service manual / *edited by* C.E. Dobson. - *Published by* Radio College Publications. 461 King St. W., Toronto, Ont. M5V 1K8, 1949-
Monthly. Trade publication, magazine format, 112 p. Includes cumulative index.
$6.40 per issue : $76.80 per year.

T.V. in psychiatry newsletter and progress report (February 1969 to April 1970) *See* TV in psychiatry newsletter and continuing dialogue

TV basics - *Published by* Television Bureau of Canada. Suite 2015, 65 Queen St. W., Toronto, Ont. M5H 2M5.
Annual. Trade publication, pamphlet format, 32 p. Language: English and French.

TV guide / *edited by* Alex. Joseph, (Executive ed.). - *Published by* McMurray Publishing Co. Ltd. 124 Merton St., Toronto, Ont. M4P 1K5 (Subscription address: P.O. Box 189, Postal Station K, Toronto, Ont)
Editions: Montreal-St. Lawrence, Toronto-Lake Ontario, Western Ontario Manitoba-Saskatchewan, Alberta, Eastern B.C., Western B.C.
Weekly. Magazine format, 112 p. Language: English and French. Includes film reviews. Circulation: 973,000
$.30 per issue : $10.00 per year.

TV hebdo / *édité par* Jacques Lina. - *Publié par* Roger Chabot. Les Publications eclair ltée. 9393, ave. Edison, Montréal, Qué. H1J 1T5, 1960-
Hebdomadaire. Intérêt général, magazine, 192 p. Comprend critique de films, publicité. Tirage: 290,000
$.35 le numéro : $16.00 par année : $18.00 par année, E.U. : $20.00 par année, l'europe. Tirage contrôlé. Abonnements payables à l'avance.

TV in psychiatry newsletter and continuing dialogue / *edited by* L. Tyhurst. - *Published by* Instructional Resources Division. Department of Psychiatry. University of British Columbia. Vancouver, B.C., February 1969-
Former title(s): T.V. in psychiatry newsletter and progress report (February 1969 to April 1970)
Quarterly. Institutional publication (Universities, schools, etc.), newsletter format, 25-30 p. supplements issued.
Indexed in Resources in educ.
$2.50 per issue : $10.00 per year. Prepayment required.

TV journal / *edited by* J.C. Metcalfe. - *Published by* The Ottawa Journal. 365 Laurier Ave. W., Ottawa, Ont. K1G 3K6.
Weekly. General interest, magazine format, 47 p. Includes advertising. Circulation: 103,000
Issued as a supplement to the Ottawa Journal.

TV times. Central B.C / *edited by* J.P. Hartnett. - *Published by* Spartan Printing and Advertising Ltd. 466 Reid St., Quesnel, B.C. V2J 2M6, 1967-
Issued every other week. Magazine format, Includes advertising. Circulation: 12,809
$.25 per issue : $9.50 per year.

TV-film filebook / *edited by* Art C. Benson. - *Published by* TV-Film Filebooks. 2533 Gerrard St. E., Scarborough, Ont. M1X 1X3.
Annual. Includes advertising.

TV/times - *Published by* Southam Press. 321 Bloor St. E., Toronto, Ont. M4W 1G9, 1969-
Weekly. Magazine format, Includes advertising.

Ta han kung pao = The Chinese times / *edited by* Regino Yip. - *Published by* The Chinese Freemasons in Canada Ltd. Suite 3, 116 East Pender St., Vancouver, B.C., 1907-
Daily. Ethnic press, newspaper format, 8 p. Language: Chinese. Includes advertising. Circulation: 4500
$.15 per issue : $36.00 per year. Prepayment required.

Take one / *edited by* Peter Lebensold. - *Published by* Peter Lebensold. Unicorn Pub. Corp. P.O. Box 1778, Postal Station B, Montreal, Que. H3B 3I3, September 1966-
Issued every other month. General interest, magazine format, 45 p. Includes book reviews, film reviews, advertising. available in microform. Circulation: 25,000
Indexed in Int. ind. film period., Multi-media rev. ind., Can. ind.
ISSN 0039-9132 $.50 per issue : $5.00 12 issues : $7.50 per year, foreign (airmail extra).

Tallyboard / *edited by* Geraldine V. Lightfoot. - *Published by* Forest Products Accident Prevention Association. P.O. Box 270, North Bay, Ont. P1B 8H2, 1954-
Issued every other month. Association publication, newsletter format, 4 p. Circulation: 1600
Free.

The Tamarack review / *edited by* Robert Weaver. - *Published by* The Tamarack Review Ltd. P.O. Box 159, Postal Station K, Toronto, Ont., 1956-
Quarterly. Special interest, magazine format, 112 p. Includes book reviews, advertising. available in microform. Circulation: 1800
Indexed in Can. ind., M.L.A. int. bib., Annu. bibl. Engl. lang. and lit.
ISSN 0039-9256 $1.95 per issue : $7.50 per year. Prepayment required.

Tape / *edited by* Nancy MacDonald. - *Published by* Nova Scotia Teachers Union. 160 Dutch Village Rd., Halifax, N.S., November 1973-
Monthly. Association publication, newsletter format, 25 p.
$5.00 per year.

La Taupe rouge / *édité par* Michel Mill. - *Publié par* Groupe Marxiste révolutionnaire. 342 est, rue Ontario, Montréal, Qué., novembre 1972-
Intermittent (approximativement 8-9 éditions par an). Publication d'association, journal, 15 p. parution de suppléments. Tirage: 2000
$.25 le numéro : $3.00 par année.

Tax memo - *Published by* Canadian Tax Foundation. 100 University Ave., Toronto, Ont. M5J 1V6, 1954-
Irregular. Association publication, 25-35 p. Subscription included in membership fee
$30.00.

Taylor's industry digest - *Published by* Gladys Taylor. Tall-Taylor Publishing Ltd. 532 Cleveland Cres. S.E., Calgary, Alta. T2G 4A9, 1973-
Monthly. Trade publication. Includes advertising. Circulation: 5000
$3.50 per year : $6.00 for 2 years : $9.00 for 3 years.

Taylor's trade index - *Published by* Gladys Taylor. Tall-Taylor Publishing Ltd. 532 Cleveland Cres. S.E., Calgary, Alta. T2G 4A9, 1971-
Annual. Trade publication. Includes advertising. Circulation: 2900

Tchebec / *edited by* Jack Steeves. - *Published by* Province of Quebec Society for the Protection of Birds, Inc. P.O. Box 43, Postal Station B, Montreal, Que., 1971-
Annual. Association publication, booklet format, 50 p.
$8.00 per issue : $8.00 per year.

The Teacher / *edited by* C.L. Fillmore. - *Published by* Nova Scotia Teachers Union. 106 Dutch Village Rd., Halifax, N.S., 1963-
Former title(s): NSTU newsletter; NSTU teacher; The Bulletin.
Issued every other week. Association publication, newsletter format, 12 p. Includes book reviews, advertising. Circulation: 14,500
$6.00 per year.

Teacher education / *edited by* James M. Paton. - *Published by* Faculty of Education. University of Toronto. 371 Bloor St. W., Toronto, Ont. M5S 2R7, Spring 1968-
Annual. Institutional publication (Universities, schools, etc.), journal format, 84 p.
Circulation: 4500
Indexed in Can. educ. ind.
$2.00.

The Teachers' magazine - *Published by* Provincial Association of Protestant Teachers of Quebec. 245 Hymus Blvd., Pointe Claire, Que. H9R 1G6, 1919-
Annual. Association publication, magazine format,

Teaching atypical students in Alberta / *edited by* Gerard Kysela. - *Published by* Special Education Council. Alberta Teachers' Association. 11010 - 142 St., Edmonton, Alta. T5N 2R1, January 1972-
Annual. Association publication, journal format, 80 p.
Indexed in Can. educ. ind.
ISSN 0315-1808 $1.50 per issue : $7.50 per year. Subscription includes Its newsletter.

Teaching forum / *edited by* J.A. Neill. - *Published by* Senate Committee on Learning and Teaching. University of Guelph. Guelph, Ont., 1971-
Irregular (approximately 2-6 issues per year). Institutional publication (Universities, schools, etc.), newsletter format, 4 p. Includes book reviews. Circulation: 1200
Free.

Teaching mathematics *See* Vector: newsletter/journal

Technical Journal - National Volleyball Coaches Association *See* Canadian Volleyball Association. Volleyball technical journal

Le Technicien - *Publié par* Corporation des techniciens professionnels de la province de Québec. 4152, rue St-Denis, Montréal, Qué. H2W 2M5, 1964-
Bimestriel. Comprend publicité. Tirage: 10,068

Le Technicien forestier (octobre 1972-juillet 1974) *Voir* Foresterie à tout

Techniques municipales : le règlement de lotissement / *édité par* Michel Cliche. - *Publié par* Division du Québec. L'Association canadienne d'urbanisme. 635, rue St-Jean, Québec, Qué. G1R 1P7, juin 1972-
Intermittent (approximativement 10 éditions par an). Publication d'association, bulletin, 5 p.
Tirage: 3000
gratuit.

Technocracy digest / *edited by* Rupert N. Urquhart. - *Published by* Technocracy Inc. 3642 Kingsway, Vancouver, B.C. V5R 5M2, September 1934-
Quarterly. Special interest, magazine format, 24 p.
$.50 per issue : $2.00 per year.

Techno-information / *édité par* Claude Montgrain. - *Publié par* La Corporation professionnelle des technologistes médicaux de Québec. 182 est, boul. St-Joseph, Montréal, Qué.
Bimestriel. Comprend publicité. Tirage: 3178
$5.00 par année : $10.00 par année, l'étranger.

Teeoff / *edited by* Jack Marks. - *Published by* Sport Media Inc. 4969A Yonge St., Willowdale, Ont. M2N 5N6, May 1974-
Issued twice a month April-September, every other month October-April. Special interest, newspaper format, 16 p. Circulation: 25,000
$.50 per issue : $4.00 per year : $5.00 per year, foreign. Controlled circulation. Special rates offered.

Teiresias : a review and continuing bibliography of Boiotian studies / *edited by* John M. Fossey and Albert Schachter. - *Published by* Department of Classics. McGill University. P.O. Box 6070, Postal Station A, Montreal, Que. H3C 3G1, 1971-
Issued twice a year. Bibliography, Bibliography, 30 p. supplements issued. Circulation: 250
$7.50 per year. Free to individuals.

Tekawennake : Six Nations - new credit reporter / *edited by* Carolyn Beaver. - *Published by* Carolyn Beaver. R.R. 6, Hagersville, Ont. N0A 1H0, 1968-
Issued twice a month. Special interest, newspaper format, 24 p. Includes book reviews, advertising, available in microform. Circulation: 750
$.40 per issue : $8.80 per year. Prepayment required.

Tel que nous le pensons et avons envie de le dire / *édité par* Michelle Asselin et Marie Boulanger. - *Publié par* Productions Bourgeons. 1300, ave 8ème, Québec, Qué. G1J 2N1, 1975-
Intermittent (approximativement 2 éditions par an). Intérêt général, revue, 100 p. Tirage: 1000
$2.10 le volume.

The Telegram / *edited by* Vladimir Valenta. - *Published by* Vladimir Valenta. P.O. Box 636, Edmonton, Alta. T5J 2K8, January 1969-
Issued every other month. Ethnic press, newspaper format, 12 p. Language: Czech and Slovak. Includes book reviews. Circulation: 1000
$1.00 per issue : $6.00 per year : $8.00, per year, overseas air mail.

Telenation / *edited by* K.W. Brooker. - *Published by* Canadian Broadcasting League. P.O. Box 1504, Ottawa, Ont. K1P 5R5, January 1973-
Irregular (approximately 10-11 issues per year). Newsletter format, 4-6 p.
ISSN 0315-8989 $8.00 per year. Controlled circulation.

Telephone echo / *edited by* Ken Cherney. - *Published by* Manitoba Telephone System. Department 70-B, 489 Empress St., Winnipeg, Man. R3C 0A2., May 1921-
Issued twice a month. House/company organ, newsletter format, 4 p. Circulation: 6000
Free. Controlled circulation.

Le Téléphone rouge / *édité par* Pierre Lemelin. - *Publié par* Editions le téléphone rouge inc. Chambre 602, 71, St. Pierre, Québec, Qué. G1K 4A4, 1972-
Annuel. Magazine, Comprend publicité. Tirage: 171,514

Telephone talk (1910-1960) *See* B.C. Tel news

Télé-presse / *edited by* Roger Lemelin. - *Published by* La Presse ltée. 7, rue St-Jacques, Montréal, Qué. H2Y 1K9.
Hebdomadaire. Magazine, Includes publicité.

Télé-scout / *edited by* Pierre D. Gagnon. - *Published by* Pierre D. Gagnon. La Cordée. 3057, rue Lacombe, Montréal, Qué. H3T 1L5, 1969-
Bimestriel. Magazine, Includes publicité.
$2.00 par année (Membres $1.00).

Telesis / *edited by* Dave Hamilton. - *Published by* Bell-Northern Research. P.O. Box 3511, Postal Station C, Ottawa, Ont. K1Y 4H7, 1967-
Irregular (approximately 4 issues per year). House/company organ, magazine format, 32 p. Language: English and French. Includes volume index.
Indexed in Eng. ind.
Free.

The Teller / *edited by* Helen C. Major. - *Published by* Credit Union Federation of Alberta Limited. 1400 - 1st St. S.W., Calgary, Alta. T2R 0V8, February 1968-
Quarterly. Association publication, newsletter format, 12 p. Includes advertising. Circulation: 1700
$2.00 per year. Free to specific groups. Controlled circulation.

Tema / *sponsored by* Saskatchewan Teachers of Ukrainian ; *edited by* Sonia V. Cipywnyk. - *Published by* Saskatchewan Teachers' Federation. 2317 Arlington Ave., Saskatoon, Sask., December 1968-
Quarterly. Association publication, magazine format, 30-35 p. Language: English and Ukrainian. Includes book reviews, film reviews, record reviews. Circulation: 200-225
Indexed in Can. educ. ind.
Subscription included in membership fee: $5.00, full member, $2.50 associate member. Controlled circulation.

The Temperance advocate (June 1928 to December 1955) *See* Concerns

La Terre de chez nous / *édité par* Pierre Courteau. - *Publié par* Jean Marc Kirouac. Union des producteurs agricols. 515, ave Viger, Montréal, Qué. H2L 2P2, 1929-
Hebdomadaire. Publication d'association, journal, 20 p. Comprend critique de livres, critique de films, critique de pièces de théâtre, publicité.Aussi sous microform. parution de suppléments. Tirage: 58,310
$5.00 par année : $8.00 2 ans : $10.00 3 ans. Tirage contrôlé.

Il Tevere - *Published by* Augusto Serafini. 1951 Eglinton Ave. W., Toronto, Ont. M5E 2J7, 1972-
Weekly. Ethnic press. Language: Italian. Includes advertising. Circulation: 1500
$.15 per issue.

Teviskes ziburiai = The Lights of homeland / *edited by* P. Gaida. - *Published by* Lithuanian Canadian R.C. Cultural Society Inc. "Ziburiai". 2185 Stavebank Rd., Mississauga, Ont. L5C 1T3, December 1949-
Weekly. Ethnic press, newspaper format, 8 or 10 p. Language: Lithuanian. Includes book reviews, advertising. available in microform. Circulation: 6329
$.25 per issue : $10.00 per year. Prepayment required.

Texaco tempo / *edited by* Robert Cameron. - *Published by* Texaco Canada Ltd. 90 Wynford Dr., Don Mills, Ont.
Quarterly. House/company organ, magazine format, 20 p. Language: English and French. Circulation: 4000

Textile apparel review - *Published by* Textile/Apparel Department. Canadian Imperial Bank of Commerce. 1115 Dorchester W., Montreal, Que., Spring 1974-
Quarterly. House/company organ, newsletter format, 4 p. Language: English and French. Free.

Thai news-letter / *edited by* Royal Thai Embassy, Ottawa. - *Published by* Royal Thai Embassy. Suite 704, 85 Range Rd., Ottawa, Ont. K1N 8J6., 1969-
Irregular. Newsletter format, 3-5 p. Language: English and French ; summaries: English and French.
Free.

The / *edited by* Paddy Gardener. - *Published by* Bell-Northern Research. P.O. Box 3511, Postal Station C, Ottawa, Ont. K1Y 4H7, 1969-
Irregular (approximately 2 issues per year). House/company organ, magazine format, 50 p.

The Alliancer *See* Zwiazkowiec

The Canadian courier *See* Corriere Canadese

The Canadian farmer *See* Kanadiysky farmer

The Canadian srbobran *See* Kanadski srbobran

The Chinese times *See* Ta han kung pao

The Christian herald *See* Khrystiansky visnyk

The Insurance broker = Le Courtier d'assurances *Voir* Le Courtier d'assurance

The Light *See* Svitlo

The Light almanac *See* Kalendar svitla

The Lights of homeland *See* Teviskes ziburiai

The New republic *See* Hsin min kuo

The Norseman *See* Norrona

The Orthodox Church calendar *See* Pravoslavnyi tserkovnyi kalendar'

The Redeemer's voice *See* Holos spasytels

The Times *See* Czas

The voice of Atlantic Canada's fishing and marine industry *See* Sou'wester

The Word of God *See* Bozja beseda

Thémis (1951-1965) *Voir* La Revue juridique thémis de l'Université de Montréal

Theosphere: journal de faculté / *édité par* Gilles Baril. - *Publié par* Agetus (association des étudiants). Université de théologie. Sherbrooke, Qué., septembre 1972-
Hebdomadaire. Publication des anciens étudiants, journal, 10 p.

The Thermogram - *Published by* Canadian Union of Operating Engineers. P.O. Box 698, Windsor, Ont., January 1961-
Former title(s): Canadian power plant worker (1961-1975)
Quarterly. Association publication, newsletter format, 4 p. Includes book reviews.
Circulation: 2000
Controlled circulation.

Thesa journal / *sponsored by* Teachers of Home Economics Specialists Association. - *Published by* British Columbia Teachers' Federation. 105-2235 Burrard St., Vancouver, B.C., June 1963-
Annual. Association publication, magazine format, 40-75 p.
Indexed in Can. educ. ind.
$5.00.

Thèses canadiennes en science politique *See* Theses in Canadian political studies

Theses in Canadian political studies = Thèses canadiennes en science politique - *Published by* Canadian Political Science Association. c/o University of Ottawa, 30 Stewart St., Ottawa, Ont. K1N 6N5., 1970-
Bi-annual. Abstracts/summaries. Language: English and French. Includes volume index, updating service.
$3.50 (1st two updatings $2.50; last updating $3.00).

This is Algoma *See* Visit Algoma

This is Calgary (1969-1971) *See* Calgary magazine

This is Ontario - *Published by* Art Howard and John Whytall. Suite 17, 1262 Don Mills Rd., Don Mills, Ont. M3B 2W7, 1972-
Irregular (approximately 4 issues per year). Magazine format, Includes advertising.
Circulation: 113,000
Free.

This magazine : education, culture, politics / *edited by* D. Drache (and others). - *Published by* The Red Maple Publishing Co. Ltd. 3 Church St., Toronto, Ont., 1966-
Former title(s): This magazine is about schools (1966-1973)
Issued every other month. General interest, magazine format, 36 p. Includes book reviews, advertising. Circulation: 9000
Indexed in Alt. press ind., Can. educ. ind.
$1.00 per issue : $6.00 per year : $7.50 per year, foreign. Prepayment required.

This magazine is about schools (1966-1973) *See* This magazine : education, culture, politics

This month / *edited by* D.L. Wenham. - *Published by* Registered Psychiatric Nurses Association of British Columbia. 7790 Edmonds St., Burnaby, B.C. V3N 1B8, January 1969-
Monthly. Association publication, newsletter format, 24 p.
Available to members and complimentary list only.

This week - *Published by* Davidson Advertising Ltd. Suite 203, 1062 Austin Ave., Coquitlam, B.C. V3K 3P3, 1971-
Weekly. Magazine format, Includes advertising. Circulation: 225,000
$5.00 per year.

This week in Halifax *See* Metro guide

This week times two / *edited by* Carol Irving. - *Published by* Information Office. Carleton University. Room 605, Administration office, Carleton University, Colonel By Dr., Ottawa, Ont. K1S 5B6., August 1971-
Issued twice a week. Institutional publication (Universities, schools, etc.), newspaper format, 4 p. Includes book reviews. Circulation: 5000
ISSN 0315-3614 Free : $3.00 per year, 1st class mail.

3¢ pulp : famous magazine - *Published by* Pulp Press. P.O. Box 48806, Station Bentall, Vancouver, B.C., 1972-
Issued twice a month. Special interest, magazine format, 4 p. Includes book reviews, film reviews. supplements issued. Circulation: 1100
$.03 per issue : $10.00 per year. Free to bookstores.

The Three link news / *edited by* J. Main. - *Published by* Grand Lodge of British Columbia. Independent Order of Odd Fellows. 1433 W., 8th Ave., Vancouver, B.C. V6H 1C9.
Issued every other month. Magazine format, 24 p. Circulation: 825
$2.00 per year.

3 M info / *edited by* Dan Coxon. - *Published by* Public Relations Dept. 3 M Canada Limited. P.O. Box 5757,London, Ont. N6a 4T1, February 1974-
House/company organ, 4 p. Language: English and French. Circulation: 2150
Free. Controlled circulation

Three M today (Spring 1952-December 1973) *See* 3 M info

The Thumper *See* Rabbits in Canada

Thunder Bay guest - *Published by* Donald F. McQuat. 837 Fort William Rd., Thunder Bay, Ont., 1963-
Irregular (approximately 17 issues per year). Magazine format, Includes advertising. Circulation: 12,083

Thunder Bay guide - *Published by* Donald F. McQuat. 837 Fort William Rd., Thunder Bay, Ont., 1965-
Weekly. Magazine format, Includes advertising. Circulation: 13,740
$10.00 per year.

Thursday (1969-1973) *See* New Thursday

Thursday's child / *edited by* Shirley Henderson. - *Published by* Calgary Association for the Mentally Retarded. Suite 402, 330 - 9th Ave. S.W., Calgary, Alta. T2P 1K7.
Monthly. Association publication, newsletter format, 20 p. Circulation: 400
Free. Controlled circulation.

Tides of change / *edited by* V. Hill. - *Published by* Prince Rupert Fishermen's Co-operative Association. P.O. Box 520, Prince Rupert, B.C. V8J 3R7.
Annual. House/company organ, 279 p.
$3.00 per issue.

Tidings / *sponsored by* United Baptist Woman's Missionary Union of the Atlantic Provinces ; *edited by* Mrs. Harry Crouse. - *Published by* Kentville Publishing Co. Ltd. Kentville, Kings Co., N.S. (Subscription address: c/o Mrs. D.M. Spinney, P.O. Box 1000, R.R. 1, Yarmouth, N.S)
Monthly except July. Church publication, magazine format, 16 p. Circulation: 7000
$.25 per issue : $1.50 per year.

The Tikinagan (1968-1969) *See* The Bookmark

Timely station topics (1943-1950) *See* Gulf Canada dealer news

The Times / *edited by* Corinne Noonan. - *Published by* Saint Mary's University. Halifax, N.S.
Issued 3 times a year. Institutional publication (Universities, schools, etc.), newspaper format, Free.

Titles in the humanities and social sciences - University of Windsor. Library (1966-1974) *See* University of Windsor. Library. List of serials held in the University of Windsor Library

Titmouse review / *edited by* Avron and Linda Hoffman. - *Published by* Titmouse Review. 720 W. 19th Ave., Vancouver, B.C., Summer 1972-
Irregular. Special interest, magazine format, 48-64 p. Circulation: 500
$1.00 per issue (Institutions $1.75) ; $3.00 per year (Institutions $5.00).

Today's generation / *sponsored by* Generation - Mailbag ; *edited by* Jim Smith. - *Published by* Douglas B. Love. 62 Shaftesbury Ave., Toronto, Ont. M4T 1A4.
Former title(s): Canadian high news.
Irregular (approximately 10 issues per year). Magazine format, 48 p. Includes film reviews, record reviews, advertising. Circulation: 140,000
$.35 per issue : $3.00 per year. Free to students. Controlled circulation. Special rates offered.

Toike oike / *edited by* Richard Pearse. - *Published by* Undergraduate Engineering Society. University of Toronto. 2nd floor, Engineering Annex, University of Toronto, Toronto, Ont. M5S 1A4, 1906-
Irregular (approximately 9 issues per year). Student publication. Includes advertising. Circulation: 19,389

Tom Graham's electronic workshop / *edited by* J.R. 'Tom' Graham. - *Published by* J.R. 'Tom' Graham. Walgram Publishing Ltd. 18 Cedarbank Cres, Don Mills, Ont.
Irregular (approximately 10 issues per year). Includes advertising. Circulation: 6271

Tom Thomson Memorial Gallery and Museum of Fine Art. Bulletin - *Published by* Tom Thomson Memorial Gallery and Museum of Fine Art. P.O. Box 312, 840 1st Ave. W., Owen Sound, Ont. N4K 5P5.
Monthly. House/company organ, newsletter format, 3 p. Circulation: 425
Free.

Top titles (1972-1973) *See* The Bookmark

The Torch / *edited by* National CGIT Committee. - *Published by* National Committee. Canadian Girls in Training. Rm. 201, 40 St. Clair Ave. E., Toronto, Ont. M4T 1M9, 1924-
Issued twice a year. House/company organ, magazine format, 32 p. Includes book reviews, film reviews.
$1.25 per year. Controlled circulation. Special rates offered.

The Torch and trumpet (1935-1950) *See* The Canadian Gideon

Torch runner / *edited by* Tom Swan. - *Published by* Christian Service Brigade. 1254 Plains Rd. E., Burlington, Ont. L7S 1W6, 1968-
Quarterly. Association publication, newspaper format, 16 p.
ISSN 0316-2931

Toronto Area Library Technicians Association. TALTA newsletter / *edited by* S. Brockhurst. - *Published by* Toronto Area Library Technicians Association. 162 Pandora Circle, Scarborough, Ont. M1H 1W1, January 1975-
Irregular (approximately 5 issues per year). Association publication, newsletter format, 5 p. Circulation: 150
$2.00 per year.

Toronto calendar magazine / *edited by* Kerry Dean. - *Published by* Calendar Magazines Ltd. 65 Front St. E., Toronto, Ont. M5E 1B6, April 1969-
Irregular (approximately 16 issues per year). Calendar of events, magazine format, 80 p. Includes film reviews, play reviews, advertising. Circulation: 173,291
$1.00 per issue : $16.00 per year. Controlled circulation.

Toronto club news / *edited by* Jerry Tutunjian. - *Published by* Toronto Club. 2 Carlton St., Toronto, Ont. M5B 1K4, January 1973-
Issued every other month. Association publication, newsletter format, 6 p.
Circulation: 160,000
Free.

Toronto Colostomy Association. T.C.A. newsletter / *edited by* Ron Maitland. - *Published by* Colostomy Association of Toronto and District. P.O. Box 5624, Terminal A, Toronto, Ont. M5W 1N8.
Monthly. Association publication, newsletter format, 10 p. Circulation: 600
Free to members.

Toronto Construction Association. TCA news - *Published by* Toronto Construction Association. Construction Centre, 1 Sparks Ave., Willowdale, Ont. M2H 2W1.
Monthly. Association publication, newsletter format, 12 p. Includes advertising, updating service.
Free to members. Controlled circulation.

The Toronto Construction Association Membership roster *See* Who's who in Toronto construction

Toronto Dominion Bank. TD bank notes / *edited by* Cassandra Sanders. - *Published by* Toronto Dominion Bank. P.O. Box 1, Toronto Dominion Centre, Toronto, Ont. M5K 1A2.
Monthly. House/company organ, tabloid format, 8 p. Circulation: 16,350

Toronto Field Naturalists Club. Toronto Field Naturalists Club newsletter / *edited by* Elmer Talvila. - *Published by* Toronto Field Naturalists' Club. 1164 Broadview Ave., Toronto, Ont. M4K 2S5.
Monthly, October to May. Association publication, newsletter format, 16 p. Includes book reviews.
$7.00 per year (Family membership $10.00). Subscription included in membership fee.

Toronto Film Society. Newsletter / *edited by* Ronald R. Anger. - *Published by* Toronto Film Society. 128 Glen Rd., Toronto, Ont. M4W 2W3, 1956-
Irregular (approximately 3 issues per year). Association publication, newsletter format, 10 p. Includes book reviews, film reviews. Subscription included in membership. Exchanges made with other film periodicals. Controlled circulation.

Toronto hemo comm / *edited by* F.B. Bott. - *Published by* Toronto Auxiliary. Canadian Hemophilia Society. Suite 508, 30 Bloor St. W., Toronto, Ont. M4W 1A2.
Quarterly. Association publication, newsletter format, 6 p.
Free.

Toronto homes magazine (1970-1974) *See* Ontario homes buyers guide to private sales

Toronto insurance directory / *edited by* Kieran Simpson. - *Published by* University of Toronto Press. 5201 Dufferin St., Downsview, Ont. M3H 5T8, 1927-
Annual. Directory. Includes advertising.
Circulation: 2567
$4.50 per year.

Toronto Jewish voice *See* Canadian Jewish chronicle review

Toronto legal directory / *edited by* Kieran Simpson. - *Published by* University of Toronto Press. 5201 Dufferin St., Downsview, Ont. M3H 5T8, 1925-
Annual. Directory. Includes advertising.
Circulation: 10,960
$6.30 per year.

Toronto life / *edited by* Alexander Ross. - *Published by* Michael de Pencier. Key Publishers Ltd. 59 Front St. E., Toronto, Ont.
Monthly. General interest, magazine format, 104 p. Includes film reviews, play reviews, advertising. Circulation: 40,000
$.75 per issue : $7.00 per year. Special rates offered.

The Toronto Life restaurant and gourmet guide / *edited by* Alexander Ross. - *Published by* Michael de Pencier. Key Publishers Ltd. 59 Front St. E., Toronto, Ont. M5E 1B3, 1974-
Quarterly. Magazine format, Includes advertising. Circulation: 10,000
$.50 per issue.

Toronto life travel guide / *edited by* Alexander Ross. - *Published by* Michael de Pencier. Key Publishers Ltd. 59 Front St. E., Toronto, Ont. M5E 1B3, 1975-
Quarterly. Magazine format, Includes advertising.

Toronto month magazine / *edited by* Dawn Osborne. - *Published by* Calendar Magazines Ltd. 65 Front St. E., Toronto, Ont. M5E 1B6, November 1973-
Monthly. Calendar of events, magazine format, 48 p. Includes film reviews, play reviews, advertising. Circulation: 150,000
$.75 per issue : $9.00 per year. Controlled circulation.

Toronto office (1969-March 1975) *See* Canadian office

Toronto office redbook *See* Canadian office redbook

Toronto Public Libraries. Toronto Boys and Girls House. Subscription reviews - *Published by* Boys and Girls Services. Toronto Public Library. 40 St. George St., Toronto, Ont. M5S 2E4.
Quarterly. Book reviews, sheets, 50 p. Includes book reviews.
$20.00 per year. Prepayment required.

Toronto Public Library. TPL News - *Published by* Toronto Public Library Board. 40 Orchard View Blvd., Toronto, Ont. M4R 1B9.
Irregular (approximately 10 issues per year). Institutional publication (Universities, schools, etc.), newsletter format, 4 p.
ISSN 0039-8470 Free.

Toronto real estate / *edited by* Wes Lore. - *Published by* Toronto Real Estate Board. 1883 Yonge St., Toronto, Ont. M4S 1Y7.
Weekly. Trade publication, newspaper format, 48 p. Circulation: 95,000
Free. Controlled circulation.

Toronto Stock Exchange. Daily record sheet / *edited by* David Marcus-Roland. - *Published by* Toronto Stock Exchange. 234 Bay St., Toronto, Ont. M5J 1R1.
Daily. Daily market quotations, 8 p.
$112.08 per year : $133.08 per year, foreign.

Toronto Stock Exchange. Indices - *Published by* Toronto Stock Exchange. 234 Bay St., Toronto, Ont. M5L 1H2, 1934-
Annual. House/company organ, newspaper format, 100 p. supplements issued.
$2.00.

Toronto Stock Exchange. Members manual - *Published by* Toronto Stock Exchange. 234 Bay St., Toronto, Ont. M5J 1R1.
Irregular. House/company organ. Includes updating service.
$20.00 per volume : $5.00 updating service.

Toronto Stock Exchange. Notice to members - *Published by* Toronto Stock Exchange. 234 Bay St., Toronto, Ont. M5J 1R1.
Irregular (approximately 25-40 issues per year). Special interest, 1 p. Circulation: 100
Controlled circulation.

Toronto Stock Exchange. Review / *edited by* Patricia Bustine. - *Published by* Toronto Stock Exchange. 234 Bay St., Toronto, Ont. M5J 1R1.
Monthly. Special interest, magazine format, 70 p.
Indexed in Can. B.P.I.
$1.00 per issue : $10.00 per year.

Toronto Stock Exchange. Weekly summary / *edited by* Public Information Section. Research and Market Development Department. - *Published by* Toronto Stock Exchange. 234 Bay St., Toronto, Ont. M5J 1R1.
Weekly. Stock market summary, newsletter format, 4 p. Language: English and French.
$17.00 per year : $17.50 per year, U.S. : $20.00 per year, foreign.

Toronto symphony news / *edited by* Andrea Alexander. - *Published by* Toronto Symphony Women's Committee. 215 Victoria St., Toronto, Ont. M5B 1V1.
Issued every other month. Special interest, pamphlet format,

Toronto Typographical Union. Bulletin / *edited by* Balfour MacKenzie. - *Published by* Typographical Union (Toronto) No. 91. 430 King St. W., Toronto, Ont. M5V 1L5.
Monthly. Association publication, newsletter format, 4 p.
Free to members.

Toronto Vegetarian Association. Newsletter / *edited by* Barbara Jackson. - *Published by* Toronto Vegetarian Association. 28 Walker Ave., Toronto, Ont. M4V 1G2, 1954-
Former title(s): Toronto vegetarian newsletter.
Issued every other month. Association publication, newsletter format, 6 p.
Circulation: 350
$.50 per issue : $3.00 per year.

Toronto vegetarian newsletter *See* Toronto Vegetarian Association. Newsletter

Toronto-Courier / *edited by* Bernd Laengin. - *Published by* Courier Press Ltd. Suite 304, 455 Spadina Ave., Toronto, Ont. M5S 2G9, 1907-
Weekly. Ethnic press, newspaper format, 24 p.
Language: German. available in microform.
Circulation: 10,038
$.25 per issue : $9.00 per year : $12.00 per year, foreign. Prepayment required.

The Toronto-Dominion Bank chartbook (1959-1968) *See* Canada's business climate

Torontoer Zeitung / *edited by* Rosel Greinwald. - *Published by* Erich O. Reprich. P.O. Box 278, Pickering, Ont. L1V 2R4, 1952-
Weekly. Ethnic press, newspaper format, 16 p.
Language: German.
$7.50 per year : $11.50 per year, foreign.

Touring and travel / *edited by* Allan E. McPhee. - *Published by* Groupmark Canada Limited. 170 University Ave., Toronto, Ont. M5H 3B3, May 1975-
Former title(s): Driving (1972-1974) Track and traffic.
Issued 8 times a year. Special interest, magazine format, 48 p. Circulation: 100,000
ISSN 0318-4390 $1.00 per issue : $6.00 per year : $6.50 per year, foreign. Controlled circulation.

Tourist guide = Guide touristique / *edited by* Lucien Fontaine. - *Published by* Editour Ltée/Ltd. 300 Arran Ave., Saint-Lambert, Que. J4R 1K5.
Annual. Magazine format, Language: English and French. Includes advertising. Circulation: 50,000
$2.50 per year.

Tourist talk / *edited by* J.P. Hamilton and J. Plemel. - *Published by* Saskatchewan Tourist Association. P.O. Box 1910, Saskatoon, Sask. S7K 3S5, June 1975-
Monthly. Special interest, newsletter format, 8 p. Circulation: 1000
Free.

Tout sur la danse / *édité par* Michel Côté. - *Publié par* Fédération des loisirs-danse du Québec. 1052 ouest, rue Laurier, Montréal, Qué. H2V 2K8.
Mensuel. Publication d'association, bulletin, 6 p. Tirage: 1000
$5.00.

The Tower / *edited by* John Ferns (chairman of the editorial board). - *Published by* Tower Poetry Society Press. c/o Tower Poetry Society, School of Adult Education, McMaster University, Hamilton, Ont., 1952-
Issued twice a year. Association publication, magazine format, 40 p.
$1.25 per issue : $2.50 per year. Controlled circulation. Special rates offered.

Towline *See* Alberta towline

Town and country librarian / *edited by* Fran Whiteway. - *Published by* Middlesex County Library Branch. Arva, Ontario. N0M 1C0, November 1964-
Issued three times a year. House/company organ, newsletter format, 12 p.
Free.

Town talk about Toronto / *edited by* Eanswythe Flynn. - *Published by* Mrs. G.W. Flynn. 89 Oriole Parkway, Toronto, Ont. M5P 2G7, 1960-
Quarterly. General interest, magazine format, 16-20 p. Includes book reviews, advertising.
$1.50 per year : $2.00 per year, foreign.
Controlled circulation.

Towns and cities magazine / *edited by* Keith Pearson. - *Published by* René Lejeune. Sentinel Publishing Co. 27 Centrale St., La Salle, Que. H8R 3K2, 1954-
Quarterly. Includes advertising. Circulation: 2868
$10.00 (Municipal executives $5.00).

Townships sun / *sponsored by* Eastern Townships Citizens Association ; *edited by* Robert Dawson. - *Published by* Russell Pocock. 105 Gordon, Sherbrooke, Qué, 1974-
Monthly. Newspaper format, 16 p. Includes book reviews, record reviews, advertising.
Circulation: 18,500
$3.00 per year. Free.

Toxicomanies / *édité par* Rosaire Gingras. - *Publié par* Rénald Chabot, Optat l'alcoolisme. L'Office de la prévention de l'alcoolisme et des autres toxicomanies. 969, route de l'Église, Québec, Qué., janvier 1968-
Trimestriel. Publication d'association, revue, 90 p. Langue(s): français. Tirage: 2000
Indexé dans Periodex, RADAR.
$3.00 le numero : $10.00 par année.

Toxophilus (March 1959-June/July 1963) *See* The Canadian archer

Toys and games / *edited by* William Schabas. - *Published by* Gwen Dempsey. Campbell-Wells Publishing Co. Ltd. Suite 401, 542 Mount Pleasant Rd., Toronto, Ont. M4S 2M7, 1973-
Issued every other month. Includes advertising. Circulation: 6604

Tracings (Vol. 1 1967-1968-Vol. 3 1969-1968) *See* University of Windsor. Main Library. Office of the University Librarian. News and views

Track and traffic *See* Touring and travel

Tractor farming (1918-1939) *See* Canadian farming

Trade and commerce : a monthly report on western industry / *edited by* Robert Tyre. - *Published by* Sanford Evans Publishing Ltd. P.O. Box 6900, 1077 St. James St., Winnipeg, Man. R3C 3R1, 1906-
Monthly. Trade publication, magazine format, Circulation: 9404
Indexed in P.A.I.S., Can. B.P.I., North. tit.
$3.00 per issue : $9.00 per year : $25.00 per year, foreign. Controlled circulation.

Trade news letter / *edited by* The Canadian German Chamber of Industry and Commerce Inc. - *Published by* Montreal Office. Canadian German Chamber of Industry and Commerce Inc. Suite 1110, 2015 Peel St., Montreal, Que. H3A 1T8, 1971-
German edition has title : Nachrichten aus Kanada.
Monthly. Book format, 15 p.
$25.00 per year.

The Trader *See* Canadian jeweller : the jewellery and giftware magazine

Trader's post / *edited by* Doug Blair. - *Published by* Toronto Junior Board of Trade. 11 Adelaide St. W., Toronto, Ont.
Quarterly. Association publication, magazine format, 16-24 p. Includes advertising.
$1.00 per issue : $5.00 per year. Controlled circulation. Prepayment required.

Tradewinds from Japan (June 1970-February 1975) *See* JETRO communique

Traffic notes / *edited by* T.J. McTague. - *Published by* The Canadian Industrial Traffic League. Suite 708, 67 Yonge St., Toronto, Ont. M5E 1S8, January 1926-
Weekly. Association publication, newsletter format, 10 p. Language: English (French). Includes book reviews, volume index, cumulative index. Circulation: 1200
Free to members and to institutions and associations in the transportation field. Controlled circulation.

Trail and landscape / *edited by* Anne Hanes. - *Published by* Ottawa Field Naturalists' Club. P.O. Box 3264, Postal Station C, Ottawa, Ont. K1Y 4J5, March 1967-
Issued 5 times a year. Association publication, magazine format, 28 p. Includes volume index. Circulation: 850
ISSN 0041-0748 $5.00 per year. Prepayment required.

Trail blazers - *Published by* Early Childhood Education Council. Alberta Teachers' Association. 11010-142 St., Edmonton, Alta., 1966-
Former title(s): Newsletter - Early Childhood Education Council.
Irregular (approximately 6-8 issues per year). Association publication, newsletter format, 6 p. Circulation: 700
Subscription included in membership fee $7.00 per year. Controlled circulation.

Trail Riders of the Canadian Rockies. The Bulletin / *edited by* Kathie Orr. - *Published by* Trail Riders of the Canadian Rockies. P.O. Box 6742, Postal Station D, Calgary, Alta. T2P 2E6.
Irregular (approximately 1 issue per year). Association publication, newsletter format, 36 p. Circulation: 450
$1.00 per volume. Prepayment required.

Trailblazer / *edited by* Tom Gibbs. - *Published by* Mountain Region. Canadian Youth Hostels Association. 455 12th St. N.W., Calgary, Alta. T2N 1Y9.
Quarterly. Newsletter format, 8 p.
Subscription included in membership fee.

The Trailsman / *edited by* H.C. Northcott. - *Published by* New Brunswick Provincial Council. Boy Scouts of Canada. 151 King St. E., Saint John, N.B. E2L 1G9, 1950-
Issued every other month. Association publication, newsletter format, 6 p. Circulation: 1750
Free. Controlled circulation.

Trainmen news in Canada (1959-1969) *See* United Transportation Union. UTU news Canada

Le Trait d'union (avril 1971 - décembre 1974) *Voir* L'Assureur-vie du Québec

Trait d'union : revue de la Communauté Melkite / *édité par* Lily Sabella, Noha Bitar et Gérard Rehban. - *Publié par* Georges Coriaty. Communauté Melkite du Canada. 329, rue Viger, Montréal, Qué.(adresse d'abonnement: C.P. 578, Succursale C, Montréal, Qué. H2L 4K4) mars 1964-
Trimestriel. Publication d'association, magazine, 36 p. Langue(s): français et anglais. Comprend critique de livres, publicité.
$5.00 par année : $10.00 par année, l'étranger. Tarifs spéciaux disponibles. Abonnements payables à l'avance.

The Tranquillian (August 1921-July 1937) *See* Your health

Transactions of the Canadian Ophthamological Society (1949, 1954-1966) *See* Canadian journal of ophthalmology

Transcript (September 1974-April 1975) *See* FYI (For your information)

Transcultural psychiatric research review / *edited by* E.D. Wittkower. - *Published by* McGill-Queen's University Press. 1020 Pine Ave. W., Montreal, Que. H3A 1A2 (Subscription address: 1266 Pine Ave. W., Montreal, Que. H3G 1A8) March 1956-
Former title(s): Transcultural research in mental health problems (Nos. 1-13, May 1956 to October 1962)
Issued twice a year. Scholarly publication, journal format, 100 p. Includes book reviews. available in microform. Circulation: 600
ISSN 0041-1108 $6.00 per issue : $12.00 per year. Prepayment required.

Transcultural research in mental health problems (Nos. 1-13, May 1956 to October 1962) *See* Transcultural psychiatric research review

Transit Canada magazine / *edited by* C.H. Prentice. - *Published by* Transit Canada. P.O. Box 6103, Postal Station A, Toronto, Ont., November 1965-
Former title(s): Canadian Coach Magazine (October 1965-December 1974)
Issued every other month. Special interest, magazine format, 24 p. Includes volume index. available in microform.
ISSN 0045-4559 $2.00 per issue : $10.00 per year : $12.00 per year, foreign. Prepayment required.

Transit fact book / *edited by* H.E. Brown. - *Published by* Canadian Urban Transit Association. 1138 Bathurst St., Toronto, Ont. M5R 3H2, September 1969-
Annual. Association publication, pamphlet format, 24 p. Includes updating service. Circulation: 250
ISSN 0082-5913 $2.50. Free to members. Controlled circulation.

Transit topics / *edited by* H.E. Brown. - *Published by* Canadian Urban Transit Association. 1138 Bathurst St., Toronto, Ont. M5H 3H2, January 1955-
Monthly. Association publication, newsletter format, 14-15 p. Circulation: 300-350
Free to members.

Transition - *Published by* Transition Society. 136 Avenue F, South, Saskatoon, Sask.
Quarterly.
$.75 per issue : $6.00 per year. Free to federal penetentiary inmates and ex-inmates.

Transition / *edited by* Bert Prime. - *Published by* The Vanier Institute of the Family. Suite 207, 151 Slater St., Ottawa, Ont. K1P 5H3.
Irregular (approximately 4 issues per year). Institutional publication (Universities, schools, etc.), newsletter format, 6 p. Language: English and French. Includes book reviews, film reviews, play reviews. Circulation: 14,000
Free.

Transition 3 / *édité par* Bill Bantey. - *Publié par* Musée des beaux-arts de Montréal. 1193, place Phillips, Montréal, Qué. H3B 3E1, février 1974-
Trimestriel. Publication d'institution (universités, écoles..), bulletin, 4 p. Langue(s): français et anglais. Tirage: 6000
$2.00 par année. Abonnements payables à l'avance.

Transport commercial / *édité par* Roger Allard. - *Publié par* John Bates. Maclean-Hunter Ltd. 481 University Ave., Toronto, Ont., janvier 1952-
Mensuel. Revue d'entreprise, magazine, 50 p. Comprend publicité. parution de suppléments. Tirage: 5000
$1.00 le numéro : $8.00 par année : $25.00 par année, l'étranger. Tirage contrôlé. Abonnements payables à l'avance.

Transport routier du Québec = Québec road transport / *édité par* Camille Archambault. - *Publié par* Camille Archambault. Association du camionnage du Québec inc. 8575, boul. Pascal-Gagnon, Montréal, Qué. H1P 1Y5.
Mensuel. Publication d'association, magazine, 50 p. Tirage: 5900
$5.00 par année. Abonnements payables à l'avance.

Transportation Safety Association of Ontario. Bulletin - *Published by* Transportation Safety Association of Ontario. 9th floor, 2 Bloor St. E., Toronto, Ont. M4W 3C2.
Monthly. Association publication, newsletter format, 4 p. Circulation: 11,000
Free. Controlled circulation.

Le Travail : le magazine du monde ordinaire, publié par la CSN / *édité par* Guy Ferland. - *Publié par* Confédération des syndicats nationaux. 1001, rue St-Denis, Montréal, Qué. H2X 3J1.
Intermittent (approximativement 5 éditions par an). Intérêt général, magazine, 48 p. Tirage: 30,000
$.75 le numéro : $5.00 par année.

Le travailleur canadien *See* Canadian labour

Le Travailleur social *See* The Social worker

Travaux de recherches sur le bilinguisme *See* Working papers on bilingualism

Travaux mécanisés du Québec *Voir* Revue machinerie lourde

Travel Toronto / *edited by* S. McDowell. - *Published by* W.H. Pepper Parr. Green Tree Publishing Co. 70 Bathurst St., Toronto, Ont. M5V 2P5.
Issued twice a year. Magazine format, Includes advertising.
$1.50 per issue.

Travel/leisure (July 1969-June 1972) *See* Leisurewheels

Treated wood perspectives = Perspectives des bois traités / *edited by* D.R. Douglas. - *Published by* Canadian Institute of Timber Construction. 100 Bronson Ave., Ottawa, Ont. K1R 6G8, 1973-
Former title(s): Modern wood (1959-1973)
Irregular. Association publication, 2-4 p. Language: English and French. Circulation: 4200
Controlled circulation.

Trellis / *edited by* Art C. Drysdale. - *Published by* Civic Garden Centre. 777 Lawrence Ave. E., Don Mills, Ont. M3C 1P2, January 1974-
Monthly. General interest, magazine format, 24-32 p. Includes book reviews, advertising. Circulation: 10,000
$5.00 per year. Prepayment required.

Trend / *edited by* P.M. Nobbs. - *Published by* Pulp and Paper Research Institute of Canada. 570 St. John's Blvd., Point Claire, Que. H9R 3J9, Autumn 1963-
House/company organ, magazine format, 20 p. Circulation: 3500
Indexed in Abstr. bull. inst. pap. chem.
ISSN 0041-2295 Irregular (approximately 2 issues per year). Free. Controlled circulation.

Trend / *edited by* J.K. Davy. - *Published by* The Steel Co. of Canada Ltd. 100 King St. W., Hamilton, Ont. L8N 3T1, 1962-
Issued twice a year. Trade publication, magazine format, 16 p. Language: English and French.

Trend construction report / *edited by* J.K. Davy. - *Published by* The Steel Co. of Canada Ltd. 100 King St. W., Hamilton, Ont. L8N 3T1, 1967-
Former title(s): Trend report.
Annual. Trade publication, magazine format, 16 p. Language: English and French.

Trend report *See* Trend construction report

Trente pour cent / *sponsored by* Mission Québec '76 ; *edited by* Denis Poulet. - *Published by* Michel Bédard. 881 est, de Maisonneuve, Montréal, Qué., janvier 1974-
Mensuel. Publication spécialisée, bulletin, 8 p. Language: français et anglais.
Envoi gratuit.

The Triangle / *edited by* Derek J. Wing. - *Published by* Public Affairs Department. International Nickel Company of Canada Ltd. Copper Cliff, Ont. P0M 1N0, 1936-
Monthly. House/company organ, magazine format, 32 p. Circulation: 28,000

The Italian tribune *See* La Tribuna Italiana

Tribuna portuguesa / *sponsored by* Tribuna Portuguesa and Enterprises ; *edited by* Frank Valadas. - *Published by* Frank Valadas. 3867 Colonial Ave., Montreal, Que. H2W 2B7, 1972-
Weekly. Ethnic press, newspaper format, 8-12 p. Language: Portuguese. Includes advertising, updating service. supplements issued.
$.25 per issue : $10.00 per year : $18.00 per year, foreign. Prepayment required.

Tricolor - *Published by* Alma Mater Society. Queen's University. Kingston, Ont.
Annual. Institutional publication (Universities, schools, etc.), book format, 304 p.
$7.00 : $8.00, foreign. Controlled circulation.

Trident press annual - *Published by* Trident Press. 842 Main St., Winnipeg, Man (Subscription address: P.O. Box 3629, Postal Station B, Winnipeg, Man. R2W 3R6)
Annual. Ethnic press. Language: Ukrainian. Includes advertising.
$3.00 per issue.

The Trillium *See* Civil Service Association of Ontario. CSAO news

Trim *See* Hair

The Trinity University review : a journal of literature, college thought and events / *sponsored by* Trinity College, University of Toronto ; *edited by* Richard G.R. Lawrence. - *Published by* The Coach House Press. 401 Huron St., (rear), Toronto, Ont. (Subscription address: Trinity College (The Review), 2 Hoskin Ave., Toronto, Ont. M5S 1H8) 1888-
Former title(s): Rouge et noir (1880-1888)
Irregular (approximately 2 issues per year). Scholarly publication, magazine format, 30 p. Includes book reviews, advertising, volume index, cumulative index. Circulation: 1200
$1.00 per issue : $1.50 per year, foreign. Controlled circulation. Prepayment required.

Le Troisième âge / *édité par* Claire H. Perreault. - *Publié par* Club social des lecteurs du Troisième âge inc. 4624, rue Garnier, Montréal, Qué. H2J 3S7.
Mensuel. Publication spécialisée, revue, 8 p. Comprend critique de livres, critique de films. Tirage: 5000
$3.00 par année. Abonnements payables à l'avance.

Truck Canada - *Published by* Don Quick Publications. 297 Old Kingston Rd., West Hill, Ont. M1C 2B4, 1953-
Monthly. Includes advertising.

Truck data book / *edited by* C.B. Wagner. - *Published by* Sanford Evans Publishing Ltd. P.O. Box 6900, 1077 St. James St., Winnipeg, Man. R3C 3B1.
Annual. Statistics, book format, 500 p. Circulation: 32,000

Truck logger (1943-) *See* B.C. logging news

Truck transport guide *See* Guide du transport par camion

Trust Companies Association of Canada. General information bulletin - *Published by* The Trust Companies Association of Canada. Suite 400, 11 Adelaide St. W., Toronto, Ont. M5H 1L9.
Annual. Association publication, magazine format, 18 p.

The Truth about China newsletter / *edited by* Patrick Walsh. - *Published by* The Canadian Friends of Free China Association. P.O. Box 130, Flesherton, Ont. N0C 1E0.
Monthly. Association publication, newsletter format, 6 p.

Truth on fire / *edited by* Wesley H. Wakefield. - *Published by* The Bible Holiness Movement Inc. P.O. Box 223, Postal Station A, Vancouver, B.C. V6C 2M3, January 1949-
Issued every other month. Church publication, magazine format, 32 p. Includes book reviews. Circulation: 1000

Twenty cents magazine / *sponsored by* The Twenty Cents Pub. Co ; *edited by* Robert C. McKenzie. - *Published by* Robert C. McKenzie. P.O. Box 151, Postal Station B, London, Ont., September 1966-
Monthly except July and August. General interest, magazine format, 40 p. Includes book reviews, film reviews, play reviews, record reviews, advertising.
$.50 per issue : $6.00 per year : $7.50 per year, foreign. Prepayment required.

U.B.C. legal notes (1949-1958) *See* University of British Columbia. Law Review Society. UBC law review

The UBC chronicle (December 1948-Winter 1974) *See* University of British Columbia. Alumni Association. UBC alumni chronicle

UFO-Quebec : informations recherches / *édité par* Claude MacDuff. - *Publié par* Norbert Spehner et Marc Leduc. C.P. 53, Dollard-des-Ormeaux, Qué. H9G 2H5, mars 1975-
Trimestriel. Publication spécialisée, magazine, 24 p. Tirage: 1000
ISSN 0317-9311 $1.00 le numéro : $4.00 par année : $5.00 par année, l'étranger.

U.S. news bulletin / *edited by* J.D. Moore. - *Published by* Canadian Export Association. Suite 1020, 1080 Beaver Hall Hill, Montreal, Que. H2Z 1T7.
Quarterly. Association publication, newsletter format, 4 p.
$25.00 per year. Subscription includes Export news bulletin and Review and digest bulletin. Controlled circulation.

UWO news (to 1972) *See* Western news

The Ubyssey - *Published by* AMS Publications Board. University of British Columbia. Vancouver, B.C.
Issued 3 times a week. Student publication. Includes advertising. Circulation: 1200

L'Ugam / *édité par* Huguette Roberge. - *Publié par* Service de l'information des relations publiques. Université du Québec à Montréal. C.P. 8888, Montréal, Qué. H3C 3P8, septembre 1974-
Hebdomadaire. Publication d'institution (universités, écoles..), journal, 8 p.
Envoi gratuit.

The Ukrainian Canadian : window on a cultural heritage / *edited by* Mitchell John Sago and Mary Skypnyk. - *Published by* Kobzar Publishing Company, Ltd. 1164 Dundas St. W., Toronto, Ont. M6J 1X4, September 1947-
Monthly. Ethnic press, magazine format, 48 p. Includes book reviews, film reviews, play reviews, record reviews, advertising. supplements issued. Circulation: 2500
$.50 per issue : $5.00 per year : $6.00 per year, foreign. Prepayment required.

Ukrainian Canadian Committee. Bulletin - *Published by* Ukrainian Canadian Committee. 456 Main St., Winnipeg, Man. R3B 1B6, January 1953-
Quarterly. Ethnic press, 24 p. Language: Ukrainian.
$5.00 per year.

Ukrainian Canadian pioneer library / *edited by* J.B. Rudnyckyi. - *Published by* Ukrainian Canadian Pioneer Library. P.O. Box 3504, Postal Station B, Winnipeg, Man., 1956-
Issued twice a year. Ethnic press, magazine format, 32-160 p. Language: Ukrainian ; summaries: English. supplements issued. Circulation: 500
$12.00 per year.

Ukrainian echo *See* Homin ukrainy

Ukrainian Free Academy of Sciences-UVAN (1949). Byuleten' humanistychnoho viddilu uvan / *edited by* J.B. Rudnyckyj. - *Published by* Ukrainian Free Academy of Sciences - UVAN (1949). P.O. Box 3504, Postal Station B, Winnipeg, Man., 1949-
Former title(s): Byuleten' prezydiyi UVAN; Byleten' UVAN u kanadi.
Annual. Association publication, newsletter format, 16 p. Language: Ukrainian.
Free to members.

Ukrainian gospel field *See* Ukrainska nyva

Ukrainian Professional and Business Men's Club. News bulletin - *Published by* Ukrainian Professional & Business Men's Club. P.O. Box 1144, Winnipeg, Man.
Monthly. Association publication, mimeographed, 4-6 p.
Free. Controlled circulation.

Ukrainian voice *See* Ukrainskyj holos

Ukrainska nyva = Ukrainian gospel field / *edited by* James Hominuke. - *Published by* Ukrainian Missionary and Bible Society, Inc. P.O. Box 1331, 539 20th St. W., Saskatoon, Sask., January 1945-
Quarterly. Ethnic press, magazine format, 48 p. Language: Ukrainian and English. Includes book reviews. Circulation: 1800
$.25 per issue : $3.00 per year.

Ukrainskyj holos = Ukrainian voice / *edited by* Michael Hykawy. - *Published by* Trident Press. 214 Dufferin Ave. Winnipeg, Man. (Subscription address: P.O. Box 3629, Postal Station B, Winnipeg, Man. R2W 3R4) 1910-
Weekly. Ethnic press, newspaper format, 12 p. Language: Ukrainian. Includes book reviews, advertising. Circulation: 12,175
$.20 per issue : $10.00 per year. Prepayment required.

Ultra-haute fréquences - *Publié par* CTVO. 259, boul. St. Joseph, Hull, Qué. J8Y 3X7, novembre 1973-
Intermittent (approximativement 4 éditions par an). Organe interne/officiel, journal, 4 p.
Tirage: 8000
Envoi gratuit.

The Uncertified human / *edited by* Denyse Handler. - *Published by* The Uncertified Human Publishing Co. Ltd. 1295 Gerrard St. E., Toronto, Ont. M4L 1Y8, June 1973-
Special interest, 16 p. Includes book reviews, advertising. supplements issued. Circulation: 4000
ISSN 0319-2008 $.25 per issue : $3.00 per year : $4.00 per year, foreign (except the U.S.).

Undergraduate awards / *sponsored by* Canadian Scholarship Trust Foundation ; *edited by* S.H. Deeks. - *Published by* National Student Aid Information Services. 1554 Knareswood Dr., Mississauga, Ont.
Annual. Special interest, 600 p. supplements issued.
$40.00.

Underwriters' Laboratories of Canada. List of equipment and materials. volume 1, general / *edited by* Gilbert L. Toppin. - *Published by* Underwriters Laboratories of Canada. 7 Crouse Rd., Scarborough, Ont. M1R 3A9.
Full volume issued. Directory, 400-500 p.
Circulation: 14,000
$5.00 per volume.

Underwriting results : the blue chart = Resultats techniques - *Published by* Stone and Cox Ltd. 203 Adelaide St. W., Toronto, Ont. M5H 1X4.
Annual. Statistics, 100 p.
$25.00.

Undzer weg *See* View

Unima Canada newsletter - *Published by* UNIMA Canada. c/o Pat Overgaard, 886 Keith Rd., Vancouver, B.C., 1969-
Irregular (approximately 4-6 issues per year). Association publication, newsletter format, 12-18 p. Language: English and French. Includes book reviews, play reviews. Circulation: 32
Subscription included in membership fee $6.00 per year.

Union Carbide Canada Ltd. Progress report / *edited by* Malcolm Greenhalgh. - *Published by* Union Carbide Canada Ltd. 123 Eglinton Ave. E., Toronto, Ont. M4P 1J3, 1967-
Quarterly. House/company organ, newsletter format, 4 p. Language: English and French. Free.

Union farmer / *edited by* Stuart A. Thiesson (Acting Editor). - *Published by* National Farmers Union. 250-C 2nd Ave., S. Saskatoon, Sask.
Monthly. Association publication, newspaper format, 12 p. Circulation: 23,000
$3.00 per year (Institutions $5.00).

Union list of serials in Montreal hospital libraries = Catalogue collectif des périodiques dans les bibliothèques médicales des hôpitaux de Montréal / *edited by* Elaine Waddington. - *Published by* Elaine Waddington. Chairman, Union List Committee, Women's Pavilion Library, Royal Victoria Hospital, 687 Pine Ave. W., Montreal, Que. H3A 1A1, 1974-
Irregular. Association publication, book format, 322 p.
ISSN 0316-5043 $5.00 per issue. Prepayment required.

L'Union médicale du Canada / *édité par* Edouard Desjardins. - *Publié par* L'Union médicale du Canada. 5064, ave du Parc, Montréal, Qué. H2V 4G2, 1872-
Mensuel. Edition savante, revue, 180 p. Langue(s): français ; sommaires: français et anglais. Comprend critique de livres, publicité, Mises à jour. Tirage: 9095
Indexé dans RADAR, Ind. med.
$2.00 le numéro : $20.00 par année : $2.50 le numéro, l'étranger : $25.00 par année, l'étranger. Tirage contrôlé. Abonnements payables à l'avance.

Union of British Columbia Municipalities. Minutes of annual convention - *Published by* Union of British Columbia Municipalities. Suite 204, 604 Blackford St., New Westminster, B.C.
Annual. Proceedings of an annual convention, 105 p.
Controlled circulation.

Unité nationale (1954) *Voir* Serviam : organe interne du parti de l'Unité nationale du Canada

United Baptist Convention of the Atlantic Provinces. Year book / *edited by* Keith R. Hobson. - *Published by* Keith R. Hobson. P.O. Box 1053, Saint John, N.B. E2L 4E7.
Annual. Annual reports and church directory, Part 1 - 160p.; Part 2 - 130 p. Circulation: 1500
ISSN 0082-7843

United Breeders Inc. News / *edited by* Don Fortune. - *Published by* United Breeders Inc. R.R. 5, Guelph, Ont. N1H 6J2, 1958-
Other title: United news.
Issued every other month. House/company organ, newsletter format, 8 p. Circulation: 25,000
Free. Issued to members only. Controlled circulation.

United Church of Canada. Committee on Archives. Bulletin / *sponsored by* Committee on Archives, United Church of Canada and Victoria University ; *edited by* C.G. Lucas. - *Published by* United Church Publishing House. c/o United Church Archives, Victoria University, Queen's Park, Toronto, Ont., 1948-
Former title(s): Records and proceedings of the Committee on Archives of the United Church of Canada.
Annual. Church publication, magazine format, 60 p. Back issues available. Circulation: 908
$1.25 to $2.50.

United Church of Canada. Committee on the Church and International Affairs. Report to the General Council of the United Church of Canada / *edited by* Norman K. Vale. - *Published by* The United Church of Canada. Room 711, 85 St. Clair Ave. E., Toronto, Ont. M4T 1M8, August 1974-
Former title(s): Little justice little joy.
Biennial. Church publication, booklet format, 45 p.

United Church of Canada. General Council. Record of proceedings / *edited by* The Secretary of the General Council, The United Church of Canada. - *Published by* General Council. United Church of Canada. Room 915, The United Church House, 85 St. Clair Ave. E., Toronto, Ont. M4T 1M8.
Biennial. Church publication, 300 p. Circulation: 3000
Prepared for distribution to our ministers and pastoral charges.

United Church of Canada. Newsletter / *edited by* Norman K. Vale. - *Published by* Division of Communications. United Church of Canada. 85 St. Clair Ave. E., Toronto, Ont. M4T 1M8, 1959-
Irregular (approximately 5 issues per year). House/company organ, newsletter format, 8 p. Circulation: 3200
Free.

United Church of Canada. Year book / *edited by* The Secretary of the General Council. The United Church of Canada. - *Published by* United Church of Canada. Rm. 915, The United Church House, 85 St. Clair Ave. E., Toronto, Ont. M4T 1M8.
Annual. Yearbook, 375 p. Circulation: 3000
$2.00. Free to all ministers and pastoral charges. Sometimes sent out free to those requesting, for a valid reason. Controlled circulation.

United Co-operatives of Ontario. UCO leader / *edited by* Michael Alaouze. - *Published by* United Cooperatives of Ontario. 151 City Centre Dr., Mississauga, Ont.
Former title(s): Director's newsletter - United Co-operatives of Ontario.
Monthly. House/company organ, newsletter format, 4 p. Language: English and French. Circulation: 2500
Free to co-operatives leaders in Ontario. Controlled circulation.

United Co-operatives of Ontario. UCO news / *edited by* Michael Alaouze. - *Published by* United Co-operatives of Ontario. P.O. Box 527, 151 City Centre Dr., Mississauga, Ont.
Issued every other month. House/company organ, magazine format, 16 p. Language: English and French. Includes book reviews, updating service. available in microform. Circulation: 63,000
Free. Controlled circulation.

United Electrical, Radio and Machine Workers of America. UE news / *edited by* Stan Bullock. - *Published by* United Electrical, Radio and Machine Workers of America (UE). 10 Codeco Court, Don Mills, Ont., 1937-
Issued every other week. House/company organ, newspaper format, 4 p. Includes book reviews. Circulation: 18,000
Free.

United florists news / *edited by* Larry Fenwick. - *Published by* United Flowers by Wire Service. Suite 804, 161 Eglinton Ave. E., Toronto, Ont. M4P 1J6.
Monthly. Directory, magazine format, 220 p. $1.00 per issue : $12.00 per year.

United Nations Association in Canada. Bulletin / *edited by* Geoffrey Grenville-Wood. - *Published by* United Nations Association in Canada. Room 808, 63 Sparks St., Ottawa, Ont. K1P 5A6, May 1975-
Irregular (approximately 6 issues per year). Association publication, newsletter format, 6 p. Language: English and French.
ISSN 0317-6460 Free.

United Transportation Union. UTU news Canada - *Published by* G.K. Strickland. Professional Towers, #108, 1729 Bank St., Ottawa, Ont., 1969-
Former title(s): Trainmen news in Canada (1959-1969)
Monthly. Association publication, newspaper format, 8 p. Language: English and French.
Free.

The United way / *edited by* A.W. Oaks. - *Published by* United Way of Canada. P.O. Box 3505, Postal Station C, 55 Parkdale Ave., Ottawa, Ont. K1Y 4G1.
Monthly. House/company organ, newsletter format, 2 p. Language: English and French. Circulation: 275
Controlled circulation.

United Way of Canada. Conference. Proceedings. - *Published by* United Way of Canada. P.O. Box 3505, Postal Station C, 55 Parkdale Ave., Ottawa, Ont. K1Y 1E5 4G1.
Irregular. Papers given at the biennial conferences. Language: English and French.
ISSN 0315-7571 $5.00 per volume.

Uniter / *sponsored by* University of Winnipeg Students Association ; *edited by* John Bowman. - *Published by* University of Winnipeg Publication Board. Room 216, 515 Portage Ave., Winnipeg, Man.
Weekly. Student newspaper, newspaper format, 12 p. Includes book reviews, film reviews, record reviews, advertising. supplements issued. Circulation: 3000
$5.00 per year. Free.

Unitt's Canadian price guide to antiques and collectables / *edited by* Doris J. Unitt. - *Published by* Clock House Publications. P.O. Box 103, Peterborough, Ont. K9J 6Y5, 1967-
Annual. Catalogue, book format, 304 p. Vol. 3, 4, 5 available.
$8.95.

Univers / *édité par* Jean-Louis Brouillé. - *Publié par* Conseil de Québec. L'Oeuvre pontificale de la propagation de la foi. 1145, chemin de la Canardière, Québec, Qué. G1J 2C3(adresse d'abonnement: C.P. 220, Limoilou, Québec, Qué. G1L 4V7) janvier-février 1971-
Ancien titre: Propagation de la foi (février 1924-novembre-décembre 1970)
Bimestriel. Publication ecclésiastique, magazine, 36 p. Tirage: 58,000
$2.00 par année. Tirage contrôlé.

Universal inquirer / *edited by* Ron Marr. - *Published by* International Christian Communications. P.O. Box 339, Ridgeway, Ont. L0S 1N0.
Monthly. Church publication, newspaper format,

Université de Moncton. La Revue de l'Université de Moncton / *édité par* Serge J. Morin. - *Publié par* Université de Moncton. Moncton, N.B., mai 1968-
Ancien titre: La Revue économique de l'Université de Moncton.
Intermittent (approximativement 3 éditions par an). Edition savante, revue, 150 p. Comprend critique de livres, index de volumes, index cumulatif. Tirage: 1200
$3.00 par année. Abonnements payables à l'avance.

Université de Montréal. Bibliothèque de chimie. Collections de périodiques - *Publié par* Université de Montréal. Succursale A, Montréal, Qué. H3C 3J7, juillet 1971-
Biennal. Publication d'institution (universités, écoles..), 18 p.
ISSN 0316-7348

Université de Montréal. Centre d'études et de documentation européennes. Bulletin d'information documentaire / *édité par* Marielle Dionne-Cartier. - *Publié par* Centre d'études et de documentation européennes. Université de Montréal. 5255, ave. Decelles, Montréal, Qué. H3T 1V6, novembre 1974-
Ancien titre: Catalogue sélectif de la documentation européenne; Bibliographie Canada-CEE (1970-1974)
Intermittent (approximativement 3 éditions par an). Edition savante, bulletin, 50 p. Comprend critique de livres. Tirage: 200
ISSN 0316-6694 $5.00. Envoi gratuit. Abonnements payables à l'avance.

Université de Montréal. Ecole de bibliothéconomie. Bibliothèque. Liste des périodiques - *Publié par* Ecole de Bibliothéconomie. Université de Montréal. C.P. 6128, Montréal, Qué. H3G 3J7, 1970-
Catalogue, 90 p.
Envoi gratuit. Tirage contrôlé.

Université de Montréal. Service des bibliothèques. Direction des services techniques. Sertek / *édité par* Ginette Darbon. - *Publié par* Service des bibliothèques. Université de Montréal. C.P. 6128, Montréal, Qué., mars 1975-
Intermittent. Publication d'institution (universités, écoles..), bulletin, 20 p.
ISSN 0317-0322

Université d'Ottawa. Facultés de médecine et des sciences. Bibliothèque Vanier. Liste des périodiques / *édité par* Maurice Alsrie. - *Publié par* Bibliothèque Vanier. Université d'Ottawa. 11 est, rue Somerset, Ottawa, Ont. K1N 6N5, 1967-
Paraît tous les 2-3 ans. Publication d'institution (universités, écoles..), 280 p. Langue(s): français et anglais ; sommaires: français et anglais. Comprend index de volumes.
Tirage contrôlé.

Université du Québec. Ecole nationale d'administration publique. Annuaire - *Publié par* Université du Québec. 2875, boul. Laurier, Ste-Foy, Qué. G1V 2M3, septembre 1970-
Annuel. Publication d'institution (universités, écoles..), 75 p.

Université du Québec à Rimouski. Les Cahiers éthicologiques de l'UQAR / *édité par* Rodrigue Belanger. - *Publié par* Départment des sciences religieuses. Université du Québec à Rimouski. 300, ave des Ursulines, Rimouski, Qué. G5L 3A1, mai 1974-
Intermittent. Publication d'institution (université, écoles..), magazine, 40 p.
Envoi gratuit.

Université et coopération / *édité par* Jean Marc Léger. - *Publié par* Association des universités partiellement ou entièrement de langue française. Université de Montréal, C.P. 6128, Montréal, Qué. H3C 3J7, 1968-
Bimestriel. Bulletin, Tirage: 2000
Compris dans la cotisation de membre.

Université laurentienne. Journal laurentien
See Laurentian University. Laurentian journal

Université Laval. Gazette officielle. Résolutions du conseil / *édité par* Nicole Le Blanc. - *Publié par* Office d'information. Université Laval. Cité Universitaire, Québec, Qué. G1K 7P4, septembre 1969-
Intermittent (approximativement 6 éditions par an). Publication d'institution (universités, écoles..), bulletin, 8 p. Tirage: 1500
Envoi gratuit.

Universities Art Association of Canada. Journal / *edited by* James Davies. - *Published by* Universities Art Association of Canada. 5163 Duke St., Halifax, N.S. B3J 3J6, April 1972-
Irregular (approximately 3-4 issues per year). Association publication, newsletter format, 8-12 p. Language: English and French. supplements issued. Circulation: 329
ISSN 0315-940X $10.00 per year. Prepayment required.

University affairs = Affaires universitaires / *edited by* Gloria Pierre. - *Published by* Association of Universities and Colleges of Canada. 151 Slater St., Ottawa, Ont. K1P 5M1., 1959-
Monthly (except May and June). Association publication, Newsmagazine, 28 p. Language: English and French. Includes advertising. Circulation: 43,300
Indexed in Can. educ. ind.
ISSN 0041-9257 $1.00 per issue : $5.30 per year (3rd class mail) : $7.00 per year (1st class mail) : $5.00 per year, foreign (surface mail) : $10.00 per year, foreign (airmail). Free to members. Prepayment required.

University gazette (1962-1971) *See* University of British Columbia. UBC gazette

University monthly (1865-1921) *See* The Brunswickan

University news / *edited by* Derek R. Mann. - *Published by* Information Office. Dalhousie University. Coburg Rd., Halifax, N.S. (Subscription address: Information Office, Old Law Building, Dalhousie University, Halifax, N.S. B3H 3J5) January 1975-
Irregular (approximately 17 issues per year). Institutional publication (Universities, schools, etc.), newspaper format, 16 p. Circulation: 7800

University of Alberta. Educational Media Division. Catalog of 16 mm educational motion pictures - *Published by* Educational Media Division. University of Alberta. Room 132, Corbett Hall, Edmonton, Alta. T6G 2G4, 1974-
Issued every 3 years. Catalogue, 150 p. Includes film reviews. supplements issued. Supplements issued every 6-8 months.
$3.00 per issue. Controlled circulation.

University of Alberta. Nuclear Research Centre. Progress report - *Published by* Nuclear Research Centre. University of Alberta, Edmonton, Alta. T6G 2N5, 1969-
Annual. Institutional publication (Universities, schools, etc.), 150 p.
ISSN 0318-0603 Free.

University of Alberta, Edmonton. Computing Services. Bulletin / *edited by* R. Sharpe. - *Published by* The Department of Computing Science. University of Alberta. Edmonton, Alta. T6G 2H1, December 6, 1968-
Former title(s): Computing Centre bulletin (December 6, 1968 - April 16, 1971)
Issued every other week. Institutional publication (Universities, schools, etc.), newsletter format, 20 p. Includes advertising, volume index. Circulation: 1300
Free.

University of Alberta, Edmonton. Library. Library staff bulletin / *edited by* Roy Barter. - *Published by* The Library. University of Alberta. Edmonton, Alta. T6G 2E1, March 8, 1972-
Former title(s): Library staff information (bulletin) (June 15, 1960, no. 1, - December 17, 1971)
Irregular. Institutional publication (Universities, schools, etc.), newsletter format, 5 p.
Free. Controlled circulation.

University of Alberta theses - *Published by* Special Collections Division. Library. University of Alberta. Edmonton, Alta. T6G 2J8, Fall 1971-
Issued twice a year. Bibliography, magazine format, 30 p. Circulation: 170
ISSN 0315-5870

University of British Columbia. Alumni Association. UBC alumni chronicle / *edited by* Susan Jamieson McLarnon. - *Published by* Alumni Association. University of British Columbia. 6251 N.W. Marine Dr., Vancouver, B.C. V6T 1A6, 1931-
Former title(s): The UBC chronicle (December 1948-Winter 1974) The Graduate chronicle (April 1931-October 1948)
Quarterly. Alumni publication, magazine format, 40 p. Includes book reviews, advertising. Circulation: 54,512
Indexed in Can. educ. ind.
$3.00 per year ($1.00 for students). Free to alumni. Controlled circulation.

University of British Columbia. Computing Centre. Newsletter / *edited by* Sieglinde L. Hogg. - *Published by* Computing Centre. University of British Columbia. UBC Campus, Vancouver, B.C. V6T 1W5, March 1969-
Monthly. Penal press, newsletter format, 8 p. Includes volume index. Circulation: 1800
Free.

University of British Columbia. Faculty Association. UBC Faculty Association newsletter / *edited by* N.E. Omelusik. - *Published by* Faculty Association. University of British Columbia. 112 West Mall Annex, University of British Columbia, Vancouver, B.C.
Irregular (approximately 7 issues per year). Association publication, newsletter format, 3 p. Circulation: 1700
Available to members only.

University of British Columbia. Faculty of Education. The Journal of education of the Faculty of Education / *edited by* L.F. Ashley. - *Published by* Faculty of Education. University of British Columbia. 2075 Westbrooke Pl., Vancouver, B.C. V6T 1W5, 1957-
Former title(s): Education bulletin.
Annual. Scholarly publication, journal format, 130 p. Includes book reviews. Circulation: 1000
$1.25 per year.

University of British Columbia. Forestry Club. UBC forester / *edited by* F.G. Farris. - *Published by* Forest Club. University of British Columbia. McMillan Building, Vancouver, B.C., 1950-
Annual. Yearbook, 100 p. Includes advertising.
$4.00. Prepayment required.

University of British Columbia. Law Review Society. UBC law review - *Published by* Law Review Society. University of British Columbia. Vancouver, B.C. V6T 1W5, 1959-
Former title(s): U.B.C. legal notes (1949-1958)
Issued twice a year. Association publication, journal format, 230-250 p. Includes book reviews, volume index. Circulation: 900
Indexed in Can. leg. per. lit., Leg. per.
ISSN 0068-1849 $6.00 per issue : $12.00 per year.

University of British Columbia. Library. Asian Studies Division. List of catalogued books / *edited by* Tung-King Ng. - *Published by* Asian Studies Division. Library. University of British Columbia. 2075 Wesbrooke Place, Vancouver, B.C. V6T 1W5, February 1964-
Issued 3 times a year (February, June and October). Institutional publication (Universities, schools, etc.), 50 p. Language: Chinese, Japanese and Korean. Circulation: 150
ISSN 0041-9427 Free or for exchange. Controlled circulation.

University of British Columbia. Library. Asian Studies Division. List of catalogued books. Supplement / *edited by* Tung-King Ng. - *Published by* Asian Studies Division. Library. University of British Columbia. 2075 Westbrook Place, Vancouver, B.C. V6T 1W5.
Institutional publication (Universities, schools, etc.). Circulation: 150
ISSN 0068-1687 Free.

University of British Columbia. Library. Serial holdings - *Published by* Library. University of British Columbia. 2075 Wesbrook Place, Vancouver, B.C. V6T 1W5, 1966-
Irregular. Bibliography.
ISSN 0084-8050 $20.00 per volume.

University of British Columbia. Library. UBC Library bulletin - *Published by* Library. University of British Columbia. Vancouver, B.C.
Institutional publication (Universities, schools, etc.), newsletter format, 6 p.

University of British Columbia. Library. UBC Library news / *edited by* M. Kasper. - *Published by* Library. University of British Columbia. Vancouver, B.C., August 1968-
Quarterly. Institutional publication (Universities, schools, etc.), newsletter format, 4-6 p.
Controlled circulation.

University of British Columbia. Physics Society. Journal / *edited by* Eric R. Brown. - *Published by* The Physics Society. Department of Physics. University of British Columbia. Vancouver, B.C.
Annual. Institutional publication (Universities, schools, etc.), journal format, 100 p. Circulation: 300
$5.00.

University of British Columbia. Summary of senate proceedings / *edited by* T.A. Myers. - *Published by* University of British Columbia. 2075 Wesbrook Place, Vancouver, B.C. V6T 1W5, December 13, 1967-
Irregular (approximately 10 issues per year). Institutional publication (Universities, schools, etc.), newsletter format, 3 p.
Free. Controlled circulation.

University of British Columbia. This week at UBC - *Published by* Information office. University of British Columbia. 2075 Westbrook Place, Vancouver, B.C. V6T 1W5.
Weekly. Institutional publication (Universities, schools, etc.), newsletter format, 2 p.
Free. Controlled circulation.

University of British Columbia. UBC gazette - *Published by* University of British Columbia. Vancouver, B.C. V6T 1W5, January 1962-
Former title(s): University gazette (1962-1971)
Irregular (approximately 10 issues per year). Institutional publication (Universities, schools, etc.), newsletter format, 3 p.
Free.

University of British Columbia. UBC reports / *edited by* J.A. Banham. - *Published by* University of British Columbia, Information Office. 2075 Westbrook Pl., Vancouver, B.C. U6T 1W5, 1951-
Issued twice a month. House/company organ, newspaper format, 12 p.
Free. Controlled circulation.

University of British Columbia. Varsity Outdoor Club. The Varsity Outdoor Club journal - *Published by* Varsity Outdoor Club. University of British Columbia. Vancouver, B.C.
Annual. Association publication, paperbound book, 150 p. Circulation: 350
$1.50.

University of Calgary Archaeological Association. Paleo-Environmental Workshop. Proceedings / *sponsored by* University of Calgary. Archaeological Association. - *Published by* Department of Archaeology. University of Calgary. Calgary, Alta. T2N 1N4, 1969-
Annual. Association publication, book format, 250 p.
Price varies.

The University of Calgary gazette / *edited by* Dorothy R. Patterson. - *Published by* The University of Calgary. Rm. 219, Public Relations Office, Social Service Bldg., The University of Calgary, Calgary, Alta., May 1971-
Issued every other week September to April, monthly May to August. Institutional publication (Universities, schools, etc.), newspaper format, 4-8 p. Includes advertising. supplements issued. Circulation: 8000
ISSN 3000-4333 Free.

University of Guelph. Arts and sciences alumni news / *edited by* Judith Main. - *Published by* Department of Alumni Affairs and Development. University of Guelph. Guelph, Ont. N1G 2W1.
Quarterly. Alumni publication, newsletter format, 4 p. Circulation: 3500
$4.00 per year.

University of Guelph. News bulletin / *edited by* Ann Middleton. - *Published by* Department of Information. University of Guelph. 4th floor E., University Centre, University of Guelph, Guelph, Ont.
Weekly. Institutional publication (Universities, schools, etc.), newsletter format, 8 p. supplements issued. Circulation: 8400

University of Manitoba. Awards bulletin / *edited by* R.J. Baizley. - *Published by* Fort Garry Campus. The University of Manitoba. Winnipeg, Man. R3T 2N2.
Annual. Institutional publication (Universities, schools, etc.), newsletter format, 200 p.

University of Manitoba. Center for Settlement Studies. Bibliography and information / *sponsored by* Central Mortgage and Housing Corporation. - *Published by* Center for Settlement Studies. University of Manitoba. Winnipeg, Man. (Subscription address: P.O. Box 5, University of Manitoba, Winnipeg, Man. R3T 2N2) April 1969-
Annual. Bibliography, 100-150 p.
$2.00 - $4.00. Controlled circulation.

University of Manitoba. Center for Transportation Studies. Seminar Series on Transportation. Proceedings - *Published by* Centre for Transportation Studies. University of Manitoba. Winnipeg, Man., June 1968-
Former title(s): Colloquium series on transportation (June 1968-June 1970)
Annual. Institutional publication (Universities, schools, etc.), 150 p.
ISSN 0076-3993 $3.00.

University of Manitoba. Medical journal - *Published by* Faculty of Medicine. University of Manitoba. Dept. of Physiology, New Basic Medical Science Bldg., 770 Bannatyne Ave., Winnipeg, Man. R3E 0W3.
Irregular (approximately 4 issues per year). Institutional publication (Universities, schools, etc.), journal format, 40 p. Language: English and French. supplements issued. Circulation: 1500
ISSN 0076-4108 $6.00 per year. Free to students.

University of Manitoba. The Alumni journal / *edited by* John M. Gordon. - *Published by* The Alumni Association. The University of Manitoba. Room 139, University Centre, University of Manitoba, Winnipeg, Man. R3T 2N2, October 1936-
Quarterly. Alumni publication, magazine format, 24 p. Includes book reviews. Circulation: 33,000
$6.00 per year. Free to members of the Alumni Association.

University of New Brunswick. Faculty of Forestry. Information for principals, guidance counsellors, teachers and students - *Published by* Faculty of Forestry. University of New Brunswick. Fredericton, N.B. E3B 5A3, 1964-
Annual. Institutional publication (Universities, schools, etc.), 45 p. Circulation: 2000

University of New Brunswick. Research Grants Office. The University of New Brunswick research inventory - *Published by* Research Grants Office. School of Graduate Studies. University of New Brunswick. Fredericton, N.B. E3B 5A3, 1969-
Annual. Institutional publication (Universities, schools, etc.).
ISSN 0316-6228

University of Regina Library serials list - *Published by* The Library. Regina Campus. University of Saskatchewan. Regina, Sask. S4S 0A2.
Catalogue.
ISSN 0317-8439

University of Saskatchewan. Continuing Medical Education. CME news / *edited by* Margaret P. Sarich (associate ed.). - *Published by* Continuing Medical Education. Saskatchewan Medical Association. University of Saskatchewan, 408 Ellis Hall, Saskatoon, Sask. S7N 0W8, September, 1969-
Issued every 6 weeks. Institutional publication (Universities, schools, etc.), newsletter format, 8 p. Includes book reviews, cumulative index. Circulation: 1400
$5.00 per year : $1.00 per volume. Controlled circulation.

University of Saskatchewan. Division of Continuing Medical Education. CME news / *edited by* M.P. Sarich (managing editor) and J.K. Wood (medical editor). - *Published by* Division of Continuing Medical Education. University of Saskatchewan. Room 408, Ellis Hall, University of Saskatchewan, Saskatoon, Sask. S7N 0W8.
Issued every 6 weeks. Institutional publication (Universities, schools, etc.), newsletter format, 8 p. Includes book reviews. Circulation: 2000
$5.00 per year. Controlled circulation.

University of Saskatchewan. University news / *edited by* News and Publication Office. - *Published by* University of Saskatchewan. Saskatoon, Sask. S7N 0W0 (Subscription address: 20.2 Education Bldg., Saskatoon, Sask.) 1967-
Issued every other month. Institutional publication (Universities, schools, etc.), newsletter format, 4 p. Circulation: 22,000
Free.

University of Toronto. Centre of Criminology. Alumni Association. Alumni Association newsletter / *sponsored by* Centre of Criminology Alumni Association ; *edited by* A.A. Nield. - *Published by* Department of Alumni Affairs. University of Toronto. 47 Willcocks St., Toronto, Ont. M5S 1C7, September 1974-
Quarterly. Alumni publication, newsletter format, 12 p.
Free. Controlled circulation.

University of Toronto. Forestry Alumni Association. Directory and newsletter - *Published by* Forestry Alumni Association. University of Toronto. Alumni House, University of Toronto, 47 Willcocks St., Toronto, Ont. M5S 1C7.
Biennial. Alumni publication, newsletter format, 65 p.
Free. Controlled circulation.

University of Toronto. Institute for the Quantitative Analysis of Social and Economic Policy. Newsletter - *Published by* Publications Office. Institute for the Quantitiative Analysis of Social and Economic Policy. University of Toronto. 150 St. George St., Toronto, Ont., 1967-
Irregular (approximately 1 issue per year). Institutional publication (Universities, schools, etc.), newsletter format, 20 p. Circulation: 1200
Free.

University of Toronto. School of Physical and Health Education. Alumni newsletter / *edited by* S. Romeiko. - *Published by* Department of Alumni Affairs. University of Toronto. 47 Willcocks St., Toronto, Ont. M5S 1A1.
Issued twice a year. Alumni publication, newsletter format, 24 p.
Free.

University of Toronto. Student Administrative Council. The SAC handbook - *Published by* The Student Administrative Council. University of Toronto. Toronto, Ont.
Annual. Student publication.
Free.

University of Toronto. University College. Bulletin / *edited by* D.C. King. - *Published by* University College. University of Toronto. Toronto, Ont. M5S 1A1.
Annual. Institutional publication (Universities, schools, etc.), magazine format, 44 p.

University of Toronto bulletin - *Published by* Department of Information Services. University of Toronto. 45 Willcocks St., Toronto, Ont. M5S 1C7, September 1968-
Weekly during the academic year, irregular during the summer. Institutional publication (Universities, schools, etc.), newspaper format, 4 p. Includes book reviews. supplements issued. Circulation: 10,000
Free. Controlled circulation.

University of Toronto Centre of Criminology. Alumni Association. Newsletter / *edited by* Al Nield. - *Published by* Alumni House. University of Toronto. 47 Wilcocks St., Toronto, Ont. M5S 1A1 (Subscription address: 47 Wilcocks St., Toronto, Ont. M5S 1A1)
Institutional publication (Universities, schools, etc.).

University of Toronto Faculty of Law review / *sponsored by* Students' Law Society of the Faculty of Law at the University of Toronto ; *edited by* Randall Scott Echlin. - *Published by* Samuel, Stevens, Hakkert and Co. 554 Spadina Cres., Toronto, Ont. M5S 2J9, 1973-
Annual. Legal articles, journal format, Back issues available.
Indexed in Can. leg. per. lit., Leg. per.

University of Toronto law journal / *edited by* R.C.B. Risk. - *Published by* University of Toronto Press. 5201 Dufferin St., Downsview, Ont. M3H 5T8, 1935/1936-
Quarterly. Special interest, journal format, 150 p.
Indexed in Can. leg. per lit., Soc. sci. cit. ind.
$16.50 per year.

The University of Toronto medical journal / *edited by* M.J. Howcroft. - *Published by* Medical Society. Faculty of Medicine. University of Toronto. Rm. 2141, Medical Sciences Bldg., University of Toronto, Toronto, Ont. M5S 1A8, 1923-
Issued 5 times a year November-March. Scholarly publication, journal format, 20 p. Includes book reviews, advertising. Circulation: 1300
$1.50 per issue : $6.00 per year.

University of Toronto monthly (1900) *See* Graduate

University of Toronto news (1956-1963) *See* Graduate

University of Toronto quarterly : a Canadian journal of the humanities / *edited by* W.J. Keith and B.Z. Shek. - *Published by* University of Toronto Press. 5201 Dufferin St., Downsview, Ont. M3H 5T8, 1931-
Quarterly. Scholarly publication, journal format, 96 p. Language: English and French. Includes book reviews, advertising. Circulation: 1400
Indexed in Hum. ind., M.L.A. int. bib., Annu. bibl. Engl. lang. and lit., Curr. ind. j. educ., Hist. abstr.; Amer. hist. and life.
ISSN 0042-0247 $3.50 per issue : $12.50 per year.

The University of Victoria. Alumni quarterly - *Published by* Alumni Association. The University of Victoria. Building "J", Victoria, B.C.
Quarterly. Alumni publication, journal format, 28-32 p.

University of Victoria gazette / *edited by* M.N. Cownden. - *Published by* University of Victoria. P.O. Box 1700, Victoria, B.C. V8W 2Y2, December 1963-
Monthly. Institutional publication (Universities, schools, etc.), newsletter format, 3 p. Circulation: 1300
Controlled circulation.

University of Waterloo. Alumni courier - *Published by* Alumni Association. University of Waterloo. Waterloo, Ont. N2L 3G1, May 1970-
Quarterly. Alumni publication, newspaper format, 8 p. Circulation: 14,000

University of Waterloo. Library. Serials list - *Published by* Library. University of Waterloo. Waterloo, Ont. N2L 3G1, December 1965-
Annual. Catalogue, 815 p.
Controlled circulation.

University of Waterloo. Quarterly *See* Gazette

University of Western Ontario. Alumni gazette / *edited by* David F. Green. - *Published by* Nigel Bellchamber. Department of Alumni Affairs. The University of Western Ontario. London, Ont.
Quarterly. Alumni publication, magazine format, 36 p. Includes book reviews, advertising, volume index. Circulation: 42,830
ISSN 0042-0344 Free.

The University of Western Ontario. Computing Centre newsletter / *edited by* Jim Stevens. - *Published by* Computing Centre. University of Western Ontario. London, Ont., September 1967-
Monthly. Institutional publication (Universities, schools, etc.), newsletter format, 6 p. Includes volume index. Circulation: 1000
Free.

University of Western Ontario dental journal / *edited by* Charles Consky. - *Published by* Dental Students Society. Faculty of Dentistry. University of Western Ontario. London, Ont.
Annual. Student publication, magazine format, 40 p.
Free. Controlled circulation.

University of Windsor. Library. List of serials held in the University of Windsor Library / *edited by* Idalia H. Rappé. - *Published by* Library. University of Windsor. Windsor, Ont. N9B 3P4 (Subscription address: Gifts and Exchanges Section, The Library, University of Windsor, Windsor, Ont. N9B 3P4) June 1975-
Former title(s): Titles in the humanities and social sciences - University of Windsor. Library (1966-1974) Serial titles in the pure and applied sciences - University of Windsor. Library (1963-1974)
Annual. Bibliography, 400 p.
$10.00. Controlled circulation.

University of Windsor. Main Library. Office of the University Librarian. News and views / *edited by* Kathy Lea. - *Published by* Gifts and exchange section. Library. University of Windsor. 400 Sunset Ave., Windsor, Ont., November 1973-
Former title(s): Tracings (Vol. 1 1967-1968-Vol. 3 1969-1968)
Monthly. Institutional publication (Universities, schools, etc.), newsletter format, 8 p. Includes book reviews. Circulation: 200
ISSN 0316-4926 Free.

University of Windsor review / *edited by* Eugene McNamara. - *Published by* University of Windsor Press. Windsor, Ont. N9B 3P4, Spring 1965-
Issued twice a year. Journal format, 110 p. Includes book reviews. Circulation: 300
ISSN 0042-0352 $2.75 per issue : $5.50 per year.

University of Winnipeg. Alumni bulletin / *edited by* Joy S. McDiarmid. - *Published by* Alumni Association. University of Winnipeg. 421 Wesley Hall, 515 Portage Ave., Winnipeg, Man.
Quarterly. Alumni publication, magazine format, 56 p. Includes book reviews.
Circulation: 6500
Free to graduates. Available to others on request.

Unmuzzled ox / *edited by* Michael Andre. - *Published by* Nathaniel Mandarin. P.O. Box 1581, Kingston, Ont., November 1971-
Quarterly. Special interest, magazine format, 128 p.
ISSN 0049-5557 $2.00 per issue : $8.00 per year.

Up - *Published by* Women's Place. 1120 - 7 Ave. S., Lethbridge, Alta., May 1974-
Issued every other month. Special interest, newsletter format, 25 p. Circulation: 500
ISSN 0318-0115 $3.00 per year.

Up to the neck - action - *Published by* Urban Social Redevelopment Centre. Room 304, 3553 St. Urbain St., Montreal, Que. H2G 2N6, April 1968-
Former title(s): Up to the neck, 'the citizens' paper (April 1968 - April 1974)
10 issues per year. Institutional publication (Universities, schools, etc.), newspaper format, 12-14 p. Includes book reviews, film reviews. Circulation: 1000
ISSN 0315-8624 \$.25 per issue : \$3.50 per year (Institutions \$10.00). Special rates offered.

Up to the neck, 'the citizens' paper (April 1968 - April 1974) *See* Up to the neck - action

Update *See* British Columbia English Teachers' Association. Journal

Update from OTF *See* Interaction

Urban forum = Colloque urbain / *edited by* Michael Berns. - *Published by* Urban Research Council of Canada. 251 Laurier Ave. W., Ottawa, Ont. K1P 5J6, 1975-
Former title(s): Urban research bulletin (1969-1974)
Quarterly. Scholarly publication, magazine format, 50 p. Language: English and French. Includes book reviews.
\$3.00 per year.

Urban research bulletin (1969-1974) *See* Urban forum

VE6 / *sponsored by* Amateur Radio League of Alberta ; *edited by* Basil Barnes. - *Published by* Basil Barnes. P.O. Box 1226, Bonnyville, Alta. T0A 0L0 (Subscription address: Roy Ellis, P.O. Box 2, R.R. 1, Fort Saskatchewan, Alta. T0B 1P0) 1964-
Former title(s): Alberta amateur.
Monthly. Association publication, magazine format, 28 p. Circulation: 370
\$4.00 per year.

Vaba Eestlane = Free Estonian / *edited by* Karl Arro. - *Published by* Free Estonian Publishers Ltd. 135 Tecumseth St., Toronto, Ont. M6J 2H2, January 1952-
Issued twice a week. Ethnic press, newspaper format, 8 p. Language: Estonian. Includes book reviews, play reviews, advertising: Circulation: 3000
\$.30 per issue : \$25.00 per year : \$26.00 per year, foreign. Prepayment required.

Vacation *See* Selling travel

The Valley echo (December 1919-December 1969) *See* Saskatchewan Anti-Tuberculosis League. Saskatchewan Anti-Tuberculosis League news quarterly

VanCity working dollars / *edited by* R.B. Spooner. - *Published by* Vancouver City Savings Credit Union. P.O. Box 33979, Postal Station D, 1030 W. Broadway, Vancouver, B.C., 1959-
Irregular (approximately 4 issues per year). House/company organ, newspaper format, 4 p. Circulation: 40,000
Free to members.

Vancouver Art Gallery. Exhibition catalogues - *Published by* The Vancouver Art Gallery. 1145 W. Georgia St., Vancouver, B.C. V6E 3H2.
Irregular (approximately 4 issues per year). Institutional publication (Universities, schools, etc.), 30 p.

Vancouver calendar magazine / *edited by* Sally Reukauf Warren. - *Published by* Calendar Magazines Ltd. 65 Front St. E., Toronto, Ont. M5E 1B6, 1971-
Monthly. Calendar of events, magazine format, 64 p. Includes film reviews, play reviews, advertising. Circulation: 100,000
\$.75 per issue : \$9.00 per year. Controlled circulation.

Vancouver City College news *See* Savant

Vancouver Coin Club news bulletin (July 1958-December 1960) *See* The Vancouver Numismatic Society news bulletin

Vancouver educational research bulletin : VERB / *edited by* E.N. Ellis and A.G. Moodie. - *Published by* Evaluation and Research. Vancouver School Board. 1595 W. 10th Ave., Vancouver, B.C. V6J 1Z8, March 1970-
Irregular (approximately 4 issues per year). Institutional publication (Universities, schools, etc.), newsletter format, 4 p.
Free.

Vancouver Historical Society. Newsletter / *edited by* Edmund and Garry Colchester. - *Published by* Vancouver Historical Society. P.O. Box 3971, Vancouver, B.C. V6B 3X6, 1961-
Irregular (approximately 10 issues per year). Association publication, newsletter format, 6 p.
\$7.00 per year (Institutions \$10.00). Prepayment required.

Vancouver Island Cage Bird Society. Annual show bulletin / *sponsored by* Vancouver Island Cage Bird Society ; *edited by* Joanne Albion. - *Published by* Doreen Albion. 3631 Cedar Hill Rd., Victoria, B.C. V8P 3Z3, 1951-
Annual. Association publication, magazine format, 26 p. Circulation: 300
ISSN 0317-0160 \$1.00 per issue.

Vancouver Island Cage Bird Society. Bulletin / *edited by* Joanne Albion. - *Published by* Vancouver Island Cage Bird Society. c/o Mrs. F. Cadwallader, 1208 Pearce Cres., Victoria, B.C. V8X 3S9, 1960-
Association publication, newsletter format, 24 p. Circulation: 306
ISSN 0316-8239 $.50 per issue : $4.00 per year : $.60 per issue, foreign.

Vancouver Island Netherlands Association. Newsletter / *edited by* The Secretary. - *Published by* Vancouver Island Netherlands Association. P.O. Box 5162, Postal Station B, Victoria, B.C. V8R 6N4.
Monthly. Association publication, newsletter format, 1 p.

Vancouver Island's outdoor journal / *edited by* Jan Blake. - *Published by* Frank M. Lee. Wilderness Publications Ltd. 1014 Government St., Victoria, B.C.
Weekly. Magazine format, Includes advertising. Circulation: 5310

Vancouver leisure magazine *See* Vancouver magazine

Vancouver magazine / *edited by* Malcolm F. Parry. - *Published by* Ronald W. Stern. 1008 Hornby St., Vancouver, B.C., 1957-
Former title(s): Vancouver leisure magazine; Dick MacLean's guide.
Monthly. Calendar of events, magazine format, 48 p. Includes advertising. Circulation: 75,000
$.50 per issue : $5.00 per year : $9.00 for 2 years : $12.00 for 3 years : $6.00 per year, foreign. Controlled circulation.

The Vancouver Numismatic Society news bulletin / *edited by* G.J. Dickie. - *Published by* Vancouver Numismatic Society. P.O. Box 2467, Vancouver, B.C. V6B 3W7, January 1961-
Former title(s): Vancouver Coin Club news bulletin (July 1958-December 1960)
Monthly. Association publication, newsletter format, 6-10 p. Circulation: 225
ISSN 0049-5824 $4.00 per year.

Vancouver Public Aquarium. Newsletter / *edited by* Sharon J. Proctor. - *Published by* Vancouver Public Aquarium Association. P.O. Box 3232, Stanley Park, Vancouver, B.C. V6B 3X8, October 1957-
Issued every other month. Association publication, magazine format, 8 p. Circulation: 4200
Free to members.

Vancouver realtor / *edited by* Anne Broadfoot. - *Published by* Real Estate Board of Greater Vancouver. 1101 W. Broadway, Vancouver, B.C. V6H 1G2, 1963-
Monthly. House/company organ, magazine format, 20 p. Circulation: 4000
Free to members of the Real Estate Board and special industrial mailing list. Controlled circulation.

Vancouver Resources Board. Inside the VRB / *edited by* D. John Lynn. - *Published by* Vancouver Resources Board. 1675 West Tenth Ave., Vancouver, B.C. V6J 2A3, April 1975-
Former title(s): C.A.S. news.
Irregular (approximately 8 issues per year). House/company organ, magazine format, 8 p.
Free in Vancouver : restricted elsewhere.

Vancouver Status of Women newsletter *See* Kinesis

Vancouver symphony VSO / *edited by* Vicky Parr. - *Published by* Vancouver Symphony Society. 873 Beatty St., Vancouver, B.C. V6B 2M6, 1968-
Irregular (approximately 12 issues per year). Program. Includes advertising. Circulation: 16,938
$3.00 per year.

Vanguard / *edited by* Norah Kembar. - *Published by* Vancouver Art Gallery. 1145 W. Georgia St., Vancouver, B.C. V6E 3H2, 1932-
Former title(s): Bulletin - The Vancouver Art Gallery.
Monthly. House/company organ, newsletter format, 16 p.
ISSN 0315-5226 $3.00 per year. Controlled circulation.

Vanguard / *edited by* Norah Kembar. - *Published by* Vancouver Art Gallery. 1145 W. Georgia St., Vancouver, B.C. V6E 3H2, January 1972-
Former title(s): Bulletin - The Vancouver Art Gallery.
Issued 10 times a year. Institutional publication (Universities, schools, etc.), newspaper format, 16 p. Includes advertising.
ISSN 0315-5226 $.10 per issue (Issues containing criteria $.25) : $3.00 per year. Controlled circulation. Prepayment required.

Vanguard : Christian vision for the seventies / *edited by* Bonnie M. Greene. - *Published by* Wedge Publishing Foundation. 229 College St., Toronto, Ont. M5T 1R4, November 1970-
Issued every other month. Magazine format, 32 p. Includes book reviews, film reviews, record reviews, advertising. Circulation: 2000
ISSN 0009-5680 $1.00 per issue : $6.50 per year. Prepayment required.

Vanishing rural community - *Published by* Better Read Graphics. Hart House, Toronto (Subscription address: P.O. Box 701, Kingston, Ont.) September 1973-
Irregular. Special interest, magazine format, 32 p. Circulation: 2000
$.35 per issue.

Vapaa sana = Free press / *edited by* Lauri Toiviainen. - *Published by* Vapaa Sana Press Ltd. 400 Queen St. W., Toronto, Ont. M5V 2A6, December 1937-
Issued twice a week. Ethnic press, newspaper format, 8 p. Language: Finnish. available in microform. Circulation: 4500
$.20 per issue : $15.00 per year.

Varrak / *edited by* H. Riga. - *Published by* H. Riga. R.R. 4, Warkworth, Ont. K0K 3K0, 1971-
Irregular. Ethnic press, journal format, 40 p. Language: Estonian and English. Includes book reviews. Circulation: 200
$1.00 per issue. Special rates offered.

Varsity / *edited by* David Simmonds. - *Published by* Students Administrative Council. University of Toronto. 12 Hart House Circle, University of Toronto (Subscription address: 91 St. George St., Toronto, Ont.) 1880-
Issued 3 times a week. Student publication, newspaper format, 16 p. Includes book reviews, film reviews, play reviews, record reviews, advertising. Circulation: 18,000
$14.00 per year : $14.00 per volume. Free.

Varsity graduate (1948-1967) *See* Graduate

Vector *See* Vector: newsletter/journal

Vector: newsletter/journal / *sponsored by* British Columbia Association of Mathematics Teachers ; *edited by* Bill Kokoskin. - *Published by* B.C. Teachers' Federation. 105-2235 Burrard St., Vancouver, B.C. V6J 3H9, 1962-
Former title(s): Vector; Teaching mathematics; B.C.A.M.T. journal.
Irregular (approximately 4 or 5 issues per year). Association publication, magazine format, 60 p. Includes book reviews. Circulation: 900
Indexed in Can. educ. ind.
$10.00 per year. $5.00 to members of the British Columbia Teachers Federation.

Vegetable Growers Association of Manitoba. Technical and scientific papers presented at the annual meeting - *Published by* Vegetable Growers Association of Manitoba. 9th Floor, Norquay Building, Winnipeg, Man. R3T 0P8, 1954-
Annual. Association publication, magazine format,
ISSN 0083-5307 Controlled circulation.

Véhicules de récréation : trade ISSN 0317-5294 (1971-1972) *See* Recreational vehicles trade

Veillée d'armes *Voir* Avec 'lui'

Le Veneur / *édité par* Serge Dupré. - *Publié par* Les Veneurs de Drummondville inc. C.P. 128, St-Germain, Co. Drummond, Qué., février 1975-
Trimestriel. Publication d'association, bulletin, 8 p. Tirage: 2000
Envoi gratuit.

Ventilator (1959-1963) *See* The Dime bag

Venture forth / *sponsored by* Early Childhood Education Council ; *edited by* Gayle Hughes. - *Published by* Saskatchewan Teachers' Federation. P.O. Box 1108, Saskatoon, Sask. S7K 3N3, 1969-
Former title(s): It's our bag (1969-1972)
Quarterly. Association publication, journal format, 30-40 p. Includes book reviews. Circulation: 750
Subscription included in membership fee $5.00 per year (Libraries $4.00). Controlled circulation. Prepayment required.

The Veterans advocate / *edited by* N.E. Doward. - *Published by* The National Prisoners of War Association. 2470 Lakeshore Rd. W., Oakville, Ont., 1947-
Quarterly. Association publication, magazine format, Includes advertising.
$2.00 per year.

Vexillum / *sponsored by* British Columbia Association of Teachers of Classics. - *Published by* British Columbia Teachers Federation. 105 - 2235 Burrard St., Vancouver, B.C. V6J 3H9, October 1972-
Former title(s): Newsletter - B.C. Association of Teachers of Classics.
Irregular (approximately 2 issues per year). Special interest, newsletter format, 6 p. Members only. Controlled circulation.

Vibrations - *Published by* The Canadian Hearing Society. 60 Bedford Rd., Toronto, Ont. M5R 2K2, March 15, 1973-
Irregular (approximately 6 issues per year). Association publication, newsletter format, 6 p.

Victoria Humanist (1964-1967) *See* Humanist in Canada

Victoria report / *edited by* John H. Davidson. - *Published by* Alumni Association. Victoria College. 150 Charles St. W., Toronto, Ont. M5S 1K7, January 1973-
Quarterly. Alumni publication, newspaper format, 12 p.
Free.

Victorian periodicals newsletter / *edited by* Hans de Groot and Peter Morgan. - *Published by* Research Society for Victorian Periodicals. Dept. of English, University College, Toronto, Ont. M5S 1A1, 1968-
Quarterly. Association publication, magazine format, 42 p. Includes book reviews. available in microform. Back issues available.
Circulation: 800
ISSN 0049-6189 $5.00 per year (Institutions $7.00). Prepayment required.

Vidéo-presse : le seul grand magazine canadien pour les jeunes / *édité par* Pierre Guimar (directeur de la publication). - *Publié par* Editions Paulines. 3965 est, boul. Henri-Bourassa, Montréal, Qué. H1H 1L1, octobre 1971-
Mensuel. Intérêt général, magazine, 68 p.
Tirage: 75,000
Indexé dans Periodex, RADAR.
ISSN 0315-3975 $.85 le numéro : $7.50 par année : $10.00 par année, l'étranger (Par avion $14.50). Tarifs spéciaux disponibles. Abonnements payables à l'avance.

La Vie chrétienne : journal mensuel de l'Eglise presbytérienne ou réformée au Canada / *édité par* André Poulain. - *Publié par* Eglise Presbytérienne au Canada. 6316 - 30ème ave, Montréal, Qué. H1T 3G4, janvier 1952-
Mensuel. Publication ecclésiastique, journal, 4 p. Comprend critique de livres, critique de films. Tirage: 1000
Envoi gratuit.

Vie des arts / *édité par* Andrée Paradis. - *Publié par* Société des arts. Suite 409, 360, McGill, Montréal, Qué., janvier-février 1956-
Trimestriel. Publication d'association, revue, 90 p. Langue(s): français ; sommaires: anglais. Comprend critique de livres, critique de films, publicité. Tirage: 8500
Indexé dans Periodex, Can. ind., RADAR.
ISSN 0042-5435 $2.50 le numéro : $9.00 par année : $10.00 par année, l'étranger. Envoi gratuit. Tarifs spéciaux disponibles. Abonnements payables à l'avance.

La Vie des communautés religieuses / *édité par* Laurent Boisvert. - *Publié par* Les Franciscains. 5750, boul. Rosemont, Montréal, Qué.
Mensuel. Publication ecclésiastique, magazine, 32 p. Comprend critique de livres.
$.60 le numéro : $6.00 par année : $9.00 par année, l'étranger (Par avion). Abonnements payables à l'avance.

La Vie médicale au Canada francais / *édité par* G.A. Bergeron. - *Publié par* G.A. Bergeron. 2860, des Quatre Bourgeois, Québec, Qué. G1V 1Y3, 1899-
Revue d'entreprise. Comprend publicité.
Tirage: 7275
$20.00 par année : $25.00 par année, l'étranger.

La Vie montante : sanctification et rayonnement des aînés / *parrainé par* Le Mouvement de vie spirituelle La Vie montante ; *édité par* François Sailler. - *Publié par* Clément Loiselle. 21, rue Ste-Elizabeth, Longueil, Qué. J4H 1J3, août 1973-
Intermittent (approximativement 5 éditions par an). Publication ecclésiastique, journal, 4 p.
Tirage: 6000
$2.00 par année. Envoi gratuit. Abonnements payables à l'avance.

Vie oblate = Oblate life / *édité par* Gaston Carrière. - *Publié par* Les Missionnaires Oblats de Marie Immaculée. 175, rue Main, Ottawa, Ont. K1S 1C3, janvier - mars 1942)-
Ancien titre: Etudes oblates (1942-1973)
Trimestriel. Publication d'association, publication ecclésiastique, revue, 80 p. Langue(s): français et anglais ; sommaires: français et anglais. Comprend critique de livres. Tirage: 500
$1.25 le numéro : $5.00 par année. Abonnements payables à l'avance.

Vieil escolier / *édité par* Léonard Bacleau. - *Publié par* Association des anciens. Université Laval. Cité Universitaire, Québec, Qué. G1K 7P4.
Trimestriel. Publication des anciens étudiants, journal, 16 p.

Vient de paraître / *édité par* Jacques de Roussan. - *Publié par* Edi-Québec inc. 436 est, rue Sherbrooke, Montréal, Qué. H2L 1J6(adresse d'abonnement: Periodica, 7045, ave du Parc, Montréal, Qué. H3N 1X8) 1964-
Trimestriel. Bibliographie, magazine, 64 p. Comprend critique de livres, critique de pièces de théâtre, publicité, index de volumes. Tirage: 10,000
ISSN 0042-5656 $5.00 par année. Abonnements payables à l'avance.

View / *sponsored by* B.C. Shop Teachers Association. - *Published by* B.C. Teachers' Federation. 105 - 2235 Burrard St., Vancouver, B.C. V6J 3J2.
Irregular (approximately 3 issues per year). Association publication, newsletter format, 10 p. Includes book reviews, advertising.
Circulation: 350
Subscriptions are not available. Controlled circulation.

View = Undzer weg / *sponsored by* Achdut - HaAvoda Poale Zion ; *edited by* Joseph Kligman and Yahuda Tyberg. - *Published by* Max Federman. 547 Douglas Ave., Toronto, Ont. (Subscription address: 272 Codsell Ave., Downsview, Ont) 1946-
Issued every other month. Ethnic press, magazine format, 24 p. Language: Yiddish and English. Includes book reviews. Circulation: 3500
$.50 per issue : $5.00 per year.

Viewpoint / *edited by* Joanne McGarry. - *Published by* Canadian Mental Health Association. 355 Princess Ave., London, Ont. N6B 2A7.
Issued every other month. Association publication, newsletter format, 18 p. Circulation: 1400
Free to members.

Viewpoint / *edited by* Hannah Polowy. - *Published by* Faculty of Education. University of British Columbia. 2855 Acadian Rd., Vancouver, B.C.
Quarterly. Institutional publication (Universities, schools, etc.), magazine format, 20 p. Includes book reviews. Circulation: 500
$1.00 per issue : $4.00 per year. Prepayment required.

The Viking / *edited by* Fred Hatfield. - *Published by* Fundy Group Publications Ltd. 2 Second St., Yarmouth, N.S., 1968-
Irregular (approximately 8 issues per year). Newspaper format, 50-60 p.
Controlled circulation.

Village squire - *Published by* Keith Roulston. The Blyth Standard. P.O. Box 10, Blyth, Ont., 1973-
Monthly. Magazine format, Includes advertising. Circulation: 4214
$2.00 per year.

Vilne slovo = Free word / *edited by* Stephen Rosocha. - *Published by* Toronto Free Press Publications Ltd. 196 Bathurst St., Toronto, Ont. M5T 2R8.
Weekly. Ethnic press, newspaper format, 8 p. Language: Ukrainian. Includes book reviews, film reviews, play reviews, record reviews, advertising. supplements issued. Circulation: 9500
$.25 per issue : $10.00 per year. Prepayment required.

Vilne slovo annual = Calendar almanach "slovo" / *edited by* Stephen Rosocha. - *Published by* Toronto Free Press Publications Ltd. 196 Bathurst St., Toronto, Ont. M5T 2R8.
Annual. Ethnic press, 144 p. Language: Ukrainian. Includes book reviews, film reviews, play reviews, advertising. Circulation: 5000
$3.50.

Vision / *édité par* Michèle Drouin-Martineau. - *Publié par* Association des professeurs d'arts plastiques du Québec. C.P. 424, Station Youville, Montréal, Qué. H2P 2V6, 1969-
Trimestriel. Publication d'association, magazine, 30 p.
$1.25 le numéro : $5.00 par année : $46.00 par année, l'étranger. Abonnements payables à l'avance.

Vision / *edited by* T.H. Drillen. - *Published by* Northern Regional Development Council. P.O. Box 5, Bathurst, N.B. E2A 3Z1, March 1968-
Irregular (approximately 10 issues per year). Magazine format, 14 p.
Free.

Visit Algoma / *edited by* Nancy Fitzpatrick. - *Published by* Sault Ste. Marie & District Chamber of Commerce. 360 Great Northern Rd., Sault Ste. Marie, Ont. P6B 4Z7, 1971-
Former title(s): This is Algoma.
Annual. Trade publication, pamphlet format, 48 p. Circulation: 50,000
Free.

Visitor's guideline / *edited by* Wm. J. Claus. - *Published by* Guideline Publishing. Lawsco Holdings Ltd. Suite 111, 415 W. Cordova St., Vancouver, B.C. V6B 1E5, 1971-
Weekly. Magazine format, Includes advertising. Circulation: 25,684
Free.

Visnyk = Herald / *sponsored by* Ukrainian Greek-Orthodox Church of Canada ; *edited by* Stephan Jarmus. - *Published by* Ecclesia Publishing Co. 9 St. Johns Ave., Winnipeg, Man., 1924-
Issued twice a month. Ethnic press, newspaper format, 16 p. Language: Ukrainian. Includes a bi-monthly English supplement. Circulation: 5500
$7.00 per year : $7.50 per year, foreign.

Visnyk Svitovoho kongresu vil'nykh ukraîntsiv
See World Congress of Free Ukrainians

Vista / *sponsored by* Saskatchewan Home Economics Teachers' Association ; *edited by* Vera M. Sylvester. - *Published by* Saskatchewan Teachers' Federation. 2317 Arlington Ave., Saskatoon, Sask., December 1968-
Quarterly. Association publication, 30-40 p. Includes book reviews, volume index.
Circulation: 186
Indexed in Can. educ. ind.
$2.00 per year. Subscription included in membership fee.

Vita Italiana / *edited by* Mario Caligiure. - *Published by* Italian Life Publishing Ltd. P.O. Box 163, Postal Station L, Toronto, Ont. M6E 4Y5.
Issued every other week. Ethnic press. Language: Italian. Includes advertising.
Circulation: 18,000

Vivre d'amour / *édité par* Michel Verret. - *Publié par* Association des frères et soeurs de Ste-Thérèse de l'Enfant-Jésus. 1a, ave du Sacré-Coeur, Quebéc, Qué., mai 1973-
Trimestriel. Publication ecclésiastique, magazine, 32 p. Tirage: 2200
Envoi gratuit.

Vivre en santé et en beauté / *édité par* Jean-Paul Ostiguy. - *Publié par* Magazine vivre. Québecor inc. Suite 108, 450 est, rue Sherbrooke, Montréal, Qué., 1969-
Intermittent (approximativement 11 éditions par an). Publication spécialisée, magazine, Comprend publicité.
$7.50 par année.

Le V'la. - *Publié par* Collège de Maisonneuve. 3800 est, rue Sherbrooke, Montréal, Qué.
Intermittent (approximativement 20 éditions par an). Publication d'institution (universités, écoles..), bulletin, 8-12 p.

Vocational guidance *Voir* Orientation professionnelle

The People's voice *See* La Voce del popolo

The Voice / *edited by* J.V. VanWaggoner. - *Published by* United Senior Citizens of Ontario Inc. 99 - 17th St., Toronto, Ont.
Monthly (10 issues a year). Association publication, magazine format, 40 p.
$1.50 per year.

Voice of Canadian Serbs *See* Glas Kanadskih srba

The Voice of motordom (1950) *See* Alberta motorist

Voice of Portugal *See* Voz de Portugal

Voice of the Kent farmer / *edited by* Gordon W. Clauws. - *Published by* Leader Publications. Main St., Dresden, Ont., 1963-
Issued twice a month. Includes advertising.
Circulation: 6800

The Voice of the Mennonite Brethren Bible College (1952-1971) *See* Direction

The Voice of the Ontario gasoline retailer / *edited by* G.H. Coates. - *Published by* Ontario Retail Gasoline and Automotive Service Association. Suite 210, 312 Dolomite Dr., Downsview, Ont., 1952-
Monthly. Trade publication. Includes advertising.
$5.00 per year.

Voice of the vaad / *edited by* Rabbi I.L. Hechtman. - *Published by* Jewish Community Council of Montreal. Suite 117, 5491 Victoria Ave., Montreal, Que., 1961-
Quarterly. Magazine format, Includes advertising.

Voici Ottawa *See* What's on in Ottawa

La Voix (avril 1971-février 1973) *Voir* L'Association nationale des camionneurs artisans inc. : La Voix de l'ANCAI

La voix de la construction / *édité par* Terry McAuliffe. - *Publié par* Southam Business Publications Ltd. 1450 Don Mills Rd., Don Mills, Ont.(adresse d'abonnement: 34 St. Patrick St. Toronto, Ont. M5T 1V2) 1927-
Publié en anglais : Daily commercial news and construction records.
Revue d'entreprise, journal, 16 p. Comprend publicité. parution de suppléments. Tirage: 8050
$95.00 par année : $120.00 par année, l'étranger. Tarifs spéciaux disponibles.

Volleyball technical journal / *edited by* Lorne Sawula. - *Published by* Canadian Volleyball Association Publications. 78 Tedford Dr., Scarborough, Ont. M1R 1M4, January 1974-
Irregular (approximately 3 issues per year). Association publication, magazine format, 88-100 p. Language: English and French. Includes book reviews. Circulation: 1000
ISSN 0315-0887 $5.00 per issue : $15.00 per year.

Volume retail merchandising / *edited by* Jack Watson. - *Published by* Weston Publishing Co. Ltd. Suite 102, 109 Railside Rd., Don Mills, Ont. M3A 1B5, 1948-
Monthly. Trade publication, magazine format, 16-24 p. Includes advertising.
Indexed in Can. B.P.I.
$8.00 per year : $12.00 per year, foreign. Controlled circulation.

Vorwärts = Forward : democratic monthly / *edited by* Henry Weisbach. - *Published by* Sudetenclub Club Forward, Toronto. 179 Durant Ave., Toronto, Ont. M4J 4W5, June 1947-
Issued every other month. Ethnic press, newsletter format, 26-28 p. Language: German. Includes book reviews. Circulation: 400
$3.00 per year : $4.00 per year, foreign. Controlled circulation. Prepayment required.

Votre église (mars 1967-décembre 1967) *Voir* L'Eglise de Montréal

Votre pharmacien *Voir* Famille d'aujourd'hui

Voxair / *edited by* G.E. Robertson. - *Published by* Canadian Forces Base, Winnipeg. Westwin, Man. R2R 0T0, 1952-
Issued every other week. House/company organ, newspaper format, 16 p. Language: English (French). Includes play reviews, record reviews, advertising. Circulation: 3300
ISSN 0300-3213 $3.50 per year. Free to CFB, WPG and SUC outlets. Controlled circulation.

Voz de Portugal = Voice of Portugal / *edited by* Armando Barqueiro. - *Published by* Carlos Sousa. P.O. Box 9, Postal Station G, Montreal, Que., 1960-
Weekly. Ethnic press. Language: Portuguese. Includes advertising.
$4.00 per year.

Vues et propos / *édité par* Mireille Harris. - *Publié par* Service des communications. CEGEP du Vieux Montréal. C.P. 444, Succursale N, 200 ouest, rue Sherbrooke, Montréal, Qué., avril 1971-
Hebdomadaire. Publication d'institution (universités, écoles..), bulletin, 16 p. Tirage: 4000

Wah Ying Yat Pa *See* Chinese times

War cry / *sponsored by* The Salvation Army ; *edited by* Eric Coward. - *Published by* Wyvel Crozier. 455 North Service Rd. E., Oakville, Ont., November 1884-
Weekly. Religious publication, magazine format, 16 p. Includes book reviews. Circulation: 73,000
$.10 per issue : $6.00 per year : $6.50 per year, U.S. : $8.00 per year, foreign.

Wascana review / *edited by* H.C. Dillow. - *Published by* Wascana Press. Department of English, University of Saskatchewan, Regina Campus, Regina, Sask., Fall 1966-
Issued twice a year. Special interest, magazine format, 100 p. Includes book reviews. Circulation: 250
Indexed in Can. essay and lit. ind.
$2.00 per issue : $3.50 per year.

Wastes handling / *edited by* Walter Jones. - *Published by* Maclean-Hunter Ltd. 481 University Ave., Toronto, Ont. M5W 1A7, 1974-
Irregular. Trade publication, magazine format, Supplement to Civic : the public works magazine.
$3.00 per issue.

Watchmaking news and views - *Published by* Canadian Jewellers' Association. 663 Yonge St., Toronto, Ont. M4Y 2A4.
Association publication.

Water and pollution control / *edited by* L.F. Webster. - *Published by* Southam Business Publications Ltd. 1450 Don Mills Rd., Don Mills, Ont. M3B 2X7, 1893-
Monthly. Includes advertising. Circulation: 8646

Water pollution research in Canada / *sponsored by* Canadian Symposium on Water Pollution Research ; *edited by* Jean S. Seddon. - *Published by* Mrs. J.S. Seddon. Room 314, Haultain Bldg., University of Toronto, Toronto, Ont. (Subscription address: Executive Editor, Water Pollution Research in Canada, Institute for Environmental Studies, University of Toronto, Toronto, Ont. H5S 1A4) 1966-
Annual. Proceedings of the annual symposium, book format, 250 p.
Indexed in Biol. abstr., Pollut. abstr.
$10.00.

Water polo in Canada / *edited by* Razso Gallow. - *Published by* Canadian Water Polo Association. 333 River Rd., Ottawa, Ont. K1L 8B9, March 1974-
Quarterly. Association publication, newsletter format, 24 p. Circulation: 300
ISSN 0317-0543 $.25 per issue : $1.00 per year.

Waterloo Campus (June 1962-December 1974) *See* Laurier campus

Waterloo Historical Society. Annual volume / *edited by* Publication Committee. - *Published by* Waterloo Historical Society. 131 William St. W., Waterloo, Ont. N2L 1K2, 1913-
Annual. Association publication, 90 p. Circulation: 550
ISSN 0315-5021 $2.00. Controlled circulation.

Waves / *edited by* Bernice Lever, Robert Casto and Kenneth Sherman. - *Published by* York University. Room 141, Petrie Science Bldg., York University, 4700 Keele St., Downsview, Ont., 1970?-
Issued 3 times a year. Special interest, magazine format, 80 p. available in microform. Back issues available.
Indexed in Can. essay and lit. ind.
$2.00 per issue : $4.00 per year (Libraries $5.00).

We and the world *See* My i svit

Weather timetable : how to foretell your weather = La Couleur du temps: comment prévoir le temps dans votre région / *edited by* Eric Neal. - *Published by* Eric Neal. 3500, Henri-Bourassa, E., Montréal, Qué. H1H 4Y9, September 1956-
Monthly. Special interest, newsletter format, 4 p. Language: English and French.
$5.00 per year. Prepayment required.

Webster's community press directory - *Published by* Warwick Webster Ltd. 319 Canice St., Orillia, Ont. L3V 4J6, 1974-
Issued twice a year. Trade publication, 64 p.
$15.00 per issue : $25.00 per year : $15.00 per volume : $30.00 per year, foreign. Controlled circulation. Prepayment required.

The Wedding guide / *edited by* Peter Mack. - *Published by* Peter Mack. Pacific Programs Ltd. 1186 Nicola St., Vancouver, B.C. V6G 2E5, 1973-
Quarterly. Magazine format, Includes advertising.

Weekend magazine / *edited by* Sheena Paterson. - *Published by* Derek A. Price. Montreal Standard (1973) Ltd. 231 St. James St. W., Montreal, Que. H2Y 1M6, September 1951-
Weekly. General interest, magazine format, 24 p. Includes advertising. Circulation: 1.7 million (3 cities)
Distributed in 23 newspapers.

Weekly labour press service / *edited by* Morden Lazarus. - *Published by* Co-operative Press Associates. P.O. Box 174, Postal Station R, Toronto, Ont.
Special interest, newsletter format,

Wellington County Historical Research Society. Newsletter / *edited by* Mrs. Thos. J. Hutchinson. - *Published by* Wellington County Historical Research Society. 176 Smith St., Elora, Ont., 1972-
Irregular (approximately 3 issues per year). Association publication, newsletter format, 2-3 p.

The Welsh black bulletin / *edited by* Nancy Phal. - *Published by* The Welsh Black Bulletin. Site 5, Box 6, Hanna, Alta. T0J 1P0.
Quarterly. Trade publication, newsletter format, 6 p.

WesTrade traffic directory - *Published by* J.B. Tompkins. WesTrade Publications Ltd. Suite 202, 1089 W. Broadway, Vancouver, B.C.
Trade publication. Includes advertising.

Wescoreb interim - *Published by* Westminster County Real Estate Board. P.O. Box 99, 15483 - 104th Ave., Surrey, B.C. V3T 4W4, 1973-
Former title(s): Westminster county crier (1959-1972)
Issued every other month. House/company organ, newsletter format, 4 p. supplements issued. Circulation: 800
Free.

West Coast review / *sponsored by* Simon Fraser University ; *edited by* Frederick H. Candelaria. - *Published by* West Coast Review. Simon Fraser University, Burnaby, B.C. V5A 1S6, 1966-
Quarterly. Special interest, magazine format, 64 p. Language: English and others. Includes book reviews, volume index. Circulation: 750
Indexed in Can. essay and lit. ind.
$1.50 per issue : $6.00 per year.

West Van bookman - *Published by* West Vancouver memorial library. 1950 Marine Dr., West Vancouver, B.C., July 1973-
Institutional publication (Universities, schools, etc.), newsletter format, 4 p. Includes book reviews. Circulation: 1000
ISSN 0317-0446 Controlled circulation.

Western angling / *edited by* J.L. Grundle. - *Published by* Western Fish and Game Magazine Ltd. Suite 205, 1591 Bowser Ave., North Vancouver, B.C., 1965-
Former title(s): Western fish and wildlife.
Monthly. Magazine format, Includes advertising. Circulation: 10,347
$.75 per issue : $7.50 per year.

Western Canada District news (to January 1968) *See* KiwaNews : Western Canada district

Western Canada reclamation *See* Reclamation

Western Canada skier / *edited by* Ian F. Brown. - *Published by* Ian F. Brown. Western Ski Promotions Ltd. P.O. Box 2531, Vancouver, B.C.
Irregular (approximately 6 issues per year). Magazine format, Includes advertising.
$2.00 : $3.00 for 2 years : $4.00 for 3 years.

Western Canada Water and Sewage Conference. Bulletin - *Published by* Western Canada Water and Sewage Conference. P.O. Box 194, Postal Station C, Winnipeg, Man.
Quarterly. Association publication, newsletter format, 4-6 p. Includes advertising.
Subscription included in membership fee ($10.00). Controlled circulation.

Western Canadian journal of anthropology / *edited by* Douglas Hudson and Patricia A. McCormack. - *Published by* Department of Anthropology. University of Alberta. Edmonton, Alta. T6G 2E1.
Quarterly. Institutional publication (Universities, schools, etc.), magazine format, 75 p. Includes book reviews, volume index.
Circulation: 585
Indexed in Soc. sci. cit. ind., North. tit.
$7.50 (Institutions $15.00). Prepayment required.

Western Canadian lumber worker / *edited by* P.S. Kerr. - *Published by* Western Canadian Regional. International Woodworkers of America - AFL, CIO, CLC. 2859 Commercial Dr., Vancouver, B.C. V5N 4C7, 1939-
Monthly. Magazine format, Includes advertising.
$2.00 per year.

Western Canadian Society for Horticulture. Report of proceedings of annual meetings / *edited by* E.W. Toop. - *Published by* Western Canadian Society for Horticulture. Room 350, Horticulture Division, Agriculture Building, University of Alberta, Edmonton, Alta. (Subscription address: L.M. Lenz, Department of Plant Science, University of Manitoba, Winnipeg, Man.) 1943-
Annual. Association publication, proceedings of the annual meeting, journal format, 120 p.
ISSN 0083-8810 $5.00.

Western Canadian tidings (to 1932) *See* Canadian union messenger

Western Catholic *See* Western Catholic reporter

Western Catholic reporter / *edited by* Victor Misutka. - *Published by* Joseph N. MacNeil. 10044-113 St., Edmonton, Alta. (Subscription address: 9537-76 Ave., Edmonton, Alta. T6C 4H7) January 1965-
Former title(s): Western Catholic.
Weekly. Church publication, newspaper format, 16 p. Includes book reviews, film reviews, advertising. Circulation: 28,000
ISSN 0512-5235 $6.00 per year : $7.00 per year, foreign. Controlled circulation.

Western commerce and construction / *edited by* Peter Maarsman. - *Published by* David B. Johnson. Trans West Publishers Ltd. Suite 4, 119 W. Broadway, Vancouver, B.C. V5Y 1P4, 1973-
Issued every other month. Trade publication. Includes advertising. Circulation: 6966
$1.00 per issue : $4.50 per year.

Western construction and industry / *edited by* King Kearns. - *Published by* Mercury Publications Ltd. 200-633 Portage Ave., Winnipeg, Man. R3B 2Z9, 1949-
Monthly. Trade publication. Includes advertising. Circulation: 5352
$.50 per issue : $8.00 per year : $12.00 for 2 years : $16.00 for 3 years.

Western fish and wildlife *See* Western angling

Western fisheries / *edited by* Henry Frew. - *Published by* Roy Wrigley Publications Ltd. 1104 Hornby St., Vancouver, B.C., 1929-
Monthly. Trade publication. Includes advertising. Circulation: 2272
Indexed in Can. B.P.I.
$6.00 per year : $10.00 for 2 years.

Western geographical series / *edited by* Harold D. Foster. - *Published by* Leon and Thea Koerner Foundation. Department of Geography. University of Victoria. P.O. Box 1700, Victoria, B.C. (Subscription address: c/o Mrs. Alison Griffith, P.O. Box 1700, Victoria, B.C) January 1970-
Irregular (approximately 3-4 issues per year). Institutional publication (Universities, schools, etc.), 300 p. Circulation: 750
ISSN 0315-2022 $4.00 per issue : $12.00 per year.

Western grocer and food store manager / *edited by* King Kearns. - *Published by* Mercury Publications Ltd. 84 Isabel St., Winnipeg, Man.
Issued every other month. Trade publication, business, Includes advertising. Circulation: 5204
$.50 per issue : $4.00 per year : $6.00 for 2 years : $8.00 for 3 years.

Western horizons / *edited by* T.H. Glenwright. - *Published by* National Drugs Ltd. P.O. Box 758, 1586 Wall St. Winnipeg, Man. R3C 2M5, 1966-
Quarterly. Trade publication, magazine format, 40 p. Circulation: 3500
$1.00 per issue. Controlled circulation.

Western Institute for the Deaf. W.I.D. news / *edited by* G.W. Magarrell. - *Published by* Western Institute for the Deaf. 2125 West 7th Ave., Vancouver, B.C., 1967-
Irregular (approximately 8 issues per year). Association publication, newsletter format, 4 p. Circulation: 600
Subscription included in membership fee $3.00.

Western law review *See* Western Ontario law review

Western livestock and agricultural news - *Published by* D. Homersham. Homersham Advertising Agency Ltd. 215 Inglewood Bldg., 11802-124 St., Edmonton, Alta. T5I 0M3, 1970-
Monthly. Newspaper format, 16 p. Includes advertising. Circulation: 11,950
$2.00 per year.

Western living / *edited by* Liz Bryan. - *Published by* John Bryan. Bryan Publications Ltd. Suite 200, 1104 Hornby St., Vancouver, B.C., 1971-
Irregular (approximately 10 issues per year). Magazine format, Includes advertising. Circulation: 51,305
$6.00 per year : $7.00 per year, U.S. : $12.00 per year, foreign.

Western management/Pattern and probe / *edited by* Doreen Sanders. - *Published by* School of Business Administration. University of Western Ontario. London, Ont.
Former title(s): Pattern and probe.
Issued twice a year. Institutional publication (Universities, schools, etc.), magazine format, 36 p.
Free.

Western Mine and Oil Charts *See* Canadian mining and oil stock charts

Western miner / *edited by* Peter C. Bell. - *Published by* Western Miner Press Ltd. Suite 305, 1200 West Pender St., Vancouver, B.C. V6E 2S9, 1928-
Former title(s): Western miner and oil review.
Monthly. Magazine format, 60 p. Includes book reviews, advertising, volume index. Circulation: 6500
Indexed in North. tit., Arct. bibl.
$1.50 per issue : $5.00 per year : $10.00 per year, foreign. Controlled circulation. Prepayment required.

Western miner and oil review *See* Western miner

Western mining and oil charts *See* Canadian weekly mining and oil stock charts

Western motor fleet / *edited by* King Kearns. - *Published by* G.R. Yeo. Mercury Publications Ltd. 200-633 Portage Ave., Winnipeg, Man. R3B 2Z9.
Monthly. Trade publication. Includes advertising. Circulation: 4349
$.50 per issue : $6.00 per year : $9.00 for 2 years : $12.00 for 3 years.

Western motordom (1930-1950) *See* Alberta motorist

Western news / *edited by* Alan B. Johnston. - *Published by* L.T. Moore. University Relations and Information. University of Western Ontario. Alumni Hall, UWO, London, Ont. N6A 3K7, November 1972-
Former title(s): UWO news (to 1972)
Weekly. Institutional publication (Universities, schools, etc.), newspaper format, 8-12 p. Includes book reviews. supplements issued. Circulation: 10,500
ISSN 0316-8654

Western Ontario farmer / *edited by* S.M. Barker. - *Published by* James O. Johnston. Bowes Publishers Ltd. 994 Adelaide St. S., London, Ont. N6E 1R6, 1968-
Weekly. Includes advertising. Circulation: 22,681
$7.00 per year.

Western Ontario historical notes / *edited by* Edward Phelps. - *Published by* The D.B. Weldon Library. University of Western Ontario. 1151 Richmond St., London, Ont., 1942-
Irregular (approximately 1 issue per year). Magazine format, 64 p. Includes cumulative index. available in microform. Circulation: 800
$2.00 per issue. Prepayment required.

Western Ontario law review - *Published by* Carswell Company Ltd. 2330 Midland Ave., Agincourt, Ont. M1S 1P7, 1967-
Former title(s): Western law review.
Annual.
ISSN 0083-8950

Western potter / *edited by* Ruth Meechan. - *Published by* Guild of B.C. Potters. 315 W. Cordova, Vancouver, B.C. V6V 1E5.
Issued twice a year. Magazine format, Includes book reviews, advertising.
$.75 per issue : $7.50 per year. Subscription included in membership fee.

The Western producer (1924-1974) *See* Western producer : a weekly newspaper serving Western Canadian farmers

Western producer : a weekly newspaper serving Western Canadian farmers / *sponsored by* Saskatchewan Wheat Pool ; *edited by* R.H.D. Phillips. - *Published by* R.H.D. Phillips. P.O. Box 2500, Saskatoon, Sask. S7K 2C4, 1923-
Former title(s): The Western producer (1924-1974) The Progressive (1923-1924)
Weekly. Newspaper format, 54 p. Includes advertising. Magazine supplement issued weekly. Circulation: 154,504
$.20 per issue : $5.00 per year : $10.00 per year, foreign. Prepayment required.

Western racing review / *edited by* P.A. McMahon. - *Published by* Western Racing Revue. P.O. Box 2234, Calgary, Alta. T2P 2M7.
Annual. Magazine format, Includes advertising.
$2.50 per issue.

Western regular Baptist *See* The B.C. regular Baptist

Western retailer (1912-1962) *See* National retailer

Western thoroughbred / *edited by* Don Fleming. - *Published by* W.W. Acton. Western Thoroughbred. 727-33A St. N.W., Calgary, Alta. T2N 2X2.
Annual. Magazine format, Includes advertising.
$3.75 per year.

Western tract news / *edited by* R.W. Rice. - *Published by* Western Tract Mission. 401-33rd St. W., Saskatoon, Sask. S7L 0V5, 1943-
Issued every other month. Church publication, magazine format, 20 p. Circulation: 5000
Free.

Western wheatman (Spring 1970-June 1971) *See* Palliser Wheat Growers Association. Newsletter

Westminster county crier (1959-1972) *See* Wescoreb interim

Westworld : the magazine of travel, leisure and living / *edited by* Bill Mayrs. - *Published by* Bill Mayrs. Westworld Publications Ltd. P.O. Box 6680, Vancouver, B.C. V6B 4L4, January 1, 1975-
Former title(s): BC motorist (1961-1974)
Issued every other month. General interest, magazine format, 68 p. Includes book reviews, advertising, volume index. Circulation: 180,000
ISSN 0316-1315 $1.00 per issue : $4.50 per year : $6.00 per year, U.S. : $8.00 per year, foreign.

What the mining industry means to Canada (1964-1967) *See* Mining : what it means to Canada

Whatchamacallit (1970-1973) *See* Ontario water skier

What's new / *edited by* Carol Winter. - *Published by* Public Information Department. Hospital for Sick Children. 555 University Ave., Toronto, Ont. M5G 1X8, 1968-
Former title(s): Paediatric patter (1968-1969)
Monthly. House/company organ, newsletter format, 12 p. Circulation: 4700
Controlled circulation.

What's on in Ottawa = Voici Ottawa / *edited by* Edna Hall and Ann Heard. - *Published by* What's On Publishing Co. 77 Maclaren St., Ottawa, Ont. K2P 0K5.
Monthly. Calendar of events, magazine format, 100 p. Language: English and French. Includes book reviews, advertising.
$5.00 per year (1st class) : $3.00 per year (2nd class). Controlled circulation.

"What's your gas Q" - papers - *Published by* Canadian Gas Association. 55 Scarsdale Rd., Don Mills, Ont. M3B 2R3, 1960-
Irregular (approximately 3 issues per year). Trade publication, newsletter format, 3 p.
$10.00 for the series to date. Controlled circulation.

Wheat pool budget / *edited by* Manager of Publicity. - *Published by* The Public Relations Department. Alberta Wheat Pool. P.O. Box 2700, Calgary, Alta. T2P 2P5, 1927-
Weekly. House/company organ, newsletter format, 4 p. Circulation: 21,000
Free.

Wheelspin news : Canada's autosport newsmagazine / *edited by* Doug Mephan (editorial director) and Paul Ogden (managing director). - *Published by* Wheelspin News Inc. 3057 Universal Dr., Mississauga, Ont. L4X 2E2, April 1965-
Former title(s): International wheelspin news.
Irregular (approximately 20 issues per year). Special interest, magtab format, 28 p. Includes book reviews, advertising.
ISSN 0020-9104 $.50 per issue : $10.00 per year : $15.00 per year, foreign. Prepayment required.

White bulletin (September 1958-November 1966) *See* The Canadian Bankers' Association. CBA bulletin

The Whiteshell echo / *edited by* Wes Rowson. - *Published by* L.A. Leech. Lance Publishing Co. Ltd. 620 Dakota Dr., Winnipeg, Man. R2M 3K2.
Monthly. Magazine format, Includes advertising. Circulation: 24,600
$3.00 per year.

Who's who biographical service : Canada - *Published by* Who's who Canadian Publications. 171 Yonge St., Toronto, Ont. M5C 2N4, June 1973-
Issued twice a year. Biography, 38 p.
ISSN 0068-9963 $11.00 per issue : $38.00 for 2 years.

Who's who in Canadian placement? / *edited by* Phil Renouf and Emile Simard. - *Published by* University and College Placement Association. 254A Main St. N., Markham, Ont. L3P 1Y7, 1966-
Annual. Directory, 135-150 p. Language: English and French. Circulation: 1000
$6.00. Controlled circulation.

Who's who in Canadian talent *See* Canadian music industry who's who

Who's who in Toronto construction - *Published by* Toronto Construction Association. 1 Sparks Ave., Willowdale, Ont. M2H 2W1.
Former title(s): The Toronto Construction Association Membership roster.
Annual. Directory, 200 p. Circulation: 2400
ISSN 0316-8026 $12.50. Prepayment required.

Widget / *edited by* Jeffrey D. Sherman. - *Published by* Commerce Students' Association. University of Toronto. Room 2005, 100 St. George St., Toronto, M5S 1A1, October 1974-
Former title(s): Commerce journal (1933-1970)
Monthly. Student publication, newsletter format, 2 p. Circulation: 2000
$.25 per issue. Free.

Wildland news / *edited by* P.A. Hardy. - *Published by* Algonquin Wildlands League. P.O. Box 114, Postal Station Q, 1430 Yonge St., Toronto, Ont. M4T 1Y6, September 1968-
Irregular (approximately 4 issues per year). Association publication, newsletter format, 6 p. Includes book reviews. Circulation: 2500
ISSN 0316-3350 Subscription included in membership fee $5.00. Controlled circulation.

Wildlife crusader / *edited by* Paul F. Murray. - *Published by* Manitoba Wildlife Federation. 1870 Notre Dame Ave., Winnipeg, Man., 1944-
Monthly. Association publication, magazine format, 48 p. Includes book reviews, advertising. Circulation: 35,610
$5.00 per year : $6.00 per year, foreign. Prepayment required.

Wildlife news *See* Wildlife report : the Canadian scene

Wildlife report : the Canadian scene / *edited by* Frank Ratcliffe. - *Published by* Canadian Wildlife Federation. 1419 Carling Ave., Ottawa, Ont. K1Z 7L7, January 1974-
Former title(s): Wildlife news.
Issued every other month. Association publication, newsletter format, 8 p. Includes book reviews. A supplement to International wildlife magazine. Circulation: 40,000
Indexed in North. tit.
$10.50 per year with CWF membership only.

The Windmill herald / *edited by* Albert Vanderheide. - *Published by* A.A. Vanderheide. Vanderheide Publishing Co. Ltd. P.O. Box 533, New Westminster, B.C. V3L 4Y8, April 1958-
Former title(s): Goed nieuws (May 1958-January 1971)
Issued every other week. Ethnic press, newspaper format, 24 p. Language: Dutch. Includes advertising. available in microform. Circulation: 7813
$.20 per issue : $4.25 per year. Prepayment required.

Windsor and Essex County development news / *edited by* J.R. Moore. - *Published by* Windsor-Essex County Development Commission. 500 Riverside Dr. W., Windsor, Ont. N9A 5K6, December 1974-
Quarterly. House/company organ, newsletter format, 4 p. Circulation: 4000
Free. Controlled circulation.

Windsor and Essex county manufacturers directory - *Published by* Windsor-Essex County Development Commission. 500 Riverside Dr. W., Windsor, Ont. N9A 5K6, 1927-
Former title(s): Greater Windsor manufacturers directory (1969-1972)
Annual. Directory, 114 p.
$5.00.

Windsor poésie *See* Poetry - Windsor

Windsor this month / *edited by* Scott Clarke Cuthbert. - *Published by* Thomas M. Harris. Metro Plaza. Suite 502, 2260 University Ave. W., Windsor, Ont. N9B 1E5, 1974-
Monthly. Magazine format, Includes advertising.
$.75 per issue : $7.00 per year : $8.00 per year, U.S. : $9.00 per year, foreign.

The Windwing / *edited by* Lucide Rioux. - *Published by* New Brunswick Antique Auto Club. P.O. Box 25, R.R. 6 (Silverwood), Fredericton, N.B. E3B 4X7, September 1966-
Former title(s): The Maritime singer.
Quarterly. Association publication, magazine format, 25 p. Includes advertising. Circulation: 246
$5.00 per year. Members only. Prepayment required.

Winnipeg industrial topics / *edited by* G.E. Paris. - *Published by* Winnipeg Economic Development Board Inc. 515-305 Broadway, Winnipeg, Man. R3C 0R9, July 1972 (vol. 32, 3)-
Former title(s): Greater Winnipeg industrial topics (July 1952-May 1972) Manitoba industrial topics (May 1941-August 1950)
Issued every other month. Special interest, magazine format, 12 p. Circulation: 4500
ISSN 0316-3458 Free. Controlled circulation.

Wise owl news / *edited by* Brent Thrall. - *Published by* The Canadian National Institute for the Blind. 1929 Bayview Ave., Toronto, Ont. M4G 3E8, 1967-
Irregular (approximately 3 issues per year). Institutional publication (Universities, schools, etc.), newsletter format, 4 p. Language: English and French.

Woman : Lithuanian women's magazine *See* Moteris : lietuviy motery zurnalas

Woman's world *See* Zhinochy svit

Women, sport, and leisure - *Published by* SIRLS. Faculty of Human Kinetics and Leisure Studies. University of Waterloo. Waterloo, Ont. N2L 3G1.
Quarterly. Bibliography, computer printout, $20.00 per year. $100.00 subscription to SIRLS required.

The Wood duck / *edited by* Hazel Broker. - *Published by* Hamilton Naturalists' Club. P.O. Box 182, Postal Station E, Hamilton, Ont. L8S 4L5, 1950-
Irregular (approximately 9 issues per year). Newsletter format, 7-10 p. Includes book reviews. Circulation: 450-500
ISSN 0049-7886 Free. Mailed free to members, exchange, and complimentary lists.

Woodsworth College. Arts and Science Alumni Association. Newsletter / *edited by* Dianne Haist. - *Published by* Alumni House. University of Toronto. 49 Willcocks St., Toronto, Ont. M5S 1A1, June 1974-
Annual. Alumni publication, newsletter format, 6 p.
Free to alumni.

Word on guard = La parole en gard *See* Slovo na storozhi

Wordjock (1967-70) *See* Empty belly : a magazine of poetry and communication

Words from inside / *edited by* George McWhirter. - *Published by* Prison Arts Foundation. 143 - 5th Ave., Brantford, Ont. N3S 1A3, 1971-
Annual. Penal press, magazine format, 40 p. Language: English and French.
$2.00.

Work and leisure - *Published by* SIRLS. Faculty of Human Kinetics and Leisure Studies. University of Waterloo. Waterloo, Ont. N2L 3G1.
Quarterly. Bibliography, computer printout, $20.00 per year. $100.00 subscription to SIRLS required.

The Worker = L'Ouvrier - *Published by* Canadian Party of Labour. P.O. Box 1151, Adelaide Postal Station, Toronto, Ont., September 1973-
Former title(s): Canadian worker (1969-1973)
ISSN 0316-3199

Working papers on bilingualism = Travaux de recherches sur le bilinguisme / *edited by* Merrill Swain and Guy Dumas. - *Published by* Ontario Institute for Studies in Education. 252 Bloor St. W., Toronto, Ont. M5S 1V6, November 1973-
Irregular (approximatley 4 issues per year). Spiral bound format, 100 p. Language: English and French ; summaries: English and French.
Free upon request. Controlled circulation.

Working safely / *edited by* Paige Ormandy. - *Published by* New Brunswick Industrial Safety Council. P.O. Box 2315C, Saint John, N.B., 1962-
Issued every other month. Newsletter format, 6 p. Language: English and French. Circulation: 8000
Free.

World affairs (1935-1970) *See* Canada and the world : for students of world affairs

World air transport statistics - *Published by* International Air Transport Association. 1155 Mansfield St., Montreal, Que. H3B 4A4, 1956-
Annual. Statistics, 70 p.
$6.00. Prepayment required.

World Congress of Free Ukrainians = Visnyk Svitovoho kongresu vil'nykh ukraîntsiv / *edited by* Jurij Darewych. - *Published by* World Congress of Free Ukrainians. Suite 1701, 2200 Yonge St., Toronto, Ont. M4S 2C6, June 1974-
Irregular (approximately 3-4 issues per year). Ethnic press, magazine format, 35 p. Language: Ukrainian and English. Circulation: 7000
ISSN 0316-9081 $25.00 per year.

World Federalist. Canadian ed - *Published by* World Federalists of Canada. 46 Elgin St., Ottawa, Ont.
Former title(s): Canadian World Federalist (1961-1968)
Issued every other month.
Indexed in Peace research abstr. j.

World Marxist review: problems of peace and socialism - *Published by* Progress Books. 487 Adelaide W., Toronto, Ont. M5Y 1T4, 1968-
Monthly. Special interest, journal format, 144 p.
Indexed in Soc. sci. ind., P.A.I.S., Hist. abstr.; Amer. hist. and life.
$.50 per issue : $5.00 per year : $8.50 per year, foreign.

Wrigley's hotel-motel directory - *Published by* R.C. Gray. Wrigley Directories Ltd. 1104 Hornby St., Vancouver, B.C., 1910-
Annual. Trade publication. Includes advertising.
$8.50 per year.

Write / *edited by* Roger Greenwald. - *Published by* Writ Magazine. c/o Innis College, University of Toronto, 63 St. George St., Toronto, Ont., Spring 1970-
Irregular (approximately 1-2 issues per year). Magazine format, 104 p. Includes book reviews. Back issues available. Circulation: 500
ISSN 0316-3768 $7.00 for 2 issues.

Xaverian weekly / *edited by* Cathy Kerr. - *Published by* Student Union. St. Francis Xavier University. P.O. Box 924, Antigonish, N.S. B0H 1C0, 1895-
Weekly. Student publication, newspaper format, 24 p. Includes book reviews, play reviews. Circulation: 2500
$3.00 per year. Controlled circulation.

X-ray (1919 to 1927) *See* Health rays

YW resource / *edited by* Sheila Ward. - *Published by* Young Women's Christian Association of Canada. National Board, 571 Jarvis St., Toronto, Ont. M4Y 2J1, February 1974-
Former title(s): National newsletter - YWCA of Canada.
Issued every other week, irregular during the summer. House/company organ, newspaper format, 4 p. Language: English (French). Includes book reviews, advertising.
Free.

Y-Canada / *edited by* R.G. Rogers. - *Published by* National Council of YMCA's of Canada. 2160 Yonge St., Toronto, Ont. M4S 2A9, September 1971-
Irregular (approximately 1-2 issues per year). House/company organ, newsletter format, 12 p. Language: English and French. Circulation: 4800
ISSN 0315-095X Free.

Yes, there is Canadian music = Oui, notre musique existe - *Published by* BMI Canada Ltd. 41 Valleybrook Dr., Don Mills, Ont. M3B 2S6, January 1971-
Monthly. A list of all Canadian music licensed by BMI Canada Limited that has been recorded, sheets, 10 p. Circulation: 500
Controlled circulation.

Yevanhel's'kyi ranok = Evangelical morning / *edited by* Weadimir Borowsky. - *Published by* Ukrainian Evangelical Alliance of North America. 5610 Trowbridge Dr., Dunwoody, Georgia 30338, U.S.A. (Subscription address: "Ev. morning", P.O. Box 185, Postal Station E, Toronto, Ont. M6H 4E2)
Former title(s): Ranok = Morning; Kanadiysky ranon = Canadian morning.
Quarterly. Church publication, magazine format, 16 p. Language: Ukrainian with two pages in English. Includes book reviews, record reviews, advertising. Circulation: 800
$3.00 per year.

Yiddish press / *edited by* S.B. Tauber. - *Published by* The Yiddish Press Inc. P.O. Box 3616, 230 Cathedral Ave., Winnipeg, Man., 1910-
Weekly. Special interest. Language: Yiddish. Includes advertising.
$8.00 per year.

Yonge-Bloor-Bay Association Inc. The Bulletin / *edited by* John L. Adam. - *Published by* Yonge-Bloor-Bay Association Inc. Room 231, Manulife Centre, 55 Bloor St. W., Toronto, Ont. M4W 1A6.
Issued 8 times a year. Association publication, newsletter format, 16-18 p. Includes advertising. Circulation: 400
Subscription included in membership fee.

The York Communiqué (October 1967-May 1970) *See* Communique

The York pioneer / *edited by* Diana K. Park. - *Published by* York Pioneer and Historical Society. P.O. Box 481, Postal Station K, Toronto, Ont. M4P 2G9, 1904-
Annual. Association publication, magazine format, 90-100 p. Back issues available. Circulation: 1000
ISSN 0513-2711 $2.00. Controlled circulation.

York University. Institute for Behavioural Research. Newsletter - *Published by* Institute for Behavioral Research. York University. 4700 Keele St., Downsview, Ont. M3J 2R6, September 1975-
Former title(s): Bulletin - York University. Institute for Behavioral Research (1968-1972)
Quarterly. Institutional publication (Universities, schools, etc.), newsletter format,

York University Alumni Association communiqué (1970-1972) *See* Communique

Young companion / *edited by* Elmo Stoll. - *Published by* Pathway Publishers. Route 4, Aylmer, Ont., January 1971-
Former title(s): Ambassador of peace (January 1966-December 1970)
Monthly. Church publication, magazine format, 28 p. Circulation: 13,000
$2.50 per year.

Young family magazine - *Published by* Myroslava Baker. P.O. Box 8, Postal Station C, Toronto, Ont. M6J 3M8, November 1975-
Quarterly.

Young Men's Christian Association. Vancouver Downtown. Department of Health and Physical Education. The Weekly news / *edited by* T.W. Connolly. - *Published by* Y.M.C.A. 955 Burrard St., Vancouver, B.C. V6Z 1Y2.
Weekly. House/company organ, newsletter format, 2 p. Circulation: 750
Free.

The Young naturalist / *edited by* Paul Sanagan. - *Published by* Federation of Ontario Naturalists. 1262 Don Mills Rd., Don Mills, Ont. M3B 2W7, 1959-
Monthly except July and August. Association publication, magazine format, 16 p. Circulation: 19,000
$3.50 per year. Bulk rates to teachers. Special rates offered. Prepayment required.

The Young Naturalist (to 1975) *See* Owl

Young pilot / *edited by* T.S. Rendal. - *Published by* Prairie Bible Institute. Three Hills, Alta. T0M 2A0.
Monthly. Church publication, magazine format, 48 p. Circulation: 24,000
$2.00 per year.

Young socialist / *edited by* Katie Curtin. - *Published by* Young Socialist. P.O. Box 517, Postal Station A, Toronto, Ont., September 1970-
Former title(s): Young socialist forum (December 1963-August 1970)
Issued every other month. Student publication, newspaper format, 12 p. Includes book reviews.
$.25 per issue : $1.00 per year.

Young socialist forum (December 1963-August 1970) *See* Young socialist

The Young soldier / *edited by* Eric Coward. - *Published by* The Salvation Army Triumph Press. 455 North Service Rd., Oakville, Ont. L6H 1A5, January 1895-
Weekly. Church publication, magazine format, 8 p. Circulation: 18,000
$.05 per issue : $2.50 per year.

Young Ukraine *See* Moloda Ukraina

Young worker / *edited by* Daniel Hammond. - *Published by* Young Worker Publishing Co. 24 Cecil St., Toronto 2B, Ont., October 1970-
Irregular (approximately 7 times per year). Special interest, newspaper format, 8 p. Includes film reviews. Circulation: 5000
$.10 per issue.

Your community news / *sponsored by* Allied Jewish Community Services ; *edited by* Joe King. - *Published by* Manuel Batshaw. 5151 Cote St. Catherine Rd., Montreal, Que., H3W 1M6, 1948-
Irregular (approximately 9 issues per year). Ethnic press, newsletter format, 24 p. Includes book reviews, play reviews, advertising. supplements issued. Circulation: 18,900

Your health / *edited by* Scott R. McDonald. - *Published by* British Columbia Tuberculosis-Christmas Seal Society. 906 W. Broadway, Vancouver B.C., August 1937-
Former title(s): The Tranquillian (August 1921-July 1937)
Quarterly. Association publication, magazine format, 16 p. Circulation: 10,000
Free.

Your host around Hamilton / *edited by* Howard G. Fairclough. - *Published by* Howard Fairclough Associates. P.O. Box 850, Hamilton, Ont. L8N 3N9, July 1960-
Monthly. Calendar of events, pamphlet format, 12 p.
$.50 per issue : $6.00 per year. Free.

Your school reports *See* Across the board

Youth for Christ happening / *edited by* Marv Wall and Craig Kelman. - *Published by* Greater Winnipeg Youth for Christ. P.O. Box 385, 186 Furby, Winnipeg, Man., 1970-
Monthly. Church publication, newsletter format, 4 p.
Free.

Youth on the spot : job description for teen volunteers - *Published by* Social Planning and Research Council of Hamilton and District. 153 1/2 King St. E., Hamilton, Ont. L8N 1B1.
Issued twice a year. Association publication, magazine format, 38 p. Includes updating service.
$1.00 per issue.

Youth profile : the Christ's ambassadors magazine / *edited by* Tom Wright. - *Published by* Youth Department of the Pentecostal Assemblies of Canada. 10 Overlea Blvd., Toronto, Ont. M4H 1A5, April 1974-
Monthly 10 times a year. Church publication, magazine format, 16 p. Includes book reviews, film reviews, record reviews, advertising. Circulation: 85
ISSN 0315-1328 $5.00 per year.

Youth science news - *Published by* Youth Science Foundation. 302 - 151 Slater St., Ottawa, Ont. K1P 5H3, September 1975-
Monthly except July and August. Special interest, newspaper format, 8 p.
$.25 per issue : $2.00 per year. Prepayment required.

Yunak / *sponsored by* Plast - Ukrainian Youth Association ; *edited by* Mrs. O. Kuzmowycz. - *Published by* Plast Publication. 2445a Bloor St. W., Toronto, Ont. M6S 1P7, January 1963-
Issued 10 times a year. Ethnic press, magazine format, 28 p. Language: Ukrainian. Circulation: 3100
ISSN 0044-1384 $.90 per issue : $9.00 per year. Prepayment required.

Die Zeit. North American edition / *edited by* Haug von Kuenheim. - *Published by* Courier Press Ltd. Suite 304, 455 Spadina Ave., Toronto, Ont. M5S 2G9, 1945-
Weekly. Ethnic press, newspaper format, 24 p. Language: German. available in microform. Circulation: 8048
$.40 per issue : $18.00 per year : $21.00 per year, foreign.

Zero Population Growth. ZPG newsletter / *edited by* Janice Palmer. - *Published by* Toronto Branch. Zero Population Growth. Department of Zoology, University of Toronto, Toronto, Ont., January 1970-
Monthly. Association publication, newsletter format, 12 p. Includes book reviews. Circulation: 250
$1.50 per issue : $1.50 per issue foreign : $10.00 per year.

Zhinochy svit = Woman's world / *edited by* Yaraslava Zorych. - *Published by* Ukrainian Women's Organization of Canada. 18 Leland Ave., Toronto, Ont. M8Z 2X5, 1950-
Monthly. Ethnic press. Language: Ukrainian. Includes advertising. Circulation: 3100
$.60 per issue : $6.00 per year.

Zoolog (1966-1972) *See* Manitoba nature

Zpravodaj / *edited by* Jan Klinka. - *Published by* Jan Klinka. 2720 Oyama Court, Vancouver, B.C., 1969-
Irregular (approximately 6 issues per year). Ethnic press, newsletter format, 12 p. Language: Czech and Slovak. Includes book reviews, record reviews, advertising.
$.30 per issue : $2.00 per year. Free to members.

Zwiazkowiec = The Alliancer / *edited by* B. Heydenkorn. - *Published by* Polish Alliance Press Ltd. 1636 Bloor St. W., Toronto, Ont.
Issued twice a week. Ethnic press, newspaper format, 8 p. Language: Polish.
$.15 per issue : $12.00 per year.

16mm films = Films 16mm / *edited by* The Ottawa Public Library. - *Published by* The Ottawa Public Library. 120 Metcalfe St., Ottawa, Ont. K1P 5M2.
Annual. Catalogue, 63 p. Language: English and French.
$1.00 per issue.

16mm sound films available from the public libraries of Metropolitan Toronto (1968) *See* 16mm films available from the public libraries of Metropolitan Toronto

SUBJECT INDEX

INDEX DES MATIÈRES

List of Subject Headings (English-French)

Accounting Comptabilité
Administration & Government Administration
Advertising Publicité
Aerospace Aérospatial
Agriculture Agriculture
Anthropology Anthropologie
Antiquary Antiquariat
Archaeology Archéologie
Architecture Architecture
Archives Archives
Arctic Arctique
Art Art
Astronomy Astronomie
Atlantic Provinces Provinces atlantiques
Atmospheric Sciences Sciences atmosphériques
Atomic Energy Energie atomique
Automation Automatisation
Automotive Automobile
Aviation Aviation

Banking & Finance Banque & finance
Bibliography Bibliographie
Biology Biologie
Boats Bateaux
Botany Botanique
British Columbia Colombie-Britannique
Building & Construction Construction
Business & Industry Affaires & Industries

Canadian Life Vie canadienne
Cartoons and Caricatures Caricatures et dessins humoristiques
Chemistry Chimie
Children's Periodicals Littérature enfantine – Periodiques
Civil Service Fonction publique
Classical Studies Etudes classiques
Clothing Vêtements
College & University Universités
Conservation Conservation
Consumer Consommation
Co-operatives Coopératives

Dairy Laiterie
Dental Art dentaire

Earth Sciences Science de la terre
Economics Economique
Education Education
Electrical Electrique
Engineering Génie
Environment Environnement
Ethnic Vie ethnique

Family Famille
Film Film
Fire Prevention Prévention des incendies
Fisheries Pêcheries
Food & Nutrition Alimentation & nutrition
Forestry Sylviculture
French Canadian Culture Culture canadienne-française
Fruit Growing Culture fruitiere

Gardening Jardinage
Genealogy Généalogie
Geography Géographie

Hardware Trade Quincaillerie
Health Santé
History Histoire
Home Economics Economie familiale
Horses Chevaux
Hospitals Hôpitaux
Hotels Hôtels
Housing Logement
Humanities Humanités
Hydroelectric Power Energie hydro-électrique

Industrial Relations Relations industrielles
Information Science Service de l'information
Insurance Assurances
International Affairs Affaires internationales
Investment Investissement

Jewellery Bijouterie

Labour Travail
Legal Légal
Librarianship Bibliothécariat
Libraries Bibliothèques
Linguistics Linguistique
Literature Littérature
Lumber & Wood Bois de construction

Liste des vedettes-matière (francaise-anglaise)

Aborigenès Native People
Administration Administration
Aérospatial Aerospace
Affaires & industries Business & Industry
Affaires internationales International Affairs
Agriculture Agriculture
Alimentation & nutrition Food & Nutrition
Animaux d'agrément Pets
Anthropologie Anthropology
Antiquariat Antiquary
Archaéologie Archaeology
Architecture Architecture
Archives Archives
Arctique Arctic
Art Art
Art dentaire Dental
Assurances Insurance
Astronomie Astronomy
Automatisation Automation
Automobile Automotive
Automobilisme Motoring
Aviation Aviation

Banque & finance Banking & Finance
Bateaux Boats
Bibliographie Bibliography
Bibliothécariat Librarianship
Bibliothèques Libraries
Bien être social Social Welfare
Bijouterie Jewellery
Biologie Biology
Bois de construction Lumber & Wood
Botanique Botany
Brevets et marques déposées Patent & Trademark

Canada du nord Northern Canada
Caricatures et dessins humoristiques Cartoons and Caricatures
Chevaux Horses
Chimie Chemistry
Colombie-Britannique British Columbia
Commerce Trade & Commerce
Commercialisation & achat Marketing & Purchasing
Comptabilité Accounting
Conservation Conservation
Consommation Consumer
Construction Building & Construction
Coopératives Co-operatives
Croix-Rouge Red Cross
Culture canadienne-française French Canadian Culture
Culture fruitière Fruit Growing

Écoles Schools
Economie familiale Home Economics
Economique Economics
Edition et impression Publishing and Printing
Education Education
Education physique Physical Education
Electrique Electrical
Energie atomique Atomic Energy
Énergie hydro-électrique Hydro-electric Power
Environnement Environment
Etudes classiques Classical Studies

Fabrication Manufacturing
Famille Family
Femmes Women
Film Film
Fiscalité Taxation
Fonction publique Civil Service

Genéalogie Genealogy
Génie Engineering
Géographie Geography
Gestion Management

Histoire History
Histoire naturelle Natural History
Hôpitaux Hospitals
Hôtels Hotels
Humanités Humanities

Immeuble Real Estate
Industries navales Marine Industry
Investissement Investment

Jardinage Gardening
Jeunesse Youth

Laiterie Dairy
Légal Legal

Linguistique Linguistics
Littérature Literature
Littérature enfantine – Periodiques Children's Periodicals
Logement Housing

Mathématiques Mathematics
Médecine Medical
Médecine vétérinaire Veterinary
Méthodes/matériel de bureau Office Equipment/Methods
Militaire Military
Mines & métallurgie Mining and Metallurgy
Montréal Montreal
Musées Museums
Musique Music

Normes Standards
Nouvelle-Écosse Nova Scotia
Numismatiques Numismatics

Ottawa Ottawa
Ouest canadien Western Canada

Paix Peace
Pâtes et papiers Pulp & Paper
Pêcheries Fisheries
Pétrole & essence Petroleum & Gas
Pharmacologie Pharmaceuticals
Philatélie Philately
Philosophie Philosophy
Photographie Photography
Physique Physics
Planification Planning
Plastiques Plastics
Plein air Outdoors
Police Police
Politique Political
Prévention des incendies Fire Prevention
Provinces atlantiques Atlantic Provinces
Psychologie Psychology

Publicité Advertising

Quincaillerie Hardware Trade

Récréation Recreation
Réhabilitation Rehabilitation
Relations industrielles Industrial Relations
Religion Religion
Ressources hydrauliques Water Resources

Santé Health
Sciences Science
Sciences atmosphériques Atmospheric Sciences
Sciences de la terre Earth Sciences
Sciences infirmières Nursing
Sciences sociales Social Sciences
Sécurité Safety
Service de l'information Information Science
Socialisme Socialism
Sports Sports
Sylviculture Forestry

Technologie Technology
Télécommunications Telecommunications
Textiles Textiles
Théâtre Theatre
Toronto Toronto
Transports Transport
Travail Labour

Universités College & University

Vancouver Vancouver
Vie rurale Rural Life
Vie urbaine Urban Life
Vie ethnique Ethnic Life
Vie canadienne Canadian Life
Vêtements Clothing
Volaille Poultry
Voyages Travel

Corn-soy guide
Country guide : the farm magazine
Country life in British Columbia
Crops guide
Eastern Ontario farmer
Economic planning
Farm and country
Farm focus
Farm journal
Farm news, views and comments
Farm report
Farm trends
Farmer forums
Feed and farm supply dealer
Feeders' day
Focus on beef
Free Press weekly report of farming : the farmer's business publication
Fur trade journal
Good farming
The Grower
Le Guide génétique de l'éleveur
Hog guide
Hog marketplace quarterly
Holstein-Friesian journal
Huron soil : crop news
The Kyloe cry
The Limousin leader and stockman's recorder
The MacDonald journal
Maineline : all about Maine-Anjou
Management digest
Mémoire présenté au Premier Ministre du Canada et membres du cabinet
Le Meunier québécois
National Chinchilla Breeders of Canada. Monthly bulletin
National Farmers Union. Newsletter
North and South Saanich Agricultural Society. Fall exhibition. Prize list
Notes on agriculture
Nova Scotia farmer
The Open door newsletter
Organic Growers Co-operative. Newsletter
Palliser Wheat Growers Association. Newsletter
Presentation to the Prime Minister and members of parliament
Quebec Farmers' Association. Newsletter
Rabbits in Canada
Rapeseed Association of Canada. Meeting. Proceedings
Rapeseed digest
Saskatchewan Red Poll Cattle Club. Annual newsletter
Saskatchewan Stockgrowers Association. Publication
Seed scoop
Shorthorn news
Simmental scene
Statistical handbook
La Terre de chez nous
Union farmer
United Breeders Inc. News
Vegetable Growers Association of Manitoba. Technical and scientific papers presented at the annual meeting
Voice of the Kent farmer
The Welsh black bulletin
Western livestock and agricultural news
Western Ontario farmer
Western producer : a weekly newspaper serving Western Canadian farmers
Wheat pool budget

Anthropology

Anthropologica
Anthropological journal of Canada
Kumtuks review
Napao : a Saskatchewan anthopology journal
Western Canadian journal of anthropology

Antiquary

Antiques in Ontario : Canadian antiques year book
Association for Preservation Technology. Communique = Association pour la préservation et ses techniques. Communiqué
Canadian antiques collector : a journal of antiques and fine art
Collectors' choice newsletter
The Glory hole
Gun talk
The Ontario showcase
Unitt's Canadian price guide to antiques and collectables
The Vancouver Numismatic Society news bulletin

Archaeology

Arch notes
Archaeological newsletter
Canadian Archaeological Association. Bulletin
Manitoba archaeological newsletter
The Midden
Ontario archaeology
Saskatchewan archaeology newsletter
Teiresias : a review and continuing bibliography of Boiotian studies

Architecture

Architecture concept
L'architecture de paysage Canada
Association des architectes de la province du Québec. Bulletin
Association for Preservation Technology. APT bulletin
The Canadian architect
The Canadian architect product bulletin directory
Canadian architect yearbook
The Canadian architect's yardstick for costing
Industrialization forum = IF
Landscape architecture Canada
Ovo. English ed

Atmospheric Sciences
Atmosphere
Climatological bulletin
The Forecaster = Le Prévisionniste
Weather timetable : how to foretell your weather = La Couleur du temps: comment prévoir le temps dans votre région

Atomic Energy
Nuclear Canada = Canada nucléaire
Nuclear science research report
University of Alberta. Nuclear Research Centre. Progress report

Automation
The Big byte
Canadian computer census
Canadian data processing directory
Canadian datasystems
Computernews
Computing Canada
Data Processing Institute. Proceedings
McGill University. Computing Centre. Newsletter
Répertoire des entreprises canadiennes de services informatiques = Directory of Canadian data processing services firms
University of Alberta, Edmonton. Computing Services. Bulletin

Automotive
AFV news magazine
Antics
Autoclub
L'automobile
Automotifs
Black book used truck guide
Black book vehicle indentification guide
Body shop
C.A.R. weekly : Canadian auto racing news
Canadian automotive trade
Canadian klaxon
Canadian service data book
Canadian special truck equipment manual
The Cart
Cycle Canada : for and about motorcycling in Canada
Facts and figures of the automotive industry
The Flying quail
Motor in Canada
Motor truck
Motor vehicle data book
The Reflector beam
Revue moteur
Sanford Evans gold book of snowmobile data and used prices
Sanford Evans gold book of used car prices
Senior cylinders
Service station and garage management
Western motor fleet
The Windwing

Aviation
Abbotsford International Air Show. Newsletter
Alberta towline
Canadian Air Traffic Control Association, Inc. CATCA journal
Canadian aircraft operator
Canadian aviation
Canadian Aviation Historical Society. The C.A.H.S. journal
Canadian flight
Canadian wings
Canadian wings : aviation directory
Free flight
From the ground up
Happy landings
International Air Transport Association. IATA news review
Model aviation Canada
Pilot
World air transport statistics

Banking & Finance
Article of the month
Bank directory of Canada
Bank of Montreal business review
The Bank of Nova Scotia. Monthly review
Banque Canadienne Nationale. Bulletin mensuel
La Banque Canadienne Nationale. Le point BCN
Banque de Montréal. B de M revue des affaires
Banque Royale. Bulletin mensuel
Le Banquier et revue IBC
The Bond record
Bulletin économique
Canada's business climate
The Canadian banker and ICB review
The Canadian Bankers' Association. CBA bulletin = L'association des banquiers canadiens. ABC bulletin
Canadian financial E-Z directory
Commercial letter
Credit management review
Directory of Canadian trust companies
The Financial post
Financial statistics : Canada's provinces and representative municipalities
Financial times of Canada perspective on money
Impetus magazine
Institute of Canadian Bankers. Educational programs
Institute of Chartered Life Underwriters. C.L.U. comment
Lettre commerciale
The National finances : an analysis of the revenue and expenditures of the Government of Canada
Programmes d'éducation = Educational programs

Biology

Boats

Botany

Canadian Life

Contact
Council of Atlantic Provincial Employees. CAPE journal
The Dome
Livre de poche du fonctionnaire
New Brunswick Public Employees Association. Newsletter
Newfoundland Association of Public Employees. Nape news
NewsNewsNews
Ottawa Civil Service Recreational Association. R A news
Prince Edward Island Public Service Association, Inc. Association news
The Professional Institute of the Public Service of Canada. Journal of the Professional Institute = l'Institut professionnel du service public du Canada. Journal de l'institut professionnel
Public Service Alliance of Canada. Weekly newsletter
Syndicat des fonctionnaires provinciaux du Québec inc. Journal SFPQ

Classical Studies
Echos du monde classique = Classical news and views
Phoenix

Clothing
Buyers' market
Canadian clothing journal
Canadian footwear and leather directory
Ego
Fem ego
Men's wear of Canada
Shoe and leather journal
Style : for Canadian fashion merchandisers

College & University
The Acadia bulletin
L'Acayen
Alumni
The Alumni journal
Alumni news, Ottawa = Bulletin des anciens, Ottawa
The Ambassador
Argosy weekly
Argus
Around the ring
Arthur
Arts and sciences alumni news
Association des collèges communautaires de Canada. Recueil d'études
L'Association des universités partiellement ou entièrement de langue française. Bulletin de nouvelles brèves
Association des universités partiellement ou entièrement de langue française. Séminaire
Association of Canadian Community Colleges. Yearbook
Association of Universities and Colleges of Canada. Proceedings of the annual meeting = Association des universities et colleges du Canada. Délibérations de l'assemblée annuelle
At Guelph
The Athenaeum
Atlantic Provinces Inter-University Committee on the Sciences. A.P.I.C.S. newsletter
Au fil des événements
Balcony square
Bandersnatch
Between times
Le Binocle
Le Borroméen : organe de l'Association des anciens du Séminaire de Sherbrooke
Bricklayer
British Columbia Institute of Technology. BCIT developments
The Brunswickan
Cadre
Les Cahiers de Cap-Rouge
Campus
The Campus
Campus : the national magazine for graduating students
Canadian Association for University Continuing Education. Bulletin = L'Association pour l'éducation permanente dans les universités du Canada. Bulletin
Canadian Association of College and University Libraries. Workshop on Automation. Papers
Canadian Association of College and University Student Services. The Bulletin = L'association des services aux étudiants des collèges et universités du Canada. Le Bulletin
Canadian Association of University Business Officers. Bulletin = Association canadienne du personnel administratif universitaire. Bulletin
Canadian Association of University Business Officers. Directory = Association canadienne de personnel administratif universitaire. Répertoire
Canadian Association of University Teachers. C.A.U.T. bulletin = Association canadienne des professeurs d'université. Bulletin de l'A.C.P.U
Canadian Association of University Teachers. Handbook = Association canadienne des professeurs d'université. Guide de l'ACPU
Canadian journal of university continuing education
The Capilano review
Carillon
Carleton University. Alumni Association. The Carleton alumneye
Carrefour
Cégepropos

Press-information
Pro tem
The Quad : student yearbook of Bishop's University
Quartier libre
Queen's gazette
Queen's journal
The Queen's University alumni review
Quill
Reflector
Répertoire des cours d'été (et cours permanents pour étrangers)
Répertoire des études supérieures et des équivalences de titres, de diplômes et de périodes d'études entres les universités de langue française
Répertoire général des universités membres de l'A.U.P.E.L.F
Requirements for secondary school leaving certificates and for admission to university and teacher training
Research McGill
Réseau
La Rotonde
Ryersonian
Saint Francis Xavier University. St. F.X. newsletter
Saison : rapport des stages
Savant
Seer
Senca
The Sheaf
The Sheridan sun
The Shillelagh
Silhouette
Simon Fraser University : SFU information for secondary school and college students
Spectrum
Spoke
Student statistics
Summer gazette
The Sword
Teaching forum
Theosphere: journal de faculté
The Times
The Ubyssey
L'Ugam
Undergraduate awards
Uniter
Université du Québec. Ecole nationale d'administration publique. Annuaire
Université du Québec à Rimouski. Les Cahiers éthicologiques de l'UQAR
Université et coopération
Université Laval. Gazette officielle. Résolutions du conseil
University affairs = Affaires universitaires
University news
University of British Columbia. Alumni Association. UBC alumni chronicle
University of British Columbia. Computing Centre. Newsletter
University of British Columbia. Faculty Association. UBC Faculty Association newsletter
University of British Columbia. Summary of senate proceedings
University of British Columbia. This week at UBC
University of British Columbia. UBC gazette
University of British Columbia. UBC reports
The University of Calgary gazette
University of Guelph. Arts and sciences alumni news
University of Guelph. News bulletin
University of Manitoba. Awards bulletin
University of Manitoba. Medical journal
University of Manitoba. The Alumni journal
University of New Brunswick. Research Grants Office. The University of New Brunswick research inventory
University of Saskatchewan. University news
University of Toronto. School of Physical and Health Education. Alumni newsletter
University of Toronto. Student Administrative Council. The SAC handbook
University of Toronto. University College. Bulletin
University of Toronto bulletin
University of Toronto Centre of Criminology. Alumni Association. Newsletter
University of Toronto quarterly : a Canadian journal of the humanities
The University of Victoria. Alumni quarterly
University of Victoria gazette
University of Western Ontario. Alumni gazette
The University of Western Ontario. Computing Centre newsletter
University of Windsor review
University of Winnipeg. Alumni bulletin
Varsity
Victoria report
Vieil escolier
Le V'la.
Vues et propos
Western news
Who's who in Canadian placement?
Woodsworth College. Arts and Science Alumni Association. Newsletter
Xaverian weekly

Conservation

Alberta Wilderness Association. Newsletter
B. C. Wildlife Federation. BCWF newsletter
Canadian conservation directory = Guide de la conservation du Canada
Canadian wolf defenders
Defending all outdoors
Duckological
Eco log information services
Eco/log week

Saskatchewan Teachers' Federation. Saskatchewan bulletin
School guidance worker
Secondary Learning Assistance Teachers' Association. Bulletin
Short courses and seminars
Special education in Canada
The Spotlight: news and views on Catholic education
Le Stagiaire
Student mathematics
Summer in Canada
Summer programmes abroad = Programmes d'été à l'étranger
Synoptic
The Teacher
Teacher education
The Teachers' magazine
Teaching atypical students in Alberta
Tema
Trail blazers
University of British Columbia. Faculty of Education. The Journal of education of the Faculty of Education
Vancouver educational research bulletin : VERB
Vector: newsletter/journal
Venture forth
Vexillum
View
Viewpoint

Electrical

Audio scene Canada
CEDA. current
CEE electronics directory and Buyers' guide
Canadian Electrical Association. Bulletin = Association canadienne de l'élecricité. Bulletín
Canadian Electrical Association. Newsletter
Canadian Electrical Association. Proceedings
Canadian electronics engineering
Circuit
The Electric power communicator
The Electric power communicator
Electrical business
Electrical contractor and maintenance supervisor
Electrical equipment news
Electronic procurement index for Canada
Electronics and communications
Electronics communicator
Farm light and power
International Microwave Power Institute. IMPI newsletter
The Line
Le Monde de l'électricité
Relay
Semiconductor devices
Tom Graham's electronic workshop
United Electrical, Radio and Machine Workers of America. UE news

Engineering

Applicator
Automatic control theory and applications
The B.C. professional engineer
Canadian consulting engineer
Canadian controls and instrumentation
Canadian Council of Professional Engineers. Newsbrief = Conseil canadien des ingénieurs. Communiqué
Canadian engineering and industrial year book
Canadian Society for Mechanical Engineering. Transactions
Cipher
Design engineering
Design product news
Drainage Engineers' Conference. Proceedings
Engineering
Engineering and contract record
Engineering digest
The Engineering journal
L'Ingénieur
Institute of Chartered Engineers of Ontario. News letter
McGill University. Mechanical Engineering Laboratory. Technical note
Main d'oeuvre en génie bulletin = Engineering manpower news
The Manitoba professional engineer
The McGill engineer
Mini pegg
Modern power and engineering
The Ontario digest
The Ontario technologist
PLAN
The Pegg
The Professional engineer in New Brunswick
The Professional engineer in Nova Scotia
The Saskatchewan professional engineer
Society of Manufacturing Engineers. Chapter 42. Monthly programme
Statistical review of plumbing and heating in Canada
The Thermogram
Toike oike

Environment

Air Pollution Control Association. Quebec Section. Annnual symposium
Alternatives : perspectives on society and environment
Beale, Colin. Beale's letter
Canadian environmental law news
Citizen's Committee for Pollution Control. Newsletter
Contact : bulletin of urban and environmental affairs
Ecospeak : a quarterly publication of Winnipeg Pollution Probe

Ethnic

Il Cittadino canadese = Canadian citizen = Le Citoyen canadien
India star
Informator
Insieme : mensile d'informazione e di attualita
Isien usko = Faith of our fathers
Iskra = Spark
Italian Chamber of Commerce. Bulletin
ItalyCanada trade
Japanese Canadian Citizen's Association. Bulletin
Jewish eagle
The Jewish post
Jewish standard
Kalendar svitla = The Light almanac
Kanadai magvarsag = Canadian Hungarian
Kanadiysky farmer = The Canadian farmer
Kanadské listy = Canadian news
Kanadski srbobran = The Canadian srbobran
Kanadsky Slovák = Canadian Slovak
Kaszebe
Kepes vilaghirado = Illustrated world review
Khristianin (the Christian)
Khrystiansky visnyk = The Christian herald
Kitchener journal
Koinotiki foni = Hellenic community voice of Ottawa
Kolping Society. Kolping bulletin
The Korean journal
Kredytova Kooperatyva Pivnichnoho Vinnipegu. Biuleten = North Winnipeg Credit Union Limited. Bulletin
Krzyk = Outcry
Kurier polsko-kanadyjski = Polish Canadian courier
La Tribuna Italiana = The Italian tribune
La Voce del popolo = The People's voice
Lâânekaare postipoiss
Latvija Amerika
L'Eco d'Italia
Lemko news
Lemko news annual
Liaudies balsas = People's voice
Liscio e busso
Liubystok : a Ukranian magazine of literature, arts and literary criticism
Logberg - heimskringla = Law mountain globe
Logos
L'ora di Ottawa
Lusitano
Magyar Elet = Hungarian life
Magyar hirlap = Hungarian journal
Meie elu = Our life
Mennonitische Rundschau = Mennonite review
Menorah - egyenloseg
Modersmaalet = Mother tongue
Moloda Ukraina = Young Ukraine
Il Mondo
Montreal - Courier
Montrealer Nachrichten
Montrealer Zeitung
Il Mormoratore
Mosaico
Moteris : lietuviy motery zurnalas = Woman : Lithuanian women's magazine
My i svit = We and the world
Narodniarsky kalendar = National calendar
Nase hlasy = Our voices
Nasha meta = Our aim
Nepriklausoma Lietuva = Independent Lithuania
The New Canadian
New Korea times
New pathway annual
New republic
Nor serount = New generation
Norrona = The Norseman
The North American Scotsman
Nouy domov = New homeland
Nowi dni = New days
Nya Svenka pressen = Swedish press
O Jornal portugues
O Mensageiro
Occidente
Ontario - Courier
Orah magazine
Ottawa ethnic groups directory
Ottawa jewish bulletin and review
Panjab
Parikiaka news
Pazifische Rundschau = Pacific review
Philippine-Canadian free press
Pioneer Christian monthly
Pivnichne siayvo = Northern lights: almanac
Placowka nad pacifikem:
El Planeta
Plastovy shliakh
The Polish Canadian courier = Kurier Poisko-Kanadyjski
El Popular
Postup = Progress
Promin
Quincentario Hispano
Reflexion 2 : primera revista de cultura hispanica en Canada
Il Rincontro
SPK W Kanadzie
Il Samaritano : la voca cattolica
Scandinavian centre news
The Scotian
Sentinela
La Settimana
Shing Wah daily news
Slovenska drzava = Slovenian country
Slovenski Jezuiti v Kanade
Slovensky hlas = Slovak voice
Slovo na storozhi = Word on guard = La parole en gard
Sovremennik (the contemporary) : Russian national review in Canada

Family

Film

Fire Prevention

Fisheries

International Commission for the Northwest Atlantic Fisheries. Annual report
International Commission for the Northwest Atlantic Fisheries. List of vessels fishing in the ICNAF convention area
International Commission for the Northwest Atlantic Fisheries. Research bulletin
International Commission for the Northwest Atlantic Fisheries. Statistical bulletin
Pacific Trollers' Association. Newsletter
Redbook
Salt water salmon fishing guide
Sou'wester = The voice of Atlantic Canada's fishing and marine industry
Tides of change
Western angling
Western fisheries

Food & Nutrition

Alimentation du Quebec
Bakers journal : the national merchandising and management magazine serving the Canadian baking industry
The Canadian Federation of Retail Grocers. Bulletin
Canadian food and packaging directory
Canadian Institute of Food Science and Technology. Journal
Corporation professionnelle des diététistes du Québec. Bulletin
Food in Canada
Frozen foods / Canada
Guide to good food in Metro Vancouver
Healthful living digest
The Holiday host
Labatt news
Les Nouvelles de la brasserie
Nutrition forum = Forum de nutrition
Retail food report
Toronto Vegetarian Association. Newsletter

Forestry

Association of B.C. Professional Foresters. Annual meeting
Association of Registered Professional Foresters of New Brunswick. Papers and reports
L'Aubelle
British Columbia lumberman's greenbook : a directory of B.C.'s forest industry
Canadian forest industries
Canadian forest industries. Directory
Canadian Forestry Association. C.F.A. news = Association forestière canadienne. Le courrier A.F.C
Foresterie à tout
The Forestry chronicle
Forêt-conservation
MacMillan Bloedel Ltd. MacMillan Bloedel news
Ontario forests
L'Ordre des ingénieurs forestiers du Québec. Textes des études présentées au congrès annuel
Prévenir
The Professional forester
University of British Columbia. Forestry Club. UBC forester
University of New Brunswick. Faculty of Forestry. Information for principals, guidance counsellors, teachers and students
University of Toronto. Forestry Alumni Association. Directory and newsletter

French Canadian Culture

L'action nationale
Association canadienne-française de l'Ontario. ACFO-Info
Centre de recherche en civilisation canadienne-française Bulletin
Conseil de la vie française en Amérique. Le bottin des sociétés patriotiques
Ebauches
Ecrits du Canada français
La Fournée
Hobo-Québec : journal d'écritures et d'images
L'Information nationale
Liberté
Le Maclean
La Maison (Centre francophone de Toronto)
Le Mirabel
Notre langue, notre culture
Nous
Pleins feux sur la francophonie...
Présence francophone : revue littéraire
Le Rempart
Revue d'histoire de l'Amérique française
Sociologie et sociétés : revue thématique

Fruit Growing

British Columbia Fruit Growers Association. Horticultural conference proceedings
Canadian Fruit Wholesalers' Association. Yearbook
Canadian fruitgrower
The Grower
The Ontario grape grower
Le Producteur de raisin d'Ontario

Gardening

Association des paysagistes et pépiniéristes du Québec inc. Bulletin
Canadian florist, greenhouse and nursery
Canadian florist, Keith's directory and horticultural guide
Canadian Gladiolus Society. Annual
Fleuriste du Québec
Garden clippings
Greenhouse newsletter
Keith's florist directory and horticultural guide
Landscape
Landscape = Paysage Canada
Landscape = Paysage Canada
Landscape Ontario

Bruce County Historical Society. Year book
Canadian Catholic Historical Association. Study sessions
Canadian Church Historical Society. Journal
Canadian frontier : a Canadian national history magazine
Canadian historical review
Canadian journal of history = Annales canadiennes d'histoire
Canadian plains bulletin
Canadian Quaker history
Canadian rail
Canadian treasure
The Charlottes
Chateauguay Valley Historical Society. Journal = Socitété historique de la vallée de la Châteauguay. Journal
Colloquium on Scottish studies. Proceedings
Dan Brock's historical almanack of London
German-Canadian yearbook = Deutsch-kanadisches Jahrbuch
Glenbow
The Grand Manan historian
Heraldry in Canada
L'Histoire au'pays' de Matane : généalogie, biographie, anecdotes, folklore
Histoire sociale = Social history
Historic Kingston : journal of the proceedings of the Kingston Historical Society
Historical and Scientific Society of Manitoba. Transactions
Historical reflections = Réflexions historiques
Historical Society of Alberta. Whoop-up Country Chapter. Newsletter
The History and social science teacher
Huguenot trails
Huron historical notes
Journal of Canadian studies
Lennox and Addington Historical Society. Paper and records
Lillooet District Historical Society bulletin
The Loyalist gazette
Lustucru
Manitoba Historical Society. Newsletter
Manitoba Historical Society. Transactions
Manitoba pageant
The Maritime express
Missisquoi County Historical Society. Missisquoi
New review of East-European history
North wind
Nova Scotia historical quarterly
Nova Scotia Historical Society. Collections of the Nova Scotia Historical Society
Ontario Historical Society. Bulletin
Ontario history
Peterborough Historical Society. Bulletin
Prince Edward Island Heritage Foundation
Regroupement de chercheurs en histoire des travailleurs québécois. Bulletin RCHTQ
Revue d'histoire de la Gaspésie
Revue d'histoire de la Société historique Nicolas-Denys
St. Thomas More College. Library. History collection : Canadian Catholic Church
Saskatchewan history
Scottish tradition
Social history = Histoire sociale
La Société historique acadienne. Les Cahiers
Stanstead County Historical Society. Journal
Vancouver Historical Society. Newsletter
Waterloo Historical Society. Annual volume
Wellington County Historical Research Society. Newsletter
Western Ontario historical notes
The York pioneer

Home Economics

Alberta Home Economics Association. AHEA newsletter
B.C. Teachers' Federation. Teachers of Home Economics Specialist Association. Newsletter
Canadian home economics journal
Home economics newsletter
Homemakers magazine
Thesa journal
Vista

Horses

Annuaire des courses = Racing year book
Annual sale of yearlings and mixed stock
British Columbia thoroughbred : an official review of the season
Canada rides
The Canadian Appaloosa journal
The Canadian horse magazine
Canadian quarter horse journal
The Canadian western rider
Cayuse conserver
The Corinthian
The Equestrian Image : Canadian all breeds magazine
Harness world = Monde du harnais
Horsing around (newsletter)
Northwestern Alberta gymkhana
La Revue hippique
Western racing review
Western thoroughbred

Hospitals

Administration hospitalière et sociale
British Columbia Health Association. Proceedings of the annual conference
British Columbia Hospital Association. BCHA news
Canadian courier
Canadian hospital directory
Catholic hospital
Catholic Hospital Association of Canada. C.H.A.C. annual directory = Annuaire de l'A.H.C.C

L'Assurance vie et le fisc
Assurances
Les assurances I.A.R.D. du Canada
L'Assureur-vie du Québec = The Quebec life underwriter
Automobile insurance experience
British Columbia insurance directory of insurance companies, agents and adjusters
The Builder
The Bulletin
CLU comment
The Canadian independent adjuster
Canadian Institute of Actuaries. Reports
Canadian Institute of Actuaries. Year book = Institut canadien des actuaires. Annuaire
Canadian insurance claims directory
Canadian insurance (incorporating Insurance agent and broker in Canada)
The Canadian insurance law service
Canadian insurance statistics (annual)
Canadian life insurance facts
Canadian risk management and business insurance
Canadian underwriter
Comment
The Continent
Corporate insurance in Canada
Le Courtier d'assurance
Current topics
Dividend
Dominionaire
F.I.I.C. program syllabus
Facts of the general insurance industry in Canada
Field news
Field record
Forum
IAC rendezvous
L'Institut d'assurance du Canada. Communiqué de l'Institut d'assurance du Canada
Institute of Chartered Life Underwriters. Commentaires CLU
The Insurance broker
The Insurance Institute of Alberta. Calgary Chapter. Newsletter
The Insurance Institute of Canada. Newsletter of the Insurance Institute of Canada
The Insurance marketer
Lien
Life insurance and taxation
Life insurance in Canada
Life Underwriters Association of Canada. The LUAC monitor
Manufacturers Life Insurance Company. ManuLife news
Manufacturers Life Insurance Company. News letter
Mercer actuarial bulletin
Metropolitan life
Mutualist
Mutualiste
Northern news
Ontario Insurance Agents' and Brokers' Association. News
L'Orbite
Palmarès
The Pelican
Power protection
Provincial results general insurance report : the brown chart = Données provinciales
Service and indemnity
Stone and Cox general insurance year book
Stone and Cox life insurance tables = Stone and Cox tables d'assurance-vie
Sun Life du Canada compagnie d'assurance-vie. Nouvelles
Sun life orbit
Toronto insurance directory
Underwriting results : the blue chart = Resultats techniques

International Affairs

Actionews : world vision's heartline to needy world
L'Amérique latine
Association canadienne des études latino-américaines. Bulletin
Australian news weekly round-up
CUSSnews
Canada and the world : for students of world affairs
Canada-Belgium-Luxembourg
Canadian Arab world review = La Revue du monde arabe
Canadian Association of Latin American Studies. CALAS newsletter
Canadian Bureau for International Education. Communications = Bureau canadien de l'éducation internationale. Communications
Canadian Commission for UNESCO. Bulletin = Commission canadienne pour l'Unesco. Bulletin
Canadian far eastern newsletter
Canadian journal of African studies = Journal canadien des études africaines
Canadian review of American studies
Canadian University Service Overseas. CUSO forum
Canadian-American seminar
El Chaski
Chili-Québec informations
Cooperation Canada
Echo d'Afrique "se connaître pour s'unir"
L'Escargot
Etudes françaises dans le monde : bulletin de liaison des départements et centres d'études françaises
Etudes internationales
German press review
International Canada
International journal

Ontario Federation of Labour. Convention. Report of proceedings
Ontario Federation of Labour. Convention. Resolutions
Ontario Federation of Labour. Legislative proposals to the government of Ontario
Opportunities unlimited
Pacific tribune
The Provincial
Retail wages and salaries in Canada
Summer weekend seminar
Le Travail : le magazine du monde ordinaire, publié par la CSN
Ukrainian Free Academy of Sciences-UVAN (1949). Byuleten' humanistychnoho viddilu uvan
Weekly labour press service
The Worker = L'Ouvrier
Working safely

Legal

Alberta corporation manual
Alberta law review
The Ansul
Barreau
British Columbia corporation manual
Butterworth's Ontario digest : being a statement of the case law of Ontario from 1901 with full annotations
Les cahiers de droit
Canada. Laws. Statutes, etc. Martin's annual criminal code
Canada corporation manual
Canada legal directory
Canadian Association of Law Teachers. Directory of law teachers = Association canadienne des professeurs de droit. Annuaire des professeurs de droit
The Canadian bar review = La Revue du barreau canadien
Canadian criminal cases
The Canadian law list
Canadian Society of Forensic Science. Journal
Canadian weekly law sheet
Canadian yearbook of international law = Annuaire canadien de droit international
Chitty's law journal
Le Conseiller juridique
Corporate developments
Cours de perfectionnement
Court house echo
Criminal law quarterly
Criminologie made in Canada
Crown's newsletter
Current legislative digest : an index-digest of current legislation
Digest business and law journal
Directory of law teachers = Annuaire des professeurs de droit
Dominion law reports
Estates and trusts quarterly
Federal court of Canada service
Labour arbitration cases
Land compensation reports
The Law Society of Upper Canada. Gazette
The Lawyer's phone book
The Legal secretary's newsletter
McGill law journal
Manitoba law journal
National
Obiter dicta
The Ontario annual practice
Ontario Association of Corrections and Criminology. Bulletin
Ontario business corporations act and regulations
Ontario corporation manual
Ontario reports
Ontario statute citator. Bill service
Osgoode Hall law journal
Ottawa law review
The Philanthropist = Le Philanthrope
Provincial Judges Association of British Columbia. Newsletter
Quebec corporation manual
Queen's law journal
Reports on family law
Revue de droit
La Revue du notariat
Revue générale de droit
La Revue juridique thémis de l'Université de Montréal
St. Leonard's Society of Canada. News & views
Saskatchewan law review
Studia canonica
Supreme Court of Canada reports service
Toronto legal directory
University of British Columbia. Law Review Society. UBC law review
University of Toronto. Centre of Criminology. Alumni Association. Alumni Association newsletter
University of Toronto Faculty of Law review
University of Toronto law journal
Western Ontario law review

Librarianship

Agora
Argus
L'Association des bibliothécaires du Québec. Bulletin A B Q = Quebec Library Association. QLA bulletin
Association of Canadian Map Libraries. Bulletin = Association des cartothèques canadiennes. Bulletin
Association of Canadian Map Libraries. Proceedings of the annual conference = Association des cartothèques canadiennes. Comptes rendus de la conférence annuelle

Libraries

Linguistics

Canadian Council of Teachers of English. Newsletter
Canadian journal of linguistics = La Revue canadienne de linguistique
The Canadian journal of research in semiotics = Le Journal canadien de recherche sémiotique
Canadian Linguistic Association. Membership directory and data book memento
The Canadian modern language review
Classmate
Elan
The English quarterly
English studies in Canada
Glossa : an international journal of linguistics
Linguistic Circle of Manitoba and North Dakota. Proceedings
Lumo
Meta
Newsletter for ugaritic studies
RLS : Regional language studies....Newfoundland
Res gestae
Saskatchewan Association of Teachers of French. Bulletin = Bulletin de service
Saskatchewan Association of Teachers of French. SATF newsletter
Seminar : a journal of Germanic studies
Slipara vortaro
Working papers on bilingualism = Travaux de recherches sur le bilinguisme

Literature

Alberta poetry yearbook
Amber
Applegarth's folly
Ariel: a review of international English literature
Aspects
The Black fly
Black images
The British Columbia monthly : Canada's national magazine
CV / II
Canadian authors : creative writings by children of Northern Alberta
Canadian Authors Association. Vancouver Branch. Bulletin
Canadian Authors Association. Winnipeg Branch. Newsletter
Canadian drama = L'Art dramatique canadien
The Canadian fiction magazine
Canadian literature = Littérature canadienne
Canadian review of comparative literature = Revue canadienne de littérature comparée
Canadian short story magazine
Captain George's penny dreadful
Catalyst
The Chesterton review
Co-ïncidences
Contemporary literature in translation
Copperfield : an independent Canadian literary magazine of the land and the North
Critère
Critical studies in Canadian poetry
Cross country : a magazine of Canadian-U.S. poetry
Cul Q
DA Vinci
Dem days Labrador
Dérives : tiers-monde Québec, une nouvelle conjoncture culturelle
Descant
The Dime bag
Diversions
ERBivore
Ellipse
Empty belly : a magazine of poetry and communication
Essays on Canadian writing
Etudes littéraires
Event
Exile
The Fiddlehead
First encounter
Four decades of poetry 1890-1930
Freelance
Germano-Slavica : a Canadian journal of Germanic and Slavic comparative studies
Golden taffy
Grain
Gut : magazine of prose, reviews and poetry
Innis herald : "lets go nummies"
Inscape : a journal of new Canadian writing
The International fiction review
Introductions from an island
Is
It needs to be said : a new look at Canadian literature
Jewish dialogue
Journal of Canadian fiction
Joyceville journal
Jubilee : a magazine of Canadian writing
Karaki
Link
Lodgistiks
The Malahat review
Matrix : new Canadian writing
The Mill news letter
The Missing link magazine
Modernist studies
Modicum
Moko
Moongoose
Mosaic : a journal for the comparative study of literature and ideas
Mudcreek magazine
Natural fauna
Nebula
The New Captain George's whizzbang : the Canadian magazine of popular culture

Marine Industry

Canadian ports and seaway directory
Canadian shipping and marine engineering
Harbour and shipping
Marine and outdoor trades
The Maritimes shipping herald and marine engineering journal = Le Journal de la marine marchande des Maritimes
Seaports and shipping world
Shipping register

Marketing & Purchasing

L'Acheteur
Action
Appliance and home entertainment business
Automotive mass marketer
Black book : official used car market guide
Byers Canadian merchandise mart
Canadian coin box magazine
Canadian consumer
Canadian electronics engineering annual buyers guide and catalog directory
Canadian municipalities buyers' guide
Canadian packaging
Canadian process equipment and control news
Canadian retailer
Canadian toy retailing
Canadian trade index = Index commercial canadien
Canadian variety merchandise directory
Centre d'équipement et machinerie : le mart
Decision
Financial post survey of markets
Fraser's Canadian trade directory
Government purchasing guide
Guide annuaire des représentants de commerce
Home goods retailing
Jobber news
Luggage and leathergoods news
Market research facts and trends
Marketing
Le Marketing social
Materials handling handbook and directory of buying sources
Modern purchasing
Operating results of independent specialty and department stores
Outdoor power products = Equipement motorisé plein air
Purchasing in Western Canada
Retailers' group service bulletin
Revue machinerie lourde
Volume retail merchandising
Western grocer and food store manager

Mathematics

Association mathématique du Québec. Bulletin
Canadian journal of mathematics = Journal canadien de mathématiques
Canadian mathematical bulletin = Canadien de mathématiques
Historia mathematica : international journal of history of mathematics
The Manitoba mathematics teacher
Metric message = Message métrique
Notes, news and comments
Ontario mathematics gazette
Saskatchewan Mathematics Teachers' Society. News/journal

Medical

Academy of Medicine, Toronto. Bulletin
Alberta medical bulletin
Association des conseils des médecins et dentistes du Québec. Bulletin de l'A.C.M.D.Q
Association of Canadian Medical Colleges. ACMC/AFMC forum
Backtalk
British Columbia medical journal
Cahiers pédopsychiatriques
Canada physiology = Physiologie Canada
Canadian Anaesthetists' Society. CAS newsletter
Canadian Anaesthetists' Society. The Canadian Anaesthetists' Society journal = Société canadienne d'anesthésistes. Journal de la Société canadienne d'anesthésistes.
Canadian Association of Pathologists. Newsletter
Canadian Association of Radiologists. Journal
Canadian Chiropractic Association. Journal of Canadian Chiropractic Association
The Canadian Dietetic Association. Journal of the Canadian Dietetic Association
Canadian doctor
Canadian family physician
The Canadian journal of medical technology
The Canadian journal of neurological sciences = Le Journal canadien des sciences neurologiques
Canadian journal of ophthalmology
The Canadian journal of optometry
Canadian journal of otolaryngology = Journal canadien d'otolaryngologie
Canadian journal of surgery
The Canadian Medical Association. Journal
The Canadian Medical Association. Newfoundland Division. Newsletter
Canadian medical directory
Canadian Osteopathic Association. Newsletter
The Canadian podiatrist
Canadian Psychiatric Association. Bulletin = Association des psychiatres du Canada. Bulletin
Canadian Psychiatric Association. Canadian Psychiatric Association journal = L'Association des psychiatres du Canada. La Revue de L'Association des psychiatres du Canada
Canadian Society for Immunology. Bulletin

Military

Mining & Metallurgy

Les Mines au Canada : renseignements et statistiques
Mining : what it means to Canada
Mining exploration and development review, British Columbia-Yukon
The Northern miner
Le Producteur d'amiante = Asbestos producer
Scope
Steel in transportation
The Triangle
Western miner

Montreal
Current events magazine. Montreal edition = Actualitiés Montréal
Montreal calendar magazine
Montréal ce mois-ci : l'agenda du mieux-vivre
Montreal scene
Olympresse 1976 = Olympress 1976

Motoring
The Accelerator
Alberta motorist
Autoclub : le journal de l'automobiliste du Québec
Bonne route
Canadian motorist
Communique
Crossroads
Gulf Canada cartalk
Hamilton Automobile Club. H.A.C. news
Manitoba motorist
Mobile home and recreational vehicle industry
Mobile living in Canada
Ontario Motor League news
The Running board
The Saskatchewan motorist
Scope : recreational vehicle and camping news
Toronto club news

Museums
Arms collecting : the Canadian journal of arms collecting
The Badlands of the Red Deer River Valley
Gazette
The Grande new Dawson and hind quarterly epistle
The Latest word from the Nova Scotia Museum
M
Museogramme = Muséogramme
Museum round-up
Ontario Historical Society. Museums Section. Newsletter
Rotunda
SNAUQ
Syesis
Tom Thomson Memorial Gallery and Museum of Fine Art. Bulletin
Transition 3
Vancouver Public Aquarium. Newsletter

Music
Alberta music calendar
Association canadienne des écoles universitaires de musique. Journal de l'association canadienne des écoles universitaires de musique
Beetle
Le Bouscueil
British Columbia music educator
British Columbia Music Educators Association. Newsletter
British Columbia Registered Music Teachers' Association. Provincial newsletter
CAMAC. Montreal Committee. Newsletter/bulletin
Les Cahiers canadiens de musique = The Canada music book
Canadian Amateur Musicians Southern Ontario Region. CAMMAC newsletter
The Canadian Band Directors. Newsletter
The Canadian composer = Le Compositeur canadien
Canadian Folk Music Society. Newsletter
Canadian Folk Music Society journal
Canadian music directory
Canadian music educator
Canadian Music Educators Association. Newsletter
Canadian music industry directory
Canadian music industry who's who
Canadian String Teachers Association. Newsletter
Canadian Talent Library. Bulletin
Coda : Canada's jazz magazine
Come all ye
Contemporary music showcase
Encore
Jeunesses musicales du Canada. Bulletin JMC
Jeunesses Musicales of Canada. JMC bulletin
M C Q : music Canada quarterly magazine
The Manitoba music educator
Musical notes
The National music teacher
The Ontario Registered Music Teachers' Association. Ormata notes
Orchestra Canada
Orchestra letter
RPM weekly
Record week
The Recorder
The Royal Canadian College of Organists. Quarterly
Royal Conservatory of Music of Toronto. Bulletin
Saskatchewan Music Educators' Association. Saskatchewan Music Educators newsletter
La Scène musicale
Sound Canada
Sur une note d'information
Toronto symphony news
Vancouver symphony VSO

Nursing papers
Ordre des infirmières et infirmiers du Québec. Notes et nouvelles = Order of Nurses of Quebec. News and notes
Registered Nurses Association of British Columbia. RNABC news
Registered Nurses Association of Nova Scotia. R.N.A.N.S. bulletin
Saskatchewan Psychiatric Nurses' Association. Newsletter
Saskatchewan Registered Nurses' Association. News bulletin
Statistiques : les infirmières au Canada
This month

Office Equipment & Methods
Le Bureau
Canadian office
Canadian office products and stationary
Canadian office products and stationery : dealer's guide
Canadian office redbook
Comda key
Comdagram
Institute of Chartered Secretaries and Administrators. Canadian Division. Newsletter
Institute of Chartered Secretaries and Administrators. ICSA opportunities bulletins
The Institute of Chartered Secretaries and Administrators. Newsletter
Office equipment and methods

Ottawa
Byword
This week times two
What's on in Ottawa = Voici Ottawa

Outdoors
Alpine Club of Canada. Montreal Section. Newsletter
Alpine Club of Canada. Ottawa Section. Bulletin
B.C. outdoors
The Bruce Trail news
Campgrounds in Canada
Camping, caravaning plein air : magazine québecois de l'aventure au grand air
Camping Canada
Canadian alpine journal
Canadian Association for Humane Trapping. CAHT update
The Canadian camper
Canadian camping magazine
Canadian trapper
Canadian Youth Hostels Association. Mid-West Area. Newsletter
Canoe
Fish and game sportsman
The Hosteller = L'Ajiste
Leisurewheels and mobile homes
Leisurewheels campgrounds directory
Mobile home directory
Mobile homes Canada
Motoneige magazine
Motoneigiste canadien
Motosports : cycling-camping-snowmobiling
The Mountain breeze
Orienteering Canada
Outdoor Canada
Outdoor careers
Park news
Parks for tomorrow
Plein air
Pools, parks and rinks
Québec chasse et pêche
Recreational vehicle life
Rock climbing in Ontario
Snowmobile annual
Snowmobile trade
Trail Riders of the Canadian Rockies. The Bulletin
University of British Columbia. Varsity Outdoor Club. The Varsity Outdoor Club journal
Vancouver Island's outdoor journal

Patent & Trademark
Canadian patent reporter
Inventions catalog: inventions for industry
Patent and Trademark Institute of Canada. Bulletin
Patent and Trademark Institute of Canada. Newsletter

Peace
Canadian Peace Research Institute. News report
Peace research
Peace research abstracts journal
Peace research reviews

Petroleum & Gas
Bulletin of Canadian petroleum geology
Canadian Gas Association. Manufacturers' directory
Canadian gas facts
Canadian oil and gas
Canadian oil register
Canadian oil register directory
Canadian petroleum
Canadian Petroleum Association. Statistical yearbook
Canadian Society of Petroleum Geologists. C.S.P.G. reservoir
Directory of Canadian gas utilities
The Financial post survey of oils
Home Oil Company. Library bulletin
Imperial oil review
The Journal of Canadian petroleum technology
Nouvelles Gulf Canada
Oilweek
Okuruk
Ontario Petroleum Institute. Annual conference proceedings
Propane/Canada

Community Planning Association of Canada. National Library. Accessions list
Community Planning Association of Canada. Saskatchewan Division. Saskatchewan Division newsletter
Community planning in British Columbia
Community planning review = Revue canadienne d'urbanisme
Info-estrie
PLAN Canada
Plan Canada
Planning Institute of British Columbia. PIBC newsletter
Plans : planning information exchange for N.S.
Saskatchewan Coordinating Council on Social Planning. Newsletter

Plastics

Canadian plastics
Canadian plastics directory and buyer's guide
Plastatistics
Plastics directory of Canada
Plasticwords
Polyfacts
Polysar progress. Plastics edition
Polysar progress. Rubber and latex edition
Random thoughts

Police

Association de bienfaisance et de retraite de la police de Montréal. Comité de préparation à la retraite
Canadian police chief
Comité de préparation à la retraite
The National police gazette : America's oldest magazine
Police : revue des agents de police = Constables review
Police dossiers
Scarlet and gold

Political

British Columbia Civil Liberties Association. B.C.C.L.A. news digest
Canadian Political Science Association. Annual general meeting. Papers
Canadian Political Science Association. Bulletin = Société canadienne de science politique. Bulletin
The Commonwealth
Democrat
L'Electeur
Liberation Support Movement. LSM news
Libertarian option : freedom or tyranny
MPs at work
Manitoba New Democrat
Monarchy Canada
New Alberta Liberal
The New Democrat
Next year country : Saskachewan's only newsmagazine
The Nutcracker
Ottawa report
P.C. bulletin
Progressive Conservative Association of Canada. P.C. bulletin
Regards : official organ of the Social Credit Party of Canada
Saskatchewan Liberal
Serviam : organe interne du parti de l'Unité nationale du Canada
South of tuk
Speak up : for political and economic realism
The Truth about China newsletter

Poultry

Canada poultryman
Canada's who's who of the poultry industry
Canadian poultry review
Feather fancier
Shaver focus

Psychology

Association of Psychologists of the Province of New Brunswick. Journal of The Association of Psychologists of the Province of New Brunswick
Association pour l'analyse et la modification du comportement. Bulletin
Canadian journal of behavioural science = Revue canadienne des sciences du comportement
Canadian journal of psychology
Canadian psychological review = Psychologie canadienne
Clarke Institute of Psychiatry. Clarke Institute tabloid
Directory of psychologists registered in the Province of Ontario
Here and Now = D'ores et déjà
L'Institut de recherches psychologiques. L'Actualité à l'IRP d'ores et déjà = The Institute of Psychological Research. Here and now : a brief of news from the IPR
The Ontario psychologist
Le Psychologue québécois
Revue de modification du comportement
York University. Institute for Behavioural Research. Newsletter

Publishing & Printing

Association internationale des presses universitaires de langue francaise. AIPULF information
Canadian author and bookman
Canadian Book Publishers' Council. Newsletter
The Canadian community publisher
Canadian Periodical Publishers' Association. Newsletter
Canadian printer and publisher
Canadian publishers directory
Lifeline : a meeting place for writers, illustrators and publishers
Livre canadien
Le Maître imprimeur

L'Ami des sourds
Aquarius
Association des rencontres culturelles avec les détenus. Information-ARCAD
Bluebird bulletin
Break through
British Columbia Association for the Mentally Retarded. Conference. Annual conference
The B.C. mental retardation advisor
The Calgary cord
Caliper
Canadian Arthritis and Rheumatism Society. C.A.R. scope
Canadian Cancer Society. Ontario Division. Quarterly newsletter
The Canadian Council of the Blind. The C.C.B. outlook
Canadian Criminology and Corrections Association. Bulletin
Canadian Diabetic Association. Quarterly newsletter
The Canadian Diabetic Association. Toronto and District Branch. The Toronto District Diabetic Branch bulletin
Canadian journal of criminology and corrections = Revue canadienne de criminologie
Canadian journal of occupational therapy = Revue canadienne d'ergothérapie
The Canadian National Institute for the Blind. Kitchener Office. Annual bulletin of services
Canadian Tuberculosis and Respiratory Disease Association. Bulletin = Association canadienne contre la tuberculose et les maladies respiratoires. Bulletin
Cancer in Ontario
Candid facts
Carscope
Cerebral palsy news
Churchwood bulletin
Concerns
The Council bulletin
Courier
Criminologie
Crippled civilians quarterly
Cultural horizons of the deaf in Canada
The Deaf Canadian magazine
Dialogue
Edmonton monthly newsletter
The Elizabeth Fry Society. Peel-Halton Branch. Newsletter
Epigram
Epilepsy Association of Metropolitan Toronto. Newsletter
Feux verts : nous les marginaux
Forward
Horizons
In a nutshell
Involvement : the family resource magazine
John Howard Society of Ontario. Newsletter
MS Canada
Mental retardation = Défience mentale
Mouthpiece
Muscular dystrophy reporter
National news of the blind
New horizon
The Northern light
Ontario Cancer Treatment and Research Foundation. Proceedings of The Clinical Conference
Ontario Speech and Hearing Association. Journal
Organization for Rehabilitation through Training. Canadian ORT reporter
Paraelite
Paragraphic
The Post
The Rehab tab
Rehabilitation digest
Le Secours aux lépreux : Foundations Raoul Follereau
The Supplement
Survivre
Thursday's child
Toronto Colostomy Association. T.C.A. newsletter
Toronto hemo comm
Toxicomanies
Transition
Vibrations
Western Institute for the Deaf. W.I.D. news
Wise owl news

Religion

Action
Africa now
Alberta Catholic directory
L'Ami de Saint-Benoît-du-Lac
L'Ami du Frère André
The Anglican
Anglican Church of Canada. Anglican Church yearbook
Anglican Church of Canada. General Synod. Journal of proceedings
Animateur
The Annals of good St. Anne du Beaupré
Apostolat
L'Appel du Sacré-Coeur
Appoint
Archidiocèses de Sherbrooke. Annuaire
L'Armée de Marie
Atlantic Baptist
Au rythme de notre église
Automotive Christian
Aux amis du Père Prévost
Avec 'lui'
The B.C. regular Baptist
La Bagatelle
Baobab
The Baptist beacon
Baptist Convention of Ontario and Quebec. Year book

Foreign focus
The Friend of Brother André
Glad Tidings Missionary Society. G.T.M.S
Good tidings
Gospel herald
Le Héraut de Saint-Paul
The High-way
Homiletic service
Huron Church news
In touch
Information : pastorale du diocèse de Mont-Laurier
Insight
Intercom
Inter-Varsity in action
Issue
Je crois : magazine populaire catholique
The Journal of automatic writing : communications from the spiritual forces
Kateri. Edition française
Kerygma
La Lettre de l'Abbé Gravel
The Link and visitor
The Little paper
Liturgie de glorie. Edition complète
Liturgie de glorie. Edition dominicale
Liturgie et vie chrétienne
Living message
Living with Christ
Lodestone
Lutheran Church in America. Canada Section. Convention minutes
Lutheran Church in America. Central Canada Synod. Convention. Minutes
Lutheran Church in Canada. Directory
Maintenant
Mandate
Manitoba Buddhist bulletins
The Mariner
Mennonite Brethren herald
Mennonite mirror
Mennonite reporter
Message de vérité
Le Messager de Saint-Antoine
Messenger of the Sacred Heart of Jesus
Mission '75
The Missionary messenger
The Missionary Sisters of the Immaculate Conception. MIC mission news
Missions d'Afrique
Missions des franciscains
Missions étrangères : magazine d'information missionnaire
Missions Saint-Viateur
Mon frère et moi
Monchanin
My brother and I
The New freeman
The New life
News of Québec
Northwest Canada echoes
Notre ministère du royaume
Les Nôtres
Nouveau dialogue
Observer
Oecuménisme
L'Oeuvre de Terre-Sainte = The Good work of the Holy Land
Ontario Catholic directory
The Ontario churchman
L'Oratoire : au service de la famille chrétienne
Order of divine service
Orient
Our Lady of the Cape
Parole-dimanche
The Pastoral visitor
Pastorale - Québec : revue de l'église de Québec
Pax regis
The Pentecostal testimony
Le Phare
Philippines
Le Point
Points west
Postal Christian witness
Prairie messenger : Saskatchewan Catholic weekly
The Prairie overcomer
Pravoslavnyi tserkovnyi kalendar' = The Orthodox Church calendar
Le Précurseur
Presbyterian Church in Canada. General Assembly. Acts and proceedings
Presbyterian comment
Presbyterian record
Le Prêtre
Prêtre et pasteur : revue eucharistique du clergé
Prions en église. Edition complète
Prions en église. Edition dominicale
RND (Revue Notre-Dame)
Rassembler
Rassembler
Real living
Redeemer's voice almanac = kalendar holosu spasytelia
Regard de foi : revue mariale d'actualité
Réveil missionnaire
La Revue franciscaine
Roundtable
Saint-Sulpice du Canada
Salam
Scarboro missions
Science et esprit : revue théologique et philosophique
Scope = Envergure
Scripture search program inc.
Search lamp
The Second mile
Semeuse de joie
Service de préparation à la vie. Bulletin S.P.V.
The Shantyman

Le Nouveau cosmos-express
Ontario Research Foundation. Newsletter
Ottawa R and D report
Québec science
Research and studies
Science affairs
Scitec bulletin
Service canadien des forêts. Revue bimestrielle de recherches
Youth science news

Social Sciences

Annuaire des sociologues et anthropologues au Canada et leur recherche courante = A Directory of sociologists and anthropologists in Canada and their current research
Cahiers québécois de démographie
Canadian journal of social work education
Canadian review of sociology and anthropology = Revue canadienne de sociologie et d'anthropologie
Canadian review of studies in nationalism
Democratic commitment
The Intelligence crediter
Journal of comparative sociology
Lavalin
One world
Onomastica
Our generation
Perspectives
The Quarterly of Canadian studies : for the secondary school
Recherche et documentation
Recherches sociographiques
Relations : revue d'intérêt général
Service social
Société canadienne de sociologie et d'anthropologie. Bulletin. = Canadian Sociology and Anthropology Association. Bulletin
Sociological inquiry
Theses in Canadian political studies = Thèses canadiennes en science politique
University of Toronto. Institute for the Quantitative Analysis of Social and Economic Policy. Newsletter

Social Welfare

Allocations to national organizations = Allocations aux organismes nationaux
Annoosch
The Bangladesh
CW
Canadaid : a news report to sponsors and friends
Canadian Association of Social Workers. Information
Canadian Council on Social Development. Canadian Conference on Social Welfare. Proceedings
The Children's Aid Society of Ottawa. The C.A.S. Record
Circle
Communiqué
Community Fund and Councils of Canada. Proceedings of biennal conference
Community Funds and Councils of Canada. Allocations to national organizations
Community services in Metropolitan Toronto
Community services in Saskatoon : services for the elderly in Saskatoon
Corporation professionnelle des travailleurs sociaux du Quebéc. Bulletin
Digeste social
Directory of Canadian United Ways and Social Planning Councils = Le répertoire des Centraides Canada et des conseils de planification sociale
Directory of Canadian welfare services = Répertoire des services sociaux canadiens
Directory of community services of Hamilton and district
Directory of services for Greater Vancouver
The Elder statesman
The Fragment
Horizons
Information
Intervention
Journal epiK-KaKouna
K Ray
Manitoba social worker
Mothercraft newsletter
National Pensioners and Senior Citizens Federation. National pensioners and senior citizens news
The Observer = L'Observateur
On record
Ontario Association of Children's Aid Societies. Journal
Our children
Partners in child care
Perhaps you can help : volunteer job description for all ages
Plan Canada news
Prism
Répertoire des services communautaires de la région de Québec
Répertoire des services communautaires du grand Montreal = Directory of community services of Greater Montreal
The Reporter
Resources Exchange Project. Newsletter
Resources exchange project (British Columbia). Library list
Resources Exchange Project (N.S.). Newsletter
Resources exchange project newsletter
Saskatchewan care
Social development
The Social worker = Le Travailleur social
Le Troisième äge
The United way
United Way of Canada. Conference. Proceedings.

Sporting goods Canada
Sports/Famille
Sportsland magazine
The Standardbred record
The Stanley Cup records and statistics
Sweep
Synchro Canada
Teeoff
Trente pour cent
Volleyball technical journal
Water polo in Canada
Western Canada skier
Wheelspin news : Canada's autosport newsmagazine

Standards

Canadian Standards Association. C.S.A. quarterly review
Canadian Standards Association. CSA and the consumer
Canadian Standards Association. Directory of CSA certified plumbing products
Consensus
List of certified fuel burning equipment and fuels handling equipment
Standards Canada

Taxation

Assessors review
British Columbia taxation service
Canada. Laws, statutes, etc. Income tax act annotated
Canada income tax regulations service
Canada tax cases
Canada tax manual
Canada tax service
Canada tax service letter
Canadian Tax Foundation. Conference report : report of proceedings of the Annual Tax Conference
Canadian tax journal
Canadian tax news
Corporate Management Tax Conference
McGoldrick's handbook of Canadian customs tariff and excise duties
Ontario taxation service
Provincial succession duties and gift tax service
Provincial taxation service
Quebec taxation service
Succession duty and gift tax handbook
Tax memo

Technology

The Canadian journal of radiography, radiotherapthy, nuclear medicine = Le Journal canadien de radiographie, radiothérapie, nucléographie
Canadian Operational Research Society. CORS bulletin
Canadian Society of Laboratory Technologists. Nova Scotia Branch. The Newsletter
Canadian steam magazine
Cassette gazette
Filter
KVP news
Laboratory guide : directory issue of Laboratory product news
Laboratory product news
Man underwater
Respiratory technology
The Respiratory Technology Society of Ontario. Quarterly newsletter
Science forum : a Canadian journal of science and technology = Revue canadienne des sciences pures et appliquées
Sono : sonorisation au Canada
Specification associate
The Summary
Le Technicien
Techno-information

Telecommunications

Actrascope news
Association for Public Broadcasting in British Columbia. Newsletter
The Audio retailer
Audio Scene Canada
B.C. Tel news
Bell news. Eastern ed
B.C. Tel news careers
Broadcaster
Cable communications magazine
The Canadian amateur
Canadian communications reports
Canadian interconnection
Canadian International DX Radio Club. The CIDX messenger
Capt. Lillie's coast guide and radiotelephone directory : British Columbia, Puget Sound and S.E. Alaska Coast Guide
Circuit fermé
Communications and cable TV business
Communitronics
Conseil de développement des média communautaires. Bulletin de liason
The FM guide
Face to face with talent
Ici Radio Canada : programme de la télévision
Les Innovateurs
The Innovators
Le journal Bell
Journal of microwave power
Media Club of Canada. Newspacket
Metro telecaster and entertainment guide
National Association of Broadcast Employees and Technicians. Canadian Office. NABET news = Association nationale des employés et techniciens en radio diffusion. Nouvelles NABET
The Newfoundland amateur

Trader's post
U.S. news bulletin
Visit Algoma
Wastes handling
Yonge-Bloor-Bay Association Inc. The Bulletin

Transport

Alberta Motor Transport Association. AMTA news bulletin
Alberta motor transport directory
Association des routes et transports du Canada. Nouvelles de l'ARTA
L'Association nationale des camionneurs artisans inc. : La Voix de l'ANCAI
Atlantic truck transport review
Bulletin Montraffic = Montraffic news
Bus and truck transport
Canadian driver/owner
The Canadian forwarder
Canadian guide : Canada's up-to-the minute gazetteer and shipper's directory
Canadian highway carriers guide
Canadian Pacific Ltd. CP rail news
Canadian road knight
Canadian transport
Canadian transportation and distribution management
Canadian Truck Body and Equipment Association. Newsletter
Canadian Urban Transit Association. Proceedings of the annual meeting
Christian railroader
Coupler
Guide du transport par camion = Truck transport guide
Highway Transport Board. Highway Transport Board Bulletin
Joint Program in Transportation. Newsletter
Manitoba Highway News
Manitoba Trucking Association. M.T.A. ship by truck directory
Motor carrier
Motor transport factbook
Motorways miler
Nation on the move = Nation en mouvement
Official Ontario 'ship by truck' directory
Ontario Trucking Association. OTA news round-up
Road runner
Roads and Transportation Association of Canada. Proceedings
Roads and Transportation Association of Canada. RTAC news
Roads and Transportation Association of Canada. Technical bulletin
Routes et transports
Traffic notes
Transit Canada magazine
Transit fact book
Transit topics
Transport commercial
Transport routier du Québec = Québec road transport
Truck Canada
Truck data book
United Transportation Union. UTU news Canada
University of Manitoba. Center for Transportation Studies. Seminar Series on Transportation. Proceedings
WesTrade traffic directory

Travel

The Arrow
Asta-Canada notes
Bluewater circle drives : one-day and weekend outings in Southwestern Ontario
Bluewater vacation guide : Lake Huron, Georgian Bay and Manitoulin Island
Bon voyage
CTM weekly bulletin
Canadian host
Canadian travel courier
Canadian travel news
Canadian travel news weekly
Canadian travel press
The Canadian traveller
Cariboo calling : supplement to the 100 Mile House Free press
The Globe and Mail vacation guide
Hospitalité Laurentides
Huronia tourist guide book
Huronia winter adventures
Leisurewheels
Manitoba Farm Vacations Association. Newsletter
Metro guide
Personnel guide to Canada's travel industry
Selling travel
South east Alberta
Thunder Bay guide
Toronto life travel guide
Touring and travel
Tourist guide = Guide touristique
Tourist talk
The Viking
Westworld : the magazine of travel, leisure and living
Your host around Hamilton

Urban Life

Bureau of Municipial Research. BMR comment
City magazine
Community Planning Association of Canada. Ontario Division. Ontario division newsletter
The London hi riser
The Municipal news
Municipal open line
Municipal report
Saskatoon

PUBLISHER AND SPONSOR INDEX

INDEX DES ÉDITEURS ET DES PARRAINS

Alberta Hog Producers Marketing Board.
Alberta hog journal

Alberta Home Economics Association.
Alberta Home Economics Association. AHEA newsletter

Alberta Hospital Association.
HospitAlta

Alberta Law Review.
Alberta law review

Alberta Medical Association.
Alberta medical bulletin

Alberta Motor Association.
Alberta motorist

Alberta Motor Transport Association.
Alberta Motor Transport Association. AMTA news bulletin
Alberta motor transport directory

Alberta Native Communications Society.
The Native people

Alberta Polled Hereford Club.
Alberta Polled Hereford Club. Newsletter

Alberta Rehabilitation Council for the Disabled. John Mockler.
The Alberta handicapped forum

Alberta School Trustees' Association.
The Alberta school trustee

Alberta Social Studies Specialist Council.
One world

Alberta Teachers' Association.
Alberta English
Alberta English notes
Alberta learning resources journal
Alberta science education journal
Alberta Teachers' Association. English council. Newsletter
Alberta Teachers' Association. Health and Physical Education Council. HPEC runner
Alberta Teachers' Association. The ATA magazine
Alberta Teachers' Association. The ATA news
Challenge in educational administration
Fine
One world
Professional development bulletin
Synoptic

Alberta Teachers' Association. Le Conseil français.
Notre langue, notre culture

Alberta Teachers' Association. Early Childhood Education Council.
Early childhood education
Trail blazers

Alberta Teachers' Association. Guidance Council.
The Alberta counselor

Alberta Teachers' Association. Home Economics Council.
Home echos

Alberta Teachers Association. Industrial Teachers' Council.
The Communicator

Alberta Teachers' Association. Learning Resources' Council.
Alberta Teachers' Association. Learning Resources Council. Newsletter

Alberta Teachers' Association. Mathematics Council.
Delta-K

Alberta Teachers' Association. Modern Language Council.
Alberta modern language journal

Alberta Teachers' Association. Special Education Council.
Alberta Teachers' Association. Special Education Council. Newsletter
Teaching atypical students in Alberta

Alberta Wheat Pool. The Public Relations Department.
Wheat pool budget

Alberta Wilderness Association.
Alberta Wilderness Association. Newsletter

Alberta Women's Institute.
Home and country

Albert-Westmorland-Kent Regional Library.
Albert-Westmorland-Kent Regional Library. News = Nouvelles

Doreen Albion.
Avicultural journal
Vancouver Island Cage Bird Society. Annual show bulletin

Alcan.
L'Equipe

Alcan. Service des relations publiques.
Le Lingot

Alcan Canada Limitée. Câblerie-Tréfilerie de Shawinigan.
Filo cable

Alcan Canada Products Ltd.
Alcan Canada Products Ltd. Alcan news

Alcohol and Drug Concerns Inc.
Concerns

The Alcuin Society.
Amphora

Ralph Alfonso.
Moongoose

Apostleship of Prayer.
Messenger of the Sacred Heart of Jesus

Apostolic Church of Pentecost of Canada, Inc.
End times messenger

Appaloosa Horse Club of Canada.
The Canadian Appaloosa journal

Applegarth Follies.
Applegarth's folly
Dan Brock's historical almanack of London

Appraisal Institute of Canada.
Appraisal Institute of Canada. Appraisal Institute digest
Appraisal Institute. Directory

Arab Information Centre.
Arab - Canada newsletter

Arbutus Publications Ltd.
British Columbia insurance directory of insurance companies, agents and adjusters

Archaeological Society of British Columbia.
The Midden

Archival Association of Atlantic Canada.
Archival Association of Atlantic Canada. Newsletter

Archway Publishers Ltd. Harold Schiel.
Playboard

Joseph D. Armand.
Service canadien des forêts. Revue bimestrielle de recherches

Armée de Marie.
L'Armée de Marie

Armenian Youth Federation. "S. Zavarian" Toronto Chapter.
Echo : Armenian tabloid

Armenian Evangelical Church.
Canada Armenian press : newsletter

J.H. Arnott and Son.
Canadian beekeeping

Art Gallery of Ontario.
Art Gallery of Ontario. Extension Department. Circulating exhibition catalogue

Art Magazine Incorporated.
Art magazine

Artdata enr.
Parachute : revue d'art contemporain

The Arthritis Society.
Carscope

Arthurs Publications Ltd.
Canadian boating
Canadian hairdresser
Canadian men's hairstylist and barber
Marine and outdoor trades

Art-Official Inc.
File magazine

Arts and Science Alumni Association. University of Guelph.
Arts and sciences alumni news

Arts Council of the Nanaimo Regional District.
The Arts counsellor

Asia Publications.
India star

Aslin Advertising Company.
Metro guide

L'Association canadienne de la construction.
Construction

Association canadienne d'éducation de langue française.
Association canadienne d'éducation de langue française. Bulletin
Pleins feux sur la francophonie...

Association canadienne des détaillants en quincaillerie.
Association canadienne des détaillants en quincaillerie. A.C.D.Q. journaliste

Association canadienne des écoles universitaires de musique.
Association canadienne des écoles universitaires de musique. Journal de l'association canadienne des écoles universitaires de musique

Association canadienne des éducateurs de langue française.
Association canadienne d'éducation de langue française. ACELF revue

Association canadienne des entraîneurs.
Association canadienne des entraîneurs. Bulletin
Communiqué

Association canadienne des études latino-amèricaines.
Association canadienne des études latino-américaines. Bulletin

L'Association canadienne des producteurs de pätes et papiers.
Rapport sur l'industrie des pätes et papier

L'Association canadienne d'urbanisme. Division du Québec.
Techniques municipales : le règlement de lotissement

Association canadienne-française de l'Ontario.
Association canadienne-française de l'Ontario. ACFO-Info
Ebauches

Association des infirmières catholiques du Canada.
Association des infirmières catholiques du Canada. Bulletin des infirmières catholiqués du Canada

Association des inspecteurs en santé publique du Québec.
Associcomportement.
Le Maître imprimeur

Association des mines d'amiante du Québec.
Le Producteur d'amiante = Asbestos producer

L'Association des outfitters du Québec.
Bulletin des outfitters = Bulletin of the outfitters

Association des paysagistes et pépiniéristes du Québec inc.
Association des paysagistes et pépiniéristes du Québec inc. Bulletin

Association des pharmaciens des établissements de santé du Québec.
Association des pharmaciens des établissements de santé du Québec. Bulletin d'information

Association des pharmaciens détaillants de la province de Québec.
L'Echo

Association des photographes professionnels de la province de Québec.
Le Photographe professionnel

Association des professeurs d'arts plastiques du Québec.
Vision

Association des professeurs du campus Notre-Dame-de-Foy de Cap Rouge.
Les Cahiers de Cap-Rouge

Association des professionels de l'activité physique du Québec.
Mouvement

L'Association des professionnels de l'activité physique du Québec.
Mouvement

Association des propriétaires de machinerie lourde du Québec, inc. Gérard Privé.
Machinerie lourde = Heavy equipment
Revue machinerie lourde

Association des religieuses enseignantes du Québec.
Association des religieuses enseignantes du Québec. AREQ
Association des religieuses enseignantes du Québec. AREQ informations

Association des rencontres culturelles avec détenus.
Association des rencontres culturelles avec les détenus. Information-ARCAD

Association des routes et transports du

Revue de modification du comportement

Association des techniciens forestiers du Québec.
Foresterie à tout

L'Association des technologistes agricoles inc. G. Vincent.
Québec horticole

L'Association des universités et colleges du Canada.
L'Association des universities et colleges du Canada. Bibliographie sur l'enseignement supérieur

Association des universités partiellement ou entièrement de langue française.
L'Association des universités partiellement ou entièrement de langue française. Bulletin de nouvelles brèves
Association des universités partiellement ou entièrement de langue française. AUPELF cahiers
Association des universités partiellement ou entièrement de langue française. AUPELF revue
Association des universités partiellement ou entièrement de langue française. AUPELF assemblée générale, compte rendu de la conférence triennale
Association des universités partiellement ou entièrement de langue française. Séminaire
Catalogue des publications périodiques universitaires francophones
Etudes françaises dans le monde : bulletin de liaison des départements et centres d'études françaises
Répertoire des études supérieures et des équivalences de titres, de diplômes et de périodes d'études entres les universités de langue française
Répertoire des thèses de doctorat soutenues devant les universités de langue française
Répertoire général des universités membres de l'A.U.P.E.L.F
Université et coopération

Association of Certified Survey Technicians & Technologist of Ontario.
Northpoint

Association of Community Theatres, Central Ontario.
Act news

The Association of Faculties of Pharmacy.
The Association of Faculties of Pharmacy. Proceedings of the annual meeting

The Association of Kinsmen Clubs.
Kin

Association of Manitoba Museums.
The Grande new Dawson and hind quarterly epistle

Association of Newfoundland Land Surveyors.
Newfoundland surveyor

The Association of Ontario Land Surveyors.
The Ontario land surveyor

Association of Polish Engineers in Canada.
Association of Polish Engineers in Canada. Bulletin

Association of Professional Engineers, Geologists, and Geophysicists of Alberta.
Mini pegg
The Pegg

Association of Professional Engineers of B.C.
The B.C. professional engineer

Association of Professional Engineers of Nova Scotia.
The Professional engineer in Nova Scotia

Association of Professional Engineers of Ontario.
The Ontario digest

Association of Professional Engineers of Saskatchewan.
The Saskatchewan professional engineer

Association of Professional Engineers of the Province of Manitoba.
The Manitoba professional engineer

Association of Professional Engineers of the Province of New Brunswick.
The Professional engineer in New Brunswick

Association of Psychologists of the Province of New Brunswick.
Association of Psychologists of the Province of New Brunswick. Journal of The Association of Psychologists of the Province of New Brunswick

Association of Registered Nurses of Newfoundland.
Association of Registered Nurses of Newfoundland. News bulletin

Association of Registered Professional Foresters of New Brunswick.
Association of Registered Professional Foresters of New Brunswick. Papers and reports

The Association of Superintendents of Insurance of the Provinces of Canada. The Office of the Secretary.
Association of Superintendents of Insurance of the Provinces of Canada. Conference. Minutes of Proceedings

Association of Teachers of Exceptional Children.
Association of Teachers of Exceptional Children

Association of the Scientific, Engineering & Technological Community of Canada.
Scitec bulletin

Association of Translators and Interpreters of Ontario.
Association of Translators and Interpreters of Ontario. Inform-ATIO

Association of Universities and Colleges of Canada.
Association of Universities and Colleges of Canada. Proceedings of the annual meeting = Association des universities et colleges du Canada. Délibérations de l'assemblée annuelle
Fellowships and scholarships offered by private donors and foreign governments
Inventory of research into higher education in Canada = Inventaire des recherches sur l'enseignement supérieur au Canada
Select bibliography on higher education
University affairs = Affaires universitaires

Association pour la protection automobile.
Communiqué aux consommateurs = Consumer communique

Association pour l'avancement de l'administration scolaire.
Bulletin d'administration scolaire

Association pour l'avancement des sciences et des techniques de la documentation.
Association pour l'avancement des sciences et des techniques de la documentation. ASTED nouvelles
Documentation et bibliothèques

L'Association professionnelle des meuniers du Québec.
Le Meunier québécois

Association provinciale de l'enseignement commercial. Marcel Blondeau.
Informapec

Brandon University. Student's Union Inc.
Quill

Brandon University Alumni Association.
Alumni

Brandstead Press.
Modicum

La Brasserie Labatt Ltée au Québec.
Les Nouvelles de la brasserie

Bratstvo/Fraternity.
Bratstvo. Fraternity

Brave Beaver Pressworks Ltd. Martin Levesque.
Cycle Canada : for and about motorcycling in Canada

Brereton Field Naturalists Club of Barrier.
The Blue heron

Briercrest Bible Institute.
Echo

British America Publishing Co. Ltd.
Sentinel

British Columbia Aberdeen Angus Association.
British Columbia Aberdeen Angus Association. Newsletter

British Columbia & Yukon Chamber of Mines.
Mining exploration and development review, British Columbia-Yukon

B.C. Art Teachers' Association.
British Columbia Art Teachers' Association. BCATA journal for art teachers

B.C. Art Teachers' Association.
British Columbia Art Teachers' Association. Newsletter

British Columbia Artificial Insemination Centre.
B.C. Artificial Insemination Centre. B.C.A.I. newsletter

British Columbia Association for the Mentally Retarded.
British Columbia Association for the Mentally Retarded. Conference. Annual conference
The B.C. mental retardation advisor

British Columbia Association of Mathematics Teachers.
Vector: newsletter/journal

B.C. Association of School Supervisors of Instruction.
British Columbia Association of School Supervisors of Instruction. Newsletter of the British Columbia Association of School Supervisors

British Columbia Association of Teachers of Classics.
Vexillum

British Columbia Association of Teachers' of Modern languages.
Elan

B.C. Business Educators' Association.
British Columbia Business Educators' Association. Newsletter

British Columbia Chamber of Commerce.
British Columbia Chamber of Commerce. General policy statements and resolutions

British Columbia Chiropractic Association.
Backtalk

British Columbia Civil Liberties Association.
British Columbia Civil Liberties Association. B.C.C.L.A. news digest
Democratic commitment

British Columbia Corrections Association.
Courier

British Columbia English Teachers' Association.
British Columbia English Teachers' Association. Journal

British Columbia Fruit Growers Association.
British Columbia Fruit Growers Association. Horticultural conference proceedings

British Columbia Genealogical Society.
The British Columbia genealogist

B.C. Goat Breeders Association.
B.C. dairy goat news

British Columbia Government Employees' Union.
The Provincial

B.C. Health Association.
BC Health Association. BCHA activity bulletin
British Columbia Health Association. Proceedings of the annual conference
British Columbia Hospital Association. BCHA news

British Columbia Historical Association.
British Columbia historial news

British Columbia Institute of Agrologists.
B.C. agrologists

British Columbia Institute of Technology.
British Columbia Institute of Technology. BCIT developments
Link

British Columbia Library Association.
British Columbia library quarterly

British Columbia Medical Association.
British Columbia medical journal

Provincial Intermediate Teachers' Association. PITA news
Secondary Learning Assistance Teachers' Association. Bulletin
Thesa journal
Vector: newsletter/journal
Vexillum
View

British Columbia Telephone Co.
B.C. Tel news
B.C. Tel news careers

British Columbia Thoroughbred Breeders' Society.
Annual sale of yearlings and mixed stock
British Columbia thoroughbred : an official review of the season

British Columbia Tuberculosis-Christmas Seal Society.
Your health

British Columbia Voice of Women.
B.C. voice

British Columbia Wildlife Federation.
B. C. Wildlife Federation. BCWF newsletter

British North America Philatelic Society.
BNA topics

Brock Publishers Ltd.
Mennonite mirror

Brock University.
The Press

Brock University. Students Union Inc.
Press

Brotherhood of Locomotive Engineers.
The Locomotive engineer

Logan Brown Communications.
Building management and maintenance news
Copperfield : an independent Canadian literary magazine of the land and the North
Dimensions nouvelles

Browndale.
Involvement : the family resource magazine

Bruce County Historical Society.
Bruce County historical notes
Bruce County Historical Society. Year book

The Bruce Trail Association.
The Bruce Trail news

Bryan Publications Ltd. John Bryan.
Western living

Bryon Lawes and Assoc.
The Elder statesman

R.M. Bucke Memorial Society.
The R.M. Bucke Memorial Society. Conference. Proceedings
The R.M. Bucke Memorial Society newsletter

The Building Centre.
Select home designs

Les Buissonnets inc.
Carrefour chrétien

Bureau canadien de l'éducation internationale.
L'Amérique latine
Eté au Canada

Bureau d'assurance du Canada.
Les assurances I.A.R.D. du Canada

Bureau de Presse IMC.
Réveil missionnaire

Bureau of Municipal Research.
Bureau of Municipial Research. BMR comment
Civic affairs
Directory of municipal governments in Metropolitan Toronto

Louis Burke.
Canadian short story magazine

Burlington Fine Arts Association.
Burlington Fine Arts Association. Newsletter

Burnaby Creative Writers Society.
Diversions

Burnaby Public Library.
Book news

Business Education Council. Teachers' Association.
Synoptic

Tom Butters.
The Drum

Butterworth and Co. (Canada) Ltd.
Butterworth's Ontario digest : being a statement of the case law of Ontario from 1901 with full annotations
Canadian Labour Relations Boards. Reports
Canadian oil and gas
Canadian weekly law sheet
Federal court of Canada service
Supreme Court of Canada reports service

Buyers' Market of Canada.
Buyers' market

Byelorussian Kastus Kalinouski Institute.
Byelorussian in Canada = Bielarusy u Kanadzie : Fotodocumentation

Byelorussian Literary Society, Bayavaya Uskalos.
Bayavaya uskalos = Literary magazine

Byers Associates.
Byers Canadian merchandise mart
Byers national industrial directory
Byers trade directory
Byers western industrial directory

Canada Bonded Attorney and Legal Directory Ltd.
Canada legal directory

Canada Centre Holdings Ltd. Asia Publications.
Asia times
Bharati
Panjab

Canada Committee.
Opinion canada

Canada Council.
Greenhouse newsletter
Historia mathematica : international journal of history of mathematics

Canada Council and Ontario Arts Council.
artscanada

The Canada Council and the University of British Columbia.
Pacific affairs : an international review of Asia and the Pacific

Canada Goose.
Canada goose

Canada Grains Council.
The Open door newsletter
Statistical handbook

Canada Japan Trade Council.
Canada Japan
Canada Japan Trade Council. Newsletter

The Canada Jaycees.
Canadian jaycee

Canada Law Book Ltd.
Canada. Laws. Statutes, etc. Martin's annual criminal code
Canadian criminal cases
The Canadian law list
Canadian patent reporter
Criminal law quarterly
Dominion law reports
Estates and trusts quarterly
Labour arbitration cases
Land compensation reports
The Lawyer's phone book
The Ontario annual practice
Ontario reports
Ontario statute citator. Bill service

The Canada Life Assurance Company.
The Pelican

Canada Rides Publications.
Canada rides

Canada Safety Council.
Accident fatalities - Canada
Safety Canada

Canada Sociological Research Centre.
Journal of comparative sociology

The Canada Starch Company Ltd.
The Kernel

Canada West Publications.
Canada west magazine

Canada's 10 Chartered Banks.
The Canadian Bankers' Association. CBA bulletin = L'association des banquiers canadiens. ABC bulletin

Canadian Aberdeen Angus Association. R.H. Turner.
Canadian Aberdeen Angus news

Canadian Aeronautics and Space Institute.
Canadian Aeronautics and Space Institute. C.A.S.I. transactions
Canadian aeronautics and space journal

Canadian Agricultural Economics Society.
Canadian journal of agricultural economics

Canadian Air Line Pilots' Association, Montreal.
Pilot

Canadian Air Traffic Control Association Inc.
Canadian Air Traffic Control Association, Inc. CATCA journal

Canadian Aircraft Operator Publishing Ltd. Robert G. Halford.
Canadian aircraft operator

Canadian Amateur Boxing Association.
Canadian Amateur Boxing Association. C.A.B.A. news

Canadian Amateur Football Association.
Canadian Amateur Football Association. CAFA football journal

Canadian Amateur Musicians.
CAMAC. Montreal Committee. Newsletter/bulletin

Canadian Amateur Musicians. Southern Ontario Region.
Canadian Amateur Musicians Southern Ontario Region. CAMMAC newsletter

Canadian Amateur Radio Federation.
The Canadian amateur

Canadian Amateur Synchronized Swimming Association.
Synchro Canada

Canadian Anaesthetists' Society.
Canadian Anaesthetists' Society. CAS newsletter
Canadian Anaesthetists' Society. The Canadian Anaesthetists' Society journal = Société canadienne d'anesthésistes. Journal de la Société canadienne d'anesthésistes.

Canadian & Ontario Nursery Trades Association.
Landscape = Paysage Canada

Canadian Association of Geographers.
Canadian geographer = Le Géographe canadien

Canadian Association of Hospital Auxiliaries.
Courier

Canadian Association of Latin American Studies.
Canadian Association of Latin American Studies. CALAS newsletter
Directory of Canadian scholars and universities interested in Latin American studies = Repertoire des universitaires et universités se spécialisant dans études latino - américaines au Canada

Canadian Association of Law Libraries.
Canadian Association of Law Libraries. Newsletter = Association canadienne des bibliothèques de droit. Bulletin
Index to Canadian legal periodical literature

Canadian Association of Law Teachers.
Canadian Association of Law Teachers. Directory of law teachers = Association canadienne des professeurs de droit. Annuaire des professeurs de droit

Canadian Association of Medical Clinics.
Group practice in Canada

Canadian Association of Medical Record Librarians.
Canadian Association of Medical Record Libraries. Camrl recorder

Canadian Association of Occupational Therapists.
Canadian journal of occupational therapy = Revue canadienne d'ergothérapie

The Canadian Association of Optometrists.
The Canadian journal of optometry

Canadian Association of Pathologists.
Canadian Association of Pathologists. Newsletter

Canadian Association of Physicists.
Physics in Canada = La Physique au Canada

Canadian Association of Psychiatric Nurses.
Canadian journal of psychiatric nursing

Canadian Association of Public Libraries.
Canadian Association of Public Libraries. Newsletter

Canadian Association of Radiologists.
Canadian Association of Radiologists. Journal

Canadian Association of School Administrators.
Casagram
Casagram : quarterly supplement

Canadian Association of Schools of Social Work.
Canadian journal of social work education

Canadian Association of Sheet Metal and Air Handling Contractors.
Canadian Association of Sheet Metal and Air Handling Contractors. CASMAHC news bulletin

Canadian Association of Slavists.
Canadian Association of Slavists. Newsletter = Association canadienne des Slavistes. Newsletter
Canadian Slavonic papers = Revue canadienne des Slavistes

Canadian Association of Social Workers.
Canadian Association of Social Workers. Information
Information
The Social worker = Le Travailleur social

Canadian Association of Special Libraries and Information Services.
Agora
Canadian Association of Special Libraries and Information Services. Art Libraries Committee. Newsletter

Canadian Association of University Business Officers.
Canadian Association of University Business Officers. Bulletin = Association canadienne du personnel administratif universitaire. Bulletin
Canadian Association of University Business Officers. Directory = Association canadienne de personnel administratif universitaire. Répertoire

Canadian Association of University Teachers.
Canadian Association of University Teachers. C.A.U.T. bulletin = Association canadienne des professeurs d'université. Bulletin de l'A.C.P.U
Canadian Association of University Teachers. Handbook = Association canadienne des professeurs d'université. Guide de l'ACPU

Canadian Association of University Teachers of German and The Germanic Section of the Australian Universities Language and Literature Association.
Seminar : a journal of Germanic studies

Canadian Athletic Program Service Ltd.
Racquets Canada

Canadian Authors Association. Edmonton Branch.
Alberta poetry yearbook
Canadian author and bookman

Canadian Chiropractic Association.
Canadian Chiropractic Association. Journal of Canadian Chiropractic Association

Canadian Church Growth Centre.
Church growth : Canada

Canadian Church Historical Society.
Canadian Church Historical Society. Journal

Canadian Clothing Journal.
Canadian clothing journal

Canadian College of Health Service Executives.
Contact

The Canadian College of Teachers.
The Canadian College of Teachers. Newsletter
Canadian College of Teachers. The Journal of the Canadian College of Teachers

Canadian Commission for UNESCO.
Canadian Commission for UNESCO. Bulletin = Commission canadienne pour l'Unesco. Bulletin

Canadian Committee for Geography.
Canadian Committee for Geography. Newsletter

Canadian Community Newspapers Association.
The Canadian community publisher
Publisher

Canadian Comparative Literature Association.
Canadian review of comparative literature = Revue canadienne de littérature comparée

Canadian Conference of Mennonite Brethren Churches.
Mennonitische Rundschau = Mennonite review

Canadian Construction Association.
Construction

Canadian Contractors Equipment Magazine.
Canadian contractors equipment magazine

Canadian Co-operative Wool Growers Limited.
Canadian wool grower

Canadian Copper and Brass Development Association.
Canadian copper = Cuivre canadien

Canadian Corporation for Studies in Religion/Corporation canadienne des sciences religieuses.
Studies in religion = Sciences religieuses

Canadian Correspondence Chess Association.
Check

Canadian Council of Christians and Jews.
Scope = Envergure

Canadian Council of Churches.
Council communicator

Canadian Council of Professional Engineers.
Canadian Council of Professional Engineers. Newsbrief = Conseil canadien des ingénieurs. Communiqué

Canadian Council of Teachers of English.
Canadian Council of Teachers of English. Newsletter
The English quarterly

The Canadian Council of the Blind.
The Canadian Council of the Blind. The C.C.B. outlook

Canadian Council on Social Development.
CW
Canadian Council on Social Development. Canadian Conference on Social Welfare. Proceedings
Correctional literature published in Canada = Ouvrages de criminologie publiés au Canada
Directory of Canadian welfare services = Répertoire des services sociaux canadiens
Housing and people
Social development

Canadian Council on Social Development. Community Funds and Councils of Canada.
Community Fund and Councils of Canada. Proceedings of biennal conference
Community Funds and Councils of Canada. Allocations to national organizations

Canadian Crafts Council.
Canadian Crafts Council. Newsletter = Conseil canadien de l'artisan. Bulletin de nouvelles

Canadian Credit Institute.
Article of the month
Credit management review

Canadian Criminology and Corrections Association.
Canadian Criminology and Corrections Association. Bulletin
Canadian journal of criminology and corrections = Revue canadienne de criminologie
Correctional literature published in Canada = Ouvrages de criminologie publiés au Canada

Canadian Cultural Society of the Deaf.
Cultural horizons of the deaf in Canada

Canadian Cycling Association.
Canadian cyclist = Cycliste canadien

Canadian Cystic Fibrosis Foundation.
Candid facts

Canadian Daily Quotation Service Ltd.
The Bond record
Canadian financial E-Z directory

Canadian Figure Skating Association.
Canadian skater

Canadian Film Editors' Guild.
The Canadian film editor

Canadian Film Institute.
Film canadiana. Part 1 - Film, Part 2 - Television
Images

Canadian Flight Publishing Co.
Canadian flight

Canadian Folk Music Society.
Canadian Folk Music Society journal
Canadian Folk Music Society. Newsletter

Canadian Forces Base, Calgary.
The Roundup

Canadian Forces Base, Edmonton.
Sealandair

Canadian Forces Base, Moose Jaw. Base Commander.
The Plainsman

Canadian Forces Base, Summerside Base Commander.
Gulf wings

Canadian Forces Base, Winnipeg.
Voxair

Canadian Forestry Association/ Association forestière canadienne.
Canadian Forestry Association. C.F.A. news = Association forestière canadienne. Le courrier A.F.C

Canadian Forestry Association of British Columbia.
Fire Control Course. Fire control notes

Canadian Foundation for Economic Education.
Canadian Foundation for Economic Education. Rapport

Canadian Friends Historical Association.
Canadian Quaker history

The Canadian Friends of Free China Association.
The Truth about China newsletter

Canadian Friends Service Committee.
Canadian Friends Service Committee = Secours Quaker Canadien

Canadian Fruit Wholesalers' Association.
Canadian Fruit Wholesalers' Association. Yearbook

The Canadian Gallup Poll Ltd.
The Gallup report

Canadian Gas Association.
Canadian Gas Association. Manufacturers' directory
Directory of Canadian gas utilities
"What's your gas Q" - papers

Canadian Gas Association. Statistics Department.
Canadian gas facts

Canadian German Chamber of Industry and Commerce Inc. Montreal Office.
Nachrichten aus Kanada
Trade news letter

Canadian Girls in Training. National Committee.
The Torch

Canadian Gladiolus Society.
Canadian Gladiolus Society. Annual

Canadian Guernsey Breeders' Association.
Canadian guernsey breeders' journal

Canadian Guidance and Counselling Association.
Canadian counsellor

Canadian Guild of Crafts. Ontario Chapter.
Craft dimensions artisanales

Canadian Gymnastics Federation.
Canadian Gymastics Federation. C.G.F. monthly bulletin

Canadian Health Education Specialists Society.
Annotated guide to health instruction materials in Canada

The Canadian Hearing Society.
Vibrations

Canadian Heart Foundation. New Brunswick Division.
N.B. heart beat

Canadian Hemophilia Society. Ontario Chapter.
Canadian Hemophilia Society. Ontario Chapter. Bulletin

Canadian Hemophilia Society. Toronto Auxiliary.
Toronto hemo comm

Canadian Highland Cattle Society.
The Kyloe cry

Canadian Historical Association.
Register of post-graduate dissertations in progress in history and related subjects

Canadian Home Economics Association.
Canadian home economics journal

Canadian Home Leaguer.
The Canadian home leaguer: a magazine for women

Canadian Honey Council.
Canadian beekeeping

Canadian Jewish Outlook.
Canadian Jewish outlook

Canadian Jewish Weekly.
Canadian Jewish weekly

Canadian Journalism Foundation.
The Last post

Canadian Kodak Co. Ltd.
Canadian Kodakery

Canadian Labour Congress.
Canadian labour = Le travailleur canadien
Canadian Labour Comment = Information syndicale
Canadian Labour Congress. Report of proceedings of the convention
Canadian Labour Congress. Memorandum to the Government of Canada
Notes on unions

Canadian Lacrosse Association.
Lacrosse-the Canadian game

Canadian Ladies Golf Association.
Canadian Ladies Golf Association. Year book

Canadian Lawn Bowling Council.
The Green

Canadian Lawn Tennis Association : Canadian Squash Racquets Association.
Racquets Canada

The Canadian Leprosy Relief Association Inc.
Help for the leper : Raoul Fallereau foundations

Canadian Liberation Movement.
New Canada

Canadian Library Association.
Agora
Canadian Association of College and University Libraries. Newsletter
Canadian Association of Public Libraries. Newsletter
Canadian Association of College and University Libraries. Workshop on Automation. Papers
Canadian Library Association. Proceedings
Canadian library journal
Canadian Library Trustees' Association. Newsletter
Canadian materials
Canadian periodical index = Index des périodiques canadiens
Feliciter
Moccasin telegraph

Canadian Library Trustees Association.
Canadian Library Trustees' Association. Newsletter

The Canadian Life Insurance Association.
Canadian life insurance facts
Current topics

Canadian Linguistic Association.
Canadian journal of linguistics = La Revue canadienne de linguistique
Canadian Linguistic Association. Membership directory and data book memento

Canadian Liquid Air Ltd.
Liquid air review

The Canadian log house.
The Canadian log house : a yearbook of current log builder information

Canadian Manufacturers' Association.
Canadian trade index = Index commercial canadien

Canadian Manufacturers' Association (Quebec division) : La Chambre de commerce du district de Montréal.
Annual survey of clerical employees = Enquête annuelle sur les employés de bureau

Canadian Mathematical Congress.
Canadian journal of mathematics = Journal canadien de mathématiques
Canadian mathematical bulletin = Canadien de mathématiques
Notes, news and comments

Canadian Medical Association.
Canadian journal of surgery
The Canadian Medical Association. Journal

Canadian Mennonite Brethren Conference. Board of Publications.
Mennonite Brethren herald

Canadian Mental Health Association.
Viewpoint

Canadian Meteorological Society.
Atmosphere

The Canadian Metric Association.
Metric message = Message métrique

Canadian Micrographic Society.
Micro notes

Canadian Mothercraft.
Mothercraft newsletter

Canadian Murray Grey Association.
Canadian Murray Grey news
Canadian Murray Grey Association. Yearbook and breeder's directory

Canadian Museums Association.
Gazette
Museogramme = Muséogramme

Canadian Music Educators.
Canadian music educator

Canadian Music Educators. Wallace Laughton.
Canadian Music Educators Association. Newsletter

Peace research reviews

Canadian Periodical Publishers' Association.
Canadian Periodical Publishers' Association. Newsletter

Canadian Petroleum Association.
Canadian Petroleum Association. Statistical yearbook

Canadian Pharmaceutical Association.
Canadian journal of pharmaceutical sciences
Canadian pharmaceutical journal
Compendium of pharmaceuticals and specialities (Canada)
Price book for community pharmacy

Canadian Philosophical Association.
Dialogue : Canadian philosophical review = Dialogue : revue canadienne de philosophie

Canadian Photopress Publishing Ltd.
Krzyk = Outcry

The Canadian Physiological Society.
Canada physiology = Physiologie Canada

The Canadian Physiotherapy Association.
Physiotherapy Canada = Physiothérapie Canada

Canadian Phytopathological Society.
Canadian Phytopathological Society. Proceedings
Canadian Phytopathological Society. C.P.S. news

Canadian Plains Research Center.
Canadian plains bulletin

Canadian Plastics.
Plastics directory of Canada

Canadian Polish Congress.
Canadian Polish Congress. Information bulletin = Congrès canadien polonais. Bulletin

Canadian Political Science Association.
Canadian Political Science Association. Annual general meeting. Papers
Canadian Political Science Association. Bulletin = Société canadienne de science politique. Bulletin
Theses in Canadian political studies = Thèses canadiennes en science politique

Canadian Postmasters Association.
The Canadian postmaster = Le Maître de poste canadien

Canadian Process Equipment and Control News.
Canadian process equipment and control news

Canadian Progress Club.
The Progression

Canadian Psychiatric Association.
Canadian Psychiatric Association. Canadian Psychiatric Association journal = L'Association des psychiatres du Canada. La Revue de L'Association des psychiatres du Canada
Canadian Psychiatric Association. Bulletin = Association des psychiatres du Canada. Bulletin

Canadian Psychological Association.
Canadian journal of behavioural science = Revue canadienne des sciences du comportement
Canadian journal of psychology
Canadian psychological review = Psychologie canadienne

Canadian Public Health Association.
Canadian journal of public health = Revue canadienne de santé publique

Canadian Public Policy.
Canadian public policy = Analyse de politiques

The Canadian Public Relations Society, Inc.
Communication

Canadian Publications.
Fortnightly crescent Toronto

Canadian Pulp and Paper Association.
Canadian Pulp and Paper Association. Reference tables
Canadian Pulp and Paper Association. Technical Section. Proceedings
Canadian Pulp and Paper Association. Statistical bulletin
Canadian Pulp and Paper Association. Environmental Services Office. Review
Monthly newsprint report
Newsprint data
Pulp and paper report

Canadian Pulp and Paper Association. Technical Section.
Canadian Pulp and Paper Association. Technical Section. Transactions

Canadian Pulp and Paper Association. Woodlands Section.
Canadian Pulp and Paper Association. Woodlands Section. News bulletin

Canadian Racing Pigeon Union.
Canadian Racing Pigeon Union. Yearbook

Canadian Railroad Historical Association.
Canadian rail

Canadian Real Estate Association.
Canadian Real Estate Association. C.R.E.A. reporter

Canadian Red Cross Society.
Circle
Despatch. English ed.

Canadian Society for the Study of Education. Yearbook = Sociéte canadienne pour l'étude de l'éducation
Canadian Society for the Study of Education. Bulletin

Canadian Society for the Study of Higher Education.
Canadian journal of higher education = La Revue canadienne d'enseignement supérieur

Canadian Society of Biblical Studies.
Canadian Society of Biblical Studies. Bulletin = Société canadienne des études bibliques. Bulletin
Newsletter for ugaritic studies

Canadian Society of Clinical Chemists.
Canadian Society of Clinical Chemists. CSCC newsletter
Clinical biochemistry

Canadian Society of Exploration Geophysicists.
Canadian Society of Exploration Geophysicists. Journal

Canadian Society of Forensic Science.
Canadian Society of Forensic Science. Journal

Canadian Society of Hospital Pharmacists.
The Canadian journal of hospital pharmacy

Canadian Society of Hospital Pharmacists. Ontario Branch.
Hospital pharmacy in Ontario

Canadian Society of Laboratory Technologists.
The Canadian journal of medical technology
Canadian Society of Laboratory Technologists. News bulletin = L'association canadienne des technologistes de laboratoire. Bulletin nouvelles

Canadian Society of Laboratory Technologists. Nova Scotia Branch.
Canadian Society of Laboratory Technologists. Nova Scotia Branch. The Newsletter

Canadian Society of Landscape Architects.
L'architecture de paysage Canada
Landscape architecture Canada

Canadian Society of Microbiologists.
Canadian Society of Microbiologists. Newsletter

Canadian Society of Military Medals and Insignia (1965-1971).
Canadian military medals and insignia journal

Canadian Society of Painters in Water Colour.
Canadian Society of Painters in Water Colour. Annual exhibition catalogue

Canadian Society of Petroleum Geologists.
Bulletin of Canadian petroleum geology
Canadian Society of Petroleum Geologists. C.S.P.G. reservoir

Canadian Society of Radiological Technicians.
The Canadian journal of radiography, radiotherapthy, nuclear medicine = Le Journal canadien de radiographie, radiothérapie, nucléographie

Canadian Society of Radiological Technicians. Alberta Division.
Cassette gazette

Canadian Society of Radiological Technicians. Manitoba Division. M.A. Lunn.
KVP news

Canadian Society of Respiratory Technologists.
Respiratory technology

Canadian Society of Wildlife and Fishery Biologists.
Canadian Society of Environmental Biologists. Newsletter = Société canadienne des biologistes de l'environnement. Bulletin

Canadian Society of Zoologists.
Canadian Society of Zoologists. Bulletin

Canadian Sociology and Anthropology Association.
Canadian review of sociology and anthropology = Revue canadienne de sociologie et d'anthropologie

Canadian Sport Parachuting Association.
Canadian parachutist : canpara

Canadian Stage and Arts Publications Ltd. George Hercz.
Performing arts magazine

Canadian Standards Association.
L'Association canadienne de normalisation. ACNOR et le consommateur
Canadian Standards Association. CSA and the consumer
Canadian Standards Association. C.S.A. quarterly review
Canadian Standards Association. Directory of CSA certified plumbing products
List of certified fuel burning equipment and fuels handling equipment
Standards Canada

Canadian String Teachers Association.
Canadian String Teachers Association. Newsletter

The Canadian Studies Foundation.
Contact

Canadian Sunshine Club for Shut-ins & Invalids.
Canadian sunshine friend

Canadian Swine Breeders' Association.
Canadian swine

Canadian Youth Hostels Association. Maritime Region.
The Atlantic hosteller

Canadian Youth Hostels Association. Mid-West Area.
Canadian Youth Hostels Association. Mid-West Area. Newsletter

Canadian Youth Hostels Association. Mountain Region.
Trailblazer

Canadian Youth Hostels Association. North West Region.
Pathfinder

Canadian Youth Hostels Association. Pacific Region.
The Pacific hosteller

Canadian Youth Hostels Association. St. Lawrence Region.
The Hosteller = L'Ajiste

The Canadian Zionist Federation.
Canadian Zionist

Canadian-Hungarian Authors' Association.
Antológia: Kanadai magyar irók könyve

Candra Courier.
Holos Instytutu. Mohyla Institute. Newsletter

Cape Breton's Magazine.
Cape Breton's magazine

Capilano College. Humanities Division.
The Capilano review

Capital Communications Ltd.
Canadian energy news
Interface-1
The Multinational
Northern reporter
Ottawa commercial report
Ottawa R and D report

Capucins canadiens.
Capucins canadiens

Carleton Board of Education.
Carleton education bulletin

Carleton University, Alumni Association.
Carleton University. Alumni Association. The Carleton alumneye

Carleton University, Information Office.
Research and studies
This week times two

Carleton University. St. Patrick's College. The Student Association.
The Shillelagh

Carleton University. School of Social Work.
Prism

Carleton University Students' Association.
The Charlatan

Carlisle Business Service. Gwen Stupple.
Landscape

Donald Carlson.
Financial times of Canada

G. Carrero.
Reflexion 2 : primera revista de cultura hispanica en Canada

Carswell Company Ltd.
Reports on family law
Western Ontario law review

Carswell/Methuen Publications.
Canadian tax news

Cash Crop Farming Publications Ltd.
Cash crop farming
The Grower

Cash Crop Farming Publications Ltd. E. De Sutter.
Canadian fruitgrower

Cash Crop Farming Publications Ltd. M.K. Glendinning.
Canadian tobacco grower

Catholic Children's Aid Society of Metropolitan Toronto.
Partners in child care

Catholic Church. Archdiocese of Vancouver.
The B.C. Catholic

Catholic Hospital Association of Canada.
Catholic hospital
Catholic Hospital Association of Canada. C.H.A.C. annual directory = Annuaire de l'A.H.C.C
Catholic Hospital Association of Canada. Directory of member hospitals and homes = Association des hôpitaux catholiques du Canada. Annuaire des hôpitaux et des foyers membres
L'Hôpital catholique

The Catholic Womens' League of Canada.
The Canadian league

Cause Père Prevost, Pères de la fraternité sacerdotale.
Aux amis du Père Prévost

Cegep-Saint-Jean-sur-Richelieu.
Info-parents

Centax of Canada.
The Saskatchewan motorist

Centennial College of Applied Arts and Technology. College Bibliocentre Division.
Film catalogue : a union catalogue of films, videotapes and filmloops used in the Ontario colleges of applied arts and technology

Centraide - Québec.
Répertoire des services communautaires de la région de Québec

Cerebral Palsy Association of British Columbia.
Cerebral palsy news

The Certified General Accountants Associations of Canada.
CGA : the certified general accountant

Paul-Henri Chagnon.
Lustucru

Chambre de Commerce Belgo-Luxembourgeoise au Canada.
Canada-Belgium-Luxembourg

La Chambre de commerce de la province de Québec.
Action : chambre de commerce

Chambre de commerce du Canada.
Chambre de commerce du Canada. Déclaration de principes
Le Lien

Chambre de Commerce française au Canada.
Chambre de commerce française au Canada. Revue de la Chambre de commerce française au Canada

Chambre des notaires du Québec.
Cours de perfectionnement
La Revue du notariat

Champlain Regional College. The English Department.
Matrix : new Canadian writing

La Chancellerie de Montréal.
Eglise catholique. Archidiocèse de Montréal. Bottin

Chancellerie du diocèse de Trois-Rivières.
Eglise catholique. Diocèse de Trois-Rivières. Annuaire

G.C. Chapman.
Canadian sportsman
Management compensation in Canada

Fernande Charbonneau.
Entretiens d'oraison : message spirituel
Protect yourself

Roger Charland.
Kiro santé : le magazine des gens en santé

Charlottetown Group Publishing Inc.
City magazine

Charlton International Publishing Inc.
Charlton coin guide
Charlton liste de valeur

Chatair.
Chatair

Chateauguay Valley Historical Society.
Chateauguay Valley Historical Society. Journal = Socitété historique de la vallée de la Châteauguay. Journal

The Chemical Institute of Canada.
Canadian chemical education
Canadian journal of chemical engineering
Chemistry in Canada
Clinical biochemistry

Chemical Institute of Canada. Hamilton Section.
Chemistry in Hamilton

Chemical Institute of Canada. Toronto Section.
The Catalyst

Chess Federation of Canada.
Chess Federation of Canada. Chess Federation of Canada bulletin

Chesswood House Publishing Ltd.
Canadian training methods
Elements of technology

Chesswood House Publishing Ltd. Richard Guerrier.
Learning resources

The Chesterton Review.
The Chesterton review

Children's Aid Society of Metro Toronto.
Our children

The Children's Aid Society of Ottawa.
The Children's Aid Society of Ottawa. The C.A.S. Record
Communiqué

Chimo Media Ltd.
Sound Canada

Chinese Express Ltd.
Chinese express

Chinese Express Ltd. P. Mor.
New republic

The Chinese Freemasons in Canada Ltd.
Ta han kung pao = The Chinese times

The Chinese Freemasons Publisher Ltd.
Chinese times

Chinese Publicity Bureau Ltd.
Chinatown news

The Chinese Voice Publishing & Printing Co. Ltd.
The Chinese voice

Chrétiens d'aujourd'hui.
Animateur

Christian Children's Fund of Canada.
Canadaid : a news report to sponsors and friends

Christian Labour Association of Canada.
The Guide

Christian Press.
Direction

The Conference Board in Canada.
The Canadian business review
Canadian business trends : quarterly indicators
Canadian business trends : monthly indicators
Canadian business trends : regional indicators
Survey of consumer buying intentions

Conférence catholique canadienne.
Oecuménisme

Conférence catholique canadienne. Claire Dubé.
Conférence catholique canadienne. Annuaire = Canadian Catholic Conference. Directory

Conference of Mennonites in Canada.
Conference of Mennonites in Canada. Bulletin
Conference of Mennonites in Canada. Yearbook

Conference on Scottish Studies.
Scottish tradition

La Conférence religieuse canadienne.
Conference religieuse canadienne. Bulletin

Congregational Libraries Association of British Columbia.
The Rare bird

Congres du travail du Canada.
Cahiers syndicaux
Congrès du travail du Canada

Conseil canadien de développement social.
Digeste social

Conseil canadien de la main d'oeuvre en génie.
Main d'oeuvre en génie bulletin = Engineering manpower news

Conseil canadien de la musique/ Canadian Music Council.
Les Cahiers canadiens de musique = The Canada music book

Conseil canadien de la sécurité.
Des accidents Canada
La prévention au Canada

Conseil canadien des arts populaires.
Le Portage

Conseil de développement des média communautaires.
Conseil de développement des média communautaires. Bulletin de liason

Conseil de la jeunesse scientifique.
Camp aérospatial
Conseil de la jeunesse scientifique. Bulletin de liaison du Conseil de la jeunesse scientifique
Jeunes scientifique
Stage de biochimie

Conseil de la santé et des services sociaux région du Saguenay-Lac-St-Jean.
Le Centre

Le Conseil de la vie française en Amérique.
Conseil de la vie française en Amérique. Le bottin des sociétés patriotiques

Conseil des écoles séparées catholiques d'Ottawa.
Nos écoles

Conseil des écoles séparées catholiques d'Ottawa. Service de l'information.
Nos jeunes

Conseil des producteurs de pâtes et papiers du Québec.
Le Papetier

Conseil du Québec de l'enfance exceptionnelle.
L'Enfant exceptionnel

Conseil du statut de la femme.
Conseil du statut de la femme. Bulletin

Construction Alberta News Ltd.
Construction Alberta news

Construction Specifications Canada.
Specification associate

Consulat General of Switzerland.
Swiss Canadian review = Revue Suisse-Canada

Consumer Press Ltd.
Co-operative consumer

Consumers Association of Canada.
Canadian consumer

Contemporary Music Showcase Association.
Contemporary music showcase

Contrast Publications Ltd. A.W. Hamilton.
Contrast

Convention of Regular Baptist Churches of British Columbia.
The B.C. regular Baptist

R.J. Cooke Ltd.
The MacDonald journal
Resort and motel

Coopérateur féderée de Québec.
Coopérateur agricole

La Coopérative des producteurs de lait de Montréal. Noël Fortin.
Le Producteur de lait

Co-operative Press Associates.
Weekly labour press service

Co-operative Union of Canada.
Co-op commentary

Coopers and Lybrand.
Canadian tax news

Leslie Cowger.
Jabberwocky

Cowley-Bracebridge Press. Society of St. John the Evangelist.
Order of divine service

Craftsmen's Association of British Columbia.
Craft contacts

Charles Crane Memorial Library.
Crane Library. Crane Library news
Crane Library. Crane Library update circular

Crawley Films Ltd.
Crawley commentary

Creative Arts Co.
The Canadian composer = Le Compositeur canadien

Creative Writing Program.
The Dime bag

Credit Union Federation of Alberta Limited.
The Teller

Credit Union National Association Inc.
Everybody's money. Canadian edition

Criminilogie made in Canada.
Criminologie made in Canada

Crisis Intervention and Suicide Prevention Centre of Canada. Community Information Centre.
Directory of services for Greater Vancouver

Critical Studies in Canadian Poetry.
Critical studies in Canadian poetry

Croatian Republicans.
Hrvatski put = Croatian way

Croation Peasant Society of Canada.
Hrvatski glas = Croation voice

Croation Voice Publishing Co. Ltd.
Croation voice annual = Hrvatski glas kalendar
Hrvatski glas = Croation voice

John S. Crosbie.
Canada report

George Cross.
George Cross news letter: Western Canadian investments

Cross Country Press.
Cross country : a magazine of Canadian-U.S. poetry

Cruikshank Communications Ltd.
Gastown and Vancouver today

Crusader Department.
Chivalry

Culture Vulture Publishing Ltd.
The Edmonton culture vulture

Current Events Publishing Co. Ltd. Robert D. Simpson.
Current events. West coast ed

Current Legislative Digest.
Current legislative digest : an index-digest of current legislation

Philip J. Currie.
ERBivore

Currie Coopers and Lybrand Ltd./Ltée.
Répertoire des entreprises canadiennes de services informatiques = Directory of Canadian data processing services firms

James Custy.
Current events magazine. Montreal edition = Actualitiés Montréal

Cycle Canada. Martin Levesque.
Introduction to motorcycling
Moto journal

Dairy Farmers of Canada.
Dairy facts and figures at a glance
Dairy policy = Politique laitière

Dalhousie Labour University Committee and Institute of Public Affairs.
Dalhousie Labour Institute for the Atlantic Provinces. Proceedings

Dalhousie Law School.
The Ansul

Dalhousie Medical Alumni Association.
MeDal

Dalhousie University. Alumni Association.
Dalhousie University. Dalhousie alumni news

Dalhousie University. Council of the Students.
The Dalhousie gazette

Dalhousie University. Information Office.
University news

Dalhousie University. Institute of Public Affairs.
Dalhousie Labour Institute for the Atlantic Provinces. Proceedings

Dalhousie University. Institute of Public Affairs. Library.
Dalhousie University. Institute of Public Affairs. Library. Industrial Relations Reference Library. Accessions list
Dalhousie University. Institute of Public Affairs. Library. Municipal reference library
Dalhousie University. Institute of Public Affairs. Library. Urban community and regional development accession list

Dalhousie University Press Ltd.
Dalhousie review

Dominion Life Assurance Company. Sales Promotion Department Head Office.
Dominionaire

Domtar Limited. Corporate Communications.
The News

Don Quick Publications.
Canadian wood products
Construction materials specifier
Truck Canada

Pat Donaldson.
Canadian golden west

Donovan Ltd.
Canadian poultry review
Holstein-Friesian journal

Dorchester Jaycees.
The Echo

Douglas College. Department of English.
Event

Dow Chemical of Canada, Ltd. Sarnia Division.
Dow Chemical of Canada Ltd. Sarnia Division. SDN Sarnia Division news

Doyens des facultés francophones des sciences de l'éducation.
Revue des sciences de l'éducation

Duca (Toronto) Credit Union Ltd.
Duca-post newsletter

Ducks Unlimited (Canada).
Duckological

Raymond Dulude.
Sport illustré

David Dunlap Observatory.
David Dunlap doings

Elizabeth M. Dunn.
Dogs in Canada

Durham College. Journalism Department.
The Chronicle

The Dutch-Canadian Association.
De nieuwe weg

EM Publications.
Scandinavian Canadian businessman

W. Eames and J.S. Griffith.
Ontario mathematics gazette

Earle Whynot and Associates Ltd.
Dartmouth chamber news

Early Childhood Education Council.
Venture forth

Eastern Canada Centre of Slavic and East European Specialists.
Slavic and East-European studies = Etudes slaves et est-européennes

Eastern Townships Citizens Association.
Townships sun

Ecclesia Publishing Co.
Visnyk = Herald

The Echo.
The Echo

L'Echo du Norc. Inc. Marc Fortin Nord.
Hospitalité Laurentides

L'Eco d'Italia Company.
L'Eco d'Italia

Ecole de médecine vétérinaire. Bibliothèque.
Ecole de médecine vétérinaire. Bibliothèque. Nouvelles acquisitions

Ecole de service social de l'Université Laval.
Service social

Ecole des hautes études commerciales.
L'Actualité économique
L'Actualité économique

Ecole nationale de théâtre du Canada.
Ecole nationale de théâtre du Canada

Ecology Action Centre.
Fine print

Ecrits du Canada français.
Ecrits du Canada français

The Ecumenical Institute of Canada.
The Fish-eye lens

Edi-Québec inc.
Répertoire de l'édition au Québec
Vient de paraître

Les Editions Bellarmin.
Education et société
Philosophiques : revue de philosophie
Relations : revue d'intérêt général
Science et esprit : revue théologique et philosophique

Editions champs d'application inc.
Champs d'application

Les éditions cinéma Québec. Jean-Pierre Tadros.
Le Cinéma au Québec : bilan d'une industrie

Les Editions de la Femme Inc. Robert Juster.
Madame

Les Editions de la femme inc.
Magazine madame : le magazine de la québécoise

Les Editions de l'Aurore.
Brèches : analyse/fiction

Les Editions de l'homme nouveau. Centre américain de l'homme nouveau.
L'Homme nouveau. Edition canadienne

Eglise catholique. Diocèse de Chicoutimi. Office des communications sociales. L'abbé Yves Gagnon.
En église : vie de l'église du diocèse de Chicoutimi

Eglise catholique. Diocèse de Montréal. L'Oeuvre des vocations.
Le Prêtre

Eglise catholique. Diocèse de Québec.
Diocèse de Québec. Annuaire

Eglise catholique. Diocèse de St-Jean. Gilles Roy.
Au rythme de notre église

Eglise Presbytérienne au Canada.
La Vie chrétienne : journal mensuel de l'Eglise presbytérienne ou réformée au Canada

Eglise unie du Canada.
Credo

Elchaski enr.
El Chaski

Electrical Contractors Association of British Columbia.
Relay

Electrical Utilities Safety Association of Ontario Inc.
Safe-t-line bulletin

The Elizabeth Fry Society. Peel-Halton Branch.
The Elizabeth Fry Society. Peel-Halton Branch. Newsletter

Ellipse.
Ellipse

Ellis Publishing Co. Ltd.
The Canadian traveller

Embassy of the Federal Republic of Germany.
German press review

The Empire Club of Canada.
Empire Club of Canada. Addresses

Empire Life Insurance Co.
The Builder

Employers' Association of Saskatchewan.
Employers' Association of Saskatchewan. Bulletin

James G. Endicott.
Canadian far eastern newsletter

Engineering and Contract Record.
Government and the contractor

The Engineering Institute of Canada.
The Engineering journal

English Council of The Alberta Teachers' Association.
Alberta English
Alberta English notes
Alberta Teachers' Association. English council. Newsletter

Entertainer Magazines Inc.
Entertainer

Entertainment Atlantic Publications Ltd.
Entertainment Atlantic

Entertainment Publications Incorporated. Moe Wortzman.
Beetle

Entomological Society of British Columbia.
Entomological Society of British Columbia. Journal of the Entomological Society of British Columbia

Entomological Society of Canada.
The Canadian entomologist
Entomological Society of Canada. Bulletin
Entomological Society of Canada. Memoirs

Entomological Society of Manitoba.
Manitoba entomologist

L'Entraide missionnaire inc.
Le Dossier du missionnaire

Environmental Centre of Greater Victoria.
Environmental Centre of Greater Victoria. Newsletter

Epilepsy Association of Calgary.
Epigram

Epilepsy Association of Metropolitan Toronto.
Epilepsy Association of Metropolitan Toronto. Newsletter

The Equestrian Image.
The Equestrian Image : Canadian all breeds magazine

Ero Talvila.
Inner life : Toronto's aquarian age newsletter

Esperanto Press.
Slipara vortaro

Esprit Publishing Co. Limited.
Esprit

Essays on Canadian Writing.
Essays on Canadian writing

Essex County Automobile Club. Craig Ainslie.
Ontario Motor League news

Estonian Publishing Co. Toronto Ltd.
Meie elu = Our life

The Eternal Network.
Is
Only paper today : a bi-monthly devoted to writing about art in Ontario

Ethnic Publications Ltd. R. Schlyecner.
De Hollandse krant : the Dutch newsletter

Federation of Catholic Education Associations of Ontario.
The Spotlight: news and views on Catholic education

Federation of Free Byelorussian Journalists.
Bielaruski holas = Byelorussian voice

Federation of Independent School Associations in British Columbia.
Federation of Independent School Associations in British Columbia. Fisa spokesman

Federation of Ontario Naturalists.
Ontario naturalist
The Young naturalist

Federation of Saskatchewan Indians.
The Saskatchewan Indian

Federation of Women Teachers' Associations of Ontario.
Educational courier
Federation of Women Teachers' Associations of Ontario. FWTAO newsletter

Max Federman.
View = Undzer weg

Fellowship of Evangelical Baptist Churches in Canada.
Evangelical Baptist
Fellowship year book
Intercom

Fellowship Publishers Resources Pool.
Our cultural mosaic

Feminist Communication Collective.
Feminist communication collective

The Fiddlehead.
The Fiddlehead

Filmcraft Publications & Productions.
Canadian professional film directory

The Financial Post.
Meetings, conferences and conventions: a Financial post guide

The Financial Post. Corporation Service.
Corporation service
Dividend record
Record of new issues
Record of predecessor and defunct companies

Financial Times of Canada. Donald Carlson.
Financial times of Canada perspective on money
Industrial locations in Canada

Fine Arts Council, Alberta Teachers Association.
Fine

Fisheries Association of B.C.
Facts on fish

The Fisherman Publishing Society.
The Fisherman

Fitness and Sports Publishing Ltd.
Sports, recreation and fitness

Five Windsors Publishing Co. Ltd. George H. Windsor.
Production machinery and equipment

Flintcom Publishing Co. Dieter Thelen.
Bowline sail and power

Mrs. G.W. Flynn.
Town talk about Toronto

Fondation canadienne d'éducation économique.
Fondation canadienne d'éducation économique. Rapport

Fondation Cosmos.
Les Cahiers de cours de l'holanthrope

Foothills Lutheran Press.
The Shepherd

Forest Products Accident Prevention Association.
Tallyboard

Forze Nuove Inc.
Forze nuove

Foster Parents Plan of Canada.
Plan Canada news

Four Decades of Poetry.
Four decades of poetry 1890-1930

Les Franciscains.
La Vie des communautés religieuses

Franciscains. Procure des missions.
Missions des franciscains

Fraser Valley Milk Producers' Association.
Butter fat
Milk break

Fraser's Trade Directories. R.C. Freeman.
Fraser's construction and building directory

Fraternité des policiers de la communauté urbaine de Montréal inc.
Police : revue des agents de police = Constables review

Free Estonian Publishers Ltd.
Vaba Eestlane = Free Estonian

The Free Methodist Church in Canada. Jurisdictional Conference.
The Canadian Free Methodist herald

Free Press Weekly Ltd.
Free Press weekly report of farming : the farmer's business publication

R.C. Freeman.
Fraser's Canadian trade directory

Gospel Herald Foundation.
Gospel herald

Gospel Text Publishers.
The Mariner

Gossip Ltd.
Gossip

Graduate Centre for Study Drama. University of Toronto.
Modern drama

Graduate Christian Fellowship.
Crux

Granby Leader-Mail Reg'd. Fred Aston.
Farm journal

Grand Manan Historical Society.
The Grand Manan historian

Grand Manon Museum.
Grand Manan Museum newsletter

Grands ballets canadiens.
L'Envol de la danse

M. le curé Pierre Gravel.
La Lettre de l'Abbé Gravel

Walter Grealis.
RPM weekly

Greater Barrie Chamber of Commerce.
The Magnet

Greater Vancouver Japanese Canadian Citizens Association.
Japanese Canadian Citizen's Association. Bulletin

Greater Welland Chamber of Commerce.
Business beat

Greater Winnipeg Youth for Christ.
Youth for Christ happening

Jerry Green.
The Critical list

Green Tree Publishing Co. W.H. Pepper Parr.
Travel Toronto

Greencrest Industrial Publications Ltd. L. Paul Masse.
The Greenleaves. B.C. edition

Greey de Pencier Publications Ltd.
Building development

Greey de Pencier Publications Ltd. Fiona Mee.
Books for everybody
Canadian publishers directory
Quill and quire

Mme Alfred Grenier.
La Bagatelle

Grobar Publishing. V. Ricciardi.
La Settimana

Groupe Lavalin.
Lavalin

Groupe Marxiste révolutionnaire.
La Taupe rouge

Groupmark Canada Limited.
Touring and travel

Growing Room Collective.
Room of one's own : a feminist journal of literature and criticism

Victor C. Grunean & Sydney Rosen.
Caribbean business news

Guardian Publishing Co. Ltd.
Calvinist contact

Guérin.
Le Québec littéraire

Guide du transport par camion inc.
Guide du transport par camion = Truck transport guide

Guide Magazines Ltd.
Alberta new homes
B.C. new homes

Guideline Press Ltd.
Canadian Dental Nurses and Assistants Association. Journal

Guild of B.C. Potters.
Western potter

Gulf Oil Canada Ltd.
Automotifs
Gulf Canada cartalk
Gulf Canada dealer news
Nouvelles Gulf Canada

Stylianos Gusmas.
Greek Canadian action = Drassis

B.V. Gutsell.
Canadian cartographer
Cartographica

H.B. Publishers Ltd. Cy Young.
Hiballer magazine

A.M. Hackkert Ltd.
Modern drama

Hadassah-WIZO Organization of Canada.
Orah magazine

Halifax Antique Car Club.
Antics

Halifax Board of Trade.
Commercial news

Hamilton and Regional Arts Council. George A. Harrison.
Art-i-fact

Hamilton Automobile Club.
Hamilton Automobile Club. H.A.C. news

Ray Holman.
The Running board

Holman Island Eskimo Co-operative.
Holman Eskimo prints 1974 = Estampes esquimaudes d'Holman

Holstein-Friesian Association of Canada.
Holstein-Friesian journal

Holt, Rinehart and Winston of Canada, Limited.
Canada : an historical magazine

Holy Trinity Armenian Church.
Nor serount = New generation

Home Oil Company. Library.
Home Oil Company. Library bulletin

Homersham Advertising Agency Ltd. D. Homersham.
Western livestock and agricultural news

Homin Ukrainy Publishing Co. Ltd.
Homin ukrainy = Ukrainian echo

Hôpital de Chicoutimi inc. Wilfrid Lachance.
Le Saguenay médical

Hôpital Sainte-Justine. Département de Psychiatrie. Comité d'organisation du carrefour scientifique.
Cahiers pédopsychiatriques

Hôpital St-Jean-de-Dieu. Service de psychologie.
Association pour l'analyse et la modification du comportement. Bulletin

The Hopkins Club.
Inscape : a journal of new Canadian writing

Horticulture Publications Ltd.
Canadian florist, greenhouse and nursery
Canadian florist, Keith's directory and horticultural guide
Keith's florist directory and horticultural guide

Hospital for Sick Children. Public Information Department.
What's new

Serge Housseaux.
L'Actualité joliettaine

Houstons Standard Publications Ltd.
Bank directory of Canada

Art Howard and John Whytall.
This is Ontario

Howard Fairclough Associates.
Your host around Hamilton

Howes, Waldon Associates Ltd.
Manitoba motorist
Motorways miler

Hudson's Bay Company.
The Beaver
Moccasin telegraph

The Huguenot Society of Canada.
Huguenot trails

Humanist-Association of Canada.
Humanist in Canada

The Humanities Association of Canada.
The Humanities Association. The Humanities Association review. = L'association des humanités. La Revue de l'Association des humanités

Humanities Research Council of Canada.
Humanities Research Council of Canada Canada. Bulletin = Conseil canadien de recherche sur les humanities. Bulletin

Humber College of Applied Arts and Technology. Journalism Department.
Coven

Hungarian Journal Publishing Co.
Magyar hirlap = Hungarian journal

J.L. Hunt Publications. Donald Gordon Baker.
Best wishes

Huron County Historical Society.
Huron historical notes

Huronia Tourist Association.
Huronia tourist guide book
Huronia winter adventures

Huxley Institute for Biosocial Research (New York) and Canadian Schizophrenia Foundation.
Canadian Schizophrenia Foundation. Huxley Institute - CSF newsletter

IAC Ltd.
IAC rendezvous

I.O.D.E.
Echoes

Dan Iannuzzi.
Corriere Canadese = The Canadian courier

Illustrated World Review. Andrew Laszlo.
Kepes vilaghirado = Illustrated world review

Imperial Oil Ltd.
Imperial oil review

Imprimerie Drouin Inc.
Le feuillet paroissial

Independent Lithuania Printing Company Ltd.
Nepriklausoma Lietuva = Independent Lithuania

Independent Order of Odd Fellows. Grand Lodge of British Columbia.
The Three link news

Jewish Community Council of Ottawa.
Ottawa jewish bulletin and review

John Abbot College.
Bandersnatch

John Howard Society of Ontario.
John Howard Society of Ontario. Newsletter

John Milton Society for the Blind in Canada.
Insight

Johoso Club of Hamilton.
Break through

Jonah Publications Ltd.
Chitty's law journal

Jean Jonassaint et Jean-Pierre Durand.
Dérives : tiers-monde Québec, une nouvelle conjoncture culturelle

Paul A. Joncas Inc.
Guide des institutions Joncas = Joncas institutional guide

Le Journal Les enseignements ltée. Fernand Houde.
Les Enseignants

Journal of Canadian Fiction Association.
Journal of Canadian fiction

Journal of Commerce. J.L. Whitehead.
Journal of commerce

Journal of Commerce. Tony McDonnell.
British Columbia lumberman's greenbook : a directory of B.C.'s forest industry

Journal of History Co. Ltd.
Canadian journal of history = Annales canadiennes d'histoire

The Journal of Rheumatology Publishing Co. Ltd.
The Journal of rheumatology

Joyceville Institution.
Joyceville journal

Junior League of Halifax.
Ahoy : an Atlantic magazine for children

K.W. Probe.
Kitchener-Waterloo Probe. K.W. Probe news

Kabalarian Philosphy.
Kabalarian courier

Ron Kaighin.
Outdoor Canada

Kalay Foundation Society.
Out front

Kanada Esperanto Association.
Lumo

Kanader Adler Inc. The Jewish Eagle.
Jewish eagle

Kanata-Beaverbrook Community Association.
The Kanata standard

Karaki.
Karaki

Kenroy Publishers Ltd. Roy Kenneth Cooke.
Bakers journal : the national merchandising and management magazine serving the Canadian baking industry

Kentville Pub. Co. Ltd. Jean U. Matheson.
A Selection of choice inns and restaurants of Nova Scotia and en route

Kentville Publishing Co. Ltd.
Home economics newsletter
Tidings

Kerrwil Publications Ltd.
Appliance and home entertainment business
CEDA. current
Communications and cable TV business
Electrical business
Government and military business

Key Advertising Service Ltd.
Semiconductor devices

Key Publishers Ltd.
Key to Toronto

Key Publishers Ltd. Michael de Pencier.
Toronto life
The Toronto Life restaurant and gourmet guide
Toronto life travel guide

Killaly Press.
Index to little magazines of Ontario, 1967-
Stuffed crocodile

The Kingston Arts Council.
ARTiculator

Kingston Historical Society.
Historic Kingston : journal of the proceedings of the Kingston Historical Society

Kitchener Public Library.
Direction

Kitchener-Waterloo Jaycees.
Dynamo

Kitchener-Waterloo Probe.
Kitchener-Waterloo Probe. K.W. Probe news

Kitchener-Waterloo Woman's Place.
Strength

Kiwanis International. Eastern Canada and the Caribbean District.
K Ray

Jan Klinka.
Zpravodaj

The Legal Secretary's Reverence Service.
The Legal secretary's newsletter

Guy Léger.
Dialogue : the voice of the bilingual diocese of Yarmouth, Nova Scotia

Leisure Publications.
Snowmobile annual

Lennox and Addington Historical Society.
Lennox and Addington Historical Society. Paper and records

Lethbridge Herald.
Home and country

Cliff Letovsky.
Impulse

Letter Service.
The Mariner

Martin Levesque.
L'ABC du motocyclisme

R.G. Lewis Co. Ltd.
Broadcaster

Lewven Publishing Co. Ltd.
Canadian teacher

The Liberal Party in Alberta.
New Alberta Liberal

Libération enr.
Libération

Libertarian Enterprises of Canada.
Libertarian option : freedom or tyranny

Liberté.
Liberté

Librairie Beauchemin ltée.
Almanach du peuple
Famille d'aujourd'hui

Librairie de l'Université de Montréal.
Etudes pastorales : l'évangélisation et ses défis

Librairie Gagné ltée.
L'action nationale

The Library, Association of Universities and Colleges of Canada.
Select bibliography on higher education

Life Underwriters Association of Canada.
Forum
Life insurance and taxation
Life Underwriters Association of Canada. The LUAC monitor

La Ligue de sécurité de la province de Québec.
Signal

Ligue de sécurité de la province de Québec. Guy Mathieu.
Famille avertie

Lillooet District Historical Society.
Lillooet District Historical Society bulletin

Linguistic Circle of Manitoba and North Dakota.
Linguistic Circle of Manitoba and North Dakota. Proceedings

Lions International. District A.
Lionage

Lithuanian Canadian R.C. Cultural Society Inc. "Ziburiai".
Teviskes ziburiai = The Lights of homeland

Lithuanian Catholic Women's Association.
Moteris : lietuviy motery zurnalas = Woman : Lithuanian women's magazine

Lithuanian League of Canada = Remejy Klubas.
Nepriklausoma Lietuva = Independent Lithuania

Lithuanian Press Association.
Liaudies balsas = People's voice

J.M. Livingston.
Canadian Air Traffic Control Association, Inc. CATCA journal

Lloyd Publications of Canada.
Canadian chemical, pharmaceutical and product directory
Canadian engineering and industrial year book
Canadian food and packaging directory
Canadian footwear and leather directory
Canadian furniture and furnishings directory
Canadian hardware, electrical and building supply directory
Canadian hotel, restaurant, institution and store equipment
Canadian jewellery and giftware directory
Canadian music directory
Canadian sporting goods and playthings directory
Canadian textile directory
Canadian variety merchandise directory

Lodestone Security Society.
Lodestone

Logan Brown Communications Ltd.
Decor : the Canadian journal for decorating retailers

Lögberg-Heimskringla Publishing Co. Ltd.
Logberg - heimskringla = Law mountain globe

Clément Loiselle.
La Vie montante : sanctification et rayonnement des aînés

London Board of Education.
The Advocate

McGill University. Information office.
McGill reporter

McGill University. Medical Students Society.
McGill medical journal

McGill University. Osler Library.
Osler Library newsletter

McGill University. Research McGill.
Research McGill

McGill University. Students' Society.
McGill daily

McGill-Queen's University Press.
Arctic
Transcultural psychiatric research review

McGraw-Edison of Canada Ltd. Power System Division.
The Line

R.W. McGuire.
Hog guide

Cosmo Maciocia. Mario Barone.
La Voce del popolo = The People's voice

Norman Mackenzie Art Gallery.
Norman Mackenzie Art Gallery. The NMAG
Twenty cents magazine

McLaren Micropublishing.
Books in Canada. : index and microtext

Maclean-Hunter Ltd.
L'Acheteur
The Audio retailer
Audio Scene Canada
Bätiment
CEE electronics directory and Buyers' guide
Canada and the world : for students of world affairs
Canadian building
Canadian controls and instrumentation
Canadian driver/owner
Canadian electronics engineering
Canadian electronics engineering annual buyers guide and catalog directory
Canadian grocer
Canadian hotel and restaurant
Canadian interconnection
Canadian machinery and metalworking
Canadian packaging
Canadian photo annual
Canadian premiums and incentives
Canadian printer and publisher
Canadian special truck equipment manual
Canadian travel courier
Chatelaine
Civic : the public works magazine
Design engineering
Educational digest
Electrical contractor and maintenance supervisor
The Financial post
The Financial post directory of directors
The Financial post survey of industrials. V. 1 Manufacturing Co. V. 2 Sales and Service Co
Financial post survey of markets
The Financial post survey of mines
The Financial post survey of oils
Food in Canada
Hardware handbook
Hardware merchandising
Home goods retailing
Ideas
Maclean's
Men's wear of Canada
Miss Chatelaine
Modern power and engineering
Monday report on retailers
Office equipment and methods
A Report on Canada
Sporting goods Canada
Style : for Canadian fashion merchandisers
Wastes handling

Maclean-Hunter Ltd. A. Bert Sevink.
Heavy construction news
Spec index international = International specification index

Maclean-Hunter Ltd. Alan J. Waters.
Canadian advertising rates and data
Canadian industry shows and exhibitions
The National list of advertisers

Maclean-Hunter Ltd. Andrew L. Rodgers.
Marketing

Maclean-Hunter Ltd. Business Publications Division.
Canada

Maclean-Hunter Ltd. Canadian Hotel and Restaurant. Norman A. Goldie.
Frozen foods / Canada

Maclean-Hunter Ltd. Charles T. Turner.
Canadian aviation

Maclean-Hunter Ltd. Chuck O'Hearn.
Canadian automotive trade
Canadian service data book
Revue moteur

Maclean-Hunter Ltd. D.G. Brydges.
Real estate development annual

Maclean-Hunter Ltd. Douglas Dingeldein.
Canadian research and development

Maclean-Hunter Ltd. E.A. Welling.
Audio scene Canada

Maclean-Hunter Ltd. F. Maurice Shore.
L'Epicier

Maclean-Hunter Ltd. The Financial Post.
The Financial Post survey of funds
Survey of industrials

David MacWilliam.
Natural fauna

Madoc Review Ltd. Maurice Golah.
Contemporary music showcase

Magazine Association of Canada.
Magazine advertising summary service

John Magor.
Canadian UFO report

Maine-Anjou Canada Ltd.
Maineline : all about Maine-Anjou

La Maison (Centre francophone de Toronto). Jeanne Bryan.
La Maison (Centre francophone de Toronto)

Nathaniel Mandarin.
Unmuzzled ox

Manitoba Archaeological Society.
Manitoba archaeological newsletter

Manitoba Association of Licensed Practical Nurses.
Nurses news

Manitoba Association of Mathematics Teachers.
The Manitoba mathematics teacher

Manitoba Association of Registered Nurses.
Nurscene

Manitoba Association of School Trustees.
Manitoba Association of School Trustees. Newsletter

Manitoba Association of Social Workers.
Manitoba social worker

Manitoba Association of Teachers of English.
Classmate

Manitoba Buddhist Association, Inc.
Manitoba Buddhist bulletins

Manitoba Business Education Teachers' Association.
Manitoba Business Education Teachers Association. BETA journal
Manitoba spectra

Manitoba Educational Research Council.
Manitoba journal of education

Manitoba Farm Vacations Association.
Manitoba Farm Vacations Association. Newsletter

Manitoba Government Employees' Association.
Contact

Manitoba Historical Society.
Historical and Scientific Society of Manitoba. Transactions
Manitoba Historical Society. Newsletter
Manitoba Historical Society. Transactions
Manitoba pageant

Manitoba Library Association.
Manitoba Library Association. Bulletin

Manitoba Métis Federation.
Le Métis

Manitoba Motor League.
Manitoba motorist
Motorways miler

Manitoba Music Educators' Association.
The Manitoba music educator

Manitoba Naturalists' Society.
Manitoba nature

Manitoba Pool Elevators.
The Manitoba co-operator

Manitoba School Library - Audio Visual Association.
Manitoba School Library Audio Visual Association. M.S.L.A.V.A. journal

Manitoba Teachers Society.
Classmate
Manitoba Business Education Teachers Association. BETA journal
The Manitoba counsellor
The Manitoba mathematics teacher
The Manitoba music educator
Manitoba School Library Audio Visual Association. M.S.L.A.V.A. journal
Manitoba social sciences teacher
Manitoba spectra
The Manitoba teacher

Manitoba Telephone System.
Telephone echo

Manitoba Theatre Centre.
Manitoba theatre centre

Manitoba Trucking Association.
Manitoba Highway News
Manitoba Trucking Association. M.T.A. ship by truck directory

Manitoba Underwater Council. Gary Tennenhouse.
Man underwater

Manitoba Wildlife Federation.
Wildlife crusader

Manitoba Women's Institute.
Manitoba Women's Institute. Institute news

George Mannion.
The Clansman news

Manoir Notre-Dame de Grâce.
Manoir-écho

Jackie Manthorne.
Long time coming : Canadian Lesbian-Feminist newspaper

Mercury Publications Ltd.
Western construction and industry
Western grocer and food store manager

Mercury Publications Ltd. G.R. Yeo.
Western motor fleet

Roy D. Merritt. H. Ralph Perry.
Gospel herald

Merton Publications Ltd.
Scope : recreational vehicle and camping news

Messagers catholiques de la Bible.
Je crois : magazine populaire catholique

Métiers d'Art du Québec Inc.
Signe

Metis Society of Saskatchewan.
New breed

Metro Plaza. Thomas M. Harris.
Windsor this month

Metropolitan Life. Public Relations Division.
Metropolitan life

Metropolitan Toronto Central Library.
Bulletin of outstanding acquisitions

Metropolitan Toronto Central Library. Fine Art Section.
Selected list of reference acquisitions

Metropolitan Toronto Central Library. General Information Centre.
Selected list of new titles

Metropolitan Toronto Central Library. Municipal Reference Library.
Selected list of new titles

Metropolitan Toronto Central Library. Music Library.
Selected list of recent acquisitions

Metropolitan Toronto Central Library. Science and Technology Library.
Selected list of new titles

Metropolitan Toronto Central Library. Social Sciences Section.
Selected list of new titles

Metropolitan Toronto Central Library. Theatre Section.
A selected list of acquisitions for reference use

Metropolitan Toronto Hospital Planning Council.
Health facilities in Metropolitan Toronto

Metropolitan Toronto Library Board.
Continuing education directory : courses, programs and activities, September through December
Guide to periodicals and newspapers in the public libraries of Metropolitan Toronto
Metropolitan Toronto Library Board. Business Library. Selected list of new titles
Metropolitan Toronto Library Board. Languages Co-ordinator. Books...
16mm films available from the public libraries of Metropolitan Toronto

Charles Meunier.
Plein air

Micromedia Limited.
Profile index to Canadian provincial and municipal publications

Microscopical Society of Canada.
Microscopical Society of Canada. Bulletin = Société de microscopie du Canada. Bulletin

Middlesex County Library Branch.
Town and country librarian

Mills Memorial Library, McMaster University.
Library research news

Mil-Mac Publications Ltd.
Official Ontario 'ship by truck' directory

The Mineralogical Association of Canada.
The Canadian mineralogist
Mineralogical Association of Canada. Newsletter

The Mining Association of Canada.
Facts and Figures : mining in Canada
Mining : what it means to Canada

Le Mirabel.
Le Mirabel

Missing Link Press.
Link
The Missing link magazine

Mission Québec '76.
Trente pour cent

Missionary Association of Mary Immaculate.
My brother and I

The Missionary Sisters of the Immaculate Conception.
The Missionary Sisters of the Immaculate Conception. MIC mission news

Missionnaire Oblats de Marie Immaculée.
Apostolat

Missionnaires comboniens.
Baobab

Les Missionnaires de la Consolata.
Réveil missionnaire

Les Missionnaires du Sacre-Coeur.
RND (Revue Notre-Dame)

Les Missionnaires Oblats de Marie Immaculée.
Vie oblate = Oblate life

Missions des Pères de Sainte-Croix.
Orient

Multiscience Publications Ltd.
Canadian journal of spectroscopy

Municipal Officers' Association of British Columbia.
Municipal Officers' Association of British Columbia. Proceedings and minutes of the annual conference

Municipal World Ltd.
Municipal world

The Muscular Dystrophy Association of Canada. British Columbia Chapter.
Muscular dystrophy reporter

Musée des beaux-arts de Montréal.
M
Transition 3

Museum Restoration Service.
Arms collecting : the Canadian journal of arms collecting

The Mutual Life Assurance Co. of Canada.
Dividend
Field record
Mutualist

Mutual Press Ltd., Ottawa.
Canadian service employee

La Mutuelle du Canada.
Palmarès

N.R.D.C. Agriculture Committee.
Farm news, views and comments

Nathanael Literature Distributors.
Come and see

National Action Committee on the Status of Women in Canada.
Status of women news

National and Provincial Parks Association of Canada.
Park news
Parks for tomorrow

National Association for Photographic Art.
Camera Canada
Foto flash

National Association of Broadcast Employees and Technicians.
National Association of Broadcast Employees and Technicians. Canadian Office. NABET news = Association nationale des employés et techniciens en radio diffusion. Nouvelles NABET

National Association of Canadian Credit Unions.
National Association of Canadian Credit Unions. NACCU briefs

National Auto Research Canada.
Black book : official used car market guide
Black book vehicle indentification guide

National Auto Research Canada. Wm. G. Ward.
Black book used truck guide

National Aviculture Association of Canada.
Avicultural journal

National Business Publications Ltd.
Pulp and paper Canada

National Centre for Sport and Recreation, Ottawa.
The Canadian archer

National Chinchilla Breeders of Canada.
National Chinchilla Breeders of Canada. Monthly bulletin

National Council of Canadian Labour.
National Council of Canadian Labour. NCCL briefs
National Council of Canadian Labour. NCCL information

National Council of Jewish Women of Canada.
Canadian Council woman : keeping you posted

The National Council of Women of Canada.
The National Council of Women of Canada. Annual year book
The National Council of Women of Canada. Yearbook
The National Council of Women of Canada. NCWC newsletter

National Council of YMCA's of Canada.
Y-Canada

The National Dairy Council of Canada.
Resumé

National Democratic Party of British Columbia.
Democrat

National Drugs Ltd.
Western horizons

National Farmers Union.
National Farmers Union. Newsletter
Union farmer

National Hockey League.
National Hockey League. National Hockey League guide
National Hockey League. Official rule book of the National Hockey League

National Honor Society.
Sociological inquiry

National Indian Brotherhood.
National Indian Brotherhood of Canada. Library and Information Services. Weekly acquisitions

National Northern Development Conference.
National Northern Development Conference. Proceedings

Newfoundland Medical Board.
Newfoundland medical directory

Newfoundland Public Libraries Board.
Newfoundland and Labrador Provincial Libraries. Newsletter

Newfoundland Status of Women Council.
Newfoundland Status of Women Council. Newsletter

Newfoundland Teachers' Association.
Newfoundland Teachers' Association. N.T.A. journal
Newfoundland Teacher's Association. School Library/Audio Visual Council. Newsletter

Newfoundland Tuberculosis & Respiratory Disease Association Inc.
The Northern light

Newman Foundation of Toronto.
Ontario Catholic directory

Next Year Country.
Next year country : Saskachewan's only newsmagazine

Niagara College. Journalism Department.
Niagara news

Niagara College of Applied Arts. A. Jelbert.
Niagara news

Niagara Construction Association.
Plans on display bulletin

C.O. Nickle Publications Co. Ltd.
Canadian oil register
Canadian oil register directory

Nightingale Arts Council.
Only paper today : a bi-monthly devoted to writing about art in Ontario

Nimrod Publications Ltd.
Fish and game sportsman

Norbry Publishing Ltd. M. Pembry.
Country estate magazine

Richard Norman.
The Kensington market

Norman Bethune Institute.
New literature and ideology
People's Canada daily news

Nor-Rand Publishing. J.K. Norris.
Canadian wings : aviation directory

Nor-Rand Publishing. J.K. Norris.
Canadian wings

Norrona Publishing Company.
Norrona = The Norseman

North American Life Assurance Company.
The Continent

North and South Saanich Agricultural Society.
North and South Saanich Agricultural Society. Fall exhibition. Prize list

North Central Saskatchewan Regional Library.
Northern air

North Hill News Ltd.
The Emery weal
Okuruk

North Shore Publications.
Bright leaf tobacco journal

The North Wind (Society for Creative Anachronism in B.C.).
North wind

North Winnipeg Credit Union Ltd.
Kredytova Kooperatyva Pivnichnoho Vinnipegu. Biuleten = North Winnipeg Credit Union Limited. Bulletin

The Northern Alberta Institute of Technology.
Nugget

Northern Electric Company Ltd.
The Innovators

Northern Journey Press.
Northern journey

The Northern Life Assurance Company of Canada.
Northern news

Northern Lights.
Northern lights

Northern Miner Press Ltd.
Canadian mines handbook
The Northern miner

Northern Neighbours Publishing Association.
Northern neighbours : the magazine of socialism in action

Northern Ontario Art Association.
Northern Ontario Art Association. Bulletin

Northern Regional Development Council.
The Guiding light
Vision

Northern Stores Dept. - Hudson's Bay Company.
Moccasin telegraph

Northwest Canada Conference Evangelical Church. A.W. Riegel.
Northwest Canada echoes

Northwest Digest Ltd.
B.C. outdoors

Northwest Printing & Lithographing Ltd.
The Right hand

Oblats de Marie-Immaculée. Jacques Lemay.
Dossiers "vie ouvrière" au service des militants chrétiens du monde ouvrier

Occidente.
Occidente

L'Oeuvre pontificale de la propagation de la foi. Conseil de Québec.
Univers

Office canadien des provendes.
Chroniques des grains

L'Office de la prévention de l'alcoolisme et des autres toxicomanies. Rénald Chabot, Optat l'alcoolisme.
Toxicomanies

Office de la protection du consommateur. Roland Charbonneau.
Protégez-vous

Office des communications sociales.
Films à l'écran
Livre canadien
Office des communications sociales. OCS-nouvelles
Office des communications sociales. OCS nouvelles

Office Franco-Québécois pour la jeunesse.
Le Journal des stages (stages accessibles aux résidents québécois)
Le Stagiaire

Office national d'oecuménisme.
Ecumenism: a quarterly information bulletin

Old Cabin Crafts Society.
The Craftsman

Old Order Amish.
Blackboard bulletin

A.L. O'Neill.
The Fourth estate

Ontario Agricultural College.
Notes on agriculture

Ontario Agricultural College. Alumni Association.
Ontario Agricultural College. Alumni news

Ontario Amateur Softball Association.
Ontario Amateur Softball Association. O.A.S.A. bulletin

Ontario Archaeological Society.
Arch notes
Ontario archaeology

Ontario Arts Council.
Jabberwocky

Ontario Association for Children with Learning Disabilities.
Communique

Ontario Association for Continuing Education.
Oracle

Ontario Association for Curriculum Development.
Ontario Association for Curriculum Development. Annual conference. Proceedings

Ontario Association for Geographic and Environmental Education.
The Monograph

Ontario Association of Certified Engineering Technicians and Technologists.
The Ontario technologist

Ontario Association of Children's Aid Societies.
Ontario Association of Children's Aid Societies. Journal

Ontario Association of Corrections and Criminology.
Ontario Association of Corrections and Criminology. Bulletin

The Ontario Association of Education Administrative Officials.
Newscap

Ontario Association of Mathematics Education.
Ontario mathematics gazette

Ontario Association of School Business Officials.
The Advocate

Ontario Beef Improvement Association.
Breeder and feeder

Ontario Bible College.
Evangelical recorder

Ontario Board of Examiners in Psychology.
Directory of psychologists registered in the Province of Ontario

Ontario Business Education Association.
Ontario Business Education Association. OBEA newsletter

Ontario Campus Cultural Association.
Ontario campus culture newsletter

The Ontario Cancer Treatment and Research Foundation.
Cancer in Ontario
Ontario Cancer Treatment and Research Foundation. Proceedings of The Clinical Conference

The Ontario Chamber of Commerce.
Exchange

The Ontario Churchman.
The Ontario churchman

Ontario Industrial Arts Association.
Ontario industrial arts bulletin

Ontario Industrial Development Council Inc.
Ontario Industrial Development Council Inc. OIDC newsletter and press clippings
Ontario Industrial Development Council Inc. Newsletter

Ontario Institute for Studies in Education.
Curriculum theory network
Interchange : a journal of educational studies
Ontario Institute for Studies in Education. News and notes
Ontario Institute for Studies in Education. Office of the Coordinator of Field Development. Newsletter
Orbit : ideas about teaching and learning
Working papers on bilingualism = Travaux de recherches sur le bilinguisme

Ontario Institute for Studies in Education. Department of Measurement and Evaluation.
Evaluation and measurement newsletter

Ontario Institute for Studies in Education. Northwest Centre.
Corridor

Ontario Insurance Agents' & Brokers' Association.
Ontario Insurance Agents' and Brokers' Association. News

Ontario Lawn Tennis Association.
Ontario tennis

Ontario Library Association.
Expression
Focus

Ontario Library Association. School Libraries Division.
The Reviewing librarian
The Revolting librarian

Ontario Medical Association.
Ontario medical review

Ontario Medical Wives' Association.
The Ontario doctor's wife

Ontario Métis and Non-Status Indian Association.
Dimensions

Ontario Milk Marketing Board.
Ontario milk producer

Ontario Ministry of Agriculture and Food.
Ontario Agricultural College. Department of Land Resource Science. Research and Advisory Service. Progress report

Ontario Modern Language Teachers' Association.
The Canadian modern language review

Ontario Mortgage Brokers Association.
Ontario Mortgage Brokers Association. Monthly letter

Ontario Motor League.
Canadian motorist
Crossroads

Ontario Motor League. Ottawa Club.
The Accelerator

Ontario Municipal Recreation Association.
Ontario Municipal Recreation Association. OMRA newsletter

Ontario Music Educators' Association.
The Recorder

Ontario Nursing Home Association.
Ontario nursing home news

Ontario Parks Association.
Greensward

Ontario Petroleum Institute Inc.
Ontario Petroleum Institute. Annual conference proceedings

Ontario Pharmacists' Association.
Ontario pharmacist

Ontario Physiotherapy Association.
Intouch

Ontario Plumbing Inspectors Association.
Ontario Plumbing Inspectors Association. Annual conference. Report

Ontario Professional Foresters Association.
The Professional forester

Ontario Psychological Association.
The Ontario psychologist

Ontario Public School Men Teachers' Federation.
Educational courier
Ontario Public School Men Teachers' Federation. News

Ontario Public School Trustees' Association.
Ontario education

Ontario Puppetry Association.
The Opal

The Ontario Registered Music Teachers' Association.
The Ontario Registered Music Teachers' Association. Ormata notes

Ontario Report Editorial Board.
Ontario report

Ontario Research Council on Leisure.
Catalogue of Ontario recreation and leisure research

Ontario Research Foundation.
Ontario Research Foundation. Newsletter

L'Ordre séculier franciscain.
La Revue franciscaine

Ordre séculier franciscain. Gabriel Dextraze.
Bonne nouvelle

Ordres des arpenteurs-géomètres du Québec.
La Revue de l'arpenteur-géomètre

Organic Growers Co-Operative.
Organic Growers Co-operative. Newsletter

L'Organisation du commerce du Japan.
Communiqué de JETRO

Organization for the Defence of Lemkivschyna.
Lemko news
Lemko news annual

Origins.
Origins : a magazine based on creative writing

Orphan Universe Press.
Empty belly : a magazine of poetry and communication

Osgoode Hall Law School.
Continuum

Osgoode Hall Law School. Legal and Literary Society.
Obiter dicta

The Other Woman.
The Other woman

Ottawa Board of Trade.
Byword

Ottawa Civil Service Recreational Association.
Ottawa Civil Service Recreational Association. R A news

Ottawa Field Naturalists' Club.
Canadian field-naturalist
Trail and landscape

The Ottawa Journal.
TV journal

Ottawa Public Library.
Ottawa Public Library. Periodicals = Ottawa bibliothèque publique. Périodiques
Ottawa Public Library. Bulletin = Bibliothèque publique d'Ottawa. Bulletin
16mm films = Films 16mm

Ottawa Roman Catholic Separate School Board.
Ottawa's Catholic schools

Ottawa Valley Western Horse Association.
Horsing around (newsletter)

Our Aim Publishing Company.
Nasha meta = Our aim

Our Country Publishing Company.
Batkivschyna = Our country

Our Generation.
Our generation

Our Voices Publishing and Printing.
Nase hlasy = Our voices

Ousia publishing.
Seed

The Outdoor news.
The Outdoor news

Outdoors Unlittered (Alberta).
Newslitter

Outdoors Unlittered (B.C.) Incorp.
Newslitter

Ovo Magazine.
Ovo. Edition français
Ovo. English ed

Ovul.
Ovul : revue socio-culturelle de l'Outaouais

Owl's Head Press.
The Journal of Canadian art history : studies in Canadian art, architecture and the decorative arts

Pace Publishing Ltd. E.E. Abel.
Equipment journal

Pacific Association for Continuing Education.
Pacific Association for Continuing Education. P.A.C.E. newsletter

Pacific Community Self-Development Society.
Resources Exchange Project. Newsletter
Resources exchange project newsletter

Pacific Great Eastern Railway Co. Employees.
Coupler

Pacific Northwest Humanist Publications.
Humanist in Canada

Pacific Programs Ltd. Peter Mack.
The Wedding guide

Pacific Rim Publications Ltd.
B.C. business

Pacific Trollers' Association.
Pacific Trollers' Association. Newsletter

The Pacific Women's Graphic Arts Co-operative Association.
Makara

Page Publications Ltd.
Crafts Canada

Page Publications Ltd. Gwen P. Demsey.
Luggage and leathergoods news

Guy Paiement.
Communauté

Palliser Wheat Growers Association.
Palliser Wheat Growers Association. Newsletter

Photo-Atlantic Productions Ltd.
Axiom
Fore and aft
Photo Atlantic

Alexandra Pidhainy.
New review of East-European history

Pinpoint Publications. Lorne Millar.
The London hi riser

Planning Institute of British Columbia.
Planning Institute of British Columbia. PIBC newsletter

Claire Plante-Lambin.
La Barrique : la seule revue française servant l'industrie des boissons alcooliques au Canada

Plast - Ukrainian Youth Association.
Hotuys
Plastovy shliakh
Yunak

Plast Publication.
Hotuys
Plastovy shliakh
Yunak

Plaza Advertising. A.M. Bougie.
Executive's directory = Annuaire de l'exécutif

Plesman Publications Ltd.
Computing Canada

Plumbing and Mechanical Contracting Industry in British Columbia.
Mechanical contractor

Russell Pocock.
Townships sun

Polish Alliance Press Ltd.
Zwiazkowiec = The Alliancer

Polish Canadian Courier.
Kaszebe

Polish Canadian Women's Federation.
Informator

Polish Combatant's Association in Canada. B.C. Branch.
Placowka nad pacifikem:

Polish Combatant's Association in Canada Inc.
SPK W Kanadzie

Polish Press Ltd.
Czas = The Times

Polish Voice Publishing Co.
Glos Polski-gazeta Polska = Polish voice gazette

Pollution Probe.
Environmental education

Pollution Probe at the University of Toronto.
Probe bulletin

Pollution Probe London.
The Probe

Polysar Limited.
Polysar progress. Plastics edition
Polysar progress. Rubber and latex edition

Pomeroy, Carter and Associates Ltd.
The Canadian review

Pontifical Institute of Mediaeval Studies.
Mediaeval studies

Pontifical Missionary Union.
Mission '75

Potlatch Publications.
Canadian children's annual

J.M. Pouliot.
La Semaine commerciale : organe officiel des intérêts commerciaux et financiers du grand Québec

Henri Poupart.
Québec chasse et pêche

Prairie Bible Institute.
The Prairie overcomer
Young pilot

Premier Printing Ltd.
The Clarion : Canadian reformed magazine

Presbyterian Church in Canada.
Presbyterian Church in Canada. General Assembly. Acts and proceedings
Presbyterian record

La Presse ltée.
Télé-presse

Les Presses de L'Université de Montréal.
Criminologie
Meta
Revue canadienne de biologie
La Revue de géographie de Montréal
Sociologie et sociétés : revue thématique

Les Presses de l'Université du Québec.
Cahier des études anciennes

Les Presses de l'Université du Québec. Jean-Marc Gagnon.
Québec science

Les Presses de l'Université Laval.
Les cahiers de droit
Cahiers de géographie de Québec
Etudes littéraires
Index de l'actualité
Laval théologique et philosophique
Livre et auteurs québécois : revue critique
Le Naturaliste canadien : revue d'écologie et de systématique
Recherches sociographiques
Relations industrielles = Industrial relations

Provincial Association of Geography Teachers.
Geoscope

Provincial Association of Protestant Teachers of Quebec.
The Teachers' magazine

Provincial Bank of Canada. Economic Research Department.
Economic review

Provincial Intermediate Teachers' Association.
Intermediate teacher
Provincial Intermediate Teachers' Association. PITA news

Provincial Judges Association of British Columbia.
Provincial Judges Association of British Columbia. Newsletter

Provincial Lawn Bowling Association of Ontario.
Provincial Lawn Bowling Association of Ontario. P.L.B.A. annual

Pryde Publications.
Cable communications magazine

The Psychiatric Hospital Patients' Welfare Association.
Psychiatric Hospital Patients' Welfare Association. Newsletter

Public Archives of Canada and the Canadian Historical Association.
Register of post-graduate dissertations in progress in history and related subjects

The Public Press Ltd. R.W. McGuire.
Cattlemen : the beef magazine
Corn-soy guide
Country guide : the farm magazine
Crops guide
Dairy guide

Public Service Alliance of Canada.
Argus-journal
The Civil service review = La revue du service civil
Public Service Alliance of Canada. Weekly newsletter

Publications chrétiennes.
Message de vérité

Les Publications Cousin-Poupart-Turmel inc.
Nous fiances

Les Publications Décormag inc. Ginette Gadoury.
Décormag : le magazine québécois de décoration

Les Publications des grands lacs.
Le Rempart

Les Publications eclair ltée. Roger Chabot.
TV hebdo

Les Publications éclaire ltée.
Almanach moderne

Les Publications industrielles ltée. F. Guibert.
Le Monde de l'électricité

Les Publications L & L, inc.
L'Association nationale des camionneurs artisans inc. : La Voix de l'ANCAI

Publications les affaires inc.
Les affaires
Québec construction

Les Publications mon bébé inc.
Mon bébé

Les Publications Norco Inc.
Ski-mag

Publications plein air inc.
Québec chasse et pêche

Les Publications québecor inc.
Le Grand journal illustré

Les Publications SEM inc.
SEM (service des écrivains de Montréal)

Publications Wadham Ltd. French Commercial Publications Division.
L'automobile

Publinova.
The Olympians

Publisysteme Inc. Canadian Ski Association. Quebec Division.
Ski Quebec

Carlos Puitti.
Correo Hispano-Americano

Pulp and Paper Canada.
Canadian Pulp and Paper Association. Technical Section. Gadget competition entries

Pulp and Paper Research Institute of Canada.
Trend

Pulp Press.
3¢ pulp : famous magazine

Purchasing Management Association of Canada.
Action

Purchasing Management Association of Canada. B.C. District.
Purchasing in Western Canada

Quarry Magazine.
Quarry

Quarterly Committee of Queen's University.
Queen's quarterly: a Canadian review

Redeemer's voice almanac = kalendar holosu spasytelia

The Redemptorist Order. Ste Anne de Beaupre Province.
The Annals of good St. Anne du Beaupré

Reflections Creative Art. James Hargittay.
Canadian jester

Regina Chamber of Commerce.
Regina
Regina : visitor information guide

Registered Nurses Association of British Columbia.
Registered Nurses Association of British Columbia. RNABC news

The Registered Nurses' Association of Nova Scotia.
Registered Nurses Association of Nova Scotia. R.N.A.N.S. bulletin

Registered Psychiatric Nurses Association of British Columbia.
This month

Regroupement de chercheurs en histoire des travailleurs québécois.
Regroupement de chercheurs en histoire des travailleurs québécois. Bulletin RCHTQ

The Rehabilitation Society of Calgary for the Handicapped.
The Rehab tab

W. Stanford Reid.
Presbyterian comment

Religious Society of Friends (Quakers). Home Mission and Advancement Committee.
The Canadian friend : Quaker news and thought

La Rencontre.
Signal pour l'évangélisation par des communautés évangéliques

Repository Press.
Repository

Erich O. Reprich.
Hamilton journal
Kitchener journal
Montrealer Zeitung
Torontoer Zeitung

Research Institute of Northern Canada.
Canada North almanac

Research Society for Victorian Periodicals.
Victorian periodicals newsletter

Resources Exchange Project (B.C.).
Resources Exchange Project. Newsletter
Resources exchange project (British Columbia). Library list

Resources Exchange Project (N.S.).
Resources Exchange Project (N.S.). Newsletter

The Respiratory Technology Society of Ontario.
The Respiratory Technology Society of Ontario. Quarterly newsletter

Retail Council of Canada.
Canadian retailer
Operating results of independent specialty and department stores
Retail food report
Retail wages and salaries in Canada

Retail Gasoline Dealers Association of Nova Scotia.
Station reporter

Retail Merchants' Association of Canada (Saskatchewan) Inc.
National retailer
Retailers' group service bulletin

La Revue commerce.
Le Point
La Revue commerce

La Revue du notariat.
La Revue du notariat

Revue littéraire les chroniques inc. Laurent-Michel Vacher.
Chroniques

La Revue municipale inc.
Le Revue municipale

Rexwood Publishing Co.
The Canadian horse magazine

Riegel Publications Ltd.
Curling review

H. Riga.
Varrak

Rino Citarella.
Comunita' viva

Riviera Printers and Publishers Inc.
Liscio e busso

Roads and Transportation Association of Canada.
Nation on the move = Nation en mouvement
Roads and Transportation Association of Canada. Proceedings
Roads and Transportation Association of Canada. Technical bulletin
Roads and Transportation Association of Canada. RTAC news

Jacques Robert.
L'Éclair

Fred Roberts.
Canada ski

Ryerson Polytechnical Institute. J.D. MacFarlane.
Ryersonian

Ryerson Polytechnical Institute. Student Union.
Eyeopener

SCOC/CGCA.
Cognica

Le Sablier inc.
Grains de sel, grains de sable

The Sacro Occipital Research Society International.
Dispatcher

Sage Brush Ventures Ltd.
The Limousin leader and stockman's recorder

Sagitawa Friendship Centre.
Achimowin

St. Bernard Enterprises.
Challenge magazine

St. Catharines and District Arts Council.
St. Catharines and District Arts Council. Bulletin

St. Francis Theatre Corp.
Festival Lennoxville

Saint Francis Xavier University.
Saint Francis Xavier University. St. F.X. newsletter

St. Francis Xavier University. The Public Relations Department.
The Antigonish review

St. Francis Xavier University. Student Union.
Xaverian weekly

St. John Ambulance.
St. John Ambulance in Canada. St John news

St. John Ambulance. Ontario Council.
Order of St. John. Ontario Council. Bulletin
St. John Ambulance. Ontario Council. Bulletin

Saint John Regional Library. Extension Services Dept.
New season

Saint John School of Marine Technology.
The Maritimes shipping herald and marine engineering journal = Le Journal de la marine marchande des Maritimes

St. John's Board of Trade.
St. John's Board of Trade. News and Views

Saint John's Edmonton Report Ltd. Keith Bennett.
Saint John's Edmonton report

St. Joseph's Oratory.
The Friend of Brother André

The Saint Leonard's Society of Canada.
St. Leonard's Society of Canada. News & views

Saint Mary's University.
The Atlantic Provinces book review
Between times
The Journal
The Times

St. Michael's College. The Student Council.
Rune

St. Patrick's German Congregation.
Der Deutsche Katholik in Kanada

Saint Paul Society.
Christian communications

St. Paul University.
Homiletic service
Living with Christ

Saint Paul University. Faculty of Canon Law.
Studia canonica

St. Peter's Abbey, Muenster, Sask.
Prairie messenger : Saskatchewan Catholic weekly

St. Peter's Press.
Prairie messenger : Saskatchewan Catholic weekly

St. Theresa Missionary Center.
Capuchins missions : bulletin of the St-Theresa Missionary Center

St. Thomas More College. Library.
St. Thomas More College. Library. History collection : Canadian Catholic Church
St. Thomas More College. Library. Periodicals and serials in the Shannon Library

Gérard-Roger Saint Victor.
Kombe

Salah Allam.
Arc Arabic Journal = Le journal "ARC" arabe

Sales and Marketing Executives of Montreal Inc.
Decision

Sales & Markets Inc.
Sports/Famille

Salmon Arm Observer.
The High-way

The Salvation Army.
War cry

Salvation Army Triumph Press.
The Crest : the Salvation Army's youth magazine
Insight
The Young soldier

Saskatchewan Mathematics Teachers' Society.
Saskatchewan Mathematics Teachers' Society. News/journal

Saskatchewan Medical Association.
Saskatchewan medical quarterly

Saskatchewan Medical Association. Continuing Medical Education.
University of Saskatchewan. Continuing Medical Education. CME news

Saskatchewan Music Educators' Association.
Saskatchewan Music Educators' Association. Saskatchewan Music Educators newsletter

Saskatchewan Natural History Society.
Blue jay : a journal of natural history and conservation for Saskatchewan and adjacent regions
Saskatchewan Natural History Society. Newsletter

Saskatchewan Physical Education Association.
Leisure and movement

Saskatchewan Poetry Society.
The Saskatchewan poetry book

Saskatchewan Psychiatric Nurses' Association.
Saskatchewan Psychiatric Nurses' Association. Newsletter

Saskatchewan Reading Council.
Query

Saskatchewan Registered Nurses' Association.
Saskatchewan Registered Nurses' Association. News bulletin

Saskatchewan Research Council.
Industrial business management

Saskatchewan School Trustees Association.
Saskatchewan School Trustees Association. SSTA newsletter
The School trustee

Saskatchewan Science Teachers Society.
Accelerator

Saskatchewan Society for Education through Art.
Discovery through art

Saskatchewan Society for Prevention of Cruelty to Animals.
Saskatchewan humanitarian

Saskatchewan Stock Growers Association.
Saskatchewan Stockgrowers Association. Publication

Saskatchewan Teachers' Education Association,.
Saskatchewan Physical Education Association. SPEA newsletter

Saskatchewan Teachers' Federation.
The Administrative scene
Discovery through art
Golden taffy
Guidelines
Insite
Intercom
Leisure and movement
Perspectives
Query
The Saskatchewan administrator
Saskatchewan Association of Teachers of French. Bulletin = Bulletin de service
Saskatchewan Mathematics Teachers' Society. News/journal
Saskatchewan Music Educators' Association. Saskatchewan Music Educators newsletter
Saskatchewan Physical Education Association. SPEA newsletter
Saskatchewan Science Teachers' Society. SSTS newsletter
Saskatchewan Teachers' Federation. Saskatchewan bulletin
Skylark
Tema
Venture forth
Vista

Saskatchewan Teachers of Ukrainian.
Tema

Saskatchewan Telecommunications.
Sask Tel news

Saskatchewan Tourist Association.
Tourist talk

Saskatchewan Waffle.
Next year country : Saskachewan's only newsmagazine

Saskatchewan Wheat Pool.
Western producer : a weekly newspaper serving Western Canadian farmers

Saskatchewan Wildlife Federation.
Saskatchewan Wildlife Federation. S.W.F. news

Saskatchewan Women's Institutes.
Second penny

Saskatchewan Writer's Guild.
Grain

Saskatchewan Writers' Guild and Saskatchewan Arts Board.
Freelance

Saskatoon Board of Trade.
Saskatoon

Saskatoon Environmental Society.
Environment probe : Saskatchewan's environment magazine

Saskatoon Horticultural Society.
Garden clippings

Service de police de la communauté urbaine de Montréal.
Le Conseiller juridique

Service de préparation à la vie.
L'Envolée dans l'aujourd'hui l'église

Service de psychologie, Hôpital St-Jean-de-Dieu, att: M. J.-M. Boisvert.
Revue de modification du comportement

Service de recherches economique de la Banque provinciale.
Bulletin économique

Service des bibliothèques : Service des centres de documentation.
Le Polariseur

Service des Loisirs St. Francois de Sales de Laval, att: M. J.-P. Messier.
Boileau babillard

Service d'information de Cacouna.
Journal epiK-KaKouna

Service diocésain de pastorale.
Eglise catholique. Diocèse de Mont-Laurier. Annuaire diocésain
Information : pastorale du diocèse de Mont-Laurier

Service incroyance et foi.
Nouveau dialogue

Service mond-ami.
AmiSol
Amigo

Service universitaire canadien outre-mer.
L'Escargot

Sex Information and Education Council of Canada.
Sex Information and Education Council of Canada. Sieccan newsletter

Shantymen's Christian Association of North America.
The Shantyman

Shaver Poultry Breeding Farms Ltd.
Shaver focus

Shell Canada Ltd.
Sphere
Sphère

Sheridan College of Applied Arts and Technology.
The Sheridan sun

Shing Lea Association.
Shing Wah daily news

Shing Wah Association. William C. Wong.
Shing Wah daily news

Sidbec-Dosco Ltée.
La Coulée

Silverwood Industries Ltd.
About us

José Simoes Silvestre.
Lusitano

Simmental Canada Ltd.
Simmental scene

Simon Fraser University.
West Coast review

Simon Fraser University. Admissions Office.
Simon Fraser University : SFU information for secondary school and college students

Simon Fraser University. Department of Modern Languages.
Glossa : an international journal of linguistics

Simon Fraser University. Library.
Simon Fraser University. Library. Information bulletin

Simon Fraser University. University News Service.
Comment

Sir George Williams University. Alumni Association.
Garnet

Sir Wilfred Laurier University. Student Union.
Cordweekly

Ski East Association.
Ski ventures

Slavuta Publishers.
Pivnichne siayvo = Northern lights: almanac

Slovak Jesuit Fathers.
Slovenski Jezuiti v Kanade

Slovenian National Federation of Canada.
Slovenska drzava = Slovenian country

Karen Smith.
On line

Smith Publishing Co.
Bon voyage

Soaring Association of Canada.
Free flight

Social Credit Party of Canada.
Regards : official organ of the Social Credit Party of Canada

Social Planning and Research Council of Hamilton and District.
Youth on the spot : job description for teen volunteers

Social Planning Council of Hamilton.
Directory of community services of Hamilton and district

The Society for the Propagation of the Faith and The National Missionary Council.
Mission '75

Society for the Study of Architecture in Canada.
Society for the Study of Architecture in Canada. News = Société pour l'étude de l'architecture au Canada. Nouvelles

The Society of Canadian Artists.
Art magazine

Society of Canadian Cine Amateurs.
Panorama

Society of Industrial Accountants.
RIA digest = RIA news

The Society of Industrial Accountants of Alberta.
The Accounter

Society of Industrial Accountants of Canada.
Cost and management

Society of Manufacturing Engineers. Hamilton District Chapter No. 42.
Society of Manufacturing Engineers. Chapter 42. Monthly programme

Society of Newfoundland Radio Amateurs Inc.
The Newfoundland amateur

The Society of Saint John the Evangelist.
The Little paper

The Society of the Plastics Industry of Canada.
Plastatistics
Plasticwords

Society to Overcome Pollution.
Stop press

Soeurs missionnaires de l'Immaculée Conception.
Le Précurseur

Sokeédit ltée.
La Semaine commerciale : organe officiel des intérêts commerciaux et financiers du grand Québec

Il Sole Publications Ltd.
Corriere illustrato

Solidaire.
Solidaire

Sons of Scotland Benevolent Association.
The Scotian

Sons of Temperance of Nova Scotia. Grand Division.
Forward

Sound Publishing Ltd.
Canadian coin box magazine

Gabriel Sousa.
Sentinela
Voz de Portugal = Voice of Portugal

South Central Regional Library System.
Scurrilous news letter

South Western Ontario Square Dance Association.
South Western Ontario Square Dance Association. S.W.O.S.D.A. bugle

Southam Business Publications Ltd.
Administrative digest
Administrative digest reference manual
The Canadian architect
Canadian architect yearbook
Canadian chemical processing
Canadian consulting engineer
The Canadian dairy farmer
Canadian doctor
Canadian farm equipment dealer
Canadian highway carriers guide
Canadian industrial equipment news
Canadian mining journal's reference manual & buyers' guide
Canadian office products and stationary
Canadian office products and stationery : dealer's guide
Canadian petroleum
Canadian plastics
Canadian plastics directory and buyer's guide
Canadian pool and patio
Canadian sales meetings and conventions
Canadian travel news
Dental guide
Electrical equipment news
Electronic procurement index for Canada
Electronics and communications
Furniture and furnishings
Furniture and furnishings buyers' guide and directory
Génie construction
Good farming
Health car digest
Hospital administration in Canada
Laboratory guide : directory issue of Laboratory product news
Laboratory product news
Médecine moderne du Canada
Modern medicine of Canada
Oral health
Plastics directory of Canada
Pulp and paper Canada business directory
Pulp and paper Canada reference manual and buyers' guide
Shop
Southam building guide
La voix de la construction
Water and pollution control

The Thorne Group Ltd.
Fringe benefit costs in Canada

3 M Canada Limited. Public Relations Dept.
3 M info

Three Schools.
Doings

Thunder Bay Chamber of Commerce.
Chamber chat

Titmouse Review.
Titmouse review

Toby Nakamura and Associates Ltd.
Ski trails west

Tom Thomson Memorial Gallery and Museum of Fine Art.
Tom Thomson Memorial Gallery and Museum of Fine Art. Bulletin

Toronto Academy of Veterinary Medicine.
Fur and feathers

Toronto Area Library Technicians Association.
Toronto Area Library Technicians Association. TALTA newsletter

Toronto Board of Education. Education Centre Library.
Additions and accessions

The Toronto Camera Club.
Focus

Toronto Christian Mission.
Khristianin (the Christian)

Toronto Club.
Toronto club news

Toronto Construction Association.
Toronto Construction Association. TCA news
Who's who in Toronto construction

Toronto Dominion Bank.
Toronto Dominion Bank. TD bank notes

Toronto Dominion Bank. Department of Economic Research.
Canada's business climate

Toronto Field Naturalists' Club.
The Ontario field biologist
Toronto Field Naturalists Club. Toronto Field Naturalists Club newsletter

Toronto Film Society.
Toronto Film Society. Newsletter

Toronto Film-makers Co-op.
Rushes

Toronto Free Press Publications Ltd.
Vilne slovo = Free word
Vilne slovo annual = Calendar almanach "slovo"

Toronto Home Builders' Association.
Houses for sale
New homes and apartments guide

Toronto Humane Society.
Humane viewpoint

Toronto Junior Board of Trade.
Trader's post

Toronto Public Library.
Catalogue of replacement books for children's library collections
Marguerite G. Bagshaw Theatre Committee. Newsletter
150 books of the last three years

Toronto Public Library. Boys and Girls Services.
Toronto Public Libraries. Toronto Boys and Girls House. Subscription reviews

Toronto Public Library Board.
Books for young people
Toronto Public Library. TPL News

Toronto Real Estate Board.
Listings magazine
Toronto real estate

Toronto Ski Club.
Ski runner

Toronto Stock Exchange.
The Spread
Toronto Stock Exchange. Daily record sheet
Toronto Stock Exchange. Indices
Toronto Stock Exchange. Members manual
Toronto Stock Exchange. Notice to members
Toronto Stock Exchange. Review
Toronto Stock Exchange. Weekly summary

The Toronto Sun. Douglas Creighton.
Sunday sun television

Toronto Symphony Women's Committee.
Toronto symphony news

Toronto Vegetarian Association.
Toronto Vegetarian Association. Newsletter

Tower Poetry Society Press.
The Tower

Town Planing Institute of Canada.
Plan Canada

J.F. Traff.
Cariboo calling : supplement to the 100 Mile House Free press

Traffic Club of Montreal Inc.
Bulletin Montraffic = Montraffic news

Trail Riders of the Canadian Rockies.
Trail Riders of the Canadian Rockies. The Bulletin

Unicorn Pub. Corp. Peter Lebensold.
Take one

Unifarm. Len J. Bland.
Farm trends

Union Carbide Canada Ltd.
Union Carbide Canada Ltd. Progress report

Union des producteurs agricols. Jean Marc Kirouac.
La Terre de chez nous

Union générale des étudiants africains à Québec. Layachi Howsnia.
Echo d'Afrique "se connaître pour s'unir"

L'Union médicale du Canada.
L'Union médicale du Canada

Union of British Columbia Municipalities.
Union of British Columbia Municipalities. Minutes of annual convention

Union of Nova Scotia Municipialities.
Municipal open line

The Union of Spiritual Communities of Christ.
Iskra = Spark

United Baptist Woman's Missionary Union of the Atlantic Provinces.
Tidings

United Baptists Convention of the Atlantic Provinces. The Board of Publications.
Atlantic Baptist

United Breeders Inc.
United Breeders Inc. News

The United Church of Canada.
Canadan viesti = Canadian messenger
Issue
Observer
United Church of Canada. Year book
United Church of Canada. Committee on the Church and International Affairs. Report to the General Council of the United Church of Canada

United Church of Canada. Division of Communications.
United Church of Canada. Newsletter

United Church of Canada. Division of Communications. Committee on Education and Stewardship. R.C. Plant.
Mandate

United Church of Canada. The Division of Mission in Canada.
COMBO

United Church of Canada. General Council.
United Church of Canada. General Council. Record of proceedings

United Church Publishing House.
United Church of Canada. Committee on Archives. Bulletin

The United Church Publishing House. A.C. Forrest.
Observer

The United Church Renewal Fellowship.
The Small voice

United Cooperatives of Ontario.
United Co-operatives of Ontario. UCO leader
United Co-operatives of Ontario. UCO news

United Electrical, Radio and Machine Workers of America (UE).
United Electrical, Radio and Machine Workers of America. UE news

The United Empire Loyalists' Association of Canada. E.J. Chard.
The Loyalist gazette

United Flowers by Wire Service.
United florists news

United Nations Association in Canada.
United Nations Association in Canada. Bulletin

United Nurses Inc.
Dialogue

United Senior Citizens of Ontario Inc.
The Voice

United Way of Canada.
Allocations to national organizations = Allocations aux organismes nationaux
Directory of Canadian United Ways and Social Planning Councils = Le répertoire des Centraides Canada et des conseils de planification sociale
The United way
United Way of Canada. Conference. Proceedings.

Université Concordia. Sir George Williams Campus. Departement d'économie.
Revue canadienne d'économie publique et coopérative = Canadian journal of public and cooperative economy

Université de Moncton.
Université de Moncton. La Revue de l'Université de Moncton

Université de Montréal.
Chercheurs : bulletin des activités de recherche de l'Université de Montréal
Revue canadienne de biologie
La Revue de géographie de Montréal
Sociologie et sociétés : revue thématique
Université de Montréal. Bibliothèque de chimie. Collections de périodiques

Université Laval. Association des anciens.
Vieil escolier

Université Laval. Bibliothèque. La Cartothèque.
Cartologica

Université Laval. Faculté des sciences de l'administration.
Laval administration

Université Laval. Office d'information.
Université Laval. Gazette officielle. Résolutions du conseil

Université Laval. Service des Loisirs. Yvon Lirette.
Revue annuelle de photographie de l'Université Laval

Université Laval. Service des relations publiques.
Au fil des événements

Université Saint-Paul. Institut des sciences missionnaires.
Kerygma

Universities Art Association of Canada.
Universities Art Association of Canada. Journal

The University and College Placement Association.
Employment opportunities handbook, Canada. English ed.
Employment opportunities handbook = Répertoire des possibilités d'emploi Canada. Bilingual edition
Employment opportunities handbook Canada. Western ed.
Who's who in Canadian placement?

University of Alberta.
Alberta Information Retrieval Association. A.I.R.A. - Western Canada A.S.I.S. newsletter

University of Alberta. Department of Educational Foundations Intercultural Education Program.
Indian-ed

University of Alberta. Faculty of Law.
Alberta law review

University of Alberta. Boreal Institute for Northern Studies.
Boreal Institute for Northern Studies Library. Accessions list

University of Alberta. Boreal Institute for Northern Studies. Mrs. N. Cooke.
Alberta Information Retrieval Association. A.I.R.A. - Western Canada A.S.I.S. newsletter

The University of Alberta. Department of Animal Science.
Feeders' day

University of Alberta. Department of Anthropology.
Western Canadian journal of anthropology

University of Alberta. The Department of Computing Science.
University of Alberta, Edmonton. Computing Services. Bulletin

University of Alberta. Department of Educational Administration.
Canadian administrator

The University of Alberta. Department of Elementary Education.
Elements : translating theory into practice

University of Alberta. Department of English.
Modernist studies

University of Alberta. Department of Entomology.
Quaestiones entomologicae

University of Alberta. Department of Geography.
The Albertan geographer

University of Alberta. Education Centre Alberta Department.
Indian-ed

University of Alberta. Educational Media Division.
University of Alberta. Educational Media Division. Catalog of 16 mm educational motion pictures

University of Alberta. Faculty of Agriculture and Forestry. Public Relations and Publications Committee.
Agriculture bulletin

University of Alberta. The Faculty of Education.
The Alberta journal of educational research
Canadian Society for the Study of Education. Bulletin
Perspectives on curriculum

University of Alberta. Intercultural Education Program.
Indian ed

University of Alberta. The Library.
Library information bulletin
University of Alberta, Edmonton. Library. Library staff bulletin

University of Alberta. Library. Special Collections Division.
University of Alberta theses

University of British Columbia. Varsity Outdoor Club.
University of British Columbia. Varsity Outdoor Club. The Varsity Outdoor Club journal

University of British Columbia Press.
B.C. studies
Canadian literature = Littérature canadienne
Canadian yearbook of international law = Annuaire canadien de droit international
Pacific affairs : an international review of Asia and the Pacific

University of Calgary.
Ariel: a review of international English literature
The University of Calgary gazette

University of Calgary. Archaeological Association.
University of Calgary Archaeological Association. Paleo-Environmental Workshop. Proceedings

University of Calgary. Department of Archaeology.
University of Calgary Archaeological Association. Paleo-Environmental Workshop. Proceedings

University of Calgary. Department of Computer Services.
The Big byte

University of Calgary. Department of Sociology and Anthropology.
Journal of comparative family studies

University of Calgary. Faculty of Education.
Journal of education thought

University of Calgary. Research Centre for Canadian Ethnic Studies.
Canadian ethnic studies = Etudes éthniques du Canada

University of Calgary, Students' Union.
Gauntlet

University of Guelph.
Notes on agriculture
The Ontarian

University of Guelph. Department of Alumni Affairs.
Guelph alumnus

University of Guelph. Department of Alumni Affairs and Development.
Arts and sciences alumni news
Macdonald Institute - Family and Consumer Studies. Alumni Association. Alumni news
Ontario Agricultural College. Alumni news
University of Guelph. Arts and sciences alumni news

University of Guelph. Department of Geography.
Ontario Association of Geomorphologists. Handbook

University of Guelph. Department of Information.
At Guelph
University of Guelph. News bulletin

University of Guelph. Department of Soil Science.
Ontario Agricultural College. Department of Land Resource Science. Research and Advisory Service. Progress report

University of Guelph. Interdepartmental Committee on Scottish Studies.
Colloquium on Scottish studies. Proceedings

University of Guelph. Ontario Agricultural College. School of Engineering.
Drainage Engineers' Conference. Proceedings

University of Guelph. Senate Committee on Learning and Teaching.
Teaching forum

University of Lethbridge. Student Society Council. Production Department.
Meliorist

University of Lithbridge. Students' Union.
Meliorist

University of Manitoba.
Mosaic : a journal for the comparative study of literature and ideas

University of Manitoba. Alumni Association.
The Alumni journal
University of Manitoba. The Alumni journal

University of Manitoba. Center for Settlement Studies.
University of Manitoba. Center for Settlement Studies. Bibliography and information

University of Manitoba. Centre for Transportation Studies.
University of Manitoba. Center for Transportation Studies. Seminar Series on Transportation. Proceedings

University of Manitoba. Faculty of Agriculture. Plant Science Department.
Greenhouse newsletter

University of Manitoba. Faculty of Arts.
Linguistic Circle of Manitoba and North Dakota. Proceedings

University of Manitoba. Faculty of Law.
Manitoba law journal

University of Manitoba. Faculty of Medicine.
University of Manitoba. Medical journal

University of Western Ontario. Computing Centre.
The University of Western Ontario. Computing Centre newsletter

University of Western Ontario. The D.B. Weldon Library.
Western Ontario historical notes

The University of Western Ontario. Department of Alumni Affairs. Nigel Bellchamber.
University of Western Ontario. Alumni gazette

University of Western Ontario. Department of Geography.
Ontario geography

University of Western Ontario. Faculty of Dentistry. Dental Students Society.
University of Western Ontario dental journal

University of Western Ontario. Office on International Education.
International view

University of Western Ontario. School of Business Administration.
The Business quarterly : Canadian management journal
Western management/Pattern and probe

University of Western Ontario. University Relations and Information. L.T. Moore.
Western news

University of Windsor.
Canadian journal of history of sport and physical education
Canadian-American seminar

University of Windsor. French Department.
Poetry - Windsor = Windsor poésie

University of Windsor. Library.
University of Windsor. Library. List of serials held in the University of Windsor Library

University of Windsor. Library. Gifts and exchange section.
University of Windsor. Main Library. Office of the University Librarian. News and views

University of Windsor. Students Administrative Council. Publications Commission.
The Ambassador
The Lance

University of Windsor Press.
Canadian-American seminar
University of Windsor review

University of Winnipeg. Alumni Association.
University of Winnipeg. Alumni bulletin

University of Winnipeg Publication Board.
Uniter

University of Winnipeg Students Association.
Uniter

University Press of New Brunswick.
The Atlantic advocate

Upper Canada College.
College times

Upper Canada College. Alumni Association.
Old times

Urban Research Council of Canada.
Urban forum = Colloque urbain

Urban Social Redevelopment Centre.
Up to the neck - action

Frank Valadas.
Tribuna portuguesa

Luis S. Valdés.
El Planeta

Vladimir Valenta.
The Telegram

The Vancouver Art Gallery.
Vancouver Art Gallery. Exhibition catalogues
Vanguard
Vanguard

Vancouver Board of Trade.
The Sounding board

Vancouver City College. Journalism Department.
Savant

Vancouver City Savings Credit Union.
VanCity working dollars

Vancouver Community College.
Faculty affairs

Vancouver Estonian Society.
Lâânekaare postipoiss

Vancouver Folk Song Society.
Come all ye

Vancouver Historical Society.
Vancouver Historical Society. Newsletter

Vancouver Island Cage Bird Society.
Vancouver Island Cage Bird Society. Annual show bulletin
Vancouver Island Cage Bird Society. Bulletin

Vancouver Island Netherlands Association.
Vancouver Island Netherlands Association. Newsletter

Vancouver Island Real Estate Board.
The Islander

Vancouver Island Western Square Dance Association.
Cross trail news

Vancouver Museums & Planetarium Association.
SNAUQ

J.P. Wearing. L.W. Conolly.
Nineteenth century theatre research

Webber Pharmaceuticals.
The Summary

Wedge Publishing Foundation.
Vanguard : Christian vision for the seventies

Dr. F. Weinstein.
The Canadian podiatrist

Wellington County Historical Research Society.
Wellington County Historical Research Society. Newsletter

The Welsh Black Bulletin.
The Welsh black bulletin

WesTrade Publications Ltd. J.B. Tompkins.
Motor transport factbook
WesTrade traffic directory

West Coast Review.
West Coast review

West Vancouver memorial library.
West Van bookman

Western Canada District.
KiwaNews : Western Canada district

Western Canada Water and Sewage Conference.
Western Canada Water and Sewage Conference. Bulletin

Western Canadian Society for Horticulture.
Western Canadian Society for Horticulture. Report of proceedings of annual meetings

Western Canadian Sudeten, German Alliance.
Sudentenbote = Sudeten herald

Western Catholic Reporter.
Alberta Catholic directory

Western Fish and Game Magazine Ltd.
Western angling

Western Guard Party.
Straight talk!

Western Institute for the Deaf.
Western Institute for the Deaf. W.I.D. news

Western Miner Press Ltd.
The B.C. professional engineer
Purchasing in Western Canada
Western miner

Western Racing Revue.
Western racing review

Western Ski Promotions Ltd. Ian F. Brown.
Western Canada skier

Western Thoroughbred. W.W. Acton.
Western thoroughbred

Western Tract Mission.
Western tract news

Westminster Abbey.
Pax regis

Westminster County Real Estate Board.
Wescoreb interim

Weston Publishing Co. Ltd.
Mark 11 : the sales and marketing management magazine
Volume retail merchandising

Westrade Publications Ltd.
Motor carrier

Westroc Industries Ltd. 2650 Lakeshore Highway, Mississauga, Ont. L5J 1K4.
Dimensions nouvelles

Westworld Publications Ltd. Bill Mayrs.
Westworld : the magazine of travel, leisure and living

What's On Publishing Co.
What's on in Ottawa = Voici Ottawa

Wheatland Regional Library.
Harvestings from the wheatland

Wheelspin News Inc.
Autosport Canada
Wheelspin news : Canada's autosport newsmagazine

Terry M. Whelpton.
Ski Canada journal

Whitehouse. Lynn Whitehouse.
B.C. dairy goat news

Whitsed Publishing Ltd.
Campus : the national magazine for graduating students
Canadian data processing directory
Canadian Information Processing Society. CIPS computer magazine
Canadian office
Canadian office redbook

Who's who Canadian Publications.
Who's who biographical service : Canada

Wilderness Publications Ltd. Frank M. Lee.
Vancouver Island's outdoor journal

Wilfrid Laurier University.
Laurier campus

Wilfrid Laurier University. Board of Publications.
Keystone

Wilfrid Laurier University Press.
Ontario archaeology

David E. Williams.
Le Beaver

Harold L. Willis and Assoc.
Collective bargaining : statistics in education

NOTES

NOTES

NOTES

NOTES

NOTESV

NOTES

www.ingramcontent.com/pod-product-compliance
Lightning Source LLC
LaVergne TN
LVHW082157080826
844660LV00046B/1259